New Testament Commentary

New Testament Commentary

Exposition
of the Acts
of the Apostles

Simon J. Kistemaker

BAKER BOOK HOUSE
Grand Rapids, Michigan 49516

Copyright 1990 by
Baker Book House Company

ISBN: 0-8010-5290-4

Library of Congress Catalog Card Number: 54-924

Printed in the United States of America

Contents

Abbreviations   vii
Preface   xi
Introduction   1
Commentary   41

1. Before Pentecost **(1:1–26)**   43

2. The Church in Jerusalem, *part 1* **(2:1–47)**   71

3. The Church in Jerusalem, *part 2* **(3:1–26)**   117

4. The Church in Jerusalem, *part 3* **(4:1–37)**   143

5. The Church in Jerusalem, *part 4* **(5:1–42)**   179

6. The Church in Jerusalem, *part 5* **(6:1–15)**   217

7. The Church in Jerusalem, *part 6* **(7:1–8:1a)**   235

8. The Church in Palestine, *part 1* **(8:1b–40)**   285

9. The Church in Palestine, *part 2* **(9:1–43)**   325

10. The Church in Palestine, *part 3* **(10:1–48)**   367

11. The Church in Palestine, *part 4* **(11:1–18)**
    and The Church in Transition, *part 1* **(11:19–30)**   405

12. The Church in Transition, *part 2* **(12:1–25)**   429

13. The Church in Transition, *part 3* **(13:1–3)**
    and The First Missionary Journey, *part 1* **(13:4–52)**   451

14. The First Missionary Journey, *part 2* **(14:1–28)**   501

15. The Council at Jerusalem **(15:1–35)**
    and The Second Missionary Journey, *part 1* **(15:36–41)**   531

16. The Second Missionary Journey, *part 2* **(16:1–40)**   575

17. The Second Missionary Journey, *part 3* **(17:1–34)**   609

18. The Second Missionary Journey, *part 4* **(18:1–22)**
    and The Third Missionary Journey, *part 1* **(18:23–28)**   645

19. The Third Missionary Journey, *part 2* **(19:1–41)**   673

20. The Third Missionary Journey, *part 3* **(20:1–38)** 709

21. The Third Missionary Journey, *part 4* **(21:1–16)**
    and In Jerusalem and Caesarea, *part 1* **(21:17–40)** 741

22. In Jerusalem and Caesarea, *part 2* **(22:1–30)** 777

23. In Jerusalem and Caesarea, *part 3* **(23:1–35)** 805

24. In Jerusalem and Caesarea, *part 4* **(24:1–27)** 831

25. In Jerusalem and Caesarea, *part 5* **(25:1–27)** 857

26. In Jerusalem and Caesarea, *part 6* **(26:1–32)** 881

27. Voyage to and Stay in Rome, *part 1* **(27:1–44)** 911

28. Voyage to and Stay in Rome, *part 2* **(28:1–31)** 943

Select Bibliography 971
Index of Authors 981
Index of Scripture 989

Abbreviations

ASV	American Standard Version
AUSS	*Andrews University Seminary Studies*
Bauer	Walter Bauer, W. F. Arndt, F. W. Gingrich, and F. W. Danker, *A Greek-English Lexicon of the New Testament*, 2d edition
BEB	*Baker Encyclopedia of the Bible*
Beginnings	F. J. Foakes Jackson and Kirsopp Lake, eds., *The Beginnings of Christianity*
BF	British and Foreign Bible Society, *The New Testament*, 2d edition
Bib	*Biblica*
BibRes	*Biblical Research*
BibToday	*Bible Today*
BibTr	*Bible Translator*
BJRUL	*Bulletin of John Rylands University Library of Manchester*
BS	*Bibliotheca Sacra*
BZ	*Biblische Zeitschrift*
CBQ	*Catholic Biblical Quarterly*
CJT	*Canadian Journal of Theology*
I Clem.	First Epistle of Clement
ConcJourn	*Concordia Journal*
ConcThMonth	*Concordia Theological Monthly*
CT	*Christianity Today*
EDT	*Evangelical Dictionary of Theology*
EphThL	*Ephemerides théologicae lovaniensis*
Esd.	Esdras
EvQ	*Evangelical Quarterly*
ExpT	*Expository Times*
GNB	Good News Bible
GTJ	*Grace Theological Journal*
HTR	*Harvard Theological Review*
IDB	*Interpreter's Dictionary of the Bible*
Interp	*Interpretation*
ISBE	*International Standard Bible Encyclopedia*, rev. ed.
IsrExJ	*Israel Exploration Journal*
JB	Jerusalem Bible
JBL	*Journal of Biblical Literature*

JETS	*Journal of the Evangelical Theological Society*
JJS	*Journal of Jewish Studies*
JSNT	*Journal for the Study of the New Testament*
Jth.	Judith
JTS	*Journal of Theological Studies*
Jub.	Jubilees
KJV	King James Version (= Authorized Version)
LB	Living Bible
LCL	Loeb Classical Library edition
lit.	literal, literally
LXX	Septuagint
Macc.	Maccabees
Majority Text	Arthur L. Farstad and Zane Hodges, *The Greek New Testament: According to the Majority Text*
Merk	Augustinus Merk, ed., *Novum Testamentum Graece et Latine,* 9th ed.
MLB	The Modern Language Bible
Moffatt	*The Bible—A New Translation,* James Moffatt
NAB	New American Bible
NASB	New American Standard Bible
NEB	New English Bible
NedTTs	*Nederlands theologisch tijdschrift*
Neotest	*Neotestamentica*
Nes-Al	Eberhard Nestle and Kurt Aland, *Novum Testamentum Graece,* 26th edition
NIDNTT	*New International Dictionary of New Testament Theology*
NIV	New International Version
NKJV	New King James Version
NovT	*Novum Testamentum*
n.s.	new series
NTS	*New Testament Studies*
PEQ	*Palestine Exploration Quarterly*
Phillips	*The New Testament in Modern English,* J. B. Phillips
RefThR	*Reformed Theological Review*
RelStudRev	*Religious Studies Review*
ResQ	*Restoration Quarterly*
1QS	Manual of Discipline
RB	*Revue biblique*
RevThom	*Revue thomiste*
RSPT	*Revue des sciences philosophiques et théologiques*
RSV	Revised Standard Version
RV	Revised Version
SB	H. L. Strack and P. Billerbeck, *Kommentar zum Neuen Testament aus Talmud und Midrasch*
SEB	Simple English Bible

SecCent	*Second Century*
Sir.	Sirach
Talmud	The Babylonian Talmud
TDNT	*Theological Dictionary of the New Testament*
Thayer	Joseph H. Thayer, *Greek-English Lexicon of the New Testament*
TheolZeit	*Theologische Zeitschrift*
Tob.	Tobit
TynB	*Tyndale Bulletin*
VigChr	*Vigiliae christianae*
VoxRef	*Vox Reformata*
Wis.	Wisdom of Solomon
WTJ	*Westminster Theological Journal*
ZNW	*Zeitschrift für die Neutestamentliche Wissenschaft*
ZPEB	*Zondervan Pictorial Encyclopedia of the Bible*

Preface

With this volume, the sequence of the four Gospels and Acts in the New Testament Commentary series is complete. My predecessor, Dr. William Hendriksen, wrote the commentary on Luke's Gospel and I have the distinct privilege of presenting the reader with the volume on Acts. Although I have adopted Hendriksen's format, it is apparent that I differ from him in style and presentation.

While composing the commentary on Acts, I kept in mind the needs of the pastor and the teacher of Scripture. Throughout this volume I have attempted to give an adequate description of the historical times, the cultural influences, and the geographic features mentioned by the writer of Acts. Limitations of space often forced me to restrict discussions on historical, cultural, and linguistic problems. These issues, then, I have left for further treatment in scholarly journals. My aim has been to stay with the text and to explain it as clearly as possible.

In the sections called **Greek Words, Phrases, and Constructions,** basic helps are given for a better understanding of the text. These sections have been set apart, so that the reader who lacks a knowledge of the Greek is not intimidated and the pastor and teacher who know Greek grammar will be assisted in understanding this portion of Scripture.

Further, this volume aids the reader in receiving insights into the doctrinal and practical considerations of particular passages. Even though Luke wrote a history of the church and not a doctrinal discourse, Acts has a decidedly theological emphasis. For this reason, I have summarized the theology of Acts in Section F of the Introduction and in individual sections throughout the commentary.

I am giving the reader my own translation of Acts. Wherever relevant I have recorded the readings of the Western text, which frequently are additions to and embellishments of the passages in question. In those cases, I have rejected these readings. Sometimes the Western text provides a wording that appears to be genuine and acceptable. Such a reading I have incorporated in my translation, as, for instance, in the text of 24:6–8 (see the commentary).

May this commentary prove to be a blessing to the pastor and student of the Bible in proclaiming and teaching the riches of God's Word.

Spring 1990   *Simon J. Kistemaker*

ppi
Neapolis

A
E
G
E
A
N

S
E
A

Troas
Assos
Mitylene
Antioch
Iconium
Sardis
Tarsus
ens
Ephesus
Lystra
Derbe
Miletus
Perga
Antioch
Myra
Attalia
Patara
SYRIA
Cos
Rhodes
Crete
CYPRUS
Salamis
Paphos
Damascus
Fair Havens
Tyre
Ptolemais
Caesarea
Antipatris
Jerusalem

Introduction

Outline

A. Title
B. Sources
C. Speeches
D. Historicity
E. Author, Date, and Place
F. Theology
G. Characteristics
H. Text
I. Purpose
J. Themes
K. Outline

In length, Acts surpasses nearly all the books in the New Testament canon. With its twenty-eight chapters that comprise a total of 1,007 verses, it forms an inseparable link between the Gospels and the Epistles. Indeed, without Acts the canon would be incomplete. Acts is the continuation of the Gospel account and establishes the basis for the epistolary literature.

A. Title

The title of Acts, probably added in the second century, is problematic in many respects. Some Bible translations feature the designation *Acts of the Apostles* and have the support of early church fathers.[1] But apart from listing the twelve apostles in chapter 1, Luke discusses only the ministry of Peter and Paul. To be sure, John accompanies Peter to the temple "in the afternoon for prayer" (3:1) and to Samaria (8:14), but Luke records no specific words or deeds of John. Obviously, this descriptive title of the book is too broad. The suggestion to resort to the name *Acts of Peter and Paul* has not met any favorable response because in this book Luke also relates the ministry of Stephen, Philip, Barnabas, Silas, and Timothy.

Next, a proposal to label the book *The Acts of the Holy Spirit* fails in its bid to gain support.[2] Notwithstanding Luke's emphasis on the outpouring of the Holy Spirit in Jerusalem (2:1–4), Samaria (8:17), Caesarea (10:44–46), and Ephesus (19:6), the content of the book is much broader than the proposed title conveys. Moreover, in the first verse of Acts, Luke implies that he is writing a continuation of his Gospel. He indicates that his first volume is a book of "all that Jesus *began* both to do and to teach" (1:1). By implication he says that in Acts Jesus continues his work. The emphasis, then, falls not so much on the Holy Spirit but rather on what Jesus is doing in developing the church in Jerusalem, Samaria, Asia Minor, Greece, and Italy.

Still another choice is to name the book *Acts*.[3] The brevity of this title is

---

1. Irenaeus *Against Heresies* 3.13.3; Clement of Alexandria *Stromata* 5.82; Tertullian *Fasting* 10. Codices Sinaiticus, Vaticanus, and Bezae also have this reading. Minuscule manuscripts provide expansions: "Acts of the Holy Apostles" and "Acts of the Holy Apostles of Luke the Evangelist."

2. Compare John Albert Bengel, *Gnomon of the New Testament*, ed. Andrew R. Fausset, 5 vols. (Edinburgh: Clark, 1877), vol. 2, p. 512.

3. NIV, SEB.

attractive. Although it avoids the objections raised against the other names, it is nevertheless nondescript and colorless. Ancient writers commonly used the expression *Acts* to describe the deeds of illustrious heroes, including Cyrus and Alexander the Great.[4] The title for Acts, accordingly, whether long or short, remains problematic.

The sequence of Luke-Acts from the hand of Luke can be compared with the sequence of Paul's two letters to the Corinthians. The difference, however, is that Christians in the first century placed Luke's "first book" with the Gospels and considered Acts a history of the church. Thus they placed Acts in the category of historical books. In short, Acts relates the history of the early church.

B. Sources

1. Selectivity

Is Luke a historian who presents a complete description of the development of the early church? No, because he depicts only the church's growth that begins in Jerusalem and moves in a northerly and westerly direction. He relates what occurred in Palestine, Syria, Asia Minor, Macedonia and Greece, and Rome, but omits what happened elsewhere. Luke bypasses many names of the countries which he lists as a table of nations (2:9–11). People from these countries had come to Jerusalem to celebrate the feast of Pentecost, heard the gospel proclaimed, and returned to their homelands. But in portraying the developing church, Luke follows a path that leads him to countries to the north and to the west of Jerusalem. He disregards what happened in countries to the south and east of Israel.

Further, from all the available material Luke selects only certain incidents, and when he describes them he deliberately chooses to be brief. For instance, his report on the deaths of Ananias and Sapphira (5:1–11) raises numerous questions because of its brevity; he relates that Peter, who is the leader of the Jerusalem church, simply leaves for another place (12:17); and he states that at the conclusion of Paul's second missionary journey, Paul "went up and greeted the church," by implication, at Jerusalem (18:22). Historians in the ancient world "were compelled to set quite strict limits to the narrative material which came down to them from oral tradition or from written sources."[5]

2. Tradition

Luke had to be brief in view of the wealth of material and the length of the period he covered. If we place Jesus' ascension (described in 1:9–11) in A.D. 30 and Paul's release from house arrest in about A.D. 63, then Luke covers a

---

4. Xenophon *Cyropaed* 1.2.16; Diogenes Laertius 2.3; Diodorus Siculus 16.1.1; Josephus *Antiquities* 14.4.3 [68].

5. Martin Hengel, *Acts and the History of Earliest Christianity*, trans. John Bowden (Philadelphia: Fortress, 1980), p. 10.

thirty-three-year period. Incidentally, Luke relates that Jesus began his public ministry when he was about thirty years old (Luke 3:23); this ministry lasted three years. Thus the period that the Gospel of Luke covers is also thirty-three years. The total span for both Gospel and Acts is sixty-six years.

Because Luke's Gospel and Acts are a continuous account, the words of the introduction to the Gospel also apply to Acts. Luke writes that his information was handed down to him by "eyewitnesses and ministers of the word" (Luke 1:2). As he had gathered his material for the Gospel from the apostles and other eyewitnesses, he obtained his facts for the composition of Acts from Peter, Paul, James, Silas, and Timothy. In Acts, he reveals by the use of the pronouns *we* and *us* that he himself was present as an eyewitness.[6] He indicates that he was in Jerusalem when Paul was arrested and that he met James and the elders (21:17–18). We assume that during Paul's imprisonment, Luke had ample time to gather factual material from eyewitnesses who related to him the birth, development, and extended influence of the Jerusalem church. From both Peter and Paul, he was able to obtain numerous oral accounts which he arranged in a more or less chronological sequence. Did Luke have access to written documents? Were the speeches of Peter, Stephen, Paul, and others available in written form? We have no evidence that Luke relied on written sources and any scholar who states that Luke used such accounts must necessarily work with hypotheses.[7] Luke's Gospel can be compared with the other canonical Gospels, but Acts as a historical account is unique in the New Testament: it is the only history book of the early church in the canon.

3. Eyewitness Account

When Luke listened to eyewitnesses who told him about the events that occurred beginning with Jesus' appearances and ascension, he undoubtedly took written notes. Subsequently he edited these summaries which he had gathered from personal interviews.[8] Luke mentions many persons in a manner that seems to suggest a personal acquaintance with them. According to tradition, supported by the anti-Marcionite prologue of the second half of the second century and by Eusebius, Luke hailed from Antioch in Syria.[9] Luke developed a friendship with Barnabas, whom the apostles had sent to aid the fledgling church of Antioch (11:22). He describes Barnabas as "a good man, full of the Holy Spirit" (11:24). Because of his connection

---

6. See 16:10–17; 20:5–21:18; 27:1–28:16. These passages refer to Paul's second and third missionary journeys and to his voyage to Rome.

7. Jacques Dupont concludes, "Despite the most careful and detailed research, it has not been possible to define any of the sources used by the author of Acts in a way which will meet with widespread agreement among the critics." *The Sources of the Acts,* trans. Kathleen Pond (New York: Herder and Herder, 1964), p. 166.

8. Colin J. Hemer, "Luke the Historian," *BJRUL* 60 (1977–78): 49. See his *Book of Acts in the Setting of Hellenistic History,* ed. Conrad H. Gempf (Tübingen: Mohr, 1989), pp. 335–36.

9. Eusebius *Ecclesiastical History* 3.4.6.

with Antioch, Luke describes Nicolas as being from Antioch and a convert to Judaism (6:5). In addition, he provides some details concerning the Antiochean prophets and teachers: Barnabas, Simeon called Niger, Lucius of Cyrene, Manaen who had been brought up with Herod the tetrarch, and Saul (13:1). In Antioch he perhaps encountered Judas, called Barsabbas, and Silas (15:22, 32); but certainly he came to know Silas in Philippi (16:19–40). There he also knew Lydia, the seller of purple cloth from Thyatira (16:14).

Luke stayed at the home of Philip the evangelist in Caesarea (21:8; and see 6:5). It is logical to think that from him Luke received information about the beginning and development of the church in Samaria (8:5–25), the conversion of the Ethiopian eunuch (8:26–40), and the admission of the household of Cornelius to the church in Caesarea (10:1–11:18). In Jerusalem, Luke became acquainted with John Mark whose mother, Mary, had a large home (12:12). Here he may have met the servant girl Rhoda (12:13).

In Acts, Luke cites more than a hundred personal names, and he lists some of them with titles. For example, he notes that Sergius Paulus was a proconsul in Cyprus (13:7) and Gallio a proconsul in Achaia (18:12). Archaeological inscriptions testify to the accuracy of these titles.[10] If we know that today many officials in our government fill a certain post for no more than a year or two, we concede that only an astute historian is able to keep an accurate record. Consequently, Luke appears to be a meticulous historiographer.

In numerous instances, Luke reveals the place where certain persons lived by specifying their home town or province: Aquila, a native of Pontus, with his wife, Priscilla, had been driven from Rome and settled in Corinth (18:1–2). Titius Justus lived next door to the synagogue in Corinth (18:7); Crispus was the ruler of that synagogue (18:8; see also I Cor. 1:14); and Sosthenes became Crispus's successor (18:17; I Cor. 1:1). Luke elaborately describes Apollos, who was a native of Alexandria and a learned man (18:24–26). He relates that at Troas he met Sopater son of Pyrrhus from Berea, Aristarchus and Secundus from Thessalonica, Gaius and Timothy from Derbe, Tychicus and Trophimus from the province of Asia (20:4).

Geographical information, especially in relation to Paul's journeys, is remarkably detailed; Luke cites no fewer than a hundred place names in Acts. As a companion of Paul at the conclusion of the third missionary journey, Luke mentions all the places along the route from Greece to Jerusalem and the length of time they stayed at each place. Paul spent three months in Greece (20:3), five days traveling to Troas, and seven

---

10. Kirsopp Lake, "The Chronology of Acts," *Beginnings*, vol. 5, pp. 445–74. "The normal length of office appears to have been one year, but two years was not unprecedented" (p. 463). See also A. N. Sherwin-White, *Roman Society and Roman Law in the New Testament* (1963; reprint ed., Grand Rapids: Baker, 1978), pp. 99–107.

days in Troas (20:6). On the first day of the week Paul and company worshiped in Troas (20:7). Paul walked to Assos while the others took a boat to get there. Luke writes a day-by-day description of the voyage along the western coast of Asia Minor to the ports of Tyre, Ptolemais, and Caesarea (20:15–16; 21:1–8). Again, Luke gives detailed time references of Paul's stay and arrest in Jerusalem, his nighttime journey to Caesarea, and his imprisonment there (21–26). And last, with many nautical, climatic, and geographical terms Luke has given a reliable account of Paul's voyage to Rome (27–28).[11]

In a word, Luke's presentation of historical and geographical data is superb. He demonstrates that in many episodes, he himself was an eyewitness. And wherever he was not present, he consulted people who had been on the scene and could furnish an accurate account of the incidents that happened.[12]

Luke begins the Book of Acts with the first person singular pronoun *I* (1:1) and in the second half of his book he uses the first person plural *we*. Since his style is the same from beginning to end, we draw the conclusion that the personal pronouns refer to the author of this book. Moreover, the early recipients of Acts were acquainted with Paul and his fellow worker Luke (Col. 4:14; II Tim. 4:11; Philem. 24) and were able to check the accuracy of his historical and geographical reports. Church members in Ephesus and Colosse would know the names of the places Luke mentions in connection with Paul's journeys along the western and southern coasts of Asia Minor. They would have rejected the book as fraudulent should Luke have presented fiction instead of fact. Critics claim that the writer of Acts originated the "we" and "us" pronouns "in order to make it clear that he himself took part in Paul's journeys."[13] But they have been unable to prove that Luke himself could not have been an eyewitness.

We conclude, therefore, that Luke depended not on written sources but on oral tradition which he received from persons who had personal knowledge of the events that had occurred.

---

11. Angus Acworth, "Where Was St. Paul Shipwrecked? A Reexamination of the Evidence," *JTS* n.s. 24 (1973): 190–93; and Colin J. Hemer, "Euraquilo and Melita," *JTS* n.s. 26 (1975): 100–111. Consult also Colin J. Hemer, "First Person Narrative in Acts 27–28," *TynB* 36 (1985): 79–109.

12. Consult W. Ward Gasque, "The Historical Value of the Book of Acts. The Perspective of British Scholarship," *TheolZeit* 28 (1972): 177–96. See also W. Ward Gasque, "The Historical Value of the Book of Acts. An Essay in the History of New Testament Criticism," *EvQ* 41 (1969): 68–88.

13. Martin Dibelius, *Studies in the Acts of the Apostles* (London: SCM, 1956), p. 105. See also Ernst Haenchen, *The Acts of the Apostles: A Commentary,* trans. Bernard Noble and Gerald Shinn (Philadelphia: Westminster, 1971), p. 85. Haenchen calls the use of "we" in Acts "the author's last minute embellishment." Consult Hans Conzelmann, *Acts of the Apostles,* trans. James Limburg, A. Thomas Kraabel, and Donald H. Juel (1963; Philadelphia: Fortress, 1987), p. xxxix.

C. Speeches

Luke is able to express himself in excellent Greek, but in Acts he varies the choice of words with reference to the locale. He reflects the diction, vocabulary, and culture of the area he describes. Hence, in the chapters that depict Palestine (1–15), Luke's Greek has an Aramaic coloring. The second half of the book (16–28) reflects a Gentile setting and is written in fluent Greek that, at times, rivals classical Greek. To illustrate, of the sixty-seven times that the optative mood occurs in the New Testament, seventeen are in Acts. These seventeen instances appear mostly in the second half of the book and often come from the lips of speakers who know Greek well.[14]

1. Classification

Acts is filled with direct speech which constitutes about half of the entire book. Counting both the short and the long addresses, we number at least twenty-six speeches. They are made by apostles and Christian leaders on the one hand and by non-Christians (Jews and Gentiles) on the other. Luke presents eight addresses delivered by Peter,[15] a lengthy sermon of Stephen before the Sanhedrin (7:2–53), a brief explanation by Cornelius (10:30–33), a short address by James at the Jerusalem Council (15:13–21), the advice to Paul by James and the elders in Jerusalem (21:20–25), and nine sermons and speeches by Paul.[16] The rest of the discourses were given by Gamaliel the Pharisee (5:35–39), Demetrius the silversmith (19:25–27), the city clerk in Ephesus (19:35–40), Tertullus the lawyer (24:2–8), and Festus the governor (25:24–27).[17] Additionally, Luke relays the text of two letters: one from the Jerusalem Council to the Gentile churches (15:23–29), and the other written by Claudius Lysias to Governor Felix (23:27–30).

The speeches make the Book of Acts fascinating, because when people speak we learn something about their personalities. Luke portrays people as they are, and as we listen to their speech, we come to know them. Luke heard Paul proclaim the Good News in Philippi, his address to the Ephesian elders, his speech in Jerusalem, his defense before Felix, and his defense before Festus and Agrippa. We presume that from Paul Luke received the wording of Paul's sermon in Pisidian Antioch and his Areopagus address. From Peter, Luke gathered information on the addresses of Peter in the upper room, at Pentecost, near Solomon's Colonnade, before the Sanhe-

---

14. Greek philosophers in Athens (17:18), Paul at the Areopagus (17:27 [twice]), Governor Festus (25:16 [twice], 20), Paul addressing King Agrippa (26:29). The other instances are 5:24; 8:20, 31; 10:17; 17:11; 20:16; 21:33; 24:19; 27:12, 39.

15. 1:16–22; 2:14–36, 38–39; 3:12–26; 4:8–12, 19–20; 5:29–32; 10:34–43; 11:5–17; 15:7–11.

16. 13:16–41; 14:15–17; 17:22–31; 20:18–35; 22:1–21; 24:10–21; 26:2–23, 25–27; 27:21–26; 28:17–20.

17. H. J. Cadbury, "The Speeches in Acts," *Beginnings,* vol. 5, p. 403. See also John Navonne, "Speeches in Acts," *BibToday* 65 (1973): 1114–17.

drin, and at the Jerusalem Council. Perhaps Paul and other witnesses provided information on Stephen's speech before the Sanhedrin.

If Luke received his information from eyewitnesses, does he faithfully reproduce the speeches that they and others made? As expected, the context reveals that Luke presents the addresses in summary form. But are these summaries true to fact or have they been placed on the lips of speakers? Some scholars are of the opinion that the speeches are the creation of the writer of Acts. By comparison, they point to the Greek historian Thucydides and claim that Luke adopted the methodology of Thucydides, who averred that in composing his speeches he "adhered as closely as possible to the general sense of what was actually said."[18] The apparent intention of this ancient writer is to state that the speeches he wrote were historically accurate and not based on his own imagination. Even though the words of Thucydides have been a topic of much debate,[19] the inclination to take his saying at face value prevails. The task which the ancient historian assumed was to give an account of the events just as they happened. He reported facts, not fiction.

If we listen to Luke's own words in the preface to his Gospel, we learn that he gives an account of the things that have happened and which people have accepted as true (Luke 1.1). Thus at the beginning of his writings, Luke informs the reader that his reporting as a historian is true to fact.

The question that concerns the student of Acts is whether in this historical account Luke is giving a truthful presentation. Are the speeches which he himself did not hear accurately reported? This question can be answered by reading and comparing the speeches of Peter with Peter's writings and the speeches of Paul with the epistles Paul composed.

2. Peter

In the speeches of Peter, Luke consistently presents Greek grammatical constructions that seem to reveal the speaker's inability to speak fluently and correctly. In literal translations, the incoherent constructions are obvious. Following are two examples, the first one from Peter's address to the Jews at the temple and the second from Peter's sermon at the house of Cornelius:

> And on the basis of faith of his name, his name has strengthened this man whom you see and know, and the faith which is through him has given him this perfect health which is before all of you. [3:16][20]

---

18. Thucydides *History of the Peloponnesian War* 1.22.1.

19. See Dibelius, *Studies in the Acts of the Apostles*, p. 141, expressing doubt; and W. Ward Gasque, accepting the statement as true, in "The Speeches of Acts: Dibelius Reconsidered," *New Dimensions in New Testament Study*, ed. Richard N. Longenecker and Merrill C. Tenney (Grand Rapids: Zondervan, 1974), pp. 243–44. Compare T. F. Glasson, "Speeches in Acts and Thucydides," *ExpT* 76 (1964–65): 165.

20. For a discussion on a possible translation from an Aramaic text, consult F. J. Foakes Jackson and Kirsopp Lake, "The Internal Evidence of Acts," *Beginnings*, vol. 2, pp. 141–42.

Introduction

> The word which he sent to the sons of Israel, preaching peace through Jesus Christ, this one is Lord of all, you yourselves know the thing which took place throughout all Judea, beginning from Galilee, after the baptism which John proclaimed. [10:36–37][21]

These contorted sentences resemble some of the verses in Peter's writings, in which we have to supply words to complete the clauses so as to give us an unambiguous presentation. In the following example the italicized words have been added for clarity:

> If anyone speaks, *let him speak,* as it were the *very* words of God; if anyone serves, *let him do so* as it were with the strength God supplies. [I Peter 4:11]

An example from Peter's second epistle demonstrates the difficulty the writer had in expressing himself clearly and correctly:

> By the word of God, the earth was formed out of water and by water, through which the world at that time was destroyed deluged with water. [II Peter 3:5b–6]

Another aspect that reveals similarities is the word choice of Peter in his speeches and letters. Examining these similarities, we find some instances that not only in the Greek but even in translation are striking:

Acts	I Peter
by the set purpose and foreknowledge of God [2:23]	according to the foreknowledge of God [1:2]
as judge of the living and the dead [10:42]	to judge the living and the dead [4:5]

When Peter addresses the household of Cornelius, he tells the Gentile audience that "God shows no favoritism" (10:34). Next, he repeats this thought in slightly different wording when he speaks at the Jerusalem Council in favor of admitting the Gentiles to membership in the church. He says that God "made no distinction between us and them" (15:9, NIV). And last, in I Peter he writes that God "impartially judges each man's work" (1:17). Further, when Peter proclaims the Good News to the crowd at Solomon's Colonnade, he instructs the people to repent in order to hasten the coming of Christ (3:19–21). He expresses the same sentiment in a brief sentence in II Peter: "You ought to live holy and godly lives as you look forward to the day of God and speed its coming" (3:11b–12a, NIV).

We admit that the parallels and resemblances we have noted in Peter's

---

21. Consult Max Wilcox, *The Semitisms of Acts* (Oxford: Clarendon, 1965), pp. 151–53.

speeches and letters are only straws in the wind.[22] And we realize that Luke's vocabulary is wider and broader in scope than the words we have listed in the comparisons. Nevertheless, in these speeches Luke appears to represent Peter as we know him from the Gospels and from his epistles.

3. Paul

In his epistles, Paul refers to names and circumstances mentioned by Luke in Acts. Luke describes the first acquaintance Paul had with the tentmaker Aquila and his wife, Priscilla (18:2). And Paul in various letters mentions the names of this faithful couple (Rom. 16:3; I Cor. 16:19; II Tim. 4:19). Luke mentions the names of Crispus, Sosthenes, and Apollos with reference to Corinth (18:8, 17, 24). These names appear frequently in Paul's epistles.[23]

In Acts, Luke reports how Paul chose Silas and Timothy to accompany him as fellow workers (15:40; 16:1–3). In his letters to the churches, Paul recognizes them as preachers of the gospel message (II Cor. 1:19; I Thess. 1:1; II Thess. 1:1). Some of the other names that occur in both Acts and Paul's epistles are Barnabas, James, Mark, Tychicus, Aristarchus, and Trophimus.

Furthermore, Paul reminds Timothy of the things that happened to him in Pisidian Antioch, Iconium, and Lystra (II Tim. 3:11)—the persecutions and stoning Paul had to endure in these places (Acts 13:14, 50–51; 14:4–6, 19; see also II Cor. 11:25). And in his letter to the Thessalonians, Paul pointedly refers to the persecution the believers had to endure from their own countrymen who were incited by local Jews. These Jews were successful in driving Paul from the city of Thessalonica and in thwarting his effort to bring the message of salvation to the Gentiles (I Thess. 2:14–16; and see Acts 17:1–9). We conclude from this brief survey that there are connecting links between the reports in Acts and the cross-references to Paul's epistles. Paul, then, corroborates the historical evidence Luke presents in Acts.

In the sermons and speeches of Paul, aspects of his epistolary teaching are discernible. When Paul preached in the synagogue of Pisidian Antioch, he ended his sermon by mentioning the doctrine of justification: "Everyone who believes in [Jesus] is justified from all things from which you could not be justified through the law of Moses" (13:39). Paul expresses the doctrine of justification in his epistles to the Romans, the Galatians, and the Ephesians.[24] This fundamental tenet he taught both in sermons and in letters.

---

22. Cadbury expresses skepticism in regard to these parallels. "The Speeches in Acts," *Beginnings*, vol. 5, p. 413.

23. I Cor. 1:1, 12, 14; 3:4, 5, 6, 22; 4:6; 16:12; Titus 3:13.

24. Rom. 3:20–21, 28; Gal. 3:16; Eph. 2:9. Rejecting that Luke wrote Acts, Jürgen Roloff says that in general the speeches which the writer places on the lips of Paul have nothing in common with the Pauline theology and characteristics known from his epistles. *Die Apostelgeschichte*, Das Neue Testament Deutsch series, vol. 5 (Göttingen: Vandenhoeck und Ruprecht, 1981), p. 3. But see Hemer, *Book of Acts*, p. 426.

Incidentally, the sermon Paul preached in Pisidian Antioch apparently served as a pattern for other places where Paul taught the gospel but for which Luke has not recorded any sermon summaries.

Paul's farewell address to the Ephesian elders on the beach at Miletus has a number of phrases that occur also in his epistles. These are a few illustrations:

serving the Lord with all humility [20:19]	serving the Lord [Rom. 12:11] with all humility [Eph. 4:2]
that I may finish the race [20:24]	I have finished the race [II Tim. 4:7]
complete the task I received from the Lord [20:24]	complete the task you received in the Lord [Col. 4:17]

Luke presents a number of sermons and speeches of Paul, but he shows no knowledge of the Pauline epistles. He reports nowhere in his historical survey that Paul wrote letters to churches. Nevertheless, we assume that Luke was acquainted with the existence and influence of these writings in the church. How do we explain this peculiar phenomenon? The answer must be sought in the respective purposes of Paul and Luke. Paul wrote theological and pastoral epistles to correct, rebuke, exhort, and teach. Usually his letters originated because of controversies or questions within the churches. Luke's purpose in Acts, however, is different. He is writing Acts to present a history of the birth, development, and growth of the church. Without Acts there would have been a chasm in the New Testament canon; hence, Acts is the bridge between the four Gospels and the epistles of Paul, Peter, John, James, Jude, and the Epistle to the Hebrews. (Revelation serves as the capstone of Scripture.) Because of his purpose to present the history of the early church, Luke circumvents the theological epistles of Paul and provides a chronological review of the apostle's ministry.

4. Stephen

The major speech in Acts is the one Stephen delivered before the members of the Sanhedrin (7:2–53). In this speech, Stephen traces the history of the people of Israel from the time of Abraham to that of Solomon's temple. But the speech is much more than a chronicle of historical events. Stephen reveals that he, like the writer of the Epistle to the Hebrews, is an expert theologian, thoroughly acquainted with the Scriptures, and knowledgeable in drawing implicit conclusions. Stephen shows that God is not bound by an earthly temple built by human hands: God revealed himself to Abraham in Mesopotamia, to Joseph in Egypt, and to Moses in the flames of the burning bush. Stephen proves that the Jews are unable to confine God's dwelling place to the temple in Jerusalem.

In his speech, Stephen develops the theological themes of God, worship, the law, the covenant, and the person and message of the Messiah. Through the work of the Messiah, the house of Israel is able to worship God in truth and justice. Stephen avoids mentioning the name of Jesus, but teaches that God has raised up a Savior for the house of Israel.

We are unable to ascertain from whom Luke received the substance of Stephen's speech. We surmise that Luke gained access to the speech that Stephen delivered before the Sanhedrin from Paul and those members of the Sanhedrin who became Christians. The speech came to Luke's attention through a fixed tradition in either oral or written form. With reference to Acts 7, a study of word choice, references to the temple and to Moses, the absence of typical Lucan constructions—all these facts indicate that Stephen's speech did not originate in the mind of Luke.

Thus, the words *promise* and *affliction* have their own significance in the context of Acts 7 and do not correspond to their usages in the rest of Acts. Next, Stephen's manner of speaking about Moses and the temple is confined to this particular discourse. Luke writes nowhere else in Acts in a similar manner. And last, in Stephen's speech are at least twenty-three words that do not occur again either in Acts or in the other books of the New Testament; also, numerous literary forms, peculiar to both the Gospel of Luke and Acts, are absent from Stephen's speech.[25] We cannot assume that Luke has presented a verbatim account of Stephen's speech, but we confidently assert that he allows the original speaker, Stephen, to be heard in words and concepts that belong to him, the first Christian martyr.

We infer that as a faithful historian Luke has incorporated the discourse of Stephen at this juncture of Acts to prepare the reader for the persecution subsequent to Stephen's death and for the extension of the church beyond the confines of Jerusalem. It was Stephen, and not Luke, who provided the impetus to further the church's development. Luke, therefore, is reporting factual information based on historical events.[26] He is a historian who, in the manner of Thucydides, reports as closely as possible the sense of what the speakers actually said.

D. Historicity

In his Gospel, Luke provides a few time references to demonstrate that his Gospel message is founded on historical fact:

In the days of Herod king of Judea [1:5]

In those days, a decree went out from Caesar Augustus [2:1]

---

25. Martin H. Scharlemann, "Stephen's Speech: A Lucan Creation?" *ConcJourn* 4 (1978): 57. See also A. F. J. Klijn, "Stephen's Speech—Acts VII. 2–53," *NTS* 4 (1957–58): 25–31; L. W. Barnard, "Saint Stephen and Early Alexandrian Christianity," *NTS* 7 (1960–61): 31.
26. Compare Martin H. Scharlemann, *Stephen: A Singular Saint,* Analecta Biblica 34 (Rome: Biblical Institute, 1968), pp. 52–56; John J. Kilgallen, *The Stephen Speech. A Literary and Redactional Study of Acts 7, 2–53,* Analecta Biblica 67 (Rome: Biblical Institute, 1976), p. 113.

Introduction

> And in the fifteenth year of the reign of Tiberius Caesar, when Pontius
> Pilate was governor of Judea, Herod tetrarch of Galilee, his brother
> Philip tetrarch of Iturea and Traconitis, and Lysanias tetrarch of Abi-
> lene [3:1]

Luke's history is devoid of any exact dates. Nevertheless, historical precision is more pronounced implicitly in Acts than in Luke's Gospel. We are
able to ascertain some time references in Acts. The book itself appears to be
written as a chronology of events that, with few exceptions, are listed in
sequential order.

1. Ascension and Pentecost

From historical and archaeological sources we glean sufficient information concerning the life of Paul to enable us to construct a chronology for
Acts. However, scholars differ in their assessment of these dates and frequently show little unanimity. We begin with the opening verses of Acts,
which relate Jesus' appearances during the forty-day period before his
ascension. The resurrection, appearances, and ascension of Jesus presumably took place in the spring of A.D. 30. Subsequently, the outpouring of the
Holy Spirit at Pentecost occurred ten days after Jesus' ascension.

2. Paul in Damascus

The first few chapters of Acts provide no references to events that point
to verifiable dates. Not until Paul's escape over the city walls of Damascus
do we gather tentative chronological evidence (9:23–25; II Cor. 11:32–33).
Aretas IV, king of the Nabataeans, ruled Damascus for a few years from
A.D. 37 to 40; "whether he seized it by force or obtained it by imperial
favor" remains a question.[27] Nevertheless, no Roman imperial coins of the
era of Caligula (A.D. 37–41) and Claudius (A.D. 41–54) have been found in
Damascus. This fact seems to suggest that Damascus was ruled by the
Nabataeans beginning in A.D. 37 and, consequently, we surmise that Paul
escaped from Damascus in that year.

3. The Famine in Jerusalem

In Acts 11:27–28, Luke records a prophecy from Agabus that "there
would be a severe famine all over the Roman world." And he asserts that
"this happened during the reign of [Emperor] Claudius." The expression
all over the Roman world ought not to be taken literally, for then Antioch,
which sent aid to Jerusalem (11:29), would also have been stricken by that
famine. However, in the New Testament the Greek term *oikoumenē* (the
inhabited world) is often used as a mere generalization. (For example, Paul

---

27. Emil Schürer, *The History of the Jewish People in the Age of Jesus Christ (175 B.C.–A.D. 135)*,
rev. and ed. Geza Vermes and Fergus Millar, 3 vols. (Edinburgh: Clark, 1973–87), vol. 2, pp.
129–30.

and Silas are accused of "causing trouble all over the world" [17:6] when, in fact, they are preaching the gospel in Macedonia.) Therefore, we presume that Luke knew that the effects of the famine were more severe in one place than another.[28]

The information we glean from writers in the first few centuries of the Christian era seems to suggest that the famine took place in the second half of the fifth decade, A.D. 46. In that year, Queen Mother Helena from Adiabene (a state east of the Tigris River in ancient Assyria) and her son, King Izates, both converts to Judaism, came to Jerusalem. When they became aware of a severe famine in that city, they bought grain from Egypt and figs from Cyprus for the famine-stricken people of Jerusalem.[29] Likewise, the Christians in Antioch extended their loving concern to fellow believers of the mother church in Jerusalem by commissioning Barnabas and Saul (Paul) to bring them relief (11:29–30).

4. Peter's Release

Luke reports this incident in the context of the founding and development of the Antiochean church. Next, he continues his chronological sequence and relates the demise of the apostle James (12:2), the imprisonment and release of Peter (12:3–17), and the death of King Herod Agrippa I (12:21–23).

Herod Agrippa I spent some time in Rome, where he eventually befriended Gaius Caligula, who after the death of Tiberias in A.D. 37 became emperor. Caligula gave him the tetrarchies of Iturea, Traconitis, and Abilene: an area east and north of Galilee.[30] He also conferred on Agrippa the right to call himself king. Falsely accusing his uncle Antipas of conspiracy before the emperor, Agrippa contrived his uncle's downfall and obtained Antipas's tetrarchy of Galilee and Perea in A.D. 39.[31] When Emperor Caligula was assassinated in A.D. 41, Agrippa was in Rome, befriended Claudius the new emperor, and received from him the rule over Judea and Samaria. The territory of Agrippa was as large as that of his late grandfather Herod the Great.[32]

In Jerusalem, Agrippa killed James and then arrested Peter with the intention of killing him after the Passover (12:2–4). After Peter's release

---

28. Conzelmann opines that "Luke did not note the inconsistency that Antioch would also have been involved in such a famine." *Acts of the Apostles*, p. 90 n. 7. For a similar comment, see Gerd Luedemann, *Paul, Apostle to the Gentiles: Studies in Chronology*, trans. F. Stanley Jones (Philadelphia: Fortress, 1984), p. 11.

29. See especially Josephus *Antiquities* 3.15.3 [320]; 20.2.5 [51–52]; 20.5.2 [101]; and consult Suetonius *Claudius* 18.2; Tacitus *Annals* 12.43; Dio Cassius *Roman History* 60.11; Eusebius *Ecclesiastical History* 2.8.

30. Josephus *War* 2.9.6 [181]; *Antiquities* 18.6.10 [237].

31. Josephus *War* 2.9.6 [181–83]; *Antiquities* 18.7.1–2 [240–56].

32. Josephus *War* 2.11.5 [214–15]; *Antiquities* 19.5.1 [274–75] and 19.8.2 [351].

from prison, Agrippa left for Caesarea and there faced a delegation from Tyre and Sidon. This delegation came to Caesarea to settle a dispute with Agrippa; they desired to seek reconciliation because they depended on Agrippa to sell them grain (12:20). Luke writes that "on the appointed day Herod wore his royal robe and sat on his throne" (12:21). And Josephus, whose account of this event corresponds closely with that in Acts, says:

> After the completion of the third year of his reign over the whole of Judaea [A.D. 44], Agrippa came to the city of Caesarea, which had previously been called Strato's Tower. Here he celebrated spectacles in honour of Caesar, knowing that these had been instituted as a kind of festival on behalf of Caesar's well-being.[33]

These games were held either on March 5 (the anniversary of the city of Caesarea) or on the first of August (known as the emperor's month).[34] Here the king was acclaimed as a god and not as a man. And as a consequence, divine justice caused his sudden death.

Of these two dates (March 5 or August 1), the second is preferred for two reasons. First, Agrippa deliberately attacked two of God's servants by killing James and imprisoning Peter. When the guards were unable to explain Peter's escape, Agrippa meted out swift judgment and had them killed (12:19). Besides, when the king arrived in Caesarea, he incurred God's wrath, met swift judgment, and died a painful death. Second, the delegation from Tyre and Sidon sought peace in order to buy grain. August was the time when grain purchases would be made after the wheat harvest came to an end in June and July.

We conclude that Peter was released from prison during the Passover feast (April) of A.D. 44, and that Agrippa died in August of that same year. Should we set the date for the games in Caesarea five months earlier on March 5, we would have to say that Peter's imprisonment and release occurred in the spring of A.D. 43.[35]

5. First Missionary Journey

After the interlude of Peter's escape from prison and Agrippa's death, Luke mentions the return of Barnabas and Saul (Paul) to Antioch (12:25). The Antiochean church ordained these men as missionaries to the Gentiles and sent them on their way to Cyprus. There they met the proconsul Sergius Paulus, who became a Christian (13:7, 12). Archaeological evidence, discovered at Kythraia in north Cyprus, points to Quintus Sergius

---

33. Josephus *Antiquities* 19.8.2 [343] (LCL). Compare *War* 2.11.6 [219].

34. Consult Lake, "The Chronology of Acts," *Beginnings*, vol. 5, p. 452. See also Suetonius *Claudius* 2.

35. Consult F. F. Bruce, "Chronological Questions," *BJRUL* 68 (1985–86): 277. Compare F. F. Bruce, *The Book of the Acts*, rev. ed., New International Commentary on the New Testament series (Grand Rapids: Eerdmans, 1988), pp. 241–42.

Paulus, who was proconsul during the reign of Claudius (A.D. 41–54). Because proconsuls usually served only one year in a certain area, this particular person could have held office in A.D. 46 at the beginning of the first missionary journey.

6. Second Missionary Journey

Paul's second journey must be viewed in the light of two incidents: the expulsion of the Jews from Rome by Claudius (18:2), and Paul's appearance before the judgment seat of the proconsul Gallio (18:12).

Population estimates of Jews dwelling in Rome during the middle of the first century are placed at least at forty thousand. When Christians began to acquaint the Jewish people in Rome with the message of the gospel, reaction set in and tumults broke out in the streets. Suetonius, a Roman historiographer, relates that Claudius "expelled the Jews because they were continually rioting at the instigation of Chrestus."[36] Unfamiliar with the Greek name *Christos,* this writer misspelled it; and being unfamiliar with Christianity, he thought that "Chrestus" himself led the riots.

Suetonius gives no date of this incident. Orosius, a writer in the fifth century, states that the expulsion occurred in the ninth year of Claudius's reign.[37] If Orosius is correct, Claudius's ninth year is A.D. 49. This date fits the chronology of Paul's second missionary journey. Orosius records that he received his information from Josephus, but in the extant writings of Josephus this incident is not reported. Although the information from Orosius cannot be verified, the date itself is credible in view of Paul's arrival in Corinth about A.D. 50.[38]

While Paul stayed in Corinth, "the Jews rose up together against Paul and brought him before the judgment seat" of Gallio, the proconsul (18:12). Paul had met fierce opposition from the Jews who refused him entrance to the local synagogue. With a following of Corinthians, Paul founded a church and stayed in the city a year and a half. During this time, Gallio came to Achaia as proconsul. Inscriptions reveal that he served in that capacity in A.D. 51–52, possibly from July of 51 to June of 52. "It is a near certainty, then, that Paul's eighteen months in Corinth lasted from the Fall of A.D. 50 to the Spring or early Summer of 52 (according to the Western text of Acts 18:2 he attended a festival in Jerusalem soon after leaving Corinth.")[39]

---

36. *Judaeos impulsore Chresto assidue tumultuantes expulit;* Suetonius *Claudius* 25.4. See also Dio Cassius *Roman History* 60.6.6.

37. Paulus Orosius, *The Seven Books of History Against the Pagans,* Fathers of the Church series, trans. Roy J. Deferrari (Washington, D.C.: Catholic University Press, 1964), p. 297.

38. Luedemann asserts that Claudius's edict was issued in A.D. 41; *Paul, Apostle to the Gentiles,* p. 170. But E. M. Smallwood, *The Jews under Roman Rule* (Leiden: Brill, 1976), pp. 210–16, suggests that Claudius addressed the issue twice: in 41 and 49.

39. Bruce, "Chronological Questions," p. 283. Compare Colin J. Hemer, "Observations on Pauline Chronology," in *Pauline Studies,* ed. Donald A. Hagner and Murray J. Harris (Exeter: Paternoster; Grand Rapids: Eerdmans, 1980), pp. 6–9.

7. Paul's Imprisonment

At Paul's return to Jerusalem on concluding his third missionary journey, he was imprisoned for two years in Caesarea (24:27). Governor Felix, married to the Jewess Drusilla, frequently talked to Paul but left him in prison when Felix was succeeded by Governor Festus.

Josephus records interesting details about Drusilla. She was born in Rome in A.D. 38, the third child and younger daughter of Herod Agrippa I. When Agrippa died in A.D. 44, the six-year-old Drusilla had already been promised in marriage to Epiphanes, the son of Antiochus, king of Commagene.[40] Since Epiphanes refused to submit to circumcision and thus rejected the marriage, Drusilla was given in marriage by her brother Agrippa II to Azizus, king of Emesa in northern Syria.[41] This occurred when she was fourteen years old. The following year, Governor Felix persuaded her to leave her husband and become his wife. Suetonius notes that Drusilla became Felix's third wife.[42] Felix and Drusilla had one son, Agrippa, who died when Vesuvius erupted in A.D. 79. We infer that Paul spoke to the governor and his wife about Jesus Christ (presumably in the second half of the sixth decade, certainly after A.D. 54).

Felix became procurator of Judea in A.D. 52, after Claudius had deposed Ventidius Cumanus. Josephus reports that this took place in the twelfth year of Claudius's reign.[43] But how long was Felix in office? Guided by a comment of Tacitus (that Pallas, the influential brother and protector of Felix at Nero's court, fell from grace in A.D. 55),[44] some scholars contend that Felix's governorship lasted from 52 to 55 and that the downfall of Pallas caused Felix's recall to Rome (24:27).[45] But in light of a number of factors we favor a longer term of office. First, in his speech before Felix, the lawyer Tertullus praises the governor for giving the Jews "lasting peace" (24:2). Paul, in a similar vein, notes that Felix had been governor for "a number of years" (24:10). Next, Felix kept Paul for two years in the Caesarean prison. We can hardly refer to a three-year term as a long period that produced lasting peace, especially not when Paul's initial trial before Felix was slated at the beginning of Paul's imprisonment. Last, the removal of Pallas need not be understood as a cessation of his influence at Nero's court. Pallas wielded considerable influence because of his wealth, which Nero eventually appropriated in A.D. 62 when he killed Pallas.[46]

We are unable to pinpoint the date of Felix's recall to Rome and the

---

40. Josephus *Antiquities* 19.9.1 [354–55].
41. Josephus *Antiquities* 20.7.1 [137–39].
42. Suetonius *Claudius* 28.
43. Josephus *Antiquities* 20.7.1 [137]; compare Tacitus *Annals* 12.54.7.
44. Tacitus *Annals* 13.14.1.
45. Haenchen, *Acts*, p. 71; Conzelmann, *Acts of the Apostles*, pp. 194–95.
46. Tacitus *Annals* 14.65.1.

arrival of Porcius Festus in Caesarea (25:1). But two indications suggest a date of A.D. 59 or 60. First, coins marking the fifth year of Nero's reign (A.D. 58/59) began to circulate in Judea. We surmise that the introduction of these coins resulted from the arrival of the newly appointed Governor Festus.[47] Second, Felix assumed office in A.D. 52 and Festus's successor, Albinus, became governor in A.D. 62. Therefore, the governorships of both Felix and Festus fill a ten-year period. Josephus reports a number of events relating to Felix but hardly any referring to Festus. He leaves the unmistakable impression that Festus's term in office was short, perhaps three years, because Festus died in office.[48]

Granted that Josephus furnishes no time references, we are inclined to say that Felix's term as governor lasted seven years and that of Festus three years. To be precise, Festus became procurator in A.D. 59.[49] By contrast, if Felix were recalled by Nero to Rome in the summer of A.D. 55 within nine months after Nero became emperor, the numerous incidents that Josephus records of Nero's administration would have to be crowded into this nine-month period.[50] And that seems unlikely. Hence, we opt for an seven-year span of Felix's rule.

Within weeks of Festus's arrival in Caesarea, the new governor sought the advice of Agrippa II in regard to Paul the prisoner (25:1, 6, 13–22), arranged passage for Paul aboard a ship, and sent him to Rome. Paul was shipwrecked on the island of Malta in October of 59 and in February of 60 continued his trip to Rome. There, as a prisoner, he spent two years in his own rented house and was released in A.D. 62.

8. Chronology

On the basis of a few fixed dates and a number of likely hypotheses I venture to draw up the following chronological list:

Event	Date
Birth of Paul	A.D. 5
Pentecost	30
Paul's conversion	35
Escape from Damascus	37
Death of Agrippa I	44
Famine relief for Jerusalem	46

47. Consult Smallwood, *The Jews under Roman Rule*, p. 269 n. 40.
48. Josephus *War* 2.12.8–13.1 [247–71]; *Antiquities* 20.8.9–11 [182–96]. Consult Robert Jewett, *A Chronology of Paul's Life* (Philadelphia: Fortress, 1979), pp. 43–44.
49. Hemer, *Book of Acts*, p. 171. Schürer opts for A.D. 60. *History of the Jewish People*, vol. 1, p. 465 n. 42.
50. Josephus *War* 2.13.1–7 [250–70]; *Antiquities* 20.8.1–8 [148–81].

First missionary journey	46–48
Jerusalem Council	49
Jews expelled from Rome	49
Second missionary journey	50–52
Third missionary journey	52–55
Paul in Macedonia	56–57
Arrest and imprisonment	57–59
Voyage and shipwreck	59
House arrest in Rome	60–62
To Spain, Crete, Macedonia	63–67
Arrest and imprisonment	67
Death of Paul	67 or 68

E. Author, Date, and Place

1. Who Wrote Acts?

The early church of the first and most of the second century is silent on the authorship of Acts. In A.D. 175, the Muratorian Canon records these words: "However, the Acts of all the Apostles were written in one volume. Luke addresses it to the most excellent Theophilus." From this era we have the anti-Marcionite prologue to Luke, which notes that Luke himself wrote the Acts of the Apostles. Around A.D. 185 Irenaeus speaks in similar terms. And at the beginning of the third century, Clement of Alexandria, Origen, and Tertullian declare that Luke is the author of both the Gospel and Acts. The external evidence, accordingly, is unanimous and strong in declaring Luke the author of Acts.

As is evident from the anti-Marcionite prologue, which was written between A.D. 160 and 180, tradition reveals certain aspects of Luke's life:

> Luke is a Syrian, a native of Antioch, by profession a physician. He was a disciple of the apostles and afterwards accompanied Paul until the martyrdom of Paul. He served the Lord without distraction, without a wife, without children, and at the age of eighty-four he fell asleep in Boeotia, full of the Holy Spirit.

Paul also notes that Luke was a physician by profession (Col. 4:14). From an analysis of Luke's vocabulary in both the Gospel and Acts, we learn that the writer could have been a medical doctor who in his writings reflects his profession.[51] Both Eusebius and Jerome testify that Luke hailed from Antioch. In Acts, the writer seems to have a proclivity for mentioning Antioch.

---

51. Refer to H. J. Cadbury, *The Style and Literary Method of Luke*, 2 vols. (Cambridge: Harvard University Press, 1919–20).

Out of the fifteen times that Antioch in Syria is mentioned in the New Testament, fourteen instances occur in Acts.[52] For Luke, Antioch is important because here the church had the vision to send forth missionaries to the Greco-Roman world. If he resided in Antioch, Luke would have met Barnabas (11:22), Paul (11:26), and Peter (Gal. 2:11). And in this city he undoubtedly heard the gospel message, was converted, and became a disciple of the apostles.

Luke's Gospel and Acts are closely related because of the dedication of these two books to Theophilus (Luke 1:3; Acts 1:1). Incidentally, the address *most excellent Theophilus* seems to imply that Theophilus belonged to a high-ranking social class (compare 23:26; 24:3; 26:25). Also, the introductory verse of Acts (1:1) reveals that it is the second volume Luke has written and a continuation of the first volume (the Gospel).

The name *Luke,* however, is absent from both his Gospel and Acts. The Gospel became known as "the Gospel according to Luke," yet the major manuscripts omit the name of Luke in the title of Acts. This is no obstacle if we consider that none of the evangelists mentions his own name in the Gospel account he wrote.

Luke became a follower of Paul, as we are able to ascertain from the "we" passages in the second part of Acts (16:10–17; 20:5–21:18; 27:1–28:16). He was with Paul on the second missionary journey, accompanied him from Macedonia to Jerusalem at the conclusion of the third missionary journey, apparently stayed in Judea and Caesarea while Paul was in prison, and finally traveled with Paul to Rome. In his epistles, Paul himself testifies to the fact that Luke was his companion and fellow worker (Col. 4:14; II Tim. 4:11; Philem. 24).

Paul's helpers included Timothy, Silas, Titus, Demas, Crescens, and Luke, but as the author of Acts we have to rule out everyone except Luke. Crescens is relatively unknown (II Tim. 4:10); Demas was Paul's fellow worker (Col. 4:14; Philem. 24) but later deserted him (II Tim. 4:10). Although Titus accompanied Paul and Barnabas to Jerusalem and worked in the churches of Corinth, Crete, and Dalmatia, he appears not to have been one of Paul's companions whom the apostle mentions in the greetings of his epistles. The names of Silas and Timothy appear in the "we" passages of Acts, but both men are referred to in the third person. By process of elimination, we arrive at the conclusion that Luke is the most likely person to have composed the books attributed to him.

2. When Was Acts Written?

The earliest possible date for the composition of Acts is A.D. 62, which is the year of Paul's release from Roman imprisonment and is the last time reference ("two full years" [28:30]) in Acts. A terminal date for the writing

---

52. 6:5; 11:19, 20, 22, 26 [twice], 27; 13:1; 14:26; 15:22, 23, 30, 35; 18:22.

of this book is A.D. 96, because Clement of Rome was acquainted with Acts. The composition date, therefore, lies in that thirty-four-year period.[53]

Scholars who have adopted the late-date theory advance three points. First, they call attention to Luke 19:43–44 and 21:20–24, where the writer is describing the fall and destruction of Jerusalem in A.D. 70. This means that the composition of the sequence Luke-Acts must be placed after the devastation of Jerusalem. Next, the Gospel of Mark, written about A.D. 65, is basic to Luke's Gospel. Sequentially, then, Luke's Gospel and Acts must have been composed after Mark's Gospel appeared, and thus originated in the seventies or eighties. And last, Luke relied on the writings of the Jewish historian Josephus, who completed the *Jewish War* in the early seventies and his *Antiquities* around A.D. 93.

The objections to a date after A.D. 70 are numerous and weighty and seriously undermine the late-date theory. We list and discuss these objections seriatim.

1. Proportionally in Acts, Luke devotes more space to Paul than to any other person. This is understandable because he became Paul's travel companion and fellow worker. Yet Luke breaks off his chronology of Paul's life with the message that the apostle spent two years under house arrest in Rome (28:30). He reports nothing about Paul's continued journeys, his second arrest and imprisonment in Rome (where Luke was present [II Tim. 4:11]), and Paul's death.

The argument that Luke intended to write a third volume to complete a trilogy is speculation and has no support in antiquity and history. If, according to the pastoral Epistles, Paul visited Ephesus after his Roman imprisonment (I Tim. 3:14), Luke would not have described Paul's emotional parting from the Ephesian elders (20:25, 38) without some additional clarification.[54] And if indeed Paul visited Spain (Rom. 15:24, 28), as Clement of Rome seems to assert when he writes that Paul "reached the limits of the West,"[55] Luke undoubtedly would have noted this in the conclusion of Acts to show that Jesus' command (to bear his witness to the ends of the earth) had been fulfilled. If Luke was present with Paul in prison, we would expect that he also knew of Paul's death. But Luke reports nothing about the apostle's arrest, imprisonment, and execution.

2. The last word (in the Greek) in the Book of Acts is "unhindered."

---

53. J. C. O'Neill puts the date of composition well into the second century, but this view lacks support. *The Theology of Acts in its Historical Setting* (London: SPCK, 1970), pp. 21, 26.

54. Conzelmann tries to solve this problem by stating that "the wording [of Acts 20:25] excludes the possibility that [Paul] was set free from Roman imprisonment (and succeeded in making another visit to the East). This also agrees with the Pastorals, which know only *one* imprisonment of Paul"; *Acts of the Apostles*, p. 174. But Eusebius writes that Paul was released after his first Roman imprisonment. Refer to *Ecclesiastical History* 2.22.2–3.

55. I Clem. 5.7 (LCL). See also the Muratorian Canon, lines 34–39.

That is, in Rome Paul preached the gospel of God's kingdom and the message of Jesus Christ "boldly and unhindered" (28:31). By implication, Luke tells the reader that the Roman government did not prohibit the proclamation of the gospel and the founding of the church. Luke ends his second volume on a joyful note: the state does not object to the work of the church. He reflects the social and political conditions of Rome at the time of Paul's release. While Paul was in Roman custody, Roman officials protected him from physical harm (21:30–36). They gave him opportunity to defend himself and allowed him to explain the gospel message (22:1–21). They were kindly disposed to Paul during the voyage to Rome (27:43) and his house arrest in the imperial city (28:30–31). Indeed, Rome did not hinder the progress of the gospel in those years. This changed when Nero began to persecute the Christians after Rome was burned in A.D. 64.

If Luke had written Acts in the seventies, he would have done violence to his sense of historical integrity by not reflecting these cruel persecutions instigated by Nero. "For any Christian to write, thereafter, with the easy optimism of Acts 28 would require an almost subhuman obtuseness."[56]

3. The Book of Acts reflects a theology that is reminiscent of the first three decades after Pentecost. Consider the following points: First, Luke identifies Jesus as Jesus of Nazareth (3:6; 4:10; 6:14; 10:38–40; 22:8; 26:9), and he calls converts "disciples" in Jerusalem, Damascus, Joppa, Antioch, Lystra, and Ephesus. Next, the church itself consisted of numerous congregations that met in individual homes. "Each group came to be known as an *ekklesia* in a local area."[57] Last, the content of Acts does not exhibit any theological and ecclesiastical concerns that pertained to the church of the last decades of the first century.

4. The historical accounts of Acts at times have a parallel in the works of Josephus. But this fact does not signify that Luke depended on Josephus to furnish him with historical details. On the contrary, a comparison of parallels from Luke and Josephus clearly indicates that the two writers relied on independent traditions. For instance, both authors have a reference to the Egyptian revolutionary who led his followers into the desert. Luke writes that there were four thousand terrorists (21:38), but Josephus relates that the Egyptian had an army of thirty thousand men of whom four hundred were killed and two hundred were taken prisoner. In another report he writes that most of the Egyptian's force were killed or imprisoned.[58] With respect to these numbers, Josephus's historical accuracy is definitely called into question. Conclusively, a careful analysis of Josephus's writings shows that Luke did not depend on Josephus for historical accounts.

---

56. Pierson Parker, "The 'Former Treatise' and the Date of Acts," *JBL* 84 (1965): 53.

57. Donald Guthrie, *New Testament Theology* (Downers Grove: Inter-Varsity, 1981), p. 741.

58. Josephus *War* 2.13.5 [261–63]; *Antiquities* 20.8.6 [169–71].

5. If Luke wrote his Gospel after A.D. 70, then his words concerning the destruction of Jerusalem (Luke 19:43–44; 21:20–24) are descriptive history. If we acknowledge that Luke received from tradition (Luke 1:2) the words of Jesus' prophecy about Jerusalem and if we assume that he knew their fulfillment, Luke could have composed his books after Jerusalem's ruin. But if this assumption is true, we would have expected striking details concerning the historic event of Jerusalem's destruction.

Luke's writings on this point are devoid of any hint that the author is presenting history instead of prophecy. If we believe that Jesus spoke words of genuine prophecy concerning Jerusalem some forty years before its destruction, we are able to date the composition of both the Gospel and Acts before A.D. 70.

If scholars were able to express genuine unanimity on ascribing exact dates to the composition of the other synoptic Gospels, they would have no difficulty assigning a date to Luke's Gospel and Acts. Because of this lack of consensus, we submit that an early date for Luke's writings is plausible. We accept as genuine prophecy the words recorded in the discourse on the destruction of Jerusalem, as spoken by Jesus himself (Matt. 24; Mark 13; Luke 19:41–44; 21:5–36). And for the composition of Acts, we suggest a date prior to July 19, A.D. 64, when Rome was burned and the Neronian persecutions against the Christians began. A date later than the summer of 64 would have caused Luke to alter the ending of Acts.

3. Where Was Acts Written?

We have no indication where Luke composed Acts. Had he written parts of it already before he accompanied Paul on his voyage to Rome? Was he able to keep his documents safe during the shipwreck at Malta? Did he complete the book in Rome during the two years of Paul's house arrest? We can multiply the questions but cannot give definitive answers. Some scholars point to Achaia as a possible place of composition, others to Rome.

F. Theology

Even though Luke served Paul as his faithful companion, in his writings Luke shows no knowledge at all of the epistles Paul sent to various churches and individuals. By the time Luke wrote the Book of Acts, many of Paul's letters were composed and had begun to circulate in the early church. Paul wrote his epistles to the Galatians and to the Thessalonians during his second missionary journey, and he composed his major epistles (I and II Corinthians and Romans) near the end of his third missionary journey. He drafted the so-called prison Epistles (Colossians, Philemon, Ephesians, and Philippians) while he was under house arrest in Rome. Paul urged the recipients of these epistles to have them read in other churches (see Col. 4:16; I Thess. 5:27). Luke, then, must have known Paul's epistles. But in Acts, Luke's purpose is to write as a historian and not as a theologian. That

24

does not mean, however, that there is no theology in this history book. Rather, we find a number of theological subjects that are featured in the various speeches Luke has recorded.

1. God in Word and Deed

At Pentecost, Peter stresses the work of God in Jesus Christ. God accredited Jesus of Nazareth, who was put to death according to God's set purpose and foreknowledge, yet God raised him from the dead, exalted him to a place of honor in heaven, and made Jesus both Lord and Christ (2:22–24, 32–36). At Solomon's Colonnade, Peter affirms that the God of the patriarchs had glorified Jesus and raised him to life (3:13–15). Jesus came, says Peter, as a fulfillment of the promise that God would raise up a prophet like Moses (3:22). Peter and the other apostles repeat these theological motifs before the members of the Sanhedrin (4:10; 5:30–32).

In the house of Cornelius, Peter testified that God commissioned him to go to a Gentile (10:28). He assured his audience that God shows no favoritism, for he anointed Jesus with the Holy Spirit, raised him from the dead, caused him to be seen by witnesses whom God had chosen, and appointed him to be judge of the living and the dead (10:34–42; see 15:7–10).

In his sermon delivered in the Jewish synagogue of Pisidian Antioch, Paul echoed the themes of God's electing grace, promise, and purpose (13:17–37). Paul's Areopagus address focuses on God the Creator, the Designer, and the Judge in Christ (17:24–31). And his farewell address to the Ephesian elders has references to both God's purpose and church (20:27–28).

Concerning God's work of saving sinful man, Leon Morris observes, "One of the things Luke is making abundantly clear is that this is not to be regarded as just another human movement. We are not to think that some garrulous Galileans managed to persuade people to throw in their lot with them. Rather there was a great divine act: *God* sent Jesus to be Savior. We do not understand this movement unless we see that God is in it."[59] God saves a person according to his predestined plan. Thus, the Gentiles whom God in eternity had appointed for eternal life gladly received the gospel from Paul and Barnabas and believed (13:48). When Paul shook the dust off his clothes in protest to the Jews and was ready to leave Corinth, the Lord told him to stay there because he had many people in that city (18:6–10). At that time, these people had not yet received the gift of salvation even though they belonged to God.

Throughout Acts, Luke repeatedly uses the expressions *the word of God* (thirteen times), *the word of the Lord* (ten times), or simply *the word* (thirteen times). Twice Luke uses the phrase *the word of his grace*, once the descriptive

---

59. Leon Morris, *New Testament Theology* (Grand Rapids: Zondervan, Academie Books, 1986), p. 150.

term *the word of this salvation,* and once *the word of the gospel.* In total, there are forty references to God's Word.[60] These terms denote God's revelation made fully known in his Son Jesus Christ. The terms, then, refer to Christ's gospel.

Jesus sends his apostles with the same message he himself proclaimed during his earthly ministry. To illustrate, in his Gospel Luke reports that in the evening hours of resurrection day Jesus opened the Scriptures for the disciples. Jesus taught them that everything had to be fulfilled in accordance with what was written about him in the Law of Moses, the Prophets, and the Psalms (Luke 24:44). Jesus referred to the three parts of the Hebrew Scriptures and thus by implication to the entire Old Testament. When Peter delivered his sermons on Pentecost and at Solomon's Colonnade, he likewise quoted from these three parts of God's Word to prove that Jesus indeed had fulfilled the Scriptures.

2. Jesus Christ

In his speeches, Peter alludes to the humanity of Jesus. He portrays him as a man who performed miracles and wonders (2:22) and who was known as Jesus of Nazareth (4:10). Jesus demonstrated the reality of his human body after the resurrection by eating and drinking with the apostles (10:41). Next, Peter expresses Jesus' divinity by calling him the Holy and Righteous One (3:14). This theme occurs also in the speeches of Stephen and Paul respectively (7:52; 17:31; 22:14).[61]

Among the various names for Jesus in Acts are the following designations: "Lord" (1:24; 2:36; 10:36), "Christ" (2:36; 3:20; 5:42; 8:5; 17:3; 18:5), "servant" (3:13, 26; 4:27, 30), "prophet" (3:22), "Prince and Savior" (5:31), "Son of man" (7:56), "Son of God" (9:20) and many others. In general, Luke ascribes names to Jesus in the first half of his book but not in the second. We suggest that, first, these names reflect the Aramaic setting in which they originated; and, second, these names were new to the Gentile audiences that Paul met on his missionary journeys.

According to Luke, the focal point of Jesus' ministry is to bring salvation to his people. In the Gospel Luke describes what Jesus began to do and to teach, and in Acts he continues to relate the work of salvation that Jesus accomplished. By emphasizing the concept *salvation,* Luke depicts Jesus, the giver of salvation, as the central figure in his theology.[62]

3. The Holy Spirit

A prominent motif in Acts is that of the Holy Spirit. Promised by Jesus prior to his ascension, poured out on the day of Pentecost, promised to all the

---

60. Ibid., p. 219.

61. Guthrie, *New Testament Theology,* p. 231. See also F. F. Bruce, "The Theology of Acts," *TSF Bulletin* 10 (1987): 15.

62. I. Howard Marshall, *Luke: Historian and Theologian* (Grand Rapids: Zondervan, 1971), p. 94. Consult Robert H. Smith, "The Theology of Acts," *ConcThMonth* 42 (1971): 531.

people and given as a gift to every one who is baptized, the person and work of the Holy Spirit are evident everywhere in Acts. The Spirit gave believers the ability to speak in other tongues (2:4, 11; 10:46; 19:6). Further, the Spirit filled the believers when they prayed together after the release of Peter and John (4:31). Stephen was full of faith and the Holy Spirit and thus boldly proclaimed the gospel to the Hellenistic Jews in Jerusalem synagogues (6:5, 8–10). The Holy Spirit was poured out on the Samaritans to indicate that the wall of separation between Jewish Christians and Samaritan Christians was effectively removed (8:14–17). The same thing happened to the Gentile audience in the house of Cornelius (10:44). As a consequence, the Jewish believers in Jerusalem had to accept Peter's word that God gave them the same gift as he gave those who in Jerusalem believed in the Lord Jesus Christ (11:17). And last, the Spirit descended on the disciples of John the Baptist in Ephesus so that they, too, became part of the Christian communion (19:1–7).

The Holy Spirit spoke through the prophet Agabus and predicted a severe famine (11:28) and the arrest of Paul (21:10–11). The Spirit appointed Barnabas and Paul to become missionaries to the Greco-Roman world (13:1–2) and directed Paul and his companions to go to Macedonia instead of the province of Asia and Bithynia (16:6–7). The Spirit is identified with the Father (1:4–5) and with Jesus (16:7). Implicitly, Luke teaches the doctrine of the Trinity.

The Spirit also spoke through the Old Testament Scriptures. Peter said that the Scriptures had to be fulfilled, for "through the mouth of David" the Holy Spirit voiced a prophecy that, in effect, pertained to Judas (1:16). Next, note that the prayer of the Jerusalem church reveals the same wording: "You have spoken by the Holy Spirit through the mouth of our father and your servant, David" (4:25). Last, addressing the Jews in Rome, Paul said that the Spirit spoke to the forefathers through the prophet Isaiah (28:25). The presence of the Holy Spirit was evident in the time of the Old Testament saints but also at the time of the Jerusalem Council. In the letter to the Gentile churches, the members of the Council testified that their decision seemed good to the Holy Spirit (15:28). In brief, the Spirit guides and directs the church.

4. The Church

Although the word *ekklēsia* (church) occurs only three times in the four Gospels (Matt. 16:18; 18:17 [twice]), it appears twenty-three times in Acts. Luke uses the word in the singular to express the unity of the body. The plural appears with reference to churches in Syria and Cilicia (15:41) and Paul's visit to the Gentile churches when he delivers the letter from the Jerusalem Council (16:5). For Luke, the Jerusalem church is and remains the mother church that gives leadership and direction to developing daughter churches in Samaria, Caesarea, Antioch, and elsewhere. The Jerusalem church plays a leading part when the Council convenes (15:4, 12, 22). At the conclusion of his third missionary journey, Paul reports to James and the elders of the church in Jerusalem (21:17–19). Luke, then, exhibits an aspect of the centrality of this church.

The basis for the church is the teaching of Jesus' resurrection; the apostles proclaimed this teaching everywhere to both the Jews and the Gentiles. The doctrine of Christ's resurrection became the fundamental tenet of the church. Peter proclaimed it before the multitudes in the temple courts, before the members of the Sanhedrin, and in the house of Cornelius. No other teaching divided the believers from the unbelievers as much as the doctrine of the resurrection. Both Jewish Christians and Gentile Christians joyfully confessed that Jesus died and rose again from the dead, while opponents to the gospel vehemently rejected this teaching. The crucial point in Paul's Areopagus speech came when he introduced the doctrine of the resurrection of the dead (17:32). Some sneered at Paul's teaching while few people accepted it. Later, when Paul addressed both Governor Festus and King Agrippa and mentioned the resurrection of Christ, Festus shouted, "Paul, you are out of your mind. Your great learning is driving you insane" (26:24).

In Acts, fellowship in the church depends on personal faith in Jesus Christ, repentance, remission of sins, baptism, and the indwelling of the Holy Spirit (2:38–39). Church membership comes to expression in being trained in the apostolic teaching, attendance at worship, partaking of communion, and dedication to prayer (2:42). Love for one's neighbor reaches its peak when the members abolish poverty within the fellowship of the church (4:34). Deacons help in distributing food to the needy (6:1–6) and elders tend to the spiritual needs of the church (14:23; 20:28). The apostles spend their time in prayer and in teaching God's Word.

5. Eschatology

Luke's Gospel contains Jesus' discourse on the destruction of Jerusalem and the consummation at the end of cosmic time (Luke 19:42–44; 21:5–36). But in Acts, Luke refrains from referring to the end of time. For him, the progress of the gospel is of supreme importance. True, Luke's description of Jesus' ascension reveals that Jesus will return in the same way in which he left (1:11; compare 3:19–20); and both Peter and Paul call attention to the judgment day (10:42; 17:31). But the historical nature of Acts does not lend itself to the doctrinal issue of Jesus' return, the general resurrection of believers, the day of judgment, the life hereafter, heaven and hell. Luke writes a history of the birth, development, and progress of the New Testament church. In brief, he composes Acts not as a plain history book but as a book that opens theological windows to the future. Luke affirms that Christ's gospel advanced from Jerusalem via Antioch to Rome. And he sees that from this imperial city, the Good News spreads to the ends of the earth (1:8). The conclusion of Acts is directed to the future, for "the gospel cannot be stopped."[63]

---

63. F. F. Bruce, "The Holy Spirit in the Acts of the Apostles," *Interp* 27 (1973): 183.

G. Characteristics

One of the characteristics of Luke's style is his approach to writing the church's history. He gathered an album filled with pictures, as it were, and now he gives a running commentary while explaining the individual snapshots. As he moves from one picture to the next, he omits details that give rise to many questions. Here are a few. Where did the rest of the apostles do mission work? When was the gospel proclaimed in Alexandria, Egypt, to the Jewish community of about one million people? What did the Ethiopian eunuch accomplish in his native land? What happened to Cornelius of Caesarea? If Paul spent three years of his life pastoring the church in Ephesus (20:31), why did Luke fail to relate the growth and development of that church?

At a fast pace, Luke takes the reader through the historical gallery of the early church. He overlooks details and often quickly summarizes the events that took place. These summaries, however, are of great importance because in their brevity they convey the purpose of Luke's work, namely, to present an account of the message of salvation.[64] Luke captures this thought in the last verse of Acts: it is the work of preaching the kingdom of God and teaching the things concerning the Lord Jesus Christ (28:31). Acts, then, is the continuation of the work Jesus began to do and to teach while on earth (1:1).

1. Continuation of the Gospel

The close connection between Luke's Gospel and Acts is obvious not only in the dedication to Theophilus, the account of the appearance of Jesus, and the repetition of the ascension account. It also becomes apparent when we closely examine the parallel of the last segment of Luke 24 and the first half of Acts 1, which describe Jesus' ascension. These two passages reveal an inherent interrelation.[65]

The following points are prominent:

Luke 24:42–53	*Acts 1:4–14*
Jesus ate fish, 42–43	eating with apostles, 4
promise of the Father, 49	promise of the Father, 4
clothed with power, 49	you will receive power, 8
witnesses of these things, 48	my witnesses, 8
near Bethany, 50	the Mount of Olives, 12
he was taken up to heaven, 51	he was lifted up, 9
disciples returned to Jerusalem, 52	disciples returned to Jerusalem, 12
praising God, 53	constantly in prayer, 14

---

64. W. C. van Unnik, "The 'Book of Acts' the Confirmation of the Gospel," *NovT* 4 (1960): 58.
65. Consult M. D. Goulder, *Type and History in Acts* (London: SPCK, 1964), pp. 16–17.

Some characteristics of Luke's Gospel also appear in Acts. For instance, Luke's interest in people is evident in his Gospel. He mentions more personal names in his Gospel than any of the other evangelists do in their Gospel accounts. He cites the names of husbands and wives (Zachariah and Elizabeth, Joseph and Mary), he often refers to people other than Jews (the widow of Zarephath, Naaman the Syrian, the Samaritans), and he describes social relationships (e.g., meals at the homes of Mary and Martha, Zaccheus, Pharisees). The same thing is true in Acts, which includes more than a hundred personal names. He depicts husbands and wives (Ananias and Sapphira, Aquila and Priscilla), he highlights the inclusion of Samaritans and Gentiles, and he delineates countless social relationships.

2. Repetition

Acts is noted for parallelism and repetition. Remarkable incidents in the life of Peter are repeated in the account of Paul's life. Peter healed the cripple at the temple gate of Jerusalem (3:1–10); Paul healed the cripple of Lystra (14:8–10). Peter raised Dorcas from the dead in Joppa (9:36–42) and Paul restored Eutychus to life in Troas (20:9–12). Imprisoned in Jerusalem, Peter was released by an angel (12:3–11); and Paul, jailed in Philippi, was set free when an earthquake shook the prison (16:26–30).

The sermon Paul preached in the synagogue of Pisidian Antioch (13:16–41) has many parallels in the Pentecost sermon of Peter (2:14–36). In fact, both Peter and Paul quote the same passage from the Old Testament (Ps. 16:10) to prove Jesus' resurrection. And both sermons conclude with an emphasis on forgiveness of sins through Jesus Christ (2:38; 13:38).

Luke relates Paul's conversion experience three times: the actual event (9:1–19), Paul's address in Jerusalem (22:3–16), and Paul's audience with King Agrippa (26:12–18). Three times Luke alludes to Peter's vision on the roof at Joppa (10:9–16; 10:28; 11:5–10). Twice Peter addressed the Sanhedrin and said that he must obey God instead of men (4:19; 5:29). And twice Paul appealed to his status as a Roman citizen (16:37–38; 22:25–28). These are a few examples of Luke's peculiar characteristics in Acts. By repeating the same features of an incident or saying, Luke seeks to emphasize and advance the cause of the gospel.

3. Style and Language

Luke is an able writer who, compared with other Greek authors, deserves respect and admiration for composing a book that in style, word choice, grammar, and vocabulary takes a place between writers of Koine Greek and those of the classical period. In addition to excellent Greek (including use of the optative and numerous instances of the genitive absolute construction),[66] Luke records many Aramaisms in his account. Some of these are names of places and individuals: Akeldama (1:19), Barsabbas (1:23), Tabitha (9:36, 40), Bar-Jesus (13:6).

Perhaps because Luke was recording accounts that were reported to him orally, he often adjusted his style to write popular instead of literary Greek. As a result, in many places the syntax in a sentence or clause lacks clarity and precision.[67] These are a few examples in literal translations from the Greek:

> "Then the captain with his officers brought them not with force, for they feared the people that they not be stoned" (5:26). The meaning of the last clause is "for they feared that the people would stone them."

> "For many of those who had unclean spirits crying with a loud voice went out, and many who had been paralyzed and [many who] were lame were healed" (8:7). The meaning of the first part of the sentence is, "Evil spirits shrieking loudly were coming out of many people."

> "You know that from earlier days among you God chose through my mouth the Gentiles to hear the message of the gospel and to believe" (15:7). Peter is the speaker and he means to say, "You know that in earlier days God chose me from among you that from my lips the Gentiles might hear the message of the gospel and believe."

These examples are a few from countless others throughout the entire book. In some sentences Luke neglects to give the subject of the sentence, so that its meaning is obscure. For instance, "And there after his father died, he made him move to this land in which you now dwell. And he did not give him an inheritance" (7:4–5). The subject of these two sentences is God, which the translator must supply to clarify the meaning.

We are unable to explain why Luke, who proves that he is capable of writing excellent Greek, presents grammar that is incomplete and defective. The grammatical irregularities seem to reflect the sources Luke consulted for the composition of his book. Yet these peculiarities enhance, not diminish, the stature of Acts. The book itself is a piece of literary art that occupies a place among the classics.

---

66. J. de Zwaan tabulates sixty-three proper usages of the genitive absolute in Acts, twelve that are dubious, and twenty which he evaluates as faulty. "The Use of the Greek Language in Acts," *Beginnings*, vol. 2, p. 12.

67. For an extensive list of irregularities in Greek syntax, see F. W. Grosheide, *De Handelingen der Apostelen,* Kommentaar op het Nieuwe Testament series, 2 vols. (Amsterdam: Van Bottenburg, 1948), vol. 2, p. xxv.

H. Text

The reader who compares the King James Version (1611) and the New King James Version (1979) with any other Bible version immediately observes differences in wording. Both the old and new King James Versions present a text that is longer and diverse. Thus they transmit the full text of verses that have been either deleted or shortened in all other translations.[68] Translators have omitted these verses completely or in part because the better Greek manuscripts, known as the Alexandrian text, do not have them. They have followed this text and regard it as authentic and true. The differences in translation depend largely on the Western text, of which Codex Bezae is the best representative. This text varies in numerous respects, of which length is the most prominent characteristic. Bruce M. Metzger, following the account of Albert C. Clark, writes, "The Western text is nearly one-tenth longer than the Alexandrian text, and is generally more picturesque and circumstantial, whereas the shorter text is generally more colorless and in places more obscure."[69] For example, Luke relates that in Ephesus Paul rented the lecture hall of Tyrannus and daily lectured there (19:9). Codex Bezae at this point adds the interesting note that Paul lectured "from the fifth to the tenth hour," which is from 11:00 A.M. to 4:00 P.M. during the heat of the day. Even if this addition is genuine, translators hesitate to incorporate it into the text.

If we survey the long list of numerous short additions that Codex Bezae makes to the traditional text, we get the distinct impression that the Western text takes a secondary place. Here are only a few illustrations:

Simon the sorcerer "did not stop weeping copiously" (8:24).

Peter and the angel "descended seven steps" (12:10).

The jailer "secured the rest" of the prisoners before he brought Paul and Silas out of the jail (16:30).[70]

Nonetheless, in some verses of the Western text the question of genuineness is real. One instance pertains to the addition of the pronoun *we* of Codex Bezae in 11:27–28, "Now at that time some prophets came down from Jerusalem to Antioch. *And there was much rejoicing; and when we were gathered together,* one of them named Agabus stood up and predicted through the Spirit that there would be a severe famine all over the Roman world." Should we adopt the Western text (the italicized words) in this

---

68. Here is a brief list: 2:30b; 8:37; 9:5b–6a; 15:18, 34; 24:6b–8a; 28:16b, 29.

69. Bruce M. Metzger, *A Textual Commentary on the Greek New Testament,* 3d corrected ed. (London and New York: United Bible Societies, 1975), p. 260; Albert C. Clark, *The Acts of the Apostles: A Critical Edition with Introduction and Notes on Selected Passages* (1933; Oxford: Clarendon, 1970), p. xxxii.

70. Consult F. F. Bruce, *The Acts of the Apostles: The Greek Text with Introduction and Commentary,* 3d (rev. and enl.) ed. (Grand Rapids: Eerdmans, 1990), p. 107.

verse, we indeed would have the first "we" passage and thus give additional support to the view that Luke, an eyewitness, was a native of Antioch.

What is the origin of the Western text? Toward the close of the nineteenth century (1895), the German scholar Friedrich Blass proposed that Luke made a copy of his original draft of Acts and altered a number of phrases and deleted some sentences. The first draft is the Western text and the altered and shortened copy is the Alexandrian text. Another theory is that as scribes in the first few centuries were copying the text, they introduced clarifying phrases and added complete sentences derived from oral tradition. James Hardy Ropes concludes that "the 'Western' text was made before, and perhaps long before, the year 150, by a Greek-speaking Christian who knew something of Hebrew, in the East, perhaps in Syria or Palestine. . . . The reviser's aim was to improve the text, not to restore it, and he lived not far from the time when the New Testament canon in its nucleus was first definitely assembled."[71]

None of the hypotheses that have been suggested has proved to be convincing or has taken a leading position. In general, scholars adopt the Alexandrian text and follow the rule that the shorter text is preferred: scribes are more likely to add to the text, ostensibly to improve it, than to decrease its length. This does not mean that the Western group of witnesses lacks credibility; rather, each verse has to be judged on its own merits.

Scholars who have researched the Western text of Acts discover evidence of anti-Semitism.[72] Moreover, F. F. Bruce comments that if we say the Alexandrian text is superior to the Western text, "it does not follow that the [Alexandrian] text is equivalent to the original text."[73] On the contrary, the third-century papyrus manuscript P[45] may very well be older than both the Alexandrian and the Western texts.

I. Purpose

Was it Luke's purpose to write Acts as a history of the early church? As we have already noted earlier, we hardly think so, because Luke's work is not a carefully constructed chronicle of historical incidents. True, Luke traces the birth, growth, and development of the church but, strictly speaking, Acts is not a history book as such. Even the title of Acts fails to show that it is a history book. It is known as the "Acts of the Apostles."

Granted that Luke has composed a book on the early history of the church, he has never been regarded as the father of church history. Instead, Luke is known as an evangelist. Eusebius has composed church history and because of his works he is called a historian. Luke, however, as one

---

71. James Hardy Ropes, "The Text of Acts," *Beginnings*, vol. 3, p. ccxliv–cclv. For a comprehensive survey of the various hypotheses, see Metzger, *Textual Commentary*, pp. 260–70.

72. Consult Eldon J. Epp, *The Theological Tendency of Codex Bezae Cantabrigiensis in Acts* (Cambridge: Cambridge University Press, 1966), p. 64.

73. F. F. Bruce, "Acts of the Apostles," *ISBE*, vol. 1, p. 35; his *Acts* (Greek text), p. 109.

of the four Evangelists presents the good news of Jesus Christ.[74] Luke addresses his Gospel to Theophilus for the purpose of giving him certainty in the things he has been taught (Luke 1:4). He teaches his friend Theophilus the words and deeds of Jesus Christ. Upon completing the Gospel, he composes Acts and dedicates it also to Theophilus. Luke wants to tell him that the message of the gospel cannot be restricted to the nation Israel, for the gospel which Jesus first proclaimed to the Jews must be proclaimed to the entire world.

The purpose of Acts, then, is to convince Theophilus that no one is able to hinder the victorious march of Christ's gospel. For that reason, Luke relates to Theophilus the progress of the Good News from Jerusalem to Rome. He does this in harmony with the Great Commission which Jesus gave his followers (Matt. 28:19). In Acts, Luke shows Theophilus that the apostles indeed exerted themselves to fulfill Jesus' mandate (compare 1:8). Luke demonstrates that God desired the spread of the gospel and sent the Holy Spirit to advance the gospel's cause. In his first book, Luke reveals that Jesus is the Messiah whom the Old Testament prophets predicted and who would come to fulfill the messianic promises. In his second book, Luke depicts how the gospel enters the world and how the name of Jesus is proclaimed to all the nations.[75]

Just as Luke had to be selective with his material when he composed the Gospel, so he painstakingly chose the elements he needed for the composition of Acts. He sketches the progress of the gospel and therefore devotes much time and energy to Peter's Caesarean visit. He fills a chapter and a half with the account of Peter's visit to the house of Cornelius (10:1–11:18). For Luke, who is a Gentile Christian, this is the point in history at which the Gentiles receive the good news of salvation and become part of the community of believers.

Also, Luke elaborately describes Paul's voyage to Rome in nearly two chapters (27 and 28). His aim is to delineate Satan's attempts to thwart Paul's mission to the church in Rome. When Paul arrived in the imperial city, for two years he made his rented house the mission headquarters of the early church. From his home, missionaries went forth into the entire Roman world. Conclusively, Luke fulfilled the purpose of his book when he brought it to completion with his reference to Paul's work in Rome.

J. Themes

Acts displays a number of themes that the author weaves into its structure. We can trace the themes throughout the book and, recognizing them, gain a clearer understanding of Luke's intent when he composed Acts.

---

74. van Unnik, "The 'Book of Acts' the Confirmation of the Gospel," p. 42.
75. Consult Jacques Dupont, *The Salvation of the Gentiles: Essays on the Acts of the Apostles*, trans. John R. Keating (New York: Paulist, 1979), p. 33.

Introduction

1. The theme of the Holy Spirit is summarized in 1:8, "But you will receive power when the Holy Spirit has come upon you, and you will be my witnesses both in Jerusalem, in all Judea and Samaria, and to the ends of the earth." The Holy Spirit is poured out on the Jews in Jerusalem at Pentecost. The Samaritans receive the Holy Spirit when Peter and John arrive, pray, and place their hands on them. Next, the Holy Spirit instructs Peter to accompany the servants of Cornelius, travel to Caesarea, and preach the gospel to the Gentiles, represented by Cornelius and his household. The Holy Spirit descends upon them also. And last, in Ephesus Paul encounters disciples of John the Baptist, who are unaware of the coming of the Spirit. When Paul places his hands on these disciples, they receive the gift of the Holy Spirit.

2. The next topic is the missionary theme. Peter and the Eleven proclaim the gospel in Jerusalem chiefly to Aramaic-speaking Jews. Stephen preaches the Good News in the Synagogue of the Freedmen to Jews whose native tongue is Greek. Philip goes to Samaria, preaches the word, and baptizes the people. When the apostles arrive to accept the Samaritans as members of the church, Philip travels toward Gaza and tells the Ethiopian eunuch the meaning of Isaiah 53. After baptizing the Ethiopian, Philip preaches the gospel in numerous places along the Mediterranean coast and arrives in Caesarea. Peter extends his ministry beyond the city of Jerusalem and travels to Lydda and Joppa to strengthen the churches. From Joppa he journeys to Caesarea to teach the gospel in the house of Cornelius and to welcome the Gentiles into the church.

Paul, converted on the way to Damascus, preaches in the local synagogues of that city, goes to Jerusalem, where he debates with Greek-speaking Jews, voyages via Caesarea to Tarsus, and presumably starts churches in Cilicia and northern Syria. Barnabas is sent to Antioch to organize a church of Jewish and Gentile Christians. He and Paul are sent to Cyprus and to Asia Minor to preach the gospel to the Gentiles. On his second missionary journey, Paul extends his ministry to cross the Aegean Sea and begin mission work in Europe (Macedonia and Greece). During his third missionary journey, he writes a letter to the church in Rome in which he expresses the wish to visit the believers there. After two years of imprisonment, Paul arrives in the imperial city.

3. The authority of the apostles and the Jerusalem church is another theme. The apostles are instrumental in organizing the church in Jerusalem, teaching the people the apostolic doctrine, receiving gifts for the poor, and appointing seven men to supervise the daily distribution of food. They also oversee the extension of the church among the Samaritans in Samaria and the Gentiles in Caesarea. The Jerusalem church commissions Barnabas to go to Antioch, and this church also gives leadership at the Jerusalem Council. And last, at the conclusion of every missionary tour, Paul visits Jerusalem to inform the church about the work he has performed.

4. The theme of opposition to the spread of the gospel is evident from beginning to end. The scoffers at Pentecost accuse the apostles of being intoxicated. The Sanhedrin arrests Peter and John for preaching at Solomon's Colonnade. Ananias and Sapphira seek to undermine the integrity of the church through deception. The apostles are arrested, jailed, released by an angel, and scourged by order of the Sanhedrin. Stephen is stoned and dies; but Paul, experiencing a similar fate in Lystra, lives. Paul and Silas, flogged and jailed in Philippi, are driven from Thessalonica and Berea. But wherever the apostles meet opposition, the gospel is preached and the church flourishes. Satan's efforts to block the spread of the gospel are not only futile; indeed, they aid the growth of the church.

5. A last theme is the defense of the gospel. Jesus informed his disciples that they would be dragged before local councils, flogged in synagogues, and brought before governors and kings. He told them not to be afraid, because God would give them his Spirit who would speak for them and through them (Matt. 10:17–20). Peter addresses a crowd of thousands of Jews on Pentecost with the result that three thousand repent, believe, and are baptized. Standing in the half circle and facing the members of the Sanhedrin, Peter and John defend the cause of the gospel. They speak with such boldness that the members of the Sanhedrin have to acknowledge that the men had been disciples of Jesus. Peter rebukes Simon the sorcerer for desiring to purchase the gift of the Holy Spirit and Paul opposes the deceit of Bar-Jesus. Paul ably defends the gospel before Athenian philosophers and seeks to persuade two governors (Felix and Festus) and King Agrippa to become Christians. From one of Paul's epistles we learn that, while in Rome under house arrest, Paul was instrumental in converting the palace guard and Caesar's household (Phil. 1:13; 4:22). Luke depicts both Peter and Paul as defenders of the gospel of Christ.

K. Outline

First, here is a ten-point outline of Acts that, because of its simple arrangement, presents no difficulty to the student who commits it to memory:

1:1–26	Before Pentecost
2:1–8:1a	The Church in Jerusalem
8:1b–11:18	The Church in Palestine
11:19–13:3	The Church in Antioch
13:4–14:28	The First Missionary Journey
15:1–35	The Council at Jerusalem
15:36–18:22	The Second Missionary Journey
18:23–21:16	The Third Missionary Journey
21:17–26:32	In Jerusalem and Caesarea
27:1–28:31	Voyage to and Stay in Rome

Introduction

Second, a full outline with all the details is as follows:

I.	1:1–26	Before Pentecost	
	1:1–8	A. Before Jesus' Ascension	
		1. Introduction	1:1–5
		2. Purpose	1:6–8
	1:9–11	B. Jesus' Ascension	
	1:12–14	C. After Jesus' Ascension	
	1:15–26	D. Matthias's Appointment	
		1. Scripture Fulfilled	1:15–20
		2. Apostolic Requirements	1:21–22
		3. Divine Appointment	1:23–26
II.	2:1–8:1a	The Church in Jerusalem	
	2:1–47	A. Pentecost	
		1. Outpouring of the Spirit	2:1–13
		2. Peter's Sermon	2:14–41
		3. Christian Community	2:42–47
	3:1–5:16	B. The Power of Jesus' Name	
		1. Healing of the Cripple	3:1–10
		2. Address of Peter	3:11–26
		3. Before the Sanhedrin	4:1–22
		4. Prayers of the Church	4:23–31
		5. Love of the Christians	4:32–37
		6. Deception of Ananias	5:1–11
		7. Healing Miracles	5:12–16
	5:17–42	C. Persecution	
		1. Arrest and Release	5:17–20
		2. Freedom and Consternation	5:21–26
		3. Accusation and Response	5:27–32
		4. Wisdom and Persuasion	5:33–40
		5. Rejoicing	5:41–42
	6:1–8:1a	D. Stephen's Ministry and Death	
		1. Seven Men Appointed	6:1–7
		2. Stephen's Arrest	6:8–15
		3. Stephen's Speech	7:1–53
		4. Stephen's Death	7:54–8:1a
III.	8:1b–11:18	The Church in Palestine	
	8:1b–3	A. Persecution	
	8:4–40	B. Ministry of Philip	
		1. In Samaria	8:4–25
		2. To the Ethiopian	8:26–40
	9:1–31	C. Conversion of Paul	
		1. Paul to Damascus	9:1–9
		2. Paul in Damascus	9:10–25

37

	3.	Paul in Jerusalem	9:26–30
	4.	Conclusion	9:31
9:32–11:18	D.	Ministry of Peter	
	1.	Miracle in Lydda	9:32–35
	2.	Miracle in Joppa	9:36–43
	3.	Peter's Call	10:1–8
	4.	Peter's Vision	10:9–23a
	5.	Peter's Visit to Caesarea	10:23b–48
	6.	Peter's Explanation	11:1–18
IV. 11:19–13:3		The Church in Transition	
11:19–30	A.	Ministry of Barnabas	
	1.	Spread of the Gospel	11:19–21
	2.	Mission of Barnabas	11:22–24
	3.	Christians in Antioch	11:25–26
	4.	Prediction and Fulfillment	11:27–30
12:1–19	B.	Peter's Escape from Prison	
	1.	Arrest by Herod	12:1–5
	2.	Release by an Angel	12:6–11
	3.	Church in Prayer	12:12–17
	4.	Reaction of Herod	12:18–19
12:20–25	C.	Death of Herod Agrippa I	
13:1–3	D.	Paul and Barnabas Commissioned	
V. 13:4–14:28		The First Missionary Journey	
13:4–12	A.	Cyprus	
	1.	Jewish Synagogue	13:4–5
	2.	Bar-Jesus	13:6–12
13:13–52	B.	Pisidian Antioch	
	1.	Invitation	13:13–15
	2.	Old Testament Survey	13:16–22
	3.	Coming of Jesus	13:23–25
	4.	Death and Resurrection	13:26–31
	5.	Good News of Jesus	13:32–41
	6.	Invitation Renewed	13:42–45
	7.	Effect and Opposition	13:46–52
14:1–7	C.	Iconium	
	1.	Message Proclaimed	14:1–3
	2.	Division	14:4–5
	3.	Escape	14:6–7
14:8–20a	D.	Lystra and Derbe	
	1.	Miracle	14:8–10
	2.	Response	14:11–13
	3.	Reaction	14:14–18
	4.	Revulsion	14:19–20a

	14:20b–28	E. Antioch in Syria	
		1. Strengthening the Churches	14:20b–25
		2. Reporting to Antioch	14:26–28
VI.	15:1–35	The Council at Jerusalem	
		A. The Chronology	
	15:1–21	B. The Debate	
		1. The Controversy	15:1–5
		2. Peter's Address	15:6–11
		3. Barnabas and Paul	15:12
		4. James's Address	15:13–21
	15:22–35	C. The Letter	
		1. Messengers	15:22
		2. Message	15:23–29
		3. Effect	15:30–35
VII.	15:36–18:22	The Second Missionary Journey	
	15:36–16:5	A. Revisiting the Churches	
		1. Separation	15:36–41
		2. Derbe and Lystra	16:1–5
	16:6–17:15	B. Macedonia	
		1. Macedonian Call	16:6–10
		2. Philippi	16:11–40
		3. Thessalonica	17:1–9
		4. Berea	17:10–15
	17:16–18:17	C. Greece	.
		1. Athens	17:16–34
		2. Corinth	18:1–17
	18:18–22	D. Return to Antioch	
VIII.	18:23–21:16	The Third Missionary Journey	
	18:23–28	A. To Ephesus	
	19:1–41	B. At Ephesus	
		1. John's Baptism	19:1–7
		2. Paul's Ministry	19:8–12
		3. Jesus' Name	19:13–20
		4. Paul's Plan	19:21–22
		5. Demetrius's Grievance	19:23–41
	20:1–21:16	C. To Jerusalem	
		1. Through Macedonia	20:1–6
		2. At Troas	20:7–12
		3. At Miletus	20:13–38
		4. Travel	21:1–16
IX.	21:17–26:32	In Jerusalem and Caesarea	
	21:17–23:22	A. At Jerusalem	
		1. Paul's Arrival	21:17–26
		2. Paul's Arrest	21:27–36

	3. Paul's Address	21:37–22:21
	4. Paul's Trial	22:22–23:11
	5. Paul's Protection	23:12–22
23:23–26:32	B. At Caesarea	
	1. Paul's Transfer	23:23–35
	2. Paul Before Felix	24:1–27
	3. Paul Before Festus	25:1–12
	4. Paul and Agrippa II	25:13–27
	5. Paul's Speech	26:1–32
X. 27:1–28:31	Voyage to and Stay in Rome	
27:1–44	A. Caesarea to Malta	
	1. To Crete	27:1–12
	2. The Storm	27:13–44
28:1–16	B. Malta to Rome	
	1. At Malta	28:1–10
	2. To Rome	28:11–16
28:17–31	C. Roman Imprisonment	

Commentary

1

Before Pentecost

1:1–26

Outline

1:1–26	I. Before Pentecost
1:1–8	A. Before Jesus' Ascension
1:1–5	1. Introduction
1:6–8	2. Purpose
1:9–11	B. Jesus' Ascension
1:12–14	C. After Jesus' Ascension
1:15–26	D. Matthias's Appointment
1:15–20	1. Scripture Fulfilled
1:21–22	2. Apostolic Requirements
1:23–26	3. Divine Appointment

1

1 The first book, Theophilus, I composed concerning all that Jesus began both to do and to teach 2 until the day he was taken up, after he had instructed through the Holy Spirit the apostles whom he had chosen. 3 To them he also presented himself alive, after his suffering, by many convincing proofs, appearing to them over a period of forty days and speaking the things concerning the kingdom of God. 4 And while eating with them, he commanded them: "Do not leave Jerusalem, but wait for the promise my Father made, of which you heard me speak. 5 For John baptized with water, but you will be baptized with the Holy Spirit within a few days."

6 And so when they came together, they were asking him: "Lord, at this time are you restoring the kingdom to Israel?" 7 He said to them: "It is not for you to know the times or seasons which the Father has fixed by his own authority. 8 But you will receive power when the Holy Spirit has come upon you, and you will be my witnesses both in Jerusalem, in all Judea and Samaria, and to the ends of the earth."

9 After he said these things, he was lifted up while they were looking. And a cloud hid him from their sight. 10 As they were looking intently toward the sky while he was going, instantly two men dressed in white stood beside them. 11 They said, "Men of Galilee, why do you stand looking into the sky? This same Jesus, who has been taken from you into heaven, will come back in just the same way as you have seen him go into heaven."

12 Then they returned to Jerusalem from the Mount of Olives, which is a Sabbath day's journey from Jerusalem. 13 And when they had entered, they went to the upper room where they were staying; they were Peter, John, James and Andrew, Philip and Thomas, Bartholomew and Matthew, James son of Alphaeus and Simon the Zealot, and Judas son of James. 14 These were all with one mind constantly devoting themselves to prayer along with the women and Mary the mother of Jesus and with his brothers.

15 And in those days, Peter stood up in the midst of the brothers (a gathering of about a hundred and twenty people) and said: 16 "Men and brothers, the Scripture had to be fulfilled which the Holy Spirit foretold through the mouth of David concerning Judas, who became a guide for those who arrested Jesus. 17 Because he was numbered among us and he shared in this ministry."

18 (This man bought a field with the reward received for his wickedness; and falling headlong, he burst open in the middle and all his intestines spilled out. 19 And it became known to all that live in Jerusalem, so that they called that field in their own language Akeldama, that is, field of blood.)

20 "For it is written in the Book of Psalms:

> 'Let his place be a desert
> and let no one dwell in it.'

And,

> 'And let someone else take his office.'

21 It is therefore necessary that one of the men who have accompanied us all the time that Jesus went in and out among us— 22 beginning from the baptism of John until the day in which he was taken up from us—be a witness of his resurrection with us."

23 And they proposed two men, Joseph called Barsabbas (who was also known as Justus), and Matthias. 24 They prayed, "Lord, you know the hearts of all men. Show us which one of these two you have chosen 25 to receive this ministry and apostleship from which Judas strayed to go to where he belongs." 26 And they cast lots and the lot fell to Matthias, and he was added to the eleven apostles.

I. Before Pentecost
1:1–26

A. Before Jesus' Ascension
1:1–8

1. Introduction
1:1–5

In the first sentence of this book, Luke makes it abundantly clear that he is the author of the third Gospel. He dedicates both his Gospel and Acts to Theophilus, a Gentile convert to Christianity. Although Luke refrains from mentioning his own name in either the Gospel or Acts, the style, vocabulary, and choice of words point to the same author for both books.

The first two verses of Acts serve as a bridge between the Gospel account of Jesus' life and ministry and the historical account of the developing church. In effect, Luke's Gospel and Acts form one book in two parts; Acts is the continuation of the Gospel.

1. The first book, Theophilus, I composed concerning all that Jesus began both to do and to teach.

Note the following points:

a. *Gospel.* Luke refers to the third Gospel as "the first book."[1] In the Greek, the expression *former* or *first* signifies the first of either two or more items. In this case, Luke writes only two books, the Gospel and Acts. He distinguishes between the two documents by calling the first one the "former." To ask whether he planned a third volume about the history of the church after Paul's release from house arrest in Rome leads to mere speculation and utter futility.

b. *Name.* Luke dedicates both his Gospel and Acts to Theophilus. The name means "friend of God" and applies to both Jew and Gentile.[2] In the Gospel prologue, Luke calls Theophilus "most excellent." This description also occurs in addresses to the Roman governors Felix and Festus (see Acts 23:26; 24:3; 26:25). We assume that Theophilus belongs to the educated, ruling class of society. He is a God-fearer who attends the worship services in a Jewish synagogue but objects to circumcision. Hence, he is not a con-

---

1. Bauer (p. 477) gives three examples from Herodotus, Plato, and Philo that are similar in wording to the first phrase in 1:1.
2. Consult SB, vol. 2, p. 588. And see Josephus *Antiquities* 17.4.2 [78]; 18.5.3 [124], who records the name *Theophilus* belonging to Jewish people.

vert to Judaism, but like the Roman centurion Cornelius (10:1–2) he worships the Lord God. By dedicating his Gospel to Theophilus (Luke 1:3), Luke introduces him to Jesus Christ in word and deed. And although Luke gives no further details about him in Acts, we surmise that by reading the Gospel Theophilus has become a Christian.

c. *Person.* "Concerning all that Jesus began both to do and to teach." Even though Luke's Gospel is more extensive than the other three Gospels, Luke does not mean that he has recorded everything Jesus said and did (compare John 21:25). He uses the adjective *all* to include all the things that he has mentioned about Jesus in the third Gospel. In the first eleven verses of chapter 1, the predominant subject is Jesus.[3] With the clause "all that Jesus began to do and to teach," Luke implies that his account in Acts is a continuation of what Jesus said and did as recorded in the Gospel. Luke writes about Jesus, who is the subject of both the Gospel and Acts.

2. Until the day he was taken up, after he had instructed through the Holy Spirit the apostles whom he had chosen.

In this verse, Luke presents three distinct topics. They are:

a. *Ascension.* Of the four evangelists, only Luke presents a descriptive account of Jesus' ascension. He concludes his Gospel with a brief report on the event (Luke 24:50–53), returns to the subject in the first chapter of Acts (1:2), and presents a more detailed record later in the chapter (vv. 9–11). With the ascension narrative, Luke ties together the Gospel and Acts, for this narrative marks the end of the Gospel and the beginning of Acts.

In the New Testament, the Greek verb meaning "was taken up" frequently describes Jesus' ascension to heaven.[4] Without the qualifying phrase *into heaven,* the verb itself "testifies to the familiarity of the apostolic church with the Ascension as a formal and recognized event in our Lord's course."[5] Here Luke briefly mentions the ascension and thus summarizes a topic he intends to expand in the rest of the chapter.

b. *Instruction.* Luke writes, "after he had instructed through the Holy Spirit the apostles whom he had chosen." Obliquely, Luke relates Jesus' ascension to an element in the Great Commission. Before he was taken up to heaven, Jesus instructed the eleven disciples to make disciples of all the nations by teaching them "to pay attention to everything I have commanded you" (Matt. 28:20). During the forty-day period between Jesus' resurrection and his ascension, Jesus instructed his disciples in the teaching

---

3. In Acts, Jesus is the subject of numerous other passages also (e.g., 2:33; 7:55, 59; 9:5, 10–16, 34; 10:13–15; 16:7; 18:9; 20:35; 22:7–10, 18–21; 23:11; 26:14–17).

4. Compare Mark 16:19; Acts 1:2, 11, 22; I Tim. 3:16; consult Burghard Siede, *NIDNTT,* vol. 3, p. 749; Gerhard Delling, *TDNT,* vol. 4, p. 8. Also refer to Jacques Dupont, " 'Anelēmphthē (Act. i.2)," *NTS* 8 (1962): 154–57.

5. Henry Alford, *Alford's Greek Testament: An Exegetical and Critical Commentary,* 7th ed., 4 vols. (1877; Grand Rapids: Guardian, 1976), vol. 2, p. 2.

of the gospel. Accordingly, he prepared them for the tremendous task that awaited them on and after Pentecost.

In the Greek, the phrase *through the Holy Spirit* can be taken with either the preceding words *had instructed* or the following verb *he had chosen.* In view of Luke's emphasis on the work of the Spirit in chapter 1, scholars prefer to link the phrase to that which precedes. Writes Donald Guthrie, "Luke clearly shows that he sees his book as the outcome of revelations of the Spirit from the risen Lord to the apostles."[6] The Holy Spirit dwelled in Jesus, for Jesus breathed on his disciples and gave them the Holy Spirit (John 20:22). In their ministry, he directed his apostles through the Holy Spirit (see, e.g., 16:7). The Spirit of Jesus is the Holy Spirit.

c. *Election.* "The apostles whom he had chosen." Luke employs the term *apostles,* for in Acts he characterizes believers as disciples (learners) and the apostles as teachers. In fact, these disciples receive instruction in the apostles' teaching (2:42); also, Jesus' apostles teach with authority in the name of Jesus Christ.[7] Jesus himself chose the twelve apostles (the Eleven and Matthias) and sent them forth as his ambassadors to proclaim the gospel and to perform miracles in his name. The Holy Spirit confirmed the election of these twelve, for he filled them on the day of Pentecost (2:4).

3. To them he also presented himself alive, after his suffering, by many convincing proofs, appearing to them over a period of forty days and speaking the things concerning the kingdom of God.

In one short clause, "after his suffering," Luke sums up the events of the Passion Week that he has described in detail in the Gospel. He also deems a mere reference to Jesus' postresurrection appearances sufficient to prove that Jesus is alive. According to the four Gospel accounts, Acts, and Paul's first epistle to the Corinthians, Jesus appeared ten times in the period between Easter and Ascension Day. He showed himself to

1. The women at the tomb (Matt. 28:9–10)
2. Mary Magdalene (Mark 16:9–11; John 20:11–18)
3. Two men of Emmaus (Mark 16:12; Luke 24:13–32)
4. Peter in Jerusalem (Luke 24:34; I Cor. 15:5)
5. Ten disciples (Luke 24:36–43; John 20:19–23)
6. Eleven disciples (John 20:24–29; I Cor. 15:5)
7. Seven disciples fishing in Galilee (John 21:1–23)
8. Eleven disciples in Galilee (Matt. 28:16–20; Mark 16:14–18)
9. Five hundred persons (presumably in Galilee; I Cor. 15:6)
10. James, the brother of the Lord (I Cor. 15:7)

---

6. Donald Guthrie, *New Testament Theology* (Downers Grove: Inter-Varsity, 1981), p. 536.

7. For a comprehensive study on the concept *apostle,* see especially Karl Heinrich Rengstorf, *TDNT,* vol. 1, pp. 407–45; Dietrich Müller, *NIDNTT,* vol. 1, pp. 128–35.

The last appearance of Jesus occurred when he ascended to heaven from the Mount of Olives near Jerusalem. All these appearances show, says Luke, that "[Jesus] presented himself alive, after his suffering, by many convincing proofs." The work that Jesus began to do during his earthly ministry continues because Jesus lives.

Jesus' ascension took place on the fortieth day after his resurrection and ten days before Pentecost, which is a Greek word meaning "fiftieth." During these forty days, Jesus instructed the disciples in the things pertaining to "the kingdom of God." With this summary statement, Luke once again calls the reader's attention to his Gospel account. Luke's Gospel has more than thirty occurrences of the expression *kingdom of God;* Luke also mentions it several times in Acts (1:6; 8:12; 14:22; 19:8; 20:25; 28:23, 31). By comparison, however, Matthew develops the kingdom concept and uses the expression *kingdom of heaven* (or, *God*) at least fifty times.

What is the message of God's kingdom? This idiom summarizes the heart of Jesus' teaching. The kingdom is God's rule in the hearts and lives of his people, who as citizens of this kingdom receive remission of sins and eternal life.[8] Moreover, for the apostles the phrase *the kingdom of God* meant preaching the good news of Jesus' death and resurrection and making disciples of all nations. "It follows that the church can take up the message of Jesus, as recorded in the Gospels, and make it part of its own."[9]

4. And while eating with them, he commanded them: "Do not leave Jerusalem, but wait for the promise my Father made, of which you heard me speak. 5. For John baptized with water, but you will be baptized with the Holy Spirit within a few days."

Translations vary for the first part of this verse. Many versions have the reading "and being assembled together with them" (e.g., NKJV). This translation derives from the crucial Greek word *sunalizomenos*. But this expression occurs only once in the New Testament and therefore the translator must exercise caution. The primary meaning of the Greek term is "eating [salt] with someone." Although objections have been raised, this version appears to be supported by the words of Peter: "God caused [Jesus] to be seen, not by everyone but by witnesses who were appointed beforehand by God; that is, to us who ate and drank with him after he rose from the dead" (10:40–41). In other words, Jesus ate with the disciples as visible proof that he was not a ghost but a human being of flesh and bones (see Luke 24:36–43). By eating with his disciples, Jesus demonstrates to them the reality of his resurrection.

"Do not leave Jerusalem, but wait for the promise my Father made." We

---

8. Refer to John Calvin, *Commentary on the Acts of the Apostles,* ed. David W. Torrance and Thomas F. Torrance, 2 vols. (Grand Rapids: Eerdmans, 1966), vol. 1, pp. 24–25.

9. I. Howard Marshall, *The Acts of the Apostles: An Introduction and Commentary,* Tyndale New Testament Commentary series (Leicester: Inter-Varsity; Grand Rapids: Eerdmans, 1980), pp. 57–58.

should see this command which Jesus gives his apostles in the light of the historical context. After his resurrection, Jesus instructed the disciples to return to Galilee (Matt. 28:10; Mark 16:7). They readily complied for two reasons. First, they would be able to see Jesus again in Galilee, as he had said. Next, they had no desire to remain in Jerusalem, the place where the Jews had killed Jesus. Nevertheless, on Easter Sunday Jesus already had told them that, beginning in Jerusalem, they would proclaim repentance and forgiveness in his name to all nations. He said, "And I will bestow on you the promise of my Father, but stay in the city until you are clothed with power from on high" (Luke 24:49).

During his ministry, Jesus instructed the disciples that the Father would send the Spirit.[10] At Pentecost Peter asserts that the gift of the Holy Spirit originates with the Father (compare 2:33). Jesus points to the Father and not to himself, for, like the Holy Spirit, he has been sent by the Father. As spokesman for the Father, Jesus promises the gift of the Spirit (John 14:26).

Because the apostles had been with Jesus from the time of his baptism (compare 1:22), they knew the words spoken by John the Baptist concerning Jesus. John declared that even though he baptized with water, Jesus would baptize with the Holy Spirit and with fire (Matt. 3:11; Luke 3:16). Jesus reminds the disciples of the words John had spoken and says, "For John baptized with water, but you will be baptized with the Holy Spirit within a few days." Peter later repeats this saying of Jesus verbatim when he reports to the Jewish Christians in Jerusalem about his visit to the house of Cornelius (11:16). Notice that Jesus does not say he will baptize the apostles with the Spirit; instead, they will be baptized and God the Father is the implied agent.

The time between Jesus' ascension and the outpouring of the Holy Spirit on Pentecost is short, only ten days. In the words of Jesus, the period is only "a few days." In that time, the disciples must fill the vacancy left by Judas Iscariot with a person who had been with Jesus from the time Jesus was baptized by John. The repeated references to John the Baptist in this chapter indicate the beginning of the New Testament era.

Doctrinal Considerations in 1:3

As forerunner of Jesus, John the Baptist proclaims that "the kingdom of heaven is near" (Matt. 3:2). When Jesus begins his ministry, he preaches that same message (Matt. 4:17), for he announces that the kingdom of God is a present reality. Thus, Jesus informs the Pharisees, "The kingdom of God is within you" (Luke 17:21).

What is the effect of the kingdom of God? First, Jesus breaks the power of Satan, who is the prince of this world. Figuratively, he enters Satan's house, binds him, and

---

10. Matt. 10:20; John 14:16–17, 26; 15:26; 16:7–8, 12–13.

robs him of his possessions (see Matt. 12:29). Then, Jesus discloses that he has seen Satan falling like lightning from heaven (Luke 10:18) and implies that Satan has yielded place to Jesus. The kingdom belongs to the Father, to whom Christ will present it when he has subdued all his enemies (I Cor. 15:24–28).

Jesus gives his followers authority to oppose the forces of Satan, to usher in the kingdom of God, and to apply the kingdom principles of righteousness, justice, love, mercy, and peace. The message of the kingdom includes remission of sin, the gift of eternal life, the declaration of Jesus' authority over everything in heaven and on earth, and the promise that Jesus is near his people to the end of time (Matt. 28:19–20). Clearly, Jesus Christ is at the center of God's kingdom, because he is King of kings and Lord of lords (Rev. 19:16).

Greek Words, Phrases, and Constructions in 1:1–4

Verse 1

πρῶτον—in his Gospel and Acts, "Luke does not use πρότερος [former] (adjective or adverb) so that πρῶτος [first] in Ac[ts] 1:1 with λόγος [account] does not imply τρίτος [third]."[11]

Verse 3

δι' ἡμερῶν—the genitive case denotes time. The preposition appears to mean "after" in a construction that is idiomatic (compare Matt. 26:61; Acts 24:17; Gal. 2:1).

Verse 4

συναλιζόμενος—in Hellenistic Greek the verb συναλίζω spelled with a long α means "I assemble," but spelled with a short α it means "I eat [salt] with another."[12] The use of the singular instead of the plural in the participle is strange indeed when it means "to assemble." For this reason, many translators have chosen the reading *to eat*.

2. Purpose
1:6–8

In the first section of this chapter, Luke writes two verses of introduction (vv. 1–2) that are historical in nature. Then he refers to the forty-day period in which Jesus appeared to his followers and during which he instructed his disciples (vv. 3–5). Next he relates a specific question of the eleven disciples and adds Jesus' comprehensive reply which, in fact, indicates Luke's purpose in writing Acts.

11. A. T. Robertson, *A Grammar of the Greek New Testament in the Light of Historical Research* (Nashville: Broadman, 1934), p. 663.
12. Refer to Bruce M. Metzger, *A Textual Commentary on the Greek New Testament,* 3d corrected ed. (London and New York: United Bible Societies, 1975), pp. 278–79.

6. And so when they came together, they were asking him: "Lord, at this time are you restoring the kingdom to Israel?"

Before Jesus' ascension, when the apostles realized that the appearances of Jesus would soon come to an end, they asked him a question about the future. As in Greek the verb *to ask* indicates repetition, we understand that the disciples unanimously posed the question that was foremost in their minds: "Lord, at this time are you restoring the kingdom to Israel?"

How do we interpret this question? The usual explanation is that the disciples are still thinking in terms of a political kingdom of the nation Israel in which Jesus would be their earthly king. During Jesus' earthly ministry, the mother of James and John requested that her two sons might receive a special place in his kingdom. Shortly before Jesus' triumphal entry into Jerusalem, she asked Jesus whether James and John might sit at his left and right in his kingdom (Matt. 20:21). In spite of Jesus' emphasis on a spiritual kingdom, at the time of his ascension the disciples express their burning desire to be liberated from foreign oppression and implore him to restore the kingdom to Israel. For them, Jesus is their sovereign Lord.

Even if this explanation should be valid, we must nonetheless carefully examine the request of the apostles. First, they query whether Jesus *at this time* is going to restore Israel's kingdom. In his reply, Jesus answers the question not of restoration but of time. He tells the apostles, "It is not for you to know the times or seasons which the Father has fixed by his own authority" (v. 7). Next, if we interpret the text to mean the restoration of spiritual Israel, Jesus intimates that the disciples with their reference to Israel are too restrictive. The gospel of salvation is for all nations. Hence Jesus instructs them to be his witnesses in Jerusalem, in Judea and Samaria, and to the ends of the earth (v. 8).[13] Conclusively, then, in the light of Jesus' answer it is possible and even plausible to give a spiritual interpretation of the apostles' question.

7. He said to them: "It is not for you to know the times or seasons which the Father has fixed by his own authority."

The apostles reveal their curiosity about the future. But the future belongs to God, not to them. They should have remembered Moses' pertinent observation: "The secret things belong to the LORD our God, but the things that are revealed belong to us and to our children forever" (Deut. 29:29). Everyone has an innate longing for the ability to lift the curtain that separates the future from the present. Because we lack this ability, we need help. But even Jesus is unable to reveal the end of time for us. He declares, "But of that day or hour no one knows, not even the angels in heaven, nor the Son, but only the Father" (Matt. 24:36). Jesus does not say that he is

---

13. Consult F. W. Grosheide, *De Handelingen der Apostelen*, Kommentaar op het Nieuwe Testament series, 2 vols. (Amsterdam: Van Bottenburg, 1942), vol. 1, p. 17.

ignorant of the future; he means that the disciples have no right to know what lies in store for them.

"It is not for you to know." Jesus mildly rebukes the disciples for their limited understanding of the extent of God's kingdom. Yet his objective is not to reprove but to teach.[14] The Father is completely in control of the calendar of world events and he will bring everything to its destined end.

Jesus teaches that the disciples should avoid probing the unknown times and seasons of the future. In contrast to the Old Testament prophets who scanned the horizon of time and predicted the future, the New Testament apostles are witnesses of the life of Jesus Christ of Nazareth and speak in the present time. In short, the disciples testify to the past (namely, the life of Christ) rather than prophesy about the future.[15]

"The times or seasons which the Father has fixed by his own authority." Because God has determined the calendar of events, nothing happens by chance. As the sixteenth-century German theologian Zacharias Ursinus put it:

> All things, in fact, come to us
> not by chance
> but from his fatherly hand.[16]

Note that Jesus says "the Father" and not "my Father." He implies that the apostles, too, call God their Father. With Christ they are sons of God and can be assured that God is in complete control.

8. "But you will receive power when the Holy Spirit has come upon you, and you will be my witnesses both in Jerusalem, in all Judea and Samaria, and to the ends of the earth."

In this text, Luke presents the theme for the entire book. This text contains the promise of Pentecost and the mandate to witness for Jesus in the following geographical areas: Jerusalem, Judea and Samaria, and the world.

a. *Promise.* We see a distinct parallel between Jesus and his disciples when they are about to begin their respective ministries. When Jesus was baptized, the Holy Spirit descended upon him and strengthened him to oppose the power of Satan (see Matt. 3:16). Before the apostles are able to assume the tremendous responsibility of building the church of Jesus Christ and to conquer the strongholds of Satan, they receive the power of the Holy Spirit. In the upper room on Easter Sunday, Jesus breathed on the apostles and said: "Receive the Holy Spirit" (John 20:22). But immediately before this he told them, "As the Father has sent me, so I am sending you" (v. 21).

The Holy Spirit proceeds from the Father and the Son. For instance, Jesus informs the disciples in his farewell discourse, "When the Counselor

---

14. Compare John Albert Bengel, *Gnomon of the New Testament,* ed. Andrew R. Fausset, 5 vols. (Edinburgh: Clark, 1877), vol. 2, p. 514.

15. Consult Alford, *Alford's Greek Testament,* vol. 2, p. 4.

16. Heidelberg Catechism, answer 27.

comes, whom I will send to you from the Father, the Spirit of truth who goes out from the Father, he will testify about me" (John 15:26, NIV). The Holy Spirit, therefore, is not an inanimate power but the third person of the Trinity. And the promise of the Spirit originates with the Father: "I will bestow on you the promise of my Father" (Luke 24:49a).

b. *Mandate.* Only through the indwelling person and power of the Holy Spirit are the disciples able to witness for Jesus Christ. Not only the disciples receive the gift of the Spirit, but, as Luke shows in Acts, numerous persons are filled with the Holy Spirit and become Christ's witnesses. "Effective witness can only be borne where the Spirit is, and where the Spirit is, effective witness will always follow."[17] Jesus' word, "You will receive power," applies first to the twelve apostles and then to all believers who witness effectively for Jesus Christ.

"You will be my witnesses." In Acts, the term *witness* has a twofold meaning. First, it relates to the person who has observed an act or event. Next, it refers to the person who presents a testimony by which he defends and promotes a cause. Accordingly, the apostles choose Matthias to succeed Judas Iscariot because as an eyewitness he has followed Jesus from the time of John's baptism to the moment of Jesus' ascension. Further, Jesus commands Matthias to proclaim the message of his resurrection (1:21–22).[18]

In the strict sense of the word, the expression *witness* does not apply to Paul and Barnabas, who during their first missionary journey proclaimed the message of Jesus' resurrection to the people in Pisidian Antioch (13:31). Paul and Barnabas state that they are not witnesses; they tell the Good News.[19] Jesus sends forth the twelve apostles on the day of Pentecost as true witnesses of all that he said and did.

These twelve have seen and heard Jesus and now tell others about him (compare I John 1:1). Filled with the Holy Spirit, they begin to proclaim the Good News in Jerusalem (see Luke 24:47). Then they preach the gospel in the Judean and Samarian countryside, and eventually they take it to Rome. Rome was the imperial capital from which all roads extended, like spokes in a wheel, to the ends of the then-known world (cf. Isa. 5:26, "the ends of the earth"). In the third Gospel, Luke directs attention to Jerusalem, where Jesus suffers, dies, rises from the dead, and ascends. In Acts, he focuses on Rome as the destination of Christ's gospel. From Rome the Good News reaches the entire world.

---

17. David John Williams, *Acts,* Good News Commentaries series (San Francisco: Harper and Row, 1985), p. 8.

18. The Greek noun for "witness" occurs thirteen times in Acts (1:8, 22; 2:32; 3:15; 5:32; 6:13; 7:58; 10:39, 41; 13:31; 22:15, 20; 26:16). Incidentally, of the thirty-four occurrences in the New Testament, Acts has the highest number, followed by nine in Paul's epistles and five in Revelation.

19. Consult Hermann Strathmann, *TDNT,* vol. 4, p. 493; Lothar Coenen, *NIDNTT,* vol. 3, p. 1044.

Greek Words, Phrases, and Constructions in 1:6 and 8

Verse 6

εἰ—when this particle is used to introduce a direct question, it is not translated.
μὲν οὖν—in Acts, this combination occurs repeatedly, not to show contrast, but "to introduce a new section of the narrative, meaning 'so then.' "[20]

Verse 8

ἐπελθόντος—the aorist active participle in the genitive case is part of the genitive absolute construction. The compound form of the participle is directive because of the repetition of ἐπί (upon).
Ἰουδαία . . . Σαμαρεία—"these two Roman provinces are distinct, but adjacent."[21]

B. Jesus' Ascension
1:9–11

Jesus' ascension to heaven is a historical event. Christians observe it on the fortieth day after Easter, thus on a Thursday, and ten days before Pentecost. In fact, some churches even have a worship service on Ascension Day to celebrate the enthronement of Jesus Christ. And in their worship, they verbally confess that Jesus "sits at the right hand of God the Father almighty" (Apostles' Creed).

9. After he said these things, he was lifted up while they were looking. And a cloud hid him from their sight.

Luke records the event of Jesus' ascension in remarkably few words. At the conclusion of his Gospel account, he reports that Jesus led the disciples to the vicinity of Bethany, less than two miles from Jerusalem (Luke 24:50; John 11:18). In Acts, he reveals that the exact place of departure was the Mount of Olives (1:12). In the Gospel, he relates that "having lifted up his hands, Jesus blessed [the disciples]. As he was blessing them, he left them and was taken up to heaven" (Luke 24:50–51). But Luke's narrative in Acts merely has the words, "After [Jesus] said these things, he was lifted up while they were looking."

a. "He was lifted up while they were looking." Although in verse 9 Luke omits a reference to heaven, in the next two verses (vv. 10–11) he uses the expression *into heaven* or *sky* four times. Why does Luke omit a reference to heaven in verse 9? Luke portrays the ascension not from Jesus' point of view when he entered heaven, but from the perspective of the disciples.[22] They are witnessing Jesus' ascent from earth to heaven. They must realize

20. Robert Hanna, *A Grammatical Aid to the Greek New Testament* (Grand Rapids: Baker, 1983), p. 187.
21. Robertson, *Grammar*, p. 787.
22. Consult David E. Holwerda, "Ascension," *ISBE*, vol. 1, p. 311.

that the periodic visits of the resurrected Christ have ceased with his ascension, which marks the end of the time he was physically present with his followers. Accordingly, in subsequent chapters of Acts, Jesus appears to the apostles in visions (e.g., 18:9). Note that the passive construction of the verb *he was taken up* implies that God the Father is the agent who took Jesus back to heaven (see v. 2). This construction reveals that Jesus' task on earth has ended.

b. "And a cloud hid him from their sight." We should not discuss the ascension in terms of physics or cosmology, for Scripture does not intend to teach a lesson on the location of heaven. "The upward movement is almost the only possible method of pictorially representing complete removal."[23] What Luke conveys is that Jesus leaves this earthly scene and enters heavenly glory. From other passages of Scripture we learn that a cloud hides God's heavenly glory. A bright cloud enveloped Moses and Elijah as they were talking with Jesus at the time of his transfiguration. And from this cloud, the disciples heard God's voice (Matt. 17:5; II Peter 1:17; also compare Exod. 40:34–35).[24]

10. As they were looking intently toward the sky while he was going, instantly two men dressed in white stood beside them. 11. They said, "Men of Galilee, why do you stand looking into the sky? This same Jesus, who has been taken from you into heaven, will come back in just the same way as you have seen him go into heaven."

We make these observations:

a. *Disciples.* Even though Luke is not an eyewitness of Jesus' ascension, he gives a vivid description. He describes the apostles' continued gazing into the sky. In his Gospel, Luke states that the disciples worship Jesus and return to Jerusalem with great joy (Luke 24:52). But in Acts, he focuses attention on their constant gazing toward the sky (see also v. 11). Luke portrays the human emotion which departure evokes. However, if there is any sadness, it dissipates with the appearance of two angels.

b. *Angels.* As the disciples continue to stare heavenward, suddenly two men dressed in white apparel stand next to them. Obviously, they are angels sent by God. Notice the similarity with the appearance of two angels at the empty tomb on Easter morning, when two angels in white appear to the women and to Mary Magdalene (Luke 24:4; John 20:12). The color white symbolizes purity and joy.

The angels have been sent not to rebuke but to reveal. Hence they ask, "Men of Galilee, why do you stand looking into the sky?" We assume that all eleven disciples are from Galilee—Judas Iscariot had been the exception. The angels call the apostles Galileans to remind them of their fellowship with Jesus and his earthly ministry in Galilee. The angels have come to turn

---

23. Guthrie, *New Testament Theology*, p. 395.
24. Refer to George E. Ladd, *A Theology of the New Testament* (Grand Rapids: Eerdmans, 1974), p. 334.

possible sadness into joy; to assure the disciples that even though Jesus has ascended, from heaven he will direct them in fulfilling their task; and to tell them of Christ's return at the appointed time.

c. *Jesus.* As Jesus himself promised the apostles that he would be with them to the end of time (Matt. 28:20), so the angels stress the continuity the apostles have with Jesus. They say that "this same Jesus, who has been taken from you into heaven, will come back in just the same way as you have seen him go into heaven." The angels are not disclosing new revelation but affirming and repeating what Jesus taught during his ministry. At the end of the age, Jesus said, "[men] will see the Son of man coming in a cloud with power and great glory" (Luke 21:27). The angels place Jesus' ascension and his return in equilibrium. As he has ascended, so he will come back. Jesus will return physically, in the same glorified body with which he went to heaven. He remains true to his character and word as he directs the increase of his church and prepares a place for his followers (John 14:2–3).

Doctrinal Considerations in 1:9–11

After Jesus' ascension, the disciples "returned to Jerusalem with great joy" (Luke 24:52). Although Luke does not reveal the incentive for their rejoicing, we find a few reasons that cause every believer to rejoice in Christ's ascension.

First, Jesus' entrance into heaven with a glorified human body is our assurance that we likewise shall be glorified and with body and soul enter God's presence. In heaven, "the dust of the earth [Gen. 2:7] is on the throne of the majesty on high," where Christ sits at the right hand of God himself.[25]

Next, at the right hand of God the Father, Jesus is our advocate to plead our cause (I John 2:1). When we pray to God in Jesus' name, Jesus perfects our prayers and presents them to God. Jesus knows our longing to be with him, our daily needs, and our sins. He speaks in our behalf to the Father and procures our salvation. During his physical absence, he grants us the gift of the Holy Spirit to guide and direct us in our daily lives.

Last, Jesus' ascension and session at God's right hand mark his royal enthronement. From his royal throne, Jesus rules in this world, even if the world is unwilling to acknowledge Christ's sovereignty. When Christ "has put all his enemies under his feet" (I Cor. 15:25), he hands the kingdom to his Father and the end has come.[26]

Greek Words, Phrases, and Constructions in 1:10–11

Verse 10

παρειστήκεισαν—this compound verb from παρίστημι (I stand beside) is in the pluperfect but is equivalent to the imperfect tense.[27]

---

25. Alexander Ross, "Ascension of Christ," *EDT*, p. 87.

26. Compare Bruce M. Metzger, "The Meaning of Christ's Ascension," *CT* 10 (May 27, 1966): 863–64; see also C. F. D. Moule, "The Ascension—Acts 1.9," *ExpT* 68 (1957): 205–9.

27. Consult Robertson, *Grammar*, p. 904.

Verse 11

ὅν τρόπον—literally it means "in what manner." This construction "represents a compound adverbial phrase such as ἐκεῖνον τρόπον ὅν. . . , *in that manner in which*."[28]

C. After Jesus' Ascension
1:12–14

In obedience to Jesus' instructions (1:4; Luke 24:49), the apostles wait ten days in Jerusalem for the coming of the Holy Spirit. During this time of waiting, they meet daily in a large room for continued prayer as they prepare for the task that awaits them.

12. Then they returned to Jerusalem from the Mount of Olives, which is a Sabbath day's journey from Jerusalem.

Luke calls attention not to the angels but to the apostles who returned to Jerusalem. This city is significant in New Testament history, because near it Jesus died on the cross and rose from the dead. From it, in a broader sense, he ascended to heaven. And in it, the Holy Spirit came upon the apostles.

The place from which Jesus ascended to heaven is the Mount of Olives. Luke does not specify the exact spot from which Jesus departed, but the top of this hill is two hundred feet higher in elevation than the city of Jerusalem (compare Zech. 14:4; Mark 11:1). The view of the city is magnificent.

Writing to Theophilus, who was a Gentile, Luke assumes that he is acquainted with Jewish law and custom even though Theophilus may have been unfamiliar with Palestinian topography. Luke employs the popular expression *a Sabbath day's walk* to indicate distance and not time, for a Jew was permitted to walk from Jerusalem a distance of three-quarters of a mile on the Sabbath.[29] Jesus ascended not on a Sabbath but on a Thursday, which is the fortieth day after Easter (see v. 3).

13. And when they had entered, they went to the upper room where they were staying; they were Peter, John, James and Andrew, Philip and Thomas, Bartholomew and Matthew, James son of Alphaeus and Simon the Zealot, and Judas son of James.

The apostles return to Jerusalem and assemble in the upper room where they are accustomed to meet. Luke indicates that this is *the* room, which may have been the same place where Jesus and the disciples celebrated the Passover. Nevertheless, we lack certainty because Luke uses a different word for the Passover room; he calls it "the room above ground level" (Luke 22:12). According to the account in Acts, the disciples come to their room; the word in Greek signifies "under the roof," that is, upstairs. They come to it via a stairway on the outside of the house. We understand that an

---

28. C. F. D. Moule, *An Idiom-Book of New Testament Greek*, 2d ed. (Cambridge: Cambridge University Press, 1960), p. 132.

29. SB, vol. 2, pp. 590–94. Compare Exod. 16:29; Num. 35:5; Josh. 3:4.

upstairs room shields the occupants from outside interference and thus is ideally suited for the disciples' purpose, namely, to pray. Although we know that the early church gathered in the house of John Mark's mother for prayer (12:12), Luke provides no proof that this is the same place. The apostles continue to stay in that place until they assume their task on the day of Pentecost.

Who are the apostles? The writers of the synoptic Gospels have given a list of names (Matt. 10:2–4; Mark 3:16–19; Luke 6:14–16), yet Luke deems it necessary to present another list without the name of Judas Iscariot. He implies that the apostles must appoint a person in the place of Judas to fill up the number twelve. He lists the names in a sequence that varies from earlier lists: Peter, John, James, and Andrew. Notice that although Peter and Andrew are brothers, their names are separated by the names of the brothers John and James. Then follow Philip and Thomas, Bartholomew and Matthew. The last three have additional descriptions: James son of Alphaeus, Simon the Zealot, and Judas son of James. The last person also is known as Thaddaeus (Matt. 10:3; Mark 3:18).

14. These were all with one mind constantly devoting themselves to prayer along with the women and Mary the mother of Jesus and with his brothers.

a. *Prayer*. In the first part of this verse, Luke mentions two noteworthy items. First, the apostles are continually in prayer. This is a fundamental characteristic of the apostles and of the early Christians. After Pentecost, the believers come together for prayer (2:42) and the apostles make it known that their task is to "devote [themselves] to prayer and the ministry of the word" (6:4). And in their writings they urge the believers to "pray continually" (I Thess. 5:17). Next, the apostles pray together "with one mind" (NASB). They present their prayers unanimously and express a perfect unity that becomes a feature of the early church.[30] Presumably the apostles pray for the outpouring of the Holy Spirit, whose coming Jesus promised repeatedly during his ministry.

b. *Believers*. The believers who are together in Jerusalem form the nucleus of the Christian church. This nucleus consists of men and women, to whom are added a group of about 120 people (v. 15). We assume that the women Luke refers to are those (Mary Magdalene, Joanna, Susanna, and many others) who accompanied Jesus during his ministry and supported him financially (Luke 8:2–3). They had followed Jesus from Galilee for his last visit to Jerusalem; they stood at a distance from Jesus' cross when he died (Luke 23:49; John 19:25); they made the necessary preparations for his burial (Luke 23:55–56; 24:1); and they reported the news of Jesus' resurrection to the disciples (Luke 24:9–10).

Luke also refers to Mary, the mother of Jesus. In the first two chapters of

---

30. Consult Williams, *Acts,* p. 12; Calvin, *Acts of the Apostles,* vol. 1, p. 39.

his Gospel, Luke makes Mary a central figure.[31] Undoubtedly, she is an influential person who, with her sons, believed in Jesus. The term *brothers* denotes not sons born to Joseph in a previous marriage but sons born to Joseph and Mary after Jesus' birth. They are James, Joseph, Simon, and Judas (Matt. 13:55; Mark 6:3). From the Gospels we learn that Jesus' own brothers refused to believe in him, even in the last six months of his public ministry (John 7:5; see also Mark 3:21). After Jesus' resurrection, they believed in him. Thus we read that during the forty days before the ascension, Jesus privately appeared to James to prove to him the reality of his resurrection (I Cor. 15:7). James put his faith in Jesus. Eventually, he became the head of the Jerusalem church and wrote a letter to the dispersed Christians (James 1:1). And last, Judas, who calls himself a brother of James, also wrote a canonical epistle (Jude 1).

Greek Words, Phrases, and Constructions in 1:13–14

Verse 13

καταμένοντες—with the imperfect active ἦσαν, this construction is past periphrastic and expresses continuity. The compound in this present participle conveys the perfective idea.

ζηλωτής—Simon is a Zealot. The Gospels of Matthew and Mark call him a Κανάναιος. This word is not the equivalent of "Canaanite"; rather, it derives from an Aramaic form that means "zealot" (Matt. 10:4; Mark 3:18).

Verse 14

προσκαρτεροῦντες—this is part of a past periphrastic construction. The compound present participle is perfective and has its root in the verb καρτερέω (I am strong, steadfast).

ὁμοθυμαδόν—as an adverb, this word comes from ὁμοῦ (together) and the noun θυμός (passion; ardor).

D. Matthias's Appointment
1:15–26

1. Scripture Fulfilled
1:15–20

We know from Paul's enumeration of Jesus' post-Easter appearances that Jesus was seen by more than five hundred persons at the same time (I Cor. 15:6). This appearance may have occurred in Galilee (Matt. 28:10, 16–20).

---

31. Mary's name occurs nineteen times in the New Testament, of which five appear in Matthew (1:16, 18, 20; 2:11; 13:55), one in Mark (6:3), twelve in Luke (1:27, 30, 34, 38, 39, 41, 46, 56; 2:5, 16, 19, 34), and one in Acts (1:14). Mary not only gave birth to her Son; she also assisted with the birth of the church.

In Jerusalem, however, were some 120 believers who before Pentecost began to meet with the apostles.

15. And in those days, Peter stood up in the midst of the brothers (a gathering of about a hundred and twenty people) and said: 16. "Men and brothers, the Scripture had to be fulfilled which the Holy Spirit foretold through the mouth of David concerning Judas, who became a guide for those who arrested Jesus. 17. Because he was numbered among us and he shared in this ministry."

Between Jesus' ascension and Pentecost, the believers in Jerusalem come together not only for prayer but also to reflect on the vacancy left by the departure of Judas. Luke speaks in general terms: "in those days." He records that Peter is the spokesman for the apostles as he addresses the believers.[32] Luke adds an explanatory note and literally says, "There were at the same [place] a multitude of names of about a hundred and twenty." The names belong to persons who are true believers.

In the first twelve chapters of Acts, Peter is the unquestioned leader in the Jerusalem church. Here is the beginning of his apostolic ministry. Speaking decisively, he addresses the crowd and directs attention to the fulfillment of Scripture. He says, "Men and brethren,"[33] which is a familiar address. He begins his speech by pointing to the Scriptures that *had* to be fulfilled. Peter bases his remarks on God's Word and intimates that Scripture is authentic and inexorably must be fulfilled. He links the written Word to the Holy Spirit, who "spoke long ago through the mouth of David concerning Judas" (NIV). Scripture, then, is the product of the Spirit, as Peter eloquently states in one of his epistles (II Peter 1:20–21). He asserts that the Holy Spirit speaks by using the mouth of man. That is, the Spirit communicates to us through the mouth of David, the composer of many psalms.

What is fulfilled? Peter points to Judas, "who became a guide for those who arrested Jesus." He himself vividly remembers the night of Jesus' betrayal and his own sin of disowning Jesus. Nevertheless, he briefly articulates the charge against Judas, who willfully betrayed his Lord.

"Because he was numbered among us and he shared in this ministry." Almost as an afterthought Peter notes that Judas belonged to the circle of the twelve disciples during Jesus' earthly ministry. Throughout this period, Judas was one of the twelve whom Jesus appointed after he spent a night in prayer (Luke 6:12–16). In addition, "Peter refers to Judas having obtained

---

32. At least two translations have the reading *disciples* (KJV, NKJV). Translators, however, follow the better Greek text that has the expression *brothers*. To avoid confusion caused by the repetition of this word from the preceding verse (v. 14), where it refers to the brothers of Jesus, scribes adopted the reading *disciples*.

33. In the Greek text, this expression appears as an address thirteen times, all in Acts (1:16; 2:29, 37; 7:2; 13:15, 26, 38; 15:7, 13; 22:1; 23:1, 6; 28:17). A modern equivalent, "brothers and sisters," is proposed by SEB.

through Christ's choice a share in the apostolic ministry."[34] Judas, then, was divinely appointed to take his place among the apostles and serve Christ in the ministry.

18. (This man bought a field with the reward received for his wickedness; and falling headlong, he burst open in the middle and all his intestines spilled out. 19. And it became known to all that live in Jerusalem, so that they called that field in their own language Akeldama, that is, field of blood.)

Before Luke continues Peter's speech proving that Scripture had to be fulfilled "through the mouth of David concerning Judas" (v. 16), he gives an explanatory note about Judas's death. He provides information that is supplementary and not contradictory to what Matthew writes about Judas's demise (Matt. 27:3–10). Matthew records that Judas, after he returned the thirty silver coins to the chief priests and the elders, hanged himself. The chief priests decided to use the money to buy the potter's field for the burial of foreigners.

In an abbreviated account, Luke portrays Judas as the buyer of this field. Because the high priests considered the reward Judas had received to be blood money, they refused to accept the thirty silver coins. These belonged to Judas. Indirectly, then, Judas purchased the potter's field. This is what Luke has in mind when he writes, "This man bought a field with the reward money he got for his wickedness."

"Falling headlong, he burst open in the middle and all his intestines spilled out." Even though Luke omits the information that Judas hanged himself (Matt. 27:5), we infer that Judas's falling down headlong resulted from being suspended. The rope either broke due to the sudden stress caused by a falling body or eventually was cut by someone. The possibility is not remote that, while falling, Judas's body struck a sharp object that caused it to burst open. We also infer that Judas died on the field which the chief priests bought. Luke indicates that the residents of Jerusalem heard about Judas's gruesome death and named the field "in their own language Akeldama," which means "field of blood." From Matthew's point of view, the blood that was spilled belonged to Jesus. For that reason, the high priests called the thirty silver coins "blood money" (Matt. 27:6). But notice that whereas Matthew writes for a Jewish audience, Luke addresses Gentile Christians. Hence, the accounts of Matthew and Luke are not at variance.[35] Matthew and Luke are like two news reporters describing an event from different perspectives for different audiences.

20. "For it is written in the Book of Psalms:

---

34. J. I. Packer, *NIDNTT*, vol. 1, p. 478.
35. Consult A. B. Gordon, "The Fate of Judas According to Acts 1:18," *EvQ* 43 (1971): 97–100; Max Wilcox, "The Judas-Tradition in Acts 1.15–26," *NTS* 19 (1973): 438–52.

> 'Let his place be a desert
> and let no one dwell in it.'

And,

> 'And let someone else take his office.' "

Consider these points:

a. *Setting.* Luke returns to Peter's speech and presents two psalm citations that Peter quoted to prove his point. The first one is from Psalm 69:25 and the second from Psalm 109:8. Peter introduces the Old Testament quotations with the familiar phrase *for it is written.* That is, the Scriptures have abiding validity, are absolutely trustworthy, and must be fulfilled.

The psalms were well known to the Jews and early Christians. They were sung in local synagogues during the worship services and thus committed to memory. The Christians gave a messianic interpretation to many of the psalms, especially when they knew that Jesus himself had quoted and applied a particular psalm. In fact, when Jesus cleansed the temple he cited Psalm 69:9a: "Zeal for your house will consume me" (John 2:17).

Paul quotes Psalm 69:9b and applies it to Christ: "The insults of those who insult you have fallen on me" (Rom. 15:3, NIV).[36] This particular psalm belongs to the category that speaks of the suffering Messiah. "The passion Psalms are the part of the Old Testament Scriptures most frequently cited in the New Testament; and after Ps[alm] 22 there is no Psalm referred to in so many ways as Ps[alm] 69."[37] Not every verse in this psalm is directly messianic. Some of the verses describe God's enemies upon whom the psalmist pronounces a curse. Peter takes one of these verses and applies it to Judas. Psalm 109:8 also contains a curse that Peter directs against Jesus' betrayer.

b. *Meaning.* The wording of these quotations differs little from the Old Testament text. Instead of using the singular "his" and "it," the psalmist gives the plural "their" and "tents" ("May their place be desolate; let no one dwell in their tents" [Ps. 69:25]). He pronounces a curse upon God's enemies and implies that the expression *place* includes all the material possessions a man owns. By contrast, Peter applies the expression to Judas's name, family, and earthly possessions, which are cursed. Then he thinks of the apostolic place Judas occupied during Jesus' ministry and quotes Psalm 109:8: "Let another take his place of leadership." The apostolic office itself is not affected by the death of Judas but is given to someone else. With this psalm citation, Peter indicates that the circle of the twelve apostles must be restored. The successor of Judas Iscariot must fill the apostolic office and as

---

36. Paul quotes Ps. 69:22–23 in Rom. 11:9–10. In addition, there are at least twelve allusions in the New Testament to verses of Ps. 69.

37. Franz Delitzsch, *Biblical Commentary on the Psalms,* trans. Francis Bolton, 3 vols. (1877; Grand Rapids: Eerdmans, 1955), vol. 2, p. 277.

a person must differ radically from the betrayer. He must be able to meet the apostolic requirements that Peter enumerates in the last part of his speech.

Greek Words, Phrases, and Constructions in 1:15–20

Verse 15

ὀνομάτων—literally this word means "names," but it is translated "persons," and thus refers to both men and women.

Verse 16

ἔδει—the imperfect active indicative from the incomplete verb δεῖ (it is necessary) expresses, in this text, divine necessity.[38]

ὁδηγοῦ—with the participle γενομένου, this is the genitive absolute construction. The aorist tense of the participle denotes single action that occurs subsequent to the action of the main verb.

Verse 17

κατηριθμημένος—this perfect passive participle from the verb καταριθμέω (I number with) is a periphrastic construction to show duration of time. The word occurs once in the New Testament.

Verse 18

ἐκ μισθοῦ τῆς ἀδικίας—"from wages that caused wickedness." Here is the objective genitive construction (compare II Peter 2:13, 15).

πρηνής—"headlong." Some scholars suggest the translation "*swollen, distended.*"[39]

Verse 19

τῇ ἰδίᾳ διαλέκτῳ—the adjective means "private" and the noun "language." This is a reference to the Aramaic language spoken in Jerusalem and transliterated into Greek with the word Ἀκελδαμάχ.

Verse 20

ἐπισκοπήν—from the verb ἐπισκοπέω (I oversee), the noun signifies oversight in fulfilling the apostolic office.

ἕτερος—the word denotes another of a different kind.

---

38. Refer to R. C. Trench, *Synonyms of the New Testament* (1854; Grand Rapids: Eerdmans, 1953), p. 392.
39. Bauer, pp. 700–701. Consult Metzger, *Textual Commentary*, pp. 286–87.

2. Apostolic Requirements
1:21–22

What are the requirements for apostleship? Peter briefly defines them and expects that a candidate who is able to meet these standards will be chosen to fill the vacancy left by Judas.

21. "It is therefore necessary that one of the men who have accompanied us all the time that Jesus went in and out among us—22. beginning from the baptism of John until the day in which he was taken up from us—be a witness of his resurrection with us."

Quoting the words of the psalmist, "Let someone else take his office," Peter utters the wish that God indeed will appoint a successor. When he says that it is necessary to choose a prospective apostle, Peter reveals God's will in this matter (compare v. 16). Peter and his audience do not act on their own accord but in obedience to God's word (Ps. 109:8) and will.

a. "It is therefore necessary that one of the men who have accompanied us all the time that Jesus went in and out among us." As Jesus appointed the twelve disciples, who formed a parallel to the twelve tribes of Israel, so the eleven apostles had to choose by lot one additional person to restore the apostolic circle.[40] The number twelve denotes perfection and in the New Testament appears numerous times with reference to the disciples, the tribes of Israel, Jerusalem, and the judgment day.[41] Incidentally, no successor was chosen after the death of the apostle James (Acts 12:2), because the church at that time was well established. And Paul became an apostle as "one untimely born" (I Cor. 15:8).

During his ministry, Jesus had more disciples than the twelve he had chosen. At one time he commissioned seventy-two (or seventy) others for a mission comparable to that of the twelve disciples (Luke 10:1, 17; and see Matt. 10:5).

b. "The men who have accompanied us all the time that Jesus went in and out among us." Even though the Evangelists report that Jesus called Matthew (Matt. 9:9) and perhaps others at a later date, at least half of the twelve disciples had already begun to follow Jesus before his baptism (see John 1:35–51).

The title *Lord Jesus* occurs frequently in Acts (4:33; 11:20; 16:31; 20:21, 24, 35). It describes Jesus' earthly ministry and it serves as a confession of faith (I Cor. 12:3). The phrase *[Jesus] went in and out* is a Semitism typical of Peter's native tongue. Indeed, Luke accurately presents Peter's speech and not a more or less free composition.[42]

40. Refer to Richard N. Longenecker, *The Acts of the Apostles*, in vol. 9 of *The Expositor's Bible Commentary*, ed. Frank E. Gaebelein, 12 vols. (Grand Rapids: Zondervan, 1981), p. 265.

41. E.g., Matt. 11:1; 19:28; John 6:70; Acts 6:2; Rev. 7:5–8; 21:12, 14, 16, 21.

42. Refer to Herman N. Ridderbos, *The Speeches of Peter in the Acts of the Apostles* (London: Tyndale, 1962), p. 9.

c. "Beginning from the baptism of John until the day in which [Jesus] was taken up from us." Here is a clear reference to the beginning of the apostolic gospel (Matt. 3:1; Mark 1:1; Luke 3:1).[43] For instance, in the house of Cornelius, Peter also begins his gospel presentation with Jesus' baptism (Acts 10:37). The apostolic gospel sketches the baptism by John as the beginning of Jesus' ministry. And that ministry lasted until the day of his ascension.

d. "[It is therefore necessary that one of the men] be a witness of his resurrection with us." The qualifications for apostleship are two: the prospective apostle must have been trained by Jesus from the time of Jesus' baptism to the day of his ascension; he also must be a witness of Jesus' resurrection. Strictly speaking, no disciple was present when Jesus arose from the dead. But Jesus appeared to the apostles and to many other people and thus presented the physical evidence of his resurrection. The term *witness* has a double meaning: it refers to something that a person has observed, and it means the act of testifying (compare v. 8). The apostles had seen the resurrected Christ; now they are about to tell the world about this redemptive event. The doctrine of Christ's resurrection is fundamental to the preaching of both Peter and Paul, for their sermons culminate in proclaiming the Christian tenet: "I believe in the resurrection of the body" (Apostles' Creed).

Greek Words, Phrases, and Constructions in 1:21–22

Verse 21

ἐν παντὶ χρόνῳ—"the context strongly suggests *during the whole time,* not *on every occasion.*"[44]

Verse 22

τῆς ἀναστάσεως αὐτοῦ—"of his resurrection." The genitive is as much subjective as objective.

γενέσθαι—the aorist middle infinitive, introduced by δεῖ (it is necessary), is an indirect statement. This lengthy sentence (vv. 21–22) exemplifies excellent Greek style.

Among the numerous disciples of Jesus, only two men are candidates to fill the place that Judas left vacant. We assume that candidates are scarce, for relatively few people are able to meet the requirements. However, the apostles need only one person to restore their circle.

---

43. Consult Bengel, *Gnomon of the New Testament,* vol. 2, p. 521. The birth narratives in the first two chapters of both Matthew's and Luke's Gospels refer to a time that was not part of Jesus' official ministry.
44. Moule, *Idiom-Book,* pp. 94–95.

3. *Divine Appointment*
1:23–26

23. And they proposed two men, Joseph called Barsabbas (who was also known as Justus), and Matthias. 24. They prayed, "Lord, you know the hearts of all men. Show us which one of these two you have chosen 25. to receive this ministry and apostleship from which Judas strayed to go to where he belongs."

After Peter formulates the conditions for apostleship, the others respond and propose the names of two men: Joseph and Matthias. Joseph is also known by his Latin name *Justus* (compare 18:7; Col. 4:11) and as the Son of Sabbas (the elder) or Son of the Sabbath. Either his father's name was Sabbas or Joseph was born on a Sabbath. Probably Judas Barsabbas (15:22) was his brother. The second candidate is Matthias. His name is a shortened form of Mattathias (gift of Yahweh).

The believers are unable to make a decision on their own accord. They know that not two but only one person is needed to fill Judas's place and to regain a twelfth member of the apostolate. Jesus originally appointed the twelve; now he must elect one of the two candidates. The congregation prays,

> Lord, you know everyone's heart.
> Show us which of these two you have chosen
> to take over this apostolic ministry. [NIV]

The decision, therefore, is made not by the apostles but by the Lord himself. The expression *Lord* denotes either God or Jesus. Even if Luke elsewhere writes, "God, who knows the heart" (15:8), the context itself shows that Peter refers to the Lord Jesus (v. 21). In addition, the verb *have chosen* occurs in verse 2, where Jesus is the subject.[45]

The apostles formulate and apply the qualifications for the two men, but the Lord knows their hearts and chooses the successor to take over the apostolic ministry from Judas Iscariot. The believers conclude their prayer with the words, "from which Judas strayed to go where he belongs." These words imply that Judas has left his apostolic office to take up his place in the service of Satan.

26. And they cast lots and the lot fell to Matthias, and he was added to the eleven apostles.

The apostles resort to the Old Testament custom of casting lots to learn the will of God.

> The lot is cast into the lap,
> but its every decision is from the LORD. [Prov. 16:33]

---

45. See F. F. Bruce, *The Book of the Acts*, rev. ed., New International Commentary on the New Testament series (Grand Rapids: Eerdmans, 1988), p. 47.

The practice of casting the lot was common in Old Testament times; in the New Testament the Evangelists record that the soldiers cast lots for Jesus' clothes (Matt. 27:35; Mark 15:24; Luke 23:34; John 19:24). After the outpouring of the Holy Spirit on Pentecost, the practice ceases. In the period between Jesus' ascension and Pentecost, the apostles determine the conditions for apostleship, pray for divine guidance, and cast the lot to ascertain God's choice.

"The lot fell to Matthias." Luke does not reveal how the apostles cast lots, but writes only that Matthias is the Lord's choice. The Lord appoints him as he had earlier commissioned the twelve apostles. For that reason, the ceremony of laying hands on Matthias is not observed (e.g., 6:6). Although Matthias fills the vacancy in the circle of the twelve apostles, we do not hear from or about him in the rest of the New Testament.[46]

Apostleship as such is an intriguing subject. Paul is unable to meet the qualifications for apostleship, yet he becomes the apostle to the Gentiles. Next to Peter, Paul is the prominent apostle in the early church. However, Paul could not have filled Judas's place, for his apostleship is entirely different. The difference between Paul and the Twelve is obvious: Paul submits his work to the scrutiny of the apostles (see Gal. 1:18; 2:1–2, 7–10). Nevertheless, Paul and the apostles share a common appointment because Jesus Christ himself commissioned them.[47]

Practical Considerations in 1:26

Should a church cast lots when choosing its leaders? In Old Testament times, the high priest used the Urim and Thummim to make decisions for the Israelites (Exod. 28:30). Perhaps the Urim and Thummim were small stones that gave the high priest either a positive or negative answer to a question. Casting lots was common among the Israelites. They cast the lot to distribute the land and determine their inheritance (e.g., Num. 26:55; Josh. 14:2; 15:1; I Chron. 6:54); to disclose Achan's sin (Josh. 7:16–18); to select Saul as king of Israel (I Sam. 10:20–21); and to determine the number and time of the priests and Levites to serve at the temple (Neh. 10:34; 11:1).

The last scriptural reference to God's people casting lots is when Matthias is chosen to succeed Judas. Note that, according to the New Testament, at no time during Jesus' ministry or after the outpouring of the Holy Spirit did God's people cast lots. Furthermore, the early church provides no evidence for such practice in appointing its leaders. Because the New Testament and the early church are silent on this matter, believers ought to exercise caution and not adopt a practice that lacks firm support.

---

46. In the first few centuries, unverifiable traditions concerning Matthias circulated. Thus, Eusebius (A.D. 300) believed that Matthias was one of the seventy(-two) disciples Jesus commissioned (Luke 10:17). *Ecclesiastical History* 1.12.3 (LCL). See also David W. Wead, "Matthias," *ISBE*, vol. 3, p. 288.

47. Consult William Childs Robinson, "Apostle," *ISBE*, vol. 1, pp. 192–95; Karl Heinrich Rengstorf, *TDNT*, vol. 1, pp. 420–45.

Greek Words, Phrases, and Constructions in 1:24–26

Verse 24

ἀνάδειξον—the aorist imperative active from the verb ἀναδείκνυμι (I lift up for all to see; appoint) shows single occurrence.

ἐξελέξω—this is the second person singular aorist middle indicative of the verb ἐκλέγομαι (I choose).

Verse 25

λαβεῖν—from λαμβάνω (I take, receive), this second aorist infinitive expresses purpose.

τὸν τόπον τὸν ἴδιον—note the emphatic use of the definite articles. The adjective stands last in the sentence for emphasis. The phrase itself is a euphemism for death.

Verse 26

ἔδωκαν—instead of the verb βάλλω (I cast), the aorist indicative of δίδωμι (I give) appears to express a Hebrew idiom.

συγκατεψηφίσθη—the two prepositions σύν (with) and κατά (down) with the noun ψῆφος (pebble) connote the casting of lots by putting down pebbles together.

Summary of Chapter 1

In the first two verses, Luke writes an introduction that serves as a bridge between his Gospel and Acts. He records that Jesus appeared to the apostles during the forty-day period and gave them instructions in preparation for their task. Those instructions are to wait in Jerusalem for the gift of the Holy Spirit. The disciples ask Jesus when he will restore the kingdom to Israel. Jesus tells them that the Father has set the time and the date for establishing the kingdom, and that they will receive divine power to be witnesses for Jesus from Jerusalem to the ends of the world.

Jesus ascends as the apostles are looking at him. Then two angels announce that Jesus will return in the same way as he ascended. From the Mount of Olives the apostles return to Jerusalem, meet in a room upstairs, and show unity in constant prayer together with some women, Mary the mother of Jesus, and Jesus' brothers.

Peter addresses a group of about 120 believers and mentions the fulfillment of Scripture with respect to Judas. He states the necessity of choosing someone to fill the vacancy and to meet the requirements for apostleship. The group proposes two names, in prayer asks the Lord to choose one of them, and casts lots. Matthias is chosen and added to the eleven apostles.

2

The Church in Jerusalem, *part 1*

2:1–47

Outline

2:1–8:1a   II. The Church in Jerusalem

2:1–47   A. Pentecost

2:1–13   1. Outpouring of the Spirit

2:1–4   a. Outpouring

2:5–11   b. Gathering

2:12–13   c. Scoffing

2:14–41   2. Peter's Sermon

2:14–21   a. Events Explained

2:22–24   b. God's Word Fulfilled

2:25–28   c. David's Prophecy

2:29–36   d. God's Promise Kept

2:37–41   e. Genuine Response

2:42–47   3. Christian Community

2:42–43   a. At Worship

2:44–47   b. In the Community

2 1 When the day of Pentecost came, they were all together in one place. 2 And suddenly a noise like a violently blowing wind came from heaven and it filled the whole house where they were sitting. 3 And to them tongues as of fire appeared that separated and rested on each one of them. 4 They were all filled with the Holy Spirit and began to speak with other tongues as the Spirit was giving them ability.

5 Now there were dwelling in Jerusalem devout Jews from every nation under heaven. 6 When they heard this noise, a crowd gathered; they were confused because each one was hearing them speaking in his own language. 7 And they began to be utterly amazed, saying: "Are not all these men who are speaking from Galilee? 8 Then how is it that each of us hears them in his native tongue? 9 Parthians, Medes, and Elamites; residents of Mesopotamia, Judea, and Cappadocia, Pontus and Asia, 10 Phrygia and Pamphylia, Egypt and the parts of Libya near Cyrene, and visitors from Rome, 11 Jews and converts to Judaism, Cretans and Arabs—we hear them speaking in our own tongues the mighty deeds of God!" 12 And all were astonished and perplexed, asking one another, "What does this mean?" 13 But others were mocking and saying, "They are full of sweet wine."

14 Then Peter stood up with the Eleven, raised his voice, and addressed them: "Fellow Jews and all you who reside in Jerusalem, let this be known to you and pay attention to my words. 15 For these men are not drunk as you suppose. It is only nine in the morning! 16 But this is what was spoken by the prophet Joel:

> 17 " 'And in the last days, God says,
>   I will pour forth of my Spirit on all people;
> Your sons and your daughters shall prophesy,
>   your young men will see visions,
>   and your old men will dream dreams.
> 18 Even on my slaves, both men and women,
>   I will pour forth of my Spirit in those last days
>   and they will prophesy.
> 19 And I will show wonders in heaven above
>   and signs on the earth below,
>   blood and fire and billows of smoke.
> 20 The sun will be turned into darkness
>   and the moon into blood,
>   before the great and glorious day of the Lord will come.
> 21 And it will be that everyone who calls on the name
>   of the Lord will be saved.'

22 "Men of Israel, listen to these words: Jesus of Nazareth was a man attested by God to you with miracles, wonders, and signs, which God did through him in your midst, as you yourselves know. 23 This man was given up to you according to God's set purpose and foreknowledge, and you by using lawless men nailed him to the cross and killed him. 24 God raised him up, having freed him from the agony of death, because it was impossible for him to be kept in its power. 25 For David said about him:

" 'I saw the Lord always before me;
  for he is at my right hand,
  that I may not be shaken.
26 Therefore my heart was glad
  and my tongue rejoiced;
  even my body will dwell in hope,
27 because you will not abandon me to the grave,
  nor will you let your Holy One undergo decay.
28 You have made known to me the paths of life;
  and you will fill me with joy in your presence.'

29 "Men and brothers, I can say confidently to you that the patriarch David both died and was buried, and his tomb is with us to this day. 30 And being a prophet, he knew that God had sworn to him on oath to place one of his descendants on his throne. 31 Looking ahead, he spoke concerning the resurrection of Christ that he was neither abandoned to the grave nor did his body undergo decay. 32 This Jesus God raised up, and all of us are witnesses of it. 33 Therefore, having been exalted to God's right hand, and having received from the Father the promise of the Holy Spirit, he has poured out what you now both see and hear. 34 For David did not ascend into heaven, but he himself said,

" 'The Lord said to my Lord;
  "Sit at my right hand
35 until I make your enemies
  a footstool for your feet.'

36 "Therefore let all the house of Israel assuredly know that God has made this Jesus, whom you crucified, both Lord and Christ."

37 Now when they heard this, they were cut to the heart and said to Peter and the rest of the apostles, "Men and brothers, what shall we do?"

38 Peter answered them, "Repent and be baptized every one of you in the name of Jesus Christ for the forgiveness of your sins. And you will receive the gift of the Holy Spirit. 39 The promise is for you and your children and for all who are far off—as many as the Lord our God will call to himself."

40 And with many other words he testified and kept on exhorting them: "Save yourselves from this crooked generation." 41 Then those who accepted his word were baptized, and about three thousand people were added that day.

42 They were continually devoting themselves to the apostles' teaching and to fellowship, to the breaking of bread and to prayer. 43 Everyone was filled with awe, and many wonders and signs were being done by the apostles. 44 And all who believed were together and they shared all things. 45 They began to sell their possessions and goods and they gave to anyone who might have need. 46 Day by day continuing to meet together in the temple courts, breaking bread from house to house, they ate together with gladness and sincerity of heart, 47 praising God and enjoying the favor of all the people. The Lord continued to add daily to their number those who were being saved.

II. The Church in Jerusalem
2:1–8:1a

A. Pentecost
2:1–47

1. Outpouring of the Spirit
2:1–13

Even though Acts is a historical book, Luke omits references to exact dates. Scholars generally agree that in the chronology of Acts the feast of Pentecost was celebrated in A.D. 30 in the last week of May.[1] The word *Pentecost* derives from a Greek word that means "fiftieth." The Jews celebrated Pentecost as the Feast of Weeks on the fiftieth day after Passover (Lev. 23:15–16; Deut. 16:9–12). They also called it the Feast of Harvest (Exod. 23:16). The Jews considered Pentecost the harvest festival, at which time they presented the first fruits of the wheat harvest (Num. 28:26). After the destruction of the temple in A.D. 70, they changed this festival into a commemoration of the giving of the Decalogue at Mount Sinai. They based this on the chronological reference in Exodus 19:1.[2] Presumably the Jews reacted to the Christian observance of Pentecost.

a. Outpouring
2:1–4

1. When the day of Pentecost came, they were all together in one place.
In response to Jesus' command (1:4), the apostles wait patiently and prayerfully in Jerusalem for the gift of the Holy Spirit. The Greek text begins with the word *and* (KJV, NASB); this indicates that the event of Pentecost is closely linked to Jesus' ascension. A literal version of the Greek text has "when the day of Pentecost was being fulfilled." That is, when the fiftieth day arrives, the period of waiting is completed. For the apostles a new era dawns.

How many persons were together on the day of Pentecost? We expect that the number includes all the believers in the group of 120 (1:15). Some objections to this interpretation are raised, however. The last verse of the preceding chapter (1:26) mentions the apostles; in the second chapter, not the 120 but Peter and the Eleven occupy center stage (v. 14); and at the conclusion of Peter's sermon, the crowd addresses the apostles and not the 120 (v. 37). Conversely, we cannot limit the adjective *all* to the twelve

---

1. E.g., W. Ralph Thompson, "Chronology of the New Testament," *ZPEB*, vol. 1, p. 821. Also consult Harold W. Hoehner, *Chronological Aspects of the Life of Christ* (Grand Rapids: Zondervan, 1976), p. 143.
2. Refer to SB, vol. 2, p. 601; Arthur F. Glasser, "Pentecost," *ISBE*, vol. 3, p. 759; James D. G. Dunn, *NIDNTT*, vol. 2, pp. 784–87. In view of evidence from intertestamental literature (Jub. 6:17 and Qumran), some scholars think that the change to commemoration of the giving the Decalogue is pre-Christian.

apostles when the context of the preceding chapter stresses basic Christian harmony. Therefore, we interpret the adjective to include all the believers mentioned in the preceding chapter.

Where were the believers? Luke tersely writes that they were "in one place." If we think of the upper room (1:13), we question whether this room could accommodate a group of 120. Luke, however, indicates that they were sitting in a house (v. 2) and not in the precincts of the temple.[3] We admit that we are unable to achieve certainty, but we presume that the meeting place was near the temple, where the apostles stayed continually praising God (compare Luke 24:53).

2. And suddenly a noise like a violently blowing wind came from heaven and it filled the whole house where they were sitting. 3. And to them tongues as of fire appeared that separated and rested on each one of them. 4. They were all filled with the Holy Spirit and began to speak with other tongues as the Spirit was giving them ability.

Note these three points:

a. *Wind.* In the morning hours of Pentecost, the people suddenly hear the sound of a violent wind blowing from heaven. One important aspect of the coming of the Holy Spirit is the suddenness of his appearance. Although, as they were instructed, the disciples stay in Jerusalem to wait for the outpouring of the Spirit, nonetheless his sudden arrival is surprising. Christ's followers will experience a similar situation when Jesus suddenly returns. Despite the signs of the times Jesus reveals to his people, his return will be surprising and unexpected.

Luke states that there is the sound of the blowing of a violent wind. He does not indicate that the wind itself is making its effects known. From other parts of Scripture, we know that both in the Hebrew and in the Greek one word conveys the double meaning *wind* and *spirit* (Ezek. 37:9, 14; John 3:8). We hear and feel the effect of the wind but are unable to see it. So it is with the Spirit. The Holy Spirit comes from heaven, not from the sky, with the sound of a violent wind. He fills the house where the Christians are sitting and praying for his coming (compare 4:31).

We see the significance of the wind in Luke's account. The wind symbolizes the Holy Spirit, who fills the house where the believers are sitting. The sound of the wind denotes heavenly power, and its suddenness reveals the inception of a supernatural event.

b. *Fire.* "And to them tongues as of fire appeared that separated and rested on each one of them." This is the fulfillment of John the Baptist's description of Jesus' power: "He will baptize you with the Holy Spirit and with fire" (Matt. 3:11; Luke 3:16). In the Old Testament, fire is often a symbol of God's presence in respect to holiness, judgment, and grace. For example, Moses heard the voice of God in the burning bush and was told to

---

3. Consult Richard N. Longenecker, *The Acts of the Apostles*, in vol. 9 of *The Expositor's Bible Commentary*, ed. Frank E. Gaebelein, 12 vols. (Grand Rapids: Zondervan, 1981), p. 269.

take off his sandals (Exod. 3:2–5); fire destroyed the sacrifice of Elijah at Mount Carmel (I Kings 18:38); and a chariot of fire took Elijah to heaven (II Kings 2:11).[4]

The believers not only hear the coming of the Holy Spirit, but also see him appearing in what seem to be tongues of fire. The fire, symbol of the divine presence, takes the form of tongues that do not come out of the believers' mouths, but rest on their heads. Therefore, we should not confuse these tongues with the "other tongues" mentioned in the next verse (v. 4), where Luke introduces the miracle of tongue speaking.

The Holy Spirit appears in this external sign and rests upon each of the believers. He is not illusory, because Luke clearly indicates that they saw tongues of fire. The coming of the Spirit fulfills John the Baptist's prophecy that the disciples would be baptized with the Spirit and with fire.[5] Therefore the coming of the Holy Spirit ushers in a new era, for he comes to take up his dwelling with men not temporarily but forever.

c. *Tongues.* "They were all filled with the Holy Spirit and began to speak with other tongues as the Spirit was giving them ability." The Greek text indicates that the filling with the Spirit occurred once for all. That is, the Spirit did not come and go but stayed, as is evident from Luke's account. When Peter addresses the Sanhedrin, he is filled with the Spirit (4:8; and see 4:31). After his conversion, Saul receives the Holy Spirit (9:17; compare 13:9, 52). The outpouring of the Spirit is not repetitious, for the Spirit stays with the person who has been filled. Furthermore, the Spirit reaches out in ever-widening circles to the Samaritans (8:17), the Gentiles (10:44–46), and the disciples of John the Baptist (19:1–6). This occurs in harmony with and in fulfillment of the command Jesus gave to the apostles to witness in Jerusalem, in Judea and Samaria, and to the ends of the earth (1:8).

What is the effect of the Holy Spirit on all the believers? Luke writes, "They were all filled." We should not limit the adjective *all* as applying only to the apostles, for Peter in his sermon shows that Joel's prophecy has been fulfilled: "Your sons and daughters will prophesy" (v. 17; Joel 2:28). And when subsequently Peter and John report the remarks of the chief priests to the believers, *all* were filled with the Holy Spirit (4:31). The effect of the indwelling of the Holy Spirit is that he takes full possession of the individual believer.

The Christian who is filled with the Spirit becomes the Spirit's mouthpiece. In the case of the believers in Jerusalem, they speak in other tongues and thereby prove that the Holy Spirit controls and enables them. The word *tongue* is the equivalent of the concept *spoken language.* This is evident from Luke's comment that "each one was hearing them speaking in his own

---

4. Consult Friedrich Lang, *TDNT,* vol. 6, pp. 934–47; Hans Bietenhard, *NIDNTT,* vol. 1, pp. 653–57.

5. Refer to James D. G. Dunn, *Baptism in the Holy Spirit,* Studies in Biblical Theology, 2d series 15 (London: SCM, 1970), p. 40.

language" (v. 6); the multitude asks, "Then how is it that each of us hears them in his native tongue?" (v. 8); and they say, "We hear them speaking in our own tongues the mighty deeds of God" (v. 11). The tongues the believers speak are the known languages spoken in areas ranging from Persia in the east to Rome in the west. We cannot equate the Pentecost event with tongue speaking in the Corinthian church. The believers who speak in other tongues at Pentecost do not speak for the edification of the church (in distinction from ecstatic speech [I Cor. 14]). Whereas in the Corinthian church ecstatic speech has to be interpreted, at Pentecost the hearers do not need interpreters because they hear and are able to understand their own languages.[6] The ability to speak in tongues comes from within man as an internal sign of the Holy Spirit; the wind and the fire are external signs.

Doctrinal Considerations in 2:2 and 4

Verse 2

Here is the fulfillment of Jesus' promise to the apostles: "You will be baptized with the Holy Spirit within a few days" (1:5). On the day of Pentecost, the Spirit filled everyone sitting in the house, so that the 120 were spiritually baptized (vv. 2, 4). A study of Spirit baptism in Acts is significant. "Whenever baptism with the Spirit is mentioned after Pentecost, it is never an experience of believers who have already been baptized once with the Spirit but only of new groups of people who are brought to faith in Christ."[7]

After the outpouring of the Holy Spirit upon the Jews in Jerusalem, Jesus extended his church by adding the Samaritans, who received the Spirit (8:16–17). Next, he invited the Gentiles into his church. This occurred when Peter preached the gospel in the house of Cornelius and the Holy Spirit was poured out on the Gentiles (10:44–45). Finally, the disciples of John the Baptist, who had not heard the gospel and did not know about the Holy Spirit, were added to the church. Paul baptized them in the name of Jesus and the Holy Spirit came on them (19:6).

Peter told the Jerusalem crowd, "Repent and be baptized, every one of you, in the name of Jesus Christ for the forgiveness of your sins. And you will receive the gift of the Holy Spirit" (2:38, NIV). We conclude from a study of Acts that water baptism and Spirit baptism normally occur simultaneously.

Verse 4

Although some scholars assert that the miracle of speaking in tongues relates more to the hearers than to the speakers, this view fails to do justice to those who, filled with the Holy Spirit, spoke in tongues. The context of the Pentecost event features the remarks of those who heard the apostles speak in familiar languages, but a few questions must be faced. For instance, if we say that believers, by the

---

6. Refer to William G. MacDonald, "Glossolalia in the New Testament," in *Speaking in Tongues: A Guide to Research on Glossolalia,* ed. Watson E. Mills (Grand Rapids: Eerdmans, 1986), p. 134.

7. George E. Ladd, *A Theology of the New Testament* (Grand Rapids: Eerdmans, 1974), p. 345.

power of the Spirit, spoke to the crowd in their own languages, why did Peter address all the people in only one language (v. 14)? Next, if the multitude understood Peter, we expect that those present were able to converse in Greek or Aramaic or both. Furthermore, the words *other tongues* do not apply to Judea (v. 9), for there Aramaic and Greek were spoken. And last, if everyone present was able to hear about "the mighty deeds of God" in his native language, why did some people mock the apostles and charge them with drunkenness (v. 13)?[8] Specific questions concerning the Pentecost experience remain unanswered because of the brevity of the report. From the account, we are able to draw only general conclusions.

The Holy Spirit unites believers from many parts of the world by speaking miraculously to them in the language of faith. He makes it possible for the hearers to overcome the linguistic confusion of Babel (Gen. 11:1–9) when he calls them to respond to the gospel in repentance and faith (v. 38). As unbelievers scoff at the Pentecost miracle, three thousand believers repent, are baptized, and join the church (v. 41).

Greek Words, Phrases, and Constructions in 2:1–4

Verse 1

ἐν τῷ—with the present middle infinitive this construction denotes time and refers to the one day of Pentecost during which the Holy Spirit came.

Verse 2

φερομένης πνοῆς—from the verb φέρω (I carry, bear), the present middle participle can be either a genitive absolute construction or a descriptive participle (with the noun πνοῆς) dependent on ἦχος (sound).

Verse 4

ἐπλήσθησαν—the aorist passive indicative from πίμπλημι (I fill) complements the other two verbs that express the concept *fill*: συμπληροῦσθαι (v. 1) and ἐπλήρωσεν (v. 2).

ἑτέραις—in context, this adjective has the meaning *different*. Contrast the use of ἑτέροις in verse 40.

Among the Jewish people living in dispersion, many decided to take up residence in Jerusalem for either religious or educational purposes. They came from numerous countries and stayed permanently or temporarily in Jerusalem. Also, a number of pilgrims had come to Jerusalem to celebrate the Jewish harvest feast called Pentecost (compare 20:16; I Cor. 16:8).

---

8. Consult Richard B. Rackham, *The Acts of the Apostles: An Exposition,* Westminster Commentaries series (1901; reprint ed., Grand Rapids: Baker, 1964), p. 21; F. W. Grosheide, *De Handelingen der Apostelen,* Kommentaar op het Nieuwe Testament series, 2 vols. (Amsterdam: Van Bottenburg, 1942), vol. 1, pp. 61–63.

b. Gathering
2:5–11

5. Now there were dwelling in Jerusalem devout Jews from every nation under heaven. 6. When they heard this noise, a crowd gathered; they were confused because each one was hearing them speaking in his own language.

a. "Now there were dwelling in Jerusalem devout Jews." We observe that the gospel comes to the Jew first and not to the Gentile, as Jesus instructed his disciples when he sent them on their missionary tour: "Do not go toward the Gentiles. . . . But go rather to the lost sheep of the house of Israel" (Matt. 10:5–6). God-fearing Jews from abroad settled in the holy city. "It was the wish of pious Jews of the Dispersion to spend their last days on the soil of the holy land and to be buried there."[9]

In the New Testament, the Greek term that means "devout" is descriptive only of Jewish people: Simeon (Luke 2:25), Ananias (Acts 22:12), and the men who buried Stephen (8:2). They are the people who obey God's law faithfully and reverently.

b. "From every nation under heaven." These Jews represent the world at large. They have come to Jerusalem from every nation of the civilized world of that time. In subsequent verses, Luke provides a list of nations (vv. 9–11).

c. "When they heard this noise, a crowd gathered; they were confused." Do the people hear the noise of the violent wind or the sound of the apostles speaking in many languages? We assume that the term *noise* refers to the noise of the violent wind (v. 2) and not to the speaking of the believers. We visualize the people gathering in groups to determine the origin of the sound. As they move toward the place where the believers are, they hear them speaking in numerous tongues. The result is that they are confused.

d. "Because each one was hearing them speaking in his own language." Luke indicates not only that the multitude hears the voices of the believers but that every individual Jew who is present listens to his own language. In fact, he says that each one keeps on hearing while the speakers continue to speak.

We presume that the God-fearing Jews were at least bilingual, if not trilingual. Living in Jerusalem, they conversed in Aramaic. And if they had come from the parts of the Roman empire west and north of Israel, they would know Greek. But they also learned the languages of their native countries. They now hear these languages spoken by people who are not residents of these countries but who are Galileans. Luke reports only the fact of speaking and does not mention the content. He presents the substance of Peter's Pentecost sermon in subsequent verses.

---

9. Everett F. Harrison, *The Apostolic Church* (Grand Rapids: Eerdmans, 1985), p. 49.

7. And they began to be utterly amazed, saying: "Are not all these men who are speaking from Galilee? 8. Then how is it that each of us hears them in his native tongue?"

Language is the vehicle of communication which for each person is his native tongue. When the alien residents of Jerusalem hear the language they learned in the country where they were born and reared, they are utterly amazed. Linguistic barriers that hinder effective communication are removed when the Holy Spirit enables the believers to convey God's revelation in numerous languages.

The crowd detects that the speakers are not foreigners but Galileans. Perhaps the people recognized them as followers of Jesus, or the apparel of the apostles marked them as Galileans.[10] In the eyes of the Jews in Jerusalem, Galilee was a culturally backward area of Palestine inhabited by uneducated people. Yet these Galileans communicate God's truth in numerous languages.

As the believers are speaking, they demonstrate to the audience that they are praising God in all the languages and dialects of the world. They prove that God's revelation is not bound to one particular language but that it transcends all variations of human speech. Nevertheless, we observe that God does not repeatedly grant the miracle of speaking in a foreign language. For example, we do not read that Paul and Barnabas address the people of Lystra in their own language (14:11).

When the believers address the crowd in known languages, the alien Jews living in Jerusalem ask: "Then how is it that each of us hears them in his native tongue?" By speaking other languages, the believers provide the evidence that the Holy Spirit is performing a miracle. Those who hear their own language or dialect are dumbfounded and ask emphatically how this is possible. This question is basic, for they mention it twice after Luke has introduced the concept (see vv. 6, 8, 11). Hearing their native language or dialect, they become susceptible to accepting Christ and his gospel when Peter preaches his Pentecost sermon.

These aliens represent the countries where they were born. After the Babylonian captivity, not all the Jewish people returned to Palestine. Many remained in Persia and Mesopotamia. Others were deported from Babylon to Asia Minor during the fourth and third centuries before Christ. Still others settled in Egypt, especially in the city of Alexandria, or traveled west to Rome.[11] Jews resided everywhere in the Roman empire, from east to west, for they were a scattered people.

9. "Parthians, Medes, and Elamites; residents of Mesopotamia, Judea, and Cappadocia, Pontus and Asia, 10. Phrygia and Pamphylia, Egypt and the parts of Libya near Cyrene, and visitors from Rome, 11. Jews and

---

10. Compare Matt. 26:73; Mark 14:70; Luke 22:59.
11. Consult F. F. Bruce, *New Testament History* (1969; Garden City, N.Y.: Doubleday, 1971), pp. 135–37.

converts to Judaism, Cretans and Arabs—we hear them speaking in our own tongues the mighty deeds of God!"

Luke lists fifteen nations of the civilized world in his day. He begins with nations in the east (Parthia, Media, Elam, Mesopotamia), then moves via Judea to Asia Minor (Cappadocia, Pontus, Asia, Phrygia, Pamphylia), from there to Africa (Egypt, Cyrene), and then to Rome, Crete, and Arabia.[12] Why he lists these nations and omits others (e.g., Greece, Macedonia, Cyprus) is an open question. Luke seems to group the nations in linguistic categories, for his objective in this Pentecost account is to emphasize that the Good News transcends linguistic barriers.[13]

a. "Parthians, Medes, and Elamites." These people belonged to different nations where different languages were spoken. The Parthians lived south of the Caspian Sea, in an area now known as Iran. In the apostolic era, these people had never been conquered by the Roman armies, spoke a Persian dialect, and allowed the Jews religious freedom. The Medes, who with the Persians had consolidated an empire (refer to Esther 1:3, 18–19; Dan. 5:28; 6:8, 12, 15; 8:20), resided southwest of the Caspian Sea. The Elamites occupied the land directly north of the Persian Gulf to the east of the Tigris River. They became part of the Persian empire but kept their own language.

b. "Residents of Mesopotamia." They lived between the Tigris and Euphrates rivers. The Jews who came to Jerusalem from Mesopotamia actually were residents of Babylon, to which they had been exiled centuries earlier. They were visitors in Jerusalem because they continued to live in Mesopotamia, which is modern Iraq.

The Greek shows that the term *residents* should also include people from Judea, Cappadocia, Pontus, Asia, Phrygia, Pamphylia, Egypt, and Libya. These people, then, have come for the Pentecost feast in Jerusalem and expect to return to their native lands.

c. "Judea." The presence of Judea in this list is problematic; obviously it does not fit between Mesopotamia and Cappadocia. Luke often refers to Judea as the land of the Jews and may be thinking of the territory that David and Solomon controlled, from the Euphrates in the north to the Egyptian border in the south.[14] This eases the problem because then it includes Syria, which is absent from the list. Furthermore, in the eyes of the

---

12. Consult G. D. Kilpatrick, "A Jewish Background to Acts 2:9–11?" *JJS* 26 (1975): 48–49.

13. Refer to E. Güting, "Der geographische Horizont der sogenannte Völkerliste des Lukas (Acta 2:9–11)," *ZNW* 66 (1975): 149–69; J. A. Brinkman, "The Literary Background of the 'Catalogue of the Nations' (Acts 2, 9–11)," *CBQ* 25 (1963): 418–27; Bruce M. Metzger, "Ancient Astrological Geography and Acts 2:9–11," in *Apostolic History and the Gospel*, ed. W. Ward Gasque and Ralph P. Martin (Exeter: Paternoster; Grand Rapids: Eerdmans, 1970), pp. 123–33.

14. F. F. Bruce, *The Book of the Acts*, rev. ed., New International Commentary on the New Testament series (Grand Rapids: Eerdmans, 1988), p. 56.

Jews, Jerusalem was the capital not only of Judea but of all the places where Jews had settled. Jews coming from Judea could hardly be overlooked.[15]

d. "Cappadocia, Pontus, and Asia." Luke mentions the areas of Asia Minor next in his list. Cappadocia was located north of Syria and Mesopotamia and extended to the southeast coast of the Black Sea. Pontus with Bithynia formed a Roman province situated along the southwestern shores of the Black Sea. Asia was the name for the Roman province in western Asia Minor. To illustrate, Peter addressed his first epistle to the Jewish Christians who were scattered throughout Pontus, Galatia, Cappadocia, Asia, and Bithynia (I Peter 1:1).

Jews inhabited Asia Minor by the thousands. Therefore, Luke adds the provincial names Phrygia and Pamphylia, located in the southwestern and southern part of Asia Minor respectively. The Jewish historian Josephus records that in the second century B.C., the Syrian ruler Antiochus III deported two thousand Jewish families to Phrygia.[16] During his missionary journeys Paul traveled through Pamphylia (13:13) and Phrygia (16:6; 18:23).

e. "Egypt." In the first century of the Christian era, the Jewish population in Egypt numbered about a million people. Most of them lived in the coastal city of Alexandria.[17] In this city, the Jews had translated the Old Testament Scriptures from Hebrew into Greek. To the west of Egypt, Libya had opened its borders to Jewish people who settled in its capital city, Cyrene (6:9; 11:20; 13:1; Matt. 27:32).[18]

f. "Visitors from Rome." Luke is specific and no longer uses the word *residents* but "visitors." These Jews are not necessarily Roman citizens but Jews and converts to Judaism who lived in Rome. Jews in Rome numbered in the tens of thousands in the time of the apostles. In Rome the Jews propagated Judaism and as a result gained numerous proselytes. Among these converts were also many God-fearers, who observed the law of Moses but did not submit to circumcision (see 10:1; and Luke 7:5).

g. "Cretans and Arabs." As an afterthought Luke mentions two other groups: Cretans and Arabs. Crete is an island in the Mediterranean Sea and is located south of Greece. Paul saw the coast of Crete on his voyage to Italy (27:7) and visited the island when Titus founded the church there (Titus 1:5). The Arabs who came to Jerusalem for the feast of Pentecost presumably were Jews who resided in Nabatea. The Nabateans were desert dwellers who lived in an area that stretched in a southwesterly direction from Damascus to Egypt. Petra, situated to the southeast of Palestine, was its capital. Paul spent time in the Nabatean kingdom of Arabia (Gal. 1:17).

---

15. SB, vol. 2, p. 611.
16. Josephus *Antiquities* 12.3.4 [147].
17. Josephus *Antiquities* 14.7.2 [118]; *War* 2.18.8 [110–18].
18. Compare Josephus *Antiquities* 14.7.2 [116–18].

h. "We hear them speaking in our own tongues the mighty deeds of God!" The believers filled with the Holy Spirit proclaim the miracles God has performed. We assume that they especially declare the wonders in connection with the resurrection and ascension of Jesus. Luke states that the devout Jews who were residing or visiting in Jerusalem hear about these wonders in their native languages.

Doctrinal Considerations in 2:5–11

The New Testament church begins with the 120 who await the coming of the Holy Spirit. When he comes, he opens the floodgates by addressing Jews "from every nation under heaven" (v. 5). In all the different languages of these nations, the Holy Spirit through the mouths of his people presents the message of the wonders God has done. From these thousands of Jews who have come from numerous places, God adds three thousand to his church. God's truth is no longer confined to the city of Jerusalem. On the day of Pentecost, the church becomes worldwide.

From the Old Testament Scriptures we know that the Jews were together in Jerusalem for the harvest festival. In the New Testament, God through the outpouring of the Holy Spirit and the mission of the church reaps the first fruits of his spiritual harvest. Henry Alford, the nineteenth-century British poet and commentator, put this truth in song:

> All the world is God's own field,
> Fruit unto his praise to yield;
> Wheat and tares together sown,
> Unto joy or sorrow grown:
> First the blade, and then the ear,
> Then the full corn shall appear:
> Lord of harvest, grant that we
> Wholesome grain and pure may be.

We note that Luke gives no indication that he is acquainted with the rabbinic interpretation of commemorating the Law-giving event at Pentecost. From comments made by rabbis two hundred years after the outpouring of the Holy Spirit on the day of Pentecost, we learn that God promulgated the Law from Mount Sinai in seventy languages but that only the Israelites listened to the voice of God.[19] Even if we see a resemblance between the rabbinic tradition of the seventy languages at Mount Sinai and Luke's account of the many languages spoken at Pentecost, we do not see that with the coming of the Spirit God gave a new law.[20] Instead God presented the gift of his Spirit not only to the 120 but also to every believer. As Peter said: "Repent and be baptized, every one of you, in the name of Jesus Christ for the forgiveness of your sins. And you will receive the gift of the Holy Spirit" (v. 38, NIV).

---

19. For a list of references consult SB, vol. 2, pp. 604–5.

20. Refer to Ernst Haenchen, *The Acts of the Apostles: A Commentary*, trans. Bernard Noble and Gerald Shinn (Philadelphia: Westminster, 1971), p. 174. Also consult David John Williams, *Acts*, Good News Commentaries series (San Francisco: Harper and Row, 1985), p. 27.

Greek Words, Phrases, and Constructions in 2:5–9

Verse 5

κατοικοῦντες—this present active participle of the compound verb κατά (down) and οἰκέω (I dwell) is with the imperfect active ἦσαν (they were) a periphrastic construction that expresses duration. The compound form with the preposition κατά denotes permanence. By contrast, παρά with the verb οἰκέω points to strangers who live somewhere temporarily.

Verse 6

γενομένης—with the noun φωνῆς, this aorist middle participle forms the genitive absolute construction.

συνεχύθη—from συγχύν(ν)ω (I confuse), this verb occurs repeatedly in Acts (2:6; 9:22; 19:32; 21:27, 31) but nowhere else in the New Testament. Literally, the verb means "to pour together [in the mind]" and thus cause confusion.

ἤκουον—the imperfect active of ἀκούω (I hear) expresses continued action.

Verse 8

ἡμεῖς—as a personal pronoun, it emphasizes the subject of the verb ἀκούομεν (we hear). Word for word, the entire verse is emphatic.

Verse 9

οἱ κατοικοῦντες—this articular present participle pertains to nine countries or areas ranging from Mesopotamia to Libya.

Ἰουδαίαν—as an adjective with the understood noun γῆν (land), this word must be understood in the widest possible sense of the entire Jewish nation. However, the combination τε καί (and) links it closely to Cappadocia, which is highly unusual. Moreover, as a substantive, Ἰουδαίαν should have been preceded by the definite article τήν. Why should the inhabitants of Judea "be amazed to hear the apostles speak in their own language"?[21] Throughout the centuries, writers have proposed conjectures (e.g., Armenia, Bithynia, and Cilicia); nevertheless, the manuscript evidence for Ἰουδαίαν is exceptionally strong.

---

c. Scoffing
2:12–13

12. And all were astonished and perplexed, asking one another, "What does this mean?" 13. But others were mocking and saying, "They are full of sweet wine."

Luke resumes his account of the crowd's reaction by saying that they were "astonished." He uses the same word in verse 7, but now he adds the

---

21. Bruce M. Metzger, *A Textual Commentary on the New Testament*, 3d corrected ed. (London and New York: United Bible Societies, 1975), p. 293.

expression *perplexed*. Luke indicates that the people continue to be confused, for they are unable to explain the miracle they are witnessing. These devout people are asking one another about the meaning of the event (compare 17:20).

Not all the hearers are at a loss. Luke says that a certain group of people ridicules the apostles and those with them. He depicts them as unbelievers who oppose the advance of Christ's church. They can be equated with "the world [, which] begins with *ridicule;* then afterwards it proceeds to *questioning* (4:7); to *threats* (4:7); to *imprisoning* (5:18); to *inflicting stripes* (5:40); to *murder* (7:58)."[22] This is the devil's unchanging strategy against Jesus and his followers. God performs miracles for everyone to see and hear, yet the unbelievers refuse to accept the truth. They make fun of that which is holy and thus harden their hearts.

The scoffers assert that the apostles are intoxicated because they drank too much wine. They attack Peter and his companions with a claim that is ridiculous; the time of day to see people under the influence of an alcoholic beverage is not at its beginning. Peter responds to their charge by calling attention to the time: "It is only nine in the morning!" (v. 15).

The feast of Pentecost is the harvest festival of wheat and not of grapes. The grape harvest takes place at the conclusion of the summer. Therefore, the word *wine* refers not to new wine but to sweet wine from the harvest of the past year.

Greek Words, Phrases, and Constructions in 2:12–13

Verse 12

διηπόρουν—from διαπορέω (I am at a loss), this compound shows intensity ("thoroughly perplexed"), duration (imperfect tense), and support for the preceding verb ("amazed").

ἄλλος πρὸς ἄλλον—an idiom that is reflexive and equivalent to the pronoun ἀλλήλων.

Verse 13

ἕτεροι—this adjective is not a synonym for ἄλλοι in this sentence. Here it relates to a group of people who are entirely different from those who were amazed and perplexed.

διαχλευάζοντες—this present participle of a compound verb indicates continued and intense action. It describes the manner of mocking the apostles.

μεμεστωμένοι—the verb μεστόω (I fill) in this context refers to wine. Note that the perfect middle in this participle denotes an act that began in the past and has effect in the present. With the verb *to be,* the construction is the perfect periphrastic.

---

22. John Albert Bengel, *Gnomon of the New Testament*, ed. Andrew R. Fausset, 5 vols. (Edinburgh: Clark, 1877), vol. 2, p. 526.

2. Peter's Sermon
2:14–41

a. Events Explained
2:14–21

After enumerating the nations of the world and describing the reaction of the crowd to the Pentecost miracle, Luke focuses attention on the sermon Peter preaches that morning. The sermon itself is a model for other sermons and speeches recorded in Acts. In his address, Peter begins by explaining the event itself and quoting the prophecy of Joel. Then he preaches Christ's gospel by referring to Jesus' suffering, death, resurrection, and exaltation. Last, he exhorts the multitude to repent and to be baptized.

Some scholars are of the opinion that Peter's sermon is much more a theological discourse written by Luke than a historical report of the apostle's speech.[23] We know that Luke himself was not present in Jerusalem on the day of Pentecost, but that he received his information from "eyewitnesses and servants of the word" (Luke 1:2). Most likely Peter served as Luke's informant and gave him the pattern and wording of the sermon. In fact, "both the pattern and the basic theology are older than Luke and probably reach back into the early days of the church."[24]

14. Then Peter stood up with the Eleven, raised his voice, and addressed them: "Fellow Jews and all you who reside in Jerusalem, let this be known to you and pay attention to my words. 15. For these men are not drunk as you suppose. It is only nine in the morning!"

a. *Leadership.* Immediately after Jesus' ascension, Peter assumes the leadership role within the company of the 120 believers. Again, on the day of Pentecost, when all the people are perplexed about the miracle of speaking other languages, Peter shows the crowd that he is the leader of the twelve apostles. In earlier days, the multitudes came to listen to Jesus. Now they come to the apostles and Peter realizes that the task of giving leadership belongs to him. Supported by his fellow apostles and filled with the Holy Spirit, he faces the thousands of Jews in the temple area. Confidently and boldly he addresses them.

"Then Peter stood up with the Eleven." The pressures of uncertainty and curiosity compel the apostles to step forward and explain the significance of the Pentecost event. The unschooled, ordinary fisherman Simon Peter finds a place from which he can address the people within the reach of his voice. The verb *stand up* means not that he arises from a sitting position but

---

23. Among others, Richard F. Zehnle, *Peter's Pentecost Discourse: Tradition and Lukan Reinterpretation in Peter's Speeches of Acts 2 and 3*, Society of Biblical Literature Monograph Series 15, ed. Robert A. Kraft (Nashville: Abingdon, 1971), pp. 136–38.

24. I. Howard Marshall, *The Acts of the Apostles: An Introduction and Commentary*, Tyndale New Testament Commentary series (Leicester: Inter-Varsity; Grand Rapids: Eerdmans, 1980), p. 72.

that he faces the multitude. The presence of the other apostles next to him conveys to the crowd that Peter speaks on their behalf.

For the apostles, the miracle of speaking in numerous languages is past (compare 10:46; 19:6). After Pentecost, they proclaim Christ's gospel in the vernacular. Thus, Peter delivers his sermon in one language. We surmise that he spoke his native Aramaic, which the multitude understood. And at the conclusion of his sermon, the crowd responds (v. 37).

b. *Address.* "Fellow Jews and all you who reside in Jerusalem." As Peter develops his speech, he gradually becomes more familiar with his audience. He begins with the common address, "fellow Jews" (v. 14); then he appeals to their religious pride and says, "men of Israel" (v. 22); and last he calls them "brothers" (v. 29).[25] Peter also addresses all those who have come from other places and now reside in Jerusalem. Even though he fails to mention the converts, he undoubtedly includes them. (Incidentally, Peter does not slight the women. According to the custom of that day, the expression *brothers* includes sisters.) Peter tells them to pay close attention to what he is going to explain what they have seen and heard.

c. *Refutation.* Peter counters the unbelievers' attack with a remark that appeals to the common sense of the audience. Pointing to the apostles, he says, "These men are not drunk as you suppose. It is only nine in the morning!" The literal translation has, "It is only the third hour of the day" (NKJV). We must understand that the ancients divided the period between sunrise and sunset into twelve periods. This means that these periods were shorter in winter and longer in summer. Therefore, if Pentecost was celebrated in the last week of May, the "third hour" was not nine but eight in the morning.[26] And at this hour of the day, 120 people would not be intoxicated. Especially on the Sabbath and on festive days, a Jew would have his first meal no earlier than about noon.[27]

16. "But this is what was spoken by the prophet Joel:
17. 'And in the last days, God says,
    I will pour forth of my Spirit on all people;
Your sons and your daughters shall prophesy,
    your young men will see visions,
    and your old men will dream dreams.
18. Even on my slaves, both men and women,
    I will pour forth of my Spirit in those last days
    and they will prophesy.' "

Peter begins his sermon by quoting from the Old Testament Scriptures. He practices what Jesus taught the apostles, namely, first quote Scripture

---

25. Consult R. C. H. Lenski, *The Interpretation of the Acts of the Apostles* (Columbus: Wartburg, 1944), p. 71.

26. John Calvin, *Commentary on the Acts of the Apostles,* ed. David W. Torrance and Thomas F. Torrance, 2 vols. (Grand Rapids: Eerdmans, 1966), vol. 1, p. 56.

27. Josephus *Life* 54 [279].

and then show its fulfillment and application. Peter cites the prophet Joel, who predicts the outpouring of the Holy Spirit, and explains that the prophecy has been fulfilled. In short, he indicates that the era of the last days has come. Peter exemplifies the fulfillment of Joel's prophecy when he speaks boldly to the crowd, proclaims Christ's gospel, and visibly demonstrates that he is filled with the Holy Spirit.

The Jews present at Pentecost know that Joel prophesied the coming of the day of the Lord "in the last days." In these last days of fulfillment, God grants his blessings to his people who repent from sin. These days inaugurate the messianic age in which God pours out his Spirit on his people.

"I will pour forth of my Spirit on all people." In the prophecy from Joel, the expression *people* includes men and women, young and old. Similarly, in Acts Luke makes no distinction between men and women. Both suffer persecution (8:3); both join the church (17:4, 12); and both teach (18:26).[28]

"Your sons and daughters shall prophesy." What is the meaning of the verb *prophesy*? In Old Testament settings it connotes predicting the future. In the Pentecost event, foretelling the future is not evident. Another interpretation is that prophesying is equivalent to preaching. And last, "prophesying can mean to engage in praise to God (see I Chron. 25:3)."[29] In the early church, the prophets instructed and exhorted God's people. Thus Luke records that Philip the evangelist "had four unmarried daughters who prophesied" (21:9).

"Your young men will see visions, and your old men will dream dreams." God reveals himself in prophecy, in visions, and in dreams, as the Scriptures repeatedly testify.[30] With the outpouring of the Holy Spirit, all believers, without distinction of gender, age, and social status, receive the wisdom and ability to know God, so that even teaching one's neighbor about the Lord is no longer necessary (Jer. 31:34; Heb. 8:11).

"Even on my slaves, both men and women, I will pour forth of my Spirit in those last days." The word *slaves* signifies that God grants his Spirit to every class of society. Notice that God claims them as his own by saying, "*my* slaves." Many of these servants were not Jews but Gentiles. Gentile slaves, both male and female, receive the Spirit and know the Lord. This becomes evident especially in the epistles of the New Testament (compare Eph. 6:5–9; Col. 3:22–4:1; I Tim. 6:1–2; Titus 2:9–10; I Peter 2:18–21). God pours out his Spirit upon the slaves, so that they are able to share the gifts of the Spirit.

---

28. Donald Guthrie, *New Testament Theology* (Downers Grove: Inter-Varsity, 1981), p. 162.

29. Harrison, *The Apostolic Church*, p. 51. And see Gary V. Smith, "Prophet," *ISBE*, vol. 3, p. 1004.

30. The Old Testament is replete with examples of prophecy and dreams. In the New Testament, see Matt. 1:20; 2:12; 27:19 regarding dreams. In Acts, references to visions are many (e.g., 9:10, 12; 10:3; 12:9; 18:9).

> **19.** " 'And I will show wonders in heaven above
> and signs on the earth below,
> blood and fire and billows of smoke.
> **20.** The sun will be turned into darkness
> and the moon into blood,
> before the great and glorious day of the Lord will come.
> **21.** And it will be that everyone who calls on the name
> of the Lord will be saved.' "

a. "And I will show wonders in the heavens above and signs on the earth below." Luke reports that Peter quotes from Joel's prophecy, but Luke fails to give its application. He refrains from stating that this prophecy was fulfilled at the time of Jesus' death on the cross when darkness came over the land for three hours (Matt. 27:45). At that time the sun was no longer visible and the signs of nature were an eloquent testimony to Christ's death.

Furthermore, Luke does not indicate that at Pentecost God fulfilled Joel's prediction of the signs and wonders. He relates that the outpouring of the Holy Spirit occurred in Jerusalem (2:1–4), Samaria (8:17), Caesarea (10:44), and Ephesus (19:6). But on none of these occasions did the people see signs in nature as Joel predicted them.

And last, Luke is equally noncommittal in respect to the fulfillment of Joel's prophecy on signs and wonders. Joel predicts that all these things will take place "before the great and glorious day of the Lord will come." However, apart from the announcement by the angels at the time of Jesus' ascension (1:11), Luke places no emphasis on the doctrine of Christ's return in the Acts of the Apostles.[31] Even if the believers on the day of Pentecost expected Jesus' eventual return, Luke focuses attention on Jesus' death, resurrection, and exaltation (vv. 22–36) but not on his return. He only reports what Peter quoted from the prophecy of Joel. Hence he accomplishes the purpose of his writing, namely, to show that the apostles are witnesses from Jerusalem to the ends of the world (1:8). Conversely, in Peter's writings composed near the end of his life, Peter distinctly outlines the return of Christ as a cardinal doctrine of the church (I Peter 5:4; II Peter 3:4, 10–13). Peter appropriately designates Christ's return as "the day of the Lord," that is, the day of judgment. For the unbeliever this day means eternal punishment, but for the Christian it signifies salvation in the presence of the Lord.

b. "Everyone who calls on the name of the Lord will be saved." Peter uses the last verse of his quotation from Joel's prophecy as an introduction to his explanation of Christ's gospel (vv. 22–36). Paul cites this same text in his discussion on salvation (Rom. 10:13).[32]

---

31. Refer to Herman N. Ridderbos, *The Speeches of Peter in the Acts of the Apostles* (London: Tyndale, 1962), p. 15.

32. Allusions to the prophecy of Joel are numerous in the New Testament; most of them appear in Revelation (twelve occurrences). Refer to Nes-Al, p. 767.

The wording of this particular verse from Joel indicates that Peter no longer addresses the multitude in general. He confronts the individual listener with Christ's gospel and tells him to call on the name of the Lord. At this point the listener understands the term *Lord* to mean God; but in the conclusion of his sermon, Peter clearly states that God made Jesus "both Lord and Christ" (v. 36). When the believer calls on the Lord's name (compare 9:14), he calls on Christ.

God opens the way of salvation to all people, both Jew and Gentile. He makes his promise to individual persons and asks them to respond individually.[33] These believers as members of Christ's body constitute the Christian church.

Doctrinal Considerations in 2:17–21

After God's work of creation and the incarnation of the Son of God, the outpouring of the Holy Spirit at Pentecost is the third major divine act. From the Old Testament we know that the Spirit was present before Pentecost but always temporarily and for special purposes. For example, the Holy Spirit rested on Eldad and Medad in the camp of Israel and enabled them to prophesy (Num. 11:26; also compare I Sam. 10:6, 10). Jesus' disciples knew from the prophets that God would pour out his Spirit on the Messiah and on the house of Israel (Isa. 11:2; 44:3; Ezek. 39:29; Joel 2:28–32). Indeed, God gave the Spirit without limit to Jesus (John 3:34) and he filled John the Baptist and his parents with the Holy Spirit (Luke 1:15, 41, 67).

After his resurrection and before his ascension, Jesus breathed on his disciples and said: "Receive the Holy Spirit. If you forgive anyone his sins, they are forgiven; if you retain them, they are retained" (John 20:22–23). Then, on the day of Pentecost, the Holy Spirit descended upon the apostles, the women and Mary, the brothers of Jesus, and others, in all 120 persons (Acts 1:12–15; 2:4, 17).

God gave the Holy Spirit to be with Jesus' church forever. When Jesus gathered his twelve disciples he began to build his church (Matt. 16:18) in distinction from Judaism. As long as Jesus was not yet glorified, the Holy Spirit would not come, for Jesus himself was the divine presence in their midst (John 7:39). But when Jesus was glorified, he breathed on them the Holy Spirit in anticipation of Pentecost. In the interim between Jesus' ascension and Pentecost, they experienced the Holy Spirit's presence. With the outpouring of the Holy Spirit on Pentecost, the church assumed its own identity separate from Judaism.

In harmony with Jesus' command to the apostles to begin in Jerusalem, Peter proclaimed Christ's gospel first in the holy city. Later he preached the Good News in Samaria and Caesarea, and in these places the Holy Spirit was poured out. The result has been that from its inception Christ's church is a universal church, for every Christian confesses these words:

---

33. Henry Alford, *Alford's Greek Testament: An Exegetical and Critical Commentary*, 7th ed., 4 vols. (1877; Grand Rapids: Guardian, 1976), vol. 2, p. 22.

I believe in the Holy Spirit;
I believe a holy universal church,
the communion of saints.
—Apostles' Creed

Greek Words, Phrases, and Constructions in 2:17 and 21

Verse 17

ἐκχέω ἀπό—"I will pour out from." The verb normally takes a direct object instead of a prepositional phrase. However, the presence of the preposition is the result of literally translating the Hebrew text into the Greek.

ἐνυπνίοις ἐνυπνιασθήσονται—"will dream dreams." Here is the Hebrew infinitive absolute construction transmitted into the Greek. This Hebrew construction connotes emphasis.

Verse 21

πᾶς ὅς—"everyone who." The relative pronoun has no antecedent. Therefore, with the adjective πᾶς it serves as the subject of the sentence. The adjective includes anyone without discrimination.

---

b. God's Word Fulfilled
2:22–24

After Peter has quoted a passage from the Old Testament Scriptures (Joel 2:28–32) that explains the Pentecost miracle the people have observed, he is ready to preach Christ's gospel. He wants people to know that with the outpouring of the Holy Spirit the messianic era has arrived.

22. "Men of Israel, listen to these words: Jesus of Nazareth was a man attested by God to you with miracles, wonders, and signs, which God did through him in your midst, as you yourselves know."

a. "Men of Israel, listen to these words." First, Peter appeals to common ground, because both speaker and listeners accept the Scriptures as the Word of God. Next, he addresses his audience with the words *men of Israel*. These words do not convey a nationalistic message to the exclusion of Gentiles; they represent no male chauvinism; and they are not a mere variation of his earlier greeting, "fellow Jews" (v. 14). The word *Israel* in this context is a religious term that reminds Peter's audience of the covenant God made with his people Israel. That is, both Peter and his listeners are members of that covenant.[34] With this greeting, Peter becomes more personal and uses it to introduce Jesus of Nazareth.

b. "Jesus of Nazareth was a man attested by God to you with miracles, wonders, and signs." Peter uses Jesus' name and place of residence that are familiar to the people.[35] By this name the crowds knew Jesus (Matt. 26:71;

---

34. Refer to Grosheide, *Handelingen der Apostelen*, vol. 1, p. 73; Lenski, *Acts*, p. 80.
35. See also 3:6; 4:10; 6:14; 22:8; 24:5; 26:9. In the Greek, the wording differs slightly in 10:38.

Luke 18:37; John 18:5, 7). According to the notice on the cross, this was Jesus' name (John 19:19). Peter describes Jesus as a man attested by God throughout his earthly life, as is evident from the miracles, signs, and wonders Jesus performed. The word *attested* describes Jesus as a person who is sent out by God and who speaks on God's behalf. No person in the audience familiar with the life of Jesus can deny his miraculous deeds of giving sight to the blind, raising the dead, and preaching the gospel of the kingdom (compare Matt. 11:5; Luke 7:22). In fact, these miracles, wonders, and signs demonstrate to the listeners that the messianic era has come, for Jesus is the Messiah.

c. "[These signs] which God did through him in your midst, as you yourselves know." In his gospel proclamation, Peter places the emphasis on God.[36] He says that God accredited Jesus (v. 22), performed miracles through him (v. 22), handed him over to be killed (v. 23), raised him from the dead (vv. 24, 32), and made him Lord and Christ (v. 36). This emphasis rests on common ground, for these God-fearing Jews (v. 5) acknowledge that Jesus could not have done what he did unless God were with him (compare John 3:2; 10:38). Accordingly, Peter observes, "As you yourselves know."

23. "This man was given up to you according to God's set purpose and foreknowledge, and you by using lawless men nailed him to the cross and killed him."

We note these two points:

a. *God's purpose.* Peter intimates that the audience is fully acquainted with the trial and death of Jesus Christ. He employs the personal pronoun *you* in this verse to involve his listeners in assuming responsibility for Jesus' crucifixion. However, he views their accountability from a divine point of view. God is in complete control even though the Jews brought Jesus to trial and the Roman soldiers killed him.

Peter says that Jesus' death occurred according to "God's set purpose and foreknowledge." The expression *set purpose* denotes a plan that has been determined and is clearly defined. The author of this set purpose is God himself (see 4:28). Peter removes any doubt whether God acted rashly in formulating his purpose to hand over Jesus to the Jewish people. He adds the term *foreknowledge.* With this word, Peter points to God's omniscience by which every part of his plan is fully known to God in advance (I Peter 1:2). In his first epistle, Peter writes that "[Jesus] was chosen before the creation of the world" (I Peter 1:20, NIV). And last, through all the Old Testament prophets, God foretold that Christ would suffer (3:18).

b. *Man's responsibility.* Peter holds his audience responsible for Jesus' death. In their view, "Jesus' messianic claim and his death on the cross were irreconcilable, self-contradictory opposites."[37] They know that "any-

---

36. Consult Alford, *Alford's Greek Testament,* vol. 2, p. 22.
37. Günter Dulon, *NIDNTT,* vol. 1, p. 473.

one who is hung on a tree is cursed [by God]" (Deut. 21:23; Gal. 3:13). Peter opposes this view by pointing to God's determinate counsel and foreknowledge.

Here is an unresolved tension between God determining the death of his Son and man being held responsible for perpetrating the deed (see 3:17– 18; 4:27–28; 13:27). God himself handed Jesus over to the Jews, who put him to death by nailing him to the cross. The Jews could not exonerate themselves by blaming Jesus' death on the Romans, whom the Jews called "wicked men," for they themselves had engaged the help of the Romans. Peter teaches that the Jews must be held accountable for killing Jesus (3:15; 4:10; 5:30; 10:39). The Jews must see all the aspects of God's plan. Thus Peter says,

24. "God raised him up, having freed him from the agony of death, because it was impossible for him to be kept in its power."

Peter states the fact of Christ's resurrection. Positively he notes that God raised Jesus from the dead. He asserts the apostolic doctrine of the resurrection, a recurring theme in Acts.[38] God worked out his plan in predetermined stages: first the death of Christ and afterward his resurrection.

God raised Jesus by "having freed him from the agony of death." The literal reading of the text for "agony" is "birth pains." But what is the meaning of freeing Jesus from the birth pains of death? Some interpreters have suggested that Peter, speaking Aramaic, used another word for birth pains, namely, cords.[39] They argue that the psalmists speak of "the cords of death" (Pss. 18:4; 116:3; and see II Sam. 22:6). We are unable to determine what word Peter used in Aramaic. The Greek, however, has the expression *birth pains*, which also occurs in Jesus' discourse on the end of the age (Matt. 24:8; Mark 13:8). This expression is a figure of speech which should not be pressed (compare the phrase *the gates of hell* in Matt. 16:18). God set Jesus free from the agony that accompanies death.

Peter gives the reason for Jesus' deliverance from the agony of death: "because it was impossible for him to be kept in its power." God pronounced the curse of death upon the human race when Adam fell into sin (Gen. 3:17–18; see also Gen. 2:17). But the sinless Jesus, who took upon himself the sin of the world (John 1:29), removed the sting of death (I Cor. 15:55–56) when he died on the cross. Therefore, death no longer had any power over him.

> Death cannot keep his prey—
> Jesus, my Saviour.
> —Robert Lowry

---

38. See also 2:32; 3:15; 5:30; 10:40; 13:30, 34, 37; 17:31.
39. Compare Robert G. Bratcher, " 'Having Loosed the Pangs of Death,' " *BibTr* 10 (1959): 18–20; Haenchen, *Acts*, p. 180.

Greek Words, Phrases, and Constructions in 2:23–24

Verse 23

βουλῇ καὶ προγνώσει—these two nouns are preceded by one definite article, τῇ, and therefore are closely connected. βουλῇ (purpose) is qualified by the perfect passive participle ὡρισμένη (from the verb ὁρίζω [I set limits; determine]).

ἔκδοτον—this is a verbal adjective from ἐκδίδωμι (I give up) that expresses the passive construction *was handed over;* God is the implied agent.

διὰ χειρός—literally it is "through the hand [of]." This is a typical Hebraic construction translated into Greek.

Verse 24

ὠδῖνας—"birth pains." The Greek text has no variants for this word. However, in the Hebrew the Masoretic Text has *ḥebel* (cord) instead of *ḥēbel* (birth pains) in Psalms 18:6 and 116:3. The Septuagint [Ps. 18:6 = 17:6 and 116:3 = 114:3] has ὠδῖνες. The text of the Septuagint and the words of Peter are much earlier than the relatively late vowel pointing of the Masoretic Text and therefore are preferred.

---

c. David's Prophecy
2:25–28

25. "For David said about him:
'I saw the Lord always before me;
for he is at my right hand,
that I may not be shaken.
26. Therefore my heart was glad
and my tongue rejoiced;
even my body will dwell in hope,
27. because you will not abandon me to the grave,
nor will you let your Holy One undergo decay.
28. You have made known to me the paths of life;
and you will fill me with joy in your presence.' "

Here is the second of the three Old Testament quotations in Peter's Pentecost sermon. Peter follows the Greek translation of Psalm 16:8–11, which differs little from the Hebrew text in this passage. Peter quotes this psalm to support his teaching that God raised Jesus from the dead and thus fulfilled David's prophecy concerning Christ and his resurrection. Paul also quotes a verse from this psalm when he preaches in Pisidian Antioch and sees the fulfillment of Jesus' resurrection in Psalm 16:10, "You will not let your Holy One see decay" (13:35).

a. "I saw the Lord always before me; for he is at my right hand, that I may not be shaken." David reveals himself as a person who puts his trust completely in God. He speaks as God's child who knows that God is never far from him. In fact, David sees the Lord in front of him; the Hebrew text has, "I have set the LORD continually before me" (Ps. 16:8). God is at David's right hand and because of the Lord's nearness David is at ease. The clause "he is at my right hand" (Pss. 73:23; 109:31; 110:5; 121:5) depicts God as David's protector.

b. "Therefore my heart was glad and my tongue rejoiced." Because of the close fellowship David has with God and the confidence he places in him, his heart is filled with joy and happiness. He expresses his feelings by singing songs of praise. David refers to his heart, which is the center of his being. He believes with his heart and confesses with his mouth (Rom. 10:10). He continues, "My body will dwell in hope." The Hebrew reading of Psalm 16:9b is, "my body also will rest securely." David knows that physically he is safe and secure even in the face of death. He puts his hope in God. Here is the reason:

c. "Because you will not abandon me to the grave, nor will you let your Holy One undergo decay." Although David refers to himself in the first part of the verse (v. 27; Ps. 16:10), in the second half he prophesies about the Messiah and his resurrection. David expresses his confidence that the grave will not mark the end of his fellowship with God. He will continue to enjoy life in the Lord's presence. He repeats this thought in the next verse: "You have made known to me the paths of life" (v. 28; Ps. 16:11).

Many versions transliterate the Greek term *Hades*.[40] This is the term for the Hebrew *Sheol*, which signifies "pit" or "grave." In his sermon, Peter employs the word *Hades* not in the sense of "abode of the dead," but as the grave. Even in the grave God does not abandon his own child but gives him assurance of the resurrection. The sentence, "Nor will you let your Holy One undergo decay," is David's assurance of God's affirmation.

Paul provides a logical analysis of David's words and applies them to Christ. He says: "For David, after he served God's purpose in his own generation, fell asleep. He was buried with his fathers and underwent decay. But whom God raised from the dead did not undergo decay" (13:36–37). Peter's explanation of David's remark is even more explicit (vv. 29–32). He points to the evidence of David's tomb in Jerusalem, but Christ's tomb is empty because God raised him from the dead. And Peter himself can testify to this fact.

d. "You have made known to me the paths of life; and you will fill me with joy in your presence." In the last part of this psalm, David resorts to the literary device of contrast: negative and positive, death and life, decay and God's presence. Note also the contrast between "me" and "your Holy One." Even if the second part of verse 27 (Ps. 16:10) applies to David himself, the fact that Peter calls him a prophet points not to the psalmist but to Christ. Nevertheless, in the last verse of this psalm David speaks about himself; he sums up his intimate fellowship with God.

---

40. E.g., NKJV, JB, RSV, NASB.

David acknowledges that God has given him divine revelation that instructs him to follow the paths of life. He states, "You have made known to me the paths of life." For David, God's Word is a lamp for his feet and a light for his path (Ps. 119:105). He knows that God himself is a fountain of life, so that David is able to enjoy the fullness of life in the presence of God. David's joy consists of walking continuously in the path of life in fellowship with his Lord.

The phrase *in your presence* is a source of joy, for God's presence is the light of lights.[41] In the words of the apostle John, "And our fellowship is with the Father and with his Son, Jesus Christ. We write these things to make our joy complete" (I John 1:3–4).

Doctrinal Considerations in 2:25–28

The writers of the Old Testament know that no one can escape the power of death and that everyone descends into the grave at the appointed time. They also know that God has power over death and that in the presence of God they have eternal life. Accordingly, Job confidently states that although death destroys his skin in the grave, he will see God in his flesh (Job 19:25–27). Filled with hope, David asserts that he will see God's face and have access to him after death (Pss. 11:7; 16:9–11; 17:15). And Asaph confesses that he is always with God, who will take him into glory. Even when his physical being fails him, God is his portion forever (Ps. 73:23–26).

The early Christians applied Psalm 16:10 to Christ: "Because you will not abandon me to the grave, nor will you let your Holy One undergo decay." They interpreted David's word to mean that the grave could not destroy Jesus' body. In Hebrew, the word *destroy* (*šāḥaṭ*) has the same root as the term *grave* (*šaḥaṭ*). "The grave or pit is the place where the body is destroyed."[42] Christ's body did not see decay but was glorified at his resurrection. Therefore, God's promise was fulfilled not in David but in Christ.

Greek Words, Phrases, and Constructions in 2:25 and 27

Verse 25

εἰς αὐτόν—with the accusative the preposition is comparable to the dative of reference, "with respect to."[43]

διὰ παντός—literally the expression means "through all [time]" with the noun χρόνος supplied.

---

41. Consult Franz Delitzsch, *Biblical Commentary on the Psalms*, trans. Francis Bolton, 3 vols. (1877; Grand Rapids: Eerdmans, 1955), vol. 1, p. 229.

42. Friedemann Merkel, *NIDNTT*, vol. 1, p. 470. Haenchen and Longenecker observe that Luke omits from his Gospel Jesus' cry, "My God, my God, why have you forsaken me?" (Ps. 22:1). Luke includes Jesus' reference to Paradise (Luke 23:43) and his words, "Father, into your hands I commit my spirit" (v. 46). The parallel to Ps. 16:8 is significant. Haenchen, *Acts*, p. 181; Longenecker, *Acts*, pp. 281–82.

43. Refer to H. E. Dana and Julius R. Mantey, *A Manual Grammar of the Greek New Testament* (1927; New York: Macmillan, 1967), p. 103.

Verse 27

εἰς—with the accusative the preposition has the sense of ἐν with the dative, "in the grave."

ὅσιον—this adjective appears eight times in the New Testament, five of which are in quotations. Used of God, it connotes that he is holy in judgment (Rev. 16:5). Jesus is the Holy One (Hebrew: *ḥāsîd*), whom God raised from the dead.[44]

---

d. God's Promise Kept
2:29–36

29. "Men and brothers, I can say confidently to you that the patriarch David both died and was buried, and his tomb is with us to this day. 30. And being a prophet, he knew that God had sworn to him on oath to place one of his descendants on his throne."

Peter addresses the multitude by calling them "brothers." In the gathering of 120 believers, he used the same address (1:16). After quoting from Psalm 16, familiar to his audience because of its use in the local synagogues, Peter identifies himself with his listeners and employs the term *brothers*.[45]

a. *Patriarch.* By mentioning David and calling him "patriarch," Peter effectively relates to the Jews; the name *David* reminds them of Israel's golden era. David died and was buried in Jerusalem, and his tomb remained there even to the time of the apostles.[46] No one objects to Peter's reference, because what he says is indisputable. Everyone has visited David's tomb; therefore, Peter can speak confidently about this historical fact.

However, Peter is not so much interested in the history of David's death and burial as in the interpretation of Psalm 16:10. God made an everlasting covenant with the Israelites; he promised David his faithful love (Isa. 55:3). Yet David passed away. Peter calls him a patriarch and thus places him on the same level as Abraham, Isaac, Jacob, and Israel's twelve tribal heads. David's body buried in a tomb is mute evidence to Peter and his contemporaries that this particular psalm quotation (Ps. 16:10) remains unfulfilled.

b. *Prophet.* David himself does not fulfill the words of Psalm 16:10, but he speaks prophetically about someone else. David is king of Israel; nonetheless he functions as a prophet. In fact, with the rest of the Old Testament prophets, David is "trying to find out to what person or what time the Spirit of Christ in them was pointing when he predicted the sufferings of Christ and the glories that would follow" (I Peter 1:11). In Psalm 16 David looks

---

44. Compare R. C. Trench, *Synonyms of the New Testament* (1854; Grand Rapids: Eerdmans, 1953), p. 329.

45. The greeting *brothers* (literally "men [and] brothers") occurs only in addresses when Jews speak to Jewish audiences (1:16; 2:29, 37; 7:2; 13:15, 26, 38; 15:7, 13; 22:1; 23:1, 5, 6; 28:17).

46. See Neh. 3:16. Josephus comments that David's tomb was a building with several rooms and vaults for the burial of kings. *Antiquities* 13.8.4 [249]; 16.7.1 [179]; *War* 1.2.5 [61]. The tomb remained untouched during the destruction of Jerusalem in A.D. 70 and was still mentioned in the time of Hadrian (A.D. 117–38).

ahead to the resurrected Christ. For the composition of this psalm, David received a revelation from God and prophesied about the Messiah.

"[David] knew that God had sworn to him on oath." The use of the oath is not only to guarantee the truthfulness of a statement; swearing an oath signifies that what is asserted can never be changed.[47] Breaking an oath is perjury. Thus when God promises with an oath that he will do something, he is bound to fulfill his promise.

What did God promise David on oath? He would "place one of [David's] descendants on his throne." The Old Testament Scriptures clearly state that God swore an oath in regard to David's successors. Here is one passage:

> The LORD swore an oath to David,
> a sure oath that he will not revoke:
> "One of your own descendants
> I will place on your throne—
> If your sons keep my covenant
> and the statutes I teach them,
> then their sons will sit
> on your throne for ever and ever."
> [Ps. 132:11–12, NIV][48]

This passage indicates the conditional clause in God's promise to David, for David's descendants were obliged to keep God's covenant and obey his precepts. The Messiah, David's offspring, keeps the covenant and fulfills the law (Matt. 5:17; Rom. 10:4). Christ occupies the throne of David forever (Luke 1:32–33), not in an earthly kingdom but in an eternal and spiritual kingdom (John 18:36). Also, notice that with the oath God swears in regard to David's successor, God signifies that the Messiah fulfills the promise.[49]

31. "Looking ahead, he spoke concerning the resurrection of Christ that he was neither abandoned to the grave nor did his body undergo decay."

In verses 30 and 31, the terms *prophet, knew, looking ahead,* and *spoke* are intimately related. The terms relate to David's prophetic function and describe him scanning the horizon of the future and predicting the Messiah's resurrection. Prophetically, David knew that the Messiah would rise from the grave and have eternal life.[50] Therefore, Peter says that David spoke of the Messiah's resurrection in Psalm 16:10, "Because you will not abandon me to the grave, nor will you let your Holy One undergo decay." Peter sees

---

47. F. Charles Fensham, "Oath," *ISBE*, vol. 3, p. 573.

48. See also II Sam. 7:12–16; Ps. 89:3–4, 35–36.

49. Consult Calvin, *Acts of the Apostles*, vol. 1, p. 73.

50. "We must warn the Christian church that Peter's view clearly states that David's prophetic status allowed him to have a clear prevision of Christ's resurrection." Walter C. Kaiser, Jr., "The Promise to David in Psalm 16 and Its Application in Acts 2:25–33 and 13:32–37," *JETS* 23 (1980): 229; also published in *The Uses of the Old Testament in the New* (Chicago: Moody, 1985), p. 40.

the fulfillment of this psalm and therefore changes the tenses of the verbs from the future to the past: "[Christ] *was* neither *abandoned* to the grave, nor *did* his body undergo decay" (italics added). Hence, Peter views Christ's resurrection to eternal life as the consummation of David's spiritual kingdom in which Christ is king forever. He places the emphasis not on David, the composer of the psalm, but on Christ, who has fulfilled its words. Moreover, Peter asserts that the evidence for his observation is irrefutable. He makes the following observation:

32. "This Jesus God raised up, and all of us are witnesses of it. 33. Therefore, having been exalted to God's right hand, and having received from the Father the promise of the Holy Spirit, he has poured out what you now both see and hear."

In these two verses Peter notes the redemptive facts of Jesus' resurrection and ascension in conjunction with the outpouring of the Holy Spirit. In fact, he refers to the three Persons of the Trinity: the Father, Jesus, and the Holy Spirit. Three times in his Pentecost sermon he emphatically points to Jesus as *this* Jesus (see vv. 23, 32, 36) to recall for his audience their knowledge of and acquaintance with Jesus of Nazareth (v. 22). Once again Peter stresses the theme of the early Christian church: the resurrection from the dead (v. 24; and see 13:30, 33–34, 37; 17:31).

In verses 32 and 33, Peter makes a distinction between the apostolic witnesses ("all of us are witnesses") who have seen the resurrected Jesus and the multitude who observe the phenomena of Pentecost ("what you now both see and hear"). In another context, Peter states that Jesus appeared only to those witnesses "who were appointed beforehand by God" (10:41). Conversely, the multitude at Pentecost did not see the resurrected Christ; they saw and heard the visible and audible tokens of the Holy Spirit's presence.

Because Peter's audience had not seen Jesus in the forty-day period between his resurrection and ascension, they needed proof that what the eyewitnesses proclaimed was true. Therefore, they wanted to know the relationship between Jesus' resurrection and the coming of the Holy Spirit. To meet the questions of his audience, Peter alludes to Jesus' ascension and mentions Christ's place at the right hand of God (compare 5:31). Christians eventually formulated these truths in the Apostles' Creed and confessed that Jesus Christ

> ascended to heaven,
> and sits at the right hand
> of God the Father almighty.

From his exalted position, Jesus has fulfilled the promise that the Father would send the Holy Spirit (refer to John 7:39; 14:26; 15:26). On the day of Pentecost Jesus' words concerning the coming of the Spirit are being fulfilled. Consequently, everyone present at the temple area in Jerusalem is able to see the evidence of the outpouring of the Spirit. The listeners must know, therefore, that Jesus, seated at the right hand of God, has the authority to commission the Spirit to come and live in the hearts of the believers.

Peter approaches the end of his sermon, and at last he answers the crowd's question, "What does this mean?" (v. 12). That is, the Holy Spirit promised by Jesus as a gift from the Father has come because of Jesus' authority to send the Spirit. Peter tells his audience that Jesus indeed ascended and took the seat of honor next to God the Father. He says,

34. "For David did not ascend into heaven, but he himself said,
'The Lord said to my Lord:
Sit at my right hand
35. until I make your enemies
a footstool for your feet.' "

Peter introduces David's name once more to link Psalm 16:8–11 to Psalm 110:1. Should anyone in Peter's audience question whether the first psalm refers to Christ, the second psalm citation proves without doubt that Jesus has ascended and sits enthroned in heaven. The Jewish people interpreted Scripture with the hermeneutical rule of verbal analogy. That is, if two passages have a verbal analogy (as in the case of these two quotations from the Psalter), then the one passage must be interpreted as the other. The Jews considered Psalm 110 to be messianic, and therefore they had to interpret the passage from Psalm 16 messianically.

Psalm 110:1 does not apply to David but to Christ (see Matt. 22:41–46). In his debate with the Pharisees, Jesus demonstrates that in this psalm David speaks of Christ's exaltation in heaven and the authority entrusted to him.[51] He reigns and will not be completely victorious until all his enemies become a footstool for his feet.

36. "Therefore let all the house of Israel assuredly know that God has made this Jesus, whom you crucified, both Lord and Christ."

Here is the conclusion of Peter's sermon. Peter utters an admonition that he directs to every member who belongs to the house of Israel and tells him that Jesus is both Lord and Christ.

Observe these points:

a. *All Israel.* In this conclusion, Peter appeals to all the people who claim to be Israelites. He does so because the nation Israel considered itself the people of God. Repeatedly God had told the descendants of Abraham, "I will be [your] God, and [you] will be my people" (Jer. 31:33). Also, when Jesus sent the disciples on their first missionary journey, he instructed them not to go to the Gentiles: "Go rather to the lost sheep of the house of Israel" (Matt. 10:6). Christ addresses his gospel first to the Jews, then to the Samaritans (Acts 8:4–25), and last to the Gentiles (Acts 10:24–48). On the day of Pentecost the Jewish audience must have full assurance of the truth of the gospel.

---

51. Consult Longenecker, *Acts,* pp. 279–80.

b. *God.* What is the content of this truth? Peter says, "God made this Jesus, whom you crucified, both Lord and Christ." Throughout his sermon, Peter makes God the principal speaker and doer (vv. 17, 22–24, 30, 32, 36). At the conclusion, he shifts attention to the deity of Jesus Christ, whom he places on the same level as God. He does this with full awareness of the monotheistic creed of the Jewish people: "Hear, O Israel: The LORD our God, the LORD is one" (Deut. 6:4, NIV). Peter teaches the deity of Jesus Christ and thus places Jesus next to God. He notes that although the Jewish people crucified Jesus (v. 23), God has made Jesus Lord and Christ. When Peter states that God made Jesus Lord and Christ, he does not convey the interpretation that God exalted Jesus after his death on the cross. To the contrary, the New Testament alludes to Jesus' exaltation even before he suffered on Calvary's cross.[52] Of course, the titles *Lord* and *Christ* are used after Jesus' resurrection and ascension, when the apostles become conscious of the meaning of these redemptive events.

c. *Lord and Christ.* Here is the point. During his earthly ministry, Jesus never referred to himself as the Christ. Only at his trial did Jesus affirmatively answer the high priest's question concerning his messiahship (Mark 14:61–62). Yet in the first recorded sermon of one of Jesus' apostles, Peter calls Jesus Lord and Christ.[53] Whereas in the Old Testament Scriptures the term *Lord* denotes God, in the New Testament writings Jesus' followers call Jesus both Lord and Christ. Did the early Christian community originate these terms and ascribe them to Jesus?[54] Hardly. Notice that the angel who proclaims Jesus' birth tells the shepherds in Bethlehem's field that "[Jesus] is Christ the Lord" (Luke 2:11). The words of Peter clearly state that God, not the Christian church, made Jesus both Lord and Christ. That is, in consequence of Jesus' death and resurrection, God declares that Jesus is indeed the Christ, who is the sovereign Lord (compare Rom. 1:4).

Doctrinal Considerations in 2:36

In this verse, the two titles *Lord* and *Christ* are significant. The verse indicates that God himself gave these titles to Jesus. The title *Lord,* then, belongs to Jesus instead of God the Father, for the writers of the New Testament declare that every knee

---

52. See especially Matt. 22:44 (and parallels); 26:64. Consult Harrison, *The Apostolic Church,* pp. 51–52.

53. The literature is extensive. See, e.g., Hans Bietenhard, *NIDNTT,* vol. 2, p. 515; Richard N. Longenecker, *The Christology of Early Jewish Christianity,* Studies in Biblical Theology, 2d series 17 (London: SCM, 1970), p. 129; Vincent Taylor, *The Names of Jesus* (London: Macmillan, 1953), p. 43.

54. For a study of this view, refer to Wilhelm Bousset, *Kyrios Christos: A History of the Belief in Christ from the Beginnings of Christianity to Irenaeus,* trans. John E. Steely (Nashville: Abingdon, 1970), p. 146. See Rudolf Bultmann, *Theology of the New Testament,* trans. Kendrick Grobel, 2 vols. (New York: Charles Scribner's Sons, 1951), vol. 1, p. 51.

must bow before him and every tongue confess that he is King of kings and Lord of lords (see Phil. 2:9–11; Rev. 17:14; 19:16). Also, before ascending to heaven, Jesus revealed his royal status when he said, "All authority in heaven and on earth has been given to me" (Matt. 28:18).

In his sermon, Peter speaks about Jesus of Nazareth, whom the Jews had crucified. He mentions historical events that are well known to his audience and thus he links the names *Jesus* and *Christ* (v. 31).[55] Peter writes emphatically "this Jesus" (vv. 32, 36), who is exalted to the position of highest honor. Jesus is seated next to God the Father (v. 33), for he is the Christ, the Son of God.

Greek Words, Phrases, and Constructions in 2:30–36

Verse 30

ὅρκῳ ὤμοσεν—"[he] had sworn with an oath" (NKJV). Although the noun is redundant in English, its use in the dative perhaps reflects the Hebrew infinitive absolute construction.

καθίσαι—the aorist active infinitive of καθίζω (I seat; sit) should be taken as a transitive verb and not as an intransitive. The direct object is "one of his descendants" (RSV, NASB).

Verse 32

τοῦτον τὸν Ἰησοῦν—the demonstrative pronoun preceding the definite article and the noun signifies emphasis. See also verse 36.

ἡμεῖς—this personal pronoun has been placed for emphasis between the adjective πάντες (all) and the verb ἐσμεν (we are). The implicit contrast with ἡμεῖς (you) in the next verse (v. 33) is apparent.

Verse 33

τῇ δεξιᾷ—the noun *hand* should be supplied. The dative can be either instrumental ("by the right hand"), locative ("at the right hand"), or directive ("to the right hand"). [56]

τε—this adjunct particle connects the clause with the aorist passive participle ὑψωθείς (exalted) and the clause with the aorist active participle λαβών (received).

Verse 36

ἀσφαλῶς—used figuratively, the adverb means "beyond a doubt." It stands first in the sentence for emphasis.

πᾶς οἶκος Ἰσραήλ—"there is only one 'house of Israel.' "[57] This construction, therefore, means "the whole house of Israel."

---

55. Consult Guthrie, *New Testament Theology*, p. 246.
56. Robert Hanna, *A Grammatical Aid to the Greek New Testament* (Grand Rapids: Baker, 1983), p. 190.
57. A. T. Robertson, *A Grammar of the Greek New Testament in the Light of Historical Research* (Nashville: Broadman, 1934), p. 772.

Luke presents a summary of Peter's sermon. Nevertheless the reader is able to sense the dramatic effect of the audience's response to the preaching of the Word. The people are greatly disturbed and ask Peter and his companions, "What shall we do?" in response to Peter's address.

e. Genuine Response
2:37–41

37. Now when they heard this, they were cut to the heart and said to Peter and the rest of the apostles, "Men and brothers, what shall we do?"

a. "Now when they heard this." Peter's words reach the hearts of the people. His sermon reminds them of their refusal to listen to Jesus and to accept him as the Messiah. His accusation that they crucified and killed Jesus is justified and pierces their consciences.

b. "They were cut to the heart." The expression *cut*, in fact, implies that their hearts are pierced by guilt so that they become deeply troubled (GNB). Those who have received God's revelation know that they are guilty. Consequently they cry out, "Men and brothers, what shall we do?" On the day of Pentecost they see the evidence of the outpouring of the Holy Spirit, they hear Peter's exposition, and they realize that they have sinned against God by refusing to accept his Son. Now they turn to Jesus' immediate followers and ask the apostles for advice.

c. "[They] said to Peter and the rest of the apostles." They address Peter and those with him and use the same expression Peter had for them, "brothers" (v. 29). Thus they establish a mutual bond of spiritual kinship. Asking the question, "What shall we do?" they go to the source that provides the necessary information. They pose the same question the crowd asked John the Baptist at the Jordan (Luke 3:10; see also Acts 16:30; 22:10). This question implies that they are unable to remove their guilt and therefore they need help.[58] In response to Peter's words, they express faith in Jesus and indirectly entreat the apostles to lead them to God.

38. Peter answered them, "Repent and be baptized every one of you in the name of Jesus Christ for the forgiveness of your sins. And you will receive the gift of the Holy Spirit. 39. The promise is for you and your children and for all who are far off—as many as the Lord our God will call to himself."

We make these observations:

a. *Repentance.* The people ask Peter and the rest of the apostles how they can receive remission of sin and find salvation. What does Peter tell them? He speaks no words of rebuke. Rather, he utters the same word spoken by John the Baptist at the Jordan and by Jesus during his ministry: "Repent" (see Matt. 3:2; 4:17). The imperative *repent* implies that the Jews turn from

---

58. See Lenski, *Acts*, p. 104.

the evil they have perpetrated, have an intense abhorrence for the sins they committed, experience a complete turnabout of their lives, and adhere to Jesus' teaching.[59]

Repentance signifies that man's mind is changed completely, so that he consciously turns away from sin (3:19).[60] Repentance causes a person to think and act in harmony with Jesus' teachings. The result is that he breaks with unbelief and in faith accepts God's Word.

b. *Baptism.* Peter continues and says, "Be baptized every one of you." In Greek, the imperative verb *repent* is in the plural; Peter addresses all the people whose consciences drive them to repentance. But the verb *be baptized* is in the singular to stress the individual nature of baptism. A Christian should be baptized to be a follower of Jesus Christ, for baptism is the sign indicating that a person belongs to the company of God's people.

Repentance, baptism, and faith are theologically related. When the believer who repents is baptized he makes a commitment of faith. He accepts Jesus Christ as his Lord and Savior and knows that through Christ's blood his sins are forgiven. Indeed Peter instructs the people that baptism must be "in the name of Jesus Christ for the forgiveness of your sins." Forgiveness of sins takes place only through Christ in consequence of his death and resurrection (see Rom. 6:1–4). As forerunner of Jesus, John the Baptist preached repentance from sin and then baptized the people who turned from sin (Mark 1:4).

c. *Name.* Peter asserts that the believer must be baptized "in the name of Jesus Christ for the forgiveness of your sins." The instruction appears to go contrary to the words of the Great Commission, in which Jesus tells the apostles to baptize believers in the name of the Triune God (Matt. 28:19–20). Notice, first, that the term *name* includes the full revelation concerning Jesus Christ (see also 8:12; 10:48; 19:5). That is, this term points to his person and work and the people he redeems. In other words, Peter is not contradicting Jesus' baptism formula; rather, he stresses the unique function and place Jesus has in regard to baptism and the remission of sins. Next, Peter uses the double name *Jesus Christ* to indicate that Jesus of Nazareth indeed is the Messiah. As Jesus fulfills the prophecies concerning the coming of the Messiah, so the baptism in his name is a fulfillment of the baptism of John (see 19:1–7). John's baptism was with water only, but that of Jesus is with water and the Holy Spirit (compare Matt. 3:11; Mark 1:8; Luke 3:16; John 1:33; Acts 1:5).

d. *Gift.* "And you will receive the gift of the Holy Spirit." Within the early church, this text proved to be no contradiction to the words of John the Baptist: "I baptize you with water, but [Jesus] will baptize you with the Holy Spirit" (Mark 1:8, NIV). In the first century, Christians saw John's baptism

---

59. Thayer, p. 405; Bauer, p. 512. Also consult Jürgen Goetzmann, *NIDNTT*, vol. 1, p. 358.
60. According to Louis Berkhof, true repentance encompasses three elements: intellect, emotion, and volition. See *Systematic Theology*, 2d rev. ed. (Grand Rapids: Eerdmans, 1941), p. 486.

as the shadow and that of Jesus as reality. Accordingly, the person who was baptized in the name of Jesus pledged his allegiance to Christ, particularly with the confession *Jesus is Lord* (Rom. 10:9; I Cor. 12:3).[61]

What is this gift of the Spirit? Peter puts the noun *gift* in the singular, not in the plural. By contrast, Paul writes to the Corinthian church about the gifts of the Holy Spirit, among them wisdom, knowledge, faith, healing, prophecy, tongues, and interpretation (I Cor. 12:8–11, 28–31; 14:1–2). But to the people who were present at Pentecost Peter says that the baptized believer will receive the gift of the Holy Spirit. The expression *gift* appears in the passage about the outpouring of the Spirit on the Samaritans; Simon the sorcerer tried to buy this gift with money (8:20). The term also occurs in the account of Peter's visit to Cornelius, who with his household received the gift of the Holy Spirit (10:45; see also 11:17). From these passages we are able to learn that this gift refers to the indwelling power of the Holy Spirit. Notice, however, that in 2:38–41 Luke makes no mention of the converts speaking in tongues (2:4) or of the apostles laying their hands on the converts so that they might receive the Spirit (8:17). We assume, therefore, that "speaking in tongues and laying on of hands were not considered prerequisites for receiving the Spirit."[62]

The context of the Pentecost account indicates that the gift of the Spirit is not dependent on baptism. The two clauses "be baptized" and "you will receive the gift of the Holy Spirit" are separate statements. In a detailed study of this point Ned B. Stonehouse observes, "One may conclude with confidence that Acts 2:38 is not to be understood as teaching that the gift of the Spirit was conditional upon baptism."[63] A study in Acts on baptism and the gift of the Holy Spirit reveals that these two are related but do not necessarily follow each other. Hence, in verse 38 Peter instructs the people to repent and to be baptized; then he adds the promise (in the future tense) that they "will receive the gift of the Holy Spirit."

e. *Promise.* In the next verse (v. 39) Peter relates to his audience that "the promise is for you and your children and for all who are far off—as many as the Lord our God will call to himself."

What is the meaning of the word *promise*? Luke, who reports Peter's words, refrains from providing details. The definite article preceding the noun *promise* seems to indicate that Peter has the specific promise of the coming of the Holy Spirit in mind. The promise refers to the prophecy of Joel 2:28–32, which was fulfilled on the day of Pentecost. Before his ascension Jesus tells the apostles, "Do not leave Jerusalem, but wait for the promise my Father made, of which you heard me speak" (1:4; see also Luke

---

61. Marshall, *Acts*, p. 81.
62. Longenecker, *Acts*, p. 284.
63. Ned B. Stonehouse, "Repentance, Baptism and the Gift of the Holy Spirit," *WTJ* 13 (1950–51): 14.

24:49). And the exalted Christ pours out the promised Holy Spirit he received from God the Father (Acts 2:33).[64]

The phrase *for you and your children* is an echo of God's promise to Abraham to be a God to him and his descendants for generations to come (Gen. 17:7). Likewise, the promise of the Holy Spirit goes far beyond the Jews and their children who were present in Jerusalem at Pentecost. From the moment of arrival, the Holy Spirit remains among God's people until the end of time. The Spirit leads believers to Jesus Christ and lives within their hearts, for their physical bodies are his temple (I Cor. 6:19).

"And for all who are far off—as many as the Lord our God will call to himself." Peter and his fellow Jews consider themselves God's covenant people, who are the first to receive the blessing of salvation. But through the work of Christ the Gentiles also are included in God's covenant. Peter himself eventually realizes the import of the words he utters at Pentecost when he reports to the Jews in Jerusalem about his visit to Cornelius in Caesarea. Concludes Peter, "If then God gave them the same gift as he gave us who believed in the Lord Jesus Christ, who was I that I could stand in God's way?" (11:17). Years later, Paul writes to Gentile members of the church about their exclusion from the covenant and says, "But now in Christ Jesus you who once were far away have been brought near by the blood of Christ" (Eph. 2:13, and see v. 17).

Two concluding remarks are in order. First, the term *far off* includes both time and place. God's promise extends throughout the generations until the end of the world. It also reaches people from every nation, tribe, race, and language, wherever they dwell on the face of this earth. Peter's words are in complete harmony with those of Jesus: "Make disciples of all nations" (Matt. 28:19). And second, God is sovereign in calling his own people to himself. Salvation originates with him and he grants it to all those whom he, in his sovereign grace, effectively will call. These words of Peter correspond to and have their counterpart in Joel's prophecy: "And it will be that everyone who calls on the name of the Lord will be saved" (v. 21; Joel 2:32).

40. And with many other words he testified and kept on exhorting them: "Save yourselves from this crooked generation." 41. Then those who accepted his word were baptized, and about three thousand people were added that day.

Here is the conclusion to the Pentecost event. Even though Luke presents a brief statement, we understand that Peter continued speaking after he ended his sermon.

a. "And with many other words he testified and kept on exhorting them," writes Luke. He appears to say that the Jews asked questions about many subjects related to Peter's message. He stresses the word *other*, which in the Greek stands first in the sentence for emphasis. Luke leaves the impression

---

64. MacDonald, "Glossolalia in the New Testament," p. 130.

that Peter warned the inquirers to examine carefully the evidence he has presented. In fact, the tense of the verb *exhorting* (in Greek) indicates that Peter repeatedly appealed to his listeners with this request: "Save yourselves from this crooked generation." The request is an echo of a line in the song of Moses familiar to the audience because of its use in the synagogue worship services:

> They have acted corruptly toward [God];
> to their shame they are no longer his children,
> *but a warped and crooked generation.* [Deut. 32:5, NIV, italics added]

Who are the people of this corrupt generation? Obviously, they are the religious leaders who at Jesus' trial incited the crowd to shout, "Crucify him, crucify him" (Luke 23:21). The priests and the scribes desired full control of the Jewish people. But when Jesus taught the Scriptures with authority, they vigorously opposed him and eventually succeeded in killing him.

From a Christianized culture, we have difficulty understanding the mental agony the Jews at Pentecost experienced when they decided to break away from the power and authority of their spiritual leaders. In faith, they accepted Christ and adhered to his teachings. They took this step of faith because Peter plainly told them that the leadership of the priests and scribes was corrupt (compare Phil. 2:15). He kept pleading with them to leave these wicked people and be saved.[65] By being baptized, the Jewish believers decisively rejected the authority of the religious hierarchy, followed Jesus Christ, and were prepared to endure the hatred and scorn of their former leaders and teachers.

b. "Then those who accepted [Peter's] word were baptized." The text clearly indicates that not everyone who heard Peter's words believed. But the people who accepted his message requested baptism. Because this verse fails to provide any information about the mode of baptism, the age of the persons who were baptized, and the place where their baptism occurred, we do well to refrain from being dogmatic.

c. "And about three thousand people were added that day." Prior to Pentecost, the group of believers numbered about 120 (1:15), but when the Holy Spirit was poured forth the Lord added some 3,000 persons, both men and women, we assume. This increase is phenomenal and undoubtedly caused administrative problems, as is evident from the neglect of the Greek-speaking widows (6:1). The growth of the church continued unabated,[66] so that a conservative estimate is that there were 20,000 Christians in Jerusalem prior to the persecution following Stephen's death (8:1b).

---

65. Refer to Calvin, *Acts of the Apostles,* vol. 1, p. 84.
66. Compare 2:47; 4:4; 5:14; 6:1, 7; 9:31, 35, 42; 11:21, 24; 14:1, 21; 16:5; 17:12.

Practical Considerations in 2:40–41

In numerous churches, candidates for membership are required to have adequate knowledge of Scripture and an ability to articulate the doctrines of the church before they are baptized and accepted as members. Granted that knowledge of Scripture and doctrine is desirable for church members (so that they may be able to answer people who ask them about the Christian faith), we must raise the question whether Scripture says anything about accepting prospective members. The answer is affirmative.

Let us begin with the so-called Great Commission (Matt. 28:19–20). Literally Jesus says, "Therefore having gone forth, make disciples of all nations by baptizing them in the name of the Father and of the Son and of the Holy Spirit, and by teaching them to obey everything I have commanded you." The process of making disciples, then, is accomplished in two steps: first, by baptizing the candidate, and next, by teaching him doctrine.

Now notice that Peter follows Jesus' directives. He goes forth on the day of Pentecost, makes disciples when he preaches the Word, and immediately baptizes these believers. Then he and the other apostles continue to teach them the gospel of Christ (2:42) on a regular basis. The Jewish people who listened to Peter at Pentecost knew the Old Testament Scriptures, but such knowledge was not expected of Gentiles. Comments Richard B. Rackham, "We are surprised at the rapidity with which baptism was given in the case of a Gentile like the Philippian jailor, or even a proselyte like the Ethiopian eunuch."[67]

The New Testament seems to indicate that when a believer accepts Jesus Christ as his Lord and Savior upon hearing the gospel, he should be given the opportunity for baptism. But baptism must be followed by diligent and sustained study of the Scriptures for the rest of his earthly life.

Greek Words, Phrases, and Constructions in 2:37–39

Verse 37

κατενύγησαν—a compound verb from κατανύσσομαι (I am pierced). The compound is perfective; in form it is a second aorist passive.

τε—the adjunctive particle closely links the two verbs *pierced* and *said*.

λοιπούς—translated "the rest of" or "other," this adjective is omitted in the Western text of Codex Bezae (see JB and NEB).

Verse 38

ἐπί—this preposition precedes the term *the name* and is synonymous with ἐν (in), as, for example, in 3:6; 4:10, 17, 18; 5:28, 40.

εἰς—stressing result rather than purpose, this word has the sense of "with a view to" or "resulting in."[68]

---

67. Rackham, *Acts*, p. 33.
68. C. F. D. Moule, *An Idiom-Book of New Testament Greek,* 2d ed. (Cambridge: Cambridge University Press, 1960), p. 70.

τοῦ ἁγίου πνεύματος—this clause is an appositional genitive with τὴν δωρεάν and means "the gift, namely, the Holy Spirit."[69]

Verse 39

εἰς μακράν—the feminine noun ὁδόν (way) must be supplied. The expression appears to be a Semitism.

ὑμῖν—this dative of possession with the verb *to be* can be translated "you have the promise."[70]

---

3. Christian Community
2:42–47

a. At Worship
2:42–43

Luke describes the beauty of the growing and developing church. He portrays the spontaneity, dedication, and devotion of the early Christians in relation to God in the worship services. In the last section of this chapter, he describes the church at formal and informal worship and its influence in the community.[71]

42. They were continually devoting themselves to the apostles' teaching and to fellowship, to the breaking of bread and to prayer.

Notice these components:

a. *Teaching.* The sentence "They were continually devoting themselves to the apostles' teaching" points to the fervor and dedication of the first converts to Christianity. They steadfastly turned to the apostles for instruction in Christ's gospel, for Jesus had appointed his immediate followers to be the teachers of these learners (Matt. 28:20).

During his earthly ministry, Jesus taught with authority and "not as the teachers of the law" (Mark 1:22, NIV). Before he ascended, he delegated this authority to the apostles, who spoke in his name. Notice the double meaning of the term *teaching*. Extensively, the word refers to the good news of all that Jesus said and did. And intensively, the apostles were involved in the work of teaching an oral gospel to the converts, whom Luke calls disciples (learners) in Acts.[72] We assume that this teaching was done especially at public worship services, where the apostles taught this gospel in their preaching.

b. *Fellowship.* Three words follow the term *teaching*. The first one, fellowship, describes the enthusiasm believers demonstrated in a common bond

---

69. See Hanna, *Grammatical Aid*, p. 191.

70. Consult Friedrich Blass and Albert Debrunner, *A Greek Grammar of the New Testament and Other Early Christian Literature*, trans. and rev. Robert Funk (Chicago: University of Chicago Press, 1961), #189.2.

71. Guidelines for dividing these verses into sections or paragraphs are lacking. Scholars show no unanimity.

72. See, e.g., 6:1, 2, 7; 9:1, 10, 19, 25, 26, 38; 11:26, 29; 13:52.

at worship, at meals, and in the sharing of their material goods (v. 44). The Christians visibly showed their unity in Jesus Christ in the worship services, where they called one another brothers and sisters.

c. *Breaking of bread.* Is this a reference to a meal in a private home (see Luke 24:30, 35) or to a communion service? This question is difficult to answer.[73] The context, however, seems to suggest that it refers to a celebration of the Lord's Supper. In the Greek, the definite article precedes the noun *bread* and thus specifies that the Christians partook of *the* bread set aside for the sacrament of communion (compare 20:11; I Cor. 10:16). Also, the act of breaking bread has its sequel in the act of offering prayers (presumably in the setting of public worship). The words *breaking of bread* appear within the sequence of teaching, fellowship, and prayers in worship services. Therefore, we understand the term as an early description for the celebration of Holy Communion. In the liturgy of the Christian church, this celebration was and is usually accompanied by the teaching of the gospel and by prayers.

d. *Prayer.* Literally the text has "the prayers." Note that here also Luke uses the definite article to describe definite prayers uttered in worship; perhaps they include the formal prayers the Jews were accustomed to offer in the temple (3:1). In summary, the four elements Luke mentions in this verse (v. 42) appear to relate to public worship: apostolic teaching and preaching, fellowship of the believers, celebration of the Lord's Supper, and common prayers.

43. Everyone was filled with awe, and many wonders and signs were being done by the apostles.

A sense of awe filled the hearts of all believers because they experienced the nearness of God in their midst. The Greek attests that their awe continued unabated (see 5:5, 11; 19:17). This stemmed from the "many wonders and signs" the apostles performed (5:12).

Jesus endowed the apostles with authority to perform miracles (compare Matt. 10:8). The apostles repeatedly exercised this power either in response to the faith of the people or to increase their faith. The result was twofold: the believers were conscious of God's sacred presence among them and numberless converts were added to the church (v. 47). The words *many wonders and signs* echo Joel's prophecy and constitute its fulfillment (2:19; Joel 2:30).

Greek Words, Phrases, and Constructions in 2:42

ἦσαν—the use of the imperfect tense to express continuity is evident in this verse and the rest of the passage. For the past periphrastic construction of ἦσαν and the present active participle προσκαρτεροῦντες, see the explanation in 1:14.

---

73. Alford remarks that the interpretation given "as the celebration of the Lord's Supper has been, both in ancient and modern times, the prevalent one." *Alford's Greek Testament,* vol. 2, p. 29.

τοῦ ἄρτου—here the definite article specifies the noun, but in verse 46 it is absent.

---

b. In the Community
2:44–47

In these last few verses of the chapter Luke is more general in his description of the activities that take place in the lives of the early believers. The Christians express their spiritual beliefs in spontaneous action.

44. And all who believed were together and they shared all things. 45. They began to sell their possessions and goods and they gave to anyone who might have need.

This is the first time in Acts that Luke designates the members of the church "the believers." For lack of a definite term (for example, Christians [see 11:26]), he writes, "those who believe." The scoffers who refuse to accept Jesus in faith are excluded and have no part in the Christian community. Faith in Jesus is the principal requisite for belonging to the Christian church. Only the people who believe in him share in the unity that becomes visible in worship and communal life.

"They shared all things." When the Israelites traveled through the desert for forty years, God daily provided for them. They were all on the same economic level; no one was rich and no one was poor.[74] When the Israelites arrived in the Promised Land, everyone received his inheritance. In the course of time, they began to observe and experience both wealth and poverty in their communities. This difference was evident throughout the centuries, because we know the Jews refused to observe God's stipulations to care for the poor and to be generous to them (Deut. 15:1–11; Mic. 2:1–2).

Jesus preached the gospel and said, "Blessed are you who are poor, for yours is the kingdom of God" (Luke 6:20; Matt. 5:3). He instructed the rich young man to sell his possessions and to give the money to the poor (Matt. 19:21).

After Pentecost, the new converts in Jerusalem "shared all things. They began to sell their possessions and goods and they gave to anyone who might have need." The communal sharing of material goods was not a divestment of wealth. Rather, it was a willingness on the part of the owners to place their possessions at the disposal of all those believers who were needy.[75] The aim of the early Christians was to abolish poverty so that needy persons, as a class of people, were no longer among them (4:34a). Luke

---

74. David M. Howard, Jr., "Poverty," *ISBE*, vol. 3, p. 922.

75. In the first century, the Qumran community promoted the practice of sharing goods. In harmony with the words from Ps. 37:14, "the poor and needy," the Qumran residents viewed themselves as "the Congregation of the Poor." Consult David E. Holwerda, "Poor," *ISBE*, vol. 3, p. 908.

provides no information that the rich sold all their possessions. Instead, he alludes to the establishing of a general fund out of which the poor were supported and into which the rich placed the money gained from the sale of properties (4:34b–35; 6:1). Moreover, those who had possessions sold them on a voluntary basis (5:4).

46. Day by day continuing to meet together in the temple courts, breaking bread from house to house, they ate together with gladness and sincerity of heart, 47a. praising God and enjoying the favor of all the people.

Luke continues to depict life in the Christian community. He prefaces his description of the activities of the believers with the expression *every day*. The Christians in Jerusalem go to the temple, which for them is God's house. They consider themselves Jews who have seen the fulfillment of the Old Testament Scriptures through the life, death, and resurrection of Jesus Christ. They meet in the temple courts, presumably the area called Solomon's Colonnade (3:11; 5:12), for prayer and praise. They enjoy complete unity in a context that compares with nature bursting forth in a springtime panorama of beauty, splendor, and perfect harmony. From the Jewish people in general and their religious leaders in particular, the Christians do not as yet receive any opposition. Their lives are exemplary, so that through their conduct they are able to lead others to Christ.

Daily they come together in their private homes to eat bread and confirm the unity they possess in Christ. Of course, eating bread at home is hardly newsworthy, for this is customary and expected. However, Luke parallels the unity and harmony of the believers at the temple with their togetherness at common meals in private homes. The Christians "ate together with gladness and sincerity of heart." Although Luke does not explicitly state so, the practice of eating common meals is comparable to the love feast mentioned indirectly and directly by Paul in his letter to the Corinthian church (I Cor. 11:20–22), by Peter (II Peter 2:13), and by Jude (Jude 12).[76] Walter Bauer explains the love feast as "a common meal eaten by early Christians in connection w[ith] their church services for the purpose of fostering and expressing brotherly love."[77] In Jerusalem, the believers enjoy these meals "every day" (v. 46a), as Luke indicates in the Greek. Accordingly, we should distinguish the common meal from the celebration of the Lord's Supper (v. 42).

Luke emphasizes the unity, harmony, joy, and sincerity of the believers. These elements are the fruits of the Holy Spirit, who is at work in the hearts and lives of the early Christians. In Acts, Luke repeatedly stresses joy or gladness, many times in relation to the influence of the Holy Spirit (see, e.g., 8:8, 39; 13:48, 52; 15:3; 16:34). Conversely, the expression

---

76. Consult Simon J. Kistemaker, *Exposition of the Epistles of Peter and of the Epistle of Jude*, New Testament Commentary series (Grand Rapids: Baker, 1987), pp. 301, 392.
77. Bauer, p. 6.

sincerity occurs only once in the New Testament. It derives from a word that signifies smooth, plain land without any rocks that mar the surface or soil.[78]

"Praising God and enjoying the favor of all the people." The first phrase relates to God and the other to the people. Both phrases are structurally part of the preceding verse (v. 46) in which Luke describes the daily activities of the believers. What a testimony to true Christianity! These Christians live a life of praise to God and as a result are praised by the people. They demonstrate the power of the gospel and the presence of the Spirit. Thus they are living witnesses for Christ. Here the missionary church is at work, for the people noticing the Christian conduct of the converts speak in favor of the church and are drawn to Christ.[79]

47b. The Lord continued to add daily to their number those who were being saved.

Luke concludes this section by saying that the Lord adds new converts to the church. Note, first, that Luke uses the title *the Lord* for Jesus, not for God. Next, the Lord Jesus continues his work of extending the Christian community. From the inhabitants of Jerusalem he takes three thousand people, effects conversions, and adds them as believers to the church. Luke portrays the converts as "those who were being saved." That is, the Lord is the agent in the work of saving his people, for he fulfills Joel's prophecy: "Everyone who calls on the name of the Lord will be saved" (v. 21; Joel 2:32). And last, notice the word *daily*. This term should be taken with the descriptive phrase "those who were being saved." The phrase does not imply a gradual salvation of the individual believer but rather indicates that the miracle of salvation occurs daily. Today also the Lord continues to add to his church and calls people to be spiritual citizens of the city called Zion. With John Newton, the believer humbly yet triumphantly sings,

> Saviour, if of Zion's city
> I, through grace, a member am,
> Let the world deride or pity,
> I will glory in thy Name:
> Fading is the worldling's pleasure,
> All his boasted pomp and show;
> Solid joy and lasting treasure
> None but Zion's children know.

---

78. Thayer, p. 88.

79. Following the Greek text literally, the Vulgate has the reading *habentes gratiam ad omnem plebem* (having charity toward all the people). This translation gives an active instead of a passive interpretation to the text and thus parallels the first part of v. 47, "praising God." See also F. P. Cheetham, "Acts ii.47: *echontes charin pros holon ton laon*," *ExpT* 74 (1963): 214–15.

Practical Considerations in 2:42–45

Verse 42

From its beginning to the present, the Christian church has employed catechisms in its educational ministry. These catechisms are brief summaries of the Christian faith presented in question-and-answer form. They teach the ABCs of doctrine by explaining the meaning of the Apostles' Creed, the sacraments, the Ten Commandments, and the Lord's Prayer. In 1529, Martin Luther composed his Small Catechism to teach children the elementary doctrines of the church. Said Luther, "I have brought about such a change that nowadays a girl or boy of fifteen knows more about Christian doctrine than all the theologians of the great universities used to know." John Calvin wrote a catechism in French (1537) to instruct the people in the truths of Scripture. In Germany, Zacharias Ursinus and Caspar Olevianus wrote the Heidelberg Catechism (1563), which has been called the sweetest document of the Reformation. And in England, the Westminster Shorter and Larger Catechisms came off the press in 1647. These and many other catechisms have been and are valuable tools in teaching God's people doctrinal knowledge. They support Peter's admonition: "Always be ready to give an answer to everyone who asks you to give an account for the hope that is in you" (I Peter 3:15).

Verses 44–45

The members of the Jerusalem church exhibited a unique spontaneity in taking care of the poor. They did so in obedience to Christ and the apostles, who taught them to "remember the poor" (e.g., see Gal. 2:10). Yet the apostles never told anyone to sell property to support the needy. Instead they stressed the joy of voluntary giving. Thus Paul wrote, "Let each man give just what he has decided in his heart, not reluctantly or under compulsion, for God loves a cheerful giver" (II Cor. 9:7, NIV).

The church instituted the diaconate for the purpose of ministering to the needs of the poor because, as Jesus said, "You will always have the poor with you" (John 12:8). The church is not promoting community of goods but is stressing the biblical injunction to help the needy. "Let us do good to all people, especially to those who belong to the household of the [Christian] faith" (Gal. 6:10).

Greek Words, Phrases, and Constructions in 2:44–47

Verse 44

ἐπὶ τὸ αὐτό—this phrase also occurs in 1:15; 2:1, 44; I Cor. 11:20; 14:23. It signifies "altogether." "[The phrase] seems to have acquired a semi-technical sense not unlike ἐν ἐκκλησία ('in church fellowship')."[80]

---

80. F. F. Bruce, *The Acts of the Apostles: The Greek Text with Introduction and Commentary*, 3d (rev. and enl.) ed. (Grand Rapids: Eerdmans, 1990), p. 155. Also refer to Metzger, *Textual Commentary*, pp. 304–5.

Verse 45

τὰ κτήματα—these words refer to properties, lands, and estates; τὰς ὑπάρξεις are possessions, goods, and wealth. The verbs ἐπίπρασκον (imperfect active from πιπράσκω [I sell]) and διεμέριζον (imperfect active from the compound verb διαμερίζω [I distribute]) describe the sustained activity of selling and distributing.

Verse 47

προσετίθει—from προστίθημι (I add), this imperfect active verb connotes repetition, that is, continued action in the past tense.

τοὺς σῳζομένους—the definite article with the present passive participle from σῴζω (I save) is a description for recent converts. The literal translation is, "those who were being saved." However, some translators present their own interpretation of the Greek participle: "such as should be saved" (KJV), "those whom he was saving" (NEB), "those destined to be saved" (JB).

Summary of Chapter 2

Manifested by visible and audible signs, the Holy Spirit is poured out on the day of Pentecost. He fills the persons who are gathered and causes them to speak in other languages. Numerous devout Jews from many nations are staying in Jerusalem. They hear the noise of the wind, come together, and hear the Galileans speak to them in their native languages. Some of the people come from the east (Parthia, Media, Elam, and Mesopotamia), others are from Asia Minor and Africa, and still others are visitors from Rome. These people are filled with amazement and ask what this phenomenon means.

Some scoffers assert that the apostles are drunk, but Peter addresses the multitude and answers the scoffers. He points out that Joel's prophecy concerning the coming of the Holy Spirit has been fulfilled. He proves from the Psalms that Jesus, crucified by the Jews, was raised by God and now sits at his right hand in heaven. From his exalted position, he has sent the Holy Spirit. He is able to do this because God made him Lord and Christ.

The people are overcome with guilt and ask Peter for counsel. He admonishes his audience to repent and to be baptized. Three thousand persons accept Peter's message, are baptized, and are added to the initial group of believers. The converts are instructed in the teaching of the apostles, worship, and partake of communion. They share their material possessions, praise God, and enjoy the favor of all the people. The church continues to grow.

3

The Church in Jerusalem, *part 2*

3:1–26

Outline (continued)

3:1–5:16   B. The Power of Jesus' Name
3:1–10   1. Healing of the Cripple
3:1–5   a. Setting
3:6–10   b. Miracle
3:11–26   2. Address of Peter
3:11–16   a. Explanation
3:17–23   b. Exhortation
3:24–26   c. Promise

3 1 Now Peter and John were going up to the temple at three in the afternoon for prayer. 2 And a man who was crippled from birth was being carried to the gate of the temple called Beautiful, where they usually placed him to beg from those entering the temple. 3 When he saw Peter and John about to enter the temple, he asked them for something. 4 Peter looked at him intently, so did John, and said, "Look at us!" 5 And he fixed his attention on them, expecting to receive something from them. 6 But Peter said, "Silver and gold I do not have, but what I have I give to you: In the name of Jesus Christ of Nazareth, walk." 7 Taking him by the right hand, he pulled him up; and immediately his feet and ankles were strengthened. 8 And jumping up he stood and began to walk; he entered the temple with them, walking, and jumping, and praising God. 9 And all the people saw him walking and praising God. 10 They recognized him as the one who used to sit begging at the temple gate called Beautiful. And they were filled with wonder and amazement at what had happened to him.

B. The Power of Jesus' Name
3:1–5:16

1. Healing of the Cripple
3:1–10

In the preceding chapter, Luke states in summary form that the apostles performed many wonders and miraculous signs (2:43). What are these miracles that caused everyone to be filled with awe? Luke describes one of them, namely, the healing of the crippled beggar. This miracle was performed in response to the faith of the beggar (v. 16) and was followed by Peter's sermon to the crowd. It caused an increase in church membership to five thousand men, not counting women (4:4).

a. Setting
3:1–5

1. Now Peter and John were going up to the temple at three in the afternoon for prayer.

a. "Peter and John." Luke continues to focus attention on Peter, who is the spokesman for the twelve apostles. But now he adds the name of John, son of Zebedee. During Jesus' ministry, both Peter and John belonged to the so-called inner circle of the disciples. They were with Jesus at his transfiguration (Matt. 17:1). Jesus instructed these two disciples to prepare the

Passover feast (Luke 22:8). And Jesus took Peter and John with him into the place called Gethsemane (Mark 14:33).

Luke relates that the apostles in Jerusalem commissioned Peter and John to give directions to the growing church in Samaria (8:14). In addition, Paul considers Peter and John to be pillars in the Christian community (Gal. 2:9). These two apostles were indeed church leaders, even if—as Luke reports—Peter spoke and John listened. Furthermore, the apostles continued the practice of going out two by two (see Mark 6:7).

b. "Were going up to the temple." The New International Version adds the words *one day*, which are not in the Greek text.[1] But notice that the verb *were going up* is in the past progressive form, which indicates that they customarily went up to the temple to pray. The apostles stayed in Jerusalem, obviously to teach the multitude of believers (see 2:41–42, 47). They kept the tradition of praying at stated times in the temple.[2] The early Christians considered themselves Jews who would not think of breaking with traditional prayer times at the temple.

c. "At three in the afternoon for prayer." According to the Talmud, the people offered prayers in the temple three times per day: early in the morning, in the afternoon, and at sunset.[3] As the priests offered sacrifices, the Jews prayed. Indeed, the time for sacrifice was the time for prayer. Peter and John were going to the three o'clock meeting and entered the temple complex, but not the sanctuary. Already in the time of David, Jewish people customarily prayed three times a day. Writes David,

> But I call to the Lord God for help
>   and he will save me.
> Morning, noon, and night
>   my complaints and groans go up to him,
> and he will hear my voice.
>
> [Ps. 55:16–17, GNB]

2. And a man who was crippled from birth was being carried to the gate of the temple called Beautiful, where they usually placed him to beg from those entering the temple.

Luke relates that the man born crippled had to be carried to the temple, where he begged for money. As was common in those days, handicapped people were not taught a trade but became beggars (see John 9:1, 8). Relatives and friends daily carried the man to one of the gates of the temple where people entered for prayer. These worshipers would have pangs of

---

1. The NEB, SEB, and GNB also have this reading. The Greek text has the term *now* or *and*. Codex Bezae features the temporal phrase *and in these days*.

2. The verb *to go up* is the standard verb to describe a person going to Jerusalem or someone going to the temple.

3. *Berachoth* 1.1–2; 4.1. Josephus remarks that sacrifices were offered twice a day: "in the morning and at the ninth hour." *Antiquities* 14.4.3 [65] (LCL).

conscience when they saw the crippled beggar and consequently would give him some money. The place at the temple was a shrewd choice of the man and his carriers.

Scholars are unable to say with certainty where the temple gate called Beautiful was located. Records about the temple area after Jerusalem's destruction in A.D. 70 are lacking. Says Kirsopp Lake, "There was not only a complete destruction of buildings, but an absolute dislocation of tradition in Jerusalem."[4] Nevertheless, scholars present three theories about the location of the Beautiful gate. They are:

1. The so-called Shusan gate in the outside wall east of the temple. This gate was close to Solomon's Colonnade (3:11) on the outside of the Court of the Gentiles.
2. The Nicanor gate located east of the Court of Women. It provided access to the Court of Women from the Court of the Gentiles. Because its doors were made of Corinthian bronze and "far exceeded in value those plated with silver and set in gold,"[5] Peter's remark about not possessing silver or gold (3:6) was quite appropriate.
3. The Nicanor gate situated between the Court of Women and the Court of Men. (This information comes from rabbinic literature.) However, this gate can hardly be the same as the gate called Beautiful. Luke reports that after the invalid was healed, he accompanied the apostles into the temple courts (v. 8).

Most scholars accept the second theory and consider the gate called Beautiful to be the Nicanor gate made of Corinthian bronze.[6] An Alexandrian Jew named Nicanor donated the beautiful bronze-covered doors to the temple.

Daily the beggar sat at the temple gate and expected monetary gifts from the worshipers. This man was not a member of the Christian community, for then he would have received financial assistance from the believers. God had told the Israelites that there should not be any poor among them (Deut. 15:4, and see vv. 7–8). But the Jews ignored God's command and considered giving alms to beggars a virtue (e.g., see Matt. 6:1–2).

3. When he saw Peter and John about to enter the temple, he asked them for something. 4. Peter looked at him intently, so did John, and said, "Look at us!" 5. And he fixed his attention on them, expecting to receive something from them.

Just before the two apostles are about to enter the temple area, the beggar asks them for a monetary gift. To him, they are nameless worship-

---

4. Kirsopp Lake, "Localities in and near Jerusalem Mentioned in Acts," *Beginnings,* vol. 5, p. 486.

5. Josephus *War* 5.5.3 [201] (LCL).

6. For further study, consult Joachim Jeremias, *TDNT,* vol. 3, p. 173 n. 5; Gottlob Schrenk, *TDNT,* vol. 3, p. 236; David F. Payne, "Gate," *ISBE,* vol. 2, pp. 408–9.

ers. He expects that when they are asked to show mercy, they will stop and give him money. Instead of giving the beggar a few coins, Peter fixes his attention on the man and speaks to him. Luke records that John, too, looks intently at the crippled beggar.

We notice two things in verse 4. First, Peter is not interested in the symptoms of the man's condition, namely, his role as beggar. Peter looks at him to effect a cure so that the man can be restored physically. Next, Peter and John do not wish to perform a healing miracle without response from the man in question. The apostles have the Holy Spirit to guide them to determine whether the man has faith. And although Luke does not say so in this verse, in his subsequent sermon Peter states unequivocally that the man was healed by faith (v. 16). The beggar was over forty years of age (see 4:22) and presumably had heard Jesus, and possibly Peter, preach in the temple area. He complies with Peter's request and looks at the apostles, "expecting to receive something from them."

Greek Words, Phrases, and Constructions in 3:1–5

Verse 1

ἱερόν—this word connotes the entire temple complex, both building and grounds, whereas ναός signifies the sanctuary itself.

ἐπί—"in the expression of time here, [the preposition] indicates a more definitive period than the simple accusative would have expressed."[7]

Verse 2

ὑπάρχων—as a present active participle, this word is the equivalent of the present active participle ὤν of the verb *to be*.

ἐτίθουν—note the frequent use of the imperfect tense in this passage (vv. 1–5). The imperfect expresses repetition.

καθ' ἡμέραν—"daily." Luke has a penchant for this prepositional phrase, for he uses it five times in his Gospel and seven times in Acts. By contrast, it appears only twice in the Pauline Epistles and once in both Matthew and Mark. With a slight variation, the Epistle to the Hebrews has it four times.

τοῦ αἰτεῖν—the infinitive with the definite article in the genitive case expresses purpose.

Verse 5

ἐπεῖχεν—a compound form from ἐπί (upon) and ἔχω (I have, hold) in the imperfect tense needs the complement τοὺς ὀφθαλμούς (he was holding his eyes upon [them]).

προσδοκῶν—the present active participle denotes manner.

---

7. Robert Hanna, *A Grammatical Aid to the Greek New Testament* (Grand Rapids: Baker, 1983), p. 192. See also A. T. Robertson, *A Grammar of the Greek New Testament in the Light of Historical Research* (Nashville: Broadman, 1934), p. 602.

b. Miracle
3:6–10

6. But Peter said, "Silver and gold I do not have, but what I have I give to you: In the name of Jesus Christ of Nazareth, walk."
Peter continues to be the spokesman as John remains silent. And while the beggar eagerly waits to receive something, Peter says, "Silver and gold I do not have." That is, among my possessions I have no money. The money from the people who sold lands and valuables did not belong to Peter (refer to 2:44–45; 4:34–35; 5:1–2). In the service of Jesus, Peter was not a rich man (see Matt. 10:9–10). He lived by the Lord's command that "those who proclaim the gospel should receive their living from the gospel" (I Cor. 9:14).

What Peter gives to the crippled beggar is of far greater value to him than any amount of silver and gold. Peter heals him in the name of Jesus Christ of Nazareth and tells him to walk. For forty years this man had been immobile and now he is about to use his legs. Peter calls upon the name of Jesus to show him that the healing power of Jesus, known to all the people in Israel, flows through the apostle to the crippled man. Therefore not Peter but Jesus grants restoration.

The term *name* is significant because it comprises the full revelation of the person mentioned. Hence, the name *Jesus* refers to his birth, ministry, suffering, death, resurrection, and ascension. Next, the name *Christ* points to the Messiah, who is the exalted Son of God. Also, the place name *Nazareth* is added for further identification; this was the name Pilate had written on the sign attached to Jesus' cross (John 19:19). And last, the phrase *name of Jesus (Christ)* occurs repeatedly in Acts.[8]

Healing in the name of Jesus Christ of Nazareth calls for faith on the part of the invalid. Peter commands him to walk, but the crippled man can walk only if he puts his faith in Jesus. The New Testament teaches that miracles occur in connection with faith.[9]

7. Taking him by the right hand, he pulled him up; and immediately his feet and ankles were strengthened. 8. And jumping up he stood and began to walk; he entered the temple with them, walking, and jumping, and praising God.
When Peter takes the cripple by his right hand to help him stand up, he follows the same procedure Jesus practiced when he healed Peter's mother-in-law of a fever: "Taking her hand, Jesus helped her up. The fever left her

---

8. These are the references: 2:38; 3:6, 4:10, 18, 30; 5:40; 8:12, 16; 9:27; 10:48; 16:18; 19:5, 13, 17; 21:13; 26:9. Implicit references to the name of Jesus are numerous.
9. Consult John Calvin, *Commentary on the Acts of the Apostles*, ed. David W. Torrance and Thomas F. Torrance, 2 vols. (Grand Rapids: Eerdmans, 1966), vol. 1, p. 94.

and she began to wait on them" (Mark 1:31). In both cases, the miracle occurs after the patients are helped by extending the hand. Note that Luke, as a physician, accurately reports that Peter took hold of the man's right hand. The man instantly feels strength in his feet and ankles and knows that a miracle has taken place. The adverb *immediately* makes plain that a miracle occurred.

The man jumps up and for the first time in his life stands erect. What an experience of joy and happiness! Even though he has never been able to walk, he tries and has no difficulties. His walking turns into jumping, for he realizes that God has performed a miracle in his life. He utters words of praise and thanks to God and desires to accompany the apostles into the temple courts for prayer. (The place where his relatives and friends placed him to beg from day to day was not considered a court of the temple.) Now he enters the temple courts to express his gratitude to God (compare Luke 17:15).

The parallel of Paul healing the crippled man in Lystra is striking. Luke writes that Paul looked directly at the man and saw that he had faith to be healed. Then Paul told him to stand up on his feet, with the result that the man jumped up and began to walk (14:9–10).

Significant is the indirect reference to the arrival of the messianic age. Prophesying the time of the Messiah's coming, Isaiah said:

> Then will the eyes of the blind be opened
> and the ears of the deaf unstopped.
> *Then will the lame leap like a deer,*
> and the mute tongue shout for joy.
> [35:5–6a, NIV, italics added]

Jesus inaugurated the messianic age when he made the blind see, the lame walk, the lepers clean, and the deaf hear; when he raised the dead and preached the gospel to the poor (Matt. 11:5; Luke 7:22). After Pentecost, this messianic age continues, as Peter indicates by miraculously healing a crippled man in the name of Jesus Christ of Nazareth.

9. And all the people saw him walking and praising God. 10. They recognized him as the one who used to sit begging at the temple gate called Beautiful. And they were filled with wonder and amazement at what had happened to him.

How long the apostles and the man who was healed prayed in the temple courts is not known. Luke relates the reaction of the people who witness the effect of the miracle in the beggar who now walks, jumps, and praises God.

These are the facts:

a. For many years the people have known the crippled man as a beggar seated at the gate called Beautiful; they know that his malady was a birth defect that made it impossible for him to walk.

b. They recognize the beggar and now see him walking around and jumping for joy; they hear that he praises God for healing him.

c. They are utterly astonished and amazed in reaction to a wonderful act of God. As Jesus used to perform miracles in their midst, now his apostles perform them in his name. In short, what Jesus began during his earthly ministry is now continued through his immediate followers. In wonder and amazement the people are open to the good news of Jesus Christ, which Peter is about to proclaim.

Doctrinal Considerations in 3:6

Our names serve the useful purpose of distinguishing us from other persons. To have the same first and last names as someone else is confusing and sometimes even annoying. But our personal names do not reveal anything concerning our being, characteristics, and abilities. Scripture teaches us that when God gives names to people, their names describe their personalities. For instance, God calls Abram Abraham, which means "father of many nations" (Gen. 17:5). And the angel of the Lord instructs Joseph to call the son of Mary Jesus, "because he will save his people from their sins" (Matt. 1:21). Jesus' name reveals his being and his mission. Appearing in human flesh, Jesus as the Son of God has power to forgive sins.

Jesus' disciples prophesy, cast out demons, and perform miracles in his name (Matt. 7:22; Mark 9:39; Luke 10:17). They have received authority to preach repentance and forgiveness in Jesus' name (Luke 24:47) and to act on his behalf. When God pours out the Holy Spirit in that name (John 14:26), the apostles receive divine power and authority to perform miracles (Acts 3:6; 14:10).

Are we able to prophesy and perform exorcisms and miracles by using the name *Jesus*? Although the apostles received miraculous powers, the New Testament indicates that Jesus gives us no commands to cast out demons, heal the sick, and raise the dead in his name. What Jesus does tell us is to use the formula *in the name of Jesus* whenever we pray to God the Father (John 14:13–14; 15:16; 16:23–24). This formula should not be a formal and habitual conclusion to our prayers. It signifies that as Christ's followers we ask God to bless us in glorifying God's name, extending his kingdom, and doing his will (Matt. 6:9–10). When we pray in harmony with the prescription Jesus has given us, God will hear and answer our prayers.[10]

Greek Words, Phrases, and Constructions in 3:7–10

Verse 7

πιάσας—the aorist active participle from πιάζω (I take hold of) is followed by the accusative αὐτόν as direct object and the genitive τῆς δεξιᾶς χειρός, which is partitive.

Verse 8

ἐξαλλόμενος—the present middle (deponent) participle of the compound verb ἐξάλλομαι (I leap up) depicts continuity, intensity, and direction. The main verb

---

10. Hans Bietenhard, *NIDNTT*, vol. 2, p. 653; Gerald F. Hawthorne, "Name," *ISBE*, vol. 3, p. 483.

ἔστη is in the aorist to indicate single occurrence. But περιεπάτει is in the imperfect active: the man did not stop walking.

Verse 10

ἐπεγίνωσκον—the imperfect tense in this compound verb conveys that "they *began* to recognize him."[11] The preposition ἐπί has a directive rather than an intensive connotation (compare 4:13).[12]

συμβεβηκότι—in the perfect tense from the verb συμβαίνω (I meet, happen), this active participle is translated as a pluperfect. Not the action, which belongs to the past, but the continuing state of the miracle is important.

---

11 While he was clinging to Peter and John, all the people, full of amazement, ran together to them at the place called Solomon's Colonnade. 12 When Peter saw this, he addressed the crowd: "Men of Israel, why do you marvel at this or why do you gaze at us as if by our own power or piety we had made him walk? 13 The God of Abraham, Isaac, and Jacob, the God of our fathers, has glorified his servant Jesus, whom you handed over and disowned in the presence of Pilate, although he had decided to release him. 14 You disowned the Holy and Righteous One and asked that a murderer be released to you. 15 You killed the Prince of life, whom God raised from the dead. We are his witnesses. 16 And by faith in his name, this one whom you see and know was made strong in his name. And the faith that has come through him has given him this perfect health in the presence of all of you.

17 "And now, brothers, I know that you acted in ignorance, just as your leaders did. 18 But God fulfilled in this way the things which he had foretold through all the prophets that his Christ would suffer. 19 Repent, therefore, and turn to God, so that your sins may be wiped away, 20 that times of refreshing may come from the Lord, and that he may send the Christ appointed for you, namely, Jesus. 21 He must stay in heaven until the times of restoration of all things occur about which God spoke long ago through his holy prophets. 22 For Moses said, 'The Lord God will raise up for you a prophet like me from among your brothers; listen to everything he tells you. 23 And anyone who does not listen to that prophet will be utterly destroyed from among his people.'

24 "And all the prophets, as many as have spoken from Samuel and those succeeding him, likewise foretold these days. 25 And you are the sons of the prophets and of the covenant which God made with your fathers. He said to Abraham, 'And through your offspring all the families of the earth will be blessed.' 26 When God raised up his servant, he sent him first to you to bless you by turning each of you from your evil ways."

---

2. Address of Peter
3:11–26

a. Explanation
3:11–16

Peter is a true missionary of Jesus. He sees an opportunity to witness for his Lord and he takes it. He performs a miracle, observes its effect, and

---

11. Robertson, *Grammar*, p. 885.
12. Consult F. F. Bruce, *The Acts of the Apostles: The Greek Text with Introduction and Commentary*, 3d (rev. and enl.) ed. (Grand Rapids: Eerdmans, 1990), p. 193.

immediately speaks to the crowd that gathers. He knows that his audience is "filled with wonder and amazement," is sympathetic toward him, and wants to hear an explanation.

11. While he was clinging to Peter and John, all the people, full of amazement, ran together to them at the place called Solomon's Colonnade.

Luke provides no details about the prayer service in the Court of Men. We infer that when Peter and John tried to walk through the Court of Women and the temple gate called Beautiful into the Court of the Gentiles, the crippled man who was healed did not permit them to get out of his sight. We need not think that he prevented the apostles from walking. Rather, he stayed next to them and indicated to the crowd that Jesus' disciples had been instrumental in healing him.

The focus of attention is therefore on Peter and John. Luke writes, "All the people, full of amazement, ran together to them." When the apostles walked through the Court of the Gentiles to Solomon's Colonnade, throngs of people began to surround them. Solomon's Colonnade, located on the east side of the temple building, was thought to be a part of Solomon's temple. But this assumption is based more on honorable remembrance of this great king than on actuality. The floor plans of the respective temples of Solomon and Herod differ considerably, so that identification of the exact place is not possible.[13]

There was a three-aisled colonnade with columns that reached a height of twenty-seven feet. "The rows of columns were spaced thirty f[ee]t apart at the side aisles and forty-five f[ee]t at the center aisle."[14] In all, there were 162 columns. The colonnade was covered with a cedar roof, and the place itself afforded ample room for countless people. This was the place where Jesus met the Jewish leaders when he came to Jerusalem for the celebration of the Dedication Feast (John 10:22). And here the crowd, curious and amazed, gathered around Peter and John to find out what had happened to the crippled beggar.

12. When Peter saw this, he addressed the crowd: "Men of Israel, why do you marvel at this or why do you gaze at us as if by our own power or piety we had made him walk?"

Peter has an audience ready to hear his explanation, for the people are amazed at the miracle that has occurred. They display no skepticism; the ridicule that was heard at Pentecost is absent (compare 2:13). Therefore, Peter has a rare opportunity to proclaim the gospel. As in his Pentecost sermon, Peter first explains the circumstances of the miracle, then acquaints his hearers with the death and resurrection of Jesus Christ, and last calls them to repentance and faith.

---

13. Josephus *Antiquities* 15.11.3–5 [391–420]; 20.9.7 [219–23]. Consult William S. LaSor, "Jerusalem," *ISBE*, vol. 2, p. 1028.

14. Harold Stigers, "Temple, Jerusalem," *ZPEB*, vol. 5, p. 651.

a. "Men of Israel." Peter uses the familiar address of his Pentecost sermon (2:22), for he is speaking to a crowd of Jewish people who know the Old Testament Scriptures and who are not ignorant of the miracles Jesus performed. He addresses them as the people of God and tells them that they should not be surprised at the miracle they see in the crippled beggar. By implication he reminds them of the works of Jesus of Nazareth, whose power continues in his immediate followers.

b. "Why do you gaze at us as if by our own power or piety we had made him walk?" Peter reproves his Jewish audience by admonishing them to look not at the works of man but at the power of God. Luke provides a parallel in the account of the people of Lystra, who regarded Paul and Barnabas as gods after Paul healed a crippled man (14:8–18). Of course, the Jerusalem crowd does not worship Peter and John, but they think that Peter and John have gained inherent power and godliness and thereby earned the ability to make the lame person walk. Peter directs their attention not to man's works but to God's glory.

13. "The God of Abraham, Isaac, and Jacob, the God of our fathers, has glorified his servant Jesus, whom you handed over and disowned in the presence of Pilate, although he had decided to release him."

Luke presents only an abstract of Peter's address. Nevertheless, the record clearly shows that Peter appeals to the religious motives of his audience. After addressing them as "men of Israel," he notes that God is the God of the patriarchs Abraham, Isaac, and Jacob. Here Peter touches a basic part of Israel's religious foundation. God revealed himself to the forefathers, of whom Abraham, Isaac, and Jacob are the first three generations. Here are the same words God spoke to Moses from the burning bush: "I am the God of your fathers, the God of Abraham, the God of Isaac, and the God of Jacob" (Exod. 3:6, 15).[15] Jesus also referred to these same words when he, in his address to the Sadducees about the doctrine of the resurrection, told them that God is a God of the living and not of the dead (Matt. 22:32; Mark 12:26–27; Luke 20:37–38). And last, Stephen mentions them in his address before the Sanhedrin (7:32). The words are hallowed by reverential use. Conclusively, God is the God of Israel's forefathers (compare Matt. 8:11; Acts 22:14).

Peter continues and says, "The God of our fathers has glorified his servant Jesus." He indicates that Jesus stands in the line of the patriarchs and the spiritual forefathers of the Jewish people. God has glorified Jesus, whom Peter deliberately calls "servant" to remind his listeners of Isaiah's prophecy concerning the suffering and glory of the Lord's servant (Isa. 52:13–53:12). They should know that Jesus fulfilled this messianic prophecy (compare Matt. 12:18). Jesus is the servant of God (see v. 26; 4:27,

---

15. These words form the opening line of the well-known Jewish Eighteen Benedictions.

30).[16] During his ministry he refers to his fulfillment of Isaiah's prophecy (e.g., Isa. 53:12 and Luke 22:37). Jesus is the suffering servant, but God has glorified him; that is, he was "raised and lifted up and highly exalted" (Isa. 52:13, NIV).

Why has Jesus been raised up? Because, says Peter to his fellow Jews, "You handed [him] over and disowned [him] in the presence of Pilate, although he had decided to release him." He puts the burden of guilt where it belongs. The Jews are responsible for the death of God's servant, whom God glorified by raising him from the dead. He subsequently ascended to heaven to take his place at God's right hand.

In the presence of Pontius Pilate, the Jews disowned God's servant, who had come to his own people (John 1:11). And even when Pilate wanted to set Jesus free because he found no basis for a charge against him (Luke 23:4, 14), they put Pilate to the test. The Jews first forced him to maintain his allegiance to Caesar and then made him yield to their demand to crucify Jesus (John 19:12–16).

14. "You disowned the Holy and Righteous One and asked that a murderer be released to you. 15. You killed the Prince of life, whom God raised from the dead. We are his witnesses."

The Jews should have known from the Old Testament Scriptures that the Messiah is called holy. For example, in his Pentecost sermon (2:27) Peter reminded them of this fact by quoting Psalm 16:10, "Nor will you let your Holy One undergo decay." He pointed out that David was not speaking of himself but of the Christ (compare Isa. 41:14). And the people knew from the prophets that the Messiah is the Righteous One. Thus Isaiah wrote, "By his knowledge my righteous servant will make many righteous" (53:11; and see Jer. 23:5; 33:15; Zech. 9:9).[17]

Peter reminds his audience of their recent history and repeats the charge that they disowned and killed Jesus. They were the people who stood before Pontius Pilate and demanded the death of Jesus. They wanted the release of the prisoner Barabbas, who was an insurrectionist and murderer (Mark 15:7). Indeed, the choice Pilate put before the Jews was clear. Pilate said that he would release to them either Jesus, whom he had found to be innocent, or the rioter and murderer Barabbas (Luke 23:13–19). Even Pilate's wife told the governor not to have anything to do with that innocent man Jesus (Matt. 27:19).

"You killed the Prince of life." Peter's denunciation is directly aimed at the conscience of his audience. Note that he puts the blame not on Pontius

---

16. For a full discussion on the topic *servant of God,* see Joachim Jeremias, *TDNT,* vol. 5, pp. 684–717; Otto Michel, *NIDNTT,* vol. 3, pp. 607–13; and Richard T. France, "The Servant of the Lord in the Teachings of Jesus," *TynB* 19 (1968): 26–52.

17. New Testament references to Jesus as the Holy One are Mark 1:24; John 6:69; and as the Righteous One, Acts 7:52; 22:14; I John 2:1. Consult Herman N. Ridderbos, *The Speeches of Peter in the Acts of the Apostles* (London: Tyndale, 1962), p. 22.

Pilate, who commanded his soldiers to crucify Jesus. Peter blames the Jewish people who, incited by the chief priests and elders, demanded Jesus' death. He asserts that they themselves are the murderers. Here is the stark contrast and the depth of their crime: they asked Pilate for the release of Barabbas the murderer (v. 14) and the death of Jesus the Prince of life (v. 15). But Jesus is the giver of life (John 10:28) and therefore is its source. The Greek term translated "prince" can also mean "author" (5:31; and see Heb. 2:10; 12:2). Mortal man, however, is unable to kill the author of life, who has risen from the grave.

"God raised [him] from the dead." A characteristic theme that the apostles Peter and Paul express in their sermons appears in this sequence: you Jewish people killed Jesus; God raised him from the dead; and we apostles are witnesses.[18] If God raised Jesus from the dead, then by implication he is also able to give life to his murderers. In other words, Peter's triumphant announcement, "God raised [him] from the dead," reaches out to include his accused audience. When they see the error of their way and turn to God in repentance and faith, God is willing to forgive and restore them as his people and to grant them eternal life. Accordingly, Jesus' apostles are witnesses of Christ's resurrection and proclaim the good news of life and healing in his name.

16. "And by faith in his name, this one whom you see and know was made strong in his name. And the faith that has come through him has given him this perfect health in the presence of all of you."

Faith in the name of Jesus is the basic requirement that Peter places before his listeners. By faith in the resurrected and glorified Jesus, the apostles are able to perform miracles. Notice that the expressions *faith* and *his* [*Jesus'*] *name* appear twice in this verse. Let us look at these two concepts.

a. *Faith.* The question we must ask is whether Peter speaks about the faith of the apostles or the faith of the cripple. The answer, of course, is that both the apostles and the beggar had faith. Peter and John performed the miracle only because they fully trusted Jesus to give them the power to heal. The lame man also trusted the Lord to heal him, even if Luke refrains from suggesting anything about his faith at the time the miracle took place (vv. 3–7). This faith, as Peter puts it, comes through Jesus. Only through him is faith effective, as is evident in the healing of the lame man: "And the faith which is through Jesus has given the man this perfect health" (RSV). Faith and the name of Jesus are the two sides of the same coin that represents healing. In brief, faith is the manner and Jesus' name is the cause of the man's restoration.[19]

b. *Name.* In the Greek, verse 16 lacks polish and balance. As a resumé

---

18. Compare these references: Acts 2:23–24; 4:10; 5:30–32; 10:39–41; 13:28–31.
19. Consult Calvin, *Acts of the Apostles*, vol. 1, p. 99.

presented by Luke, it reflects Peter's emphasis on the name of Jesus, which he repeatedly mentions and even personifies. Literally the text says, "It is the name of Jesus which has strengthened this man whom you see and know" (NASB). When Peter said to the cripple, "In the name of Jesus Christ of Nazareth, walk" (v. 6), he did not merely utter a magic formula that caused a miracle. On the contrary, by faith in Jesus' name he trusted that Jesus' divine power would flow through him to heal the lame man. The seven sons of Sceva without faith invoked the name of Jesus and accomplished nothing, but received a severe beating from the evil spirit they tried to cast out (19:13–16). However, when the seventy-two disciples commissioned by Jesus returned to him, they rejoiced and said, "Lord, even the demons submit to us in your name" (Luke 10:17, NIV).

Faith in the name of Jesus calls forth a response from the beggar, who extends his right hand to Peter and realizes that his feet and ankles are strong. With this evidence, which everyone in the audience can see, Peter is now at the point of asking the Jews to put their faith in Jesus.

Practical Considerations in 3:16

Throughout the history of the church, the gift of healing the sick has never been absent. The names of Francis of Assisi, Martin Luther, and John Wesley, not to mention the names of modern-day Christians, stand out in relation to a healing ministry. Among the gifts of the Holy Spirit is the gift of healing (I Cor. 12:9, 28). Paul, however, pointedly and rhetorically asks, "Do all have gifts of healing?" (I Cor. 12:30, NIV). Paul himself performed healing miracles during his missionary tours, but he gives no indication that he healed Epaphroditus, who was so ill that he almost died (Phil. 2:27). Paul openly admits that he "left Trophimus sick in Miletus" (II Tim. 4:20). And Paul himself had to contend with a thorn in the flesh which God did not remove (II Cor. 12:7–9). In short, Paul was not able to use his gift of healing whenever he pleased and wherever he was.

James instructs us to call on the elders of the church when we are ill. These elders should pray and anoint with oil in the name of the Lord (5:14). He emphasizes that "prayer offered in faith will heal the sick person" (v. 15), for faith and prayer are requisites to which the Lord responds.[20] Sometimes healing miracles do not occur, especially when God wants to strengthen our faith to his glory. As Scripture teaches, God answers prayer at his time and in his own way. He said to Paul, "My grace is sufficient for you, for my power is perfected in weakness" (II Cor. 12:9).

---

20. For a discussion on this matter, refer to Simon J. Kistemaker, *Exposition of the Epistle of James and the Epistles of John,* New Testament Commentary series (Grand Rapids: Baker, 1986), pp. 175–77.

Greek Words, Phrases, and Constructions in 3:11–16

Verse 11

κρατοῦντος δὲ αὐτοῦ—the present active participle with the pronoun in the genitive case forms the genitive absolute construction.

ὁ λαός—in Luke's Gospel and Acts, this is a favorite expression. Of the 143 occurrences of this noun in the New Testament, 84 are in Luke's writings. The noun is collective; has a verb in the singular (συνέδραμεν, aorist active from συντρέχω [I run together]); and features a compound adjective (ἔκθαμβοι, utterly astonished) in the plural.

Verse 12

ἡμῖν—because of its position in the sentence, this personal pronoun is emphatic. It is in the dative plural as an indirect object and is explained by the perfect active participle πεποιηκόσιν (from ποιέω [I do, make]) in the dative.

τοῦ περιπατεῖν—with the definite article in the genitive the present active infinitive expresses purpose.

Verse 14

τὸν ἅγιον καὶ δίκαιον—with one definite article two epithets are applied to one person.[21] Notice the contrast between this phrase and ἄνδρα φονέα (murderer).

Verse 16

ἡ πίστις—the general context of this noun indicates that both the apostles and the cripple put their faith in Jesus Christ.

ἀπέναντι—a compound adverb from three prepositions (ἀπό, ἐν, and ἀντί) has the secondary meaning *in the sight of* instead of "opposite."

---

b. Exhortation
3:17–23

Peter has uncovered the miserable plight of his listeners, who now see their guilt before God. Although they may register excuses and plead extenuating circumstances, they remain guilty of killing Jesus Christ, the author of life. Peter addresses them with gentle words spoken with pastoral interest and concern. He places himself on their level and speaks words of comfort.

17. "And now, brothers, I know that you acted in ignorance, just as your leaders did. 18. But God fulfilled in this way the things which he had foretold through all the prophets that his Christ would suffer."

We make these observations:

a. *Ignorance.* After explaining the events of the recent past which are familiar to every listener in Peter's audience, Peter turns to the present

---

21. Consult Robertson, *Grammar*, p. 785.

situation. In gentle tones he is actually asking, "What shall we do about your sin?" Because the people look to him for guidance, Peter has a perfect opportunity to lead them to repentance and faith in Jesus Christ. As a pastor he admits that his listeners, whom he addresses as "brothers," committed their crime in ignorance. They sinned unintentionally, being led astray by a mob spirit that caused them to shout, "Crucify him." If they had sinned defiantly, they would have committed blasphemy. God says that he does not forgive a man who sins intentionally (see Num. 15:30–31). Someone who sins defiantly is actually committing the sin against the Holy Spirit (Matt. 12:31–32). The Jewish people, however, sinned unintentionally because of spiritual blindness.

The Jews did not realize that Jesus of Nazareth came to them as their Messiah. Nor did they understand the Scriptures that spoke of the suffering Servant, that is, the Messiah. In his sermon to the Jews in Pisidian Antioch, Paul says that the people of Jerusalem and their rulers did not recognize Jesus (13:27). Nevertheless, their guilt, which can be removed only by repentance and by Christ's forgiving love, remains. Christ's love is present. Even on the cross, Jesus prayed for the people who killed him: "Father, forgive them, for they do not know what they are doing" (Luke 23:34).

Peter includes the leaders of the Jewish people in his address: "And now, brothers, I know that you acted in ignorance, just as your leaders did." This general statement does not mean that every Jewish leader acted in ignorance. Remember that Jesus taught the doctrine of sinning against the Holy Spirit when Pharisees and teachers of the law said that he was casting out demons by Beelzebub, the prince of demons (see Matt. 12:24; Mark 3:22; Luke 11:15).

b. *Fulfillment.* Peter repeats the words that Jesus spoke first to the two men of Emmaus and later in the upper room when he opened the Scriptures and told the disciples that the Christ would suffer and enter his glory (see Luke 24:26–27, 45–46).

Peter bases his sermon on the Old Testament Scriptures and tells his audience that Jesus is the fulfillment of prophecy. In fact, Peter puts it pointedly when he says that "God fulfilled in this way the things which he had foretold through all the prophets." God speaks through his servants the prophets, but he fulfills his word through Jesus his Son. God, then, provides continuity in his revelation. He makes it known that the Christian community lives in the age of fulfillment.[22] Thus, the early Christians see in the Old Testament Scriptures Christ's humiliation and suffering that leads to glory.

The prophets in the Old Testament era prophesied that the "Christ

---

22. Refer to Donald Guthrie, *New Testament Theology* (Downers Grove: Inter-Varsity, 1981), pp. 736–37. And consult George E. Ladd, *A Theology of the New Testament* (Grand Rapids: Eerdmans, 1974), pp. 330–31.

would suffer" (compare Isa. 50:6; 53:3–12; I Peter 1:10–12). Because the Jews were familiar with the writings of the prophets, they should have known these facts. Jesus told the men of Emmaus that they were "slow of heart to believe all that the prophets have spoken" (Luke 24:25); and in the upper room Jesus had to open the minds of his disciples so that they could understand the Scriptures (Luke 24:45).

Now Peter follows the example that Jesus set and instructs his listeners in the teaching concerning the suffering of the Messiah. He tells them that Jesus suffered and died on the cross, because the Jews handed him over to be crucified. He also shows them the way of repentance, a turning to God, remission of sins, and a renewal of life which is refreshing.

19. "Repent, therefore, and turn to God, so that your sins may be wiped away, 20. that times of refreshing may come from the Lord, and that he may send the Christ appointed for you, namely, Jesus."

a. "Repent, therefore, and turn to God." Here is the answer to the question, "What shall we do about your sin?" On the basis of the scriptural evidence that God has fulfilled the messianic prophecies, Peter commands his hearers to repent (compare 2:38). They must renounce their former life and turn their thinking around, so that they no longer follow their old ways but listen obediently to God's Word fulfilled in Jesus Christ. Repentance affects the totality of man's existence; it reaches the inner depths of his being and touches all his external relations with God and with his neighbor. Repentance is a turning away from sin; faith is a turning to God.[23] Peter tells the people to turn to God, which in simpler language is: repent and believe.

b. "So that your sins may be wiped away." Peter presents a picture of man's sins recorded on a slate that can be wiped clean. Granted that he fails to say who cleans the slate, we know that only God through Jesus Christ forgives sins. Perhaps this is an indication of the typical Hebraic way of expressing a thought without using God's name. Peter's words are an allusion to baptism, which is the symbol of washing away man's sins. Notice that Peter uses the word *sins* in the plural to encompass the totality of the believer's sins. When God forgives man's sins, the relationship between God and man is restored. This means that man enters a new period in his life. Peter expresses this thought in characteristic terms. He says,

c. "That times of refreshing may come from the Lord."[24] This indeed is an interesting clause, which literally reads, "that there may come seasons of refreshing from the face of the Lord." What does Peter mean? The word *refreshing* occurs only once in the New Testament and once in the Septuagint text of the Old Testament (Exod. 8:15; 8:11 LXX). As a result, scholars

---

23. James D. G. Dunn, *Baptism in the Holy Spirit,* Studies in Biblical Theology, 2d series 15 (London: SCM, 1970), p. 91. See also his article "Repentance," in *Baker's Dictionary of Christian Ethics,* ed. Carl F. H. Henry (Grand Rapids: Baker, 1973), pp. 578–79.

24. The verse division differs in Greek New Testaments and in translations. Some include this clause with verse 19, others with the following verse.

are unable to ascertain the precise meaning of this word. Here are some suggestions they submit:

1. The times of refreshing are "the age of salvation, which is promised to the nation Israel if it repents."[25]
2. The phrase *times of spiritual strength* (GNB) "refers to the future and to Jesus' return."[26] In light of the context, commentators think that the phrase describes the imminent return of Jesus.
3. Because the phrase *times of refreshing* is directly linked with repentance and turning to God, it refers to times that are in the immediate, not the remote, future.[27]

In view of the uncertainty surrounding this phrase, we should refrain from being dogmatic. The word *times* is in the plural and signifies periodic seasons in which the forgiven and restored believer experiences the refreshing nearness of the Lord. Moreover, we must ask whether the term *Lord* denotes Jesus or is the Old Testament name for God. The subject of the next clause is God. This is evident, for example, in the following translation: "Then the Lord may grant you a time of recovery and send you the Messiah he has already appointed" (NEB).[28]

d. "And that he may send the Christ appointed for you, namely, Jesus." In response to man's repentance and turning to God, God is sending the Christ. But when is Christ coming? To be sure, Christ did come to his people, who rejected and killed him. At present, he comes to all who listen to him through the preaching of God's Word. And at the end of the age, God will send Christ Jesus to earth again. But what is the context in which Peter speaks?

Peter addresses Jews who, though they did not accept the God-appointed Jesus when he lived among them, now receive the opportunity to claim him as their Messiah. In his grace and love, God gives them one more opportunity to acknowledge the Christ. If they reject him a second time, they will not be able to come to repentance when Jesus eventually returns on the clouds of heaven. Their repentance, therefore, will speed Christ's return. Peter corroborates this thought in his epistle: "You ought to live holy and godly lives by looking forward to and by speeding the coming of God's day" (II Peter 3:12).

21. "He must stay in heaven until the times of restoration of all things occur about which God spoke long ago through his holy prophets."

---

25. Colin Brown, *NIDNTT*, vol. 3, p. 686. And consult Eduard Schweizer, *TDNT*, vol. 9, pp. 664–65.

26. David John Williams, *Acts*, Good News Commentaries series (San Francisco: Harper and Row, 1985), p. 55. See also Lake and Cadbury, *Beginnings*, vol. 4, p. 37.

27. Consult R. C. H. Lenski, *The Interpretation of the Acts of the Apostles* (Columbus: Wartburg, 1944), p. 142.

28. See also NAB, GNB, MLB, *Moffatt*.

a. "He must stay in heaven." In his discourse on the end of the age, Jesus told the disciples that no one but the Father knows the exact time of Jesus' return (Matt. 24:36). Therefore, God the Father determines when Jesus will come back to restore everything. In the meantime, while Christ's gospel is preached on earth, Jesus remains in heaven, from where he directs the development of his church and kingdom. He will not return until "this gospel of the kingdom [has been] preached in the whole world as a testimony to all nations, and then will come the end" (Matt. 24:14).

b. "Until the times of restoration of all things occur." What does Peter intend to say with these words? In the context of the passage, he addresses Jewish people who look forward to the restoration of all things, as the Old Testament prophets in the Scriptures told them. The times of refreshing that come as a result of repentance and faith are harbingers of the time of complete restoration. Whereas the seasons of refreshing are periodic and subjective, the time of restoration is permanent and objective.[29] According to Paul, the restoration will be completed when everything has been subjected to Jesus Christ and when he hands the kingdom to his Father (I Cor. 15:24).

c. "About which God spoke long ago through his holy prophets." Peter proves his point by referring again to the Old Testament prophecies (see also I Peter 1:10–12; II Peter 1:19–21). Notice that Peter calls the prophets holy because they conveyed divine revelation. In a sense, Peter repeats the wording of verse 18, where he says that "God fulfilled in this way the things which he had foretold through all the prophets." God made promises through his spokesmen the prophets. What did the prophets say?

22. "For Moses said, 'The Lord God will raise up for you a prophet like me from among your brothers; listen to everything he tells you. 23. And anyone who does not listen to that prophet will be utterly destroyed from among his people.' "

a. "For Moses said." From among the Old Testament prophets, Peter chooses the example of Moses. No one can dispute the prophetic status of Moses, for God himself gave him this rank (Deut. 18:18). At the burning bush God called Moses to be his prophet (Exod. 3:4); other prophets received a similar call (see I Sam. 3:1–14; Isa. 6:1–13; Jer. 1:4–19; Ezek. 1:1–3). Moses, then, is first in the line of the prophets and is the greatest.

b. "The Lord God will raise up for you a prophet." Peter quotes a familiar passage from the Old Testament. He gives an abbreviated version of the words spoken by Moses and recorded in Deuteronomy 18:15–20. The Gospel writers allude to these words numerous times[30] and Stephen in his address to the Sanhedrin partially quotes them (7:37). The exact wording,

---

29. Refer to Albrecht Oepke, *TDNT*, vol. 1, p. 391; Hans-Georg Link, *NIDNTT*, vol. 3, p. 148; John Albert Bengel, *Gnomon of the New Testament*, ed. Andrew R. Fausset, 5 vols. (Edinburgh: Clark, 1877), vol. 2, p. 545.

30. See Matt. 17:5; Mark 9:4, 7; Luke 7:39; 24:25; John 1:21; 5:46.

therefore, differs from the Hebrew text and the Septuagintal translation, but the meaning is virtually identical.

c. "Like me from among your brothers." Fulfilling the Old Testament prophecy, Christ is a prophet like Moses, speaks the words God has given him, and demands that the Jewish people listen obediently to what he has to say. The conclusion is that everyone who refuses to listen to Jesus "will be cut off from his people" (compare Lev. 23:29).

Is Christ like Moses? Moses says that God will raise up a prophet like him. The Jews considered Moses the greatest prophet on earth because God spoke to him face to face (see Num. 12:8). They also knew this eloquent testimony concerning Moses:

> There has never yet risen in Israel a prophet like Moses, whom the LORD knew face to face: remember all the signs and portents which the LORD sent him to show in Egypt to Pharaoh and all his servants and the whole land; remember the strong hand of Moses and the terrible deeds which he did in the sight of all Israel. [Deut. 34:10–12, NEB]

But Christ surpassed Moses in every respect. The writer of Hebrews puts it succinctly when he says that Moses was a servant in God's house but Christ is a son over God's house (3:5–6). Moses instituted the first covenant for the nation Israel (Exod. 24:3–8), but this covenant became obsolete (Heb. 8:13); Christ instituted the new covenant in his blood for people from every nation (Matt. 26:28; I Cor. 11:25). Yet the similarity of Christ and Moses is evident in the words, "a prophet like me from among your brothers." Christ is a prophet who, like Moses, is a physical descendant of Abraham and thus belongs to Israel. The Jews who listen to Peter must acknowledge that Christ indeed fulfilled the prophetic words of Moses.

d. "Listen to everything he tells you." With this prophecy Peter seems to tell his Jewish hearers that if they believe and obey the words of Moses, they should also believe and obey Jesus. Moses prophesied about the Christ, and Christ spoke about Moses (John 5:45–46). The Jewish people expected the coming of "*the* Prophet," as they said repeatedly during Jesus' ministry (refer to John 1:21, 25; 7:40). And many times they called Jesus a prophet or the Prophet.[31]

e. "And anyone who does not listen to that prophet will be utterly destroyed from among his people." Here is the proverbial two-sided coin. On the one hand, God gives the command to obey; on the other, he reveals the consequence of disobedience. God calls the Jews to listen to the words of Moses in which he speaks of the Christ. He commands them to listen to Christ's message. But God encountered unwillingness when the Jews refused to obey Jesus during his earthly ministry. Now once more God speaks

---

31. See Matt. 21:11; Luke 7:16, 39; 24:19; John 6:14.

to them through the mouth of one of Christ's apostles. If he finds that they continue in their disobedience, they will be cut off from God's people.

Practical Considerations in 3:22b

In English, we have two verbs that are synonyms, yet each can have its own distinct meaning. They are the verbs *to hear* and *to listen*. The first verb means, among other things, "to perceive with the ear." The second one signifies "to hear with thoughtful attention." Due to the multiplicity of noises that we hear around us, we often fail to listen. That is, our minds possess an uncanny ability to hear but not respond. Children at times demonstrate this proficiency of hearing without listening when bedtime approaches. Parents gently remind them to get ready for bed, but find that the youngsters continue to stall for time. If the children do not respond even after repeated and sometimes more persistent reminders, father or mother often asks: "Do you hear me?" Certainly they hear, but they fail to listen.

Similar episodes also occur daily in our own adult lives. Speaking to us of his Son, God says, "You must listen to everything he tells you." We nod and promise to do so. But when we examine ourselves, we confess that even though Jesus speaks to us when we read the Scriptures, we fail to act obediently. Remember, therefore, that God spoke from heaven at the time of Jesus' transfiguration and said: "This is my Son, whom I love; I am well pleased with him. Listen to him!" (Matt. 17:5).

Greek Words, Phrases, and Constructions in 3:17–23

Verse 17

καὶ νῦν—Peter makes a transition from his explanation of past events to that of present realities.

κατὰ ἄγνοιαν—instead of a participle, Luke uses a prepositional phrase to express manner: in ignorance.

Verse 20

ὅπως ἄν—the combination of adverb and particle introduces a purpose clause that is based on the aorist active imperatives μετανοήσατε (repent!) and ἐπιστρέψατε (turn!) in the preceding verse (v. 19).

καιροί—this noun is closely related to χρόνων (v. 21) and like it is without the definite article. In the verses 21 and 22, the nouns are virtually synonymous.

Verse 23

ἀκούσῃ τοῦ προφήτου—as a protasis in a conditional sentence, the verb is the aorist active subjunctive. The aorist denotes single action. Followed by the genitive case in the noun προφήτου, the verb has the following meaning: "every soul which will not hear that prophet" (i.e., "which refuses even to let a prophet speak.").[32]

---

32. Hanna, *Grammatical Aid*, p. 193.

c. Promise
3:24–26

The last three verses of Peter's sermon form the conclusion to his discourse. In these verses Peter reminds his audience of the covenant blessings which they have inherited through Abraham, their spiritual father. Now, through Jesus Christ, God continues to bless his people.

24. "And all the prophets, as many as have spoken from Samuel and those succeeding him, likewise foretold these days."

The line of reasoning Peter develops is that all the prophets, from Moses to Samuel to those who follow, have spoken about the coming of the Messiah. After quoting Moses' prophecy in the preceding verses, Peter mentions Samuel. In the intervening ages between Moses and Samuel, the prophets left no prophecies concerning the Christ. For this reason, Peter omits that period and continues with Samuel, who in Jewish writings was known as the teacher of the prophets (compare 13:20; I Sam. 3:19).[33] However, Scripture gives no indication that Samuel either prophesied or taught the prophets. If we take the name *Samuel* to refer to the period that covers the time of the books ascribed to him, we find some prophetic allusions to the Messiah. For instance, the prophet Nathan informs David that from his offspring God will establish an everlasting kingdom (II Sam. 7:12–14; Acts 2:30; Heb. 1:5). David, whom Samuel anointed king over Israel, is himself a forerunner of Jesus, king of the Jews (Matt. 2:2; 27:37).[34]

"All the prophets . . . have spoken and foretold these days." The early Christian community attentively searched the Old Testament prophecies to ascertain that Jesus Christ of Nazareth had fulfilled them. In their sermons and epistles, Peter and Paul repeatedly quote these prophecies to show that Jesus is indeed the promised Messiah.

> Lead on, O King eternal,
> Till sin's fierce war shall cease,
> And holiness shall whisper
> The sweet amen of peace;
> For not with swords' loud clashing,
> Or roll of stirring drums,
> With deeds of love and mercy
> The heavenly kingdom comes.
> —Ernest W. Shurtleff

25. "And you are the sons of the prophets and of the covenant which God made with your fathers. He said to Abraham, 'And through your offspring all the families of the earth will be blessed.' "

33. Refer to SB, vol. 2, p. 627; Lenski, *Acts,* p. 147.
34. For the references to David's kingship see I Sam. 13:14; 15:28; 16:13; 28:17.

The fact that Luke presents a resumé of Peter's sermon becomes especially evident in this verse. The connection between it and the preceding verse is the phrase *heirs of the prophets*.[35] Who are these heirs? Peter addresses his listeners and says, "you." According to Paul, the Jewish people were entrusted with the very words of God (Rom. 3:2). The phrase *heirs of the prophets*, then, implies that the Jews were recipients of the prophecies; ultimately these come from God in the form of Scripture. Moreover, the Jews are heirs of the covenant God made with Abraham and his descendants (Gen. 15:18; 17:2, 4, 7; Rom. 9:4), which was confirmed by the nation Israel in the days of Moses (Exod. 24:3–8). Hence, Peter moves from the time of Moses to an earlier period in which God made a covenant with Abraham and promised him and his descendants untold blessings. God sealed his words in a covenant that would transcend the centuries and include all the spiritual descendants of Abraham.

God said to Abraham, "And through your offspring all the families on earth will be blessed." The word *offspring* in the Greek is "seed" (in the singular) and thus calls attention to one person, namely, Christ. Paul uses the same word (seed) in the singular and writes,

> Now the promises were spoken to Abraham and to his seed. Scripture does not say "and to seeds," referring to many people, but "and to your seed," referring to one person, who is Christ. [Gal. 3:16]

In their theological discussions, both Peter and Paul call attention to Jesus Christ. Peter quotes directly from the Septuagint, which describes the scene of Abraham offering Isaac on Mount Moriah (Gen. 22:18).[36] His listeners consider themselves "heirs of the covenant" that God made with Israel and think that the Gentiles have no part in this covenant.[37] But the well-known Old Testament citation includes all the nations of the earth. Peter does not elaborate, even if the words of the Great Commission, "make disciples of all nations" (Matt. 28:19), are indelibly inscribed in his memory. He makes known to his audience, however, that Jesus has come to bless them first, for the gospel must be proclaimed first to the members of the house of Israel (Matt. 10:6; Rom. 1:16; 2:10).

26. "When God raised up his servant, he sent him first to you to bless you by turning each of you from your evil ways."

a. *Servant.* "When God raised up his servant." God appointed Jesus Christ to take the place of Abraham in order to fulfill the words spoken to Abraham: "Through your offspring [that is, Christ] all the families on earth will

---

35. The literal translation is "sons of the prophets," which is a familiar phrase in the Septuagintal translation of I Kings 20:35; II Kings 2:3, 5, 7. Consult Adolf Deissmann, *Bible Studies* (reprint ed.; Winona Lake, Ind.: Alpha, 1979), p. 163.

36. Compare also Gen. 12:3; 18:18; 26:4; 28:14. For a New Testament reference see Gal. 3:8.

37. Gerhard Schneider, *Die Apostelgeschichte*, Herders Theologischer Kommentar zum Neuen Testament series, 2 vols. (Freiburg: Herder, 1980), vol. 1, p. 330.

be blessed." Therefore, the verb *raised up* does not relate to the resurrection but rather to Christ's appointment to serve as the offspring of Abraham (compare v. 22). Note that Peter once again (see v. 13) calls Jesus God's servant, which appears to be a common appellation for him (4:27, 30). Peter derives this terminology from the Old Testament and identifies Jesus with the suffering servant of Isaiah.[38]

b. *Sent.* "He sent him first to you to bless you." Christ's mission is to bless in word and deed the spiritual descendants of Abraham. Notice that Peter, using the verb *bless*, links Jesus Christ to the quotation concerning Abraham. Whom does Jesus bless first? The text clearly states that he goes first to the Jews: "[God] sent him first to you." This is the reason Peter preaches his sermon at Solomon's Colonnade to a Jewish audience. At this moment he does not elaborate that a rejection of Christ by the Jews implies a turning to the Gentiles instead. This is what Paul told the Jews in Pisidian Antioch: "The word of God had to be spoken to you first. Since you reject it and do not consider yourselves worthy of eternal life, we are turning to the Gentiles" (13:46).

What is the blessing Jesus grants? Peter says, "[He is sent] to bless you by turning each of you from your evil ways." The blessing, then, is repentance and salvation. Here is a repetition of the command Peter uttered earlier in his sermon (v. 19), yet with the difference that we understand Christ to be instrumental in the process of turning a sinner away from evil. Note that Peter is forthright when he tells the Jews that Christ turns them "from [their] evil ways." He is the Savior of his people.

Greek Words, Phrases, and Constructions in 3:24 and 26

Verse 24

κατήγγειλαν—although the verse features two verbs, ἐλάλησαν (aorist active of λαλέω [I speak]) has ὅσοι (as many as) as subject; κατήγγειλαν (aorist active of καταγγέλλω [I proclaim]) is the main verb preceded by καί (also).

Verse 26

εὐλογοῦντα—the present active participle is "used as a future in the sense of purpose" (to send).[39]

ἐν τῷ ἀποστρέφειν—the present active infinitive preceded by the preposition and definite article in the dative case expresses duration; it is also transitive with ἕκαστον (each) as direct object; and last, the construction is instrumental, for the implied subject of the infinitive is Christ.

---

38. See Isa. 52:13 53:12. Also consult Guthrie, *New Testament Theology*, p. 461. For additional study, refer to Richard N. Longenecker, *The Christology of Early Jewish Christianity*, Studies in Biblical Theology, 2d series 17 (London: SCM, 1970), p. 105.

39. Robertson, *Grammar*, p. 891.

Summary of Chapter 3

Peter and John go together to the temple at the stated hour of prayer. There Peter heals a lame man at the gate called Beautiful. The crowd is astonished and gathers around the apostles and the former cripple. Peter seizes the opportunity and preaches a sermon. He tells the people that he does not possess inherent power to heal but that the man was healed in the name of Jesus Christ.

Peter reminds the crowd that they killed Jesus, but God raised him from the dead. He comforts the people and admonishes them to repent, so that they may be forgiven and receive the Christ. He instructs them in the Old Testament prophecies by taking an example from the testimony of Moses. Peter mentions that all the prophets speak of Christ and points out that the covenantal blessings promised to Abraham's descendants now come to them through Christ, who turns them from their evil ways.

4

The Church in Jerusalem, *part 3*

4:1–37

Outline (continued)

4:1–22	3.	Before the Sanhedrin
4:1–4		a. Arrest
4:5–7		b. Trial
4:8–12		c. Defense
4:13–17		d. Consultation
4:18–22		e. Acquittal
4:23–31	4.	Prayers of the Church
4:23–24a		a. Setting
4:24b–28		b. Address
4:29–31		c. Request and Reply
4:32–37	5.	Love of the Saints
4:32–35		a. Community of Goods
4:36–37		b. Example of Barnabas

4
1 While Peter and John were still talking to the people, the priests, the captain of the temple guard, and the Sadducees approached them. 2 They were greatly disturbed because the apostles were teaching the people and proclaiming in Jesus the resurrection of the dead. 3 And they arrested Peter and John and, because it was evening, they put them in prison until the next day. 4 But many of those who heard the message believed, and the number of men came to be about five thousand.

5 And the next day, their rulers, elders, and scribes gathered in Jerusalem. 6 Annas the high priest, and Caiaphas, John, Alexander, and all who were of high-priestly descent were there. 7 And having placed them in the center, they began to inquire: "By what power or in what name did you do this?"

8 Then Peter, filled with the Holy Spirit, said to them: "Rulers and elders of the people! 9 If we are questioned today for a good deed done to a sick man and how he was healed, 10 let it be known to all of you and to all the people of Israel that by the name of Jesus Christ of Nazareth, whom you crucified, whom God raised from the dead, this man stands before you healthy. 11 He is 'the stone, which was rejected by you, the builders, which has become the capstone.' 12 Salvation is found in no one else, for there is no other name under heaven given among men by which we must be saved."

13 When they observed the courage of Peter and John and understood that they were uneducated and untrained men, they marveled and realized that they had been with Jesus. 14 And seeing the man who had been healed standing with them, they could think of nothing to say. 15 When they ordered them to leave the Sanhedrin, they conferred together 16 and said, "What are we to do with these men? For the fact that a noteworthy miracle has occurred through them is obvious to all who live in Jerusalem. We cannot deny it. 17 But in order to stop this thing from spreading further among the people, let us warn them to speak no more to anyone in this name."

18 When they called them in, they commanded them not to speak or teach at all in the name of Jesus. 19 But Peter and John answered, "Judge whether it is right in God's sight to obey you rather than God. 20 For we cannot stop speaking about the things we have seen and heard."

21 And when they had threatened them further, they let them go—they found no basis for punishing them, on account of the people, for all were glorifying God for what had happened. 22 For the man who had been miraculously healed was more than forty years old.

---

3. Before the Sanhedrin
4:1–22

a. Arrest
4:1–4

When crowds gathered around Jesus, the authorities used to keep him under close surveillance. Likewise, when Peter and John address a large crowd in the temple area, "the priests, the captain of the temple guard, and the Sadducees" react. Who are these people and what authority do they have to arrest Peter and John?

Priests were organized into twenty-four divisions which served at the temple on a rotation basis (compare Luke 1:8).[1] The priests and Levites administered the morning and evening sacrifices. The captain of the temple guard was a priest in charge of the temple police force. His authority ranked second to that of the high priest;[2] his term of service was indefinite and uninterrupted; and his duty was to maintain order in the temple and its surrounding area. Luke often refers to the captain and the officers of the temple guard (5:24, 26; Luke 22:4, 52).

The Sadducees were of priestly descent, presumably from the line of the high priest Zadok (Ezek. 40:46; 44:15–16; 48:11). Having formed a party that controlled the temple and the high priesthood, they wielded enormous political power. They accepted as authoritative only the five books of Moses; the rest of the Old Testament had only secondary value for them. Thus they denied the doctrines pertaining to the Messiah, angels, demons, immortality, and resurrection.[3]

1. While Peter and John were still talking to the people, the priests, the captain of the temple guard, and the Sadducees approached them.

On the day of Pentecost a large crowd of people listened to Peter's sermon. The priests, temple police, and the Sadducees, who would normally refrain from exerting any influence on large crowds in the temple courts during festive days, were alerted to take action when throngs surrounded Peter and John at Solomon's Colonnade. Even if the healing of the crippled beggar was unimportant to the religious leaders, the publicity that ensued and Peter's sermon were such a cause of concern to them that they interrupted the apostles' teaching.

Luke presents a resumé of Peter's sermon delivered at the temple and writes that both Peter and John were speaking to the crowd. He depicts Peter as spokesman but indirectly notes that John also expresses himself (compare vv. 13, 17–20).

The priests, temple police, and Sadducees prevented the apostles from continuing their teaching by arresting them. The presence of three groups of people to arrest two apostles betrays either an inability to control the crowd or a fear of the Roman military command stationed at the temple. But the crowd was orderly and peaceful, in contrast with the crowd at Paul's arrest decades later (see 21:27–40). The priests, temple guards, and Sadducees, however, objected to two matters: the mere fact

---

1. Consult Josephus *Antiquities* 7.14.7 [363–65]; and see Emil Schürer, *The History of the Jewish People in the Age of Jesus Christ (175 B.C.–A.D. 135)*, rev. and ed. Geza Vermes and Fergus Millar, 3 vols. (Edinburgh: Clark, 1973–87), vol. 2, p. 247.

2. See Josephus *War* 2.17.2 [409]; 6.5.3 [294]; *Antiquities* 20.6.2 [131]; 9.3 [208]. And consult SB, vol. 2, pp. 628–31.

3. For further information refer to Donald A. Hagner, "Sadducees," *ZPEB*, vol. 5, pp. 211–16.

that Peter and John taught; and the content of their teaching, especially the doctrine of resurrection.

2. They were greatly disturbed because the apostles were teaching the people and proclaiming in Jesus the resurrection of the dead.

a. *Teaching.* In the culture of that day, the title *rabbi* commanded great respect. This Hebrew word actually means "my great one" with the word *teacher* understood. "In the gospels this term is repeatedly used in contexts where extreme deference (whether sincere or not) is intended."[4] A teacher in Israel was expected to be an educated person (see v. 13) with credentials. Although Jesus had no formal training, he was accepted as a teacher because he spoke with authority (Matt. 7:29; Mark 1:22). Yet the religious leaders questioned the source of his authority (Matt. 21:23; John 2:18). According to them, a teacher must be able to answer questions about doctrine and law and have a following of disciples. Jesus qualified on both counts, for he ably interpreted the Scriptures to the point that no one dared to ask any questions (Matt. 22:46). And Jesus had a following of twelve disciples. In the opinion of the priests, however, the apostles definitely lacked the necessary qualifications. Moreover, by the power and convincing nature of their message, the apostles were weakening the influence and authority of the priests. The apostles therefore posed a threat to the religious leaders of that day.

b. *Doctrine.* Another objection to the teaching of Peter and John came from the Sadducees, who denied the doctrine of the resurrection (23:8; Matt. 22:23). By contrast, the Pharisees taught this doctrine, and in their opposition to the Sadducees, welcomed the support they were receiving from the Christian community.[5] Some of the Pharisees (e.g., Nicodemus and Joseph of Arimathea) became followers of Jesus, and the learned Rabbi Gamaliel persuaded the Sanhedrin to set the apostles free (5:34–40).

The apostles preach the doctrine of the resurrection with respect to Jesus. Notice that in the thinking of the Sadducees, Jesus' disciples are claiming the impossible. After the Jewish leaders rid the earth of Jesus of Nazareth by nailing him to a cross, Jesus' followers begin to speak about Jesus' resurrection. And although none of the Jewish leaders saw Jesus again, suddenly some seven weeks later, in Jerusalem, multitudes of people listen to Jesus' disciples, who proclaim the doctrine of the resurrection (2:24, 32). Then once more, two of his disciples preach that doctrine with reference to Jesus.

By implication, Peter and John teach that as Jesus had been raised from the dead, so all who put their trust in him will experience the resurrection of the body (compare John 5:28–29; I Cor. 15:12–18). The doctrine of the resurrection is basic to Acts; in their sermons and speeches, Peter and Paul

---

4. Wilber T. Dayton, "Teaching of Jesus," *ZPEB*, vol. 5, p. 607.

5. See Richard B. Rackham, *The Acts of the Apostles: An Exposition*, Westminster Commentaries series (1901; reprint ed., Grand Rapids: Baker, 1964), p. 45.

proclaim this doctrine to Jew and Gentile.[6] To be a witness of Jesus' resurrection is one of the requirements for apostleship (1:22).

3. And they arrested Peter and John and, because it was evening, they put them in prison until the next day. 4. But many of those who heard the message believed, and the number of men came to be about five thousand.

Acts is a book that lists numerous first experiences. For instance, among the first experiences are the healing of a cripple (3:6–7), the death of a martyr (7:60), the great persecution (8:1–4), and the raising of Dorcas (9:40). Here Luke describes the first arrest. The temple police apprehend Peter and John; because of the late hour they are taken to a jail and not to a courtroom for arraignment. We assume that the time of day must be after four o'clock in the afternoon, for after the evening sacrifices were offered the temple guards would close the gates. Luke merely reports that the apostles are taken into custody and does not elaborate on the place or conditions.

Of importance is not the imprisonment of the apostles but the effect of their teaching. "[Because] God's word is not in chains" (II Tim. 2:9), the church continued to grow. God indeed performed a miracle to cause multitudes to come to Christ after hearing one sermon.[7] The Greek indicates that the total membership of the Jerusalem church "became" five thousand men.

Furthermore, Luke writes specifically that "the number of *men* came to be about five thousand" (italics added). We assume that he means male members of the church, who often were counted as heads of households. (Elsewhere in the New Testament, the word *men* must be taken literally [compare Matt. 14:21; Mark 8:9].) In another chapter, Luke mentions that "more and more believers in the Lord, both men and women, were being added to their number" (5:14). According to one estimate, twenty thousand Christians lived in Jerusalem prior to the persecution that followed the death of Stephen (8:1–4). We see that the church continues to grow and that Christ lives in and among his people.

Additional Comments on the Sadducees

The Sadducean party flourished for more than two centuries, from the time of the Maccabees in approximately 150 B.C. to the time of the destruction of Jerusalem and the cessation of the priesthood in A.D. 70. The information we are able to gather comes primarily from the New Testament and from Josephus, who, belonging to the party of the Pharisees, writes from that perspective. During the Maccabean era the parties of the Pharisees and Sadducees were formed. The Pharisees were numerous and popular; but the Sadducees, although they formed the minority party, had

---

6. See 2:24, 32; 3:15; 4:10; 10:40; 13:30, 33, 34, 37; 17:31.

7. Consult John Calvin, *Commentary on the Acts of the Apostles,* ed. David W. Torrance and Thomas F. Torrance, 2 vols. (Grand Rapids: Eerdmans, 1966), vol. 1, p. 113.

wealth and political power. The Sadducees controlled the priesthood in Jerusalem and had the support of the Roman government. The priesthood ceased when the Roman forces destroyed Jerusalem, and the Sadducees disappeared from the scene.

The origin of the name *Sadducees* cannot be ascertained. One theory is that the name derives from the Greek word *Saddouk,* which is the equivalent of "son of Zadok." Zadok was a priest during the time of David and Solomon (II Sam. 8:17; 15:24–36; I Kings 1:32; 2:35). In later years, the sons of Zadok formed a special group of priests who remained faithful to God (Ezek. 40:45–46; 44:15–17; 48:11). They are also mentioned in the intertestamental and Qumran literature. The Qumran community, however, was opposed to the Sadducean party. Moreover, the evidence to establish a link between the priesthood of the Maccabean period and the sons of Zadok cannot be verified.

The Sadducees appear on the New Testament scene a few times. They listen to the preaching of John the Baptist, who calls them a "brood of vipers" (Matt. 3:7). They ask Jesus to show them a sign from heaven (Matt. 16:1), and Jesus warns his disciples to be on guard against the yeast (doctrine) of the Sadducees (Matt. 16:6). They question Jesus about the resurrection, which is a doctrine they reject (Matt. 22:23). Jesus answers them by quoting from one of the books of Moses (Exod. 3:6), because the Sadducees accepted only these books as authoritative. They oppose the apostles, put them in jail, and make them stand trial before the Sanhedrin (Acts 4:1–21; 5:17–18; 23:6–8).

Whenever the Sadducees perceived a threat to their authority, they reacted ruthlessly. Thus the Sadducean high priest Caiaphas found it expedient that one man die for the people rather "than that the whole nation perish" (John 11:50; 18:14) and condemned Jesus (Matt. 26:57–66). Because they were unable to cope with the rapid growth of the church, the priests and Sadducees arrested the apostles. And last, the Sadducean high priest Annas condemned to death James, who was the brother of Jesus and the writer of the epistle named after him.[8]

Greek Words, Phrases, and Constructions in 4:1

ἱερεῖς—two codices (B and C) have the reading ἀρχιερεῖς (high priests); so does the New English Bible. The word *priest* occurs only 31 times but the word *high priest* 122 times in the New Testament. "It is more likely that the scribes would have substituted the more frequently used word for the other than vice versa, especially since in this instance the modification was also in the interest of heightening the seriousness of the persecution."[9]

---

b. Trial
4:5–7

Luke is not interested in details pertaining to the apostles in prison and the whereabouts of the beggar they healed. He describes the trial that takes

---

8. Consult Josephus *Antiquities* 20.9.1 [197–200].
9. Bruce M. Metzger, *A Textual Commentary on the Greek New Testament,* 3d corrected ed. (London and New York: United Bible Societies, 1975), p. 316.

place the next day when the Sadducees and the high-priestly family convene the Sanhedrin.

5. And the next day, their rulers, elders, and scribes gathered in Jerusalem. 6. Annas the high priest, and Caiaphas, John, Alexander, and all who were of high-priestly descent were there.

a. "The next day." As in the case of Jesus, the ruling body called the Sanhedrin hastily gathered for a trial. By law, the Sanhedrin convened between the time of the morning and the evening sacrifices. Because the apostles were arrested in the late afternoon, a trial before the Sanhedrin was postponed until the next day. Accordingly, on the next day this body convened as Israel's supreme court. The rulers (who were vested with authority), the elders (who provided counsel), and the teachers of the law (who formulated doctrine) constituted the court.

The Sanhedrin did not mete out capital punishment, except in the case of a Gentile who entered the inner court of the temple. An indicator of the Sanhedrin's authority is an inscription that dates from the time of Christ: "No Gentile may enter within the railing around the sanctuary and within the enclosure. Whoever should be caught will render himself liable to the death penalty which will inevitably follow."[10] The deaths of Stephen (7:58) and of James the brother of Jesus are not normative. Therefore, the apostles could be tried but not executed.

b. "Rulers, elders, and scribes." The membership of the Sanhedrin included seventy-one persons, a number patterned after the Mosaic court of seventy (Num. 11:16–17). Although the elders were respected for their advice and the teachers for their knowledge of the Mosaic law, the Sadducees were the leaders, with the high priest serving as president (and seventy-first member) of this ruling body. At Jesus' trial, Caiaphas was the head of the Sanhedrin and at the trial of Paul the high priest Ananias presided (23:2). At the trial of Peter and John, the high priest and his family members were prominent figures.

c. "[They] gathered in Jerusalem." Presumably the high priest convened the meeting by calling together all the Sanhedrin members. This could be done without difficulty, for all of them resided in Jerusalem, where the meeting was held. The Jewish historian Josephus writes that the meeting place of the Sanhedrin was west of the temple area.[11]

d. "Annas the high priest, and Caiaphas, John, Alexander, and all who were of high-priestly descent were there." According to the Gospels, Caiaphas was the high priest (Matt. 26:3, 57; John 11:47–53; 18:13, 14, 24, 28). Annas, however, had filled the office of high priest for nearly a decade (A.D. 6–15) but was deposed by the Roman governor Valerius. Annas was an influential person who belonged to the Sadducean party and was loath to yield authority. Therefore, by ensuring that members of his family suc-

---

10. Harold Stigers, "Temple, Jerusalem," *ZPEB*, vol. 5, p. 650.
11. Josephus *War* 5.4.2 [142–46].

ceeded him, he continued to exert his power and at the same time keep the title of high priest (Luke 3:2; John 18:13, 24). Five of his sons, as well as his son-in-law Caiaphas and a grandson, were high priests at successive intervals. Thus the family of Annas maintained and consolidated Annas's power in the Sanhedrin.[12]

Annas's son Eleazar succeeded Annas in A.D. 15 and filled the office of high priest for three years. Then son-in-law Caiaphas became high priest and served in that capacity for eighteen years (A.D. 18–36). After him, Annas's son John (Jonathan)[13] took office and eventually was followed by Alexander. Unfortunately, nothing more is known about John, Alexander, "and all who were of high-priestly descent." Perhaps the term *high-priestly descent* should not be restricted to Annas's family but should include the influential priestly families whose members filled leadership roles in the temple service and the Sanhedrin. Luke's information about the presence of the high-priestly family at the meeting of the Sanhedrin indicates that the opposition to the apostles came primarily from the Sadducees.

7. And having placed them in the center, they began to inquire: "By what power or in what name did you do this?"

Peter and John were led by the temple police to the place where the Sanhedrin met. Whether the man who was healed spent the night in jail with the apostles is not known, but according to Luke (vv. 10, 14), he was present at the trial and stood with the apostles. The three men were placed in the center of a semicircle of elevated seats which the members of the Sanhedrin occupied. These seats were purposely arranged in a semicircle so that the members could see one another.[14] They were seated, but the defendant(s) had to stand facing the rulers of the nation. The apostles faced the council members, who looked down on them from their seats.

Only a few weeks earlier, the Sanhedrin had met in the house of Annas for the trial of Jesus, where Caiaphas functioned as the presiding officer of the court. The leaders in the Sanhedrin had tried to rid themselves of Jesus Christ of Nazareth by crucifying him. But Jesus' name reappeared when his disciples used it to heal a cripple. The leaders refused to acknowledge Jesus and instead asked by what power or name the apostles had performed the miracle of healing the lame man (refer to Matt. 21:23).

In the Greek, the emphasis falls on the pronoun *you*, which is the last word in the sentence and thus receives all the stress. The apostles are addressed as if they, with the beggar as their accomplice, have perpetrated a crime. The court is trying to learn the facts of the case, even if the members already have heard the details from others. The rulers want to

---

12. Refer to Josephus *Antiquities* 20.9.1 [197–203].

13. Josephus writes that Governor Vitellius "removed from his sacred office the high priest Joseph surnamed Caiaphas, and appointed in his stead Jonathan, son of Ananus the high priest." *Antiquities* 18.4.3 [95] (LCL). The Western text (the Greek manuscript Codex D and the Old Latin versions) has the reading *Jonathan* instead of "John."

14. Mishnah, *Sanhedrin* 4.3.

know the source of the apostles' power for performing a miracle and they want to learn the name of the person who endowed the apostles with this power. Note that the leaders do not question the apostles about their authority to teach in public. Nor do they ask about the doctrine of the resurrection, for that would prove too risky in the presence of the Pharisees, who defended that teaching (compare 22:30–23:10). They wish to learn from whom the Galilean fishermen received power to perform miracles.

Greek Words, Phrases, and Constructions in 4:5 and 7

Verse 5

τοὺς ἄρχοντας—the three groups that make up the Sanhedrin are the rulers, the elders, and the scribes. Note that the definite article precedes each noun. The first constituent part, "the rulers," is equivalent to "the high priests" (compare Mark 14:53). The elders occupy a venerable position as representatives of Israel (see Exod. 3:16). And the scribes are scholars who studied the Scriptures.

Verse 7

ἐπυνθάνοντο—from the verb πυνθάνομαι (I inquire), this imperfect middle (deponent) denotes repeated action.

ποίᾳ—the interrogative pronoun conveys qualitative force: "by what kind of power?"

ὑμεῖς—last in the sentence, the pronoun is emphatic. It corresponds with the personal pronoun ἡμεῖς (v. 9).

---

c. Defense
4:8–12

8. Then Peter, filled with the Holy Spirit, said to them: "Rulers and elders of the people! 9. If we are questioned today for a good deed done to a sick man and how he was healed, 10. let it be known to all of you and to all the people of Israel that by the name of Jesus Christ of Nazareth, whom you crucified, whom God raised from the dead, this man stands before you healthy."

a. "Then Peter, filled with the Holy Spirit, said." On the day of Pentecost Peter and the others received the Holy Spirit, who continued to live in them. Nevertheless, the Spirit on special occasions enabled the apostles to speak boldly, for Jesus had told his disciples, "But when they arrest you, do not worry about what you will say or how you will say it. For what you are to say will be given to you at that time, because you are not the ones who are speaking, but the Spirit of your Father is speaking through you" (Matt. 10:19–20). Peter experienced the fulfillment of Jesus' words when he stood before the Sanhedrin.

b. "Rulers and elders of the people." Even though Luke mentions that the gathering consisted of rulers, elders, and teachers of the law, Peter addresses only the rulers and elders. Apparently only these two groups of people give leadership and ask questions (compare v. 23; 23:14; 25:15).

c. "If we are [being] questioned today for a good deed done to a sick man and how he was healed." Peter skillfully changes the trial from a possible criminal investigation to an inquiry about an act of mercy. The verb *questioned* signifies that Peter regards the trial as an inquiry and so puts it in positive form. "If we are being questioned" means that this inquiry is a fact and is actually happening at the moment. Moreover, it also indicates that Peter is in full control of the situation. He says that he and John have performed a good deed, and he implies that no one can fault them for doing good to a man who was a cripple from birth.

d. "And [asked] how he was healed." In Greek, the verb *to heal* can also mean "to save" (see v. 12). In the case of the cripple, the physical healing is obvious; we know that because of his faith in Jesus he also obtained salvation.

Peter realizes that the leaders are interested in the manner of the healing miracle. In response to their question, he gives them a direct answer concerning the source of the healing power and the name in which he and John rendered the miracle. Unafraid of the same judges who condemned Jesus and handed him over to Pontius Pilate, Peter boldly speaks and reveals to them that the man was healed in the name of Jesus Christ of Nazareth. The word *name* points to the full revelation concerning Jesus. This word appears repeatedly in Peter's addresses, for he proclaims it to all people.[15]

e. "Let it be known to all of you and to all the people of Israel." The phrase *let it be known* is similar to the injunction *pay attention to my words* (see 2:14; 13:38; 28:28). Peter expands his audience to include the Sanhedrin and the entire Jewish nation. Once again, Peter adroitly changes the focus of the inquiry from the healed beggar to Jesus Christ, who healed him. The name of Jesus Christ must be made known to every person in Israel.

f. "By the name of Jesus Christ of Nazareth." Notice that Peter utters the same words he used when he healed the lame man at the gate called Beautiful (3:6). He realizes that although Jesus' name is an offense to the rulers and elders who condemned him, they posed the question about the manner in which the apostles healed the cripple. Now Peter gives them an honest and straightforward answer. They are unable to understand that Jesus, who died on the cross, has divine power to perform an undeniable healing miracle.[16] But this is exactly the point Peter tries to make. He deliberately uses the double name to point to Jesus' earthly life and the divine mission of the Christ (the Messiah). To make the identification complete, Peter adds Jesus' place of residence by which he was known to the people: "of Nazareth."

g. "Whom you crucified, whom God raised from the dead." In his ser-

---

15. See Herman N. Ridderbos, *The Speeches of Peter in the Acts of the Apostles* (London: Tyndale, 1962), p. 29.

16. Consult Calvin, *Acts of the Apostles*, vol. 1, p. 115.

mons and speeches, Peter unabashedly tells his Jewish audiences the same thing: "you crucified Jesus, but God raised him from the dead" (2:23–24; 3:15; 5:30). Peter puts the blame for Jesus' death on the Sanhedrists. Yet he dwells not on the ignominy of condemning an innocent man to death but on Jesus' resurrection to life. The resurrection message is basic to apostolic preaching and here Peter proclaims it in the presence of Israel's supreme court.

h. "[Through Jesus' power] this man stands before you healthy." One imagines Peter pointing directly at the healed beggar, who is the living testimony to Jesus' power. Since the miracles Jesus wrought during his ministry are well known throughout Israel, the members of the Sanhedrin are unable to deny the continuing work of the resurrected Jesus. When Jesus rose from the grave, the chief priest bribed the soldiers guarding his tomb and had them say, "His disciples came at night and stole the body while we were asleep" (Matt. 28:13). But their deception is unable to match the glorious power of Jesus that is demonstrated in the healing of the cripple. The healed man is living testimony to the resurrected Christ. Jesus receives the credit for this healing miracle.

11. "He is 'the stone, which was rejected by you, the builders, which has become the capstone.' "

As in all his addresses, Peter bases his message on passages taken from the Old Testament Scriptures. Here he quotes a text from a familiar psalm sung by pilgrims on their way to Jerusalem for a religious festival (Ps. 118:22). With this quotation, Peter reminds the chief priests and Pharisees of the words Jesus spoke to them in the last week of his ministry. Jesus quoted Psalm 118:22–23 and applied the words of this psalm to his audience by saying, "Therefore I tell you that the kingdom of God will be taken away from you and given to a nation that will produce fruit. He who falls on this stone will be broken to pieces, but it will crush the one on whom it falls" (Matt. 21:43–44). At that time the chief priests and Pharisees realized that Jesus was addressing them. Now Peter tells them the same thing. The members of the Sanhedrin are the spiritual builders of God's house, for which they have to choose the building stones. They reject one of the stones, which they deem unfit; yet God who is the master builder takes this stone and makes it the capstone of the building. This psalm quotation is a graphic illustration of Jesus Christ, who, as Peter writes in his epistle, is "the living Stone, rejected by men but with God chosen and precious" (I Peter 2:4; see also vv. 6–8).[17]

The members of the Sanhedrin ought to realize that they are the spiritual builders of God's house in which God has made Jesus Christ the capstone. They are unable to avoid the name of Jesus; this name is inextricably connected with spiritual Israel. Jesus has fulfilled the psalm citation that

---

17. Consult Simon J. Kistemaker, *Exposition of the Epistles of Peter and of the Epistle of Jude,* New Testament Commentary series (Grand Rapids: Baker, 1987), pp. 84–88.

portrays him as the capstone (Ps. 118:22). Accordingly, the Sanhedrists cannot circumvent the power and the name of Jesus Christ. Salvation is found only in him.

12. "Salvation is found in no one else, for there is no other name under heaven given among men by which we must be saved."

We make these observations:

a. *Salvation proclaimed.* "Salvation is found in no one else." This text is among the well-known and cherished passages in Acts. Peter challenges his immediate audience but at the same time speaks to all people who seek salvation.[18] He addresses learned and influential men in the Sanhedrin whose work consisted of showing the people of Israel the way of salvation. They did so by telling the Jews to perform works that would earn them salvation. But Peter preaches that salvation can be obtained in no way other than through the name of Jesus Christ. The salvation he preaches comprises both physical and spiritual healing.[19] They see the evidence of physical healing in the man who used to be a cripple. But they must understand that spiritual well-being includes forgiveness of sin and a restored relationship with God. No one in Peter's audience is able to point to any person who grants salvation, because everyone needs salvation himself. Hence, they should realize that they can have peace with God only through Jesus Christ.

b. *Name given.* "There is no other name under heaven given among men." The name *Jesus* reveals the task of the Savior, because the name means "he will save his people from their sins" (Matt. 1:21). That is, he heals people physically from the effect of sin, but more than that, he removes sin itself so that people can stand before the judgment seat of God as if they had never sinned at all. Jesus makes them spiritually whole by restoring them in true relation to God the Father. Jesus says, "No one comes to the Father but through me" (John 14:6). No person but Jesus has the ability to provide remission of sin. "Through his name everyone who believes in him receives forgiveness of sins" (10:43).

Peter resorts not to an overstatement but rather to a descriptive idiom when he says that there is no other name under heaven than the name *Jesus*. Nowhere in the entire world is man able to find another name (i.e., person) that offers the salvation Jesus provides. Religions other than Christianity fail because they stress salvation by works and not by grace. The name *Jesus* has been given to men by God himself to show that salvation has its origin in God.

c. *Believers saved.* "[No other name] by which we must be saved." The

---

18. Colin Brown writes that in Acts 4:12 Peter "makes an absolute and universal claim for the Christian message of salvation." *NIDNTT*, vol. 3, p. 213.

19. Consult Ernst Haenchen, *The Acts of the Apostles: A Commentary*, trans. Bernard Noble and Gerald Shinn (Philadelphia: Westminster, 1971), p. 217. And see C. K. Barrett, "Salvation Proclaimed: XII. Acts 4:8–12," *ExpT* 94 (1982): 68–71.

Greek text is specific. It does not say that we can be saved, for this would indicate that man has inherent ability to achieve salvation. Nor does it say that we may be saved, for then the clause would convey uncertainty. The text is definite. It says: "by which we must be saved." The word *must* reveals a divine necessity which God has established, according to his plan and decree, to save us through the person and work of Jesus Christ.[20] Furthermore, this word signifies that man is under moral obligation to respond to the call to believe in Jesus Christ and thus gain salvation. He has no recourse to salvation other than through the Son of God.

Doctrinal Considerations in 4:11

The translators of the New International Version have chosen the word *capstone* for the quotation from Psalm 118:22. In the Greek, the literal rendering is "the head of the corner," which many versions have.[21] This phrase refers to the headstone of the corner. Other translations have the reading *cornerstone*.[22] In ancient times, the cornerstone was part of the foundation upon which the entire structure of a building or house rested. We use this expression when we dedicate a building and put the cornerstone in place. Figuratively, the word refers to the basic element of a policy (thus, its foundation). Still other translators prefer the word *keystone*.[23] This term is the name for either the topmost stone that fit into the arch of a doorway or the stone that held the uppermost tier of stones together.

The choice of either cornerstone or keystone (capstone) is not important when we apply the terms to Christ. The Messiah is the first and the last stone of God's house. Jewish rabbis understood the Old Testament passages that speak of the cornerstone (Ps. 118:22; Isa. 8:14 [stone]; 28:16) to refer to the Messiah. And New Testament writers, following Jesus' example (Matt. 21:42), applied them to Christ (Rom. 9:33; Eph. 2:20; I Peter 2:6).[24]

Greek Words, Phrases, and Constructions in 4:9–12

Verse 9

εἰ—the particle followed by a verb in the indicative mood introduces a simple-fact condition that expresses reality.

ἀνθρώπου—the genitive case is objective: "a good deed [is done] 'to' a sick man."[25]

---

20. Refer to Thayer, p. 126; Bauer, p. 172; Walter Grundmann, *TDNT,* vol. 2, p. 24; Erich Tiedtke and Hans-Georg Link, *NIDNTT,* vol. 2, p. 666.

21. See KJV, RV, ASV, RSV, *Moffatt, Phillips.*

22. E.g., NKJV, NASB, NAB, SEB.

23. Compare JB, NEB.

24. Edward Mack, "Cornerstone," *ISBE,* vol. 1, p. 784.

25. A. T. Robertson, *A Grammar of the Greek New Testament in the Light of Historical Research* (Nashville: Broadman, 1934), p. 500.

Verse 10

γνωστὸν ἔστω—this combination of adjective and imperative occurs four times in Acts (2:14; 4:10; 13:38; 28:28). With the present imperative, Peter gives his audience a gentle command, "Let it be known."

Verse 11

οὗτος—the demonstrative pronoun refers to Jesus, even though in the preceding clause the same pronoun applies to the cripple.

Verse 12

ἕτερον—"the point of ἕτερον is rather that no other name than that of Jesus" is meant.[26]

ἐν ἀνθρώποις—some versions have the translation *among men* (e.g., NKJV); with the verb *to give* the preposition ἐν with the dative is equivalent to εἰς with the accusative ("to men").[27]

---

d. Consultation
4:13–17

In his address to the Sanhedrin, Peter demonstrates that he is in full command. He speaks without trepidation and openly challenges the members of the court to accept Jesus Christ as their Savior. His audience is stunned and everyone refrains from asking further questions.

13. When they observed the courage of Peter and John and understood that they were uneducated and untrained men, they marveled and realized that they had been with Jesus.

a. *Perceive.* "When they observed the courage of Peter and John." Luke writes the Greek verbs of this verse in the imperfect tense to depict the continuing effect of an action. Thus, the Sanhedrists continued to be spellbound by the courage of both Peter and John, who open their mouths and boldly and frankly speak the truth. They could not know, however, that the Holy Spirit enabled the apostles to speak and gave them courage (v. 8).

b. *Realize.* How could common, ordinary fishermen from Galilee skillfully and eloquently address learned members of the supreme court? These fishermen quoted from and applied the Scriptures; they were able to preach effectively; yet they had received no formal theological training from recognized teachers. Their Galilean accent and apparel undoubtedly revealed that Peter and John belonged to an uneducated class. This does not mean that the apostles had not learned to read and write, for their writings testify that they had. However, they lacked formal theological

---

26. Ibid., p. 749.
27. Consult C. F. D. Moule, *An Idiom-Book of New Testament Greek*, 2d ed. (Cambridge: Cambridge University Press, 1960), p. 76.

schooling. Luke reports that they were regarded as "uneducated and untrained men"; that is, they were not perceived to be theological experts, for they were common folk.[28]

c. *Recognize.* "[The Sanhedrists] marveled and realized that they had been with Jesus." The members of the court began to see similarity between Jesus and the apostles. The Jewish leaders (many of whom belonged to the Sanhedrin) had been amazed when Jesus taught openly in the temple during the Feast of Tabernacles. They had asked, "How did this man get such learning without having studied?" (John 7:15, NIV). Moreover, Peter and another of Jesus' disciples had been at Jesus' trial in the high priest's courtyard, and "the other disciple . . . was known to the high priest" (John 18:16).

The high priest and the other members of the court were astonished and saw the obvious connection between Jesus and his disciples (see Matt. 26:71; Luke 22:56). The uneducated Jesus, who had been skillful in expounding Scripture, had trained disciples to continue the work cut short because of his untimely death.[29] The Sanhedrists had rid the earth of Jesus by crucifying him; now they faced Jesus' spokesmen, who possessed the same courage as their teacher. Furthermore, the members of the court avoided using the name *Jesus* during the trial, but now they had to acknowledge Jesus because of his disciples. They directed their anger against Jesus' followers Peter and John.

14. And seeing the man who had been healed standing with them, they could think of nothing to say.

The members of the Sanhedrin were unable to act—before them was the incontrovertible evidence of the healed beggar. This man was standing next to the apostles as living proof of the healing miracle that had taken place in the temple area the previous day. Luke portrays the man as standing; that is, with strong ankles and feet. Later he adds the information that the beggar was more than forty years old (v. 22).

The members of the Sanhedrin were in a quandary, for they did not have a case. They realized that Peter had turned the trial into an inquiry about a lame man who was healed. And the person in question presented live evidence by standing next to the apostles. In short, the prosecutors had nothing to say. Jesus fulfilled his promise to his disciples: "I will give you ability to speak and wisdom that none of your adversaries will be able to resist or refute" (Luke 21:15).

15. When they ordered them to leave the Sanhedrin, they conferred together 16. and said, "What are we to do with these men? For the fact that a noteworthy miracle has occurred through them is obvious to all who live in Jerusalem. We cannot deny it."

---

28. Consult Bauer, p. 370; Thayer, p. 297.

29. Compare Everett F. Harrison, *Interpreting Acts: The Expanding Church,* 2d ed. (Grand Rapids: Zondervan, Academie Books, 1986), p. 93. And see Rackham, *Acts,* p. 59.

The court is at a loss and needs time for reflection. Hence, the suggestion is made to recess for consultation (compare 5:34). The presiding officer of the Sanhedrin orders the apostles and the beggar to excuse themselves and leave the courtroom. We cannot determine how long the recess lasted, but from the verb *to confer* we are able to deduce that many words were spoken behind closed doors. Luke perhaps received his information from an eyewitness (compare Luke 1:2) who was or subsquently became a follower of Jesus. For example, Nicodemus, "who was one of their own number" (John 7:50, NIV), may have been the eyewitness who gave Luke the information about the discussion.

The question "What are we to do with these men?" reveals perplexity and inability to act. They debate whether they should release the apostles or do something to them. For the members of the court to release the apostles is a matter of losing face. Conversely, to punish them for performing a miracle would risk incurring the wrath of the people, for "the fact that a noteworthy miracle has occurred through [the apostles] is obvious to all who live in Jerusalem." As a result of this miracle and the preaching of Peter, the Christian church has increased to about five thousand men in Jerusalem (v. 4).

The court comes to the one and only conclusion: "We cannot deny [the miracle]." In their confrontations with Jesus, the Jewish leaders were unable to lay a proven charge against him. His disciples also deprive them of any evidence that points to wrongdoing. For lack of a case, the Sanhedrists are forced to release the apostles.

17. "But in order to stop this thing from spreading further among the people, let us warn them to speak no more to anyone in this name."

After deliberating the consequences of whatever decision they make, the members of the Sanhedrin resolve to set the apostles free. They stipulate that the apostles refrain from any action that influences the people. Notice, first, that the Jewish leaders show their contempt for the Christian faith and call it "this thing." Next, their initial question was, "By what power or in what name did you do this?" (v. 7). But the discussion has centered primarily on the name and secondarily on the power. Although they concluded that the apostles had been with Jesus, the Jewish leaders refused to mention his name. Third, they decide that Jesus' name must not spread any further and that the disciples should be told "to speak no more to anyone in this name." The word *further* can be understood either in terms of degree or extent. The growth and development of the Jerusalem church make it preferable to interpret the term in the sense of degree. And last, the members of the Sanhedrin fully understand that the revelation of Jesus' name constitutes the message the apostles proclaim.[30] The members of the court show their enmity toward Jesus by forbidding

---

30. See F. W. Grosheide, *De Handelingen der Apostelen*, Kommentaar op het Nieuwe Testament series, 2 vols. (Amsterdam: Van Bottenburg, 1942), vol. 1, p. 138.

the apostles to mention his name. And as Israel's spiritual leaders, they reject Peter's admonition to find salvation only in Jesus' name (v. 12). They are unable to punish or penalize Peter and John for their courage to preach to them about Jesus. Nevertheless, they are determined to stop the spread of Jesus' name.

Practical Considerations in 4:13–17

God uses two Galilean fishermen to confound the prominent judges of Israel's supreme court. In the hall of justice, Peter proclaims Christ's gospel and tells the religious and national leaders of his day that they are unable to obtain salvation except through the name of Jesus Christ. This name has been given by God to men everywhere in the world. People either curse, ignore, or adore Jesus' name. In the service of Satan, millions use this name in curses; countless people try to ignore the name, because they have the mistaken notion that Jesus does not exist; and multitudes from every nation and tongue praise the glorious name of Jesus in audible or silent prayer, with joyful song, and through the spoken word.

At times even Christians ignore Jesus' name outside the four walls of their church building. They act as if Jesus has no part in the world in which they live. Yet Jesus has redeemed the world and everything in it. This redeemed world, therefore, is the Christian's workshop in which the believer expresses his thankfulness to Jesus. The name of Jesus must be heard in all areas of life: in the halls of justice and government; in the classrooms of schools, colleges, and universities; in the places of commerce and industry; and in all places of today's workaday world. God has put ordinary people at strategic places and wants them to make Jesus' name and message known.

Greek Words, Phrases, and Constructions in 4:13

καταλαβόμενοι—as a second aorist middle from the compound verb καταλαμβάνω (I lay hold of), this participle needs the word *mind* to complete the thought.

ἀγράμματοί καὶ ἰδιῶται—A. T. Robertson has an interesting comment on these two nouns that describe Peter and John as "unschooled and ordinary" people. He writes, "This need not be pushed too far, and yet it is noteworthy that 2 Peter and Revelation are just the two books of the N[ew] T[estament] whose Greek jars most upon the cultured mind and which show most kinship to the *koine* in somewhat illiterate papyri. One of the theories about the relationship between 1 Peter and 2 Peter is that Sylvanus (I Pet. 5:12) was Peter's scribe in writing the first Epistle, and thus the Greek is smooth and flowing, while in 2 Peter we have Peter's own somewhat uncouth, unrevised Greek. This theory rests on the assumption of the genuineness of 2 Peter, which is much disputed. So also in Acts Luke refines Peter's Greek in the reports of his addresses."[31]

ἐπεγίνωσκον—all the finite verbs in this verse are in the imperfect tense, except

---

31. Robertson, *Grammar*, pp. 415–16.

for εἰσιν, which is part of an indirect statement. The imperfect shows continued action in the past tense. The verb means "to recognize" and not "to acknowledge."[32]

ἦσαν—because the verb εἰμί is incomplete and lacks the aorist, perfect, and pluperfect tenses, the imperfect is pressed into service to function as a pluperfect, "had been."

---

e. Acquittal
4:18–22

Peter and John are filled with the Holy Spirit, who enables them to address the Sanhedrin, refute their adversaries, and proclaim the Good News. The Sanhedrists, by contrast, have lost their composure and are unable to save the day.

18. When they called them in, they commanded them not to speak or teach at all in the name of Jesus. 19. But Peter and John answered, "Judge whether it is right in God's sight to obey you rather than God. 20. For we cannot stop speaking about the things we have seen and heard."

a. "When they called them in." The members of the Sanhedrin have devised a face-saving measure to give the court session a semblance of legality. They order the apostles to enter the courtroom and then sternly warn them not to utter a word about Jesus or to teach in his name. They attach no penalty in case of noncompliance, but should the apostles refuse to obey the order they would be held in contempt of court.[33] They do not forbid the apostles to perform miracles in the name of Jesus.

b. "Judge [for yourselves]." Both Peter and John reply to the verdict and boldly appeal to a higher authority that governs both the members of the Sanhedrin and the apostles. They appeal to God and challenge the court to examine its verdict to see whether it conforms to God's law. The apostles ask the judges "whether it is right in God's sight to obey you rather than God." They imply that the verdict goes contrary to the will of God, even if the Sanhedrists themselves think they are right. The courageous apostles are ready to accept a verdict from the Sanhedrin that is not contrary to God's will.[34] They assert that the judges must stand in God's presence and pass a just verdict. "The one thing the Sanhedrists need to dread is that the divine Judge should pronounce an action of theirs unjust."[35]

c. "To obey you rather than God." In this brief report, Luke omits details pertaining to God's will. We could ask, "How would the court know

---

32. Refer to Thayer, p. 237; Bauer, p. 291.

33. Consult I. Howard Marshall, *The Acts of the Apostles: An Introduction and Commentary*, Tyndale New Testament Commentary series (Leicester: Inter-Varsity; Grand Rapids: Eerdmans, 1980), p. 102.

34. John Albert Bengel, *Gnomon of the New Testament*, ed. Andrew R. Fausset, 5 vols. (Edinburgh: Clark, 1877), vol. 2, p. 552.

35. R. C. H. Lenski, *The Interpretation of the Acts of the Apostles* (Columbus: Wartburg, 1944), p. 172.

whether its verdict forced the apostles to disobey God?" But notice that sometime later the honorable Pharisee Gamaliel addresses his associates in the Sanhedrin and tells them to release the apostles. Says he, "So in this case I suggest to you: Stay away from these men and let them go! For if this plan or movement is of human origin, it will fail. But if it is of God, you will be unable to overthrow them; you will even find yourselves fighting against God" (5:38–39). Peter and John persist in stating their allegiance to God rather than men, for they are under divine authority to obey him. They exhort the Sanhedrists to do likewise, for all authority comes from God. On another occasion, Peter and his fellow apostles state the same principle: "We must obey God rather than men" (5:29).

d. "We cannot stop speaking about the things we have seen and heard." Here is the explanation of the preceding clause, "whether it is right in God's sight to obey you rather than God." As the Old Testament prophets were unable to keep from proclaiming the word God had given them (see Jer. 20:9; Amos 3:8; Jonah 3:1–3), so the apostles have to teach all that Jesus had commanded them (Matt. 28:20). They obey Jesus, who charged them to be "witnesses both in Jerusalem, and in all Judea and Samaria, and to the ends of the earth" (1:8). Filled with the Holy Spirit, the apostles have to speak and teach the good news of Jesus Christ.

21. And when they had threatened them further, they let them go—they found no basis for punishing them, on account of the people, for all were glorifying God for what had happened. 22. For the man who had been miraculously healed was more than forty years old.

The judges in the Sanhedrin cannot counter the words of Peter and John and thus dismiss the case without acquitting the apostles. The Sanhedrists refuse to take the apostles' words to heart and instead issue hollow threats. They realize that the apostles have won the day because of their desire to obey God rather than men. The judges have not been able to devise any punishment for Peter and John that will effectively stop their cause. They fear the wrath of the people in Jerusalem who are singing God's praises for the miracle that has occurred in their midst.

Sin has a blinding effect on man's judgment, as is evident in the words and deeds of the Sanhedrin. The apostles challenge the judges to examine the verdict in the presence of God, for they are responsible to him; meanwhile the people of Jerusalem are praising God for performing a healing miracle. From inside and outside the courtroom the judges are told to look at God, yet, blinded by sin, they reject the admonition and continue to grope in darkness.

The emphasis in this passage is neither on the apostles nor on the Sanhedrists. Luke places emphasis on God, who desires obedience and who receives man's praises. Accordingly, the apostles do not earn praise for having spoken courageously in the presence of the seventy-one members of the Sanhedrin. The apostles win the day in court and gain their own release, but praise belongs to God. He has sent his Holy Spirit and has caused the people to rejoice in that which has happened.[36]

No one can doubt the evidence of the miracle. Luke provides the reason by saying that "the man who was miraculously healed was more than forty years old." The man was born a cripple (3:2); he had never been able to walk. Therefore, having known the man for decades, the people acknowledge that a miracle had occurred. The evidence is irrefutable.

Practical Considerations in 4:18–22

We are citizens of God's kingdom here on earth and at the same time most of us are citizens in the land of our residence. As Christians we strive to obey the laws of God's kingdom and because of his word we know that we must be obedient to the authorities he has established (Rom. 13:1; I Peter 2:17). But when God's law and the law of the land conflict, we face a problem. We know the apostolic injunction "to obey God rather than man." We confess that God demands unconditional obedience. When the intent of a civil law is contrary to God's law, we must register our objections to the governing authorities. For example, if the law forbids Christians to preach and teach Christ's gospel, they must disobey that law and find ways to circumvent this prohibition.

In a democracy, Christians must publicly object to laws that force them to be disobedient to God. They can take a number of actions: they can protest by writing members of the legislature, advertise to arouse public awareness, organize opposition, vote against unacceptable proposals, vote elected government officials out of office, and seek to fill these offices by electing Christian legislators.

Wherever possible, Christians should resort to moral persuasion and passive resistance but not to force. They should refrain from taking the law into their own hands. Instead they should use the legal means available to change the system that opposes God's law. As they seek to obey that higher law, Christians must be prepared to pay the price of persecution. As they pay that price, they should remember Jesus' encouraging word: "Rejoice and be glad, because your reward in heaven is great" (Matt. 5:12).

Greek Words, Phrases, and Constructions in 4:18–22

Verse 18

τὸ καθόλου—the definite article precedes the adverb καθόλου (completely, [not] at all) as if it were a noun. The article is not translated. For a comparable construction see τὸ πῶς in verse 21.[37]

μὴ φθέγγεσθαι—the negative prohibition features the present infinitive from the

---

36. Grosheide, *Handelingen der Apostelen*, vol. 1, p. 140.
37. Consult Friedrich Blass and Albert Debrunner, *A Greek Grammar of the New Testament and Other Early Christian Literature*, trans. and rev. Robert Funk (Chicago: University of Chicago Press, 1961), #399.3.

verb φθέγγομαι (literally: I produce a sound). The derivative noun is φθόγγος (sound).

ἐπὶ τῷ ὀνόματι—see the explanation of 2:38.

Verse 19

εἰ—the particle introduces an indirect question and means "whether."

κρίνατε—the aorist active imperative from κρίνω (I judge) conveys the concept of a single action.

Verse 20

οὐ δυνάμεθα . . . μὴ λαλεῖν—in a sense, the two negatives cancel each other and thus present a positive meaning: "We cannot stop speaking."[38]

Verse 21

εὑρίσκοντες—this present active participle from εὑρίσκω (I find) expresses a causal connotation that explains the action of the preceding main verb ἀπέλυσαν (they let them go because . . .).

τὸ πῶς—the definite article introduces an indirect question that begins with the adverb πῶς (how). The definite article should not be translated.

Verse 22

ἐτῶν . . . πλειόνων—this is the genitive of definition, and so is the case of τῆς ἰάσεως (of healing).[39]

γεγόνει—the pluperfect active tense of γίνομαι (I am, become) often drops the augment.

---

23 As soon as they had been released, Peter and John went to their own people and told them everything the chief priests and elders had said to them. 24 When they heard this, they raised their voices together to God. They said: "Lord, you have made the heaven, the earth, the sea, and everything in them. 25 You have spoken by the Holy Spirit through the mouth of our father and your servant, David:

> 'Why did the nations rage,
> and the peoples conspire in vain?
> 26 The kings of the earth took their stand,
> and the rulers gathered together
> against the Lord and against his Anointed One.'

27 For indeed both Herod and Pontius Pilate with the nations and the peoples of Israel gathered together in this city against your holy servant Jesus, whom you anointed. 28 They did what your hand and your purpose predestined should happen. 29 And now, Lord, consider their threats and grant that your servants may speak your word with great boldness, 30 and that you may stretch out your hand to heal and to do signs and wonders through the name of your holy servant Jesus."

---

38. Ibid., #431.1.
39. Moule, *Idiom-Book,* p. 38. And see Robertson, *Grammar,* p. 498.

31 After they had prayed, the place where they had gathered shook. And they were all filled with the Holy Spirit and began to speak the word of God with boldness.

---

4. Prayers of the Church
4:23–31

Although Luke provides no details about the Jerusalem church during the imprisonment and trial of Peter and John, we need little imagination to know that the believers were in continual prayer. They prayed for the safety of the apostles, boldness to speak, and immediate release.

a. Setting
4:23–24a

23. As soon as they had been released, Peter and John went to their own people and told them everything the chief priests and elders had said to them. 24a. When they heard this, they raised their voices together to God.

As soon as the apostles are released, they rush to "their own people," as Luke reports. Who are these people? We cannot say that they constitute the entire church in Jerusalem, for then we have to think in terms of at least five thousand men (v. 4). Perhaps Luke has in mind the original group that used to meet in the upper room after Jesus' ascension (see 1:13–15).

Here we have the communion of the saints. Those who prayed for the release of the prisoners now receive a detailed report from the former prisoners themselves. Peter and John relate to their friends the proceedings of the court trial and report the questions the chief priests and elders asked and the threats these rulers made. Furthermore, all the other apostles are interested in knowing the implications of the verdict Peter and John received.

Note that Luke mentions only the chief priests and the elders, who represent the Sanhedrin and the Sadducean party. We assume that these people had led the questioning during the trial. In Acts, this is the first time that Luke writes the plural expression *chief priests,* which includes the persons who belonged to the high priest's family (see v. 6) and other representatives, including the captain of the temple guard.[40]

Notice also that Luke mentions that the apostles gave a report concerning the questions and threats from the chief priests and elders but not about their own defense. The leaders of the Jerusalem church, therefore, are looking to the future and realize the dangers they are facing from the members of the Sanhedrin. Their only recourse is to flee to God in prayer.

---

40. The plural *chief priests* occurs frequently in Acts—see 5:24; 9:14, 21; 22:30; 23:14; 25:15; 26:10, 12. Also consult Jürgen Baehr, *NIDNTT*, vol. 3, p. 40; Joachim Jeremias, *Jerusalem in the Time of Jesus* (Philadelphia: Fortress, 1969), p. 179; and Schürer, *History of the Jewish People*, vol. 2, pp. 233–36.

From ev'ry stormy wind that blows,
From ev'ry swelling tide of woes,
There is a calm, a sure retreat;
'Tis found beneath the mercy-seat.
                                        —Hugh Stowell

Together the leaders of the church pray to God, as they did after Jesus' ascension (1:14). They find their strength and courage in intimate communion with God, for they realize that he rules in this world and will overrule the threats of the Sanhedrin.

b. Address
4:24b–28

24b. They said: "Lord, you have made the heaven, the earth, the sea, and everything in them."

The prayer that Luke records is typically Jewish and is modeled after the petition Hezekiah uttered when the Assyrian army surrounded Jerusalem (Isa. 37:16–20).[41] The leaders of the Jerusalem church now pray and address God as sovereign Lord (see Luke 2:29; II Peter 2:1; Jude 4; Rev. 6:10). He is the sovereign ruler over everything he has made. He is the creator of the universe and master of all his servants (notice the term *servant* in the next verse [v. 25]).

When the apostles pray, they acknowledge God as creator of "the heaven, the earth, the sea, and everything in them." In fact, they quote from the Old Testament Scriptures, which in numerous places record these words (Exod. 20:11; Neh. 9:6; Ps. 146:6; Isa. 37:16). They know the fundamental truth that God, who created heaven, earth, sea, and everything else, has the sovereign right to rule his creation.[42] God rules in his creation; therefore, man's will cannot stand up against the sovereign Lord for one moment.

25. "You have spoken by the Holy Spirit through the mouth of our father and your servant, David:
    'Why did the nations rage,
    and the peoples conspire in vain?' "

Translations differ in regard to the introductory formula of this psalm citation (Ps. 2:1–2). Here is a shorter reading of the text: "[You] who by the mouth of your servant David have said" (NKJV).[43] The difference in translation stems from the Greek text that in this formula has many seemingly unconnected nouns. The shorter reading that omits the phrase *by the Holy*

---

41. Although the Greek term *despotēs* (sovereign Lord) is applied to God and Christ, no distinction should be made. The early Christians did not even distinguish between God and Christ when they used the expression *kyrios* (Lord).

42. See Donald Guthrie, *New Testament Theology* (Downers Grove: Inter-Varsity, 1981), p. 85.

43. See also the KJV. The NASB has, "who by the Holy Spirit, through the mouth of our father David Thy servant, didst say," and points out in a marginal note that the word *through* is not in the Greek text.

Spirit is not based on the oldest and most reliable textual witnesses.[44] Translators prefer to keep the phrase, and even though the Greek is confusing, the sense of the formula is clear. The text says that God spoke by the Holy Spirit (compare I Peter 1:11; II Peter 1:21) through the mouth of David. A similar formula, but in straightforward Greek, appears in 1:16. The early Christians had a penchant for referring to David and quoting from the Psalter.[45] In the introductory formula, David is called "our father and your servant."

The quotation from Psalm 2:1–2 is appropriate to the situation at hand, for the apostles feel the religious hierarchy and the Jewish government closing in on them. With the psalmist they ask, "Why did the nations rage and the peoples conspire in vain?" The text follows the Septuagintal translation and thus differs slightly from the Hebrew wording, "Why do the nations conspire." But the emphasis falls on the word *vain;* that is, why do the nations plot in vain? The enemies of God think that they are victorious against God's church. They crucify Jesus and imprison his apostles with impunity, and yet their actions are futile. As David endured persecution at the hands of Saul but experienced God's protecting care, so the apostles know that the Lord will not forsake them (Matt. 28:20b). Psalm 2 reveals the utter foolishness of the nations in plotting against God, for all their efforts are thwarted. The kingdom of God's Son shall last forever.

26. " 'The kings of the earth took their stand,
and the rulers gathered together
against the Lord and against his Anointed One.' "

David is a type of Christ. He sees the raging nations of his day conspiring and plotting against God; they oppose the Lord God and have set themselves against his anointed one. David is the king who was anointed by the prophet Samuel, as God instructed. So David is the anointed of the Lord. When the nations conspire against David, they rage against God. When the kings are against David, they oppose the Lord. And all their efforts are utterly futile. David, however, is only a sign that points to Christ. He speaks prophetically about Jesus Christ, who is the King and the Anointed One.

The apostles see the fulfillment of this particular psalm (Ps. 2) in Christ, whom God has anointed and installed as king on his holy hill of Zion (Ps. 2:2, 6). Since the middle of the first century before Christ, Psalm 2 has been interpreted to refer to the Messiah. For example, the context of the Psalms

---

44. Metzger discusses this difficult sentence in detail and concludes that "the earliest attainable text" is considered "to be closer to what the author wrote originally than any of the other extant forms of text." *Textual Commentary,* pp. 321–23.

45. In Acts the name *David* appears eleven times (1:16; 2:25, 29, 34; 4:25; 7:45; 13:22 [twice], 34, 36; 15:16). And the direct quotations from the Psalter are 2:1–2 (Acts 4:25–26); 2:7 (Acts 13:33); 16:8–11 (Acts 2:25–28); 16:10 (Acts 13:35); 69:25 (Acts 1:20); 109:8 (Acts 1:20); 110:1 (Acts 2:34–35); 146:5–6 (Acts 4:24). How many of these psalms David composed is difficult to say.

of Solomon 17:26 has a messianic reference to Psalm 2:9.[46] Among the Dead Sea Scrolls is a document dating from that time that includes Psalm 2 in a messianic collection of Old Testament passages.[47] In the New Testament, of course, this particular psalm is considered messianic and is quoted frequently (see 13:33; Heb. 1:5; 5:5; Rev. 2:26–27; 19:15).

27. "For indeed both Herod and Pontius Pilate with the nations and the peoples of Israel gathered together in this city against your holy servant Jesus, whom you anointed."

The apostles themselves give a current interpretation of the psalm citation because they see it fulfilled in the life of Jesus. Here is a graphic parallel of prophecy and fulfillment:

Psalm 2:1–2	*Acts 4:27*
the nations conspire (rage)	the Gentiles conspire
the peoples plot in vain	with the people of Israel
the kings and the rulers	Herod and Pontius Pilate
of the earth	in this city
against	against
the Lord	your holy servant Jesus
and his Anointed One	whom you anointed

Indeed, say the early Christians, the truth is that Jesus fulfilled the messianic words of Psalm 2, as anyone who witnessed Jesus' trial and death can testify. Herod Antipas was tetrarch of Galilee and Perea during Jesus' ministry and was known by the people as king (Matt. 14:9; Mark 6:14, 22, 25–27). Pontius Pilate, appointed by Tiberius Caesar to serve as governor, was the ruler representing Roman authority. Of the four evangelists, only Luke reports the incident of the judge Pontius Pilate sending Jesus to Herod Antipas, who was in Jerusalem at the time of Jesus' trial. Herod was delighted to see Jesus, because he hoped to see him perform a miracle. When Jesus gave him no satisfaction, Herod sent Jesus back to Pilate. Luke concludes this episode with these words: "That very day Herod and Pilate became friends; before this they had been enemies" (Luke 23:12).

Even if we can identify Pilate with the Gentiles, only in an inferential manner can we view Herod and Israel as the "people."[48] In the Greek text this term appears as a plural to correspond with the wording of Psalm 2. Notice also that the apostles call Jesus *servant*, which seems to have been a common designation for Jesus that reflects well-known passages in Isaiah

---

46. Refer to James H. Charlesworth, ed., *The Old Testament Pseudepigrapha*, 2 vols. (Garden City, N.Y.: Doubleday, 1983), vol. 2, p. 643.
47. Y. Yadin, "A Midrash on 2 Sam. vii and Ps. i–ii (4 Q Florilegium)," *IsrExJ* 9 (1959): 97.
48. Consult Hans Bietenhard, *NIDNTT*, vol. 2, p. 799.

(52:13–15; 53:1–12). In fact, in the context of his sermon at Solomon's Colonnade, Peter twice refers to Jesus as "servant" (3:13, 26). In the prayer of the Jerusalem church this term also applies to Jesus (vv. 27, 30). God anointed Jesus with the Holy Spirit at the time of his baptism in the Jordan River (compare 10:38; Isa. 61:1; Matt. 3:16). Thus, in fulfillment of prophecy, the Gentiles and the people of Israel have set themselves against God and his anointed.

28. "They did what your hand and your purpose predestined should happen."

The apostles look at the fulfillment of Psalm 2 from a divine point of view. They see that God foreordained with his "hand and purpose" the actions taken by the people who brought Jesus to his trial and death. They repeat the observation Peter made in his Pentecost speech: "This man [Jesus] was given up to you according to God's set purpose and foreknowledge; and you, by using lawless men, nailed him to a cross and killed him" (2:23; see also 3:18).

The apostles affirm the doctrine of predestination and in their prayer they specifically assert it. "This is the only place in the N[ew] T[estament] where the verb 'predestined' (*proōrizō*) occurs outside the Pauline epistles."[49] God permitted Herod, Pilate, and the people to bring his Son to trial and to kill him. Note the word order in verse 28. The Jews and Gentiles did what (and only that which) God with his power (first) and in accordance with his will (second) had planned beforehand. He did not force Jesus' adversaries to engage in acts of violence against their will, for the evidence shows that they took full responsibility. Instead, God allowed them to conspire against him that he might accomplish salvation for his people.

Greek Words, Phrases, and Constructions in 4:25 and 27

Verse 25

ὁ . . . εἰπών—the sentence as it stands is tortuous Greek compared with the same thought expressed smoothly in 1:16. Throughout the centuries, numerous emendations have been suggested; they range from deleting the phrase *by the Holy Spirit* to assuming the presence of an Aramaic original text that reads, "that which our father David, your servant, said by the mouth of the Holy Spirit."[50]

Verse 27

ἐπ' ἀληθείας—this phrase expresses reality "as opposed to mere appearance." It means "in accordance with the truth."[51]

---

49. Guthrie, *New Testament Theology*, p. 618. Refer to George E. Ladd, *A Theology of the New Testament* (Grand Rapids: Eerdmans, 1974), p. 330.

50. Robert Hanna, *A Grammatical Aid to the Greek New Testament* (Grand Rapids: Baker, 1983), p. 195.

51. Bauer, p. 36.

c. Request and Reply
4:29–31

29. "And now, Lord, consider their threats and grant that your servants may speak your word with great boldness, 30. and that you may stretch out your hand to heal and to do signs and wonders through the name of your holy servant Jesus."

Interestingly, the community of believers utters not a word of thanks to God for delivering Peter and John from prison and trial. Instead, the Christians ask the Lord to counteract the Sanhedrin's threats by granting his servants "great boldness" to proclaim Christ's gospel. They do not ask for protection from the persecution that will inevitably follow when they proclaim the Good News. They know that God is in control of every situation, as they have confessed with Psalm 2. They are confident that he will not allow his plan and purpose to be frustrated by the rulers of the people.

The word *boldness* appears three times in this chapter (4:13, 29, 31)[52] and the concept is prominent in Acts. The apostles know that they must ask God to give them courage every time they proclaim God's Word. They realize that when it is put into effect the gift of boldness causes astonishment (v. 13), strife, and division (14:1–4). When the Lord grants this gift to his servants, they are able to speak eloquently and effectively in a hostile situation. He confirms their request by giving them the ability to heal the sick and to "perform miraculous signs and wonders."[53]

Although the Sanhedrin sent Peter and John away with the prohibition not to speak or teach any more in the name of Jesus Christ (v. 18), the members of the court did not forbid them to perform healing miracles. Had they told the apostles not to heal the infirm, they would have denied the healing miracle that the beggar experienced. Unable to disavow this living testimony, they only denied the apostles the freedom to speak in Jesus' name.

The apostles, however, ask God to heal those who are afflicted. They ask him to send his healing power by stretching out his hand and touching the infirm. In brief, God, not man, works miracles. Miracles and wonders are signs that confirm the preaching of the Good News. They occur in the name of Jesus Christ and aid the proclamation of that name. Thus, the adversaries cannot deny the evidence of the miracles. The prayer of the apostles ends with the clause "through the name of your holy servant Jesus" (v. 30).

31. After they had prayed, the place where they had gathered shook.

---

52. See also 2:29; 28:31. The verb *to speak freely, openly* occurs (in varying translations) in 9:27, 28; 13:46; 14:3; 18:26; 19:8; 26:26.
53. Heinrich Schlier, *TDNT*, vol. 5, p. 882. Consult Hans-Christoph Hahn, *NIDNTT*, vol. 2, p. 736.

And they were all filled with the Holy Spirit and began to speak the word of God with boldness.

Not every prayer receives an immediate answer, but in this case God strengthens the faith of the believers by indicating that he has heard their petition. We are reminded of the experience Paul and Silas had in the Philippian jail. While they were praying and singing hymns to God in the middle of the night, suddenly a violent earthquake shook the foundation of the prison (16:26). In like fashion, God showed his divine approval to the apostles by shaking the house where they were staying, and he apparently used an earthquake to accomplish this effect. God gave the apostles a sign that as he shook the house with a quake so he would shake the world with Christ's gospel.

Look at the parallel between Pentecost and this event. On the day of Pentecost, a violent wind blew and filled the house where the believers were sitting (2:2). Then they saw tongues of fire resting on each of them; "they were filled with the Holy Spirit and began to speak with other tongues as the Spirit was giving them ability" (2:4). After the release of Peter and John, the Christians prayed. Then the place where the believers were meeting shook; "they were all filled with the Holy Spirit and began to speak the word of God with boldness."

The differences between these two events are the blowing of the wind versus the shaking of the meeting place; the external evidence of tongues of fire in the one instance and the internal manifestation of courage in the other; and last, an ability to speak in other tongues at Pentecost over against a boldness to speak the word of God now.

The similarities are striking: the Holy Spirit comes as an answer to prayer (1:14; 4:24–30); the Spirit fills all who are present (2:4; 4:31); and they all proclaim the wonders and the word of God (2:11; 4:31). The believers receive a new outpouring of the Holy Spirit, who fills them with courage so that they proclaim the Good News. Luke fails to describe to whom the believers courageously speak God's word; perhaps first in their own circle and then, in direct opposition to the threats of the Sanhedrin, to outsiders.

Thus, the term *boldly* becomes meaningful and fittingly describes the speaking of the apostles and their helpers. They are the proclaimers of "the word of God," which in the context of Acts is a synonym for the gospel of Jesus Christ. Luke provides a glimpse of their boldness when he writes in a subsequent passage, "And every day, in the temple and from house to house, they did not stop teaching and preaching the good news that Jesus is the Christ" (5:42).

Greek Words, Phrases, and Constructions in 4:29–31

Verse 29

καὶ τὰ νῦν—this phrase appears only in Acts (4:29; 5:38; 20:32; 27:22) and signifies "and as for the present situation" (NASB margin).

ἔπιδε—the aorist active imperative from the compound verb ἐφοράω (I look upon, consider). The verb is directive.

πάσης—with the noun that lacks the definite article, this adjective means "complete," that is, "with complete candor."[54]

Verse 30

ἐν τῷ—the preposition ἐν followed by the definite article τῷ and the present infinitive is one of Luke's favorite constructions. This combination holds for both the infinitives ἐκτείνειν and γίνεσθαι.[55]

Verse 31

δεηθέντων—the aorist passive participle with the pronoun αὐτῶν forms the genitive absolute construction. The participle is derived from the verb δέομαι (I ask, beg).

ἐσαλεύθη—from σαλεύω (I shake), this verb is weaker in meaning than the verb σείω (I cause to quake, agitate). The aorist passive implies that God is the agent.

ἐλάλουν—note that Luke uses the imperfect tense to indicate the continual action of the verb in the past. With this verb Luke describes the action of speaking.

τὸν λόγον τοῦ θεοῦ—"the word of God." In Acts, this construction can denote both the subjective and the objective use of the genitive: the word that belongs to God, and the word that is spoken for God.

---

32 And the community of believers was one in heart and mind. No one claimed that anything he possessed belonged to him; rather, they had all things in common. 33 With great power the apostles were giving witness to the resurrection of the Lord Jesus, and much grace was on all of them. 34 For there was no needy person among them. For those who were owners of lands or houses would periodically sell them and bring the proceeds of the sales, 35 put them at the apostles' feet, and the proceeds were distributed to anyone who had need.

36 And Joseph, a Levite born in Cyprus, who was also called Barnabas by the apostles— which means Son of Encouragement—37 and who owned a field, sold it and brought the money and put it at the apostles' feet.

---

5. Love of the Saints
4:32–37

Luke describes how the members of the Jerusalem church lived together in unity. Evident harmony prevailed among the members, and the apostles continued to preach the resurrection of Jesus Christ. Together they cared for all the spiritual and material needs of the early Christians, so that poverty was indeed abolished.

---

54. Blass and Debrunner, *Greek Grammar*, #275.3.
55. Refer to Robertson, *Grammar*, p. 417.

a. *Community of Goods*
4:32–35

32. And the community of believers was one in heart and mind. No one claimed that anything he possessed belonged to him; rather, they had all things in common.

a. "And the community of believers was one in heart and mind." Here is a picture of the extraordinary unity of the early Christian community. Despite the opposition from the Sanhedrin (perhaps because of it), the believers form a community that is "one in heart and mind." The believers, who number about five thousand men (v. 4), maintain unanimity because of the presence of the Holy Spirit in their midst, the preaching of the Word of God, and the readiness to share each other's goods. Even though we are able to explain the unity of the Christian community, we acknowledge that in such a large group of people it is indeed unique.[56]

The phrase *one in heart and mind* is typically Hebraic. It occurs frequently in Deuteronomy[57] and is part of the summary of the Decalogue: "Love the Lord your God with all your heart, with all your soul, and with all your mind" (Mark 12:30). The early Christians express this love on a horizontal plane to their brothers and sisters who are in need. Thus they fulfill the second part of this summary, "Love your neighbor as yourself" (Mark 12:31).

b. "No one claimed that anything he possessed belonged to him; rather, they had all things in common." Emphatically Luke reports that no one in the community claimed ownership of his possessions. The term *no one* underscores the prevailing unity of the Jerusalem church. In a sense, Luke repeats what he has related as the effect of Peter's Pentecost sermon: "All who believed were together and shared all things. They began to sell their possessions and goods, and they gave to anyone who might have need" (2:44–45).

Once more he illustrates the unique spirit of the early Christians as they take care of the poor in their midst. They do so by sharing their material possessions and demonstrate their willingness not to claim them as their own. They are mindful of the divine instruction not to have any poor among God's people (compare Deut. 15:4). That is, because of God's abundant blessings on his people, the Christian community ought to abolish poverty.

Note that the apostles advocate voluntary sharing of possessions, not abolition of ownership. As a community the Christians are distinct from the so-called Qumran community that was located near the northwest shore of the Dead Sea. The Essenes who lived in that community renounced the

---

56. Consult Calvin, *Acts of the Apostles*, vol. 1, p. 128.
57. See Deut. 6:5; 10:12; 11:13; 13:3; 26:16; 30:2, 6, 10.

right to private property, established a common fund, and distributed to each member an equal share to meet his needs.[58] The Christians in Jerusalem, however, lived by the principle of voluntarily sharing possessions to strengthen the unity and harmony of the community. The Essenes acted in response to a manmade rule of compulsion; the Christians acted in obedience to God's law of love. The Christians practiced common use of their possessions, not common ownership.

33. With great power the apostles were giving witness to the resurrection of the Lord Jesus, and much grace was on all of them.

The material needs and the spiritual needs go together. The entire community engages in helping each other materially, while the apostles proclaim Christ's gospel. Especially after God's confirmation in answer to their prayer, the apostles are unable to keep silent and boldly preach the resurrection of the Lord Jesus. Luke writes that they continued to do so with great power. The words *great power* do not refer to healing miracles but rather to the filling of the Holy Spirit that enabled the apostles to preach boldly (compare v. 30). The community demonstrates vibrant power in support of the apostles, who willfully disregard the threats of the Sanhedrin.

Once again, Luke stresses one of the basic themes of apostolic preaching: "the apostles were giving witness to the resurrection of the Lord Jesus" (see 1:22; 3:15, 26; 4:2, 10). They personally met Jesus after his resurrection; he is their Lord, as Luke points out. In obedience to their Lord, the apostles testify to his resurrection (2:36).

The last part of this verse (v. 33) balances the words *great power* with *much grace*. What is the meaning of "grace"? Some translators understand the term to signify "God's great blessings"[59] on all the believers. This is a free rendering of the text, particularly because it lacks the word *God*. Therefore, other translators interpret the term *grace* as "favor" in the sense that the residents of Jerusalem looked favorably upon the Christians: "they were all given great respect" (JB; also NAB, NEB). Here is a fitting translation, for the citizens of Jerusalem observed that the Christians were providing for all their people so that no one experienced poverty; they heard the apostles preach the doctrine of Christ's resurrection; and they witnessed an inherent power because of the presence of the Holy Spirit. The general public received a favorable impression of the Christian community (compare 2:47; 4:21; 5:13).

34. For there was no needy person among them. For those who were owners of lands or houses would periodically sell them and bring the

---

58. Josephus *War* 2.8.3 [122–23]. Among the Dead Sea Scrolls see 1QS1.11–13. For additional information consult Haenchen, *Acts,* pp. 234–35; and Richard N. Longenecker, *The Acts of the Apostles,* in vol. 9 of *The Expositor's Bible Commentary,* ed. Frank E. Gaebelein, 12 vols. (Grand Rapids: Zondervan, 1981), pp. 311–12.

59. Note the SEB and GNB. Also consult Deut. 15:4b. Among commentators who hold this view, see Lenski, *Acts,* p. 189.

proceeds of the sales, 35. put them at the apostles' feet, and the proceeds were distributed to anyone who had need.

Here Luke provides a few more details about the church than he gave about the community that was formed immediately after Pentecost (2:44–45). There he recorded that the Christians had everything in common and sold their possessions and goods to take care of the poor. But here he states that poverty has been eliminated and that as the need arises, believers who own property sell it and bring the money to the apostles for distribution among the needy. We observe three aspects of the developing Christian community: first, the selling of lands or houses occurred only when there was a need; second, the believers established a fund for needy persons; and third, the apostles had the task of distributing the money.

We know little about the church in Jerusalem in the period between Pentecost and the persecution following the death of Stephen (8:1). While some of the believers had possessions, others did not. But no one in the community had need, because the rich sold either lands or houses and generously gave the revenue to the apostles. With the membership increase of the church the diaconal work of the apostles equally increased. The time had come to appoint qualified men to distribute money to the needy in the developing church.

Greek Words, Phrases, and Constructions in 4:32–35

Verse 32

ἔλεγεν—notice the use of the imperfect tenses in verses 32–35. The imperfect reveals repeated action. Also note that οὐδὲ εἷς as subject of the verb is more emphatic than the simple οὐδείς (no one).

Verse 33

ἀπεδίδουν—from the compound verb ἀποδίδωμι (I give back), the imperfect tense shows repeated occurrences in the past and signifies that the apostles paid a debt.

μεγάλη—once in the dative with δυνάμει (power) and once with χάρις (grace, favor) in the nominative. The adjunct particle τε binds the two clauses intimately together.

Verses 34–35

πωλοῦντες—the present active participle signifies repetition; so does the imperfect tense of ἔφερον (they continued to bring) and ἐτίθουν (they continued to place).

καθότι ἄν—this construction appears twice in the New Testament, both times in Acts (2:45; 4:35). It expresses the comparative idea. The particle ἄν with the imperfect tense of εἶχεν reveals repetitive use.[60]

---

60. Consult Robertson, *Grammar*, p. 967.

b. Example of Barnabas
4:36–37

After describing the generosity of the Christian community in general, Luke gives a specific example and depicts an incident out of Barnabas's life. Throughout the first half of Acts, Barnabas fulfills the role of helper, mediator, and encourager. Here Luke portrays him in respect to helping the needy.

36. And Joseph, a Levite born in Cyprus, who was also called Barnabas by the apostles—which means Son of Encouragement—37. and who owned a field, sold it and brought the money and put it at the apostles' feet.

As was typical in New Testament times, Barnabas had the given name *Joseph,* which undoubtedly was used by family members and relatives. In the New Testament, he is not known by that name; in Acts and in Paul's epistles he is Barnabas. Luke informs us that the apostles called him Barnabas; perhaps when he was baptized he received a name which both he and the Christian community accepted. Luke also gives us an interpretation: that the name means Son of Encouragement. In other words, the name describes the character of this person.

The difficulty is that we are unable to trace the origin of the name *Barnabas* to a meaningful Aramaic expression. Of course, the Aramaic word *bar* means "son." But the name *Nabas* is unknown. Adolf Deissmann has attempted to find a solution with a variation on the word *Nabas.* He suggests that we accept the hypothesis *son of Nebo.*[61] Others suggest the variation *son of a prophet.* But these variations cannot serve as a base for "son of encouragement" and do not solve the difficulty we face. The fact remains that not the father of Barnabas, but Barnabas himself, was known as an encourager. We admit that the problem is insoluble and think that he received this name because of his outstanding character.

Barnabas was a Levite and was born on Cyprus, an island in the eastern part of the Mediterranean Sea. He came to Jerusalem perhaps because his cousin Mark and aunt Mary (the mother of Mark) lived there (12:12; and Col. 4:10).

Although the law of Moses prohibited the Levites from owning property (Num. 18:20; Deut. 10:9), we have no confirmation whether Levites in dispersion observed this ordinance. Barnabas could have obtained property through marriage and, knowing the Mosaic stipulation, wished to sell it. The point is that he sold a field, presumably in the vicinity of Jerusalem, and gave the proceeds to the apostles for distribution among the poor. He was one of many persons who sold property to support needy people. But

---

61. Adolf Deissmann, *Bible Study* (reprint ed.; Winona Lake, Ind.: Alpha, 1979), pp. 309–10. See also S. P. Brock, "BARNABAS; HUIOS PARAKLĒSEŌS," *JTS* 25 (1974): 93–98.

Luke portrays Barnabas because of the leadership role he held in later times.

Greek Words, Phrases, and Constructions in 4:36

ἀπό—this preposition often takes the place of the proper form ὑπό (by).[62] With the genitive it expresses agency.

τῷ γένει—"by race." The dative as a dative of reference denotes manner.

Summary of Chapter 4

Peter and John are arrested, spend the night in prison, and the next day appear before the Sanhedrin. The rulers, elders, and teachers of the law meet to question the apostles about the healing they performed the previous day.

Filled with the Holy Spirit, Peter courageously addresses the members of the Sanhedrin and informs them that the healing took place as an act of kindness in the name of Jesus Christ of Nazareth. He reminds his audience that they crucified Jesus but that God raised him from the dead. Then he tells them that Jesus is the stone rejected by men but chosen to be the capstone; in no one else but him is salvation.

The council realizes the courage of the apostles, notes that they have been schooled by Jesus, and acknowledges the miracle they performed. The Sanhedrin prohibits the apostles from speaking and teaching in Jesus' name. Nevertheless, Peter replies to the verdict and says that the Sanhedrists should judge whether it is right to obey man rather than God. After they are enjoined not to preach, the apostles are released.

The believers come together for prayer. With references to Scripture, they ask God to grant them boldness to preach the Word. God answers their prayer with the external sign of an earthquake and the internal filling of the Holy Spirit.

The community of believers demonstrates unity. They share possessions and eliminate poverty. The apostles boldly preach the Word, receive funds from property that is sold, and distribute the money to the needy. Barnabas sells a field and brings the proceeds to the apostles.

---

62. Refer to Bauer, p. 88.

5

The Church in Jerusalem, *part 4*

5:1–42

Outline (continued)

5:1–11	6. Deception of Ananias
5:1–6	a. Ananias
5:7–11	b. Sapphira
5:12–16	7. Healing Miracles
5:17–42	C. Persecution
5:17–20	1. Arrest and Release
5:21–26	2. Freedom and Consternation
5:27–32	3. Accusation and Response
5:27–28	a. Accusation
5:29–32	b. Response
5:33–40	4. Wisdom and Persuasion
5:33–34	a. Reaction
5:35–39	b. Wisdom
5:40	c. Persuasion
5:41–42	5. Rejoicing

5 1 Now a man named Ananias with his wife, Sapphira, sold a piece of property. 2 And after he kept back part of the price for himself with his wife's full knowledge, he brought the rest and placed it at the apostles' feet. 3 But Peter said, "Ananias, why has Satan filled your heart to lie to the Holy Spirit and to keep back for yourself part of the price of the land? 4 When the land remained unsold, did it not remain yours? And after it was sold, was not the money at your disposal? Then what made you think of doing this thing? You did not lie to men but to God." 5 And as Ananias heard these words, he fell down and died. Great fear came upon all who heard it. 6 Then the young men stood up, covered up his body, carried him out, and buried him.

7 And about three hours later, his wife entered, not knowing what had happened. 8 Peter said to her, "Tell me, is this the price you and Ananias received for the land?" "Yes," she said, "it is." 9 Then Peter said to her, "Why did the two of you agree to test the Spirit of the Lord? Look! The feet of those who buried your husband are at the door and they will carry you out also."

10 And immediately she fell at Peter's feet and died. When the young men came in, they found her dead, carried her out, and buried her beside her husband. 11 Great fear came upon the whole church and all who heard these things.

---

6. Deception of Ananias
5:1–11

After portraying the exemplary conduct of Barnabas, Luke describes the greedy conduct of Ananias and Sapphira. Without any introduction, he relates that this husband and wife decide to sell a field, take the money to the apostles, and make it known to them that their gift is the total amount they received for the sale of their property. Yet they surreptitiously keep part of the money for themselves. In short, Ananias and Sapphira are robbing God (compare Josh. 7:1).

a. Ananias
5:1–6

1. Now a man named Ananias with his wife, Sapphira, sold a piece of property. 2. And after he kept back part of the price for himself with his wife's full knowledge, he brought the rest and placed it at the apostles' feet.

First, Luke mentions the name of Ananias, which is a rather common Jewish name in Acts and probably means "the Lord is gracious."[1] Luke

---

1. David Miall Edwards enumerates eleven persons who bear the name *Ananias* in Acts (5:1; 9:10; 23:2) and apocryphal literature (e.g., Tob. 5:12; Jth. 8:1; I Esd. 5:16; 9:21). See "Ananias" in *ISBE*, vol. 1, pp. 120–21; and refer to D. Edmond Hiebert, "Ananias," *ZPEB*, vol. 1, pp. 153–54.

records that the name also belongs to a Christian in Damascus who is sent by Jesus to minister to Saul (9:10–17) and to the high priest who presided over Paul's trial in Jerusalem (22:30–23:5).

Next, the name *Sapphira* appears once in Scripture and signifies "beautiful." Like her husband, Ananias, she has an Aramaic name. Together they belong to the Christian community in Jerusalem and together they seek praise and admiration from the members of that community. However, they purposely plan to keep part of the income from the sale of their property, because they love not God but money. They sell a field they own, receive the money, keep part of the revenue for themselves, and give the rest to the apostles for distribution among the poor.

Luke omits details and presents a mere outline of the incident.[2] What he highlights, however, is intent. When Ananias approaches the apostles and hands them a bag of money, as Barnabas had done on an earlier occasion, the congregation audibly or silently praises Ananias and puts him on the level of Barnabas. Even if the believers are unaware of the intended deception, Peter perceives the work of Satan in the heart of Ananias.

3. But Peter said, "Ananias, why has Satan filled your heart to lie to the Holy Spirit and to keep back for yourself part of the price of the land? 4. When the land remained unsold, did it not remain yours? And after it was sold, was not the money at your disposal? Then what made you think of doing this thing? You did not lie to men but to God."

We notice some parallels to this account in the Old Testament Scriptures. In the purity of Paradise, Satan entered to entice Eve to sin against God (Gen. 3:1). Her sin affected the entire human race. When the Israelites consecrated themselves to God by observing the rite of circumcision and celebrating the Passover feast (Josh. 5:1–12), Achan's sin of stealing from God effectively destroyed Israel's moral purity. Thus his sin affected every Israelite. Ananias's deception likewise could have destroyed the purity of the early church, which was displayed through unity, love, and harmony. These three examples serve as warnings.

Guided by the Holy Spirit, Peter senses Satan at work in the heart of Ananias and thus asks a few penetrating questions.

a. "Ananias, why has Satan filled your heart?" From personal experience, Peter knows that Satan persuaded him to disown Jesus three times (Luke 22:31–32) and that Satan put into the heart of Judas Iscariot the intent to betray Jesus (Luke 22:3; John 13:2, 27). He realizes that with the initial growth of the church Satan tries to create havoc by entering the heart of a believer. Incidentally, when Satan comes to a believer to lead him into sin,

---

2. I. Howard Marshall suggests that both Ananias and Sapphira, convicted of sinning against the Holy Spirit, died of shock for "having broken a taboo." *The Acts of the Apostles: An Introduction and Commentary,* Tyndale New Testament Commentary series (Leicester: Inter-Varsity; Grand Rapids: Eerdmans, 1980), p. 111.

man is fully responsible if he gives Satan permission to enter his life.[3] The believer must be aware of the power of the devil and resist him by standing in the faith (I Peter 5:8–9).

b. "[What caused you] to lie to the Holy Spirit?" With this question Peter reveals the core of Ananias's sin. Even though Satan influences the heart of everyone from time to time, in the case of Ananias Satan has completely filled his heart. Consequently, Ananias lied to the Holy Spirit, expelled God from his life, and deliberately sinned.[4] His sin, then, is not only a lie but also utter deception. He wants the church to believe that he is donating money in order to please God. His lie, as Peter says, is not to men but to God (v. 4). Ananias acts as if God is unaware of the daily transactions in the church and is ignorant of Ananias's deception.

c. "[What caused you] to keep back for yourself part of the price of the land?" As Paul informs the Corinthian believers, "God loves a cheerful giver" (II Cor. 9:7). That is, God rejoices when a believer gives from the heart. God desires that his children give generously without compulsion. Some years ago, I attended a worship service during which the deacons passed the offering plate. A woman directly in front of me received the plate from the deacon and then politely asked him to change a bill she held in her hand. When he complied, she gave him the amount she had decided to donate and kept the rest. She was undoubtedly a cheerful giver who contributed as much as she had decided in her heart. Similarly, Ananias could have kept part of the revenue for himself when he sold his land. But because he tried to deceive God, Peter had to ask him additional questions.

d. "When the land remained unsold, did it not remain yours? And after it was sold, was not the money at your disposal?" These questions reveal that the early Christians did not practice communal possession of property but only a sharing of goods to eliminate poverty among the believers (compare 2:44–45; 4:32, 34–35).

The answer Ananias must give to Peter's questions is affirmative. As the guilty party, Ananias is unable to say anything at all. He remains speechless (compare Matt. 22:12), for he has committed a grievous sin against God and now stands condemned.

Sin is a mystery that causes man to act irrationally. If Ananias had been honest and forthright, he would have known that the property and, after the sale, the money belonged to him as long as it was in his possession. He could do with it as he pleased and would be under no obligation.[5] However,

---

3. Consult Donald Guthrie, *New Testament Theology* (Downers Grove: Inter-Varsity, 1981), p. 136.

4. Refer to John Calvin, *Commentary on the Acts of the Apostles*, ed. David W. Torrance and Thomas F. Torrance, 2 vols. (Grand Rapids: Eerdmans, 1966), vol. 1, pp. 133–34.

5. See B. J. Capper, "The Interpretation of Acts 5.4," *JSNT* 19 (1983): 117–31.

he permitted Satan to fill his heart, refused to worship God, and made money the object of his worship. While serving his idol, he nevertheless desired the praise of God's people for his feigned generosity. He should have known that man cannot serve two masters, both God and Money (Matt. 6:24; Luke 16:13).

e. "Then what made you think of doing this thing? You did not lie to men but to God." A few ancient manuscripts substitute the words *this evil* for "this thing." That is, Ananias has committed an evil in the sight of God and man. He should have known that God is truth and light and that falsehood originates with the devil. Peter draws the conclusion that Ananias tried to deceive man but actually lied to God. Man always stands in the presence of God, who sees everything (see Prov. 15:3).

Peter makes no distinction between God and the Holy Spirit. In verse 3, he states that Ananias has lied to the Holy Spirit and in the next verse he notes that Ananias has lied to God. Peter therefore identifies the Holy Spirit with God. In a subsequent verse (v. 9), he mentions the Spirit of the Lord. For him, then, the Holy Spirit is God; he is the third person of the Trinity: Father, Son, and Holy Spirit.

5. And as Ananias heard these words, he fell down and died. Great fear came upon all who heard it. 6. Then the young men stood up, covered up his body, carried him out, and buried him.

a. "And as Ananias heard these words, he fell down and died." The Greek indicates that while Ananias listened to the words Peter spoke, he fell down and expired. Here is a case of God's judgment taking immediate effect. Scripture reveals similar incidents in which God punished sinners with sudden death. For instance, when Aaron's sons Nadab and Abihu presented fire that God had not prescribed, God struck them with fire so that they died instantaneously (Lev. 10:1–2). When Uzzah tried to steady the ark of God that was placed on an ox-drawn cart instead of carried by priests, God struck him so that he died beside the ark (II Sam. 6:7). God's verdict against Ananias (and Sapphira) also resulted in swift execution. In each instance, divine infliction of capital punishment conveys a fundamental truth: God's people must know that they exist to serve him and not vice versa.

God, not Moses, killed Aaron's sons (Lev. 10:2) and God, not David, executed Uzzah (II Sam. 6:7). Accordingly, God uses Peter as spokesman, but he himself puts Ananias to death. In the case of Sapphira, Peter utters the verdict which God himself executes (see v. 9). The emphasis in the account of Ananias's death falls not on some physical or psychological factors that result in a heart attack, but on the execution of God's verdict (compare Isa. 11:4).

b. "Great fear came upon all who heard it." God wants the church to remain pure and unstained. He removes the blame of Ananias's sin by removing him and his wife from the community of the early Christians. If

God had allowed this sin to remain unpunished, the church would have no defense against the charge that God tolerated deception directed against him and his people. Now, at the beginning of its ministry, the church is free from such a charge.

Luke frequently describes the fear and awe of the people (see 2:43; 5:11; 19:17). The believers who witnessed the death of Ananias in the presence of the apostles were filled with awe, and others who heard about it from these eyewitnesses were also gripped by holy fear. All of them understood the truth that "God visits a dreadful vengeance on deceivers."[6]

c. "Then the young men stood up." Scripture provides no report that young men occupied a particular office or that burial tasks were entrusted to them. Another passage that uses the expression *young men* appears in Peter's first epistle, where Peter exhorts the young men to "be submissive to their elders" (I Peter 5:5; and see I Tim. 5:1; Titus 2:1–6).

The customs and practices of that time differed from what is conventional in our day. Because of the hot climate in Israel, burial took place the same day death occurred. Especially when a body was under divine judgment, it had to be buried immediately (compare Lev. 10:4 [see the larger context]; Deut. 21:23; Matt. 27:57–59; John 19:31; Gal. 3:13). Moreover, the dead body of someone condemned by God defiled the sanctuary where the believers were meeting. The apostles asked the young men to remove the corpse and prepare it for burial. The young men wrapped the body of Ananias and buried it, probably in a rockhewn tomb outside Jerusalem. They would then have covered the tomb with a stone.[7]

Doctrinal Considerations in 5:1–6

Two issues in the account of Ananias's death demand discussion. For one thing, why did Peter not give Ananias opportunity to repent? When Peter confronted Simon the sorcerer, who offered him money to buy the power of the Holy Spirit, he commanded the magician to repent (8:22; also compare 2:38). We venture to say that Ananias was a Jew who since childhood knew the Scriptures and then in later life came to a knowledge of the truth when he was baptized in the name of Jesus. Simon, by contrast, lived in spiritual darkness by practicing sorcery. He was baptized because he believed (8:13), even though his faith was not genuine. When he wanted to buy the Spirit's power, Peter rebuked him and called him to repentance to rescue him from the clutches of Satan.

Both Ananias and Sapphira lied to the Holy Spirit (vv. 3–4) and agreed to test the Spirit of God (v. 9). Although they did not blaspheme the Spirit, they deliberately

---

6. Ernst Haenchen, *The Acts of the Apostles: A Commentary*, trans. Bernard Noble and Gerald Shinn (Philadelphia: Westminster, 1971), p. 241.

7. For further information consult W. Harold Mare, "Burial," *ZPEB*, vol. 1, pp. 672–74; J. Barton Payne, "Burial," *ISBE*, vol. 1, pp. 556–61.

put the Holy Spirit to the test. As the Israelites who tested God perished in the desert, so Ananias and his wife died. The writer of the Epistle to the Hebrews, commenting on the death of a blasphemer, asks, "How much more severe punishment do you think a man deserves who has trampled the Son of God under foot, who has considered as unclean the blood of the covenant that sanctified him, and who has insulted the Spirit of grace?" (10:29). And he concludes that "it is dreadful to fall into the hands of the living God" (v. 31). Ananias and Sapphira insulted the Holy Spirit, lied to him, and tested him. Consequently, they perished.

A simple illustration from daily life parallels God's discipline of Ananias and Sapphira. When a father faces the task of disciplining one of his children who has been naughty, the other children in the family who witness the disciplinary action wisely keep silent. They realize that discipline is necessary and justified. They also know that there is a time to speak and a time to be silent. When discipline is applied, it is a time to be silent.

Thus we consider a second issue. Why did the apostles not notify Sapphira of Ananias's death and burial? We are unable to answer this question, because the account does not provide complete information. However, when the congregation realized that God punished Ananias with sudden death, the believers knew from Scripture that the corpse of a person cursed by God had to be removed and buried that same day (Deut. 21:23). In the case of Aaron's sons Nadab and Abihu, who died at the altar, Moses told their cousins to carry the corpses, "still in their tunics," outside the camp for burial (Lev. 10:5). Aaron and his sons Eleazar and Ithamar were not even allowed to mourn. Moreover, anyone who touched a corpse was considered unclean for seven days (Num. 19:11).

The young men removed Ananias's body from the assembly to eliminate the danger of pollution. Realizing that God's judgment had struck, they neither gave evidence of mourning nor notified the next of kin. And by burying Ananias as quickly as possible, they cleansed the meeting place of the curse that rested on Ananias.

Greek Words, Phrases, and Constructions in 5:2–6

Verse 2

ἐνοσφίσατο—from the verb νοσφίζω (I set apart), this aorist middle form means "to misappropriate."

συνειδυίης—together with the noun γυναικός (wife), the perfect active participle from σύνοιδα (I share knowledge), translated in the present tense, is in the genitive case and forms the genitive absolute construction. The compound denotes shared responsibility.

Verse 3

ψεύσασθαι—this aorist middle infinitive from the verb ψεύδομαι (I lie) expresses result.[8]

---

8. H. E. Dana and Julius R. Mantey, *A Manual Grammar of the Greek New Testament* (1927; New York: Macmillan, 1967), pp. 215, 285.

Verse 4

οὐχί—here the negative particle introduces a rhetorical question that demands an affirmative answer. The particle controls the two verbs ἔμενεν (it remained) and ὑπῆρχεν (it was). The aorist tense of the first verb is culminative.

τί ὅτι—this is a shortened form of τί γέγονεν ὅτι (what has happened that) or simply "why?" (see v. 9).

Verse 6

συνέστειλαν—the aorist active from συστέλλω (I draw together) has various interpretations: "I cover, wrap up"; "I pack, fold, snatch up"; and "I take away, remove."[9]

---

b. Sapphira
5:7–11

7. And about three hours later, his wife entered, not knowing what had happened. 8. Peter said to her, "Tell me, is this the price you and Ananias received for the land?" "Yes," she said, "it is."

The account is rather sketchy, yet Luke provides the reader sufficient detail to follow the sequence. Sapphira becomes uneasy and begins to look for her husband. Whether their home was far removed from the meeting place of the apostles is not known. But after three hours have elapsed, she approaches the apostles. No one of the Christian community has informed her of the tragic end of Ananias's earthly life; she herself, blinded by sin, has not deviated from the path of deception she and her husband agreed to take.

When she approaches Peter and apparently asks him where her husband is, Peter demands her answer to a question. "Tell me," he says and quotes a figure, "is this the price you and Ananias received for the land?" Perhaps she sees the money bag her husband has carried to the meeting place and probably Peter points to it. Already Sapphira has perceived her husband's absence. Yet these observations and Peter's pointed question concerning the price of the land do not cause her to reflect on the sin she and her husband have committed. Her spiritual blindness causes her to persist in sin. She affirms that the price Peter quotes is the amount she and Ananias have received for the sale of their property. With her affirmative reply to Peter she indicates not only persistence in sin but also refusal to admit guilt. Accordingly, with her answer Sapphira seals her own condemnation.

9. Then Peter said to her, "Why did the two of you agree to test the Spirit of the Lord? Look! The feet of those who buried your husband are at the door and they will carry you out also."

What a sad experience, especially for Peter, who learns that both husband and wife have deliberately perpetrated a lie. He asks Sapphira a

---

9. Bauer, p. 795.

question, although he does not expect her to answer. His question is actually equivalent to a factual statement. But note the significance of the question, which describes the essence of the sin that Ananias and Sapphira committed: "Why did the two of you [husband and wife] agree *to test* the Spirit of the Lord?"

God gave his people the command, "Do not test the LORD your God as you put him to the test at Massah" (Deut. 6:16). The classic example of testing the Spirit of God is that of the rebellious Israelites in the desert at Massah and Meribah. They tested God ten times and then faced the death penalty that was executed during their stay in the desert (see, e.g., Num. 14:21–23; Ps. 95:7–11; Heb. 3:16–19). Jesus, when he was tempted by Satan to jump from the pinnacle of the temple, also appealed to the command not to tempt the Lord God (Matt. 4:7).

We know that Luke presents a resumé of Peter's remarks. Listening to Peter, Sapphira probably senses that her husband has died and that his body has been removed for burial. Peter reveals to her, in a descriptive Hebraic figure of speech, that the feet of the young men who buried Ananias are at the door. The term *feet* is an idiom in which part of the body represents the whole person. That is, the men who have served as pall bearers for her husband are now returning. Peter completes his sentence by saying, "And they will carry you out also." Is Peter the executioner of Sapphira? No, not really. Peter pronounces the verdict and God executes punishment. The case of Sapphira differs from her husband's because Peter does not render judgment when he addresses Ananias. Notice, however, that Peter informs Sapphira that the men will carry her out for burial. He leaves the execution of the death penalty to God.

10. And immediately she fell at Peter's feet and died. When the young men came in, they found her dead, carried her out, and buried her beside her husband.

In the first sentence of this verse Luke stresses the immediacy of Sapphira's death. Peter informs Sapphira about the task of the young men and she collapses dead at his feet. Indeed, Isaiah prophesies about the Messiah and portrays him in his awesomeness: "With the breath of his lips he will slay the wicked" (11:4).

Here is a repeat performance for the young men who have been given the task to carry out Sapphira and bury her beside her husband. Again, Luke mentions nothing about mourning or notifying relatives. The implication is that the believers saw God's judgment meted out to wicked people. And because they realized that this was God's work of discipline, they kept silent. The positive effect is that God wants the church to remain the bastion of truth and integrity in which deception and hypocrisy have no place.

11. Great fear came upon the whole church and all who heard these things.

We make these observations:

a. *Fear*. Once again Luke uses the expression *great fear* (v. 5), which clearly refers to a state of being afraid. The divine intervention to stop deceit within the early church strikes fear in the hearts of every member of the church. All those who hear about the death of Ananias and Sapphira take note of God's judgment. The believers should know that God condemns neither wealth nor the people who possess riches. God punishes those who deceitfully try to test him when they pretend to be generous givers but in reality defraud God.

b. *Church*. This is the first time in Acts that Luke employs the term *church*. Significantly, the word appears only in two passages in the four Gospels (Matt. 16:18; 18:17). Before and immediately after Pentecost, Luke uses descriptive phrases for the concept *church*. He refers to the believers (1:15; 2:44; 4:32), their number (2:41, 47; 4:4; 5:14), and "their own people" (4:23). In the early stages of the Christian church, the believers readily called their meeting place "the synagogue" (see the Greek text of James 2:2). Only in later years, when the division between the Jews and the Christians became permanent, the Jews went exclusively to their synagogues and the Christians to church.[10] And in later stages, the expression *church* conveyed the meaning that Christians rather than Jews were the true people of God.[11] Luke writes that the whole church was seized with fear. From the Greek we understand that the adjective *whole* pertains to all the believers who belong to the universal church that met in Jerusalem, Judea, and elsewhere.

c. *Report*. By word of mouth, the report concerning the death of Ananias and Sapphira spread far and near and brought the message that God does not tolerate deceit and falsehood in the church. The report, therefore, carried a warning to anyone who wished to infiltrate the assembly of the believers for the purpose of deception. God's sudden judgment served as a deterrent and kept the church a haven of truth and integrity.

Greek Words, Phrases, and Constructions in 5:7–9

Verse 7

ὡρῶν τριῶν—"three hours." Luke frequently introduces numbers with the particle ὡς (about) to convey an approximation. The genitive case is descriptive.

Verse 8

ἀπεκρίθη—usually the idiom is fully written out: "he answered and said." But occasionally the verb *said* is omitted. The construction means "to address." Nevertheless, the possibility that Sapphira asked Peter about her husband is not remote.

τοσούτου ἀπέδοσθε—with the verb, the genitive case of the adjective *such* denotes

---

10. In Acts, Luke employs the word *ekklēsia* (church) twenty-three times: 5:11; 7:38; 8:1, 3; 9:31; 11:22, 26; 12:1, 5; 13:1; 14:23, 27; 15:3, 4, 22, 41; 16:5; 18:22; 19:32, 39, 41; 20:17, 28.
11. Lake and Cadbury, *Beginnings*, vol. 4, p. 54.

the genitive of price. The verb is the aorist middle of ἀποδίδωμι (I give back) and signifies "you gave away for your own interest," that is, "you sold."[12]

Verse 9

ὑμῖν—although Peter confronts only Sapphira, he addresses her in the plural ("you") to include her husband.

ἰδού—this particle is actually the aorist middle imperative of εἶδον (I saw). Here it "is not only a prophecy but a pronouncement of the divine judgment and its immediate execution."[13]

---

12 Many signs and wonders were done by the apostles among the people. And they all used to meet together in Solomon's Colonnade. 13 But no one else dared to associate with them, even though the people held them in high esteem. 14 Nevertheless, more and more believers in the Lord, both men and women, were being added to their number. 15 They even brought out the sick into the streets and placed them on beds and mats so that when Peter came by at least his shadow might fall on any one of them. 16 And also crowds were coming together from the towns around Jerusalem. They kept on bringing the sick and those who were troubled by unclean spirits; they were all healed.

---

7. Healing Miracles
5:12–16

Here is the third summary that Luke places within his continuous narrative (compare 2:42–47 and 4:32–35) and which displays some similarities to the other two summaries. That is, Luke seems to resort to general statements that appear contradictory, as is evident in verses 13 and 14. The flow of thought in this summary is not smooth. This has caused some scholars to rearrange the sequence of verses in this paragraph to maintain the theme of the apostles performing healing miracles among the people. These translators begin the paragraph with verse 12b, which is then followed by verses 13 and 14. They place verse 12a as a preface to verse 15 to achieve continuity.[14] Other translators regard verses 12b–14 as a parenthetical comment.[15] However, the question must be raised whether rearrangement of the verses or setting them off in parenthetical form is necessary. In spite of difficulties, most translators stay with the text as we have it.

12. Many signs and wonders were done by the apostles among the people. And they all used to meet together in Solomon's Colonnade. 13. But no one else dared to associate with them, even though the people held them in high esteem.

Luke continues his narrative by calling attention to the other apostles

---

12. A. T. Robertson, *A Grammar of the Greek New Testament in the Light of Historical Research* (Nashville: Broadman, 1934), p. 810.

13. Haenchen, *Acts*, p. 239.

14. For instance, JB, *Phillips*, and *Moffatt*.

15. See the KJV. The NEB places verse 12a with verse 11 to form the conclusion of the account concerning Ananias and Sapphira. Verse 12b, then, forms the beginning of a new paragraph.

besides Peter and John. Verse 12a literally says, "And at the hands of the apostles many signs and wonders were happening among the people." We know that the apostles in obedience to Jesus' command healed people by placing their hands on the sick.[16] We also know that the literal translation has a typical Hebraic idiom that need not be translated: the expression *at the hands of* refers to the apostles; in this sentence Luke places all the emphasis on them. However, not the apostles but God heals the sick; the apostles serve as instruments in God's hands. Also, Luke wishes to dispel the idea of featuring Peter as the miracle worker, as if the rest of the apostles do not count. All the apostles have received authority from Jesus Christ to preach and heal, and upon all of them the Holy Spirit has been poured out.

a. "Many signs and wonders were done by the apostles among the people." Here, then, is an explicit reference to the apostles. The phrase *many signs and wonders* is a repetition of 2:43,[17] where in summary form Luke mentions the work done by the apostles. He says that the apostles performed these signs and miracles among the people. With the word *people* the writer has in mind the people of Israel. The residents of Jerusalem observed the healing power demonstrated in the wonders the apostles performed.

b. "And they all used to meet together in Solomon's Colonnade." Who is included in the word *all*? Is Luke saying that all the apostles were one in heart and mind and met in a spacious area of the temple called Solomon's Colonnade (see the discussion of 3:11)?[18] Or is he saying that the more than five thousand believers (4:3) were with the apostles in the precincts of the temple? Scholars generally favor the second interpretation because the flow of the sentence is more natural. However, the problem of interpretation has only begun with verse 12. The next verse (v. 13) also presents ambiguities.

c. "But no one else dared to associate with them, even though the people held them in high esteem." The question is, to whom does the pronoun *them* refer? If the believers are separated from the apostles, then Luke has the apostles in mind when he uses the pronoun *them*. In this interpretation, the apostles stand alone in the temple area and the people of Jerusalem praise them (compare v. 26). Then the believers are afraid of the authorities and keep their distance from the apostles. But the contrary is true, for we find no indication that the believers are fearful and timid (see 4:24–30).

A second interpretation is that the expression *no one else* (or *the rest*) refers to non-Christians or the ones "from outside" (NEB). In the New Testament, the term frequently describes unbelievers (e.g., Luke 8:10; Eph. 2:3; I Thess. 4:13; 5:6).[19] This interpretation, then, calls for three categories of

---

16. See 3:7; 9:41; 28:8; and see Mark 16:18.
17. See also Acts 2:19, 22; 4:30; 6:8; 7:36; 14:3; 15:12; II Cor. 12:12.
18. The SEB translates, "The apostles were together in Solomon's Porch." Everett F. Harrison agrees that "only the apostles were in Solomon's Colonnade." *Interpreting Acts: The Expanding Church*, 2d ed. (Grand Rapids: Zondervan, Academie Books, 1986), p. 105.
19. In two passages the term *the rest* denotes believers (see Rev. 11:13; 12:17). Walther Günther and Hartmut Krienke, *NIDNTT*, vol. 3, p. 253.

people in Jerusalem: the Christians, the unbelievers, and those faithful Jewish people who were favorably inclined to the gospel. Because of the sudden judgment on Ananias and Sapphira, the unbelievers are afraid to join the church. Yet the Jewish people who love God continue to hold the Christians in high esteem (4:21). The pronoun *them* signifies the Christians.

A third explanation is to regard those who are afraid to join the Christian community as "non-joining sympathizers."[20] They are supportive of the Christians and have high regard for them, yet they hesitate to become one with the believers. The terms *the rest* and *the people* are virtually synonymous. Conclusively, although the choice remains difficult, scholars prefer the second interpretation.

14. Nevertheless, more and more believers in the Lord, both men and women, were being added to their number.

We note three items:

First, Luke has lost count of the number of Christians in Jerusalem. After the healing of the cripple, he estimates the total membership to be about five thousand men (4:3). Now he remarks that "more and more believers in the Lord, both men and women, were being added to their number." Regardless of the fear unbelievers display, the Holy Spirit is at work in the hearts of men and women. The growth of the church continues unabated. The deaths of Ananias and Sapphira keep the unbelievers from entering the church, yet at the same time large numbers of true converts join and strengthen the Christian community. In fact, Luke has abandoned his desire to be precise and now records that multitudes of people became members of the church.

Next, we observe that Luke specifically states that women joined the church. In the pre-Pentecost setting of the upper room, he records the presence of women, among them Mary the mother of Jesus (1:14). In his last tally of church membership, Luke specifically mentions only the five thousand men, not the women (4:3). But in subsequent chapters, he refers to both men and women (e.g., 8:3, 12; 9:2; 13:50).

A third observation is that the Greek allows for two translations: either "Nevertheless, more and more *believers in the Lord,* both men and women, were being added to their number" (italics added) or "And believers were increasingly *added to the Lord,* multitudes of both men and women" (NKJV, italics added; and see KJV, NEB margin). Because the verb *to believe* usually takes a direct object (in this case, "the Lord") and because of its position the verb *to believe* in the Greek sentence receives emphasis, the first translation is the better of the two choices.

15. They even brought out the sick into the streets and placed them on beds and mats so that when Peter came by at least his shadow might fall on any one of them.

How is verse 15 linked to the preceding passage? Some scholars either

---

20. D. R. Schwartz, "Non-Joining Sympathizers (Acts 5, 13–14)," *Bib* 64 (1983): 550–55.

rearrange this paragraph or consider verses 12b–14 a parenthetical statement (see the discussion of v. 12). Other translators take verses 14 and 15
together and thus see the one verse dependent on the other.[21] There is
merit in this combination, for the resultant deed of people bringing their
sick into the streets (v. 15) stems from the fact that they believe in the
Lord (v. 14). The stress, then, falls on the verb *to believe*. These people
who believe in the Lord trust in him to heal the sick. The context seems to
indicate that their faith was not contingent on the miracles the apostles
did.[22]

Here we see the principle that God performs miracles in answer to and
for the increase of faith. Miracles do not occur apart from faith. The point
is that as Jesus did miracles in Galilee and Jerusalem, so his disciples now
are performing similar miracles by his authority. That is, the people who
have put their trust in Jesus come to the apostles for healing. And we
expect that the apostles in their teaching and preaching direct the people to
Jesus.

The people bring the sick into the main streets and city squares in full
assurance that the miracles of healing will take place. Yet, because of their
faith in the Lord, there is no magic in the healing of the sick. Occupying
beds and mats, the sick wait for Peter to pass by, so that even his shadow
may fall on them. A shadow is related to the object that blocks the light,
but it is not an integral part of that object. These invalids do not even
touch an apron or handkerchief belonging to Peter (compare 19:12) or
try to touch the edge of his cloak (see Mark 6:56). The believers trust that
Peter's shadow will be sufficient to heal the sick. The text actually reads,
"so that when Peter came by, at least his shadow might fall on any one of
them." That is, not everyone who has been carried on a bed or mat to the
street will be touched by Peter's shadow. At this juncture, the so-called
Western text of Greek manuscripts has an additional sentence for clarification: "For they were set free from every ailment with which each one was
afflicted."

From the culture in which he lived, Luke is borrowing the concept that
an object has inherent power.[23] But we do not have to ask whether the
people were superstitious, for the Lord can heal a person by touching him,
speaking to him, or causing a shadow to fall on him. Henry Alford queries
and concludes,

> Cannot the 'Creator Spirit' work with any instrument, or with none, as
> pleases Him? And what is a hand or a voice, more than a shadow, except
> that the analogy of the ordinary instrument is a greater help to faith in

---

21. Refer to RSV, NASB, NKJV.
22. F. W. Grosheide, *De Handelingen der Apostelen,* Kommentaar op het Nieuwe Testament
series, 2 vols. (Amsterdam: Van Bottenburg, 1942), vol. 1, p. 167.
23. P. W. van der Horst, "Peter's Shadow: The Religio-Historical Background of Acts v. 15,"
NTS 23 (1977): 204–12.

the recipient? Where faith, as apparently here, did not need this help, the less likely medium was adopted.[24]

For the cultural significance of the concept *shadow*, consider the words of Gabriel to Mary: "The power of the Most High will overshadow you" (Luke 1:35). A shadow, therefore, is more than sufficient as a means for God to extend his healing power to man. God demands faith if there is to be healing for the sick. Faith is present, for verse 14 reveals that crowds of men and women believed in the Lord. And these crowds are not limited to the numerous inhabitants of Jerusalem.

16. And also crowds were coming together from the towns around Jerusalem. They kept on bringing the sick and those who were troubled by unclean spirits; they were all healed.

Note at least two distinct parallels. First, we detect a parallel with Jesus' healing ministry. People who heard what Jesus was doing came to Jesus from Galilee, Judea, Jerusalem, Idumea, and areas across the Jordan and around Tyre and Sidon (Mark 3:7–8). The Gospel writers speak of crowds of people coming to Jesus to hear him and of the sick who desired to touch him (see Luke 6:17–19). Now the apostles see the same thing happening to them, when crowds come from the countryside with relatives and friends who are ill. The influence of the Christian church extends far beyond the city of Jerusalem.

The second parallel is the healing of the cripple at the gate called Beautiful (3:1–10). This healing resulted in animosity from the high priest and the Sadducees, who expressed their resentment by jailing Peter and John and putting them on trial the next day (4:1–7). At this trial, the members of the Sanhedrin never sought to restrict the healing ministry of the apostles. They only commanded them not to speak or teach in the name of Jesus (4:18). Whereas the healing of the cripple was a single incident, the healings performed by all the apostles for people from the towns around Jerusalem are countless.[25] What the reaction of the Sadducees is becomes clear in the sequence of the narrative. The apostles are jailed and put on trial by the Sanhedrin. And members of the Sanhedrin vent their fury by wanting to put the apostles to death (5:33).

Luke reports that people bring not only the sick to the apostles but also those who were tormented by evil spirits (see Luke 6:18). He distinguishes between people suffering from common ailments and those who are demon-possessed. Only the writers of the Gospels and Acts mention people tormented by evil spirits in Jerusalem, Judea, Galilee, Decapolis, Samaria, Philippi, and Ephesus.[26] The rest of the New Testament is silent about this illness. During Jesus' ministry and for a few decades, the forces of evil seemed

---

24. Henry Alford, *Alford's Greek Testament: An Exegetical and Critical Commentary*, 7th ed., 4 vols. (1877; Grand Rapids: Guardian, 1976), vol. 2, p. 53.

25. Consult Haenchen, *Acts*, p. 245.

26. Refer to Guthrie, *New Testament Theology*, p. 137.

to become evident especially in persons who were afflicted with demon-possession (see, e.g., 8:7; 16:16; 19:15; Matt. 8:16; 10:1). Accordingly, like Jesus, the apostles encounter the forces of the devil in people who are tormented by unclean spirits. Luke concludes his summary by stating that the sick and those who were troubled with unclean spirits were all healed.

Greek Words, Phrases, and Constructions in 5:14–16

Verse 14

προσετίθεντο—the imperfect tense indicates continued action in the past tense. The passive voice implies that God is the agent, for God adds his people to the church. Therefore, the verb should not be taken with the dative τῷ κυρίῳ (to the Lord), which is redundant. Rather, the present active participle πιστεύοντες controls the dative case.

Verse 15

ἵνα κἄν—this combination occurs only twice in the New Testament (here and in Mark 6:56, where the sick attempt to touch the edge of Jesus' cloak). "In both instances an implied *conditional* clause may be detected."[27]

ἐρχομένου—because of the genitive case in this present middle participle and in the proper noun Πέτρου, and because of its position in the sentence, this is the genitive absolute construction.

Verse 16

συνήρχετο—the imperfect middle in the singular, dependent on its singular subject τὸ πλῆθος (the crowd), is followed by φέροντες (carrying), which is a plural present active participle.

πέριξ—an adverb obviously derived from the preposition περί (around) occurs only here.

---

17 Then the high priest and all who were with him, that is, the party of the Sadducees, were filled with jealousy. 18 They arrested the apostles and put them in the public jail. 19 But during the night an angel of the Lord opened the gates of the prison. Leading them out, he said, 20 "Go, stand and speak to the people in the temple all the words of this life." 21 And when they heard this, they entered the temple at daybreak and began to teach.

When the high priest and those with him arrived, they convened the Sanhedrin—the assembly of the elders of Israel—and sent orders to the prison house to have the apostles brought before them. 22 And when the officers arrived at the prison, they did not find the apostles. They returned and reported, 23 "We found the prison securely locked and the guards standing at the doors. But when we opened them, we found no one inside." 24 When they heard these words, both the captain of the temple guard and the chief priests were greatly perplexed, wondering what was going to happen.

25 Then someone arrived and said to them, "Look! The men you put in prison are standing

---

27. C. F. D. Moule, *An Idiom-Book of New Testament Greek*, 2d ed. (Cambridge: Cambridge University Press, 1960), p. 139.

in the temple courts and teaching the people." 26 Immediately the captain with his officers went out and brought them—not with force, because they were afraid of being stoned by the people.

27 They brought the apostles and placed them before the Sanhedrin. The high priest questioned them, 28 "We gave you strict orders not to continue teaching in his name. And look what has happened; you have filled Jerusalem with your teaching and intend to bring this man's blood upon us."

29 Peter and the other apostles replied: "We must obey God rather than men. 30 The God of our fathers raised up Jesus, whom you had put to death by hanging him on a tree. 31 He is the one whom God exalted to his right hand as Prince and Savior to give repentance to Israel and forgiveness of sins. 32 And we are witnesses of these things, and so is the Holy Spirit, whom God has given to those who obey him."

33 And when they heard this, they were stung in their hearts and wanted to kill them. 34 But a member of the Sanhedrin, a Pharisee named Gamaliel, a teacher of the law and respected by all the people, stood up and ordered that the men be put outside for a little while. 35 He said to the Sanhedrin, "Men of Israel, be careful what you intend to do with these men. 36 Some time ago, Theudas rose up saying that he was somebody. About four hundred men rallied to him; but when he was killed, all his followers were dispersed and came to nothing. 37 After this man, Judas of Galilee appeared at the time of the census and caused the people to revolt and follow him. He too was killed and all who followed him were scattered. 38 So in this case I suggest to you: Stay away from these men and let them go! For if this plan or movement is of human origin, it will fail. 39 But if it is of God, you will be unable to overthrow them; you will even find yourselves fighting against God." And they were persuaded by him.

40 After summoning the apostles, they flogged them and ordered them to speak no more in the name of Jesus; then they released them.

41 Therefore, the apostles went out from the presence of the Sanhedrin and rejoiced because they had been considered worthy to suffer disgrace for the Name. 42 And every day in the temple and from house to house they did not stop teaching and preaching the good news that Jesus is the Christ.

C. Persecution
5:17–42

The narrative in Acts is filled with recurrences. In the last part of chapter 5, Luke presents an account which in many respects is a repetition of 4:1–21. Luke reports that once again the party of the Sadducees counteracts the growth of the Christian church. Presently, however, the reaction of the Sadducees is more severe and their opposition intensifies. They have all the apostles arrested.

1. Arrest and Release
5:17–20

17. Then the high priest and all who were with him, that is, the party of the Sadducees, were filled with jealousy. 18. They arrested the apostles and put them in the public jail.

The healings of numerous people residing in Jerusalem and surrounding towns create headlines in the daily news, so to speak. Thousands crowd around the apostles, who meet the people in the streets, the city squares, and Solomon's Colonnade in the temple area. The gathering of these crowds becomes known to the high priest and his associates in the Sanhedrin. They face a problem that they were not able to solve earlier when they told Peter and John not to speak or teach in the name of Jesus.

The Greek text has the reading, "Then the high priest rose up." That is, he goes into action, for in his opinion the movement led by the apostles has gone far enough. We assume that the high priest is Annas and not Caiaphas his son-in-law (see the discussion at 4:6), and that his associates are members of the high-priestly families and the Sadducean party. The term *party* is a translation of the Greek word *hairesis,* from which we have the derivatives *heresy* and *heretic.* In Acts, this term can have either a favorable or an unfavorable connotation;[28] here its meaning is positive, because the party of the Sadducees was in effect the ruling political party in Israel. The high priest and his associates were not only spiritual overseers who controlled the temple services and grounds. They were also political rulers who gave leadership in the Sanhedrin (see the commentary on 4:1–2; and see 23:6–8) and feared local disturbances. For this reason, they objected strenuously that the apostles attracted large crowds, especially in the temple area, which they regarded as their domain of influence (compare 5:12). Luke therefore adds the telling note, "[they] were filled with jealousy."

Does the jealousy of the high priest Annas and the leading Sadducees originate in a zeal for God and his people? Not at all, for their envy is personal and vindictive. For example, the fact that Annas remained high priest when Caiaphas was appointed to that office depicts Annas's selfish ambition. The power and authority of the religious and political leaders are challenged by the apostles. Hence, they must act.

The high priest and his party order the captain of the temple guard and his officers to arrest the apostles (see v. 26). Presumably they give the order in the afternoon, for the apostles upon their arrest must spend the night in the public jail. This jail belonging to the state differs from the place where Peter and John spent a night on an earlier arrest (4:3). Now the apostles are in the public jail where thieves and murderers are kept. (Incidentally, the Greek for the word *public* can also be taken adverbially and thus mean "the apostles were put publicly in jail.") In New Testament times, prisoners were kept in a public prison for a limited period of time to await trial and sentencing. "Imprisonment itself was not considered a form of punishment under the Roman legal system."[29]

19. But during the night an angel of the Lord opened the gates of the prison. Leading them out, he said, 20. "Go, stand and speak to the people in the temple all the words of this life."

Luke reports the release of the apostles by an angel at night, but he omits the details. He reserves them for the parallel account of Peter's release

---

28. Compare the Greek text of Acts 15:5; 24:5, 14; 26:5; 28:22; see also I Cor. 11:19; Gal. 5:20; II Peter 2:1. Refer to Gerhard Nordholt, *NIDNTT,* vol. 1, p. 535.

29. Gary L. Knapp, "Prison," *ISBE,* vol. 3, p. 975.

(12:4–10). Luke reports that an angel of the Lord set the apostles free, yet ironically the Sadducees who arrested the apostles denied the existence of angels (see 23:8). Luke simply writes "an angel of the Lord" and not "the angel of the Lord," who is frequently mentioned in the Old Testament as "the personified help of God for Israel" (e.g., Exod. 14:19; Num. 22:22; Judg. 6:11–24).[30] Luke also uses the designation *an angel of the Lord* in his accounts of

Stephen's narrative of Israel's history (7:30),

Philip's encounter with the Ethiopian eunuch (8:26),

Peter's release from prison (12:7–10), and

King Herod's death (12:23).[31]

God supernaturally intervenes by sending an angel with the twofold task of opening the doors of the public prison to release the apostles and of instructing them to preach the full message of salvation. How the angel opens the doors without the guards becoming aware of it is part of the miracle of the release. He instructs the apostles to go to the temple courts, most likely Solomon's Colonnade, to "speak to the people in the temple all the words of this life." Their task of preaching and teaching the people must continue in Jerusalem. The apostles are released from prison to proclaim the word of life.

The Greek text reads, "In the temple speak to the people all the words of this life." What is the meaning of the expression *this life*? When crowds of people forsook Jesus during his ministry, Jesus asked the twelve apostles, "You do not wish to leave too, do you?" Then Peter as their spokesman said, "Lord, to whom shall we go? You have the words of eternal life" (John 6:67–68, NIV). These words, then, convey the message of salvation—eternal life through the resurrection of Christ (compare 3:15; Phil. 2:16). The Sadducees rejected the doctrine of the resurrection, yet the apostles publicly proclaim it as "the full message of this new life" (NIV).

Greek Words, Phrases, and Constructions in 5:17–20

Verse 17

ἀναστάς—this aorist active participle from the verb ἀνίστημι (I rise) in the intransitive form occurs frequently in the New Testament (seventeen times in the singular), so that its basic meaning has been weakened. It generally indicates "the beginning of an action."[32]

---

30. Hans Bietenhard, *NIDNTT*, vol. 1, p. 101.
31. See also Matt. 1:20–24; 2:13, 19; 28:2; Luke 1:11; 2:9; Acts 27:23.
32. Bauer, p. 70.

ἡ οὖσα αἵρεσις—the present participle of εἰμί actually means "existing," that is, "the existing party."

Verses 19–20

διὰ νυκτός—the preposition διά (through) adds little to the translation *during the night* (compare John 3:2).

τῆς ζωῆς ταύτης—the New International Version has the reading *this new life*. The word *life* in Aramaic and Syriac is the equivalent of "salvation" (see 3:26).

---

2. Freedom and Consternation
5:21–26

21a. And when they heard this, they entered the temple at daybreak and began to teach.

After their release from prison, the apostles had time to prepare themselves for the task the angel had given them. At the break of dawn, when people customarily went to the temple for morning prayers, the apostles were waiting to tell them about the new life in Jesus Christ. They demonstrate courage and boldness in returning to the place where the high priest and his fellow priests exercise authority. Yet they do so in obedience to the divine command they have received.

Most translators render the verb in the second part of the sentence as "[they] began to teach." In the Greek, the verb appears in the imperfect tense, which can refer to the initiation of an act. It can also mean continuation of a process; that is, the apostles kept on teaching the gospel.[33] In their prayer, they ask God to grant them the ability to teach the gospel with great boldness (4:29); filled with the Holy Spirit, they speak "the word of God with boldness" (4:31). We therefore see a continuation of the apostles' preaching and teaching the gospel of Christ.

21b. When the high priest and those with him arrived, they convened the Sanhedrin—the assembly of the elders of Israel—and sent orders to the prison house to have the apostles brought before them.

Most translators begin a new paragraph with verse 21b, because in context the verb *arrived* means that the high priest came not to the temple but to the hall of the supreme court, called the Sanhedrin. The emphasis in this verse is not on the verb *to arrive* but on the verb *to call together*.

With an implied touch of humor, Luke reports that the high priest convenes the Sanhedrin for a hasty trial and sends officers to the jail to bring the apostles to their arraignment. Luke relates the account from a divine perspective and accordingly portrays man's efforts to oppose God's work as futile. Thus the high priest sends messengers to convene the members of

---

33. In fact, two versions reflect this meaning: "they . . . went on with their teaching" (NEB) and "they resumed their teaching" (NAB).

the Sanhedrin as quickly as possible. But the apostles are teaching the people in the temple area.

Luke writes, "the Sanhedrin—the assembly of the elders of Israel." He provides an explanation at this point, perhaps to indicate that in contrast to the earlier trial for Peter and John (4:5–22), now the entire assembly is present.[34] The Sanhedrin is the ruling council not only for Jerusalem but for all Israel.

At the request of the high priest and his colleagues, temple police officers go to the public jail to bring the apostles before the Sanhedrin. We can ask whether anyone of the priestly order serving at the temple that morning could have detected the presence of the apostles in the temple courts. Luke gives no indication except to say that the captain of the temple guard was unaware of the apostles' release (v. 24). The hall of the Sanhedrin was to the west of the temple proper and Solomon's Colonnade to the east. The location of the public jail is unknown.

22. And when the officers arrived at the prison, they did not find the apostles. They returned and reported, 23. "We found the prison securely locked and the guards standing at the doors. But when we opened them, we found no one inside."

We assume that the hour of the day when the officers arrive at the jail is relatively early. They ask the jailer to release the apostles to them for arraignment, but upon investigation the officers find the doors locked and guards keeping watch over empty cells. They come to the embarrassing conclusion that the apostles are not there and in consternation they return to the Sanhedrin hall. They report to the surprised members of the supreme court that in spite of securely locked prison doors and the continual presence of the guards, the cells that had housed the apostles are empty.

24. When they heard these words, both the captain of the temple guard and the chief priests were greatly perplexed, wondering what was going to happen.

The person responsible for the security of the prisoners is the captain of the temple guard (see 4:1). He is a member of a prominent priestly family who serves permanently at the temple and is exempt from the rotation schedule which the rest of the priests must follow. He is a servant of the Sanhedrin (compare Luke 22:4, 52). He and the chief priests are thoroughly perplexed and unable to find a rational explanation for the escape of the apostles. The full assembly of the Sanhedrin is waiting in the courtroom, but the chief priests who have convened the meeting are at a loss to

---

34. Bauer, p. 156, interprets the "council of elders" to be the "Sanhedrin in Jerusalem." However, Gerhard Schneider thinks that there was a senate (council) next to the Sanhedrin. *Die Apostelgeschichte*, Herders Theologischer Kommentar zum Neuen Testament series, 2 vols. (Freiburg: Herder, 1980), vol. 1, p. 390. For more information on the Sanhedrin, see the commentary on 4:5–6; see also Emil Schürer, *The History of the Jewish People in the Age of Jesus Christ (175 B.C.–A.D. 135)*, rev. and ed. Geza Vermes and Fergus Millar, 3 vols. (Edinburgh: Clark, 1973–87), vol. 2, pp. 210–18; Donald A. Hagner, "Sanhedrin," *ZPEB*, vol. 5, p. 271.

present the apostles. They ask themselves what to make of this incident. The Sanhedrin discusses the situation, even though no one is able to explain the details the officers have reported. They fail to realize that God is protecting the apostles and is using them to foster the growth of his church.

25. Then someone arrived and said to them, "Look! The men you put in prison are standing in the temple courts and teaching the people."

God is guiding and directing the development of this event. In his providence, a messenger runs from the temple area to the hall where the Sanhedrin is assembled. Perhaps he is a priest or Levite who is acquainted with the arrest of the apostles and their scheduled trial that morning. In the commotion of the morning he is allowed to come before the Sanhedrin. Excitedly he tells the councilmen, "Look! The men you put in prison are standing in the temple courts and teaching the people." The consternation is complete, for the high priest and his associates realize that the apostles have received help from outside for their release from prison. This means the apostles have support that obviously opposes the authority of the high priest. Of course, the high priest and his colleagues know that the apostles have the support of the general public (see 4:21). Perhaps they surmise that even among the members of the Sanhedrin are Pharisees who are favorably disposed to the apostles and their cause. These supporters include Nicodemus and Joseph of Arimathea.

The prominent members of the Sanhedrin are at a loss, for they had commanded the apostles not to speak or teach in Jesus' name. Yet these Galilean fishermen continue to teach the people in the temple area. The boldness of the apostles is incredible to the high priest and his friends; the apostles have not escaped and hidden themselves but are teaching in the temple courts. Now that the temple guard and his officers know where the apostles are, they have occasion to redeem themselves.

26. Immediately the captain with his officers went out and brought them—not with force, because they were afraid of being stoned by the people.

The captain of the temple guard needs to save face. As soon as he hears the news about the apostles, he takes his officers, rushes to the temple courts, and finds the apostles teaching the people. The Greek text puts the verb *to bring* in the imperfect to describe the delicate situation. The captain is unable to take the apostles by force because the people hold them in high esteem and are ready to protect them by throwing stones at the temple guards.

The temple police officers and the prominent members of the Sanhedrin are guided by fear and not by wonder and amazement at divine miracles. Remember that the chief priests and the elders also were afraid of the people when Jesus asked them whether John the Baptist came from heaven or from men. They could not admit that he came "from heaven," for then they should have accepted John as a prophet. And they could not say "from men," because they feared the people (Matt. 21:25–26). The chief priests and the elders during Jesus' ministry and again at the arrest of the apostles show that fear has eroded their authority. The captain and his men fear that should they show any sign of force, they would be attacked by the crowd. Conversely, the apostles accompany the officers voluntarily in an effort not to be provocative. They know that God, who has delivered them from prison, will also protect them in the courtroom.

Greek Words, Phrases, and Constructions in 5:21–26

Verse 21

ἐδίδασκον—this imperfect active is either inceptive (they began to teach) or iterative (they kept on teaching). I prefer the latter because it is in harmony with the divine command the apostles received.

τὸ συνέδριον καί—the conjunction is explanatory and signifies "that is."

Verse 24

διηπόρουν—for an explanation of this verb, see 2:12. The verb introduces an indirect question that features a potential optative (γένοιτο) with the particle ἄν.[35] The direct question is "What will happen?" or the more idiomatic "What do we make of this?"

Verse 26

ἦγεν—the use of the imperfect active from the verb ἄγω (I lead, bring) is descriptive; that is, it describes an action in progress.

μὴ λιθασθῶσιν—"lest the people stone them." This negative purpose clause introduced by the verb *to fear* depends more on οὐ μετὰ βίας than on the verb ἐφοβοῦντο (they were afraid).[36]

---

3. Accusation and Response
5:27–32

Not only Peter and John but all the apostles now are standing before the full assembly of Israel's supreme court. They are mindful of Jesus' words that they do not have to worry about what they should say before a court of law. The Holy Spirit will give them the words to speak in that hour (Matt. 10:19–20).

a. Accusation
5:27–28

27. They brought the apostles and placed them before the Sanhedrin. The high priest questioned them, 28. "We gave you strict orders not to

---

35. Robertson, *Grammar*, p. 940.
36. Alford, *Alford's Greek Testament*, vol. 2, p. 55.

**continue teaching in his name. And look what has happened; you have
filled Jerusalem with your teaching and intend to bring this man's blood
upon us."**

The members of the Sanhedrin sit in a semicircle while the apostles stand
in the center facing them. For Peter and John this is a repeat performance,
but for the rest of the apostles this trial is a first experience. The high
priest, as presiding officer of the assembly, addresses them. Apparently he
is not interested in learning from the apostles how they were released from
prison, even though this caused much consternation earlier. He and the
other members of the Sanhedrin focus attention on the command they
issued when they dismissed Peter and John at the previous trial. Admittedly, at the earlier occasion he addressed only two apostles, but he and the
Sanhedrin intended the command for the entire church. The believers,
however, prayed for great courage to proclaim the gospel, and, "filled with
the Holy Spirit, [they] began to speak the word of God with boldness"
(4:31). They have failed to comply with the orders of the Sanhedrin and
thus are now accused of disobedience.

This is the point at issue: "We gave you strict orders not to continue
teaching in his name." Notice that the high priest purposely ignores the
name *Jesus* (see also 4:17) and contemptuously calls Jesus "this man."[37] But
he refrains from saying that he had given these orders with threats when
the members of the Sanhedrin were not able to punish the apostles. He
realizes that as his threats were words devoid of power, so were his orders.
He has the feeling that he is fighting a losing battle, for what he sees
happening in public is the opposite of what he commanded. He knows that
the apostles have filled Jerusalem with Jesus' teachings in open defiance of
his orders; indeed, he is unable to stop them from teaching in the name of
Jesus. And he recognizes that the Sanhedrin has no teaching to oppose the
doctrines of Christ. In his frustration, he levels two additional accusations:

1. "You have filled Jerusalem with your teaching." The high priest purposely avoids using Jesus' name and asserts that the teaching originates
with the apostles. Yet the apostles have stressed repeatedly that they do not
act in their own name but have received authority from Jesus Christ (see
3:6, 16; 4:10).

2. "[You] intend to bring this man's blood upon us." With his own words he
admits to murdering an innocent man. The high priest is unable to escape
the evidence that the Sanhedrin desired the death of Jesus, even though
Pontius Pilate found no basis for condemning him (Luke 23:22). The reference to Jesus' blood is a clear echo of the response of the Jewish people to
Pilate's assertion, "I am innocent of this man's blood. You yourselves see to it"
(Matt. 27:24). The crowd responded, "Let his blood be on us and our children" (v. 25). Now the members of the Sanhedrin realize that they must take

---

37. The Jewish leaders already ignored the name of Jesus during his ministry and referred to
him as "this deceiver" and "this man." See, e.g., Matt. 27:63; John 9:16, 24; 11:47.

the responsibility for shedding innocent blood. Nevertheless, the high priest strenuously objects to Peter's repeated reminders that the Jewish authorities and the crowd which they had aroused put Jesus to death by nailing him to a cross.[38] The evidence is overwhelmingly against the members of the Jewish court, yet the high priest accuses the apostles of being determined to assign the guilt for Jesus' death to him and his associates.

Greek Words, Phrases, and Constructions in 5:28

οὐ—this negative particle at the beginning of the sentence is part of a rhetorical question that expects an affirmative answer. Its omission turns the sentence into a positive statement. Bruce M. Metzger thinks that the particle "is a scribal addition, occasioned by the influence of the verb ἐπηρώτησεν in ver[se] 27."[39] He and many translators favor omitting this particle.

παραγγελίᾳ παρηγγείλαμεν—the combination of a noun and a verb from the same family reflects the Hebrew infinitive absolute construction. The construction is emphatic and means "we strictly commanded you."[40]

βούλεσθε—although it occurs less frequently in the New Testament than the verb θέλω (I wish), this verb expresses not a simple future but purpose.

---

b. Response
5:29–32

Peter has been the spokesman for the believers ever since Jesus ascended to heaven. He addressed the faithful in the upper room (1:15–22), the multitude at Pentecost (2:14–39), the crowd at Solomon's Colonnade (3:12–26), and the Sanhedrin (4:8–12). Once again Peter addresses that full assembly.

29. Peter and the other apostles replied: "We must obey God rather than men. 30. The God of our fathers raised up Jesus, whom you had put to death by hanging him on a tree."

Peter begins by answering the high priest's first accusation: the apostles' disobedience to the command of the Sanhedrin. Peter's response is identical to what he told the Sanhedrin the last time he addressed it. At that time he asked its members to choose: "Judge whether it is right in God's sight to obey you rather than God" (4:19). Now he plainly asserts that the apostles must obey God rather than men. The Sanhedrists are the spiritual leaders of Israel and for them there should be no choice. Their uniform reply to a question concerning obedience ought to be: "Obey God!" God is the absolute ruler in heaven and on earth.

---

38. Compare Acts 2:23; 3:13–15; 4:10–11.
39. Bruce M. Metzger, *A Textual Commentary on the Greek New Testament,* 3d corrected ed. (London and New York: United Bible Societies, 1975), p. 331.
40. See Moule, *Idiom-Book,* p. 178.

When Peter with the assent of the apostles says that they obey God rather than men, he effectively removes the high priest's objection to the apostles' alleged disobedience. Moreover, from their national history the members of the Jewish council know the validity of the principle to obey God instead of man.[41] For example, the Hebrew midwives obeyed God, not Pharaoh (Exod. 1:17); Hezekiah listened to the Lord and not to the king of Assyria (II Kings 19:14–37). Scripture teaches that God blesses obedience but abhors disobedience. Therefore, the apostles must obey God and not the orders of the high priest.

Next, Peter responds to the high priest's accusation concerning the death of Jesus. He says, "The God of our fathers raised up Jesus, whom you put to death by hanging him on a tree." Peter skillfully presents his answer to the councilmen: he brings the good news that Jesus is alive, because God raised him from the dead. Note that he calls God "the God of our fathers." With these words he reminds his audience of Moses, who was told by God to say to the Israelites in Egypt, "The LORD, the God of your fathers, the God of Abraham, the God of Isaac and the God of Jacob, has sent me to you" (Exod. 3:15). With his indirect reference to the passage recorded by Moses, Peter demonstrates unity and continuity with his fellow Israelites. He boldly refers to Jesus, because Israel's hope and consolation were bundled in the coming of the Messiah, whom God had sent in Jesus Christ.

In the courtroom, Peter reminds the members of the Sanhedrin that they are responsible for Jesus' death by "hanging him on a tree." He chooses the words of this last phrase carefully, but not because he wants to describe Jesus' death by crucifixion in poetic terms. On the contrary, Peter employs these words because they come straight from the Old Testament. When the Jewish authorities plotted Jesus' death, they incited the crowd to shout, "Crucify him." They knew the words of the Old Testament and consequently wanted God to curse him in conformity with the divine injunction: "Anyone who is hanged is under God's curse" (Deut. 21:23; Gal. 3:13; see also Acts 10:39; 13:29; I Peter 2:24). In short, they tried to use God for their own wicked purposes by denying Jesus every vestige of divine grace and favor. They said that God's curse should rest on him as he died on Calvary's cross; according to them, he was not fit to be on this earth and, because of God's curse, heaven would not have him. Peter, therefore, deliberately reminds the high priest and his colleagues of the words of Scripture that they had in mind when they asked Pilate to crucify Jesus.

31. "He is the one whom God exalted to his right hand as Prince and Savior to give repentance to Israel and forgiveness of sins."

The subject of both the preceding verse (v. 30) and this verse is God. By stressing this subject, Peter is clearly saying to the members of the Sanhedrin that they have committed their crime against the Almighty, who raised Jesus from the dead and exalted him to the choicest position in heaven,

---

41. Consult Harrison, *Interpreting Acts,* p. 108.

namely, at God's right hand. They killed Jesus, but God raised him from the dead (see 2:24; 3:15; 4:10). They condemned him by crucifying him, but God exalted Jesus to the highest degree (see 2:33). God is at work in the death, resurrection, and ascension of Jesus.

In a sense, Peter is repeating parts of the sermon he preached at Pentecost. That day he told his audience that Jesus had ascended to heaven to take his place next to God the Father in fulfillment of the messianic prophecy of Psalm 110:1 (2:34–35). Now he is telling the members of the Sanhedrin that they have killed the Messiah, whom God has raised to life and given a place in heaven next to him. That is, they are guilty before both God and Jesus.

Peter describes Jesus as Prince and Savior. He calls him Prince because of Jesus' exalted position and his status as "the Prince of life" (3:15). The term *Savior* occurs only twice in Acts, here and in 13:23. These descriptions are significant. With them, Peter informs his audience that this Prince is not only a ruler, who on the basis of his exalted position and divine authority demands man's obedience. Jesus is also Savior, by whom man must be saved. On an earlier occasion, Peter advised the rulers and elders of Israel that salvation can be received only through the name of Jesus (4:12). Now, more directly, Peter informs them that Jesus is Savior so that "[God may] give repentance to Israel and forgiveness of sins." Although salvation involves the complete turnabout of a sinner's mind, Peter declares that both repentance and remission of sins are gifts of God. The two concepts *repentance* and *forgiveness of sins* are the component parts of the good news preached by John the Baptist (Mark 1:4), by Jesus (Matt. 4:17), and by the apostles (Luke 24:47; Acts 2:38; 13:38). Of course, the significance of Jesus' name is that he saves his people from their sins (Matt. 1:21).[42]

In the courtroom setting of the Sanhedrin, Peter indicates that repentance and remission of sins are God's gifts to Israel. A few years later, the Gentiles also receive remission of sin (10:43) to validate the angelic assertion that "the good news of great joy shall be for all people" (Luke 2:10). Peter already has shown his unity and continuity with his fellow Jews by referring to the God of their fathers. Now he discloses that through Jesus, God has provided salvation for his people Israel. Thus, God offers his gifts even to the members of the Sanhedrin that they may be absolved of their heinous crime.

32. "And we are witnesses of these things, and so is the Holy Spirit, whom God has given to those who obey him."

We note these points:

a. *Witnesses.* Actually, Peter is repeating the words Jesus spoke to the disciples in the upper room on the evening of Easter Sunday. There Jesus

---

42. For further study of the words *Prince* and *Savior,* consult Richard N. Longenecker, *The Christology of Early Jewish Christianity,* Studies in Biblical Theology, 2d series 17 (London: SCM, 1970), pp. 55–58, 141–44.

explained the Scriptures to them; opened their minds that they might understand the messianic fulfillment of these Scriptures; showed them the significance of his suffering, death, and resurrection; told them about preaching in his name repentance and forgiveness of sins; commissioned them as witnesses of these things; and commanded them to wait in Jerusalem until they received power from on high, which is the gift of the Holy Spirit (Luke 24:44–49). Peter echoes Jesus' words, especially when he says that the apostles are witnesses of these things. Peter and the apostles are eyewitnesses and at the same time testify to everyone about the person and work of Jesus Christ.[43]

b. *Holy Spirit.* Peter is not saying that the apostles are on the same level as the Holy Spirit in witnessing for Jesus. Certainly not. In his epistles, Peter clarifies this matter when he writes that in the Scriptures the Holy Spirit pointed to the time and circumstances of Christ's sufferings and his glories that would follow (I Peter 1:11; also see II Peter 1:21). The Holy Spirit qualifies the apostles to testify for Jesus and works through them (Matt. 10:20; John 14:26; 15:26–27).

c. *Gift.* The Holy Spirit is God's gift to his people. Anyone who puts his trust in Jesus, repents, and is baptized and forgiven, receives the Holy Spirit (2:38–39). Peter explicitly states that God gives the Spirit "to those who obey him." Peter calls the high priest and his associates to obedience, faith, and repentance. But if they refuse to accept Jesus as their Savior, they do not receive the gift of the Holy Spirit. Then the guilt of their crime remains with them forever.

Peter uses the word *obey*, which he repeats from the beginning of his defense: "We must obey God rather than men" (v. 29). The term he employs, however, does not merely imply that his listeners should be persuaded to voluntarily assent to someone's orders. This is good in itself. But the word means that one obediently fulfills these orders without delay.[44] This is what Peter is asking of his audience. Should the Sanhedrists obey Jesus, they would experience the working of the Holy Spirit.

Doctrinal Considerations in 5:27–32

Sixteenth-century Scottish Reformer John Knox coined the motto: "With God man is always in the majority." Whether Knox looked at the life of Peter is not known, but from Scripture we learn that Peter courageously faced seventy-one members of Israel's supreme court. He had received no training in legal defense, yet Peter ingeniously answered all the charges leveled against him. As he addressed the Sanhedrin, he experienced the power of the Holy Spirit in effectively formulating and presenting his response.

---

43. See also 1:8, 22; I Peter 5:1.
44. Compare John Albert Bengel, *Gnomon of the New Testament,* ed. Andrew R. Fausset, 5 vols. (Edinburgh: Clark, 1877), vol. 2, p. 562.

The high priest realized that by teaching the gospel of Jesus Christ, the apostles continually told the crowds in Jerusalem that the Sanhedrin was guilty of shedding innocent blood. The gospel, therefore, placed them under judgment and called them to repentance, faith, and obedience. If they should listen to the preaching of the apostles, they would have to leave the priesthood. They faced the crucial decision: to cast their lot either for or against Jesus. The writer of Acts records that "a large number of priests became obedient to the faith" (6:7, NIV).

Greek Words, Phrases, and Constructions in 5:29–32

Verse 29

οἱ ἀπόστολοι—the word ἄλλοι (other) is implied;[45] thus, "Peter and the other apostles."

πειθαρχεῖν δεῖ—"it is necessary to obey." In this case, the words signify divine necessity. The compound derives from πείθομαι (I am persuaded) and ἀρχή (a leader): "to obey a ruler."[46] In his address, Peter uses the verb twice (see v. 32).

Verse 30

διεχειρίσασθε—this verb in the aorist middle occurs once in the New Testament. The compound form is perfective, "to lay violent hands on."

κρεμάσαντες—an aorist participle that expresses means or manner: "by hanging him on a tree."

Verse 31

τῇ δεξιᾷ—the dative case can be either means or place: either "with his right hand" or "to his right hand." Translators are divided on this point of grammar. See 2:33.

τοῦ δοῦναι—the aorist active infinitive from δίδωμι (I give) with the definite article in the genitive case denotes purpose.

Verse 32

τῶν ῥημάτων—literally the noun means "words" but the context demands the translation *things*.

---

4. Wisdom and Persuasion
5:33–40

Many in the courtroom reacted negatively to Peter's response, while others were sympathetic to the cause of the believers. And we assume that still others (e.g., Nicodemus) were followers of Jesus Christ. Consequently, the high priest was unable to count on full support from the members of the Sanhedrin.

---

45. Robertson, *Grammar*, p. 747.
46. Thayer, p. 497.

a. Reaction
5:33–34

33. And when they heard this, they were stung in their hearts and wanted to kill them. 34. But a member of the Sanhedrin, a Pharisee named Gamaliel, a teacher of the law and respected by all the people, stood up and ordered that the men be put outside for a little while.

The apostles who proclaim Christ's gospel can say: "To the one we are the smell of death; to the other, the fragrance of life" (II Cor. 2:16, NIV). When the Jews at Pentecost come to Peter after his sermon, they are cut to the heart and repentant (2:37). When the Sadducees in the Sanhedrin hear the words of Peter, they are cut to the heart not because of repentance, but anger. They are so furious that they want to kill the apostles (compare 7:54). They refuse to accept the gospel that calls them to obey God and instead want to rid the earth of Jesus' followers. Even though they have no power to execute the death sentence, they will try to find a way to kill them (see 7:57–58). With the help of the Roman governor, they had executed Jesus; now they want to remove his disciples.

During Jesus' ministry, his opponents were the Pharisees and the experts in the law. The Sadducees hardly ever approached him with questions (Matt. 22:23). In the post-Pentecost era, however, the Sadducees feel threatened by the growing influence of the apostles. But opposition from the Pharisees is subdued. In fact, some of the Pharisees see an ally in the Christians, who preach the doctrine of the resurrection. The Pharisees, who cherish this doctrine, oppose the Sadducees, who repudiate it; therefore, they welcome the support they receive from the Christian community.[47] In the Sanhedrin, the Pharisees hold the balance of power and one of them, Gamaliel by name, even gives counsel that favors the apostles.

"A Pharisee named Gamaliel, a teacher of the law." Gamaliel was born into a family of teachers of the Mosaic law. He was the son of Rabbi Simeon and a grandson of the influential Rabbi Hillel, who had founded a school for the Pharisees. Gamaliel became a leader in that school, which was known for a more liberal trend than its rival, the school of Rabbi Shammai. Gamaliel was a tolerant and cautious man who also served in the Sanhedrin as one of its learned members.[48] Paul was one of his students, for when Paul identified himself he said that he was educated and trained in the law by Gamaliel (22:3). Paul, however, adopted an intolerant attitude toward the early Christians and tried to destroy the church of Christ (see Gal. 1:23). We know that students sometimes disagree with their teachers and follow a course that goes contrary to what they have learned.

"[Gamaliel was] respected by all the people." In Jewish literature, Gama-

---

47. Richard B. Rackham, *The Acts of the Apostles: An Exposition*, Westminster Commentaries series (1901; reprint ed., Grand Rapids: Baker, 1964), p. 45.

48. Ronald F. Youngblood, "Gamaliel," *ISBE*, vol. 2, pp. 393–94.

liel is mentioned repeatedly as Rabban Gamaliel the Elder (in distinction from his grandson Gamaliel II), who submitted sage advice and counsel concerning matters related to a relaxation of Sabbath observance and protection for women in case of divorce. The Jews looked to him for leadership especially in the Sanhedrin. His period of influence was approximately A.D. 25–50.[49] Luke, who perhaps obtained the substance of Peter's address from a sympathetic council member, portrays Gamaliel as an outstanding leader at the trial of the apostles.

Greek Words, Phrases, and Constructions in 5:33–34

διεπρίοντο—the imperfect passive from διαπρίω (I saw in two) signifies continued action in the past tense. The compound is directive.

βραχύ—used adverbially, this word expresses time (a little while), not place or quantity.

---

b. Wisdom
5:35–39

Gamaliel calls for a closed session of the assembly and therefore orders that the apostles be dismissed for a while (compare 4:15). In the meantime, he addresses the council and gives advice.

35. He said to the Sanhedrin, "Men of Israel, be careful what you intend to do with these men. 36. Some time ago, Theudas rose up saying that he was somebody. About four hundred men rallied to him; but when he was killed, all his followers were dispersed and came to nothing."

Notice that Gamaliel separates himself from the intentions of the high priests and his Sadducaic associates. He does not use the first person plural *we* to include himself in the decisions of the Sanhedrin. Instead he addresses his colleagues of the court in the second person plural *you* and indicates that he is not party to the actions of the assembly but only serves it in an advisory role. He observes others inflamed with hatred and anger to the point of rashly committing murder, which he as a man of moderation is unable to condone. Hence, with calm words and two examples from recent history he tries to temper the excesses of the Sanhedrin.[50]

a. *Theudas.* Gamaliel mentions Theudas (the name perhaps is a contraction of Theodorus, Theodotus, or Theodosius), who set himself up as a leader. He attracted four hundred men who rallied around him. But he was killed and his followers dispersed. Luke provides no date for this incident. We assume that he presents his examples in historical sequence and that this event occurred prior to the uprising led by Judas the Galilean in

---

49. Consult SB, vol. 2, pp. 636–39.
50. Calvin, *Acts of the Apostles,* vol. 1, p. 152.

A.D. 6 (v. 37). Josephus relates an account about a certain Theudas, a self-proclaimed prophet, who persuaded masses of people to take their possessions and follow him to the Jordan; he promised them to lead them across the river dry-shod. There Cuspius Fadus, procurator of Judea (A.D. 44–46), and his soldiers killed Theudas and a number of his followers.[51]

Some scholars object that Luke mentions an event that happened more than a decade after Gamaliel addressed the Sanhedrin. But because Josephus did not write this account until A.D. 93, Luke had no recourse to the *Antiquities* of Flavius Josephus. Apart from the date, Josephus's account differs significantly in wording from the example Gamaliel presents to the Sanhedrin. The possibility is not remote, therefore, that another person named Theudas led a rebellion that took place before the time of Judas the Galilean.[52]

With this example, Gamaliel intimates that as Theudas had a following of some four hundred persons but was killed and his followers dispersed, so Jesus has adherents. Jesus, however, has been crucified and so, Gamaliel implies, his leaderless followers will eventually disband.

37. "After this man, Judas of Galilee appeared at the time of the census and caused the people to revolt and follow him. He too was killed and all who followed him were scattered."

b. *Judas.* During the reign of Emperor Augustus, a census was conducted at least twice: once in 6 B.C. (Luke 2:2) and again in A.D. 6. Since conducting a census involved not only counting the population but also paying property taxes to the Roman government, the Jewish population resented the people who conducted the census. In A.D. 6, riots broke out in protest of Roman taxation. Judas, a native of Gamala in Gaulanitis (the Golan Heights), rebelled, caused "the people to revolt," and mustered the support of the Jewish people. But Judas was killed when Roman forces squashed his revolt and scattered his followers.[53] A result of Judas's rebellion was the rise of the Zealot party, to which one of the twelve disciples, Simon the Zealot, belonged (Matt. 10:4).

Gamaliel's second example, then, is not as striking as his first illustration. Whereas the followers of Theudas were dispersed, some of those who belonged to Judas became Zealots and were part of the political fabric of first-century Judea. In a similar vein, Jesus died but his disciples altered Israel's religious configuration.

With the second example, Gamaliel advises his colleagues: as you tolerate the Zealots so tolerate the Christians.

38. "So in this case I suggest to you: Stay away from these men and let

---

51. Josephus *Antiquities* 20.5.1 [97].

52. SB, vol. 2, p. 640. An analogous situation is two separate uprisings in Ireland in 1848 and 1891. In both rebellions, a certain William O'Brien was leader. See Grosheide, *Handelingen der Apostelen*, vol. 1, p. 184 n. 3.

53. Josephus *Antiquities* 17.13.5 [354]; 18.1.1 [1]. He lists the exact date of the census as "the thirty-seventh year after Caesar's defeat of Anthony," which is A.D. 6 (see 18.2.1 [26]).

them go! For if this plan or movement is of human origin, it will fail. 39. But if it is of God, you will be unable to overthrow them; you will even find yourselves fighting against God." And they were persuaded by him.

Gamaliel applies his examples to the case before the court and advises the Sanhedrin to leave the apostles alone and to set them free. He counsels the members of the court not to get involved and implies that their involvement in the death of Jesus now rests as a burden of guilt on their consciences. He tells the Sanhedrists to release the apostles, just as they let Peter and John go free at an earlier trial.

By using two conditional sentences, Gamaliel convinces his audience that if the new movement is of human origin, it will fail. But if its origin is divine, the Sanhedrin will fail because the court will be fighting God. In the Greek, these two sentences reveal a difference in emphasis. That is, the first conditional sentence expresses Gamaliel's uncertainty: "For if this plan or movement is of human origin, it will fail." The examples from their own history are proof that manmade movements are fruitless and cause more harm than good.

From what Gamaliel has seen and heard in Jerusalem, he is not at all convinced that this new religion is of human origin in purpose and activity. He knows that the apostles themselves repeatedly teach first that their religion is the fulfillment of the Scriptures and second that they must be obedient to God (vv. 29, 32). Hence, in the second conditional sentence, Gamaliel expresses reality or simple fact: "But if it is of God, you will be unable to overthrow them; you will even find yourselves fighting against God." Gamaliel implies that Christianity originates with God. He therefore persuades the members of the court to release the apostles.

The Western text of Greek manuscripts expands verses 38 and 39 by adding words and phrases and by providing an interesting commentary on Gamaliel's advice. Here is the translation with the additions in italics:

> So in the present case, *brethren,* I tell you, keep away from these men and let them go, *without defiling your hands;* for if this plan or this undertaking is of men, it will fail but if it is of God, you will not be able to overthrow them—*neither you nor kings nor tyrants. Therefore keep away from these men,* lest you be found opposing God.[54]

The last clause, "you will even find yourselves fighting against God," is a complete sentence that is separate from the preceding. Gamaliel resorts to uttering a warning when he calls his fellow Jews to recognize a truth they know from the Scriptures: "Do not fight against the LORD God of your fathers, for you will not succeed" (II Chron. 13:12; see also Prov. 21:30).

---

54. Metzger, *Textual Commentary,* p. 335.

Greek Words, Phrases, and Constructions in 5:35–39

Verse 35

προσέχετε ἑαυτοῖς ἐπί—the present imperative with the reflexive pronoun in the dative case ("pay attention to yourselves") is followed by ἐπί, meaning "in the case of" or "against."

μέλλετε—with the present infinitive, it is the equivalent of the future tense (compare 9:44).

Verse 36

διελύθησαν—the compound has a perfective connotation: "to loose completely" or "to dissolve."

Verses 38–39

ἐὰν ᾖ–this conditional sentence with the present subjunctive denotes uncertainty. The use of εἰ with the present indicative ἐστιν expresses certainty. Comments A. T. Robertson: "Gamaliel gives the benefit of doubt to Christianity. He assumes that Christianity is of God and puts the alternative that it is of men in the third class [conditional sentence]. This does not, of course, show that Gamaliel was a Christian or an inquirer. He was merely willing to score a point against the Sadducees."[55]

---

c. Persuasion
5:40

40. After summoning the apostles, they flogged them and ordered them to speak no more in the name of Jesus; then they released them.

Gamaliel's prudent counsel calms his colleagues. He persuades them to release the apostles (see 4:21). Notice that he, a Pharisee, is able to give effective leadership in the Sanhedrin dominated by the Sadducees. His learning, knowledge of the Mosaic law, and respect from the Jewish population make him a formidable spokesman whose advice is readily accepted.

The high priest and his associates call in the apostles. Instead of hurling threats at them as they had done previously, they punish the apostles with flogging. According to the Mosaic law, a man who is guilty of a crime deserves to receive a beating. The judge orders the man to lie down and has him flogged in his presence. He punishes the man with the number of lashes he has decreed, but he may not exceed forty lashes (Deut. 25:2–3). Paul writes that he was flogged five times and that he received from the Jews the stipulated forty lashes minus one (II Cor. 11:24). Lower Jewish

---

55. Robertson, *Grammar*, p. 1018.

councils punished lawbreakers with floggings meted out in the synagogues (Matt. 10:17).

> Floggings were administered with a whip made of calfskin on the bare upper body of the offender—one third of the lashes being given on the breast and the other two thirds on the back. The offender stood in a bowed position with the one administering the beating on a stone above him and the blows were accompanied by the recital of admonitory and consolatory verses from Scripture.[56]

The court releases the apostles with the command "not to speak in the name of Jesus" (see 4:18). The members of the Sanhedrin acknowledge their inability to stop the growth of the church, for they demonstrate their weakness by submitting the apostles to floggings.

5. Rejoicing
5:41–42

The apostles' reactions seem contrary to ordinary human emotions. When Jesus leaves the disciples at his ascension, they return to Jerusalem "with great joy" (Luke 24:52). When the apostles are flogged, they leave the Sanhedrin rejoicing. The followers of Jesus look at life from a divine perspective and say that suffering for Jesus is an honor.

41. Therefore, the apostles went out from the presence of the Sanhedrin and rejoiced because they had been considered worthy to suffer disgrace for the Name.

Because the Sanhedrin ordered the apostles to be flogged, the general public would have to consider them criminals who had broken the law—to be precise, the order not to speak or teach in the name of Jesus. The flogging marks branded the apostles as lawbreakers and were meant to be signs of disgrace.

But the apostles were not ashamed of their punishment. Instead they remembered Jesus' beatitude to rejoice and be glad whenever people would utter insults and instigate persecutions against his followers. Said Jesus, "Your reward in heaven is great" (Matt. 5:12). In later years, Peter himself encourages the oppressed Christians in Asia Minor: "Rejoice insofar as you share in the sufferings of Christ" (I Peter 4:13; see also II Thess. 1:4). Paul in his epistle to the Romans also informs his readers that Christians rejoice in their sufferings (5:3). In brief, Christians are triumphant and joyous when they suffer for the name of Jesus.

The expression *name* in this verse is significant and therefore is capitalized in some translations.[57] It embraces God's truth revealed in Jesus as Savior of the world. In this abbreviated form, "the Name" refers to Jesus,

---

56. H. Cohn, "Flogging," *Encyclopaedia Judaica*, vol. 6, p. 1350.
57. E.g., NAB, NEB, NIV.

his person and work, and the good news his people proclaim (see 9:16; III John 7). Incidentally, the early Christians often employed brief terms to identify Christianity (e.g., "the Way" [9:2; 19:9, 23; 22:4; 24:14, 22]).

42. And every day in the temple and from house to house they did not stop teaching and preaching the good news that Jesus is the Christ.

The apostles had their day in court and won. Obedient to the command of the Lord to tell the people the full message of salvation (v. 20), they disregard the command of the Sanhedrin. In fact, they return to the same place where the captain of the temple arrested them. They teach in the temple courts, presumably Solomon's Colonnade, and do so in the knowledge that the high priest is unable to stop them. In the temple courts they daily meet the crowds and engage in mass communication. But they direct their evangelistic efforts also to individual people and therefore teach families from house to house. Centuries earlier, Jeremiah prophesied a word from God:

> "No longer will a man teach his neighbor,
>   or a man his brother, saying, 'Know the LORD,'
> because they will all know me,
>   from the least of them to the greatest." [Jer. 31:34, NIV]

This prophecy is being fulfilled in Jerusalem. Everywhere in the city the people know that Jesus is the Christ, who has fulfilled the messianic prophecies of the Scriptures (2:36).

Doctrinal Considerations in 5:41–42

In the words of his well-known hymn, Isaac Watts asks a penetrating question:

> Am I a soldier of the cross,
> A foll'wer of the Lamb,
> And shall I fear to own his cause,
> Or blush to speak his Name?

The apostles not only proclaimed the name of Jesus in the temple courts and from house to house; they even thanked the Lord for being found worthy to suffer for his name. This does not mean that Christians should actively seek persecution and reprisal, because suffering for the sake of a reward promotes man's ego and thus is worthless in God's sight. Nor should a Christian actively avoid suffering for Christ's sake, for that is a demonstration of cowardice. When God puts a Christian through trying times in which suffering is unavoidable, the believer ought to rejoice and be glad, for his reward will be great in heaven. Adversities are God's tools to strengthen the believer in faith and trust. The troubles the Christian experiences today are momentary and cannot be compared to the eternal glory that awaits him in heaven (II Cor. 4:17).

Greek Words, Phrases, and Constructions in 5:41–42

Verse 41

μὲν οὖν—this combination expresses a resumptive and transitional idea. It does not indicate contrast, because δέ is lacking. A simple translation is "and so."[58] The translators of the New International Version omit it.

ἐπορεύοντο—the imperfect middle is descriptive and durative. It should be taken with the present participle *rejoicing*.

ὑπέρ—with the genitive case, this preposition means "for the sake of."

Verse 42

οὐκ ἐπαύοντο—in the imperfect middle, this verb shows continued action in the past tense and controls two present participles to supplement its meaning. They are διδάσκοντες (teaching) and εὐαγγελιζόμενοι (proclaiming the good news).

Summary of Chapter 5

Ananias tries to deceive the Holy Spirit, is rebuked by Peter, and is punished with sudden death by God. His wife, Sapphira, who agreed to the deception, is questioned by Peter and meets a fate similar to that of her husband. The sudden death of these two persons brings great fear upon the church and upon the people who hear about it.

The apostles perform numerous miracles by healing the sick and the demon-possessed. Even the shadow of Peter falling upon them is sufficient to bring healing.

The high priest and his associates are filled with jealousy and have the apostles arrested and put in jail. An angel delivers them during the night and instructs them to preach the Good News in the temple courts. This they do the next morning. When officers sent by the high priest come to the jail to bring the apostles to the courtroom of the Sanhedrin, they find the jail empty. They find the apostles in the temple area and escort them to the Sanhedrin to stand trial. The high priest accuses them of disobeying the strict orders not to teach in the name of Jesus, but Peter, with the other apostles, defends their activities and proclaims Christ and his resurrection. The members of the Sanhedrin are furious to the point of killing the apostles, but Gamaliel intervenes with sage advice. He persuades the Sanhedrin to release the apostles. After being flogged, the apostles return to the temple courts and continue to teach and proclaim Christ's gospel.

---

58. Moule, *Idiom-Book*, p. 162.

6

The Church in Jerusalem, *part 5*

6:1–15

Outline (continued)

6:1–8:1a   D. Stephen's Ministry and Death

6:1–7   1. Seven Men Appointed

6:1–4   a. Problem and Proposal

6:5–7   b. Implementation and Result

6:8–15   2. Stephen's Arrest

6:8–10   a. Opposition

6:11–15   b. Arrest and Testimony

6 1 And in those days, when the number of disciples continued to increase, there was a complaint from the Greek-speaking Jews against the Aramaic-speaking Jews, because their widows were being overlooked in the daily distribution of food. 2 Then the Twelve called together the whole community of disciples and said, "It is not right for us to stop teaching the word of God to serve at tables. 3 Brothers, select from among you seven men of good reputation, who are full of the Spirit and wisdom, whom we will appoint to this task. 4 But we will devote ourselves to prayer and the ministry of the word."

5 This proposal pleased the whole community. Thus, they chose Stephen, a man full of faith and of the Holy Spirit; and Philip, Prochorus, Nicanor, Timon, Parmenas, and Nicolas of Antioch, who had been a convert to Judaism. 6 They introduced these men to the apostles, who prayed and placed their hands on them.

7 As the word of God continued to spread, the number of disciples in Jerusalem continued to increase more and more. And a great number of priests became obedient to the faith.

D. Stephen's Ministry and Death
6:1–8:1a

1. Seven Men Appointed
6:1–7

Luke introduces a new phase in the development of the church. Its incessant growth creates administrative problems that affect the unity of the church. The twelve apostles are teaching the people the apostolic doctrine (2:42) and evangelizing the neighborhoods of Jerusalem. They also have the responsibility of distributing the gifts placed in their possession to alleviate the needs of the poor. Now a problem arises among the Greek-speaking Christians whose widows suffer neglect in respect to the daily distribution of food.

a. Problem and Proposal
6:1–4

1. And in those days, when the number of disciples continued to increase, there was a complaint from the Greek-speaking Jews against the Aramaic-speaking Jews, because their widows were being overlooked in the daily distribution of food.

a. "In those days." We are unable to determine the exact year or time to which Luke refers. He evidently reports about the days that followed the trial of the apostles and their concerted effort to preach and teach the gospel throughout Jerusalem. The result of this intensive activity is that the membership of the church increased by leaps and bounds. How many Christians belonged to the Jerusalem church is difficult to say. We assume that the church doubled in size from the last figure Luke provided: "five thousand men" (4:4; see also 5:14).

Population statistics for first-century Jerusalem are nothing more than estimates. Figures from ancient sources, together with estimates provided by modern scholars, are available. But these figures reflect a disparity that ranges from an estimate of three million inhabitants to another of twenty thousand.[1] William S. LaSor aptly concludes, "Figures from ancient records, incredible as they seem, are often no more erroneous than scholarly estimates."[2]

Notice that Luke identifies the believers as disciples. In the time of Jesus' ministry, the Twelve but also the seventy were known as disciples. Now these twelve apostles have become teachers and the new converts are their disciples (e.g., 6:1, 2, 7; 9:1, 10, 19).

b. "There was a complaint from the Greek-speaking Jews." From the Pentecost account we learn that devout Jews had come from the dispersion to settle in Jerusalem (2:5–11). Many of these devout Jews were elderly people who wanted to spend the rest of their lives in the holy city. Because they had formerly resided elsewhere, their native tongue was Greek, not Aramaic or Hebrew (which was spoken by the Jews in Jerusalem). Many of these people accepted Christ's gospel and became part of the Christian church. However, each group had its own synagogue before these people became Christians, and when they became disciples the Greek-speaking and the Aramaic-speaking believers continued to have their own assemblies. Furthermore, each group used its own Bible; the Greek-speaking Jews were accustomed to the Septuagint (a Greek translation of the Hebrew Scriptures) and the Hebraic Jews read the Old Testament in the original Hebrew. Here, then, is the beginning of a division brought about by linguistic and cultural differences.

The term translated "Greek-speaking Jews" appears in the Greek text as "Hellenists." This Greek term has created much discussion among scholars from early Christianity to the present. If we discount textual variants, we find it three times in Acts. In 6:1, translators correctly give it the meaning *Greek-speaking Jewish Christians*. The term also occurs in 9:29, where it signifies Greek-speaking Jews who were not Christians. In 11:20, it refers to people who are neither Jew nor Christian but whose native tongue is Greek. Scholars generally conclude that the meaning of the expression *Hellenists* must be determined by the context in which it is used.[3]

---

1. Josephus *War* 2.14.3 [280]; Joachim Jeremias, *Jerusalem in the Time of Jesus* (Philadelphia: Fortress, 1969), p. 84.

2. William S. LaSor, "Jerusalem," *ISBE,* vol. 2, p. 1014.

3. Representative literature on this point includes H. J. Cadbury, "The Hellenists," *Beginnings,* vol. 5, pp. 59–74; E. C. Blackman, "The Hellenists of Acts vi.1," *ExpT* 48 (1937): 524–25; C. F. D. Moule, "Once More, Who Were the Hellenists," *ExpT* 70 (1959): 100–102.

c. "Their widows were being overlooked." The Aramaic-speaking Christians in Jerusalem were in the majority and the Greek-speaking believers formed a minority. Although harmony and unity were the characteristics of the Christian church, linguistic and cultural differences caused inevitable separation. Especially the widows in this minority group felt alienated and forsaken. They "were being overlooked in the daily distribution of food," but could no longer go to the local synagogue for financial aid. The wording of the text states only the fact that the widows of Greek-speaking Jews suffered neglect; it does not imply that the apostles were to blame for this oversight.

In view of their many responsibilities, the apostles are unable to do justice to caring for the financial needs of all the widows. The evidence shows that the apostles are too busy. Hence, the situation is reminiscent of Moses judging the people of Israel. Moses' father-in-law, Jethro, advised him to choose capable men and have them serve as judges for the people (Exod. 18:17–26). This eased the burden on Moses. So the apostles attempt to solve the problem of taking care of the needy.

2. Then the Twelve called together the whole community of disciples and said, "It is not right for us to stop teaching the word of God to serve at tables. 3. Brothers, select from among you seven men of good reputation, who are full of the Spirit and wisdom, whom we will appoint to this task. 4. But we will devote ourselves to prayer and the ministry of the word."

Notice these points:

a. *The Twelve.* This is the only time in Acts that Luke uses the descriptive term *the Twelve* for the apostles.[4] He employs the expression to indicate that next to the body of twelve apostles another body of seven administrators serves the needs of the growing church. Thus far the Twelve have had the full responsibility of caring for the spiritual and physical needs of the believers. But the time has come to find relief.

The twelve apostles call together the entire Christian community to make an important decision. We do not expect that all the believers were able to be present at one particular meeting, for then the proceedings would become unwieldy. The Twelve are in charge of the meeting and place before the believers a matter of priority: "It is not right for us to stop teaching the word of God to serve at tables." Their primary task is to teach and preach the gospel of salvation. Because of their leadership role, the apostles also assumed the responsibility to care for the needy. But this secondary task should not cause them to stop preaching the word of God. They must devote themselves to prayer and the ministry of the word (v. 4).

The Twelve with the help of the Christian community find a solution: appointing some men to serve at tables. The meaning of the word *tables* relates to the phrase *daily distribution,* which points to either sharing food or

---

4. In his Gospel, the term occurs six times (Luke 8:1; 9:1, 12; 18:31; 22:3, 47).

doling out money designated for buying food.[5] Qualified men in the church are able to perform this duty. Therefore, the apostles propose that seven men be appointed to this task.

b. *Seven men.* Here are a few considerations. First, the number seven represents the number of fullness. The apostles suggest the number, the church selects seven men, and the apostles ordain them. Next, in this passage Luke refrains from using the term *deacon,* yet he indicates that the apostles at this time ordained seven men to the special office of ministering to the poor (see also Phil. 1:1; I Tim. 3:8–13). Third, the men must meet two requirements: they must have a good reputation and they must be full of the Holy Spirit and wisdom. Of course, for the task of distributing food and money a person must have a reputation that is above reproach and a recommendation that his peers and superiors gladly provide (compare 10:22; 16:2; 22:12). Also, a person helping the needy must be full of the Holy Spirit and wisdom (refer to Num. 27:16–18).

There is no separation of sacred and secular for the Holy Spirit; he fills both the twelve apostles and the seven chosen men. In fact, Stephen and Philip not only distribute food and finances, but also preach the Word and perform miracles (vv. 8–10; 8:6).

c. *Prayer.* "But we will devote ourselves to prayer and the ministry of the word." The work which the apostles must do is, first, to be constantly in prayer. This is exactly how Luke portrays the apostles and the church (see 1:14; 2:42; 4:24). And the second assignment is to teach and preach Christ's gospel (see especially 5:20, 42).

Practical Considerations in 6:1 and 4

Verse 1

The New Testament, not to mention the Old Testament Scriptures, has much to say about the status and lot of the widow in Israel. Many widows in first-century Palestine faced poverty, even though the Jewish authorities had made provisions for their support (e.g., Mark 12:42–44). Within the church, the principle prevailed that there should not be any needy persons among the believers. Note that James categorizes caring for orphans and widows as a part of religion that is pure and undefiled (James 1:27). Paul also proscribes rules and regulations: for widows who really need daily support; for those who ought to be supported by children and grandchildren; for widows who are sixty years and older; for younger widows who should marry; and for Christian women who should help support widows (I Tim. 5:3–16).

---

5. Consult Kirsopp Lake, "The Communism of Acts ii and iv–vi and the Appointment of the Seven," *Beginnings,* vol. 5, pp. 148–49. And see SB, vol. 2, pp. 641–47. Other interpretations for the expression *table* are the table of the moneychanger and the Lord's table. But these two meanings do not fit the context.

Verse 4

A century ago, pastors usually put the initials *V. D. M.* after their name. This is not an abbreviation of an academic degree but a description of their task. The initials are Latin for *Verbi Domini Minister,* that is, minister of the Word of the Lord. A pastor, strictly speaking, is not a minister of the church, even if he is ordained by that body. He is not a minister of a local congregation, even though a church council or board supervises his work and pays his salary. A pastor is first and foremost a minister of Christ's gospel, for Jesus sends him forth to teach and preach the Good News (Matt. 28:19–20). The pastor, then, is a servant of God's Word. As Paul puts it, "How can the people hear unless someone preaches [the Word]?" (Rom. 10:14). But if the pastor is a servant of the Word, then he ought to devote himself fully to the task of proclaiming the glad gospel tidings. He ought to guard against attractions that take him away from his task. Genuine devotion to prayer and preaching will crown his work with untold blessings.

Greek Words, Phrases, and Constructions in 6:1–4

Verse 1

πληθυνόντων—together with the noun μαθητῶν (disciples) in the genitive case, here is the genitive absolute construction.

πρός—in context, the preposition means "against." It connotes an indirect approach rather than the direct ἀντί (face to face).

Verse 2

ἀρεστόν—the verbal adjective from the verb ἀρέσκω (I please; see v. 5) with the negative particle οὐκ (not) signifies "it is not desirable."[6]

καταλείψαντας—from the directive compound verb καταλείπω (I leave to one side, give up), the aorist active participle denotes manner. Both the pronoun ἡμᾶς (the subject of the infinitive) and the present infinitive διακονεῖν (to serve) comprise the main verbal construction.

Verse 4

τῇ—note the two definite articles preceding the nouns προσευχῇ (prayer) and διακονίᾳ (ministry). Both articles signify that the writer points to stated prayer and preaching services.

προσκαρτερήσομεν—for an explanation of the verb, see 1:14. The pronoun ἡμεῖς expresses emphasis. The position of the pronoun at the beginning of the sentence and the position of the verb at the end denote emphasis.

---

b. Implementation and Result
6:5–7

5. This proposal pleased the whole community. Thus, they chose Stephen, a man full of faith and of the Holy Spirit; and Philip, Prochorus,

---

6. Bauer, p. 105.

Nicanor, Timon, Parmenas, and Nicolas of Antioch, who had been a convert to Judaism. 6. They introduced these men to the apostles, who prayed and placed their hands on them.

The apostles propose and the church approves their suggestion. The word *pleased* denotes a basic harmony between apostles and the Christian community. The complaint has been withdrawn and the irritation concerning the financial neglect has subsided. As a result, the church enters into the work of finding seven capable men. How the people instituted and regulated the search for these men is not known. Luke says nothing about casting the lot (compare 1:26), but the verb *to choose* indicates that a selection was made based on the rules stipulated by the apostles. Incidentally, Christ chose the twelve apostles (including Matthias; see 1:24), but the church chooses the seven men whom the apostles installed.

Who are these seven men? All the names are of Greek origin. Although some native Jews had Greek names, among them the apostles Philip and Andrew,[7] scholars favor the explanation that all seven were Hellenistic Jews whose native tongue was Greek. The first name is Stephen, which actually means "a crown." In a sense, he received the crown of righteousness when he died a martyr's death. Stephen meets the requirements the apostles set, for Luke reports that he is a man "full of faith and of the Holy Spirit." He is known for his faith, as he demonstrates in his teaching and preaching. Philip is next. He is later known as the evangelist (21:8). Then follow the names of Prochorus, Nicanor, Timon, and Parmenas, of whom we know nothing. The last man is Nicolas, a native of Antioch and a Gentile who had been converted first to Judaism and now to Christianity. Perhaps Luke has a special interest in Nicolas, because, according to tradition, he himself was born and reared a Gentile in Antioch and afterward became a Christian.[8] Here, then, are seven Hellenists, of whom six were of Jewish descent. The seventh is Nicolas, a Gentile who entered the church as a proselyte. Nicolas has often been identified as the father of the Nicolaitans, who are mentioned in Revelation 2:6, 15. "The Nicolaitans certainly derived their name from some Nicolas—whether from this Nicolas or another must remain uncertain."[9] The fact that all the candidates are Hellenists undoubtedly appeases the Greek-speaking part of the Jerusalem church.

The church presents these seven men to the apostles, who approve the choice the church has made. Then the apostles present these men in prayer

---

7. Henry Alford, *Alford's Greek Testament: An Exegetical and Critical Commentary*, 7th ed., 4 vols. (1877; Grand Rapids: Guardian, 1976), vol. 2, p. 63.

8. Consult F. F. Bruce, *The Book of the Acts*, rev. ed., New International Commentary on the New Testament series (Grand Rapids: Eerdmans, 1988), p. 121.

9. Ibid.

to God and seek divine approval and blessings upon the work that awaits the seven administrators. After the prayer, the apostles ordain these seven servants by placing their hands upon them. Thus, they adopt the practice that Moses inaugurated for the ordaining of the Levites for special service and for the commissioning of Joshua as Moses' successor (Num. 8:10; 27:23). In New Testament times, not only the apostles adhere to the rite of the laying on of hands to commission qualified persons; but also the church in Antioch obediently listens to the Holy Spirit and places hands on Barnabas and Paul (13:2–3; see also I Tim. 5:22).[10]

7. As the word of God continued to spread, the number of disciples in Jerusalem continued to increase more and more. And a great number of priests became obedient to the faith.

Throughout his book, Luke records summaries that describe the phenomenal growth of the early church. For instance, at the conclusion of his Pentecost report he states that the Lord daily added people to the three thousand believers (2:41, 47).[11] Literally, the Greek text has the reading, "the word of God continued to increase." This does not mean that the New Testament Scriptures increased with the addition of certain books, but that the gospel itself became part of the spiritual lives of the people. In other words, the effect of the proclaimed word became increasingly noticeable in the lives of the inhabitants of Jerusalem. As a direct result of the preaching and teaching of the apostles, who could now devote themselves fully to prayer and the ministry of the Word, more and more people believed and joined the church.

Luke adds one more observation to this summary. "And a great number of priests became obedient to the faith." The Jewish historian Josephus relates that in his day there were four priestly tribes and that each one of them numbered some five thousand members. "These officiate by rotation for a fixed period of days."[12] On any given day, therefore, there were some five thousand priests in Jerusalem. Obviously, a large number of priests, persuaded by the preaching of the gospel, joined the church. Note that Luke uses the term *faith* as synonymous with Christ's gospel (compare 13:8). This term means the objective faith embodied in doctrinal teaching and not the subjective faith of the believer. Indeed, Luke employs various expressions to describe Christianity in this formative period of the church: the Name (5:41), the Way (9:2), and the Faith (6:7).

---

10. In addition to commissioning services, the practice in the New Testament also relates to the blessing of children (Mark 10:16), healing (Mark 1:41; Acts 28:8), receiving the Holy Spirit (Acts 8:17; 19:6), and spiritual gifts (I Tim. 4:14; II Tim. 1:6).

11. See also 4:4; 5:14; 6:1; 9:31; 12:24; 16:5; 19:20; 28:31.

12. Josephus *Against Apion* 2.8 [108] (LCL). Also compare Ezra 2:36–39 and Neh. 7:39–42, which list 4,289 priests returning after the exile. In the centuries following the return, this number increased substantially.

Doctrinal Considerations in 6:5–7

Although the term *deacon* (one who serves) does not occur in the first six verses of this chapter, the Greek word *diakonia* appears twice and is translated "distribution" (v. 1) and "ministry" (v. 4). The context discloses that the seven men are servants on behalf of Christ, that is, deacons, who help the needy. In later years Paul delineates the role of the deacon (I Tim. 3:8–13). But in Acts, both Stephen and Philip preach. In fact, Philip is called "the evangelist" (21:8). Both perform miracles (6:8; 8:6), and Philip even baptizes an Ethiopian (8:38).

Does the work of a deacon differ from that of teachers and preachers of the gospel? Certainly. Apart from the preaching and the healing ministry of Stephen and Philip, the fundamental reason for the appointment of these seven men is to alleviate the needs of the poor. In Acts, the men provide the Greek-speaking widows with the necessities of life and by doing so take this responsibility out of the apostles' hands. In turn, the apostles devote themselves completely to the task of praying and preaching. The primary responsibility of the deacon, then, is to serve the poor on behalf of Christ. Because Paul mentions elders and deacons in the church at Philippi (Phil. 1:1) and instructs Timothy about overseers and deacons (I Tim. 3:1–13), we know that the church at large recognizes the two offices of elder and deacon. Church fathers of the first and second centuries verify the existence of these offices and even refer to the seven men of Acts 6 as deacons. In the history of the church, the term *deacon* has been variously interpreted. A study of this nature, however, belongs to disciplines other than exegesis.

---

8 Now Stephen, full of grace and power, kept on doing great wonders and signs among the people. 9 Some who opposed him were members of the so-called Synagogue of the Freedmen— they were Jews from Cyrene and Alexandria, and from Cilicia and Asia. These men argued with Stephen, 10 but they were unable to stand up to his wisdom and the Spirit with which he spoke. 11 Then they secretly instigated men to say: "We have heard him speak blasphemous words against Moses and against God." 12 They stirred up the people, the elders, and the scribes. Having apprehended Stephen, they dragged him away and brought him before the Sanhedrin. 13 They presented false witnesses who said, "This man does not stop speaking things against this holy place and against the law. 14 We have heard him say that this Jesus of Nazareth will break down this place and will change the customs which Moses has handed down to us." 15 When all those seated in the Sanhedrin were looking at him attentively, they noticed that his face was as the face of an angel.

---

2. Stephen's Arrest
6:8–15

As is characteristic of his account, Luke enumerates incidents that bear the qualification *first*. In chapters 6 and 7, he features the brief ministry of the first martyr, Stephen. As the church continues to develop among the Greek-speaking Jews, the first Hellenist preacher is Stephen. Although it is brief, Stephen's ministry is a prelude to that of Paul, who in a sense assumed the work cut short by Stephen's death. Stephen enters a local synagogue of Greek-speaking Jews and meets opposition. After his conversion and return to Jerusalem, Paul also debated with Greek-speaking Jews who tried to kill him (9:29).

a. Opposition
6:8–10

8. Now Stephen, full of grace and power, kept on doing great wonders and signs among the people.

We know virtually nothing about the personal history of Stephen, except that he was a Hellenist, a Jew who became a Christian. Luke describes him as a man of faith and full of the Holy Spirit. Stephen was known for his wisdom and in view of his address before the Sanhedrin he appears to be an educated person. Presumably he attended schools of the Jewish theologians in Jerusalem and Alexandria.[13]

Stephen is a man "full of grace and power." With the words *grace* and *power,* Luke links Stephen's work of mercy, healing, teaching, and preaching to that of the apostles. In an earlier context, Luke writes that the apostles continued to proclaim Jesus' resurrection "with great power," and that they experienced "much grace" (4:33). God, then, blesses Stephen's work to the same degree as he has blessed the deeds of the apostles. To be precise, Luke seldom qualifies the miracles and wonders performed by the apostles. But in the case of Stephen, he discloses that the wonders and signs are great. In the Greek, the tense indicates that Stephen kept on doing them. Whether he already performed miracles before the apostles ordained him is not clear, but it is probable. We infer that the "great wonders and signs" describe Stephen's healing ministry. Especially because of these miracles, he was a blessing to the people. And yet, his own countrymen soon afterward killed him.

9. Some who opposed him were members of the so-called Synagogue of the Freedmen—they were Jews from Cyrene and Alexandria, and from Cilicia and Asia. These men argued with Stephen, 10. but they were unable to stand up to his wisdom and the Spirit with which he spoke.

Opposition comes not because of the miracles but because of Stephen's preaching. Luke says nothing about Stephen's diaconal task, but stresses his healing ministry and his debates with Greek-speaking Jews. He appears to indicate that this talented man served God in other capacities besides serving at the tables. Stephen went to the local synagogue of his compatriots.

We make the following observations:

a. *Synagogue.* The opposition Stephen faced came from members of the so-called Synagogue of the Freedmen. The term *freedmen* relates to a group of Jewish prisoners of war whom the Romans under the command of Pompey captured in 63 B.C. In subsequent years these prisoners were re-

---

13. Consult Richard B. Rackham, *The Acts of the Apostles: An Exposition,* Westminster Commentaries series (1901; reprint ed., Grand Rapids: Baker, 1964), p. 88.

leased and built a colony along the Tiber River in Rome. Later, their descendants were expelled from Rome and many of them presumably found refuge in Jerusalem, where they built a synagogue.[14] Scholars are divided on the veracity of a Greek inscription, referring to this synagogue, unearthed in 1913–14 in Jerusalem.[15]

Furthermore, scholars disagree on the interpretation of the phrase *Synagogue of the Freedmen*. Does Luke imply that the Freedmen had one synagogue, as did the other individual groups from Cyrene, Alexandria, Cilicia, and Asia? By this count, there would have been five different synagogues.[16] Conversely, the Greek text indicates a division between the Jews from Cyrene and Alexandria (two cities in Libya and Egypt respectively) and from Cilicia and Asia (two provinces in Asia Minor). This means that there were two synagogues (the Freedmen, Cyrenians, and Alexandrians in one group and the Cilicians and Asians in the other).[17] This later interpretation is commendable because of the support from the Greek text. Also, the geographic, cultural, and even linguistic differences between Jews from North Africa (Cyrene, Alexandria) and from Asia Minor (Cilicia, Asia) were too great to have them agree to one meeting place.

b. *Cities and provinces.* The Hellenistic Jews came from various places in the Roman empire. Cyrene was the capital of the North African province of Cyrenaica (modern Libya). A seaport located in a rich agricultural area of grain and livestock, Cyrene served as a crossroads of traffic from sea and land and became known as a trade center. It developed as a Greek colony with a substantial Jewish population. From the New Testament we learn that many of these Jews became residents of Jerusalem (2:10; Matt. 27:32; Mark 15:21; Luke 23:26).[18]

Alexandria was the capital of ancient Egypt and next to Rome the most important administrative center of the Mediterranean world. It had renowned cultural and literary attractions centered in a museum, library, and schools. Here thousands of Jews had settled in the course of the centuries; many of them assumed leading positions in the army and civil government. The Alexandrian Jews spoke Greek, so that eventually they needed a Greek translation of the Old Testament Scripture (the Septuagint).[19]

---

14. Tacitus *Annals* 2.85; Josephus *Antiquities* 18.3.5 [83].

15. Consult Hermann Strathmann, *TDNT*, vol. 3, p. 265.

16. Emil Schürer, *The History of the Jewish People in the Age of Jesus Christ (175 B.C.–A.D. 135)*, rev. and ed. Geza Vermes and Fergus Millar, 3 vols. (Edinburgh: Clark, 1973–87), vol. 2, p. 428. And see SB, vol. 2, pp. 661–65. Rabbinic literature mentions the synagogue of the Alexandrians.

17. I. Howard Marshall, *The Acts of the Apostles: An Introduction and Commentary*, Tyndale New Testament Commentary series (Leicester: Inter-Varsity; Grand Rapids: Eerdmans, 1980), p. 129. But Alford puts the Freedmen separately and sees three distinct synagogues. *Alford's Greek Testament*, vol. 2, p. 65.

18. William S. LaSor, "Cyrene," *ISBE*, vol. 1, pp. 844–45.

19. Consult E. M. Blaiklock, "Alexandria," *ZPEB*, vol. 1, pp. 100–103.

Both Cilicia and Asia were Roman provinces in Asia Minor (modern Turkey), where Greek was spoken. Cilicia was located along the Mediterranean coast in the southeastern part of Asia Minor. It included Tarsus, the birthplace of Paul, among its cities. Here a considerable number of Jewish people resided, some of whom became members of Christian churches (15:41). The province of Asia, bordering the western coast of Asia Minor, had Ephesus as a leading city. The area had numerous Jewish settlements and in many places churches were founded (e.g., the seven churches of Asia [Rev. 1:11]).

c. *Debate*. "These men argued with Stephen." Even if Luke portrays Stephen as a forerunner of Paul, he gives no indication that Paul was present among the Greek-speaking Jews from Cilicia who argued with Stephen. It is possible that Paul attended the worship services in the Synagogue of the Freedmen. Further, he was present when the Jews hurled stones at Stephen and killed him (7:58).

These Jews from many places in the dispersion were unable to stand up against Stephen. Certainly they did not argue about the healing miracles and the support of the local people. They were the figurative guards on the walls of Zion and were vigilant in their defense of the law of Moses, the temple, and religious observances; therefore they debated with Stephen points of doctrine and matters of worship. Luke merely states that Stephen spoke with wisdom and the Spirit. This is sufficient for the present, for in chapter 7 Luke relates the content of Stephen's speech. Luke repeats the apostolic requirement for the seven men appointed to office: men "who are full of the Spirit and wisdom" (v. 3). Stephen realized the fulfillment of Jesus' promise to give his followers words of wisdom so that none of their opponents would be able to refute them (Luke 21:15; compare Matt. 10:20). Notice also that the term *wisdom* occurs only four times in Acts, twice in connection with Stephen (vv. 3, 10) and twice in his speech before the Sanhedrin (7:10, 22). With the Spirit of God and wisdom from above, Stephen was capable of debating his opponents in the Jewish synagogues. And filled with the Spirit he was able to rebut the arguments leveled against him and his interpretation of the Scriptures. If the Greek-speaking Jews had realized that they were opposing the Holy Spirit, they would have known that they were fighting a battle they could not win.

Greek Words, Phrases, and Constructions in 6:8–11

Verse 8

ἐποίει—the imperfect denotes continued action. This is not an inceptive imperfect, "he began to do," but a progressive imperfect, "he kept on doing."

μεγάλα—this adjective with the nouns *wonders* and *signs* appears only here. It is not used to describe the miracles Jesus or the apostles performed.

Verse 9

τῆς λεγομένης—"the so-called." The noun Λιβερτίνων (Freedmen) is followed by the conjunction καί, which in context means "that is."

τῶν—this definite article occurs twice in the sentence. A. T. Robertson comments, "The use of τῶν twice divides the synagogues into two groups (men from Cilicia and Asia on the one hand, men from Alexandria, Cyrene and Libertines (?) on the other)."[20]

Verses 10–11

The Western text has a number of additions to these two verses. Here is the translation with the expansion in italics:

> Who could not withstand the wisdom *that was in him* and the *holy* Spirit with which he spoke, *because they were confuted by him with all boldness. Being unable therefore to confront the truth,* . . . .[21]

---

b. Arrest and Testimony
6:11–15

Satan opposes God's people by either deceit or violence. He employs both methods in the case of Stephen. First he brings false testimony against Stephen before the Sanhedrin and afterward he instigates the people to stone him to death.

11. Then they secretly instigated men to say: "We have heard him speak blasphemous words against Moses and against God."

Who are these insidious people who instigate men to give false testimony? Stephen's opponents are Hellenists who have come from the dispersion; perhaps they are trying to overcome what they perceive to be the stigma of Greek culture and, by extension, liberalism. In Jerusalem, they want to prove their allegiance to Jewish law and custom. Thus, they consider suspect anyone who deviates from strict rules and regulations. Why these zealots hire false witnesses (see v. 13) instead of stating their own objections to Stephen's words is not clear.

Stephen is a true disciple of Jesus Christ. Facing false accusations, Stephen is not above his Master, who also had to listen to charges brought against him by false witnesses (see Matt. 26:59–66 and parallel passages). The charge against Stephen is twofold: "We have heard him speak blasphemous words against Moses and against God." This is a serious matter, for the penalty for anyone who blasphemes the name of God is death by stoning (see Lev. 24:16; compare John 10:33). The word *Moses* refers to the five

---

20. A. T. Robertson, *A Grammar of the Greek New Testament in the Light of Historical Research* (Nashville: Broadman, 1934), p. 788.

21. Bruce M. Metzger, *A Textual Commentary on the Greek of the New Testament,* 3d corrected ed. (London and New York: United Bible Societies, 1975), p. 340.

books of Moses, that is, the Law. Accusations about disloyalty to the law and blaspheming God's name are effective in stirring up the people of Jerusalem. Despite all the healings performed by Stephen, the people are fickle enough to believe the false accusations and turn against him.

12. They stirred up the people, the elders, and the scribes. Having apprehended Stephen, they dragged him away and brought him before the Sanhedrin.

The instigators are successful in winning the support of the people, the elders of Israel, and the learned scribes. We assume that Stephen taught that believers can worship anywhere because God does not dwell in houses men have built (see 7:48–49). For the zealous Jew, this assertion is tantamount to blasphemy. With the crowds stirred up, the civil authorities (the elders) and teachers of the law (scribes) see an opportunity to bring Stephen to trial. Undoubtedly, many of these leaders are members of the Sanhedrin.

The people no longer favor Stephen, so the members of the Sanhedrin have no fear of an uprising. Stephen is apprehended, perhaps by the captain of the temple guard and his officers, and is brought before the Sanhedrin. This is the third time that Israel's supreme court brings followers of Jesus to trial; first Peter and John, then the twelve apostles, and now Stephen.

13. They presented false witnesses who said, "This man does not stop speaking things against this holy place and against the law. 14. We have heard him say that this Jesus of Nazareth will break down this place and will change the customs which Moses has handed down to us."

Luke presents his account in telescoped style. We must understand that the Sanhedrin needs some time for scheduling a court trial for Stephen. Also, the Hellenists need time to coach false witnesses to bring accusations that touch the heart of Israel's religion: the holy place and the law (compare 21:28). According to the law of Moses, any accusation against an individual must be supported by the combined testimony of two or three witnesses (Deut. 17:6–7). Therefore, at Jesus' trial false witnesses could not agree and were dismissed until two of them came forward and said that Jesus claimed that he would destroy the temple and rebuild it within three days (Matt. 26:60–61; 27:40; see also John 2:19).

The witnesses at Stephen's trial come with a trumped-up accusation that Stephen never stops speaking words against the law of Moses and against the temple with everything it embodies. The phrase "this man does not stop speaking" is an obvious exaggeration, for Stephen proclaims the Good News and accompanies it with great miracles. The witnesses, however, portray him as a revolutionary who subverts the Jewish religion. The emphatic "this place" refers to the temple and its services and not to the entire city of Jerusalem. The meeting place of the Sanhedrin "may have been situated on the Temple Mount on the western side of the enclosing wall."[22] And the charge that Stephen speaks against the Law (the Old Testament Scriptures) appears to be an overstatement. Jesus himself taught that he did not come to abolish the Law and the Prophets, but to fulfill them (Matt. 5:17).

The witnesses use the same accusation against Stephen that Jesus heard during his trial and at his crucifixion. They testify that they heard Stephen say that this Jesus of Nazareth would destroy the temple and change Jewish customs that reportedly originated with Moses. First, notice that the witnesses use the pronoun *this* before the name Jesus of Nazareth to express their disdain for Jesus. Next, they rely on hearsay concerning Jesus' words. If they refer to Jesus' challenge which he gave his opponents to break down the temple, they obviously misunderstood him. Jesus spoke about his body and added that he would rise from the grave within three days (John 2:19). However, Stephen's accusers distort the words of Jesus and their meaning.

In one of his discourses, Jesus predicted the overthrow of Jerusalem and its temple (Matt. 24:2, 15; Luke 19:43–44), but he spoke prophetically about the destruction of Jerusalem which occurred in A.D. 70. It is difficult to ascertain if Stephen's accusers are referring to Jesus' discourse on the last things. In that discourse Jesus merely predicts the downfall of Jerusalem.

The next accusation is that Jesus spoke against the customs Moses had handed down. The witnesses utter generalities but fail to give details. Apparently, a mere reference to changing Jewish customs is sufficient evidence to label someone a lawbreaker. Jesus opposed traditions that nullified the clear teachings of Scripture (Matt. 15:6), but he always taught the fulfillment of God's Word. Jesus revealed to the Samaritan woman that in the messianic era true worshipers did not have to go to the Samaritan temple on Mount Gerizim or to the temple in Jerusalem. True believers worship the Father anywhere in spirit and truth (John 4:21–24). We expect that Stephen, too, proclaimed this good news to the people of Jerusalem to set them free from cumbersome customs and traditions (refer to 21:21).

15. When all those seated in the Sanhedrin were looking at him attentively, they noticed that his face was as the face of an angel.

To stand in the semicircle and face the members of the Sanhedrin seated in elevated rows would intimidate any person on trial. Not so Peter, who in his two appearances before the Sanhedrin was filled with the Holy Spirit, spoke boldly in his own defense, and in fact was in control of the entire situation (4:8–12; 5:29–32).

Now Stephen takes the stand and, as everyone who is seated in the assembly looks at him intently, a divine glow seems to envelop him. Luke writes that Stephen's face "was as the face of an angel." We infer that Luke

---

22. Metzger, *Textual Commentary,* p. 341.

received a detailed eyewitness report from Paul, who in his address to the Jerusalem crowd freely admits his part in Stephen's death (22:20). Paul, then, was one of those who observed the transformation of Stephen's facial features. Yet in spite of the supernatural glow (see Exod. 34:29–30), the members of the Sanhedrin are unwilling to listen to the appeal of Christ's gospel.

Greek Words, Phrases, and Constructions in 6:11–15

Verse 11

ὑπέβαλον—the compound verb consisting of ὑπό (under) and βάλλω (I throw) has a sinister meaning: to instigate with evil motive.

ἀκηκόαμεν—the perfect active from ἀκούω (I hear) is the perfect of frequent action (see v. 14). The verb governs the genitive case to denote the act of hearing. By contrast, the accusative case denotes the act of understanding.[23]

εἰς—the remote meaning of this preposition is "against." See this meaning also in Luke 12:10; 15:18.

Verse 14

καταλύσει—"he will destroy." Note the future tense in this verb and in ἀλλάξει (he will change). This indirect statement is meant to report the actual spoken words of Jesus. According to their own beliefs, the accusers should have nothing to fear: Jesus had died and had not risen from the dead.

Verse 15

ἑστῶτος ἐν μέσῳ αὐτῶν—"standing in their midst." The Western text adds this phrase as an explanatory comment.

Summary of Chapter 6

The Greek-speaking Jewish Christians in Jerusalem voice their complaints against the Aramaic-speaking believers, because in the daily distribution of food the widows of the first-mentioned group suffer neglect. The apostles call the believers to a congregational meeting and suggest a division of labors: seven men who are full of the Spirit and wisdom should take care of the physical needs of the poor, and the apostles, by devoting themselves to prayer and preaching, should fulfill the spiritual needs of the people. Seven men are elected and appointed. As a result, the church continues to expand; even many of the priests join the church.

One of the seven men is Stephen, who in addition to his new responsibility performs great miracles among the people and enters the Synagogue of

---

23. Consult Robertson, *Grammar*, p. 506. See the extensive discussion in the **Greek Words, Phrases, and Constructions in 9:7.**

the Freedmen to preach God's Word. Greek-speaking Jews from North Africa (including Egypt) and Asia Minor listen to him but are unable to oppose him. However, they manage to stir up the crowd to react adversely toward Stephen, who is arrested to stand trial before the Sanhedrin. False witnesses bring charges against him by saying that Stephen has spoken blasphemous words against the Law and God. As Stephen faces the members of the Sanhedrin his face shines like that of an angel.

7

The Church in Jerusalem, *part 6*

7:1–8:1a

Outline (continued)

7:1–53	3. Stephen's Speech
7:1–8	a. Abraham
7:9–16	b. Joseph
7:17–22	c. Moses' Training
7:23–29	d. Moses' Departure
7:30–36	e. Moses' Mission
7:37–43	f. Moses' Teaching
7:44–50	g. Tabernacle
7:51–53	h. Application
7:54–8:1a	4. Stephen's Death

7 1 Then the high priest asked, "Are these things true?" 2 Stephen answered, "Men, brothers and fathers. The God of glory appeared to our father Abraham while he was still in Mesopotamia, before he settled in Haran. 3 And God said to him, 'Leave your country and your relatives, and go to the land that I will show you.' 4 Then he left the land of the Chaldeans and settled in Haran. And there, after Abraham's father died, God made him move to the land where you are now living. 5 And God gave him no inheritance in it, not even a foot of land, but he promised to give it to him for his possession and his descendants after him, although at the time he still had no child. 6 This is what God told him: 'Your descendants will live in a foreign land as strangers, where they will be enslaved and mistreated for four hundred years. 7 And I will judge the nation to which they are enslaved,' God said, 'and afterward they will come out and worship me in this place.' 8 And God gave Abraham the covenant of circumcision; and thus he became the father of Isaac, and Abraham circumcised him on the eighth day. Isaac became the father of Jacob, and Jacob became the father of the twelve patriarchs.

9 "And the patriarchs were jealous of Joseph and sold him as a slave into Egypt. But God was with him 10 and rescued him from all his troubles. He gave him favor and wisdom before Pharaoh, king of Egypt, and appointed him ruler over Egypt and all his household.

11 "Then a famine came over all Egypt and Canaan, and great affliction. And our fathers could not find food. 12 When Jacob heard that there was grain in Egypt, he sent our fathers the first time. 13 On the second visit, Joseph made himself known to his brothers and the family of Joseph became known to Pharaoh. 14 And Joseph sent for and invited his father Jacob and his whole family, in total seventy-five people. 15 Then Jacob went down to Egypt, and he and our fathers died there. 16 Their bodies were taken to Shechem and buried in the tomb Abraham bought with silver from the sons of Hamor in Shechem.

17 "When the time was approaching for God to fulfill the promise he had made to Abraham, our people became more and more numerous in Egypt, 18 until a different king began to rule over Egypt, who did not know Joseph. 19 This king took advantage of our race, mistreated our fathers, and made them abandon their infants so that they would not survive.

20 "At this time, Moses was born and he was a handsome child to God. For three months he was taken care of in his father's house. 21. And after he was abandoned, Pharaoh's daughter adopted him and brought him up as her own son. 22 Moses was instructed in all the wisdom of the Egyptians, and he was powerful in words and deeds.

23 "When Moses was about forty years old, he decided to visit his fellow countrymen, the Israelites. 24 And when he saw one of them being treated unjustly by an Egyptian, he came to his help; he avenged the oppressed by striking down the Egyptian. 25 He supposed that his fellow countrymen would understand that God was using him to deliver them, but they did not understand. 26 Then on the following day he came upon two Israelites who were fighting and he tried to reconcile them. He said, 'Men, you are brothers. Why are you hurting each other?' 27 But the one who was mistreating his fellow countryman said, 'Who made you a ruler and judge over us? 28 Do you want to kill me as you killed the Egyptian yesterday?' 29 When Moses heard this, he fled and became a refugee in the land of Midian and had two sons.

30 "And after forty years had passed, an angel appeared to Moses in the flames of a burning bush in the desert near Mount Sinai. 31 When Moses saw it, he was amazed at the sight. As he approached to look at it more closely, there was the voice of the Lord: 32 'I am the God of your fathers, the God of Abraham, Isaac, and Jacob.' Moses was trembling and did not dare to look.

33 "Then the Lord said to him: 'Remove the sandals from your feet, for the place where you are standing is holy ground. 34 I have indeed seen the mistreatment of my people in Egypt and heard their groaning. I have come down to deliver them. Come now, I will send you to Egypt.'

35 "This is the same Moses whom the Israelites rejected when they said, 'Who made you ruler and judge?' This man God sent as ruler and deliverer with the help of the angel who appeared to him in the bush. 36 He led them out of Egypt, having performed miracles and signs in Egypt, at the Red Sea, and in the desert for forty years.

37 "This is the Moses who said to the Israelites, 'God will raise up a prophet for you from your brothers as he raised me up.' 38 This is the one who was in the assembly in the desert with the angel who was speaking to him at Mount Sinai and with our fathers. He received living oracles to pass on to us.

39 "Our fathers refused to obey, however; they rejected him and in their hearts returned to Egypt. 40 They said to Aaron, 'Make for us gods who will go before us. For this Moses, who led us out of the land of Egypt, we do not know what has become of him.' 41 And they made a calf in those days; they offered a sacrifice to the idol and rejoiced in the works of their hands. 42 But God turned away and delivered them to worship the hosts of heaven, just as it is written in the book of the prophets:

> 'You did not bring me sacrifices and offerings
> for forty years in the desert,
> O house of Israel, did you?
> 43 You took along the tent of Moloch
> and the star of your god Rephan,
> and the images you made to worship them.
> I will banish you beyond Babylon.'

44 "Our fathers had the tabernacle of testimony in the desert, just as God, who spoke to Moses, had commanded him to construct it according to the pattern which he had seen. 45 And when our fathers had received it from their fathers, they with Joshua brought it along while dispossessing the Gentiles, whom God expelled before them. It stayed there until the time of David. 46 He found favor in God's sight and asked that he might provide a dwelling place for the God of Jacob. 47 But it was Solomon who built a house for him. 48 However, the Most High does not live in houses made by human hands. As the prophet says:

> 49 'Heaven is my throne,
>   and earth my footstool.
> What house will you build for me?
>   says the Lord.
> Or what place is there for my rest?
> 50 Did not my hand make all these things?'

51 "You stiff-necked people, uncircumcised in hearts and ears. You are always resisting the Holy Spirit. As your fathers did, so do you. 52 Was there any prophet your fathers did not persecute? They even killed those who foretold the coming of the Righteous One, whose betrayers and murderers you have now become, 53 you who received the law transmitted by angels, yet you did not keep it."

3. Stephen's Speech
7:1–53

His face shining with an angelic glow, Stephen answers his adversaries by reciting the history of the Israelites. He begins with the patriarch Abraham, then refers to Joseph and the beginning of the nation Israel in Egypt, and calls attention to the training, mission, and teaching of Moses. He points out that Israel's history is marred by disobedience. He mentions the construction of the tabernacle and the temple and quotes from the prophecy of Isaiah to show that God cannot be confined to a house of worship (Isa. 66:1–2). He concludes his speech by calling attention to Israel's resistance to God and his Word.

Is this speech an adequate response to the charges leveled against Stephen? From Stephen's point of view the answer is affirmative, because as a Jew Stephen appeals to the historical heritage of Scripture he has in common with his countrymen. Accordingly, Stephen declares his basic unity with fellow Jews by mentioning Abraham, the father of believers. Jewish audiences relish surveys of their historical past that originate with Abraham.[1]

a. Abraham
7:1–8

1. Then the high priest asked, "Are these things true?" 2. Stephen answered, "Men, brothers and fathers. The God of glory appeared to our father Abraham while he was still in Mesopotamia, before he settled in Haran."

After the Hellenists have brought their accusations and the false witnesses their hearsay charges, the high priest requests Stephen to tell the audience the truth of the matter.

Stephen addresses the members of the Sanhedrin as "men, brothers and fathers." At the conclusion of his third missionary journey, Paul uses the same words when he speaks to the Jews in Jerusalem (22:1). In many respects, therefore, Stephen's speech forms a bridge between the speeches of Peter and those of Paul.[2] Moreover, we do not know who accurately remembered the words of Stephen. Luke undoubtedly received this fixed tradition in either oral or written form and faithfully recorded its substance.[3]

Stephen not only considers the members of the Sanhedrin his spiritual brothers, but also shows deep respect for their age and dignity. He calls them "fathers" not because he wishes to flatter his listeners but to show

---

1. For similar surveys, see Josh. 24; Neh. 9:5–37; Pss. 78; 105; 106; Heb. 11.
2. Consult Richard B. Rackham, *The Acts of the Apostles: An Exposition*, Westminster Commentaries series (1901; reprint ed., Grand Rapids: Baker, 1964), p. 92.
3. Refer to J. Julius Scott, Jr., "Stephen's Speech: A Possible Model for Luke's Historical Method?" *JETS* 17 (1974): 91–97; Martin H. Scharlemann, "Acts 7:2–53. Stephen's Speech: A Lucan Creation?" *ConcJourn* 4 (1978): 52–57.

respect for authority. He wants their undivided attention and tells them to listen to what he has to say.

The first accusation against Stephen is that of blasphemy against Moses and against God (6:11). Stephen squarely meets this accusation when he begins his recital of Israel's history by saying, "The God of glory appeared to our father Abraham while he was still in Mesopotamia." This opening statement corresponds to Moses' account of God's dwelling among the Israelites in the Tent of Meeting and God's glory filling the tabernacle (Exod. 25:8; 40:34–35). Stephen conforms completely to Jewish expectations by displaying deep reverence for God, his divine glory, the tabernacle, and Moses.[4] Stephen is one with the people of Israel. Notice, however, that he begins and ends his speech with an indirect and direct reference, respectively, to God's dwelling place (see vv. 44–50). By doing so, Stephen emphasizes that God is not bound to a particular place, as is evident from God appearing to Abraham in Ur of the Chaldeans.

Abraham's residence in Mesopotamia is recorded in the first book of Moses (Gen. 11:31). Abraham, with his wife, Sarah, and his parents and brothers, lived in Ur. In those days, Ur was a prosperous city along the banks of the Euphrates River (the area is modern-day southern Iraq). God called Abraham in Ur (Gen. 15:7; Neh. 9:7). Here his forefathers, including his father, Terah, worshiped idols (Josh. 24:2). Abraham, his wife, his father, and his nephew Lot set out for Canaan, but they settled in Haran, which was a prominent city in the northern part of Mesopotamia. Here Terah died and here God again called Abraham to proceed to Canaan.

3. "And God said to him, 'Leave your country and your relatives, and go to the land that I will show you.' 4. Then he left the land of the Chaldeans and settled in Haran. And there, after Abraham's father died, God made him move to the land where you are now living."

Here is the first of many historical difficulties we encounter in Stephen's account. Did God call Abraham twice, once in Ur of the Chaldeans and the other time in Haran? Stephen asserts that God called Abraham in Mesopotamia, but the historical account in Genesis reveals that Terah, Abraham, Sarah, and Lot left for Canaan (Gen. 11:31). They came as far as Haran, where Terah died (v. 32). Then God spoke to Abraham and told him to leave the country and his relatives and go to the land that God would show him (Gen. 12:1). Accordingly, God called Abraham twice. Stephen, however, follows the accepted interpretation of his day, namely, that God instructed Abraham to leave Chaldea and go to Canaan.[5]

The second question is whether Abraham left Haran before or after his father died. If Abraham left when he was 75 years old, then Terah was 145. Terah lived another 60 years; he reached the age of 205 (Gen. 11:26, 32; 12:4). How do we solve this apparent discrepancy? Some scholars want to

---

4. Compare Ps. 29:1–2; I Cor. 2:8; James 2:1.

5. See Philo *On Abraham* 71; Josephus *Antiquities* 1.7.1 [154].

reverse the order of Terah's sons, Abraham, Nahor, and Haran. They say that Abraham was Terah's youngest son, born 60 years after Haran, whom they consider Terah's firstborn. This solution seems improbable. Terah would have been 130 years old when Abraham was born, yet Abraham finds it "incredible that he himself should beget a son at 99 (Gen. 17:1, 17)."[6] Other scholars suggest that Stephen relied on a Greek text that has the same reading as the Samaritan Pentateuch, which says Terah died when he was 145. But because no Greek manuscript with this reading is extant, this suggestion remains only theory.[7]

What is the answer to this problem? As in the case of God's call to Abraham, Stephen follows a popular interpretation of his day that does not take account of precise mathematical detail. "Both these discrepancies between Acts and the Old Testament are really nothing more than the natural interpretation of an ordinary reader."[8] Stephen's remark about Terah's death in Haran need not be taken as a chronology. We can understand it as a biographical note that conveys the information that Abraham leaves for Canaan without his father, who died in Haran. Notice that in referring to the account of Abraham and Terah, Stephen is not interested in specific figures. The point of his allusion to Abraham's migration is to show that God called Abraham to the land where Stephen's fellow Jews now live.

Relying on his memory, Stephen quotes almost word for word from the Greek translation of the Old Testament (Gen. 12:1). He says, "And God said to him: 'Leave your country and your relatives, and go to the land that I will show you.'" From the Septuagint Stephen deletes the words "and from your father's house." God told Abraham to depart from his relatives and to go to the land of God's choice, namely, southern Canaan.

5. "And God gave him no inheritance in it, not even a foot of land, but he promised to give it to him for his possession and his descendants after him, although at the time he still had no child."

Repeatedly God promised Abraham that he would give the land of Canaan to him and to his descendants for an everlasting possession.[9] Abraham was a nomad who moved his livestock from place to place in southern Canaan in search of green pastures, but he owned no land. When Sarah died, Abraham purchased the cave of Machpelah (Gen. 23:17–18). He could not say that God had given this cave to him, for Abraham paid a sum

6. Henry Alford, *Alford's Greek Testament: An Exegetical and Critical Commentary*, 7th ed., 4 vols. (1877; Grand Rapids: Guardian, 1976), vol. 2, p. 69.

7. Consult E. Richard, "Acts 7: An Investigation of the Samaritan Evidence," *CBQ* 39 (1977): 190–208.

8. Lake and Cadbury, *Beginnings*, vol. 4, p. 70. See also Richard N. Longenecker, *The Acts of the Apostles*, in vol. 9 of *The Expositor's Bible Commentary*, ed. Frank E. Gaebelein, 12 vols. (Grand Rapids: Zondervan, 1981), p. 340. Both Philo (*Migration of Abraham* 176–77) and Josephus (*Antiquities* 1.7.1 [154]) lend support to Stephen's popular interpretation.

9. Gen. 12:7; 13:15, 17; 15:18; 17:8.

of money to obtain it. Abraham received God's promise that the land of Canaan would be for his numerous descendants (Gen. 48:4). But both his son, Isaac, and his grandson Jacob lived in tents without owning the land where they dwelled. These three patriarchs were heirs of the Promised Land, yet all they possessed was God's promise (Heb. 11:9). Stephen states that Abraham did not possess even so much as a foot of land (compare Deut. 2:5). Although he had the promise that God would give Canaan to his offspring, he still remained childless. God gave Abraham a promise before he had made a covenant with him, prior to Abraham's circumcision, while the Canaanites lived in the land (Gen. 12:6). God severely tested Abraham's faith. In time, God gave the land to the Israelites when they came out of Egypt.

6. **"This is what God told him: 'Your descendants will live in a foreign land as strangers, where they will be enslaved and mistreated for four hundred years. 7. And I will judge the nation to which they are enslaved,' God said, 'and afterward they will come out and worship me in this place.'"**

As Stephen stands before the members of the Sanhedrin, he relies on memory for quoting and alluding to Scripture. Once again he cites from Abraham's history (Gen. 15:13–14). Except for a few minor variations, Stephen takes his quote directly from the Septuagint. Israel's stay in Egypt was not the patriarchs' choice; as Stephen says, God predicted that the Israelites would be enslaved in Egypt for four hundred years. In spite of God's promise to give Canaan to Abraham's descendants, for four centuries the Israelites had to live as resident aliens in a foreign land. Moreover, they were slaves. Stephen refrains from mentioning the name *Egypt,* perhaps out of deference to the Hellenistic Jews from Alexandria.

The number of years Israel spent in Egypt was 400, according to God's word to Abraham (Gen. 15:13). Moses writes that the duration of Israel's stay was 430 years (Exod. 12:40–41; see also Gal. 3:17). Obviously, the figure 400 is a round number, whereas 430 is more specific.[10] Stephen is not interested in precise figures. From memory he quotes the Genesis text for the purpose of pointing out that God would punish the oppressors of his people. With this clause he calls to mind the ten plagues on Egypt and the subsequent deliverance of God's people. God's prophetic words in Genesis, then, are fulfilled in the account recorded in Exodus.

The last part of verse 7 differs from its Old Testament source. Stephen says, "And afterward they will come out and worship [God] in this place." But the Old Testament text has, "And afterward they will come out with many possessions" (Gen. 15:14b). When the Israelites left Egypt, they received so many possessions from the Egyptians that they plundered them (Exod. 12:36). But Stephen deletes the clause about the material wealth the

---

10. Rabbinic exegesis explains that the period of 430 years extended from Isaac's birth to the day of the exodus. SB, vol. 2, pp. 668–71.

Israelites gained when they departed from Egypt. Instead, he adds a modified clause from Exodus 3:12, where God informs Moses in the Sinai Desert that when he has led the Israelites out of Egypt, "you will worship [me] on this mountain." But Stephen changes the words *on this mountain* to "in this place," and thus points to the Jerusalem temple instead of Mount Sinai.

Notice that Stephen begins to answer the charges of the false witnesses: that he is speaking against the holy place and that Jesus will destroy "this place" (6:13–14). Stephen demonstrates that he holds sacred the worship of God, for the Greek word for worship signifies external religious duties that are performed in a formal setting and that entail an internal commitment.

8. "And God gave Abraham the covenant of circumcision; and thus he became the father of Isaac, and Abraham circumcised him on the eighth day. Isaac became the father of Jacob, and Jacob became the father of the twelve patriarchs."

a. *Covenant.* After a brief remark about Israel in Egypt, Stephen returns to his discussion of Abraham and the days before Isaac was born. At that time, God appeared to the father of believers and made a covenant with him that was sealed with the blood of circumcision (Gen. 17:9–14).

Stephen's purpose for introducing the concept *covenant* at this juncture is to show that it precedes the temple and law and therefore is basic to Israel's religion. Thus he clears himself of the accusation that he has blasphemed against the law and against God. By establishing a covenant with Abraham and his descendants, God declares his enduring love toward his people.[11] In the historical account of God confirming his covenant with Abraham, God calls this covenant "my covenant" nine times (Gen. 17:2–21). God initiates and maintains it throughout the generations as an everlasting covenant.

b. *Circumcision.* Circumcision is the sign of the covenant that God has made with Abraham and his descendants. God requires total consecration from those who are circumcised, including Stephen and his Sanhedrin audience. As Abraham circumcised his son Isaac on the eighth day, so the Jews circumcise their male descendants throughout the generations. This covenant symbolized in the rite of circumcision is Israel's security. Not the temple (which could cease to exist, as in the days of the exile) but the covenant remains forever.[12]

c. *Service.* "And thus [Abraham] became the father of Isaac." The translators of the New International Version have deleted the word *thus* from the text. But this word is significant because it points to the covenant relationship Abraham has with God. Abraham must circumcise his son with whom God continues the same covenant (Gen. 17:12, 21). Abraham and his de-

---

11. John Calvin, *Commentary on the Acts of the Apostles,* ed. David W. Torrance and Thomas F. Torrance, 2 vols. (Grand Rapids: Eerdmans, 1966), vol. 1, p. 179.

12. F. W. Grosheide, *De Handelingen der Apostelen,* Kommentaar op het Nieuwe Testament series, 2 vols. (Amsterdam: Van Bottenburg, 1942), vol. 1, p. 215. See also Gleason L. Archer, Jr., "Covenant," *EDT,* pp. 276–78.

scendants (Isaac, Jacob, and the twelve patriarchs) are obliged to keep the covenant by living a blameless life in the presence of God (Gen. 17:1). Note that Abraham and his offspring must serve and worship God without the benefit of a tabernacle or a temple. The covenant, therefore, supersedes the temple and its services. Both Stephen and his listeners are in a covenant relationship with God. To them the everlasting covenant that came through Abraham and the patriarchs is basic. The charge that Stephen blasphemed becomes meaningless, for Stephen demonstrates that he keeps the covenant by loving and serving God.[13]

Doctrinal Considerations in 7:2–8

Should not the high priest have interrupted Stephen a number of times to tell him to answer the charges leveled against him? The high priest does not have to do this, because Stephen, in his own way, is responding to the accusations.

Throughout his address Stephen repudiates the charge of blasphemy by revealing his profound reverence for God and his high regard for God's Word. He refers to the God of glory (v. 2) and quotes God's command to Abraham to leave Mesopotamia for Canaan (v. 3). He mentions God's promise to give Abraham and his descendants the land of Canaan (v. 5). He cites God's prophetic word about Israel's stay in Egypt and the plagues (vv. 6–7). And last, he notes the institution of God's covenant of circumcision with Abraham and his progeny (v. 8).

Even though Stephen, a Greek-speaking Jew, uses not the Hebrew text but the Septuagint translation, his quotations are accurate and well chosen. He knows Scripture and has an uncanny ability to interpret its message.

One of the themes in the first part of Stephen's address is God's omnipresence. That is, God reveals himself in many places that are outside the Promised Land. In Ur of the Chaldeans God gives Abraham the promise of numerous descendants; from Ur and from Haran God sends him to Canaan. In Egypt God punishes Israel's oppressors and leads Jacob's offspring to freedom. Because God is universally present, he can be worshiped anywhere. Therefore, the temple in Jerusalem is not the only place where God's people can worship him. And Christianity is not bound to the Jerusalem temple.

Stephen's speech is delivered at a time when the Greek-speaking Jews become influential in the church (6:1–7) and when the Samaritans are about to come to the faith (8:4–25). In brief, Stephen speaks at a time when the gospel is spreading in ever-widening circles.

Greek Words, Phrases, and Constructions in 7:1–8

Verse 1

εἰ—in a direct question this particle is not translated.

ταῦτα οὕτως ἔχει—here is an idiomatic expression that means "are these things

---

13. Consult R. C. H. Lenski, *The Interpretation of the Acts of the Apostles* (Columbus: Wartburg, 1944), p. 267.

true?" Compare 17:11 and 24:9. The neuter plural subject is followed by a verb in the singular.

Verse 2

πρὶν ἤ—this combination is the same as πρίν (before) "and predominates in Koine."[14]

κατοικῆσαι—the aorist active infinitive from the compound verb κατοικέω (I dwell, settle) differs from the compound verb παροικέω (I inhabit as a stranger). See the difference between these two in verses 2, 4, and 6.

Verse 4

μετῴκισεν—the aorist active from μετοικίζω (I transfer settlers). The subject of this verb is ὁ θεός.

εἰς—the second time this preposition appears in verse 4 it should have been ἐν (in). It has a local sense and is εἰς (in) possibly by attraction.[15]

Verse 5

καί—the second καί in this verse is adversative and has the meaning *but.*

οὐκ—normally the negative particle with a participle is μή; οὐκ negates verbs in the indicative mood. The expression occurs in the Septuagint (compare I Chron. 2:30, 32).

Verses 6–7

ἔσται—this and the other future tenses in verses 6 and 7 have a progressive meaning.

ἀλλοτρίᾳ—"foreign." This is a substitute for οὐκ ἰδίᾳ (not one's own) from Genesis 15:13 (LXX). See also Exodus 2:22 (LXX).

ἐὰν δουλεύσουσιν—notice that the particle introduces a future active indicative instead of a present or an aorist subjunctive. Compare ἄν σοι δείξω (I will show you) in verse 3.

Verse 8

καὶ οὕτως—"and so." Kirsopp Lake and H. J. Cadbury comment, "Possibly the 'so' is emphatic and means 'thus, while there was still no holy place, all the essential conditions for the religion of Israel were fulfilled.' "[16]

---

b. Joseph
7:9–16

The next example from Israel's history is Joseph, but Stephen does not mention Isaac and refers to Jacob in connection with Joseph in Egypt.

---

14. Bauer, p. 701.

15. C. F. D. Moule, *An Idiom-Book of New Testament Greek,* 2d ed. (Cambridge: Cambridge University Press, 1960), p. 68. And see Robert Hanna, *A Grammatical Aid to the Greek New Testament* (Grand Rapids: Baker, 1983), p. 200.

16. Lake and Cadbury, *Beginnings,* vol. 4, p. 72.

Stephen's choice of inclusions and omissions in his historical survey, then, reflects his desire to show the members of the Sanhedrin that God cared for the patriarchs in a foreign land.

9. "And the patriarchs were jealous of Joseph and sold him as a slave into Egypt. But God was with him 10. and rescued him from all his troubles. He gave him favor and wisdom before Pharaoh, king of Egypt, and appointed him ruler over Egypt and all his household."

Jacob considered Joseph his firstborn son because he was the first son of Rachel (Gen. 30:24). Jacob loved Rachel, not Leah. Thus, in Jacob's opinion, Rachel was his first wife. Accordingly, Joseph received gifts and favors from his father and as a result was despised by his brothers. In later years, Joseph received a double portion of the inheritance when, in the name of his sons Manasseh and Ephraim, Jacob gave him a double share in the land of Canaan (Gen. 48:5; I Chron. 5:2).

The term *patriarchs* applied to the sons of Jacob became current in the intertestamental period.[17] But these sons did not display any patriarchal dignity when they decided to throw Joseph into a pit; then, for twenty pieces of silver, they sold him as a slave to Ishmaelites who took Joseph to Egypt; and finally the brothers took his beautiful robe, dipped it in goat's blood, and presented it to Jacob (Gen. 37:12–36). The parallel between the sale of Joseph and the betrayal of Jesus is obvious. The patriarchs sold their own brother to foreigners; the Jews delivered Jesus into the hands of the Romans.

Stephen avoids details and stresses the positive: "God was with Joseph and rescued him from all his troubles." God cared for Joseph, who was alone in a foreign land. Notice that in verses 9–15, the name *Egypt* occurs six times.[18] That is, God's presence in that country was real, as Joseph could testify. God blessed him by rescuing him from temptation in Potiphar's house and from a lengthy imprisonment (Gen. 39:2, 21, 23). God made him gain favor with Pharaoh and gave Joseph divine wisdom as he interpreted Pharaoh's dreams and suggested measures to deal with a predicted famine (Gen. 41:25–36). God appointed Joseph ruler over Egypt and Pharaoh's palace (Gen. 41:37–43; and see Ps. 105:20–22). Stephen says that God made Joseph Pharaoh's second-in-command in Egypt, the highest official in his palace, and his chief adviser (Gen. 45:8). Note, then, that God is in control of government in Pharaoh's land.

11. "Then a famine came over all Egypt and Canaan and great affliction. And our fathers could not find food. 12. When Jacob heard that there was grain in Egypt, he sent our fathers the first time."

---

17. See IV Macc. 16:25 and the title of the pseudepigraphal book The Testaments of the Twelve Patriarchs.

18. The suggestion has been made that the emphasis on Egypt points to Alexandria as the birthplace of the Greek-speaking Stephen. David John Williams, *Acts*, Good News Commentaries series (San Francisco: Harper and Row, 1985), p. 120.

The famine Joseph predicted when God interpreted Pharaoh's dreams became reality. It affected not only all Egypt but also neighboring Canaan. In his providence, God sent Joseph to Egypt to save the lives of his father, his brothers, and their families (Gen. 45:5, 7). The expression *great affliction* describes the suffering and death of multitudes of people and animals when for a period of seven years there were no harvests. Stephen does not elaborate but states that Joseph's relatives in Canaan were unable to find food for man and beast. The tense of the Greek verb indicates that they kept on looking for food without any result.

Egypt depends on the waters of the Nile River and not on its annual amount of rainfall to nourish its crops. Palestine, conversely, receives its precipitation from moisture-laden clouds coming from the Mediterranean Sea. A drought seldom happens in both countries at the same time, but in the days of Joseph the inhabitants of Egypt, Canaan, and all other lands (Gen. 41:54) suffered a famine. "Egyptian sources refer to numerous instances in which inhabitants from other nations, or even whole nations, sought help from Egypt during periods of famine. Against this background the seven-year famine in Joseph's day has a ring of historical accuracy."[19]

Through the wisdom God had given Joseph, wheat was stored for seven years in Egypt in anticipation of a seven-year drought. When Jacob heard that the granaries in Egypt were full and that the Egyptians sold grain to their own people and to all surrounding countries, he sent his sons on a buying expedition (Gen. 41:56–57; 42:1–3). Why Stephen deems it necessary to refer to the two visits of Joseph's brothers we are unable to answer, but we should not look for typology in this passage. In fact, there is insufficient information in Stephen's speech to parallel the two visits of Joseph's brothers with the first and second comings of Christ (Heb. 9:28).[20] Instead we should stress the central message of this passage: God saves his people from certain death in Canaan by giving them food from Egypt.

13. "On the second visit, Joseph made himself known to his brothers and the family of Joseph became known to Pharaoh. 14. And Joseph sent for and invited his father Jacob and his whole family, in total seventy-five people."

Stephen omits all the historical details concerning Joseph's brother Benjamin and states only that Joseph revealed himself to his brothers. When he was sold as a slave into Egypt, Joseph was seventeen years old (Gen. 37:2). Twenty years later (Gen. 41:46, 53), his brothers did not recognize Joseph, who wore Egyptian clothes, spoke through an interpreter, and was clean-shaven like the Egyptians. When, two years into the famine, Joseph re-

---

19. Gerhard F. Hasel, "Famine," *ISBE*, vol. 2, p. 281.
20. Lake and Cadbury are of the opinion that such a view is possible on the basis of "a common contrast in early patristic literature." *Beginnings*, vol. 4, p. 73.

vealed his identity to Jacob's sons, he was thirty-nine (compare Gen. 45:6). Because of Joseph's authority and influence, his family members were introduced to Pharaoh, who invited them with father Jacob to come and settle in Egypt. Although the famine would last for another five years, Jacob and his family could dwell in the fertile Nile Delta (Goshen; Gen. 46:28). Here their flocks and herds had sufficient food to sustain them, and Joseph provided food for all the members of Jacob's extended household. As Joseph told his brothers, "God sent me ahead of you to preserve for you a remnant on earth to keep you alive by a great deliverance" (Gen. 45:7).

Is there a discrepancy between the Old Testament account, which states that there were seventy people in Jacob's family, and the New Testament, which mentions seventy-five persons?[21] Scholars have offered solutions to this problem, but the one that is best comes from the Greek translation of the Old Testament, the Septuagint, which states that the people who entered Egypt with Jacob numbered sixty-six. The text excludes Jacob and Joseph and adds nine sons of Joseph (a total of seventy-five). The tally given in the Hebrew Bible and its translations is sixty-six persons, plus Jacob, Joseph, and Joseph's two sons; that is, seventy people.[22]

15. "Then Jacob went down to Egypt, and he and our fathers died there. 16. Their bodies were taken to Shechem and buried in the tomb Abraham bought with silver from the sons of Hamor in Shechem."

The Jews attached great significance to the fact that Jacob and his sons were buried in Canaan. Jacob instructed Joseph to bury him in the tomb of Machpelah near Mamre in Canaan (Gen. 50:5, 13). And in turn, Joseph told Jacob's descendants to remove his bones from Egypt (Gen. 50:25; Exod. 13:19); the Israelites buried him centuries later in the land Jacob bought from the sons of Hamor (Josh. 24:32).

Scripture provides no information about the death and burial of Joseph's brothers.[23] We assume that the reason for Joseph's burial in Shechem is that this is the land Joseph's descendants inherited (Josh. 24:32). Therefore, Joseph was buried in his own inheritance.

"Their bodies were taken to Shechem and buried in the tomb Abraham bought with silver from the sons of Hamor in Shechem." Here is an inconsistency—Abraham bought the cave of Machpelah from Ephron the Hittite for four hundred shekels of silver (Gen. 23:15). And Jacob bought a plot of ground from the sons of Hamor in Shechem for a hundred pieces of silver (Gen. 33:19). However, before we go any further, we should look again at the preceding verses (vv. 14–15).

---

21. See Gen. 46:27; Exod. 1:5; Deut. 10:22; Acts 7:14.

22. Josephus follows the reading in the Hebrew text (*Antiquities* 2.7.4 [183]; 6.5.6 [89]). But Philo mentions both the Hebrew and the Greek accounts and tries to reconcile the difference in numbering (*Migration of Abraham* 199–201 [36]).

23. Josephus relates that the brothers of Joseph were buried in Hebron. *Antiquities* 2.8.2 [199]. Also consult Jub. 46:8; and The Testaments of the Twelve Patriarchs.

Stephen and his audience knew the Scriptures well enough that a mere reference would be sufficient to recall the entire account. When Stephen says, "their bodies," the members of the Sanhedrin knew that he had Jacob and Joseph in mind and that these two were buried in two different places: Jacob in the cave Abraham had bought and Joseph in the plot of ground Jacob had purchased in Shechem. The name *Abraham* in verse 16b calls to mind the cave of Machpelah at Hebron, where Jacob was buried. And Shechem is the place where the Israelites buried the bones of Joseph. The two accounts have been telescoped in one short sentence.[24]

Practical Considerations in 7:9–16

"Do not trouble trouble until trouble troubles you." This well-known saying tells us to avoid trouble at all cost. Even though we admit that much of our trouble is of our own making, we know that many times we stumble into adversities for which we are not able to take responsibility. The sudden death of a dear relative or friend, the loss of a job or income, persecution, hardship, poverty—all these afflictions come to us as trials sent by God. At the age of seventeen, Joseph was sold as a slave, taken to Egypt, tempted by a seductive woman, imprisoned, and forsaken. Yet God was with him. And that knowledge was sufficient for him to flee from temptation, to be filled with divine wisdom to counsel Pharaoh, to be strong in faith amid pagan idolatry, and to be forgiving toward his brothers.

Joseph, therefore, understood that God had sent him to Egypt to save his own relatives from starvation and that his adversities were divinely designed to accomplish God's purpose: the salvation of God's people (Gen. 50:20). Troubles from the hand of God, therefore, are a source of untold blessings. And William Cowper succinctly captured this truth in the words of his hymn:

> Ye fearful saints, fresh courage take;
> The clouds ye so much dread
> Are big with mercy and shall break
> In blessings on your head.

Greek Words, Phrases, and Constructions in 7:11–13

Verse 11

οὐχ ηὕρισκον—here the imperfect indicative expresses lasting inability: "they were unable to find food."

χορτάσματα—this noun in the neuter plural means "fodder" and is a synonym of χόρτος (grass). It can also mean food "for men or flock."[25]

---

24. Refer to F. F. Bruce, *The Book of the Acts*, rev. ed., New International Commentary on the New Testament series (Grand Rapids: Eerdmans, 1988), p. 137 n. 35; R. A. Koivisto, "Stephen's Speech: A Theology of Errors?" *GTJ* 8 (1987): 101–14.
25. Thayer, p. 670.

Verses 12–13

εἰς—as a preposition with a locative sense, it takes the place of ἐν (in), which in fact is the preposition that occurs in Genesis 42:2 (LXX).[26]

ἀνεγνωρίσθη—this compound form is intensive. It is preferred to the simple form because of the attestation of the better Greek manuscripts.

---

c. Moses' Training
7:17–22

Stephen has adequately demonstrated that he has not blasphemed God and has not dishonored his worship. Now he is ready to answer the charge that he has spoken blasphemous words against Moses. Note that he devotes the greater part of his speech to the life, mission, and teaching of Moses.

17. "When the time was approaching for God to fulfill the promise he had made to Abraham, our people became more and more numerous in Egypt, 18. until a different king began to rule over Egypt, who did not know Joseph. 19. This king took advantage of our race, mistreated our fathers, and made them abandon their infants so that they would not survive."

The new phase in the history of God's people is the fulfillment of the promise God had made four hundred years earlier to Abraham. This promise, of course, related to Abraham's numerous descendants and the inheritance of Canaan (Gen. 15:5, 7). God permits four centuries to go past during which the family of Jacob increased and formed a nation (compare Exod. 1:7). (Moses reveals that at the time of the exodus there were six hundred thousand men on foot, not counting the women and children [Exod. 12:37; Num. 1:46; see also Ps. 105:24]. Scholars debate about population estimates; one possibility is that the total population was about a million and a half.) God determines the time for the growth of the nation and its eventual exodus from Egypt.

The estimated time between the death of Joseph and the rise of the Pharaoh who did not know Joseph is about two centuries. Joseph reached the age of 110 (Gen. 50:26), and when Moses was 80 years of age he led the Israelites out of Egypt and set them free from Pharaoh's rule. The Pharaoh who no longer honored Joseph and cared for his descendants belonged to the eighteenth dynasty. His name was Thutmose I. He was exceedingly cruel and issued the decree to destroy all the Hebrew male babies (Exod. 1:22). Note that Moses' older brother, Aaron, was born before the decree

---

26. Friedrich Blass and Albert Debrunner, *A Greek Grammar of the New Testament and Other Early Christian Literature*, trans. and rev. Robert Funk (Chicago: University of Chicago Press, 1961), #205.

was issued, so that the rise of Pharaoh Thutmose I took place just before Moses was born (approximately 1530 B.C.).[27]

Moses discloses that this Pharaoh put the Israelites to forced labor in building the cities of Pithom and Rameses for him (Exod. 1:11). Stephen says that Pharaoh took advantage of the Jewish people, for the forced labor caused the death of countless Jewish slaves. Pharaoh wanted to check the growth of the population, but God thwarted his purposes by giving the Israelites phenomenal numerical growth. The Egyptians were cruel to their slaves not only in making them perform all kinds of tasks but also in ordering the Hebrew midwives to kill all the Jewish male children at birth (Exod. 1:15–16). But in spite of Pharaoh's inhuman decrees, the Hebrews continued to increase in numbers. As a last resort, Pharaoh ordered that all the Hebrew male babies be thrown into the Nile (Exod. 1:22).

Two observations are pertinent. First, the destruction of the male babies in Egypt parallels the killing of the male infants in Bethlehem when Jesus was born (Matt. 2:16).[28] The lives of both Moses and Jesus are spared, and Moses serves as a type of Christ. Second, through Pharaoh's continued cruelty to the Israelites, God prepared them for their freedom and exodus and gave them a desire to travel to the Promised Land.

20. "At this time, Moses was born and he was a handsome child to God. For three months he was taken care of in his father's house. 21. And after he was abandoned, Pharaoh's daughter adopted him and brought him up as her own son. 22. Moses was instructed in all the wisdom of the Egyptians, and he was powerful in words and deeds."

In these critical days, Moses was born into the family of a Levite (Exod. 2:1–2). The family included two older children: Moses' sister, Miriam, and his brother, Aaron. The Old Testament account and the writer of Hebrews state that Moses was handsome (Exod. 2:2; Heb. 11:23). The literal translation, "[Moses] was a handsome child to God," perhaps is a Semitic idiom that means "exceedingly fair."[29] The New International Version has the reading, "he was no ordinary child."

Moses' parents accepted this beautiful child as a gift from God and therefore were not minded to abandon him. For three months, they protected him from the searching eyes and ears of Pharaoh's soldiers. But the time came to give him up. His parents fashioned a basket made of papyrus leaves sealed with tar and pitch; having put Moses in it, they hid the basket and child among the reeds of the Nile. They instructed their daughter, Miriam, to watch Moses. Incidentally, the name *Moses* sounds like a Hebrew word that means "drawn out [of the water]."

---

27. William H. Shea, "Exodus, Date of the," *ISBE*, vol. 2, p. 233.
28. Consult W. H. Gispen, *Bible Student's Commentary: Exodus,* trans. Ed van der Maas (Grand Rapids: Zondervan; St. Catharines: Paideia, 1982), p. 37.
29. Moule, *Idiom-Book,* p. 46.

The daughter of Pharaoh came to the river to bathe. When her attendants saw the baby, they drew him out of the water and brought Moses to the princess. She adopted him as her son and reared him in the royal palace (Exod. 2:10).[30] We see God's providence in protecting Moses at a time when other Hebrew infants died because of Pharaoh's cruelty. Yet Moses himself became part of Pharaoh's family when the princess adopted him. Although the Old Testament Scriptures do not relate Moses' training at the royal court, Stephen follows tradition and discloses that Moses received an education "in all the wisdom of the Egyptians."[31] In ancient times, Egypt was a great center of learning, knowledge, and wisdom (compare I Kings 4:30). Moses probably was instructed in philosophy, mathematics, literature, and rhetoric. These disciplines qualified him for a leadership role. Stephen is brief and to the point. He says only that Moses "was powerful in words and deeds."

Of course, as leader of the Israelites Moses repeatedly demonstrates his ability to speak well in the presence of Pharaoh or in addressing the people of Israel. His self-evaluation that he is slow of speech (Exod. 4:10) must be understood as an excuse to be relieved of the task God put before him. The Old Testament reveals that not Aaron but Moses speaks eloquently and performs numerous miracles. Indeed, Moses was powerful in word and deed.

Greek Words, Phrases, and Constructions in 7:17–22

Verse 17

καθώς—this compound is not translated literally ("just as") but is regarded as a temporal adverb ("when").

ὡμολόγησεν—in the early church, the verb ὁμολογεῖν was given the technical meaning *to make one's confession*. Scribes, therefore, were ready to alter this reading to either ἐπαγγελεῖν (to promise) or ὀμνύειν (to swear). However, ὁμολογεῖν in this context means "to promise."[32]

Verse 19

τοῦ ποιεῖν—the singular definite article in the genitive case with the present infinitive normally expresses purpose. Here the intention seems to be result: "so as to make."[33] Also, the combination εἰς τό with the present infinitive ζῳογονεῖσθαι in this sentence expresses hypothetical result.

---

30. Josephus *Antiquities* 2.9.7 [232].

31. Philo *Life of Moses* 1.20–22.

32. Bruce M. Metzger, *A Textual Commentary on the Greek New Testament*, 3d corrected ed. (London and New York: United Bible Societies, 1975), p. 345. See also Blass and Debrunner, *Greek Grammar*, #187.

33. A. T. Robertson, *A Grammar of the Greek New Testament in the Light of Historical Research* (Nashville: Broadman, 1934), p. 1090.

Verses 21–22

ἐκτεθέντος αὐτοῦ—the genitive case in both the aorist passive participle and the pronoun signifies the genitive absolute construction.

εἰς—with αὐτόν as a predicate accusative, this prepositional phrase means "as a son."

πάσῃ σοφίᾳ—with the noun *wisdom* in the abstract, the preceding adjective can mean either "every" or "all."[34]

---

d. Moses' Departure
7:23–29

The next paragraph in Stephen's speech reveals Moses' age and his inability to give leadership. Although Moses is forty years of age, he is not yet ready to be Israel's leader. He needs additional time to prepare himself for the task God is giving him.

23. "When Moses was about forty years old, he decided to visit his fellow countrymen, the Israelites. 24. And when he saw one of them being treated unjustly by an Egyptian, he came to his help; he avenged the oppressed by striking down the Egyptian. 25. He supposed that his fellow countrymen would understand that God was using him to deliver them, but they did not understand."

a. "When Moses was about forty years old." The Old Testament does not say how old Moses was when he fled to Midian. It merely reports that Moses was grown (Exod. 2:11; see also Heb. 11:24). However, we learn that Moses was 80 when he stood before Pharaoh with his brother, Aaron (Exod. 7:7), and that he was 120 years old when he died (Deut. 34:7). Jewish tradition relates that Moses was 40 years of age when he fled Egypt, that he lived in Midian for 40 years, and that he led the Israelites for 40 years. Therefore, his life is divided into three equal periods of 40 years each.[35]

b. "He decided to visit his fellow countrymen, the Israelites." The writer of Hebrews explains that Moses did not want to be known as the son of Pharaoh's daughter but cast his lot with the people of God, who were ill-treated by Pharaoh (Heb. 11:24–25). Moses identified himself with the descendants of Abraham, God's covenant people. In spite of his training at Pharaoh's palace, he was an Israelite at heart. Accordingly, at the age of forty Moses decided to visit his fellow Israelites. Not only did he claim to be a physical descendant of Abraham when he determined to associate with the oppressed Hebrew slaves; he also knew that he was a spiritual descendant of Abraham because of his faith in God (compare Heb. 11:26).[36] The

---

34. Robertson, *Grammar*, p. 772.

35. SB, vol. 2, pp. 679–80. Some sources say that Moses was twenty years old when he fled Egypt.

36. Refer to Simon J. Kistemaker, *Exposition of the Epistle to the Hebrews*, New Testament Commentary series (Grand Rapids: Baker, 1984), pp. 337–38.

Greek text literally has, "it came up in his heart to visit his brothers, the sons of Israel." That is, God worked in his heart so that he decided to cast his lot with the Israelites. And thus the word *visit* in this verse means more than a social meeting; it implies helping someone in need.

c. "And when he saw one of them being treated unjustly." When Moses left the royal palace to be with the Israelites, he risked the wrath of Pharaoh for breaking Egyptian family ties in favor of Hebrew identification. Moreover, he also ran the risk of being misunderstood by the Israelites, who saw him as a member of Pharaoh's family.

When Moses observed an Egyptian abusing an Israelite, he came to the rescue by striking the Egyptian oppressor so that he died. The Western text of Greek manuscripts, following the Old Testament account, adds that Moses buried him in the sand (Exod. 2:12). Apart from the question whether Moses had any justification for taking the law into his own hands, the event proved that Moses disqualified himself for the role of leadership. Moses had to learn the lesson of meekness (Num. 12:3) to become an effective leader.

d. "He supposed that his fellow countrymen would understand that God was using him to deliver them."[37] Moses was of the opinion that he was God's appointed man to deliver the Israelites and that they would acknowledge him as their leader. He was a mature person who had been fully educated in Egyptian learning. He had a genuine faith in Israel's God, who had promised to deliver his people from slavery four hundred years after he gave Abraham the promise to inherit Canaan (Gen. 15:13). The Israelites treasured this knowledge, perhaps through oral tradition, and patiently waited for their freedom. However, even if Moses was acquainted with this divine prophecy, his fellow countrymen did not accept him as their deliverer. Stephen says, "they did not understand."

26. "Then on the following day he came upon two Israelites who were fighting and he tried to reconcile them. He said, 'Men, you are brothers. Why are you hurting each other?' 27. But the one who was mistreating his fellow countryman said, 'Who made you a ruler and judge over us? 28. Do you want to kill me as you killed the Egyptian yesterday?' 29. When Moses heard this, he fled and became a refugee in the land of Midian and had two sons."

a. "Then on the following day." The next day proved to be Moses' watershed. By returning to the Israelites, he indicated that his break with the royal family was permanent. He expected his countrymen to accept him as their God-given leader who would deliver them from cruel slavery. However, he was sadly mistaken. When he returned to the Israelites, he saw two of them fighting with the intent of hurting each other. Moses tried to intervene as peacemaker. He stopped them and said, "Men, you are brothers. Why are you hurting each other?"

---

37. Josephus *Antiquities* 2.9.2–3 [205–15].

At this point, Stephen does not follow the Old Testament text but gives the drift of Moses' original question, "Why are you hitting your fellow countryman?" (Exod. 2:13). Note that Moses stressed the concept *brothers* not in the sense that these two men belonged to one family but rather that they were members of the Hebrew race. Moses, therefore, called attention to their (and his) shared nationality. When he asked why they were trying to hurt each other, he indirectly referred to wounds the Israelite slaves received from Egyptian overseers. Moreover, he inadvertently called attention to his own forceful and fatal attack on an Egyptian.

b. "Who made you a ruler and judge over us?" Instead of finding rapport with the men he was trying to help, Moses encountered repudiation and rebuff. The Israelite who was hurting his countryman pushed Moses aside, not physically but verbally, with an attack that made Moses cringe. He bluntly challenged Moses' authority to come to the Israelites as a ruler and judge. With this question, the self-appointed spokesman for the Hebrew nation rejected Moses as the man called by God to deliver his people. This rejection was both physical and spiritual. The Israelite, recognizing in Moses evidences of Egyptian culture, refused to recognize Moses as an Israelite. And in his spiritual blindness, he closed his eyes to God's plan of salvation.

c. "Do you want to kill me as you killed the Egyptian yesterday?" For the words of this Israelite, Stephen quotes exactly from the Septuagint. The answer that the Israelite expected, of course, had to be negative. This question drove Moses to despair. He could not return to Pharaoh's court after breaking ties with the royal family. He knew that when Pharaoh heard of the Egyptian's death, he would try to kill Moses (Exod. 2:15). Conversely, Moses would find no shelter among the Israelites; the rude rebuff of the Hebrew spokesman indicated as much. There was nothing left for Moses to do but flee and become a refugee in a foreign land.

d. "He fled and became a refugee in the land of Midian." Because the Midianites were nomads who with their flocks sought pasture anywhere, the exact boundaries of Midian cannot be defined accurately. Most scholars place it on the east side of the Gulf of Aqabah, in modern Saudi Arabia. Perhaps it extended to or included the Sinai Peninsula, for Moses led Jethro's flock to the far side of the desert near Horeb (Sinai). Scripture calls Jethro, who was Moses' father-in-law, the priest of Midian (Exod. 3:1). This was the place where Moses fled from the presence of Pharaoh and was an alien for forty years.[38]

e. "And had two sons." Purposely Stephen adds that Moses had two sons. In the historical context to which Stephen refers, Moses fled to Midian, was welcomed into Jethro's home, and married Zipporah, one of Jethro's seven daughters, but had only one son (Exod. 2:16–22). From a later account that describes the exodus, we learn that Moses had two sons,

---

38. Consult Robert L. Alden, "Midian, Midianites," *ZPEB*, vol. 4, pp. 220–22.

Gershom and Eliezer. Stephen calls to mind this later passage because it gives and explains the names of Moses' sons: Gershom means "an alien there," and Eliezer means "my God is [my] helper" (Exod. 18:3–4). Moses never became a Midianite during his forty-year stay with Jethro. As the names of his sons reflect, Moses remained a foreigner who put his trust in Israel's God.

Doctrinal Considerations in 7:23–29

We make three observations:

a. *Type*. The parallel between Moses and Christ is striking. Moses, the leader of Israel, was destined to deliver his people from the bondage of slavery in Egypt. Jesus was sent by God to deliver his people from the bondage of sin and death. Moses came as a native Hebrew to his own people, who flatly rejected him and caused him to flee to Midian. Jesus was born in Bethlehem, but when he came as a teacher to his own people, they rejected and killed him (compare John 1:11). Moses was exalted by God, who commissioned him in the desert to lead the Israelites out of Egypt, the land of their captivity, into the freedom of the Promised Land. God also exalted Jesus by raising him from the dead. Jesus delivers his people from the bondage of sin and spiritual death and grants them freedom in the kingdom of heaven. The difference in this parallel is that Moses came to Israel as a servant in the name of God, but in Jesus God himself comes to his people and saves them.

Stephen explains that Moses is a type and forerunner of Christ (v. 37) and quotes a prophecy given to Moses. Moses was told that God would raise up a prophet like him from among his brothers (Deut. 18:15, 18). And Jesus fulfilled that prophecy.

b. *Rejection*. Stephen clearly shows that the Israelites rejected Moses as their deliverer, and thus he touches a theme that is relevant to Israel. The theme of rejection not only appears in Stephen's speech (vv. 27, 35, 39), but also prevails throughout Israel's history. The Jewish people are notorious for rejecting the grace of God. In his address, Stephen wants to remind his audience of this negative characteristic that has obstructed Israel's relationship with God.

c. *Honor for Moses*. In this part of his speech, Stephen leaves no doubt that he has great respect for Moses. Therefore, the accusations of his opponents, who say that he blasphemed Moses, are unfounded.

Greek Words, Phrases, and Constructions in 7:23–27

Verse 23

ἐπληροῦτο αὐτῷ—this is a favorite verb in Luke's writings. Note the imperfect tense in the passive voice ("it was being fulfilled to him"). The verb form conveys a sense of approximation.

ἀνέβη—this is a typical Semitic construction: "it came up in his heart" (e.g., the Septuagint of Isa. 65:16; Jer. 3:16; Ezek. 38:10). The subject of the verb is the infinitive ἐπισκέψασθαι (to visit).

Verse 24

ἠμύνατο—from the verb ἀμύνομαι, which occurs once in the entire New Testament. In the middle voice, it is translated "to assist [a friend]."[39]

Verses 26–27

συνήλλασσεν—this is the imperfect active of συναλλάσσω (I reconcile). The imperfect is conative: "he tried to reconcile them."

ἀπώσατο—from ἀπωθέω (I push aside), the form is the aorist middle: "he pushed Moses away from himself." See also verse 39.

---

e. Moses' Mission
7:30–36

Here Stephen states that the second period of forty years in the life of Moses has come to an end. The last forty-year period comprises Moses' mission of leading the people of Israel out of Egypt, through the Red Sea, and in the desert. Moses needed forty years of schooling at Pharaoh's palace and forty years of training in the desert before he was fully prepared to serve God. (Incidentally, many other leaders spent time in the desert to prepare themselves for consecrated service [e.g., David, Elijah, John the Baptist, Jesus, and Paul].)

30. "And after forty years had passed, an angel appeared to Moses in the flames of a burning bush in the desert near Mount Sinai. 31. When Moses saw it, he was amazed at the sight. As he approached to look at it more closely, there was the voice of the Lord: 32. 'I am the God of your fathers, the God of Abraham, Isaac, and Jacob.' Moses was trembling and did not dare to look."

Stephen continues to relate the history of Moses by going through the Book of Exodus. He appears to have committed the account to memory, for in numerous places he provides word-for-word quotations from the Septuagint. Here is a man who knows the Scriptures and is able to expound them. He relates the account of Moses' mission.

a. "And after forty years had passed, an angel appeared to Moses." At the age of eighty, after being with Jethro for forty years, Moses led Jethro's flock into the southern part of the Sinai Peninsula near Mount Sinai (see Exod. 3:12; 19:11–13; Deut. 1:6). While there, he noticed a bush that continued to burn without being consumed (Exod. 3:2).[40] As he approached the bush to have a closer look at this strange spectacle, he heard the voice of God. Stephen explains that the angel is the Lord (v. 31), that is, God himself (vv. 32, 35; Exod. 3:2, 7). Some interpreters understand the angel to be the pre-

---

39. Robertson, *Grammar*, p. 805.
40. Presbyterian churches have taken their symbol of the burning bush from this text. For their motto they use the Latin words *nec tamen consumebatur* (however, it was not consumed).

incarnate Son of God. For example, John Calvin states that God never communicates with man except through Christ.[41] But in this context, the evidence is insufficient to conclude that Stephen is referring to Christ. We say rather that "the angel bears the authority and presence of God Himself."[42]

God appeared in the flames of a burning bush and does so in conformity with many of his appearances in flame. Thus, God was a pillar of fire by night to the Israelites as they traveled through the desert (Exod. 13:21); at the time of the giving of the law, God descended on Mount Sinai in fire (Exod. 19:18; also compare I Kings 18:24, 38).

b. "When Moses saw it, he was amazed at the sight." God kindled Moses' curiosity, and when Moses approached the burning bush, God spoke to him. God bridged the centuries and identified himself as the God of the three patriarchs: Abraham, Isaac, and Jacob. The covenant he made with Abraham and the promises he gave the patriarch were real. God would fulfill his word and redeem his people Israel from bondage. No wonder that Moses trembled and did not dare to look at the bush. Moses again trembled with fear when God spoke from Mount Sinai (Heb. 12:21). He realized that he stood in the presence of God. Yet God called Moses and commissioned him to the task of leading his people out of Egypt.

33. "Then the Lord said to him: 'Remove the sandals from your feet, for the place where you are standing is holy ground. 34. I have indeed seen the mistreatment of my people in Egypt and heard their groaning. I have come down to deliver them. Come now, I will send you to Egypt.' "

a. *Holiness.* Moses realized that he was standing in the presence of the holy God, whose presence sanctified even the ground where Moses stood (see Josh. 5:15). Moses was standing in the sanctuary of God, so to speak, and had to loosen and take off his sandals. Orientals still do so when they enter temples, sanctuaries, and even their own homes. They show utmost care not to defile that which is sacred and clean.

Stephen transposes the sequence the Exodus account gives. In this account, God first told Moses to take off his shoes and then revealed himself as the God of the patriarchs (3:5–6). The sequence has no bearing on the importance of the event. God showed Moses that even the area of a burning desert bush is holy when God is present. And Stephen uses this incident to tell his Sanhedrin audience that God's sacred presence is not limited to the Jerusalem temple. Elizabeth Barrett Browning captured the essence of God's presence in the burning bush when she said:

> Earth's crammed with heaven
> And every common bush afire with God;
> But only he who sees takes off his shoes,
> The rest sit round it and pluck blackberries.

---

41. Calvin, *Acts of the Apostles,* vol. 1, p. 190. See also John Albert Bengel, *Gnomon of the New Testament,* ed. Andrew R. Fausset, 5 vols. (Edinburgh: Clark, 1877), vol. 2, p. 576.
42. Alford, *Alford's Greek Testament,* vol. 2, p. 75.

Notice that before the bush began to burn, the ground was no more holy than any other place in the Sinai Peninsula. Also, the space occupied by the burning bush became holy only for the time God's glory was present.[43] Any place on earth, then, is holy when God meets man who worships him.

b. *Commission.* Moses spent forty years in Midian as a shepherd while the Israelites suffered from the cruelties of Egyptian slave drivers. He fled to the freedom of Midian; conversely, the Israelites could not escape but languished in misery. No doubt Moses thought about God's people and the promise of their deliverance. When God said that he had really taken note of their oppression and had really heard their groaning, God revealed that his covenant and his promises to Abraham were still valid. God spoke in human terms and Hebraic idiom when he said he had really seen the misery of the Israelites and had really heard their cries for deliverance. Also, God said that he had come down to deliver them. He commissioned Moses as his servant to set his people free: "Come now, I will send you to Egypt." The time for the redemption of Israel had arrived and God chose Moses as the man to achieve this task. The short command, "Come now," meant that Moses had to leave Midian and return to the people who had rejected him. He did not have to fear the Egyptians who wanted to kill him, for God revealed to Moses that they had died (Exod. 4:19).

35. "This is the same Moses whom the Israelites rejected when they said, 'Who made you ruler and judge?' This man God sent as ruler and deliverer with the help of the angel who appeared to him in the bush. 36. He led them out of Egypt, having performed miracles and signs in Egypt, at the Red Sea, and in the desert for forty years."

a. "This is the same Moses." Stephen no longer recounts the history of Moses as such. He now begins to interpret the significance of the event by showing that Moses returned to the same people who forty years earlier had rejected him with the question, "Who made you ruler and judge?" Stephen calls attention to Moses as a person by using the demonstrative pronoun *this* [one] to describe Moses. He stresses the theme of rejection to which the history of Israel's desert journey testifies. The parallel between Moses rejected by the Israelites and the Christ repudiated by the Jews is obvious.

b. "This man God sent as ruler and deliverer." The Israelite who forty years earlier asked Moses, "Who made you a ruler and judge over us?" (v. 27) represented the nation Israel that rejected God's grace. In spite of Israel's rebuff, God sent Moses with power and authority as a "ruler and deliverer." Note the difference in wording, for the word *deliverer* has taken the place of "judge." A judge is able to deliver a person from an adversary who has brought charges against him. A deliverer redeems a nation from the oppression of another nation.[44]

---

43. Consult Calvin, *Acts of the Apostles*, vol. 1, p. 194.
44. Bengel, *Gnomon of the New Testament*, vol. 2, p. 577.

Notice that the terms *ruler* and *deliverer* actually point to Christ. First, Moses was Israel's ruler as the father of this nation. The apostles proclaimed Jesus as "Prince," which in the Greek is a word related to "ruler" (e.g., 5:31). Next, the Israelites knew that God would redeem them from the yoke of the Egyptians (Exod. 6:6), for God is the redeemer of Israel (Ps. 19:14; 78:35).

When Stephen utters the expression *redeemer* in the Sanhedrin, he touches the deepest longing of his contemporaries. This longing was expressed eloquently by the two men on the way to Emmaus: "We were hoping that [Jesus] was the one who was going to redeem Israel" (Luke 24:21; and compare 2:38). By calling Moses both a "ruler and deliverer," Stephen tells his listeners that in this double aspect Moses is a type of Christ.[45]

c. "With the help of the angel." God commissioned Moses when he spoke to him from the burning bush. And God gave him divine power and authority to address Pharaoh and the elders of Israel. Moses received power to perform miracles and signs with respect to the ten plagues in Egypt, the crossing of the Red Sea and the drowning of Pharaoh's army, and the protecting care for the Israelites in the desert for forty years. The expression *miracles and signs* unmistakably points to Jesus Christ, who during his earthly ministry demonstrated in word and deed that God had commissioned him to redeem his people.

Greek Words, Phrases, and Constructions in 7:30–36

Verse 30

ἐτῶν—the genitive absolute occurs frequently in this chapter (e.g., vv. 21, 31).

ἄγγελος—here the noun is without the definite article and the qualification τοῦ κυρίου (see 5:19; Exod. 3:2 [LXX]). The angel is the voice of the Lord (v. 31), God (v. 32), and the Lord (v. 33).

Verse 31

ἐθαύμαζεν—the imperfect tense is descriptive.

κατανοῆσαι—this aorist active infinitive discloses the perfective sense of the compound form. It describes "the completion of a mental process."[46]

Verse 34

ἰδὼν εἶδον—two forms, the one an aorist participle and the other the aorist active of ὁράω (I see), are a Semitism that reflects the Hebrew infinitive absolute construction. It expresses emphasis.

---

45. Colin Brown, *NIDNTT*, vol. 3, p. 199.
46. James Hope Moulton, *A Grammar of New Testament Greek*, vol. 1, *Prolegomena*, 2d ed. (Edinburgh: Clark, 1906), p. 117. See also Hanna, *Grammatical Aid*, p. 201.

ἀποστείλω—although the future indicative is expected (I will send), the extraordinary subjunctive with futuristic meaning appears.[47]

Verse 35

τοῦτον—this demonstrative pronoun referring to Moses occurs six times in this passage (vv. 35–40). For emphasis, it stands at the beginning of each sentence (vv. 35 [twice], 36, 37, 38).

λυτρωτήν—we should not translate this noun "deliverer" without considering the meaning of λυτρόω (I free by paying a ransom). In Scripture, the noun is used twice for God (Pss. 19:14; 78:35 [LXX]), once for Moses (Acts 7:35), but never for Jesus.

ἀπέσταλκεν—in English, the perfect tense cannot be expressed in the context of this sentence. Translations have the simple past tense "sent." However, the perfect shows lasting result.

σὺν χειρί—literally "with the hand," the expression is a direct translation from the Hebrew. It means "with the help."

Verse 36

ἐξήγαγεν ποιήσας—the aorist tense of the participle should not be taken too strictly, for it also applies to the miracles and signs Moses performed during the forty-year desert journey. The aorist tense of the verb ἐξήγαγεν is culminative and refers to the entire journey.

---

f. Moses' Teaching
7:37–43

If anyone in Stephen's audience fails to realize that there is a direct parallel between Moses and Jesus, let him hear a prophecy God gave Moses. This prophecy compares Moses with another prophet whom God would raise up from the Jewish people. Quoting this prophecy, Stephen says,

37. "This is the Moses who said to the Israelites, 'God will raise up a prophet for you from your brothers as he raised me up.' "

In his remarks to the members of the Sanhedrin, Stephen is emphatic. He tells them that this Moses about whom he has been speaking is the man who gave the Israelites a divine prophecy that reveals the coming of the Prophet. To be sure, the wording of this prophecy does not have the definite article before the term *prophet*. But from the New Testament and other sources (Samaritan, Qumran, and Jewish literature) we learn that the people of Jesus' day were expecting the coming of *the* Prophet (e.g., John 1:19–21; 7:40).[48] Moreover, in the temple courts Peter proclaimed the fulfillment of Moses' prophecy (3:22). Accordingly, everyone in the Sanhedrin knew that none other than Jesus Christ of Nazareth had come as the prophet foretold by Moses.

---

47. Moule, *Idiom-Book*, p. 22.

48. Joachim Jeremias, *TDNT*, vol. 4, pp. 859–63; Longenecker, *Acts*, p. 343; Donald Guthrie, *New Testament Theology* (Downers Grove: Inter-Varsity, 1981), p. 269.

38. "This is the one who was in the assembly in the desert with the angel who was speaking to him at Mount Sinai and with our fathers. He received living oracles to pass on to us."

a. "This is the one who was in the assembly." Once again Stephen stresses that Moses is the one who reveals God's law. What did Moses do? He served as mediator between God and the people of Israel when God gave them the Ten Commandments in the desert at Mount Sinai (Exod. 20:1–17). Moses was in the assembly. The Greek at this point has the word *ekklēsia*, which literally means "church."[49] The term, of course, describes the people of Israel assembled at Mount Sinai to hear God giving them the Decalogue (see Deut. 4:10). Modern translations, therefore, have the reading *assembly* or *congregation*. F. F. Bruce observes, "As Moses was with the ἐκκλησία then, Christ is with his ἐκκλησία now, and it is still a pilgrim ἐκκλησία, 'the assembly in the wilderness.' "[50] Moses did not receive the law in the tabernacle when God dwelled among the Israelites, but he received the Decalogue on top of Mount Sinai. Notice that earlier God had commissioned Moses near this same mountain (Exod. 3:1).

b. "The angel who was speaking to him . . . and [to] our fathers." The Old Testament account reveals that God himself spoke to the Israelites from Mount Sinai (Exod. 20:1; Deut. 5:4). At a later time, God himself gave Moses two tablets of stone on which God had written the Ten Commandments (Exod. 31:18; Deut. 9:10). But Jewish tradition, which Stephen transmitted to the Sanhedrin, taught that an angel served as a mediator between God and man and thus conveyed God's law to the people.[51]

c. "He received living oracles to pass on to us." Moses received numerous commandments (in addition to the Decalogue) which he taught the people. Stephen calls these laws "living oracles." The term *oracle* signifies a short saying and aptly describes the individual commands God gave Moses. When Stephen says that these oracles are living, he proves to his audience that he has the greatest respect for the law of Moses. We should not interpret the word *living* to mean that God uttered these laws in a living voice or that the laws themselves are life-giving.[52] That is self-evident. These oracles are not fossils that time has preserved in rock. Rather, Moses tells the Israelites that the law of God is their life, for with it they are able to live their earthly lives to the fullest extent (Deut. 30:19–20; 32:46–47). Scripture repeatedly states that the Word of God is living (for example, Heb. 4:12).

39. "Our fathers refused to obey, however; they rejected him and in their hearts returned to Egypt."

Stephen calls the rebellious Israelites in the desert "our fathers," of

---

49. See KJV, RV, ASV.
50. Bruce, *Book of the Acts*, p. 142 n. 57.
51. See especially SB, vol. 3, pp. 554–56. Also compare 7:53; Gal. 3:19; Heb. 2:2.
52. Alford, *Alford's Greek Testament*, vol. 2, p. 77.

whom he and his listeners are physical descendants. Our fathers, he says, did not wish to obey Moses and the teaching of the law. Stephen is not interested in reciting the history of Israel's desert journey. He mentions that the people rejected Moses' leadership and contemplated returning to Egypt. Stephen alludes to the time when the twelve spies returned from their mission to explore Canaan. Although two spies, Caleb and Joshua, exhorted the Israelites to take possession of the land, the other ten spies spread the alarming news that Canaan was inhabited by giants. These ten so frightened the people that they told Moses and Aaron it would be better for them to return to Egypt and choose another leader (Num. 14:4).

The theme of Israel rejecting Moses is prevalent in Stephen's speech (see vv. 27, 35). Of course, the people did not return to Egypt, but, except for Caleb and Joshua, all those who were twenty years and older perished in the desert. Once again the parallel between Moses rejected by Israel in the desert and Jesus rejected by the Jews is evident. The members of the Sanhedrin were physical descendants of the Israelites who repudiated Moses and wanted to return to Egypt.

40. "They said to Aaron, 'Make for us gods who will go before us. For this Moses, who led us out of the land of Egypt, we do not know what has become of him.' 41. And they made a calf in those days; they offered a sacrifice to the idol and rejoiced in the works of their hands."

Were the Israelites momentarily deceived by the ten spies? No, says Stephen, all along they rejected God, as history clearly shows. In spite of everything God did for his people—

all the miracles performed in Egypt,

the crossing of the Red Sea,

the daily manna and the provision of drinking water,

the cloud shielding them from the hot desert sun,

the pillar of fire protecting them at night

—the Israelites nevertheless asked Aaron to make idols to lead them.

Stephen quotes almost word for word from the Greek translation of the Old Testament. While Moses was on Mount Sinai receiving the law, the people said to Aaron: "Make for us gods who will go before us. For this Moses, who led us out of the land of Egypt, we do not know what has become of him" (compare Exod. 32:1, 23). They demonstrate that they have not put their faith in Israel's God but want to worship the idols of Egypt. They reject the one true God in favor of handmade images and assert that these lifeless objects will lead them. Note that they ask for "gods," even though the only idol they make is the golden calf.

Furthermore, the Israelites renounce Moses as their leader in disparaging words: "as for this fellow Moses who led us out of Egypt" (NIV). They know that Moses has ascended to the top of Mount Sinai to receive God's law, but they express their impatience: "We do not know what has become of him." Seventy elders of Israel, Aaron, and his sons Nadab and Abihu ascended Mount Sinai with Moses. They saw God and ate a covenant meal in his presence (Exod. 24:9–11). All these people were witnesses who could testify about God's glory and Moses' mission, yet the people refused to accept their testimony.

In this state of mind, the Israelites deliberately broke the covenant God had made with them (Exod. 24:1–8) and with Abraham their spiritual father (Gen. 17:7). They spurned the rich promises God had given them and refused to accept and keep his law. The contrast between Moses receiving the Ten Commandments on top of Mount Sinai and Israel worshiping a golden calf at the foot of that mountain could not be starker.

With this illustration from Jewish history, Stephen recounts a chapter his contemporaries would rather ignore. Here is a report of an incident in which the most blatant sin of Israel is depicted: the rejection of the Lord God, whom the Israelites replaced with a golden calf.[53]

"They made a calf in those days." Not Aaron, whom they chose as leader to replace Moses, but the people themselves fashioned an idol in the form of a calf. Actually, the calf was portrayed as the male gender and a symbol of fertility. Scholars assume that the Israelites made it from wood and overlaid it with gold, for Moses burned the idol with fire and ground it to powder (Exod. 32:20).

"They offered a sacrifice to the idol and rejoiced in the works of their hands." The Israelites deliberately transgressed God's law that states not to have other gods before him, not to make an idol of anything, and not to bow down and worship it (Exod. 20:1–4; Deut. 5:7–8). They brought burnt offerings and fellowship offerings to this idol and then indulged in a time of eating, drinking, and revelry (Exod. 32:6). In the Greek, the verb *rejoiced* indicates that their festivities lasted for some time.

42. "But God turned away and delivered them to worship the hosts of heaven, just as it is written in the book of the prophets:

> **'You did not bring me sacrifices and offerings**
> **for forty years in the desert,**
> **O house of Israel, did you?**
> **43. You took along the tent of Moloch**
> **and the star of your god Rephan,**
> **and the images you made to worship them.**
> **I will banish you beyond Babylon.' "**

Note these points:

a. *God's judgment.* Here Stephen changes from following the historical

---

53. Consult the Babylonian Talmud, e.g., *Shabbath* 17a, *Megillah* 25b, *Sopherim* 35a. See also A. Pelletier, "Valeur Évocatrice d'un Démarquage Chrétien de la Septante," *Bib* 48 (1967): 388–94.

sequence of Israel's sin to making fitting observations. "God turned away," Stephen says. This clause, however, should not be understood to mean that God merely turned himself away in disgust. Although God is disgusted, he avenges himself by bringing disaster upon those who have sinned against him (compare Josh. 24:20; Isa. 63:10). Whereas he has been good to his people, he now withholds his blessing and turns his back to them.[54]

"[God] delivered them to worship the hosts of heaven." Here is a parallel with Paul's description of people who indulge in sin. God allows sin to run its disastrous course in their lives as just punishment for their disobedience (Rom. 1:24, 26, 28). The hosts of heaven represent the heavenly bodies (sun, moon, and stars), which Israel worshiped at first secretly and later openly. Instead of worshiping the Creator, the Israelites looked up to the created spheres and revered them.[55]

b. *History's record.* Stephen now turns to the book of the twelve minor prophets, which the Jews considered one book in the canon of the Old Testament. Stephen quotes almost verbatim from the Greek translation of Amos 5:25–27.[56] In this passage, the prophet reveals God's displeasure with Israel, first in the time of the desert journey, and second during the time of the kings of Israel and Judah until the exile to Babylon.

God asks a rhetorical question to which the Israelites must answer negatively. "You did not bring me sacrifices and offerings for forty years in the desert, O house of Israel, did you?" Of course, the people offered sacrifices in the desert, as is evident from the institution of the Aaronic priesthood. However, during the time of the desert journey much was lacking and neglected in true worship. The Israelites who were twenty years and older did not serve God with dedication and love, for their hearts were not right with God. They worshiped idols instead of God. Amos intimated to his contemporaries that God could do without sacrifices, as he had in the time of the exodus. Therefore, their offerings would not keep them from being exiled to Babylon.[57] By implication, the sacrifices of Stephen's listeners would not keep the Jerusalem temple from eventual destruction (compare Luke 19:42–44). Worshiping God is not dependent on sacrifices.

c. *Star worship.* "You took along the tent of Moloch and the star of your god Rephan, and the images you made to worship them." The Greek text differs from the Old Testament wording in Amos 5:26, which has

---

54. Thayer, p. 590. Bauer (p. 771) suggests the "non-literal sense . . . *God turned* the Israelites towards the heavenly bodies, so that they were to serve them as their gods."

55. See Deut. 4:19; 17:3; II Kings 21:3, 5; 23:11; Jer. 7:18; 8:2; 19:13; Zeph. 1:5.

56. Refer to E. Richard, "The Creative Use of Amos by the Author of Acts," *NovT* 24 (1982): 37–53.

57. Interpretations of Amos 5:25–27 are numerous and varied. I have followed the suggestion of J. Ridderbos, *De Kleine Profeten: Hosea, Joël, Amos,* 2d ed., Korte Verklaring der Heilige Schrift series (Kampen: Kok, 1952), p. 224.

"You have lifted up the shrine of your king,
    the pedestal of your idols,
    the star of your god—
which you made for yourselves." [NIV]

Except for pointing out the difference in the reading of this passage, we refrain from entering into a discussion on these variations. The Greek text mentions two names, Moloch and Rephan. These two names occur only once each in the New Testament. Moloch was the "Canaanite-Phoenician god of the sky and sun,"[58] or the planet Venus.[59] Rephan (with many variations in spelling) is another name for the planet Saturn. In short, both names refer to the worship of heavenly bodies.

In their worship, the Israelites had degenerated to bowing before the stars in the sky. Perhaps they did so already during the forty-year period, because the text states that the Israelites lifted up the tent of Moloch. There is a parallel between idol worshipers carrying the tabernacle of a heathen god and Levites carrying the tabernacle of the Lord in the desert.

d. *Divine verdict.* In the last sentence of Amos's quotation, "I will banish you beyond Damascus" (according to the Hebrew Bible and the Septuagint), Stephen looks at the text from a historical point of view. He freely changes the word *Damascus* to "Babylon" and obviously has in mind the exile of Judah's kingdom to Babylon (compare II Chron. 36:15–21).

Practical Considerations in 7:39–43

During his ministry, Jesus often told his followers that the spiritual fields were ripe for the harvest, even though the workers were few in number (Matt. 9:37; Luke 10:2; John 4:35). On Pentecost and afterward, these words proved to be true when thousands upon thousands accepted Jesus as their Lord. The church grew, spreading from Jerusalem to Samaria and to the ends of the earth.

Jesus instructed us to pray that the Lord of the harvest would be pleased to send out workers into that harvest field. And many believers respond to the call to serve the Lord. Countless people around the world preach and teach the gospel of Christ to untold millions. Even if this gospel has circled the globe and is proclaimed in all the major languages, the population of the world is increasing at a pace that is faster than the growth of the Christian church. Millions have not yet heard the good news of salvation in Christ.

Yet, missionaries have worked and are working in some countries of the world without any measurable results. They feel the sharp edge of rejection by people belonging to other religions that have the protection and open support of the governments of these nations. They experience Satan's enmity that is bent on eradicating the influence of the gospel. Seemingly, they stand alone in the service of the

---

58. Bauer, p. 526.
59. See J. Gray, "Molech, Moloch," *IDB*, vol. 3, p. 422b.

Lord. In the nineteenth century, Thomas Kelly eloquently expressed the rejection missionaries often experience:

> Where no fruit appears to cheer them,
> And they seem to toil in vain,
> Then in mercy, Lord, draw near them,
> Then their sinking hopes sustain;
> Thus supported,
> Let their zeal revive again.
>
> In the midst of opposition,
> Let them trust, O Lord, in Thee;
> When success attends their mission,
> Let Thy servants humbler be.
> Never leave them
> Till Thy face in heaven they see.

Greek Words, Phrases, and Constructions in 7:41–43

Verse 41

εὐφραίνοντο—the imperfect passive from εὐφραίνομαι (I rejoice in) shows continued action in the past. The cause of rejoicing lies in the prepositional phrase ἐν τοῖς ἔργοις (in the works), which has a causal connotation.

Verse 42

ἔστρεψεν—from στρέφω (I turn), the aorist active lacks a direct object. The verb is intransitive, not reflexive, and means "turned away."

Verse 43

τὴν σκηνήν—notice the same expression in the next verse (v. 44), where it signifies the tabernacle of the Lord.

ἐπέκεινα—this adverb is pressed into service as a preposition to mean "beyond." It derives from ἐπὶ ἐκεῖνα [μέρη], "to those parts."

---

g. Tabernacle
7:44–50

In this part of his speech, Stephen skillfully refutes one of the accusations leveled against him: "you teach that Jesus of Nazareth will break down the temple" (6:14). He shows that although Israel has had a tabernacle and now has a temple, God is not bound to a structure which human hands have made.

44. "Our fathers had the tabernacle of testimony in the desert, just as God, who spoke to Moses, had commanded him to construct it according to the pattern which he had seen."

a. "Our fathers had the tabernacle of testimony." In his speech, Stephen uses the expression *our fathers* eight times.[60] The term applies to the fore-fathers of Stephen and his audience, from the sons of Jacob to the Israelites who conquered Canaan. Despite the fathers' disobedience to God's instructions, Stephen still respectfully calls them "our fathers." In the application of his speech (vv. 51–53), he dissociates himself from them and his listeners and says "your fathers and you" (vv. 51–52).

Here Stephen speaks of the Israelites who constructed the tabernacle in the desert. This structure he calls the "tabernacle of testimony," which actually means the tabernacle that contains the testimony of the two tablets of stone on which God had inscribed the Ten Commandments.[61] In the books of Moses, this tent is also known as the "tabernacle of meeting" (e.g., see Exod. 27:21). Following the wording of the Septuagint translation of Exodus 27:21, Stephen uses the term *tabernacle of testimony* to call attention once more to the law of Moses (6:11, 13; 7:38). Moreover, he elucidates the point that God wanted to live with his people in the desert. God gave them a structure where the Israelites could worship him and where he had placed the testimony of the Decalogue. Indeed, the Israelites had received a great privilege, for now they had a visible structure with the testimony of God's law.

b. "Just as God, who spoke to Moses, had commanded." The plan to build a tabernacle did not originate with man but with God, who called Moses to the top of Mount Sinai. There God revealed to him a detailed pattern for constructing the tabernacle (Exod. 25:9, 40; 26:30; 27:8; Heb. 8:5). Did God show Moses an original tabernacle from which Moses received a pattern? Or did the pattern for building this structure exist only in the mind of God? We simply do not know what Moses saw when he was with God on Mount Sinai. We know that Christ Jesus, as high priest, has gone through the heavenly tabernacle that is greater and more perfect than the one Moses made in the desert (compare Heb. 8:2; 9:11, 24). But where Scripture is silent, we also must be reticent.[62]

God gave Moses all the instructions about the building of the tabernacle and revealed to him the craftsmen whom he had chosen for the work (Exod. 31:1–6). While God was instructing Moses about the tabernacle and its workmen, the Israelites were worshiping the golden calf. The implied message Stephen conveys to the Sanhedrin is that even though God wants his people to worship him, Israel turns away in unbelief. He also alludes to the fact that Israel was without a sanctuary until Moses built a movable structure called the tabernacle. He means to say that, according to Scripture, the worship of God is not limited to a tabernacle or a temple.

---

60. Acts 7:11, 12, 15, 19, 38, 39, 44, 45.
61. See Exod. 31:18; 32:15; 34:29. For the term *ark of the testimony*, see Exod. 25:22; 26:33–34; refer to Num. 1:50; 17:7 for the words *tabernacle of testimony*.
62. Consult Kistemaker, *Hebrews*, pp. 219–20.

45. "And when our fathers had received it from their fathers, they with Joshua brought it along while dispossessing the Gentiles, whom God expelled before them. It stayed there until the time of David."

For thirty-eight years, the Levites moved the tabernacle from place to place in the desert as the Israelites traveled to the Promised Land. All the Israelites twenty years and older died in that desert, but they passed on the tabernacle to the next generation. Stephen respectfully calls this generation also "our fathers." They were the people who, under the leadership of Joshua, took the tabernacle across the Jordan River (Josh. 3:14–17). They carried it into Canaan where, after dispossessing the Canaanites, they set up the tabernacle in Shiloh (Josh. 18:1).

Stephen again follows the Scriptures when he says that God expelled the Canaanites (Josh. 23:9; 24:18). Accordingly, he gives God the honor and respect for the conquest of the Promised Land. God fulfilled his covenant promise to Abraham and the patriarchs that he would cause their offspring to dwell in Canaan (Gen. 17:8; Deut. 32:49).

The tabernacle was designed so that it could be transported during the desert journey. Therefore, it gave the appearance of temporality and the hope that it would be replaced by a permanent building. As the history of Israel shows, the tabernacle remained in Shiloh until the time of Samuel (I Sam. 4:3). Then the ark of God was taken to the battlefield, captured by the Philistines, and returned to the Israelites. The people of Kiriath Jearim took the ark to the house of Abinadab (I Sam. 7:1), where it stayed until the time when David became king. During the period of the judges, the Israelites displayed little interest in worshiping the Lord.[63] The ark remained in one place (Kiriath Jearim; see II Sam. 6:3) and the tabernacle in another (Nob; see I Sam. 21:1). David brought the ark to Jerusalem and placed it in a tent he had made for it (II Sam. 6:17), while the tabernacle was placed in Gibeon (I Chron. 16:39). Gibeon was located some five miles northwest of Jerusalem.

46. "He found favor in God's sight and asked that he might provide a dwelling place for the God of Jacob. 47. But it was Solomon who built a house for him."

a. "He found favor in God's sight." When David brought the ark to Jerusalem, he expressed to the prophet Nathan his desire to build a temple for God (II Sam. 7:1–2; I Chron. 17:1). But God instructed Nathan to tell David that God wanted David's son to build the house of God (II Sam. 7:13; I Kings 8:17–19). The psalmist also reveals that it was David's desire to construct a dwelling for the God of Jacob (Ps. 132:4–5). In fact, Stephen alludes to the psalmist's words.

God did not permit David to build the temple because he was a warrior who had shed blood (I Chron. 22:8; 28:3). That is, David was defiled because of bloodshed. However, David spent the rest of his productive

---

63. Refer to Charles L. Feinberg, "Tabernacle," *ZPEB*, vol. 5, p. 578.

years in preparation for the building of the temple. He set aside silver, gold, and furnishings and dedicated them for use in God's house (I Kings 7:51). Although God highly favored David, he did not give him the honor of constructing the temple. This denial, in a sense, points out that the worship of God can take place without a permanent temple. If this building were essential, God would not have delayed its construction.[64] If God had desired the construction of a temple, he would have made it known. The idea originated with David and God gave his approval.

b. "A dwelling place for the God of Jacob." Some translations have the reading "that he might provide a dwelling place for the house of Jacob."[65] The reading *house* instead of "God" has the support of excellent Greek manuscripts, but the textual evidence for either word is divided. Of the two choices, the reading *house of Jacob* is the more difficult to explain.[66] And the time-honored rule that the harder reading is likely to be the original is significant. But even when that is said, we still ask what the word *house* means in the context. The flow of thought, especially with reference to the next verse (v. 47), appears to favor the reading *the God of Jacob*.

c. "But it was Solomon who built a house for him." David's son Solomon, a man of peace, constructed the Jerusalem temple. When the building was completed, Solomon realized that God could not be contained within the walls of a manmade structure (I Kings 8:27; II Chron. 2:6). Solomon confessed that the temple he built was only a place where the people could offer their sacrifices. Even the heavens, he said, cannot contain God.

Coming to the conclusion of his speech, Stephen summarizes his theme that the worship of God is not confined to one particular place. He says:

48. "However, the Most High does not live in houses made by human hands. As the prophet says:

49. 'Heaven is my throne,
　　and earth my footstool.
What house will you build for me?
　　says the Lord.
Or what place is there for my rest?
50. Did not my hand make all these things?' "

We make these observations:

a. *Contrast.* How great is your God? This is actually the question Stephen asks the members of the Sanhedrin. Certainly, God who created the universe cannot be confined to a building located in Jerusalem. The Scriptures clearly teach this truth.[67] In his emphatic statement, "The Most High does

---

64. Consult Grosheide, *Handelingen der Apostelen*, vol. 1, p. 232.

65. For example, JB and NAB. Some Greek New Testament editions also prefer the reading *the house of Jacob;* see Nes-Al (25th ed.), BF (2d ed.), United Bible Societies (3d ed.).

66. For a detailed discussion, see Metzger, *Textual Commentary*, pp. 351–53.

67. E.g., II Chron. 2:6; Ps. 139:7–16; Isa. 66:1–2; Jer. 23:24; Acts 17:24.

not live in houses made by human hands," Stephen contrasts the extremes. He puts God the Creator and Upholder of the universe over against humans who fashion a temple for him. Because God is everywhere, he has no need for one particular place of worship.

b. *Design.* True, in the Old Testament Scriptures God repeatedly speaks about the place where he may put his name.[68] God's name signifies his presence, which is guaranteed in the temple, yet God himself transcends all creation.[69] At the time of the exile, Solomon's temple was in ruins. Yet the people continued to worship God in Babylon and other places of exile. Moreover, the Most Holy Place in the temple Herod built was empty because the ark of the covenant and its contents were either destroyed or lost (Jer. 3:16). But note the purpose of this temple. When Jesus cleansed it because the temple courts were "a den of robbers," he said that God intended the temple as a house of prayer for all nations (Mark 11:17; and Isa. 56:7).

c. *Prophecy.* Instead of quoting the words from Solomon's prayer (I Kings 8:27), Stephen turns to Isaiah's prophecy:

> Heaven is my throne,
>   and earth my footstool.
> What house will you build for me?
>   says the Lord.
> Or what place is there for my rest?
> Did not my hand make all these things? [66:1–2]

As with all his other quotations from the Old Testament, Stephen cites almost verbatim the text of the Septuagint, which is virtually identical with the Hebrew Bible.

Isaiah's prophecy immediately follows a passage in which the prophet has spoken of a new heaven and a new earth. Isaiah now speaks of judgment and asks where the Israelites will build a house for God or where he may have a resting place. God says that he dwells in heaven and on earth and that all things have been made by him. By asking these questions, God implies that the temple will be destroyed, but worship will continue. Who are the true worshipers? God says: "I am pleased with those who are humble and repentant, who fear me and obey me" (Isa. 66:2b, GNB).[70]

d. *Proof.* What point is Stephen trying to make by quoting Isaiah's prophecy? In his speech Stephen has pointed to Abraham, Joseph, and

---

68. Deut. 12:5, 11, 21; 14:23; I Kings 3:2; 14:21; II Chron. 12:13.

69. Consult Hans Bietenhard, *NIDNTT*, vol. 2, p. 650.

70. T. C. G. Thornton suggests that an Aramaic midrash (related to the Targum Jonathan) regards Isa. 66:1 as a prophecy about the destruction of Solomon's temple. If this interpretation were known in the first century, Stephen could have used Isaiah's prophecy to predict the ruin of Herod's temple. "Stephen's Use of Isaiah LXVI. 1," *JTS* 25 (1974): 432–34.

Moses to prove that God is not bound to any particular place of worship. Thus, the prophecy of Isaiah, which records words spoken by God himself, clearly reveals that God is unlimited and omnipresent. Then why did the members of the Sanhedrin react violently to these words from Scripture? In the mind of the Jew, Israel was the center of all the nations; the center of Israel was Jerusalem, the city of God; and the center of Jerusalem was the temple where God dwelled. Anyone who dared to detract from these orthodox beliefs, even if he quoted Scripture to prove his point, would risk death by stoning. Stephen, however, opposes not the temple itself but the undue significance that the Jews of his day attached to worship at the temple.

Practical Considerations in 7:44–50

"I believe a holy universal church." This is one of the statements in the Apostles' Creed confessed by Christians throughout the world. The church is universal; that is, wherever believers meet in the name of Christ, there the church is present. In some places, believers meet in magnificent cathedrals or majestic buildings. At times, Christians gather for worship in rented quarters, storefronts, and homes. In countries where persecution is the order of the day, believers secretly congregate outdoors in forests and caves. But wherever two or three come together for worship in the name of Christ, there Jesus is in their midst (Matt. 18:20).

Liturgies in all these churches differ. Some churches have no musical accompaniment, in others the organ or piano accompanies congregational singing, and in still others guitars, flutes, or drums are part of the service. The variety of musical instruments used to praise God is reflected in the last psalm of the Psalter (Ps. 150), where the psalmist mentions the harp, lyre, tambourine, stringed instruments, flute, and cymbals.

In the Christian church, the common denominator that draws all believers together in worship is this: they worship God in spirit and truth (John 4:24). This means that in the worship service, God is the host, who invites the believers to come into his presence. To say it differently, Christ as the bridegroom and the church as the bride meet in joyful celebration.

> Jesus, where'er Thy people meet,
> There they behold Thy mercy-seat;
> Where'er they seek Thee, Thou art found,
> And every place is hallowed ground.
>
> Here may we prove the power of prayer,
> To strengthen faith and banish care;
> To teach our faint desires to rise,
> And bring all heaven before our eyes.
> —William Cowper

Greek Words, Phrases, and Constructions in 7:46 and 48

Verse 46

εὑϱεῖν—this is the aorist active infinitive of the verb εὑϱίσκω (I find). In the aorist it expresses single action. The verb does not convey the sense of discovering something but that of obtaining it.[71]

Verse 48

οὐχ—although this particle negates the verb ϰατοιϰεῖ (he dwells), it stands first in the sentence for emphasis. Moreover, it is separated from the verb by the subject of the sentence ("the Most High") and a prepositional phrase ("in [houses] made by human hands"). The result is emphatic negation.[72]

The verb ϰατοιϰεῖ is a compound in the perfective sense and conveys the sense of permanence. See also 17:24, where Paul uses virtually the same phrase.

---

h. Application
7:51–53

As any public speaker knows, the support or rejection given by an audience does not have to be expressed verbally. Stephen begins his address with the words *men, brothers and fathers*. But as he develops his speech and speaks about the Jerusalem temple, he has a hostile audience that refuses to listen to God's word. Even if he has not mentioned Jesus' name in his entire presentation, he realizes that the Jews have drawn their own conclusions concerning his view of temple worship. Stephen knows that his audience forces him to end his discourse. Therefore, he abruptly changes his style; he directly confronts the members of the Sanhedrin with a pointed conclusion; and in picturesque language he shows them that they are outside of God's covenant.

51. "You stiff-necked people, uncircumcised in hearts and ears. You are always resisting the Holy Spirit. As your fathers did, so do you."

a. "You stiff-necked people." Stephen chooses his words carefully as he addresses the supreme court. He selects an expression that God used to describe the rebellious Israelites when they worshiped the golden calf: "stiff-necked people" (Exod. 33:3, 5).[73] And his audience has no difficulty understanding that term in its historical setting. The expression *stiff-necked* originates in the agricultural world of that day, in which oxen or horses refuse to yield to the yoke the farmers try to put around their necks. The expression is synonymous with "disobedience."

b. "Uncircumcised in hearts and ears." This expression is even more telling than the preceding one. For the Jews, the term *uncircumcised* refers

---

71. Bauer, p. 325.
72. Blass and Debrunner, *Greek Grammar*, #433.1.
73. See also Exod. 32:9; 34:9; Deut. 9:6, 13; 10:16; 31:27.

to all the people who are not in the covenant made with Abraham. In the Jewish community, every male child was circumcised on the eighth day and entered that covenant. Thus, for Stephen to say that his listeners were uncircumcised was equal to calling them Gentiles. But Stephen is using the words God employed to describe the Israelites in the desert and which the prophets used when the Jews were exiled.[74] God urged the Jewish people to circumcise their hearts (Deut. 10:16; 30:6; Jer. 4:4), which means that they should open their hearts and ears to listen obediently to God's commands.

With these Old Testament terms, Stephen declares that his listeners are outside the covenant because by refusing to listen to God's Word they have broken its obligations.[75] They have the external sign on their physical bodies, but they lack the internal sign—an obedient heart regenerated by the Holy Spirit (Rom. 2:28–30).

c. "You are always resisting the Holy Spirit." Stephen emphatically addresses his audience with the personal pronoun *you*. He again alludes to the Old Testament, where Isaiah comments that in spite of God's love and mercy, his people rebelled and grieved the Holy Spirit (63:10; and see Ps. 106:33). The Jews knew that if they rebelled against the Spirit of God, they sinned grievously. Then God would turn against them and become their enemy.

d. "As your fathers did, so do you." The references to the Holy Spirit are few in the Old Testament in comparison with the New Testament. This does not mean that the Spirit was inactive. Scripture teaches that God's Spirit was at work in the Old Testament era in the children of the promise (refer to Gal. 4:28–29) and in the prophets (I Peter 1:10–11). Both the forefathers and the leaders of Stephen's day continually resisted the Holy Spirit.

52. "Was there any prophet your fathers did not persecute? They even killed those who foretold the coming of the Righteous One, whose betrayers and murderers you have now become, 53. you who received the law transmitted by angels, yet you did not keep it."

a. "Was there any prophet your fathers did not persecute?" Notice that Stephen distinctly separates himself from his audience and the Jewish forefathers. Whereas earlier in his discourse he respectfully included himself with the words *our fathers,* now he reproachfully says "your fathers." He denounces the actions of the forefathers, who willfully persecuted and even killed the prophets God had sent to them. A conspicuous example is the prophet Elijah, who complained to God that the Israelites had killed all the prophets and now wanted to put him to death (I Kings 19:10, 14; and compare II Chron. 36:16; Neh. 9:26; Jer. 2:30).

The crimes committed by the Israelites filled a shameful chapter in Is-

---

74. Lev. 26:41; Jer. 9:25–26; Ezek. 44:7, 9.
75. Refer to Calvin, *Acts of the Apostles*, vol. 1, p. 213.

rael's history, so that the Jews were unable to boast unequivocally about their forefathers (see also Matt. 5:12; 23:31). Hence, Stephen asks rhetorically whether the Sanhedrin could point to any prophet whom the fathers had not persecuted. The answer is, no one. Many prophets had died a martyr's death in the service to which God had called them.

b. "They even killed those who foretold the coming of the Righteous One." The prophets, of course, prophesied about the coming of the Messiah, who was Israel's hope and salvation. Among them was Zechariah, the son of Jehoiada, whose blood was shed in the courtyard of the temple (II Chron. 24:21; Matt. 23:35). The Jews not merely bit the proverbial hand that fed them; they severed it. They killed the messengers who brought the good news about their deliverer. Stephen calls this Deliverer the Righteous One. He calls Jesus the Righteous One in accordance with the message of the prophets who characterized the Messiah as God's righteous servant (Isa. 53:11; Jer. 23:5; 33:15; Zech. 9:9; see also Acts 3:14; 22:14). Presumably the term *Righteous One* was a messianic title.[76]

c. "Whose betrayers and murderers you have now become." Here is the reason that Stephen separates himself from his listeners. They stand in the line of murderers, but he stands in the line of the prophets. They have betrayed and killed Jesus of Nazareth, but he testifies on Jesus' behalf. As Peter reminded the Jews of their crime (see 3:14), so Stephen boldly accuses the Sanhedrin of betraying Jesus through Judas Iscariot and murdering him with the help of Roman soldiers. The judges in Israel's supreme court killed God's righteous servant.

d. "You who received the law transmitted by angels." These judges who occupied the judgment seat knew the law of God recorded in the Old Testament. They had passed the guilty verdict on Jesus, and presently they are in session to judge Stephen himself.

The Jewish people had received the law of Moses, Stephen says, through the mediation of angels (see v. 38; Gal. 3:19; Heb. 2:2). Although the historical account in Exodus 20:1 reveals that God spoke the Ten Commandments, Jewish tradition taught that angels were intermediaries sent by God to transmit the law to man. Despite the sanctity of God's law, the Jews refused to obey it. Stephen bluntly accuses the Sanhedrin of disobedience.

We shall never learn whether Stephen had planned to say anything else. His lengthy discourse came to an abrupt end when the dignified members of the supreme court lunged at him and dragged him off to kill him. Nevertheless, Stephen had cleared himself of the false accusations the witnesses had brought against him. He did not preach Christ's gospel as Peter had done on earlier occasions (4:8–12; 5:29–32). But by drawing parallels, he unmistakably pointed to Christ.

---

76. Lake and Cadbury, *Beginnings*, vol. 4, p. 83.

Main Themes of Stephen's Speech in 7:1–51

Stephen answers his accusers not in a point-by-point fashion but in narrative style. The historical sequence is Abraham, Joseph, Moses, and the building of the temple. Throughout this narrative he weaves his themes that refute the charges brought against him. Here are the themes:

a. *God.* Stephen begins his speech with the words *the God of glory.* He shows that God called Abraham, was with Joseph, commissioned Moses, blessed the Israelites with the Ten Commandments, and favored David. As he develops this theme, Stephen demonstrates his love and deep reverence for God. Hence, the charge that he blasphemed God is baseless.

b. *Worship.* Abraham worshiped God in Mesopotamia, Haran, and Canaan. Joseph served God in Egypt, as did Moses. Worship is not restricted to one particular place and building, for God's people worshiped him in various places and for centuries even without a building. And when the tabernacle was constructed, it did not remain stationary, either in the desert or in Israel. Stephen concludes that not even the temple can contain God. Therefore, he presents a comprehensive view of worship which nullifies his opponents' accusation that he speaks against the temple.

c. *Law.* Stephen devotes most of his speech to Moses and relates that Moses received the law at Mount Sinai. He shows that God desires obedience to his law, but that the Israelites refused to obey his Word. Moreover, when God sent prophets to Israel with prophecies concerning the Messiah, they persecuted and even killed him. Not Stephen, who masterfully preaches God's Word, but the Jews rejected the law.

d. *Covenant.* God made a covenant with Abraham and his spiritual descendants. God honored the promise he made to Abraham by giving descendants to the patriarch and the Promised Land to the nation Israel. The Israelites failed to keep their part of the covenant when they refused to obey God's Word. Likewise, Stephen's contemporaries had uncircumcised hearts and ears and resisted the Holy Spirit. For them, God's covenant had become meaningless.

e. *Jesus.* Although Stephen never mentions Jesus, he nevertheless draws unmistakable parallels between Moses and the Christ. He uses expressions that speak of the person and work of the Messiah: the ruler and deliverer (v. 35), the Prophet (v. 37), and the Righteous One (v. 52). As Joseph and Moses were rejected by their own people, so Jesus was rebuffed by the Jews. As the Jews murdered prophets, so they betrayed and killed Jesus.

Stephen ends his discourse by reminding his listeners that they have received the law, but that they refuse to obey it. The words seem repetitious and therefore superfluous. We would have expected Stephen to plead with his audience to believe in Christ. Not so. As John Albert Bengel aptly remarks, "he who believes [in] Christ, establishes the law: he who sets aside Christ, sets aside the law."[77] In conclusion, according to the Jews, anyone who breaks the law is placed on the same level as a Gentile.

---

77. Bengel, *Gnomon of the New Testament*, vol. 2, p. 583.

Greek Words, Phrases, and Constructions in 7:51–53

Verse 51

ὑμεῖς—note that this personal pronoun occurs twice in the nominative case and once in the genitive. The author uses the pronouns for emphasis.

Verse 52

τίνα—the interrogative pronoun is followed by the partitive genitive.

τῆς ἐλεύσεως—the noun derives from the verb ἔρχομαι (I come). As the term ὁ ἐρχόμενος (the coming one) is messianic, so is this noun. It occurs once in the New Testament.

Verse 53

οἵτινες—in the New Testament the indefinite relative pronoun often has a causal connotation. Here also, cause is implied.[78]

εἰς—this preposition is similar to ἐν (by) in the instrumental sense.

---

54 When they heard this, they were stung in their hearts and began gnashing their teeth at him. 55 But Stephen was full of the Holy Spirit and looked intently into heaven. He saw the glory of God and Jesus standing at the right hand of God. 56 He said, "Look, I see heaven open and the Son of man standing at the right hand of God." 57 With a loud voice they shouted and covered their ears. Together they rushed at him, 58 threw him out of the city, and began to stone him. The witnesses placed their cloaks at the feet of a young man named Saul. 59 As they were throwing stones at Stephen, he prayed, "Lord Jesus, receive my spirit." 60 He fell to his knees and shouted with a loud voice, "Lord, do not hold this sin against them." And when he had said this, he fell asleep.

8 1a Saul concurred in the killing of Stephen.

---

4. Stephen's Death
7:54–8:1a

If the Sanhedrin in session represents the supreme court of Israel, then it failed to abide by normal procedure and accorded Stephen no justice at all. In fact, no verdict was pronounced and the death sentence the court executed was illegal. Only the Romans could mete out the death penalty (John 18:31). In blind anger, the members of the Sanhedrin killed Stephen without a semblance of legality.

54. When they heard this, they were stung in their hearts and began gnashing their teeth at him.

If we read Stephen's speech, especially the conclusion, we have difficulty understanding the reaction of the Sanhedrin. However, we must look at the narrative from a cultural point of view in a Jewish setting.

---

78. Consult Robertson, *Grammar*, p. 728.

a. "When they heard this." Stephen was brought to trial because he allegedly had spoken against the law. But when he defends himself by relating Israel's history and summarizes his speech with the remark that the members of the Sanhedrin are guilty of breaking the law, he becomes the prosecutor and his listeners the defendants.[79] When Peter addressed the Sanhedrin on an earlier occasion, he also turned the tables on his judges (4:12).

b. "They were stung in their hearts." Stephen's trial initially produces the same reaction that the trial of the apostles had on the Jews (5:33). Then Peter and the other apostles addressed the Sanhedrin and when they were finished, the judges were furious. On that occasion, the Sanhedrists wanted to kill the apostles but were persuaded to listen to Gamaliel's advice. At Stephen's trial, the Jews begin to gnash their teeth to show their malice and contempt (compare Ps. 35:16). They are consumed by anger that incites them to murder.

55. But Stephen was full of the Holy Spirit and looked intently into heaven. He saw the glory of God and Jesus standing at the right hand of God. 56. He said, "Look, I see heaven open and the Son of man standing at the right hand of God."

Observe these points:

a. *Faith.* Amid the storm lashing the hall of the Sanhedrin, Stephen appears to be an island of serenity. Once again Luke reports that Stephen is full of the Holy Spirit (see 6:5, 10), who now causes him to look heavenward. Incidentally, Luke employs the same words for the phrase *to look intently into heaven* as he used to describe the apostles looking toward the sky at the time Jesus ascended (1:10).

Stephen is permitted to see God's glory, not in a vision, but in reality. At the beginning of the trial Stephen's face had a heavenly glow like the face of an angel (6:15). At the conclusion of the trial he sees God's glory. Although Scripture asserts that no one is able to see God and live, God's glory has often been revealed to man (compare Ps. 63:2; Isa. 6:1; John 12:41).

In addition to observing God's glory, Stephen sees Jesus standing, not sitting, at the right hand of God. We do not need to make much of the possible difference between standing and sitting.[80] The standing position possibly denotes that Jesus is welcoming Stephen to heaven (see I Kings 2:19). The expression "at the right hand of God" refers to the highest honor given to Jesus at the time of his ascension.

Stephen's trial resembles that of Jesus. When Jesus stood trial before the Sanhedrin, the high priest asked him whether he was the Son of God. Jesus answered in the affirmative and added that his audience would see "the Son of man sitting at the right hand of power and coming on the clouds of heaven" (Matt. 26:64; see also Heb. 1:3, 13).

---

79. Refer to Lenski, *Acts*, p. 301; and see Williams, *Acts*, p. 132.
80. Calvin, *Acts of the Apostles*, vol. 1, p. 219. Also note that in Rev. 5:6 Jesus is portrayed as standing, instead of sitting on his heavenly throne.

b. *Fulfillment.* "Look, I see heaven open and the Son of man standing at the right hand of God." Stephen is inviting his audience to look up to heaven and see Jesus in person at his place of honor. He calls Jesus "the Son of man," which is the title Jesus used exclusively for himself to reveal that he fulfilled the messianic prophecy that speaks about the rule of the Son of man (Dan. 7:13–14). According to the Gospel accounts, people never refer to or address Jesus by that name. Stephen's remark is the exception to that practice. Why does he use this title? Because Stephen fully recognizes that Jesus as the Son of man has fulfilled the messianic prophecy (Dan. 7:13–14) and has been given all authority, power, and dominion in both heaven and earth (Matt. 28:18).[81]

c. *Effect.* The effect of Stephen's invitation to look into heaven is not one of wonder and reverential fear on the part of the Sanhedrists but one of anger and hate. The Jews regard Stephen's words as blasphemy. Just as the high priest at Jesus' trial tore his priestly garments and cried out, "He has blasphemed" (Matt. 26:65), so the members of the Sanhedrin deem Stephen to have blasphemed the name of God. In view of their Hebrew creed, "Hear, O Israel! the LORD is our God, the LORD is one!" (Deut. 6:4), Stephen no longer teaches monotheism. When Stephen says that he sees Jesus standing next to God, they hear him say that Jesus is God. Therefore, Stephen is a blasphemer.

In conformity with the law of Moses, anyone who blasphemes the name of God must be put to death; the members of the assembly must throw stones at him so that he dies (Lev. 24:16). In short, the members of Israel's supreme court say that the charges of blasphemy, which the Hellenistic Jews have brought against Stephen, are proven to be true now that Stephen claims that Jesus is God.

d. *Heaven.* Where is heaven? If we visualize Stephen standing in the hall of the Sanhedrin, he would not have been able to look up into the sky. The text gives no indication that the meeting had moved outdoors at this point. How do we explain the appearance of Jesus to Stephen? God opened Stephen's eyes so that he could see heaven and gave him the ability to view heaven as if it were in proximity to Stephen. Somewhat of a parallel is Paul's conversion experience on the way to Damascus. Paul heard Jesus' voice but his companions heard only sound (9:7; also compare II Kings 6:17). Heaven, then, is up and around us in a dimension that we are unable to see. When God opens the eyes of believers, as some Christians experience on their deathbed, he permits them to look into heaven.

57. With a loud voice they shouted and covered their ears. Together they rushed at him, 58. threw him out of the city, and began to stone him. The witnesses placed their cloaks at the feet of a young man named Saul.

The scene is almost comical. Dignified men are shouting at the top of their voices, and at the same time they are putting fingers in their ears to

---

81. Refer to Bruce, *Book of the Acts,* p. 154.

block the noise around them. But these men are venting their anger by shouting and are indicating their refusal to hear Stephen by covering their ears. As judges they forget to pass the guilty verdict, so that the trial itself becomes meaningless.

The members of the Sanhedrin take hold of Stephen and drag him outside the city wall. There they take up stones and proceed to kill him. Notice that the Sanhedrin acts in accordance with legal form: the victim must be killed outside the city to purge the evil from the midst of Israel;[82] the witnesses who testified against the guilty party must cast the first stones (Deut. 17:7). Stones are in abundant supply in Israel, so that in ancient times death by stoning was common for transgressions ranging from worshiping other gods to blasphemy and adultery.[83]

The two or three witnesses who testified against Stephen (Deut. 17:6–7) now take up stones and begin to pelt him. They put aside their outer garments for greater facility in throwing the stones. These cloaks they lay at the feet of a young man called Saul. This is the first time Saul's name occurs in connection with the death of Stephen. Saul was a theological student whose teacher Gamaliel served as a member of the Sanhedrin (5:34; 22:3). He not only stood watching the execution; he also consented to Stephen's death (8:1a). The ascription *young man* refers to a person aged twenty-four to forty.[84] Probably Saul (Paul) was thirty.

The question of the legality of Stephen's death is a difficult one. By all appearances, his death is the result of mob action that the Romans did not prevent. Nevertheless, the Roman governor could conduct an inquiry, because the Jews might not administer capital punishment (John 18:31).[85] That power belonged to the Roman governor. To illustrate: Josephus states that the Roman procurator (governor) Coponius, sent to Judea by the emperor, was "entrusted by Augustus with full powers, including the infliction of capital punishment."

If we assume that Stephen died in A.D. 35, Pontius Pilate was still the governor of Judea. At that time Pilate's troubles, resulting from his slaughter of numerous Samaritans at Mount Gerizim, were sufficient evidence to demand his recall (A.D. 36) to Rome at the request of Syria's governor.[86] In this political climate, the Jews would not fear repercussions for killing Stephen. To be sure, in his last year in office Pilate had lost influence and authority in Judea.

Notice that already when the apostles were on trial, the members of the Sanhedrin were so angry that they wanted to kill them (5:33). Conversely, when Paul at the end of his third missionary journey was attacked by a crowd

---

82. See especially Deut. 13:5; 19:19; 21:21, 23; 24:7.
83. Consult James C. Moyer, "Stoning," *ZPEB*, vol. 5, p. 524.
84. Bauer, p. 534.
85. Josephus *War* 2.8.1 [117].
86. Josephus *Antiquities* 18.4.1–2 [85–89].

in the temple area, the commander of the Roman troops protected him (21:30–36). This was during the governorship of Felix, who was fully in control of Judea. But when Governor Festus died and his successor, Albinus, had not yet arrived in Jerusalem, the Jews, led by the high priest Ananus, put James, the brother of Jesus, to death in A.D. 62.[87] We conclude, therefore, that the Sanhedrin executed Stephen because in those days they had nothing to fear from a weak Roman governor. Moreover, Pilate resided in Caesarea, which was located a distance of two days' travel from Jerusalem.

59. As they were throwing stones at Stephen, he prayed, "Lord Jesus, receive my spirit." 60. He fell to his knees and shouted with a loud voice, "Lord, do not hold this sin against them." And when he had said this, he fell asleep.

1a. Saul concurred in the killing of Stephen.

a. "As they were throwing stones at Stephen." Stone after stone strikes defenseless Stephen. As the angel of death beckons, he utters a prayer that is similar to the one Jesus prayed on the cross: "Lord Jesus, receive my spirit." Jesus addressed his Father: "Father, into your hands I commit my spirit" (Luke 23:46). But Stephen prays to Jesus and identifies entirely with the One whom he has already seen as the Son of man standing next to God (v. 56). As Stephen prays, Jesus reaches out to the first martyr of the Christian faith and receives his spirit. Stephen, as it were, looks to Jesus and commits himself to his Lord.

In his dying moments, as he kneels down in prayer, Stephen voices virtually the same words Jesus spoke when he was crucified: "Lord, do not hold this sin against them" (see Luke 23:34). But the sequence of these two sayings from the cross has been reversed. Stephen first prays that Jesus will accept his spirit and then prays that his enemies' sin of murdering an innocent man may be forgiven. He addresses the Lord. This title in the context of the passage refers not to God but to Jesus. In his prayer, Stephen also places Jesus on the level of God and thus prays to him directly. One last remark about these prayers: Even if the wording between the sayings of Jesus and Stephen's prayers differs, the sentiment they express is the same. What is significant is Stephen's identification with Jesus.

Luke's description of Stephen's death is brief, yet in his brevity he gives the reader sufficient information about Stephen. Luke presents a picture of serenity in the midst of violence when he writes that Stephen fell asleep. He uses a euphemism for death. Throughout his account, he keeps Stephen in the center of this picture.

b. "Saul concurred in the killing of Stephen." The first sentence of the next chapter and verse (8:1a) serves as a bridge between the preceding and the following accounts. For a second time (see v. 58), Luke introduces Saul (Paul), whom he now describes as a person giving his approval to the death of Stephen. The writer implies that this death becomes a turning point for Saul

---

87. Josephus *Antiquities* 20.9.1 [200]; see Eusebius *Ecclesiastical History* 2.23.21.

(22:20). Saul is Stephen's successor in bringing the gospel to Greek-speaking Jews and Gentiles. In his missionary life, Paul suffered ten times as much for Christ as Stephen did (II Cor. 11:23–29). Reflecting on the death of Stephen and Paul's consent, Augustine made this penetrating comment:

> If Stephen had not prayed,
> the church would not have had Paul.

Greek Words, Phrases, and Constructions in 7:54–60

Verses 54–55

διεπρίοντο—for an explanatory note see 5:33.

πνεύματος ἁγίου—although the comment that Stephen is full of the Holy Spirit also appears in 6:5, the writer here mentions the three Persons of the Trinity: God, Jesus, and the Holy Spirit.

ἐκ δεξιῶν—this idiom is explained in 2:33.

Verse 56

διηνοιγμένους—the perfect tense in this participle denotes lasting effect: heaven remains open for Stephen. The use of the passive implies that God is the agent in opening heaven. And the compound form of the participle signifies that heaven is completely open for Stephen. Only in 2:34 and here the plural noun τοὺς οὐρανούς (the heavens) occurs; elsewhere in Acts, Luke always uses the singular noun *heaven*. The plural is a Hebraism.

Verses 59–60

ἐλιθοβόλουν—the imperfect tense (also see v. 58) describes the process of throwing stones.

Κύριε Ἰησοῦ—Stephen prays, "Lord Jesus." By addressing Jesus in prayer, he asserts the deity of Christ.

μὴ στήσῃς—this is a negative command that features the aorist subjunctive in place of the aorist imperative. The aorist denotes single action with lasting results.

ἐκοιμήθη—from the verb κοιμάω (I sleep), which in the passive means "I fall asleep." The aorist is ingressive. The use of this verb indirectly points to the resurrection of the body.

Summary of Chapter 7

Standing in front of the Sanhedrin, Stephen begins his speech by politely addressing the members of the court. He continues by reciting Israel's history and mentions Abraham. The patriarch was called by God out of Mesopotamia and settled in Canaan, but he did not own a foot of ground. God told him that his descendants would be slaves for four hundred years and afterward leave for Canaan to worship God there. God gave Abraham the covenant of circumcision.

Joseph was sold as a slave in Egypt, but later became ruler of that nation. During a famine, Jacob and his family went to Egypt. Although he died in Egypt, he was buried in Canaan. His descendants continued to increase in number and received cruel treatment. They were forced to abandon their newborn babies. Moses was born and placed outdoors, where Pharaoh's daughter found him. Moses was educated at Pharaoh's court, visited fellow Israelites, killed an Egyptian, and fled to Midian.

After Moses spent forty years in Midian, God called him from the flames of a burning bush. God sent him to Egypt to deliver his people from oppression. Performing miracles, Moses led the Israelites out of Egypt, through the Red Sea, and into the desert. Moses testified of the Christ, who would come as a prophet. While Moses received the law at Mount Sinai, the Israelites made an idol in the form of a golden calf and worshiped it. God told Moses to construct the tabernacle according to the pattern God had shown him. The tabernacle remained with the Israelites until Solomon built the temple.

Stephen reproves the members of the Sanhedrin for being obdurate by resisting the Holy Spirit. He reminds them of Israel's infamous history of persecuting and even killing the prophets and tells them that they are like their forefathers. The Jews become furious, hear Stephen say that he sees Jesus standing in heaven next to God, drag him outside the city, and begin to throw stones at him. In his dying moments, Stephen asks Jesus to receive his spirit and to forgive his enemies.

8

The Church in Palestine, *part 1*

8:1b–40

Outline

8:1b–11:18	III. The Church in Palestine
8:1b–3	A. Persecution
8:4–40	B. Ministry of Philip
8:4–25	1. In Samaria
8:4–8	a. Proclaiming Christ
8:9–13	b. Converting Simon
8:14–17	c. With Peter and John
8:18–23	d. Opposing Simon
8:24–25	e. Conclusion
8:26–40	2. To the Ethiopian
8:26–29	a. Traveling
8:30–33	b. Reading
8:34–35	c. Explaining
8:36–40	d. Baptizing

8 1b On that day a great persecution took place against the church in Jerusalem. All the believers, except the apostles, were scattered throughout the provinces of Judea and Samaria. 2 Devout men buried Stephen and loudly lamented him. 3 But Saul began to destroy the church. As he entered house after house, he dragged away men and women and put them in prison.

III. The Church in Palestine
8:1b–11:18

A. Persecution
8:1b–3

From the Old Testament we learn that Jerusalem is a city to which every Jew wished to go. In fact, the last verse in the Hebrew Bible records Cyrus's edict permitting every Jew to go up to Jerusalem (II Chron. 36:23).[1] But as in the Old Testament people are drawn to the holy city, so in the New Testament they are sent from Jerusalem into the world. To put it differently, in the Old Testament, Jerusalem exerts a centripetal force on the Jews; in the New Testament, it exercises a centrifugal force on the believers.

Jesus told the apostles to go into the world to make disciples of all nations (Matt. 28:19–20). They faithfully proclaimed Christ's gospel in Jerusalem, so that the number of believers ran into the thousands. However, the church could not be limited to Jerusalem, for Jesus had instructed the apostles to be witnesses in Jerusalem, Judea, Samaria, and the ends of the world (1:8). In God's providence, the persecution following Stephen's death drove the believers into Judea and Samaria and eventually as far as Phoenicia, Cyprus, and Antioch (11:19). These Christians witnessed to numberless people, with the result that the church continued to grow (11:20–21).

1b. On that day a great persecution took place against the church in Jerusalem. All the believers, except the apostles, were scattered throughout the provinces of Judea and Samaria.

Stephen's death marks the turning point for the Jerusalem church. Sud-

---

1. Bible translations follow the Septuagint in respect to the sequence of books. The Hebrew Bible begins with Genesis and ends with II Chronicles.

denly one of their leaders is maligned by Greek-speaking Jews and apprehended. He is placed before Israel's supreme court to stand trial and is put
to death without a verdict. The people in Jerusalem at one time were
favorably disposed toward the Christians, but now they are hostile to the
point of persecuting them.

a. "On that day." This phrase indicates the day during which the persecution broke out against the Christians. This persecution lasted for some
time, for Saul went from house to house in search of believers. In Acts, the
word *persecution* occurs only twice (here and in 13:50). Luke adds the descriptive adjective *great* to distinguish this incidence from the persecution
the apostles and Stephen experienced.

b. "All the believers, except the apostles, were scattered." Who is included
in the the term *all*? Three interpretations are possible.

The first interpretation is that literally every believer endured persecution and was driven from Jerusalem. But even if everyone experienced the
effect of persecution, some Christians remained in the city. The text indicates that the apostles stayed.[2] Further, we expect that Mary the mother of
Jesus continued to reside with the apostle John. John Mark's mother, who
owned a sizeable house, also either remained there or soon returned
(12:12).[3]

A second possibility is that because Hellenistic Jews brought Stephen, a
Greek-speaking Jew, to trial, these people now turned against Hellenistic
Jewish Christians and drove them out of the city.

And the third interpretation is that although the Greek-speaking Christians bore the brunt of the persecution, Aramaic-speaking believers were not
exempt. The high priest and his associates crucified Jesus, imprisoned Peter
and John, flogged the apostles, and killed Stephen. Hence, we assume that
the religious and civil leaders of the Sanhedrin were influential in both
persecuting the Hebrew Christians and expelling them from Jerusalem.

Moreover, when Saul (Paul) went from house to house searching for
believers, he probably made no distinction between Greek-speaking and
Aramaic-speaking Christians. In conclusion, we ought not to interpret the
adjective *all* too strictly. After the persecution, life in the Jerusalem church
gradually returned to normalcy, as is evident from the historical sequence
in Acts (e.g., see 9:26).

Usually the leaders of a persecuted minority are among the first to be
apprehended. Not so in the case of the apostles. They stayed in Jerusalem
to encourage the Christians who remained there and those who were scattered. The expression *scattered* is meaningful to the Jews who lived in the
dispersion, for the exile and subsequent persecutions had directly affected
their lives. Now the church enters the era of being scattered (compare

---

2. Eusebius *Ecclesiastical History* 5.18.14.

3. F. W. Grosheide, *De Handelingen der Apostelen,* Kommentaar op het Nieuwe Testament
series, 2 vols. (Amsterdam: Van Bottenburg, 1942), vol. 1, p. 249.

James 1:1; I Peter 1:1). The Old Testament prophets taught that when a Jew lived in dispersion (for example, during the Babylonian exile), he was receiving God's just punishment for earlier disobedience. Conversely, the New Testament church considered the dispersion of the Jews "the divinely ordained means of providing a beachhead for the spread of the gospel in alien territory."[4]

2. Devout men buried Stephen and loudly lamented him. 3. But Saul began to destroy the church. As he entered house after house, he dragged away men and women and put them in prison.

a. *Time.* When Luke reports that certain devout men buried Stephen, he intimates that this took place within hours after his death. That is, the persecution had not yet broken out, so that God-fearing Christians could pay their respects to Stephen and mourn his demise. Stephen's burial took place that same day, because the Jews would not permit a corpse to defile the land. Even though some Jews were known as devout (2:5),[5] they could not be expected to lament Stephen's death. Accordingly, I think that immediately after the execution, godly Christians removed Stephen's body to prepare it for burial.

b. *Custom.* The Jewish Talmud teaches that there should not be any mourning for a criminal put to death by stoning.[6] But what is probable in this instance was that the custom was not observed because Stephen's death lacked every semblance of legality. Where the men buried Stephen is unknown, for criminals were customarily buried in a common grave. Yet Jesus was buried in a private tomb, which indicates that Christians enjoyed a measure of freedom. The believers loudly mourned the death of Stephen, the first Christian martyr.

c. *Persecutor.* "But Saul began to destroy the church." This is the third time Luke mentions Saul (7:58; 8:1a, 3). Although he was a disciple of Gamaliel, Saul lacked his master's moderation. Instead, Luke portrays him as a man (perhaps thirty years of age) who was determined to eliminate the church of Jesus Christ.[7]

In his speeches, Paul indicates that, blinded by zeal, he persecuted numerous people. When they were put to death, he gave his approval (26:10). Hence his concurrence with Stephen's execution was only the beginning of a murderous career.

Luke presents Saul as the Jerusalem inquisitor who was bent on destroying the church, much the same as a wild beast pounces on his prey. By going from house to house, Saul flushed out the Christians and handed them over to the jailers. Continually he dragged both men and women to

---

4. George A. Van Alstine, "Dispersion," *ISBE*, vol. 1, p. 968.
5. See also 22:12, where Paul calls Ananias of Damascus a devout Jew. Ananias observed the law and was a disciple of Jesus.
6. *Sanhedrin* 6.6; see also SB, vol. 2, p. 686.
7. Compare 9:1, 21; 22:4, 19; 26:10–11; Gal. 1:13, 23.

prison, from where they were brought to trial, perhaps in local synagogues (Matt. 10:17), and punished. Notice that before the arrest of Stephen, only the Sadducees opposed the apostles (4:1). At Stephen's death, the Pharisees joined in persecuting the church, as is evident from the actions of Saul.

Greek Words, Phrases, and Constructions in 8:1b–3

Verse 1b

διωγμός—from the verb διώκω (I persecute), the noun with the -μος ending denotes action that is in progress.

διεσπάρησαν—this is a compound verb with directive meaning.[8] The form is aorist passive from διασπείρω (I scatter abroad).

τῆς—notice that one definite article precedes the two nouns *Judea* and *Samaria*. Because of their proximity, these two provinces are linked.

Verses 2–3

κοπετόν—the noun derived from κόπτομαι (I beat myself) describes the mourner who beats his breast to express his grief.

ἐλυμαίνετο—the imperfect tense depicts continued action in the past tense. The imperfect is inceptive: "he began to destroy."

---

4 Then those who had been scattered went from place to place preaching the word. 5 And Philip went down to the city of Samaria and preached Christ to them. 6 The multitudes were paying close attention to what Philip was saying; they listened to him and saw the miracles he was performing. 7 Evil spirits shrieking loudly were coming out of many people who had them; and many paralytics and cripples were healed. 8 So there was great joy in that city.

9 Now a certain man called Simon used to practice magic arts in that city and astounded the people of Samaria. He said that he was someone great. 10 Everyone, both high and low, paid attention to him and said, "This man is the power of God, the power that is called great." 11 They paid attention to him because for a long time he had astounded them with his magic tricks. 12 But when they began to believe Philip, who was preaching the good news concerning the kingdom of God and the name of Jesus Christ, both men and women were being baptized. 13 Even Simon himself believed and was baptized. He stayed close to Philip, and when he saw both great signs and wonders taking place, he was amazed.

14 When the apostles in Jerusalem heard that Samaria had accepted the word of God, they sent Peter and John to them. 15 They went down there and prayed for them that they might receive the Holy Spirit, 16 because the Holy Spirit had not yet fallen upon any of them. They had only been baptized in the name of the Lord Jesus. 17 Then Peter and John placed their hands on them and they received the Holy Spirit.

18 When Simon saw that the Spirit was given through the laying on of the apostles' hands, he offered them money 19 and said, "Give me also this power, so that anyone on whom I place my hands may receive the Spirit." 20 But Peter said to him: "May your silver perish with you because you thought to purchase the gift of God with money! 21 You have neither

---

8. A. T. Robertson, *A Grammar of the Greek New Testament in the Light of Historical Research* (Nashville: Broadman, 1934), p. 581.

part nor lot in this matter, for your heart is not right before God. 22 Repent, then, of this wickedness of yours and pray to the Lord. If possible, the intent of your heart may be forgiven you. 23 For I see that you are in the gall of bitterness and the bond of iniquity." 24 Then Simon said, "Pray to the Lord for me so that nothing of what you have said may come upon me."

25 Now when Peter and John had testified and spoken the word of the Lord, they returned to Jerusalem; and they preached the good news to many villages of the Samaritans.

26 Then an angel of the Lord spoke to Philip and said, "Get ready and go south on the road that goes down from Jerusalem to Gaza." (This is the desert road.) 27 And he got ready and went. Now an Ethiopian eunuch, who was a court official of Candace, queen of the Ethiopians, and her chief treasurer, had gone to Jerusalem to worship. 28 As he was returning and sitting in his carriage, he was reading the book of Isaiah the prophet. 29 And the Spirit told Philip, "Go toward this carriage and stay close to it." 30 Then Philip ran toward it and heard the Ethiopian reading from the book of Isaiah the prophet. He asked, "Do you understand what you are reading?"

31 "How can I unless someone explains it to me?" the official replied. He invited Philip to come up and sit with him. 32 Now the passage of Scripture he was reading was this:

> "He was led as a sheep to the slaughter,
> and as a lamb before its shearer is silent,
> so he did not open his mouth.
> 33 In his humiliation he was deprived of justice.
> Who will tell his descendants,
> because his life was taken from the earth?"

34 The eunuch said to Philip, "Tell me, please, about whom did the prophet say this? About himself or someone else?" 35 Then Philip began to speak, and beginning with this passage of Scripture he preached to him the good news of Jesus.

36 And as they were going along the road, they came to some water. The eunuch said, "Look! Water! What prevents me from being baptized?" 37 [See the commentary.] 38 He ordered the carriage stopped. Both Philip and the eunuch went down into the water and Philip baptized him. 39 When they came up out of the water, the Spirit of the Lord took Philip away and the eunuch saw him no more. He continued his journey rejoicing. 40 But Philip appeared in Azotus; and passing through, he kept on preaching in all the towns until he came to Caesarea.

B. Ministry of Philip
8:4–40

1. In Samaria
8:4–25

Of the seven men whom the apostles appointed to minister to the widows in Jerusalem, Stephen and Philip are the only ones whose activities Luke recounts. Both men were Greek-speaking Jews who preached Christ's gospel to people who were not Aramaic-speaking Jews. Stephen went to the Hellenistic Jews in Jerusalem (6:9–10); Philip went to Samaria.

When persecution drove the Christians from Jerusalem, they went to the rural areas of Judea and Samaria. There they testified for Jesus Christ and made his gospel known.

a. Proclaiming Christ
8:4–8

4. Then those who had been scattered went from place to place preaching the word. 5. And Philip went down to the city of Samaria and preached Christ to them.

"The blood of martyrs is the seed of the church." This time-honored proverb proved to be true for the Christians who experienced persecution after the death of Stephen. They fled Jerusalem and went from place to place in the countryside of both Judea and Samaria. Wherever they went, they preached the Good News and consequently founded churches.

Whereas Jews were accustomed to avoid any contact with Samaritans, Jesus stayed with the Samaritans for two days, proclaimed the gospel to them, and gained numerous adherents to the faith (John 4:39–42). After Stephen's death, Jewish Christians from Jerusalem came to the Samaritans with the message of salvation. One of these Jewish Christians was Philip (not the apostle), the deacon who was also called the evangelist (21:8). The apostles remained in Jerusalem while Philip traveled to a prominent city in Samaria. Philip could relate to the Samaritans, who worshiped on Mount Gerizim, for both he and the Samaritans were excluded from worshiping in the Jerusalem temple (John 4:20). Expelled from Jerusalem, Philip knew that God is not limited to one particular place but can be worshiped anywhere.

Translators have difficulties choosing the correct reading for verse 5. Textual evidence strongly supports the reading "Philip went down to *the* city of Samaria." But most translators favor another rendering: "Philip went down to *a* city of Samaria." The capital city, Samaria, renamed Sebaste by Herod the Great, was a Gentile city in apostolic times. The historical context seems to favor a less important city, perhaps Shechem (or Sychar), located near Jacob's well.[9] Luke, however, fails to name the city, so we are unable to ascertain its identity.

Philip preached Christ, Luke writes, to the Samaritans. They were no longer excluded from the Good News (Matt. 10:5), which is God's universal message to all people. Because the Samaritans were only half a step removed from the Jews, so to speak, they were the first to hear Christ's gospel now that the Jews had expelled the Christians from Jerusalem.

6. The multitudes were paying close attention to what Philip was saying; they listened to him and saw the miracles he was performing. 7. Evil spirits shrieking loudly were coming out of many people who had them; and many paralytics and cripples were healed. 8. So there was great joy in that city.

"The multitudes were paying close attention." Notice these two parallels:

---

9. Josephus *Antiquities* 11.8.6 [340]. Another possible place is the Samaritan town Gitta. Justin Martyr, born about A.D. 100 in Samaria, writes that this is Simon the sorcerer's native town (8:9). See Justin's *Apology* 1.26.

First, there is a parallel between the preaching of the apostles in Jerusalem and that of Philip in Samaria. On the day of Pentecost and on later occasions, thousands of people came to listen to the apostles, who were preaching the gospel. In Samaria, Philip preached and multitudes came to listen to him.

Second, note the parallel between the miracles performed by the apostles and Stephen and by Philip. First Peter, then the apostles, and later Stephen worked numerous great miracles among the people.[10] In Samaria, Philip also performed wonders and the crowds paid close attention to what he said and did. The special gift of preaching and performing wonders, therefore, was not limited to the apostles. Stephen and Philip, who were commissioned to aid the poor, also possessed this gift.

Philip drew crowds in Samaria as a result of his preaching and healing ministry. The Greek indicates that he kept on doing miracles while the crowds continued to listen to and watch him. The people gave Philip their undivided attention; through the preaching of the gospel and the evidence of divine miracles, they came to faith in Christ.

When Jesus began his ministry, Satan opposed him by causing his evil spirits to dwell in numerous people. Some of these demons were in the synagogue worship services and identified Jesus as the Holy One of God (Mark 1:23–26). In apostolic times, demon possession continued undiminished. Peter cast out evil spirits from people who were coming to him from the towns surrounding Jerusalem (5:16). Paul exorcised a spirit from a slave girl in Philippi (16:16–18) and cast out demons when he taught and preached in Ephesus (19:12). Philip likewise cast out evil spirits from Samaritans. He exorcised the demons, who made their exits known with loud shrieks. They knew that Philip spoke to them in the name and power of Jesus. In their outreach to Jews and Gentiles, Peter, Paul, and Philip knew that they confronted Satan's opposition to Jesus Christ.[11]

Philip also healed paralytics and those who were crippled. Through his ministry, the people received physical and spiritual healing. Hence Luke reports that there was great joy in this Samaritan city. One of the fruits of the Spirit is joy (Gal. 5:22), which Christians demonstrate especially when they first come to know Jesus Christ.

Greek Words, Phrases, and Constructions in 8:4–7

Verse 4

οἱ μὲν οὖν—this is a resumptive phrase that is transitional.[12]

---

10. See 3:6–7; 5:12, 15–16; 6:8.

11. Consult Donald Guthrie, *New Testament Theology* (Downers Grove: Inter-Varsity, 1981), p. 137.

12. C. F. D. Moule, *An Idiom-Book of New Testament Greek*, 2d ed. (Cambridge: Cambridge University Press, 1960), p. 162.

Verse 5

κατελθών—the compound verb in the aorist active participle is directive and at the same time descriptive. One either goes up to Jerusalem or goes down from it to another place.

τὴν πόλιν—the manuscript support for the inclusion of the definite article is strong and thus demands retention. However, because Luke reveals no place name, translators favor deletion.[13]

αὐτοῖς—grammatically this pronoun should have been in the singular. The plural masculine is used to refer to people.[14]

Verse 6

προσεῖχον—the imperfect tense denotes continued action; the compound signifies "pay attention to." Literally it means "they continued to hold [the mind] to."

ἐν τῷ ἀκούειν—this is a favorite construction in the writings of Luke and appears frequently. It expresses time: "while they were listening."

Verse 7

πολλοί—this nominative case in the plural cannot be the subject of the verb ἐξήρχοντο (they went out). The subject is the accusative plural πνεύματα (spirits), which is the direct object of the present participle ἐχόντων (having). Kirsopp Lake and H. J. Cadbury attribute this anacoluthon to "mental 'telescoping' to which all writers are liable."[15] That is, Luke took the noun *spirits* as a nominative case and thus as the subject of the verb. The nominative and accusative endings of this noun are identical. Luke forgot that he already had started the sentence with the nominative adjective *many*.

---

b. Converting Simon
8:9–13

Philip receives a warm reception from the Samaritans as he preaches the Good News and heals the sick. The power of Christ's gospel and Philip's divine authority to perform miracles are greater and stronger than the magic arts of Simon the sorcerer.

9. Now a certain man called Simon used to practice magic arts in that city and astounded the people of Samaria. He said that he was someone great.

In Jerusalem, Satan's opposition to the church came in the form of the deceit of Ananias and Sapphira (5:1–11), the imprisonment of the apostles (4:3; 5:18), the death of Stephen (7:60), and the great persecution (8:1b). In Samaria, Satan employs different methods to thwart the growth of the church. He uses a man named Simon, known in Samaria as the sorcerer.

---

13. Bruce M. Metzger, *A Textual Commentary on the Greek New Testament*, 3d corrected ed. (London and New York: United Bible Societies, 1975), pp. 355–56.

14. Robertson, *Grammar*, p. 684.

15. Lake and Cadbury, *Beginnings*, vol. 4, p. 90.

Luke introduces Simon as someone who practiced magic arts in that particular Samaritan city.

We need not think that Simon performed some tricks by sleight of hand (a form of deceiving the mind because the eye fails to observe correctly). Rather, we must see the magic arts as a serious threat to the Christian faith, because they represent witchcraft and sorcery. Among the vices Paul lists as acts of the sinful nature is witchcraft (Gal. 5:20). Those who practice magic arts are excluded from the Holy City and are cast into the fiery lake of burning sulfur (Rev. 21:8; 22:15). Magic arts originate with Satan and are diametrically opposed to God. Therefore, God tells his people not to become involved in any form of magic (Deut. 18:10–14).[16]

Simon the sorcerer had been able to astound the people for a long time with his magic. When Philip came to Samaria and proclaimed the Good News, Simon believed and was baptized. Before his conversion, he boasted that he was someone great. Moreover, the people paid him great respect. They regarded Simon as someone who had received divine power to perform his magic.

10. Everyone, both high and low, paid attention to him and said, "This man is the power of God, the power that is called great." 11. They paid attention to him because for a long time he had astounded them with his magic tricks.

The Scriptures of the Samaritans consisted of the five books of Moses that, in the light of the entire Old Testament, gave them only a segment of religious truth. The Jews forbade the Samaritans to worship in Jerusalem; therefore, they worshiped in their own temple on top of Mount Gerizim. They also expected the coming of the Messiah, whom they called Ta'eb. Because of their mixed racial and religious background (see II Kings 17:24–41), they were receptive to sorcery.[17]

In the second century, Justin Martyr asserted that Simon the sorcerer moved from Samaria to Rome, where, because of his magic arts, he was honored as a god. Justin probably was mistaken when he claimed that a statue in Rome was dedicated to Simon: "To Simon the Holy God"; it probably had the words *To the God Semo Sancus*. This statue, therefore, honored not Simon but a Sabine god.[18] In the second and third centuries, Simon's name was frequently mentioned. He even was regarded as the father of Gnosticism.[19] But the question remains whether the Simon who listened to Philip and Peter is to be identified with the Simon who originated the Gnostic movement. Scholars who question this point have refuted

---

16. Refer to Colin Brown, *NIDNTT*, vol. 2, p. 554.

17. Everett F. Harrison, *Interpreting Acts: The Expanding Church*, 2d ed. (Grand Rapids: Zondervan, Academie Books, 1986), pp. 144–45. Especially see Adolf Deissmann, *Bible Studies* (reprint ed.; Winona Lake, Ind.: Alpha, 1979), p. 336.

18. Justin Martyr *Apology* 1.26.56; *Dialogue* 120.

19. Irenaeus *Against Heresies* 1.23.

reports that indicate a link between Simon the sorcerer and pre-Christian Gnosticism. In spite of the strong evidence provided by writers of the first few centuries, scholars claim that the course of development of the movement known as Simonianism remains as obscure as ever.[20]

"Everyone, both high and low, paid attention to him." Before Philip came to the Samaritans, these people held Simon in high esteem. The expression translated "both high and low" or "young and old" is rather common in Scripture (see, e.g., Gen. 19:11) and indicates that Simon had numerous admirers. The Samaritans confessed their faith in him and said, "This man is the power of God, the power that is called great." The Samaritans believed in one God and presumably regarded Simon as God's representative endowed with divine power. By contrast, it could also be that Simon proclaimed himself to be God because of the magic deeds he performed.

The Greek word translated "power" can also mean "Mighty One." Then it is a circumlocution for the name of God. This is evident, for example, from Jesus' response to a question from the high priest.[21] At his trial, Jesus said to the high priest, "In the future you will see the Son of Man sitting at the right hand of the Mighty One and coming on the clouds of heaven" (Matt. 26:64, NIV). However, having said all this, we are unable to determine the exact intent of this Samaritan creedal statement and accordingly must leave it an open question.

The influence of Simon was enormous and his following immense. For a long time he had held the people in his power because of his magic arts. But when Philip appears, preaches the Good News, and performs healing miracles, the people pay close attention to what Philip has to say and to the wonders he performs. To them, Philip's message and deeds far surpass Simon's performance.

12. But when they began to believe Philip, who was preaching the good news concerning the kingdom of God and the name of Jesus Christ, both men and women were being baptized. 13. Even Simon himself believed and was baptized. He stayed close to Philip, and when he saw both great signs and wonders taking place, he was amazed.

a. "But when they began to believe Philip." The Samaritans accept the gospel Philip proclaims and begin to believe the message he brings. I have translated the verb "began to believe," indicating an action that has a starting point and then continues unabated. The Samaritans first give their intellectual assent to Philip's message and then commit themselves to Jesus by requesting baptism. We know that their commitment is genuine, especially when Peter and John arrive and the Holy Spirit comes upon the Samaritans. When the Holy Spirit chooses to dwell in them, he provides the

---

20. Wayne A. Meeks, "Simon Magus in Recent Research," *RelStudRev* 3 (1977): 137–42; Robert P. Casey, "Simon Magus," *Beginnings,* vol. 5, p. 163.

21. SB, vol. 1, p. 1006. And see Lake and Cadbury, *Beginnings,* vol. 4, p. 91; Gustaf Dalman, *The Words of Jesus,* trans. D. M. Kay (Edinburgh: Clark, 1909), p. 200.

evidence that their faith is genuine. We conclude, therefore, that the Samaritans believe Philip and the message of salvation he proclaims.[22]

b. "The good news concerning the kingdom of God and the name of Jesus Christ." Luke discloses the full content of Philip's message; that is, he first mentions the expression *kingdom of God* and then speaks of "the name of Jesus Christ." In the synoptic Gospels, especially in Matthew, the kingdom concept is prominent. But in Acts, it occurs only four times (19:8; 20:25; 28:23, 31). Here the words *kingdom of God* should not be interpreted merely as a synonym for "the gospel." Rather, Luke uses this term to illustrate that Philip stressed the kingship and sovereignty of God in this world in opposition to the powers of Satan which Simon displayed through his magic.

Moreover, Philip proclaims the name of Jesus Christ to the Samaritans. Note that the term *name* connotes the full revelation of the Son of God and that the double name *Jesus Christ* reveals both his earthly ministry and his divine office. Jesus, therefore, is king in the kingdom of God. The Samaritans hear the full gospel of salvation, something which Simon is unable to give them. And they respond to Philip with the request for baptism.

c. "Both men and women were being baptized." Luke no longer reports specific numbers of believers, but merely states that men and women profess their faith in Jesus Christ and are baptized (compare 5:14). With the verb *to baptize* in the imperfect tense, Luke indicates continued action. We presume that the baptismal ceremony was constantly repeated. Notice also that the walls separating Jews and Samaritans (see John 4:9) have been taken down. The Samaritans are being baptized by a Jew.

d. "Even Simon himself believed and was baptized." Simon acknowledges that someone greater and more powerful than he has appeared in Samaria. When the people leave him and follow Philip, he joins the crowd and accepts the presence of a superior power. He observes the miracles Philip performs, but the preaching of the gospel does not appear to change his heart (see v. 21). He is of the opinion that he is "in league with some powerful spirit."[23] He views baptism not as a sign of entering into a relationship with the Triune God but as an initiation into fellowship with that powerful spirit. He expects that through baptism he will receive the same power Philip has to perform miracles (see v. 19).

e. "When he saw both great signs and wonders taking place, he was amazed." After his baptism, Simon stays close to Philip and follows him wherever he goes. Luke discloses the reason for Simon's action: the magician's interest in the great signs and wonders that kept on occurring. The

---

22. James D. G. Dunn asserts that the verb *to believe* in this context "signifies intellectual assent to a statement or proposition rather than commitment to God." *Baptism in the Holy Spirit,* Studies in Biblical Theology, 2d series 15 (London: SCM, 1970), p. 65.

23. Henry Alford, *Alford's Greek Testament: An Exegetical and Critical Commentary,* 7th ed., 4 vols. (1877; Grand Rapids: Guardian, 1976), p. 88.

Greek word translated "wonders" actually means "powers." Simon is interested in the powerful miracles that Philip performs. He has never seen anything comparable to what Philip does. Luke writes that as Simon is observing the great signs and wonders he is amazed. Thus Simon reveals that his interest is not in knowing Jesus Christ but in the divine powers Philip displays.

We conclude this section with three brief observations. First, Philip is unable to judge Simon's heart and thus accepts his testimony of faith in Christ. Next, the account of Simon's baptism is adequate proof that baptism is not an act which effects salvation. And third, Simon was baptized with the Samaritans in order not to offend the people among whom he lived and worked.[24]

Practical Considerations in 8:9–13

Today occult practices that range from palm reading to the horoscope, fortune telling, spiritism, and magic are common. Of course, these practices go back to the beginning of human history, but in recent years the general public has accepted them as part of life. People who dabble in the occult desire information that is not available to them through normal channels; they want to communicate with supernatural or demonic powers; and they strive to acquire such power so that other people can be their servants.[25] They believe the lie that Satan told Adam and Eve in Paradise: "You will be like God" (Gen. 3:5). Thus, in their quest to acquire knowledge supernaturally, they are slaves of Satan and repudiate the claims of Christ.

What is the difference between the occult and the Christian religion? A few criteria provide an answer to this question. In the mysterious practice of magic, a professional manipulates a gullible person for his own benefit. In religion, a person prayerfully asks God to fulfill his spiritual and material needs. Magic is directed to the individual in private; religion is a group activity and is open to the public. And last, occult practices are impersonal; by contrast, religious services evoke a personal interaction between God and his people at worship.[26]

Both the Old and New Testaments denounce the abominable practices of the occult. God wants his people to put their trust in him only, for he says, "I am the Lord your God." He cares for his people and fills all their needs (compare Ps. 81:8–10).

Greek Words, Phrases, and Constructions in 8:9–11

Verse 9

προϋπῆρχεν—first, note that the imperfect tense is the customary imperfect, "he used to practice." Next, the verb is a compound consisting of the preposition πρό

---

24. John Calvin, *Commentary on the Acts of the Apostles*, ed. David W. Torrance and Thomas F. Torrance, 2 vols. (Grand Rapids: Eerdmans, 1966), vol. 1, p. 232.
25. Ronald M. Enroth, "Occult, The," *EDT*, p. 787.
26. Refer to David E. Aune, "Magic," *ISBE*, vol. 3, pp. 213–14.

(before) and the verb ὑπάρχω (to be). And third, the verb is part of a periphrastic construction with the present participle μαγεύων (practicing magic arts).

τὸ ἔθνος—Luke literally describes the Samaritans as "the nation of the Samaria." He refrains from using the term ὁ λαός, which relates to God's people (e.g., 4:27).

τινα μέγαν—this combination expresses the superlative idea, "a very great man."

Verse 11

προσεῖχον—three times (vv. 6, 10, 11) this verb occurs to show the intense interest of the Samaritans. See the explanation at verse 6.

ταῖς μαγείαις—"with these magic arts." The dative is instrumental. For the related word μάγος see 13:6, 8.

ἐξεστακέναι—the perfect active infinitive of the verb ἐξίστημι (I amaze) is a perfect of "broken continuity" to express repeated action in the past.[27]

---

c. With Peter and John
8:14–17

Do the apostles go to Samaria to approve the work that Philip has done? Does Philip lack the gift of the Holy Spirit? Is there an inadequacy in establishing the Christian church in Samaria? We ask these questions in the context of the development of the church as Luke portrays this development in Acts.

Before his ascension, Jesus told the apostles to remain in Jerusalem and to await the coming of the Holy Spirit. When they received the power of the Holy Spirit, they began to be witnesses for Jesus in Jerusalem, Judea and Samaria, and the ends of the world (1:8).

The theme that Luke unfolds is one of ever-widening circles comparable to those created by a stone thrown into a placid pond. The Spirit is poured out on Jewish people in Jerusalem and the church there begins to develop. When Philip preaches in Samaria and Samaritans believe and are baptized, the apostles come from Jerusalem to welcome these believers into the Christian church. God binds Jewish Christians and Samaritan Christians together in one church.[28] He breaks down the wall of separation that has existed between the Jew and the Samaritan. And he abolishes any animosity between these two groups (compare 11:17). He also causes the Holy Spirit to descend, so that the Samaritans experience their own Pentecost, so to speak, and Jew and Samaritan know that they are one in Christ.

14. When the apostles in Jerusalem heard that Samaria had accepted the word of God, they sent Peter and John to them.

The apostles in Jerusalem hear about the work Philip has performed in Samaria and now deliberate what to do. In harmony with Jesus' command

---

27. Robertson, *Grammar*, p. 909.
28. Calvin, *Acts of the Apostles*, vol. 1, p. 234; see also David John Williams, *Acts*, Good News Commentaries series (San Francisco: Harper and Row, 1985), p. 142.

to be witnesses in Samaria, they commission Peter and John to travel to the city where Philip is preaching Christ's gospel. They instruct Peter and John to be their official representatives to welcome the Samaritan believers into the Christian church. Incidentally, this is the last time Luke mentions John's name in Acts. Also note that at one time, John and his brother James asked Jesus if they might call down fire from heaven to destroy the Samaritans (Luke 9:54).

Luke writes that the apostles heard that Samaria received God's word. The word *Samaria* is a general term that signifies not the country as such but the Samaritans as a people. And the expression *the word of God,* which in Acts and the rest of the New Testament is similar to the phrases *the word of the Lord* or simply *the word,* is equivalent to the message and witness of Jesus embodied in the gospel of Christ.[29]

15. They went down there and prayed for them that they might receive the Holy Spirit, 16. because the Holy Spirit had not yet fallen upon any of them. They had only been baptized in the name of the Lord Jesus.

Peter and John leave Jerusalem (see v. 5) and travel to the town where Philip is preaching to and baptizing the Samaritans. When the apostles arrive, they pray for the Samaritans and ask God to send the Holy Spirit to these recent converts (compare 2:38; 10:44). Luke records that the Samaritans have not had the experience of the Holy Spirit falling upon them and that they are baptized not in the name of the Triune God but in the name of Jesus.

Is Philip, because he is an evangelist and not an apostle, unable to pray for the gift of the Holy Spirit? Is not the Spirit at work as Samaritans turn in faith to Christ? And why does Philip baptize only in the name of Jesus? I will try to answer these questions one by one.

First, did Philip have the ability to pray for the gift of the Holy Spirit? Certainly he had the ability, for he himself was full of the Spirit (6:3). However, God sent the apostles Peter and John to Samaria to signify that through the apostles he officially approved a new level of development in the church: adding the Samaritan believers. God confirmed this new phase by sending the Holy Spirit as a visible sign of his divine presence. As he declared his presence among the Jewish Christians in Jerusalem, so he affirmed his nearness to the Samaritan believers.

Notice also that when Peter preached in the house of Cornelius and baptized Gentile believers, God once again approved of a new period in the growth of the church by sending his Spirit (10:44). I conclude, then, that as the apostles fulfilled the mandate to be witnesses in Jerusalem, Samaria, and the Gentile world (1:8), God sanctioned every initial stage with the

---

29. Gerhard Kittel, *TDNT*, vol. 4, pp. 114–15.

outpouring of the Holy Spirit. God affirmed this new phase in Samaria through the apostles and not through Philip.

Second, is not the Spirit at work among the Samaritans when they accept Christ in faith? Definitely; these believers are baptized externally with water and internally experience rebirth and renewal through the Holy Spirit (Rom. 8:9; I Cor. 12:3; II Thess. 2:13; Titus 3:5; I Peter 1:2). The significance of the outpouring of the Spirit on the Samaritan believers, accordingly, lies in the visible signs that result from the Spirit's arrival (compare 10:45–46; 19:6; I Cor. 14:27). The power of the Holy Spirit, evident in the lives of Jewish believers after Pentecost, now becomes reality in the hearts and lives of believers in Samaria. In other words, the outpouring of the Spirit upon the Samaritans is proof of their equality with the Jerusalem believers.

Third, why did Philip baptize the Samaritans only in the name of Jesus? We see an inconsistency with the Great Commission formula that prescribes baptism in the name of the Father, the Son, and the Holy Spirit (Matt. 28:19). But note that the emphasis in this formula is on the word *name*, which refers to God's full revelation in word and deed. Philip baptized the people in this full revelation and specified the name *Jesus* (see v. 12). He followed the common contemporary formula for baptism (see 2:38; 10:48; 19:5). This particular formula should be understood in the historical context of apostolic preaching in which the expression *the name of Jesus* occurs numerous times.[30]

We should not place more emphasis on the baptism formula than the historical circumstances warrant. Concludes Donald Guthrie, "There is no support for the view that the use of the triune name would be regarded as any more or less effective than the simple name of Jesus."[31] The context shows that Philip proclaims Jesus to the Samaritans (v. 12); hence, their baptism in that name means that their baptism is the same as that of the Jewish Christians.

17. Then Peter and John placed their hands on them and they received the Holy Spirit.

Peter and John, representing the twelve apostles, place their hands on the Samaritan believers, who consequently receive the Holy Spirit. This event marks the full Samaritan participation in the Christian church (also see 19:6). The event itself is lucid and simple. Interpreting its meaning, however, has always been problematic because of varying theological views.[32] We are unable to discuss these views at length and will limit ourselves to a few comments.

---

30. E.g., see Acts 3:6; 4:10, 17–18, 30; 5:40; 8:12; 9:27; 16:18; 19:13, 17; 21:13; 26:9.

31. Guthrie, *New Testament Theology*, p. 719.

32. In a chapter entitled "The Riddle of Samaria," Dunn provides a detailed and thorough study on this matter. *Baptism in the Holy Spirit*, pp. 55–72.

In certain segments of the church, theologians derive the sacrament or rite of confirmation from this passage. For example, in harmony with a papal letter, Roman Catholic theologians teach that "the imposition of hands is designated by the anointing of the forehead which by another name is called confirmation, because through it the Holy Spirit is given for an increase [of grace] and strength."[33] They say that as the apostles in the early church confirmed the Samaritans by placing their hands on them, so the church as successor to the apostles today confirms the faithful.

However, in apostolic times Philip baptized the Ethiopian eunuch, who did not receive apostolic confirmation (8:36–39). Conversely, Ananias placed his hands on Saul, who then received the Holy Spirit (9:17). Yet Ananias was not an apostle. Peter did not place his hands on those who were baptized in Cornelius's household (10:44–48). And Paul did not lay his hands on the Philippian jailer and the members of his household, even though they were baptized (16:30–34).

Except for 19:6, the historical context in Acts fails to lend support to the teaching that the church must have a sacrament of confirmation that is administered by placing hands on every believer, so that he or she may receive the Holy Spirit. In fact, the New Testament does not command the church to follow the practice of Peter and John in Samaria. "On the other hand, there is no reason why the scriptural practice of laying on of hands with prayer should not be continued as such, [that is,] so long as there is no thought of a necessary bestowal of spiritual gifts by this means."[34]

What does the New Testament teach us about the reception of the Holy Spirit? The outpouring of the Spirit occurred in Jerusalem (2:1–4) and was repeated when the church added new groups: the Samaritans (8:11–17), the Gentiles (10:44–47), and the disciples of John the Baptist (19:1–7). But apart from these special manifestations, the New Testament is devoid of references to Jews or Gentiles receiving the Holy Spirit by the laying on of apostolic hands. Because of Pentecost, the Holy Spirit remains with the church and lives in the hearts of all true believers (see Rom. 5:5; 8:9–11; Eph. 1:13; 4:30). Paul reveals that the bodies of believers are the temple of the Holy Spirit (I Cor. 3:16; 6:19). Therefore, from these New Testament passages we learn "that those who believe and are baptized have also the Spirit of God."[35]

---

33. Heinrich J. D. Denzinger, *The Sources of Catholic Dogma,* trans. Roy J. Deferrari (St. Louis and London: B. Herder Book Co., 1957), p. 165. See also Charles Gregg Singer, "Confirmation," *EDT,* pp. 266–67; L. S. Thornton, *Confirmation. Its Place in the Baptismal Mystery* (London: Dacre, 1954), p. 73.

34. E. Y. Mullins and Geoffrey W. Bromiley, "Baptism of the Holy Spirit," *ISBE,* vol. 1, p. 428.
35. F. F. Bruce, *The Book of the Acts,* rev. ed., New International Commentary on the New Testament series (Grand Rapids: Eerdmans, 1988), p. 169.

Greek Words, Phrases, and Constructions in 8:14–17

Verse 14

δέδεκται—although this form is passive, it is translated as an active. The perfect tense from the verb δέχομαι (I receive, accept) signifies lasting effect.

Verse 15

πνεῦμα ἅγιον—Luke intends no distinction between this form and the form that has definite articles: τὸ πνεῦμα τὸ ἅγιον.[36]

Verses 16–17

ἦν ἐπιπεπτωκός—this is the past periphrastic construction that consists of the imperfect tense of the verb *to be* with the perfect participle. The perfect from the compound ἐπιπίπτω (I come upon) denotes abiding result.

ἐλάμβανον—note the use of the imperfect tense to depict duration. The subject of this verb, of course, is the understood noun *Samaritans* and not the noun *apostles*.

---

d. Opposing Simon
8:18–23

Here is the second part of the account about Simon (see vv. 9–13) that stands in direct contrast to God's gift of the Holy Spirit to the Samaritans. Luke skillfully places Barnabas's generosity (4:36–37) over against the deceit of Ananias and Sapphira (5:1–11). He compares God's majestic power with Satan's wicked influence. Accordingly, Luke depicts the Samaritans receiving the Holy Spirit in the expanding church and Satan using Simon to make a mockery of the Christian faith.

Simon's actions reveal that he has not experienced a genuine conversion and has not received the Spirit. Seeing the external evidence of the Spirit, Simon evaluates gifts on a commercial basis and offers the apostles money for the presence of the Spirit.

18. When Simon saw that the Spirit was given through the laying on of the apostles' hands, he offered them money 19. and said, "Give me also this power, so that anyone on whom I place my hands may receive the Spirit."

When the Samaritans receive the Holy Spirit, the Spirit's presence is evident in external signs. Although Luke's terse description omits details, we assume that some signs, perhaps in the form of miracles, were visible to the people. For Simon, who thinks in terms of the magic arts, possession of

---

36. Consult the detailed study of Dunn, *Baptism in the Holy Spirit*, pp. 69–70; see also Moule, *Idiom-Book*, pp. 112–13.

these extraordinary gifts becomes imperative. He, too, wishes to have at his disposal the power that Philip displayed when he healed the sick and cast out demons. Simon noticed that the Jerusalem apostles placed their hands on the Samaritans, who then received the miraculous power of the Holy Spirit. The fact that he was by-passed because of his lack of genuine faith does not occur to him.

In earlier days, Simon had obtained magical formulas from other practitioners by paying them certain amounts of money. And he had charged the people fees for the services he rendered. Now he approaches Peter and John, whom he considers agents of the Holy Spirit, and offers them money. If he is able to purchase this supernatural power, he will rise to even greater heights than he achieved before his conversion to the Christian faith. Thus, Simon tries to purchase spiritual gifts. Incidentally, in English the term *simony* means the buying or selling of an ecclesiastical office or obtaining an ecclesiastical promotion by offering money.

When Simon offers Peter and John money, he is not trying to bribe them or pay them an honorarium for becoming their associate. Instead, he is of the opinion that he can purchase a priesthood from Peter and John in much the same manner as he is able to obtain a priesthood in any pagan religion. In the first half of the first century, such priesthoods were often sold by auction.[37]

"Give me also this power, so that anyone on whom I place my hands may receive the Spirit." Simon has intentions of being a leader in the Samaritan church with authority to place hands on people to give them the Holy Spirit. He wants to function as a priest who is subordinate to the apostles. For him, the Holy Spirit is a power that can be subjected to the will of man.

Simon offends God by placing the Holy Spirit on the same level as his magic arts. Because he wants to buy the Spirit of God, he demonstrates that he has no knowledge of spiritual matters. He fails to see that the apostles possess heavenly power to glorify God. He wants to have supernatural powers to promote himself.[38]

20. But Peter said to him: "May your silver perish with you because you thought to purchase the gift of God with money!"

Note the contrast between God's servants and Simon the sorcerer. Although Jesus instructed his disciples that the worker deserves his wages (Luke 10:7) and that those who proclaim the gospel should receive adequate remuneration for their work (I Cor. 9:4), he never told them to charge people for their services. Listen to Paul, who states categorically that he has not desired any gold, silver, or clothing from anyone, but has

---

37. Consult J. Duncan M. Derrett, "Simon Magus (Acts 8:9–24)," *ZNW* 73 (1982): 52–68 (see especially p. 61).
38. Calvin, *Acts of the Apostles,* vol. 1, p. 238.

worked with his own hands to meet his needs (Acts 20:33–35; II Cor. 11:7; see also I Peter 5:2).

Believers who receive spiritual benefits are not charged and do not pay for them, because Jesus said, "Freely you have received, freely give" (Matt. 10:8). This is in harmony with the Old Testament example of Elisha, who refused to accept a gift for healing Naaman from leprosy. But his servant, Gehazi, who took money and clothes from Naaman, contracted leprosy—punishment for his greed (II Kings 5:15–16, 23–27). Similarly, Simon approaches spiritual matters from a commercial point of view and thus hears Peter pronounce a curse over him.

"May your silver perish with you because you thought to purchase the gift of God with money." Peter zealously guards God's glory and honor and rebuffs the attacks of Satan, who, through Simon, seeks to pervert the truth. He utters a curse that has an Old Testament echo, for he tells Simon that he and his money are on the way to hell. Peter's curse has far-reaching significance that relates not merely to the elimination of money and to Simon's physical death, but even to his state after death.[39] Simon's sin is that he values God's Spirit in terms of a given sum of money, that money as such is of chief importance to him, and that he worships the creature (money) rather than God.

21. "You have neither part nor lot in this matter, for your heart is not right before God."

Peter excludes Simon completely from the Christian community by saying that Simon has neither part nor lot in receiving the Holy Spirit. If Simon had part or lot in this matter, he would not have to ask for it. The word *part* points to partnership and the term *lot* to ownership. The words are an idiom that was well known to the Levites, because they had no share or inheritance in the real estate of Israel.[40] Simon the sorcerer, however, has no share or lot in the Lord (contrast Isa. 57:6). He is completely unqualified to receive the Holy Spirit and to become a teacher of the Good News. The words *this matter* refer to the work of teaching and preaching Christ's gospel.

Why is Simon excluded? With spiritual discernment Peter looks at Simon and says, "Your heart is not right before God." Peter is actually quoting from Psalm 78:37, where the psalmist records the unfaithfulness of the rebellious Israelites who perished in the desert. Peter looks at the wellspring of Simon's life and knows that spiritually Simon is serving not God but himself. There is only one way to effect a change in this condition and that is to repent. By implication, Simon's earlier confession of faith and subsequent baptism (v. 13) are meaningless because of this unrepentant heart. Therefore, Peter shows him the way of salvation and says,

39. Hans-Christoph Hahn, *NIDNTT*, vol. 1, p. 463.
40. See Deut. 10:9; 12:12; 14:27; 18:1.

22. "Repent, then, of this wickedness of yours and pray to the Lord. If possible, the intent of your heart may be forgiven you. 23. For I see that you are in the gall of bitterness and the bond of iniquity."

a. *Contrast.* Comparing the account about Ananias and Sapphira (5:1–11) with that about Simon the sorcerer, we see a number of differences. Ananias and Sapphira were Jewish Christians who professed to know the Lord and to be filled with the Holy Spirit. They belonged to the true Israel; they were baptized and instructed in the faith by the apostles. They sinned against the Holy Spirit by purposely deceiving and testing him. So God took the lives of Ananias and Sapphira as a sign of his displeasure but also as a measure to keep the early church pure.

Conversely, Simon was a Samaritan who made a verbal confession of faith but whose heart was not right with God. He did not receive the gift of the Holy Spirit. Formerly he had been the sorcerer known as "the power of God," but now, after observing Philip's miracles, joined the believers. Simon grievously sinned against God by desiring to buy the gift of the Holy Spirit. Although Peter pronounced a curse on Simon, he also showed him the way of deliverance. Hence, we conclude that Simon sinned in ignorance because he had never been set free from the bondage of wickedness. His was not the sin against the Holy Spirit.

b. *Condition.* "Repent, then, of this wickedness of yours and pray to the Lord." Peter gives Simon the opportunity to repent. He tells him to repent and ask the Lord to forgive him. Notice that Peter does not forgive his sin, even though Jesus gave him the authority to do so (John 20:23). He directs Simon to petition the Lord for remission of sin. "The apostles themselves referred the forgiveness of sins to, and left it in, the sovereign power of God, and not to their own delegated power of absolution."[41] Peter advises Simon to repent and ask the Lord to remove his sin and the curse Peter has pronounced upon Simon.

"If possible, the intent of your heart may be forgiven you." Peter prefaces his suggestion to find remission of sin with the phrase *if possible*. This conditional statement relates not to God's ability to forgive sin but to Simon's willingness to repent. Simon has to cleanse his heart from the intent to buy the gift of the Spirit, and he has to change the course of his life to be in harmony with God.

c. *Constriction.* "You are in the gall of bitterness and the bond of iniquity." Here Peter alludes to passages from the Old Testament. Moses warns the Israelites not to worship other gods and to avoid having a root of bitterness among them (Deut. 29:18; and see Heb. 12:15). Moses says this in the context of God's unwillingness to forgive sin should there be such bitter poison in their midst. Peter likewise warns Simon not to have "the gall of bitterness." The metaphor relates to the bitter spirit in a person and to the bitterness he imparts to people who meet him. In

---

41. Alford, *Alford's Greek Testament*, vol. 2, p. 91.

addition, Simon is a slave to sin through the bond of iniquity that con-
stricts him (compare Isa. 58:6).

God wants no person filled with bitterness and fettered to iniquity to be
in the company of his people, because bitterness belongs to Satan. Gall is
actually the fruit of bitterness and thus the exact opposite of the fruit of the
Spirit: love, joy, peace, and so on (Gal. 5:22–23). God wants his people to be
happy and free.

Doctrinal Considerations in 8:18–23

Was Simon the sorcerer ever a true believer? Luke reports that Simon believed
and was baptized (v. 13). He uses the same verb for the Samaritans who accepted the
good news of salvation and the message of Christ's kingdom (v. 12). But if Simon
had experienced genuine conversion, he would have provided evidence of true
faith. Sixteenth-century theologian Zacharias Ursinus asked, "What is true faith?"
and answered:

> True faith is
>   not only a knowledge and conviction
>   that everything God reveals in his Word is true;
>   it is also a deep-rooted assurance
>   created in me by the Holy Spirit through the gospel
>   that, out of sheer grace earned for us by Christ,
>   not only others, but I too,
>   have had my sins forgiven,
>   have been made forever right with God,
>   and have been granted salvation.[42]

Simon never experienced genuine conversion and never had true faith. His faith
was never rooted in regeneration and therefore it was temporary (see Matt. 13:21).
For this reason, Peter told Simon to repent, because faith and repentance are the
two sides of the same coin. When there is true faith, there is genuine repentance.
Peter admonished Simon to repent because he lacked true faith.

Greek Words, Phrases, and Constructions in 8:18–23

Verse 18

διά—with the genitive this preposition signifies "by means of."[43]
ἐπιθέσεως—this noun in the genitive (from the verb ἐπιτίθημι [I put upon]) has a
-σις ending in the nominative case that denotes continuous activity.

Verse 20

εἴη—the present optative occurs in a construction that connotes a curse (see Mark
11:14).

---

42. Heidelberg Catechism, question and answer 21.
43. Moule, *Idiom-Book,* p. 57.

τὴν δωρεάν—"the gift of God" is the presence of the Holy Spirit operative in the hearts and lives of God's people. See also Matthew 10:8.

Verse 21

σοι—here is an instance of the dative of possession.

ἔναντι—the double preposition ἐν (in) with ἀντί (opposite) means "*in* that part of space which is *opposite*."[44]

Verse 22

κακίας—notice the difference between this noun, "wickedness," and πονηρία, which has the same translation. "κακία denotes rather the vicious disposition, πονηρία the active exercise of the same."[45]

εἰ ἄρα—this combination expresses an element of doubt in a conditional clause.

Verse 23

εἰς—in this construction, the preposition is similar to ἐν (in). It is possible to explain the preposition as "destined for."

ὁρῶ—the present active of ὁράω (I see) with ὅτι conveys "intellectual apprehension, an opinion or judgment."[46]

---

e. Conclusion
8:24–25

Even though Luke briefly describes Simon's reaction to Peter's curse and counsel, he is sufficiently clear. Yet, the Greek manuscript known as Codex Bezae differs from the text we follow. It has supplemented the passage (as indicated by the italicized words):

> And Simon answered and said *to them,*
> '*I beseech you,* pray for me to *God,*
> that none *of these evils* of which you have spoken
> *to me* may come upon me'—*who did not stop weeping
> copiously.*[47]

24. Then Simon said, "Pray to the Lord for me so that nothing of what you have said may come upon me."

25. Now when Peter and John had testified and spoken the word of the Lord, they returned to Jerusalem; and they preached the good news to many villages of the Samaritans.

a. "Pray to the Lord for me." We are unable to determine whether Simon's repentance is genuine. With this verse (v. 24), Luke discontinues the

---

44. Thayer, p. 213.
45. Ibid., p. 320.
46. Robertson, *Grammar*, p. 1041.
47. Metzger, *Textual Commentary*, pp. 358–59.

account about Simon. Nevertheless, Simon's request is telling because of its similarity to that of Pharaoh. Many times Pharaoh asked Moses and Aaron to pray to the Lord for him, but he never repented (Exod. 8:8, 28; 9:28; 10:17).

Some commentators think that the evidence Luke provides is sufficient to assume Simon's salvation. For example, John Calvin states that Simon submits to Peter's rebuke, is moved by his sin, fears God's judgment, seeks the mercy of God, and asks for the prayers of the apostles. Thus Calvin conjectures that Simon repented.[48] However, we must be careful not to read into the text what Luke purposely disregards.

Other writers ask whether Simon in requesting the prayers of the apostles was motivated by fear. That is, Simon wanted to escape punishment rather than turn in repentance to the Lord.[49] Some support for this view comes from the history of the church.

Scripture has revealed to us only Simon's request for the prayers of the church. We are not asked to pass judgment on the eternal destiny of Simon and, therefore, we do well to leave this matter to the day of God's last judgment.

b. "Peter and John had testified and spoken." The apostles conclude their visit to Samaria. They achieved their objective: the full recognition of Samaritan believers as members in the Christian church. The apostles and even Philip now have the freedom to leave Samaria and entrust to leaders of the Jerusalem and Judean churches the task of encouraging and teaching the Samaritan Christians. Even as they travel from Samaria to Jerusalem, the apostles proclaim the Good News everywhere in many Samaritan villages. In time, the apostles return to Jerusalem to give a report of their work.

We do not know if Philip accompanied Peter and John to Jerusalem. The text does not specify, except to indicate that Philip left Samaria. In the next segment of Luke's account, Philip is told to travel south of Jerusalem to Gaza (v. 26). In brief, Luke features Philip as the prominent figure in the accounts of the Samaritan church and the Ethiopian official.

Greek Words, Phrases, and Constructions in 8:24–25

Verse 24

ὑμεῖς—note the use of the plural personal pronoun. Simon presents his request to the apostles, Philip, and the Samaritan believers.

ὑπέρ—followed by the genitive case, this preposition means "for one's benefit" or "for the sake of."

---

48. Calvin, *Acts of the Apostles,* vol. 1, p. 241.
49. Consult Williams, *Acts,* p. 143.

Verse 25

μὲν οὖν—this frequently occurring combination in Acts is a resumptive phrase of Luke that indicates transition: "and so" or "now."[50]

ὑπέστρεφον—the imperfect tense in this verb and in the verb εὐηγγελίζοντο is inceptive: "they began to return and preach the good news."

---

2. To the Ethiopian
8:26–40

Now Luke relates the second phase of Philip's ministry. Philip's first mission was to preach the gospel to the Samaritans and his second is to explain the Scriptures to a Gentile who is a convert to Judaism. Guided by the Holy Spirit, Philip proclaims the Good News in ever-widening circles radiating from Jerusalem. As a Greek-speaking Jew from the dispersion, he has a distinct role in the expanding ministry of the Christian church. And as a Jew from the dispersion, he bridges the gap between the Jew and the non-Jew. He goes from Samaria, perhaps via Jerusalem, to the southern part of Judea and travels toward Gaza.

a. Traveling
8:26–29

26. Then an angel of the Lord spoke to Philip and said, "Get ready and go south on the road that goes down from Jerusalem to Gaza." (This is the desert road.)

a. "An angel of the Lord." Luke is rather brief in his report about Philip's travels. He gives no information about where Philip was when an angel spoke to him. It could be that while he accompanied the apostles to Jerusalem or in one of the Samaritan towns he received the angelic command. Philip's location is unimportant in the story. What is important is his next assignment, which comes to him through an angel of the Lord.

Who is this angel of the Lord? In Acts Luke mentions four actions of the angel:

appearing to Moses in the burning bush (Stephen's speech, 7:30–38),

instructing Philip (8:26),

setting Peter free (12:7–10),

and striking down Herod (12:23).

In the case of Philip, Luke reveals that this angel is actually the Spirit of the Lord (vv. 29, 39). Philip is in the service of the Lord, whose Spirit communicates to him through an angel. Whether the angel appeared to Philip or spoke to him in a vision is not known. The message, however, is clear.

---

50. Moule, *Idiom-Book*, p. 162.

b. "Get ready and go south on the road that goes down from Jerusalem to Gaza." The Greek text literally says, "Arise." But because the verb occurs frequently in the New Testament, the context determines its meaning. Here it signifies "get ready."[51]

In other words, the angel instructs Philip to make arrangements for a journey. He tells him the direction he must travel, namely, along the road that winds in a southerly direction from Jerusalem along the Judean hills and then angles westward to the coastal city of Gaza.

A traveler could take either of two roads from Jerusalem to Gaza. The first one went straight west to the coastal plains via the village of Lydda and linked with the caravan route between Egypt and Damascus; the other extended southward from Jerusalem to Hebron and then westward to Gaza. Philip's instructions are to take the second route. In fact, Luke adds an explanatory note and says, "This is the desert road." It was a road that was not much in use in those days, which indeed made the angel's command unique.[52]

What makes the angel's command doubly curious is an alternative translation for the expression *south* in "go south on the road." This term in Greek can also mean "at midday" (see 22:6). Should this translation be adopted, then the angel would have given Philip the peculiar command to travel at high noon—that is, in the heat of the day—and to take the desert road that was seldom used. The strangeness of this command fits in well with the task that awaits Philip, who is told to travel along a road that leads to Gaza.

Translators, however, must determine whether the word *desert* refers to the road or to the city of Gaza. Strictly speaking, the desert itself begins south of Gaza and extends into Egypt. The term *desert* could be a reference to the ruins of old Gaza over against the new Gaza. At the beginning of the first century before Christ, the Jews completely destroyed this city. In 57 B.C., by order of the Roman general Pompey, Gaza was rebuilt at a new location along the coast.[53] The ruins of the old city were known as "desert Gaza." The context, however, seems to favor the translation *desert road*. The emphasis in the account falls not on cities (Jerusalem and Gaza) but on an Ethiopian official who by reading Scripture becomes a Christian. And Philip meets him along a seldom-traveled road.

27. And he got ready and went. Now an Ethiopian eunuch, who was a court official of Candace, queen of the Ethiopians, and her chief treasurer, had gone to Jerusalem to worship.

Philip listens obediently to the instructions he receives, gets ready for an extended journey, and travels along the desert road toward Gaza. Because of the unusual direction, Philip realizes that something extraordinary is

---

51. Bauer, p. 70.

52. W. C. van Unnik, "Der Befehl an Philippus," *ZNW* 47 (1956): 181–91.

53. Josephus *Antiquities* 13.3 [358–64]; 14.4.4 [76]. And see Anson F. Rainey, "Gaza," *ISBE*, vol. 2, p. 417.

about to happen. He notices a carriage occupied by a Negro traveling from Jerusalem to Gaza. The traveler is from the African nation of Ethiopia, south of Egypt. Ethiopia stretched from the modern Aswan Dam in the Nile River southward into the Sudan as far as Khartoum. In the Old Testament, Ethiopia is known as Cush (e.g., Ezek. 29:10). Its main cities located along the Nile were Meroë, Napata, and Kerma, populated by people of the Nubian race.

We assume that Philip is able to identify the Ethiopian because of his race, speech, and dress. And the carriage possibly indicates that it belongs to the Ethiopian royal house. Luke notes that the occupant of the carriage is a eunuch, which normally refers to a keeper of the harem. Such a person was emasculated. However, the term is also used of government officials of that day and perhaps should not be taken literally, for it does not mean that these men were deprived of their male functions.[54]

If we understand the word *eunuch* literally, then we see Christianity removing the barriers that Judaism had erected. A foreigner could become a convert to Judaism, but, because the Ethiopian was a eunuch, he could not fully participate in the temple worship (see Deut. 23:1). Although he traveled to Jerusalem for worship, he was still considered a semiproselyte. Nevertheless, the Old Testament predicted the day when foreigners and eunuchs would no longer be excluded from the fellowship of God's people (Isa. 56:3–7; also compare I Kings 8:41–43). We observe that Philip first brings the Samaritans, who were in between the Jew and the Gentile, into the church. Now he leads the Ethiopian, who was a half-convert to Judaism, into the assembly of the Lord.

The Ethiopian is a court official of Candace, queen of Ethiopia. (Incidentally, Candace is not the name of a person but the title of the queen mother, who ruled in the place of her son.)[55] The official serves at the royal court as the chief treasurer. He has the prominent position of chancellor of the exchequer, or finance minister, in charge of the royal treasury and national revenue.

This Ethiopian man traveled to Jerusalem for worship. He not only worshiped God in his local Jewish synagogue; he also took his religion seriously and went on a pilgrimage to Jerusalem (compare John 12:20). Historical records show that numerous Jews had taken up residence in Egypt and Ethiopia. These Jews worshiped Israel's God and invited the Gentiles to their religious services, with the result that many Gentiles became God-fearers (see also Acts 10:2).

28. As he was returning and sitting in his carriage, he was reading the book of Isaiah the prophet. 29. And the Spirit told Philip, "Go toward this carriage and stay close to it."

In Jerusalem, the official presumably purchases a copy of the Greek

---

54. Johannes Schneider, *TDNT*, vol. 2, p. 766; Hans Baltensweiler, *NIDNTT*, vol. 1, p. 560.
55. Therefore, the NEB has the reading "a high official of the Kandake, or Queen, of Ethiopia."

translation of Isaiah's prophecy and, on his way home, passes the time by reading it. In ancient times, people read out loud and thought it strange when a reader would not do so. Indeed, the Jewish rabbis were of the opinion that reading a manuscript aloud was an aid to memorization and silent reading a cause of forgetfulness.[56] The Ethiopian knows that the Word of God will lead him to salvation and is eagerly reading the text of Isaiah's book. Even though he is unable to understand the full meaning of the text, he is confident that the Jewish people in his homeland will explain it to him. The Holy Spirit now instructs Philip to approach the royal carriage of the official and to stay close to it. Then Philip hears the familiar words of Isaiah from the lips of the Ethiopian and realizes that this man is a God-fearing person who is seeking the way of salvation.

Greek Words, Phrases, and Constructions in 8:26–28

Verse 26

μεσημβρίαν—this is a combination of μέσος (middle) and ἡμέρα (day). It signifies either time (midday) or place (south).

αὕτη—the feminine demonstrative pronoun relates either to the nearest antecedent Γάζαν (Gaza) or to τὴν ὁδόν (the road). The latter is more probable.

Verse 27

Αἰθίοψ—the etymology of this word is interesting: αἴθω (I burn) and ὤψ (face).[57]

προσκυνήσων—the future active participle denotes purpose. The Ethiopian had come (ἐληλύθει, pluperfect from ἔρχομαι) to Jerusalem to worship.

Verse 28

ἦν ὑποστρέφων—the periphrastic construction of the imperfect tense of the verb *to be* with the present participles of the verbs *to return* and *to sit* is descriptive. Also note the imperfect tense of the verb ἀνεγίνωσκεν (he continued to read).

---

b. Reading
8:30–33

In his providence, God is leading Philip to the Ethiopian dignitary just at the time when the official is reading aloud a messianic prophecy from Isaiah's book. The eunuch who is reading the prophecy is unable to understand Isaiah's message and needs someone to explain it to him. Furthermore, he is reading from the Greek, which is Philip's native tongue. This is

---

56. SB, vol. 2, p. 687. Augustine mentions that Ambrose by reading silently failed to explain the text. *Confessions* 6.3.
57. Thayer, p. 14.

the point of contact that Philip needs to overcome his initial hesitancy in approaching the royal carriage.

30. Then Philip ran toward it and heard the Ethiopian reading from the book of Isaiah the prophet. He asked, "Do you understand what you are reading?"

31. "How can I unless someone explains it to me?" the official replied. He invited Philip to come up and sit with him.

The Ethiopian official had purposely chosen the less-traveled road from Jerusalem to Gaza to allow him time to read the Scriptures. Undoubtedly, the carriage was driven by a servant who was told to travel at a walking speed. Thus, Philip could easily keep up with the carriage and listen closely to what the official was reading. Philip knew the messianic prophecies of Isaiah by heart and immediately recognized the words that were read aloud.

What a marvelous opportunity to teach Christ's gospel! Here is a man who eagerly reads God's Word but is unable to understand its meaning. Then, guided and prompted by the Holy Spirit, Philip hears the words spoken by this person. He knows that God has placed him here at this moment to lead the Ethiopian eunuch to Christ. Thus he asks the engaging question, "Do you understand what you are reading?" In the Greek, the question has a play on words which is apparent even in transliteration: *ginoskeis ha anaginoskeis.* The idiom reveals that the conversation is conducted in Greek, the language common to both men. And a possible linguistic barrier has been removed.

Philip actually interrupts the reading exercise of the Ethiopian, but he expects that the man will not take offense. On the contrary, with his question, he suggests a readiness to help the reader in understanding the Scriptures. And the official responds affably to what Philip asks. His response is interesting, for he answers Philip with a counterquestion: "How can I unless someone explains it to me?" He openly admits his ignorance and his inability to grasp the meaning of the text he is reading. Differences in rank, race, and nationality disappear when the Ethiopian acknowledges his need for an interpreter. Neither pride nor shame mars the relationship that is developing between these two men.

The eunuch turns to Philip, who as a Jew knows the prophecies of Scripture and as a Christian knows how to explain their fulfillment. Jesus Christ is at the core of these prophecies, for he is the one about whom the prophet Isaiah speaks. Christ's gospel begins with these messianic prophecies and demonstrates that Jesus has fulfilled them. Further, Christ sends out his servants to interpret the message of salvation for people who are ready to receive the Good News.

The wording of the official's question expresses perplexity ("How can I?") and a need for a guide ("unless someone *guides* me"). This is "a very obvious metaphor for a teacher, when life is thought of as a road, and the church is called 'the way.' "[58] Philip is ready to open the Scriptures to lead the Ethiopian to Christ. Notice the distinct parallel with the account of the two men on the way to Emmaus when Jesus met them. Jesus explained to them what the Scriptures said about him (Luke 24:27). Moreover, in the upper room Jesus promised the eleven disciples the coming of the Holy Spirit, who would guide them in all truth (John 16:13). But let us return to the Ethiopian eunuch.

The visit to Jerusalem has not been a rewarding experience for the Ethiopian official. He has failed to find answers to spiritual questions, and even though he heard the name of Jesus mentioned, he has not come to an understanding of the truth. When Philip offers to interpret the Scriptures for him, the seeker is ready. Philip is invited to come up into the carriage, sit next to the official, and explain the text of the Scripture passage.

32. Now the passage of Scripture he was reading was this:
> **"He was led as a sheep to the slaughter,**
> **and as a lamb before its shearer is silent,**
> **so he did not open his mouth.**
> **33. In his humiliation he was deprived of justice.**
> **Who will tell his descendants,**
> **because his life was taken from the earth?"**

a. "Now the passage of Scripture." The book of Isaiah's prophecy that the Ethiopian owned did not consist of pages but was in the form of a scroll. This scroll was made of papyrus leaves glued together sheet by sheet. Then each end of this lengthy strip of paper was fastened to a stick; by simultaneously rolling and unrolling these ends, the reader was able to find the passage he wanted to read. The scroll probably contained the entire text of Isaiah and showed only one column of the text at a time.[59]

The column which the official was reading happened to be Isaiah 53:7–8. The wording of this passage recorded by Luke is identical with that of the Septuagint. However, the Old Testament wording based on the Hebrew text differs slightly.

b. "He was led as a sheep to the slaughter." Here is a messianic passage that clearly speaks about the life and death of Jesus Christ. But because Isaiah does not mention the name of the person he introduces only as "he," the Ethiopian is unable to grasp the meaning of the text. To Philip, this passage from Isaiah's prophecy speaks volumes. He sees Jesus arrested in Gethsemane's garden and led to the house of the high priest to stand trial. While witnesses accused Jesus of wanting to break down the temple and rebuild it in three days, Jesus remained silent (Matt. 26:60–63).

c. "As a lamb before its shearer is silent." Philip is familiar with the words

---

58. Richard B. Rackham, *The Acts of the Apostles: An Exposition*, Westminster Commentaries series (1901; reprint ed., Grand Rapids: Baker, 1964), p. 122.

59. Consult Bruce M. Metzger, *The Text of the New Testament: Its Transmission, Corruption, and Restoration*, 2d ed. (New York: Oxford University Press, 1968), p. 6.

John the Baptist spoke to his disciples when Jesus approached him: "Behold the Lamb of God, who takes away the sin of the world" (John 1:29, 36). Peter also describes Jesus as the lamb that is without blemish or defect (I Peter 1:19). When the term *lamb* occurs in the Greek translation of the Old Testament, it signifies sacrificial lambs. In Scripture, the words *lamb* and *sheep* are often interchanged. This is clear in Isaiah 53:7, where the prophet speaks of a lamb that is slaughtered and a sheep that is silent when the shearer takes away its wool. (Note that adult sheep are shorn of their wool when summer approaches, but the lambs born in the spring do not have a thick fleece.) Moreover, when the expressions *lamb* and *sheep* appear in Isaiah 53:7, they refer to a human being who fulfills the function of an animal that is sacrificed.[60]

d. "In his humiliation he was deprived of justice." This is the Septuagint wording of Isaiah 53:8, but in the Old Testament the reading differs: "By oppression and judgment he was taken away." This wording prophetically points to the unjust trial and subsequent death of Jesus. We lack any and all indication why the Greek translation diverges from the Hebrew text. However, the Septuagint in this verse blends in smoothly with the preceding passage, where the reading refers to a silent lamb. Here is a picture of humility, and translators use this very word in the text.

e. "Who will tell his descendants, because his life was taken from this earth?" The prophet is speaking about a person who has descendants. But this person's life has come to an untimely end (compare Dan. 9:26). Who are these descendants? Scripture provides no parallels to elucidate this text and Luke does not relate Philip's exposition. Perhaps in this text we can see the fulfillment of Jesus' words: "And I, when I am lifted up from the earth, will draw all men to myself" (John 12:32). If we understand the text to refer to Jesus' spiritual descendants, then it fits in with the tremendous growth of the church in the first few years after the outpouring of the Holy Spirit. The reference to Jesus' descendants then means, "The number of his disciples will grow incalculably, because he has become the Exalted."[61]

Doctrinal Considerations in 8:30–33

Philip puts a penetrating question to the Ethiopian eunuch: "Do you understand what you are reading?" This question is basic to confirming the Christian faith, for the Christian knows Christ only through the Scriptures. By reading God's Word, he increases his knowledge of Jesus Christ, his Savior. Thus Philip begins with the

---

60. Johannes Gess, *NIDNTT*, vol. 2, p. 410; Richard N. Longenecker, *The Christology of Early Jewish Christianity*, Studies in Biblical Theology, 2d series 17 (London: SCM, 1970), p. 50. Compare Joachim Jeremias, *TDNT*, vol. 1, p. 339.

61. Ernst Haenchen, *The Acts of the Apostles: A Commentary*, trans. Bernard Noble and Gerald Shinn (Philadelphia: Westminster, 1971), p. 312. See also P. B. Decock, "The Understanding of Isaiah 53:7–8 in Acts 8:32–33," *Neotest* 14 (1981): 123.

Scriptures, explains their fulfillment in Christ, and leads the Ethiopian official to repentance, faith, and joy.

The task of the preacher is to show Christ to his audience. For precisely this reason, some churches have a plaque fastened to the pulpit just below the open Bible and visible only to the preacher. The plaque has the words, "Sir, we want to see Jesus" (John 12:21). The average member of a congregation listens to the preacher only on Sunday, during the worship service. He comes not to hear views on a number of topics that may or may not relate to his life; he has come to meet Jesus. And he meets Jesus through the faithful exposition of the Scriptures. The preacher must be a workman "who correctly handles the word of truth" (II Tim. 2:15, NIV) and opens the Word for his audience. The old adage is worth repeating:

> *Expound the Scriptures*
> *Exhort the sinner*
> *Exalt the Savior*

Greek Words, Phrases, and Constructions in 8:30–33

Verse 30

ἆρά γε—the combination of two particles introducing a direct question expresses a sense of doubt.[62]

ἀναγινώσκεις—the compound form of this verb in the present indicative is intensive or perfective: "do you know accurately?" That is, "do you read?"

Verse 31

δυναίμην—preceded by the particle ἄν, this verb is in the present optative. The optative expresses "what would happen on the fulfillment of some supposed condition."[63] The sentence is a condition which has the protasis with a future indicative ὁδηγήσει (he will explain) and an apodosis with the optative.

Verse 33

ταπεινώσει αὐτοῦ—the noun *humiliation* denotes not so much a state as a process. The pronoun *his* is absent in the Septuagint text. Yet its presence in this verse may be original.[64]

---

c. Explaining
8:34–35

Luke mentions the passage that the Ethiopian eunuch read while traveling from Jerusalem to Gaza. However, he fails to record the explanation Philip gave the occupant of the royal carriage. Philip interprets the messi-

---

62. Moule, *Idiom-Book*, p. 158.
63. Robert Hanna, *A Grammatical Aid to the Greek New Testament* (Grand Rapids: Baker, 1983), p. 205.
64. Metzger, *Textual Commentary*, p. 359.

anic prophecy of Isaiah 53 from the point of view that Christ has fulfilled the Scriptures. That is, all the messianic prophecies must be understood as fulfilled by Jesus Christ. The passage in which the prophet Isaiah predicts the suffering and death of the Messiah is especially significant. John Albert Bengel remarks, "By means of that [fifty-thir]d chapter of Isaiah, not only many Jews, but even Atheists, have been converted: history records the names of some of these; God knows them all."[65] This passage, then, sets the tone for evangelism and mission endeavor.

34. The eunuch said to Philip, "Tell me, please, about whom did the prophet say this? About himself or someone else?" 35. Then Philip began to speak, and beginning with this passage of Scripture he preached to him the good news of Jesus.

The Ethiopian is both receptive to the Good News and not far from the kingdom. He asks Philip to interpret for him the passage he has read, because he is unable to see the spiritual meaning of the message.

"Tell me, please, about whom did the prophet say this?" he asks. Philip's answer can be put in one word: Jesus. When Isaiah wrote his messianic prophecy, he was not writing about himself. In the broader context of this prophecy (chaps. 42–53), Isaiah speaks of the messianic king, whom God calls "my servant." This servant, says Isaiah in five sections of three verses each (52:13–53:12),

suffers on behalf of others,

is despised and rejected by men,

dies for the sins of the world,

is buried with the wicked,

and declares many people righteous.

From a Christian point of view, the text of Isaiah 53 unmistakably refers to the Messiah and not to the prophet. As far as we are able to determine, however, the Jews of the first century lacked a doctrine of a suffering Messiah. This doctrine originated with Jesus, who "saw himself fulfilling the role of the Servant."[66]

We know what passage the Ethiopian eunuch read from the Book of Isaiah, but we do not know how Philip explained the text to him and what the content of his sermon about Jesus may have been. We must assume, therefore, that because the Ethiopian official had the Book of Isaiah in his hands, Philip explained the broader context of the verses that were unclear

---

65. John Albert Bengel, *Gnomon of the New Testament,* ed. Andrew R. Fausset, 5 vols. (Edinburgh: Clark, 1877), vol. 2, p. 590.

66. I. Howard Marshall, *The Acts of the Apostles: An Introduction and Commentary,* Tyndale New Testament Commentary series (Leicester: Inter-Varsity; Grand Rapids: Eerdmans, 1980), p. 164.

to the eunuch. Luke indicates that Philip began with the passage the official had been reading and then continued to preach the good news about Jesus. Accordingly, Philip taught that Jesus fulfilled the messianic prophecies, especially those in the Book of Isaiah (compare 18:28). We conclude that selections from the Old Testament, explained in the light of Jesus' teachings, suffering, death, and resurrection, formed Philip's sermon.

Philip undoubtedly explained to the Ethiopian that baptism signifies the washing away of sin and that baptism is a sign and seal of belonging to God's people. Implicitly we know that the eunuch put his faith in Jesus, confessed his sin, and desired to be baptized.

d. Baptizing
8:36–40

36. And as they were going along the road, they came to some water. The eunuch said, "Look! Water! What prevents me from being baptized?" 37. [See the commentary.] 38. He ordered the carriage stopped. Both Philip and the eunuch went down into the water and Philip baptized him.

Luke describes the road between Jerusalem and Gaza as the desert road (v. 26). He does not indicate how long Philip preached the Good News to the Ethiopian official, but we surmise that considerable time elapsed. In a desert area, "the problem is not where to find enough water for immersion but where to find water at all."[67] Yet, closer to Gaza, a brook called Wadi el-Hashi flows north of the city into the Mediterranean Sea. Another possibility is that pools in that area provided a suitable place for baptism. It makes little sense to try to find the exact location of this baptism. The significance of baptism is what counts in this passage.

a. *Verse 36.* "The eunuch said, 'Look! Water! What prevents me from being baptized?' " (see 10:47; 11:16). Although the written text merely gives the words spoken by the Ethiopian, we can imagine excitement, joy, and happiness in his voice. He is the one who notices a body of water and poses the rhetorical question whether anything prevents him from being baptized. The obvious answer to this question is, nothing.

Through baptism, Philip accepts the man into the membership of the church. Note the parallel of Peter accepting Cornelius and his household. God communicates to Peter a vision of unclean animals and tells him to overcome his hesitancy to eat anything unclean (10:9–16). Then Peter goes to Cornelius, preaches the gospel, and baptizes the Roman centurion and his household (10:24–48). But observe the difference between Philip and Peter. Although Philip is a Jew, he has his roots in the dispersion, where the Greek language and culture are commonplace. Because of his background, Philip is cosmopolitan. Peter, however, is a Palestinian Jew from Galilee and speaks Aramaic. Philip leaves the Hellenistic group of Christians in Jerusa-

---

67. R. C. H. Lenski, *The Interpretation of the Acts of the Apostles* (Columbus: Wartburg, 1944), p. 345.

lem and brings the gospel first to the Samaritans and then, at the request of an angel, to the Ethiopian eunuch. Peter ministers exclusively to Jewish Christians in Jerusalem and Judea, and only afterward God prepares him for his mission to the Gentile Cornelius. And last, the Ethiopian official is baptized but does not receive the Holy Spirit. Cornelius and his household listen to Peter's sermon and the Spirit descends on them. Afterward they are baptized.

b. *Verse 37.* Some manuscripts of the Western text of Greek manuscripts have this reading: "Then Philip said, 'If you believe with all your heart, you may.' And he answered and said, 'I believe that Jesus Christ is the Son of God' " (NKJV). All the major textual witnesses do not have this verse. Says Bruce M. Metzger, "There is no reason why scribes should have omitted the material, if it had originally stood in the text."[68] Perhaps in the early church the need was felt to have the Ethiopian profess his faith before he was baptized. Scribes added Philip's comment and the eunuch's confession to the margin of the manuscript of Acts. The words the eunuch spoke may have been used as a baptismal formula toward the end of the second century; the words were known in those days, as is evident in the writings of the church father Irenaeus, who cites part of this formula.[69] Via late medieval manuscripts verse 37 was added to the Greek text and eventually translated into English. However, because the verse is an insertion and reveals a style differing from that of Luke, it is generally omitted in texts and translations.

c. *Verse 38.* "He ordered the carriage stopped." The Ethiopian now gives an order. He tells the driver to halt the carriage. Then with Philip he descends into the water and Philip baptizes him. Although the text itself is terse, I confidently aver that, in harmony with the practice of the early church, Philip baptized the eunuch in the name of Jesus Christ and not in the name of the Triune God (see 2:38; 8:12; 10:48; 19:5).

39. When they came up out of the water, the Spirit of the Lord took Philip away and the eunuch saw him no more. He continued his journey rejoicing. 40. But Philip appeared in Azotus; and passing through, he kept on preaching in all the towns until he came to Caesarea.

We make these observations:

a. *Text.* The account comes to an abrupt end when Philip is physically removed from the scene by the Holy Spirit. Some ancient manuscripts have an insertion of seven Greek words, which translated are, "Holy [Spirit] fell upon the eunuch, but an angel." The expanded version then reads: "When they came up out of the water, the Holy Spirit fell upon the eunuch, and an angel of the Lord took Philip away." Is this reading authentic? Hardly. Greek manuscripts support the shorter, not the longer, reading of this

---

68. Metzger, *Textual Commentary,* p. 359.
69. Irenaeus *Against Heresies* 3.12.8.

passage. Even though some scholars favor the longer text,[70] others point out that a scribe probably altered the text for purposes of harmonization. A scribe made the text agree first with the account concerning the baptism of the Holy Spirit in Samaria and next with that of the angel of the Lord calling Philip (vv. 17, 26). We conclude that as yet no translation has appeared with the longer reading.[71]

b. *Removal.* How the Spirit of the Lord snatched Philip from the baptismal site is not known. We do not have to resort to fanciful speculation: that Philip was invisible or flew through the air. Even references to the Spirit of the Lord, who transports the prophet Elijah to heaven, shed no light on this particular verse.[72] Paul's description of a man caught up to the third heaven (II Cor. 12:2, 4) fails to help us. Paul voices uncertainty whether this experience was a physical or mental rapture.

The emphasis falls on the phrase *the Spirit of the Lord.* This phrase occurs also in the account of Ananias and Sapphira (5:9). And in Luke's Gospel, the phrase appears in the sermon Jesus preaches on Isaiah 61:1: "The Spirit of the Lord is on me." Jesus says that this Scripture has been fulfilled in him. Therefore, we conclude that the Spirit of Jesus (compare 16:7) impels Philip to go elsewhere by transferring him from the scene of the baptism.

c. *Joy.* Luke reports no surprise on the part of the Ethiopian eunuch when Philip suddenly disappeared. The official continued his journey and was filled with joy. As a new creature in Christ with the Holy Spirit in his heart, he traveled to his homeland. We surmise that he was unable to keep his joy to himself but that he had to acquaint his countrymen with Jesus and the message of salvation. However, we have no knowledge about a church in Ethiopia during the first three centuries. Granted that tradition features accounts of conversions that result from the eunuch's preaching, we have evidence only of a fourth-century Ethiopic church.

d. *Proclamation.* "But Philip appeared in Azotus." Philip's next assignment is to preach Christ's gospel in the coastal towns, beginning with Azotus, until he reaches Caesarea. Azotus is one of the five ancient Philistine cities and was known as Ashdod (see I Sam. 5:1), located about eighteen miles north of Gaza. Philip brought the gospel to the coastal towns, including Joppa and Lydda, where Peter later went to visit the saints (9:32–38). Eventually Philip reached Caesarea, where he settled permanently. Years later, Paul stayed at the house of Philip the evangelist in Caesarea. Luke records that Philip had four unmarried daughters who had the gift of prophecy (21:8–9). We do not know if Philip already resided in Caesarea

---

70. Marshall, *Acts*, p. 165; Williams, *Acts*, p. 149; see also Lake and Cadbury, *Beginnings*, vol. 4, p. 98.

71. Perhaps inadvertently, the NEB omits the words *of the Lord* with this resultant reading: "the Spirit snatched Philip away."

72. I Kings 18:12; II Kings 2:16; and see Ezek. 3:14; 8:3.

when Peter preached the gospel in the home of Cornelius the Roman centurion (10:24).

Practical Considerations in 8:34–40

Do you ever feel guilty for failing to be a witness for Jesus Christ? Repeatedly you have been exhorted to introduce the Lord to your neighbors, friends, and acquaintances, but you admit that the results of your attempts have been meager. You try to witness, yet are not sure whether you choose the correct moment for your evangelistic efforts.

Many instances of witnessing for the Lord are self-made and ill-timed. Instead of following the Lord, we run ahead of him. Instead of waiting for directives from him, we boldly formulate our own orders. Instead of asking God to provide for us an opportunity to witness, we fail to ask.

Scripture tells us that we are God's fellow workers (I Cor. 3:9). This means that God rules, directs, saves, and increases his church. We are his servants and obediently take orders from him. Therefore, we humbly ask him to use us in his church and kingdom and to give us an opportunity to witness. When he answers our prayer, he opens a window of opportunity and crowns our efforts with his blessing.

> Wait for the LORD;
> be strong and take heart
> and wait for the LORD. [Ps. 27:14, NIV]

Greek Words, Phrases, and Constructions in 8:36 and 40

Verse 36

ἐπί—this preposition, preceding the words τι ὕδωρ (some water) in the accusative case, "seems not to imply strictly 'upon,' but rather 'as far as.' "[73]

Verse 40

εὑρέθη—the aorist passive of the verb εὑρίσκω (I find) means that Philip has appeared on the streets of Azotus. Hence the preposition εἰς must be understood in the local sense: "in" or "at."

Summary of Chapter 8

The church in Jerusalem endures a great persecution and consequently the believers are scattered throughout Judea and Samaria. Devout men bury Stephen and mourn for him, but Saul tries to destroy the church. Philip preaches Christ in Samaria and performs many healing miracles.

Simon the sorcerer had gained the reputation among the Samaritan people that he was the power of God, the power that is called great. The

---

73. Robertson, *Grammar,* p. 602.

people listen to Philip preach the Good News; they believe and are baptized. Simon also believes and is baptized.

The church in Jerusalem hears about the believers in Samaria and sends Peter and John to pray for them. The apostles place their hands on the Samaritan believers, who then receive the Holy Spirit. Simon offers money to the apostles in an attempt to buy the gift of the Spirit. Peter rebukes him and tells him to repent.

An angel of the Lord instructs Philip to travel along the desert road toward Gaza, where Philip meets an Ethiopian eunuch sitting in his carriage and reading a messianic passage from the prophecy of Isaiah. Philip asks the man if he understands what he is reading. The Ethiopian requests help and Philip interprets the passage for him, telling him the good news about Jesus. The eunuch notices some water, stops the carriage, and is baptized. Philip is snatched away, appears in Azotus, and preaches the gospel in coastal towns until he comes to Caesarea.

9

The Church in Palestine, *part 2*

9:1–43

Outline (continued)

9:1–31	C. Conversion of Paul
9:1–9	1. Paul to Damascus
9:1–3	a. Objective
9:4–6	b. Encounter
9:7–9	c. Effect
9:10–25	2. Paul in Damascus
9:10–12	a. Call
9:13–14	b. Objection
9:15–16	c. Command
9:17–19a	d. Response
9:19b–22	e. Propagation
9:23–25	f. Plot
9:26–30	3. Paul in Jerusalem
9:31	4. Conclusion
9:32–11:18	D. Ministry of Peter
9:32–35	1. Miracle in Lydda
9:36–43	2. Miracle in Joppa

9 1 Now Saul was still breathing murderous threats against the Lord's disciples. He went to the high priest 2 and asked him for letters to the synagogues in Damascus, so that if he found any persons who belonged to the Way, both men and women, he might lead them as prisoners to Jerusalem. 3 And as he traveled and approached Damascus, suddenly a light from heaven flashed around him. 4 He fell to the ground and heard a voice say to him, "Saul, Saul, why do you persecute me?" 5 Saul asked, "Who are you, Lord?" He answered, "I am Jesus, whom you are persecuting. 6 Now get up and enter the city, and you will be told what you must do."

7 But the men who were traveling with Saul stood speechless; they heard the voice, but saw no one. 8 Saul got up from the ground; he saw nothing even though his eyes were open. So they led him by the hand and brought him into Damascus. 9 And for three days he did not see anything nor did he eat or drink anything.

10 In Damascus was a disciple named Ananias. The Lord said to him in a vision, "Ananias." And he said, "Here I am, Lord." 11 The Lord said to him, "Go at once to Straight Street and ask at the house of Judas for a man called Saul from Tarsus, for he is praying. 12 And in a vision, he has seen a man named Ananias enter and place his hands on him so that he might regain his sight."

13 Ananias replied, "Lord, from many people I have heard about this man, how much harm he has done to your saints at Jerusalem. 14 And here he has authority from the chief priests to bind all who call upon your name."

15 The Lord said to him, "Go, for he is my chosen instrument to carry my name before the Gentiles, kings, and the people of Israel. 16 For I will show him how much he must suffer for my name."

17 And Ananias went and entered the house. He placed his hands on Saul and said, "Brother Saul, the Lord Jesus, who appeared to you on the road by which you were coming, has sent me so that you may regain your sight and be filled with the Holy Spirit." 18 And immediately something like scales fell from his eyes and he regained his sight. He stood up and was baptized. 19 After taking some food, he regained his strength.

Saul spent several days with the disciples in Damascus. 20 Immediately he began to preach in the synagogues that Jesus is the Son of God. 21 And all who heard him were amazed and said, "Is not this the man who destroyed those who called upon this name in Jerusalem? Did he not come here to lead such people as prisoners to the chief priests?" 22 Saul became increasingly stronger; he bewildered the Jews living in Damascus by proving that Jesus is the Christ.

23 After many days had passed, the Jews plotted to kill him. 24 But their plot became known to Saul. And the Jews were also watching the gates day and night so that they might kill him. 25 His converts took him by night and they lowered him in a basket through the wall.

26 When Saul came to Jerusalem, he tried to associate with the disciples. And all were afraid of him because they did not believe that he was a disciple. 27 But Barnabas took him and brought him to the apostles. He explained to them how Saul on the road had seen the Lord, who spoke to him. And he told them how in Damascus Saul had boldly spoken in the name of Jesus. 28 So Saul was with them, moving freely about Jerusalem and speaking boldly in the name of the Lord. 29 He talked and argued with Hellenistic Jews, but they were trying to kill

him. 30 And when the brothers learned of this, they brought him down to Caesarea and sent him away to Tarsus.

31 Then the church throughout Judea, Galilee, and Samaria enjoyed a period of peace and was strengthened. And it continued to increase, living in the fear of the Lord and the comfort of the Holy Spirit.

C. Conversion of Paul
9:1–31

1. Paul to Damascus
9:1–9

Luke has brought his account of Stephen and Philip to an end and now continues to relate the activities of Saul (see 7:58; 8:1, 3). He seems to indicate that Philip's evangelistic labors are an interlude and that the reader should once again focus attention on Saul (whom I will call Paul), bent on destroying the church of Jesus Christ. Conversely, Luke is not quite ready to devote himself completely to Paul's ministry; thus the report on Paul's conversion in effect also is an interlude, but in the section about Peter's ministry. The account about this ministry comes to an end when Peter is released from prison (12:17); thereafter Paul's active ministry begins (13:2).

a. Objective
9:1–3

1. Now Saul was still breathing murderous threats against the Lord's disciples. He went to the high priest 2. and asked him for letters to the synagogues in Damascus, so that if he found any persons who belonged to the Way, both men and women, he might lead them as prisoners to Jerusalem.

a. "Now Saul was still breathing murderous threats." In the preceding chapter (8:3), Luke depicts Paul as the persecutor of the Jerusalem believers. Now he gives a more fearsome portrayal of Paul in his pre-conversion state: everything Paul thinks, says, and does is dominated by his desire to destroy the followers of Jesus. He has parted company with his mentor, Gamaliel, who cautioned the members of the Sanhedrin not to find themselves in opposition to God (5:39). Paul's entire being is concentrated on destruction and murder. We have no reason to believe that Paul himself killed the Christians. But he himself confesses that he approved the executions of Christians by casting his vote against them (26:10). Blinded by his zeal, Paul unwittingly fulfilled Jesus' word to the apostles: "Anyone who kills you will think that he is offering a service to God" (John 16:2).

Not satisfied with only the Jerusalem scene, Paul now looks to other places where Christians reside. Luke calls the Christians "disciples," for they are learners who receive instruction in the apostles' teaching. Luke indicates that these disciples are found in Damascus (vv. 10, 19), Jerusalem

(v. 26), Joppa (v. 36), and Lydda (v. 38). So, with authority from the Sanhedrin, Paul intends to arrest Christ's followers in Damascus.

b. "He went to the high priest." The high priest served as head of the Sanhedrin, which as a legislative body had jurisdiction over the Jews living in Jerusalem, Palestine, and the dispersion. Thus the high priest had power to issue warrants to the synagogues in Damascus for the arrests of Christian Jews residing there (see 9:2; 22:5; 26:12).[1] Did the Romans permit religious persecution in their provinces? We are not sure whether at that time the Roman government had full control over Damascus. In the fourth decade of the first century, the Nabatean Arabs under the leadership of Aretas IV were exerting their influence on that city and gave the Damascenes temporary autonomy. The Nabateans and Jews probably collaborated because of their anti-Roman stance.

From the New Testament and other historical records we know that the high priest was Caiaphas, the son-in-law of Annas.[2] Nevertheless, Annas exercised the authority of high priest, as is evident from verse 14, where the plural term *chief priests* occurs.

c. "And asked him for letters to the synagogues in Damascus." That city gave residence to a large Jewish population, so that for centuries Damascus had its own Jewish quarter (compare v. 22).[3] Consequently, Jewish synagogues were common in the Syrian capital. From the annals of Jewish history we learn that at the time of the Jewish war against Rome (A.D. 66), no fewer than ten thousand Jews were killed in Damascus.

Scripture tells us that Damascus already existed in the time of Abraham (Gen. 14:15; 15:2), was conquered by David (II Sam. 8:6), regained independence during the reign of Solomon (I Kings 11:24–25), and became a hotbed of hostility toward Israel and eventually dominated it for some time (Amos 1:3–5). During the Roman conquest (64 B.C.), Damascus was the seat of government for Rome's Syrian province and one of the ten cities in the region known as the Decapolis (Mark 5:20; 7:31). The Nabatean Arabs ruled the Arabian desert area and under the leadership of Aretas IV, who was the father-in-law of Herod Antipas (Matt. 14:3; Mark 6:17; Luke 3:19), controlled Damascus for a few years (II Cor. 11:32).

Damascus is situated along the Abana River, from which it draws water to irrigate the sun-parched landscape in and around the city. In Paul's day, to journey on foot from Jerusalem to Damascus took about five or six days to cover the approximate distance of 150 miles. The city was a commercial center where caravans converged from all directions in the ancient world and where the Christian faith began to flourish. Paul realized that from Damascus, the gospel of Christ would spread throughout the world. For

---

1. Emil Schürer, *The History of the Jewish People in the Age of Jesus Christ (175 B.C.–A.D. 135)*, rev. and ed. Geza Vermes and Fergus Millar, 3 vols. (Edinburgh: Clark, 1973–87), vol. 2, p. 218.
2. Matt. 26:3; Luke 3:2; John 11:49; 18:13–14, 24, 28; Acts 4:6.
3. Josephus *War* 2.20.2 [561]; 7.8.7 [368].

that reason, he wanted to stop the influence of Christianity and asked the high priest for warrants to arrest Christians, both men and women, in the Damascus synagogues. He knew that among the worshipers in the local assemblies were countless followers of Jesus Christ. Here Paul intended to make multiple arrests.

d. "If he found any persons who belonged to the Way." In the beginning, Christians used a variety of names to identify themselves. The term *the Way* is one of the first names that describes the Christian faith (compare the term *the Name* [5:41]). In Acts it appears a few times (19:9, 23; 22:4; 24:14, 22). The term denotes the teaching of the gospel, the Christian's conduct directed and guided by this gospel,[4] and the Christian community in general. Granted that the believers formed a distinct group, they nevertheless continued to meet with fellow Jews in the Damascus synagogues. As a result, the rulers of these synagogues could readily identify the followers of the Way; Paul intended to depend on the rulers for help in arresting the Christians. He planned to lead Christ's followers as bound prisoners to Jerusalem, where they would have to stand trial.

3. And as he traveled and approached Damascus, suddenly a light from heaven flashed around him.

Three reports describe the conversion of Paul on the Damascus road (9:1–19; 22:4–16; 26:12–18). All of them have a common theme: "Paul saw Jesus, who spoke to him on the way to Damascus." Yet all three accounts differ, even though Luke has written them. We can explain the differences by considering their purposes, settings, and audiences. The first account reports the historical event; the second features Paul addressing a crowd of angry Jews in Jerusalem; and the third is a speech in which Paul seeks to persuade Agrippa to become a Christian.

If we believe that all three reports originate with Paul, we have no difficulty with their variations. It is a fact of life that whenever someone tells a story to diverse audiences under differing circumstances, we expect changes to occur.

Nevertheless, literature on the three accounts of Paul's conversion is extensive. Most of it is written by literary and source critics who carefully analyze the variations in each report.[5] Their conclusion is that Luke composed the three different presentations of Paul's conversion. But if Luke received his information for all three accounts from Paul himself, we must assume that the writer has recorded the content and phrasing of each report.

Further, for stylistic reasons Luke is not interested in repeating the same

---

4. Consult Wilhelm Michaelis, *TDNT*, vol. 5, p. 89; Günther Ebel, *NIDNTT*, vol. 3, p. 942.
5. Two studies are C. W. Hedrick, "Paul's Conversion/Call: A Comparative Analysis of the Three Reports in Acts," *JBL* 100 (1981): 415–32, and Gerhard Lohfink, *The Conversion of St. Paul: Narrative and History in Acts*, trans. and ed. Bruce J. Malina (Chicago: Franciscan Herald Press, 1975). Lohfink ascribes the differences of the three accounts "to the creative literary activity and composition of the author, Luke" (p. 60).

story three times in exactly the same words (9:1–19; 22:4–16; 26:12–18). Hence, we see that Luke describes the light from heaven (v. 3) as bright (22:6) and even brighter than the sun (26:13). The time of day was high noon when Paul and his companions were approaching Damascus. All of them saw a brilliant light flash around them, which caused Paul but not his companions to be blinded (v. 8).

Is Paul's experience on the Damascus road comparable to a fit of epilepsy or sunstroke? The New Testament never discloses that Paul suffered from such ailments. Instead we learn that Jesus appeared to him both in visions and when Paul was in a trance. So Jesus gave him instructions and revelations (e.g., see 18:9–10; 22:17–21; Gal. 1:12). He personally called Paul to be one of his apostles and did so outside the confines of Jerusalem to separate him from Judaism. That is, Jesus took Paul with all his training in the Scriptures, his desire to promote Judaism, and his zeal for tradition (Gal. 1:13–14). Then Jesus turned him around so that Paul with his talents, capabilities, and enthusiasm became a willing instrument to serve the cause of Christ.

Greek Words, Phrases, and Constructions in 9:1–2

Verse 1

ἐμπνέων—the present active participle of the compound verb ἐμπνέω (I breathe) expresses intensity. Also, this verb governs the genitive case of ἀπειλῆς (threat) and φονοῦ (murder). Verbs of sensation (touch, smell, taste) and emotion take the genitive case.

Verse 2

Notice the careful use of the prepositions in this verse: παρά (from the side of), εἰς (into, in), and πρός (for).

εὕρῃ—the aorist subjunctive from the verb εὑρίσκω (I find) does not express uncertainty regarding the fact that there were Christians in Damascus. The uncertainty relates to the number of believers residing there.

---

b. Encounter
9:4–6

4. He fell to the ground and heard a voice say to him, "Saul, Saul, why do you persecute me?"

Jesus brings Paul to conversion by appearing to him in heavenly glory light.[6] In this supernatural light, the only thing man can do is fall to the ground and lie face down. And this is exactly what Paul does. Then Jesus

---

6. John Calvin is of the opinion that Christ appeared to Paul in a flash of lightning or a thunderbolt, but this can hardly be correct in view of the evidence. *Commentary on the Acts of the Apostles*, ed. David W. Torrance and Thomas F. Torrance, 2 vols. (Grand Rapids: Eerdmans, 1966), vol. 1, p. 257.

personally addresses Paul by his given name. He asks Paul the penetrating question: "Why do you persecute me?" Indeed, Jesus' wording is remarkable, for with this question he identifies himself completely with the believers whom Paul seeks to destroy. Jesus and his followers are one (compare Matt. 10:40; 25:45).

The cautionary message not to oppose God, advocated by Paul's teacher, Gamaliel, now confronts Paul in stark reality. The martyred Stephen, the persecuted Christians driven from Jerusalem, the believers jailed by Paul—all these people are represented by Jesus Christ. Accordingly, Paul has been fighting against Jesus and has lost the battle. Jesus addresses Paul in Aramaic (see 26:14) and repeats his Hebrew name, Saul (compare, e.g., I Sam. 3:10). Paul knows that the repetition means that a divine voice is calling him.

5. Saul asked, "Who are you, Lord?" He answered, "I am Jesus, whom you are persecuting. 6. Now get up and enter the city, and you will be told what you must do."

Some commentators prefer the reading *"Who are you, sir?"*[7] They think that because Paul had not yet acknowledged Jesus Christ as the Messiah, he used the polite address *sir*. But the setting—Paul lying face down on the ground with brilliant light flashing around him and a heavenly voice calling to him in Aramaic—indicates that Paul realizes he is confronted by Jesus, the ascended Lord (see vv. 17, 27; 22:14; 26:15).

Of course, Paul is confused. Thinking that he is doing God's will in persecuting the Christians, he now hears Jesus' voice calling him to face reality. Although in writing to the Corinthians Paul seems to indicate that he knew Christ during his earthly ministry (II Cor. 5:16), we have no solid evidence of Paul meeting Jesus. Yet he has heard the Christians proclaiming Jesus' resurrection and ascension. These facts now become reality for Paul as Jesus calls him. Hesitatingly he asks, "Who are you, Lord?"

Jesus replies, "I am Jesus, whom you are persecuting." Notice that he uses his earthly name *Jesus* given to him on the day of circumcision (Luke 2:21). Jesus addresses Paul from heaven, and Paul discerns that the words spoken by Stephen are true: "I see heaven open and the Son of man standing at the right hand of God" (7:56). Jesus is alive, raised from the dead and seated at the right hand of God in heaven. In the Greek, Jesus is actually saying to Paul, "Yes, indeed, I am Jesus." Then he adds, "whom you yourself are persecuting," to emphasize the direct accusation. That is, what Paul has been doing to the Christians, he has perpetrated against Jesus. For that reason, Jesus declares twice that Paul has been persecuting him. In other words, Paul understands that he has sinned against Jesus,

---

7. F. W. Grosheide, *De Handelingen der Apostelen*, Kommentaar op het Nieuwe Testament series, 2 vols. (Amsterdam: Van Bottenburg, 1942), vol. 1, p. 293. See also F. F. Bruce, *The Book of the Acts*, rev. ed., New International Commentary on the New Testament series (Grand Rapids: Eerdmans, 1988), pp. 182–83.

which he acknowledges repeatedly in his letters (see I Cor. 15:9; Gal. 1:13, 23; Phil. 3:6).

Jesus instructs Paul and says, "Now get up and enter the city, and you will be told what to do." Paul hardly has time to assimilate that Jesus has appeared to him when he hears Jesus commanding him to get up and enter Damascus. Jesus is in charge and Paul, who earlier breathed death and destruction, obeys. Note that Jesus only tells Paul to enter the city, where he will receive further instructions. At this moment, Jesus says nothing about Paul's eventual role as apostle to the Gentiles. First, Paul has to be accepted by the Christians in Damascus and be one of Christ's disciples. Next, he will learn that Jesus commissions him to proclaim the name of Christ to the Gentiles, kings, and the nation Israel (v. 15). And last, he must be prepared to suffer on behalf of Jesus (v. 16).

Greek Words, Phrases, and Constructions in 9:4–6

Verse 4

Some manuscripts complete verse 4 with a clause from the parallel passage (26:14): "It is hard for you to kick against the goad." Copyists probably added this clause to harmonize it with the wording in 26:14. Moreover, some Latin, Syriac, and Coptic manuscripts also have these words: "So he, trembling and astonished, said, 'Lord, what do You want me to do?' And the Lord said to him . . ." (NKJV). In 1516, Erasmus translated these words from the Latin and put them in his Greek edition of the New Testament.[8]

Verse 5

ὁ δέ—this is an abbreviated construction; it lacks the proper noun Ἰησοῦς following the definite article ὁ, and the verb ἔφη (he said) is implied. The combination ὁ δέ always signals a change of subject in a historical account.

Verse 6

ἀλλά—this adverb is conveying not an adversative but a consecutive meaning. It signifies, "Well, get up and enter."

---

c. Effect
9:7–9

7. But the men who were traveling with Saul stood speechless; they heard the voice, but saw no one.

The men accompanying Paul are able to testify that a brilliant light flashed around them, causing them to fall to the ground (26:13–14); that

---

8. Bruce M. Metzger, *A Textual Commentary on the Greek New Testament*, 3d corrected ed. (London and New York: United Bible Societies, 1975), p. 362.

they heard a voice but did not understand what it was saying (22:9); and that they saw no one.

Translators face the problem whether to translate the Greek verb *akouō* as "hear" or "understand" and the Greek noun *phōnē* as "voice" or "sound." To illustrate, here are two passages with two translations:

Acts 9:7

"They heard the sound" (NIV)   "They heard the voice" (NEB)

Acts 22:9

"They did not understand   "[They] . . . did not hear
the voice" (NIV)   the voice" (NEB)

The approach to this problem is to indicate either that Luke contradicts himself in these two accounts of Paul's conversion narrative or that in the context of these passages Luke intimates a difference. The second approach has merit, because the context of both passages shows that Jesus addressed Paul and not those who accompanied him. Paul occupies center stage in these reports. His companions, however, heard the sound of a voice but were unable to fathom the meaning of the words Jesus spoke (compare Dan. 10:7). These men stood speechless, saw the brilliant light, heard the sound of a voice, but were unable to understand that Jesus appeared to Paul to bring him to conversion, repentance, and faith. In fact, the term *speechless* implies that they were shaken with fright.[9] They heard a voice, but could not see the speaker. In passing, I refer to the parallel in the Martyrdom of Polycarp that relates Polycarp's death in Rome (A.D. 155):

> Now when Polycarp entered into the arena there came a voice from heaven: "Be strong, Polycarp, and play the man." And no one saw the speaker, but our friends who were there heard the voice.[10]

Paul's fellow travelers saw no one but heard a sound which they could not explain. Conversely, Paul saw Jesus, listened to his voice, and understood what he told him to do: "Get up and enter the city."

8. Saul got up from the ground; he saw nothing even though his eyes were open. So they led him by the hand and brought him into Damascus. 9. And for three days he did not see anything nor did he eat or drink anything.

Only Paul comprehended Jesus' message, and only he was blinded by the light. He was unable to see anything when he got to his feet. Although his eyes were open, he stumbled about in blindness. Luke reports that God had

---

9. Bauer, p. 265; Thayer, p. 217.
10. Martyrdom of Polycarp 9.1 (LCL). See also Everett F. Harrison, *Interpreting Acts: The Expanding Church*, 2d ed. (Grand Rapids: Zondervan, Academie Books, 1986), p. 160.

placed over Paul's eyes something like scales, which fell off when Ananias placed his hands on Paul (vv. 17–18). God struck Paul with a three-day period of blindness to give him time to meditate, reflect, and pray (vv. 9, 11).

What a reversal of events! Paul, who desired to dash the believers to the ground, is lying face down on the ground. He, who wished to bring prisoners bound from Damascus to Jerusalem, now is led as a prisoner of blindness into Damascus. He, who acted with the authority of the high priest, now breaks his ties with the Jerusalem hierarchy. He, who came to triumph over the Christian faith, now submits to the Captain of this faith (Heb. 12:2).

Even though Luke refrains from describing the return trip of Paul's companions, who perhaps were members of the temple guard (4:1; 5:22, 26), we conclude that they returned empty-handed to Jerusalem and reported to the high priest that Paul had taken up residence with a Jew named Judas, living on Straight Street in Damascus.

"For three days he did not see anything nor did he eat or drink anything." Separated from society by his blindness and left to himself for three days, Paul has time to cope with the greatest crisis of his life: conversion. Note the symbolism of the three days Paul spent in solitary confinement. "He is crucified with Christ, and the three days of darkness are like the three days in the tomb."[11] And notice the contrast of light and darkness in the account of Paul's conversion. In spiritual blindness Paul sees Jesus in brilliant glory light. Physically blinded, Paul prays and begins to see spiritually.

For three days, Paul neither ate nor drank anything. He fasted because of the emotional disturbance he experienced. In repentance and faith he sought reconciliation with God and thus earnestly prayed. Whereas he was accustomed to utter form prayers, now as a convert he prayed from the heart.

In a sense, Paul's conversion was sudden when Jesus arrested him on the way to Damascus and addressed him personally. But if we look at the broader context (vv. 10–19), we see a gradual development of his conversion and calling.[12] In his loneliness, no one proclaimed the gospel to him until Ananias, sent by Jesus, extended to him the welcome of the Christian community.

Doctrinal Considerations in 9:4–9

Paul saw Jesus, not in an apparition that can be described as a figment of his imagination, but in an actual encounter. When he stayed in the house of Judas on

---

11. Richard B. Rackham, *The Acts of the Apostles: An Exposition*, Westminster Commentaries series (1901; reprint ed., Grand Rapids: Baker, 1964), p. 133.
12. Consult Grosheide, *Handelingen der Apostelen*, vol. 1, p. 296.

Straight Street, Jesus appeared to him in a vision to tell him about the arrival of Ananias (v. 12). On the road near Damascus, Paul did not have a vision but saw Jesus in heavenly glory.

The New Testament reveals that Jesus in his glorified state appeared only four times. First, before his suffering, death, resurrection, and ascension, Jesus appeared to Peter, James, and John on the Mount of Transfiguration (Matt. 17:1–8). Next, after his ascension, he showed himself to Stephen (7:55). Then he appeared to Paul near Damascus (9:1–9). And last, on the island of Patmos John saw the glorified Jesus coming to him on the Lord's Day (Rev. 1:9–20).

Therefore, when Jesus appeared to Paul, he singularly honored him. Jesus granted him this honor because Paul was his chosen instrument to bring the gospel to the Gentiles (v. 15).

Greek Words, Phrases, and Constructions in 9:7–9

Verse 7

ἀκούοντες τῆς φωνῆς—in verse 4 the verb ἀκούω occurs with the noun φωνή (accusative case) referring to Paul; here the verb appears with the noun *voice* (genitive case) in relation to Paul's companions. In 22:7, Paul says that he heard the voice (genitive case) of Jesus speaking to him. Then he asserts that his fellow travelers did not understand the voice (accusative case [22:9]). Does the verb *to hear* with the accusative mean "to understand" and with the genitive "to hear a sound"? Some scholars assert that the two constructions were used interchangeably in the Hellenistic world of the first century.[13] Others, however, argue that the nuances of these two case distinctions are significant.[14]

The evidence, however, is inconclusive. Take, for example, the scene of Jesus' trial, where the high priest tells the members of the Sanhedrin: "You have heard the blasphemy." This text is the same in Matthew 26:65 and Mark 14:64, except that in the Greek the word *blasphemy* is in the accusative case in Matthew and in the genitive case in Mark.[15] The grammatical rule of classical Greek does not even apply: the accusative relates to the thing that is heard and the genitive to the person who is heard.

To return to Luke's use of the genitive and accusative cases with the verb *to hear:* Did he consciously contradict himself? Hardly. We must find the solution in the context of the verse in question and judge each case on its own merits. Thus, Paul's companions heard a voice, did not see Jesus, and consequently did not understand what he was saying. Jesus addressed Paul and not his companions, so we conclude that Luke intends to convey a difference in meaning.

---

13. H. R. Moehring, "The Verb AKOYEIN in Acts IX 7 and XXII 9," *NovT* 3 (1959): 80–99; Robert G. Bratcher, "*Akouō* in Acts ix. 7 and xxii. 9," *ExpT* 71 (1960): 243–45.

14. A. T. Robertson, *A Grammar of the Greek New Testament in the Light of Historical Research* (Nashville: Broadman, 1934), p. 506.

15. Consult Nigel Turner, *Grammatical Insights into the New Testament* (Edinburgh: Clark, 1965), pp. 88–90.

Verse 8

ἀνεῳγμένων—with the noun ὀφθαλμῶν (eyes) the participle forms the genitive absolute construction. The perfect passive participle from the verb ἀνοίγω (I open) denotes lasting result. That is, blindness caused Paul's eyes to remain open.

• Verse 9

μή—the negative particle precedes the participle; οὐκ and οὐδὲ negate the verb. The construction ἦν βλέπων is periphrastic.

---

2. Paul in Damascus
9:10–25

Jesus brings Paul to conversion, but Paul still has to face entrance into the church that he came to destroy. This is not one of Paul's concerns, however, for Jesus opens the way for him to enter the church and to be welcomed by the believers. One of the lessons we learn from Paul's conversion is that salvation originates with God and not with man. God takes the initiative and brings salvation to its destined end.

a. Call
9:10–12

10. In Damascus was a disciple named Ananias. The Lord said to him in a vision, "Ananias." And he said, "Here I am, Lord."

Blinded near the city of Damascus, Paul has to rely on his companions to take him by the hand and lead him to the house of a Jew named Judas, who lives on Straight Street. Judas provides lodging for Paul, who stays with him for three days. During that period, Jesus appears to Paul and tells him that a man named Ananias will visit him to lay his hands on him and restore his sight.

Jesus also appears to a Jew named Ananias, whose name is rather common in Israel (see 5:1; 23:2). Luke describes Ananias as a disciple, that is, a Christian. Indirectly he indicates that this disciple is not a refugee driven from Jerusalem during the great persecution. He reports that Ananias relies on hearsay concerning the hardship that the saints in Jerusalem endure (v. 13). Further, in later years Paul speaks of Ananias in glowing terms when he informs his audience that Ananias keeps the law and is respected by fellow Jews (22:12). Jesus chooses Ananias to introduce Paul to the Christian community in Damascus.

Jesus calls Ananias by name in a vision. Whether this was in the form of a dream at night or in a trance during the day (compare 10:10) is not known. Ananias, like the child Samuel in earlier times, obediently responds to Jesus' call by saying, "Here I am, Lord."

11. The Lord said to him, "Go at once to Straight Street and ask at the house of Judas for a man called Saul from Tarsus, for he is praying. 12.

And in a vision, he has seen a man named Ananias enter and place his hands on him so that he might regain his sight."

a. "Go at once." Respected among the Jewish people of Damascus, Ananias has no objections to going to the house of Judas along Straight Street. This street in the oldest city mentioned in Scripture is still a major thoroughfare of modern Damascus. In distinction from crooked oriental streets, it extends straight in a westerly direction from the East Gate for approximately one mile.

b. "Ask at the house of Judas for a man called Saul from Tarsus." Imagine the fear and revulsion that arise in Ananias's mind when he hears the name of the great persecutor of the Christian church. Paul's reputation has preceded him to Damascus, so that the believers are on full alert. Now Jesus instructs Ananias to meet Paul. To avoid misunderstanding, Jesus adds the name of the city where Paul is from: Tarsus. Located in southeast Asia Minor (modern Turkey), Tarsus had a population of half a million inhabitants and is mentioned repeatedly in Acts.[16] The city was situated along the banks of the Cydnus River and was surrounded by fertile farmland. Near the city, in the Taurus mountain range, were the Cilician Gates, through which traffic from the north had to pass. The gates controlled access to the central and western parts of Asia Minor and protected the city from marauding forces.

Moreover, Tarsus, as the capital of the province of Cilicia, was no ordinary city (21:39). It enjoyed the privilege of granting Roman citizenship to all those born within its walls (22:28). In the first century, Tarsus was an influential city, known for its commercial interests, strategic location, agricultural products, and educational facilities.

Paul was born in this city and received part of his education there (22:3). Because of his education and citizenship (and because he was in the service of the Sanhedrin) Paul of Tarsus was a prominent person in the Jewish world. No wonder that when Paul became the persecutor of Christians, fear and dread preceded him even before he came to Damascus.

c. "For he is praying." Prayer is the bridge between God and man and between individual believers. When Paul, struck by blindness, begins to pray earnestly to Jesus, Jesus comes to him in a vision and prepares him for his entrance into the Christian community. Jesus puts to rest Ananias's fear by telling him that Paul is praying. With these words, Jesus indicates that all along Paul has been in continual prayer. And he intimates that Paul, by praying to him, has put his trust in him and that Jesus has accepted Paul. Therefore, the time has come for Paul to meet a spiritual brother in Christ.

Jesus prepares both Paul and Ananias by appearing to each one in a vision and giving them instructions. Thus Jesus himself removes the barrier that separates the former persecutor from the persecuted Christians. In a related account, Jesus does the same for Peter and Cornelius as he bridges

---

16. 9:11, 30; 11:25; 21:39; 22:3.

the gap between Jew and Gentile. Through an angel and a heavenly voice, Jesus instructs both men in separate visions (10:3–6, 9–16).

d. "And in a vision, he has seen a man named Ananias." Jesus informs Ananias what he has been doing to prepare the way for him. That is, Paul is ready to receive Ananias, for in a vision he has seen a man by that name come to him, place his hands on him, and restore his sight. This vision is Jesus' answer to Paul's prayer. Through this vision, Paul receives Jesus' assurance that Ananias will accept and acknowledge him as a believer. Through another vision, Jesus intimates to Ananias that he has already accepted Paul as a believer and that Ananias must accept Paul, too, by placing his hands on him. Last, Paul learns that Ananias is the Lord's instrument to restore his eyesight.

In other words, Jesus informs Ananias that Paul is blind, that the destroyer of the church is a believer who prays, that Paul expects him to come to the house of Judas to accept him as a Christian, and that Jesus will grant Ananias the power to remove Paul's blindness.

b. Objection
9:13–14

13. Ananias replied, "Lord, from many people I have heard about this man, how much harm he has done to your saints at Jerusalem. 14. And here he has authority from the chief priests to bind all who call upon your name."

We should not fault Ananias for registering his objections to the Lord's command. The reports concerning the great persecution at Jerusalem are circulating in the dispersion and the believers in Damascus are prepared for an onslaught against the Christian community there. The believers are on guard especially against Paul, sent to Damascus with authority from the chief priests.

Ananias takes exception to the divine command to visit Paul. The history of redemption teaches us that other saints in the Old and New Testaments were given instructions and that they also made their objections known to God. Think of Moses, who was called by God to go to Pharaoh's court in Egypt (Exod. 3); Jonah, who was instructed to preach repentance to the inhabitants of Nineveh (Jonah 1); and Zechariah, who was told that his wife, Elizabeth, would bear a son (Luke 1:11–20). God exercises utmost patience with his people when they register objections that arise from ignorance. When Jesus speaks to Ananias in a vision, Ananias is unaware that the danger of persecution has disappeared. He is revealing not a lack of faith, but consternation and fear.

a. "I have heard about this man." When the Christians were driven from Jerusalem, they traveled to Judea and Samaria (8:1b) and eventually to Phoenicia, Cyprus, and Antioch (11:19). We assume that some also went to Damascus, where they informed the Christian community about the horrors of the persecution. They pointed out that one of the chief persecutors in Jerusalem was Paul. Ananias, therefore, was not a refugee himself but received his information from others.

b. "How much harm he has done to your saints." Paul has tried to devastate the church and has inflicted incalculable damage on the saints. This is the first time in the New Testament that the followers of Christ are called "saints."[17] They are the holy ones of God, who share in his holiness because God's Spirit dwells in them. Ananias, then, asserts that Paul has inflicted harm on God's holy ones.

c. "[Paul] has authority from the chief priests." Presumably, believers recently come to Damascus have reported that Paul received authority from the chief priests to conduct persecutions in the synagogues of Damascus. They know that he wants to arrest the followers of Jesus Christ, bind them, and lead them to Jerusalem. Now Ananias speaks as a defender of the believers, who come together to call on the name of the Lord. The expression "call on the name of the Lord" points to regular meetings in which Christians claim the spiritual presence of Jesus.[18] Accordingly, the objection Ananias voices is valid and timely. In his reply, Jesus utters no rebuke, refrains from speaking a word of understanding; instead, he presents additional information that is preceded by a single command: "Go."

c. Command
9:15–16

15. The Lord said to him, "Go, for he is my chosen instrument to carry my name before the Gentiles, kings, and the people of Israel. 16. For I will show him how much he must suffer for my name."

A second time Jesus tells Ananias to go to Paul. Jesus reveals three illuminating facts about the future life of Paul. In a sense, these three facts form a synopsis of the second part of Acts.[19] They portray Paul's life after his conversion:

1. Paul becomes Christ's chosen instrument.
2. He will present the gospel to both Jews and Gentiles.
3. In doing so, he will suffer for the name of Christ.

Jesus removes all doubt from the mind of Ananias and instructs him to go to Paul. He says:

a. "He is my chosen instrument." For five reasons Paul is a choice person for the task Jesus has set before him: Paul is a Jew who has been thoroughly trained in the Old Testament Scriptures by Gamaliel in Jerusalem; he grew

---

17. In the Greek, the term occurs four times in Acts (9:13, 32, 41; 26:10), thirty-nine times in Paul's epistles, twice in Hebrews, twice in Jude, and thirteen times in Revelation.

18. E.g., see Matt. 18:20; 28:20; Acts 2:21, 38; 22:16; Rom. 10:13; I Cor. 1:2.

19. Richard N. Longenecker, *The Acts of the Apostles*, in vol. 9 of *The Expositor's Bible Commentary*, ed. Frank E. Gaebelein, 12 vols. (Grand Rapids: Zondervan, 1981), p. 373.

up in a Greek-speaking environment; he is familiar with Hellenistic culture; he knows how to interpret the gospel in terms the Hellenistic world can understand; and he is a Roman citizen who realizes that the vast network of roads in the Roman empire facilitates travel, so that the gospel can reach the ends of the world. Writes E. M. Blaiklock, "No other man known to history from that time combined these qualities as did Paul of Tarsus. It is difficult to imagine any other place [than Tarsus] whose whole atmosphere and history could have so effectively produced them in one person."[20] When Jesus uses the word *chosen,* he is referring not to election but to office. This is Paul's task:

b. "To carry my name before the Gentiles." Paul is Jesus' personal representative to the Gentile world. In his epistles, Paul repeatedly points out that he was called to be an apostle to the Gentiles.[21] On the way to Damascus, Jesus personally called him to this task. Although the commission to be an apostle did not come until a few days later, nevertheless the charge to carry Christ's gospel before the Gentiles remained the same. Moreover, Paul proclaimed the gospel first to the Jews in their local synagogues, but afterward he routinely went to the Gentiles. He considered himself first and foremost Jesus' apostle to the Gentiles.

c. "Before . . . kings and the people of Israel." In time, Paul would stand before King Agrippa and try to persuade him to become a Christian (26:28). He would appeal to Caesar and eventually be judged by Nero's court in Rome (25:11–12, 21, 25; 26:32; 28:19). And numerous times he would address the Jews, as his speech from the steps of the Roman barracks in Jerusalem attests (22:1–21).

d. "I will show him how much he must suffer for my name." Jesus gives Ananias only partial information and reserves for himself the privilege to inform Paul about the suffering he would have to endure for the sake of Christ's gospel. Perhaps Jesus anticipates a question from Ananias whether a task so demanding as Paul's ambassadorship for Christ would involve suffering. Jesus' answer is affirmative and reassuring. Jesus is fully in control of the situation, and he will inform Paul in due time.

Doctrinal Considerations in 9:15

Paul claims to be an apostle "not from men nor through man but through Jesus Christ" (Gal. 1:1). At first glance, the evidence in Acts does not seem to support Paul's claim to apostleship. First, the three accounts of Paul's conversion (9:1–19; 22:6–21; 26:12–18) say nothing about Paul's appointment to apostleship. Next, Luke only once describes Paul as an apostle, and that in a broader sense to include Barnabas (14:14). Third, Peter clearly states the requirements for apostleship when the believers meet to choose a successor to Judas Iscariot (1:21–22). That is, an

---

20. E. M. Blaiklock, "Tarsus," *ZPEB*, vol. 5, p. 602.
21. Rom. 11:13; 15:15–16; Gal. 1:16; 2:7–8; see also Acts 13:2, 46; 22:21.

apostle had to be a follower of Jesus from the time when John baptized Jesus in the Jordan to the day of his ascension. And an apostle had to be a witness of Christ's resurrection.

Nonetheless, Paul is an apostle because Jesus himself appointed him to apostolic rank. Even though he is not numbered with the Twelve, the apostles in Jerusalem accepted him as Christ's apostle to the Gentiles. Their reasons were five:

Paul saw the resurrected Jesus and thus became a witness of his resurrection (26:16–18; I Cor. 9:1). Like the other apostles, Paul possessed the power to perform signs and wonders. As the apostles received the gift of the Holy Spirit, so did Paul (9:17). Paul proclaimed the same gospel the apostles proclaimed (Gal. 2:2). And last, with the rest of the apostles Paul became an interpreter of the gospel. In short, from Paul's own testimony in his letters and speeches we know that he fulfilled the apostolic requirements. Paul was personally called by Jesus.[22]

Greek Words, Phrases, and Constructions in 9:15–16

Verse 15

σκεῦος ἐκλογῆς—literally translated, the expression *instrument of choice* is a Hebraism. Grammarians explain the genitive as an attributive and treat it as a descriptive adjective: "a choice instrument."[23]

τοῦ βαστάσαι—the definite article in the genitive case followed by the aorist infinitive denotes purpose.

Verse 16

ὅσα—the implied antecedent of this indefinite pronoun is πάντα (compare 14:27).[24]

---

d. Response
9:17–19a

Ananias understands that Jesus himself has paved the way for him to go to Paul and for Paul to meet a brother in Christ. He has nothing to fear from the persecutor of the believers, for he will find Paul, a blind person, in the house of Judas on Straight Street.

17. And Ananias went and entered the house. He placed his hands on Saul and said, "Brother Saul, the Lord Jesus, who appeared to you on the road by which you were coming, has sent me so that you may regain your sight and be filled with the Holy Spirit."

a. "And Ananias went." Obedient to Jesus' command, Ananias walks

---

22. Consult Everett F. Harrison, "Apostle, Apostleship," *EDT*, pp. 70–72; William Childs Robinson, "Apostle," *ISBE*, vol. 1, pp. 192–95.

23. Robertson, *Grammar*, p. 496.

24. Friedrich Blass and Albert Debrunner, *A Greek Grammar of the New Testament and Other Early Christian Literature*, trans. and rev. Robert Funk (Chicago: University of Chicago Press, 1961), #304.

along Straight Street to the house of Judas, enters it, and meets Paul. Granted that Luke provides only the bare outline of this encounter, we expect that Judas welcomes Ananias when he enters the house and that he acquaints Ananias with Paul's physical and spiritual condition. Instead of finding a ferocious man, Ananias looks at a person in need of Christian fellowship.

b. "He placed his hands on Saul." The exact meaning of this gesture is not clear and Luke gives no explanation. Because of a degree of ambiguity at this point, we should avoid interpretations that cannot be substantiated from the context. Thus we venture to say that the purpose of Ananias laying hands on Paul is, first, to acknowledge Paul as a fellow believer; then, to restore his sight; and, last, to effect the outpouring of the Holy Spirit. The interesting fact is that Ananias, who is a disciple but not an apostle, serves as Jesus' instrument to work a healing miracle and to confer the Holy Spirit.[25]

c. "Brother Saul." Touched by Paul's meekness, Ananias demonstrates his genuine love in greeting Paul. As the transliterated word *Saoul* in the Greek indicates, he addresses Paul in either Hebrew or Aramaic. Not only that, he also calls him "brother." For Paul, this one word more than anything else speaks volumes. Now he knows that with the greeting *brother*, Ananias has accepted him and is welcoming him into the church.[26] This servant of the Lord, therefore, spans the gap between Judaism and Christianity. By touching Paul, he indicates that he recognizes Paul as a believer. And then he delivers the message Jesus has given him.

d. "The Lord Jesus, who appeared to you ... has sent me." Ananias mentions Jesus, whom he calls Lord, and thus establishes a point of contact with Paul. He implies that Jesus has acquainted him with Paul's conversion experience near Damascus. And he avers that Jesus has commissioned Ananias to go to Paul. By contrast, Jesus told Paul that Ananias would come to him to restore his sight (v. 12). The verbal portrait Luke paints is vivid yet lacking in detail. In descriptive language he reveals that Paul received his eyesight, but the words concerning the filling with the Spirit are sketchy. Luke gives no sequence of events, so we are unable to ascertain when the coming of the Holy Spirit occurred. He states that after Paul received his sight, he was baptized.

18. And immediately something like scales fell from his eyes and he regained his sight. He stood up and was baptized. 19a. After taking some food, he regained his strength.

Even though Luke is a medical doctor, he reports the restoration of Paul's eyesight in short measure. A parallel to the phrase *something like scales* appears in the apocryphal book of Tobit, where we read that when

---

25. Donald Guthrie, *New Testament Theology* (Downers Grove: Inter-Varsity, 1981), pp. 541–42.
26. Lake and Cadbury even suggest that this greeting "really would be given better by 'my fellow-Christian.' " *Beginnings*, vol. 4, p. 104.

Tobias sprinkled the gall of a fish into the blind eyes of his father, Tobit, the blind man regained his sight: "And when his eyes began to smart he rubbed them, and the white films scaled off from the corners of his eyes."[27]

In the second account of Paul's conversion (22:13), Ananias says to Paul, "Brother Saul, receive your sight!" And after that, he instructs Paul with these words:

> The God of our fathers has appointed you to know his will and to see the Righteous One and to hear a message from his mouth, because you will be a witness for him to all men of the things you have seen and heard. And now why are you delaying? Get up, be baptized and wash away your sins, calling on his name. [22:14–16]

We understand that in the first account Luke presents a brief and factual description of the meeting between Ananias and Paul. In the second account, Paul himself relates the meeting and vividly recalls the words Ananias spoke.

Paul gets up and makes known his wish to be baptized. Luke omits the details of the place of baptism, the mode of baptism, and the person who baptizes Paul. The River Abana, flowing through Damascus to the north of and parallel with Straight Street, is possibly the place where Paul was baptized. What is significant, however, is the fact that spiritual matters precede physical needs. After three days of fasting, Paul is in no hurry to still hunger pains. He desires to be known as a disciple of Jesus Christ by being baptized. We assume that Ananias administered the sacrament of baptism to Paul. Following this ceremony, Paul takes some food to end his fast and to regain physical strength.

Practical Considerations in 9:18

One of the tasks of an ordained clergyman is to perform the rite of baptism whenever he is asked to do so. In some of the larger congregations, baptismal services are scheduled for a specified Sunday of the month. At these services, the pastor of the local church usually officiates.

The New Testament often mentions baptism and indicates that an apostle (I Cor. 1:14–16), an evangelist (Acts 8:38; 21:8), and a member of the Christian church (Acts 9:18) administer baptism. No hard-and-fast rule existed in the early church. Paul even states that his primary task is to preach the gospel and not to baptize (I Cor. 1:17). The custom of allowing unordained church members to administer the rite of baptism, therefore, has prevailed throughout the centuries. In most churches, primarily those of Reformed persuasion, this practice has been discontinued. To promote order and dignity, only ordained pastors perform baptisms.

---

27. Tob. 11:12–13 (RSV).

Greek Words, Phrases, and Constructions in 9:17–19a

Verse 17

ὁ κύριος . . . Ἰησοῦς—the word *Lord* is separated from the name *Jesus* to indicate emphasis.

Verse 18

ἐβαπτίσθη—the aorist passive intimates an implied agent, namely, Ananias. In 22:16, the first aorist middle imperative βάπτισαι occurs. The middle does not mean "to baptize oneself," but rather "to allow oneself to be baptized."[28]

Verse 19a

ἐνίσχυσεν—from the verb ἐνισχύω (I strengthen), this compound form is intensive.

e. Propagation
9:19b–22

Translators divide the text in the middle of verse 19. They see that Paul entered a new phase in his life, one event of which is Paul's reclusion in the Arabian desert. According to the information Paul supplies in his letter to the Galatians, he spent three years in Arabia and Damascus before he went to Jerusalem (1:17–18). We do not know whether this period is the full term of three years or one full year plus parts of both the preceding and the following year. The Jews consider part of a year equivalent to a full year.

Paul's reclusion in the desert is significant for more than one reason: first, a long-term stay in a solitary place prepared him for the task awaiting him;[29] next, because time heals all wounds, an extended absence from Jerusalem was beneficial for both him and the church; and last, Paul did not rush to Jerusalem to meet the apostles because Jesus himself, not the apostles, had appointed him to apostleship.

After his stay in the wilderness, which may have been anywhere in the Nabatean kingdom that extended from Damascus to the borders of Egypt, Paul returned to Damascus. From his own testimony (Gal. 1:16–24) and from Luke's account in Acts, one can posit the following sequence of events in Paul's life:

28. Nigel Turner, *A Grammar of New Testament Greek,* 4 vols. (Edinburgh: Clark, 1963), vol. 3, p. 57. See also C. F. D. Moule, *An Idiom-Book of New Testament Greek,* 2d ed. (Cambridge: Cambridge University Press, 1960), p. 26.
29. Both John the Baptist (Luke 1:80) and Jesus (Matt. 4:1–11) spent time in the desert in preparation for their tasks.

1. conversion on the way to Damascus (9:1–19a)
2. brief stay in Damascus (9:19b–22)
3. seclusion in Arabia (Gal. 1:17)
4. return to Damascus for some time (9:23)
5. escape to Jerusalem (9:23–25; II Cor. 11:32–33)
6. meeting with the apostles (9:26–28; Gal. 1:18–19)
7. departure for Syria and Cilicia (9:30; Gal. 1:21)

The information supplied by Luke and Paul is insufficient to formulate an accurate chronology of this particular phase in Paul's life. Therefore, we are compelled to resort to the use of hypotheses. One of these is that in respect to the expressions *several days* (v. 19b) and *many days* (v. 23) Luke telescopes events that include Paul's seclusion in the Arabian desert.[30]

19b. Saul spent several days with the disciples in Damascus. 20. Immediately he began to preach in the synagogues that Jesus is the Son of God.

Although Luke deletes the account of Paul meeting the Damascus believers, we are confident that Ananias served as Paul's spokesman, removed barriers of fear and resentment, and caused the church to accept its former persecutor. We also assume that Paul had to prove himself as a disciple of Christ and had to gain the confidence of the Christian community.

We see that Paul, delegated by the Jerusalem Sanhedrin to go to the Damascus synagogues, immediately begins to preach in these synagogues.[31] In his preaching he convincingly states that Jesus is the Son of God. Admittedly, this message is the core of Christianity, but to the Jew it is blasphemous. He confesses the Hebrew creed: "Hear, O Israel! The LORD our God, the LORD is one!" (Deut. 6:4, NIV).

Significant is the fact that only in the verse which describes Paul's initial preaching does the phrase *Son of God* appear in Acts. That is, Paul's preaching begins with the assertion that Jesus is the Son of God, who has fulfilled the Old Testament prophecies. Even if the term *Son of God* applies to the Israelites or to the nation Israel (see, e.g., Jer. 3:19–20; Hos. 11:1), the idea of sonship applies specifically to a royal descendant of David (II Sam. 7:14) and the Messiah (Ps. 2:7).[32] Jesus never used the title himself except when, on trial, he was asked by the high priest whether he was the Son of God (Matt. 26:63). When Jesus answered affirmatively, he was accused of blasphemy. Now Paul continues to preach in the Damascus synagogues that Jesus is the Son of God and thus reveals the heart of the Christian faith.

---

30. Some commentators aver that Luke was not aware of Paul's stay in Arabia. But then they have to assume that Luke had never seen Paul's letter to the Galatians. See Gerhard Schneider, *Die Apostelgeschichte*, Herders Theologischer Kommentar series, 2 vols. (Freiburg: Herder, 1982), vol. 2, p. 34. Also consult Ernst Haenchen, *The Acts of the Apostles: A Commentary*, trans. Bernard Noble and Gerald Shinn (Philadelphia: Westminster, 1971), p. 334.

31. Preaching in Jewish synagogues became an established practice of Paul. See 13:5, 14; 14:1; 17:2, 10, 17; 18:4, 19; 19:8.

32. Guthrie, *New Testament Theology*, p. 302; see also Bruce, *Book of the Acts*, p. 190.

21. And all who heard him were amazed and said, "Is not this the man who destroyed those who called upon this name in Jerusalem? Did he not come here to lead such people as prisoners to the chief priests?"

Luke describes the reaction of the Jews attending the synagogue worship services. They ask themselves whether they are listening to a representative of the high priest or to a Christian. They expect to hear a message from the high priest in Jerusalem and instructions on persecuting Christians. Instead they hear that Jesus of Nazareth is the Christ, the Son of God. They query, "Is not this the man who destroyed those who called upon this name in Jerusalem?" They wonder what has happened to him. The complete reversal takes them by surprise and thus in a sense deprives them of the faculty of raising objections.

Luke appears to be familiar with Paul's biographical comments in his epistle to the Galatians. For example, he reports that the Damascene Jews use the word *destroy* to describe Paul's persecution of the church. In the New Testament, this word occurs only here (v. 21) and in Galatians 1:13 and 23. Next, the title *Son of God,* which appears only once in Acts (9:20), is a name Paul incorporates in preaching the gospel to the Gentiles (Gal. 1:16).

Paul proclaims the name of Jesus Christ, the Son of God. And by doing so, he places himself among the disciples who call upon this name. Hence, in utter amazement his listeners ask whether he is the same man who was sent to Damascus to arrest such people and take them as prisoners to the high priest. They begin to realize that Christianity has gained one of Judaism's most gifted persons. Paul has left the authoritative circles in Jerusalem and now takes his orders from Christ.

22. Saul became increasingly stronger; he bewildered the Jews living in Damascus by proving that Jesus is the Christ.

Reaction to Paul's preaching is inevitable and Paul seems to thrive on the opposition he receives. The word *stronger* refers not to his physical powers but to his ability to prove from the Scriptures that Jesus is the Messiah. Manuscripts of the Western text add the prepositional phrase *in the Word* to the clause *Saul became increasingly stronger.* Thus, the text "refers to his power in preaching and not merely to his recovery of physical strength" after his three-day fast.[33] Paul has received extensive training in the Old Testament and now uses his education to explain the fulfillment of these Scriptures to his audiences. And the more he opens the Word of God, the more he sees the Christ personified in Jesus of Nazareth.

The Jews treasure the sacred Word, but they become confused and bewildered when Paul shows them the fulfillment of these messianic prophecies. They are unable to oppose this scholar who, filled with the Holy Spirit, shows them the truth of Scripture. Their feeble efforts to defend themselves result in contradiction, confusion, and defeat. They must admit that Paul is correct in his teaching and that everything he says

---

33. Metzger, *Textual Commentary,* p. 365.

is in harmony with God's Word. Paul proves "that Jesus is the Christ." In the Greek, the verb *prove* actually means to bring together many parts from which a person is able to draw a conclusion.[34] Paul brings together numerous Old Testament passages and proves the teaching that Jesus of Nazareth is the Messiah.

Greek Words, Phrases, and Constructions in 9:20–21

Verse 20

ἐκήρυσσεν—the imperfect tense denotes continued action in the past; it is also ingressive: "He began to preach."[35]

συναγωγαῖς—because of the large Jewish community in Damascus, the city had many synagogues.

ὅτι—the conjunction introduces an object clause, "that this one is the Son of God."

Verse 21

τὸ ὄνομα τοῦτο—these words are translated "this name" and refer to Jesus. F. F. Bruce comments, "Perhaps 4:17; 5:28 should be compared for the vagueness of τὸ ὄνομα τοῦτο."[36]

ἐληλύθει—the pluperfect active from the verb ἔρχομαι (I come) is translated in English as a past tense. The pluperfect in this context has lost its true meaning because the action is an accomplished fact.

---

f. Plot
9:23–25

At this juncture, Paul's seclusion in the Arabian desert fits in. The prepositional phrase *after many days* differs from the phrase *several days* in verse 19b. Luke seems to indicate a break in Paul's stay in Damascus. As we have seen in the commentary on verse 21, Luke is familiar with Paul's life and letters. Yet he does not deem it necessary to relate details about Paul's solitary sojourn in Arabia.

23. After many days had passed, the Jews plotted to kill him. 24a. But their plot became known to Saul.

The general time description, "many days had passed," relates to Paul's autobiographical comment: "Then after three years [since my conversion near Damascus] I went up to Jerusalem" (Gal. 1:18). The time period need not be three full years but may even be less than two years. In that case, we count one full year with the two partial years that precede and follow it

---

34. Bauer, p. 777.
35. Robertson, *Grammar*, p. 885.
36. F. F. Bruce, *The Acts of the Apostles: The Greek Text with Introduction and Commentary*, 3d (rev. and enl.) ed. (Grand Rapids: Eerdmans, 1990), p. 327.

(compare 20:31). This period of time includes his stay in Arabia and his days in Damascus.

Paul continues his preaching in the Damascene synagogues, where he meets stiff opposition from those Jews who refuse to accept the gospel. Indeed, Paul runs the risk of being killed by his fellow Jews. What a reversal of events! The persecutor who breathed murderous threats against the Christians (9:1) now receives his own death warrant. The religious zealot who made the followers of Christ suffer now suffers himself for the sake of Christ (see v. 16). At this point, his life of suffering has only begun (refer to II Cor. 11:23–29).

The Jews devise a plan to kill Paul, but through contacts in the community Paul receives information about their plot (compare 23:16, 30). They are not interested in a sniper attack on Paul's life. Rather, the Jews work through official channels of local government and intend to achieve their objective to eliminate Paul.[37] According to the parallel passage (II Cor. 11:32–33), the official government representative in Damascus is not the Roman governor but the ethnarch (governor) appointed by Aretas IV, king of the Nabatean Arabs (9 B.C.–A.D. 40). In the last few years of his life, this Nabatean king took Damascus from Roman control and temporarily ruled it.[38] His governor now gives orders to watch the city gates of Damascus, because he and the Jews want to capture and kill Paul.

24b. And the Jews were also watching the gates day and night so that they might kill him. 25. His converts took him by night and they lowered him in a basket through the wall.

Why are the Jews able to persuade the Nabatean governor of Damascus to put out an arrest warrant for Paul? Although we think that Paul spent time in the Arabian desert to meditate and prepare, we should not rule out the possibility that he tried to evangelize the Nabatean Arabs. For more than a year Paul proclaimed the gospel to the Nabateans and perhaps to the king himself. The probability is not remote that King Aretas no longer tolerated Paul but tried to capture him. When the governor under Aretas learned that Paul resided in Damascus, he guarded the city in order to arrest Paul.[39]

Paul's converts, however, protect him and help him escape. In an overhanging house built on the city wall, typical in oriental cities, they put Paul into a basket and lower it, through a window, to ground level outside the city (II Cor. 11:33; Josh. 2:15). This takes place under cover of darkness. Paul's mission efforts have not been in vain, because he has gained a number of converts (disciples, in Greek). The owner of the house on the wall

---

37. Consult Grosheide, *Handelingen der Apostelen,* vol. 1, p. 306.

38. Schürer, *History of the Jewish People,* vol. 2, pp. 129–30. Refer to F. F. Bruce, *New Testament History* (1969; Garden City, N.Y.: Doubleday, 1971), p. 242. Contrast Kirsopp Lake, "The Conversion of Saul," *Beginnings,* vol. 5, p. 193.

39. Refer to Lake, "Conversion of Saul," p. 194; and consult Bruce, *Book of the Acts,* pp. 191–92.

may have been a Christian. Nevertheless, Paul's time in Damascus has come to an end and he returns to Jerusalem.

Before we leave the subject of Paul's escape from Damascus, we should look once more at the two accounts (vv. 23–25; II Cor. 11:32–33), because the one clarifies the other. For instance, the expression *through the wall* (v. 25) becomes meaningful when it is compared with the words *a window in the wall* (II Cor. 11:33). Also, the verb *lowered* is the same in both passages. Even though these indications are but straws in the wind, they nevertheless point in the direction of Luke's acquaintance with Paul's second letter to the Corinthians.[40]

Greek Words, Phrases, and Constructions in 9:23–25

Verse 23

ἐπληροῦντο—the use of the imperfect passive of the verb πληρόω (I fill) conveys the sense of a gradual passing of time: "they were being filled."

ἱκαναί—referring to time, this adjective shows that considerable time has passed (see also 27:7).[41]

Verse 24

παρετηροῦντο—this is the imperfect middle of the compound verb παρατηρέω (I watch closely). The imperfect denotes constant activity, the middle means "to watch for one's self,"[42] and the compound reflects intensity.

ἡμέρας καὶ νυκτός—the genitive of time—that is, the time within which an event occurs.

Verse 25

διά—the preposition followed by a noun in the genitive case signifies "through" in the sense of "through a window opening."

---

3. Paul in Jerusalem
9:26–30

This section presents Paul's return to Jerusalem, which he had left as a relentless persecutor of the Christians and an envoy of the high priest. He knows that as a convert to the Christian faith and an apostle to the Gentiles—appointed by Jesus himself—he must meet the church and the apostles. The passage contains some difficulties. To illustrate, Luke reports that Barnabas introduced Paul to the apostles, but Paul in his letter to the

---

40. C. Masson, "A propos de Act. 9.19b–25. Note sur l'utilisation de Gal. et de 2 Cor. par l'auteur de Actes," *TheolZeit* 18 (1962): 161–66.
41. Bauer, p. 374.
42. Thayer, p. 486.

Galatians writes that he met none of the apostles except Peter and James (1:18–19).

Conversely, this section also displays a remarkable similarity to the parallel preceding section (vv. 19b–25): Paul's introduction to the churches, his preaching in the local synagogues, the threat to his life, and the escape to other places.

26. When Saul came to Jerusalem, he tried to associate with the disciples. And all were afraid of him because they did not believe that he was a disciple.

a. "Saul came to Jerusalem." Luke apparently overlooks Paul's emotional and psychological frame of mind, yet we can readily imagine the tremendous pressure Paul endures when he approaches the city of Jerusalem. For all practical purposes, this city more than Tarsus is home to him. In Jerusalem Paul may have stayed with his sister (23:16). But as a former Pharisee (Phil. 3:5), Paul will have to face his erstwhile colleagues, teachers, and superiors. They will regard him as a traitor to Judaism and some of them do not shrink from trying to kill him (v. 29). Indeed, when Paul explains how the Lord called him near Damascus, they refuse to accept his testimony about Jesus; the Lord himself has to tell Paul to leave Jerusalem immediately (22:17–18).

b. "He tried to associate with the disciples." As a Christian, Paul will have to meet with the members of the Jerusalem church at worship and prayer. But he knows no one who will serve as an intermediary to introduce him to the members of the Jerusalem church. In Damascus, Ananias performed this loving deed for him, but here he stands alone. He fully realizes that the Christians in Jerusalem are afraid of him. They regard him as the persecutor of the church who is not worthy of their trust.

c. "All were afraid of him." Repeatedly Paul attempts to worship with the believers, whom Luke calls "the disciples," but he endures rebuff and rejection. In his preconversion days, Paul had planned to return to Jerusalem with numerous imprisoned disciples of Jesus from the Christian community in Damascus. Presently he comes to the Jerusalem church as a disciple of Christ. What a reversal! The church is not ready to accept him and refuses to believe that he has become a disciple.

In his letter to the Galatians, Paul reveals that three years after his conversion he went to Jerusalem (1:18). But would not the Jerusalem church have heard about Paul's conversion? The fact is that after these three years the Jerusalem church is still suffering the results of the great persecution (8:1a). Paul does not mention the Jerusalem church but discloses that the churches in Judea did not know him personally (Gal. 1:22). Because Paul spent more time in the Arabian desert than in Damascus itself, the news concerning him has been indefinite, sketchy, and perhaps untrustworthy. Paul stands alone between two religious bodies, Judaism and Christianity, for neither accepts him.

27. But Barnabas took him and brought him to the apostles. He ex-

plained to them how Saul on the road had seen the Lord, who spoke to him. And he told them how in Damascus Saul had boldly spoken in the name of Jesus.

Once again Luke introduces Barnabas (4:36–37), a Levite from Cyprus, whom the apostles called "Son of Encouragement." He had sold a field and had given the proceeds to support the poor in Jerusalem. Luke also describes him as "a good man, full of the Holy Spirit and faith" (11:24).

Barnabas lives up to his name when he takes an interest in Paul. He understands Paul's need for acceptance by the Christian church and therefore reaches out to Paul. Similar backgrounds facilitate the initial contact between Barnabas and Paul. Both hail from Jewish communities in the dispersion, Cyprus and Tarsus, respectively; both speak Greek as their native tongue. We should refrain from speculating whether these two men had met each other in earlier days either in the dispersion or in Jerusalem. Scripture provides no indication that these two knew each other. If this were the case, we would have expected Paul to go directly to Barnabas when he arrives in Jerusalem.[43]

Barnabas believes the account of Paul's conversion and is convinced of its authenticity. He brings Paul to the apostles, where he functions as Paul's spokesman, much the same as Ananias had been Paul's supporter in Damascus. Barnabas's record of trustworthiness causes the apostles to listen to what he has to say about Paul. Barnabas relates the story of Paul's experience on the way to Damascus, his conversion to the Christian faith, and his boldness to preach in the local synagogues of Damascus about the name of Jesus. Barnabas persuades the apostles of Paul's genuine conversion.

Who are those apostles in Jerusalem? Paul himself states that during his visit to Jerusalem, he saw only Peter and James, the Lord's brother, but none of the other apostles (Gal. 1:18–19). James, of course, does not belong to the Twelve but to the broader circle of apostles. What does Paul mean when he says that he met only Peter and James? Paul means to say that Peter was in Jerusalem but all the others were engaged in giving leadership in "many Christian communities scattered throughout the country."[44] Luke's remark that Barnabas brought Paul to the apostles is a general statement that refers to at least two representatives, Peter and James.

28. So Saul was with them, moving freely about Jerusalem and speaking boldly in the name of the Lord. 29. He talked and argued with Hellenistic Jews, but they were trying to kill him.

What did Paul do when he was with Peter in Jerusalem? He certainly did not talk about the weather for fifteen days (Gal. 1:18). In the Damascene

---

43. "It is very probable that Barnabas and Saul may have been personally known to each other in youth," writes Henry Alford, *Alford's Greek Testament: An Exegetical and Critical Commentary*, 7th ed., 4 vols. (1877; Grand Rapids: Guardian, 1976), vol. 2, p. 105.

44. William Hendriksen, *Exposition of Galatians*, New Testament Commentary series (Grand Rapids: Baker, 1968), p. 61.

synagogues, Paul had proclaimed Jesus as the fulfiller of the Old Testament messianic prophecies. On the basis of his training in the Scriptures and his encounter with Jesus, Paul was able to preach the name of Jesus. However, Paul had not followed Jesus from the time of the Lord's baptism to the time of his ascension (1:21–22). Although he states that he did not receive the gospel from any man but by revelation from Jesus Christ (Gal. 1:12), he nevertheless needed confirmation and insight to preach Christ's gospel. As a fellow apostle, Paul did not work independently of the other apostles (see Gal. 2:1–2). He proclaimed a gospel in harmony with that of the Twelve.

To prove to the Christians that he really is a convert, Paul takes up a preaching ministry among the Greek-speaking Jews. In short, he continues the work begun by Stephen. He boldly presents the name of Jesus Christ to the Hellenists (see 6:1, 9), who consider him no longer a respectable scholar of the Scriptures but a traitor to the cause of Judaism. As they did with Stephen, so they try to kill Paul.

30. And when the brothers learned of this, they brought him down to Caesarea and sent him away to Tarsus.

The parallel between Paul's experiences in Damascus and in Jerusalem is pronounced: he has to flee for his life. Note also that in both instances fellow believers, here called "brothers," protect Paul from harm. In Damascus they help him escape by lowering him in a basket outside the city wall. The brothers in Jerusalem accompany him to Caesarea, where they put him aboard ship and send him to his native town of Tarsus.

We raise two questions concerning Paul's stay in Jerusalem and his years in Tarsus. First, Paul writes that he stayed with Peter fifteen days (Gal. 1:18), but Luke relates that Paul talked and debated with Greek-speaking Jews in Jerusalem. This difficulty disappears when we realize that Paul's impetuous nature did not allow him merely to sit still and learn quietly from Peter and James as they related to him the numerous details about the life and ministry of Jesus. During the span of two weeks, Paul went to the synagogues Stephen had visited. There, within a few days, the Hellenistic Jews were unable to counteract the skilled debate of the former Pharisee. In their opposition, accordingly, they resorted to threats on his life. And those plots to take his life limited his stay in Jerusalem to fifteen days.

Next, what did Paul do when he returned to his native town of Tarsus? He stayed there for many years until Barnabas came and invited him to help him teach and preach in the church at Antioch (11:25–26). Although Luke writes about Paul's missionary journeys and the churches Paul visited, he never mentions the existence of a church in Tarsus. Yet we know that numerous Jews lived in that city and undoubtedly had built synagogues.

In his native province, Cilicia, Paul must have been active as a missionary. He himself writes that after leaving Jerusalem, he went to Syria and Cilicia (Gal. 1:21). The advice of the Jerusalem Council to the Gentile believers was addressed to those living in Antioch, Syria, and Cilicia (15:23). When Paul began his second missionary journey, he and Silas visited the churches in Syria and Cilicia for the purpose of strengthening them (15:41).[45] All appearances, therefore, indicate that Paul used his time to proclaim Christ's gospel in the provinces of Syria and Cilicia.

Humanly speaking, Paul was a failure who, because of his rash approach in preaching the gospel, created enmity wherever he went. He did little to advance Christ's church and kingdom. What he needed was a period of maturation and reflection in Tarsus to gain confidence and learn patience. From a divine perspective, we say that Jesus removed Paul from the scene of conflict and confrontation in Damascus and Jerusalem. In due time, Jesus called Paul as his chosen instrument to proclaim the gospel to the Gentiles.

Practical Considerations in 9:26–30

"Perfect love drives out fear," John writes in one of his epistles (I John 4:18). Perfect love comes to expression when we love the Lord with all our heart, soul, and mind, and love our neighbor as ourselves. When we love God and our neighbor, then fear in the sense of alarm or fright is banished from our hearts. Jesus tells us to love even our enemies and to pray for them (Matt. 5:44). He places enemies, therefore, on the same level as our neighbors.

Barnabas not only listened to this teaching of Jesus but also applied it. When Paul arrived in Jerusalem and was rejected by the believers because they doubted his sincerity, Barnabas reached out in love and accepted Paul as a brother in Christ. With a heart filled with love for Paul, Barnabas was unafraid of the former persecutor of the Jerusalem church. Barnabas became the bridge for Paul when he led him to the apostles and the members of the church to gain their acceptance. He motivated the brothers to accept Paul. When within two weeks the situation in Jerusalem became precarious for Paul, these brothers accompanied Paul to Caesarea. Barnabas and the brothers demonstrated their genuine love to Paul and thus lived without fear. In the words of a ninth-century hymn writer:

> Faith they had that knew not shame,
> Love that could not languish;
> And eternal hope o'ercame
> Momentary anguish.
> —trans. John Mason Neale

Greek Words, Phrases, and Constructions in 9:26–28

Verse 26

ἐπείραζεν—notice the imperfect tense of this verb and the verb ἐφοβοῦντο in this verse. The imperfect depicts repeated action. The verb πειράζω means "to attempt."

---

45. E. A. Judge, "Cilicia," *ISBE*, vol. 1, p. 699. See also R. C. H. Lenski, *The Interpretation of the Acts of the Apostles* (Columbus: Wartburg, 1944), p. 378.

πιστεύοντες—this present active participle suggests the cause for the action of the preceding verb *to fear*.

ὅτι—used as a conjunction, the word introduces indirect discourse in which the present tense of the verb ἐστίν is translated in the past.

Verse 27

ἐπιλαβόμενος—the basic meaning of this aorist participle is "to take hold of." The figurative meaning, "to take an interest in," is preferred.

πῶς . . . ὅτι . . . πῶς—the phrasing switches from an indirect question to an indirect assertion and then back to an indirect question.[46]

Verse 28

εἰσπορευόμενος καὶ ἐκπορευόμενος—here is an idiom that actually means "moving about freely." The words should not be understood as a periphrastic construction with the verb ἦν, "he was going in and out of Jerusalem." Rather, the verb *to be* is construed with μετ' αὐτῶν (he was with them). Also, the preposition εἰς is equivalent to ἐν (in).

---

4. Conclusion
9:31

Throughout his book, Luke gives short summaries that alert the reader to a transition. For example, Luke provides a transitional summary between his Pentecost report and the account of Peter and John healing the cripple in the temple area (2:44–47).[47] Before he writes about Peter's missionary outreach in Lydda and Joppa, Luke reports that the churches in Palestine entered a peaceful period.

31. Then the church throughout Judea, Galilee, and Samaria enjoyed a period of peace and was strengthened. And it continued to increase, living in the fear of the Lord and the comfort of the Holy Spirit.

a. "The church throughout Judea, Galilee, and Samaria." Luke focuses his attention on the ultimate goal: the ends of the earth. For that reason, he reveals next to nothing about the missionary work in Palestine. We assume that the believers who were scattered throughout Judea and Samaria (8:1) taught the Good News and were instrumental in establishing churches. Only here in Acts Luke mentions the word *Galilee*. We would expect that the five hundred brothers to whom Jesus appeared after his resurrection and before his ascension (I Cor. 15:6) witnessed for Christ in Galilee. Now, in a summarizing statement, Luke divulges that the church in Judea, Galilee, and Samaria enjoyed a period of peace. Notice that he uses the word *church* in the singular to indicate the unity of the body of

---

46. Robertson, *Grammar*, p. 1047; and see Moule, *Idiom-Book*, p. 153.
47. See also 4:32–35; 5:12–16.

Christ.[48] Jewish Christians from the south (Judea) and the north (Galilee) lived in perfect harmony with Samaritan Christians.

b. "[The church] enjoyed a period of peace and was strengthened." In this text, Luke indicates that the entire church in Palestine enjoyed peace. He leaves the impression that the attention of those Jews antagonistic toward the Christian church was diverted by other matters. In other words, the religious and political news of that day captured attention, with the result that the church received respite from persecution.

If we assume that Luke's summary reflects the years A.D. 36–37, then we know from the Jewish historian Josephus that these years were marked by change. To illustrate, in A.D. 36 the Roman governor Vitellius succeeded Pontius Pilate. As soon as he assumed office, he deposed Caiaphas the high priest and gave the high priesthood to Jonathan; one year later, Jonathan was replaced by his brother Theophilus.[49] Vitellius, in contrast to Pilate, promoted order and stability. Furthermore, in A.D. 37 emperor Tiberius died and was succeeded by Caligula. In that year, Caligula gave his friend Herod Agrippa I the authority to rule as king in Palestine.[50] Herod Agrippa I, who was the grandson of Herod the Great, ruled from A.D. 37–44. He was stricken by an angel of the Lord and died a painful death (12:23). These changes caused the Jews who were bent on persecuting the Christians to desist and listen to their new rulers. Accordingly, the church enjoyed a period of peace and tranquillity, and it was strengthened in the faith. Not only did the church increase in spiritual strength, but also it increased numerically.

c. "It continued to increase." In all the areas of Palestine, the church showed substantial gains in membership. When the fear of persecution subsided, countless people openly confessed their faith in Jesus Christ. Luke mentions two reasons for this increase: first, the Christians were living in the fear of the Lord. That is, they revered and honored Jesus Christ as their Savior and Lord in their daily conduct. Second, they experienced the comfort of the Holy Spirit. In brief, these early believers demonstrated to the world the joy of living a Christian life. Through their Spirit-filled lives, they attracted countless people to a saving knowledge of Christ.

Greek Words, Phrases, and Constructions in 9:31

μὲν οὖν—see the explanation of this recurring idiom in Acts in 8:25.

τῆς—the one definite article is followed by three nouns (Judea, Galilee, Samaria) and thus refers to the entire country of Palestine.[51]

---

48. At least two translations (KJV, NKJV) have the plural *churches*. However, "the range and age of the witnesses which read the singular number are superior to those that read the plural." Metzger, *Textual Commentary*, p. 367.

49. Josephus *Antiquities* 18.4.3 [95]; 18.5.3 [123].

50. Josephus *War* 2.9.6 [181]; *Antiquities* 18.6.10 [237].

51. Robertson, *Grammar*, p. 787.

εἶχεν—this verb (it was having) and the next, ἐπληθύνετο (it was increasing), are in the imperfect tense that describes a continued action in the past tense.

τῷ φόβῳ—the dative case is a dative of place with the verb πορεύομαι (I walk, live).

---

32 Once while Peter was traveling through various regions, he went down to the saints who lived at Lydda. 33 There he found a man named Aeneas, who had been bedridden for eight years as a paralytic. 34 And Peter said to him, "Aeneas, Jesus Christ heals you. Get up and make your bed." Immediately Aeneas got up. 35 And all who lived at Lydda and Sharon saw him and turned to the Lord.

D. Ministry of Peter
9:32–11:18

1. Miracle in Lydda
9:32–35

In Acts, Luke moves quickly through the history of the Christian church in the first decade of its existence. After relating the conversion of Paul near Damascus and his brief ministry there and in Jerusalem, Luke once more chronicles the ministry of Peter. Peter, of course, met Paul in Jerusalem for a two-week period. When the churches throughout Palestine enjoyed respite from persecution and continued to increase in spirit and in number, Peter left Jerusalem and began to travel throughout the country. Perhaps his mission tour took place in the last year of the fourth decade.[52]

Peter's tour is a prelude to his call to visit the Roman centurion Cornelius in Caesarea. Incidentally, Jesus commissioned Paul to be his apostle to the Gentiles, but he instructs Peter to preach the gospel to the Gentile family of Cornelius. Peter, not Paul, is the first to welcome Gentiles into the Christian church.

Prior to his trip to Caesarea, Peter visits churches located along the borders of Judea. He travels to the coastal region to meet with the believers in Lydda.

32. Once while Peter was traveling through various regions, he went down to the saints who lived at Lydda.

We know nothing about Peter's travels except what Luke reports in Acts. Paul notes that Peter took his wife along on missionary journeys (I Cor. 9:5). We presume that Peter visited the churches in Galilee and Samaria. Luke gives a general description and says that Peter traveled through various regions. How far and wide Peter traveled is not important to Luke, who is interested in reporting about Peter's visit to Lydda.

---

52. Alford contends that Peter visited the churches before Paul came to visit him in Jerusalem. *Alford's Greek Testament*, vol. 2, p. 107.

From the higher locations of either Jerusalem or Samaria, Peter went down to the fertile fields in the plain of Sharon along the Mediterranean coast. The city of Lydda, formerly known by its Hebrew name *Lod*,[53] was located eleven miles southeast of Joppa. It was situated at the intersection of the trade route between Egypt and Damascus and the road from Jerusalem to Joppa. Julius Caesar gave the city of Lydda to the Jews, who ruled it until the time of the Jewish revolt in A.D. 66. Then, while the people were in Jerusalem for the celebration of the Feast of Tabernacles, the Roman commander Cestius burned Lydda to the ground.[54]

Who evangelized the people of Lydda and Joppa? We infer from the evidence Luke provides that the evangelist Philip, after baptizing the Ethiopian eunuch, appeared in Azotus and brought the gospel to all the towns in the coastal regions; eventually he came to Caesarea (8:40).

Peter visited the saints in Lydda, Luke writes. Interestingly, the word *saints* occurs only a few times in Acts (vv. 13, 32, 41; 26:10). In the first decade of the Christian era, believers were known as disciples of Jesus Christ. A few years later, the believers in Antioch are called Christians (11:26). But in the closing years of the fourth decade, followers of Jesus still lacked identity, so that the name *saints* served the purpose.

The saints in Lydda welcome Peter. As a result of the healing miracle he performs, the membership of the churches in Lydda and in the plain of Sharon increases (v. 35). Whenever we read in the New Testament about a miracle performed by either Jesus or the apostles and evangelists, we see that these miracles are designed to create and strengthen faith. This certainly is the case in Lydda, where Aeneas places his trust in the words Peter speaks and is healed. I assume that Peter has related this miracle and the miracle of raising Dorcas from the dead to Luke. In both instances Luke mentions the names of the people involved (Aeneas and Dorcas) and thus is able to give these stories vividness and color.

33. There he found a man named Aeneas, who had been bedridden for eight years as a paralytic.

The saints in Lydda acquaint Peter with Aeneas, who has suffered a stroke or paralysis and for the last eight years has been bedridden. This man is unable to rise from his lowly bed even when Peter approaches him. Whether the man is a fellow believer or not cannot be determined, because the narrative is too brief. Perhaps Aeneas has heard that Peter healed people in Jerusalem; now he waits expectantly for Peter to speak.

34. And Peter said to him, "Aeneas, Jesus Christ heals you. Get up and make your bed." Immediately Aeneas got up. 35. And all who lived at Lydda and Sharon saw him and turned to the Lord.

---

53. Israel's international airport bears the name *Lod*. It has been built eleven miles due east of Tel Aviv (ancient Joppa).

54. Josephus *War* 2.19.1 [515–16]; *Antiquities* 14.10.6 [205–8]. Also refer to William Ewing and R. K. Harrison, "Lydda," *ISBE*, vol. 3, p. 151.

Peter heals people only by calling on the name *Jesus Christ* (compare 3:6), for the Lord, not Peter, performs the healing miracles. Peter calls Aeneas by name and then announces that Jesus Christ heals him. He uses the present tense in a declarative sentence. Peter announces a fact that comes true the moment he utters the words. Then he commands Aeneas to get up and to make his bed. The literal wording of the Greek is "prepare for yourself." The object of the verb *prepare* is lacking and may either be "bed" or "table." Translators prefer to take the verb with the noun *bed*.[55]

The adverb *immediately* reveals that, without a moment's delay, Aeneas stands up and arranges his bed to demonstrate to the people that he has been healed. He has received the full use of his limbs.

The people in Lydda and in the surrounding countryside of Sharon see and hear what has happened and put their faith and trust in Jesus Christ. The plain of Sharon extends from Joppa along the coast past Caesarea to Mount Carmel. Here Luke is speaking in general terms to convey the news that the church continues to increase numerically.

Greek Words, Phrases, and Constructions in 9:32 and 34

Verse 32

κατελθεῖν—the aorist infinitive depends on the verb ἐγένετο, which is followed by Πέτρον (accusative) as the subject of the infinitive. The compound form of the infinitive indicates that Peter came down to the plain of Sharon from geographic places that were at a higher elevation.

Verse 34

ἰᾶται—this present active indicative—the perfect active is ἴαται—is an aoristic present. That is, healing takes place when Peter speaks.

στρῶσον—the aorist active imperative takes the implied noun κλίνην (bed) as direct object. The word *bed* can also refer to a couch that is placed next to a table.

---

36 In Joppa was a woman, a disciple named Tabitha (which translated is Dorcas). She continually performed many works of kindness and compassion. 37 And in those days she became sick and died. When they had washed her body, they laid it in an upper room. 38 Because Lydda was near Joppa and the disciples heard that Peter was there, they sent two men asking him, "Without delay, please come along."

39 Peter went with them. When he arrived, they brought him to the upper room. All the widows stood around him; they were weeping and showing him all the coats and other clothes that Dorcas had made while she was still with them. 40 Peter sent them all outside the room, knelt down, and prayed. He turned to the body and said, "Tabitha, get up." She opened her eyes, saw Peter, and sat up. 41 Extending his hand, he helped her stand up. Then he called the saints and the widows and presented her to them alive. 42 And this became known all over Joppa, and many believed in the Lord. 43 Peter stayed in Joppa for some time with Simon the tanner.

---

55. Bauer, p. 771.

2. Miracle in Joppa
9:36–43

36. In Joppa was a woman, a disciple named Tabitha (which translated is Dorcas). She continually performed many works of kindness and compassion. 37. And in those days she became sick and died. When they had washed her body, they laid it in an upper room.

Along the blue waters of the Mediterranean Sea lies the town of Joppa (modern Jaffa), some thirty-five miles northwest of Jerusalem. A harbor town, Joppa had served Solomon when timber was shipped by rafts from Lebanon (II Chron. 2:16). In Joppa, the prophet Jonah boarded ship (Jonah 1:3). Through the centuries many countries had controlled the city, but in the first century B.C. Julius Caesar gave it to the Jews.[56] It remained in Jewish hands until the Jews waged war against Rome (A.D. 66–70).

Residents of Joppa heard the Good News proclaimed by the evangelist Philip (8:40), and among those who believed was a disciple named Tabitha. This lady was a true disciple of Jesus Christ, for she lived her Christianity in all that she said and did. She was known for her tireless work among the poor; she kept on doing deeds of kindness and compassion. Apparently, she was blessed with material possessions. Whenever she had opportunity, she lived by the divine injunction to care for the poor (compare Deut. 15:11; Matt. 26:11; Gal. 6:9–10).

The name *Tabitha* is Aramaic and means "gazelle." In Greek her name is Dorcas. Like many people in first-century Palestine, Dorcas had two names (one in Aramaic, the other in Greek). Because she was known for her numerous kind deeds to the poor in that area, her sickness and death came as a shock to them and created a void in the Christian community. Details about her illness and death are lacking, but Luke relates that Christians came to prepare her body for burial. They washed her body and placed it in the upper room located on the roof of the house where she had lived (see I Kings 17:19; II Kings 4:10, 21). The upper room often served as a guest room to house visitors. Luke records these facts to show that Dorcas had died and that her death had occurred that day. Burial in the hot climate of the Middle East takes place on either the day of death or the following day. Both the Jews and the Greeks practiced the custom of washing the dead in preparation for burial. In fact, the Jews still observe the custom known as "Purification of the Dead."[57]

Bodies normally were anointed prior to burial. Luke mentions only that the body of Dorcas was washed, and therefore he seems to imply that the Christians had a hidden motive. Having heard that Peter performed the

---

56. Josephus *War* 1.20.3 [396]; *Antiquities* 14.10.6 [202–5]; 15.7.3 [217].
57. Lake and Cadbury, *Beginnings,* vol. 4, p. 110.

miracle of healing a paralytic in nearby Lydda, they wanted to ask him to raise Dorcas from the dead.

38. Because Lydda was near Joppa and the disciples heard that Peter was there, they sent two men asking him, "Without delay, please come along."

The distance between Joppa and Lydda was relatively short and Peter's presence became known to the Christians in that region. Thus, the believers in Joppa sent two of their men to Peter. They knew that since Jesus had raised people from the dead and Peter had received the authority from Jesus to do similar miracles, the possibility of Peter bringing Dorcas back to life was real. The Christians acted in faith by sending two of their men to ask Peter to come without delay to Joppa. These men demonstrated faith in action when they persuaded Peter to accompany them to Joppa. Although Luke records only the men's request to come, they probably were unable to hide their grief. We suppose that Peter immediately heard of Dorcas's death. He learned that the poor people in Joppa experienced the acute loss of their benefactress.

The request is couched in words that are courteous ("Please come at once" [NIV]), and the urgency of the invitation is linked to the imminent burial of Dorcas. The request is not that Peter should conduct Dorcas's funeral service. On the contrary, the Christians in faith hope for the miracle of Dorcas returning to them alive and well.[58]

39. Peter went with them. When he arrived, they brought him to the upper room. All the widows stood around him; they were weeping and showing him all the coats and other clothes that Dorcas had made while she was still with them.

The distance between Lydda and Joppa was at least a three-hour walk. The two men sent by the believers in Joppa had already spent that number of hours on the road. The need for action was urgent and Peter, continuing his tour to visit churches, took leave of the Christians in Lydda and immediately accompanied the two men to Joppa.

When Peter arrived there, the believers took him upstairs to the room where the body of Dorcas lay in state. The room was filled with widows who, according to Jewish custom, were weeping. Widows of that day were identified by special garments and commonly they belonged to the poorer class of society. The widows in Joppa had depended on Dorcas, who had made numerous tunics and other articles of clothing which she had given them. These poor widows showed the garments to Peter and by doing so paid tribute to the memory of Dorcas.

John Calvin observes that God could have kept Dorcas alive to care for the widows. But by raising her from the dead, God gave her two lives. At

---

58. Refer to Harrison, *Interpreting Acts*, pp. 172–73.

the same time, he showed the widows the power of his Son as the author of life.[59]

40. Peter sent them all outside the room, knelt down, and prayed. He turned to the body and said, "Tabitha, get up." She opened her eyes, saw Peter, and sat up.

a. "Peter sent them all outside the room." No one had asked Peter to perform a miracle, even though Jesus at one time had given him the power to raise people from the dead (see Matt. 10:8). Peter could not act on his own initiative but felt the need to ask the Lord for guidance. Following the practice of Jesus when the Lord raised the daughter of Jairus from the dead,[60] he sent all the people out of the upper room. He needed to be alone with Jesus and pray in private. Peter knelt down in humble adoration and dependence on God. He understood the need for Dorcas to continue her work among the poor. And now he prayed for power to perform a miracle in harmony with God's will.

b. "He turned to the body and said, 'Tabitha, get up.' " Unlike the two prophets Elijah and Elisha, who raised children from the dead by touching them (I Kings 17:19–23; II Kings 4:32–35), Peter spoke to the body of Dorcas (compare John 5:25). He followed the example of Jesus, who said to the daughter of Jairus, "Talitha koum!" (Mark 5:41). These Aramaic words mean "Little girl, get up." We have reason to believe that Peter spoke Aramaic when he raised Dorcas. Calling her by her Aramaic name, he said, "Tabitha koum!" ("Tabitha, get up!"). The difference between Jesus' command to the daughter of Jairus and that of Peter to Dorcas is only one letter. The similarity, however, which is only coincidental, does not go any further. In addition, the manuscripts of the Western text lengthen Peter's command. They have the reading, "Tabitha, in the name of our Lord Jesus Christ, get up" (compare 4:10).[61] The additional phrase is extraneous.

c. "She opened her eyes, saw Peter, and sat up." Notice that not Peter but Jesus brought about Dorcas's resurrection. By opening her eyes and sitting up, she proved that she was alive and well. Her former ailment that had terminated her life had disappeared. She looked at Peter. Luke does not indicate what she said to him. But Peter helped her to her feet.

41. Extending his hand, he helped her stand up. Then he called the saints and the widows and presented her to them alive.

Peter did not touch Dorcas until she showed that she was alive. Perhaps the Jewish fear of contamination had kept him from taking hold of Dorcas's hand and making her stand up. After Peter performed the miracle of restoring Dorcas to life, he walked out of the room and called the Christians

---

59. Calvin, *Acts of the Apostles*, vol. 1, p. 280.
60. Matt. 9:25; see also Luke 7:11–17; John 11:44.
61. Translators reject this reading, but Lake and Cadbury call it "the right formula." *Beginnings*, vol. 4, p. 111.

and the widows to come and see Dorcas alive. What joy among the believers! What thanksgiving to God! What faith triumphant!

42. And this became known all over Joppa, and many believed in the Lord. 43. Peter stayed in Joppa for some time with Simon the tanner.

Look at the tremendous impact of this miracle and that in Lydda. Luke reports that the people in Lydda and those living in the plain of Sharon turned to the Lord after Aeneas was healed (v. 35). After Dorcas was raised from the dead, many people in Joppa believed in the Lord. The Christian church now had congregations in Ashdod, Lydda, Joppa, and all along the coast, "almost as far as Caesarea."[62] Luke has already referred to the church in Judea, Galilee, and Samaria (v. 31). The time has come to bring the Good News to the Gentiles.

Not Peter but the Lord received the praise, for the people in Joppa put their faith in Jesus. Peter stayed in that harbor city and took up residence with a tanner named Simon, who lived next to the seashore (10:6, 32). Here Simon had a plentiful supply of water for flaying and soaking the hides; here he removed hair and dirt from these hides.[63] Perhaps Luke's information tells us something about the members of the Joppa congregation. The general population may have avoided Simon, for the tanning materials and the dead animals and their hides created a stench. Moreover, the Jews considered the occupation of the tanner to be ceremonially unclean. Shunned by the Jews in the local synagogue, Simon was accepted by the members of the Christian church. Peter's decision to live with Simon the tanner reflects his readiness to separate himself from Jewish legalism and engage in mission work among the Gentiles. In short, his residence with Simon the tanner prepares him for his call to proclaim the gospel in the home of Cornelius the Roman centurion.

Practical Considerations in 9:35 and 42

The New Testament church was born in a single day—the day of Pentecost, when three thousand believers were added to the initial group of Christians (2:41). The next figure Luke reveals is five thousand men belonging to the church. If these are family men, then we add their wives and come to a total of ten thousand (4:4). Subsequently, increasing numbers of men and women believe in Jesus (5:14; 6:1, 7; see also 21:20).

The gospel brings together people whose native tongues differ: Greek-speaking Jews and Aramaic-speaking Jews (6:1). It overcomes barriers of culture: common people embrace the Christian faith, as do a large number of priests (6:7); the Samaritans and Jews are part of the same church; and Christ accepts both the rich and the poor (e.g., Dorcas and the widows).

---

62. Haenchen, *Acts*, p. 341.
63. Howard M. Jamieson, "Tanner," *ZPEB*, vol. 5, p. 595.

As the water of a flood inundates the land, so the gospel covers the land of Israel within ten years after Pentecost. Christ's gospel touches all areas and all classes of people. In a sense, mission work in Palestine has been brought to completion, so that Peter and Paul must go to the Gentiles and to the Jews in dispersion. However, guided by the teaching of Jesus' parables of the mustard seed and the yeast, we observe that externally the church continues to increase. Internally, the gospel must penetrate every layer, segment, and sector of society. As the yeast affects every particle of the dough, so the gospel of Christ's kingdom penetrates the spheres of family life, occupation, school, and government. We rejoice when the church increases numerically, but we should not neglect to pray that we obediently apply God's Word to everything we do and say. The Christian ought to live his life in the presence of God.

Greek Words, Phrases, and Constructions in 9:36–39

Verse 36

μαθήτρια—occurring only here, this form is the feminine of the noun μαθητής (disciple). Notice that in the case of Dorcas, Luke explicitly states that she is a disciple; he does not specify that Aeneas is a disciple.

Ταβιθά—a transliterated Aramaic word, the name is related to the name *Zibiah* in II Kings 12:1.

Verse 38

οὔσης Λύδδας—both participle and noun in the genitive case reveal the genitive absolute construction.

δύο—Luke states that two messengers are sent out, in harmony with Near Eastern customs of sending out disciples two by two (compare 8:14; 11:30; 13:2; 15:27; 19:22; 23:23).[64]

μὴ ὀκνήσῃς—from the verb ὀκνέω (I hesitate, delay), this is the aorist subjunctive, preceded by μή, in the form of a negative command. The prohibition expects the answer, "I will avoid doing so."[65] See also Numbers 22:16.

Verse 39

ἐπιδεικνύμεναι—this present participle in the middle voice means "to display by wearing." There is no need to interpret the participle as active, because "a valid meaning can be derived from the middle voice."[66]

ἐποίει—the tense of the verb that precedes this imperfect active form influences its translation. Therefore, the tense appears as a pluperfect ("had made").

---

64. Refer to Bruce, *Acts* (Greek text), p. 199.

65. James Hope Moulton, *A Grammar of New Testament Greek,* vol. 1, *Prolegomena,* 2d ed. (Edinburgh: Clark, 1906), p. 125.

66. Robert Hanna, *A Grammatical Aid to the Greek New Testament* (Grand Rapids: Baker, 1983), p. 207.

Summary of Chapter 9

Paul travels to Damascus to persecute the church, arrest the believers, and take them as prisoners to Jerusalem. As he approaches Damascus, brilliant light from heaven flashes around him. He hears the voice of Jesus, who asks him why he is persecuting him. Blinded by the light, Paul is led to Damascus, where he fasts for three days.

Jesus calls Ananias and sends him to the house of Judas on Straight Street, where Paul is staying. After objecting to the assignment and hearing reassuring words from Jesus, Ananias goes to Paul. He places his hands on Paul, who then receives his sight and is filled with the Holy Spirit. Paul is baptized, ends his fast, and is strengthened.

Paul preaches in the synagogues of Damascus, but in time experiences so much opposition that he fears for his life. His converts let him down in a basket on the outside of the city wall. He escapes to Jerusalem, where he is introduced to the apostles through the tactful words of Barnabas. Paul debates the Greek-speaking Jews in Jerusalem, again is threatened, and travels to Caesarea and Tarsus.

Peter performs two miracles, one in Lydda, where he heals bedridden Aeneas, and the other in Joppa, where he brings Dorcas back to life. Many people believe in the Lord, and Peter stays with Simon the tanner.

10

The Church in Palestine, *part 3*

10:1–48

Outline (continued)

10:1–8	3. Peter's Call
10:1–3	a. Setting
10:4–6	b. Message
10:7–8	c. Action
10:9–23a	4. Peter's Vision
10:9–13	a. Vision
10:14–16	b. Instruction
10:17–20	c. Call
10:21–23a	d. Reception
10:23b–48	5. Peter's Visit to Caesarea
10:23b–29	a. Arrival
10:30–33	b. Explanation
10:34–43	c. Sermon
10:44–48	d. Response

10 1 In Caesarea was a man named Cornelius, an officer of what was called the Italian Regiment. 2 He was devout and feared God with his household; he gave generously to the people and prayed continually to God. 3 About three in the afternoon, he distinctly saw in a vision an angel of God, who came to him and said, "Cornelius!" 4 Gazing at him intently and fearfully, Cornelius said, "What is it, Lord?" The angel answered, "Your prayers and generous gifts to the poor have ascended and are remembered before God. 5 And now send men to Joppa and summon a man named Simon who is called Peter. 6 He is staying with a certain tanner named Simon, whose house is by the sea." 7 And when the angel who spoke to him had departed, Cornelius called two of his servants and a devout soldier of those who were continually with him. 8 He explained everything to them and sent them to Joppa.

---

3. Peter's Call
10:1–8

In the closing years of its first decade, the Christian church continued to gain adherents among both the Jews in Judea and Galilee and the Samaritans. The church increased along the Mediterranean coast where Philip had preached the gospel in Azotus and towns as far north as Caesarea. Moreover, after visiting the Christians in Lydda, Peter stayed with the believers in Joppa.

The time had come to preach the gospel to people who were not of Jewish or Samaritan descent; the gospel had to be brought to the Gentiles (Matt. 28:19–20). Not Paul, whom Jesus had commissioned to be the apostle to the Gentiles (9:15), but Peter was the first to break the barrier between Jew and Gentile. This action of Peter is understandable. First, he was the spokesman in Jerusalem when at Pentecost he proclaimed the gospel to the Jews. Next, he and John went to Samaria to welcome the Samaritans into the Christian church. And last, Peter opened the way for the Gentiles to enter the church when God called him to go to Cornelius in Caesarea.

a. Setting
10:1–3

1. In Caesarea was a man named Cornelius, an officer of what was called the Italian Regiment.
This is the third time that Luke mentions Caesarea. First, Philip settled

369

there after he preached the gospel while traveling northward from Azotus (8:40). Next, when Paul had to escape from Jerusalem, his Christian friends took him to Caesarea to board ship and sail to Tarsus (9:30). And third, Cornelius resided in Caesarea.

Caesarea was known originally as Strato's Tower, which Caesar Augustus gave to Herod the Great in 30 B.C.[1] In turn, Herod wanted to please Caesar Augustus and named the city after him. He rebuilt Caesarea to make it a showcase of the East. In a twelve-year period (22–10 B.C.), Herod constructed a theater, an amphitheater, public buildings, a racecourse, a palace, an aqueduct, and a magnificent harbor.

The city flourished; Greek culture and Roman influence drew a mixed population to this beautiful harbor city. Among these people was the Roman governor, who had his residence and headquarters in Caesarea. Even though Greeks, Romans, and other nationalities represented the majority of the population, Jews constituted an influential and powerful minority.

Under the authority of the Roman governor were some three thousand troops, among them the Italian Regiment. Its members belonged to the second cohort of Roman citizens who had volunteered their services (Cohors II. Miliaria Italica Civium Romanorum Voluntariorum).[2] This regiment served in Caesarea in A.D. 69, and presumably also before that date, to protect Roman interests.

Serving with the Italian Regiment was a centurion, in essence a noncommissioned officer who commanded a hundred soldiers, named Cornelius. The name *Cornelius* was common in Roman circles and points to Roman citizenship; also, we know that a centurion had to be a Roman citizen. Further, we understand from Luke's description that Cornelius lived in a large house and had many servants. During his years of service in the armed forces, he had no doubt accumulated financial assets (compare Luke 7:1–6) and had some measure of prestige.

2. He was devout and feared God with his household; he gave generously to the people and prayed continually to God.

During his military career, Cornelius had become acquainted with the Jewish religion and had embraced it as one who feared God. That is, he attended the Sabbath worship services in the local synagogue and observed the Sabbath as a day of rest. He kept the Jewish dietary laws, generously gave material gifts to alleviate the needs of the poor, and daily prayed at set times.[3] However, he did not consent to circumcision and baptism, and he refrained from offering sacrifices. Thus he followed the example of

---

1. Josephus *Antiquities* 13.12.2 [324]; 13.15.4 [395]; 15.7.3 [215–17].

2. T. R. S. Broughton, "The Roman Army," *Beginnings*, vol. 5, p. 437.

3. P. L. Schoonheim, "De Centurio Cornelius," *NedTTs* 6 (1964): 462; see F. F. Bruce, *The Acts of the Apostles: The Greek Text with Introduction and Commentary*, 3d (rev. and enl.) ed. (Grand Rapids: Eerdmans, 1990), p. 342.

numerous Gentiles who worshiped God but who were not admitted to the Jewish community.[4]

"[Cornelius] was devout and feared God with his household." The officer did not consider his religion a personal matter but acquainted his household with spiritual truths. Indeed, at least one of his soldiers was known as a devout man (v. 7). Cornelius sought to live in harmony with the Ten Commandments and, by observing them, expressed his love for God. Luke writes that Cornelius prayed faithfully to God, expressed his loving concern to the poor, and made generous provisions available to them. His gifts to the poor were acceptable to God and were remembered by him as offerings (v. 4). Cornelius possessed a genuine faith in Israel's God, had true knowledge of God's precepts, and expected the coming of the Messiah. Without the virtues that Luke mentions, Cornelius could not have become a believer. In short, Cornelius was ready to hear the gospel and accept Jesus Christ as Lord and Savior.

3. About three in the afternoon, he distinctly saw in a vision an angel of God, who came to him and said, "Cornelius!"

We see a parallel in the visions of Ananias and Paul in Damascus (9:11–16 and 9:12, respectively) and those of Cornelius and Peter in Caesarea and Joppa (vv. 3 and 10–16). Appearing to Ananias and Paul in separate visions, Jesus prepared them for their eventual meeting. The same thing is true for Cornelius and Peter.

For the Jews, the customary hour of prayer was three in the afternoon (see 3:1). At this hour one day, Cornelius was on his knees in prayer and suddenly saw an angel. Luke uses the word *vision* to describe the appearance of "an angel of God." When the apostles were set free from their Jerusalem prison, an angel of the Lord opened the doors for them (5:19). Likewise, Peter was released from prison by an angel of the Lord (12:7–10). But the angel who came to Cornelius appeared in a vision (see also 8:26).

Presumably, Cornelius had been told about the existence and the task of angels. For the centurion, however, the appearance of an angel who called him by name was a unique experience. Even if the officer was unfamiliar with angelic visits, he was not deceived by his senses. He was in full control of his faculties.[5] The angel called him and said, "Cornelius."

---

4. Emil Schürer, *The History of the Jewish People in the Age of Jesus Christ (175 B.C.–A.D. 135)*, rev. and ed. Geza Vermes and Fergus Millar, 3 vols. (Edinburgh: Clark, 1973–87), vol. 3, pp. 173–74; Max Wilcox, "The 'God-fearers' in Acts—A Reconsideration," *JSNT* 13 (1981): 102–22; A. T. Kraabel, "The Disappearance of the 'God-Fearers,' " *Numen* 28 (1981): 113–26, and his "Roman Diaspora: Six Questionable Assumptions," *JJS* 33 (1982): 445–64; T. M. Finn, "The God-Fearers Reconsidered," *CBQ* 47 (1985): 75–84; J. A. Overman, "The God-Fearers: Some Neglected Features," *JSNT* 32 (1988): 17–26; Colin J. Hemer, *The Book of Acts in the Setting of Hellenistic History*, ed. Conrad H. Gempf (Tübingen: Mohr, 1989), pp. 444–47.

5. John Albert Bengel, *Gnomon of the New Testament*, ed. Andrew R. Fausset, 5 vols. (Edinburgh: Clark, 1877), vol. 2, p. 599.

Greek Words, Phrases, and Constructions in 10:2

φοβούμενος τὸν θεόν—"fearing God." The expression occurs four times in Acts (10:2, 22; 13:16, 26). In addition, the verb σέβομαι (I worship) with participial forms refers to Gentiles who worship God (13:43, 50; 17:4, 17; 18:7).

οἴκῳ—this noun ("house") is virtually identical with the noun οἰκία. Depending on the context, the noun οἶκος means "household" (e.g., in this verse and in 16:31, 34; 18:8); so does οἰκία in John 4:53.[6]

διὰ παντός—an idiomatic expression meaning "always" or "regularly." It lacks the noun χρόνου (time).

---

b. Message
10:4–6

4. Gazing at him intently and fearfully, Cornelius said, "What is it, Lord?" The angel answered, "Your prayers and generous gifts to the poor have ascended and are remembered before God."

Two worlds meet in the encounter of the angel and Cornelius: the sinless world in which the angel moves and the sinful world to which Cornelius belongs. As soon as Cornelius sees the angel, he perceives the divine presence of God represented by one of his messengers. No wonder, then, that Cornelius is afraid when he looks intently at the angel.[7] Zechariah and Mary, to whom the angel Gabriel appeared in the Jerusalem temple and in Nazareth, respectively, were also greatly perturbed. As a result the angel had to tell them not to be afraid (Luke 1:13, 30). Similarly, Cornelius has nothing to fear.

Cornelius asks, "What is it, Lord?" Note the similarity between Paul and Cornelius: Jesus called Paul by name on the way to Damascus, and the angel addressed Cornelius by name in Caesarea; Paul answered Jesus with the word *Lord* (9:5), and Cornelius used the same word for the angel.[8] The officer knows that he faces a holy angel and, therefore, his response is more than a polite address.

The angel continues, "Your prayers and generous gifts to the poor have ascended and are remembered before God." The message of the angel reassures this Roman centurion that his prayers to Israel's God are not offered in vain. God has accepted the love Cornelius shows to him through his generous gifts to the poor. Therefore, the angel tells Cornelius that God has remembered his prayers and generosity.

---

6. Jürgen Goetzmann, *NIDNTT*, vol. 2, pp. 248, 250.

7. Consult John Calvin, *Commentary on the Acts of the Apostles*, ed. David W. Torrance and Thomas F. Torrance, 2 vols. (Grand Rapids: Eerdmans, 1966), vol. 1, p. 287.

8. David John Williams, *Acts*, Good News Commentaries series (San Francisco: Harper and Row, 1985), p. 172.

For the Jew, remembrance meant that he could appeal to God in prayer, because he had the assurance that he could count on God for help.[9] Since Cornelius was a God-fearer and not a Jewish convert, he was barred from presenting offerings to God in the Jerusalem temple. But his prayers and his acts of generosity to his fellow man had been accepted by God.

5. "And now send men to Joppa and summon a man named Simon who is called Peter. 6. He is staying with a certain tanner named Simon, whose house is by the sea."

What was the content of the prayers Cornelius presented to God? Even though Luke fails to relate these details, the content of Cornelius's prayers is implied in the message of the angel. Cornelius had learned from a study of the Scriptures about the promised Messiah. We assume that since his arrival in Palestine, he had heard about the life and death of Jesus, but not about his resurrection, appearances, and ascension. He now prayed that God would grant him salvation through the promised Messiah, whom the apostles and the evangelists proclaimed. Although the biblical text does not specifically indicate (see 8:40), by this time Philip perhaps had reached Caesarea and, having settled there, preached Christ's gospel.

"And now send men to Joppa and summon a man named Simon who is called Peter." We make two observations. First, the angel does not reveal to Cornelius what God's answer to his prayers is. He tells him only how God will answer his requests. In other words, God desires that Cornelius exercise his faith. Next, God does not instruct the officer to travel to Joppa to meet Peter. Rather, Cornelius must send his men to Peter and ask him to come to a Gentile home in Caesarea. This is significant: as the apostles Peter and John went to Samaria and welcomed the Samaritans as full members of the Christian church, so Peter travels to Caesarea and welcomes the Gentiles as full members in the church. Thus, in fulfillment of Christ's mandate to the apostles (1:8), God ordains new phases in the growth of the church through the apostles of Christ.

The directions Cornelius received from the angel were clear. As centurion and head of his household, he was to send men to Joppa, a city located about halfway between Gaza to the south and Mount Carmel to the north. To be precise, Joppa was situated thirty-five miles northwest of Jerusalem and thirty miles south of Caesarea. The men would invite Simon, who is called Peter, to the home of Cornelius. Note that the angel used the Hebrew name *Simon* to indicate that Cornelius would ask a Jew to enter his home. Further, the men would have no difficulty finding Simon. They would meet him in the home of Simon the tanner, who lived by the sea. They would readily be able to locate the tanner's house, which was situated outside the confines of the city (see the commentary on 9:43).

---

9. Colin Brown, *NIDNTT,* vol. 3, p. 238. See Lev. 2:2, 9, 16; 5:12; Sir. 35:6; 38:11; 45:16.

Doctrinal Considerations in 10:1–6

When Christian missionaries brought the gospel to the Gentiles, they met a group of people called God-fearers. These people were Gentiles who had not fully embraced the Jewish religion and therefore could be classified as neither pagan nor proselyte. They were acquainted with the Septuagint translation of the Scriptures, but had not been incorporated into Judaism because they had not submitted to the Mosaic regulations pertaining to circumcision, baptism, and sacrifices.[10] Many God-fearers accepted the teachings of the gospel, adhered to the Christian faith, and believed in Jesus as their Savior. Among these God-fearers were Lydia, who was a seller of purple cloth in Philippi (16:14), Greeks in Athens (17:4), and Titius Justus in Corinth (18:7).

As Cornelius prayed to Israel's God, he did not know Jesus Christ. Yet God heard and answered his prayer. The point is that Cornelius could not have prayed unless he prayed in faith.[11] Cornelius, then, prayed to God and asked for the gift of salvation in anticipation of knowing Christ. He lived in the expectation of Christ coming into his life, much as the Old Testament saints awaited the Messiah. Luke provides no evidence that Cornelius offered prayers to God and showed his generosity to the poor for the purpose of meriting salvation. Devoted to God, he strove to keep the summary of God's commandments with a heart filled with love for God and his needy neighbors.

Greek Words, Phrases, and Constructions in 10:4–6

Verse 4

ἀτενίσας—the verb ἀτενίζω (I look intently at) appears fourteen times in the New Testament; twelve are in the writings of Luke (Luke 4:20; 22:56; Acts 1:10; 3:4, 12; 6:15; 7:55; 10:4; 11:6; 13:9; 14:9; 23:1). See also II Corinthians 3:7, 13.

κύριε—the vocative, but it denotes more than a polite address. In context, it means "Lord."

ἐλεημοσύναι—with the verb ποιεῖν this noun signifies "to practise the virtue of mercy or beneficence." Here it means to make "a donation for the poor."[12]

Verses 5–6

μετάπεμψαι—this is the aorist active infinitive of the verb μεταπέμπω (I send after or for). The preposition in this compound verb means "after."[13]

βυρσεῖ—the dative is in apposition to the name *Simon*, thus, "Simon, the tanner."

---

10. Kirsopp Lake, "Proselytes and God-fearers," *Beginnings*, vol. 5, pp. 74–96.

11. Henry Alford, *Alford's Greek Testament: An Exegetical and Critical Commentary*, 7th ed., 4 vols. (1877; Grand Rapids: Guardian, 1976), vol. 2, p. 111; see Calvin, *Acts of the Apostles*, vol. 1, p. 290.

12. Thayer, p. 203.

13. A. T. Robertson, *A Grammar of the Greek New Testament in the Light of Historical Research* (Nashville: Broadman, 1934), p. 609.

c. Action
10:7–8

7. And when the angel who spoke to him had departed, Cornelius called two of his servants and a devout soldier of those who were continually with him. 8. He explained everything to them and sent them to Joppa.

The angel had one task and that was to deliver God's message to Cornelius. Having accomplished his task, the angel left. But Cornelius in faith obeyed the instructions God had given him. He called two of his household servants who were thoroughly reliable, were acquainted with their master's devotion to God, and were spiritual men (see v. 2). In addition, Cornelius charged a soldier to accompany the two servants, obviously for protection. This soldier was a devout man who attended the worship services Cornelius conducted for the benefit of his household. All three men possessed a spiritual treasure and thus were united in purpose.

Then Cornelius sent the two servants and the soldier on their way to Joppa. If this happened on a Monday, Cornelius would expect them to return on Thursday (see vv. 9, 23, 24, 30). If the men walked along the sandy and level road next to the Mediterranean Sea, they would have to allow themselves about ten hours to cover the distance between Caesarea and Joppa. They probably walked four hours on that first day and, starting out early the next morning, arrived in Joppa about noon on the second day.

Greek Words, Phrases, and Constructions in 10:7–8

ὁ λαλῶν—the present participle is translated in the past tense ("spoke") because of the aorist tense of ἀπῆλθεν (he departed).

ἅπαντα—the word is equivalent to πάντα (all). For Luke, the term is a favorite in both his Gospel and Acts. It occurs seventeen times in Luke's Gospel, thirteen times in Acts, four times in Mark, four times in Paul's Epistles, and once in James.

---

9 The next day at noon as they were traveling and approaching the city, Peter went up on the roof to pray. 10 He became hungry and wanted to eat; but while the food was being prepared, he fell into a trance. 11 And he saw heaven opened and a certain object like a large sheet being lowered to earth by its four corners. 12 In it were all the four-footed animals, reptiles of the earth, and birds of the air. 13 Then a voice said to him, "Get up, Peter. Kill and eat."

14 Peter replied, "Certainly not, Lord. I have never eaten anything impure and unclean." 15 And the voice spoke to him a second time, "Do not consider unclean what God has made clean." 16 This happened three times; and immediately the object was taken up into heaven.

17 While Peter was wondering what the vision he had seen might mean, the men sent by Cornelius, after asking directions to Simon's house, stood at the gate. 18 They called out and asked whether Simon called Peter was staying there. 19 While Peter was reflecting on the vision, the Spirit said to him, "Three men are looking for you. 20 But get up and go downstairs. Accompany them without hesitation, for I myself have sent them." 21 So Peter went down to the men and said, "I am the one you are looking for. What brings you here?" 22 They said, "Cornelius, an officer, a man who is righteous and fears God and is respected by all the

Jewish people, has sent us. A holy angel told him to summon you to the house of Cornelius to hear a message from you." 23a Peter invited them to enter the house and gave them lodging.

---

4. Peter's Vision
10:9–23a

Luke discloses that God prepares Cornelius for entering the Christian church and Peter for receiving Gentiles into the church as full members. Luke devotes about a chapter and a half (10:1–11:18) to the subject of the first Gentiles accepting Jesus Christ as their Savior, receiving the gift of the Holy Spirit, and being baptized. In these chapters, Luke notes that God commissions Peter to open the door to the Gentiles; Peter represents the apostles and is the leader of the Jerusalem church. For that reason, Peter, not Paul, is the person who extends a welcome to the Gentiles.

Peter is a Jew who since childhood has learned not to enter the home of a Gentile and not to have table fellowship with a non-Jew. He must now learn to overcome his prejudice and accept as brothers and sisters God-fearing Gentiles who believe in Jesus. Through a vision, God prepares Peter for the meeting with Cornelius and his household.

a. Vision
10:9–13

9. The next day at noon as they were traveling and approaching the city, Peter went up on the roof to pray.

The messengers of Cornelius have not lost any time while traveling. Within ten hours they arrive in Joppa. We surmise that after resting during the night, they continued their journey at daybreak and came to Joppa at noon. From Luke's reference to Peter being on the roof, we infer that the time of year was summer, which gave the travelers extended periods of daylight.

While the messengers approach Joppa, Peter seeks privacy on the flat roof of the tanner's house where he is staying. Palestinian houses in those days had outside staircases that led to flat roofs, where the people could either sleep during the hot summer nights or, in the case of Peter, enjoy the cool breezes from the Mediterranean Sea during the day. The house of the tanner apparently lacked an upper room. Peter ascends the roof at noon that day for the purpose of spending time in private prayer.

The times of private prayer in Israel were morning, noon, and evening (see, e.g., Ps. 55:17; Dan. 6:10). The Jews in Jerusalem participated in public prayers at the temple during the time of the morning sacrifice and the mid-afternoon offering at three (see 3:1).[14] In Joppa, Peter observes the hour of prayer at noon while he awaits the noon meal.

---

14. SB, vol. 2, pp. 696–702; Schürer, *History of the Jewish People*, vol. 2, p. 481.

10. He became hungry and wanted to eat; but while the food was being prepared, he fell into a trance.

The Greek indicates that Peter becomes very hungry, perhaps because he had fasted. Indeed, his body demands something to eat. Meanwhile, Peter's hostess is busy preparing the noon meal. While Peter endures the hunger pangs, his senses are keen as he focuses his thoughts in prayer to God. Then he falls into a trance, which the Greek expresses with the word *ekstasis* (from which we have the derivative *ecstasy*). When Peter is in a trance, he neither loses control of his senses nor dreams. During a similar ecstatic experience Paul sees the Lord speaking to him and telling him to leave Jerusalem immediately (22:17–18). In either instance, the apostle enters into the presence of God to receive instructions for his ministry. In a profound state of concentration, both men are partially or completely oblivious to external sensations but fully alert to subjective influences coming to them by sight and sound.

In the case of Peter, all his senses are directed to God in anticipation of divine directives. God himself induces Peter's trance so that God is able to communicate visually and audibly with him.[15] Note, then, that Peter's hunger pangs relate directly to the vision he receives when he falls into a trance. His physical senses are stimulated because of his desire to eat, yet, in spite of his keen appetite, he is fully prepared to decline the invitation to eat.

11. And he saw heaven opened and a certain object like a large sheet being lowered to earth by its four corners. 12. In it were all the four-footed animals, reptiles of the earth, and birds of the air. 13. Then a voice said to him, "Get up, Peter. Kill and eat."

Peter sees that heaven opens and a large sheet filled with all kinds of animals comes down. This is interesting indeed, because we would have expected the opposite to take place, namely, that all the animal species would come together on the earth and then be taken to heaven. But an object descends from heaven to earth, and Peter observes that it is lowered by its four corners. The agents who are lowering this large sheet are not mentioned but undoubtedly they are angels. The purpose of this presentation is to indicate that the spectacle originates in heaven and not on earth.[16] In other words, it is ordained by God.

When the sheet comes closer to view, Peter discerns that it contains all kinds of four-footed animals, reptiles, and birds of the air. Except for the fish of the sea, all the creatures God has made are present in this large and open container and thus, by comparison, are similar to those that were in Noah's ark (Gen. 6:20). The sheet contains clean and unclean animals—the sheep and the swine, the cow and the coney (compare Lev. 11; Deut. 14:3–

---

15. Everett F. Harrison, *Interpreting Acts: The Expanding Church*, 2d ed. (Grand Rapids: Zondervan, Academie Books, 1986), p. 177.
16. Bengel, *Gnomon of the New Testament*, vol. 2, p. 601.

21). When Peter takes note of all these animals, he revolts as he hears a voice from heaven commanding him to kill and eat.

God instructed the Jew to separate himself from the Gentile by eating ritually prepared kosher food. Jewish people would not think of entering the home of a Gentile and eating or drinking with him (see 11:3; John 18:28). Jews also refused to buy their meat from a Gentile butcher and thus avoided polluting themselves with something that was ritually unclean.[17] These strict laws of separation offended the Gentiles, who could not see harm in eating unclean animals. Accordingly, by observing the Mosaic command not to eat with Gentiles, Peter considered himself clean and all the Gentiles unclean (compare Gal. 2:12–14).

The lesson God teaches Peter in this vision of the clean and unclean animals is that God has removed the barriers he once erected to separate his people from the surrounding nations. The barrier between the Jewish Christian and the Samaritan Christian had been removed when Peter and John went to Samaria to accept the Samaritan believers as full members of the church. Now the time has come to extend the same privilege to Gentile believers. Not man but God removes the barrier that separates the Jew from the Gentile. God instructs Peter to accept Gentile believers in the Christian church. God, not Peter, opens the gates of heaven to the Gentiles. God himself inaugurates a new phase of gospel ministry for Peter (11:18).

Doctrinal Considerations in 10:9–13

Before Jesus ascended to heaven, he told the apostles to make disciples of all nations by baptizing and teaching believers regardless of race and color (Matt. 28:19–20). Of course, the apostles understood the mandate they received to proclaim Christ's gospel everywhere. Their training, culture, and background directed them first to the Jews: they went to the lost sheep of the house of Israel (Matt. 10:6). But Jesus told them to be witnesses for him in Jerusalem, Judea, Samaria, and the ends of the world. Except for admitting Samaritans to the Christian church, the apostles understood the mandate to include only Jews living in countries other than Palestine (see, e.g., 11:19).

God guided the apostles step by step as the church continued to develop. First, at Pentecost devout Jews repented, were baptized, and received the Holy Spirit (2:38). Then, after the persecution following the death of Stephen, the Good News entered Samaria, where Philip preached the word. Representing the apostles, Peter and John went to Samaria, prayed that the Samaritan believers might receive the Holy Spirit, and baptized them (8:14–17).

Next, through a vision of clean and unclean animals, God prepared Peter to preach the gospel to the household of the Roman officer Cornelius. These representative Gentiles received the Holy Spirit and were baptized. But the matter of full acceptance of the Gentiles into the Christian church was not settled until Paul and

---

17. Richard B. Rackham, *The Acts of the Apostles: An Exposition*, Westminster Commentaries series (1901; reprint ed., Grand Rapids: Baker, 1964), p. 150.

Barnabas returned from their first missionary journey to the Gentiles and reported their experiences to the members of the Jerusalem Council (15:4).

At this council meeting, those present debated whether Gentile believers had to submit to circumcision. For the Jew, circumcision signified that he belonged to the covenant God had made with Abraham (Gen. 17:7). Thus, the Jewish Christians questioned whether the Gentiles who did not submit to circumcision were members of Abraham's covenant. Guided by the Holy Spirit, the Jerusalem Council determined that the Gentiles did not have to submit to circumcision but only to regulations that were already considered sacred prior to the Mosaic laws (15:19–20). For the Gentiles, therefore, baptism was sufficient.

When Peter preached the gospel in Caesarea and baptized the household of Cornelius, the question of circumcision was not raised. God himself guided Peter, the apostles, and the Jewish believers in Jerusalem to accept the Gentiles. And in later years, God led the church to admit the Gentiles without circumcision. We conclude that God determines the church's direction and development.

---

b. Instruction
10:14–16

14. Peter replied, "Certainly not, Lord. I have never eaten anything impure and unclean." 15. And the voice spoke to him a second time, "Do not consider unclean what God has made clean." 16. This happened three times; and immediately the object was taken up into heaven.

a. "Certainly not, Lord. I have never eaten anything impure and unclean." When Peter sees the animals and hears the voice saying, "Get up, Peter. Kill and eat," he responds by using some of the words that the prophet Ezekiel uttered when Jerusalem was in a state of siege:

> "Not so, Sovereign Lord! I have never defiled myself. From my youth until now I have never eaten anything found dead or torn by wild animals. No unclean meat has ever entered my mouth." [Ezek. 4:14, NIV]

Peter hears the voice of God addressing him; in his reply he addresses God as Lord. He knows that whenever God speaks from heaven, an important event is taking place. Two instances were the baptism and the transfiguration of Jesus (Matt. 3:17; 17:5). But the event of God addressing Peter is also significant. It marks the entrance of the Gentiles into the church in accordance with God's will, plan, and purpose.[18]

Peter's ingrained cultural objections are so strong that he forcefully refuses to obey God's command to kill and eat. Alluding to Scripture (Ezek. 4:14), he feels that he is on safe ground to object to the divine directive. Peter tells the Lord that he has never eaten anything impure and unclean and thus indicates that he observes the barrier between the Jew and the Gentile.

---

18. F. W. Grosheide, *De Handelingen der Apostelen*, Kommentaar op het Nieuwe Testament series, 2 vols. (Amsterdam: Van Bottenburg, 1942), vol. 1, p. 331.

What is the meaning of the words *impure* and *unclean*? The Jew could eat the meat of only those animals which God had declared clean, that is, ruminants and those with cloven hoofs. All other animals were impure and unclean. The large sheet let down to earth contained clean and unclean animals. When God told Peter to kill and eat, he did not make a distinction between these two categories. By contrast, Peter distinguished between clean and unclean; he regarded the clean animals defiled because of their association with the unclean animals.[19]

b. "Do not consider unclean what God has made clean." This is the second time a voice speaks from heaven and answers Peter's legitimate objection. The voice conveys the message that God, who formulated the dietary laws for his people Israel, can also revoke them according to his sovereign will. God has made the animals clean; therefore, Peter with his fellow Jewish Christians can disregard the food laws that have been observed since the days of Moses (compare Rom. 14:14). Literally the Greek text can be translated, "What God has made clean, do not continue to call unclean."

When does God abolish the dietary laws for Jewish Christians? The moment God removes the barrier between the Jew and Gentile, the validity of the food laws ceases. Abolition of these laws means that Jewish and Gentile Christians enter into a new relationship and accept one another as equals in the church. God himself removes the barrier, for he is the lawmaker.

c. "This happened three times." The heavenly voice is unable to convince Peter until he has heard it three times. Peter should have remembered Jesus' teaching that food does not make man unclean when it enters his mouth (Matt. 15:11). Three times the heavenly voice speaks to Peter to tell him that God has made all foods clean. By implication, God is teaching Peter that with the abolition of food laws Peter can now associate with Gentiles and have table fellowship. After hearing the heavenly voice three times, Peter is convinced. When the chief spokesman for the twelve apostles and the leader of the Jerusalem church heeds the voice, the sheet is suddenly taken up to heaven. This return to heaven once again indicates that God himself has opened the way for the gospel ministry to the Gentiles.

Greek Words, Phrases, and Constructions in 10:14–15

Verse 14

μηδαμῶς—the intensive adverb is a negative compound that signifies "by no means." It is a combination of μηδέ (and not) and ἅμα (to a man).

---

19. Colin House, "Defilement by Association: Some Insights from the Usage of KOINÓS-KOINÓŌ in Acts 10 and 11," *AUSS* 21 (1983): 143–53.

οὐδέποτε . . . πᾶν—the negative adverb negates the verb, yet it pointedly means "nothing."[20]

Verse 15

πάλιν ἐκ δευτέρου—the construction is redundant, but the prepositional phrase is idiomatic (see Matt. 26:42; and compare John 4:54; 21:16).

ἐκαθάρισεν—the aorist active denotes a single occurrence during which God declared all animals clean.

μὴ κοίνου—the present imperative with the negative particle conveys the message "stop considering unclean what God has declared clean."[21]

---

c. Call
10:17–20

17. While Peter was wondering what the vision he had seen might mean, the men sent by Cornelius, after asking directions to Simon's house, stood at the gate. 18. They called out and asked whether Simon called Peter was staying there.

When God removes the sheet, he also causes Peter's trance to cease. The significance of the vision God has given Peter, however, is not at all clear to Peter. The apostle meditates; he ponders the meaning of that which he has seen.

Peter realizes that God is at work in his life and that he will make the meaning of the vision plain to him. He knows that the extraordinary vision has something to do with his ministry of the gospel. And indeed, God himself immediately provides the explanation of the vision. He sends Gentiles from Cornelius in Caesarea to Peter in Joppa.

The three men sent by Cornelius have arrived in Joppa and have asked here and there for the address of Simon the tanner. We conjecture that they have no difficulty finding the house, which was situated along the seashore. When they arrive at the gate, they inquire whether Simon, who is also known as Peter, is staying with the tanner. The appearance of the Roman soldier probably is unsettling to Peter's host. Further, the clothing and speech of the two servants indicate that they are non-Jews. The men stand at the gate, call the owner of the house, and inquire where Simon Peter resides.

19. While Peter was reflecting on the vision, the Spirit said to him, "Three men are looking for you. 20. But get up and go downstairs. Accompany them without hesitation, for I myself have sent them."

Peter is still in deep thought and has not heard any of the conversation between his host and the visitors. The Spirit of God addresses him and tells

---

20. Robertson, *Grammar*, p. 752.
21. James Hope Moulton, *A Grammar of New Testament Greek*, vol. 1, *Prolegomena*, 2d ed. (Edinburgh: Clark, 1906), p. 125.

him that three men are at the door and want to meet him. Luke often records that the Spirit instructs God's servants to go somewhere or do something (e.g., 8:29, 39; 11:12; 13:2; 21:11). The Spirit informs Peter how many men are looking for him, but not who they are. However, to calm Peter's mind, the Spirit instructs him to go downstairs and not to show any hesitation. The Spirit assures Peter that he has sent these men to Joppa to meet the apostle.

Peter has to overcome at least two causes for hesitation when he meets the men at the gate. First, he knows that they are Gentiles who have traveled and need accommodation. That is, Peter and his host must lay aside the Jewish restrictions on associating with Gentiles. They must feed these men and provide shelter for one night. Second, Peter ought to lay aside any fear of being in the presence of a Roman soldier and two servants of a Roman officer at a time of political tension between the Jews and the Romans.[22]

When the Holy Spirit removes Peter's fears by telling him that God has sent the three men to him, the meaning of the vision becomes clear to Peter. God himself has assured Peter that what he has declared clean, Peter ought not to call unclean. God wants Peter to associate with these Gentiles. And they, in turn, will relate to him the account of the angel of God who visited Cornelius. This is the confirmation Peter receives, namely, to know that God is interpreting the vision for him in terms relating to gospel ministry.

Greek Words, Phrases, and Constructions in 10:17–20

Verse 17

τί ἂν εἴη—introduced by the imperfect active διηπόρει (he was thoroughly perplexed), the indirect question features the present optative of the verb εἰμί with the particle ἄν: "as to what the vision might mean."[23] Note the use of the present, imperfect, aorist, and perfect tenses in the verbs and participles of this verse.

Verse 18

ἐπυνθάνοντο εἰ Σίμων—the imperfect middle of πυνθάνομαι (I inquire) is followed by an indirect question. "But the fact that εἰ can be used to introduce a *direct* question and that ἐνθάδε, *here*, is strictly incorrect for an *indirect* question, which requires ἐκεῖ, *there*, may point to this not being intended to be indirect at all, but a direct quotation: *they were enquiring, Does Simon . . . lodge here?*"[24]

---

22. Josephus *Antiquities* 18.8.2 [261]; Suetonius *Gaius Caligula*, in *The Lives of the Caesars*, trans. John C. Rolfe, 2 vols., vol. 1, bk. 4, pp. 405–97 (LCL).

23. Robertson, *Grammar*, p. 940.

24. C. F. D. Moule, *An Idiom-Book of New Testament Greek*, 2d ed. (Cambridge: Cambridge University Press, 1960), p. 154. See Lake and Cadbury, *Beginnings*, vol. 4, p. 116.

Verse 19

τοῦ Πέτρου—with the present middle participle in the genitive (διενθυμουμένου) this personal noun forms the genitive absolute construction.

τρεῖς—Codex Vaticanus has the reading δύο (two). This reading is based on verse 7 and refers to the two servants, who are accompanied by a soldier as a guard. Scribes supposedly harmonized the reading with 11:11, where the word τρεῖς appears. However, a broad range of textual witnesses supports the reading τρεῖς.[25]

---

d. Reception
10:21–23a

21. So Peter went down to the men and said, "I am the one you are looking for. What brings you here?" 22. They said, "Cornelius, an officer, a man who is righteous and fears God and is respected by all the Jewish people, has sent us. A holy angel told him to summon you to the house of Cornelius to hear a message from you."

Peter meets the men at the gate and introduces himself as the person they want to see. He asks them why they have come to Joppa and why they want to meet him. Then he hears the details concerning the spiritual and moral life of Cornelius, a Roman military officer in Caesarea. The messengers portray Cornelius as a righteous man who fears God. In other words, they tell Peter that Cornelius worships God in the local synagogue and also in his home. They add that Cornelius has the respect of all the Jewish people, specifically, those residing in Caesarea. This last point is significant, for the Jews would not testify to his godliness if the officer did not worship Israel's God.[26]

Then the men inform Peter about the angelic visit to Cornelius some two days earlier. They relate that in obedience to the message that the centurion received, they have come to meet Simon Peter in Joppa. They describe the angel as "holy." By respecting the holiness of the angel, they show their sincerity and faithfulness. They also relay the meaningful information that the angel gave to Cornelius, namely, to invite Simon Peter to deliver the gospel message in the officer's home in Caesarea. Here, then, is the purpose of their mission, and they look to Peter for a reply.

Unfortunately, Luke is brief in his account and fails to describe Peter's reaction. How the apostle must have marveled at God's guiding care and purposeful design! What a realization it must have been for him that the church was about to enter a new phase of its ministry! To be sure, the vision and the visit of the three men from Caesarea testify to the changes that are about to happen.

23a. Peter invited them to enter the house and gave them lodging.

---

25. Bruce M. Metzger, *A Textual Commentary on the Greek New Testament,* 3d corrected ed. (London and New York: United Bible Societies, 1975), p. 373.
26. Calvin, *Acts of the Apostles,* vol. 1, p. 298.

Peter understands that he must accept the visitors and, implicitly, Simon the tanner concurs. These two men now serve as hosts to the visitors and provide for them the meal that has been prepared (v. 10). We have no information whether Peter breaks bread with the Gentiles, but we have reason to believe that, in obedience to the vision, he does. As soon as he leaves Joppa he will have to eat a number of meals with non-Jews. The men spend the afternoon conversing with one another, and Peter makes preparations to travel to Caesarea. They stay with Simon the tanner that night, and the next day they are ready to return to Cornelius.

Greek Words, Phrases, and Constructions in 10:22

τοῦ ἔθνους—"the nation." These words come from the lips of Gentiles. A Jew would have used the term λαός (God's own people).

23b The next day Peter, accompanied by some of the brothers from Joppa, went out with them. 24 And the following day he arrived at Caesarea. Cornelius was waiting for them and had invited his relatives and close friends. 25 As Peter entered the house, Cornelius met him, fell at his feet, and worshiped him. 26 But Peter made him get up and said, "Stand up! I, too, am only a man." 27 And talking to him, Peter entered and found the many people who had gathered. 28 He said to them, "You yourselves know it is unlawful for a Jew to associate with or visit a Gentile. Yet God has shown me not to call any man impure or unclean. 29 That is why I came without raising any objection when I was summoned. So I ask why have you summoned me?"

30 Cornelius said, "Four days ago at this hour, at three in the afternoon, I was in my house praying. Suddenly a man in radiant clothes stood before me 31 and said, 'Cornelius, your prayer has been heard and your generous gifts to the poor have been remembered before God. 32 Send, therefore, to Joppa and invite Simon who is called Peter. He is staying in the house of Simon the tanner by the sea.' 33 So immediately I sent for you, and you did well in coming. Now, then, we are all here before God to hear everything that you have been instructed by God to tell us."

34 Peter said: "I truly understand that God shows no favoritism. 35 But in every nation, the man who fears him and does what is right is accepted by God. 36 You know that the message which proclaims peace through Jesus Christ, that he is Lord of all, was sent to the people of Israel. 37 And you know what happened throughout Judea, beginning in Galilee after the baptism that John preached. 38 You know about Jesus of Nazareth, how God anointed him with the Holy Spirit and power, and how he went around doing good and healing all who were dominated by the devil, for God was with him. 39 And we are witnesses of everything he did both in the land of the Jews and in Jerusalem. They put him to death by hanging him on a tree, 40 but God raised him on the third day. God caused him to be seen, 41 not by everyone but by witnesses who were appointed beforehand by God, that is, to us who ate and drank with him after he rose from the dead. 42 He commanded us to preach to the people and to testify that Jesus is the one whom God appointed judge of the living and the dead. 43 All the prophets bear witness to him that through his name everyone who believes in him receives forgiveness of sins."

44 While Peter was still speaking these words, the Holy Spirit fell upon all who were hearing the message. 45 And all the circumcised believers who had come with Peter were amazed that the gift of the Holy Spirit had been poured out on the Gentiles also. 46 For they heard them speaking in tongues and praising God.

Then Peter said, 47 "Can anyone prevent these people from being baptized with water? Because they have received the Holy Spirit as we have." 48 So he ordered that they be baptized in the name of Jesus Christ. Then they asked him to remain with them a few days.

---

5. Peter's Visit to Caesarea
10:23b–48

In the first part of chapter 10, Luke relates that God has made possible the meeting between Cornelius and Peter. Accordingly, Peter has authority to preach the gospel to Gentiles and to accept them as Christians. Peter realizes that this step is significant for the church and therefore requests that six Jewish Christians from Joppa accompany him (see 11:12). Likewise, Cornelius is fully aware of the importance of this event and invites his relatives and intimate friends to his house.[27]

a. Arrival
10:23b–29

23b. The next day Peter, accompanied by some of the brothers from Joppa, went out with them. 24. And the following day he arrived at Caesarea. Cornelius was waiting for them and had invited his relatives and close friends.

Peter makes final preparations for his visit to Caesarea: he invites six members of the church in Joppa to go along with him. He wants eyewitnesses to report accurately his visit to the home of a Gentile so that the church can learn the details of this extraordinary visit (11:1–18).

We have no indication when Peter and his companions left Joppa, but a party of ten people needs more time to get ready than two or three messengers. Luke notes that they leave, travel all day, and arrive in Caesarea the next day. On foot the trip takes about ten hours. No doubt the travelers spend the night somewhere and come to Caesarea during the course of the following day. If Cornelius received the angel's instructions on a Monday and immediately sent his messengers to Joppa, these men arrived there on Tuesday. The next day, Peter left for Caesarea and entered the house of Cornelius on Thursday (see v. 30).

Luke writes that Cornelius is waiting anxiously for Peter's arrival. The officer has made all the preparations for this important visit by gathering relatives and close friends in his home. Evidently he has lived many years in Caesarea, for his extended family has come to reside there. In the course of time, Cornelius has been able to build up lasting friendships with residents in the area. All these people respond to Cornelius's invitation to meet Simon Peter and to hear him proclaim Christ's gospel. With Cornelius they are waiting to greet the returning messengers, the six Jewish Christians from Joppa (see v. 45; 11:12), and Peter. When the party of ten persons

---

27. Rackham, *Acts,* p. 153.

enters his home at the expected hour, Cornelius meets Peter at the gate and welcomes him.[28]

25. As Peter entered the house, Cornelius met him, fell at his feet, and worshiped him. 26. But Peter made him get up and said, "Stand up! I, too, am only a man."

How did Cornelius know the exact time of Peter's arrival in Caesarea? We do not know. The Western text has an expansion of this passage and provides an explanation: "And as Peter was drawing near to Caesarea, one of the servants ran ahead and announced that he had arrived. And Cornelius jumped up and [met him]."[29] But this reading is regarded to be a later explanation of the text and thus lacks authenticity.

When Peter enters the home of Cornelius, he is astonished to see that this military officer puts his authority aside and falls to the ground to pay respect to Peter. From his Gentile background, Cornelius knows no other way to honor Peter than by prostrating himself. Cornelius is of the opinion that the person pointed out by the angel of God "must be deserving of the highest respect."[30] By contrast, Peter shuns any action that resembles idolatry, for one of God's commandments is to worship only God (Exod. 20:3–4; Deut. 5:7–8). Scripture teaches that whenever man seeks to worship either an angel or a fellow man, he is told not to do so but to worship God (see 14:14–15; Rev. 19:10; 22:8–9). Consequently, when Cornelius and Peter meet, their initial encounter causes embarrassment.

Peter realizes that Cornelius wishes to show him deep respect, but he tells the officer to get up on his feet. He seeks to rectify the situation with an appropriate response and says, "Stand up! I, too, am only a man." In other words, Peter reveals himself as an ordinary man who in the sight of God is on the same level as Cornelius. He teaches the centurion the equality of all believers in God's presence.

27. And talking to him, Peter entered and found the many people who had gathered. 28. He said to them, "You yourselves know it is unlawful for a Jew to associate with or visit a Gentile. Yet God has shown me not to call any man impure or unclean. 29. That is why I came without raising any objection when I was summoned. So I ask why have you summoned me?"

a. "Talking to him, Peter entered." Luke describes the initial meeting of Peter and Cornelius and indicates that the two men have many things to discuss. Cornelius invites Peter to enter a large room, where he meets the relatives and close friends of Cornelius. Peter, then, faces a Gentile audience of many people. If he has any doubt about the significance of his vision, in the presence of these Gentiles that doubt disappears.

---

28. Manuscript evidence gives equal support to the readings *they entered* and *he entered*. Hence, translators are divided on this point: KJV, NKJV, RV, ASV, RSV, MLB, and SEB have the plural; the singular is preferred by GNB, JB, NAB, NASB, NEB, NIV, and *Moffatt*.

29. Metzger, *Textual Commentary*, pp. 374–75.

30. Alford, *Alford's Greek Testament*, vol. 2, p. 116.

b. "It is unlawful for a Jew to associate with or visit a Gentile." At first glance, Peter's remark lacks friendliness and appears to be a verbal lesson on alienating himself from prospective converts to the Christian faith. However, Cornelius and his relatives and friends are personally acquainted with the strict separation rules that the Jews observe. Even though some Gentiles worship with the Jews in the local synagogue, they are unable to socialize with them because of the Jewish laws on table fellowship (see 11:2–3). The Jews recognize only converts to Judaism; only these people have attained full recognition in the Jewish community (see Isa. 56:3); they are permitted to visit Jews and eat with them. The Gentiles know that the Jews do not even buy their food from the Gentiles for fear of contamination. They have experienced that Jews are unwilling to set foot in the home of a Gentile (compare Matt. 8:8; Luke 7:6).

By entering Cornelius's house and perhaps eating something presented to him as refreshment after the journey, Peter must explain to his Gentile audience why he differs from other Jews. From infancy, every Jew has been told that being in the house of a Gentile and eating with him constitutes a violation of Jewish law.[31] The Gentiles know this from their association with Jews in business and work. Should Peter now neglect to explain his conduct that goes contrary to all Jewish practice, he would be regarded as insincere and unreliable. Therefore, at the outset Peter addresses himself to this particular point, and he explains his social conduct by informing his listeners about God's revelation to him.

c. "Yet God has shown me not to call any man impure or unclean." When Peter relates that he has come because of a revelation from God and thus at God's command, the Gentiles are satisfied. Peter is the bridge between Jew and Gentile, for he announces that God himself has removed the race barrier (Eph. 2:11–22). As a Jewish Christian, Peter can no longer separate himself from Gentiles and call them "impure and unclean" (v. 14). He informs these Gentiles, who worship God but are not full converts to Judaism, that God accepts them as pure and clean. With this statement, Peter implicitly reveals that God does not require them to submit to circumcision.[32] In the setting of the first century, the Jews apply the words *impure* and *unclean* to the Gentiles in respect not only to food laws but also to circumcision. This issue eventually becomes explicit when the apostles, elders, and the church meet at the Jerusalem Council (see especially 15:1, 7–11).

d. "I came without raising any objection when I was summoned." Because Luke often presents discourses in abridged form, we assume that Peter describes the vision he had in Joppa. On the basis of this vision, Peter is now able to state freely that he has come to the Gentiles without any objections. He knows that his visit to Cornelius and his household is according to God's will.

---

31. Compare Exod. 34:15–16; refer to SB, vol. 4, pt. 1, pp. 352–414.
32. Schürer, *History of the Jewish People*, vol. 3, p. 173.

e. "Why have you summoned me?" From the messengers, Peter has learned that Cornelius wants to hear a message from the apostle. Further, the servants have told Peter about Cornelius's vision some days earlier; but now Peter wants to hear the reason for calling him to Caesarea. He waits for an explanation from Cornelius.

Practical Considerations in 10:23–29

The apostles gave the Christian church the simple truth that God shows no favoritism, for every believer is equal in his presence.[33] In the days of the apostles, the Jews were told to respect the high priest (see 23:1–5). They also paid respect to the teachers of the law and the Pharisees, who enjoyed being called Rabbi (Matt. 23:7). However, Jesus took a different approach and taught his people humility:

> "But you are not to be called Rabbi [my great teacher], for only one is your Teacher and all of you are brothers. And do not call anyone on earth your 'father,' for only one is your Father in heaven. And do not be called 'teachers,' for only one is your Teacher, namely, Christ. He who is the greatest of you shall be your servant." [Matt. 23:8–11]

Certainly, leaders who serve the church well deserve respect and "are worthy of double honor" (I Tim. 5:17). Scripture teaches that we must obey our leaders because of the authority entrusted to them (Heb. 13:17). But the leader ought to set the example of being a servant who obediently listens to Jesus' word: "If anyone wants to be first, he must be the very last, and the servant of all" (Mark 9:35, NIV).

Greek Words, Phrases, and Constructions in 10:23b–29

Verse 23b

ἀναστάς—see the discussion at 5:17.

Verses 24–25

συγκαλεσάμενος—the middle aorist of the participle has the same meaning as the active aorist participle: "he summoned."

ἀναγκαίους—"necessary." This adjective is related to the noun ἀνάγκη (necessity). It has a secondary meaning: "connected by bonds of nature or of friendship."[34] An acceptable translation is "intimate."

τοῦ εἰσελθεῖν—the definite article preceding the aorist infinitive is superfluous.

Verses 27–28

εὑρίσκει—"he finds." Luke's use of the historical present lends vividness to his account.

---

33. E.g., see v. 34; Rom. 2:11; Eph. 6:9; Col. 3:25; James 2:1.
34. Thayer, p. 36.

ὡς—this particle is the equivalent of ὅτι (that).

κἀμοί—formed by combining καί and ἐγώ, the word in this context is adversative: "but to me."

---

b. Explanation
10:30–33

30. Cornelius said, "Four days ago at this hour, at three in the afternoon, I was in my house praying. Suddenly a man in radiant clothes stood before me 31. and said, 'Cornelius, your prayer has been heard and your generous gifts to the poor have been remembered before God.' "

a. "Four days ago." The time has come for Cornelius to explain why he summoned Peter to his home. In a few sentences he relates the incident that happened "four days ago at this hour." Strictly speaking, the time between Cornelius's vision and the moment he addresses Peter is only three days. But in first-century Palestine, the people regarded part of a day as a full day. Hence, the day of Cornelius's vision is the first day; the day of Peter's vision and the arrival of the messengers in Joppa, the second; the day the travelers left Joppa, the third; the day they arrived in Caesarea, the fourth.

b. "At three in the afternoon." We surmise that the men from Joppa arrived about noon on the fourth day, and that they were provided with food and drink and a refreshing bath. When they came together to hear Cornelius answer Peter's question, the time of day was three o'clock. At this hour of the day, Cornelius customarily had his devotional hour.

A literal translation of the Greek gives the interpreter difficulties: "From the fourth day until this hour I was praying at three in my house."[35] In fact, the text becomes unintelligible. Although we have insufficient proof, we suppose that the Greek wording features two idiomatic expressions relating to time; they should not be taken literally but must have their counterparts in our expression of time.[36] "From the fourth day" actually means "four days ago"; and "until this hour" signifies "at this hour."

c. "A man in radiant clothes stood before me." Cornelius describes the angel in human terms. In the New Testament, the writers portray angels as men dressed in white garments that often show a supernatural radiance.[37]

d. "Cornelius, your prayer has been heard." Although Luke does not disclose the content of the prayer, we infer that Cornelius had asked God for spiritual guidance and understanding of his word especially in regard to the messianic prophecies (see v. 4). The angel tells him that God has remembered his generosity to the poor and needy as he helped them with material gifts.

---

35. The KJV and NKJV read, "Four days ago I was fasting until this hour; and at the ninth hour I prayed in my house."

36. Metzger mentions the possibility "that the Greek may be explained as colloquial koine or as Semitized Greek." *Textual Commentary*, p. 376.

37. 1:10; Matt. 28:3; Mark 16:5; Luke 24:4; John 20:12.

32. " 'Send, therefore, to Joppa and invite Simon who is called Peter. He is staying in the house of Simon the tanner by the sea.' **33.** So immediately I sent for you, and you did well in coming. Now, then, we are all here before God to hear everything that you have been instructed by God to tell us."

Luke repeats almost word for word the historical account recorded in verses 5–6. When the messengers come to Peter in Joppa, they report that the angel asked Cornelius to summon Peter because he would have a message for him (v. 22). Luke disregards this additional note in view of the fact that in the present situation Cornelius expects Peter to preach the gospel.[38]

In response to the call of the messengers, Peter has come to Cornelius's house. He hears words of thanks from the lips of his host, for Cornelius commends him by saying, "You did well in coming." He continues and reveals the eager desire of all those present to hear a message from Peter. Cornelius says, "Now, then, we are all here before God to hear everything that you have been instructed by God to tell us."

What an opportunity to preach God's Word! What an audience! What an intense desire to listen to the gospel! What a joy and satisfaction for Peter to proclaim it! Cornelius asserts that this gathering of people has come to hear the Word of God and for that reason everyone in the audience stands in God's sacred presence. That is, God is going to speak to them through the mouth of his servant, the apostle Peter.

Greek Words, Phrases, and Constructions in 10:30 and 33

Verse 30

τὴν ἐνάτην—the accusative case for the reference *the ninth hour* (three in the afternoon) expresses not so much length of time as point of time.[39]

Verse 33

καλῶς ἐποίησας παραγενόμενος—the action of the aorist participle and that of the main verb occurred simultaneously. The first two words of the Greek phrase convey gratitude: "thank you for coming." The expression καλῶς ποιήσεις means "please, will you do [this]."

---

c. Sermon
10:34–43

In the first part of Peter's address (vv. 34–35), he explains God's intention to save people from every nation. Next, he reminds his listeners of

---

38. Numerous ancient manuscripts add, "When he comes, he will speak to you" (NKJV). The words are a reflection of 11:14 and thus may be an expansion of the text.
39. Moule, *Idiom-Book*, p. 34.

God's message in word and deed through Jesus Christ (vv. 36–38). Then, he reveals Christ's death, resurrection, and appearances (vv. 39–41). And last, proclaiming the message of salvation, he calls his audience to faith in Christ and forgiveness of sin (vv. 42–43). While Peter is still preaching, he is interrupted by the coming of the Holy Spirit (v. 44). Nevertheless, his sermon as such is complete.

34. Peter said: "I truly understand that God shows no favoritism."

This is Peter's first address to a Gentile audience.[40] As a representative of the Christian church, he is fully aware of the uniqueness of this situation. He realizes the significance of his vision in Joppa and knows that he is doing God's will. He says, "I truly understand that God shows no favoritism." The Jews of Peter's day lived by the doctrine that God had made a covenant with Abraham and his descendants and that they were God's chosen people. They despised the Gentiles because, according to the Jews, God had rejected the Gentiles and had withheld his blessings from them.

The Jews also knew that God had told Abraham that in him all the nations of the earth would be blessed (Gen. 12:3; 18:18; 22:18; 26:4). So, then, believers of all nations would claim Abraham as their spiritual father. Interestingly, in his sermon at Solomon's Colonnade Peter had quoted the words God had spoken to Abraham: "And through your offspring all the families of the earth will be blessed" (3:25). But at that time, Peter had not fully fathomed the depth of this divine saying. Now, however, Peter sees the fulfillment of God's word to Abraham. The Roman centurion, the members of Cornelius's household, and all his invited relatives and guests receive God's blessing.

Peter appeals to the Scriptures when he says that God shows no favoritism. For instance, Moses tells the Israelites in the desert, "For the LORD your God is God of gods and Lord of lords, the great God, mighty and awesome, who shows no partiality nor takes bribes" (Deut. 10:17, NIV).[41]

God does not look at a person's external appearance, nationality, wealth, social status, and achievements. In the light of God's teaching given in a vision, Peter sets aside his ingrained bias against the Gentiles and, as he states, truthfully accepts the doctrine of God's impartiality. He is convinced that salvation belongs to all nations and not merely to Israel. He knows that his earlier view of God was defective.[42]

> There's a wideness in God's mercy,
> Like the wideness of the sea;

---

40. The Greek literally reads, "Having opened his mouth, Peter said." This is an Aramaic idiom for which translators try to find an equivalent in English. The text conveys the meaning *Peter said.* Compare the translations of 8:35; Matt. 5:2; 13:35.

41. See Job 34:19; Mark 12:14; Rom. 2:11; Gal. 2:6; Eph. 6:9; Col. 3:25; James 2:1; I Peter 1:17.

42. Consult Donald Guthrie, *New Testament Theology* (Downers Grove: Inter-Varsity, 1981), p. 101.

There's a kindness in his justice,
Which is more than liberty.
For the love of God is broader
Than the measure of man's mind;
And the heart of the Eternal
Is most wonderfully kind.
                                        —Frederick W. Faber

35. "But in every nation, the man who fears him and does what is right is accepted by God."

The expression *in every nation* stands first in the sentence for emphasis. God excludes no country on the face of this earth but accepts believers from every nation into the church. God has removed the barrier between the nation Israel and the Gentiles. Nevertheless, God accepts a Gentile only when such a person fears him and obediently does his will. God accepts no sinner on his own merit; everybody, be he Jew or Gentile, must be saved through the atoning work of Jesus Christ. If Cornelius were acceptable on the basis of his own moral purity and personal religiosity, Peter would not have to preach Christ's gospel in the officer's home.[43]

What is the meaning of Peter's remark that God accepts a man who fears God and does what is right? Peter is saying that a person who seeks God and strives to keep his law is, on that account, eager to hear the good news of salvation. In Acts, Luke shows that God-fearers who earnestly do what is right readily place their trust in Jesus. When the apostles preach the gospel to them, they believe (see 16:14–15; 17:4, 12; 18:7–8). God receives people from every race, tribe, or tongue, not on the basis of their reverence for God and their striving after righteousness, but because they put their faith in Jesus. Thus, Peter reminds his audience of their knowledge of the Christ.

36. "You know that the message which proclaims peace through Jesus Christ, that he is Lord of all, was sent to the people of Israel."

a. "You know." Peter intimates that the people in his audience have heard the reports concerning Jesus Christ as the supreme ruler and his message of peace. This message, of course, was proclaimed in Jewish circles and as yet was not made known to Gentiles. The evangelist Philip had preached the Good News in the local synagogues along the Mediterranean coast and perhaps even in Caesarea.

b. "The message which proclaims peace." The Gentiles know that God sent his message of peace through Jesus Christ, for people living in Palestine in those days had heard about Jesus' preaching. Jesus proclaimed the biblical concept of peace, which is not merely an absence of hostility. Peace is a comprehensive concept that refers to the restoration of man's relationship with God (see Isa. 52:7; Rom. 5:1). Peace is evident when man enters

---

43. Alford, *Alford's Greek Testament*, vol. 2, p. 118.

the presence of God and receives his favor and grace. Peace means that God blesses man, shields him from danger and harm, and makes him whole again.[44]

c. "Through Jesus Christ." The proclamation of peace is not limited to Jesus' earthly ministry but extends to all his servants who faithfully preach the gospel of salvation (Eph. 2:17; 6:15). This peace can be obtained only from God through Jesus Christ (compare John 14:6).

d. "He is Lord of all." Peter's message to his Gentile audience is that Jesus is Lord of the Jews and Gentiles (Rom. 10:12). Indeed, Christ's authority extends to everyone and everything (Matt. 28:18). Jesus Christ, therefore, is Lord of Cornelius and his companions.

e. "[The message] was sent to the people of Israel." Literally, the Greek text has "the sons of Israel." As sons, the Jews are the heirs of God's promise to Abraham and his descendants; this promise includes the coming of the Messiah. "These [sons] were the legal heirs of Israel who inherited [Israel's] position and prerogatives in the covenant" (compare 5:21).[45]

The gospel came first to the Jews and then to the Gentiles (Rom. 1:16), yet both are equal in God's sight. Peter stands before the Gentiles to proclaim to them the gospel of peace.

37. "And you know what happened throughout Judea, beginning in Galilee after the baptism that John preached."

Here Peter preaches his gospel message, which Luke records in skeletal form. Actually, Peter provides us with an outline of the oral gospel that seems to correspond with a summary of Mark's Gospel.[46] Hence, Christian leaders of the second century write that Mark served as Peter's interpreter when Mark composed his Gospel. In simple form, Peter tells Cornelius and his friends about the words Jesus spoke and the miracles he performed in Galilee and Judea after Christ's baptism in the River Jordan.

a. "You know what happened throughout Judea." The four Gospels indicate that the news concerning Jesus' words and deeds spread far and wide. People came from everywhere to hear him (see, e.g., Matt. 4:24). With the term *Judea* Luke often refers to the entire land of the Jews, from Galilee in the north to the Negev desert in the south.[47]

Peter can confidently and even emphatically say to his listeners that they are acquainted with the events that occurred in Israel during Jesus' ministry. We imagine that the messengers informed Peter about the spread of the gospel in Caesarea. Thus, Peter is able to assert that his audience knows about Jesus.

---

44. Hartmut Beck and Colin Brown, *NIDNTT*, vol. 2, pp. 776–83; see Werner Foerster, *TDNT*, vol. 2, pp. 406–20.

45. R. C. H. Lenski, *The Interpretation of the Acts of the Apostles* (Columbus: Wartburg, 1944), p. 420.

46. C. H. Dodd, "The Framework of the Gospel Narrative," *ExpT* 43 (1932): 396–400. See his *Apostolic Preaching and Its Developments* (New York and Evanston: Harper and Row, 1964), p. 28.

47. See Luke 1:5; 4:44; 7:17; 23:5; Acts 1:8; 2:9.

b. "Beginning in Galilee after the baptism that John preached." Notice that the ministry of John the Baptist was not unknown to the Gentiles, for Peter merely speaks of "the baptism that John preached" and does not identify the Baptist. Peter mentions John the Baptist to mark the distinction between the Old Testament era and the beginning of New Testament times.[48] He says that Jesus began his work in Galilee, a fact that is evident from the Gospels.[49]

38. "You know about Jesus of Nazareth, how God anointed him with the Holy Spirit and power, and how he went around doing good and healing all who were dominated by the devil, for God was with him."

a. "You know about Jesus of Nazareth." Peter repeats the name of Jesus and unmistakably asserts that his audience is familiar with the name *Jesus of Nazareth*. This is the name by which Jesus was known as he taught the crowds and healed the sick (see Matt. 21:11; John 1:45).

b. "God anointed him with the Holy Spirit and power." Peter presents his gospel account in chronological order, for at the baptism of Jesus the Holy Spirit descended on him like a dove (Matt. 3:16). God anointed Jesus with the Spirit and with power to enable him to fulfill the messianic prophecy (Isa. 61:1; see also Luke 4:18).[50] That is, God equipped Jesus for the special task of preaching and healing. The term *power* points to the work Jesus was able to do through the indwelling Spirit. Jesus withstood Satan, cast out demons, healed the crippled and the sick, cleansed the lepers, raised the dead, and proclaimed the gospel (compare Matt. 11:4–5).

c. "He went around doing good and healing all who were dominated by the devil." Jesus set people free from the bondage of sin, sickness, and Satan (e.g., see Luke 13:16). Wherever Jesus went, he was a benefactor to the people. He reclaimed territory from Satan, so that the devil had to yield his power to Jesus. He liberated all those who were in Satan's power.

d. "God was with him." Luke presents only an outline of Peter's sermon. He intimates that Peter recounted numerous incidents about Jesus' healing ministry. Note also that Peter has not yet spoken of Christ's divinity. Peter recounts only the external manifestations of Jesus' power, which he explains by saying that God was with Jesus. God enabled Jesus to perform miracles and signs, because of the Father's presence in his Son (compare John 10:30, 38; 14:9–10).

39. "And we are witnesses of everything he did both in the land of the Jews and in Jerusalem. They put him to death by hanging him on a tree, 40. but God raised him on the third day. God caused him to be seen, 41. not by everyone but by witnesses who were appointed before-

---

48. Bengel, *Gnomon of the New Testament*, vol. 2, p. 607.

49. Matt. 4:12; Mark 1:14; Luke 4:14; John 1:43; 2:1.

50. Consult W. C. van Unnik, "Jesus the Christ," *NTS* 8 (1962): 113–16; Richard N. Longenecker, *The Christology of Early Jewish Christianity*, Studies in Biblical Theology, 2d series 17 (London: SCM, 1970), pp. 79–80.

hand by God, that is, to us who ate and drank with him after he rose from the dead."

Note these points:

a. *Death*. Peter now acquaints his audience with the part that the immediate followers of Jesus have in proclaiming the Good News. Emphatically he says that he and the rest of the apostles are eyewitnesses of all that Jesus did throughout the land of Israel. By telling his audience that he is an eyewitness, Peter portrays himself as a source of information about Jesus. However, Peter implies that he is only a servant of his Sender and as such is on the same level as any other follower of Jesus.

With the inclusive phrase *in the land of the Jews,* Peter refers to Jesus' entire ministry in Galilee and Judea. He mentions Jerusalem to identify the place where Jesus died on the cross. His reference to Jesus' death by crucifixion is brief; Peter is not interested in casting any blame on the Roman military for executing Jesus. In earlier speeches, he blamed the Jews, not the Romans, for this crime (2:23; 3:15; 4.10; 5:30).

b. *Resurrection*. "God raised him on the third day." Peter proclaims the good news of Jesus' resurrection and thus introduces his apostolic office. With the other apostles, Peter is a witness of the resurrection (1:22). He is a witness to Jesus' entire ministry, but this witness culminates in testifying to his resurrection.[51] Peter has received the task to proclaim the news that Jesus rose from the grave on the third day. He must tell the people that God himself raised Jesus from the dead. Apart from the references in the Gospels, the phrase *on the third day* occurs only here and once in Paul's epistles (I Cor. 15:4).

c. *Appearances*. God gave only a few people the privilege of seeing Jesus after the resurrection. Except for his appearance to the five hundred brothers at one time (I Cor. 15:6), Jesus showed himself exclusively to his immediate followers.[52] These followers must be Jesus' witnesses of his resurrection. Accordingly, the possibility is not remote that Cornelius and his friends had not heard anything about the appearances of Jesus during the forty-day period between his resurrection and ascension. The Jews in the local synagogue in Caesarea were not able to tell Cornelius anything about Jesus' appearances, for they could testify only about his death on the cross.[53]

d. *Proof*. Peter removes any semblance of skepticism about Jesus' resurrection. We know that the apostles met with derision and doubt whenever they taught the resurrection doctrine in first-century society (e.g., 17:32). Peter, however, speaks as an eyewitness and recalls that Jesus often ate and drank with the apostles after he rose from the dead. He undoubtedly recounts that Jesus broke bread with the two men from Emmaus (Luke 24:30), ate a piece of broiled fish in the upper room (Luke 24:42–43), and had breakfast

---

51. Rackham, *Acts*, p. 158.
52. See the commentary on 1:3.
53. Grosheide, *Handelingen der Apostelen*, vol. 1, p. 349.

with seven disciples on the beach of the lake of Galilee (John 21:13). Peter provides absolute proof that Jesus' physical body has been raised from the dead and that the Lord is alive.[54] The comforting assurance Peter proclaims is that the apostles have fellowship with Jesus not only during his earthly life but also after his resurrection (Matt. 28:20).

42. "He commanded us to preach to the people and to testify that Jesus is the one whom God appointed judge of the living and the dead. 43. All the prophets bear witness to him that through his name everyone who believes in him receives forgiveness of sins."

a. *Command.* "He commanded us to preach to the people." Here is the charge that Jesus gave the apostles, namely, to preach in his name the gospel of salvation to all nations (Matt. 28:19; Mark 16:15; Luke 24:47). Notice that Peter employs the Greek word for "people," which until that time referred to the people of Israel; it is an expression used for those who are in God's covenant. But now God has broken down the wall of separation between Jew and Gentile with the result that Gentiles, too, belong to the people of God. And these Gentiles become part of the Christian church; they believe in Jesus Christ but do not have to submit to the rite of circumcision.

Nevertheless, Peter and his Jewish companions from Joppa are amazed when the Gentiles receive the gift of the Holy Spirit (v. 45). They need time to accept that Gentile believers are equal to the Jewish and Samaritan Christians.

Peter informs his audience that Christ gave his apostles a second command: "to testify that Jesus is the one whom God has appointed judge of the living and the dead." That is, the apostles must warn the people that God has set a judgment day and has already appointed Jesus to serve as judge in that day. This is significant because, by having appointed Jesus as judge, God declares that Jesus is equal to himself. Both God the Father and God the Son will judge the people on the judgment day.[55]

In his address before the Athenian philosophers, Paul makes the same assertion: "For God has appointed a day on which he is going to judge the world in righteousness through a man whom he has appointed. He furnished proof to all men by having raised him from the dead" (17:31; and see 24:25).

No person is able to escape judgment, for everyone must appear before God. Peter uses the idiomatic expression *the living and the dead* to indicate that everyone is included when Christ judges the people. Here, then, Peter warns the members of his audience to seek forgiveness of sin through faith

---

54. Jesus' resurrection body was not angelic. A reference to the tradition about angels (Tob. 12:19) highlights the contrast: The archangel Raphael reveals to Tobit and Tobias that all the days Raphael appeared to them he did not eat or drink.

55. Compare Gen. 18:25; Judg. 11:27; John 5:22, 27; 9:39; Rom. 2:16; 14:9–10; II Tim. 4:1; I Peter 4:5.

in Jesus Christ, so that when they appear before the God-appointed judge they may be acquitted.

b. *Commitment.* "Everyone who believes in him receives forgiveness of sins." This is the heart of the gospel: Christ cleanses every sinner who comes to him in faith and repentance. He commits himself to this truth, so that the believer who has been forgiven has nothing to fear in the judgment day. Peter adds that the remission of sins takes place only through Christ's name. The word *name* means more than a title, for it includes the complete revelation of Jesus Christ, especially with reference to his life, works, and words. For whom is the cleansing from sin through the name of Christ? Peter says that it is for everyone who believes. He places no restrictions and limitations: both Jew and Gentile receive remission of sin. Everyone, then, who continues to put his faith and trust in him belongs to Jesus. The converse is also true; that is, everyone who refuses to believe in Jesus will face him as judge on the judgment day. Then he will hear his sentence of condemnation for his refusal to accept the offer of salvation.

Peter bases his announcement of Christ's cleansing work on the Old Testament Scriptures. He refrains from giving chapter and verse but asserts that "all the prophets bear witness to [Christ]" and have spoken about his forgiving love.[56] He tells Cornelius that the knowledge the centurion has gathered from the Scriptures in the synagogue worship services is true. The prophets indeed testify to the person and work of the Christ, who had fulfilled the messianic promises.

Doctrinal Considerations in 10:34–43

Luke records how Peter presents the gospel of Christ to a Gentile audience. In doing so, Peter displays skill in removing possible misunderstandings. He announces the good news of salvation and traces the history of Jesus' life, death, and resurrection. He also reveals his role as an eyewitness who has been told to proclaim the gospel. And last, by referring to the Old Testament Scriptures, he calls the people to repentance and faith.

Pastors, evangelists, and missionaries who preach the gospel from week to week must know their audience to be effective in their ministry. In their sermons, they should begin by establishing rapport with their listeners. When they have their attention, they must minister to the people by reading and explaining God's Word. In every sermon they must point to Jesus Christ as the author and perfecter of faith. In the conclusion of their preaching, they should call the worshipers to faith in Christ and exhort them to repent of sin. They should tell them that continuance in sin ends in perdition, but forgiveness of sin ends in eternal life.

---

56. Isa. 33:24; 53:5–6, 10–11; Jer. 31:34; 33:8; 50:20.

Greek Words, Phrases, and Constructions in 10:34–43

Verse 34

ἐπ' ἀληθείας—this phrase is Luke's rendering of the Aramaic expression in transliterated form (ἀμήν, ἀμήν), which occurs twenty-five times in John's Gospel. It introduces a solemn statement.

προσωπολήμπτης—the compound form from πρόσωπον (face) and λαμβάνω (I receive, accept) occurs once in the New Testament.

Verses 36–38

Translators differ in their approach to rendering a smooth translation for the unusually harsh and disjointed syntax of these verses. Some take ὁ θεός (v. 34) as the controlling subject of verse 36 and delete the relative pronoun ὅν (which). I have taken the verb οἴδατε (you know) as the main verb for verses 36, 37, and 38, and thus I incorporate the relative pronoun in the construction of the sentence. Nevertheless, the nominative case of ἀρξάμενος (v. 37) and the accusative case of Ἰησοῦν (v. 38) remain problematic.[57]

Verse 38

πνεύματι and δυνάμει—these two datives express the means with which Jesus was anointed.

διῆλθεν—from διέρχομαι (I go through), this aorist is constative because it encompasses the action of the verb in its entirety.[58]

Verse 39

κρεμάσαντες—see the explanation of 5:30. The tense of the aorist active participle coincides with that of the main verb.[59]

Verse 41

ἡμῖν—the dative of the personal pronoun is in apposition to μάρτυσιν (witnesses) and is emphatic.

οἵτινες—this indefinite relative pronoun has a casual connotation. At the end of this verse, the Western manuscripts expand the text by adding the italicized words: "who ate and drank with him *and accompanied (him)*, after he rose from the dead, *for forty days.*"[60]

---

57. For another approach see F. Neirynck, "Acts 10, 36a *ton logon*," *EphThL* 60 (1984): 118–23; and Bengel, *Gnomon of the New Testament*, vol. 2, p. 606. Consult Harald Riesenfeld, "The Text of Acts 10:36," in *Text and Interpretation: Studies in the New Testament Presented to Matthew Black*, ed. E. Best and R. McL. Wilson (Cambridge: Cambridge University Press, 1979), pp. 191–94.

58. H. E. Dana and Julius R. Mantey, *A Manual Grammar of the Greek New Testament* (1927; New York: Macmillan, 1967), p. 196.

59. Robertson, *Grammar*, p. 1113.

60. Metzger, *Textual Commentary*, p. 381.

Verse 42

τῷ λαῷ—in the preceding verse, this expression refers to the Jews; here it refers to the Gentiles.

οὗτος—a number of important manuscripts have the reading αὐτός (he). On the basis of external evidence, the choice is difficult.

ὡρισμένος—the perfect passive participle from ὁρίζω (I appoint) shows action that began in the past and continues through the present into the future.

Verse 43

Note the tenses in this verse: μαρτυροῦσιν (they testify) is the durative present; λαβεῖν (to receive) is the constative aorist; and πιστεύοντα (is believing) is the present active participle that denotes continued action.

---

d. Response
10:44–48

The Holy Spirit was poured out in Jerusalem on the Jews (2:1–4), in Samaria on the Samaritans (8:15–17), and in Caesarea on the Gentiles (10:44–46). The circle of the Christian church expanded with every additional group, so that the mandate given to the apostles at Jesus' ascension might be fulfilled (1:8).

44. While Peter was still speaking these words, the Holy Spirit fell upon all who were hearing the message.

Peter is not yet finished with his sermon when he is interrupted by the outpouring of the Holy Spirit. To be sure, Peter himself explains to the church in Jerusalem what happened. He says, "As I began to speak the Holy Spirit fell on them just as he fell upon us at the beginning" (11:15). Peter had experienced the outpouring in Jerusalem on the day of Pentecost. At that time, the apostles and those with them heard a noise as it were of a violent wind, saw tongues of fire on their heads and, filled with the Holy Spirit, "began to speak with other tongues" (2:4).

In the house of Cornelius, Peter once more observes the outpouring of the Holy Spirit. But now the Spirit descends on Gentiles and thereby indicates that the Gentiles are part of the church and on equal footing with the Jewish Christians.

The Holy Spirit comes to the Gentiles before they are baptized. If any of the Jewish Christians who accompany Peter to Caesarea were to raise the question whether the Gentiles should be baptized before they received the Holy Spirit, the Spirit's sudden coming prevents that question. Further, the coming of the Spirit makes the rite of circumcision obsolete,[61] a rite which indeed the Jerusalem Council later abolishes (15:8–11).

Peter preaches the word to the Gentiles, who hardly have time to respond to the gospel. Suddenly God sends his Spirit as a sign that God

---

61. Bengel, *Gnomon of the New Testament*, vol. 2, p. 609.

accepts those Gentile believers as his people. Notice that the Holy Spirit descends on Cornelius, his household, and his invited guests but not on the six Jewish Christians who accompanied Peter (see v. 46). Thus, God demonstrates that he is ushering in a new phase in the development of the Christian church.

45. And all the circumcised believers who had come with Peter were amazed that the gift of the Holy Spirit had been poured out on the Gentiles also. 46a. For they heard them speaking in tongues and praising God.

Although Jesus had commanded the apostles to preach the gospel to all the nations, Peter's associates nevertheless are astonished when God accepts the Gentiles by giving them the gift of his Spirit. Because this outpouring of the Holy Spirit is identical to the Pentecost experience in Jerusalem, the Jewish believers now see that Gentiles and Jews are equal in God's sight.[62] And even though Peter himself began his sermon by saying that God does not show favoritism (see vv. 34–35), Peter's friends are amazed that God himself verifies this truth by pouring out his Spirit on the Gentile believers. At that moment, Peter remembers the saying of Jesus, "John baptized with water, but you will be baptized with the Holy Spirit" (11:16, NIV; see also 1:5; Matt. 3:11; Mark 1:8; Luke 3:16).

The six members of the delegation from Joppa (11:12) hear the Gentiles speaking in tongues and praising God. They see the evident signs of the outpouring of the Holy Spirit (compare 2:4, 11; 19:6). Luke does not explain the manner of this speaking in tongues; he only records Peter's report to the church in Jerusalem. Peter relates that the Spirit came on the Gentiles exactly as he did on the apostles at Pentecost (11:15) and that God gave the Gentiles the same gift he gave the Jews (11:17). The only difference between Luke's Pentecost account and his narrative about the Caesarean Gentiles is the word *other*. That is, in Jerusalem the apostles spoke in other tongues (languages), but Cornelius and his friends were "speaking in tongues." Luke fails to explain whether the Gentiles expressed themselves in known languages or in ecstatic speech. We are unable to ascertain the precise meaning of the term *tongue speaking* in this text and in 19:6.[63] Indeed, the difficulty with which we wrestle lies in the extreme rarity of this expression in New Testament writings.

With the use of verb tenses in the Greek, Luke indicates that the outburst of joy and happiness took time. The Jewish Christians continued to listen as the Gentiles were raising their voices in praise to God (see 13:48). Luke

---

62. Compare 11:1, 18; 13:48; 14:27; 15:7, 12.

63. "Aside from its occurrences in Acts and I Corinthians the only instances . . . which are earlier in date than the fourth century are found in Mark 16:17 and in Irenaeus, *Against Heresies* (V vi I)." Stuart D. Curric, "Speaking in Tongues: Early Evidence Outside the New Testament Bearing on *Glossais Lalein,*" *Interp* 19 (1965): 277. Also published in *Speaking in Tongues: A Guide to Research in Glossolalia,* ed. Watson E. Mills (Grand Rapids: Eerdmans, 1986).

seems to suggest that the Jews heard the Gentiles speak in tongues but that they did not need interpreters to understand the spoken words.[64]

46b. Then Peter said, 47. "Can anyone prevent these people from being baptized with water? Because they have received the Holy Spirit as we have." 48. So he ordered that they be baptized in the name of Jesus Christ. Then they asked him to remain with them a few days.

When Peter has heard the Gentiles speaking and singing praise to God, he knows that no one is able to prevent them from being baptized and seeking membership in the church. He asks a rhetorical question that demands a negative answer. In other words, no Jewish or Samaritan Christian is able to bar the Gentile Christians from full-fledged membership in the church. The saying "Can anyone prevent these people from being baptized with water?" perhaps is a formulaic question uttered at the time of baptism. The Ethiopian eunuch asked Philip a similar question before being baptized (8:36).

When Peter and John came to Samaria, they prayed that the Samaritans might receive the Holy Spirit. Afterward they placed their hands on the Samaritans, who then received the Spirit (8:15–17). But in Caesarea, God interrupts Peter's sermon by causing the Spirit to fall on the Gentiles. After Cornelius and his household have completed their praise to God, Peter asks whether there are any objections to baptism. We conclude that the reversal in the sequence of baptism and the descent of the Spirit reveals God's sovereign pleasure.

Peter, as the Greek text implies, orders the six Jewish Christians to baptize the Gentile converts. In Samaria, not the apostles but Philip baptized the people. Paul, writing to the Corinthians, states that he did not baptize any believers in Corinth except Crispus, Gaius, and the household of Stephanas (I Cor. 1:14, 16; and compare John 4:2). Paul even writes that he does not want his name to be associated with baptism (I Cor. 1:15). The apostles, then, place the emphasis not on themselves but on the name of Jesus; thus, Peter instructs his companions to baptize the Gentiles in the name of Jesus Christ. He follows the common baptismal procedure of that day (2:38; 8:16; 19:5).

The name *Jesus Christ* signifies the full revelation of everything Jesus did and said. Further, it denotes all that the Scriptures disclose about the coming, the office, and the function of the Messiah. Accordingly, when in apostolic times a believer was baptized in the name of Jesus Christ, he declared that as a baptismal candidate he completely identified with this name.[65]

Cornelius and his friends invite Peter to stay with them in Caesarea for a few days. They ask numerous questions and desire instruction in

---

64. Anthony A. Hoekema, *Holy Spirit Baptism* (Grand Rapids: Eerdmans, 1972), pp. 48–49.
65. Leon Morris, *New Testament Theology* (Grand Rapids: Zondervan, Academie Books, 1986), p. 166.

the Christian faith. Luke implies that Peter's travel companions also remain in Caesarea and later accompany Peter to Jerusalem. He explicitly states that they were in Jerusalem (11:12) when Peter reported to the church there. By staying in Gentile homes, Peter and his Jewish friends demonstrate that they fully accept their hosts as equal members of the Christian church. And thus their presence in these homes strengthens the Gentile believers.[66]

Practical Considerations in 10:44–48

"When in Rome, do as the Romans do." This proverbial saying is applicable especially to the men and women who preach and teach the gospel in countries and cultures other than their own. They must not only learn the language so that they are able to communicate fluently and be worthy ambassadors of Jesus Christ. They should also submerge themselves completely in the culture in which they live and work. That is, they are obligated to identify as much as possible with the people to whom they minister. Their message ought to be clear and forthright: to tell the people to repent from sin and evil and to turn in faith to Jesus Christ. E. T. Cassel cogently formulated this thought in the words of a hymn:

This is the King's command:
that all men, everywhere,
Repent and turn away
from sin's seductive snare;
That all who will obey,
with him shall reign for aye—
And that's my business for my King.

This is the message that I bring,
A message angels fain would sing:
"O be ye reconciled,"
thus saith my Lord and King,
"O be ye reconciled to God."

Greek Words, Phrases, and Constructions in 10:44–48

Verse 44

λαλοῦντος—with the name *Peter* in the genitive case, this present active participle forms the genitive absolute construction.

τὸ πνεῦμα τὸ ἅγιον—the two definite articles make plain that this is the Holy Spirit (in distinction from a spirit) and refer to his outpouring on the Gentiles.[67]

---

66. Peter was wrong when later he refused to eat with Gentile Christians in Antioch. Paul, therefore, openly rebuked Peter for his erring behavior (Gal. 2:11–14).

67. Friedrich Blass and Albert Debrunner, *A Greek Grammar of the New Testament and Other Early Christian Literature,* trans. and rev. Robert Funk (Chicago: University of Chicago Press, 1961), #257.2.

Verse 45

ἐκ—the preposition describes the party of the Jewish Christians, who stressed the rite of circumcision.

ὅτι καί—translators are divided whether to take ὅτι as causal ("because") or as the conjunction *that*. The conjunction καί is either ascensive or adjunctive and is translated "even" or "also."

δωρεὰ τοῦ ἁγίου πνεύματος—see the comment on 2:38.

ἐκκέχυται—this perfect passive form from the verb ἐκχέω (I pour out) is translated in the pluperfect tense due to the past tense of the main verb ("they were amazed").

Verse 47

μήτι—the interrogative particle introduces a rhetorical question that expects a negative reply. The negative particle μή before the infinitive *to be baptized* is redundant because of the verb *to prevent*.

οἵτινες—this indefinite relative pronoun has a causal sense. See verse 41.

Verse 48

All the tenses in this verse are in the aorist and signify single occurrence. The aorist infinitive βαπτισθῆναι implies that Jewish Christians officiated at the baptismal ceremony.

Summary of Chapter 10

Cornelius, who serves as centurion in the Italian Regiment stationed in Caesarea, is a devout God-fearer. He supports the poor materially and spends much time in prayer. At one of his prayer sessions, an angel appears to him and instructs him to summon Simon Peter from Joppa. Cornelius dispatches two trusted servants and a devout soldier to Joppa to request that Peter come to Caesarea.

In Joppa, Peter spends time on the flat roof of the house where he is staying. As he prays, he falls into a trance and in a vision sees a large sheet filled with all kinds of animals coming down from heaven. Peter hears a voice telling him to kill and eat. He objects, saying that he has never eaten anything unclean. But the voice informs him that God has removed the distinction between clean and unclean. Three times this happens, and while Peter puzzles over the meaning of his vision, the messengers from Caesarea arrive. They invite Peter to come to the house of Cornelius.

Two days later, Peter and his fellow travelers enter Caesarea, where Cornelius welcomes them. A large circle of Cornelius's friends awaits Peter. He explains that God has told him that he should not call anybody unclean; that is, Peter should accompany the messengers. Cornelius relates the visit and the message of the angel. Then Peter preaches the Good News to his Gentile audience. Suddenly the Holy Spirit descends on the Gentiles, which amazes the Jewish Christians. The Gentiles speak in tongues, glorify God, and are baptized. Peter stays with them for a few days.

11

The Church in Palestine, *part 4*

11:1–18

and The Church in Transition, *part 1*

11:19–30

Outline (continued)

11:1–18	6. Peter's Explanation
11:1–3	a. Critique
11:4–10	b. Vision
11:11–14	c. Visit
11:15–18	d. Conclusion
11:19–13:3	IV. The Church in Transition
11:19–30	A. Ministry of Barnabas
11:19–21	1. Spread of the Gospel
11:22–24	2. Mission of Barnabas
11:25–26	3. Christians in Antioch
11:27–30	4. Prediction and Fulfillment

11

1 The apostles and brothers throughout Judea heard that the Gentiles also had received the word of God. 2 And when Peter went up to Jerusalem, those who were circumcised took issue with him. 3 They said, "You entered a house of uncircumcised men and ate with them."

4 Peter began to explain to them point by point what had happened. He said: 5 "I was in the city of Joppa praying, and in a trance saw a vision. I saw a certain object like a great sheet being lowered by four corners from heaven and it came down to me. 6 I looked intently to observe what was in it and I saw four-footed animals of the earth, wild beasts, reptiles, and birds of the air. 7 Then I heard a voice saying to me, 'Get up, Peter. Kill and eat.' 8 But I said, 'Certainly not, Lord. Nothing impure and unclean has ever entered my mouth.' 9 The voice from heaven spoke a second time, 'Do not consider unclean what God has made clean.' 10 This happened three times and then the whole thing was pulled up to heaven.

11 "Immediately three men who had been sent to me from Caesarea stood at the house in which we were staying. 12 The Spirit told me to have no qualms about going with them. These six brothers also went with me, and we entered the man's house. 13 He reported to us how he had seen an angel standing in his house and saying, 'Send to Joppa for Simon called Peter, 14 who will speak words by which you and all your household will be saved.'

15 "As I began to speak, the Holy Spirit fell on them just as he fell upon us at the beginning. 16 Then I remembered the word of the Lord, how he used to say, 'John baptized with water, but you will be baptized with the Holy Spirit.' 17 If then God gave them the same gift as he gave us who believed in the Lord Jesus Christ, who was I that I could stand in God's way?"

18 When they heard these things, they quieted down and glorified God, saying, "Then also to the Gentiles God has granted repentance that leads to life."

---

6. Peter's Explanation
11:1–18

In numerous places throughout Acts, Luke provides only a few details of the historical accounts he records. We receive the impression that because of the vast history of the Christian church, Luke is forced to be selective and concise. However, when he records Peter's visit to Cornelius, Luke is purposely elaborate. He devotes about one and a half chapters (10:1–11:18) to this incident. As a Gentile Christian, he attaches considerable importance to the entrance of Gentiles into the church.

When Peter arrives in Jerusalem, the Jewish Christians demand an explanation concerning his visit to the Gentiles. Peter has to inform the Jerusalem church that God himself has opened the way for the Gentiles to be members of the church. When the Samaritans entered the church, the Jewish Christians in Jerusalem had no objections. But now that Gentiles turn to Christ in faith, Peter has to tell the Jerusalem church that God has accepted them.

In his account, Luke refrains from giving any indication when Peter traveled to Caesarea. Let us assume, however, that Peter's visit took place near the end of the fourth decade or even the beginning of the fifth (A.D. 39–41). We know that in those years the political situation in Jerusalem was tense. Emperor Caligula, whose insanity had caused untold turmoil and death,[1] had decreed that a statue of the emperor be placed in the Jerusalem temple. Caligula had issued this decree after he received a Jewish delegation that wished to explain why the Jews in Alexandria, Egypt, had no altar to Caesar. At this meeting, Caligula was offended by the Jews and became angry with them. Josephus reports:

> Indignant at being so slighted by the Jews alone, Gaius dispatched Petronius [Governor of Syria, A.D. 39–42] as his legate to Syria to succeed Vitellius in this office. His orders were to lead a large force into Judaea and, if the Jews consented to receive him, to set up an image of Gaius in the temple of God. If, however, they were obstinate, he was to subdue them by force of arms and so set it up.[2]

When Petronius eventually came to Tiberias, located along the shore of Lake Galilee, tens of thousands of Jews met him and persuaded him not to erect the emperor's statue in Jerusalem. Risking his own life, Petronius wrote to Caligula and asked him to rescind the order. Shortly afterward, the emperor died at the hands of assassins (A.D. 41) and the calamity that threatened the Jews was averted.

If we are correct in assuming that Peter's visit to Caesarea occurred at the time of Caligula's decree, we can imagine that the Jews in Jerusalem took exception to Peter visiting a Roman military officer. In any case, relations between the Jews and the Romans were tense.

a. Critique
11:1–3

1. The apostles and brothers throughout Judea heard that the Gentiles also had received the word of God.

The Jewish Christians living in Caesarea had heard that Peter and six Jews from Joppa had entered the house of Cornelius and had stayed with him for some time. They relayed this news to the Jews in Judea and especially in Jerusalem. Moreover, they reported that Gentiles in Caesarea had received God's word and had put their faith in Jesus Christ.

Luke first mentions the apostles and then adds the word *brothers*, which in New Testament usage means "fellow believers." The apostles consulted the

---

1. Refer to Suetonius *Gaius Caligula*, in *The Lives of the Caesars*, trans. John C. Rolfe, 2 vols., vol. 1, bk. 4, pp. 403–97 (LCL).
2. Josephus *Antiquities* 18.8.2 [261]; *War* 2.10.1 [184–87].

members of the church and sought to understand the news they had heard. They knew that the Gentiles had become Christians, for the expression *word of God* was synonymous with the apostolic preaching of the gospel.[3] This preaching was rooted in the history of Jesus Christ (10:36–43).

Suddenly the Jewish Christians had to face a new phase in the development of the church: the entrance of Gentiles into membership. No longer did the Jews have a monopoly on God's grace, for God had also invited the Gentiles to be full participants in his grace. Although the Jews had heard the news of this recent development, they lacked detailed information and at the same time were unwilling to adjust to the unavoidable changes that were occurring in the church. They demanded an explanation from Peter.

2. And when Peter went up to Jerusalem, those who were circumcised took issue with him. 3. They said, "You entered a house of uncircumcised men and ate with them."

Soon after leaving Caesarea, Peter returns to Jerusalem, where he has to report to the apostles and the church about his visit to the house of Cornelius. Incidentally, some Western manuscripts (Greek, Latin, Syriac, and Coptic) have an expanded text which indicates that Peter spent considerable time on his way to Jerusalem.[4] We are unable to say how long Peter took to reach the city; we know, however, that when he arrived he faced "those who were circumcised."

Some commentators interpret the phrase *those who were circumcised* to refer to a separate Jewish party in the Christian church.[5] Others are of the opinion that the phrase refers to people of Jewish birth (see NEB). They say that "there is no suggestion that there was a definite 'party' in the church at this stage, especially before the issue of circumcision had arisen in such a way as to lead to people taking sides on it."[6]

Peter himself had expressed his aversion to entering the home of a Gentile until God told him to do so (10:28). Thus, in general we can say that every Jew who avoided social contact with Gentiles belonged to "those who were circumcised." But Luke has in mind Jewish Christians, not all the Jews in Israel and in the dispersion. He uses the same phrase to describe the six Jewish Christians who accompanied Peter (10:45). Further, as a Gentile Christian himself, Luke views the entire Jerusalem church of that time as circumcised Christians. He points out that all the Jewish Christians in Jerusalem and Judea at the time of Peter's visit were opposed to accepting

---

3. See 4:29, 31; 6:2, 7; 8:14; 13:5, 7, 44, 46, 48; 16:32; 17:13; 18:11. Bertold Klappert, *NIDNTT*, vol. 3, p. 1113.

4. Bruce M. Metzger, *A Textual Commentary on the Greek New Testament*, 3d corrected ed. (London and New York: United Bible Societies, 1975), pp. 382–83.

5. E.g., R. C. H. Lenski, *The Interpretation of the Acts of the Apostles* (Columbus: Wartburg, 1944), p. 438.

6. I. Howard Marshall, *The Acts of the Apostles: An Introduction and Commentary*, Tyndale New Testament Commentary series (Leicester: Inter-Varsity; Grand Rapids: Eerdmans, 1980), p. 195.

Gentile Christians into the church.[7] He introduces the party of the Judaizers (15:5) in a later setting, but not at this time.

The objection of the church members is that Peter entered the home of Gentiles and ate with them. The Jews avoided visiting Gentiles (see John 18:28) for fear of becoming ceremonially unclean. And they refused table fellowship with Gentiles because they were commanded not to eat anything unclean. This strict law of separation compelled them to reject contacts with Gentiles; pressure from fellow Jews who were not members of the Christian church also was a decisive factor.

Jews would travel on land and sea to win converts to their faith, as Jesus remarked (Matt. 23:15), but they scrupulously avoided contamination by eating only kosher foods. Note that the Jewish Christians in Jerusalem, even though they have heard that the Gentiles accepted Christ's gospel, do not question Peter's evangelistic mission to the Gentiles. They do not inquire about faith in Christ or baptism; they probe Peter's reasons for entering a Gentile home and eating unclean food.

Greek Words, Phrases, and Constructions in 11:1–3

Verse 1

κατά—in context this preposition means "in." See 13:1; 15:23; 24:12; Heb. 11:13.[8]

τὰ ἔθνη—normally the neuter plural noun is the subject of a verb in the singular. Here it occurs in the plural. Despite the textual variant, the plural ἐδέξαντο (they received) is preferred.

Verse 2

διεκρίνοντο—this is the imperfect middle of the compound verb διακρίνομαι (I dispute) and has an ingressive sense: "they began to dispute."[9]

περιτομῆς—the lack of the definite article generalizes the phrase in which this noun appears. Therefore, without the definite article, the phrase hardly refers to a party.

Verse 3

ὅτι—some translators understand ὅτι as an interrogative (RSV, JB). It can mean "Why did you enter . . . ?" This conjunction, then, has the meaning *why*, which occurs also in Mark 2:16; 9:11, 28. However, most translators favor the recitative use, which introduces direct speech.[10]

---

7. Refer to F. W. Grosheide, *De Handelingen der Apostelen,* Kommentaar op het Nieuwe Testament series, 2 vols. (Amsterdam: Van Bottenburg, 1942), vol. 1, p. 360.

8. H. E. Dana and Julius R. Mantey, *A Manual Grammar of the Greek New Testament* (1927; New York: Macmillan, 1957), p. 107.

9. A. T. Robertson, *A Grammar of the Greek New Testament in the Light of Historical Research* (Nashville: Broadman, 1934), p. 885.

10. C. F. D. Moule, *An Idiom-Book of New Testament Greek,* 2d ed. (Cambridge: Cambridge University Press, 1960), p. 132.

b. *Vision*
11:4–10

Luke has a penchant for recounting the same incident more than once (compare 9:1–19; 22:3–16; 26:9–18).[11] Here he repeats the story of Peter's vision and his visit to Caesarea. Even though he omits some details, he adds others to stress certain points in the incident. Nevertheless, in many verses the accounts are identical.

4. Peter began to explain to them point by point what had happened. He said: 5. "I was in the city of Joppa praying, and in a trance saw a vision. I saw a certain object like a great sheet being lowered by four corners from heaven and it came down to me."

In his defense, Peter refrains from citing relevant passages from the Old Testament and pertinent sayings of Jesus. Instead he recounts his personal history and begins from the time of his vision in Joppa. He is completely at ease, for he knows that God himself has told him, through a vision, to proclaim Christ's gospel to the Gentiles.

Obviously, Luke presents an abbreviated version of Peter's experience, because he omits references to Peter being on the roof at noon and being hungry while a meal was being prepared. He relates Peter's explanation that, while he was praying, God gave him a vision of a large sheet held by its four corners and descending toward him.

6. "I looked intently to observe what was in it and I saw four-footed animals of the earth, wild beasts, reptiles, and birds of the air. 7. Then I heard a voice saying to me, 'Get up, Peter. Kill and eat.' 8. But I said, 'Certainly not, Lord. Nothing impure and unclean has ever entered my mouth.' 9. The voice from heaven spoke a second time, 'Do not consider unclean what God has made clean.' 10. This happened three times and then the whole thing was pulled up to heaven."

Peter reports the vision in the first person singular to give the audience a vivid description of what he saw. He stresses that he intently observed the contents of the large sheet: the living creatures of this earth (he adds a specific reference to wild animals), reptiles, and birds of the air (compare Ps. 148:10).

As a Jew, Peter avoids using the name *God* and thus recalls that a voice from heaven told him to get up, to kill, and to eat. Further, he implies that the sheet contained clean and unclean animals; this fact relates directly to his Jewish refusal to eat something unclean. Adhering to the Old Testament laws, Peter objects to defiling himself. But the heavenly voice reveals that he should not consider unclean anything that God has made clean. In

---

11. Luke refers four times to Cornelius (10:3–6, 22, 30–32; 11:13), four times to Peter's stay with Simon the tanner (9:43; 10:6, 17, 32), and twice to Peter's vision in Joppa (10:9–16; 11:5–10).

other words, God removed the distinction between clean and unclean animals. After God had spoken three times in succession, the sheet was pulled back to heaven and the vision ended. Obviously, the purpose of the vision was to prepare Peter for his mission to Caesarea.

Greek Words, Phrases, and Constructions in 11:6

ἀτενίσας—this aorist active participle from the verb ἀτενίζω (I look intently at) is followed by the imperfect active κατενόουν (I was observing) and the aorist active εἶδον (I saw). The use of the verb tenses in this verse is significant.

---

c. Visit
11:11–14

Next, Peter describes his visit to the house of Cornelius. This man is the first Gentile convert to the Christian faith, yet Peter neglects to mention his name in his report. Peter simply calls him "the man" (v. 12), and perhaps purposely excludes any reference to Cornelius's military status.

11. "Immediately three men who had been sent to me from Caesarea stood at the house in which we were staying. 12. The Spirit told me to have no qualms about going with them. These six brothers also went with me, and we entered the man's house. 13. He reported to us how he had seen an angel standing in his house and saying, 'Send to Joppa for Simon called Peter, 14. who will speak words by which you and all your household will be saved.' "

Peter reveals to his audience that immediately after he had seen the vision, three men from Caesarea came to the house where he and some companions were staying. Even though he does not disclose that these visitors were Gentiles, his listeners knew that Gentiles invited him to come to Caesarea. Notice that Peter informs the members of his audience that God instructed him to visit the household of Cornelius. That is, Peter did not of his own accord decide to go to the Gentiles. On the contrary, first in a vision and then by speaking to him through the Holy Spirit, God told Peter to accept the invitation. Peter correctly places the emphasis on God and not on himself.

We learn that the six Jewish Christians who went with Peter to Caesarea are now in Jerusalem to verify Peter's report. Peter confirms that he and his six Jewish companions entered the house of a Gentile and stayed there for some days.

Peter reports that an angel instructed this Gentile to send messengers to Peter and to invite him to the man's house. Note that Luke presents a version of the angelic message that varies from the report in the preceding chapter (10:4–6, 31–32). The angel promised salvation to Cornelius and all his household. The term *household* includes all the members of Cornelius's family, his servants, and even his soldiers (16:15, 31–34; 18:8; see John

4:53; I Cor. 1:11, 16). Moreover, when the angel promised Cornelius and all his household salvation, he implicitly referred to the author of salvation, Jesus Christ. Although Cornelius received religious instruction in the synagogue and worshiped God in private devotions at home, he had not yet received the gift of salvation. Only through faith in Jesus Christ would he and the members of his household be granted this gift.

Greek Words, Phrases, and Constructions in 11:11–14

Verse 11

ἦμεν—some manuscripts have the singular ἤμην (I was) instead of the plural ἦμεν (we were). The plural form is the more difficult reading and therefore preferred.

Verses 13–14

τὸν ἄγγελον—although the flow of the story demands the deletion of the definite article, its presence nevertheless appears to be original. Scribes would be more inclined to delete the article than to add it.

σωθήσῃ σύ—note the emphatic use of the personal pronoun in the second person to strengthen the future passive verb in the second person singular.

---

d. Conclusion
11:15–18

Peter declares that he visited the Gentiles because God was giving them the gift of salvation. He confesses that he ought not to interfere when God is giving presents to whomever he pleases. Thus Peter directs the attention of the audience to God. He points out that when God pours out his Spirit on the Gentiles, as he did on the Jews at Pentecost, Gentiles and Jews become equals in the Christian church.

15. "As I began to speak, the Holy Spirit fell on them just as he fell upon us at the beginning. 16. Then I remembered the word of the Lord, how he used to say, 'John baptized with water, but you will be baptized with the Holy Spirit.' 17. If then God gave them the same gift as he gave us who believed in the Lord Jesus Christ, who was I that I could stand in God's way?"

The words *as I began to speak* should not be taken literally but rather figuratively. What Peter intends to convey is that he had only begun to preach an outline of Christ's gospel and that in the succeeding days of his visit he continued to explain the way of salvation to his Gentile audience. Hence, at the outset of his stay the Holy Spirit descended upon Cornelius and his household. The outpouring of the Spirit on the Jews in Jerusalem was a major event in the history of the church. Now Peter explains that the Gentiles also have received the gift of the Spirit. Accordingly, the Christian church now consists of Jews, Samaritans, and Gentiles.

At this point in his story, Peter introduces a word spoken by Jesus: "John baptized with water, but you will be baptized with the Holy Spirit" (1:5; Mark 1:8). The verb *remembered* is interesting because Jesus told his disciples that he would send the Holy Spirit to help them remember everything that Jesus had said to them (John 14:26). When the Holy Spirit came upon the Gentiles, he caused Peter to remember Jesus' words concerning the baptism of the Holy Spirit.

The conclusion Peter draws from this historical incident is that God is sovereign in granting salvation to Jews and Gentiles. When God places the Gentile Christians on the same level as the Jewish Christians, and both Jew and Gentile believe in the Lord Jesus Christ, Peter is unable to entertain even the thought of denying the Gentiles entrance into the church. Peter asks the pertinent question, "Who was I that I could stand in God's way?" To ask the question is to answer it. Peter says nothing about circumcision. He and the members of the Jerusalem church see the hand of God in the development of the church. The Jerusalem church is unwilling to oppose God's work among the Gentiles.

18. When they heard these things, they quieted down and glorified God, saying, "Then also to the Gentiles God has granted repentance that leads to life."

When age-old patterns of conduct suddenly become obsolete and have to yield to a new way of life, the people who are intimately affected by this change must adapt. The Jerusalem church accepted Peter's explanation of his visit to Caesarea and recognized God's sovereignty in granting salvation to the Gentiles. Nevertheless, the greater part of a decade passed before the Jerusalem Council met to lay down the basic requirements which the Gentiles had to follow (15:20, 28–29).

The people who listened to Peter's explanation are satisfied and have no further objections to permitting the Gentiles to enter the church. They acknowledge that God himself had instructed Peter to go to Caesarea, and consequently they are praising God for his mercy and grace. In a sense, the believers in Jerusalem have raised the same objections Peter had when in a vision God told him to eat unclean food. But as God assured Peter that he had made all things clean, so he makes the people in Jerusalem understand that he has accepted the Gentiles and has granted them the gift of salvation.

Praising God, the Jewish Christians in Jerusalem conclude, "Then also to the Gentiles God has granted repentance that leads to life." The Jerusalem church accepts the Gentiles on the twofold basis of God's gift of the Spirit to the Gentiles and their repentance. These two facts present sufficient evidence that the Christian church (in distinction from Judaism) depends not on legalistic observances but on divine guidance.[12]

At the conclusion of his Pentecost sermon, Peter exhorted his audience to repent of their sins (2:38). In his sermon at Solomon's Colonnade, deliv-

---

12. Donald Guthrie, *New Testament Theology* (Downers Grove: Inter-Varsity, 1981), p. 686.

ered after he healed the cripple, Peter called the people to repentance (3:19). Castigating Simon the sorcerer, Peter told him to repent of his wickedness (8:22). However, repentance is not something that originates in man's heart on his own initiative. Repentance, as the believers in Jerusalem confess, is a gift of God: "God has granted repentance that leads to life" (see also 5:31; II Tim. 2:25). That is, God grants his people the gifts of repentance, forgiveness of sin, and eternal life.

Doctrinal Considerations in 11:18

When John the Baptist preached his baptism of repentance, he confronted the clergy of his day, the tax collector and the soldier in Roman employ, and Herod Antipas, who had married his brother Philip's wife. He told them to repent and be baptized (Luke 3:7–20). John commanded sinners to turn from a life bent on sin to a life dedicated to God. He even taught them how to live a God-glorifying life.

Can the sinner who repents declare that he should receive credit for turning away from evil? No, not really. The sinner who knows that God through Christ has cleansed him from sin and has granted him life gives God the credit. He realizes that he has been saved, not by works but by grace through faith (Eph. 2:8–9). Thus he accepts repentance as a gift of God, who through his Son secured salvation and who through his Spirit has raised him from spiritual death. In one of his epistles, Paul ascribes salvation to both God and man: "With fear and trembling work out your own salvation, for it is God who works in you both to will and to act according to his pleasure" (Phil. 2:12–13). God grants his grace by raising man to a new life in Christ and then calls him to repent from everything that is evil.[13] The believer, therefore, sees repentance as God's gift to him and in return wishes to express his thankfulness to God by obeying his precepts.

Greek Words, Phrases, and Constructions in 11:15–18

Verse 15

ἐν τῷ ἄρξασθαι—the articular aorist infinitive in the dative (because of the preposition ἐν) denotes the time during which Peter began to speak. The wording should not be pushed to a logical extreme (see 10:44).

ἐν ἀρχῇ—the prepositional phrase refers to the Pentecost experience, which for the Jewish Christians marked the beginning of the Christian faith. The outpouring of the Holy Spirit in Caesarea is the Pentecost of the Gentiles.

Verse 16

ἐμνήσθην—from μιμνήσκομαι (I remember), this verb in the aorist passive is followed by the genitive case. Verbs of remembering and forgetting have their direct object in the genitive.

---

13. Leon Morris, *New Testament Theology* (Grand Rapids: Zondervan, Academie Books, 1986), p. 181.

ἔλεγεν—the imperfect tense ("he used to") is customary.[14] The saying, first uttered by John, appears to be proverbial; all four evangelists quote it, with variations (Matt. 3:11; Mark 1:8; Luke 3:16; John 1:26).

Verse 17

εἰ—this particle introduces a conditional sentence that states a simple fact and depicts reality.

πιστεύσασιν—in the dative plural, this aorist active participle refers to both Jewish and Gentile believers. At the conclusion of the verse, Western manuscripts add: "that he should not give them the Holy Spirit after they had believed on him."[15]

Verse 18

ἡσύχασαν—the aorist active of ἡσυχάζω (I am quiet) conveys the constative sense. The verb "describes a quiet condition . . . inclusive of silence."[16]

ἄρα—the inferential particle signifies "accordingly, so."[17]

---

19 So those who had been scattered because of the persecution that happened in connection with Stephen made their way as far as Phoenicia, Cyprus, and Antioch, telling the word only to Jews. 20 Some of them, men who were from Cyprus and Cyrene, came to Antioch and began to speak to the Greeks also, proclaiming the Lord Jesus. 21 And the hand of the Lord was with them, and a large number believed and turned to the Lord.

22 The news about them reached the ears of the church in Jerusalem and they sent Barnabas to go to Antioch. 23 When he arrived and witnessed the grace of God, he rejoiced and began to encourage them all to remain true, with a resolute heart, to the Lord. 24 He was a good man, full of the Holy Spirit and faith. And a large crowd was added to the Lord. 25 Barnabas left for Tarsus to look for Saul. 26 When he found him he brought him to Antioch. And for a whole year they met with the church and taught a great number of people. The disciples were called Christians first in Antioch.

27 Now at that time some prophets came down from Jerusalem to Antioch. 28 One of them, named Agabus, stood up and predicted through the Spirit that there would be a severe famine all over the Roman world. This happened during the reign of Claudius. 29 And the disciples, each of them as he was financially able, decided to send help for the relief of the brothers living in Judea. 30 They did this by sending their gift to the elders by Barnabas and Saul.

IV. The Church in Transition
11:19–13:3

A. Ministry of Barnabas
11:19–30

Luke resumes his account of the Jewish Christians who had been driven from Jerusalem after the death of Stephen (8:1–4). These persecuted Christians moved from Judea and Samaria in a northerly direction to Phoenicia

---

14. Dana and Mantey, *Manual Grammar*, p. 188.
15. Metzger, *Textual Commentary*, p. 386.
16. Thayer, p. 281.
17. Robertson, *Grammar*, p. 1190.

(modern Lebanon), Cyprus, and Antioch in Syria. Luke may have had a special interest in providing this account, for the oldest prologue to Luke, written between A.D. 160 and 180, states that Luke was a Syrian, a native of Antioch, and a physician (Col. 4:14) by profession.[18] Although we do not know when Luke was converted, it is possible that he was among the first Gentiles to acknowledge Christ as his Savior and Lord.

The city of Antioch, located about twenty miles inland from the Mediterranean Sea, was founded in 300 B.C. by Seleucus I Nicator, who named the city after his father, Antiochus. When the Romans conquered Syria in 64 B.C., Antioch became the capital of western Syria and prospered as an important commercial center. In the Roman empire, Antioch ranked third in importance after Rome in the west and Alexandria in the east.[19] To this city, Jewish settlers came in great numbers. They were influential and secure, having received citizenship rights that were equal to those of the Greeks.[20] However, Antioch was known not for its virtues but for its vices: it was a city of moral depravity, as a Roman author points out.[21] Here the Jewish people had their synagogues, taught the Law and the Prophets on the Sabbath, and even evangelized the local population. (For example, Nicolas converted to Judaism in Antioch. He came to Jerusalem, where he became a Christian and one of the seven deacons [6:5].) Converts had to fulfill three requirements: submit to circumcision to establish the covenant relationship through Abraham (Gen. 17:11–12); accede to baptism to cleanse a person from moral impurities and thus demonstrate obedience to Jewish law; and offer an appropriate sacrifice.[22] The Greeks, however, adored their bodies and objected to circumcision. People who refused to be circumcised could not become converts to Judaism and were called God-fearers by the Jews. It is logical to suppose that some of these God-fearing Gentiles became Christians, contributed to the mission of the church, and received honorable mention in Acts.

1. Spread of the Gospel
11:19–21

19. So those who had been scattered because of the persecution that happened in connection with Stephen made their way as far as Phoenicia, Cyprus, and Antioch, telling the word only to Jews.

After Stephen's death, mission work among the population in Jerusalem came to a halt. In God's providence, the Christians who were driven out of

---

18. Albert Huck, *Synopsis of the First Three Gospels*, rev. Hans Lietzmann, 9th ed. (Oxford: Blackwell, 1957), pp. vii–viii.

19. Josephus *War* 3.2.4 [29].

20. Josephus *War* 7.3.3 [43–45].

21. Juvenal *Satires* 3.62. See also Richard N. Longenecker, *The Acts of the Apostles*, in vol. 9 of *The Expositor's Bible Commentary*, ed. Frank E. Gaebelein, 12 vols. (Grand Rapids: Zondervan, 1981), p. 399.

22. Everett F. Harrison, *The Apostolic Church* (Grand Rapids: Eerdmans, 1985), p. 54.

the city brought the gospel to the people in Palestine. Wherever they went, they proclaimed the gospel of salvation and caused the church to expand. Accordingly, God used the death of Stephen and the subsequent persecution to enlarge the church through the mission work of persecuted Christians. Hellenistic Jews who embraced the teachings of Christ returned to their homelands; some settled in the coastal cities and towns of Phoenicia. These believers, by associating with Jewish people and not with Gentiles, told the Good News only to members of their own race.

20. Some of them, men who were from Cyprus and Cyrene, came to Antioch and began to speak to the Greeks also, proclaiming the Lord Jesus.

Hellenistic Jews who resided in Cyprus and Cyrene made their way to Antioch and communicated the gospel to the Greeks. We know that numerous Jews lived in both places.[23] Because the distance between Cyprus and Antioch is relatively short and direct, we can understand that Jews traveled from one place to the other. But we are unable to explain why Jewish people from Cyrene in North Africa came to Antioch.

Nevertheless, when these Hellenistic Jews arrived in Antioch, they preached the gospel to the Greeks. As the Jews in Antioch customarily taught the Old Testament Scriptures to the Gentiles, so the Christians brought the gospel to the Greeks. And these Greeks were ready to put their faith in Jesus Christ.

Some scholars favor the translation *Greeks* in the text, while others opt for the reading *Hellenists*. The problem stems from a variant in the text: the word for "Greeks" is *Hellēnas* and that for "Hellenists" is *Hellēnistas*. The problem of the variant in the Greek text is reflected in translations, which try to convey the significance of the underlying Greek word. Here are a few examples:

Gentiles (GNB)

Grecians (KJV)

non-Jews (SEB)

How do we approach this matter? First, the textual variant has strong external support, so we are unable to make a choice on the basis of manuscript evidence. Consequently, we are forced to rely on internal evidence. Luke states that Greek-speaking Jewish Christians from Cyprus proclaimed the gospel, not to the Jews, but to people either who were born in Greece or whose native tongue was Greek. With this stark contrast, he intimates that the Jewish Christian missionaries addressed not the Greek-speaking Jews,

---

23. For Cyprus, see 4:36; 13:4–5; 21:16; and for Cyrene, see 2:10; 6:9; 13:1; Matt. 27:32.

whom he elsewhere calls *Hellēnistas*,[24] but the non-Jewish Greeks, whom he repeatedly classifies as *Hellēnas*.[25] The internal evidence, therefore, seems to favor the reading *Greeks*.

Next, how should we interpret this reading? In the New Testament, the term *Greeks* denotes either natives of Greece and Macedonia or non-Jewish Hellenized residents of major cities, including Antioch, Iconium, Ephesus, Thessalonica, and Corinth.[26]

Luke indicates that the Jewish Christians, in addition to preaching the gospel to Jews in Antioch, proclaimed Jesus Christ to the Gentiles. Not only Luke in Acts, but also Paul in his writings, stresses that the gospel is first for the Jew and then for the Greek, that is, the Gentile (Rom. 1:16, see especially the NIV).[27]

21. And the hand of the Lord was with them, and a large number believed and turned to the Lord.

In this text, Luke sounds a note of triumph. As a Gentile Christian, he describes the growth of the Christian church among the Gentiles. They listened to the message, believed in the Lord Jesus, and joined the fellowship of the church. Luke ascribes the increase to the hand of the Lord (see 4:30; 13:11). That is, in his providence God blessed the labors of the missionaries when numerous Gentiles were converted. Perhaps Luke was one of these early converts.

Striking is the emphasis on the word *Lord*. It occurs three times in succession (vv. 20–21) and presents a marked emphasis in the proclamation of the Good News. This does not mean that the term *Lord* originated in Antioch among Gentile believers.[28] On the contrary, Jesus applied Psalm 110:1, "The LORD said to my Lord," to himself, as did his apostles (Matt. 22:41–44; Acts 2:34). Both Jews and Gentiles accepted Jesus Christ as their Lord; by confessing his name they became his disciples.

On the basis of verse 19, we assume that the initial ministry of the Jewish Christians among Jews and Greeks took place in the confines of Antiochean synagogues. The news of the great number of converts soon reached the apostles in Jerusalem (see 2:47; 6:7; 9:31; 12:24; 14:1; 16:5; 19:20). They

---

24. The term *Hellēnistas* occurs twice in Acts, referring to Jews (either Christian or non-Christian) whose native language was Greek (6:1; 9:29). But apart from these two instances and the variant reading in 11:20, the word does not occur elsewhere in known literature.

25. See 14:1; 17:4; 18:4; 19:10, 17; 20:21; 21:28; and 16:1, 3 in the singular.

26. Refer to Hans Windisch, *TDNT*, vol. 2, p. 510; Hans Bietenhard, *NIDNTT*, vol. 2, p. 126; Martin Hengel, *Between Jesus and Paul*, trans. John Bowden (Philadelphia: Fortress, 1983), p. 58.

27. Metzger favors the reading *Hellēnistas* but understands the term "in the broad sense of 'Greek-speaking persons.'" *Textual Commentary*, pp. 388–89.

28. This is the view of Wilhelm Bousset, *Kyrios Christos: A History of the Belief in Christ from the Beginning of Christianity to Irenaeus*, trans. John E. Steely (Nashville: Abingdon, 1970), pp. 146–47. But see Richard N. Longenecker, *The Christology of Early Jewish Christianity*, Studies in Biblical Theology, 2d series 17 (London: SCM, 1970), p. 122.

realized that the age of preaching the gospel to the Gentiles had come and that appropriate action should be taken to welcome them into the church.

2. Mission of Barnabas
11:22–24

22. The news about them reached the ears of the church in Jerusalem and they sent Barnabas to go to Antioch. 23. When he arrived and witnessed the grace of God, he rejoiced and began to encourage them all to remain true, with a resolute heart, to the Lord. 24. He was a good man, full of the Holy Spirit and faith. And a large crowd was added to the Lord.

We make these observations:

a. *News.* Good news travels fast! Travelers who arrived in Jerusalem reported to the church the phenomenal influence of the Christian faith and the resultant increase of believers in the city of Antioch. First, the Jerusalem church received the news about the Samaritans who had accepted the gospel. In consequence, its members sent Peter and John to them (8:14). Next, the mother church heard about the Gentiles in Antioch who accepted the gospel. In response, the church commissioned Barnabas as the representative of the apostles. Note, then, that the Jerusalem church remained in charge of developments abroad.

When the news came to the ears of the church in Jerusalem, the apostles were perhaps in other regions (compare v. 30). The Jewish Christians had no objections to Gentiles entering the church, primarily because Peter had told them about his experience in Caesarea. Although Caesarea was located in Palestine, in the minds of the Jews the city of Antioch was the capital of a heathen nation. Nevertheless, the church in Jerusalem voiced no dissent. Instead the church leaders looked for a person who could represent them and who would understand the situation in Antioch. They appointed Barnabas.

Finally, the Jerusalem church could not take lightly the increase of the church in Antioch. In time, the Antiochean church became the mission center for the Christian faith and overtook the mother church of Jerusalem. Even though Jerusalem provided leadership and direction, Antioch had vision and ambition. From Antioch, the gospel sounded forth throughout the countries that bordered the Mediterranean Sea. Antioch became the Gentile church that occupied a strategic position between the Jewish center in Jerusalem and the Gentile churches Paul had founded.[29] After the fall of Jerusalem in A.D. 70, Antioch filled the leadership vacuum in the church at large.

b. *Action.* As a Greek-speaking Jewish Christian and a native of Cyprus, Barnabas is the right person to promote the development of the church in Antioch. He comes not to exert authority, but to help the believers grow in faith.

---

29. Richard B. Rackham, *The Acts of the Apostles: An Exposition,* Westminster Commentaries series (1901; reprint ed., Grand Rapids: Baker, 1964), p. 167.

Perhaps traveling along the coastal area, visiting and strengthening churches along the way, Barnabas eventually arrives in Antioch. He is amazed at the grace of God when he observes the harmony that exists between Jew and Gentile in the Antiochean church. With spiritual eyes, he looks at the development of the church and gives God the glory. Barnabas rejoices when he sees the effect of Christ's gospel among the people and, true to his name—Son of Encouragement (4:36)—he immediately begins to encourage the believers to remain true to the Lord. He realizes that these recent converts may become an easy prey of Satan. Therefore, on a daily basis Barnabas instructs them to be true to Jesus. He urges them to cling to Christ with determination (compare 13:43; 14:22).

c. *Result.* Luke expresses his admiration for the spiritual characteristics of Barnabas. He calls him "a good man, full of the Holy Spirit and faith." The description matches that of Stephen (6:5; 7:55) and thus puts Barnabas on the same level as Stephen. The adjective *good*, applied to Barnabas, denotes the quality of excellence. Luke describes Barnabas as good in the sense that this person is of sterling character, wholesome, capable, and helpful. Filled with the Holy Spirit and faith, Barnabas lives in daily fellowship with God the Father and the Lord Jesus Christ (I John 1:3). The presence of the Holy Spirit and complete trust in Jesus furnish him with serene stability, genuine love for his fellow man, and unparalleled dedication to the work of the Lord.

As a result, the church at Antioch continues to increase in numbers. Writes Luke, "A large crowd was added to the Lord." In fact, this is the second time that Luke reports the growth of the Antiochean church (v. 21). The church experiences a development that is unique in the Gentile world and in a sense indicates still greater things to come.

Greek Words, Phrases, and Constructions in 11:22–23

εἰς τὰ ὦτα—this is a Semitic idiom that occurs frequently in the Septuagint. See also Matthew 10:27.

τῇ προθέσει—the noun in the dative case modifies the verb. The dative is used adverbially to express manner, that is, how to remain true to the Lord.[30]

---

3. Christians in Antioch
11:25–26

Barnabas proves to be the right man in the right place. He relates well to the people living in the capital city of Antioch, is bilingual, is familiar with Greek culture, and perhaps works at a trade to support himself. Due to the numerical increase of the Antiochean church, Barnabas needs assistance. He knows that Paul resides in Tarsus and is a capable teacher.

---

30. Robertson, *Grammar,* p. 530.

25. Barnabas left for Tarsus to look for Saul. 26. When he found him he brought him to Antioch. And for a whole year they met with the church and taught a great number of people. The disciples were called Christians first in Antioch.

a. "Barnabas left for Tarsus to look for Saul." The geographic distance between Antioch and Tarsus was relatively short and by traveling on foot could be covered in a few days. Tarsus was a major city in Cilicia, a Roman province in the southwest corner of Asia Minor (modern Turkey). It was a university city that ranked higher academically than Alexandria and Athens. In this city Paul was born; he describes himself as "a Jew, from Tarsus in Cilicia, a citizen of no unimportant city" (21:39). E. M. Blaiklock suggests that influential Jews in that city had petitioned Rome to confer on them Roman citizenship with the provision that this privilege be transmitted by birth to their descendants.[31] Rome granted their request and as a consequence Paul enjoyed the protection of Roman citizenship (16:37; 22:28).

After Paul left Jerusalem and traveled via Caesarea to Tarsus (9:30), he seemed to have disappeared. However, in view of Luke's reference to churches in Cilicia (15:41), we presume that Paul, as the energetic missionary to the Gentiles, proclaimed and taught the gospel in that area. No wonder that Barnabas chose Paul to be his right-hand man to teach the Word to the Gentile Christians in Antioch.

b. "When he found him he brought him to Antioch." Luke does not disclose how long Barnabas had to look for Paul in Tarsus and its vicinity. He merely states that he found Paul and brought him to Antioch. Barnabas knew that Jesus had called Paul to be an apostle to the Gentiles (9:27). And even if many years had elapsed since they both had been in Jerusalem, Paul's call remained intact. Barnabas informed Paul about the influx of the Gentiles into the Antiochean church and invited him to be their teacher.[32] When Paul agreed to accompany Barnabas and work with him in Antioch, he made his debut as a teacher of Gentile Christians.

c. "And for a whole year they met with the church." Both Barnabas and Paul taught the believers in Antioch for a year. Moreover, Luke adds that these two men taught a great number of people. This information is indicative of the tremendous growth of the Christian church in that city. Obviously, Paul was well qualified to teach the people that the Old Testament Scriptures were fulfilled in Jesus Christ. He had been schooled in the Scriptures at the feet of Gamaliel in Jerusalem (22:3), and following his conversion near Damascus, he interpreted the Old Testament messianic prophecies from a fulfillment motif.

---

31. E. M. Blaiklock, *Cities of the New Testament* (Westwood, N.J.: Revell, 1965), p. 21; see also "Tarsus," *ZPEB*, vol. 5, p. 602; William M. Ramsay, *The Cities of St. Paul: Their Influence on His Life and Thought* (1907; reprint ed., Grand Rapids: Baker, 1963), pp. 197–98.

32. Henry Alford, *Alford's Greek Testament: An Exegetical and Critical Commentary*, 7th ed., 4 vols. (1877; Grand Rapids: Guardian, 1976), vol. 2, p. 127.

d. "The disciples were called Christians first in Antioch." Since the outpouring of the Holy Spirit on the day of Pentecost in Jerusalem, Jesus' followers referred to themselves as brothers, disciples, believers, saints, and those who belonged to the Way. The time had come, however, to adopt a definitive and descriptive name for the people who accepted Jesus as their Lord and Savior. The name *Christians* was used first in Antioch in the multicultural setting of that city. In Acts, the name occurs only twice, here and in 26:28 (where Herod Agrippa II chides Paul for trying to make him a Christian). The word also appears in I Peter 4:16. Peter puts it in the context of suffering and urges his readers not to be ashamed of bearing that name. We are unable to determine if antagonists to the Christian faith coined the Greek name *Christianoi* to defame the followers of Christ. In the light of Agrippa's remark to Paul and the context of Peter's comments to his readers, we are inclined to think that the enemies of the faith ascribed this name to the Christians.

The other possibility is that the believers carefully chose the name. They did not designate themselves followers of Jesus, nor did they adopt the name that the Jews gave them, "the Nazarene sect" (24:5). Instead they used the official title *Christ* and, adding the ending *-ians* (Greek *-ianoi*), indicated that they completely identified themselves with Christ.[33] Similarly, members of Caesar's household, soldiers, and public officials called themselves *Kaisarianoi* to demonstrate their allegiance to the Roman emperor.

Although Jewish Christians could stay under the protective umbrella of the "freedom of religion" that the Roman government had granted the Jews, with the influx of Gentiles into the church the Christians had to distinguish themselves from the Jews and assume a new name. Nonetheless, we are unable to prove that the Christians themselves coined the term *Christianoi*. The absence of this term from early Christian literature (except in the letters of Ignatius) "suggests that as a matter of fact it was not a name early accepted by the Christians themselves."[34] As the Christians in Antioch dedicated themselves completely to Jesus Christ so we ought to reflect Christ's virtues, glory, and honor. As Christians, we are brothers and sisters in the household of faith, citizens in the kingdom of heaven, and soldiers in the army of Christ.

Practical Considerations in 11:26

Why are you called a Christian? The name *Christian* means that you identify completely with Christ because you are his disciple. But for many Christians this identification seems to apply only in a Sunday worship service. During the week,

---

33. A variant spelling that originated with Roman historiographers is "Chrestianoi." Tacitus *Annals* 15.44; Suetonius *Life of Claudius* 25.4, and *Nero* 16.2; Pliny *Epistles* 10.97. Codex Sinaiticus also features this spelling.
34. H. J. Cadbury, "Names for Christians and Christianity in Acts," *Beginnings*, vol. 5, p. 386.

many Christians appear to have put aside the Christian nametag that they display on Sundays when they sing praises to God, read Scripture, pray, and listen to a sermon. How do some Christians live? Some live for the sake of money; others are in the process of destroying their bodies through chemical dependence; and still others use vile and profane language as part of their daily speech. The question, "Why are you called a Christian?" is personal and to the point. It makes many Christians blush.

In the sixteenth century, German theologian Zacharius Ursinus asked this same question and formulated the following answer:

> Because by faith I am a member of Christ
> and so I share in his anointing.
>   I am anointed
>   to confess his name,
>   to present myself to him as a living sacrifice of thanks,
>   to strive with a good conscience against sin and the devil in this
>   life,
>   and afterward to reign with Christ
>   over all creation
>   for all eternity.[35]

Greek Words, Phrases, and Constructions in 11:25–26

Codex Bezae and other Western manuscripts have an expanded text. The italicized clauses and phrases indicate variations:

> And *having heard that Saul was at Tarsus,* he went out to seek him; and *when he had met him, he entreated him to come* to Antioch. *When they had come,* for a whole year a large company of people *were stirred up,* and *then* for the first time the disciples in Antioch were called Christians.[36]

ἀναζητῆσαι—the compound aorist infinitive expresses purpose and, at the same time, thoroughness. That is, Barnabas went to Tarsus to make a diligent search.[37]

ἐγένετο αὐτοῖς—this simplistic phrase, literally translated "it was to them," introduces three infinitives: first, συναχθῆναι (they met), then, διδάξαι (they taught), and last, χρηματίσαι (they received a name).

---

4. Prediction and Fulfillment
11:27–30

As a historian, Luke speaks in general terms (compare 12:1) and fails to give exact dates. From the information about a famine and the historical

---

35. Heidelberg Catechism, question and answer 32.
36. Metzger, *Textual Commentary,* p. 390.
37. Thayer, p. 37.

context in Acts and other sources, we conjecture that Agabus predicted the famine in the first part of the fifth decade. Scholars differ on an exact date, but historical evidence seems to support the view that this famine took place about A.D. 46.[38]

27. Now at that time some prophets came down from Jerusalem to Antioch. 28. One of them, named Agabus, stood up and predicted through the Spirit that there would be a severe famine all over the Roman world. This happened during the reign of Claudius.

We make these comments:

a. *Prophets.* The link between the churches in Jerusalem and Antioch appears to be strong, for in time some prophets come down from Jerusalem to visit the believers in Antioch. They are Christian prophets who have the gift of the Holy Spirit (v. 28) and come to strengthen the Christians in their faith (13:1). Even though this is the first time Luke mentions prophets, we know from other New Testament passages that prophets interpreted and preached God's Word, encouraged the people, and predicted events.[39] They differed from the Old Testament prophets in respect to their function. Old Testament prophets primarily foretold the birth and coming of Christ. But after Jesus' coming, messianic prophecy had ceased and New Testament prophets preached the gospel and predicted events. Furthermore, Christ's gospel had been entrusted to the apostles, who filled a primary role in the Christian church. Thus Paul lists the apostles first and then the prophets (see Eph. 4:11).

b. *Prediction.* One of the prophets was Agabus, who predicted that a famine would strike the Roman empire. Agabus merely predicts; he does not prophesy. Likewise, when Paul arrived at Caesarea at the conclusion of his third missionary journey, Agabus came from Judea and predicted Paul's imprisonment (21:10–11). The fact that this prophet was filled with the Holy Spirit means that God wished to communicate with his people regarding an event in the future. This event touched the lives not only of Christians but of all those living in the Roman empire.

The famine that Agabus predicted occurred during the reign of Emperor Claudius, who ruled from A.D. 41 to 54. Luke calls it a severe famine, for in varying degrees it affected the entire Roman empire. Egypt sold grain for the benefit of the people in famine-stricken Jerusalem, Cyprus supplied figs,[40] and the Christians in Antioch sent aid to the believers in Judea (v. 29). Different parts of the Roman empire suffered famines. Therefore, we interpret Luke's description, "a severe famine all over the Roman world," not in a literal but in a broad sense.

---

38. Josephus *Antiquities* 3.15.3 [320]; 20.2.5 [51–52]; 20.5.2 [101]; Suetonius *Claudius* 18.2; Tacitus *Annals* 12.43; Dio Cassius *Roman History* 60.11; Eusebius *Ecclesiastical History* 2.8.

39. See especially 15:32; 19:6; 21:9–10; Rom. 12:6; I Cor. 12:10; 13:2, 8; 14:3, 6, 29–37.

40. Josephus *Antiquities* 20.2.5 [51–52]. See also Kenneth S. Gapp, "The Universal Famine under Claudius," *HTR* 28 (1935): 258–65.

29. And the disciples, each of them as he was financially able, decided to send help for the relief of the brothers living in Judea. 30. They did this by sending their gift to the elders by Barnabas and Saul.

The purpose for the visit of the Jerusalem prophets was to inform the Antiochean believers that a severe famine would occur in Judea with detrimental consequences for the Christians in that area. The church in Antioch did not receive the message for information but made immediate plans to alleviate the need of the believers in Judea.

Luke describes the loving care of the Christians in Antioch in glowing terms: "And the disciples, each of them as he was financially able, decided to send help for the relief of the brothers living in Judea." The Antiochean Christians decided to establish a relief fund to which each person contributed as much as his resources permitted. On a voluntary basis, the believers donated their gifts to show their love for needy brothers. Indeed, "God loves a cheerful giver" (II Cor. 9:7). The Gentile church broke down the wall of separation between Jew and Gentile by sending famine relief to the Jewish church in Jerusalem.

For decades, perhaps as a result of the persecution following the death of Stephen, the Jerusalem church became impoverished. During his missionary journeys Paul asked the Gentile churches for donations to help the poor in Jerusalem.[41] The Gentile Christians wished to thank the Jewish Christians for sharing their spiritual blessings. Returning a kindness, the Gentiles shared material blessings with the Jewish Christians in Jerusalem (compare Rom. 15:27).

In his report, Luke is extremely brief. He does not indicate what kind of help the believers in Antioch sent to Jerusalem and when they dispatched it. We surmise that they entrusted a monetary gift to Barnabas and Paul, who served as their emissaries (see v. 30). Further, we believe that the two envoys arrived in Jerusalem before the famine took effect. We must keep in mind that the prophets came to Antioch for the purpose of informing the Christians about a need among the believers in Judea. When this news reached the Antiocheans, their response was immediate and spontaneous. They commissioned Barnabas and Paul to take a gift to the elders in Jerusalem and thus demonstrated the visible unity of Christ's church.

Two items need a word of explanation. First, the believers in Antioch sent their foremost teachers to Jerusalem to act as their representatives. Barnabas used the occasion to report to the church in Jerusalem about the work he and Paul performed in Antioch (see v. 22). For Paul, this trip was a homecoming of sorts. Years earlier he had left Jerusalem because local Jews were seeking to kill him (9:29–30). He returned not knowing whether his enemies would allow him to stay safely in the city. Was this visit Paul's return to Jerusalem "fourteen years later" (Gal. 2:1)? We keep this question

---

41. Refer to 24:17; Rom. 15:25–28, 31; I Cor. 16:1; II Cor. 8:1–6.

in abeyance, for it relates to Paul's visit at the time of the Jerusalem Council (see the commentary on 15:2).[42]

Next, verse 30 is the first mention of elders in the Jerusalem church. When Paul and Barnabas established churches in Asia Minor, they appointed elders in each church (14:23; see also 20:17). And when Paul wrote a letter to Titus, who was a pastor on the island of Crete, he instructed him to appoint elders in every town (Titus 1:5). Luke introduces the Greek expression *presbyteroi* (elders) in connection with the leaders of the Jerusalem church. This leadership was patterned after the Jewish synagogue, in which a council of elders filled a leading role.[43]

Greek Words, Phrases, and Constructions in 11:28–30

Verse 28

The text of Codex Bezae and a few other manuscripts indicate that Luke was present in Antioch. Here is the first "we" passage: "And there was much rejoicing; and when *we* were gathered together one of them named Agabus spoke, signifying. . . ."[44]

διὰ τοῦ πνεύματος—"Christian prophecy was a gift of the Holy Spirit himself, and Agabus spoke directly from God."[45]

μέλλειν ἔσεσθαι—these two infinitives introduced by the aorist active ἐσήμανεν (he indicated) show redundancy. The first infinitive conveys a future connotation; the second infinitive is in the future tense.

ἐπί—this preposition conveys a temporal idea, "in the time of."

Verses 29–30

εὐπορεῖτο—the imperfect middle of εὐπορέομαι (I am well off) is significant because it describes financial status.

αὐτῶν—this pronoun in the genitive case, redundant in view of the genitive case ("of the disciples"), expresses emphasis.

ὅ—the relative pronoun is in the accusative case and refers to the entire verbal clause of the preceding sentence.

διά—not "through" but "by means of."

Summary of Chapter 11

When Peter arrives in Jerusalem, he is accused of entering the house of Gentiles and eating with them. Peter fully explains to the members of the Jerusalem church the events as they occurred. He tells them about his

---

42. Some scholars equate the famine visit with that of Gal. 2:1; see, e.g., Longenecker, *Acts,* p. 405. Consult also P. Benoit, "La deuxième visite de Saint Paul à Jérusalem," *Bib* 40 (1959): 778–92.

43. Lothar Coenen, *NIDNTT,* vol. 1, p. 199; Günther Bornkamm, *TDNT,* vol. 6, p. 662.

44. Metzger, *Textual Commentary,* p. 391 (italics added).

45. Nigel Turner, *Grammatical Insights into the New Testament* (Edinburgh: Clark, 1965), p. 21.

vision in Joppa when he saw a sheet filled with animals come down from heaven; when he heard a voice commanding him to kill and eat; and when, after hearing the voice three times, he saw the sheet pulled back to heaven.

Peter reports that three men sent from Caesarea asked him to come with them. Commanded by the Spirit to do so and in the company of six Jewish believers from Joppa, Peter traveled to Caesarea. There he spoke to the Gentiles and witnessed the coming of the Spirit on the Gentiles. Peter states that he was unable to oppose God. His listeners have no further objections and praise God.

Refugees from Jerusalem proclaim the gospel to Jews in Phoenicia, Cyprus, and Antioch. But a few from Cyprus and Cyrene also preach the good news about Jesus to the Greeks in Antioch. As a result, many of them believe. The news concerning the growth of the church in Antioch comes to the attention of the Jerusalem church. Barnabas is delegated to go to Antioch. When he arrives, he rejoices in the evident grace of God. He goes to Tarsus in search of Paul, who accompanies him to Antioch. These two teach the believers for an entire year. The church increases numerically and the disciples are called Christians first in Antioch.

Agabus comes from Jerusalem and predicts a severe famine in the Roman empire. The Antiochean believers extend their loving concern to the believers in Jerusalem and delegate Barnabas and Paul to bring a gift to the elders in Judea.

12

The Church in Transition, *part 2*

12:1–25

Outline (continued)

12:1–19   B. Peter's Escape from Prison

12:1–5   1. Arrest by Herod

12:6–11   2. Release by an Angel

12:12–17   3. Church in Prayer

12:18–19   4. Reaction of Herod

12:20–25   C. Death of Herod Agrippa I

12 1 Now about that time King Herod arrested some who belonged to the church to mistreat them. 2 He had James, the brother of John, killed with a sword. 3 And when he saw that it pleased the Jews, he proceeded to arrest Peter also. It was during the Feast of Unleavened Bread. 4 Having seized Peter, Herod put him in prison. He handed him over to four squads of four soldiers each to guard him. He intended to bring him before the people after the Passover. 5 So Peter was kept in prison, but fervent prayer for him was offered by the church to God.

6 The night before Herod was about to bring him to trial, Peter was sleeping between two soldiers. Peter was bound with two chains, and guards were before the door watching the prison. 7 Suddenly an angel of the Lord appeared and a light shone into the cell. He struck Peter's side and woke him up. He said, "Get up quickly." And the chains fell off Peter's hands.

8 The angel said to him, "Get dressed and put your sandals on." And Peter did so. The angel said, "Wrap your cloak around you and follow me." 9 He went out and followed the angel, but he did not know that what the angel was doing was real. He thought he was seeing a vision. 10 And when they had passed the first and second guard, they came to the iron gate that leads into the city. The gate opened for them by itself and they went through it. They walked along one street and suddenly the angel left him.

11 When Peter came to himself, he said, "Now I know for sure that the Lord has sent his angel and rescued me from Herod's clutches and from all that the Jewish people were expecting." 12 When he realized this, he went to the house of Mary, the mother of John called Mark, where many people were gathered and praying. 13 Peter knocked at the door of the gate and a servant girl named Rhoda came to answer. 14 When she recognized Peter's voice, because of her joy she did not open the gate. But she ran in and announced that Peter was standing in front of the gate. 15 They said to her, "You are out of your mind." But she kept insisting that it was so. But they said, "It is his angel." 16 Peter continued knocking; when they opened the door, they saw him and were astonished. 17 But after he motioned to them with his hand to be silent, he described to them how the Lord had led him out of the prison. He said, "Report these things to James and the brothers." Then he went out and departed to another place.

18 Now when daylight came, there was no small commotion among the soldiers as to what had happened to Peter. 19 Herod had a search made for him but did not find him. Then he examined the guards and ordered that they be led away to execution. Herod went down from Judea to Caesarea and was spending time there.

B. Peter's Escape from Prison
12:1–19

Luke begins a new episode in the life of Peter, who becomes a prisoner, is released from prison by an angel, and leaves Jerusalem for another place. Even though Luke introduces the chapter with the general phrase *now about that time*, questions concerning chronological sequence must be raised. Does Luke present a strictly chronological account, or is the report about

Peter's imprisonment an interlude that occurred before the famine? Luke's wording, "now about that time," seems to preclude a chronological sequence of chapters 11 and 12. He simply uses the introductory phrase to pick up a historical incident that has bearing on the development of his account.[1] We must assume, then, that the famine occurred after Herod's death in A.D. 44 and that Barnabas and Saul made their relief visit to the brothers in Judea subsequent to that date.

1. Arrest by Herod
12:1–5

1. Now about that time King Herod arrested some who belonged to the church to mistreat them. 2. He had James, the brother of John, killed with a sword. 3. And when he saw that it pleased the Jews, he proceeded to arrest Peter also. It was during the Feast of Unleavened Bread.

a. *History.* The Christians in Jerusalem had been relatively free from persecution since the death of Stephen (8:1). Although Paul had received threats on his life (9:29), he had been allowed to move about freely in Jerusalem. In later years, the church received a threat not from the religious leaders of the Jews, nor from the common people, but from a person whom Luke describes as King Herod.

Who was this king? He was Herod Agrippa I (born in 10 B.C.), a grandson of Herod the Great (Matt. 2:1) and of Mariamne, a Jewess. He was the son of Aristobulus, who died in 7 B.C. His mother sent him to Rome, where Herod Agrippa was educated and where he befriended Gaius (Caligula), who in A.D. 37 became emperor. This emperor proclaimed Herod Agrippa king over Iturea, Traconitis, and Abilene (Luke 3:1), the tetrarchies east of Galilee.[2] In A.D. 39, Herod Agrippa's uncle, Herod Antipas, like his nephew, petitioned the emperor for a royal title. Antipas had ruled the tetrarchy of Galilee and Perea since the death of his father in 4 B.C. However, instead of receiving the coveted title, Antipas was deposed and exiled, and Herod Agrippa, who obviously had influenced the emperor, obtained Antipas's tetrarchy.[3] After Caligula's death in A.D. 41, Herod Agrippa appealed to Emperor Claudius and received from him Judea and Samaria.[4] By that time, King Herod Agrippa ruled over territories that equalled those of his grandfather Herod the Great.

b. *James.* Through his grandmother Mariamne, Herod Agrippa could claim Jewish ancestry. He exploited this distinction to full advantage. For example, he made it known that he enjoyed living in Jerusalem; while there he scrupulously observed Jewish law and tradition. Daily he offered sacrifices at the temple; during the Feast of Tabernacles the Jewish authorities

---

1. Lake and Cadbury, *Beginnings,* vol. 4, p. 132.
2. Josephus *Antiquities* 18.6.10 [225–39].
3. *Antiquities* 18.7.1–2 [240–55]; *War* 2.9.6 [181–83].
4. *Antiquities* 19.5.1 [274–75]; *War* 2.11.5 [214–15].

gave him the honor of reading publicly a passage from the law.[5] He did so in harmony with the Mosaic law that the king read a copy of the law all the days of his life (Deut. 17:19). In short, the Jews accepted King Herod Agrippa as one of their number.

Thus, Herod Agrippa continued his scheming and decided to lay hands on several members of the church with the intention of mistreating them and thereby gaining the favor of the Jews. Luke fails to indicate how many persons were arrested but mentions the name of James the brother of John and son of Zebedee. In fact, Herod had the apostle James killed with the sword. The king apparently acted in collusion with the Sanhedrin, which served as a court of law. According to Deuteronomy 13:6–18, if someone entices a Jew to engage in idolatry, he must be put to death by stoning. But if such a person persuades a whole city to serve other gods, then he must be killed with the sword. In the eyes of Herod Agrippa, James had led the city of Jerusalem astray. Ironically, according to the Mosaic law all the inhabitants of Jerusalem should have been put to death (Deut. 13:15).[6]

Luke records a series of first events in Acts: the first Pentecost (2:1–11), the first persecution (4:1–4), the first martyr (7:54–60), and now the first apostle to die by the sword. Note that, although the church selected Matthias to fill the place of Judas Iscariot, the church appointed no successor for James. From the time of Pentecost until his death in A.D. 44, James (unlike Judas) fulfilled his apostolic office. Because he fulfilled his office he was not replaced. And, even though James was a prominent disciple who belonged to the inner circle of Jesus' followers (Peter, James, and John), Luke mentions him only in the list of the apostles (1:13) and here. The focus is not on James but on Peter.

c. *Peter.* Spurred by the approval of the Jews, King Herod Agrippa took even bolder steps and arrested Peter, the leader and chief spokesman of the twelve apostles. He determined to put Peter to death, but delayed until the Jewish Feast of Unleavened Bread had passed. In New Testament times the feast had merged with Passover (see Luke 22:1). The people observed this week-long celebration during the end of March or the beginning of April.[7] We presume that Peter was in Jerusalem for this feast. As leader of the church, he had become vulnerable and had fallen into Herod Agrippa's hands.

4. Having seized Peter, Herod put him in prison. He handed him over to four squads of four soldiers each to guard him. He intended to bring him before the people after the Passover. 5. So Peter was kept in prison, but fervent prayer for him was offered by the church to God.

---

5. Mishnah, *Sota* 7.8.

6. Consult J. Blinzler, "Rechtsgeschichtliches zur Hinrichtung des Zebedäiden Jakobus," *NovT* 5 (1962): 191–206.

7. Gleason L. Archer, Jr., *Encyclopedia of Bible Difficulties* (Grand Rapids: Zondervan, 1982), pp. 375–76.

Herod judged it expedient to delay Peter's execution. Therefore, he put Peter in prison, which served as a place of detention. In the Roman empire, imprisonment itself was not considered punishment. Prisoners were kept in custody to await their trial, which could result in release, flogging, exile, or death. Peter's trial would come when the Passover feast had ended. Moreover, the execution of James had whetted the Jews' desire for Peter's trial and execution.

We surmise that Herod placed Peter in the prison located in the Fortress of Antonia at the northwest corner of the temple area. Herod assigned sixteen soldiers to guard Peter: four squads of four soldiers each. The soldiers were subject to execution if their prisoner escaped (v. 19); Peter's treatment was approximately equivalent to that of a modern maximum-security prisoner.

Why did Herod Agrippa set such a close guard on Peter? It is possible that the Sanhedrin had informed him about the earlier arrest of all the apostles, who escaped from prison during the night (5:19). Moreover, Peter himself had performed numerous miracles in Jerusalem and elsewhere and, consequently, had demonstrated that he at times possessed supernatural power. Therefore, Herod Agrippa wanted to be absolutely certain that this time Peter could not escape.

Herod failed to realize the power of prayer that the entire church wielded on behalf of Peter. That is, through the prayers of his people, God himself intervened and showed Herod Agrippa that his opposition was insignificant and futile. As long as Peter was kept in prison the church offered continuous prayer for him. The text speaks of *fervent* prayer, which signifies that the church prayed ardently and with heart, soul, and mind implored God for Peter's release.[8]

Greek Words, Phrases, and Constructions in 12:1–5

Verse 1

κατ' ἐκεῖνον δὲ τὸν καιρόν—this phrase simply means "at that time." The noun καιρόν connotes a definite and limited time "with the added notion of suitableness."[9]

ἀπό—denoting adherents of a party, the preposition points to church members.

Verse 3

προσέθετο—from the verb προστίθημι (I add), this form in the aorist middle followed by the aorist active infinitive συλλαβεῖν (to apprehend) means "he did it again"; precisely, "Herod also arrested Peter."[10]

τῶν ἀζύμων—the plural is a Hebrew idiom that is syntactically transferred into Greek. The word refers to a Jewish festival.

---

8. Cf. Luke 22:44; James 5:16; Jth. 4:9.
9. Thayer, p. 319.
10. C. F. D. Moule, *An Idiom-Book of New Testament Greek*, 2d ed. (Cambridge: Cambridge University Press, 1960), p. 177.

Verse 4

ἔθετο—although the form is aorist middle (from τίθημι, I put), in this verb the distinction between the active and the middle has disappeared (see 4:3; 5:18, 25). This verb, therefore, should not be translated "put for himself" in prison.

Verse 5

μὲν οὖν—the combination of these two words occurs frequently in Acts and generally is a resumptive phrase.

ἦν γινομένη—notice that this periphrastic construction with a present participle features both the verb εἰμί (I am) and the verb γίνομαι (I am, become). It probably places "special emphasis . . . on the continuousness of the praying."[11]

---

2. Release by an Angel
12:6–11

6. The night before Herod was about to bring him to trial, Peter was sleeping between two soldiers. Peter was bound with two chains, and guards were before the door watching the prison. 7. Suddenly an angel of the Lord appeared and a light shone into the cell. He struck Peter's side and woke him up. He said, "Get up quickly." And the chains fell off Peter's hands.

Luke relates Peter's escape from prison in detail. By contrast, he describes the release of the twelve apostles in few words (5:19–20). As a literary artist, he pictures the scene, describes the actions, and records the conversations that took place. He makes every word count to heighten the effect of Peter's miraculous release.

Herod Agrippa had scheduled Peter's trial and execution for the day following the conclusion of the Jewish festival. In accordance with the Roman practice of guarding prisoners in maximum security, Herod Agrippa ordered that two soldiers be chained to Peter, one soldier to Peter's right hand, the other to his left.[12] Guards were also posted at the door. Consequently, the possibility of escape was completely ruled out.

However, Luke places the emphasis not on Herod Agrippa or the soldiers, but on Peter. He portrays Peter sound asleep between two guards and paints a picture of complete trust and faith in God: on the eve of his trial and death, Peter sleeps. The Old Testament counterpart is recorded in one of David's psalms. When David fled from his son Absalom, he said:

> I lie down and sleep;
> I wake again, because the LORD sustains me. [Ps. 3:5, NIV]

---

11. F. F. Bruce, *The Acts of the Apostles: The Greek Text with Introduction and Commentary*, 3d (rev. and enl.) ed. (Grand Rapids: Eerdmans, 1990), p. 381.
12. In A.D. 37, Herod Agrippa himself had been a prisoner in Rome, where he was chained to a soldier. Josephus *Antiquities* 18.6.7 [196]. See also 28:16; Eph. 6:20; II Tim. 1:16.

God intervenes at the last moment when the situation is critical. He is in control of every situation and watches over his people. And God hears and answers the prayers of the believers who petition him in faith.

"Suddenly," Luke says, "an angel of the Lord appeared and a light shone into the cell." Notice that, as in other places in Acts, Luke writes "an angel," not "the angel."[13] This angel stood next to Peter and did not perform his task in the dark, but caused his heavenly light to illumine the cell. The implication is that the guards were overcome by sleep and did not notice the light. The angel struck Peter on his side to wake him. Undoubtedly Peter was confused to see someone standing over him and commanding him to get up. How could he do so when chains bound him to two soldiers? But the chains fell off his wrists and he was free. Obviously, a miracle happened that defies human logic and a plausible explanation.[14] When the angel told Peter to get up quickly, he did not mean that the time for escape was short. Rather, the word *quickly* denotes that a drowsy Peter had to come to his senses to obey the angel's instructions.

8. The angel said to him, "Get dressed and put your sandals on." And Peter did so. The angel said, "Wrap your cloak around you and follow me." 9. He went out and followed the angel, but he did not know that what the angel was doing was real. He thought he was seeing a vision.

The angel had to tell Peter, who was still trying to wake up, what to do: "Get dressed and put your sandals on." A literal translation indicates that the angel instructed Peter to put his belt around his waist so that his long flowing robe would not impede him in walking. And Peter's sandals had been placed aside, perhaps at the entrance of the cell. The angel then told Peter to wrap his cloak around him; they were about to leave the prison.

Peter did exactly as the angel said. When he had dressed himself, he followed. The tense of the Greek verb actually indicates that he kept on following. In amazement, he looked around, for "he had no idea that what the angel was doing was really happening" (NIV). Already he had seen one vision; Peter thought that he saw another vision. As he continued to follow the angel through the corridors of the building, the doors opened automatically and the guards appeared to be asleep. Peter realized that a miracle was taking place and he himself was its object.

10. And when they had passed the first and second guard, they came to the iron gate that leads into the city. The gate opened for them by itself and they went through it. They walked along one street and suddenly the angel left him.

---

13. See 5:19; 8:26; 10:3; 12:23; 27:23.

14. Ernst Haenchen calls the account a legend (*The Acts of the Apostles: A Commentary*, trans. Bernard Noble and Gerald Shinn [Philadelphia: Westminster, 1971], p. 391). But if the account of Peter's release from prison is considered legendary, Christ's resurrection from the dead can be regarded mythical. "Then our faith," says Paul, "is useless" (I Cor. 15:14).

Luke depicts sentinels standing at two separate doorways. Perhaps we ought to think in terms of eight soldiers on duty and eight off duty. Of the eight on duty, two were chained to Peter, two were the first guard, two were the second guard, and the last two were at the iron gate.[15] The angel and Peter passed through the gates as if someone opened them. In the Greek, Luke uses the word *automatē*, from which we derive the expression *automatically*.[16] This heavy gate opened by itself. On the other side of it was the city street that signaled freedom for Peter.

Some manuscripts have an additional reading. When the angel and Peter left the prison, they "walked down the seven steps" of the building. If Peter was imprisoned in the Fortress of Antonia—which seems likely, as Paul also was imprisoned in these barracks and guarded by soldiers—he would have to descend a number of steps (see 21:40).[17]

Suddenly the angel came into Peter's cell, and suddenly he left Peter while they were walking together on the streets of Jerusalem. The angel had accomplished his task (Heb. 1:14). This was according to God's plan. John Calvin remarks that God could have transferred Peter instantaneously to the room where the believers were praying for his release. If God had removed Peter from one place to another, he would have performed only one miracle. As Luke indicates, God performed a series of miracles in releasing Peter and answering the prayers of the saints.[18]

11. When Peter came to himself, he said, "Now I know for sure that the Lord has sent his angel and rescued me from Herod's clutches and from all that the Jewish people were expecting."

We are unable to explain the miracle of Peter's escape. We know that we can query why God permitted James to be killed but rescued Peter. We can question why Herod, following Peter's release, killed his soldiers (v. 19). Even if we are unable to provide answers, we nevertheless confess our faith in a sovereign God. And with the eighteenth-century poet William Cowper, we sing:

> God moves in a mysterious way
> His wonders to perform.
> He plants his footsteps in the sea
> And rides upon the storm.

---

15. F. W. Grosheide, *De Handelingen der Apostelen*, Kommentaar op het Nieuwe Testament series, 2 vols. (Amsterdam: Van Bottenburg, 1942), vol. 1, pp. 386–87.

16. Josephus uses the word *automatos* when he recounts that shortly before the fall of Jerusalem (A.D. 70), the temple gate "was observed at the sixth hour of the night to have opened of its own accord." *War* 6.5.3 [293] (LCL).

17. Bruce M. Metzger, *A Textual Commentary on the Greek New Testament*, 3d corrected ed. (London and New York: United Bible Societies, 1975), p. 394. See Lake and Cadbury, *Beginnings*, vol. 4, p. 136.

18. John Calvin, *Commentary on the Acts of the Apostles*, ed. David W. Torrance and Thomas F. Torrance, 2 vols. (Grand Rapids: Eerdmans, 1966), vol. 1, p. 341.

When Peter suddenly realized that the angel had disappeared, he came to his senses and knew that he had not seen a vision. He instantly experienced the reality of his rescue and knew that God had performed a miracle. He understood that his task on earth would continue, that he would receive a broader ministry away from Jerusalem, and that he was about to enter a new phase in his work of preaching the gospel of salvation.

"Now I know for sure that the Lord has sent his angel and rescued me from Herod's clutches and from all that the Jewish people were expecting," said Peter to himself. (By recording this soliloquy, Luke indicates that he heard the account of Peter's rescue from the apostle himself and then accurately transmitted Peter's words.) Peter expressed his thanks to God for sending an angel to deliver him from prison. Peter was fully aware not only of Herod Agrippa's evil intentions but also of the Jewish people's knowledge of his imprisonment and pending trial. The Jews sided with Herod Agrippa and were awaiting Peter's execution following his trial.

Doctrinal Considerations in 12:6–11

When the Jewish people celebrated the Feast of Unleavened Bread, they literally disrupted and ended the cycle of fermentation in the baking process. The old yeast, which had to be purged from every home and then burned, represented evil and wickedness (I Cor. 5:8). Because the Feast of Unleavened Bread and Passover were two names for the same festival in New Testament times, the Jews not only symbolically broke with their sinful past but also commemorated their deliverance from Egyptian bondage.

The Jews in Jerusalem at the time of Peter's imprisonment symbolically removed evil from their hearts and lives when they burned the old yeast. At the same time, they were anticipating Peter's trial and his subsequent death. And thus the symbolism of purging evil and wickedness from their hearts was meaningless. Conversely, the symbolism of deliverance in the celebration of Passover became reality for Peter when the angel delivered him from prison. While man failed to cleanse himself from sin and evil, God demonstrated his faithfulness by delivering Peter.

Greek Words, Phrases, and Constructions in 12:6–11

Verse 6

ἦν κοιμώμενος—with the verb *to be* and the present middle participle, this is the periphrastic construction that indicates duration of time.

δεδεμένος—from δέω (I bind), the perfect passive participle signifies that an action which took place in the past continues into the present. In brief, Peter had been bound for some time.

ἐτήρουν—the imperfect active from τηρέω (I keep) denotes continued action in the past tense. In this particular verse, Luke uses the Greek tenses to full advantage.

Verses 7–8

ἐκ—here the preposition does not mean "out of" but "from" and thus is equivalent to ἀπό.

περιβαλοῦ—the aorist middle imperative connotes single action: "wrap your cloak around you." But ἀκολούθει, the present active imperative, expresses linear action: "keep following me."

Verse 10

ἥτις—the indefinite relative pronoun in this case signifies "this very door."

αὐτομάτη—although the word is an adjective, it is used adverbially. It modifies the verb *opened* and not the noun *door*.

Verse 11

ἐν ἑαυτῷ γενόμενος—the pronoun in the dative case indicates that Peter was no longer sleeping, dreaming, or in a trance. Literally, the text says, "he came in himself."[19]

---

3. Church in Prayer
12:12–17

Indirectly, Luke records a contrast between the Jewish people, who were celebrating the Passover feast while anticipating Peter's public trial and death, and the Christians, who spent their time in continuous prayer petitioning God to release Peter. For their own safety, the Christians stayed together behind a locked gate that controlled entrance to the house. They tried to prevent any unexpected intruders from entering this house and making arrests.

12. When he realized this, he went to the house of Mary, the mother of John called Mark, where many people were gathered and praying.

Peter went to the church that was praying in Mary's house. He knew where some of the believers had gathered and went to them to reveal that God answers prayer and to thank them for their support. He also knew that he was a refugee who had to seek safety elsewhere.

Luke identifies the meeting place as "the house of Mary, the mother of John called Mark." It seems that Mary's house was spacious and could accommodate a large number of people. She belonged to the well-to-do class of citizens, for her house had an outer gate in the wall that surrounded the house. Even though Mary was a Christian and probably a widow, she had been able to keep her house during and after the persecution that followed the death of Stephen. Paul relates that she was the aunt of Barnabas (Col. 4:10), and Luke calls her the mother of John Mark.[20] The only

---

19. Moule, *Idiom-Book,* p. 75.
20. A. van Veldhuizen, *Markus. De Neef van Barnabas* (Kampen: Kok, 1933), pp. 18–19.

mention of Mary in Scripture relates to her readiness to make her house available to the Christians who gathered there for worship and prayer.

We have no proof that Mary's house was the place where Jesus instituted the Lord's Supper (Mark 14:13–15), where the apostles gathered after Jesus' ascension (1:13), and where the Christians gathered after Peter and John were released from prison (4:23–31). Luke reports, however, that Peter went to Mary's house, where the Christians spent the night to pray for Peter's release. Two members of Mary's household were there also: Rhoda the servant girl and probably John Mark.

Mary's son had been given the name *John;* he subsequently became known as Mark. He accompanied Paul and Barnabas on their first missionary journey to Cyprus (13:4–5) but decided not to go with them to Asia Minor (13:13). Although Paul expressed negative feelings toward Mark (15:37–40), he later made peace with him (Col. 4:10; II Tim. 4:11; Philem. 24). And Peter affectionately called Mark his son (I Peter 5:13). According to sources that go back to the beginning of the second century, Mark composed the second Gospel with Peter's help and approval.[21]

13. Peter knocked at the door of the gate and a servant girl named Rhoda came to answer. 14. When she recognized Peter's voice, because of her joy she did not open the gate. But she ran in and announced that Peter was standing in front of the gate.

Here is a subtle touch of humor which breaks the tension that holds the Christians in its tenacious grip. Picture, first, the apostle Peter standing at the outer gate of Mary's house, cautiously knocking, and longing for safety and shelter; next, the servant girl Rhoda, fearfully approaching the gate and reluctant to open it; and last, the believers, weary and worn, yet intensely praying for Peter's release. When these three parties eventually meet, they realize that God indeed has heard and answered prayer.

The fact that Luke mentions Rhoda by name indicates that Peter personally knew the members of Mary's household. We assume that in later years Luke received a detailed account from Peter himself. Rhoda was either a slave or a servant who in the employ of Mary had become a Christian. Incidentally, we would have expected a man instead of a servant girl to guard the outer entrance to Mary's house. But in those days the custom seems to have been to appoint servant girls as gatekeepers (John 18:16–17).

When Rhoda approached the outer entrance, she recognized Peter's voice. But instead of opening the gate, she left Peter standing outside. In bewilderment, she rushed back into the house and in a voice trembling with emotion joyfully exclaimed: "Peter is standing at the gate." Notice that God gradually reveals the miracle of Peter's release. Instead of having Peter rush into the group of praying Christians, God causes a short delay to prepare the believers for answered prayer.

---

21. Eusebius *Ecclesiastical History* 2.15.1–2; 3.24.7; 3.39.15; 5.8.3; 6.14.6–7; 6.25.5; see also Ralph P. Martin, *Mark: Evangelist and Theologian* (Grand Rapids: Zondervan, 1972), pp. 80–83.

15. They said to her, "You are out of your mind." But she kept insisting that it was so. But they said, "It is his angel." 16. Peter continued knocking; when they opened the door, they saw him and were astonished.

Note that Luke records no words of rebuke for the unbelief the Christians expressed. He depicts a normal human reaction to the suddenness of the good news concerning Peter's release. Vividly he portrays the reaction of the Christians by recording their exclamations: "You are out of your mind." A colloquial rendering of the Greek verb would be, "You are crazy." However, the opposite is true. Of all the people in the house, only Rhoda kept her sanity and steadfastly insisted that Peter was standing outside at the gate.[22]

The Christians refused to believe that Peter was alive and free. They told Rhoda: "It is his angel." Interestingly, an angel of the Lord set Peter free, but then left him (v. 10). Yet the people at Mary's house were unaware at this point that an angel had liberated Peter. However, we know that the Jews believed that guardian angels protected them (see Ps. 91:11; Matt. 18:10). And from the Jewish Talmud, which reflects a slightly later period in time, we learn that the Jews taught that guardian angels assumed the appearance of the persons they protected and thus served as their doubles.[23]

Meanwhile Peter was standing at the gate and possibly heard the commotion inside. He longed to be with his friends, and thus kept knocking at the gate. Eventually the Christians realized that Peter himself was standing there; they opened the door, saw him, and with utter amazement welcomed him into their midst. Fear and tension instantly vanished and gave place to laughter, happiness, joy, and gratitude.

17. But after he motioned to them with his hand to be silent, he described to them how the Lord had led him out of the prison. He said, "Report these things to James and the brothers." Then he went out and departed to another place.

We make these observations:

a. *Account.* Following the custom of his day, Peter moved his hand back and forth as a sign to his audience to become quiet (see 13:16; 21:40; 26:1). He told them about the prison where he was chained to two soldiers. He related the impossibility of escape, his complete trust in God, and his sound sleep until he was roused by an angel of the Lord. He described how the chains fell off his wrists, how the doors of the prison opened without any resistance from the guards, and how the angel left him in one of the streets of Jerusalem.

b. *James.* Peter said, "Report these things to James and the brothers." This short statement is filled with meaning, for in effect, Peter is appoint-

---

22. R. C. H. Lenski, *The Interpretation of the Acts of the Apostles* (Columbus: Wartburg, 1944), p. 480.

23. SB, vol. 1, pp. 781–83; vol. 2, pp. 707–8; C. P. Thiede, *Simon Peter: From Galilee to Rome* (Exeter: Paternoster, 1986), pp. 153–58.

ing his successor while he himself becomes a fugitive. James is the half-brother of Jesus, not the son of Zebedee whom Herod Agrippa killed (v. 2).

From Scripture we know that during Jesus' ministry James did not believe in him (John 7:5); that after his resurrection, Jesus appeared to James (I Cor. 15:7); and that subsequent to Jesus' ascension, James was present in the upper room (1:14). Already in these early years, James had become an influential leader in the Jerusalem church and was regarded as an apostle even though he was not one of the Twelve (compare Gal. 1:19). With Peter and John, James was counted one of the "pillars" of the church (Gal. 2:9). He was a man blessed with natural leadership ability, for he took an active role in presiding over the Jerusalem Council (15:13–21). And at the conclusion of his third missionary journey, Paul went to Jerusalem and reported to James "all the things God had done among the Gentiles" (21:19). We surmise that during Peter's imprisonment, James had gone into hiding and therefore had to receive Peter's message indirectly. Nevertheless, by implication Peter appointed James to be his successor.

In the New Testament, the word *brothers* normally signifies "fellow believers." Therefore, in this verse the term should be applied not to the biological brothers of James, but to his spiritual brothers and sisters.

c. *Place.* Peter "went out and departed to another place." Although Luke deletes the name of the place to which Peter went, he is explicit in stating that Peter left Jerusalem. Some scholars suggest that Peter went to Rome and, as tradition reports, was Rome's first bishop for twenty-five years.[24] However, the evidence for this tradition is insufficient. Scripture indicates that Peter was in Jerusalem at the time of the Jerusalem Council (15:7–11). Later, he was in Antioch (Gal. 2:11–14). Paul indicates that Peter had spent time in Corinth (I Cor. 1:12; 3:22) and was a traveling apostle whose wife accompanied him (I Cor. 9:5). We conclude that the place to which Peter went is unknown, but the text indicates he was an itinerant missionary.

Doctrinal Considerations in 12:15

Do we have guardian angels? Scripture clearly teaches that God commissions his angels to guard and to serve us. The psalmist writes, "God has commanded his angels to guard you wherever you go" (Ps. 91:11). Jesus warns us not to despise little children, for "their angels in heaven always see the face of my Father in heaven" (Matt. 18:10, NIV). And the writer of Hebrews asks a rhetorical question that implies a positive answer: "Are not all angels ministering spirits sent to serve those who are about to inherit salvation?" (1:14, NIV).[25]

What, then, is the message Scripture gives us? The Bible teaches that God has commissioned his angels—to be precise, a particular class of angels—to protect the believ-

---

24. For example, see John Wenham, "Did Peter go to Rome in AD 42?" *TynB* 23 (1972): 92–102; R. E. Osborne, "Where Did Peter Go?" *CJT* 14 (1968): 274–77.

25. See also Tob. 12:12–15.

ers on earth. Scripture nowhere indicates that every believer throughout his earthly life is protected by one particular angel. Angels are God's servants who take care of believers. To say more than Scripture reveals results in conjecture and speculation.

Greek Words, Phrases, and Constructions in 12:14 and 17

Verse 14

ἀπὸ τῆς χαρᾶς—"because of her joy." The preposition ἀπό expresses cause.

τὸν πυλῶνα—the word πύλη (gate, door) is not used, but a term that signifies the gateway of a city or, in this case, a house.[26]

Verse 17

ὁ κύριος—note that Peter credits the Lord, not an angel, with the miracle of delivering him from prison.

ἕτερον—here the adjective denotes a place that is entirely different from the environment familiar to Peter.

---

4. Reaction of Herod
12:18–19

18. Now when daylight came, there was no small commotion among the soldiers as to what had happened to Peter. 19. Herod had a search made for him but did not find him. Then he examined the guards and ordered that they be led away to execution. Herod went down from Judea to Caesarea and was spending time there.

God's ways are inscrutable and his judgments unsearchable. He protects his servant Peter and causes him to escape to a haven where Herod Agrippa is unable to apprehend him. But God does not shield and protect the soldiers, who by order of Herod perform their duty to guard a prisoner in a maximum-security cell. They suffer the dire consequences of Peter's nocturnal escape. Similarly, when Jesus was born in Bethlehem, Herod the Great told his soldiers to go there and kill all the boys who were two years old and younger (Matt. 2:16). These infants were innocent, and yet they were killed. God grants life but also takes it away.

a. "There was no small commotion among the soldiers." The next morning, consternation struck the soldiers. The two soldiers within the cell woke with chains still on their wrists, but the chains were not binding Peter. They knew that Roman law stipulated the death penalty for guards who permitted their prisoners to escape (see also 16:27; 27:42). The guards placed at the doors were also filled with fear because they, too, would be killed.

b. "Herod had a search made." The news of Peter's escape spread and within a short time reached Herod Agrippa. As commander-in-chief of the

---

26. Refer to Matt. 26:71; Luke 16:20; Acts 10:17. David Hill, *NIDNTT*, vol. 2, p. 30; Joachim Jeremias, *TDNT*, vol. 6, p. 921.

armed forces, he immediately ordered his soldiers to make a diligent search for Peter. Perhaps he cherished the secret hope that if Peter had miraculously escaped from prison, he would still remain in Jerusalem (5:25). Undoubtedly, the soldiers searched the houses of prominent believers and questioned numerous Christians about Peter's escape. However, the search proved to be futile, for Peter had fled.

c. "Then he examined the guards." During the course of that day, the guards were ordered to appear before Herod Agrippa to explain Peter's escape. Their only explanation was that during the night they had fallen asleep. And even though the doors were locked and Peter had been chained to two soldiers, he had disappeared. They assured Herod that they were free from complicity.

d. "[He] ordered that [the guards] be led away to execution." The verb *to be led away* can refer to committing a person to jail,[27] but in this instance the term points to capital punishment. From a human point of view, Herod's verdict seems cruel and unjust. However, this human act of injustice serves as a contrast to a divine act of justice (Herod's miserable end; see v. 23).

e. "Herod went down from Judea to Caesarea." Caesarea served as headquarters for the Roman governors who ruled Palestine, but King Herod Agrippa had decided to live in Jerusalem. After Peter's miraculous escape, Herod Agrippa left the Jewish capital and took up residence in Caesarea.

In Jerusalem, Herod had lifted his hand against God's people, learned that God fought on the side of the believers, and thus experienced disappointment. In Caesarea Herod would experience divine judgment.

---

20 Herod was very angry with the people of Tyre and Sidon. With one accord they came to him; having won over Blastus, a chief officer of the king, they sought peace because they depended on the king's land for food.

21 On the appointed day, Herod wore his royal robe and sat on his throne. He began to deliver a public address. 22 Then the people shouted, "The voice of a god and not of a man." 23 Immediately an angel of the Lord struck him because he did not give glory to God. He was eaten by worms and died.

24 But the word of God continued to increase and multiply. 25 When Barnabas and Saul returned after they had fulfilled their mission at Jerusalem, they took with them John, also called Mark.

C. Death of Herod Agrippa I
12:20–25

Luke connects the account of Peter's escape and that of Herod's death with the transitional statement, "Herod went down from Judea to Caesarea and was spending time there" (v. 19). The tense of the Greek verb for "spend" indicates that he stayed for an undetermined period of time in Caesarea. Nevertheless, from a divine point of view, his days were numbered.

---

27. Calvin, *Acts of the Apostles*, vol. 1, p. 344.

20. Herod was very angry with the people of Tyre and Sidon. With one accord they came to him; having won over Blastus, a chief officer of the king, they sought peace because they depended on the king's land for food.

Why does Luke introduce secular history into his account that describes the development of the Christian church from Jerusalem to Caesarea and Antioch, and eventually to Rome? First, God punishes Herod Agrippa by taking his life. He does so in response to Herod's attack on two of the twelve apostles: James, whom Herod killed, and Peter, whom he imprisoned. God judged Herod Agrippa, who knew the Old Testament Scriptures and who had touched the apple of God's eye (Zech. 2:7–9). Next, Luke indicates that God blessed the church: "the word of God continued to increase and multiply" (v. 24).

Herod had been angry with the people of Tyre and Sidon for some time. The inhabitants of these two harbor cities of Phoenicia (modern Lebanon) were rivals of Caesarea in the world of commerce, but for their food supply they depended on Israel's grain harvests. We assume that Herod denied the Phoenicians access to Israel's grain markets and thus made their life miserable. In short, Herod conducted economic warfare with the Phoenicians, who for centuries had been Israel's trading partners.[28]

Luke is not interested in providing details about Herod's quarrel. He merely relates that the common desire of the citizens of Tyre and Sidon was to seek peace with Herod. To achieve this end, a delegation persuaded Blastus, who was Herod's chief officer, to ask Herod to lift the grain embargo and to establish normal relations between Israel and Phoenicia. The word *peace* is the equivalent of "reconciliation" and signifies that the quarrel ended.[29] Because of the brevity of the account, we do not know whether the delegation returned immediately to Tyre and Sidon or stayed for the scheduled festivities in Caesarea.

21. On the appointed day, Herod wore his royal robe and sat on his throne. He began to deliver a public address. 22. Then the people shouted, "The voice of a god and not of a man." 23. Immediately an angel of the Lord struck him because he did not give glory to God. He was eaten by worms and died.

The Jewish historiographer Josephus relates that Herod Agrippa had come to Caesarea to celebrate a festival held in honor of Emperor Claudius.[30] The festival consisted of games that were held every five years, presumably scheduled for the first of August to coincide with the emperor's birthday.[31] This date would be significant—it came after the grain harvest had been completed and thus merchants would buy wheat.

---

28. Refer to I Kings 5:11; Ezra 3:7; Ezek. 27:17.
29. Henry Alford, *Alford's Greek Testament: An Exegetical and Critical Commentary*, 7th ed., 4 vols. (1877; Grand Rapids: Guardian, 1976), vol. 2, p. 136.
30. Josephus *Antiquities* 19.8.2 [343].
31. Suetonius *Claudius* 2.1.

Josephus writes that on the second day of these games, Herod entered the arena at daybreak. He was dressed in a garment woven from silver thread. When the first rays of the sun touched his cloak, Herod was illumined by the sun's reflected light.

> Straightway his flatterers raised their voices from various directions— though hardly for his own good—addressing him as a god. "May you be propitious to us," they added, "and if we have hitherto feared you as a man, yet henceforth we agree that you are more than mortal in your being." The king did not rebuke them nor did he reject their flattery as impious.[32]

Both Luke and Josephus describe Herod Agrippa's appearance before the crowd. The two writers differ only on a few points: Luke states that Herod began to deliver a public address, but Josephus omits this detail; Luke reports that the people shouted, "The voice of a god, and not of a man"; Josephus says that the Gentile crowd addressed Herod as a god; Luke mentions that an angel of the Lord struck Herod down, while Josephus notes that Herod saw "an owl perched on a rope over his head." Fourth-century church historian Eusebius, having quoted extensively from the account of Josephus, blends this detail with the biblical record and says that Herod "saw an angel seated above his head."[33]

In numerous passages in Scripture, we read that God commissioned an angel to execute punishment. For instance, an angel killed 185,000 Assyrian soldiers in one night (II Kings 19:35).[34] God publicly punished Herod Agrippa for accepting honors that were due to God himself. God is a jealous God, as he himself asserts. He does not allow anyone to take his place (Exod. 20:5; Deut. 5:9).

Luke graphically describes Herod's demise by saying that he was eaten by worms and died. Although scholars have suggested a number of causes of death, ranging from appendicitis to poisoning, we rely on Luke's medical analysis of the king's decease. We do so in the knowledge that, because of his divine intervention, God reveals Herod Agrippa's punishment: he had to be devoured by worms and thus suffer an extremely painful and utterly despicable end. Calvin remarks that Herod's body reeked because of decay, so that he was nothing more than a living carcass.[35] Other sources describe the excruciating death of being consumed by worms; one account refers to Antiochus Epiphanes, a tyrant who had persecuted the Jews and who therefore was struck with an incurable disease: "And so the ungodly man's body swarmed with worms, and while he was still living in anguish and pain, his flesh rotted away, and because of his stench the whole army felt revulsion at his decay" (II Macc. 9:9, RSV).

---

32. Josephus *Antiquities* 19.8.2 [345] (LCL).
33. Eusebius *Ecclesiastical History* 2.10.6 (LCL).
34. See also Exod. 33:2; Pss. 35:5–6; 78:49; Matt. 13:41.
35. Calvin, *Acts of the Apostles*, vol. 1, p. 347.

Josephus supplies the information that Herod died after five days in pain, "in the fifty-fourth year of his life and the seventh of his reign."[36] That is, Herod died in A.D. 44. A persecutor of the church, he came to a shameful death relatively soon after he had killed James and incarcerated Peter.

24. But the word of God continued to increase and multiply.

After Herod's death, the Roman emperor appointed a governor to rule the land of the Jews. The Christians once again enjoyed freedom from persecution. As a result, the church continued to increase numerically. Luke implies that the messengers of the gospel went everywhere with the Good News. Wherever these ministers proclaimed the message of salvation, there the church was strengthened in the faith and supported by numerous additional believers. At the beginning of his book, Luke mentions figures to indicate the phenomenal growth of the church. But as the church expanded in ever-widening circles, Luke speaks only in generalities and states that "the word of God continued to increase and multiply" (see 6:7; 19:20).

25. When Barnabas and Saul returned after they had fulfilled their mission at Jerusalem, they took with them John, also called Mark.

Luke has come to the end of his historical survey of Herod Agrippa's influence on the church. After this interlude, he returns to his account of Barnabas and Paul (11:30). These two men had traveled from Antioch to Jerusalem with relief for the famine-stricken population of that city. They made this trip after Herod Agrippa had died. Luke does not link the return of Barnabas and Paul to Herod's rule in Jerusalem. Rather, he completely separates the two reports and uses verse 25 as an introduction to his account of Paul's first missionary journey (13:1–3).

Luke writes the verb *returned* and by implication suggests that Barnabas and Paul went to Antioch. From Luke's point of view, the men returned to his native town. Therefore, he feels no need to be explicit and mention Antioch by name. For him, not Jerusalem but Antioch is the mission center that occupies a strategic place in the growth and development of the church. Antioch sent missionaries into the Greco-Roman world.

John Mark, who in later life became known as Mark, accompanied his cousin Barnabas and Paul. He revealed an interest in spreading the good news of salvation and became a helper of the two missionaries whom the Antiochean church sent to Cyprus (13:5).

Doctrinal Considerations in 12:21–23

When God says in the Decalogue, "I, the LORD your God, am a jealous God" (Exod. 20:5; Deut. 5:9), he speaks no idle words. He jealously guards his honor. In fact, examples abound of people meeting divine punishment when they knowingly

---

36. Josephus *Antiquities* 19.8.2 [350] (LCL).

tried to take honor from him. Two sons of Aaron, Nadab and Abihu, put aside God's instructions regarding their duties at the altar and decided to follow their own inclinations. God punished them with sudden death (Lev. 10:1–2). Uzziah, king of Judah, was filled with pride and wanted to burn incense in the temple. He set aside God's precepts that only priests could offer incense. Therefore, God struck him with leprosy, which made him an outcast, and in isolation Uzziah died (II Chron. 26:16–21). King Herod Agrippa knew the Scriptures, which he publicly read to the people in the temple area during a Jewish feast. Yet, when the crowd in Caesarea addressed him as if he were divine, Herod did not rebuke them but claimed for himself honor that belonged only to God.

Note the contrast in the lives of Paul and Barnabas, who healed a crippled man in Lystra. In their excitement, the people exclaimed that the gods had come down to them; the Lycaonians regarded Barnabas as Zeus and Paul as Hermes (14:11–12). Moreover, the priest of Zeus wanted to honor Paul and Barnabas by offering sacrifices to them. However, the missionaries strenuously objected to this misplaced honor. They expressed their anguish by tearing their clothes and emphatically stated that they were not gods but only men (14:13–15). They told the people about the living God, the maker of heaven and earth, and thus exalted God's name and honor. Indeed, they knew that God is a jealous God.

Greek Words, Phrases, and Constructions in 12:20 and 25

Verse 20

ἦν θυμομαχῶν—the periphrastic construction of the verb *to be* with the present participle indicates that Herod's quarrel was not a momentary outburst of anger but a continuing dispute. The compound participle derives from the noun θυμός (rage) and the verb μάχομαι (I fight). The second part of the compound controls the first part and thus means "to be very angry."[37]

κοιτῶνος—literally, the noun refers to "the one in charge of the bed-chamber."[38] However, in context the word signifies a highly trusted official.

Verse 25

εἰς—the reading *into Jerusalem* is indeed troublesome. The context demands the translation *from Jerusalem,* especially because John Mark, a resident of Jerusalem, accompanied Barnabas and Paul. The better manuscripts have the preposition εἰς instead of ἀπό and ἐξ (away from; from). But the verb ὑποστρέφειν (to return) in Acts frequently specifies the place to which a person returns.[39] The preposition εἰς can take the place of ἐν (at). Bruce M. Metzger, therefore, suggests the following translation: "Barnabas and Saul returned, after they had fulfilled at Jerusalem their

---

37. Friedrich Blass and Albert Debrunner, *A Greek Grammar of the New Testament and Other Early Christian Literature,* trans. and rev. Robert Funk (Chicago: University of Chicago Press, 1961), #191.1.

38. Bauer, p. 440.

39. E.g., 1:12; 8:25; 12:25; 13:13, 34; 14:21; 21:6; 22:17; 23:32.

mission, bringing with them John whose other name was Mark."[40] Even so, difficulties remain.

πληρώσαντες—from the verb πληρόω (I fulfill), the particple is an effective aorist that emphasizes completion of a task. The participle συμπαραλαβόντες (taking along) is a constative aorist that "contemplates the action in its entirety."[41]

Summary of Chapter 12

King Herod Agrippa I persecutes the church by killing the apostle James, the brother of John. He arrests Peter and places him in prison during the Feast of Unleavened Bread (Passover). He has Peter guarded by four squads of four soldiers each. While Peter is in prison, the church is praying for his release.

On the eve of Peter's trial, an angel enters Peter's prison cell. Sound asleep, Peter is shackled to two guards. Awakened by the angel and set free from his fetters, Peter follows the angel through the doors and gate to the street outside. The angel disappears and Peter comes to his senses. He quickly goes to the house of John Mark's mother, where he knocks on the door. Many Christians are praying and Rhoda, a servant girl, comes to the door. She recognizes Peter's voice but fails to open the door. The Christians give entrance to Peter and are astonished. Peter relates the story of his release and, after giving instructions, leaves Jerusalem.

Herod examines the report of the soldiers. He orders that they be executed and then leaves for Caesarea. He settles a dispute with the people of Tyre and Sidon. On a given day he is dressed in royal robes, addresses a crowd, and accepts their claim that he is a god and not a man. An angel of the Lord strikes him down, so that he is eaten by worms and dies.

The church continues to increase and multiply. Barnabas and Paul, accompanied by John Mark, journey from Jerusalem to Antioch.

---

40. Metzger, *Textual Commentary*, p. 400.

41. H. E. Dana and Julius R. Mantey, *A Manual Grammar of the Greek New Testament* (1927; New York: Macmillan, 1967), p. 196. See also A. T. Robertson, *A Grammar of the Greek New Testament in the Light of Historical Research* (Nashville: Broadman, 1934), p. 859.

13

The Church in Transition, *part 3*

13:1–3

and The First Missionary Journey, *part 1*

13:4–52

Outline (continued)

13:1–3	D.	Paul and Barnabas Commissioned
13:4–14:28	V.	The First Missionary Journey
13:4–12	A.	Cyprus
13:4–5		1. Jewish Synagogue
13:6–12		2. Bar-Jesus
13:13–52	B.	Pisidian Antioch
13:13–15		1. Invitation
13:16–22		2. Old Testament Survey
13:23–25		3. The Coming of Jesus
13:26–31		4. Death and Resurrection
13:32–41		5. Good News of Jesus
13:42–45		6. Invitation Renewed
13:46–52		7. Effect and Opposition

13 1 In the church at Antioch were prophets and teachers: Barnabas, Simeon called Niger, Lucius of Cyrene, Manaen who had been brought up with Herod the tetrarch, and Saul. 2 As they were worshiping the Lord and fasting, the Holy Spirit said, "Appoint for me Barnabas and Saul for the work to which I have called them." 3 Then after having fasted and prayed, they laid their hands on them and sent them away.

D. Barnabas and Paul Commissioned
13:1–3

In the first three verses of this chapter, Luke continues the account about the church in Antioch and portrays it as an important center of the Christian faith (11:19–30). One of its first ministries was to send relief to the famine-stricken believers in Jerusalem (11:27–30). Antioch next gained prominence when the church sent missionaries to the Gentile world, initially to Cyprus and Asia Minor and later to Macedonia and Greece. Luke mentions Antioch fourteen times,[1] while Paul refers to it once (Gal. 2:11). As the church develops, Luke calls attention to Antioch instead of Jerusalem as the center of activity. He decisively places the church in Antioch on the same level as the church in Jerusalem when he relates the principal names of those who gave leadership in the Antiochean church.

1. In the church at Antioch were prophets and teachers: Barnabas, Simeon called Niger, Lucius of Cyrene, Manaen who had been brought up with Herod the tetrarch, and Saul.

We make these observations:

a. *Church.* In the first twelve chapters of Acts, the word *church* consistently refers to the gathering of Christians in Jerusalem. But when the believers in Antioch received instruction from Barnabas and Paul, Luke refers to them as a church (11:26). The Christians in Antioch became a church when they regularly heard the gospel preached, received instruction in the faith, appointed church leaders, and implemented their vision for mission to the world. However, we know that the church is one body even if its members gather in different places and countries. The believers in Antioch, therefore, belonged to the same church as those in Jerusalem.

b. *Office.* The church at Antioch had a number of prophets and teachers.

---

1. See 11:19, 20, 22, 26 [twice], 27; 13:1; 14:26; 15:22, 23, 30, 35; 18:22, 23.

From the Greek we are unable to discern whether the words *prophets* and *teachers* signify two separate offices or if a person can be both prophet and teacher. Paul, for example, speaks of "pastors and teachers" (Eph. 4:11); in his view, a person fills one office that has a dual function. Further, he places the prophets in a separate category, which is listed after that of apostleship. We must conclude that the New Testament reveals a difference between prophets and teachers. "Whereas teachers expound Scripture, cherish the tradition about Jesus and explain the fundamentals of the catechism, the prophets, not bound by Scripture or tradition, speak to the congregation on the basis of revelations" (see I Cor. 14:29–32).[2] Luke describes both Barnabas and Paul as teachers in the Antiochean church (11:26), but in the list of five names (13:1) he refrains from specifying who is a teacher and who is a prophet and thus leaves the matter unresolved.

c. *Names.* Of the five church leaders, Barnabas is listed first. This is understandable, because the Jerusalem church commissioned him to minister to the spiritual needs of the believers in Antioch (11:22).

The next person listed is Simeon called Niger. We assume that others bore the name *Simeon,* so that further identification became necessary. The word *niger* (Latin: black) undoubtedly refers to Simeon's complexion and descent. Because Luke lists him with Lucius of Cyrene, the possibility is not remote that Simeon also was a native of North Africa. We are unable to ascertain whether Simeon is the same person as Simon of Cyrene, who carried Jesus' cross (Matt. 27:32), or if Lucius is the one for whom Paul extended greetings to Rome (Rom. 16:21).[3] Both men probably were among those refugees who, having fled Jerusalem because of the persecution following the death of Stephen, came as far as Antioch and were originally from Cyprus and Cyrene (11:19–20).

Manaen is next. His name is a Greek form of the Hebrew word *Menaḥem,* which means "comforter." Luke describes him as a man "who had been brought up with Herod the tetrarch." This description denotes that Manaen was a foster brother of Herod Antipas, the tetrarch of Galilee and Perea (4:27; Matt. 14:1–12; Mark 6:14–29; Luke 3:1). Manaen, an influential person of royal descent and a Christian in Antioch, provided Luke with information about Herod Antipas and possibly about other members of the Herodian family.[4]

The last person is Paul, here listed with his Hebrew name, Saul. At the invitation of Barnabas, he had come to the Antiochean church as a teacher when the work became too taxing for Barnabas (11:25–26). "Among the

---

2. Gerhard Friedrich, *TDNT*, vol. 6, p. 854; see also Carl Heinz Peisker, *NIDNTT*, vol. 3, p. 84. Jacques Dupont understands the terms *prophets* and *teachers* to refer to the same persons. *Nouvelles Études sur les Actes des Apôtres,* Lectio Divina 118 (Paris: Cerf, 1984), p. 164.

3. Consult H. J. Cadbury, "Lucius of Cyrene," *Beginnings*, vol. 5, pp. 489–95.

4. See Richard Glover, " 'Luke the Antiochene' and Acts," *NTS* 11 (1964–65): 101.

veterans at Antioch, with remarkable modesty, he was content with the lowest place."[5]

2. As they were worshiping the Lord and fasting, the Holy Spirit said, "Appoint for me Barnabas and Saul for the work to which I have called them." 3. Then after having fasted and prayed, they laid their hands on them and sent them away.

a. "As they were worshiping the Lord and fasting." The term *worship*, a typical Old Testament religious term, formerly described the service of the priests at the temple in Jerusalem (see, e.g., Luke 1:23). But in verse 2 Luke for the first time applies the word to Christian practice. By his use of the word *worship* Luke shows continuity with the past but also subtly indicates a different, spiritualized emphasis.[6] In the new form of worship, we see not the priests at the altar but every believer at church in prayer.

In these verses Luke also indicates that the Christians in Antioch combined prayer with the Jewish custom of fasting; the two practices were linked only on special occasions (see 14:23).

The immediate context of verses 2 and 3 seems to restrict the reference to worship to the five prophets and teachers Luke has mentioned (v. 1). But there are at least three objections to this interpretation. First, a worship service is meant for all the believers in the church. Next, the entire Antiochean church was involved in commissioning Barnabas and Saul, for upon their return the missionaries reported to the church what God had done (14:27). And last, the Holy Spirit moves the church and not merely five people to engage in mission work.[7]

b. "The Holy Spirit said, 'Appoint for me Barnabas and Saul for the work to which I have called them.' " While the church prayed, the Holy Spirit spoke through the prophets and made his will known. Through his Spirit God enlarges the church and appoints his servants to the tasks he gives them.[8] God, then, appoints Barnabas and Paul as missionaries.

Jesus had called Paul to be an apostle to the Gentiles, but both Barnabas and Paul had been teaching in the Antiochean church. Now the Holy Spirit called the believers to appoint these two men to a specific task: to proclaim the Good News to the world. For the church in Antioch this meant that these believers, by commissioning Barnabas and Paul, would lose two able teachers; that they would promise prayer support for the missionaries; and that Antioch would continue to be a mission center.

Both Paul and Barnabas had been called to be apostles to the Gentiles. In fact, when Luke refers to these men on their first missionary journey,

---

5. John Albert Bengel, *Gnomon of the New Testament*, rev. and ed. Andrew R. Fausset, 5 vols. (Edinburgh: Clark, 1877), vol. 2, p. 618.

6. Hermann Strathmann, *TDNT*, vol. 4, p. 226; Klaus Hess, *NIDNTT*, vol. 3, p. 552.

7. Compare Everett F. Harrison, *Interpreting Acts: The Expanding Church*, 2d ed. (Grand Rapids: Zondervan, Academie Books, 1986), p. 216.

8. E.g., 8:39; 9:31; 10:19, 44.

he calls them "apostles" (14:14; and see I Cor. 9:1–6). The work that the Holy Spirit assigns to Barnabas and Paul is to acquaint the world with Christ's gospel and to extend the church to the ends of the earth (compare 1:8).

c. "They laid their hands on them and sent them away." After a period of fasting and prayer, leaders of the Antiochean church placed hands on Barnabas and Paul. In Damascus, Ananias had laid his hands on Paul and thus Paul received the gift of the Holy Spirit (9:17). Although both Barnabas and Paul had taught Christ's gospel for many years, the church in Antioch officially ordained these two men to be missionaries to the Gentiles. After God called them to the special task of proclaiming the gospel to the Greco-Roman world (compare Gal. 1:16), the Antiochean church conducted the external ceremony of ordaining Barnabas and Paul.[9] The ordination service plainly denotes that the missionaries and the church are united in mission work.

Doctrinal Considerations in 13:1–3

In light of the work performed by Barnabas and Paul, what is the significance of their ordination in Antioch? First, thus far neither Paul nor Barnabas has been called an apostle, but when Luke recounts their first missionary tour he gives them the title *apostles* (14:14). Second, the two missionaries display miraculous healing powers, preach the gospel to Jew and Gentile, and possess authority that is equal to that of the apostles Peter and John. And third, the parallel between Peter and Paul is evident in healing a cripple (3:1–10 and 14:8–10), rebuking a magician or sorcerer (8:18–24 and 13:6–12), and organizing churches (8:14–17 and 14:21–25). What does the ordination of Barnabas and Paul signify? The two men "were consecrated to a work which would be recognized as the work of apostles and in which they would act with apostolic authority, holding a position corresponding to that of the Twelve."[10]

Furthermore, let us note the parallel between the twelve apostles and Barnabas and Paul. The Holy Spirit fills the twelve apostles in Jerusalem on the day of Pentecost so that they are able to address the Jewish multitudes (2:1–41). And the Holy Spirit directs the church in Antioch to appoint Barnabas and Paul to proclaim the gospel to the Gentile multitudes. The Twelve are involved in the formation of the rapidly increasing Jerusalem church, while Barnabas and Paul are sent forth by the Antiochean church to organize churches to the ends of the earth (1:8).

---

9. John Calvin, *Commentary on the Acts of the Apostles*, ed. David W. Torrance and Thomas F. Torrance, 2 vols. (Grand Rapids: Eerdmans, 1966), vol. 1, p. 355. Compare Ernest Best, "Acts xiii. 1–3," *JTS* 11 (1960): 344–48.

10. Richard B. Rackham, *The Acts of the Apostles: An Exposition*, Westminster Commentaries series (1901; reprint ed., Grand Rapids: Baker, 1964), p. 192.

Greek Words, Phrases, and Constructions in 13:1–2

Verse 1

κατὰ τὴν οὖσαν ἐκκλησίαν—"in the local church" (11:22) is a technical term.[11] Nevertheless, the unity of the church prevails.

Verse 2

λειτουργούντων—the genitive absolute construction of this present participle and the pronoun αὐτῶν separates the clause from the subject of the main sentence ("the Holy Spirit said"). The pronoun, however, is indefinite, while the participle shows continued action. The word *liturgy* is derived from the verb λειτουργέω (I serve).

δή—this particle has the force of an invitation: "Come, appoint for me. . . ."[12]

προσκέκλημαι—here the perfect middle points to an action that occurred in the past but has full significance in the present.

---

4 Having been sent by the Holy Spirit, they went down to Seleucia. From there they sailed to Cyprus. 5 When they arrived at Salamis, they began to proclaim the word of God in the synagogues of the Jews. They also had John as a helper. 6 After traveling through the whole island as far as Paphos, they met a certain Jewish magician and false prophet named Bar-Jesus. 7 He was with the proconsul Sergius Paulus, an intelligent man, who summoned Barnabas and Saul and wanted to hear the word of God. 8 But Elymas the magician—for this is what his name means—opposed them, seeking to turn the proconsul from the faith. 9 Then Saul, also known as Paul, filled with the Holy Spirit, fixed his gaze on Elymas 10 and said: "You are full of deceit and trickery, you son of the devil, you enemy of all righteousness; will you not cease to pervert the right ways of the Lord? 11 And now the hand of the Lord is against you. You will be blind and unable to see the light of the sun for a while."

Immediately a mist and darkness fell upon him, and he went about and sought someone to lead him by the hand. 12 When the proconsul saw what had happened, he believed and was amazed at the teaching of the Lord.

13 Paul and his companions put out to sea from Paphos and went to Perga in Pamphylia, where John left them and returned to Jerusalem. 14 But going on from Perga, they came to Pisidian Antioch. On the Sabbath they entered the synagogue and sat down. 15 After the reading of the Law and the Prophets, the synagogue officials sent this message to them: "Men and brothers, if you have any word of exhortation for the people, please speak."

16 Paul stood up and motioning with his hand he said: "Men of Israel and you who fear God, listen to me! 17 The God of this nation Israel chose our fathers and made the people great during their stay in the land of Egypt. With an uplifted arm he led them out from there. 18 He put up with them for about forty years in the desert. 19 He destroyed seven nations in the land of Canaan and apportioned their land as an inheritance. 20 All this took about four hundred and fifty years.

"After these things, God gave them judges until the time of Samuel the prophet. 21 Then

---

11. Friedrich Blass and Albert Debrunner, *A Greek Grammar of the New Testament and Other Early Christian Literature,* trans. and rev. Robert Funk (Chicago: University of Chicago Press, 1961), #474.5c.

12. A. T. Robertson, *A Grammar of the Greek New Testament in the Light of Historical Research* (Nashville: Broadman, 1934), p. 1149.

they asked for a king, and God gave them Saul son of Kish, a man of the tribe of Benjamin, for forty years. 22 After he had removed him, God raised up David to be their king. Concerning him God testified, 'I have found David the son of Jesse to be a man after my heart, who will do everything I desire.' 23 From this man's descendants, God brought to Israel a savior, Jesus, according to the promise. 24 Before Jesus came, John preached a baptism of repentance to all the people of Israel. 25 As John was completing his work, he repeatedly said, 'Who do you suppose I am? I am not the Christ. No, but someone is coming after me whose sandal I am not worthy to untie.'

26 "Men and brothers, sons of Abraham's family, and those among you who fear God, to us the word of this salvation has been sent. 27 Those who live in Jerusalem and their rulers did not recognize Jesus, and by condemning him they fulfilled the words of the prophets that are read every Sabbath. 28 And though they found no ground for execution, they asked Pilate that he be killed. 29 When they accomplished everything that had been written about him, they took him down from the cross and laid him in a tomb. 30 But God raised him from the dead. 31 For many days, he appeared to those who had come up with him from Galilee to Jerusalem. They are now his witnesses to the people.

32 "And we proclaim this good news to you. This promise made to the fathers 33 God has fulfilled to us, their children. He raised Jesus, as it was written in the second psalm,

> 'You are my Son;
> today I have become your Father.'

34 Namely, God raised him from the dead, never to decay, as God said: 'I will give you the holy and sure blessings of David.' 35 For this reason, God says in another psalm,

> 'You will not let your Holy One undergo decay.'

36 For David, after he served God's purpose in his own generation, fell asleep. He was buried with his fathers and underwent decay. 37 But whom God raised from the dead did not undergo decay.

38 "Therefore, men and brothers, let it be known to you that through him forgiveness of sins is proclaimed to you. 39 Everyone who believes is justified through him from all the things from which you could not be justified through the law of Moses. 40 Be careful that what was spoken by the prophets does not come upon you:

> 41 'Look, you scoffers,
> be amazed and perish!
> Because I am going to do a work
> in your days, a work which you will never believe
> even if someone would describe it to you.' "

42 When Paul and Barnabas were leaving, the people begged them that these things be spoken to them the next Sabbath. 43 After the synagogue meeting had ended, many Jews and God-fearing proselytes to Judaism followed Paul and Barnabas, who spoke to them and urged them to continue in the grace of God.

44 On the next Sabbath, nearly the whole city assembled to hear the word of the Lord. 45 But when the Jews saw the crowds, they were filled with jealousy. And abusively they began to contradict the things that Paul was saying. 46 Paul and Barnabas boldly answered them: "The word of God had to be spoken to you first. Since you reject it and do not consider yourselves worthy of eternal life, we are turning to the Gentiles. 47 For this is what the Lord commanded us:

> 'I have placed you as a light to the Gentiles,
> to bring salvation to the ends of the earth.' "

48 When the Gentiles heard this, they began to rejoice and glorify the word of the Lord. And as many as were ordained to eternal life believed.

49 The word of the Lord spread through the whole region. 50 But the Jews aroused the

God-fearing and honorable women and the leading men of the city. They instigated a persecution against Paul and Barnabas and drove them out of their region. 51 So Paul and Barnabas shook the dust off their feet in protest against them and went to Iconium. 52 And the disciples were filled with joy and the Holy Spirit.

V. The First Missionary Journey
13:4–14:28

A. Cyprus
13:4–12

The missionary task to which the Holy Spirit has called Barnabas and Paul is exacting. The missionaries frequent Jewish synagogues but in addition they actively seek new converts from the Gentile population. This new aspect to the task of the missionaries is challenging, for it results eventually in the need to formulate principles of conduct for Gentile believers (15:1–35).

1. Jewish Synagogue
13:4–5

4. Having been sent by the Holy Spirit, they went down to Seleucia. From there they sailed to Cyprus. 5. When they arrived at Salamis, they began to proclaim the word of God in the synagogues of the Jews. They also had John as a helper.

a. "Having been sent by the Holy Spirit." Luke emphasizes that the missionaries are sent out not by the church in Antioch but by the Holy Spirit. The Spirit told the church to appoint Barnabas and Paul, and he himself sent them to their field of labor. Accordingly, Paul is able to say that he has been "sent not from men nor by man, but by Jesus Christ and God the Father" (Gal. 1:1, NIV). That is, the Triune God sent Paul and Barnabas first to Cyprus and then to Asia Minor.

b. "They went down to Seleucia." Located on the Orontes River and near the Mediterranean coast, Seleucia served as the seaport for the city of Antioch. Because Antioch is in mountainous territory, Barnabas and Paul had to travel a relatively short distance down to Seleucia.

c. "From there they sailed to Cyprus." On a clear day in Seleucia, the apostles would be able to see the coastline and the mountain complex of Cyprus. The voyage across the water would take less than a day.[13] Cyprus was Barnabas's birthplace (4:36), and so he had intimate knowledge of the inhabitants, the Jewish synagogues, and the culture. This knowledge proved to be an asset. Barnabas was not the first Christian to visit the island; Christian refugees from Jerusalem had traveled as far as Cyprus, Luke relates (11:19).

d. "When they arrived at Salamis, they began to proclaim the word of God in the synagogues of the Jews." Salamis was a harbor town on the east coast of Cyprus and was situated directly north of the modern city of

---

13. Refer to E. M. Blaiklock, "Seleucia," *ZPEB*, vol. 5, p. 334.

Famagusta. It was a trading center where merchants from Cilicia, Syria, Phoenicia, and Egypt traded olive oil, wool, wine, and grain. In the course of time, this port city attracted a large number of Jews who belonged to the merchant class and who had established several synagogues there. When Barnabas and Paul arrived in Salamis, the Jews welcomed them to their synagogues.

In his brief report, Luke neglects to mention the effect of the message the missionaries proclaimed. However, with the tense of a Greek verb he indicates that Barnabas and Paul continued to preach the Word of God for some time. We surmise that the apostles proved from the Old Testament Scripture that Jesus fulfilled the messianic promises. The Word of God, therefore, served as a common denominator for both parties. Perhaps in their initial contacts with the people, Barnabas and Paul spent their time with the Jewish population of Salamis, for nothing is said about Gentiles frequenting the synagogue worship services. The missionaries applied the rule which in time became their trademark: first to the Jew and then to the Gentile.

e. "They also had John as a helper." As an afterthought, Luke inserts the information that John Mark accompanied the missionaries to the island of Cyprus (see 12:25). Perhaps Luke wants to place the emphasis on the mission of Barnabas and Paul; in passing, he also mentions their travel companion John Mark. Indeed, Mark was not called by the Holy Spirit and was not ordained by the Antiochean church. For this reason, Luke describes him as a helper to the missionaries. We are not told what the nature of his assistance was, but his work was not limited to providing physical necessities (e.g., food and lodging) for his companions. Luke literally uses the word *underling* to describe Mark, which means that he did whatever the missionaries asked him to do.

Greek Words, Phrases, and Constructions in 13:5

κατήγγελλον—from the verb καταγγέλλω (I proclaim publicly), this form is the ingressive imperfect: "they began to proclaim."

ὑπηρέτην—translated "servant" or "attendant" (see Luke 4:20), the noun is an accusative of apposition.

---

2. Bar-Jesus
13:6–12

6. After traveling through the whole island as far as Paphos, they met a certain Jewish magician and false prophet named Bar-Jesus. 7. He was with the proconsul Sergius Paulus, an intelligent man, who summoned Barnabas and Saul and wanted to hear the word of God.

The island of Cyprus had been conquered by the Romans and made an imperial province that was under the jurisdiction of the Roman senate. Avoiding the mountainous interior areas of the island, the missionaries walked through the level plains and along the southern seacoast of Cyprus. They traveled about one hundred miles from the east coast of the island to the west coast, where they arrived at the city of Paphos. This city was noted for its beautiful buildings and a temple dedicated to the goddess Aphrodite. During the reign of Emperor Augustus, Paphos was destroyed by an earthquake (15 B.C.) but was soon rebuilt with Roman government funds. The city became the administrative and religious center of the island, as well as the residence of the Roman proconsul. Proconsuls, who were appointed by the Roman senate, usually ruled for one year and had absolute military and judicial authority (see 18:12; 19:38).

On his missionary journeys, Paul usually visited capital cities, especially those where officials of the Roman government resided. In Paphos, Paul and Barnabas met a Roman proconsul, Sergius Paulus. He employed a magician—a man who interpreted dreams and dabbled in the occult— named Bar-Jesus. The name *Bar-Jesus* is Aramaic and means "son of Jesus," or in Old Testament terms, "son of Joshua." Luke reports that this man was a false prophet and a Jew. As a Jew, Bar-Jesus was acquainted with God's condemnation of prophets who had not been called by God (see Jer. 14:14– 16). But in spite of God's teachings concerning sorcerers and false prophets, Bar-Jesus was one of them (compare 19:13).[14] Both the Talmud and the postapostolic literature contain stern warnings not to practice magic (and see Rev. 22:15).[15]

In verse 7 Luke says that Sergius Paulus, the proconsul, was an intelligent man who desired to hear the word of God. He was open to religious instruction from Jewish teachers; thus, he employed Bar-Jesus and listened to Barnabas and Paul preach the gospel. He was not a God-fearer, but he desired to hear the word of God and become acquainted with the teachings of the apostles.

In the northern part of Cyprus, archaeologists have discovered a fragment of a Greek inscription that bears the name *Quintus Sergius Paulus,* who presumably was a proconsul during the reign of Emperor Claudius (A.D. 41–54). If we accept that Paul began his first missionary journey in the second half of the fifth decade (A.D. 46), the archaeological find points to the proconsul Luke describes in Acts.[16]

8. But Elymas the magician—for this is what his name means—opposed them, seeking to turn the proconsul from the faith. 9. Then Saul, also known as Paul, filled with the Holy Spirit, fixed his gaze on Elymas

---

14. Refer to Arthur Darby Nock, "Paul and the Magus," *Beginnings,* vol. 5, pp. 182–83.

15. *Shabbath* 75a; *Didache* 2.2.

16. Bastiaan Van Elderen, "Some Archaeological Observations on Paul's First Missionary Journey," in *Apostolic History and the Gospel,* ed. W. Ward Gasque and Ralph P. Martin (Exeter: Paternoster; Grand Rapids: Eerdmans, 1970), pp. 151–56.

10. and said: "You are full of deceit and trickery, you son of the devil, you enemy of all righteousness; will you not cease to pervert the right ways of the Lord? 11a. And now the hand of the Lord is against you. You will be blind and unable to see the light of the sun for a while."

a. "But Elymas the magician . . . opposed them." Luke indicates that Bar-Jesus had a Greek name, Elymas, which is a transliteration of an Aramaic or Arabic word that means "magician."[17] At the court of Sergius Paulus, Bar-Jesus used his Greek rather than his Aramaic name. Note that in this context, Paul also preferred his Greek name to his Hebrew name (v. 9).

b. "[He sought] to turn the proconsul from the faith." While the preaching of the gospel intrigued Sergius Paulus, it mobilized Elymas into opposition. Elymas was a magician who realized that if Sergius Paulus became a Christian, his services would no longer be needed and he would lose his source of income. Further, Elymas was a Jew who bitterly opposed the gospel and its messengers. When he saw that Sergius Paulus had summoned the missionaries to hear the gospel explained, Elymas did everything possible to dissuade the proconsul from accepting the Christian faith (compare II Tim. 3:8). The situation reached the critical stage, for the veracity of the gospel was at stake. Either Elymas or Barnabas and Paul were imposters.

c. "Then Saul, also known as Paul, filled with the Holy Spirit, fixed his gaze on Elymas." We observe at least four distinct changes.

First, from this moment Luke gives prominence to Paul. That is, Paul is no longer the person who accompanies Barnabas; the roles are reversed. Yet at times the order *Barnabas and Paul* is retained (see 14:14; 15:12).

Next, Paul adopts the Greek name *Paulus,* which as a loan word from Latin literally means "the little one." Paul no longer uses his Hebrew name. Augustine believed that Paul adopted his new name to indicate that he was "the least of the apostles" (I Cor. 15:9; and see Eph. 3:8). But this view has no support. Nor do we have proof that Paul used his Greek name as a compliment to Sergius Paulus. Paul, a Roman citizen, already had two, if not three, names. (Roman citizens usually had three names; for example, Quintus Sergius Paulus.) And Paul used his Greek name even before Sergius Paulus became a believer.[18]

Third, even though Paul received the Holy Spirit when Ananias put his hands on him (9:17) and was sent out by the Holy Spirit (v. 4), this is the first explicit statement that Paul is filled with the Spirit.

And last, empowered by the presence of the Holy Spirit, Paul cursed Elymas with blindness and thus exerted his apostolic authority. In passing, we call attention to the parallel between two apostles: Peter rebuking Simon the sorcerer (8:20–23) and Paul cursing Elymas.

---

17. S. F. Hunter, "Bar-Jesus," *ISBE,* vol. 1, p. 431; see also L. Yaure, "Elymas—Nehelamite—Pethor," *JBL* 79 (1960): 297–314.

18. Compare Colin J. Hemer, "The Name of Paul," *TynB* 36 (1985): 179–83.

d. "Paul . . . said: 'You are full of deceit and trickery, you son of the devil.'" When Paul denounced Elymas in front of Sergius Paulus, a verbal explosion erupted. He called Elymas "son of the devil" (compare John 8:44) instead of "son of Jesus" (Bar-Jesus). Paul was filled with the Holy Spirit, but Elymas was full of deceit and trickery.[19] Paul represented Jesus Christ and Elymas represented the devil. Therefore, in this spiritual conflict, Paul addressed Elymas directly and Satan indirectly: "You son of the devil, full of all deceit and all trickery." In Acts, Luke refers to Satan twice (5:3; 26:18) and to the devil once (13:10).

Paul could not be more explicit in his denunciation. According to him, Elymas practiced deceit and wickedness to the highest degree. Paul continued and thundered, "You enemy of all righteousness." He regarded Elymas as a servant of Satan and therefore as an enemy. What kind of an enemy was Elymas? This false prophet had set himself against everything that was right, just, and true. Elymas was actively and persistently perverting "the right ways of the Lord." From the Old Testament Scriptures, Elymas knew that God's ways are perfect, right, and just.[20] But he relentlessly opposed the teachings of the Lord. For Elymas, the expression *Lord* meant the Lord God of Israel. And this God, whom he personally opposed, chastened him with temporary blindness. Paul rebuked Elymas and said,

e. "And now the hand of the Lord is against you. You will be blind and unable to see the light of the sun for a while." Note, first, that not Paul but the Lord punished Elymas for his blatant opposition to the teaching of the gospel. With his hand, the Lord set limits (Judg. 2:15; I Sam. 12:15). Next, the Lord extended his grace and mercy to Elymas by telling him that his punishment would be only temporary. And third, God afflicted Elymas with the scourge of blindness and thus caused him to live in confinement. Paul could relate to this condition; in his state of physical blindness, his spiritual blindness was removed so that he was able to understand God's purposes (9:8–18).

11b. Immediately a mist and darkness fell upon him, and he went about and sought someone to lead him by the hand. 12. When the proconsul saw what had happened, he believed and was amazed at the teaching of the Lord.

What a pitiful sight to see the magician Elymas stumble around, unable to see, and to hear him ask people to lead him by the hand from place to place. In the sharp conflict between Paul and Elymas, Paul triumphed while his opponent groped in darkness. The immediacy of divine punishment descending upon Elymas astounded the proconsul, who saw that Paul was the true prophet of the Lord and Elymas the fraud.

Whenever the New Testament reveals that God performs a miracle, the

---

19. F. W. Grosheide, *De Handelingen der Apostelen*, Kommentaar op het Nieuwe Testament series, 2 vols. (Amsterdam: Van Bottenburg, 1942), vol. 1, p. 411.
20. Refer to Deut. 32:4; II Sam. 22:31; Ps. 18:30; Hos. 14:9.

result is that people turn to him in faith. For example, Peter healed the cripple at the temple gate and numerous worshipers believed in Jesus (3:6; 4:4). When God struck Elymas with blindness, he brought Sergius Paulus to faith in Christ. We are not told that Elymas repented and believed. But Sergius Paulus, set free from the snares with which Elymas had bound him, now believed the teaching of Christ's gospel which he earlier had been told to doubt.[21]

Doctrinal Considerations in 13:4–12

"Faith comes by hearing, and hearing comes through the word of Christ," Paul writes (Rom. 10:17). Luke reveals that people accept Christ when they listen to his gospel. The Samaritans believe when Philip proclaims the Good News to them (8:12). Philip teaches the Ethiopian eunuch, who goes on his way rejoicing (8:39). Cornelius and his household hear the gospel from Peter and receive the gift of the Holy Spirit (10:44). And Sergius Paulus sees what happens to Elymas and believes. Luke adds that he continued to be amazed at the teaching of Christ's gospel; however, we have no reason to doubt the genuineness of his faith.[22] Nothing more is said about this Roman official who, upon completing his term in office, would leave Cyprus. Sergius Paulus serves as the Holy Spirit's mark of approval on the church's missionary purpose to proclaim the Good News to the Greco-Roman world.

Greek Words, Phrases, and Constructions in 13:10

ὦ—an interjection that expresses emotion. It prefaces an announcement of impending divine judgment: the punishment of temporary blindness. With the accompanying vocatives υἱέ (son) and ἐχθρέ (enemy), the particle is intensely personal.[23]

οὐ παύσῃ—the second person singular of the future indicative of the verb παύομαι (I stop) is followed by the present active participle διαστρέφων (perverting). The phrase is almost an imperative and certainly expresses a wish: "Will you not stop perverting?"[24]

B. Pisidian Antioch
13:13–52

We see an interesting development in the route Paul and Barnabas take on the first missionary journey. Because Barnabas was born and raised on the island of Cyprus, the travelers visit Cyprus first. But when they have

---

21. Calvin, *Acts of the Apostles*, vol. 1, p. 361.
22. A number of scholars doubt that Sergius Paulus had a true conversion. See Lake and Cadbury, *Beginnings*, vol. 4, p. 147.
23. Blass and Debrunner, *Greek Grammar*, #146.1.
24. Robertson, *Grammar*, p. 874.

crossed the island from east to west, they board ship and sail to Asia Minor, the birthplace of Paul. And although they do not visit Tarsus, Paul's native town, they land at Perga in Pamphylia, travel north to Pisidian Antioch, and from there go eventually to Iconium, Lystra, and Derbe, where they organize churches. These churches, located in the heartland of the Roman province of Galatia, received a letter from Paul known as the Epistle to the Galatians.

For the last two centuries, some scholars have maintained that on his third missionary journey Paul traveled through northern Galatia on his way to Ephesus (18:23). These scholars consider that the Epistle to the Galatians was addressed to congregations in northern Galatia. But we have no evidence that Paul visited areas in the northern part of Galatia, so the objections to this theory (called the northern Galatian theory) are formidable. Therefore, we are inclined to defend what is called the southern Galatian theory. We consider the churches Paul founded during his first missionary tour to be the recipients of his Galatian epistle.[25]

1. Invitation
13:13–15

13. Paul and his companions put out to sea from Paphos and went to Perga in Pamphylia, where John left them and returned to Jerusalem.
We face two problems in this text:

a. *Location.* Paul, Barnabas, and Mark decided to leave Paphos in Cyprus, board a ship, and sail in a northwesterly direction to Asia Minor. To be precise, they set sail for Perga, a chief city in the coastal province of Pamphylia. Paul and his companions undoubtedly knew that some Jews from Pamphylia had heard Peter's Pentecost sermon in Jerusalem (2:10) and had brought the gospel to their native province. This province, bordering Cilicia to the east, Lycia to the west, and Pisidia and the Taurus Mountains to the north, possessed fertile fields along the Mediterranean coast. The River Cestrus flowed down the mountains to the sea and provided water for the agricultural plains along its banks. "The land was rich in fruit and crops and was a center of pharmaceutical products."[26] Perga was located slightly inland and a short distance west of the River Cestrus.

Paul and his fellow workers did not organize a church in Perga, even though they proclaimed the gospel there upon their return from Pisidian Antioch (14:25). Paul and Barnabas went instead to the interior and preached the Good News to the Galatians in Pisidia. William M. Ramsay suggested that at Perga Paul became ill with malaria and thus moved to the

25. A full discussion of the northern and southern Galatian theories is presented by Herman N. Ridderbos, "Galatians, Epistle to the," *ISBE*, vol. 2, pp. 380–81; and by William Hendriksen, *Exposition of Galatians*, New Testament Commentary series (Grand Rapids: Baker, 1968), pp. 5–14.
26. E. A. Judge, "Pamphylia," *ISBE*, vol. 3, p. 650.

cooler climate in the higher elevation of Pisidian Antioch,[27] for Paul refers to being ill when he first came to the Galatians (Gal. 4:13; and compare II Cor. 12:7). Even if we adopt Ramsay's suggestion, we still face a second problem. Why did John Mark leave Paul and Barnabas in Perga and return to Jerusalem?

b. *Return*. Once again, the text is obscure. Perhaps, because the information concerns his friend Mark, Luke remains silent. Scholars have speculated about Mark's homesickness, the dangers of travel in the mountainous regions of Pamphylia and Pisidia (see II Cor. 11:26), the uncertainty of travel in territory unknown to Mark, and his possible objection to preaching the gospel primarily to Gentiles.

If we take a comprehensive look at chapters 13 and 14, we notice that the emphasis falls on proclaiming Christ's gospel to the Gentiles. When Paul and Barnabas were rejected by the Jews in Pisidian Antioch, they announced that they would turn to the Gentiles (13:46; see also 14:27).[28] This purpose became objectionable to Mark, who said goodbye to the missionaries and returned to Jerusalem. We assume that there he reported that the overriding concern of Paul was to convert the Gentiles to the Christian faith. When, some time later, Barnabas wanted to take Mark along on another missionary journey, he ruptured his friendship with Paul. Because Mark had deserted the missionaries in Pamphylia, Paul refused to have him as a partner (15:37–39). The break in relations between Paul and Barnabas can be explained best if Mark's desertion originated from his objection to preaching to the Gentiles.[29]

14. But going on from Perga, they came to Pisidian Antioch. On the Sabbath they entered the synagogue and sat down. 15. After the reading of the Law and the Prophets, the synagogue officials sent this message to them: "Men and brothers, if you have any word of exhortation for the people, please speak."

Luke reports only that the missionaries continued their journey from Perga to Pisidian Antioch. But we know that they had to travel for many days, following the River Cestrus, and climb to an altitude of thirty-six hundred feet. Moreover, the route was dangerous because local bandits attacked travelers in the narrow mountain passes (compare II Cor. 11:26). The missionaries entered territory which the Romans called the province of Galatia. In the southern part of this province, the Romans had founded a colony at Antioch (25 B.C.).

The name *Antioch* was common to many cities in the ancient world that

---

27. William M. Ramsay, *St. Paul the Traveller and the Roman Citizen* (1897; reprint ed., Grand Rapids: Baker, 1962), pp. 89–97.

28. Consult Dupont, *Nouvelles Études*, p. 344.

29. Richard N. Longenecker, *The Acts of the Apostles*, in vol. 9 of *The Expositor's Bible Commentary*, ed. Frank E. Gaebelein, 12 vols. (Grand Rapids: Zondervan, 1981), p. 421.

were founded by either the Syrian ruler Seleucus Nicator (301–281 B.C.) or his son Antiochus I. Luke writes that Paul and Barnabas went to Pisidian Antioch and thus distinguishes it from Antioch in Syria. Pisidian Antioch, located on the right bank of the Anthius River,[30] was in western central Asia Minor (modern Turkey). The city was home to numerous Greeks, Phrygians, Romans, and Jews. The Jews had been brought to Antioch by the Seleucids in the third century before Christ. The Jewish population had built a synagogue and had acquainted the Gentiles with the teaching of the Old Testament Scriptures.

Further, the synagogue in dispersion was a center of learning, a source of help in community needs, a place for meetings, and a court of justice. The synagogues became a part of public life in Gentile communities. Numerous Gentiles attended the worship services in the local synagogue, observed the Jewish law, and believed in God. But some Gentiles, because of their refusal to be circumcised, were called God-fearers. Accordingly, at least four groups of people worshiped together on any given Sabbath: Jews who were born either in dispersion or in Israel, converts to Judaism, God-fearers, and Gentiles who displayed an interest but did not make a commitment.

After the missionaries arrived in Pisidian Antioch, they entered the synagogue on the following Sabbath. They sat down and waited for the people to welcome them to the worship service. Luke writes that Paul's custom was to go to local synagogues and teach from the Scriptures.[31]

Luke describes the liturgy of the Sabbath service. He relates that the Law and the Prophets were read; that is, members of the congregation in dispersion were appointed to read selections from the Old Testament Scripture in the Greek translation (the Septuagint). Of course, other parts of the liturgy were the recitation of the Shema (Deut. 6:4–9; 11:13–21; see also Num. 15:37–41), prayer, a sermon, and a concluding benediction. The important part of the worship service always was the sermon.[32]

The rulers of the synagogue invited Paul and Barnabas to give the people "a word of exhortation." These rulers were in charge and often participated in the various parts of the liturgy. They welcomed the visitors and expected that either Paul or Barnabas would accept their request to deliver a sermon. In the local synagogue, visitors were regularly asked to speak.

---

30. Bastiaan Van Elderen, "Antioch (Pisidian)," *ISBE*, vol. 1, p. 142; Colin J. Hemer, *The Book of Acts in the Setting of Hellenistic History*, ed. Conrad H. Gempf (Tübingen: Mohr, 1989), pp. 201, 228.

31. See v. 5; 14:1; 17:1, 2, 10, 17; 18:4, 19, 26; 19:8.

32. Emil Schürer, *The History of the Jewish People in the Age of Jesus Christ (175 B.C.–A.D. 135)*, rev. and ed. Geza Vermes and Fergus Millar, 3 vols. (Edinburgh: Clark, 1973–87), vol. 2, p. 448. Consult also Robert F. O'Toole, "Christ's Resurrection in Acts 13, 13–52," *Bib* 60 (1979): 361–72.

Greek Words, Phrases, and Constructions in 13:13–15

Verse 13

ἀναχθέντες—from ἀνάγω (I lead up), in the aorist passive this participle is a nautical term that denotes "set sail."

οἱ περὶ Παῦλον—this is a classical idiom meaning "Paul and his companions."[33]

Verses 14–15

σαββάτων—the plural form derives from the Hebrew idiom *shemaim* (heavens) but is translated in the singular.

ἀνάγνωσιν—from the verb ἀναγινώσκω (I read), this noun has the -σις ending to indicate the activity of reading the Scriptures.

---

2. Old Testament Survey
13:16–22

Paul had opportunity to survey the Old Testament Scriptures and show that Jesus Christ of Nazareth fulfilled the messianic prophecies. He addressed a mixed audience in which the God-fearing Gentiles became not only listeners but also followers of Christ. These people realized that the Christian faith was based on the Old Testament Scriptures but was free from the demands placed on them by the Jews.

16. Paul stood up and motioning with his hand he said: "Men of Israel and you who fear God, listen to me!"

Worship services in the local synagogues were marked by undue noise, especially during a short intermission. Men and women used the opportunity to exchange news and opinions; they were ready to express their likes and dislikes. When the rulers of the synagogue sent a message to Paul and Barnabas, who presumably occupied a seat far from the front, the worshipers were engaged in animated conversation. They met not only to worship God; they also used the synagogue as an informal meeting place. Consequently, when Paul accepted the invitation to speak "a word of exhortation," he had to ask for attention and did so according to the custom of that day. He motioned with his hand and thus called for order in the building (see also 12:17; 19:33; 21:40; 26:1).

Luke chose to record the sermon that Paul preached to an audience of Jews and Gentiles in Pisidian Antioch. In summary form, this sermon is a type that Paul delivered throughout Asia Minor, Macedonia, and Greece (refer to 14:15–17; 17:22–31). Moreover, in many respects the sermon resembles those which Peter delivered at Pentecost (2:14–36) and at Solomon's Colonnade (3:12–26) and the one Stephen preached before the

---

33. Robertson, *Grammar*, p. 766.

Sanhedrin (7:2–53). Paul's sermon in Pisidian Antioch consists of three parts: a survey of Israel's history; the life, death, and resurrection of Jesus; and the application of the gospel message.

In his Gospel and in Acts, Luke describes two synagogue worship services. In one, Jesus sits down to preach (Luke 4:20), and in the other, Paul stands up when he begins his sermon (Acts 13:16). The difference stems from two separate cultures: in the synagogues of Israel the teacher sat and in those of the dispersion he stood.

Paul begins his address with familiar words: "Men of Israel and you who fear God." Notice that he addresses the Jew first and then the Gentile. The Gentiles are the God-fearers, who willingly lend a listening ear to what Paul has to say. Among them are many prominent Gentile ladies (v. 50).

17. "The God of this nation Israel chose our fathers and made the people great during their stay in the land of Egypt. With an uplifted arm he led them out from there. 18. He put up with them for about forty years in the desert. 19. He destroyed seven nations in the land of Canaan and apportioned their land as an inheritance. 20a. All this took about four hundred and fifty years."

a. "The God of this nation Israel." Like Stephen before the Sanhedrin, Paul begins his sermon with a historical survey of the nation Israel. In his opening statement, he first declares that God is Israel's God. In fact, Paul specifies that God claims the people of Israel as his own—in this case those who worship him in the local synagogue of Pisidian Antioch (see v. 15).

Next, Paul declares that "God . . . chose our fathers." God does the choosing, not man. And God had chosen the forefathers, that is, the patriarchs Abraham, Isaac, and Jacob (see Deut. 4:37; 10:15). God's electing grace extends to the people of Israel: "In his eternal will and purpose *God chose Israel,* when as yet Israel was not, as he had chosen Paul (9:15; 22:14), and as he had fore-ordained the Christ before the foundation of the world (Luke 9:35; 23:35; compare Acts 3:20)."[34] Luke provides only a summary of Paul's address and quickly moves from the period of the patriarchs to the formation of Israel as a nation.

b. "[He] made the people great." With this one remark that Luke records, Paul refers to the descendants of Jacob who became a nation while they lived in Egypt. The Israelites were despised by the Egyptians and reduced to living in slavery. But God himself provided for the downtrodden Israelites and brought them to nationhood (compare, e.g., Exod. 1:20; 5:5; 33:13; Isa. 1:2). God regarded the Israelites as his covenant people and promoted them to prominence in a foreign country. He made them great in numbers and strength, and caused the Israelites to prosper during their stay in Egypt.

c. "With an uplifted arm he led them out from there." Paul borrows Old

---

34. Rackham, *Acts,* p. 211.

Testament language when he speaks of God's powerful hand or arm.[35] He uses the term *uplifted* to show that God's arm was the overarching power that controlled every event in Egypt. He ascribes glory and honor to the God of Israel, who delivered his people from the yoke of slavery and led them out of Egypt by signs and miracles.

d. "[God] put up with them for about forty years in the desert." After God had led his people out of Egypt, he continued to provide for them. For forty years God daily gave them food in the form of manna (Exod. 16:35), supplied them with water (Exod. 17:6), kept their clothes and sandals from wearing out (Deut. 8:4; 29:5), and protected them from enemies (Exod. 17:8–13). He carried his people as a father carries his son (Deut. 1:31).

In spite of God's miracles, goodness, and love, the Israelites grumbled, complained, and rejected God. In the desert, they disobeyed and tested God ten times (Num. 14:22). Yet God continued to put up with them for forty years. Incidentally, the Greek text has a variant reading that features a change of one letter in the verb *put up with* (v. 18). One translation has adopted the variant reading: instead of "put up with them," the Jerusalem Bible reads "took care of them."[36]

e. "[God] destroyed seven nations in the land of Canaan." Paul closely follows the Old Testament narrative and relates that not the Israelites but God conquered Canaan and dispossessed and destroyed its inhabitants. The seven nations were the Hittites, Girgashites, Amorites, Canaanites, Perizzites, Hivites, and Jebusites (Deut. 7:1; Josh. 3:10; 24:11). Not all the people in Canaan were killed during the conquest. Indeed, David finally destroyed the Jebusites when he conquered Jerusalem and made it the City of David (II Sam. 5:6–7; I Chron. 11:4–8).

f. "[God] apportioned their land as an inheritance." Paul refers to the fulfillment of God's promise to Abraham (Gen. 15:18–21) to give his descendants the land because of the covenant God had made with him. Centuries later, when the conquest had been completed, Joshua allotted the promised land to the Israelites, tribe by tribe (Josh. 14–21). The land of Canaan became the sacred inheritance of God's people Israel.

g. "All this took about four hundred and fifty years." Paul ventures to give a round number for the period that began with Jacob and his children entering Egypt and ended with the Israelites receiving their inheritance in Canaan. God told Abraham that his descendants would be oppressed in a foreign country for 400 years (Gen. 15:13). Add to this number the 40 years the Israelites spent in the desert and allow 10 years for the conquest of Canaan; the total comes to 450 years.

---

35. Refer to Exod. 6:1, 6; 13:3; Deut. 4:34; 5:15; 7:8; 9:26, 29; Pss. 77:15; 118:15; 136:12; Ezek. 20:33.

36. The variant derives from the Septuagint text of Deut. 1:31. See the discussion in Bengel, *Gnomon of the New Testament*, vol. 2, pp. 622–25; Lake and Cadbury, *Beginnings*, vol. 4, p. 149.

However, the reading of this text (vv. 19b–20a) can be rendered in varying ways:

> After that he gave them judges for about four hundred and fifty years, until Samuel the prophet. [v. 20][37]

> He gave them their land as an inheritance, for about four hundred and fifty years. And after that he gave them judges until Samuel the prophet. [vv. 19b–20a][38]

In the Greek text, no paragraph division appears; therefore, translators have to determine where one verse ends and the other begins. If we choose the first translation, we have to count the total number of years (410) that judges ruled Israel. If we add to this number the 40 years the priest Eli ruled, the total is 450. But I Kings 6:1 speaks of 480 years from the exodus to the fourth year of Solomon's reign. Furthermore, Josephus calculates the period from the exodus to the building of the temple to be 592 years.[39] In short, we meet a confusing array of figures. We do well to interpret 450 as a round number and apply it to Israel's stay in Egypt, the desert journey, and the conquest of Canaan. Hence we suspect that Paul begins to count from the time Israel became a nation.

20b. "After these things, God gave them judges until the time of Samuel the prophet. 21. Then they asked for a king, and God gave them Saul son of Kish, a man of the tribe of Benjamin, for forty years."

Despite Israel's disobedience, God continued to give the people spiritual leadership (Judg. 2:16). This spiritual leadership came from six minor judges (Shamgar, Tola, Jair, Ibzan, Elon, and Abdon) and six major judges (Othniel, Ehud, Deborah, Gideon, Jephtha, and Samson). Because he had made a covenant with them, God kept his promise to care for his people.

Paul mentions Samuel by name but calls him a prophet. To be precise, God called Samuel to serve him as priest and prophet (I Sam. 2:35; 3:20), but commissioned him to be a prophet who bridged the transitional period between the judges and the kings of Israel. Samuel had to provide leadership for the Israelites, who rejected God as their King and asked for a human king.[40] God instructed Samuel to listen to the request of the people, even though the Israelites broke their covenant relation with God and sinned.

God appointed Saul, the son of Kish, of the tribe of Benjamin, to be Israel's king. (Note the personal references: Paul's Hebrew name *Saul* and the tribe of Benjamin, to which Paul belonged [see Rom. 11:1; Phil. 3:5].) Paul says that King Saul ruled forty years. We learn not from the Old

---

37. NKJV; and see KJV.

38. RSV; see also NASB, NAB, NEB, NIV, SEB, JB, GNB, MLB.

39. Josephus *Antiquities* 8.3.1 [61]. Consult Eugene H. Merrill, "Paul's Use of 'About 450 Years' in Acts 13:20," *BS* 138 (1981): 246–57.

40. See Deut. 17:14–17; I Sam. 8:6–7; 10:19; 12:17, 19.

Testament but from Josephus that Saul was king for eighteen years while Samuel was alive, and for twenty-two years after the prophet's death.[41] But the information concerning Saul's age and duration of his reign (I Sam. 13:1) is uncertain. John Albert Bengel suggests that "the years of Samuel *the prophet* and Saul *the king* [be] brought together into one sum: for between the anointing of king Saul and his death there were not *twenty*, much less *forty* years: I Sam[uel] 7:2."[42]

22. "After he had removed him, God raised up David to be their king. Concerning him God testified, 'I have found David the son of Jesse to be a man after my heart, who will do everything I desire.'"

When Saul rejected God's instructions and placed himself above the law, God rejected him. Samuel told Saul:

> For rebellion is like the sin of divination,
>   and arrogance like the evil of idolatry.
> Because you have rejected the word of the LORD,
>   he has rejected you as king. [I Sam. 15:23, NIV]

Saul lost his kingship and the possibility of founding a dynasty. No one of his sons would ever occupy the throne. God directed Samuel to go to Jesse in Bethlehem and anoint David king over Israel (I Sam. 16:1, 13), which led to fulfillment of Jacob's prophecy that the scepter would not depart from Judah (Gen. 49:10).[43] Not Saul, a descendant of Benjamin, but David, a native of Bethlehem in the tribal territory of Judah, was the forerunner of the messianic King.

Even though Samuel and the psalmist Ethan the Ezrahite spoke words concerning David, Paul ascribes these words to God and says that God testified concerning David (I Sam. 13:14; Ps. 89:20). God said, "I have found David the son of Jesse to be a man after my heart, who will do everything I desire." The verb *testify* means that God spoke favorably about David. Yet David sinned grievously against God and his fellow man when he committed adultery with Bathsheba and had her husband, Uriah, killed in battle. David, however, earnestly sought remission and cleansing (Ps. 51). God heard his cry, accepted his confession, and restored him. David showed that he was willing to obey God's commands and that he was a man after God's own heart.

Doctrinal Considerations in 13:22

We believe that the Bible is the Word of God, because through the Scriptures God reveals himself and communicates with us. We realize that even though human

---

41. Josephus *Antiquities* 6.14.9 [378]. But in contrast see 10.8.4 [143], which states that Saul reigned twenty years.
42. Bengel, *Gnomon of the New Testament*, vol. 2, p. 628. And see SB, vol. 2, p. 725.
43. Calvin, *Acts of the Apostles*, vol. 1, p. 367.

authors wrote the books of the Old and New Testaments, their words are indeed the Word of God. Paul tells us that every word in Scripture is God-breathed (II Tim. 3:16), and Peter writes that the human authors spoke from God and were carried along by the Holy Spirit (II Peter 1:21). Consequently we assert that Scripture teaches the doctrine of inspiration.

How do the New Testament writers view the Old Testament? They have a high view of the Scriptures, for in these books they hear not the voice of man but the voice of God. Even when they quote passages in which man is the speaker, they attribute the words not to man but to God.

The writer of the Epistle to the Hebrews ascribes the words "You are my Son, today I have become your Father" (Ps. 2:7) not to the psalmist but to God (Heb. 1:5). The lines from David's psalm, "I will proclaim your name to my brothers / In the midst of the congregation I will sing your praise" (Ps. 22:22), are the words of Jesus (Heb. 2:12). And the psalmist's warning against unbelief, "Today, if you hear his voice, do not harden your heart . . ." (Ps. 95:7–11), is introduced by the phrase *the Holy Spirit says* (Heb. 3:7). The author of Hebrews treats the words written by men as words spoken by God.[44]

What the Old Testament Scriptures convey is not the voice of men but the voice of God. Hence Paul identifies the words of Scripture with the voice of God. For example, the angry words Sarah spoke to Abraham about Hagar—"Get rid of this slave woman" (Gen. 21:10)—are attributed to God in Paul's discussion on the roles of Hagar and Sarah (Gal. 4:30). Similarly, Paul attributes Samuel's condemnation of King Saul to God as if God personally had addressed the king (I Sam. 13:14). In conclusion, the writers of the New Testament demonstrate that they regard Scripture as divinely inspired and fully authoritative because God himself is the speaker.

> God writes with a pen
> that never blots,
> Speaks with a tongue
> that never slips,
> Acts with a hand
> that never fails.
> —Charles Haddon Spurgeon

Greek Words, Phrases, and Constructions in 13:16–22

Verse 16

οἱ φοβούμενοι—the articular present middle participle is dependent on the implied personal pronoun ὑμεῖς (you who fear God).

Verse 18

χρόνον—here is the accusative of extent of time: "for a period of time."
ἐτροποφόρησεν—this verb ("he put up with them") has manuscript support equal

---

44. Donald Guthrie, *New Testament Theology* (Downers Grove: Inter-Varsity, 1981), p. 974.

to that of the reading ἐτροφοφόρησεν (he cared for them). The latter reading appears in the Septuagint text of Deuteronomy 1:31. Translators apply the rule that the more difficult reading is the better. That is, accommodation to the Septuagint text is easier to explain than divergence from it. Accordingly, the translation *he put up with them* is preferred.[45]

Verses 19–20a

κατεκληρονόμησεν—this verb has a causative significance: "[God] caused them to inherit."

ἔτεσιν—although classical Greek would feature the accusative case (accusative of extent), Koine Greek employs the dative of time to express duration.

Verse 22

μεταστήσας—from the verb μεθίστημι (I remove), this aorist active participle can refer to either Saul's deposition or his death.

εἰς βασιλέα—this construction is the predicate accusative that signifies "to be a king for them."

πάντα τὰ θελήματά μου—the plural noun is used idiomatically and means "all that I desire."[46]

---

3. The Coming of Jesus
13:23–25

After providing a brief historical survey of the Old Testament Scriptures, Paul is going to show their fulfillment in Jesus. He is ready to point out that God has fulfilled the promise of the Messiah's coming through Jesus Christ.

23. "From this man's descendants, God brought to Israel a savior, Jesus, according to the promise."

We make these observations:

a. *Ancestry.* Jesus descended from David's royal line, a truth Matthew clearly shows in Jesus' genealogy (Matt. 1:1–17). Jesus indeed fulfilled the Scriptures which foretold the royal ancestry of the Messiah (Mic. 5:2; Matt. 2:5–6; Luke 2:4; John 7:42). When the angel Gabriel announced Jesus' conception and birth to Mary, he told her that God would give Jesus David's royal throne. Further, he said that Jesus' kingdom would never end (Luke 1:32–33; compare II Sam. 7:12–13; 22:51; I Chron. 17:11–14; Ps.

---

45. Bruce M. Metzger, *A Textual Commentary on the Greek New Testament*, 3d corrected ed. (London and New York: United Bible Societies, 1975), pp. 405–6. Refer also to R. Gordon, "Targumic Parallels to Acts XIII 18 and Didache XIV 3," *NovT* 16 (1974): 285–89.

46. The clause *all that I desire* is a paraphrase of "after my own heart" (see I Sam. 13:14). Consult F. F. Bruce, "Paul's Use of the Old Testament in Acts," in *Tradition and Interpretation in the New Testament*, ed. Gerald F. Hawthorne (Grand Rapids: Eerdmans; Tübingen: Mohr, 1987), p. 72.

132:11–12). "The rationale for the genealogies of Matthew and Luke is the conviction that Jesus' ancestry is demonstrably Davidic."[47]

b. *Promise.* God promised the people of Israel that he would give them a savior. Thus, God brought Jesus into the world to fulfill the promise he made to his people. Some passages in the Old Testament indicate that God indeed would bring the Redeemer, the Holy One of Israel, to be with his people (Isa. 48:15–17). To illustrate, to the high priest Joshua and his fellow priests God said: "I am going to bring my servant, the Branch" (Zech. 3:8, NIV).

c. *Function.* In Pisidian Antioch, Paul informs his audience that the savior whom God had promised came in the person of Jesus. His listeners applied the word *savior* (deliverer) to the judges who ruled Israel (e.g., Judg. 3:9, 15); to God who in time led his people out of exile (see Isa. 45:15); and to the coming Messiah who, according to popular opinion, would liberate Israel from foreign rule. But Paul proclaims Jesus as the savior who redeems his people from the shackles of sin (see Matt. 1:21), the One whom God has appointed and equipped to save his people.[48] By designating Jesus savior, Paul removes the possibility of seeing Jesus as a political deliverer.

24. "Before Jesus came, John preached a baptism of repentance to all the people of Israel. 25. As John was completing his work, he repeatedly said, 'Who do you suppose I am? I am not the Christ. No, but someone is coming after me whose sandal I am not worthy to untie.' "

a. "Before Jesus came, John preached." The Baptist apparently was known among Jews and God-fearers in Palestine and the dispersion. Peter referred to him in his sermon to Cornelius and his family; disciples of John the Baptist resided in Ephesus (19:1–6); and in this sermon Paul notes that John, the forerunner of Jesus of Nazareth, preached a message of repentance and baptism. The Baptist proclaimed this message to all Israel: the Pharisees and Sadducees, the crowds, the tax collectors and soldiers, and even Herod Antipas (Matt. 3:7–12; Luke 3:7–20).

When John preached the message of repentance and encountered a receptive audience, he baptized the people. His baptism differed from the washings of the Jews, for repentance from sin was a prerequisite to the rite of baptism. Josephus provides a brief description of John the Baptist's view and states that "he had exhorted the Jews to lead righteous lives, to practise justice towards their fellows and piety towards God, and so doing to join in baptism. In his view this was a necessary preliminary if baptism was to be acceptable to God."[49]

b. "As John was completing his work." Paul intimates that John's task was only temporary; with Jesus' arrival, the work of John ended. But during his

47. Richard N. Longenecker, *The Christology of Early Jewish Christianity,* Studies in Biblical Theology, 2d series 17 (London: SCM, 1970), p. 110. See also Otto Glombitza, "Akta xiii. 15–41. Analyse einer Lukanischen Predigt vor Juden," *NTS* 5 (1959): 306–17.
48. Johannes Schneider and Colin Brown, *NIDNTT,* vol. 3, p. 219.
49. Josephus *Antiquities* 18.5.2 [117].

brief ministry, he had to answer questions which priests and Levites asked him concerning his unauthorized preaching and baptizing at the River Jordan (John 1:19–27).

The messengers sent by the Sanhedrin asked John to identify himself, and John responded by saying, "Who do you suppose I am?" They wanted to know whether John was the Messiah, Elijah, or the Prophet. To these inquiries John answered in the negative. Emphatically he stated that he was not the Christ. Pointing away from himself, he said that he was not worthy even to untie the sandal of the one coming after him (see Mark 1:7; John 1:27; the Jews used the expression *the coming one* to refer to the Messiah [compare Matt. 11:3]). John depicts the work of a slave who removed the sandals and washed the feet of the people entering the house of his master, and thus implied that in the presence of the "coming one" he was not even on the level of a slave. He asserted that Christ must increase and he himself must decrease in importance (John 3:30). Accordingly, John identified the person of whom he spoke as Jesus and made it known that the Messiah had come.

Paul uses these well-known words of John the Baptist to introduce Jesus to his audience. He conveys the news that John's announcement about the arrival of the Messiah is true, for the Messiah has come in the person of Jesus Christ.

Greek Words, Phrases, and Constructions in 13:23–25

Verses 23–24

τούτου—note the unusual position of this pronoun. Because of its place at the beginning of the sentence, it denotes emphasis.

προκηρύξαντος—with the noun Ἰωάννου in the genitive case, this aorist participle forms the genitive absolute construction. The preposition πρό in the compound participle is temporal and depicts the time prior to Jesus' coming.

πρὸ προσώπου τῆς εἰσόδου—"before the face of his entering." Here is a Hebraic circumlocution that means "before his coming."[50]

Verse 25

τί—the pronoun can be relative ("I am not *what* you think I am," NEB) or interrogative ("*What* do you suppose I am?"). Translators prefer the interrogative.[51]

---

4. Death and Resurrection
13:26–31

Paul follows the customary practice of addressing the synagogue audience first as "men of Israel," and then, in the second half of his sermon, as

---

50. Robertson, *Grammar*, p. 94.
51. Consult Metzger, *Textual Commentary,* p. 408; C. F. D. Moule, *An Idiom-Book of New Testament Greek,* 2d ed. (Cambridge: Cambridge University Press, 1960), p. 124.

"brothers." When Peter delivered his Pentecost sermon and his speech at Solomon's Colonnade he adhered to the same custom (2:22, 29; 3:12, 17). Paul knows that his audience at Pisidian Antioch is diverse and therefore he addresses both Jew and Gentile.

26. "Men and brothers, sons of Abraham's family, and those among you who fear God, to us the word of this salvation has been sent."

a. "Men and brothers." Paul's tone of voice is intimate because he speaks to fellow Jews. He is at home among the Jews and in his desire to acquaint them with Jesus Christ, he calls them "men and brothers." Paul uses an acceptable Jewish cliché and his intent is not to exclude the women. We know that numerous and prominent God-fearing Gentile ladies attended the synagogue worship service (v. 50).

b. "Sons of Abraham's family." The Jews in the audience claimed Abraham as their physical ancestor. Yet Paul is stressing not their natural relationship but rather their spiritual affiliation. By placing the connection with Abraham on a spiritual level, Paul is able to include those believers who are not of Jewish descent.

c. "Those among you who fear God." These are the Gentiles who have been evangelized by the local Jewish population. They have come to the synagogue for instruction in the Scriptures but have not consented to submit to circumcision. Their refusal kept them from being converts; instead they are called "God-fearers" (see v. 16; 10:2, 35).[52]

d. "To us the word of this salvation has been sent." What unites the Jew and the God-fearer in common fellowship is to seek the salvation God has promised in his Word. Because God gave Abraham the promise meant for all his spiritual descendants, Paul is able to say "to *us*." Therefore, Paul includes himself as a recipient of the message of salvation God has sent from heaven. What is this message? Simply stated, it is the fulfillment of God's promise in his Son Jesus. God provides salvation through the one and only Savior, namely, Jesus Christ, to the believing Jew and Gentile (compare vv. 16, 23).

27. "Those who live in Jerusalem and their rulers did not recognize Jesus, and by condemning him they fulfilled the words of the prophets that are read every Sabbath."

Paul is among the first to admit that he used to be part of the Jerusalem elite with whom he vigorously opposed the message of salvation. He used to persecute the believers in Jerusalem and Judea. He was even sent to Damascus to arrest the Christians there and deliver them as prisoners to the Jewish authorities in Jerusalem (9:2). Paul, however, was converted on the way to Damascus, was called by Jesus to be an apostle to the Gentiles, and is now proclaiming the gospel of salvation to both Jews and Gentiles in Pisidian Antioch.

---

52. Compare Max Wilcox, "The 'God-Fearers' in Acts—A Reconsideration," *JSNT* 13 (1981): 102–22; Hemer, *Book of Acts*, p. 183.

a. "Those who live in Jerusalem and their rulers." Paul faces the difficulty of addressing an audience that regards Jerusalem as headquarters of the Jewish faith and therefore honors the religious rulers of that city. He has to guide his listeners from the position he himself occupied while he was associated with the high priest in Jerusalem to the position of freedom he now possesses in Christ. The people living in Jerusalem were the first to reject Jesus and his message; they were influenced by their religious leaders, who urged the crowds to condemn Jesus.

b. "[They] did not recognize Jesus [but condemned him]." How does Paul guide his audience to accept the fact that Jesus is the savior? First, he notes that the people in Jerusalem acted in ignorance when they rejected the Christ. Both Peter and Paul testify to this truth (3:17; I Tim. 1:13; see also Luke 23:34; John 16:3). The Jewish people did not know what they were doing. Conversely, the inhabitants of Jerusalem and the religious leaders could not shirk responsibility; if they had not handed Jesus over to Pilate, the Roman governor would never have killed him.[53] Peter in his Jerusalem sermons and speeches also held the Jews responsible for Jesus' death by saying that they killed him (2:23, 36; 3:14–15; 4:10). Moreover, the Scriptures themselves were sufficiently clear.

c. "They fulfilled the words of the prophets that are read every Sabbath." The Scriptures were read in the synagogues throughout Israel and in the dispersion. No devout Jew could ever say that he was ignorant of the words of the prophets. Part of the liturgy of every worship service on the Sabbath was the reading of the Law and the Prophets (v. 15; 15:21) with which every Jew became familiar. The prophets foretold that the Messiah would suffer, die, and yet be the savior of his people (see Isa. 52:13–53:12). On the basis of the prophetic message, then, Jesus could be their savior who died a shameful death as their substitute. Paul intimates that by condemning Jesus, the Jews in Jerusalem fulfilled the words that the prophets had spoken concerning the Messiah.

28. "And though they found no ground for execution, they asked Pilate that he be killed. 29. When they accomplished everything that had been written about him, they took him down from the cross and laid him in a tomb."

By asking Pontius Pilate to crucify Jesus of Nazareth, the Jews in Jerusalem fulfilled the Old Testament Scriptures. Leon Morris observes, "The whole unfolding panorama is a fulfillment of what God has set in motion."[54] Nevertheless, God holds the Jews accountable for condemning an innocent man to death. They tried to find a charge that would require

---

53. R. C. H. Lenski, *The Interpretation of the Acts of the Apostles* (Columbus: Wartburg, 1944), p. 528.
54. Leon Morris, *New Testament Theology* (Grand Rapids: Zondervan, Academie Books, 1986), p. 175.

Jesus' execution but were unable to do so. In fact, Pilate repeatedly said that he found no basis for executing Jesus.[55]

In the Roman colony of Pisidian Antioch, Paul is placing the blame for Jesus' death not on the Romans but on the Jews. He purposely shows that the members of the Sanhedrin, the supreme court of Israel, had acted against their own laws by condemning Jesus and asking Pilate for the death penalty. Paul differentiates the Jews in his audience from the Jews in Jerusalem and implies that they should denounce the action taken by the Sanhedrin and separate themselves from those Jews who reject Jesus and his message. In a sense, Paul risked everything, because his listeners might decide to continue their allegiance to the religious rulers in Jerusalem.

Paul points out that "[the Jews] accomplished everything that had been written about [Jesus]." Paul once more calls attention to the Scriptures that reveal the fulfillment of prophecy about Jesus Christ. He shows that Jesus' death was divinely ordained (2:23). Paul teaches that Jesus came to fulfill the Scriptures that reveal the coming, suffering, death, and burial of the Messiah (compare Luke 18:31). And by twice referring to the Scriptures (vv. 27, 29), Paul seeks to convince the audience that Jesus of Nazareth indeed is the Messiah.

When Paul says that "they took [Jesus] down from the cross" and placed his body in a tomb, he is not saying that the Jewish authorities did this. Rather, he implies that Jesus' friends asked Pilate for permission to remove the body from the cross and lay it in a tomb (Matt. 27:57–60; John 19:38–39) These friends of Jesus, Nicodemus and Joseph of Arimathea, were members of the Sanhedrin and religious rulers in Jerusalem. Paul is correct, therefore, when he states that they took the body from the cross. We surmise that his audience was familiar with the historical details of Jesus' death and burial. In the original, Paul uses the word *tree* to represent the cross (see 5:30). For the Jew, this term refers to God's curse placed upon anyone who has been put to death and impaled on a pole (Deut. 21:23; Gal. 3:13).

How could a person cursed by God be placed in a new tomb and so, as Isaiah prophesied, be with the rich in his death (Isa. 53:9)? The Jews had to acknowledge the hand of God in Jesus' burial. They had to see that if God made Jesus descend to the lowest level of humiliation (burial), he would also remove the curse and exalt him by raising him from the dead.

30. "But God raised him from the dead. 31. For many days, he appeared to those who had come up with him from Galilee to Jerusalem. They are now his witnesses to the people."

Note these points:

a. *Resurrection.* The Jews asked Pilate to secure Jesus' tomb so that Jesus'

---

55. Matt. 27:23; Luke 23:4, 14, 22; John 18:38; 19:4, 6.

disciples could not remove his body. To this end the tomb was sealed and a guard posted. Robert Lowry remarks in poetic verse:

> Vainly they watch His bed—Jesus, my Savior;
> Vainly they seal the dead—Jesus, my Lord.
>
> Up from the grave He arose,
> With a mighty triumph o'er His foes.
> He arose a Victor from the dark domain,
> And He lives forever with His saints to reign.
> He arose! He arose! Hallelujah! Christ arose!

Although the Jews spread the lie that Jesus' disciples had stolen the body during the night, the evidence proved the opposite. God raised Jesus from the dead—an act which no human force could prevent (see 3:15). Further, after his resurrection Jesus physically appeared to numerous people.

b. *Appearances.* Paul makes a general observation about the time during which Jesus appeared, by whom he was seen, and where the revelations took place. Paul says that "for many days" Jesus appeared. Luke provides the information that the length of time between Jesus' resurrection and ascension was forty days (1:3). Counting the appearances mentioned in the Gospels, Acts, and Epistles (excluding the parallels), we have a total of ten.[56] At one time, more than five hundred people saw Jesus. Moses said that the testimony of two or three witnesses was sufficient to establish a case (Deut. 19:15), but a multitude of eyewitnesses testified to Jesus' resurrection. Paul adds that these observers were the people who traveled with Jesus from Galilee to Jerusalem. He refers to the twelve apostles (1:21–22). They had received Jesus' instruction and now are his ambassadors. Perhaps for reasons of modesty, Paul excludes any references to his own encounter with Jesus on the Damascus road and refrains from introducing himself as the apostle to the Gentiles. Nevertheless, in the next verse (v. 32), he declares that Barnabas and he are messengers of Christ's gospel.

c. *Witnesses.* The people to whom Jesus appeared are now his witnesses. Because they have seen him, they testify to the truth of Jesus' resurrection (compare I John 1:1–3). By implication, Paul conveys that these witnesses have openly proclaimed the apostolic doctrine (2:42) in the city of Jerusalem. And after the persecution following the death of Stephen, they with numerous other believers spread the Good News to the Jews living in dispersion. As every eye can see and every ear can hear, Paul and Barnabas are in Pisidian Antioch to proclaim the message of salvation.

---

56. Matt. 28:1–10, 16–20; Mark 16:9–11; Luke 24:13–49; John 20:19–25, 26–31; 21:1–23; Acts 1:3–8; I Cor. 15:5–7.

Doctrinal Considerations in 13:29

The cross is the worldwide symbol of Christianity, for it signifies the death of Jesus Christ outside the walls of Jerusalem. Symbolizing Christ's death, the cross is an emblem of assurance for every believer. However, in Paul's day it became a stumbling block for the Jew who was unable to identify the cross with the Messiah. For such a person, the Messiah was victorious, but the cross meant death. The Jew could not accept the apostolic teaching that the Messiah had to die on a cross and thus be placed under God's curse (Deut. 21:23). For the Gentile of the first century, the cross was foolishness. He knew that only political rebels and villainous slaves were crucified (I Cor. 1:23). For him, Jesus Christ was a criminal.

When the missionaries proclaimed the message of the cross, they faced an audience that had immense difficulty in accepting the gospel. They had to convince the Jew and the Gentile that Jesus died on the cross for their sins, endured the wrath of God on their behalf, removed the curse that rested on them, provided life eternal for every believer, restored the relationship between God and his people, and opened the way to heaven. In brief, Jesus paid the debt of sin by dying on the cross.

For these reasons, the cross of Christ is a precious symbol to the Christian who joyfully sings:

> In the cross of Christ I glory,
> Towering o'er the wrecks of time;
> All the light of sacred story
> Gathers round its head sublime.
> —John Bowring

Greek Words, Phrases, and Constructions in 13:26–31

Verse 26

ἡμῖν—although some manuscripts have the second person plural pronoun ὑμῖν, the context calls for the first person plural.

ἐξαπεστάλη—the compound verb ἀποστέλλω (I send) with the preposition ἐκ (out of) is directive; that is, the message of salvation did not originate among men in Jerusalem but came from God. The passive voice in the aorist tense implies that God is the agent.

Verse 27

κατοικοῦντες—the compound present participle from κατά (down) and the verb οἰκέω (I dwell in) denotes permanence, in contrast to the people who are temporary residents (παροικοῦντες; compare 7:6, 29).

τοῦτον—this pronoun refers either to ὁ λόγος (the message, v. 26) or to Jesus. In view of the context, in which two aorist active participles take this pronoun as their direct object, translators understand the pronoun to refer to Jesus. The participles are ἀγνοήσαντες (being ignorant) with a causal connotation, "because they did not recognize him," and κρίναντες (judging) with a modal sense, "by condemning him."

κατά—the context demands the distributive use of this preposition: "every Sabbath."

Verse 28

θανάτου—the genitive is objective and resembles the dative: "for death."

εὑρόντες—the aorist active participle from the verb εὑρίσκω (I find) is concessive: "although they found no cause. . . ."

Verses 30–31

ὁ δὲ θεός—note the adversative strength of the particle δέ to indicate a change of subject. Paul places God over against the Jews.

ἐπί—the preposition fills out the idea of the accusative of time: "for many days."[57]

οἵτινες—the indefinite relative pronoun is not causal but emphatic. It is the equivalent of ὅσπερ (in the plural) and means "these very people are now witnesses."

---

5. Good News of Jesus
13:32–41

Like Peter in his sermons delivered at Pentecost and at Solomon's Colonnade, Paul supports his sermon by quoting from the Old Testament Scriptures. He turns to the Psalter and the Prophets to strengthen his message. After his survey of Jesus' life, death, and resurrection, he expects his listeners to ask why God made the Messiah suffer and die. They would ask about the significance of the resurrection. Therefore, Paul tells his audience the meaning of the good news of salvation in Christ.

a. Psalm 2:7

32. "And we proclaim this good news to you. This promise made to the fathers 33. God has fulfilled to us, their children. He raised Jesus, as it was written in the second psalm,
> **'You are my Son;**
> **today I have become your Father.' "**

Paul becomes personal with the use of the pronoun *we*, by which he means Barnabas and himself. Without any introduction, he asserts that they are witnesses for Jesus Christ and proclaim his gospel. The Jews and God-fearing Gentiles are receiving a first-hand report of messengers whom God himself has sent. In the Greek, the pronouns in this verse are pronounced: *"we ourselves* proclaim this good news *to you."* Implicit is the idea that Paul and Barnabas want the listeners to claim for themselves the riches of the Good News.

---

57. Robertson, *Grammar*, p. 602.

What is the good news the missionaries bring? The news comes forth from the Old Testament Scriptures. It is a good news that God long ago proclaimed to the spiritual forefathers and which would be fulfilled in time. The prophets announced God's message of peace and salvation, of the coming of the Messiah and his reign (Isa. 40:9; 52:7). The promise to which Paul refers comprises all the messianic prophecies in the Scriptures, including those that speak of the resurrection.

Before Paul turns to the written Word, he states unequivocally that God has fulfilled this messianic promise to descendants of the spiritual forefathers. What is the meaning of the phrase *to . . . their children*? At Pisidian Antioch, Paul is addressing an audience of Jews, converts, and God-fearing Gentiles. He includes all these worshipers as spiritual heirs of the patriarchs and even expresses the inclusiveness in these words: "This promise . . . God has fulfilled to *us*."

The New American Standard Bible has the reading *to our children*, which is based on the text of the best Greek manuscripts. But if the pronoun *our* refers to Paul and Barnabas, it is incongruous with the context and must be excluded. Lesser Greek witnesses have the pronoun *their* ("to their children"). But even if this reading lacks strong manuscript support and is even slightly awkward in the sequence *to us, their children*, it is nevertheless preferred.[58]

Paul turns to the second psalm for his first quotation. He does so because this psalm was part of the liturgy of the synagogue worship service and the people had committed the words to memory. By quoting words from a familiar psalm, Paul has immediate rapport with his audience. Further, we know that the Jews in the first century interpreted certain well-known passages messianically (II Sam. 7:14; Ps. 2:7).[59] From the second psalm they knew that God brought his Son into the world. Paul says, "He raised Jesus." The verb *to raise* when used in a general sense means "to bring forth." In the development of Paul's sermon, he already mentioned that God brought Jesus forth from David's royal family (see v. 23).

Falling into repetition, the apostle now quotes Psalm 2:7, where God says to his Son, "You are my Son; today I have become your Father." Among Christians of that era, this quotation applied unmistakably to Jesus, the Son of God (see, e.g., Heb. 1:5; 5:5). God brought forth his Son for the purpose of redeeming this sinful world. Accordingly, in this psalm citation Jesus' entire earthly mission, from birth to death and resurrection, is included. To be sure, the quotation itself does not specifically speak of the Son's resurrection from the dead but of Christ's enthronement and, in succeeding verses, of his universal rule over the nations. From the New Testament we learn that Christ uttered his enthronement speech after his resurrection and

---

58. Consult Metzger, *Textual Commentary*, pp. 410–11.

59. SB, vol. 3, pp. 675–77; Longenecker, *Christology of Early Jewish Christianity*, pp. 80, 95; Simon J. Kistemaker, *The Psalm Citations in the Epistle to the Hebrews* (Amsterdam: Van Soest, 1961), p. 17.

before his ascension, when he said, "To me all authority has been given in heaven and on earth" (Matt. 28:18).

In Psalm 2, the psalmist portrays a son ascending the royal throne of his father, who installs him as king and says: "You are my Son, today I have become your Father" (v. 7). The psalm is a coronation song and the particular citation is a decree of enthronement. The word choice tells the reader that the King is God himself, who appoints a Davidic king to royal office. But the wording informs the reader that this royal son of David is Jesus Christ, the Messiah.

With this psalm citation, Paul teaches that God raised Jesus for his messianic task. We assume that when Paul in his sermon first related the facts concerning the resurrection of Christ, the audience wanted proof from the Old Testament. The people desired to know whether the Scriptures predict that God would raise Jesus from the dead. Now they accept Paul's messianic reference to the second psalm and believe his verbal report that Jesus has physically appeared to numerous witnesses. But they wish to hear additional proof that the resurrection has been foretold in the messianic prophecies. Consequently, Paul once more turns to the Scriptures.

b. Isaiah 55:3

34. "Namely, God raised him from the dead, never to decay, as God said: 'I will give you the holy and sure blessings of David.' "

Paul is specific and now states that God is the agent in raising Christ from the dead. Jesus' resurrection is the basis of the Christian faith and this fundamental truth has been proclaimed ever since the time of Pentecost. Peter made it the central part of all his sermons and speeches and Paul preached the doctrine of Christ's resurrection to both Jews and Gentiles. In Pisidian Antioch, Paul turns to the prophecy of Isaiah, which implicitly states that God continued his everlasting covenant with David, whose royal family would terminate in the Messiah, the eternal King. If Jesus is the Messiah, as the Scriptures clearly show, then death has no power over him because God has raised him from the dead.[60]

Before Paul quotes Isaiah's prophecy, he states that Christ's body would never see decay. In a sense, Paul gives his audience a preliminary introduction to a subject which he will explain with a third Old Testament citation. For the moment he wants to convey the thought that, although Jesus died on the cross, Christ arose and his body will never decay. In another place Paul writes, "We know that because Christ was raised from the dead, he cannot die again; death no longer has power over him" (Rom. 6:9). Christ has a glorified body and lives forever.

In harmony with this thought, Paul quotes a text from the Greek translation of Isaiah 55:3, where God says to Israel, "I will give you the holy and sure blessings of David." The Old Testament text in the Hebrew differs

---

60. See D. Goldsmith, "Acts 13:33–37: A *Pesher* on II Samuel 7," *JBL* 87 (1968): 321–24.

considerably: "I will make an everlasting covenant with you, my unfailing love toward David." The differences in translation need not detain us at this point. Instead we look at the wording of the citation that Paul quotes and ask what Paul means to convey with this particular Scripture passage. At first glance we admit that the text has nothing in common with the doctrine of Christ's resurrection, for the context relates to David. However, Isaiah's reference to David is more than sufficient for Paul to show that God's "holy and sure blessings" did not cease after David died. When Paul says that God will give his people "the holy and sure blessings of David," he does not use the text to prove that Christ rose from the dead. Rather, he emphasizes the benefits that accrue from Jesus' resurrection.[61]

The Greek in this quotation is incomplete. A literal version reads: "I will give you the holy [things], the sure [things] of David." Translators take the adjectives *holy* and *sure* as modifiers of the supplied noun *blessings*. If we look at the Old Testament citation (Ps. 16:10) in the following verse (v. 35), we see the phrase *your Holy One*, which clearly refers to Christ. Holy and sure blessings belong to the holy descendant of David, namely, Jesus Christ. How does Christ make these blessings available to his people? He cleanses them from sin and sanctifies them. "Both the one who makes men holy and those who are being made holy, all have the same Father" (Heb. 2:11). Indeed, through Jesus Christ God never fails to fulfill his promises to his people. Decisively, then, God raised Christ from the dead to extend holy and sure blessings to the believers.

c. Psalm 16:10

35. "For this reason, God says in another psalm,

'You will not let your Holy One undergo decay.' "

Paul begins with the phrase *for this reason*. In the Jewish manner of interpreting the Old Testament, Paul looks for a key word, which in this case is the term *holy*, and then places the two citations next to each other. He makes this quotation, which is of greater importance than the first, dependent on its predecessor and thus writes, "For this reason." Paul applies the exegetical rule of analogy: explain an obscure word by finding an analogous text that has the same word but is clear.[62] Hence, the meaning of the expression *Holy One* in Psalm 16:10 serves to clarify the phrase *holy* (*things*) of Isaiah 55:3 in the Greek translation. The two quotations are intimately connected, because together they present the message that the Holy One, who will never again experience death and decay, will make his holy and sure blessings available to his people. Jesus Christ is the Holy One, whom God has raised from the dead. In short, he is the Messiah.

---

61. Jacques Dupont, "TA OSIA DAVID TA PISTA (Ac XIII 34 = Is LV 3)," *RB* 68 (1961): 91–114.
62. Longenecker, *Acts*, p. 426; Kistemaker, *Psalm Citations*, p. 62.

The messianic significance of Psalm 16 was well-known among Christians; Peter in his Pentecost address (2:27, 31) quotes the same passage Paul chooses. The Christians used the text to prove that Christ was resurrected and that in his glorified state he would never again experience death and decay. God raised him from the dead and did not permit corruption to take permanent hold of his Son, who is the Holy One. This psalm citation, originally applied to David, was fulfilled in the Messiah.

36. "For David, after he served God's purpose in his own generation, fell asleep. He was buried with his fathers and underwent decay. 37. But whom God raised from the dead did not undergo decay."

a. "For David . . . fell asleep." Interestingly, Paul's presentation of scriptural proof coincides with that of Peter (see 2:29–35). This coincidence is not at all surprising in view of Paul's desire, expressed after his first missionary journey was completed, to compare the gospel he preached with that of the apostles in Jerusalem (Gal. 2:2). Here is evidence that Paul preaches the same gospel Peter proclaimed at Pentecost.

The difference between the presentations of Peter and Paul is one of emphasis. Peter stresses David's tomb as evidence of the king's death and burial, but Paul adds that David's ministry was limited to his own time. Says Paul, "He served God's purpose in his own generation." Everything David accomplished in harmony with God's plan ended when death removed him from this earthly scene. By implication, Jesus' ministry lasts forever.

How do we interpret verse 36? The text can be read either as "[David] served God's purpose in his own generation"[63] or as "[David] served his own generation."[64] If we use the principle of interpreting one text with the help of a parallel passage, we turn to verse 22 and read that God says, "[David] will do everything I desire." The direct object of this verse is God's desire, that is, God's purpose. For that reason, translators and interpreters favor the reading, "He served God's purpose in his own generation."

b. "He was buried with his fathers and underwent decay." The euphemism *fell asleep* was common to the early Christians. For example, Stephen "fell asleep" when crushing stones ended his earthly life (7:60). Paul refers to David's remains resting peacefully in a Jerusalem tomb. Despite the skills of the embalmer, his body was subject to decay and awaits the day of the resurrection.

c. "But whom God raised from the dead did not undergo decay." Jesus, too, was buried in a tomb outside the walls of Jerusalem. And although his mangled body would be subject to disintegration while it remained in the grave from Friday afternoon until Sunday morning, God did not permit the forces of decay to have a permanent hold on him. God set him free

---

63. See NASB, RSV, NEB, NIV, JB, MLB, GNB, SEB.

64. NKJV, KJV. For additional translations of this text, see Ernst Haenchen, *The Acts of the Apostles: A Commentary,* trans. Bernard Noble and Gerald Shinn (Philadelphia: Westminster, 1971), p. 412.

from the power of death and the grave (2:24; 3:15) and gave him power over them (Rev. 1:18). Jesus Christ is victorious and as David's royal descendant lives eternally. By contrast, David died in the city of Jerusalem, was buried next to his forefathers in a tomb, and in his decayed state awaits the general resurrection of the dead. Not David, the composer of Psalm 16:10, but Jesus Christ, the Messiah, fulfilled the prophetic word.

38. "Therefore, men and brothers, let it be known to you that through him forgiveness of sins is proclaimed to you. 39. Everyone who believes is justified through him from all the things from which you could not be justified through the law of Moses."

Consider these points:

a. *Pardon.* Paul comes to the conclusion of his sermon. He touches a subject that goes to the heart of every listener in his audience: "How do I obtain forgiveness of sin?" Jews and God-fearing Gentiles had to adhere to Old Testament ceremonial and moral laws to achieve spiritual relief from the pressing burden of sin. Now Paul comes to them and teaches that their attempts at fulfilling the demands of the law will never relieve them of that burden. Proclaiming to the people the good news of Jesus Christ, Paul tells them that Jesus forgives sin. This is the message that the apostles preach to both Jews and Gentiles.[65]

In the Greek, Paul introduces this news first by a weighty statement, "Therefore, . . . , let it be known to you" (see 4:10; 28:28), and then by the familiar address *men and brothers*. The statement actually means that Paul is about to proclaim something of utmost importance. Further, the repetitious address means that Paul and his listeners are on the same level in respect to finding remission of sin.

"Through [Jesus] forgiveness of sins is proclaimed." Paul reminds his audience of John the Baptist, who preached "a baptism of repentance for the forgiveness of sins" (Mark 1:4, NIV). The Jews knew that through repentance, they would receive forgiveness and salvation. Peter's audience at Pentecost asked him, "What shall we do?" Peter told them to repent and be baptized in the name of Jesus for remission of sin (2:37–38). Both Peter and Paul proclaim the same message: man finds forgiveness of sins only through Jesus Christ! John the Baptist served as the forerunner of Jesus Christ and could only exhort the people to repent and be baptized. But the risen Lord and Savior has the power to forgive the sins of anyone who comes to him in repentance and faith.

b. *Faith.* Paul presents the offer of salvation to everyone who believes in Jesus Christ. He makes no distinction between Jew and Gentile, for God justifies anyone who pleads for remission of sin. He declares that everyone who puts his faith in Christ is made right with God. By using the literally translated phrase *the one who is believing,* Paul is able to issue a universal call to find remission of sins in Jesus Christ.

---

65. See 2:38; 3:19; 5:31; 10:43; 26:18.

c. *Justification.* In reporting the sermon Paul delivered in Pisidian Antioch, Luke reflects the apostle's teaching on justification by faith and not by law. Paul presents this teaching in his sermon and in some of his epistles.[66] For example, in his letter to the Galatians he writes,

> [We] know that a man is not justified by observing the law,
>   but by faith in Jesus Christ.
> So we, too, have put our faith in Christ Jesus
>   that we may be justified by faith in Christ
>   and not by observing the law,
> because by observing the law no one will be justified. [2:16, NIV]

Paul tells his listeners that when they put their faith in Jesus Christ, God declares them righteous, that is, without guilt. Their sins are forgiven, not on the basis of diligently observing the law of Moses but through Christ's atoning work. Paul's contemporaries know that they are unable to fulfill the demands of Moses' law and realize that their attempts to obtain righteousness on their own lead to frustration and futility. For this reason, Paul preaches that faith in Christ sets them free.

Except for the final exhortation, Paul has virtually come to the end of his sermon. If we summarize this message, we see a gradual development in his presentation, which can be summarized point by point. Paul has testified that

1. God raised Christ from the dead, according to the Scriptures;
2. eyewitnesses verified Jesus' resurrection;
3. his listeners are unable to keep the Mosaic law;
4. through faith in Christ sinners are made right with God;
5. consequently, forgiveness of sins is intimately related to Christ's resurrection.[67]

40. "Be careful that what was spoken by the prophets does not come upon you:
> **41. 'Look, you scoffers,**
>   **be amazed and perish!**
> **Because I am going to do a work**
>   **in your days, a work which you will never believe**
>   **even if someone would describe it to you.' "**

As a fitting end to his sermon, Paul first exhorts his listeners to pay attention to what the Old Testament prophets have declared. Then he

---

66. Consult Theodor Zahn, *Die Apostelgeschichte des Lucas,* Kommentar zum Neuen Testament series, 2 vols. (Leipzig: Deichert, 1921), vol. 1, p. 447; Lake and Cadbury, *Beginnings,* vol. 4, p. 157.
67. Grosheide, *Handelingen der Apostelen,* vol. 1, pp. 437–38; Zahn, *Apostelgeschichte des Lucas,* vol. 1, pp. 447–48.

quotes directly from the prophecy of Habakkuk, who lived a few decades prior to the destruction of Jerusalem and the subsequent exile of Judah (in 586 B.C.). A contemporary of Jeremiah, Habakkuk warned the people in Judah and Jerusalem that God would do something extraordinary, namely, the Babylonians would take them captive. God would do this because of unbridled violence, social corruption, and spiritual bankruptcy in Judah. Paul's contemporaries knew that the people of Judah had spurned the prophet's warnings and continued to live in sin. Eventually, God's patience ran its course and the Babylonian army conquered Jerusalem and exiled its inhabitants.

Likewise, Paul warns the worshipers in Pisidian Antioch to listen to the message of salvation and to put their faith in Jesus Christ. He realizes that some of the Jews in his audience are about to ridicule his words. They need a direct word from the Scriptures and therefore with minor variations Paul quotes the Greek text of Habakkuk 1:5. The words of this prophecy are purposely harsh:

a. "Look, you scoffers, be amazed and perish!" Like Habakkuk of old, Paul instructs his audience to take a close look at what is happening. Those who scoff at the message of salvation are rejecting God himself. And when they spurn God, they will be filled with utter amazement when God's judgment suddenly strikes and they perish. In Greek, the verb *to perish* actually means "to disappear from sight." For instance, the word is used to describe cities that have been demolished by an earthquake.[68]

b. "Because I am going to do a work in your days." The speaker in this prophecy is God, who tells the people that he will do something astounding in their midst and in their lifespan. In fact, Roman forces utterly destroyed the city of Jerusalem and its temple in A.D. 70, killed or dispersed its inhabitants, and prohibited Jews from resettling Jerusalem and rebuilding the temple.

Abruptly Paul ends his sermon to attain maximum effect. Never before had this audience heard such "a message of encouragement" (v. 15). According to the Greek text of Codex Bezae, Paul's listeners are silent.

Doctrinal Considerations in 13:39

When legislators formulate and enact laws for their nation, they often modify or even annul them in the course of time. At times they admit that a given law no longer functions or has serious flaws. Are the laws God has made for his people also subject to change? God gave Israel ceremonial laws that were set aside when Christ fulfilled his mediatorial work. The Ten Commandments, however, remain unaltered, are valid for all people, and are applicable to any culture and era.

If God's law is perfect (Ps. 19:7), why is it unable to make the believer right with God? The law is without flaw but the sinner is not. That is, the problem is inherent

---

68. Bauer, p. 124.

not in the law but in the lawbreaker (Rom. 7:12–13). Jesus Christ fulfilled the demands of the law and through his obedience made the believer righteous in God's sight. A Christian is justified not through observing the law, but through the merits of Christ. Through his Son, God grants eternal life to everyone who believes in him (John 3:16). As a result, the Christian wants to obey God's law and express his thankfulness to God for sending his own Son into the world.

Greek Words, Phrases, and Constructions in 13:32–41

Verse 32

ἡμεῖς ὑμᾶς—these two personal pronouns are juxtaposed for emphasis and inclusiveness.

Verse 33

ἐκπεπλήρωκεν—the compound from the verb ἐκπληρόω (I fulfill completely) is in the perfect tense to show an action in the past with lasting significance for the present.

τοῖς τέκνοις αὐτῶν ἡμῖν—"to their children, to us." Manuscript evidence for this reading is weak, yet contextual support is strong. Conversely, the best manuscripts present the reading τοῖς τέκνοις ἡμῶν (to our children), but the context militates against it. Still another reading is τοῖς τέκνοις αὐτῶν (to their children), but its external support is insignificant.

τῷ δευτέρῳ—the reading *the second psalm* has solid strength, yet Codex Bezae features the words τῷ πρώτῳ (the first). According to writers of the first few centuries, the first two psalms were often combined and regarded as one. Many scholars support the reading *the second psalm.*[69]

Verses 34–35

τὰ ὅσια—the translation from the Hebrew (Isa. 55:3) is "the mercies." Translators of the Septuagint interchanged the plural forms of the words ḥēsēd (mercy) and ḥasid (holy) and presented the reading *the holy* (*things*).

ἐν ἑτέρῳ—because Paul regarded the quotation in verse 34 and this one a sequence of two citations, he used this adjective as "the second" in a pair.[70]

Verses 38–39

διὰ τούτου—the preposition is instrumental ("through this [man]"). The demonstrative pronoun, which refers to Jesus, links these two verses. The Western text supplies some additions that are indicated by italics: "Through this man forgiveness of sins is proclaimed to you, and *repentance* from all those things from which you could not be freed by the law of Moses; by him *therefore* everyone that believes is freed *before God.*"[71]

---

69. Metzger, *Textual Commentary,* p. 414.
70. Robertson, *Grammar,* p. 748.
71. Metzger, *Textual Commentary,* p. 415.

ἐν νόμῳ—this phrase ("through the law") is balanced by the phrase ἐν τούτῳ (through him). The preposition is instrumental.

Verses 40–41

βλέπετε—"be careful." The present imperative is followed by the aorist imperative ἴδετε (look!). Both verbs serve to warn the people of impending judgment if they fail to heed the warning.

ἐκδιηγῆται—in the protasis of a conditional sentence, this present middle subjunctive expresses probability. The compound is perfective and can be translated "declare."[72]

---

6. Invitation Renewed
13:42–45

A characteristic of Luke's style is its brevity. He emphasizes and enlarges upon items that are relevant to the development of his account. He leaves the rest to the imagination of the reader. And this is exactly what happens when we try to depict the conclusion of the service and the exit from the synagogue.

42. When Paul and Barnabas were leaving, the people begged them that these things be spoken to them the next Sabbath. 43. After the synagogue meeting had ended, many Jews and God-fearing proselytes to Judaism followed Paul and Barnabas, who spoke to them and urged them to continue in the grace of God.

At first appearance, these two verses seem repetitious. Both indicate that the worship service had ended and that Paul and Barnabas were leaving. Customs and traditions vary from country to country and people to people. Hence we ought not to interpret these verses as if they reflect our practices. We assume that immediately after the formal worship service had ended, the worshipers remained in the building for social reasons (see the commentary on v. 16). When finally the informal part of the meeting came to an end, the caretaker closed the doors of the synagogue and the people went home. Luke, then, describes customs that prevailed at that time in Pisidian Antioch.

Paul and Barnabas make their way out of the synagogue but are stopped by the worshipers who want to hear them speak again. Most translators add the subject *Paul and Barnabas* for clarification, while others literally follow the indefinite Greek wording: "As they went out, the people begged . . ." (RSV). Still others, relying on the Majority Text of Greek manuscripts, expand the reading with two different subjects: "And when the Jews went out of the synagogue, the Gentiles begged . . ." (NKJV; also the KJV).[73]

The people are favorably impressed with Paul's message and invite him

---

72. Robertson, *Grammar*, p. 597.

73. The better Greek witnesses have the shorter reading for the first clause and omit the subject *the Gentiles* in the second clause. See also Metzger, *Textual Commentary*, pp. 416–17.

and Barnabas to return the following Sabbath. They want to hear more about the things pertaining to Jesus Christ and his gospel. Luke reports that many people, both Jews and Gentiles, continue to converse with the missionaries. By implication, other Jews avoid speaking to the visitors and are waiting for further developments (see v. 45). Luke describes the Gentile believers as God-fearing proselytes (incomplete converts to Judaism).[74] Paul, the apostle to the Gentiles, has an immediate understanding with these proselytes and leads them to Christ. Conversely, the Jews had crossed land and sea to make one convert (Matt. 23:15) and now see that Paul and Barnabas attract the God-fearing Gentiles to the Christian faith. Not unexpectedly, many of the Jews are annoyed and regard the missionaries as unwelcome rivals.

Paul and Barnabas, however, both extend the conversation and exhort the Jews and converts who eagerly listen to them "to continue in the grace of God." Paul and his companions know that after the first flush of enthusiasm has faded, the believers need words of encouragement. The verb *to continue* indicates that the people already have put their trust in Jesus and have accepted him as their Messiah (compare 11:23; 14:22). They are in fellowship with Jesus Christ and now Paul and Barnabas urge them to continue in that relationship, remain loyal to the Lord, and "expose themselves to God's grace."[75] "Grace" is a word Paul uses repeatedly in his epistles; it connotes God's decisive act to save man in Jesus Christ.

44. On the next Sabbath, nearly the whole city assembled to hear the word of the Lord. 45. But when the Jews saw the crowds, they were filled with jealousy. And abusively they began to contradict the things that Paul was saying.

We surmise that throughout the week, the Christians in Pisidian Antioch kept talking about their faith in Christ; also, Paul and Barnabas did not silently wait until the next Sabbath for an opportunity to speak. The Western text (Codex Bezae and two other manuscripts) adds an introductory sentence to this verse: "So it happened that the word of God spread throughout the whole city." The consequences of Paul's preaching are overwhelming. Luke generalizes and says that on the following Sabbath "nearly the whole city assembled to hear the word of the Lord." Luke does not relate whether this took place in the local synagogue with multiple meetings or in an outdoor gathering at the city's amphitheater. The Gentile population was not accustomed to observing the Sabbath day, yet the people take time to hear Paul and Barnabas preach Christ's gospel. The Greek text at this point has a variant reading which many translators have adopted: "to hear the word of God."[76] Both the phrase *word of God* and the phrase *word of the Lord* have equal manuscript support. Scholars favor the second choice

---

74. Compare 16:14; 17:4, 17; 18:7; and see 2:11; 6:5. For a detailed discussion, see Kirsopp Lake, "Proselytes and God-fearers," *Beginnings*, vol. 5, pp. 74–96.

75. Guthrie, *New Testament Theology*, p. 106. See also Rackham, *Acts*, p. 220.

76. See, e.g., KJV, NKJV, RSV, NEB, NASB, NAB, JB, MLB.

because it appears less often than the phrase *word of God.* The difference in meaning is negligible.

The response that the missionaries receive from the Gentile population proves that God is blessing them as missionaries to the Greco-Roman world. For the Jews, however, this tremendous reaction proves too much. Already irritated by Paul's address on the previous Sabbath, they are now filled with jealousy. We note that not the God-fearing Gentiles but the Jews set themselves against Paul and Barnabas. The Jews realize that the missionaries reap an evangelistic harvest after the Jews had witnessed for years to the Gentile population. From a human point of view, their jealousy is understandable. But from a divine perspective, the Jews should have been first in accepting the gospel of salvation. Instead of obeying the teachings of God's word, they begin to contradict the words spoken by Paul. Luke even adds that they do so abusively. The term Luke uses to describe their abusive action is the verb *to blaspheme.* That is, the Jews blaspheme the Christ proclaimed by Paul and Barnabas (compare 26:11). Undoubtedly, they tell the crowds that the crucified man Jesus is a criminal cursed by God.[77] And they deride and revile Paul for speaking about Jesus. Luke omits the details of the verbal attacks by the Jewish leaders of the local synagogue, but the account is sufficiently clear for a reader to form a mental image of the proceedings.

Greek Words, Phrases, and Constructions in 13:42–45

Verse 42

ἐξιόντων αὐτῶν—the genitive absolute construction separates the pronoun from the subject of the main verb. The present participle derives from the verb ἔξειμι (I go out). In the Majority Text, however, the subject of the genitive absolute clause is τῶν Ἰουδαίων (the Jews) and the subject of the main verb is τὰ ἔθνη (the Gentiles).[78]

μεταξύ—normally this adverb, referring to space or time, means "between." Here it signifies "afterward" or "next."

Verse 44

ἐρχομένῳ—modifying the noun σαββάτῳ (Sabbath), the present middle participle means "the coming one" or "the following one." Some manuscripts have the reading ἐχομένῳ (next).

ἀκοῦσαι—the aorist infinitive denotes purpose.

Verse 45

ζήλου—the genitive with the verb ἐπλήσθησαν (they were filled) is the genitive with verbs of sharing, partaking, and filling.[79]

---

77. Rackham, *Acts,* p. 220.

78. Arthur L. Farstad and Zane C. Hodges, *The Greek New Testament According to the Majority Text* (Nashville: Nelson, 1982), p. 420.

79. Robertson, *Grammar,* pp. 509–10.

ἀντέλεγον—the imperfect tense describes continued action in the past. The compound is directive.

---

7. Effect and Opposition
13:46–52

46. Paul and Barnabas boldly answered them: "The word of God had to be spoken to you first. Since you reject it and do not consider yourselves worthy of eternal life, we are turning to the Gentiles."

a. *Boldness.* One word that appears repeatedly in Luke's description of the disposition of the apostles is the word *boldly* or *courageously.*[80] The apostles know that Jesus told them never to be afraid when they are called to speak for him. Says Jesus, "You are not the ones who are speaking, but the Spirit of your Father is speaking through you" (Matt. 10:20). Thus both Paul and Barnabas speak boldly on behalf of Jesus and observe their basic rule to proclaim the gospel first to the Jews and then to the Gentiles (v. 26; 1:8; 3:26; Rom. 1:16; 2:9; see also Matt. 10:5–6).

b. *Priority.* Paul and Barnabas state unequivocally to the Jews, "The word of God had to be spoken to you first." The missionaries point out the necessity of their action. Because of God's love and concern for the Jews (see Rom. 11:1), the missionaries feel obliged to reveal the message of salvation first to them. The Jews are the recipients and guardians of God's revealed word (Rom. 3:2). They are God's adopted children; they have received the Law, the covenants, and the promises; they have the temple worship; and they honor the patriarch from whom the Messiah descends (Rom. 9:4–5). God, then, compels Paul and Barnabas to go first to the Jews and proclaim to them the good news of salvation in Christ. But if the Jews refuse to listen to God's ambassadors, Paul and Barnabas will go to the Gentiles. Paul had been called to serve as an apostle to the Gentiles and without doubt Barnabas had the same calling (see v. 2).

c. *Rejection.* In the prologue of his Gospel, John writes that Jesus came to his own heritage, but his own people refused to accept him (John 1:11). Jesus' ambassadors experience the same thing in Pisidian Antioch. Since the Jews reject the message of Christ's gospel, the Gentiles become the recipients of God's favor.[81] The Jews purposely forfeit their place in God's household and can no longer be considered worthy of eternal life. They can no longer count on their privileges, for God has taken them away. Paul and Barnabas look to the Gentiles and work among them. The Gentiles, then, are the wild olive branches that are grafted into the olive tree; some of the natural branches (i.e., the Jews) are broken off (Rom. 11:17–21). In his

---

80. See 2:29; 4:13, 29, 31; 9:27, 28; 13:46; 14:3; 18:26; 19:8; 26:26; 28:31.
81. Calvin, *Acts of the Apostles,* vol. 1, p. 391.

ministry, Paul repeatedly experiences rejection by the Jews and then turns
to the Gentiles (see 18:6).

47. "For this is what the Lord commanded us:
    'I have placed you as a light to the Gentiles,
      to bring salvation to the ends of the earth.' "

Paul bases his teaching on the Old Testament Scripture and thus follows
the example of Jesus Christ. He defends his decision to go to the Gentiles
by quoting a prophecy from the Book of Isaiah (49:6). From this quotation,
the Jews are able to see for themselves that centuries earlier God had
planned to grant salvation to the Gentiles. In other words, the Scriptures
prove the missionaries correct and the Jews wrong.

In Paul's reply, Scripture has the last word. Says Paul, "This is what the
Lord commanded us." The words originally spoken by God through the
prophet Isaiah, more than seven centuries before the birth of Christ, now
are claimed by Paul. Incidentally, Paul read the Old Testament Scriptures
in the light of Jesus calling him to be an apostle to the Gentiles. The words
of Isaiah, therefore, are fulfilled in Paul as he turns away from the Jews and
works among the Gentiles.

What are the words of Isaiah's prophecy? Isaiah describes the task of the
messianic servant of God, whom God appoints to free the descendants of
Jacob from the shackles of sin and bring them back to God. The task of the
Messiah is to restore the tribes of Jacob and to bring back a remnant of
faithful Israel (Isa. 49:6a). But the additional task of the Messiah is to be a
light for the Gentiles and thus grant salvation to the ends of the earth (Isa.
49:6b). This particular messianic prophecy was well known to Paul's Jewish
contemporaries. By citing this passage, Paul points out that when the Messiah makes salvation available to the Gentiles, Paul as his servant must do
likewise. Succinctly put, this text is often called "the great commission of the
Old Testament."[82] When Simeon took the baby Jesus in his arms in the
temple courts, he was filled with the Holy Spirit and spoke prophetically.
He said that his eyes had now seen "a light for revelation to the Gentiles and
for glory to your people Israel" (Luke 2:32, NIV; compare Isa. 42:6).

Paul wisely chooses a passage from the Old Testament that clearly speaks
of the Messiah's task to bring salvation to the Gentiles. None of Paul's
opponents is able to contradict the explicit teaching of Scripture. Although
the Jews remain silent after Paul's remarks, the Gentiles are filled with joy.
They know that the prophecy Paul quoted applies to them.

**48. When the Gentiles heard this, they began to rejoice and glorify the
word of the Lord. And as many as were ordained to eternal life believed.**

---

82. Consult Edward J. Young, *The Book of Isaiah*, New International Commentary on the Old
Testament series, 3 vols. (Grand Rapids: Eerdmans, 1972), vol. 3, p. 276. Refer to Pierre
Grelot, "Note sur Actes, XIII, 47," *RB* 88 (1981): 368–72.

a. "When the Gentiles heard this." The gospel always has a twofold effect on the people who listen to it. For some listeners, the gospel message is like a sweet-smelling aroma; it is the fragrance of life, as Paul writes to the Corinthians. But to others that same gospel is an evil-smelling odor that carries the stench of death (II Cor. 2:14–16). In Pisidian Antioch some of the Jews vociferously object to the preaching of Christ's gospel and reject it. The Gentiles, however, listen to Paul's exposition and respond joyously with praise for what they have heard.

b. "[The Gentiles] began to rejoice and glorify the word of the Lord." The reaction of the Gentiles is exuberant: they are filled with joy because they know that the salvation God has promised he has granted to them also.

Variations of the phrase *glorify the word of the Lord* appear in ancient manuscripts. To illustrate, one manuscript has the verb *receive*, because people receive rather than glorify the word of the Lord (compare 8:14; 11:1; 17:11). Another deletes the phrase *the word of the Lord* and substitutes the word *God*, with the resultant reading *glorify God*. Elsewhere in Acts, this reading is common, while the wording *glorify the word of the Lord* occurs only here (see 4:21; 11:18; 21:20). Incidentally, the variations *word of God* (RSV) and *word of the Lord* are insignificant (see v. 44).

A true and tested principle is that the more difficult reading is correct, for scribes would often present a more pleasing rendering of the text in an effort to clarify its meaning. The harder reading *glorify the word of the Lord* has substantial manuscript support and is therefore preferred by translators. The Gentiles glorified the word of the Lord by accepting it with great joy.

c. "And as many as were ordained to eternal life believed." Luke adds a sentence in which he uses the passive voice *were ordained.* The implication is that God is the agent, for only he grants eternal life (Matt. 25:46; John 10:28; 17:2). In the Greek, the form *were ordained* is a passive participle in the perfect tense. The perfect denotes action that took place in the past but is relevant for the present. In the past, God predestined the salvation of the Gentiles. In many places in the Old Testament Scriptures God reveals that the blessing of salvation is for the Gentiles also (e.g., Gen. 12:1–3; Isa. 42:6; 49:6). When they in faith accept Christ, he grants them the gift of eternal life.

When the Gentiles in Pisidian Antioch put their faith in Jesus Christ, they appropriate eternal life for themselves. The text reveals the proverbial two sides of the same coin: God's electing love and man's believing response (compare Phil. 2:12–13). Even though this text features the main verb *to believe,* it also teaches the doctrine of divine election (refer to Rom. 8:29–30). Note that Luke says "[The Gentiles] were ordained to eternal life." He does not say that they were ordained to believe. "What concerns him is that eternal life is not only received by faith, but is essentially the plan of God."[83]

---

83. Guthrie, *New Testament Theology,* p. 618. Consult Calvin, *Acts of the Apostles,* vol. 1, p. 393; and see Lake and Cadbury, *Beginnings,* vol. 4, p. 160.

49. The word of the Lord spread through the whole region. 50. But the Jews aroused the God-fearing and honorable women and the leading men of the city. They instigated a persecution against Paul and Barnabas and drove them out of their region.

The effect of Paul's presentation of the gospel is phenomenal: everywhere the people talk about "the word of the Lord." By word of mouth the Good News is spreading in the city of Antioch and the countryside of Pisidia. Gentile Christians filled with enthusiasm proclaim the gospel message to anyone who wishes to listen. The Christian church is rapidly growing and developing. From Paul's point of view, he can say that God is blessing the missionary labors.

After some time passes,[84] a violent persecution ensues. The Jews of the local synagogue are envious of Paul and Barnabas because of the unexpected response they have received from the Gentiles. These Jews realize that their religious influence is waning, because the Gentile converts have now accepted the teachings of Christ. As someone has said, "Jealousy is the raw material of murder" (compare 14:19). Jealousy poisons the minds of the Jews and impels them to seek support from high-ranking women who are still frequenting the synagogue worship services. (In the first century, Gentile women of prominence often attended the services of the local Jewish synagogue. They were God-fearing converts who were often present in goodly numbers [see 17:4].)[85] The Jews have these influential women persuade the leading men of the city to instigate a persecution against Paul and Barnabas.

The Jews want the city fathers to take their side, stir up a persecution against the missionaries, and banish Paul and Barnabas from Pisidia. They do not seem to realize that the gospel has taken root in their region and cannot be eradicated. The church of Jesus Christ continues to develop (14:21-24). The persecution instigated by the Jews and permitted by the city authorities not only touches the lives of the new Christians but also leads to the expulsion of the two missionaries. Among the rulers are Roman officials who champion the Roman policy of promoting peace and order. Even if Paul and Barnabas themselves do not create turmoil, the Jewish agitators generate sufficient unrest that the governing authorities are compelled to intervene. The local rulers expel Paul and Barnabas from the region, although the expulsion itself seems to have been temporary. Some time later the missionaries are back in Antioch, strengthening the believers and appointing elders in the church.

51. So Paul and Barnabas shook the dust off their feet in protest against

---

84. Ramsay thinks that the missionaries stayed in Pisidian Antioch at least two to six months. As the administrative center of that region, Antioch attracted people from other cities; the result was that the gospel was disseminated in south-central Asia Minor. *St. Paul the Traveller*, p. 105.

85. Josephus reports that in Damascus the Gentile women, "with few exceptions, had all become converts to the Jewish religion." *War* 2.20.2 [560]. See also Max Wilcox, "The 'God-Fearers' in Acts—A Reconsideration," *JSNT* 13 (1981): 102-22.

**them and went to Iconium. 52. And the disciples were filled with joy and
the Holy Spirit.**

Here is a vivid description of a Jewish custom that symbolizes a renuncia-
tion of persons or things. Pharisees, for example, would shake the dust off
their feet when they left Gentile soil so that they would not be defiled.[86]
However, Paul and Barnabas have objections not against the Gentiles but
against the Jews. They use the symbolic act of shaking the dust off their feet
to indicate that they will have nothing to do with the Jews in Pisidian
Antioch (compare 18:6).

The missionaries now leave the region of Pisidia and the city of Antioch
and travel in an easterly direction to Iconium.[87] This city, which today is
known as Konya, actually was part of Phrygia, even though it bordered
Lycaonia. Situated on a plateau, Iconium was surrounded by fertile fields
that received sufficient water from streams flowing down from the nearby
mountains. It was a commercial center that served the agricultural communities of that area. It became an important city along a major highway, and
from this center at least five roads spread into the countryside.[88]

Luke closes this segment of the account about the first missionary journey by describing the attitude of the Christians in Antioch. He says, "The
disciples were filled with joy and the Holy Spirit." As is customary in Acts,
Luke calls the recent converts to Christianity disciples (that is, they are
learners). We would expect these fledgling believers to be disheartened by
the departure of Paul and Barnabas. Instead they are filled with joy and
with the Holy Spirit. God fills the vacuum created by the sudden exit of the
teachers by giving the disciples the gift of joy, which is a fruit of the Holy
Spirit (Gal. 5:22). The presence of the Holy Spirit in the hearts of the
believers is in itself indescribable joy.

Practical Considerations in 13:52

Missions! The word reminds us to contribute to the collection of used clothes that
are sent to mission fields. We think of second-hand equipment that we no longer use
but which workers in distant lands will treasure. We designate sums of money to
support those missionaries who proclaim the gospel in faraway places. We have
heard of people who encountered academic difficulties but were told that if they did
not make the grade, they could always go to the mission fields. We have known
ministers who opted to become missionaries to avoid the stress of the local pastorate.

But does the mission field always have to be the recipient of used clothing, second-
hand equipment, leftover money, and mediocre missionaries? What would happen if
we sent brand-new merchandise, if we gave more to missions than to the needs of our

---

86. The expression *to shake the dust off one's feet* occurs five times in the New Testament: Matt.
10:14; Mark 6:11; Luke 9:5; 10:11; Acts 13:51.
87. Consult M. F. Unger, "Archaeology and Paul's Visit to Iconium, Lystra, and Derbe," *BS*
118 (1961): 107–12.
88. Donald A. Hagner, "Iconium," *ISBE*, vol. 2, p. 792.

local church, and if we recruited the best pastors as missionaries? In Syrian Antioch, the Holy Spirit said to the church, "Appoint for me Barnabas and Paul for the work to which I have called them" (v. 2). The members of the congregation fasted, prayed, and then commissioned its best teachers to do mission work. And God blessed that church beyond measure. In Pisidian Antioch, Paul and Barnabas were invaluable for building the infant church. Because of persecution, they had to leave. But instead of sorrow and sadness, the members of that church were filled with joy and the Holy Spirit. God blessed them abundantly with his sacred presence and provided for them in their needs. "God loves a cheerful giver" (II Cor. 9:7).

Greek Words, Phrases, and Constructions in 13:46–52

Verse 46

τε καί—the position of these two particles in the clause demonstrates that both Paul and Barnabas were speaking boldly. The aorist middle participle παρρησιασάμενοι derives from the words πᾶν (all) and the verb ῥέω (I say) or the noun ῥῆσις (word). The participle functions as an independent verb: "Paul and Barnabas spoke boldly and said."[89]

ἀπωθεῖσθε αὐτόν—the middle voice in this present verb means "you push yourselves away from the word of God."[90]

Verse 48

ἔχαιρον—the use of the imperfect tense in this verb and in ἐδόξαζον is inceptive and signifies "the initiation of a process."[91] That is, "they began to rejoice and praise." Note the uses of the various tenses in this verse. The participle ἀκούοντα is present: "they continued to listen." Then, two verbs in the imperfect denote continuity in the past. They are followed by the aorist ἐπίστευσαν (they believed). The last verb is the periphrastic construction of the verb *to be* (ἦσαν) in the imperfect with the perfect passive participle τεταγμένοι. The perfect indicates an action in the past that has lasting significance for the present.

Verse 52

ἐπληροῦντο—the imperfect tense of πληρόω (I fill) signifies extended action in the past tense. The passive voice implies that God is the agent.

Summary of Chapter 13

The Holy Spirit tells the church in Antioch to commission Barnabas and Paul to be missionaries to the Gentiles. After a period of fasting and prayer, the church ordains them as missionaries. They travel via Seleucia to Cy-

---

89. Blass and Debrunner, *Greek Grammar*, #420.3.
90. Robertson, *Grammar*, p. 810.
91. H. E. Dana and Julius R. Mantey, *A Manual Grammar of the Greek New Testament* (1927; New York: Macmillan, 1967), p. 190.

prus, where they preach the gospel first in Salamis and then in Paphos. At Paphos they meet a Jewish sorcerer, Bar-Jesus, also known as Elymas, and the proconsul Sergius Paulus. Because of Elymas's opposition to the gospel, the sorcerer is struck with blindness, but Sergius Paulus believes.

The missionaries leave Cyprus and sail to Asia Minor. They come to Perga in Pamphylia and then travel to Antioch in Pisidia. There they attend the worship service in the local Jewish synagogue. They are invited to speak a word of encouragement. Paul accepts the invitation and preaches a sermon in which he traces the history of the people of Israel from the time of their stay in Egypt to that of King David's reign. Paul proves that the promise God made concerning David's royal descendant has been fulfilled in the Savior Jesus. The message of salvation to both the children of Abraham and the God-fearing Gentiles is that Jesus has been crucified but God raised him from the dead. Paul shows from Scripture that the Holy One would not see corruption but would rise from the grave. Everyone who believes in Jesus is justified. Paul urges his listeners not to scoff at the gospel, but to believe so that they will not perish.

Many of the Jews and the God-fearing Gentiles believe. They invite Paul and Barnabas to return the next Sabbath with an additional message. Other Jews, filled with jealousy, verbally attack and oppose Paul. Once again, Paul quotes from the Scriptures and proves that, because they are rejected by the Jews, he and Barnabas must go to the Gentiles. With the help of the governing authorities, the Jews instigate a persecution. They succeed in their effort to expel Paul and Barnabas from that region. The missionaries travel to Iconium and the members of the church are filled with joy and the Holy Spirit.

14

The First Missionary Journey, *part 2*

14:1–28

Outline (continued)

14:1–7	C.	Iconium
14:1–3		1. Message Proclaimed
14:4–5		2. Division
14:6–7		3. Escape
14:8–20a	D.	Lystra and Derbe
14:8–10		1. Miracle
14:11–13		2. Response
14:14–18		3. Reaction
14:19–20a		4. Revulsion
14:20b–28	E.	Antioch in Syria
14:20b–25		1. Strengthening the Churches
14:26–28		2. Reporting to Antioch

14 1 A similar incident happened at Iconium. Paul and Barnabas entered the synagogue of the Jews and spoke in such a way that a great multitude believed, both Jews and Greeks. 2 But the Jews who would not believe stirred up and poisoned the minds of the Gentiles against the brothers. 3 So Paul and Barnabas remained a long time speaking boldly for the Lord, who testified to the message of his grace by performing signs and wonders through them. 4 The people of the city were divided; some sided with the Jews and others with the apostles. 5 An attempt was made by both the Gentiles and the Jews with their rulers to mistreat and stone them. 6 When Paul and Barnabas became aware of it, they fled to the cities of Lycaonia, namely, Lystra and Derbe, and to the surrounding region, 7 where they continued to preach the gospel.

C. Iconium
14:1–7

1. Message Proclaimed
14:1–3

As Paul and Barnabas proclaimed the gospel, they selected cities situated along major Roman highways. From Pisidian Antioch they traveled eighty miles east to Iconium, which at that time was an influential city. Here Paul and Barnabas spent considerable time in preaching the Good News (v. 3). They stayed longer in Iconium than in any other place on this first missionary journey.[1] Perhaps the decision to travel east instead of west or north related to Paul's geographical knowledge of Lycaonia, which bordered his native province of Cilicia. Indeed, their journey led them closer to Cilicia, where churches had been established (15:41).

1. A similar incident happened at Iconium. Paul and Barnabas entered the synagogue of the Jews and spoke in such a way that a great multitude believed, both Jews and Greeks.

Luke relates that in Iconium Paul and Barnabas follow the pattern set at Pisidian Antioch. Accordingly, his report is brief and to the point. Paul and his fellow missionary arrive in this commercial city and immediately look for the local Jewish synagogue. Here they worship with the Jews and the God-fearing Gentiles. They are invited to preach and when both Paul and Barnabas accept the invitation, they effectively proclaim the good news of

---

1. Refer to William M. Ramsay, *The Cities of St. Paul: Their Influence on His Life and Thought* (1907; reprint ed., Grand Rapids: Baker, 1963), p. 370.

salvation. We suspect that the missionaries are invited to return. Luke recounts the effect that the message had on the synagogue audience. He says that "a great multitude believed, both Jews and Greeks." He seems to indicate that the response in Iconium was much greater than that in Pisidian Antioch. By implication he conveys that the Jews in Iconium had acquainted the Gentile population with the teachings of the Old Testament. Because of this instruction, innumerable Gentiles worshiped regularly in the Iconium synagogue.

When Paul and Barnabas explained the fulfillment of the messianic prophecies through Jesus Christ, not only numerous Jews but also a large crowd of God-fearing Gentiles believed. The missionaries preached the gospel message to both Jews and Gentiles and told them to "turn in repentance to God and faith in [the] Lord Jesus Christ" (20:21).[2]

2. But the Jews who would not believe stirred up and poisoned the minds of the Gentiles against the brothers.

What happened in Pisidian Antioch is repeated in Iconium. Some Jews reject the gospel and refuse to accept Jesus as their Messiah. Literally, the text reads: "But the Jews who disobeyed." In a sense, the verb *to disobey* is the substitute for the verb *to express unbelief* and thus has a double meaning. Faith demands obedience; otherwise it lacks the characteristics of trust, confidence, and dependence. Faith without obedience is dead (James 2:17), while the essence of unbelief is disobedience.[3] The proclamation of the Good News demands a positive response of joyful compliance, but a negative response demonstrates willful defiance. Just as the believer expresses his faith in honorable deeds, so the unbeliever communicates his defiance in evil deeds.

Undoubtedly inflamed by envy because Paul and Barnabas won countless adherents to the Christian faith, the Jews now begin to work among the Gentile population. They stir up the Gentiles and persuade them to take action against Paul and his companion. More than that, they are able to poison the minds of the Gentiles against the Christians in Iconium.

The Jews use the native population in an effort to turn the people against the believers, whom Luke calls "brothers." In other words, Luke specifically states that the hostilities engendered by the Jews envelop both the church and its leaders. The recent converts to Christianity now endure the brunt of Jewish-instigated harassment. No wonder that Paul and Barnabas some time later encourage them with these instructive words: "Through many hardships we must enter the kingdom of God" (v. 22). Yet the more the opposition tries to hinder the growth and development of the church, the more boldly the missionaries preach the word.

3. So Paul and Barnabas remained a long time speaking boldly for the

---

2. Compare 18:4; 19:10, 17.

3. Consult R. C. H. Lenski, *The Interpretation of the Acts of the Apostles* (Columbus: Wartburg, 1944), p. 560.

Lord, who testified to the message of his grace by performing signs and wonders through them.

Harassing the missionaries and the church creates an effect opposite of that which the Jews intended. Instead of leaving the area, Paul and Barnabas stay with the congregation for a considerable period of time and boldly continue to preach the Good News. They demonstrate the truth that the church thrives in times of oppression. The cause of Christ attracts people who notice the boldness and courage of the believers. The work of preaching and teaching continues unabated while the Lord grants his indispensable blessings on the growth of his church. The apostles experience the power of the Lord as they boldly proclaim his name. The expression *Lord* refers to either God or Jesus. Although Luke often links apostolic boldness with the cause of Christ,[4] we do well to interpret the expression as pointing to Jesus and to God. This becomes clear when we understand the phrase *the message of his grace* to be synonymous with Christ's gospel,[5] proclaimed by the apostles, and to the word of God (see 20:32).

Indirectly Luke suggests that the church in Iconium developed rapidly. He writes, "Paul and Barnabas . . . [spoke] boldly for the Lord, who testified to the message of his grace by performing signs and wonders through them." The Lord, then, enables the missionaries to execute extraordinary deeds that caused the people of Iconium to take note. God performs miracles in answer to and for the increase of faith. The apostles receive from God the charismatic gifts to heal the sick and raise the dead so that the faith of God's people is strengthened (5:12; 6:8; Heb. 2:4). When God works a miracle, he does so in harmony with his Word and thus fortifies the believer spiritually. Luke, however, eliminates the details regarding these signs and wonders that perhaps pertained to a healing ministry. In his epistle to the Galatians, Paul notes that God worked miracles among the recipients of his letter (3:5), among whom were the inhabitants of Iconium (located in the Roman province of Galatia).

Greek Words, Phrases, and Constructions in 14:1–3

Verse 1

κατὰ τὸ αὐτό—this phrase means either "together" (KJV, NKJV, NASB, RSV) or "in the same way" (with variations, GNB, NAB, NEB, NIV, JB, MLB).[6] Modern translators prefer the second choice, as it emphasizes that the apostles followed their usual practice in Iconium.

ὥστε πιστεῦσαι—the particle ὥστε (so that) succeeded by the aorist active infinitive expresses actual result.

---

4. See 4:29, 31; 9:27–28; 19:8; 28:31.
5. Consult Donald Guthrie, *New Testament Theology* (Downers Grove: Inter-Varsity, 1981), p. 617.
6. Bauer, p. 123, also lists "at the same time." But this translation does not fit the context.

πολὺ πλῆθος—"a great multitude." The preceding genitives ("both Jews and Greeks") depend on this phrase. Usually the genitive follows the noun on which it depends.[7] The position of these genitives shows emphasis.

Verse 2

ἀπειθήσαντες—the compound from ἀ (not) and the verb πείθω (I persuade) signifies "I do not allow myself to be persuaded." In the New Testament, the compound means "to refuse to believe" and thus stands in opposition to the verb πιστεύω (I believe). As such it connotes disobedience.

ἐκάκωσαν—this verb has two meanings: "to mistreat" and "to embitter." In the New Testament, the second sense occurs only here.

Codex Bezae has an extended reading of this verse. The additions are in italics: "But *the chiefs of the synagogue of the Jews and the rulers of the synagogue stirred up for themselves persecution against the righteous,* and poisoned the minds of the Gentiles against the brethren. *But the Lord soon gave peace.*"[8]

The additions represent an attempt to provide greater coherence in the text, but the result is not encouraging. The redundance of the phrases *chiefs of the synagogue* and *rulers of the synagogue* is obvious. Moreover, the sentence *but the Lord soon gave peace* appears to be an incomplete transition between verses 2 and 3. Scholars prefer to stay with the usual text of these two verses in spite of the apparent lack of coherence.

Verse 3

μὲν οὖν—the combination of a particle and a conjunction conveys an adversative sense: "however."[9]

διέτριψαν—from the intensive compound διατρίβω (I spend time), the aorist active imparts the constative idea that views the action from beginning to end.

---

2. Division
14:4-5

4. The people of the city were divided; some sided with the Jews and others with the apostles. 5. An attempt was made by both the Gentiles and the Jews with their rulers to mistreat and stone them.

Luke introduces the word *apostles.* A study of Acts reveals that Luke employs that term consistently of the twelve apostles and only twice (vv. 4, 14) of Paul and Barnabas. The Twelve, with Peter at their head, are bearers and guardians of Christ's gospel in Jerusalem (8:1, 14). The next in line to claim the title are Paul and Barnabas, who were commissioned by the

---

7. A. T. Robertson, *A Grammar of the Greek New Testament in the Light of Historical Research* (Nashville: Broadman, 1934), p. 502.

8. Bruce M. Metzger, *A Textual Commentary on the Greek New Testament,* 3d corrected ed. (London and New York: United Bible Societies, 1975), pp. 419–20.

9. C. F. D. Moule, *An Idiom-Book of New Testament Greek,* 2d ed. (Cambridge: Cambridge University Press, 1960), p. 162.

church in Antioch to proclaim the gospel to the Gentiles (13:1–3). And last, in a wider sense Paul mentions Andronicus and Junias, who are preachers of the gospel and are recognized by the churches as apostles (Rom. 16:7). Nevertheless, an apostle had to be a witness of Christ's resurrection and had to be commissioned by Christ himself.[10] Thus Matthias is appointed by Christ in Jerusalem and Paul near Damascus. But Apollos and Timothy are never called apostles.

Even though in Acts Luke twice designates Paul an apostle, he thrice records Paul's call and commission to be an apostle to the Gentiles (9:1–19; 22:1–21; 26:2–18). Further, Jesus says that Paul is his chosen instrument to bring his name before the Gentiles and kings (9:15). Jesus sends him forth as an apostle (22:21; 26:16–17; the word derives from the Greek verb *apostellō* [I send]). Paul met the apostolic requirement set forth by the apostles when they chose Matthias to succeed Judas Iscariot (1:21–22). Because of his conversion experience near Damascus, Paul saw Jesus and became a witness of Christ's resurrection. Although Paul did not follow Jesus from the time of John's baptism to that of Christ's ascension, the Twelve accepted him as a genuine apostle. How does Luke depict Paul? "The picture that Acts paints is not that Paul was not an apostle, but that he was an apostle extraordinary which is consonant with Paul's own account (I Cor. 9:1–3; 15:5–9; Gal. 1:12–17)."[11] And last, Paul indirectly calls Barnabas an apostle (I Cor. 9:6; Gal. 2:9–10).

The teachings of the Christian faith divide the inhabitants of Iconium so that numberless people take the side of the unbelieving Jews and others support Paul and Barnabas. Clashes result; the authorities have to intervene. Once again, Luke depicts a situation that is reminiscent of Pisidian Antioch. There the Jews with the help of prominent God-fearing Gentile women influenced the local government authorities to expel the missionaries. Here the Jews are successful in procuring the help of the local officials.

The Jews are able to convince the Gentiles that an attack should be made on the lives of Paul and Barnabas. They plot and scheme with the result that the Gentiles take the lead. Luke mentions them first in his report: "Both the Gentiles and the Jews with their rulers [plotted] to mistreat and stone [the missionaries]." The Jews cleverly present themselves as supporters of a cause the Gentiles champion but which the Jews themselves originated. In Greek, the text is not clear whether the words *their rulers* refer to the Jewish synagogue rulers, the Gentile city fathers, or both.[12]

---

10. See the commentary on pp. 67–68; Karl Heinrich Rengstorf, *TDNT*, vol. 1, p. 423.

11. Colin Brown, *NIDNTT*, vol. 1, p. 136.

12. Commentators are divided. Some assert that the leaders were Jews (e.g., Lenski, *Acts*, pp. 567–68). Others think of Gentile rulers (e.g., F. W. Grosheide, *De Handelingen der Apostelen*, Kommentaar op het Nieuwe Testament series, 2 vols. [Amsterdam: van Bottenburg, 1942], vol. 1, p. 453). And still others state that the authorities came from both the Jewish and Gentile camps; see Everett F. Harrison, *Interpreting Acts: The Expanding Church*, 2d ed. (Grand Rapids: Zondervan, Academie Books, 1986), p. 231.

In harmony with the parallel occurrences in Pisidian Antioch and Iconium, the term *their rulers* most logically connotes both the local authorities and the leaders of the Jewish synagogue. The city officials seeking to maintain order and stability are on the side of the Gentiles and the Jews. They actually view Paul and Barnabas as troublemakers. The attack on the missionaries comes in the form of insolence; that is, invective and personal insults are hurled at Paul and Barnabas. But the threat becomes real when the schemers attempt murder by hurling stones at the envoys of the gospel. (Incidentally, throwing stones appears to be characteristic in the Middle East, where the supply of stones is virtually unlimited.) Once again, the time has come for Paul and Barnabas to depart suddenly (compare 13:50).

Greek Words, Phrases, and Constructions in 14:4–5

Verse 4

τὸ πλῆθος—literally the noun denotes "the multitude," but here it means "the people."

σύν—not "in company with," but "on the side of." Codex Bezae expands the text to read, "But the people of the city were divided; some sided with the Jews, and some with the apostles, *cleaving to them on account of the word of God*" (the addition is in italics).[13]

Verse 5

ὁρμὴ τῶν ἐθνῶν—although the noun ὁρμή in context means "attempt," the idea of rush, assault, or attack should not be neglected.

σὺν—in this verse, the preposition σύν is equivalent to καί (and).[14]

---

3. Escape
14:6–7

6. When Paul and Barnabas became aware of it, they fled to the cities of Lycaonia, namely, Lystra and Derbe, and to the surrounding region, 7. where they continued to preach the gospel.

Fleeing from dangerous situations became a way of life for Paul. He escaped from Damascus with the help of Christian friends (9:25; II Cor. 11:33). When the Jews in Jerusalem tried to kill Paul, he fled to Caesarea, where he boarded ship for his hometown, Tarsus (9:30). He was expelled from Pisidian Antioch (13:50) and now must leave Iconium for his own safety.

We imagine that the apostles received information from fellow Christians who learned about the plot to kill Paul and Barnabas. Weighing the advantages and disadvantages, the missionaries decide to move to a new location.

---

13. Metzger, *Textual Commentary*, p. 420.
14. Robertson, *Grammar*, p. 628.

They travel in a southerly direction to the Lycaonian region. Lycaonia is situated on a mountainous plateau in the southern part of Asia Minor at an elevation of thirty-three hundred feet. It borders the Taurus Mountains and was part of the Roman province of Galatia. "Lycaonia is a flat, dry, and almost treeless plain, extremely dusty at the end of the summer, and inhospitably cold in winter."[15]

The missionaries came first to Lystra, which is about twenty miles from Iconium, and then to Derbe, which is still farther to the southeast. The Romans had colonized Lystra much as they had Pisidian Antioch. However, the presence of the Roman population appeared to have been nonessential to Paul and Barnabas. "Beside the Roman colonists the population of Lystra consisted of the class which was educated in Greek manners and the Greek language, and the uneducated Lycaonian population."[16] We know that Timothy, who was born and reared in Lystra, was of Greek descent. His mother was a Jewess but his father a Greek, presumably of the educated class (16:1–3). The Romans belonged to the ruling class, while the Greeks, also called Hellenes, were educated and generally well-to-do people.

The common people of Lystra spoke the Lycaonian language and thereby proved that linguistically they were not influenced by Roman or Greek culture (although they did worship the Greek gods Zeus and Hermes [see v. 12]). Rural people came to the regional marketing center where they met the Jewish merchants, the Greek gentlemen, and the Roman officers.[17] Indeed, Paul and Barnabas were visiting a small country town where they tried to acquaint a mixed audience with Christ's gospel.

Practical Considerations in 14:1–7

The historical account of Acts reveals a pattern in the missionaries' experience. God appoints his servants and sends them out to proclaim the gospel of salvation. These men boldly preach and teach his Word with the result that numerous people listen, are converted, and become members of the church. Then, Jewish antagonists, aided at times by Gentiles, instigate persecutions, banishment, and even imprisonment of God's servants. But God delivers his workers from their predicaments and blesses the church.[18]

Wherever God directs his ministers and missionaries to speak boldly in his behalf, the forces of Satan try to interfere and create opposition to them and to the Word.

---

15. William S. LaSor, "Lycaonia," *ISBE*, vol. 3, p. 188.

16. Ramsay, *Cities of St. Paul*, p. 417.

17. Consult E. M. Blaiklock, *Cities of the New Testament* (Westwood, N.J.: Revell, 1965), p. 31; Ramsay, *Cities of St. Paul*, pp. 324–25; Colin J. Hemer, *The Book of Acts in the Setting of Hellenistic History*, ed. Conrad H. Gempf (Tübingen: Mohr, 1989), pp. 228–30.

18. Leland Ryken, *Words of Life: A Literary Introduction to the New Testament* (Grand Rapids: Baker, 1987), p. 79. See also M. D. Goulder, *Type and History in Acts* (London: SPCK, 1964), p. 16.

Ministers are harassed, ridiculed, and mocked not only by the world but sometimes by members of the church. In spite of the difficulties God's servants face, God's grace is sufficient. He sustains them in their task.

> In the midst of opposition,
> Let them trust, O Lord, in Thee;
> When success attends their mission,
> Let Thy servants humblest be.
> Never leave them
> Till Thy face in heaven they see.
> —Thomas Kelly

Greek Words, Phrases, and Constructions in 14:6–7

Verse 6

συνιδόντες—the aorist active participle from συνοράω (I understand, perceive) signifies "getting wind of it."

κατέφυγον—the compound form of this verb in the aorist is stronger than the simple verb φεύγω (I flee). It means "they fled for refuge."

Verse 7

The Western text (Codex Bezae) amplifies the text: "And there they preached the gospel, *and the whole multitude was moved by the teaching. And Paul and Barnabas stayed on in Lystra*" (the addition is italicized).[19]

---

8 In Lystra sat a man who was unable to use his feet because he was born a cripple and had never walked. 9 This man heard Paul speaking. Paul looked at him intently and, seeing that he had faith to be healed, 10 loudly said, "Stand up on your feet!" The man jumped up and began to walk. 11 When the crowds saw what Paul had done, they shouted in the Lycaonian language, "The gods have become like men and have come down to us." 12 They began calling Barnabas Zeus, and Paul they called Hermes, because Paul was the main speaker. 13 The priest of Zeus, whose temple was just outside the city, brought bulls and garlands to the gates. He wanted to offer sacrifices with the crowds.

14 But when the apostles Barnabas and Paul heard it, they tore their robes. They rushed out into the crowd, shouting: 15 "Men, why are you doing this? We also are men with the same nature as you. We preach the gospel to you in order to turn you from worthless things to the living God, who made the heaven and the earth and the sea, and all that is in them. 16 In the past, God allowed all nations to go their own way. 17 And yet he did not leave himself without witness. God conferred benefits by giving you rains from heaven and fruitful seasons. He filled your hearts with food and gladness." 18 Even though they said this, they were hardly able to stop the crowds from sacrificing to them.

19 But the Jews from Antioch and Iconium came and, having persuaded the crowds, stoned Paul and dragged him outside the city, supposing that he was dead. 20a But while the disciples stood around him, Paul got up and entered the city.

---

19. Metzger, *Textual Commentary*, p. 420.

D. Lystra and Derbe
14:8–20a

In Acts, Luke indirectly draws a parallel between Peter and Paul. For example, Peter heals the cripple at the temple gate called Beautiful (3:1–10) and Paul restores a lame man in Lystra (14:8–10). Peter raises Dorcas in Joppa (9:36–42) and Paul restores Eutychus (20:9–12). Peter was released from prison (12:6–11); so was Paul (16:25–28).

Luke reports that the cripple at the gate called Beautiful was healed because of his faith in the name of Jesus (3:16). Likewise, when Paul miraculously restored the crippled man in Lystra, he saw that "the man had faith to be healed" (v. 9).

1. Miracle
14:8–10

8. In Lystra sat a man who was unable to use his feet because he was born a cripple and had never walked. 9. This man heard Paul speaking. Paul looked at him intently and, seeing that he had faith to be healed, 10. loudly said, "Stand up on your feet!" The man jumped up and began to walk.

We assume that the Jews in Lystra had no synagogue, for in the account no God-fearing Gentiles are mentioned. Paul and Barnabas thus traveled to Lystra to find a refuge from Jewish synagogue officials. The missionaries proclaim the gospel to anyone who desires to listen to them.

Among the listeners to the preaching of Paul is a man born with a handicap. He is unable to use his feet and, consequently, has never walked. Luke describes the man's condition in detail and even uses a phrase that is identical to his description of the lame man at the temple gate in Jerusalem: "crippled from birth" (3:2, NIV). Luke briefly reports that during their ministry in Iconium, the apostles performed many healing miracles (14:3); he fully portrays the first miracle Paul rendered in Lystra and contrasts the severity of the man's condition with the magnitude of the miracle.

We presume that the absence of a synagogue necessitated a point of contact that would give Paul an opportunity to reach the local population. Everyone knew the cripple, who most certainly made his living by begging. Paul heals this lame man for the purpose of gaining the interest of the people. When they see the result of the miracle, they are ready to listen to the gospel.

The lame man has been carried to a public meeting place and seated perhaps in front of a temple or in a marketplace. Here crowds of people usually gathered to hear a speaker and here the beggar collected his monetary gifts. In this place, Paul preaches the gospel of salvation. Even though the native people speak the Lycaonian language, they are able to understand Paul, who communicates the gospel in Greek. The lame man listens to the sermon Paul is preaching. In fact, one reading of the Greek text indicates

511

that the man listened frequently.[20] Whatever that record may be, Paul notices the cripple and focuses his attention on him. Note, again, the similarity between this account and that of Peter healing the lame man in Jerusalem. There, Peter looked intently at a cripple (3:4); in Lystra Paul does the same.

Luke adds that "the man had faith to be healed." What kind of faith is this? Simply put, it is faith that is necessary for salvation. The verb *to be healed* can also mean *to be saved* (refer to 4:12; Rom. 5:10). The synoptic evangelists (Matthew, Mark, and Luke) often link faith to healing miracles; these three record Jesus' repeated refrain, "Your faith has saved you," spoken to those whom he healed miraculously.[21] The Gospel writers place emphasis on the healing miracle, yet we should not minimize the genuine faith of those who were healed. The lame man in Lystra, listening to Paul's sermon, puts his faith in Jesus. His authentic faith is necessary for the healing of his crippled feet (compare James 5:15).[22] How does Paul know that the man has faith? Guided by the Holy Spirit, Paul is able to detect that the cripple has faith in Jesus, which perhaps the man expressed verbally.

Paul addresses the cripple and commands him in a loud voice, so that not only the lame man but also the crowds may hear: "Stand up on your feet!" Actually, the Greek text has, "Stand straight up on your feet!" No sooner has Paul uttered the words than the man puts his faith to the test. He stands erect, jumps up, and for the first time in his life begins to walk. We can imagine the joy and happiness, the shouts of jubilation coming from the man and the cries of amazement from the crowd. Everyone is able to see that indeed a miracle has occurred, for the man himself testifies to it.

Greek Words, Phrases, and Constructions in 14:8–10

Verse 8

ἀδύνατος—this adjective does not mean "impossible" (Heb. 6:4) but "unable" or "incapable."

τοῖς ποσίν—the dative case is the dative of respect, especially with reference to the adjective *unable*.

ἐκάθητο—the use of the imperfect tense of the verb *to sit* points to the continued and habitual sitting position of the cripple at a given location.

Verses 9–10

ἤκουσεν—manuscript evidence for the aorist tense ("he heard") and the imperfect tense (ἤκουεν, he repeatedly heard) is equally strong. Textual editors are divided at this point.

---

20. Some manuscripts have the aorist tense, implying single occurrence; others have the imperfect tense that denotes continued or frequent action.
21. See Matt. 9:22; Mark 5:34; 10:52; Luke 7:50; 8:48; 17:19; 18:42. Also consult Leon Morris, *New Testament Theology* (Grand Rapids: Zondervan, Academie Books, 1986), p. 198.
22. Colin Brown, *NIDNTT*, vol. 3, p. 212.

πίστιν τοῦ σωθῆναι—the articular infinitive has a consecutive sense: the intent of the infinitive is the result of the preceding noun *faith*. Hence, "the necessary faith for salvation."

ὀρθός—the position of this adjective in this imperatival sentence makes it equivalent to an adverb: "Stand up straight!"

ἥλατο καὶ περιεπάτει—note that the first verb (from ἅλλομαι, I jump) is in the aorist tense while the second verb is in the imperfect tense.

---

2. *Response*
14:11–13

11. When the crowds saw what Paul had done, they shouted in the Lycaonian language, "The gods have become like men and have come down to us." 12. They began calling Barnabas Zeus, and Paul they called Hermes, because Paul was the main speaker.

a. "When the crowds saw what Paul had done." The citizens of Lystra and the surrounding countryside are assembled in considerable numbers which perhaps run into the hundreds if not thousands, for Luke uses the plural form *crowds*. They are amazed at what has happened and in great agitation express themselves in their native Lycaonian language. Paul and Barnabas are at first unable to understand what is being said.

b. "The gods have become like men and have come down to us," the people shout. The local population, steeped in religious lore, looks upon Paul and Barnabas as two gods who have come down to Lystra in human form. We infer that the people based this observation on the legend that both Zeus, the chief of the gods, and Hermes, the messenger of the gods, had visited an area in the province of Phrygia but had been denied lodging by the local people. Finally, an elderly man and his wife welcomed the gods to their humble dwelling. The gods amply rewarded the couple's hospitality by turning their house into a temple and, at the couple's request, appointing them priests in this temple. The gods punished the rest of the people by destroying their homes. The legend has been recorded by the Roman poet Ovid, who lived from 43 B.C. to A.D. 17 and who called the gods by their Latin names: Jupiter (Zeus) and Mercury (Hermes).[23]

(In passing, I point out that we should not interpret Paul's compliment to the Christians in Galatia, among whom were those in Lystra, as a reference to this incident. Paul writes, "You received me as an angel of God" [Gal. 4:14]. However, the Lystrans obviously considered Paul and Barnabas to be gods, not angels.)

The inhabitants of Lystra worshiped Zeus, whom they regarded as their guardian deity. Outside the city they had erected a temple in his honor. In addition, they worshiped Hermes as the patron deity of speakers and travelers and as the god of fortune and fertility.[24] Hermes, whose task was to

---

23. Ovid *Metamorphoses* 8.626–724. For the use of the Latin names, see KJV, ASV, NEB, *Phillips*.
24. "Hermes," *ISBE*, vol. 2, pp. 687–88.

relay messages from the gods to men, was the son of Zeus and Maia. His name is reflected in the word *hermeneutics*, which derives from the Greek term *hermēneutēs* (interpreter).

Archaeological evidence—inscriptions about the "priests of Zeus" and to a statue of Hermes discovered in the vicinity of Lystra—has clearly demonstrated that the gods Zeus and Hermes were worshiped in that city. Moreover, the inscriptions are in the Lycaonian language.[25]

c. "They began calling Barnabas Zeus, and Paul they called Hermes, because Paul was the main speaker." We would have expected the people to designate Paul, because of his decisive leadership ability, as Zeus, and Barnabas, who served as Paul's associate and helper, as Hermes. But this is not the case. Undoubtedly, the community of Lystra believes that the highest deity ought not to work but be served by lower gods. In view of Barnabas's reticence, the people consider him to be the chief god Zeus and they regard Paul, who appears to do all the work, as Hermes the servant god of Zeus.[26] Although the apocryphal book The Acts of Paul and Thecla presents a description of Paul, I do not think that it has any bearing on this particular passage and frankly question its accuracy:

> And a man named Onesiphorus, who had heard that Paul was come to Iconium, . . . went along the royal road which leads to Lystra, and stood there waiting for him. . . . And he saw Paul coming, a man of small stature, with a bald head and crooked legs, in a good state of body, with eyebrows meeting and nose somewhat hooked, full of friendliness; for now he appeared like a man, and now he had the face of an angel.[27]

13. The priest of Zeus, whose temple was just outside the city, brought bulls and garlands to the gates. He wanted to offer sacrifices with the crowds.

a. "The priest of Zeus." Paul and Barnabas know that they are in a pagan environment where the people worship Zeus and where his temple is "just outside the city." The man who holds religious authority and who receives the respect of the people is the priest of Zeus. In other words, the apostles have to submit to his authority, for they are visitors who enter his territory. How soon the missionaries understood the shouts of the people, "The gods have become like men and have come down to us," is difficult to determine. But when the priest of Zeus hears these shouts, he knows that he has a task to perform: to offer sacrifices to the gods who have come to visit the people of Lystra. Obviously, the priest wants to please the gods and thus avoid any

---

25. Consult F. F. Bruce, *The Book of the Acts*, rev. ed., New International Commentary on the New Testament series (Grand Rapids: Eerdmans, 1988), pp. 274–75.

26. Consult Grosheide, *Handelingen der Apostelen*, vol. 1, p. 457.

27. The Acts of Paul and Thecla 3.2–3. Edgar Hennecke, *New Testament Apocrypha*, ed. Wilhelm Schneemelcher, 2 vols. (Philadelphia: Westminster, 1963–64), vol. 1, pp. 353–54.

repetition of the earlier punishment the gods meted out to the inhospitable citizens of Phrygia.

b. "Just outside the city." Historical evidence points to the pagan practice of building temples dedicated to Zeus outside the city walls. In brief, the temple was named "the temple of Zeus-outside-the-city."[28] The priest takes bulls decked with garlands made of wool and leads them outside the city to the temple of Zeus. The word *gates* describes either the gates of the city or the gates of the temple. Here the priest and the crowds of people wish to honor Paul and Barnabas.

Greek Words, Phrases and Constructions in 14:13

πυλῶνας—because of the plural form, the word probably does not refer to a house but to the gates of the city.

3. Reaction
14:14–18

Luke's account leaves the impression that some time elapsed between the healing of the cripple and the appearance of the priest and his sacrificial animals. Apparently Paul and Barnabas were not told what the crowds were saying in the Lycaonian language and did not initially realize that the sacrifices were meant for them.

14. But when the apostles Barnabas and Paul heard it, they tore their robes. They rushed out into the crowd, shouting: 15. "Men, why are you doing this? We also are men with the same nature as you. We preach the gospel to you in order to turn you from worthless things to the living God, who made the heaven and the earth and the sea, and all that is in them."

Observe the following points:

a. *Torn garments.* Eventually the apostles hear what the crowds led by the priest of Zeus are planning to do for them. Presumably some of the disciples of the apostles serve as informants and interpreters (v. 20). When they realize what is happening, Paul and Barnabas tear their clothes as a sign of deep emotional turmoil.[29] They are greatly troubled because as God's servants they know that only the Most High should receive all glory and honor. Indeed, when Peter at God's command entered the home of Cornelius in Caesarea, Cornelius fell at Peter's feet to pay his respects. But Peter said: "Stand up! I, too, am only a man" (10:26; see also Rev. 19:10; 22:8–9).

---

28. Ernst Haenchen mentions that this name "was a widely current designation." *The Acts of the Apostles: A Commentary,* trans. Bernard Noble and Gerald Shinn (Philadelphia: Westminster, 1971), p. 427 n. 2.

29. This typically Jewish practice (e.g., Mark 14:63) was not unknown in the Greco-Roman world. See Bauer, p. 188, with reference to the verb *to tear.*

Further, the apostles know that when the people praised King Herod Agrippa I by saying his voice was that of a god, God struck him down so that soon afterward he died (12:21–23).

No wonder that Paul and Barnabas tear their clothes to indicate the mental agony they experience. They fling aside the temptation to succumb to the crowd's adulation and turn away in great distress. They have come to preach the gospel of salvation to people serving pagan gods, but now the apostles perceive that these people pervert the gospel by considering the proclaimers of that gospel to be gods and seek to worship them.

Note, first, that Luke again uses the expression *apostles* (see v. 4) for both missionaries. Also, he lists Barnabas first, perhaps because the Lycaonian people consider Barnabas to be Zeus.

b. *Similar men.* At once, Paul and Barnabas put the matter in its right perspective. Both of them rush out into the crowd of people and shout at the top of their voices: "Men, why are you doing this? We also are men with the same nature as you" (compare James 5:17). The apostles lose no time in getting to the heart of the matter and ask for an explanation. They wish to know why the people are preparing the sacrifices. And because these people customarily offer sacrifices to their gods, both Paul and Barnabas declare that they themselves are ordinary people and are not divine. They explain that they are not god-men but messengers sent out by God. They have to teach the people of Lystra the elementary truths about the living God.

c. *Gospel message.* "We preach the gospel to you." The speech of Paul and Barnabas differs substantially from the sermon Paul preached to the Jewish-Gentile audience in Pisidian Antioch. There the God-fearing Gentiles had been instructed in the teaching of the Scriptures. Here the missionaries have to begin with fundamental truths and are unable to assume that the crowds have any knowledge about God and his works. Paul's speech to the Areopagus in Athens (17:24–28) resembles the remarks the apostles make in Lystra. Both here and in Athens, Paul teaches that God is the creator and sustainer of the universe. He begins not with the nation Israel but with nature and its creation by the one God who upholds and governs this world. Paul and Barnabas must teach people who have not had the benefit of religious instruction by resident Jews. Unlike the God-fearing Gentiles in Pisidian Antioch and Iconium, the people in Lystra have had no preparation for receiving the gospel.

The missionaries directly confront the people with the pagan practice of idolatry by saying that idols are "worthless things." Throughout the Old Testament, this expression refers to the worthless idols of Gentile nations.[30] Paul and Barnabas avoid offending their audience but contrast the "worthless things" with the living God. Implicitly, they indicate that idols are

---

30. For example, see Deut. 32:21; I Kings 16:13, 26; II Kings 17:15; Ps. 31:6; Jer. 2:5; 8:19; 10:8.

inanimate objects—they are dead (refer to Ps. 115:4–8). In contrast, God is a living God "who made the heaven and the earth and the sea, and all that is in them." This is a direct quotation from an Old Testament creation account (Exod. 20:11; Ps. 146:6). In a sense, the apostles teach the Gentiles about the origin of the world and indirectly point out that their idols are unable to do anything.

Accordingly, the apostles challenge the people to turn from their idols to the living God, to know him, and to be converted (compare I Thess. 1:9). If they turn away from worthless idols, they ought to turn to God who has created heaven, earth, and sea. The Gentiles had three classes of gods for the visible universe.[31] However, the apostles teach that the one God who created everything is alive and gives life.

16. "In the past, God allowed all nations to go their own way. 17. And yet he did not leave himself without witness. God conferred benefits by giving you rains from heaven and fruitful seasons. He filled your hearts with food and gladness."

We suppose that the speaker is Paul who, on this occasion, teaches the people not about Jesus Christ the Savior but about the one God who created all things. When he tells the Lycaonians about God the Creator, he expects them to ask why God did not reveal himself to them. Paul anticipates this question and answers that for past generations, God permitted the nations to go their own way.

The phrase *in the past* should be understood in the broadest possible sense, for it refers to the time of Noah. God saved eight people from the waters of the deluge; both God's people and the unbelieving nations descended from these eight. The expression *all nations* does not include Israel, because God constantly called his own people to repentance. Throughout the long centuries, while the patriarchs and Israel received God's special revelation, the nations of the world were living apart from God.

Paul says only that God allowed all nations to go astray. All through the ages God was fully aware of what they were doing, but he permitted them to live in sin. Paul implies that the Gentiles did not fulfill God's commands. They chose their own way of life and thus must take full responsibility for their actions. They are unable to plead ignorance, for Paul asserts that God made himself plain to them since the creation of the world; hence they are without excuse (Rom. 1:19–20). In his Areopagus address, Paul tells the Athenian philosophers the same truth: "Having overlooked the times of ignorance, God is now commanding all men everywhere to repent" (17:30; see also I Peter 4:3). The period of ignorance has come to an end now with the proclamation of the Good News by the apostles.

In answer, the Lycaonians might point to the many years that have elapsed since God's revelation to Israel and to the countless numbers of

---

31. John Albert Bengel, *Gnomon of the New Testament,* ed. Andrew R. Fausset, 5 vols. (Edinburgh: Clark, 1877), vol. 2, p. 641.

ignorant Gentiles. They would perhaps plead that they were unaware of God's existence. God's truth is eternal and unchangeable,[32] and Paul proves to them that God "did not leave himself without witness." The witness, of course, is the eloquent testimony of nature. All creation sings God's praise and testifies to his goodness. Paul gives three examples that prove God's clear testimony to the Gentiles:

a. *Showing kindness.* God confers benefits on the Gentiles by giving them rain from heaven at the proper time. The rain is responsible for providing them with harvests to feed them and their animals. The recurring cycle of rains and crops is abundant proof that God, who has created all things, upholds what he has made.

b. *Providing food.* God opens his hand and feeds man and beast without reluctance or discrimination. As the psalmist puts it, "God is good to all" (Ps. 145:9). Similarly, Jesus said that "God makes his sun to rise on the evil and the good and he sends rain on the righteous and the unrighteous" (Matt. 5:45). God sends rain to replenish the earth, so that the earth brings forth abundant crops (see Lev. 26:4; Ps. 65:9–13; Jer. 5:24). The word *rains* is an implicit reference to the sea that provides water through evaporation; the sky that carries the clouds which release the rain; and the earth that receives precipitation in the form of rain, ice, or snow.

God gives his creatures crops at the proper time: grass for fodder and grain for human consumption. Periods of drought and occasional crop failures occur, but God does not abandon his creation. He always provides some crops to sustain man and beast.

c. *Joyful hearts.* God not only provides plenty of food for all his creation, but also fills man's heart with joy. Even if sinful man neglects or refuses to express thanks for all God's blessings, God nevertheless satiates the sinner's heart with pleasure and delight. Man himself does not create joy, but God grants him this gift. In short, God supplies man with everything he needs and makes him happy, too.

The Lycaonians must acknowledge that they themselves have no control over the annual rainfall and over the agricultural yield. Even their joy is dependent on external circumstances. They are dependent on God, who opens his hand and supplies them in their needs. Paul, then, preaches to the citizens of Lystra the message that God, who created the world, faithfully cares for them by giving them rains, crops, food, and happiness.

18. Even though they said this, they were hardly able to stop the crowds from sacrificing to them.

Both Paul and Barnabas are preaching to the crowds at Lystra and are trying to dissuade the people from offering sacrifices. They have to exert all their common sense, strength, tact, and talent to show the crowds that God, not the apostles, deserves honor and respect. Since in Greek a nega-

---

32. John Calvin, *Commentary on the Acts of the Apostles,* ed. David W. Torrance and Thomas F. Torrance, 2 vols. (Grand Rapids: Eerdmans, 1966), vol. 2, p. 12.

tive particle precedes the verb, we infer that the crowds have not yet begun the ceremonies. The missionaries do everything in their power to persuade the crowds not even to start the ritual. A few Greek manuscripts feature an additional clause ("but to go each to his own home"). The intent is to provide a smooth ending for the sentence, but the endeavor fails, for the extra clause gives a strained juncture.[33] Furthermore, the support for this reading is weak.

Luke portrays the parallel between Peter and Paul and their respective ministries. Peter heals a cripple in Jerusalem and Paul restores the lame man in Lystra. But notice the difference: After healing the man, Peter preaches to a multitude of Jewish people and the church in Jerusalem increased in membership to about five thousand men. Paul performs the same miracle in Lystra and the Gentile crowds regard him and Barnabas as gods whom they wish to honor with sacrifices. The effect of Paul's message is minimal in comparison with the effect of Peter's sermon in Jerusalem. Yet the church that is founded at Lystra demonstrates the triumph of faith (see vv. 21–23). With this account, Luke depicts the difficulties Paul and Barnabas face while preaching to a Gentile audience.[34]

Doctrinal Considerations in 14:14–18

When Paul preaches the gospel to Jews, he generally begins with either Abraham or the formation of the nation Israel in Egypt. But when he addresses a Gentile audience, he starts with the creation account. Thus, he teaches the Gentiles that God is the creator of heaven, earth, and sea. Paul instructs them in the elementary knowledge of the formation of the world (refer to 17:22–31; Rom. 1:19–20; 2:14–15).

In effect, the doctrine of creation is fundamental to the message of redemption.[35] By faith man ought to know God in Jesus Christ as both his Creator and Redeemer (Eccl. 12:1–7). The writer of the epistle to the Hebrews, by repeatedly mentioning faith, pointedly states: "By faith we understand that the universe was formed at God's command," and "without faith it is impossible to please God" (11:3, 6, NIV). Man is unable to comprehend redemption apart from the Scriptures. He must know the revealed Word of God to understand his fallen condition, his need for salvation, and his deliverance from sin and spiritual death through Jesus Christ. A basic knowledge of nature leads him to God the Creator, but knowledge of the Scriptures leads him to Christ his Redeemer. Briefly put, only the Bible teaches him the doctrine of sin, salvation, and service.

---

33. Metzger, *Textual Commentary*, p. 424.

34. E. Lerle contends that the sermon in Lystra did not originate with Paul; and he denies that Luke composed it. Instead he considers this sermon an example of early Christian preaching. His argument, however, lacks cogency and fails to prove that Paul was not the speaker. "Die Predigt in Lystra (Acta xiv. 15–18)," *NTS* 7 (1960): 46–55.

35. Consult Charles W. Carter and Ralph Earle, *The Acts of the Apostles* (Grand Rapids: Zondervan, 1973), p. 200; Willem A. VanGemeren, *The Progress of Redemption: The Story of Salvation from Creation to the New Jerusalem* (Grand Rapids: Zondervan, Academie Books, 1988), p. 40.

Greek Words, Phrases, and Constructions in 14:15–18

Verse 15

τί—the translation of this interrogative sentence is "Why are you doing this?" not "What are you doing?"[36]

ἐπιστρέφειν—this present active infinitive ("to turn") expresses purpose.

Verses 16–17

πάντα τὰ ἔθνη—"all the nations." However, Israel is not included in this category, because God's people received his special revelation (Rom. 3:2).

καίτοι—this adversative particle ("and yet") is followed by a double negative (οὐκ ἀμάρτυρον, not without witness) to indicate emphasis.

By using three present active participles, Paul demonstrates God's continual care for creation in general and man in particular: ἀγαθουργῶν (doing good), διδούς (giving), and ἐμπιπλῶν (filling).

Verse 18

κατέπαυσαν—the preposition κατά in this compound verb has a perfective force and gives the verb the meaning *restrain.*[37]

τοῦ μὴ θύειν—after the verb *to restrain,* the negative particle μή before the infinitive θύειν is redundant in an English translation. The infinitive ("to sacrifice") is equivalent to an infinitive of result.

---

4. Revulsion
14:19–20a

Paul and Barnabas had fled from Pisidian Antioch and Iconium to Lystra to find shelter from Jewish-instigated threats on their lives (v. 5). They sought safety in the rural city of Lystra, far removed from Jewish population centers. However, the news concerning the apostles reached the ears of the Jews in Antioch and Iconium. Their hatred was so intense that they traveled to Lystra to fulfill their threat and stone Paul.

19. But the Jews from Antioch and Iconium came and, having persuaded the crowds, they stoned Paul and dragged him outside the city, supposing that he was dead. 20a. But while the disciples stood around him, Paul got up and entered the city.

We guess that some time elapsed since the episode that followed the healing of the lame man. Paul and Barnabas continue their missionary work and are able to form the nucleus of a church. They gain a number of

---

36. Friedrich Blass and Albert Debrunner, *A Greek Grammar of the New Testament and Other Early Christian Literature,* trans. and rev. Robert Funk (Chicago: University of Chicago Press, 1961), #299.1.

37. Robertson, *Grammar,* p. 606.

disciples (vv. 20a, 22), of whom some become elders (v. 23). In a few Greek manuscripts, whose support is weak, the transition between verses 18 and 19 is smoothed with the following sentence: "But while [the apostles] were staying there and teaching, certain Jews came from Iconium and Antioch."[38]

Imagine the fanaticism of a few determined Jews! Those from Pisidian Antioch travel about one hundred miles to Lystra[39] to carry out their plan to kill Paul. They persuade the Lycaonian crowds to listen to them instead of the missionaries. And although the Jews would be unable to object to anything Paul and Barnabas had either done or said in Lystra, they nevertheless slander the apostles and oppose their work. They are able to convince the Gentiles to rid the city of these intruders. Unimpeded by the Roman military, they pick up stones and hurl them in the direction of Paul. Perhaps the Jews singled out Paul because he was the main speaker.

Luke indicates that the stoning occurs within the city itself, for after the assailants see the effect of their murderous assault and think that Paul is dead, they drag him outside the city. Of course, we wonder why the crowds are so fickle when first they accept the apostles as visiting gods and then stone Paul. But the unpredictable whims of crowds are proverbial. Think, for example, of the Jews in the synagogue of Nazareth who were amazed at the pleasing words Jesus spoke. Yet these same people wanted to throw him down the cliff (Luke 4:22, 29). The Jerusalem crowds shouted "Hosanna" on Palm Sunday but cried "Crucify him" on Friday (Matt. 21:9; Luke 23:21).

Stones hurled at Paul knock him unconscious, so that he appears to have died. His attackers drag Paul outside the city, where they abandon him without any thought of burial. Paul, however, is not dead. God miraculously restores him. The experience itself changed Paul's life, for now he knows what it means to suffer for the sake of the gospel. More than ever before, Paul presses the claims of Christ in his ministry to Jews and Gentiles.

In his epistle to the Corinthians Paul mentions that once he was stoned (II Cor. 11:25; see also II Tim. 3:11). And in his epistle to the Galatians, among whom were the believers in Lystra, he records that on his body he bore the marks of Jesus (Gal. 6:17). For Paul, the experience of being stoned was reminiscent of Stephen, whose cruel demise he himself had approved (8:1a). Stephen died, but God spared Paul's life so that he could continue to preach the gospel of salvation.

I picture Paul's disciples forming a circle around his body and protecting him from any further abuse. They are overjoyed when they detect that Paul is alive and that after some time has elapsed he is able to stand up and walk. Perhaps under cover of darkness,[40] Paul courageously returns to Lystra and

---

38. Metzger, *Textual Commentary*, p. 425.

39. Archaeological evidence shows that Antioch and Lystra were sister colonies in the Roman empire. See William M. Ramsay, *The Church in the Roman Empire Before A.D. 170* (London: Hodder and Stoughton, 1907), p. 50; see also Donald A. Hagner, "Lystra," *ISBE*, vol. 3, p. 193.

40. The Western manuscripts add the explanatory clause, "when the crowd had left and evening had come."

spends the night in the city. His ministry in that city has been terminated temporarily, and the next day Paul and Barnabas decide to go elsewhere.

Practical Considerations in 14:19–20

In Luke's writings, we find a number of unfolding developments. In his Gospel, he lists three parables: the lost sheep, the lost coin, and the lost son (Luke 15:4–32). In his first parable he stresses one sheep out of one hundred, in the second one coin out of ten, and in the third one son out of two.

In Acts, Luke also features threefold developments of incidents. For example, the Sanhedrin first imprisons Peter and John and, with a stern warning not to preach the name of Jesus, releases them (4:3–21). Then the Sanhedrin arrests all the apostles, but flogs them before setting them free (5:18–40). Last, the members of the Sanhedrin, after listening to Stephen, express their anger by having him stoned to death (7:54–60).

In his account of the first missionary journey, Luke once again profiles a threefold development. In Pisidian Antioch, the apostles are expelled (13:50); in Iconium they flee from a hostile crowd intent on stoning them (14:5); and in Lystra Paul survives after his opponents stone him and think that they have killed him (14:19).

Greek Words, Phrases, and Constructions in 14:19–20a

Verse 19

Note that Luke uses two verbs and two participles in the aorist tense to stress single occurrence: the verb ἐπῆλθαν (they appeared), the participle πείσαντες (they persuaded), the participle λιθάσαντες (they stoned), and the verb ἔσυρον (they dragged). The participles should be translated as finite verbs.

τεθνηκέναι—the perfect infinitive is the object of the present participle νομίζοντες (they were thinking). The infinitive is part of an incomplete verb θνήσκω (I die), which in the perfect means "I have died" or "I am dead."

Verse 20a

κυκλωσάντων—with the noun μαθητῶν (disciples) this aorist active participle (from κυκλόω, I surround, encircle) forms the genitive absolute construction.

20b And the next day he went away to Derbe with Barnabas. 21 After they preached the gospel in that city and made many disciples, they returned to Lystra, Iconium, and Antioch. 22 Paul and Barnabas strengthened the disciples and encouraged them to continue in the faith, saying, "Through many hardships we must enter the kingdom of God." 23 They appointed elders for them in every church, and having prayed with fasting, they commended them to the Lord in whom they had put their trust. 24 And they passed through Pisidia and came into Pamphylia. 25 Having spoken the word in Perga, they went down to Attalia. 26 From there they set sail to Antioch, the place where they had first been entrusted to the grace of God for the work they had now accomplished. 27 When they had arrived and gathered the church, they began to report all that God had done through them and that he opened a door of faith to the Gentiles. 28 Paul and Barnabas stayed with the disciples for a long time.

E. Antioch in Syria
14:20b–28

1. Strengthening the Churches
14:20b–25

20b. And the next day he went away to Derbe with Barnabas.

Paul and Barnabas realize that their mission efforts in Lystra have ended temporarily. Therefore, the next morning they once again begin their travels. They decide to go in a south-southeasterly direction to visit the city of Derbe, a distance of some sixty miles from Lystra. By walking without any interruptions, the apostles probably arrived in Derbe within two or three days.

On the basis of two inscriptions, archaeologists have been able to identify the site of Derbe near or at the mound of Kerti Hüyük about thirty miles east of Gudelisin. (For nearly half a century scholars had considered Gudelisin to be the probable site of Derbe). Now that archaeologists have verified the exact location of Derbe, earlier information concerning the site has been revised or discarded.[41]

21. After they preached the gospel in that city and made many disciples, they returned to Lystra, Iconium, and Antioch.

Luke fails to give an account of the work Paul and Barnabas performed in Derbe. He concisely states that the apostles preached the gospel, that as a result many people became disciples (learners), and that Paul and Barnabas retraced their steps and visited the three congregations in Lystra, Iconium, and Antioch, respectively. In Derbe, where the apostles preached in the city itself, no unnerving incidents occurred. In fact, Paul recounts the persecutions in Antioch, Iconium, and Lystra (II Tim. 3:11), but he excludes Derbe.

Luke gives no reason why Paul and Barnabas did not continue on to Tarsus, Paul's hometown, in the province of Cilicia. Even if he were inclined to visit the churches in Cilicia, Paul had a pastoral heart for the recently converted Christians in the cities from which he had been evicted. Because of his harrowing experience in Lystra, he proved to be an even more determined apostle for Jesus Christ than in previous days. His was the task to strengthen the believers and organize the churches.

In Acts, Derbe is mentioned three additional times. On his second missionary journey Paul traveled from Syrian Antioch through Cilicia to

---

41. Bastiaan Van Elderen, "Derbe," *ISBE,* vol. 1, pp. 924–25; see his article "Some Archaeological Observations on Paul's First Missionary Journey," in *Apostolic History and the Gospel,* ed. W. Ward Gasque and Ralph P. Martin (Exeter: Paternoster; Grand Rapids: Eerdmans, 1970), pp. 156–61. See also E. M. Blaiklock, "Derbe," *ZPEB,* vol. 2, p. 103; Ramsay, *Cities of St. Paul,* p. 395; and George Ogg, "Derbe," *NTS* 9 (1963): 367–70.

strengthen the churches. From there he continued his journey to Derbe and later to Lystra (15:41–16:1). A disciple named Timothy was a member of the church in either Lystra or Derbe (16:1), where Gaius also made his home (20:4). Although we know little about the churches in Lystra and Derbe, we are acquainted with at least two of their workers.

Luke implicitly describes the courage of the two apostles in returning to the cities that had shown such fanatical hostility. Further, Luke records the loving concern which the missionaries displayed for the fledgling churches in these cities. Indeed, pastoral concern for the believers in these cities compelled Paul and Barnabas to return. The missionaries perceived that the disciples could lose heart in the face of persecution and hardship, which the believers would have to endure from their compatriots. The small congregations could readily be disbanded and their failure would then prove the futility of the apostles' efforts. In brief, Satan and his cohorts would be victorious.

22. Paul and Barnabas strengthened the disciples and encouraged them to continue in the faith, saying, "Through many hardships we must enter the kingdom of God."

From the context we gather that the apostles spend much time with these disciples for two reasons: they continue to strengthen the new Christians in their faith and they keep on encouraging them (compare 15:32, 41; 16:5; 18:23). These recent converts in Lystra are unprepared for the harassment they have to endure. Although many of the Jewish Christians in Palestine, Phoenicia, Syria, and Cyprus could speak of the persecution they had endured following the death of Stephen (8:1), suffering for their faith would be a new and unsettling experience for Gentile Christians. We imagine that they could ask the legitimate question: "Why does God not protect his own people?"

Paul and Barnabas are able to answer questions relating to mistreatment and hardship. They know that God uses adversities to keep his people true to the faith. Remember that Paul rebukes these same Gentile Christians in Galatia for turning quickly away from the gospel to a different gospel, one that cannot even bear the name *gospel* (Gal. 1:6–7).[42] Therefore, to have them remain true to their Christian confession and put their trust in Jesus Christ, God sends his people many trials.

Accordingly, the apostles tell these recent converts: "Through many hardships we must enter the kingdom of God." The preposition *through* is descriptive of the life Christians must live; they must go through hardships and must personally experience them to enter God's kingdom. The concept *kingdom of God* appears numerous times in the Gospels of Matthew, Mark, and Luke. But in Acts, the expression occurs seldom and then only with reference to preaching (1:3; 8:12; 14:22; 19:8; 28:23, 31). That is, the

---

42. Some commentators interpret the word *faith* objectively: faith is the equivalent of Christianity. See Lake and Cadbury, *Beginnings*, vol. 4, p. 167. Others understand the term subjectively: personal faith in Christ. Consult Grosheide, *Handelingen der Apostelen*, vol. 1, p. 469.

believer who responds to Christ's gospel enters the kingdom. Note that the apostles place themselves on the same level as the disciples when they declare that "we must enter the kingdom."[43]

23. They appointed elders for them in every church, and having prayed with fasting, they commended them to the Lord in whom they had put their trust.

a. *Appointment.* In Greek, the term *to appoint* actually means to approve by a show of hands in a congregational meeting. With the approval of an assembly, individuals were appointed to serve in a particular office. In other words, the showing of hands was equivalent to choosing officials, in this case to serve in the government of the local church. Even though the text says that the apostles appointed elders for the believers in every church, we would be hard pressed to indicate that they did so without any participation by the local congregation. As the believers collectively participated in prayer and fasting, so they took part in choosing elders for their churches.[44] However, the text clearly says that Paul and Barnabas appointed elders for the believers. Some commentators aver that the congregations were excluded from choosing elders. "While it is true that the word [*appointed*] could indicate congregational choice, such is not the case in this context."[45]

The issue is difficult. In view of II Corinthians 8:19, where Titus was chosen by the churches, the practice in the churches as set forth by the apostles appears to be that the local congregation nominated and commissioned church officials. The *Didache* (also known as *The Teaching of the Twelve Apostles*), which presumably dates from the first century, gives this rule to the churches: "Appoint [by a show of hands] therefore for yourselves bishops and deacons worthy of the Lord."[46]

By following the analogical rule of comparing Scripture with Scripture, we learn that in Acts Luke presents "three typical pictures of election and ordination in the cases of Matthias (1:23–26), the Seven (6:1–6), and Paul and Barnabas (13:1–3)."[47] These analogies demonstrate that the assemblies chose the candidates, then prayed and fasted, and afterward ordained them. Likewise, in the case of the elders in Lycaonia and Pisidia, the apostles approved the selections made by the churches and, after prayer and fasting, appointed them.

---

43. Henry Alford alludes to the possibility of taking the pronoun *we* to refer to "the narrator" Luke. *Alford's Greek Testament: An Exegetical and Critical Commentary,* 7th ed., 4 vols. (1877; Grand Rapids: Guardian, 1976), vol. 2, p. 160.

44. Lenski, *Acts,* p. 586. See also Grosheide, *Handelingen der Apostelen,* vol. 1, pp. 470–71; Jacques Dupont, *Nouvelles Études sur les Actes des Apôtres,* Lectio Divina 118 (Paris: Cerf, 1984), pp. 352–55.

45. Harrison, *Interpreting Acts,* p. 237; see also Haenchen, *Acts,* p. 436. Bauer categorically states that "the presbyters in Lycaonia and Pisidia were not chosen by the congregations," p. 881. Consult Eduard Lohse, *TDNT,* vol. 9, p. 437.

46. *The Apostolic Fathers,* vol. 1, *Didache* 15.1 (LCL).

47. Richard B. Rackham, *The Acts of the Apostles: An Exposition,* Westminster Commentaries series (1901; reprint ed., Grand Rapids: Baker, 1964), p. 237.

b. *Elders.* The Greek expression *presbyteros* is actually a comparative adjective that means "elder." Paul uses this term interchangeably with *episkopos* (bishop, overseer). The word *elder* refers to the age of a person and the expression *overseer* to the function of his office. In his pastoral Epistles, Paul at times uses both terms in the same context (I Tim. 3:1–2; 5:17; Titus 1:5–7). The word *elder* stems from the Jewish practice of governing the religious and political life in Israel (see 4:5). But even in Greece and in Egypt, elders ruled and advised as representatives in local and state government.[48] In Jerusalem, the early church adopted the practice of appointing elders to govern the church (11:30).

c. *Trust.* Luke writes, "[The apostles] commended them to the Lord in whom they had put their trust." Do the words *them* and *their* relate to the elders or to all the Christians in these churches? At first glance, we would be inclined to apply the words to the elders only. However, because in Greek the phrase *in whom they had put their trust* is in the pluperfect tense (which denotes action in the past with significance for the present), we do well to apply the pronouns *them* and *their* to both elders and members of the churches. After having spent some time with these churches, Paul and Barnabas entrust them to the care of the Lord.

24. And they passed through Pisidia and came into Pamphylia. 25. Having spoken the word in Perga, they went down to Attalia.

After spending time with the Christians in Antioch, the apostles travel in a southerly direction through Pisidia and into Pamphylia. They are retracing their steps and arrive in Perga, where John Mark had left them (13:13). Luke is rather brief in describing the activities of Paul and Barnabas in Perga. He reports nothing about the journey itself, although the area through which the missionaries had to travel was unsafe (II Cor. 11:26). He merely writes that the missionaries preached the gospel there but says nothing about opposition or indifference on the part of the population. Apparently, the apostles are unable to form a nucleus for the founding of a church. Thus, they continue their travels and board ship in the harbor town of Attalia to return to Syrian Antioch.

Greek Words, Phrases, and Constructions in 14:22–23

Verse 22

ἐπιστηρίζοντες—this present active participle denotes purpose and depends on the introductory verb of the preceding verse (ὑπέστρεψαν, they returned to strengthen).[49]

τῇ πίστει—the dative case is locative. The word *faith* can have both an objective (Christian doctrine) and a subjective (personal belief) connotation in this verse.

---

48. Lothar Coenen, *NIDNTT*, vol. 1, p. 193. And consult Adolf Deissmann, *Bible Studies* (reprint ed., Winona Lake, Ind.: Alpha, 1979), p. 156.

49. Blass and Debrunner, *Greek Grammar*, #339.3a; see also Robertson, *Grammar*, p. 892.

ἡμᾶς—the personal pronoun refers to both the apostles and the members of the churches.

χειροτονήσαντες—as an aorist in compound form derived from the noun χείρ (hand) and the verb τείνω (I stretch, extend), this participle depicts the manner in which the appointing took place. Strictly speaking, the subject of the participle is the apostles. Yet we infer that the people raised their hands in the voting procedure.

αὐτοῖς—the plural pronoun refers to the church members. The form αὐτούς includes both believers and elders.

πεπιστεύκεισαν—without the augment, this is the pluperfect tense of the verb πιστεύω (I believe).

---

2. Reporting to Antioch
14:26–28

26. From there they set sail to Antioch, the place where they had first been entrusted to the grace of God for the work they had now accomplished.

When Paul and Barnabas come to the Syrian port of Seleucia, they travel inland to Antioch. In a sense, they come home, for the Christians in Syrian Antioch had commissioned them to preach the gospel to the Gentiles in the Greco-Roman world (13:1–3). How long the apostles had been away is difficult to determine, but we estimate that this first missionary journey lasted approximately two years (A.D. 46–48).

With carefully chosen words, Luke remarks that Antioch was "the place where they had first been entrusted to the grace of God for the work they had now accomplished." By implication, he is saying that the members of the church in Syrian Antioch were aware of the difficulties and perils Paul and Barnabas would have to encounter on their journey. The church had committed the missionaries to the grace of God, supported them in prayer, and trusted the Lord to extend his church through their work. In fact, the Lord had answered their prayers and the task given to the apostles had been fulfilled. From Acts, we learn that Antioch was missionary headquarters for Paul (see 15:35; 18:23). From this place he set out on his successive journeys.

27. When they had arrived and gathered the church, they began to report all that God had done through them and that he opened a door of faith to the Gentiles.

Two years earlier, the Antiochean church had commissioned the apostles. Presently Paul and Barnabas return to Antioch and call together the members of the church to hear their report. Note that Luke speaks of the church and not of individual congregations or house churches. He stresses the unity of the church, for the Christians in Antioch wish to hear about the expansion of that same church in Cyprus and Asia Minor. Luke employs the imperfect tense of the verb *to report* to indicate that the story Paul and Barnabas had to tell was too lengthy for one sitting. Moreover, he adds that the apostles tell about *all* their work. Repeatedly, then, they meet with the believers and relate in detail the inroads that the gospel made among the Jews and Gentiles. They give God the honor and the glory (see 15:4). God had worked powerfully through them by performing miracles, giving them the words to speak, blessing their work, and protecting them from danger and death.

The initial objective of the missionaries was to proclaim the Good News to the Gentiles. This objective they fully achieved, for Paul and Barnabas report that God had "opened a door of faith to the Gentiles." Although Cornelius and the people in his house had been welcomed into the Christian church by Peter some years earlier (see 10:45), no Gentile churches had been founded. Now Paul and Barnabas, as apostles to the Gentiles, had organized non-Jewish churches.

The expression *open a door* appears to be one of Paul's favorites. In his epistles, he resorts to it at least three times (I Cor. 16:9; II Cor. 2:12; Col. 4:3). The term *faith* is descriptive and serves to emphasize the importance that Paul attaches to belief in Jesus Christ. Through this door of faith the Gentiles now enter and thus are members of the household of faith. Together with Jewish Christians and Samaritan Christians they form the family of God.

28. Paul and Barnabas stayed with the disciples for a long time.

Here is the conclusion to the first missionary journey. The apostles stay in Antioch, teach and preach in the local church, and regain their strength. They still face the task of integrating Gentile churches into the mainstream Christianity of that day. We presume that they remain in Antioch for at least one year.

Greek Words, Phrases, and Constructions in 14:27–28

Verse 27

ἀνήγγελλον—here is the imperfect tense in the midst of participles and verbs in the aorist tense. The use of this tense signifies repeated action; that is, the apostles frequently met with the believers in the Antiochean church.

ὅσα—this correlative adjective is equivalent to the words πάντα ἅ (all things which).

μετ' αὐτῶν—"all that God has done in fellowship (or 'cooperation') with them."[50] The preposition μετά (with) has a plain Greek usage.

πίστεως—the noun *faith* in this verse can be either an objective genitive ("leading to faith") or a subjective genitive ("where faith enters").[51]

---

50. Moule, *Idiom-Book*, p. 61.
51. Nigel Turner, *A Grammar of New Testament Greek*, 4 vols. (Edinburgh: Clark, 1963), vol. 3, p. 212.

Verse 28

διέτριβον—the imperfect tense indicates that considerable time elapsed before Paul and Barnabas departed from Antioch. Luke completes the sentence with one of his characteristic understatements—χρόνον οὐκ ὀλίγον (not a short time).

Summary of Chapter 14

Paul and Barnabas speak boldly in the name of the Lord and perform many signs and miracles in Iconium. As a result, numerous Jews and Gentiles believe. Unbelieving Jews stir up the Gentile population, and so the city is divided on the preaching of the apostles. A plot is hatched to mistreat and stone Paul and Barnabas; when they learn about it, they flee to the cities of Lystra and Derbe.

In Lystra Paul heals a cripple. The people of Lystra consider the apostles to be gods in human form. Led by the priest of Zeus, they wish to offer sacrifices to Paul and Barnabas. But the apostles tear their clothes, rush into the crowds, and prevent them from making these sacrifices. In the meantime, hostile Jews from Pisidian Antioch and Iconium arrive at Lystra and stir up the people, who turn against Paul and stone him. Thinking that Paul is dead, they drag him outside the city and leave him. Paul's disciples gather around him and he miraculously stands up. He enters the city to spend the night there. The next morning he and Barnabas continue their journey and travel to Derbe. After a fruitful ministry in that city, they return to Lystra, Iconium, and Antioch to strengthen the believers and to appoint elders in every church. The apostles leave Pisidian Antioch and go down to Perga in Pamphylia. Then they set sail from Attalia and eventually arrive in Syrian Antioch, where they report to the church all that the Lord has done through them. They stay in Antioch for some time.

15

The Council at Jerusalem

15:1–35

and The Second Missionary Journey, *part 1*

15:36–41

Outline

15:1–35	VI.	The Council at Jerusalem
		A. The Chronology
15:1–21		B. The Debate
15:1–5		1. The Controversy
15:6–11		2. Peter's Address
15:12		3. Barnabas and Paul
15:13–21		4. James's Address
15:22–35		C. The Letter
15:22		1. Messengers
15:23–29		2. Message
15:30–35		3. Effect
15:36–18:22	VII.	The Second Missionary Journey
15:36–16:5		A. Revisiting the Churches
15:36–41		1. Separation

VI. The Council at Jerusalem
15:1–35

A. The Chronology

In Acts, Luke refrains from giving the historical references which he provides in his Gospel; see, for instance, the details about the beginning of John the Baptist's public ministry (Luke 3:1–2). With the help of parallels from the first-century Jewish writer Josephus, the Roman historiographer Suetonius, and archaeological discoveries, we are able to determine at least three dates that relate to Acts: the death of Herod Agrippa I in A.D. 44, the expulsion of Jews from Rome at the order of Emperor Claudius in A.D. 49, and the presence of the proconsul Gallio at Corinth in A.D. 51. In addition, we are able to approximate the beginning of Festus's term as governor of Judea (A.D. 59; on the basis of Paul's autumn journey after the fast.) On these four pegs of history the chronology of Acts depends. We place the first peg in 12:19b–23, the second in 18:2, the third in 18:12–17, and the fourth in 24:27 and 27:9. The rest of Acts we place around these dates.

Paul went to Jerusalem a number of times, the first visit being after his Damascus-road conversion (9:26–29). We assume that this visit occurred in the late thirties. Paul's second visit to Jerusalem took place when the church in Antioch commissioned him and Barnabas to bring famine offerings to Judea in the mid-forties (11:27–30; 12:25). Together with Barnabas, Paul visited Jerusalem a third time when the Council convened (A.D. 49) prior to the beginning of Paul's second missionary journey (15:4).

In Galatians, Paul presents a chronological account of his post-conversion life. He recounts that three years after becoming a believer, he went up to Jerusalem (Gal. 1:18). This is his first visit, recorded by Luke in Acts 9:26–29. He continues, "Then fourteen years later I again went up to Jerusalem with Barnabas; we took Titus with us" (Gal. 2:1). The fourteen years may either include or exclude the three years after his conversion. That is, these two time periods may be either concurrent or successive.

Is the visit "fourteen years later" the same as that of Paul and Barnabas to the Jerusalem Council? Many scholars respond affirmatively to this question, while others say that it corresponds with the so-called famine visit (11:27–30; 12:25). How can we tell whether Luke in Acts and Paul in Galatians are referring to the same event?

Here are a few considerations that can help us in understanding the chronology of Paul's visits to Jerusalem:

1. Paul's mention of "fourteen years" after his first Jerusalem visit meshes with the traditional date (A.D. 49) for the Jerusalem Council. But if the remark about "fourteen years" is applied to the famine visit (A.D. 46), the first visit to Jerusalem is too early and the chronology too compressed. Some scholars place Paul's conversion in A.D. 32–34, take the periods of three years (Gal. 1:18) and fourteen years (Gal. 2:1) as a concurrent lapse of time, and put the famine visit in A.D. 46–47.[1]

2. Paul writes that Barnabas and Titus accompanied him to Jerusalem (Gal. 2:1). In Acts 15, Luke mentions that Paul and Barnabas were appointed by the Antiochean church to go to Jerusalem and that "some other believers" (NIV) went along with them. Although Luke does not list Titus by name, it is possible that Titus was one of those believers.

These believers from Antioch went to Jerusalem to settle the question of circumcising the Gentiles (15:1–2). The issue is stated by Christians belonging to the Pharisaic party: "It is necessary to circumcise the Gentiles and to instruct them to keep the law of Moses" (15:5). (Some scholars maintain that Titus, an uncircumcised Gentile [Gal. 2:3], served as a test case for the council. Certainly Paul indicates that Titus was an uncircumcised Gentile Christian who was not forced to be circumcised [Gal. 2:3].) If the matter of circumcision had been settled by the time of the famine visit, the council would not have had to convene.[2]

Moreover, Scripture itself does not say whether Titus accompanied Barnabas and Paul during the famine visit (see 11:30; for the larger context, 11:27–30). One could ask why Titus would accompany Barnabas and Paul on that visit, especially since Acts 15:5 and Galatians 2:1 seem to refer to another visit.

3. In Galatians, Paul notes that he went to Jerusalem to put before the apostles the gospel he had preached and to check its accuracy (2:2, 6–7). This remark fits better in a context after the first missionary journey (Acts 13–14) than in a context when Paul and Barnabas went to Judea with funds for relief of the famine (Acts 11:27–30; 12:25).[3]

4. Paul and Barnabas met the reputed pillars of the church (James, Peter, and John), who extended the right hand of fellowship to them (Gal. 2:9). At the Jerusalem Council, Peter and James were present with other apostles and elders (Acts 15:4, 6–7, 13). But in his description of the famine visit, Luke recognizes only the elders (11:30). Moreover, the historical context of that time hardly makes it possible for Peter to have been present in Jerusa-

---

1. E.g., Colin J. Hemer, *The Book of Acts in the Setting of Hellenistic History*, ed. Conrad H. Gempf (Tübingen: Mohr, 1989), p. 264.

2. William Hendriksen, *Exposition of Galatians*, New Testament Commentary series (Grand Rapids: Baker, 1968), p. 73. For an extensive discussion of the arguments, see pp. 70–74.

3. Martin Hengel, *Acts and the History of Earliest Christianity*, trans. John Bowden (Philadelphia: Fortress, 1980), p. 111.

lem after his release from prison and his departure to another place (12:17; A.D. 44).

Nevertheless, we encounter a few problem areas:

1. If we identify the Jerusalem visit of Galatians 2 with that in Acts 15, why does Paul in his letter to the Galatians not refer to the decisions the council reached? Although we realize the importance of this question, we refer to Luke's report that Paul and Silas visited the Galatian churches and from town to town personally delivered these decisions (Acts 16:4). Further, the emphasis in Paul's letter to the Galatians is such that he is not so much concerned with the prescriptions for Gentile Christians as with the calling and responsibilities of Jewish Christians.[4]

2. Paul states in Galatians 2 that his meeting in Jerusalem was a private meeting with the leaders of the church. But in Acts 15, Luke reports that Paul met with the church, the apostles, and the elders (vv. 4, 12, 22). Even though the gathering in Jerusalem was a public meeting, Paul and Barnabas undoubtedly first met privately with Peter, James, and John.

3. How could Peter and Barnabas refuse to eat with the Gentile Christians (Gal. 2:11–14)? If this particular incident occurred some time prior to that of the council in Jerusalem (for example, soon after Peter's escape from prison), the difficulty concerning table fellowship can be explained.[5] If not, the problem of Peter and Barnabas eating only with Jews remains.

The point of the incident in Antioch, however, is the hypocrisy that ensnares Peter and Barnabas in spite of the decisions of the apostolic council (15:20). They were led astray by law-abiding Judaizers, who constituted a formidable camp. Those Jewish Christians who zealously kept the Mosaic law were still a major force a decade later, when Paul, at the conclusion of his third missionary journey, returned to Jerusalem (21:20–21). Luke writes that their number was in the thousands. We surmise that in Antioch these Jewish Christians from Jerusalem had a persuasive influence even on Peter and Barnabas. They were able to cause a division between Jew and Gentile in the Christian church by stressing the dietary laws of the Old Testament. "It only goes to show how strong a hold the old ways still had on these people and how hard it was for them to adopt a new way of life."[6]

4. Both Barnabas and Paul were commissioned by the church in Antioch to take famine relief to the believers in Judea (11:27–30). Paul writes that fourteen years later he went to Jerusalem with Barnabas because of a revela-

---

4. Jakob van Bruggen, *"Na Veertien Jaren": De Datering van het in Galaten 2 genoemde Overleg te Jeruzalem* (Kampen: Kok, 1973), pp. 163, 237; Pierson Parker, "Once More, Acts and Galatians," *JBL* 86 (1967): 175–82.

5. Refer to F. F. Bruce, *The Book of the Acts,* rev. ed., New International Commentary on the New Testament series (Grand Rapids: Eerdmans, 1988), pp. 284–85. See also his *Commentary on Galatians,* New International Greek Testament Commentary series (Exeter: Paternoster; Grand Rapids: Eerdmans, 1982), p. 128.

6. David John Williams, *Acts,* Good News Commentary series (San Francisco: Harper and Row, 1985), p. 249.

tion (Gal. 2:1–2). In addition, Paul reports that the reputed pillars James, Peter, and John asked him and Barnabas to remember the poor (Gal. 2:10).

The suggestion that the famine visit took place fourteen years after Paul's conversion has merit, but the difficulties that surround it are numerous. First, during the famine visit Barnabas and Paul met only the elders, but not the apostles. Next, the revelation Paul mentions comes from the Lord, but the prophecy about the famine comes from Agabus. According to his Galatian epistle, Paul is sent by the Lord to Jerusalem. By contrast, Luke relates that the Antiochean church commissioned Barnabas and Paul to go to the brothers in Judea. Third, the teaching to remember the poor is a Mosaic law that was well known among the Jewish people (see Deut. 15:11). And last, in Acts 11:30 and 12:25 Barnabas, not Paul, gives leadership, but in Galatians 2:1–10 the reverse is true.

To summarize, no theory is without its flaws and every hypothesis has its own set of problems. Yet we favor the view that Paul's account in Galatians 2 generally harmonizes with Luke's description of the Jerusalem Council. We believe that this conviction remains tenable and is preferable to the one that identifies the famine visit (11:27–30) with Galatians 2:1–10. Subsequent exegetical points are discussed at pertinent places in the commentary on Acts 15.

15

1 Some men came down from Judea and began teaching the brothers, "Unless you are circumcised according to the custom of Moses, you cannot be saved." 2 Paul and Barnabas had no small discussion and debate with those men. The brothers appointed Paul and Barnabas and some others from them to go up to Jerusalem to the apostles and elders concerning this issue. 3 Having been sent by the church, they were passing through both Phoenicia and Samaria. They were describing in detail the conversion of the Gentiles and were causing great joy to all the brothers. 4 When they arrived at Jerusalem, they were received by the church, the apostles, and the elders. Paul and Barnabas reported all that God had done through them. 5 However, some who belonged to the party of the Pharisees but were believers stood up and said, "It is necessary to circumcise the Gentiles and to instruct them to keep the law of Moses."

6 The apostles and elders met to discuss this matter. 7 After much debate, Peter stood up and said to them: "Men and brothers, you know that in earlier days God chose me from among you that from my lips the Gentiles might hear the message of the gospel and believe. 8 And God, who knows the heart, testified to them by giving the Holy Spirit just as he did to us. 9 He made no distinction between us and them, having purified their hearts by faith. 10 Now therefore, why do you test God by placing on the necks of the disciples a yoke which neither our fathers nor we have been able to bear? 11 But we believe that we are saved through the grace of the Lord Jesus, just as they are."

12 The whole assembly was quiet and listened to Barnabas and Paul as they were relating the signs and wonders God had done through them among the Gentiles. 13 After they were finished speaking, James said: "Men and brothers, listen to me. 14 Simon has related how God at first concerned himself to take from among the Gentiles a people for himself. 15 And the words of the prophets agree with this, as it is written:

> 16 " 'After this, I will return
> and I will rebuild the tent
> of David which has fallen.
> And I will rebuild its ruins

and I will restore it.
17 In order that the rest of mankind
    may seek the Lord,
    and all the Gentiles who are called by my name,
18 says the Lord, who makes these things known
    from of old.'

19 "Therefore, I judge that we do not trouble those Gentiles who are turning to God, 20 but that we write them to abstain from things polluted by idols, and from fornication, and from what is strangled, and from blood. 21 For Moses has been preached in every city since days of old and is read every Sabbath in the synagogues."

22 Then the apostles and elders with the whole church decided to choose some of their men and send them to Antioch with Paul and Barnabas. They chose Judas called Barsabbas and Silas, men who were leaders among the brothers. 23 They sent this letter with them:

"The apostles and elders, from your brothers to the Gentile brothers in Antioch, Syria, and Cilicia.
Greetings.
24 "We heard that some people went out from us without our instructions. They disturbed you with their words and unsettled your minds. 25 So it seemed good to us, having come to an agreement, to send some men to you with our friends Barnabas and Paul, 26 men who have dedicated their lives in behalf of the name of the Lord Jesus Christ. 27 Therefore, we have sent Judas and Silas who themselves will report these same things by word of mouth. 28 For it seemed good to the Holy Spirit and to us not to burden you with more than these essentials: 29 To abstain from things sacrificed to idols, from blood, from strangled animals, and from fornication. If you keep yourselves away from these things, you do well.
Farewell."

30 Then the men who departed went down to Antioch, and having gathered the multitude, they delivered the letter. 31 When they read the letter, they rejoiced because of its encouraging message. 32 Judas and Silas, who also were prophets, encouraged and strengthened the brothers with many words. 33 After they had spent some time there, they departed from the brothers in peace and returned to those who had sent them. 35 Paul and Barnabas remained in Antioch, teaching and preaching with many others the word of the Lord.

B. The Debate
15:1–21

Paul and Barnabas taught and preached the gospel in Antioch for a considerable length of time, perhaps for as long as one year. While they were there, they met Jews from Jerusalem who objected to the work the missionaries had performed in Cyprus and Asia Minor. They encountered Jews who wanted every Gentile Christian to be subject to Mosaic teaching on circumcision and thus become, in effect, Jewish converts. Paul and Barnabas strenuously objected to this teaching.

1. The Controversy
15:1–5

1. Some men came down from Judea and began teaching the brothers, "Unless you are circumcised according to the custom of Moses, you cannot be saved." 2. Paul and Barnabas had no small discussion and debate

with those men. The brothers appointed Paul and Barnabas and some others from them to go up to Jerusalem to the apostles and elders concerning this issue.

Note the following points:

a. *Demand.* Luke introduces some unidentified men from Judea. We suppose that they are Jewish Christians who belong to the party of the Pharisees (v. 5). In earlier days, the church appointed Barnabas to help the Christians in Antioch (11:22–23). By contrast, without authority these men come to Antioch to impose their own rules and regulations on the believers and state: "Unless you are circumcised according to the custom of Moses, you cannot be saved."

The text indicates that the men begin to teach these precepts and thus are self-appointed teachers who stay in Antioch for some time. Their presence in the Antiochean congregation is not to extend the church through evangelism; nor do they come to encourage the believers in their faith. Their purpose is to place a strict requirement on the brothers that specifies whether or not they can be saved: they insist that the Jewish rite of circumcision is necessary for the salvation of Gentile Christians. This Jewish stipulation is sufficient to alarm both Paul and Barnabas. These two missionaries had taught the Gentile Christians in Antioch, Cyprus, and Asia Minor that Gentiles were set free from the ceremonial laws of Moses; that is, the Gentiles did not have to submit to circumcision.

Now agitators from Jerusalem contend that every male believer must be circumcised to obtain salvation. They base their arguments on the Mosaic law, which for the Christian, whether Jew or Gentile, was the Word of God. They assert that God had never abrogated the requirement of circumcision. However, the practice of the apostles was not to demand circumcision of Gentile Christians, because they knew that the Greeks and the Romans were offended by this rite. Accordingly, Peter had required only baptism and not circumcision of Cornelius and his household when they became members of the Christian church (10:47). And in their travels to Cyprus and Asia Minor, Paul and Barnabas never pressed the God-fearing Gentiles to conform to this practice.

b. *Debate.* The issue at hand runs contrary to the work of Paul and Barnabas, who teach that only faith in Jesus Christ saves a person from sin and damnation. They assert that the practice of circumcision, as taught by the Jerusalem Judaizers, is unable to secure anyone's salvation. But the visiting Jewish Christians maintain that, as in the Jewish synagogue so in the Christian church, membership depends on circumcision in particular and the Mosaic law in general. The Judaizers stress that every Gentile Christian ought to adhere to and fulfill the law of Moses in order to be saved. They understand observance of the law from a Jewish, not a Christian, point of view.[7] In effect,

---

7. Donald Guthrie, *New Testament Theology* (Downers Grove: Inter-Varsity, 1981), p. 686.

these Judaizers practice racial discrimination within the context of the Christian church. For example, on the basis of Old Testament law they bar a Gentile Christian from entering the temple area because he is uncircumcised (compare 21:28–29).

The vigorous debate between the Judaizers and the missionaries ends when the Antiochean church decides to ask the apostles and elders in Jerusalem for a decision in regard to the matter of circumcision. Overseers in the church must not be quarrelsome or contentious (I Tim. 3:3; II Tim. 2:24) but must settle disputes peaceably. Even in the face of the bold assertion that a believer cannot be saved without being circumcised, the Antiochean church preserves the peace by appealing to the leaders in Jerusalem. The church appoints Paul and Barnabas to travel to Jerusalem and to learn from the apostles and elders whether faith in Christ is sufficient for salvation.

When Peter returned from his visit to Cornelius and his household in Caesarea, the Jerusalem church accepted the Gentile Christians as equals into the Jewish Christian church (11:18). The apostles and elders at that time did not formulate rules about accepting Gentiles into the church. Now the time has come to convene the church and, guided by the Holy Spirit (15:28), state the necessary requirements for Gentile believers.

The Western manuscripts of the Greek text have expanded verses 1 and 2 and state that the Judaizers order Paul and Barnabas to travel to Jerusalem:

> [1] And some men *of those who had believed from the party of the Pharisees* came down from Judea and were teaching the brethren, "Unless you are circumcised *and walk* according to the custom of Moses, you cannot be saved." [2] And when Paul and Barnabas had no small dissension and debate with them—*for Paul spoke maintaining firmly that they* [i.e., the converts] *should stay as they were converted; but those who had come from Jerusalem ordered them,* Paul and Barnabas and certain others, to go up to Jerusalem to the apostles and elders *that they might be judged before them* about this question.[8]

From a grammatical point of view, we agree that the Greek text[9] on which we base our translation states that the Judaizers ordered Paul and Barnabas to go to Jerusalem. However, the immediate context (v. 3) confirms that the Antiochean church, not the Judaizers, dispatched the missionaries to Jerusalem.

Notice that the Antiochean church, obedient to the request of the Holy Spirit (13:2), had sent Paul and Barnabas on a missionary journey. After the missionaries returned and related the account of numerous Gentiles entering the Christian church in many places, the Antiochean believers

---

8. Bruce M. Metzger, *A Textual Commentary on the Greek New Testament*, 3d corrected ed. (London and New York: United Bible Societies, 1975), pp. 426–27. The additions are italicized.
9. Nes-Al, 26th ed.

commission Paul and Barnabas to go to Jerusalem with the same account. The missionaries, therefore, want to receive support for their work from the apostles and elders in Jerusalem, not only from the Antiochean church.

3. Having been sent by the church, they were passing through both Phoenicia and Samaria. They were describing in detail the conversion of the Gentiles and were causing great joy to all the brothers.

Paul, Barnabas, and others, among whom possibly was Titus (Gal. 2:1), were officially delegated by the church in Antioch. (Incidentally, Luke never mentions Titus in Acts. Some scholars ingeniously conjecture that because Titus was Luke's brother, Luke modestly refrained from using both his own and his brother's name.)[10]

The delegates travel overland from Antioch to Jerusalem and in passing visit a number of churches in Phoenicia (modern Lebanon) and Samaria. In every church the missionaries recount the great deeds God has done among the Gentiles and how the Christian church has expanded in the world at large. The believers in Phoenicia (11:19) and Samaria (8:1) voice no objections to the news that the missionaries have brought the gospel to the Gentiles and have founded Gentile Christian churches. On the contrary, wherever Paul and Barnabas narrate the story of their missionary experiences, the believers rejoice and are glad.

God, who called Paul and Barnabas to preach the gospel to the Gentiles, confirms their work through the response of the individual churches in Phoenicia and Samaria. Indeed, God prepares the missionaries for their meeting with the apostles and elders in Jerusalem and gives them the support of the church at large. After the persecution following the death of Stephen, the Jerusalem church assumed a distinct Hebraic appearance. Yet this church must give leadership and so come to a decision that resolves the matter of admitting Gentile Christians.

4. When they arrived at Jerusalem, they were received by the church, the apostles, and the elders. Paul and Barnabas reported all that God had done through them.

The missionaries and their companions arrive in Jerusalem and are officially welcomed by the apostles and elders of the church. We presume that the apostles were proclaiming the gospel in numerous places. For this meeting, however, they had been asked to convene in Jerusalem. For instance, Peter, who had departed for another place (12:17), returns to the holy city and assumes a leadership function there. James is present, and so is John (Gal. 2:9).

Notice that the Antiochean church appointed Paul and Barnabas to meet with the apostles and elders in Jerusalem. Upon their arrival at Jerusalem, the missionaries are officially received as equals by the church, the apostles, and the elders. This indicates the fundamental unity of the Christian church.

---

10. Refer to Lake and Cadbury, *Beginnings*, vol. 4, p. 171.

The missionaries reveal what God has done among the Gentiles. They place emphasis not on their own work but on what God has performed through them (see v. 12). Consequently, the Jerusalem church, as well as the apostles and elders, realizes that God himself is enlarging the universal church through his appointed missionaries, Paul and Barnabas (compare 14:27; 21:19). Implicitly, Luke indicates that the reaction of those who listen to this oral mission report is favorable. In other words, the Judaizers who had come to Antioch with their demand for circumcising Gentile Christians had not represented the entire Jerusalem church (see v. 24).

5. However, some who belonged to the party of the Pharisees but were believers stood up and said, "It is necessary to circumcise the Gentiles and to instruct them to keep the law of Moses."

We are unable to ascertain whether the Judaizers who had visited the church in Antioch had returned to Jerusalem. By itself this point is irrelevant, but members of the Pharisaic party who had become Christians immediately respond negatively to the report of the missionaries. They do not even wait for the apostles and elders to formulate a response to the missionaries who represent the Antiochean church. They determine that all Christians, whether Jew or Gentile, are obligated to obey the entire law of Moses, and that includes circumcision. John Albert Bengel observes, "It was an easier thing to make a Christian of a Gentile than to overcome Pharisaic false teaching."[11]

Before his conversion, Paul belonged to the party of the Pharisees (compare 23:6; 26:5; Phil. 3:5). He now faces this same party in a Christian context. But the Christianity of these Pharisees is overshadowed by their emphasis on the Mosaic law. They assert that the development of the church can take place only when believers adhere to all the stipulations of the Old Testament. They virtually demand that every Gentile become a Jew before he can be a Christian.

Further, the Pharisaic Christians completely disregard Peter's earlier report concerning Cornelius in Caesarea and the favorable reaction of the apostles and the church at Jerusalem. At that time the church postponed formulating any decision concerning the Mosaic law and circumcision. Now the time has come to resolve this matter and to maintain harmony and unity in the church at large.

Doctrinal Considerations in 15:1–5

In response to Peter's proclamation of the gospel in the home of Cornelius, Gentile believers rejoiced, received the Holy Spirit, and were baptized. However, Peter did not demand that these believers be circumcised. For them, baptism was sufficient. The admission of one group of Gentiles in Caesarea caused no disagree-

---

11. John Albert Bengel, *Gnomon of the New Testament*, ed. Andrew R. Fausset, 5 vols. (Edinburgh: Clark, 1877), vol. 2, p. 643.

ment in the Jerusalem church after Peter explained that he could not oppose God (11:17–18). Some years later Paul informed the Jerusalem church that he had founded entire Gentile churches and had not demanded circumcision. This was unacceptable to the Jewish Christians who belonged to the party of the Pharisees, for they vehemently objected to admitting any uncircumcised Gentile believers into the church.

These Jewish Christians contended that every convert must first be circumcised and then be taught to observe the law of Moses. Now notice the parallel and, at the same time, the distinct contrast given by Jesus in the Great Commission. Jesus told his followers to make disciples of all nations, first, by baptizing them and, second, by teaching them to observe all that he had commanded (Matt. 28:19–20).

Greek Words, Phrases, and Constructions in 15:1–5

Verse 1

ἐδίδασκον—the imperfect tense is inceptive, that is, it denotes that an action has started: "they began to teach."

περιτμηθῆτε—from the verb περιτέμνω (I cut [off] around, circumcise), the aorist signifies single occurrence; the passive implies an agent who acts upon the subject; the subjunctive indicates uncertainty in the context of a conditional sentence; and the second person plural is direct and inclusive.

τῷ ἔθει—"according to the custom." The use of the dative expresses manner, not cause.[12]

Verse 2

γενομένης—with two genitive nouns, this aorist participle in the genitive case constitutes the genitive absolute construction.

στάσεως—from ἵστημι (I stand up), the noun στάσις means "strife, discord, discussion." The noun ζήτησις implies action in progress in the form of vigorous debate.

οὐκ ὀλίγης—"no small." This is one of Luke's characteristic understatements (12:18; 14:28; 17:4, 12; 19:23, 24).

ἔταξαν—"they appointed." Grammatically the subject is τινες (v. 1). However, the context demands that "the brothers" serve as subject (see vv. 1, 3).

Verse 3

μὲν οὖν—this phrase is resumptive and transitional. It may be translated "so."[13]

προπεμφθέντες—literally this aorist passive participle means "having been sent on their way." But the verb προπέμπω conveys much more than this translation; the travelers were given food and money, and arrangements for lodging were made for them (compare III John 5–8).[14]

διήρχοντο and ἐποίουν—the imperfect tense in these two verbs is descriptive.

---

12. C. F. D. Moule, *An Idiom-Book of New Testament Greek*, 2d ed. (Cambridge: Cambridge University Press, 1960), p. 45; Robert Hanna, *A Grammatical Aid to the Greek New Testament* (Grand Rapids: Baker, 1983), p. 218.

13. Moule, *Idiom-Book*, p. 162.

14. Bauer, p. 709.

Verse 5

πεπιστευκότες—the Judaizers have been Christians for some time, as the perfect tense of the active participle indicates. Nonetheless, as true Pharisees they follow the letter of the law.

δεῖ—"it is necessary." This verb controls the infinitives *to circumcise* and *to instruct*. The infinitive τηρεῖν is an infinitive of purpose.

---

2. Peter's Address
15:6–11

Considerable time had elapsed between Peter's return from Caesarea and the convening of the council. We estimate that in this period the greater part of a decade had expired. God had told Peter to go to Cornelius in Caesarea; God also inspires Peter to address the Jerusalem Council.

6. The apostles and elders met to discuss this matter.

We make these observations:

a. *Debate.* All indications are that the council met for many days to discuss the matter at hand and to come to a resolution that would maintain unity and unanimity in the church. We discern at least three separate meetings: first, a general meeting during which Paul, Barnabas, and other delegates from Antioch are welcomed and at which time the missionaries give their report (vv. 4–5); next, a separate meeting of the apostles and elders with Paul and Barnabas (vv. 6–11); and third, the full assembly meets to hear the missionaries and James. During this last meeting the four requirements for Gentile Christians are formulated and approved (vv. 12–22).

The information supplied by both Luke (Acts 15:6–11) and Paul (Gal. 2:1–10) is incomplete and insufficient. We are unable to prove or disprove whether Paul's separate meeting with the apostles and elders was the one to which he refers in his Galatian report. Should these meetings be the same, then the presence of Titus, who was not circumcised, undoubtedly underscored the urgency of the debate. The apostles and elders met to discuss the freedom which Gentile Christians experienced in Christ.

7. After much debate, Peter stood up and said to them: "Men and brothers, you know that in earlier days God chose me from among you that from my lips the Gentiles might hear the message of the gospel and believe. 8. And God, who knows the heart, testified to them by giving the Holy Spirit just as he did to us. 9. He made no distinction between us and them, having purified their hearts by faith."

b. *Message.* As a Gentile Christian, Luke himself has a personal interest in the discussion, proceedings, and outcome of the meeting. He indicates that the action taken by the council affects the future of the worldwide church; therefore, he not only notes that the apostles and elders engaged in much debate but also that God through his Spirit led the apostles and the church in formulating their decision.

God led Peter to the house of Cornelius in Caesarea to admit Gentiles into the church. At the Jerusalem Council Peter addresses his fellow apostles and elders to remind them of God's guiding care in accepting these Gentiles. After the familiar cliché, "men and brothers," Peter says, "You know that in earlier days God chose me from among you that from my lips the Gentiles might hear the message of the gospel and believe." He recalls that a decade earlier, God's Spirit directed him to the Gentiles in Caesarea. God's Spirit descended on these Gentiles and thus gave them a Pentecost experience equal to that of the Jews in Jerusalem (2:1–4). The outpouring of God's Spirit, then, made Jewish Christians and Gentile Christians equals. Peter reminds the apostles and elders that when he returned from Caesarea, they had agreed that God himself had called the Gentiles to salvation (11:18). He points out that God chose him for the task of preaching the message of the gospel to Gentiles. The phrase *God chose me* refers to this specific incident in Caesarea. Although Paul is known as the apostle to the Gentiles and Peter the apostle to the Jews, these designations ought not to be taken too narrowly (Gal. 2:7–9). From Paul's farewell address to the Ephesian elders we know that he preached the gospel to both the Jews and the Greeks (20:21). Correspondingly, Peter did not restrict his ministry to the Jews. He traveled extensively to Corinth, Asia Minor, and Rome and met Jew and Gentile alike, as both his and Paul's epistles testify.

Peter notes that he brought "the message of the gospel" to the Gentiles, with the result that they believed. Not he as preacher but God as Savior opened their hearts and made them receptive to the Good News. The message of the gospel therefore is synonymous with salvation. In brief, the Gentiles heard the word and believed.

c. *Knowledge*. Salvation is a gift of God. This truth is evident from Peter's remark when he says, "God, who knows the heart, testified to them by giving the Holy Spirit just as he did to us." Because man is unable to provide salvation, the stipulation "unless you are circumcised . . . you cannot be saved" (v. 1) is hollow. Only God saves his people.

God knows man's heart and imparts to him the gift of the Holy Spirit. Accordingly, not man but God chooses the recipients of salvation, for God tests the hearts of men. The heart of man is the place where God implants and increases faith that comes to expression in obedience and perseverance (Rom. 6:17; II Thess. 3:5).[15] God does not look at external signs but examines the heart. By comparison, in the middle of the first century Jewish Christians judged the external appearance of the Gentiles and consequently rejected them. But God testified to the Jewish Christians that when the Gentiles hear the Good News, they respond in faith and receive the Holy Spirit.

---

15. Theo Sorg, *NIDNTT*, vol. 2, p. 183.

The Spirit breathes upon the Word,
And brings the truth to sight;
Precepts and promises afford
A sanctifying light.

      —William Cowper

The outpouring of the Holy Spirit in both Jerusalem and Caesarea demonstrates God's acceptance of the Gentile believers. Furthermore, as God gives his Spirit equally to Jew and Gentile in the church, so the Lord removes the barrier of hostility that divides them in worship (Eph. 2:14). "There is no distinction, therefore, between Jew and Greek, for the same Lord is Lord of all, rich and generous to all who call on him" (Rom. 10:12). Peter intimates that anyone who opposes the external sign of the outpouring of the Holy Spirit on the Gentiles resists God. And if God does not insist on circumcision, neither should the Jewish Christians.[16]

d. *Sanctification*. God has removed the distinction between Jew and Gentile. By describing God as the agent, Peter clearly states that this is not a human innovation to extend the boundaries of the church. God himself has removed the barriers of race and ethnicity, for in Christ all believers are the same. The implication is that if God sets the example we should follow.

Peter says that God made no distinction between *us* (the Jews) and *them* (the Gentiles). In our language we modestly place ourselves last in either a comparison or a sequence, but in Greek the opposite occurs. If God, then, has chosen the Gentile believers to be his people, he has sanctified them in the blood of Christ and declared them purified and cleansed from sin.

If God has accepted the Gentile believers as his own people, fellow Christians may not impose conditions that the Gentiles must fulfill before they can obtain salvation. Yet the Jewish Christians who belong to the party of the Pharisees turn to the Scriptures and say, "God told Abraham that the sign of the covenant is circumcision. The covenant God made with Abraham and his descendants is eternal. Therefore, throughout the ages circumcision remains the sign of this eternal covenant and cannot be abrogated (see Gen. 17:7, 9–14)."[17]

But in the New Testament era, circumcision lost its significance because God sanctifies the believer through the atoning work of Christ (see, among other passages, Gal. 5:2–6). In addition, Jesus commanded the apostles to baptize every new disciple; by implication, baptism takes the place of circumcision. Ever since Pentecost, the church has observed the sacrament of bap-

---

16. F. W. Grosheide, *De Handelingen der Apostelen*, Kommentaar op het Nieuwe Testament series, 2 vols. (Amsterdam: Van Bottenburg, 1948), vol. 2, p. 29.

17. John Calvin, *Commentary on the Acts of the Apostles*, ed. David W. Torrance and Thomas F. Torrance, 2 vols. (Grand Rapids: Eerdmans, 1966), vol. 2, p. 35.

tism in obedience to Christ's command. When Gentile Christians eventually entered the church, circumcision was abolished (compare Col. 2:11–12).[18]

Of course, by itself the ceremony of baptism in New Testament times does not cleanse a person, any more than did circumcision in Old Testament days. On the basis of the believer's true faith in Christ, God cleanses his heart without demanding that he be circumcised. From the New Testament we learn that Christ cleanses the consciences of believers through his blood (Heb. 9:14). To be precise, the Old Testament teaches that circumcision as the sign of the covenant also had to be supported by true faith. Nevertheless, the act of cleansing from sin in the Old Testament setting remained intimately tied to external ceremonies.

10. "Now therefore, why do you test God by placing on the necks of the disciples a yoke which neither our fathers nor we have been able to bear? 11. But we believe that we are saved through the grace of the Lord Jesus, just as they are."

e. *Restrictions.* Peter concludes his address to his fellow apostles and elders by advising them to cancel the demand for obeying Old Testament regulations that include circumcision. These are Peter's last words recorded by Luke in Acts and as such they are weighty. He sums up his remarks about God's work among the Gentiles and then queries whether the Judaizers realize that they are putting God to the test.

Scripture teaches that when man tests God, he approaches God in a spirit of unbelief and disobedience. Testing God is the opposite of worshiping God with singleness of heart (Deut. 6:16).[19] The example of the Israelites in the desert is telling. God had provided water for them at Marah and Elim (Exod. 15:22–27). But when they came to Rephidim and found no water, they complained and asked, "Is the LORD among us or not?" (Exod. 17:7, NIV). They tested God by openly doubting his proven ability to supply water. Similarly, Peter asserts, the Judaizers are testing God, who has clearly shown that Gentile Christians are free in Christ.

"Why do you [place] on the necks of the disciples a yoke which neither our fathers nor we have been able to bear?" This penetrating question of Peter echoes comparable words Paul writes in his epistles (e.g., Gal. 5:1; for Jesus' teaching, see Matt. 23:4; Luke 11:46). What is this yoke that no one is able to bear? Obviously, it is the Mosaic law. The Jews defined God's law as "the yoke" which every Jew and proselyte had to bear willingly and joyfully. Even Jesus uses Jewish imagery when he invites those who are weary and burdened to take his yoke upon themselves; but he tells them that his yoke is easy and his burden is light (Matt. 11:28–30).[20]

---

18. Consult Marten H. Woudstra, "Circumcision," *EDT,* p. 245.

19. Heinrich Seesemann, *TDNT,* vol. 6, p. 27. See also Walter Schneider and Colin Brown, *NIDNTT,* vol. 3, p. 801.

20. Consult M. Maher, " 'Take My Yoke upon You' (Matt. xi. 29)," *NTS* 22 (1975–76): 97–103; Hans-Georg Link and Colin Brown, *NIDNTT,* vol. 3, pp. 1160–65.

In the case before the Jerusalem Council, Peter regards the yoke a burden that gives the believer no delight. No Jew gained salvation by trying to keep the law. It had become a burden to him because his attempts at keeping the law had resulted in failure.[21] By itself, however, the law that God had given was good. But man's inability to observe God's law oppressed Peter's contemporaries and had burdened his forefathers. Further, the ceremonial part of the law and the regulations taught by the rabbis had become an impossible burden to bear. "There is no denying that though traditional Jews could regard the mass of commandments—six hundred and thirteen in all, consisting in three hundred and forty-eight positive precepts—as a means provided by God of acquiring merit, they could also arouse a misguided zeal for external observance alone."[22] Peter expresses what Paul had proclaimed in the synagogue of Pisidian Antioch, namely, that a believer cannot be justified by the law of Moses (13:39). A person, whether Jew or Gentile, can be justified only through faith in Jesus Christ.

f. *Salvation.* "But we believe that we are saved through the grace of the Lord Jesus, just as they are." Through his atonement, Christ fulfilled the law. Consequently, from the penalty of transgressing the law, he releases everyone who trusts in him. For this reason, the law has assumed a different meaning. That is, through the grace of the Lord Jesus Christ both Jewish and Gentile believers obtain salvation.

Peter does not suggest that the council should abrogate the law. He objects to making the law a precondition to salvation. Whereas the law is unable to save a person, faith in Jesus Christ indeed saves him. Both Jew and Gentile are equal before the Lord and both gain their salvation through him "as an objective gift of grace."[23]

Peter reflects on his experience in Caesarea and as a result is in full agreement with the teaching of Paul and Barnabas: do not demand circumcision from Gentile believers and do not subject them to the yoke of the Mosaic law. Neither Peter nor Paul and Barnabas contrived this strategy. God himself directed them to proclaim freedom in Christ to Gentile Christians.

Doctrinal Considerations in 15:6–11

In his historical survey of the early Christians, Luke depicts them as observers of the law. The Jews accused Stephen of speaking against the law (6:13), but in his speech before the Sanhedrin he shows his respect for the law God gave to Moses and the Israelites (7:38). Stephen, however, boldly states that the members of the Sanhedrin, having received this law, refused to obey it (7:53).

---

21. Refer to John Nolland, "A Fresh Look at Acts 15.10," *NTS* 27 (1980): 111–12.

22. Emil Schürer, *The History of the Jewish People in the Age of Jesus Christ (175 B.C.–A.D. 135)*, rev. and ed. Geza Vermes and Fergus Millar, 3 vols. (Edinburgh: Clark, 1973–87), vol. 2, p. 466.

23. Guthrie, *New Testament Theology*, p. 617; Hengel, *Acts and the History*, p. 125.

After completing his third missionary journey, Paul went to the temple, where Jews from Asia Minor accused him of teaching the people not to keep the law (21:28). In his defense before Governor Felix, Paul confessed that he believed everything that is written in the law (24:14); he told Governor Festus that he had done nothing contrary to it (25:8). Nonetheless, in Jerusalem thousands of Jewish Christians remained zealous for the law (21:20).

What, then, is the significance of the law for the Christian? Simply put, obedience to the law is not meant to obtain salvation but rather serves as evidence of the sanctified life of a Christian.[24] We admit that for countless Jewish Christians strict observance of the law was more a matter of custom than a matter of striving to please God in thankfulness for his gift of salvation.

Greek Words, Phrases, and Constructions in 15:7–11

Verse 7

ὑμεῖς ἐπίστασθε—the personal pronoun is intensive: "you yourselves." The verb is the present middle from ἐπίσταμαι and signifies "to know, be acquainted with, understand." For example, "the king understands these things" (26:26).

ἀκοῦσαι—"to hear." This ingressive aorist infinitive is followed by the accusative case; it denotes hearing obediently. The aorist infinitive πιστεῦσαι is also ingressive.

Verses 8–9

δούς—the aorist participle points to a single occurrence; the action is simultaneous with that of the main verb ἐμαρτύρησεν (he testified).

μεταξύ—the adverb *between* strengthens the preposition διά in the compound verb διέκρινεν (he made a distinction).

Verses 10–11

ἐπιθεῖναι—this aorist infinitive from the verb ἐπιτίθημι (I place upon) is epexegetical; that is, it explains the manner by which the Judaizers test God: "by placing a yoke upon the necks."

πιστεύομεν σωθῆναι—notice that the aorist passive infinitive *to be saved* is the direct object of the main verb: "we believe that we are saved."

---

3. Barnabas and Paul
15:12

A study of the sequence of the names *Barnabas* and *Paul* reveals that Barnabas's name always precedes Paul's when an activity occurs in Jerusalem (see v. 25). But abroad, in Gentile surroundings, the order is always

---

24. Consult I. Howard Marshall, *The Acts of the Apostles: An Introduction and Commentary,* Tyndale New Testament Commentary series (Leicester: Inter-Varsity; Grand Rapids: Eerdmans, 1980), p. 250.

reversed. In Jerusalem, Barnabas enjoyed greater esteem than Paul. Elsewhere Paul, because of his ability to speak, received increased recognition.[25]

12. The whole assembly was quiet and listened to Barnabas and Paul as they were relating the signs and wonders God had done through them among the Gentiles.

We presume that in the course of the meetings, the entire council comes together after the apostles and elders had met (vv. 6–11). The phrase *the whole assembly was quiet* can be interpreted to mean that "the meeting came to order."[26] Now the main part of the deliberations has come, and the entire council is ready to listen to the testimony of Barnabas and Paul.

Note how Luke describes the message which the two missionaries deliver before the entire assembly. The emphasis does not fall on what Paul and Barnabas did during their missionary journey but on what God did through them. Therefore, the missionaries refrain from mentioning circumcision but elaborate on God extending the boundaries of the church in the Gentile world. Therefore, the assembly has to realize that the growth of the church is God's work and that the matter of admitting the Gentiles into the church must be settled definitively by the Jerusalem Council.

In the Greek, Luke indicates that the audience listened to the missionaries for an extended period of time. Barnabas and Paul not only relate their experiences in Cyprus and Asia Minor; they also explain the significance of these events. They do the same thing Peter had done when he returned to Jerusalem from his mission to Cornelius in Caesarea. He recounted the event and explained what God had done. Similarly, Barnabas and Paul show that God was working through them with signs and wonders. We suspect that they mentioned the miracles of blinding the false prophet Bar-Jesus in Cyprus (13:6–12) and healing the cripple in Lystra (14:8–10). By mentioning these miracles, they testify to the fact that God himself had approved their ministry among the Gentiles.[27]

Greek Words, Phrases, and Constructions in 15:12

ἐσίγησεν—this aorist can be either constative (referring to the action in its totality) or inceptive (pointing to the beginning of the action).

The singular forms πᾶν τὸ πλῆθος (the whole multitude) control the plural verb ἤκουον (they heard). The imperfect denotes an extended period of time.

ἐξηγουμένων—the present middle participle from the verb ἐξηγέομαι (I explain)

---

25. The exception is 14:14, where the people of Lystra honor Barnabas as Zeus and Paul as Hermes, the messenger of Zeus.

26. Lake and Cadbury, *Beginnings,* vol. 4, p. 175. Compare 12:17; I Cor. 14:28, 30, 34. The Western witnesses add this clause at the beginning of verse 15: "And when the elders assented to what had been spoken by Peter." Metzger, *Textual Commentary,* p. 429.

27. Henry Alford, *Alford's Greek Testament: An Exegetical and Critical Commentary,* 7th ed., 4 vols. (1877; Grand Rapids: Guardian, 1976), vol. 2, p. 165.

is in the genitive case because (1) it follows the verb ἀχούω (I hear); or (2) it is part of a genitive absolute construction (with the genitive nouns *Barnabas* and *Paul*).

---

4. James's Address
15:13–21

When Peter, Paul, and Barnabas have spoken, the leader of the Jerusalem church assumes the task of addressing the assembly and formulating a decision that meets the approval of the entire council. This person is James, the half-brother of Jesus, who succeeded Peter as head of the church (12:17) and who was highly respected for his authority (compare 21:17–19).[28] When he speaks to the assembly, he literally has the last word.

a. Introduction

13. After they were finished speaking, James said: "Men and brothers, listen to me. 14. Simon has related how God at first concerned himself to take from among the Gentiles a people for himself."

The Jewish Christians who belong to the party of the Pharisees have to agree with Peter that God himself had opened the door to admit Gentiles into the church. They have to acknowledge that God had blessed the mission work performed by Paul and Barnabas. Yet they still are not satisfied. They pin their hopes and expectations on James the Just. They know that he scrupulously keeps the law and they recognize him as their spiritual leader (compare Gal. 2:12). However, James is broadminded and attuned to God's guiding care for the church universal in which Jewish and Gentile Christians accept each other as brothers and sisters.

James functions as the chairman of the assembly. Everyone present is eager to listen to what James has to say on the subject of adherence to the law, namely, circumcision. His opening remarks are, "Men and brothers, listen to me." The similarity between these words and those of the Epistle of James is remarkable. In his epistle James writes, "Listen, my beloved brothers" (2:5). The command *listen to me* occurs nowhere else in the entire New Testament.[29] It reveals that James has respect and authority in the church and that apostles, elders, and delegates to the council value his leadership.

James refers to Peter's address but not to the account of Paul and Barnabas: "Simon has related how God at first concerned himself to take from among the Gentiles a people for himself." In the original, James calls Peter *Simeon*, which is also the name Peter uses in the address of his second epistle (1:1). Probably the use of this typical Jewish name denotes a close relationship between James and Peter. By calling Peter by his Jewish name, James

---

28. Eusebius asserts that James "was the first to receive from the Saviour and the apostles the episcopate of the church at Jerusalem." *Ecclesiastical History* 7.19.1 (LCL); see also 2.1.3; 2.23.1–19.

29. Refer to Simon J. Kistemaker, *Exposition of the Epistle of James and the Epistles of John,* New Testament Commentary series (Grand Rapids: Baker, 1986), pp. 9–10.

demonstrates that he agrees wholeheartedly with Peter's account of his visit to Cornelius in Caesarea. Perhaps the use of Peter's Jewish name is meant to influence the Judaizers.

Further, James mentions Peter's experience because through the apostle Peter God first caused the Gentiles to become part of the church. And at the time of his experience, Peter served as leader in the Jerusalem church and was the spokesman for the apostles. James indicates that Peter did not command any changes in relation to the Gentiles but only explained what God had done. Like Peter, James places the emphasis on God, who concerned himself with the Gentiles. That is, God took them to be a people for himself.

Unfortunately, translations fall short in conveying the meaning of the Greek text. In Greek, a verb is used that often denotes visiting. Although the word *visit* can be understood in the sense of punishment (see Exod. 32:34; Jer. 14:10), the expression usually conveys the idea of God's blessing on his people.[30] This text indicates God does not extend his blessing to the Jews but to the Gentiles. Moreover, the Greek term *ethnos*, translated "Gentiles," symbolizes the nations of the world: they are not God's covenant people.[31] In Greek, the New Testament uses the word *laos* for the people that are in God's covenant, to be precise, Christians of Jewish descent. Of course, the covenant concept originates in the Old Testament: only the people of Israel (Hebrew: *'am*) are in the covenant; the Gentiles (Hebrew: *gôyîm*) are not.

Century after century, the Hebrews laid claim to the covenant because, of all the nations on the earth, they alone were God's people. But now God has visited the Gentiles and taken from them a number to be his covenant people. God has not taken all the nations, but from them he has elected his own. Whereas in former times God chose one people from all the peoples, now he chooses from all the people to make one people for himself.[32]

The Greek text has the words *a people for his name*. The name of God, however, is the revelation of his person and his power. The phrase *for his name*, in an idiomatic and interpretive sense, is equivalent to "himself."[33]

b. Scripture

15. "And the words of the prophets agree with this, as it is written:
16. " 'After this, I will return
    and I will rebuild the tent
    of David which has fallen.

30. Consult Leon Morris, *New Testament Theology* (Grand Rapids: Zondervan, Academie Books, 1986), p. 156.
31. The term appears 162 times in the New Testament. "In about 100 instances *ethnos* is used in contrast to Jews and Christians." Hans Bietenhard, *NIDNTT*, vol. 2, p. 793.
32. Grosheide, *Handelingen der Apostelen*, vol. 2, p. 38.
33. See especially Nils A. Dahl, " 'A People for His Name' (Acts xv. 14)," *NTS* 4 (1958): 319–27; Jacques Dupont, "Un Peuple d'entre les Nations," *NTS* 31 (1985): 321–25.

> **And I will rebuild its ruins**
>   **and I will restore it.**
> **17. In order that the rest of mankind**
>   **may seek the Lord,**
>   **and all the Gentiles who are called by my name,**
> **18. says the Lord, who makes these things known**
> **from of old.' "**

James introduces this quotation from the prophecy of Amos by using the plural form *words* for one Scripture passage (Amos 9:11–12) and the plural noun *prophets* for one writer (Amos). Many commentators understand the expression *prophets* as a reference to the twelve minor prophets.[34] Yet the term probably includes all the prophets of the Old Testament and thus James speaks of "words" in the introductory formula.[35]

Why did James choose this particular passage from Scripture to affirm his support for admitting Gentiles into the church? The prophets of the Old Testament agree with the message of Amos and, in effect, speak the same thing. Indeed, the Holy Spirit is speaking through them.[36] Throughout the Old Testament, beginning with Genesis 3:15, God proclaims the message of hope. Even though God chastises his people, he does not reject them, for he gives them the promise of restoration. The passage in Amos, then, is messianic and teaches that God fulfills the covenant promises he made to Abraham and to David. When the Messiah comes, he will rule over all the nations that bear his name. In other words, the prophecy of Amos depicts the universalistic rule of the Messiah.

1. *Textual variations.* In this study, I will point out a few differences between the wording in Amos 9:11–12 and the quotation in Acts 15:16–18.[37] A cursory look at the wording of these passages is sufficient to see that James did not follow the text of the Old Testament passage:

> "In that day I will restore
>   David's fallen tent.
> I will repair its broken places,
>   restore its ruins,
>   and build it as it used to be,
> so that they may possess the remnant of Edom

---

34. For example, Marshall, *Acts,* p. 252; F. F. Bruce, *The Acts of the Apostles: The Greek Text with Introduction and Commentary,* 3d (rev. and enl.) ed. (Grand Rapids: Eerdmans, 1990), p. 454.

35. Consult Walter C. Kaiser, Jr., "The Davidic Promise and the Inclusion of the Gentiles (Amos 9:9–15 and Acts 15:13–18): A Test Passage for Theological Systems," *JETS* 20 (1977): 97–111.

36. Calvin, *Acts of the Apostles,* vol. 2, p. 46. Michael A. Braun, however, contends that "James' choice of Amos 9 was a rather arbitrary one." See "James' Use of Amos at the Jerusalem Council: Steps Toward a Possible Solution of the Textual and Theological Problems," *JETS* 20 (1977): 113.

37. For a detailed study, see Braun, "James' Use of Amos," pp. 114–17.

and all the nations that bear my name,"
declares the LORD, who will do these things.
[Amos 9:11–12, NIV]

Apart from a few variations, the Septuagint translation comes close to the quotation in Acts 15. Here is a translation of the Greek text of Amos 9:11–12:

> "In that day I will raise up David's fallen tent, and I shall rebuild its ruins, and its remains I will raise up. And I shall rebuild it even as in the days of old, so that the remnant of men may seek and all the nations upon whom my name is called," says the Lord who will do these things.

The Septuagint differs from the quotation in Acts in some places. Among the major divergences are these three: the introduction *in that day* instead of "after this"; the lack of a direct object after the phrase *the remnant of men may seek;* the abbreviated clause *the Lord who will do these things* for "the Lord, who makes these things known from of old."[38] A Dead Sea Scroll (4QFlor 1.12) of Amos 9:11–12 features this text in Hebrew in wording that corresponds with the quotation in Acts. Nevertheless, even if we should say that James quoted from a Hebrew manuscript for the benefit of his Jewish Christian audience, we are unable to prove whether the proceedings of the council were conducted in Aramaic or in Greek. No doubt both languages were spoken.

2. *Exegetical nuances.* Let us look at the exegesis of these verses and take them one by one.

**16. "After this, I will return
and I will rebuild the tent
of David which has fallen.
And I will rebuild its ruins
and I will restore it."**

Only James has the words *after this,* while both the Hebrew text and the Septuagint have "in that day." Apparently, James refers to the time of the prophet Amos, who indicates that the temple in Jerusalem will be destroyed. Amos predicts that God will destroy the sinners, but will not totally destroy the house of Jacob (Amos 9:1–10). The expression *after this* signifies "in that day" and refers to the rebuilding of the tent of David.[39] The clause *I will return and . . . rebuild* means that after Jerusalem has

---

38. J. de Waard, *A Comparative Study of the Old Testament Text in the Dead Sea Scrolls* (Leiden: Brill, 1965), pp. 24–26. For a comprehensive study of Amos 9:11–15 in the context of Acts 15:14–20, see O. Palmer Robertson, "Hermeneutics of Continuity," in *Continuity and Discontinuity: Perspectives on the Relationship Between the Old and New Testaments,* ed. John S. Feinberg (Westchester, Ill.: Crossway, 1988), pp. 89–108.

39. Kaiser, "Davidic Promise," pp. 105–6; Robertson, "Hermeneutics of Continuity," p. 97.

been destroyed, God will cause his people to return to rebuild and restore its ruins.

The phrase *the tent of David* is a prophetic reference to the temple of the Lord to which all the nations go to worship God (compare, e.g., Isa. 2:2–4; Zech. 14:16). The prophets predict that both Jews and Gentiles together worship God. Note that Amos links the word *tent* to David, not to Levi or Aaron. David is a witness to the peoples on this earth, so that nations who do not know God will run to him (Isa. 55:3–5). These prophecies, which David's descendant, Jesus Christ, eventually fulfills, are messianic. By mentioning David's tent, Amos sees the panorama of Gentile nations coming to know and worship God. At the time of the Jerusalem Council, James indicates that this messianic prophecy of Amos has been fulfilled with the entrance of Gentiles into the church. James teaches that Israel, restored through Jesus Christ, extends a welcome to the rest of mankind in spiritual fellowship.

17. "In order that the rest of mankind may seek the Lord, and all the Gentiles who are called by my name."

The textual differences of the Hebrew text, the Septuagint reading, and the wording in Acts probably result from a misunderstanding of the Hebrew text: "so that they may possess the remnant of Edom." In Hebrew, the word *Edom* was written without the vowels. The translators of the Septuagint read this word as *Adam* and interpreted it as "humanity" or "men." Further, the Septuagint translators took the phrase *that they may possess* to mean "that they may seek."[40] The Septuagint reading lacks the direct object after the verb *seek,* but the text James used supplies it: "seek the Lord."

Who are the "remnant of men"? When the Old Testament uses the expression *remnant,* it normally speaks of faithful Jewish people who experience God's protecting care (e.g., see II Kings 19:4; Isa. 37:4). However, even though the term *remnant* is not used specifically, the concept itself occurs a number of times in the Old Testament with reference to the remnant of the nations (e.g., Isa. 66:19–21; Zech. 14:16).[41]

The Septuagint text of Amos 9:12 and the wording of Acts 15:17 provide an adequate interpretation of the "remnant of men" if we read the words as follows: "that the remnant of men even all the Gentiles who are called by my name may seek the Lord."[42] The second clause explains the first clause. The

---

40. "The [Hebrew] verb *yyršw* ('they shall possess') is emended to read *ydršw* ('they shall seek'). In the history of the transmission of the O[ld] T[estament] there was a time when *d* and *y* were virtually indistinguishable." Braun, "James' Use of Amos," p. 117. See also Alford, *Alford's Greek Testament,* p. 165.

41. Volkmar Herntrich, *TDNT,* vol. 4, p. 208.

42. See GNB, MLB, JB; see also Bruce, *Book of the Acts,* p. 292; Richard N. Longenecker, *The Acts of the Apostles,* in vol. 9 of *The Expositor's Bible Commentary,* ed. Frank E. Gaebelein, 12 vols. (Grand Rapids: Zondervan, 1981), p. 449; Robertson, "Hermeneutics of Continuity," p. 104.

Gentiles, then, are the remnant who belong to the Lord (compare James 2:7). With these words from the Old Testament Scriptures, James supports his argument that God has taken a people for himself from the Gentiles. Hence, God fulfills the messianic promise by calling Gentile believers.

18. "Says the Lord, who makes these things known from of old."

This verse teaches two facts. First, God gives this prophecy to his people with the promise that he will accomplish what he has said. Accordingly, when James quotes these words from Amos, he is supporting Peter's report that God makes no distinction between Jews and Gentiles in regard to their salvation (v. 9). God himself has spoken in his Word and gives the assurance that he will do the things he has made known.

Second, the things spoken by God have been known long ago (Isa. 45:21). God made them known in the days of Amos; he does so again at the time of the Jerusalem Council. In fact, these things go back to the time when Abram received the promise that he would be the father of many nations. For that reason, God gave him the name *Abraham* (Gen. 17:5). The things spoken by God refer to David, who extended the boundaries of Israel; David conquered the surrounding nations to obtain the full extent of the Promised Land. To an infinitely greater degree, David's descendant Jesus Christ rules over all the nations of the earth.

c. Stipulations

19. "Therefore, I judge that we do not trouble those Gentiles who are turning to God, 20. but that we write them to abstain from things polluted by idols, and from fornication, and from what is strangled, and from blood."

In the council, all eyes are fixed on James, who serves as the chairman. Everyone expects him to set forth a ruling to which they can agree (v. 28). James, then, summarizes the proceedings of the council and states emphatically: "*I* judge." He as their leader gives his audience a concise recommendation: "Do not trouble those Gentiles who are turning to God." The Greek verb that I have translated "trouble" actually means "crowd in on someone."[43] This is exactly what the Judaizers are doing to the Gentile believers: they crowd into the lives of the Gentiles by demanding circumcision and the observance of the Mosaic law. James refrains from mentioning circumcision and obedience to the law, but he employs language that says: "Stop crowding in on these people."

The Jewish Christians ought to rejoice that the Gentiles are turning to God (see 14:15; 26:20). The text indicates that Gentile conversions are common.

James knows that the Judaizers will not be satisfied with a negative exhortation. Hence he suggests four recommendations that are applicable to Gentile Christians who associate with Jewish Christians, especially those

---

43. R. C. H. Lenski, *The Interpretation of the Acts of the Apostles* (Columbus: Wartburg, 1944), p. 613.

who live in dispersion. He seeks to promote unity among believers of both Jewish and Gentile backgrounds. James wants the Christians to live together in wholesome relationships. He desires that they observe certain prescribed rules which preclude any offense arising from table fellowship or social contacts. James proposes that the council write a letter to the Gentile Christians and tell them what they must do.

1. *Polluted food.* In our present-day societal structures, the first stipulation is almost unintelligible. But for Gentile believers during the middle of the first century, every word in the command "to abstain from things polluted by idols" was meaningful. From two other places where the stipulation is repeated, we learn that food, expressly meat, was sacrificed to idols (v. 29; 21:25).[44]

Jews compared meat sacrificed to an idol with a corpse. Anyone touching a corpse was considered defiled; consequently, no Jew ate polluted meat. Further, Jewish and Gentile Christians regarded partaking of food sacrificed to idols as tantamount to showing allegiance to a pagan deity. Gentiles who had embraced the Christian faith, for example in Corinth, had repeatedly observed the sacrificial rituals at the temples of the numerous pagan gods. These people now pledged their allegiance to Jesus Christ by disavowing their pagan heritage and shunning all forms of idolatry (see I Cor. 10:14).

2. *Sexual immorality.* Gentile believers knew that at pagan temple rituals sexual immorality was the order of the day. From Paul's epistles, we learn that Gentile Christians needed repeated reminders to flee from sexual immorality (e.g., I Cor. 6:9, 18; II Cor. 12:21; Gal. 5:19). John Calvin thinks that the apostolic stipulation to avoid living a sexually immoral life referred to the pagan practice of keeping a common-law wife.[45]

3. *Strangled animals.* A Jew refuses to eat the meat of an animal that has been strangled. Whenever an animal is not butchered and its blood properly drained from the body, the meat is defiled (Lev. 17:13; see also Gen. 9:4). This animal, then, is a cadaver unfit for human consumption. The apostolic injunction to Gentile believers not to eat any meat of strangled animals teaches them basic sanitation. Compliance with the injunction gives them social acceptability among Jewish believers in the Christian community.

4. *Blood.* This last stipulation concerns the Jewish abhorrence of blood. The Mosaic law forbids consumption of blood and states that life is in the blood (Gen. 9:4; Lev. 3:17; 7:26; 17:10, 13–14).

Gentile Christians were fully aware of the Jewish religious, moral, and dietary restrictions. Hence, the apostolic decrees were not a shock to them. The four stipulations formulated by James would not be a burden to them,

---

44. See also Exod. 34:15; I Cor. 8:1, 4, 7, 10; 10:19; Rev. 2:14, 20; Wilhelm Mundle, *NIDNTT*, vol. 2, p. 286; Colin Brown, *NIDNTT*, vol. 3, p. 432; Friedrich Büchsel, *TDNT*, vol. 2, p. 378; David R. Catchpole, "Paul, James and the Apostolic Decree," *NTS* 23 (1977): 428–44.
45. Calvin, *Acts of the Apostles*, vol. 2, p. 51.

even though they were presented in negative form ("to abstain"). At the same time their Jewish friends would approve their willingness to observe these four stipulations. In short, as leader of the Jerusalem Council, James suggested a course of action that would not hinder the Gentile's longing for salvation by God with a demand for circumcision and a strict observance of the Levitical law. The suggested course also would satisfy Jewish Christians who called for adherence to the law.

Some courts in the temple were closed to Gentiles (compare 21:28–29), but aside from this limitation, Jewish and Gentile Christians were mingling freely since Peter's visit to Cornelius in Caesarea (10:25–48; see also 11:19–26). The recommendation of James, then, constitutes a plea to both Jewish and Gentile believers to accept one another and promote the unity of the Christian church. James attempts to appease both parties; as the rest of this chapter reveals, he succeeds in doing so.

21. "For Moses has been preached in every city since days of old and is read every Sabbath in the synagogues."

What is James trying to say with these words that conclude his address? Is he speaking to the Jews or to the Gentiles? Is he pleasing the Judaizers who demand the Gentile believers' circumcision and adherence to the Mosaic law? Is he divesting the Gentiles of the freedom they have just received? We can ask additional questions and find answers to each of them, but the fact remains that this particular verse is difficult to interpret.[46]

James begins by saying, "For Moses has been preached in every city since days of old." The conjunction *for* introduces the reason for the four stipulations. That is, the Jewish Christians could require additional demands, but James looks at the reality of the situation and points to the dispersion of the Jews. After the exile, probably in the time of Ezra, synagogues were built so that people could receive religious instruction in the law of Moses.[47] In every city throughout the known world of that day, the Jewish people acquainted the Gentile population with the teaching of God's Word. Gentiles who received instruction were called God-fearers.

"And [Moses] is read every Sabbath in the synagogues." James argues that these Gentiles are not unfamiliar with the Mosaic precepts. Should they wish to know more about these precepts, they are able to hear them explained once a week in the synagogues. Accordingly, James is addressing the Judaizers who do not wish to hinder the evangelistic task of the Jews who are living in dispersion. But he also faces the Gentile Christians and implicitly tells them to respect the Jews who observe the Mosaic ordinances. In brief, James appeases both Jews and Gentiles with his concluding remarks and consequently preserves the unity of the church.

46. Martin Dibelius avers, "Thus the contents of the decree are regarded virtually as a concession by the people of Jerusalem to the Gentile Christians, and not the reverse." *Studies in the Acts of the Apostles* (London: SCM, 1956), p. 97.
47. Schürer, *History of the Jewish People*, vol. 2, p. 427.

Textual Note on 15:20

Our translations take the Greek text that belongs to the Alexandrian family of text types. The reading features the fourfold prohibition to abstain from food sacrificed to idols, sexual immorality, meat of strangled animals, and blood. These four prohibitions are restated in verse 29 and 21:25.

However, the Western text has a peculiar variation; in 15:20, 29, and 21:25 it omits the reference to strangled animals; and in 15:20, 29 it adds the Golden Rule in negative form: "And whatever you do not wish to happen to you, do not do these things to others." The three stipulations in the Western text are that Gentile Christians should abstain from idolatry, immorality, and blood (that is, murder). They should also observe the negative Golden Rule. "But this reading can scarcely be original, for it implies that a special warning had to be given to Gentile converts against such sins as murder, and that this was expressed in the form of asking them to 'abstain' from it—which is slightly absurd!"[48]

Last, the Caesarean text deletes the reference to sexual immorality in 15:20, 29. The omission possibly reflects an attempt to avoid the awkwardness of grouping a moral law with three food laws.[49]

The collective evidence appears to favor the reading that has the four stipulations (to abstain from polluted food, immorality, strangled meat, and consumption of blood). The New Testament indicates that the Gentile churches complied with the apostolic injunctions for an extended period (for example, see the references in Rev. 2:14, 20).

Greek Words, Phrases, and Constructions in 15:14–21

Verses 14–15

ἐθνῶν λαὸν—notice the juxtaposition of these two nouns: from the heathen nations (ἔθνη) God has taken a people (λαός) for himself.

τούτῳ—here is the neuter, not the masculine, of the demonstrative pronoun: "to this fact."

Verse 17

καί—the conjunction is ascensive and should be translated "even." The clause that follows καί explains the clause that precedes it.

πάντα—"all." God calls the Gentiles without any qualification.

Verse 19

ἐγὼ κρίνω—the presence of the personal pronoun adds emphasis so that the verb, now qualified, means "I for one judge."

---

48. Metzger, *Textual Commentary*, pp. 431–32.
49. Kirsopp Lake, "The Apostolic Council of Jerusalem," *Beginnings*, vol. 5, pp. 206–7.

μὴ παρενοχλεῖν—the present active infinitive preceded by the negative particle μή intimates that an action which is in progress should be stopped: "stop troubling them."

Verse 20

τοῦ ἀπέχεσθαι—"to abstain from." The present middle infinitive with the definite article in the genitive case denotes a purpose clause. The compound verb controls the genitive case of the nouns in all four prohibitions.

Verse 21

κηρύσσοντας αὐτὸν ἔχει—the subject of the main verb *has* is Moses. The main verb is in the present tense and describes continuing action.[50] The present tense of the active participle *preaching* expresses action in progress.

C. The Letter
15:22–35

1. Messengers
15:22

Even though Luke fails to report the assembly's reaction to the proposal James made, from the context we learn that the council accepted the four stipulations James presented (vv. 28–29). After adopting the recommendation, the gathering had to appoint men who were able to convey the apostolic decrees to the Gentile churches and compose the letter that embodied the apostolic decrees.

22. Then the apostles and elders with the whole church decided to choose some of their men and send them to Antioch with Paul and Barnabas. They chose Judas called Barsabbas and Silas, men who were leaders among the brothers.

We make these observations:

a. *Unity*. In the Greek, Luke shows that the early church had two distinct groups of leaders: the apostles and the elders.[51] We are unable to determine how many of the apostles were present at the council. For some unknown reason, the council did not appoint apostles to inform the church in Antioch about the decision that had been made. The apostles and elders work together with the entire church, that is, with representatives of individual congregations present at the Jerusalem Council, not only the mother church in Jerusalem.

The decision to send qualified men to Antioch is weighty because these men must convey and explain the deliberations of the council. Moreover,

---

50. Moule, *Idiom-Book*, p. 8.
51. See 15:2 (one definite article in Greek with the two nouns *apostles* and *elders*), 4, 6, 22, 23; 16:4. Consult Guthrie, *New Testament Theology*, p. 740.

they must ask the Antiochean church to accept the decisions and maintain the unity of the church. Their task is to create harmony between the Jewish believers who demand circumcision and the Gentile Christians who demand freedom. Hence, the council comes to a unanimous agreement to elect men who are able to fulfill this task. They do not have to go alone; they will accompany Paul and Barnabas.

b. *Named.* The council appoints two men, Judas Barsabbas and Silas. The name *Barsabbas* means "son of Sabbas" (the elder) or "son of the Sabbath," that is, born on the Sabbath. From other literature we know that Barsabbas was a common name, yet in the New Testament it occurs only here and in 1:23, where Joseph Barsabbas is mentioned. We do not know whether Judas and Joseph are related, because their names appear only in Acts. Luke describes Judas as a leader (v. 22) and a prophet (v. 32). The name *Silas* is the abbreviated form of Silvanus. This man is a recognized leader among the believers, a prophet (v. 32), a Roman citizen (16:37), a preacher (II Cor. 1:19), and a writer who assisted Peter in the composition of his first epistle (5:12). He accompanied Paul on the second missionary journey and is mentioned last when Paul founded the church in Corinth (18:5).[52]

These two men receive the charge to deliver the letter, which presumably James composed. Although James does not sign the letter, we conjecture that he wrote it. The similarity between the address of James before the council and the content of the letter is evident. From the address, however, we know that the apostles and the elders approved the exact wording of the epistle and that they are responsible for sending it.

2. Message
15:23–29

23. They sent this letter with them:

"The apostles and elders, from your brothers to the Gentile brothers in Antioch, Syria, and Cilicia.
Greetings."

Because the letter is addressed to the church in Antioch, it was probably written in Greek. We have no reason to suppose that Luke himself composed the letter, although he perhaps had access to a copy and could include it in his narrative. That Judas and Silas assisted in composition of the letter is plausible.

Notice that the address differs from that of the epistles written by Peter or Paul. Yet the Epistle of James and this address show some resemblance. For example, the word *greetings* appears in both; the term *brothers,* which occurs here twice in the address, is used by James fifteen times as an address in his epistle.[53]

---

52. Refer to B. N. Kaye, "Acts' Portrait of Silas," *NovT* 21 (1979): 13–26.
53. James 1:2, 16, 19; 2:1, 5, 14; 3:1, 10, 12; 4:11; 5:7, 9, 10, 12, 19.

Significant is the fact that the Jerusalem apostles and elders place themselves on the same level as the Gentile believers in Antioch. The address is from one group of Christian brothers to another group of brothers in Christ. The superscription, therefore, clearly indicates that the apostles and elders are free from racial discrimination.

The senders address "the Gentile brothers in Antioch, Syria, and Cilicia," although many Jewish Christians were members of the Antiochean church, too. The apostolic decrees, however, affect the Gentile Christians who live in Antioch, Syria, and Cilicia (v. 41). To be precise, prior to A.D. 72 Antioch served as the capital of Syria and the eastern part of Cilicia.[54] Paul and Silas also delivered the letter to the churches in southern Galatia (16:4).

24. "We heard that some people went out from us without our instructions. They disturbed you with their words and unsettled your minds. 25. So it seemed good to us, having come to an agreement, to send some men to you with our friends Barnabas and Paul, 26. men who have dedicated their lives in behalf of the name of the Lord Jesus Christ. 27. Therefore, we have sent Judas and Silas who themselves will report these same things by word of mouth."

The first two sentences in this letter are revealing: they candidly state the problem that caused the Jerusalem Council to convene, and they put the origin of the cause on the shoulders of unauthorized Judaizers who went from Jerusalem to Antioch. These sentences declare that the men came from the Jerusalem church but went out on their own accord. Without the approval of the apostles and elders, they caused a disturbance in the Antiochean church with their words about circumcision and the Mosaic law. Note, however, that the letter itself avoids any reference to circumcision or the law. With their insistence on correct procedure, these Judaizers upset the minds of the Gentile Christians in Antioch. The apostles and elders make it known that they distance themselves from these troublemakers (compare Gal. 1:7; 5:10). By implication, they advise the Gentile believers to pay no attention to these Judaizers who seek to divide instead of unify the church.

"So it seemed good to us." The next sentence in the letter explains the unanimity of the Jerusalem leadership: to send some men from Jerusalem along with Barnabas and Paul to explain the decisions the council made. The wording of this sentence indicates that the apostles and elders attach great importance to sending messengers along with Barnabas and Paul—they mention Paul last because he is not as well known as Barnabas. The intent is to show that the initiative comes from the apostles and elders and not from the Antiochean delegates, Barnabas and Paul, who are portrayed as "our [mutual] friends." The letter reveals that these two are held in high regard, for they are "men who have dedicated their lives in behalf of the name of the Lord Jesus Christ" (see 5:41). The leaders in Jerusalem are impressed with the dedication and fervor of these two apostles to the Gen-

---

54. E. M. B. Green, "Syria and Cilicia—A Note," *ExpT* 71 (1959): 52–53.

tiles. Indeed, the missionaries have endeared themselves to the church in Jerusalem because they have risked their lives in behalf of Christ's gospel (9:23–25; 14:19; I Cor. 15:30).

The men who are accompanying the missionaries are Judas and Silas. No further identification is given; they are the letter carriers who will speak for themselves. Possibly, these two men were not unknown to the Antiochean church. They are responsible for reporting orally the proceedings of the council and explaining the wording of the letter.

28. "For it seemed good to the Holy Spirit and to us not to burden you with more than these essentials: 29. To abstain from things sacrificed to idols, from blood, from strangled animals, and from fornication. If you keep yourselves away from these things, you do well. Farewell."

The first word *for* links the decision made by the Jerusalem Council to the task of Judas and Silas. The letter states that the decision has been made by the Holy Spirit and by the assembly. It reveals that the apostles, the elders, and the church were fully aware of the presence of the Holy Spirit to guide and direct them. The Spirit revealed what the leaders of the church should say and do. For example, at an earlier occasion Peter said: "We are witnesses of these things, and so is the Holy Spirit, whom God has given to those who obey him" (5:32, NIV). And in later years, Paul was compelled by the Spirit to go to Jerusalem (20:22).[55]

Guided by the Holy Spirit, the assembly is free to say that the Gentile Christians need not be burdened with various nonessential requirements. Notice, then, that the letter is silent about the matter of circumcision, which occasioned the convening of the council (vv. 1, 5). Nothing is said about the ceremonial laws which Jewish Christians continued to observe. And no reference is made to keeping the Sabbath as the last day of the week. The essential part for their salvation is their faith in God.

The letter specifies that Gentile Christians should comply with four regulations that are expressed in negative form: to abstain from sacrificial food offered to idols, from blood, from meat of strangled animals, and from sexual immorality. These four stipulations, however, have not been given as a universal law applicable to all Christians of all times. Rather, the prohibitions should be seen in the light of the council's desire to maintain unity and harmony between the Jewish Christians and the Gentile believers. Conversely, no Christian, whether Jew or Gentile, objects to the first stipulation if it relates to his allegiance to Jesus Christ. Next, the Christian who seeks to live in accordance with God's law instinctively abstains from sexual immorality. And last, the prescriptions not to eat meat from strangled animals and not to consume blood are general hygienic rules that the Jews for countless centuries have observed to safeguard their own physical well-being.

"To abstain from things sacrificed to idols." In a letter to the Corinthians,

55. Consult Morris, *New Testament Theology*, p. 194.

Paul discusses this stipulation, albeit in different wording and in another context (I Cor. 8:4–10, 13; 10:1–22). The apostle had been asked to give his advice on eating food sacrificed to idols. In the situation in Corinth, Paul refers not to food that was taken from pagan temples and sold to the general public in the marketplace. He alludes to "the eating of sacrificial food at the cultic meals in the pagan temples."[56] Nevertheless, the general rule enacted by the Jerusalem Council applies to Gentile Christians everywhere.

The sequence of the four stipulations differs slightly from the proposal James made during the Jerusalem Council: fornication appears last in the letter (v. 29) but takes second place in the address of James (v. 20). In the written message the first three stipulations have been grouped together as food regulations, whereas the last one is a moral injunction.[57]

These four rules are known as the apostolic decrees, which conclude with the admonition, "If you keep yourselves away from these things, you do well." By observing these rules, the Gentile Christians should not think that they are able to earn their salvation. God grants salvation by grace alone. However, God wants his people to do (that is, practice) the right things. The letter concludes with the customary goodbye of that day: "Farewell."

Doctrinal Considerations in 15:23–29

When Peter and John were sent to Samaria by the apostles, they prayed with the Samaritan believers and asked God to send his Spirit upon them. The Jewish Christians accepted the believers in Samaria because they were only half a step removed from them. The Samaritans had at least the first five books of the Old Testament; they worshiped God at Mount Gerizim (John 4:20–23); and they heard Jesus preach in Sychar (John 4:40–42).

But when Gentile Christians asked for admission to the church, the apostles and elders convened the church in general assembly. The Jewish Christians had to make a major decision: either demand that every Gentile become a Jew before he could be a Christian or preserve the unity of the church and admit Gentile believers to full membership without any preconditions. The council chose the second option. It advised the Gentiles to observe four stipulations, three pertaining to dietary laws and one to morality.

Through the steady guidance of the Holy Spirit, the apostles and elders permitted the gospel to go forth unhindered to the Jew and the Gentile. Because of the far-reaching ruling of the Jerusalem Council, the Gentile churches continued to grow and develop. These churches gave direction and leadership as the Jewish segment began to diminish and disappear. All Gentile churches, therefore, owe their origin to the decision made by the Jerusalem Council.

---

56. Gordon D. Fee, *The First Epistle to the Corinthians*, New International Commentary on the New Testament series (Grand Rapids: Eerdmans, 1987), p. 359.

57. For the textual variations of verse 29, see the **Textual Note on 15:20** after the explanation of verse 21. Also refer to M. Simon, "The Apostolic Degree and Its Setting in the Ancient Church," *BJRUL* 52 (1970): 437–60.

Greek Words, Phrases, and Constructions in 15:23–29

Verse 23

γράψαντες—grammatically, this aorist active participle has no connection with the preceding context. Translated "having written," it stands alone and is called a nominative absolute.

διὰ χειρός—a Semitism translated from the Hebrew into the Greek, the expression simply means "by."[58]

ἀδελφοί—without a definite article, this noun stands in apposition to the articular nouns *apostles* and *elders* and should be translated "your brothers."

τὴν Ἀντιόχειαν—note that one definite article τὴν applies to three nouns: the names of the city Antioch and the provinces Syria and Cilicia.[59]

χαίρειν—here is the absolute infinitive rather than the imperatival infinitive. It expresses a wish, not a command.

Verses 24–25

ἀνασκευάζοντες—"upsetting." Even though this is a present participle, in force it is identical to the main verb in the aorist indicative (ἐτάραξαν, troubled).

ἔδοξεν—from δοκέω (I think, seem), the form is impersonal in the third person singular aorist, "it seemed good" (vv. 22, 25, 28).

Verse 27

διὰ λόγου—the combination of the preposition with the noun ("word") is equivalent to the adverb *orally*.

ἀπαγγέλλοντας—the present participle expresses purpose. Judas and Silas were sent "to report," that is, "to explain."

Verse 28

πλήν—an adverb used as a preposition that controls the genitive case, it means "except." In a sentence that has a comparative adjective (πλέον, greater), the use of a preposition with the genitive is redundant.

τῶν ἐπάναγκες—the genitive case relies on the preceding preposition ("except"). However, the word ἐπάναγκες grammatically is not a noun but an adverb that means "necessarily." In translation, the adverb becomes a noun ("necessary things"). This adverb occurs only once in the New Testament.

Verse 29

ἀπέχεσθαι—see the explanation of verse 20. Here the infinitive lacks the definite article.

εἰδωλοθύτων—the genitive case of this noun depends on the preceding verb that demands a genitive of separation.

---

58. In Greek, see 2:23; 5:12; 7:25; 11:30; 14:3; 19:11, 26.
59. A. T. Robertson, *A Grammar of the Greek New Testament in the Light of Historical Research* (Nashville: Broadman, 1934), p. 787.

διατηροῦντες—the compound form intensifies this verb ("to keep carefully").[60] The present active participle is conditional: "if you keep."

---

3. Effect
15:30–35

The task of the two emissaries, Judas and Silas, is facilitated greatly through the introduction Paul and Barnabas give them at the church in Antioch. Nonetheless, the two men who have been commissioned by the Jerusalem Council have full authority to deliver the letter and explain it. In fact, on Paul's second missionary journey Paul and Silas read this letter to the people as they travel from town to town through Syria, Cilicia, and Galatia (16:4).

30. Then the men who departed went down to Antioch, and having gathered the multitude, they delivered the letter. 31. When they read the letter, they rejoiced because of its encouraging message.

Luke gives no indication that the missionaries visited the churches in Samaria and Phoenicia, as they did on their way to Jerusalem (v. 3). Yet it is possible that Paul, Barnabas, and the others traveled northward along the coastal area and communicated the council's message to the churches along the way. When the messengers reach Antioch, they convene the entire church in that city and deliver the letter to its leaders. These church officials read the communication from the Jerusalem Council in the hearing of all the people. Now the Gentile believers learn firsthand that the council has adopted the views of Paul and Barnabas and has rejected the demands of the Jewish Christians who belonged to the party of the Pharisees (v. 5). The effect of the letter and the satisfactory explanation given by Judas and Silas is joy and gladness in the hearts of believers. Undoubtedly, Paul and Barnabas also render their words of insight. In brief, the people are encouraged by the letter and the words of the messengers.[61] Apparently, they have no objections to the four stipulations of the council. Like the Christians in Jerusalem, they wish to maintain the unity of the church; thus they are willing to do their part to promote harmony and peace.

32. Judas and Silas, who also were prophets, encouraged and strengthened the brothers with many words. 33. After they had spent some time there, they departed from the brothers in peace and returned to those who had sent them.

The council's reason for choosing Judas and Silas as emissaries to Antioch is obvious. First, these two speak Greek fluently, so they are able to address the Gentile Christians in that language. Next, they are prophets who use

---

60. Thayer, p. 142.
61. The Greek has the word *paraklēsis,* which can mean either "consolation" (KJV), "exhortation" (RSV), or "encouragement" (NKJV). Translators, however, prefer the last choice. Compare 13:15.

their gift of preaching to encourage and strengthen the believers in Antioch.[62] We know that the church there already had a number of prophets, among whom were Barnabas and Paul (13:1). Luke is fully aware of this fact, but in this verse he calls attention to the two prophets from Jerusalem who have come to encourage and support the Antiochean believers. These two go about and orally make known the riches of salvation in Christ.

Both Judas and Silas remain in Antioch for some time and continue their preaching ministry. They are in the employ of the Antiochean church, so to speak. And as the text indicates (v. 33), the brothers there send them back to the body that had commissioned them. In one short clause, Luke describes the relationship between the two prophets and the church in Antioch: "They departed from the brothers in peace." The expression *in peace* is actually a farewell greeting that was in common use at that time.[63]

Because Silas is present in Antioch when Paul begins his second missionary journey, copyists in later centuries of the Christian era added explanatory notes that were incorporated in the text. To illustrate, one Greek text has the reading: "However, it seemed good to Silas to remain there" (NKJV). Another has a further expansion, "But it seemed good to Silas that they remain, and Judas journeyed alone" (Western text).[64] Scholars are of the opinion that these notes are not original; therefore they delete verse 34.

35. Paul and Barnabas remained in Antioch, teaching and preaching with many others the word of the Lord.

From the Greek text we learn that Paul and Barnabas continued their stay in Antioch and thus took up the work they were doing before they made their journey to Cyprus and Asia Minor (11:26; and see 13;1; 14:28). They have a full ministry of teaching and preaching and they do their work with many others. They teach the people the word of the Lord, much the same as the apostles used to do in Jerusalem in earlier days (2:42; 5:42). In view of the leadership talent in the Antiochean church, we must say that Antioch, not Jerusalem, gradually became the center for ecclesiastical growth, development, and missionary outreach.

Greek Words, Phrases, and Constructions in 15:30–33

Verse 30

οἱ μὲν οὖν—with Judas, Silas, Paul, and Barnabas were also some others from Antioch (v. 2).

τὸ πλῆθος—"multitude." In context, this word at times means "the church" (6:2, 5; 15:12).

---

62. Refer to Everett F. Harrison, *The Apostolic Church* (Grand Rapids: Eerdmans, 1985), p. 134.
63. Refer to Ronald F. Youngblood, "Peace," *ISBE*, vol. 3, p. 733. And compare Mark 5:34; Luke 7:50; 8:48; Acts 16:36; I Cor. 16:11; James 2:16 (NASB).
64. Metzger, *Textual Commentary*, p. 439.

Verse 32

διὰ λόγου πολλοῦ—the preoposition διά expresses attendant circumstance and conveys a precise meaning: "at length (with much talk)."[65]

Codex Bezae supplements the text. After the present participle ὄντες, it adds: "filled with the Holy Spirit." This particular manuscript includes many references to the Holy Spirit (see 11:16; 15:7, 29; 19:1; 20:3).

Verse 33

ἀπελύθησαν—the aorist passive of ἀπολύω (I dismiss) suggests that the Antiochean church is the agent.

All the leading manuscripts read, "to those who had sent them." The Textus Receptus and the Majority Text prefer the shorter reading *to the apostles*.[66] However, in view of the broader context (apostles, elders, and the entire church, v. 22), the shorter version lacks necessary support.

---

36 After some time Paul said to Barnabas, "Let us return and visit the brothers in every city in which we preached the word of the Lord and see how they are." 37 But Barnabas wanted to take John, also called Mark, with them. 38 Paul insisted that they should not take him along, because he had deserted them in Pamphylia and had not accompanied them to that work. 39 And there arose such a sharp disagreement that they separated. Barnabas took Mark with him and sailed to Cyprus, 40 while Paul chose Silas and departed, commended by the brothers to the grace of the Lord. 41 Paul went through Syria and Cilicia, strengthening the churches.

VII. The Second Missionary Journey
15:36–18:22

A. Revisiting the Churches
15:36–16:5

As a historian, Luke traces the development of the Christian church and describes how the results of Paul's first missionary journey prompted the convening of the Jerusalem Council. During Paul's first outreach into Gentile territory, numerous Gentiles came to the faith but were not welcomed by some of the Jewish members of the church. After the Jerusalem Council, Paul commences his second journey with the apostolic decrees in hand (see 16:4) and openly welcomes Gentile Christians to full membership.

Not everyone present at the Jerusalem Council agreed to the decisions that had been made. In reality, Judaizers followed Paul and Barnabas to Antioch and went as far as the churches in Galatia. In all these places, they disregarded the apostolic decrees and demanded from the Gentile converts circumcision and strict adherence to the Levitical law.[67]

---

65. Moule, *Idiom-Book*, p. 57.
66. Arthur L. Farstad and Zane C. Hodges, *The Greek New Testament According to the Majority Text* (Nashville: Nelson, 1982), p. 428.
67. Compare Gal. 2:11–12; 3:10–12; 5:2–3; 6:12.

According to Paul, Peter came to Antioch, ate with the Gentile Christians, and thus fully supported the decisions made by the Jerusalem Council (Gal. 2:12). However, when some men came from James, Peter was influenced by them and decided no longer to have table fellowship with Gentile Christians. The reference to James does not mean that James had delegated these men to sow discord in the church at Antioch. "Far more natural would seem to be the explanation that they came from the church at Jerusalem, a church in which James occupied a position of special prominence."[68] All indications seem to be that these people are of the same mold as those who earlier had insisted on making circumcision a prerequisite for salvation (v. 1). When they came to Antioch, they were able to influence not only Peter but also other Jewish Christians, including Barnabas (Gal. 2:13). Paul immediately saw through their hypocrisy. He openly rebuked Peter and told him to forsake the error of his way. Paul did not reveal what he said to Barnabas, but we surmise that he addressed him in a similar manner.

In a sense, Paul stood alone in keeping the right course. Perhaps from his perspective, this incident adversely affected the splendid relationship that had existed between him and Barnabas. Further, this episode probably induced the sharp disagreement that resulted in a break between these two friends (v. 39). We know that Paul's unwillingness to take John Mark along on the second missionary journey stemmed from Mark's decision to desert Paul and Barnabas. But we assume that Paul had additional reasons for his unhappiness with Mark. Unfortunately, we lack factual evidence about what these reasons may have been.

1. Separation
15:36–41

36. After some time Paul said to Barnabas, "Let us return and visit the brothers in every city in which we preached the word of the Lord and see how they are."

We are unable to determine how long the missionaries stayed in Antioch. Possibly they remained there for a number of months—in the Greek text Luke writes the general reference *after some time*. The spiritual needs of the newly founded churches in Asia Minor, however, were on the minds and in the prayers of Paul and Barnabas. Whereas the Holy Spirit initiated the first missionary journey, the plan to return to Asia Minor originated with Paul. That is, Paul's calling to be an apostle to the Gentiles did not cease after completing the first journey: once a missionary, always a missionary! Moreover, his life's calling was not to minister to the spiritual needs of the believers in Antioch but to those of the Gentiles in Asia Minor, Greece, and Italy.[69]

---

68. Hendriksen, *Galatians,* p. 93. Also consult Herman N. Ridderbos, "Galatians, Epistle to the," *ISBE,* vol. 2, pp. 382–83.

69. Grosheide, *Handelingen der Apostelen,* vol. 2, p. 71.

Paul addresses Barnabas as his missionary partner and suggests to him that they return to the believers in the various cities where they earlier had preached the gospel. He calls the believers brothers who had heard "the word of the Lord," and intimates that these Gentile Christians need pastoral guidance, counsel, and help. Throughout Acts, Luke interchanges the terms *word of God* and *word of the Lord* (see, for example, 8:14, 25).

37. But Barnabas wanted to take John, also called Mark, with them. 38. Paul insisted that they should not take him along, because he had deserted them in Pamphylia and had not accompanied them to that work.

Barnabas agrees with Paul's suggestion, but he adds that Mark should accompany them. First, remember that Barnabas and Mark were cousins (Col. 4:10). Next, although Mark had left the missionaries during the journey in Asia Minor and returned to Jerusalem, we infer that now he had traveled to Antioch and wished to serve Paul and Barnabas again as an assistant. Barnabas wanted to give Mark a second chance to prove himself a worthy companion. And third, at the outset of the first missionary journey, Barnabas was the leader who ranked first in importance (13:1, 7). But when the second journey is planned, Paul is in command and reacts negatively to the suggestion to take along John Mark.

Many people in the first century had two names: the one acceptable to Greeks and Romans, the other reflecting the person's Semitic heritage (e.g., Matthew and Levi, Paul and Saul). Likewise, John Mark seems to have been called John by his Jewish friends but was known as Mark in the Gentile world. In the Roman empire, the name *Marcus* (Mark) was very common. For some reason, Luke stresses this double name: three times he indicates that John is also called Mark (12:12, 25; 15:37).

When Luke writes the Book of Acts, he considers Mark a friend and fellow worker in preaching and teaching Christ's gospel (Col. 4:10, 14; Philem. 24). He has difficulty reporting that Mark was the object of contention that led to a separation between Paul and Barnabas. Understandably, Luke merely states the essentials and excludes the details. He reports the controversy but fails to delineate the basic causes. Thus we could ask whether Paul was too harsh when Barnabas, who had distinguished himself as an encourager (4:36; 9:27; 11:24–25), spoke on behalf of Mark. Should not Paul have shown a forgiving spirit and reinstated Mark as a fellow worker? From Paul's perspective, however, Mark had broken his pledge to be a bond servant of Jesus Christ when he forsook the missionaries and returned to Jerusalem (13:13).[70] We must answer that Paul doubted whether Mark could function as a missionary who, regardless of the consequences, had dedicated his life to Christ.

"Paul insisted[71] that they should not take [Mark] along." He considers Mark unsuitable for the task that lies before them. From Paul's letters we

---

70. Calvin, *Acts of the Apostles*, vol. 2, p. 62.
71. Bauer, p. 78.

know that reconciliation took place and that Paul even recommended Mark to the church at Colosse (Col. 4:10). At the end of Paul's life, he requests that Mark come to his prison cell in Rome. He adds that Mark has been helpful to him in his ministry (II Tim. 4:11). Moreover, Peter calls him his son (see I Peter 5:13).

In other words, Mark has the necessary qualifications but Paul is not yet convinced that this is so. The Greek indicates that Paul kept insisting that they not take Mark because he had deserted them in Pamphylia and had not accompanied them to Pisidian Antioch, Iconium, Lystra, and Derbe.

39. And there arose such a sharp disagreement that they separated. Barnabas took Mark with him and sailed to Cyprus.

Luke uses strong language when he reports the rupture in the relationship between Paul and Barnabas. In Greek, the expression translated "sharp disagreement" comes from a word that means "to provoke to anger" (see 17:16; I Cor. 13:5).[72] Luke only states the fact but leaves its interpretation to the reader. In this verse, he mentions Barnabas for the last time when he writes that Barnabas and Mark sail for Cyprus.

Nevertheless, Paul does not harbor any lingering animosity, for in his epistles he writes words of appreciation. He asks the Corinthians whether he and Barnabas have the right to work at a trade (I Cor. 9:6). And if we aver that Paul composed Galatians from Corinth on his second missionary journey, we read that the apostle does not denigrate Barnabas but merely mentions his name (Gal. 2:13).

Barnabas and Mark leave for Cyprus, which is the native land of Barnabas and perhaps of Mark also. Luke does not relate that the church in Antioch commended them to the task at hand (although it may have done so). He simply notes that the two missionaries left for Cyprus.

40. While Paul chose Silas and departed, commended by the brothers to the grace of the Lord. 41. Paul went through Syria and Cilicia, strengthening the churches.

In God's providence, not one team of missionaries but two teams leave from Antioch. Even if we know nothing about the result of the work performed by Barnabas and Mark, we still see God's marvelous care for the believers in Cyprus. God also tends to the needs of the Christians in Asia Minor by sending Paul and Silas.

The name *Silas* has its counterpart in the Latin form *Silvanus*. The shorter name was in vogue among Jewish people, because it seemed to be related to the name *Saul*. In the Greek text, both Paul and Peter prefer the longer form.[73] "Like Paul (also called Saul), Silas probably used both names and had them from birth."[74] Paul had become acquainted with Silas at the Jerusalem Council (v. 22) and had traveled with him to Antioch. With his

---

72. Heinrich Seesemann, *TDNT*, vol. 5, p. 857.
73. II Cor. 1:19; I Thess. 1:1; II Thess. 1:1; I Peter 5:12.
74. Robert C. Campbell, "Silas," *ISBE*, vol. 4, p. 509.

ability to preach (v. 32) and his status as Roman citizen (16:37), Silas became a prime candidate to accompany Paul on his second missionary journey.

The relationship between Paul and Silas is different from that of Paul and Barnabas. Luke never calls Silas an apostle, yet he refers twice to the apostle Barnabas. Silas accompanied Paul not as an equal but as a subordinate. By contrast, Paul always regarded Barnabas as his equal and in earlier days as his leader and mentor.

The Antiochean church commends Paul and Silas "to the grace of the Lord." The church in Antioch, in effect, commissions Paul and Silas for this second missionary journey. Nonetheless, at this time Paul is only planning to visit the believers in the towns where he and Barnabas had preached the gospel. After commending the missionaries to the Lord's grace, the brothers in Antioch send them on their way.

This second journey proves to be far more significant than Paul's first one: he brings the gospel from the continent of Asia to that of Europe when he eventually leaves Asia Minor and travels to Macedonia.

Luke is brief in his description of Paul's visit to the churches in Syria and Cilicia. First, the route leads through the city of Tarsus, which is home for Paul. Next, Silas is the letter carrier and is able to explain the apostolic decrees to the various churches they visit. And last, the mountain pass, the Cilician Gates, that provided access from Cilicia to the north and east must have been sufficiently safe that Paul and Silas were able to travel to Derbe and Lystra.

Practical Considerations in 15:36–41

Since the sixteenth-century Reformation, the church has suffered numerous divisions along either denominational, cultural, geographical, nationalistic, linguistic, doctrinal, ecclesiastical, or administrative lines. Justifications for a schism often reveal a declaration of adherence to truth at the expense of unity. Jesus' prayer for the unity of the church, "that they may be one" (John 17:22, NIV), sad to say, frequently goes unheeded. Separation seems to be the rule and unification the exception. Mergers at times occur only after years of consultation and review, while schisms emerge with surprising rapidity.

Sometimes ecclesiastical controversies arise not from doctrinal issues but from personality conflicts. The clash between Paul and Barnabas is a case in point. No one owed more to Barnabas for introducing him to the apostles in Jerusalem (9:27), for inviting him to teach in Antioch (11:25–26), and for providing companionship in Cyprus and Asia Minor than Paul. In the church of Jerusalem, the apostles had called Barnabas the "son of encouragement" (4:36). In turn, Barnabas depended on Paul to lead, preach, teach, and exhort. Barnabas knew that Paul had vision and adhered to principles.

Yet both men were human, as they themselves had said in Lystra (14:15).[75] They permitted anger to disrupt a friendship and bitterness to cause a division. Notwithstanding God's care and providence in using this incident for the progress of the

---

75. Bruce, *Book of the Acts*, p. 301.

gospel, Paul and Barnabas had to entertain sad memories of a fracture that both would rather have avoided.

Do we promote unity at the expense of truth? Not at all. As an anonymous writer put it: "When the Bible speaks about church unity, it speaks of unity not at the expense of truth but on the basis of it."

Greek Words, Phrases, and Constructions in 15:36–41

Verse 36

ἐπιστρέψαντες—this aorist participle assumes the same function as the main verb ἐπισκεψώμεθα (aorist active subjunctive). Together they convey the meaning of the hortatory subjunctive: "Let us return and visit."

αἷς—the antecedent of this relative pronoun in the feminine plural is the singular noun πόλιν (city). It is used distributively with the preposition κατά (in [every city]).[76]

Verses 37–38

συμπαραλαβεῖν—"to take along." This is the constative aorist, that is, it refers to the action in its entirety.[77] Note that Luke uses the same verb but in the present tense in verse 38.

The imperfect tense in the main verbs of both verses—ἐβούλετο (wanted) and ἠξίου (insisted)—indicates that the altercation was not limited to a momentary flash of anger.

Verse 39

ὥστε—with the aorist passive infinitive ἀποχωρισθῆναι (to separate) the adverb expresses actual result: "so that they separated."[78]

Verse 41

διήρχετο—the descriptive imperfect of the verb διέρχομαι (I go through) depicts Paul and Silas visiting and strengthening many churches.

Codex Bezae adds a clause: "delivering [to them] the commands of the elders."[79] But the authenticity of this addition is undermined by parallels in verses 22 and 23 and 16:4.

Summary of Chapter 15

In the church at Antioch some men from Judea teach that believers must be circumcised and adhere to the Mosaic law before they can be saved. Paul and Barnabas object to this teaching. The Antiochean church appoints

---

76. Moule, *Idiom-Book*, pp. 59–60.
77. H. E. Dana and Julius R. Mantey, *A Manual Grammar of the Greek New Testament* (1927; New York: Macmillan, 1967), p. 196.
78. Robertson, *Grammar*, p. 1091.
79. Metzger, *Textual Commentary*, p. 440.

them and others to present this matter to the apostles and elders in Jerusalem. On the way, the delegation travels through Phoenicia and Samaria and tells the churches about the conversion of Gentiles. And in Jerusalem its members report the work God has done through the missionaries.

The apostles and elders meet to discuss the question of circumcision and adherence to the law of Moses. Peter addresses them and points to the work God is doing among the Gentiles. He states that God makes no distinction between Jews and Gentiles. Hence, the yoke of the law, which even the Jews are unable to bear, ought not to be placed on the Gentiles. Salvation is through the grace of Jesus Christ.

After Paul and Barnabas have spoken, James addresses the assembly and declares that he agrees with Peter's presentation. James refers to the teaching of the Scriptures and then suggests that the Gentiles be asked to abstain from polluted food, fornication, meat from animals that were strangled, and blood. The entire council approves of this suggestion and appoints Judas and Silas to accompany Paul and Barnabas to Antioch to deliver the letter from the council. In Antioch, the people receive the letter, hear it read, and are glad. Judas and Silas leave but Paul and Barnabas stay.

Paul and Barnabas speak words of discord because John Mark, who had deserted the missionaries in Pamphylia, now wishes to accompany them. Their discord results in separation, so that Barnabas takes Mark and goes to Cyprus. Paul takes Silas and visits the churches in Syria and Cilicia.

16

The Second Missionary Journey, *part 2*

16:1–40

Outline (continued)

16:1–5	2. Derbe and Lystra
16:6–17:15	B. Macedonia
16:6–10	1. Macedonian Call
16:11–40	2. Philippi
16:11–12a	a. Arrival
16:12b–15	b. Worship
16:16–18	c. Exorcism
16:19–21	d. Arrest
16:22–24	e. Beating
16:25–30	f. Earthquake
16:31–34	g. Salvation
16:35–40	h. Departure

16 1 Paul came to Derbe and Lystra, where a certain disciple named Timothy lived. His mother was a Jewish believer and his father a Greek. 2 He was highly respected by the brothers in Lystra and Iconium. 3 Paul wanted Timothy to accompany him, so he took and circumcised Timothy, because the Jews in those places knew that his father was a Greek.

4 As they were traveling from town to town, they delivered the decisions that had been reached by the apostles and elders in Jerusalem, and which the people must observe. 5 So the churches were strengthened in the faith and were daily increasing in number.

---

2. Derbe and Lystra
16:1–5

In this section, Luke introduces Timothy, who becomes one of Paul's fellow workers, and relates the delivery of the apostolic decrees to the churches. He omits details that pertain to travel and to Paul's reception in Derbe and Lystra. Instead he records the development and growth of the churches.

1. Paul came to Derbe and Lystra, where a certain disciple named Timothy lived. His mother was a Jewish believer and his father a Greek. 2. He was highly respected by the brothers in Lystra and Iconium.

Luke's focus is on Paul, whom he portrays as in charge of the mission. Even though Silas is Paul's travel companion, Luke does not mention him until he records that these two missionaries are apprehended in Philippi (v. 19). He briefly reports that Paul arrives in Derbe (compare 14:6, 20) and later in Lystra (see 14:6, 8), a city located to the northwest of Derbe.

Lystra is the birthplace of Timothy (compare 20:4), whose mother was a Jewess and whose father was a Greek. Luke notes that Timothy was a disciple, that is, a Christian, and that Timothy's mother was a believer. From another source we know that his mother, Eunice, and grandmother Lois demonstrated sincere faith and taught Timothy, from infancy, the Holy Scriptures (II Tim. 1:5; 3:15). Possibly, Eunice and Lois became Christians when Paul and Barnabas preached the gospel in Lystra on their first missionary journey. In turn, they instructed Timothy, who, despite his youth, was held in high regard by the believers in both Lystra and Iconium. Paul seems to have had personal knowledge of Timothy's family, for he mentions his mother and grandmother by name.

Paul adopted Timothy as his spiritual son.[1] Timothy was fully acquainted with the persecutions Paul endured in Pisidian Antioch, Iconium, and Lystra (II Tim. 3:10–11). Perhaps he saw Paul being stoned in Lystra. This incident would have left an indelible mark on Timothy's memory.

How old was Timothy when Paul met him in Lystra? In his pastoral epistles, Paul admonishes Timothy not to take offense when people look down on him because of his youth (I Tim. 4:12). Paul wrote his first epistle to Timothy after his release from Roman imprisonment, probably in A.D. 64. This is fourteen years after Timothy became Paul's travel companion in Lystra. If Timothy was about twenty years of age at that time, then he would still be regarded a young man when he served the church at Ephesus and received Paul's epistle.

Luke writes that Timothy's mother was a Jewess who married a Greek. He provides no further information about Timothy's father, but he probably was an educated man who held a prominent position in Lystra. He was not a Jewish convert, for he had not allowed his son to be circumcised. Nor was he a Christian.

The Jews considered a mixed marriage illegal.[2] Similarly, Paul taught the Christians not to be yoked together with unbelievers but to marry in Christ (see II Cor. 6:14). Timothy's mother had married a Greek even though she knew the Scriptures.[3] As a daughter of Abraham, she had not fulfilled the law, for she neglected to have her son circumcised. Although the Christian brothers in Lystra and Iconium spoke well of Timothy, the Jews took offense because Timothy was not circumcised. The Jews regarded him to be outside the covenant God had made with Abraham and his descendants.

3. Paul wanted Timothy to accompany him, so he took and circumcised Timothy, because the Jews in those places knew that his father was a Greek.

Whenever Luke introduces a person who is an asset to the spread of the gospel, he provides a detailed introduction. (It is surprising, therefore, that Luke never mentions Titus, who, according to Paul's writings, proved to be a diligent and capable worker in Corinth and later in Crete.)[4] Luke indicates that Paul had an interest in young Timothy and wanted to take him along. Perhaps while he was in Lystra, Paul had already decided to extend his mission work beyond Iconium and therefore needed the services of Timothy.

Paul reminds Timothy that he had received the gift of prophecy when

---

1. I Cor. 4:17; I Tim. 1:2, 18; II Tim. 1:2.

2. SB, vol. 2, p. 741.

3. Refer to Gerald F. Hawthorne, "Timothy," *ISBE*, vol. 4, p. 857; Everett F. Harrison, *Interpreting Acts: The Expanding Church*, 2d ed. (Grand Rapids: Zondervan, Academie Books, 1986), p. 261.

4. II Cor. 2:13; 7:6, 13, 14; 8:6, 16, 23; 12:18; Gal. 2:1, 3; II Tim. 4:10; Titus 1:4. See also W. O. Walker, "The Timothy-Titus Problem Reconsidered," *ExpT* 92 (1981): 231–35.

the elders, including Paul, laid their hands on him and ordained him for missionary service.[5] The elders in Lystra and Iconium set Timothy aside for preaching and teaching the gospel.

However, Timothy, who was considered a Jew because of his Jewish mother and grandmother, was not acceptable to the Jews in that area. They knew his Greek father and also were aware that Timothy was uncircumcised. If both of his parents had been Gentiles, he would have encountered no difficulties. But as a son of a Jewess, Timothy was obliged to submit to circumcision. Without the mark of the covenant, he could not become an effective missionary to the Jews. To avoid any opposition from the Jews, Paul circumcised Timothy.

What an aberration for Paul, the apostle of Christian liberty! Consider for a moment the issues Paul had to face: the apostolic decrees did not demand circumcision (15:20, 29); Titus remains uncircumcised (Gal. 2:3); and Paul himself charged the Galatians (among whom were the people of Lystra) not to let themselves be circumcised (Gal. 5:2–3, 6; 6:15; see also I Cor. 7:19). Let us consider these issues one by one.

First, the Jerusalem Council did not demand circumcision of the Gentiles who turned to God (15:19). It exempted Gentile Christians, but not necessarily Jewish Christians, from the requirements of the Mosaic law.

Next, Paul took Titus to Jerusalem as a test case at the time of the Jerusalem Council. The council exempted Titus from the requirement of circumcision because he was a Gentile Christian. Titus's presence at the council proved the point: the Gentiles obtain salvation without becoming Jews.

Last, Paul tells the Galatians (including the believers in Lystra) that they are free in Christ and are not in bondage to the law of circumcision. God accepts a believer not on the basis of circumcision but because of faith expressed through love (Gal. 5:6, 13–14). Paul teaches the Galatians the same message: the Gentiles are free from the yoke of the law (15:10; Gal. 5:1).

In the case of Timothy, "being a good Christian did not mean being a bad Jew."[6] Paul himself wanted to be all things to all people, so that he might win both Jew and Gentile for Christ (I Cor. 9:19–23). He expected that Timothy, a fellow missionary, would do the same. Hence, Paul circumcised him to remove any hindrance to furthering the cause of Christ.[7]

4. As they were traveling from town to town, they delivered the decisions that had been reached by the apostles and elders in Jerusalem, and which the people must observe.

---

5. I Tim. 1:18; 4:14; II Tim. 1:6–7.

6. Richard N. Longenecker, *The Acts of the Apostles*, in vol. 9 of *The Expositor's Bible Commentary*, ed. Frank E. Gaebelein, 12 vols. (Grand Rapids: Zondervan, 1981), p. 455.

7. Ernst Haenchen contends that Luke depended on "unreliable tradition" when he wrote that Paul circumcised Timothy. *The Acts of the Apostles*, trans. Bernard Noble and Gerald Shinn (Philadelphia: Westminster, 1971), p. 482. But this is unlikely. Luke himself was a fellow traveler with Paul, Silas, and Timothy (16:10). Refer to Harrison, *Interpreting Acts*, p. 262.

Luke writes a general statement when he says that Paul and his companions traveled from town to town and delivered the apostolic decrees. We infer that the Judaizers, who had visited the church in Antioch and had been able to dissuade Peter and Barnabas from having table fellowship with Gentile Christians (Gal. 2:12–13), eventually followed Paul to the churches in south Galatia. In these churches, they insisted that Gentile Christians should observe the Mosaic law and be circumcised (Gal. 5:2–3; 6:12).[8]

To be precise, the Jerusalem Council had formulated a letter primarily for the benefit of the believers in Antioch. Yet Paul and Silas also took the letter to the churches in south Galatia to acquaint the Christians with the actions taken by the council. When the Judaizers visited the churches and led them astray, Paul had to write his epistle to the Galatians. We venture to say that Paul wrote his letter to the Galatian churches during his second missionary journey, presumably from Corinth, to avert the threat to the well-being of the Galatian Christians.[9]

The missionaries deliver the letter and instruct the readers to obey the apostolic decrees. In other words, they tell the believers to put into practice what the apostles and elders prescribed for Gentile Christians.

5. So the churches were strengthened in the faith and were daily increasing in number.

Here is a typical progress report that Luke often gives at the conclusion of a segment of his narrative (see, e.g., 2:47; 6:7; 9:31; 12:24). During their stay in south Galatia, the missionaries continue to instruct and encourage the believers. As a result, the believers are strengthened in the doctrines of the church. The word *faith* refers to objective faith, that is, doctrinal teaching, not the subjective faith of the individual believer.

The Greek indicates that both the strengthening in faith and the numerical increase of believers steadily progressed. No numbers are mentioned, but the result of the outreach among Gentiles is phenomenal. The Gentile church is rapidly developing.

Greek Words, Phrases, and Constructions in 16:1–5

Verses 1–2

Δέρβην—this city is mentioned first and Λύστραν second, for the missionaries are traveling in a westerly direction (see the reverse order in 14:6). Note that the plural form Λύστροις is used in verse 2. The plural is common with reference to cities.

ἐμαρτυρεῖτο—the imperfect tense of μαρτυρέω (I testify) is descriptive.

---

8. William Hendriksen, *Exposition of Galatians*, New Testament Commentary series (Grand Rapids: Baker, 1968), p. 19.

9. Although problems remain with the interpretation of this text, there is no reason to doubt its authenticity. All Greek manuscripts support the reading of this text. For an opposite view see F. F. Bruce, *The Book of the Acts*, rev. ed., New International Commentary on the New Testament (Grand Rapids: Eerdmans, 1988), p. 305.

Verses 3–4

ᾔδεισαν—the pluperfect tense takes the place of the imperfect tense in the verb οἶδα (I know). It introduces an indirect statement with the conjunction ὅτι (that) followed by the imperfect tense of ὑπῆρχεν (he was). The imperfect in this statement conveys the information that Timothy's father had died.[10] The use of the present tense in an indirect statement would have indicated that his father was living.

διεπορεύοντο—if Luke had written the preposition διά (through) after this compound verb, the direct object τὰς πόλεις (the cities) would have been in the genitive case. This verb ("they were going through") expresses direction but takes the object in the accusative.[11]

The Western manuscripts have an expanded version; the additions are italicized: "And while going through the cities *they preached [and delivered to them], with all boldness, the Lord Jesus Christ,* delivering *at the same time also* the commandments of the apostles. . . ."[12]

Verse 5

αἱ μὲν οὖν—the combination of the definite article and the two particles μὲν οὖν (therefore) occurs eighteen times in Acts and generally introduces summary statements.

---

6 They went through the region of Phrygia and Galatia, having been prevented by the Holy Spirit from speaking the word in the province of Asia. 7 And when they came to Mysia, they tried to enter Bithynia, but the Spirit of Jesus did not permit them to go. 8 Having bypassed Mysia, they went down to Troas.

9 One night Paul had a vision of a Macedonian man who was standing and begging him, "Come over to Macedonia and help us." 10 After Paul had seen the vision, we immediately prepared to leave for Macedonia, concluding that God had called us to preach the gospel to them.

11 We put out to sea from Troas and sailed straight to Samothrace, and on the next day to Neapolis. 12 From there we went to the Roman colony of Philippi, which is a leading city of that district of Macedonia. We stayed in that city for several days. 13 On the Sabbath, we went outside the city gate to the river, where we thought we would find a place of prayer. We sat down and spoke with the women who had assembled there. 14 And a woman named Lydia, a seller of purple cloth from the city of Thyatira, was listening as a worshiper of God. The Lord opened her heart to respond to the words spoken by Paul. 15 After she and the members of her household had been baptized, she urged us, "If you consider me to be faithful to the Lord, enter my house and stay." And she convinced us.

16 While we were on our way to the place of prayer, a slave girl who had a spirit of divination met us. She was bringing her masters much profit by fortune-telling. 17 She followed Paul and us, crying out, "These men are servants of the Most High God, who are proclaiming to you the way of salvation." 18 She continued to do this for many days. But Paul

---

10. Friedrich Blass and Albert Debrunner, *A Greek Grammar of the New Testament and Other Early Christian Literature,* trans. and rev. Robert Funk (Chicago: University of Chicago Press, 1961), #330.

11. C. F. D. Moule, *An Idiom-Book of New Testament Greek,* 2d ed. (Cambridge: Cambridge University Press, 1960), p. 91.

12. Bruce M. Metzger, *A Textual Commentary on the Greek New Testament,* 3d corrected ed. (London and New York: United Bible Societies, 1975), p. 441. Consult Édouard Delebecque, "De Lystres à Philippes (Ac 16) avec le *codex Bezae,*" *Bib* 63 (1982): 395–405.

became greatly annoyed, turned, and said to the spirit, "I command you in the name of Jesus Christ to come out of her." And the spirit left her that very moment.

19 When her masters realized that their hope of profit was gone, they seized Paul and Silas and dragged them into the market before the authorities. 20 They brought them to the magistrates and said, "These men as Jews are throwing our city into confusion. 21 They are proclaiming customs which we as Romans cannot accept or observe." 22 The crowd joined in the attack against Paul and Silas. The magistrates ordered them to be stripped and beaten with rods. 23 And when they had inflicted many blows on them, they threw them into prison. They commanded the jailer to guard them securely. 24 When he received these orders, the jailer threw Paul and Silas into the inner prison and fastened their feet in the stocks.

25 At midnight Paul and Silas were praying and singing hymns to God, while the other prisoners were listening. 26 Suddenly there was a violent earthquake so that the foundations of the prison were shaken. At once, all the doors were opened and all the chains were loosed. 27 When the jailer woke up and saw the opened prison doors, he drew his sword, intending to kill himself. He thought that the prisoners had escaped. 28 Paul loudly cried out, "Do yourself no harm, for we are all here." 29 The jailer called for lights and rushed in, trembling with fear. He fell down before Paul and Silas. 30 He brought them out and asked, "Sirs, what must I do to be saved?"

31 Paul and Silas replied, "Believe in the Lord Jesus, and you and the members of your household will be saved." 32 And they proclaimed the word of the Lord to him and all who were in his household. 33 At that hour of the night the jailer took them and washed their wounds. Immediately he and all his household were baptized. 34 The jailer brought Paul and Silas into his house and fed them. He rejoiced greatly because he and his family believed in God.

35 When it was day, the magistrates sent their officers with the message, "Release those men." 36 The jailer reported these words to Paul and said, "The magistrates have sent to release you. Now, then, go in peace." 37 But Paul said to them, "They have beaten us publicly without a trial and thrown us into prison, even though we are Roman citizens. And now do they send us away secretly? No, let them come themselves and bring us out!"

38 The officers reported this to the magistrates. When they heard that Paul and Silas were Roman citizens, they began to worry. 39 They came to the prison and apologized. They brought them out and begged them to leave the city. 40 And after Paul and Silas left the prison, they went to the house of Lydia, where they met with the brothers. Then they encouraged them and departed.

B. Macedonia
16:6–17:15

1. Macedonian Call
16:6–10

Paul, Silas, and Timothy work in the churches of south Galatia and then decide to preach the gospel in areas other than south-central Asia Minor. Their plans are to travel in a westerly direction and, dependent on the Holy Spirit for guidance, to extend Christ's church in a predominantly Gentile world.

Paul's missionary strategy is to preach the gospel in important cities, preferably in commercial and administrative centers from which the Word of God can radiate in all directions. From the text we learn that Paul had planned to go west into the province of Asia (the western part of Turkey).

We surmise that he wanted to visit Ephesus, a city located south of the Cäyster River near the Aegean Sea. But Luke reports that the Holy Spirit prevented the missionaries from entering this province. Some years later, during his third missionary journey, Paul would minister to the people of the province of Asia and particularly to those living in Ephesus (19:1–12).

6. They went through the region of Phrygia and Galatia, having been prevented by the Holy Spirit from speaking the word in the province of Asia. 7. And when they came to Mysia, they tried to enter Bithynia, but the Spirit of Jesus did not permit them to go. 8. Having bypassed Mysia, they went down to Troas.

We discuss the following areas:

a. *Phrygia and Galatia.* Instead of going straight west, Paul, Silas, and Timothy, obedient to the Spirit's direction, travel through the region known as Phrygia and Galatia. Scholars posit two explanations of the phrase *Phrygia and Galatia.* Those who support what is called the northern Galatian theory assert that Phrygia was a distinct district in which the cities of Pisidian Antioch and Iconium were located. Traveling north, the missionaries would then enter the Roman province of Galatia, also known as Old Galatia. Presumably they visited the cities of Pessinus, Ancyra [modern Ankara], and Tavium on their way to Troas (v. 8) and established churches in these places. However, the New Testament does not mention any churches in this part of Galatia. Writes Herman N. Ridderbos, "The possibility that the North Galatian hypothesis concerns itself with fictitious congregations cannot be ruled out."[13]

Proponents of the southern Galatian theory point out that the Greek uses the words *Phrygia* and *Galatia* as adjectives that describe the noun *region:* "the Phrygian and Galatian region."[14] The adjectives refer to a region in the southern half of the Roman province of Galatia, which was inhabited by Phrygians.

Evidence for the southern Galatian theory is decisive. First, Phrygia was an area populated by thousands of Jews,[15] who introduced the teaching of the Old Testament to Gentiles. This knowledge and teaching of the Scriptures contributed to the spread of the gospel. Second, Luke mentions Phrygia as one of the nations represented at Pentecost (2:10). Galatia was settled by people who, in the third century B.C., had migrated from Gaul in Europe to Bithynia in Asia Minor. The Romans made the area in which the Galatians lived into a province which extended from Bithynia and Pontus

---

13. Herman N. Ridderbos, "Galatians, Epistle to the," *ISBE,* vol. 2, p. 380; see also Lorman M. Petersen, "Galatians, Epistle to," *ZPEB,* vol. 2, p. 634.

14. Colin J. Hemer, "The Adjective 'Phrygia,' " *JTS* 27 (1976): 122–26; "Phrygia: A Further Note," *JTS* 28 (1977): 99–101; *The Book of Acts in the Setting of Hellenistic History,* ed. Conrad H. Gempf (Tübingen: Mohr, 1989), p. 112; "Phrygia," *ISBE,* vol. 3, pp. 862–63.

15. Josephus reports that Antiochus III (223–187 B.C.) transported two thousand Jewish families from Mesopotamia and Babylon to Phrygia. *Antiquities* 12.3.4 [149].

in the north to Phrygia and Lycaonia in the south. Southern Galatia, then, was a multiracial area, and Paul's mission strategy was to preach the gospel primarily in such areas. For this reason many scholars are reluctant to suggest that Paul brought the gospel exclusively to Gentiles in the northern part of Galatia.

b. *Mysia and Bithynia.* The Holy Spirit guides the missionaries in their travels. How he communicated his will to the travelers is not known; perhaps Silas, who was a prophet (15:32), received directives from the Spirit. Even though Luke uses the phrase *Spirit of Jesus* as a synonym for the Holy Spirit, the phrase itself is "indicative of the continued work of the risen Christ through the Spirit. The Spirit is the representative of Jesus."[16]

Traveling in a northwesterly direction, the missionaries come to the border of Mysia, a region in the northwest corner of Asia Minor. From there they try to go northward to Bithynia (compare I Peter 1:1), but the Spirit, who had already prevented them from entering the province of Asia, keeps them from going to Bithynia as well. (In time, however, Bithynia became a stronghold of the Christian church and the site of significant church council meetings [e.g., First Council of Nicaea, A.D. 325; Fourth General Council of Chalcedon, A.D. 451].) Paul and his companions must travel to the harbor city of Troas on the Aegean Sea.

c. *Troas.* The city of Troas, situated some ten miles south of ancient Troy, was in the western part of Mysia. A Roman colony, it served as the European gateway to Asia Minor and the departure point for Macedonia. Luke relates that the missionaries went down to Troas; that is, they left the higher elevations of Mysia and descended to sea level. They bypassed Mysia, in the sense that they did not stay to proclaim the Word in that region. The Spirit told them to travel west to Troas instead of going east into Bithynia. In later years, Paul frequently visited Troas and preached the gospel (20:5–6; II Cor. 2:12; II Tim. 4:13).

9. One night Paul had a vision of a Macedonian man who was standing and begging him, "Come over to Macedonia and help us." 10. After Paul had seen the vision, we immediately prepared to leave for Macedonia, concluding that God had called us to preach the gospel to them.

a. "Paul had a vision of a Macedonian man." The command to go down to Troas comes from the Spirit of Jesus, who, by blocking the way to the provinces of Asia and Bithynia, directs the missionaries to develop the church elsewhere. He is fully in control and in Troas informs Paul what to do next. Jesus gives Paul instructions that are sufficient for the need of the hour.

During the night Paul has a vision—an experience common to Peter,

---

16. Donald Guthrie, *New Testament Theology* (Downers Grove: Inter-Varsity, 1981), p. 547. Consult also W. P. Bowers, "Paul's Route Through Mysia: A Note on Acts XVI. 8," *JTS* 30 (1979): 507–11.

Paul, and others.[17] In Paul's vision at Troas, Jesus neither speaks to him directly nor sends an angel. Instead Paul sees a man who calls out to him, "Come over to Macedonia and help us." We suspect that Paul ascertained the man's nationality from his speech and dress.

Macedonia in the first century extended east to west from the Aegean Sea to the Adriatic Sea. To the north were Illyricum and Thracia and to the south, Achaia (Greece). Ruled by the Romans, the people of Macedonia spoke Greek and so were able to communicate with the inhabitants of Asia Minor. For Paul and his associates, therefore, the adjustment of moving from one continent (Asia) to the next (Europe) was relatively smooth.

b. "Come over to Macedonia and help us." What is the meaning of the Macedonian's request? The first part of his plea ("come over to Macedonia") refers to crossing the Aegean Sea (see v. 11). The second part of the plea is a request for help. The verb has the connotation of coming to one's aid; for instance, the father of the epileptic boy beseeched Jesus, "Help me in my lack of faith" (Mark 9:24). The request, then, is for spiritual help. The Macedonian man indicates that he is not alone; he is speaking on behalf of his countrymen. This plea comes from people who are ready to receive the gospel.

c. "We immediately prepared to leave for Macedonia." Paul relates the vision to his companions and together they follow the divine direction to go to Macedonia.

In this verse, the hand of the writer of Acts is obvious: with the pronoun *we* he identifies himself as a participant in the missionaries' deliberations. How Paul and Luke met is not known; modesty prevents Luke from providing personal information about his faith, skills, and talents. From a second-century source (the anti-Marcionite Prologue to Luke's Gospel) we know that Luke was a native of Antioch in Syria; from Scripture we know that he was a physician (see Col. 4:14). Perhaps Luke met Paul in Antioch, although Luke does not indicate that fact in the text. The phrase *God had called us* seems to convey that Luke was not a recent convert who first associated with Paul in Troas.[18] But Luke fails to relate further details, and so we must stay with the text.

Beginning with this reference to Troas, Luke uses the pronoun *we* in numerous places.[19] Even in those passages in which Luke writes in the third person, he nevertheless shows that he witnessed the events he records (see, e.g., Acts 20:4–5).[20]

---

17. Acts 9:10, 12; 10:3, 17, 19; 11:5; 12:9; 16:9, 10; 18:9.

18. Richard B. Rackham, *The Acts of the Apostles: An Exposition*, Westminster Commentary series (1901; reprint ed., Grand Rapids: Baker, 1964), p. 273.

19. Acts 16:10–17; 20:1–15; 21:1–18; 27:1–28:16.

20. Henry Alford, *Alford's Greek Testament: An Exegetical and Critical Commentary*, 7th ed., 4 vols. (1877; Grand Rapids: Guardian, 1976), vol. 2, p. 176; Otto Glombitza, "Der Schritte nach Europa: Erwägungen zu Act 16, 9–15," *ZNW* 53 (1962): 77–82.

Practical Considerations in 16:6–10

God's call to Isaiah at the time of King Uzziah's death, "Whom shall I send? And who will go for us?" (Isa. 6:8a, NIV), is heard today by many Christians. Some of them respond with the same word spoken by Isaiah: "Here am I. Send me!" (Isa. 6:8b, NIV). They demonstrate a willingness to serve the Lord and advance his cause.

However, the danger is that some Christians begin working for the Lord without waiting patiently for his orders. Thus, these willing laborers are of the opinion that the Lord should be pleased with their services. Yet they have failed to pause in prayer and ask where God wants them to work and what he expects them to do.

Paul and his companions waited for the Spirit of Jesus to tell them where to minister. They were prevented from going either west or north; they had to go to Troas. There in a vision Paul received instructions to sail for Europe. By waiting patiently for divine directions, Paul and his associates were recipients of God's indispensable blessings.

> Patient waiting is often
> the highest way
> of doing God's will.
> —Jeremy Collier

Greek Words, Phrases, and Constructions in 16:6 and 9

Verse 6

τὴν . . . χώραν—the definite article modifies the noun *region*. The noun is qualified by the adjectives *Phrygian* and *Galatian*.

κωλυθέντες—this aorist passive participle from κωλύω (I hinder) can be taken either as an action that happened prior to that of the main verb ("they went through") or as a causal clause ("because they were prevented").[21]

Verse 9

Western witnesses elaborate on the reading of this verse. The changes are in italics: "And *in* a vision in the night, there appeared to Paul, *as it were* a man from Macedonia, standing *before his face*, beseeching and saying."[22]

2. Philippi
16:11–40

Paul and his partners are about to enter Macedonia and travel to a leading city, Philippi, where they worship with God-fearing women on the Sabbath. They also cast out a demon from a slave girl and suffer the consequences. In this city the gospel takes root and a church is formed.

---

21. Moule, *Idiom-Book*, p. 100.
22. Metzger, *Textual Commentary*, p. 443.

a. Arrival
16:11–12a

11. We put out to sea from Troas and sailed straight to Samothrace, and on the next day to Neapolis. 12a. From there we went to the Roman colony of Philippi, which is a leading city of that district of Macedonia.

1. "From Troas." Paul and his companions apparently encounter no difficulty in obtaining passage aboard a ship that will take them to Neapolis (modern Kavalla). The wind is favorable, so that by the evening of the first day they arrive at the island called Samothrace. Comments Howard F. Vos, "The island had no harbor—only an unsafe anchorage on its north side— but the hazards of sailing by night generally forced mariners to anchor somewhere if possible."[23] This mountainous island, which is about halfway between Europe and Asia Minor, has a peak that rises fifty-nine hundred feet above sea level and serves as a landmark.

On the next day the ship continues its voyage and arrives at Neapolis, a harbor city in Macedonia. Favorable winds shorten the voyage to two days; contrary winds can lengthen it to five days (see, e.g., 20:6). The missionaries set out for Philippi, which lies about ten miles northwest of Neapolis.

2. "The Roman colony of Philippi." The travelers journey along the Roman-built Egnatian Road, a highway that extended four hundred miles from the east coast to the west coast of Macedonia. After leaving Neapolis, Paul and his companions ascend to a broad plateau that is exceptionally fertile and in summer lush and green. Within a few hours, they see Philippi (literally, "of Philip"; Philip II, the father of Alexander the Great, had renamed the city). At one time, the area was known for its gold mines that produced more than one thousand talents of gold annually.[24] The Romans conquered Philippi in 168 B.C. and garnered the revenue from the mines.

In 42 B.C. Philippi was the site of a decisive battle in which Mark Antony and Octavian defeated Brutus and Cassius, the assassins of Julius Caesar. Octavian, who later assumed the name *Augustus,* became the first Roman emperor. Philippi became a Roman colony. Augustus granted the right of Italian law to Philippi, and the city's administration was modeled after that of Rome. Many military veterans settled in this Roman colony. As Roman citizens, they were protected by Roman law, were exempt from scourging, and had the right of appeal in case of arrest (see v. 37). In brief, "the colonists enjoyed the same rights and privileges as if their land were part of Italy."[25]

3. "A leading city." The Greek text is ambiguous at this point: the word *leading* can be taken with either the term *city* (e.g., "Philippi . . . *the* leading city of that district of Macedonia" [NIV, italics added]) or the noun *district.*

---

23. Howard F. Vos, "Samothrace," *ISBE,* vol. 4, p. 309.
24. Diodorus Siculus 16.8.6.
25. Lake and Cadbury, *Beginnings,* vol. 4, p. 187.

Translators usually opt for the first alternative because the manuscript evidence is strong. But the objection to this reading is that Thessalonica, not Philippi, was the capital of Macedonia. The suggestion that Philippi was the *first* city Paul visited is definitely inaccurate. Paul came first to Neapolis, if we assume that this municipality was in the same district as Philippi.

According to the Roman historiographer Livy, the Romans had divided Macedonia into four districts and Amphipolis was the capital of the first district.[26] Thus, scholars prefer to accept the second alternative: "Philippi, a city in the first district of Macedonia" (GNB).[27] Although this reading is preferred, it lacks Greek manuscript support and thus is nothing more than a conjecture. A basic rule of interpretation is to accept a conjecture only when the original text is unintelligible. This is not quite the case in this instance, for it is possible to translate the text: "Philippi, *a* leading city in the region of Macedonia."[28] The expression *leading* perhaps refers to the educational facilities (a famous school of medicine) and the flourishing economy (proceeds from the gold mines) of Philippi, rather than its administrative function.

Greek Words, Phrases, and Contructions in 16:11–12a

Verse 11

τῇ ἐπιούσῃ—"the next day." However, the phrase *the first day* is understood.

Νέαν Πόλιν—instead of the single word Νεάπολιν, the classical form of two words is preferred.

Verse 12a

πρώτη μερίδος τῆς Μακεδονίας πόλις—this reading has strong support from Greek manuscripts. Without the definite article before πρώτη, this adjective can be interpreted as indefinite: "a leading city." The definite article preceding μερίδος is equivalent to the demonstrative pronoun *that:* "of that division of Macedonia."[29]

---

b. Worship
16:12b–15

12b. We stayed in that city for several days. 13. On the Sabbath, we went outside the city gate to the river, where we thought we would find a place of prayer. We sat down and spoke with the women who had assembled there.

---

26. Livy *Annals* 45.29.
27. For instance, Bruce, *Book of the Acts,* pp. 308–9; see also his article "St. Paul in Macedonia," *BJRUL* 61 (1979): 337–54; and consult Hemer, *Book of Acts,* p. 113.
28. Lake and Cadbury, *Beginnings,* vol. 4, p. 188. Consult Bauer, p. 505; and Metzger, *Textual Commentary,* p. 446.
29. Moule, *Idiom-Book,* p. 111.

The construction of the Greek text suggests that Paul and his fellow workers remained in Philippi for some time. The translation *for several days* apparently signifies a longer period than four or five days. In context, Luke is interested in relating the missionaries' experience on the first Sabbath in Philippi. He shows that after this experience, Paul and his companions continued their stay.

In Philippi the missionaries encountered a population that was overwhelmingly Roman. We conclude that Jews were noticeably few, for there is no mention of a local synagogue. According to the rabbis, ten Jewish (male) heads of families were able to establish a synagogue.[30]

On the Sabbath, the missionaries go outside the city and proceed to the Gangites River, where they expect people to meet for prayer. "The Jews' place of worship may have been determined by the Roman practice of tolerating, but sometimes excluding from colonial limits, religious practices that were inconsistent with their state."[31] (Moreover, synagogues outside the city limits usually were built near water, which was necessary for ablutions.)

At the river Paul and his friends meet a number of women who gather for Sabbath prayer. Where are the men to conduct the worship service? Consider that about this time, in A.D. 49, Emperor Claudius had expelled the Jews from Rome because they had been blamed for creating a religious disturbance (18:2). We surmise that the Roman colony of Philippi had followed Claudius's example and banished the Jews.[32] When Paul and Silas eventually are arrested in Philippi, they are accused of being Jews who are throwing the city into confusion (v. 20). This accusation parallels the charges made against the Jews in Rome.

The women welcome the visiting missionaries and expect from them an exposition of the Scriptures. With his friends, Paul sits down and begins to teach the gospel to these women. Although the group is small, the presence of the Lord is powerful, as Luke relates in the next verse.

14. And a woman named Lydia, a seller of purple cloth from the city of Thyatira, was listening as a worshiper of God. The Lord opened her heart to respond to the words spoken by Paul.

1. *Lydia's response.* One of the women present at the place of prayer is called Lydia. Her roots are in Thyatira (Rev. 1:11; 2:18, 24), a city located in the district of Lydia in western Asia Minor. We suspect that Lydia's name derived from the descriptive phrase *the Lydian lady.* We are unable to determine what her real name was. And we resist the temptation to speculate that she was either Euodia or Syntyche, whom Paul admonished to be at peace with each other in the Philippian church (Phil. 4:2).

Lydia had left Thyatira, crossed the Aegean Sea, and taken up residence

---

30. Mishnah, *Sanhedrin* 1.2a; *Aboth* 3.6.
31. Gerald L. Borchert, "Philippi," *ISBE*, vol. 3, p. 836.
32. Compare R. C. H. Lenski, *The Interpretation of the Acts of the Apostles* (Columbus: Wartburg, 1944), p. 655.

in Philippi as a seller of purple cloth. The purple dye applied to fine linen was obtained from the secretion of shellfish (mollusks) that live in the eastern part of the Mediterranean Sea. "Since approximately eight thousand molluscs were required to produce one gram of purple dye, purple cloth was extremely expensive."[33] Purple garments were worn by emperors and by private citizens as a status symbol. In Rome, purple stoles were attached to senatorial togas. We conclude, then, that Lydia belonged to the class of wealthy merchants and was the owner of a large house (vv. 15, 40).

In Thyatira, Lydia had become a believer in Israel's God and, as a Gentile, was classified as a God-fearer (10:2; 13:16, 26, 50). That is, the Jews had not fully accepted her as a convert. In Philippi, she faithfully worshiped on the Sabbath at the place of prayer. When Paul taught the gospel of Christ, she listened attentively to his words.

2. *The Lord's work.* The exalted Christ prepared Lydia through the synagogue teaching of the Old Testament. Now he sent Paul and the other missionaries to Philippi so that Lydia was able to hear the message of salvation. Luke ascribes to the Lord, not to Paul, the act of saving Lydia. Salvation, then, is not man's work but the Lord's. Not the word itself, but the Lord himself (Luke 24:45), opens the human heart. The result is that Lydia responds to Paul's message and accepts the Lord as her Savior.

15. After she and the members of her household had been baptized, she urged us, "If you consider me to be faithful to the Lord, enter my house and stay." And she convinced us.

Luke's description of the events is rather brief. Therefore, we assume that after the missionaries hear a profession of faith in Jesus Christ from the lips of Lydia, she and the members of her household are baptized in the Gangites River. Who performed the baptism? Perhaps Silas, Timothy, or Luke, for Paul himself baptized few people (I Cor. 1:14–16). And who are the members of Lydia's household? They are her immediate family members, but also her servants who reside under her roof. The fact that she and the members of her extended family come to the place of prayer depicts Lydia as a God-fearing woman whose spiritual influence permeates her entire household. She is the head of the family and teaches God's Word to her children (refer to I Cor. 7:14) and servants. Lydia professes her faith and is baptized, and the members of her household follow her example. Luke is interested not in providing details about Lydia's family but in portraying Lydia's household as the core of the emerging church of Philippi. The building blocks of the church are families and individuals.

Lydia wants to express her gratitude to Paul and his companions and urges them to stay with her. Note that a Gentile woman is asking four men

---

33. Dorothy Irvin, "Purple," *ISBE*, vol. 3, p. 1057. For the contrasting view that purple was made from the root of the Eurasian herb called madder, see Robert North, "Thyatira," *ISBE*, vol. 4, p. 846. See also Rosalie Ryan, "Lydia, A Dealer in Purple Goods," *BibToday* 22 (1984): 285–89.

(three Jews and one Gentile) to be her guests. She says, "If you consider me to be faithful to the Lord, enter my house and stay." In Greek, this conditional sentence conveys a positive fact. Lydia indicates that the missionaries indeed consider her a believer in the Lord Jesus Christ because they have accepted her testimony sealed by her baptism. Lydia prevails and the missionaries take up lodging in her house. Here they continue teaching Christ's gospel and enlarge the church.

Doctrinal Considerations in 16:14

Luke clearly teaches that salvation is the work of the Lord, for he saves his people according to his eternal plan. Recording Peter's Pentecost sermon, Luke states that Jesus suffered on the cross "according to God's set purpose and foreknowledge" (2:23; and see 4:28). When the Gentiles in Pisidian Antioch hear the saving Word of God and express their happiness, Luke observes: "And as many as were ordained to eternal life believed" (13:48). Luke truthfully conveys the teaching that God, in accomplishing his work of salvation, fulfills his eternal plan.

Salvation originates with God. Thus, the Lord opened Lydia's heart to have her pay close attention to the words Paul was speaking. God granted Lydia a receptive heart to understand spiritual things. He gave her the gift of faith and the illumination of the Holy Spirit. Concludes John Albert Bengel, "The heart is in itself closed, but it is the prerogative of God to open it."[34]

In Greek, Luke employs different verb tenses to emphasize God's work in salvation. In this translation, the changes in tense are italicized: "While Lydia *continued to listen,* God *once for all opened* her heart *to have her apply* her mind to the things that *were being said* by Paul." Conclusively, God is the author of her salvation.

Greek Words, Phrases, and Constructions in 16:12b–15

Verse 12b

ἦμεν—the position of the verb *to be* in the imperfect is emphatic. Further, with the present participle διατρίβοντες (spending), the imperfect forms a periphrastic construction and denotes a protracted period.

Verse 13

σαββάτων—in plural form, the word is a Hebraic plural that refers to a single day (see 13:14).

οὗ ἐνομίζομεν προσευχὴν εἶναι—"where we thought would be a place of prayer." The variations in the manuscripts are overwhelming. The New King James Version adopts the reading οὗ ἐνομίζετο προσευχὴ εἶναι and translates, "where prayer was customarily made." The noun προσευχή means "prayer" or "place of prayer."

34. John Albert Bengel, *Gnomon of the New Testament,* ed. Andrew R. Fausset, 5 vols. (Edinburgh: Clark, 1877), vol. 2, p. 657; see also John Calvin, *Commentary on the Acts of the Apostles,* ed. David W. Torrance and Thomas F. Torrance, 2 vols. (Grand Rapids: Eerdmans, 1966), vol. 2, p. 73; Guthrie, *New Testament Theology,* p. 618.

Verse 14

The sequence of Greek tenses is unique and purposeful—ἤκουεν (imperfect: she kept listening), διήνοιξεν (aorist: [the Lord] opened), and προσέχειν (present infinitive of purpose: to pay attention to).

Verse 15

παρεκάλεσεν—from παρακαλέω (I beseech), the aorist tense implies insistence. Lydia insisted, as is evident from the aorist verb παρεβιάσατο (she urged strongly).

εἰ—this particle, followed by the perfect indicative κεκρίκατε (you have judged) is the protasis of a simple-fact condition. Lydia confidently expresses reality.

---

c. Exorcism
16:16–18

Indirectly Luke reveals that Paul and his associates continued their work for an extended period. He indicates that on a given day, the missionaries went to the place of prayer. But instead of describing the service, he relates the incident of Paul casting out a demon from a slave girl.

16. While we were on our way to the place of prayer, a slave girl who had a spirit of divination met us. She was bringing her masters much profit by fortunetelling. 17. She followed Paul and us, crying out, "These men are servants of the Most High God, who are proclaiming to you the way of salvation."

We make two observations:

1. *Opposition.* Luke writes that the missionaries are on their way to "the place of prayer." In the Greek, he says "*the* prayer," which refers not to the act of praying but to the place of meeting (see v. 13).

Wherever the church develops, Satan tries to obstruct the work of God's servants. For instance, in Samaria Simon the sorcerer offered Peter and John money to obtain the gift of the Holy Spirit (8:18–19); on the island of Cyprus, Elymas opposed Paul and Barnabas by trying to persuade the proconsul Sergius Paulus not to believe in Jesus Christ (13:7–8). Likewise, in Philippi Satan uses a demon-possessed girl to thwart the work of the missionaries.

On the way to the place of prayer, a slave girl who has a spirit of divination meets the missionaries. In the Greek, Luke writes that she has a spirit called Python, which translators render "divination."[35] The word *Python* referred to the legendary snake that guarded the Delphic Oracle, a sanctuary in central Greece, but was slain by the god of prophecy, Apollo. In later years, the term denoted a spirit of divination that dwelled in a medium. As the priestess of Apollo at Delphi was able to predict the future, so this slave girl served her masters in Philippi as a fortuneteller. She was an instrument

---

35. J. Stafford Wright, *NIDNTT*, vol. 2, pp. 558–59; Werner Foerster, *TDNT*, vol. 6, p. 920; Bauer, pp. 728–29.

of demons who used her as a mouthpiece,[36] and she was a lucrative source of income for her owners (see **Greek Words, Phrases, and Constructions in 16:16–18**). In this demon-possessed slave girl at Philippi, we see a parallel to the demoniacs Jesus encountered during his ministry (e.g., Mark 1:24).

2. *Acknowledgment.* The slave girl follows the missionaries; shouting loudly, she informs the public about the identity of Paul and his companions: "These men are servants of the Most High God, who are proclaiming to you the way of salvation." In itself, this confession is noble, provided it comes from the heart of a believer and in the form of a declaration of faith. But the acknowledgment comes indirectly from Satan, who, by using this girl, is trying to diminish the effectiveness of Paul's ministry. However, Paul does not ask the girl to predict the future for him; instead, he sees the forces of Satan at work in a defenseless slave girl. Indeed, if Paul had accepted Satan's testimony without discernment, he would have given the devil credit and thus approved his motives.[37]

18. She continued to do this for many days. But Paul became greatly annoyed, turned, and said to the spirit, "I command you in the name of Jesus Christ to come out of her." And the spirit left her that very moment.

We suspect that the shouts of the girl caused numerous people to gather and listen to Paul and his friends. Everyone could hear the message of salvation. But the continual shouting of the girl became a hindrance to Paul in the preaching of the gospel, and the distraction so perturbed him that he had to intervene and address the demon residing in the girl.

Paul confronts the demon in the name of Jesus Christ. That is, on the authority Jesus has given him he tells the demon to leave the girl. Paul calls on the name of Jesus in the same way Peter did for the healing of the cripple in the temple area of Jerusalem (3:6). As Jesus healed the demon-possessed people in Israel so, through his servant Paul, he casts out the demon from the slave girl in Philippi. As Jesus gave the apostles power over unclean spirits (Mark 6:7) so he endows Paul with that same authority.[38] The result is that the demon instantly leaves the girl. Her owners lose a valuable source of income, but we assume that the girl received the gift of salvation and became a member of the Philippian church.

---

36. Hans Conzelmann rules out ventriloquism; "the use of the verb *krazō* 'to cry out,' in [verse] 17 is appropriate for spirit possession." *Acts of the Apostles,* trans. James Limburg, A. Thomas Kraabel, and Donald H. Juel (1963; Philadelphia: Fortress, 1987), p. 131.

37. Calvin, *Acts of the Apostles,* vol. 2, p. 76; F. W. Grosheide, *De Handelingen der Apostelen,* Kommentaar op het Nieuwe Testament series, 2 vols. (Amsterdam: Van Bottenburg, 1948), vol. 2, p. 96.

38. When Jesus was on earth, demons cried out because they recognized him as the Son of the Most High God (Mark 5:7; Luke 8:28). The title *Most High God* was used by both Jews and Greeks; in his Gospel and Acts, Luke uses the expression *Most High* seven times with reference to God: Luke 1:32, 35, 76; 6:35; 8:28; Acts 7:48; 16:17. In the Septuagint, the term generally refers to God. Consult Georg Bertram, *TDNT,* vol. 8, pp. 617–19.

Greek Words, Phrases, and Constructions in 16:16–18

Verse 16

πορευομένων ἡμῶν—"while we were on our way." With the personal pronoun in the genitive case, this present participle forms the genitive absolute construction.

πύθωνα—the reading in the accusative singular is harder to explain than πύθωνος (genitive) and therefore is preferred. The noun stands in apposition to πνεῦμα (a spirit, namely, a Python).

τοῖς κυρίοις—although the noun is in the masculine plural, the noun possibly refers to a husband and wife who own the slave girl.

Verse 17

Παύλῳ καὶ ἡμῖν—Luke features Paul as the leader; the pronoun *us* includes Silas, Timothy, and Luke. Compare 21:18 and 28:16.[39]

ὑμῖν—"to you." The context favors this reading; it has strong manuscript support. The alternate reading is "to us" (NKJV).

Verse 18

ἐποίει—"she kept on doing." This is the iterative use of the imperfect tense.

ἐπί—the preposition followed by the accusative denotes time and extent.[40]

παραγγέλλω—the present tense has an aoristic meaning: "I command you once for all."

---

d. Arrest
16:19–21

When Jesus cast out a demon, the people expressed their amazement at the miracle (see Mark 1:27). But when Paul set the slave girl free from her soothsaying spirit, her owners reacted violently and arrested Paul and Silas.

19. When her masters realized that their hope of profit was gone, they seized Paul and Silas and dragged them into the market before the authorities. 20. They brought them to the magistrates and said, "These men as Jews are throwing our city into confusion. 21. They are proclaiming customs which we as Romans cannot accept or observe."

Realizing that their earnings from the girl's fortunetelling have ended, the owners of the girl vent their anger on Paul and Silas. Enraged, they grab the missionaries and drag them into the marketplace to bring them before the rulers of the city. Why Paul and Silas? These two men are Jews, which cannot be said of the other two—both Timothy and Luke are considered Gentiles, even though Timothy could claim a Jewish heritage (v. 1).

---

39. Consult H. J. Cadbury, " 'We' and 'I' Passages in Luke-Acts," *NTS* 3 (1957): 128–32. Refer to Vernon K. Robbins, "The We-Passages and Ancient Sea Voyages," *BibRes* 20 (1975): 5–18.
40. Moule, *Idiom-Book*, p. 49.

In New Testament days, the marketplace served as the social center of the city. Here the unemployed waited for suitable work, the sick were healed, and the magistrates judged court cases. In those days, a plaintiff could drag a defendant into court and ask the judge to pass a verdict (James 2:6). The owners of the slave girl were acting according to Roman law when they laid their hands on Paul and Silas and put their grievance before the city authorities. (Incidentally, archaeologists have uncovered the judgment seat in Philippi's ancient marketplace.)

Luke calls these authorities magistrates. They were the chief officials in the Roman colony of Philippi; in harmony with inscriptions, they should have been called *duumviri* (a pair of magistrates).[41] The dignified title *praetors* (chiefs) also was used for these officials in Rome and its colonies.

The accusers bring a twofold charge against Paul and Silas: first, "these men as Jews are throwing our city into confusion"; second, "they are proclaiming customs which we as Romans cannot accept or observe." But with these charges they obscure the cause of their displeasure; not a word is said about the slave girl and the loss of revenue. Instead, the plaintiffs emphasize the nationality of Paul and Silas (i.e., they are Jews) and play upon fears raised by recent political events (see the commentary on 16:12b). Thus, the accusation reverberates on the ears of the magistrates, who are responsible for maintaining peace and order.

In the second part of their allegation, the accusers place the interests of the Romans against those of the Jews: "[these Jews] are proclaiming customs which we as Romans cannot accept or observe." They say nothing about the proclamation of the gospel and do not even mention the word *religion* but call attention to Roman customs. In ancient society customs were never separated from religion, and in context the term *customs* is a synonym of the word *religion*, signifying "the laws of the land."

The Romans had made Judaism a legal religion within the empire, and Christianity was not yet distinguished from Judaism. However, the Romans prohibited the Jews from making converts of Roman citizens.[42] Indirectly, Luke suggests that the work of the missionaries among the Roman citizens in Philippi was beginning to show results. Therefore, the magistrates judged that the proselytizing by these Jewish missionaries had to cease. The emphasis on the term *Romans* in the charge depicts the chauvinistic pride Romans took in their heritage. They would indeed oppose any attempt to change their customs.

If Paul had endured the cries from the demon-possessed slave girl, her owners would have tolerated him and would not have brought charges. But when Paul cast out the demon and thus deprived them of their

---

41. Bauer, p. 770.
42. Lake and Cadbury, *Beginnings,* vol. 4, p. 195. For an alternate view, consult A. N. Sherwin-White, *Roman Society and Roman Law in the New Testament* (1963; reprint ed., Grand Rapids: Baker, 1968), p. 81.

income, he effected a change in the religious practices of Roman society, including soothsaying.

e. Beating
16:22–24

In a marketplace, people mill around and quickly congregate in places where they see a disturbance. The crowd in Philippi hears the shouts of the owners of the slave girl and notices the commotion at the judgment seat.

22. The crowd joined in the attack against Paul and Silas. The magistrates ordered them to be stripped and beaten with rods. 23. And when they had inflicted many blows on them, they threw them into prison. They commanded the jailer to guard them securely. 24. When he received these orders, the jailer threw Paul and Silas into the inner prison and fastened their feet in the stocks.

a. "The crowd joined in the attack." The crowd listens to the accusers of Paul and Silas. Then they, too, raise their voices to attack the missionaries. Only the shouts and insults of the mob can be heard; the voices of the missionaries are drowned out. Influenced by the mob's emotionalism, the magistrates override legal procedure. Instead of listening to the defendants and taking them into custody for future arraignment, the two judges rashly give the order to strip Paul and Silas and beat them with rods.

In his epistles, Paul refers directly and indirectly to this incident in Philippi. He writes to the church in Thessalonica, "We had previously suffered and been insulted in Philippi" (I Thess. 2:2, NIV). And in his catalog of suffering for the sake of Christ, Paul mentions that he was beaten three times with rods (II Cor. 11:25).

b. "The magistrates ordered them to be stripped and beaten." The Roman magistrates had in their employ police officers (vv. 35, 38), in Latin called lictors (rod bearers). These officers carried the Roman symbols of law and order: fasces, a bundle of rods with an ax. With these fasces they administered corporal punishment and, at times, capital punishment. The officers, acting on the magistrates' order, tear the clothes from Paul and Silas and beat them with rods. Any semblance of proper legal procedure has disappeared. Even if Paul and Silas had raised the point that beating Roman citizens was illegal (v. 37), in the frenzy of the moment they would have been laughed to scorn.

c. "They threw them into prison." The magistrates had instructed the officers to give Paul and Silas many severe blows on their uncovered backs. When the missionaries are more dead than alive, the magistrates order that they be thrown into prison. They charge the jailer to guard them closely. This injunction seems to be superfluous because of the prisoners' physical condition. However, the jailer, who was probably an army veteran, knew that if Paul and Silas should ever break out of prison, he would have to pay with his life (see v. 27).

d. "The jailer threw Paul and Silas into the inner prison." In the outer part of the jail prisoners had freedom to walk and meet friends and relatives, but the inner part was dark and designed to keep prisoners in strict confinement. Here the jailer put the legs of Paul and Silas in the stocks to make escape impossible. Being confined to the stocks was torture, especially when the prisoner's legs were forced apart and placed in holes that were not next to each other.[43] Paul and Silas were treated as criminals unworthy of human comfort. Yet to the missionaries, God's power became evident in their darkest hour.

Practical Considerations in 16:22–24

Suffering. The word itself causes us to shy away from this unpleasant subject. When we observe others endure physical pain because of illness or abuse, pity fills our souls. We try to alleviate the suffering others have to endure by giving them our tangible tokens of loving care. We especially wish to help believers who suffer for the sake of Christ, whether our help is to remember them in daily prayer or to provide other means of comfort.

Peter says that if we suffer for doing good and endure it, God blesses us (I Peter 2:20; 3:14; 4:13–16). This does not mean that we should invite suffering, because if we do so, we are no longer serving God but ourselves. But when God sends us suffering while we are trying to do his will, and when we endure it, we receive God's commendation. Suffering for the sake of Christ comes in many forms: torment for those who suffer physically in times of persecution; affliction for patients who cope with illnesses, especially incurable diseases; and mental agony for those who silently suffer in a non-Christian environment at home, school, or place of employment.

What should the Christian do when he faces suffering? He should keep his eye of faith fixed on Jesus, who suffered for his people as the just for the unjust and left them an example to follow (I Peter 2:21).

Greek Words, Phrases, and Constructions in 16:22 and 24

Verse 22

περιρήξαντες—from the compound περί (around) and ῥήγνυμι (I rend, break), this aorist active participle refers more to the officers who received the order to beat the missionaries than to the magistrates themselves.

ἐκέλευον—the imperfect from κελεύω (I command) is equivalent to the aorist.[44]

Verse 24

ἐσωτέραν—this comparative adjective ("inner") can be understood as a superlative ("inmost").[45]

---

43. Compare Eusebius (*Ecclesiastical History* 5.1.27), who describes the suffering of imprisoned Christians in southern France.

44. A. T. Robertson, *A Grammar of the Greek New Testament in the Light of Historical Research* (Nashville: Broadman, 1934), p. 883.

45. Compare Lenski, *Acts*, pp. 671–72.

f. Earthquake
16:25–30

At first Paul and Silas try to accommodate their aching bodies to their surroundings, but they find that the stocks prevent them from falling asleep. Only one avenue is open to them and that is to go in prayer to God and to sing his praises in psalms and hymns.

25. At midnight Paul and Silas were praying and singing hymns to God, while the other prisoners were listening.

Instead of lamenting their deplorable condition of pain, loss of blood, hunger, and thirst, the missionaries turn to God. First in prayer and then in song they praise God's name. They are in tune with the psalmist who wrote:

> The LORD will command His
>   lovingkindness in the daytime,
> And in the night His song shall be with me—
> A prayer to the God of my life.
>
> [Ps. 42:8, NKJV]

Paul and Silas not only edify and strengthen themselves but also provide a witness and a source of encouragement to the other prisoners who listen to their prayers and psalms (compare Eph. 5:19; Col. 3:16; James 5:13). The tense of the verb *to listen* indicates that as the missionaries continue their singing for an extended period the other prisoners keep on listening. In place of curses, the captives hear words of adoration and praise.

We have no evidence that Paul and Silas prayed for release from prison. Yet from Scripture we know that God never forgets his people (Isa. 49:15–16). The moment of divine intervention has come.

26. Suddenly there was a violent earthquake so that the foundations of the prison were shaken. At once, all the doors were opened and all the chains were loosed.

a. "A violent earthquake." God sends not an angel but an earthquake to release the prisoners. He uses supernatural means of commissioning an angel to free the apostles (5:19) and Peter (12:7). God resorts to the natural phenomenon of an earthquake, which in Macedonia was a common occurrence, to liberate the prisoners in Philippi. God uses both supernatural and natural means as miracles that cannot be explained in detail.[46] He reveals his power and majesty in releasing his servants because not man but he rules supreme.

The earthquake comes unexpectedly. Luke writes that the tremor was violent (compare 4:31). He relates no details concerning damage, de-

---

46. Some commentators call the account of the earthquake that released the prisoners legendary: Martin Dibelius, *Studies in the Acts of the Apostles* (London: SCM, 1956), pp. 23–24; Haenchen, *Acts,* pp. 500–504; Conzelmann, *Acts,* pp. 132–33. However, we interpret the miracle as an act of God, who is free to use an earthquake to release the prisoners.

struction, and death in the city itself. He is interested in the release of the prisoners, including Paul and Silas, and the salvation of the jailer and his household.

b. "All the doors were opened and all the chains were loosed." We should not introduce the modern concepts of security locks and handcuffs into this account. William M. Ramsay observes:

> Anyone that has seen a Turkish prison will not wonder that the doors were thrown open: each door was merely closed by a bar, and the earthquake, as it passed along the ground, forced the door posts apart from each other, so that the bar slipped from its hold, and the door swung open. The prisoners were fastened to the wall or in wood stocks, *v.* 24; and the chains and stocks were detached from the wall, which was shaken so that spaces gaped between the stones.[47]

In God's protective providence, the prisoners are unhurt. Even though the chains are no longer attached to the prison walls, the prisoners still are not free from their shackles. They stay with Paul and Silas and perhaps consider them to be divine messengers endowed with supernatural strength and power.

27. When the jailer woke up and saw the opened prison doors, he drew his sword, intending to kill himself. He thought that the prisoners had escaped. 28. Paul loudly cried out, "Do yourself no harm, for we are all here."

Subtly Luke contrasts the prisoners' vigil and the jailer's sleep; the confidence of Paul and the perplexity of the jailer; the open doors of the prison and Paul's assuring word that the captives are inside the jail.

The immediate concern of the awakened jailer is the security of the prisoners. He knows that if they escape, his life will be demanded for their lives (see 12:19; 27:42). Seeing the wide-open doors of the prison—possibly by moonlight—and no prisoners near the jail entrance, the jailer draws his short sword and is ready to plunge it into his heart. He is of the opinion that most of the prisoners have fled and, now, with the death penalty hanging over his head, he is about to end the agony by taking his own life. The Greek verb denotes a moment of hesitation that comes to an abrupt end when Paul shouts from within the prison that all the prisoners are with him. Accustomed to the darkness of the jail, Paul can clearly see the jailer out in the open but the jailer is unable to see the prisoners.

We do not know how many detainees were present in the jail and what their lot was after Paul and Silas left them. The Western text at verse 30 adds that after releasing Paul and Silas, the jailer "secured the rest" of the

---

47. William M. Ramsay, *St. Paul the Traveller and the Roman Citizen* (1897; reprint ed., Grand Rapids: Baker, 1962), pp. 220–21.

prisoners.[48] Many commentators view these words as an expansion provided by a scribe who wished to explain the passage.

29. The jailer called for lights and rushed in, trembling with fear. He fell down before Paul and Silas. 30. He brought them out and asked, "Sirs, what must I do to be saved?"

The jailer turns to the members of his household and asks them to provide him with lights. He wants to enter the prison and determine whether the words spoken by Paul are true. When he has received lanterns from his servants, he rushes into the jail and sees that Paul is correct: indeed, all the prisoners are present.

Now the jailer falls trembling before the missionaries as a sign of humble submission. He knows that he is in the presence of men who are able to show him the way of salvation, even if he himself does not yet fully realize the meaning of salvation. When Cornelius welcomed Peter into his home and fell down before him, Peter objected to the centurion's show of reverence by saying that he, too, was only a man (10:25–26). By comparison, Paul and Silas voice no objection because they understand the confused mind of the jailer. They refrain from reprimanding the jailer but wait for him to speak.

The jailer had not heard the missionaries sing songs of praise at midnight because he was asleep, yet he knew that the coming of the earthquake was a divine response to the attitude of Paul and Silas. He leads Paul and Silas outside the prison into the open courtyard and there he addresses them. Stricken by a guilty conscience, he asks: "Sirs, what must I do to be saved?" Perhaps he has heard the message of salvation on an earlier occasion, has pondered its meaning, recognizes the spiritual power of Paul and Silas, and now asks them to show him the way of salvation. His question comes from a sincere heart, as is evident from the polite address *sirs*. With great respect he addresses men whom he cast into the inner part of the prison only a short time ago.

Practical Considerations in 16:30

The church of Philippi was close to Paul's heart. He wrote a special letter to its members in which he urged them to be joyful in the Lord. The word *joy* in its various forms appears sixteen times in this short epistle.[49] It reflects the attitude Paul displayed in the Philippian jail where he and Silas sang hymns in the middle of the night.

Paul had developed a special relationship with the members of that church because they repeatedly provided for his physical needs (Phil. 4:14–18). In his epistle to the Philippians, Paul mentions Epaphroditus (2:25; 4:18) and Euodia and Syn-

---

48. Metzger, *Textual Commentary*, p. 449; Bruce, *Book of the Acts*, p. 317 n. 69.
49. William Hendriksen, *Exposition of Philippians*, New Testament Commentary series (Grand Rapids: Baker, 1962), p. 20.

tyche (4:2). Yet we know from Acts that two persons from entirely different backgrounds became charter members of the congregation: Lydia the seller of purple from Thyatira (vv. 14–15) and the jailer (v. 33). It is possible that the slave girl also was part of the church. These converts, having learned the way of salvation, could testify that salvation is a gift of God. With these initial members, God continues to build his church, so that within a short time Paul writes about overseers and deacons in the church of Philippi (Phil. 1:1).

Greek Words, Phrases, and Constructions in 16:29–30

Verse 29

φῶτα—the form is the neuter plural accusative and should not be taken as a singular accusative (NKJV).

εἰσεπήδησεν—from εἰσπηδάω (I leap in), this aorist active occurs twice in the New Testament: here and in 14:14. It conveys "vigorous action."[50]

Verse 30

ἔξω—"outside." Here is an indication of the writer's accurate reporting.

σωθῶ—this is the aorist passive subjunctive of σῴζω (I save). The aorist indicates the totality of the jailer's salvation, the passive implies that God is the agent, and the subjunctive denotes the jailer's polite request.

---

g. Salvation
16:31–34

The context of the jailer's question shows that his interest is in eternal security, not job security: when Paul and Silas preach the gospel, the jailer and the members of his family believe in God, are baptized, and are filled with joy.

31. Paul and Silas replied, "Believe in the Lord Jesus, and you and the members of your household will be saved."

The missionaries show the way of salvation to the jailer by coming straight to the point and telling him what he must do: "Believe in the Lord Jesus." Anyone who confesses with his mouth and believes in his heart that Jesus is Lord is saved (Rom. 10:9).[51] That is fundamental. Thus, Paul and Silas tell the jailer to place his complete confidence and trust in Jesus and to acknowledge him as his Lord. Not the missionaries but only the Lord Jesus Christ can save him.

Paul and Silas, however, indicate that salvation is extended to all the members of the jailer's household (including the servants). In passing I point out that although God saves individuals, wherever applicable he

---

50. F. F. Bruce, *The Acts of the Apostles: The Greek Text with Introduction and Commentary*, 3d (rev. and enl.) ed. (Grand Rapids: Eerdmans, 1990), p. 486.
51. See, e.g., John 13:13; Acts 11:17; I Cor. 12:3; Phil. 2:11.

brings salvation to a person's family.[52] God works through families, for they are the building blocks of the church.

32. And they proclaimed the word of the Lord to him and all who were in his household. 33. At that hour of the night the jailer took them and washed their wounds. Immediately he and all his household were baptized.

After laying the foundation—"believe in the Lord Jesus, and you and the members of your household will be saved"—Paul and Silas explain the gospel (the exact phrase is *the word of the Lord*) in greater detail. The missionaries ache from the blows they received the previous day. Nevertheless, the opportunity to introduce a household to the Lord makes them forget the discomfort they feel. If angels in heaven rejoice when on earth one sinner repents (Luke 15:10), should not God's servants exult when all the members of a household repent and believe?

Luke provides the evidence of the jailer's change of life. Love for the Lord Jesus causes him to think of the physical needs of Paul and Silas. He realizes that their bruised and bleeding bodies need medical attention. He personally takes the missionaries to the prison well and washes their wounds. How the jailer must regret his earlier actions! Yesterday he had put Paul and Silas in the stocks; now he tenderly washes their wounds and soothes their welts.

As the missionaries are physically washed so the jailer and the members of his household are spiritually washed with the blood of Jesus, symbolized by the water of baptism. As Paul and Silas are the recipients of the jailer's kindness so the jailer and his family are the recipients of God's grace. With the sign of baptism, they are now members of God's household.

34. The jailer brought Paul and Silas into his house and fed them. He rejoiced greatly because he and his family believed in God.

After Lydia and the members of her family received the sign of baptism, she invited Paul and his companions into her home (v. 15). When the jailer, with his wife, children, and servants, is baptized, he does no less. Both Lydia and the jailer want to express their thankfulness that they now belong to God's family. Both Lydia and the jailer consider the missionaries brothers in Christ. Accordingly, the man no longer sees Paul and Silas as prisoners, and the missionaries have no desire to run away.

The jailer becomes the host and invites Paul and Silas to enter his home. The Greek indicates that he leads them up and into his abode. In other words, the prison is at a lower elevation than his residence. The jailer personally cares for the physical needs of Paul and Silas by providing them with food and drink. In everything he does for them he expresses his boundless joy in the Lord because he and his family are now believers. Once again, the Greek signifies that the jailer's faith is a lasting trust in God. He and the members of his household demonstrate not temporal faith but

---

52. Acts 11:14; 16:15, 31; 18:8; I Cor. 1:11, 16.

true faith in Jesus Christ. They join the ranks of others who, having come to faith, express their joy and happiness (see 8:39; 10:46; 13:48). Joy, then, proceeds from faith, which in itself is alive as a gift from God.[53]

Greek Words, Phrases, and Constructions in 16:31–34

Verses 31–32

ἐπί—with the accusative *the Lord Jesus* after the verb *to believe,* the preposition ἐπί (to) metaphorically designates motion toward someone.[54]

σωθήσῃ σύ—the second person singular pronoun is the subject of the verb, which is a future passive. The future is definite.

τὸν λόγον τοῦ κυρίου—some Greek manuscripts have the variant reading τοῦ θεοῦ. In Acts, Luke interchanges the phrases *the word of God* and *the word of the Lord* (e.g., see 13:5, 44).

Verses 33–34

ἔλουσεν ἀπὸ τῶν πληγῶν—"he washed their wounds." If we supply a direct object for the verb *to wash,* a literal translation reads, "he washed [impurities] from their wounds."

πανοικεί—this adverb, translated "with his whole house," agrees with both the verb *to rejoice* and the perfect participle *believed.*

---

h. Departure
16:35–40

When God miraculously releases Paul and Silas, the effect of the miracle is astounding. The magistrates who were influenced by the mob the day before now have second thoughts. Perhaps the magistrates superstitiously link the violent earthquake to the events of the previous day.[55] At any rate, they want to get rid of these two Jews as soon as possible. Therefore, at the break of day, they instruct the officers who had beaten Paul and Silas to go to the jail and order the jailer to release these two prisoners.

35. When it was day, the magistrates sent their officers with the message, "Release those men." 36. The jailer reported these words to Paul and said, "The magistrates have sent to release you. Now, then, go in peace."

So they will not create difficulties for the jailer, the missionaries voluntarily return to prison and wait for further developments. Soon they hear the voices of the officers, who tell the jailer to release Paul and Silas. While the

---

53. Calvin, *Acts of the Apostles,* vol. 2, p. 87.
54. Moule, *Idiom-Book,* p. 49.
55. The Western text features an addition that has all the earmarks of an explanation: "But when it was day the magistrates *assembled together in the market place, and recollecting the earthquake that had taken place, they were afraid; and* sent the police, saying. . . ." Metzger, *Textual Commentary,* p. 450.

officers wait, the jailer enters the prison and relays the message to Paul: "The magistrates have sent to release you. Now, then, go in peace." Note that Paul is the main figure in the unfolding of this drama.

The jailer no doubt is of the opinion that the news of their release should please the missionaries. He is surprised, therefore, when Paul is not ready to leave the prison. He hears Paul's pointed objections to the order of the magistrates.

37. But Paul said to them, "They have beaten us publicly without a trial and thrown us into prison, even though we are Roman citizens. And now do they send us away secretly? No, let them come themselves and bring us out!"

Consider these points:

1. *Injustice.* Paul has felt the rough edge of injustice administered to him and Silas by the magistrates. He wants them to know that they have greatly erred. Paul claims the right of appeal to Roman law, which in the case of Silas and himself was violated.

Roman law, passed from the sixth to the second century B.C., protected Roman citizens from public beatings, imprisonment, and death without trial. For example, the Roman historiographer Livy writes about the application of the Porcian law, probably passed in 198 B.C.: "Yet the Porcian law alone seems to have been passed to protect the persons of the citizens, imposing, as it did, a heavy penalty if anyone should scourge or put to death a Roman citizen."[56] Roman citizenship, then, should have protected Paul and Silas from beating and imprisonment. Exception to Roman law could only be made if a Roman citizen had been duly tried and convicted in a court of law.[57] The magistrates should have conducted a lawful trial instead of yielding to the pressure of the crowd to give Paul and Silas a public beating and confine them in prison.

Why did Paul keep silent when he and Silas were publicly beaten? If they had protested, the magistrates in the frenzy of the moment would not have listened. Paul's silence, whether by circumstance or design, now serves him well to call attention to the gross injustice he and Silas have experienced. If the magistrates are willing publicly to acknowledge their error, they will tolerate Christians and avoid future incidents that relate to the church.

2. *Apology.* "And now do they send us away secretly? No, let them come themselves and bring us out!" Paul is fully in control of the situation. He insists that the magistrates come to the jail and release the two Roman citizens. The two judges committed a grave error by not complying with Roman law. They had Paul and Silas publicly beaten, and publicly they must apologize before they can release the missionaries from prison.

---

56. Livy 10.9.4; see also Cicero *In Defence of Rabirius* 4.12–13; Boyd Reese, "The Apostle Paul's Exercise of His Rights as a Roman Citizen as Recorded in the Book of Acts," *EvQ* 47 (1975): 138–45.

57. Refer to Sherwin-White, *Roman Society and Roman Law*, p. 74.

38. The officers reported this to the magistrates. When they heard that Paul and Silas were Roman citizens, they began to worry. 39. They came to the prison and apologized. They brought them out and begged them to leave the city.

What Paul expects to happen indeed takes place. When the officers report to the magistrates that the two Jewish prisoners are Roman citizens, fear strikes their hearts. They know they could lose their office and be severely punished. They need not doubt the veracity of Paul's statement, because anyone who falsely claimed Roman citizenship was put to death.[58] Paul's claim is genuine and they take it as such. Luke does not indicate how Paul and Silas proved their Roman citizenship. When a Roman citizen registered the birth of a child in the presence of a Roman official, "he received a wooden diptych recording the declaration, which acted as a certificate of citizenship for the rest of his life."[59] It is possible that Paul and Silas carried such proofs of citizenship.

The magistrates personally come to the prison. We conjecture that they are accompanied by the officers and by people who wish to satisfy their curiosity.[60] Publicly they admit their error and offer their apologies. They lead Paul and Silas outside the prison and then ask them to leave the city of Philippi. From their point of view the request is advantageous, because the presence of these two missionaries is a continual reminder of evidence against them. They ask these men, who are able to teach them the way of salvation, to leave the city. The parallel of the Gadarenes asking Jesus to leave them is obvious (Matt. 8:34). In the interest of the church and its future, Paul and Silas comply with the magistrates' request, but with the provision that they first spend some time with the Christians in the home of Lydia.

40. And after Paul and Silas left the prison, they went to the house of Lydia, where they met with the brothers. Then they encouraged them and departed.

Paul and Silas leave the prison as honorable Roman citizens for whom the local Roman authorities have respect. Physically they are unable to begin their travels. Their bodies ache because of the welts, and lack of sleep depletes their reservoir of strength. They want lodging and care, and the place that can fill their needs is the house of Lydia. Here Luke the physician is waiting to add to the physical comfort of Paul and Silas, while Timothy and Lydia minister to both their spiritual and material needs.

To this point Luke has described the conversion of Lydia, the exorcism

---

58. Lake and Cadbury, *Beginnings*, vol. 4, p. 210.

59. A. N. Sherwin-White, *The Roman Citizenship*, 2d ed. (Oxford: Clarendon, 1973), p. 316.

60. The reviser of the Western text has added explanatory phrases, which are italicized: "And *having arrived with many friends at the prison*, they besought them to go forth, *saying, 'We did not know the truth about you, that you are righteous men.'* And when they had brought them out they besought them saying, 'Depart from this city, *lest they again assemble against us, crying out against you.*" Metzger, *Textual Commentary*, p. 451.

of the slave girl, and the transformation of the jailer. But he has not as yet recorded the growth of the Philippian church. In this verse he mentions that the missionaries meet the brothers at Lydia's house. Although the brothers try to minister to Paul and Silas, Luke relates, the missionaries encourage them instead. The point is that through the centuries Jews had learned to suffer for their faith. By contrast, the Gentiles for the first time see suffering for the sake of Christ. They realize that because of their relationship to Jesus Christ, they also will face opposition, persecution, and affliction (see Phil. 1:29–30). For that reason, the missionaries speak words of encouragement to them.

After a period of rest at the residence of Lydia, Paul, accompanied by Silas and Timothy, resumes his travels west along the Egnatian Way. We surmise that Luke remained in Philippi, for the personal pronoun *we* does not appear again in the narrative until 20:5–6.

Practical Considerations in 16:35–40

"No one has greater love than this, that he lay down his life for his friends" (John 15:13). We read these words of Jesus and accept them as true, but we know that only in exceptional circumstances are these words ever fulfilled. By laying down his life for his people, Jesus demonstrated his unquestionable love for them.

In a sense, while discharging their missionary duties Paul and Silas were ready to lay down their lives on behalf of the Philippian believers. God preserved their lives, but they suffered severely for the benefit of the Christians in Philippi. In turn, the Philippian Christians expressed their thankfulness to Paul by ministering to him again and again. Consequently, an unbreakable bond developed between Paul and the believers in Philippi. As is evident from Paul's letter to that church, these people were dear to Paul and Paul was dear to them:

"I have you in my heart" (1:7)

"Through your prayers I shall be set free" (1:19)

"My God will supply in all your need" (4:19)

In this epistle, Paul exhorts them to be joyful in the Lord. An anonymous author succinctly wrote: "Joy is the natural outcome of the Christian's obedience to the revealed will of God."

Greek Words, Phrases, and Constructions in 16:36–40

Verse 36

ἀπέσταλκαν—the perfect tense of ἀποστέλλω (I send) denotes lasting effect. Note that the ending -αν is used instead of the normal -ασιν (third person plural perfect active).

ἐν εἰρήνῃ—the preposition ἐν means "go into a peace in which you may live."[61]

Verse 37

δείραντες—Paul uses the aorist active participle of δέρω (I flay, skin). He is saying to the officers, "You skinned us."

ὑπάρχοντας—the present participle of ὑπάρχω (I exist, am present) is widely used as a substitute for the verb *to be*. The participle is concessive: "even though we are."

The contrast between δημοσίᾳ (publicly, in view of all) and λάθρᾳ (secretly, hidden from view) is striking.

οὐ γάρ—in context, this combination signifies "not so!"[62]

Verses 39–40

ἠρώτων—"they were requesting." The use of the imperfect indicates that they asked repeatedly.

ἀπό—this preposition follows the verb ἀπελθεῖν (to depart). Although the preposition properly means "from," here it connotes "out of."[63]

πρὸς τὴν Λυδίαν—the reference is to the house of Lydia, not to the district of Lydia in Asia Minor.

Summary of Chapter 16

Paul and Silas arrive at Derbe and Lystra, where they meet Timothy. Born of a Jewish mother and a Greek father, Timothy is a believer. Paul wants Timothy to accompany them; to enhance Timothy's effectiveness as a witness to the Jews, Paul circumcises him. As they journey, Paul and Silas deliver the apostolic decrees to the churches and strengthen these churches in the faith.

The Holy Spirit keeps the missionaries from preaching the gospel in the province of Asia and the regions of Bithynia and Mysia. In Troas Paul has a vision of a Macedonian man calling him to come over to help the people there. The missionaries board ship, sail to Neapolis, and travel to Philippi, where they stay for several days. On the Sabbath, Paul preaches to a group of women. God opens the heart of Lydia, who becomes a believer in the Lord and is baptized. Paul and his companions stay in Lydia's house.

A demon-possessed slave girl, a fortuneteller who brings her owners great profit, identifies the missionaries as God's servants. Her continual shouting annoys Paul, who drives out the evil spirit. The owners of the girl realize a loss of revenue and accuse Paul and Silas before the magistrates. The missionaries are severely beaten and thrown into prison. During the

---

61. Robert Hanna, *A Grammatical Aid to the Greek New Testament* (Grand Rapids: Baker, 1983), p. 223; Moule, *Idiom-Book*, p. 79.
62. Compare Robertson, *Grammar*, p. 1187.
63. Blass and Debrunner, *Greek Grammar*, #209.1.

night they pray and sing hymns. With an earthquake God sets the prisoners free. Paul prevents the jailer from committing suicide; the man becomes a believer and with his family is baptized.

The next morning the magistrates send officers to the jail to release Paul and Silas. But Paul informs them that he and Silas are Roman citizens who have suffered the injustice of a public beating and imprisonment without trial. Paul demands that the magistrates come to the jail to release him and Silas. The magistrates comply; at their request the missionaries leave Philippi after having spent some time at the house of Lydia.

17

The Second Missionary Journey, *part 3*

17:1–34

Outline (continued)

17:1–9	3. Thessalonica
17:1–4	a. Proclamation
17:5–9	b. Reaction
17:10–15	4. Berea
17:16–18:17	C. Greece
17:16–34	1. Athens
17:16–18	a. Setting
17:19–21	b. Request
17:22–23	c. Introduction
17:24–28	d. Content
17:29–31	e. Application
17:32–34	f. Reaction

17 1 When they had passed through Amphipolis and Apollonia, they came to Thessalonica; in that place was a synagogue of the Jews. 2 According to his custom, Paul entered the synagogue and for three Sabbaths he reasoned with them from the Scriptures. 3 He explained and demonstrated that the Christ had to suffer and rise from the dead. He said, "This Jesus, whom I am proclaiming to you, is the Christ." 4 Some of the Jews were persuaded and joined Paul and Silas, as well as a great multitude of God-fearing Greeks and not a few of the prominent women.

5 But the Jews were jealous. They took along some wicked men from the marketplace and having formed a mob, they began a riot in the city. They approached the house of Jason, seeking to bring Paul and Silas out to the people. 6 When they did not find them, they dragged Jason and some brothers before the city authorities. They shouted: "These men who have troubled the world have come here also, 7 and Jason has welcomed them. They all act contrary to Caesar's decrees, saying that there is another king, namely, Jesus." 8 They stirred up the crowd and the city officials who were paying attention to these things. 9 And when they had received a bond from Jason and the others, they let them go.

---

3. Thessalonica
17:1–9

During his second missionary journey, Paul endeavored to bring the gospel to commercial and administrative centers from which it could be disseminated to numerous places. With his companions, Paul traveled from Philippi to Thessalonica (modern Salonika). In the synagogue at Thessalonica, he proclaimed the gospel to the Jews and to the Gentiles.

a. Proclamation
17:1–4

1. When they had passed through Amphipolis and Apollonia, they came to Thessalonica; in that place was a synagogue of the Jews. 2. According to his custom, Paul entered the synagogue and for three Sabbaths he reasoned with them from the Scriptures.

We note these two points:

1. *Place.* The Egnatian Road stretched from the Aegean coast of northern Macedonia to the western coast (in modern Albania) along the Adriatic Sea. From Philippi, the missionaries traveled this road in a southwesterly direction. We are unable to determine whether they walked or rode horses; we assume that Paul and his fellow travelers covered the distance (about thirty miles) between Philippi and Amphipolis in one day to find lodging

611

for the night. We conjecture that they rode instead of walked, because Paul and Silas were still nursing their wounds from the beating they had received in Philippi.

Amphipolis, located on the banks of the Strymon River, was the capital city of the first district of Macedonia (see the commentary on 16:12). The name *Amphipolis* (around the city) intimates that the city was nearly surrounded by the river. Luke seems to indicate that because Amphipolis and neighboring Apollonia lacked a synagogue and no Jews were residing in these cities, Paul and his companions did not preach the gospel there.[1]

After traveling another day, the missionaries arrived at Apollonia, a city situated twenty-seven miles west-southwest of Amphipolis. Here they stayed for the night before continuing their journey to Thessalonica, thirty-eight miles to the west.

At Thessalonica, the traffic of the sea met the traffic of the land. The city, located on the Gulf of Salonika, is near two rivers (the Vardar and the Vistritza). In ancient times, the people used these rivers to transport the agricultural products they raised in the fertile plains along the river banks. Besides being a commercial center, the city in Paul's day was the capital of Macedonia and served the entire province as an administrative center.[2] In their campaign against Brutus and Cassius, who had assassinated Julius Caesar, the Romans placed a military garrison in Thessalonica. For its support of Mark Antony and Octavian (later known as Augustus), the Romans gave Thessalonica the status of a free city in 42 B.C.[3] When Paul and his companions stayed there, about two hundred thousand people, among them numerous Jews, lived in Thessalonica. This strategically located city became a base from which the gospel spread throughout Macedonia and Greece (I Thess. 1:8).

2. *Time*. Paul continued his customary practice of preaching the gospel first to the Jews and then to the Gentiles (compare 13:5; see also Luke 4:16). He visited a Jewish synagogue in Thessalonica and waited for the invitation to preach the gospel to the Jews and God-fearing Gentiles who worshiped there. Luke writes that "Paul entered the synagogue and for three Sabbaths he reasoned with them from the Scriptures."

Did Paul spend only a three-week period in Thessalonica? Apparently not. Paul's letters to that church and Luke's account in Acts suggest that he stayed much longer than three Sabbaths. To illustrate: the Philippian church sent him material aid on two occasions (Phil. 4:16).[4] Paul worked

---

1. David John Williams notes that archaeologists have found no evidence of a synagogue either in Amphipolis or in neighboring Apollonia. *Acts*, Good News Commentaries series (San Francisco: Harper and Row, 1985), p. 286.

2. Before the Romans made Thessalonica the provincial capital of Macedonia in 146 B.C., it was the capital of Macedonia's second district. Livy *Annals* 44.10.45; 45.29.

3. Pliny *Natural History* 4.36.

4. The translation of JB, "And twice since my stay in Thessalonika you have sent me what I needed," supports the interpretation of a brief stay. But translators do not favor supplying the phrase *since my stay*, for it is not found in the Greek text.

day and night to support himself, presumably as a tentmaker (see 18:3), for he did not want to become a burden to anyone (I Thess. 2:9; II Thess. 3:8).[5] I submit that for three Sabbaths Paul preached in the synagogue and afterward continued his ministry among the God-fearing Gentiles. He wrote that the church in Thessalonica consisted of Gentiles who had renounced idols and had turned to God (I Thess. 1:9). Paul also wrote that the church proclaimed the gospel throughout Macedonia and Achaia, which implies that the Thessalonians received thorough instruction in the message of the Lord. Such instruction would be offered if Paul himself worked in Thessalonica longer than three Sabbaths.[6]

3. He explained and demonstrated that the Christ had to suffer and rise from the dead. He said, "This Jesus, whom I am proclaiming to you, is the Christ."

In the worship service of the local synagogue, Paul tells his audience that Jesus is the Christ, who through his suffering, death, and resurrection had fulfilled the messianic prophecies of the Scriptures. Luke states only that Paul preached; he does not supply the text of the message. In Thessalonica Paul modified slightly his usual approach (see 13:16–41): "he reasoned with [the Jews] from the Scriptures." That is, he presents the teachings of Scripture that relate to the Messiah and invites the audience to ask questions.[7] Unless Paul's listeners are ready and willing to see that the person and work of Christ fulfill the scriptural prophecies, the Bible remains a closed book to them.[8]

Paul follows the example set by Jesus, who opened the Scriptures for the two men on the way to Emmaus and for the disciples in the upper room. Jesus showed them from the Law, the Prophets, and the Psalms that the Christ had to suffer and rise from the dead (Luke 24:25–27, 44–46). The term *explaining* comes from the Greek verb meaning "to open." Paul opens the Word and sets the explanation of the messianic prophecies before his listeners. By appealing to the Scriptures, he has a common basis to prove that the Messiah has come in the person and work of Jesus Christ of Nazareth.

Paul demonstrates that the Christ *had* to suffer, die, and rise from the grave. Luke, in his Gospel and Acts, also clearly illustrates that Jesus' life, death, and resurrection are governed by divine necessity (refer, e.g., to Luke 2:49; 4:43; 13:33; 24:26; Acts 3:21). "It is Luke's underlying concern not to depict Jesus' death as the tragic failure of a prophet but to present the death and resurrection of Jesus as necessary saving acts of God."[9]

---

5. Donald H. Madvig, "Thessalonica," *ISBE*, vol. 4, p. 837.

6. Consult Everett F. Harrison, *Interpreting Acts: The Expanding Church* , 2d ed. (Grand Rapids: Zondervan, Academie Books, 1986), p. 275.

7. Gottlob Schrenk, *TDNT*, vol. 2, p. 94; Dieter Fürst, *NIDNTT*, vol. 3, p. 821.

8. Richard B. Rackham, *The Acts of the Apostles: An Exposition*, Westminster Commentaries series (1901; reprint ed., Grand Rapids: Baker, 1964), p. 295.

9. Erich Tiedtke and Hans-George Link, *NIDNTT*, vol. 3, p. 667; see also Leon Morris, *New Testament Theology* (Grand Rapids: Zondervan, Academie Books, 1986), pp. 164, 174.

In his presentations, Paul discusses three facts: the Christ had to suffer, he had to rise from the dead, and he is Jesus proclaimed by Paul. The Jews objected to the teaching that Christ died on a cross, because to them a criminal hanging on a tree (cross) was under God's curse (Deut. 21:23; Gal. 3:13). The doctrine of the resurrection is the recurring theme the apostles proclaim wherever they speak (see 2:24, 32; 13:30, 33, 34, 37; 17:31). And identifying Jesus with the Messiah is Paul's personal objective ever since his conversion on the Damascus road (refer to 9:22). For that reason, Paul uses the personal pronoun *I*, "whom I am proclaiming to you." By opening the Scriptures and showing that Jesus fulfilled them, Paul convinces both Jews and Gentiles that Jesus is the promised Messiah.

4. Some of the Jews were persuaded and joined Paul and Silas, as well as a great multitude of God-fearing Greeks and not a few of the prominent women.

Luke describes the result of Paul's preaching. Although he mentions both Jews and Gentiles, he clearly contrasts the composition of the group: a few Jews and a great multitude of Gentiles. The church, then, is predominantly Gentile in character; the Jews had instructed the Gentiles in the teachings of the Old Testament. Paul is reaping a veritable harvest of Jewish mission activity in Thessalonica because numerous Gentiles had put their faith in Israel's God but objected to circumcision. Hence, the Jews did not accept them as converts but called them God-fearing Gentiles (see the commentary on 10:2). This is a repetition of what occurred in Pisidian Antioch (13:43–48).

Luke adds that among these God-fearing Gentiles were numerous women of prominent social status. He uses the characteristic device of understating the obvious: "and not a few of the prominent women." These women either filled leading positions in that city or they were the wives of city officials. The first option is more likely, for in the Greco-Roman society of that day women often achieved prominence and stature (16:14).

Luke uses the verb *to join*, which in Greek is unique. He writes, "Some of the Jews . . . joined Paul and Silas." This particular verb signifies that these Jews "*were allotted* by God *to Paul*, namely as disciples, followers."[10] In other words, they were attached to the missionaries in the sense of following them. Accordingly, these Jews and God-fearing Gentiles "through God obtained a share in the promised heritage and had been placed in it."[11]

Doctrinal Considerations in 17:1–4

Scripture teaches that salvation originates with God and not with man. Even though Paul exhorts the Philippians to work out their own salvation with fear and

---

10. Thayer, p. 547. See also Bauer, p. 716.
11. Johannes Eichler, *NIDNTT*, vol. 2, p. 302.

trembling, he nevertheless adds that God works through them to accomplish his purpose (Phil. 2:12–13). Salvation features both God's sovereignty and man's responsibility. God saves man but man must respond in faith by doing God's will in word and deed. God works out his plan of salvation through his Son and thus redeems his people.

Scripture teaches that according to God's plan, Christ had to suffer, die, and rise from the dead. Scripture expresses divine necessity in the word *must*. This term appears repeatedly in Acts and denotes God's purpose. For example, Jesus tells Paul at the time of his conversion what Paul *must* do (9:6) and informs Ananias that Paul *must* suffer for the sake of Christ (9:16). And Jesus instructs Paul that he *must* testify for the Lord in Rome (23:11). Throughout Acts, Luke never tires of depicting God as the author of man's salvation, who through man is working out his divine plan and purpose.

Greek Words, Phrases, and Constructions in 17:1–4

Verse 1

τὴν . . . τὴν—these two definite articles precede the nouns *Amphipolis* and *Apollonia*. Note that the noun *Thessalonica* lacks the definite article.[12] The Western text implies that Paul and his companions stopped at Apollonia: "Now when they had passed through Amphipolis they *went down* to Apollonia, *and thence* to Thessalonica."[13]

Verses 2–3

πρὸς αὐτούς—these words refer to the synagogue of the Jews.

σάββατα—usually translated "Sabbaths," but at least one translation (RSV) reads "weeks."[14]

ἀπὸ τῶν γραφῶν—this phrase can be taken with either the verb διελέξατο (he reasoned) or the present participles διανοίγων (he explained) and παρατιθέμενος (he demonstrated).

ἐγώ—the personal pronoun is emphatic and signifies the direct result of Paul's conversion on the Damascus road. For the change from indirect discourse to direct discourse compare 1:4–5 and 23:22.

Verse 4

προσεκληρώθησαν—the verb is a combination of the preposition πρός (to) and the noun κλῆρος (lot). It conveys the thought of receiving the privilege of having a share in the inheritance. The aorist passive implies that God is the agent.

πρώτων—the superlative adjective in this instance expresses only rank: "prominent."[15]

---

12. Friedrich Blass and Albert Debrunner, *A Greek Grammar of the New Testament and Other Early Christian Literature*, trans. and rev. Robert Funk (Chicago: University of Chicago Press, 1961), #261.2.

13. Bruce M. Metzger, *A Textual Commentary on the Greek New Testament*, 3d corrected ed. (London and New York: United Bible Societies, 1975), p. 452.

14. For a detailed discussion, consult Lake and Cadbury, *Beginnings*, vol. 4, pp. 202–3.

15. A. T. Robertson, *A Grammar of the Greek New Testament in the Light of Historical Research* (Nashville: Broadman, 1934), p. 669.

b. Reaction
17:5–9

5. But the Jews were jealous. They took along some wicked men from the marketplace and having formed a mob, they began a riot in the city. They approached the house of Jason, seeking to bring Paul and Silas out to the people.

After preaching for three Sabbaths in the Jewish synagogue of Thessalonica, Paul continues his teaching ministry in private homes. Among the Jewish believers is a man named Jason, who provides lodging for Paul and Silas and who presumably turns his home into a house church. Although the name *Jason* is Greek, it is a translation of the Hebrew form *Joshua*. Other believers in Thessalonica are Aristarchus and Secundus (20:4), who later accompany Paul on his journeys.

From Paul's writings we know that he proclaimed the gospel "with power, with the Holy Spirit and with deep conviction" (I Thess. 1:5, NIV). God blesses Paul's labors so that numerous Gentiles turn in faith to the Lord. Among them are the God-fearers whom the Jews had instructed in the basic teachings of the Scriptures. Consequently, when the Jews see that Paul is taking these God-fearing Gentiles away from the synagogue worship services, they are not merely jealous of Paul; they are angry. Jealousy and anger are the two sides of the same coin. Luke illustrates this in earlier accounts (5:17; 13:45) and shows that Paul's opponents resort to slander and verbal abuse.

The Jews go to the marketplace, where customarily some bad characters loiter. For modest pay, these men are willing to do anything they are asked. From the Jews they receive instructions to form a mob and start a riot (compare 14:4–5, 19; see also I Thess. 2:14–16). With these rabble-rousers, the Jews proceed to the house of Jason for the purpose of capturing Paul and Silas and bringing them before the assembly of the people.

Because Thessalonica was a free city, a popular assembly transacted public business.[16] In public assembly, citizens took care of court cases and legislative matters. We do not know whether the assembly was in session at the time or that the people themselves formed an assembly. Not the Jews, who were a minority in Thessalonica, but the crowd rules. In passing, notice that Luke uses the term *the Jews* to designate those people who were opposed to the gospel.

6. When they did not find them, they dragged Jason and some brothers before the city authorities. They shouted: "These men who have troubled the world have come here also, 7. and Jason has welcomed them. They all

---

16. Bauer, p. 179. Ernst Haenchen, however, avers that the Greek word *demos* is a synonym for *ochlos* (people). *The Acts of the Apostles: A Commentary,* trans. Bernard Noble and Gerald Shinn (Philadelphia: Westminster, 1971), p. 507. Compare 19:33, 35.

act contrary to Caesar's decrees, saying that there is another king, namely, Jesus."

1. *Officials.* We surmise that Paul received advance warning of an attempted arrest. The Christians hid Paul and Silas somewhere in the city and shielded them from physical harm. However, they had not expected that the mob would turn on Jason and other believers. When the crowd came to Jason's house and were unable to find the missionaries, Jason and some Christians present in his house were apprehended and literally dragged to the public assembly, before the city authorities.

The Greek term *politarchēs,* translated "city authorities," describes officials in the public assemblies of free cities in Macedonia. Because Thessalonica was a free city, the word *politarchēs* refers to Macedonian magistrates, not to Roman officials. Thessalonica had at least five politarches in the middle of the first century. In 1876, when city officials of Salonika decided to tear down the ancient arch called the Vardar Gate that spanned the Egnatian Road, they discovered an inscription with names of ancient city officials. These names were prefaced by the term *politarchēs.* The same term is found on many other inscriptions which date "from the second century B.C. to the third century A.D."[17]

2. *Charges.* The crowd levels charges against Jason and his Christian brothers, but the words they use apply primarily to Paul and Silas and only secondarily to Jason: "These men who have troubled the world have come here also, and Jason has welcomed them." The Jews accuse Paul and Silas, whom they cannot find, of troubling the world. In a sense, the charge that the missionaries are troubling the whole world is correct. The fact is that the gospel troubles, penetrates, and alters society in every part of the world. Moreover, the Jews perhaps had heard what happened to Paul and Silas in Philippi. They insinuate that a similar incident will occur in Thessalonica.[18] Nonetheless, from the perspective of the magistrates, the accusation at first must have appeared grossly overstated. Because the Jews are unable to present Paul and Silas, they place before the magistrates Jason, a fellow Jew and a local resident, whom they accuse of aiding the missionaries.

To strengthen their case, the Jews also accuse Paul, Silas, and Jason of sedition: "They all act contrary to Caesar's decrees, saying that there is another king, namely, Jesus." Whether the allegation is true or false matters not; the charge itself is serious and should be investigated by the magistrates. The decrees of Caesar were, for example, oaths of loyalty which local magistrates had to administer and enforce.[19]

During Jesus' trial, Pontius Pilate asked Jesus whether he was a king, and Jesus responded: "My kingdom is not of this world" (John 18:36, NIV). The

---

17. Lake and Cadbury, *Beginnings,* vol. 4, p. 205.
18. For the political background, see Suetonius *Life of Claudius* 25.4; commentary on 16:20–21.
19. Refer to E. A. Judge, "The Decrees of Caesar at Thessalonica," *RefThR* 30 (1971): 1–7.

motto *Caesar is Lord* prevailed throughout the Roman empire. However, in the first century Christians acclaimed not Caesar but Jesus as Lord (I Cor. 12:3), and the apostles preached the coming of God's kingdom.

In Acts, Luke does not stress the concept *kingdom of God,* perhaps in an attempt to avert possible charges of sedition. Yet Paul frequently mentions this concept.[20] From his two epistles to the church at Thessalonica we learn that Paul teaches the coming of the day of the Lord, during which the man of lawlessness is slain (I Thess. 4:16; II Thess. 2:8). These verses can be interpreted as allusions to a change in rulers. The expression *king* is used at times to describe the Roman emperor (compare Luke 23:2; John 19:15; I Peter 2:13, 17). The unbelieving Jews set Jesus against Caesar and accuse the missionaries of fomenting a rebellion against Rome. The magistrates of the free city of Thessalonica enjoy freedom from direct Roman rule and consequently wish to prevent any threat to this freedom.

8. They stirred up the crowd and the city officials who were paying attention to these things. 9. And when they had received a bond from Jason and the others, they let them go.

As was true with the trial of Jesus before Pontius Pilate, so it is here in Thessalonica: the Jews know how to manipulate the authorities. They do so by stirring up the crowd. Their objective is to cause confusion among the people and to convince the magistrates that the charges are weighty.

The city officials are not persuaded by the turmoil. In the absence of the principal characters, Paul and Silas, the charges lose their urgency, for no further proof is available. The officials listen to the evidence but are not persuaded that Jason and his friends constitute a threat to the security of Thessalonica. They dismiss Jason and his fellow Christians, but make them post a bond to guarantee peace and order in Thessalonica. The stipulation is that Paul and Silas must leave the city. If Jason and his friends should permit Paul to stay in Thessalonica and if as a result turmoil should ensue, Jason would lose his money and face imprisonment.

Even though Paul and Silas left Thessalonica, the fledgling congregation endured hardship and persecution, as Paul reveals in his first epistle to the Thessalonians (2:14). The Gentile population, possibly incited by the Jews, launched hostile attacks on the Christians. At least twice, Paul wanted to come to their aid but was prevented because of the bond Jason had posted. "This ingenious device put an impassable chasm between Paul and the Thessalonians. So long as the magistrates maintained this attitude, he could not return: he was helpless, and Satan had power."[21] Paul could do nothing but send Timothy to preach the gospel and encourage the believers in Thessalonica (I Thess. 2:18; 3:2–3).

---

20. See Acts 14:22; 19:8; 20:25; 28:23, 31; Rom. 14:17; I Cor. 4:20; 6:9, 10; 15:24, 50; Gal. 5:21; Eph. 5:5; Col. 4:11; II Thess. 1:5.

21. William M. Ramsay, *St. Paul the Traveller and the Roman Citizen* (1897; reprint ed., Grand Rapids: Baker, 1962), p. 231.

Greek Words, Phrases, and Constructions in 17:5–9

Verse 5

ζηλώσαντες—from the verb ζηλόω (I exert myself, am envious), this aorist active participle expresses the negative quality of envy. The Western text (Codex Bezae) lacks this participle and reads: "But the disbelieving Jews gathered some wicked fellows from the marketplace." The Majority Text reads: "But the Jews who did not believe took along some wicked men from the marketplace." And the Textus Receptus has: "But the Jews who were not persuaded, becoming envious, took some of the evil men from the marketplace" (NKJV; see also KJV).

ἐθορύβουν—the imperfect tense depicts the beginning of an action: "they began to throw the city into disorder." The verb θορυβέω differs from ταράσσω (I disturb). ἐτάραξαν (v. 8) is the result of ἐθορύβουν.

Verse 6

ἀναστατώσαντες—the aorist active participle of ἀναστατόω (I disturb, trouble) portrays the irony of the event. The Jews accuse Paul and Silas of disturbing the city (the world) while they themselves gathered a mob to cause a riot.

πάρεισιν—the present tense actually denotes a perfect tense: "they have arrived."

Verses 7 and 9

ἀπέναντι—this triple compound preposition (ἀπό, ἐν, ἀντί) expresses a hostile idea: "against."[22]

ἕτερον—another of a different kind.

λαβόντες τὸ ἱκανὸν—a legal term derived from the Latin *satis accipere*, that is, take security.

---

10 And the brothers immediately sent Paul and Silas away at night to Berea. When they arrived, they went into the synagogue of the Jews. 11 The Bereans were more noble-minded than the Thessalonians, for they received the word with great eagerness, examining the Scriptures daily to see whether these things were true. 12 Many of the Jews, then, believed, as well as a number of prominent Greek women and not a few men.

13 But when the Jews of Thessalonica learned that the Word of God was proclaimed by Paul also in Berea, they came even there, agitating and stirring up the crowds. 14 The brothers immediately sent Paul to travel to the sea, but Silas and Timothy remained in Berea. 15 The men who accompanied Paul brought him as far as Athens. They received instructions for Silas and Timothy to come to him as soon as possible, and then they departed.

---

4. Berea
17:10–15

The name *Berea* needs little introduction in Christian circles. It stands for serious Bible study by those who wish to learn what God has to say in his

---

22. Robertson, *Grammar*, p. 639.

Word. Whenever Christians refuse to take someone's explanation of a Scripture passage at face value but examine the exposition to see whether it is true to the biblical text, Bereans are present. For Bereans, the Scriptures are basic, relevant, and precious.

10. And the brothers immediately sent Paul and Silas away at night to Berea. When they arrived, they went into the synagogue of the Jews.

The Thessalonian Christians realize that the Jews might bring additional charges against Paul and Silas. They strongly advise the missionaries to leave the city and to do so under cover of darkness (compare 9:25; 23:23, 31; see also II Cor. 11:33). Paul and Silas reluctantly depart and travel in a west-southwesterly direction.

Instead of going to a major city, the missionaries decide to visit the town of Berea (modern Verria). From the writings of Cicero we learn that a century before Paul and his companions went to Berea, the Roman governor Piso came to Thessalonica at night and, because of strong opposition, took refuge in Berea. Cicero notes that this town lay off the road.[23] It was located a few miles south of the major highway and approximately forty miles from Thessalonica. Paul may have decided to go to Berea, and subsequently to Athens and Corinth instead of Rome, because Emperor Claudius had expelled the Jews from the imperial city in A.D. 49.[24]

After traveling for at least a night and two days, the missionaries arrive in Berea. They are true to their calling when soon after their arrival they enter the local Jewish synagogue. Unfortunately, Luke neglects to provide the primary motive for going to Berea. We surmise that one of Paul's reasons for visiting Berea was to meet Jewish people in their synagogue and preach the gospel (compare v. 2).

11. The Bereans were more noble-minded than the Thessalonians, for they received the word with great eagerness, examining the Scriptures daily to see whether these things were true. 12. Many of the Jews, then, believed, as well as a number of prominent Greek women and not a few men.

We observe these points:

1. *Noble-mindedness.* Luke compares the worshipers at the Berean synagogue with those at Thessalonica and praises the Bereans. Paul develops a close and loving relationship with the Thessalonians (see I Thess. 2:11); nevertheless, in respect to noble-mindedness the Bereans excel. They are more open to the truth of God's Word than the people of Thessalonica are.

The reason for the openness of the Bereans lies in their receptivity to and love for God's Word. For them, the Scriptures are much more than a written scroll or book that conveys a divine message. They use the Old Testament as the touchstone of truth, so that when Paul proclaims the gospel they immediately go to God's written Word for verification. They do

---

23. Cicero *Against Piso* 36.89.
24. Consult F. F. Bruce, *Paul, the Apostle of the Free Spirit* (Exeter: Paternoster, 1977), p. 235.

so, Luke adds, with great eagerness. Note well, the adjective *great* indicates that they treasure the Word of God. Luke ascribes the same diligence to the Bereans as Peter does to the Old Testament prophets, who intently and diligently searched the Word and inquired into its meaning (I Peter 1:10). The Bereans open the Scriptures and with ready minds learn that Jesus has fulfilled the messianic prophecies.

Day by day, the Bereans examine the Scriptures to see whether the teachings of Paul and Silas accord with God's written Word. They do so not from unbelief and doubt but from honest analysis and eagerness to learn the message of God's revelation. Although Luke fails to mention that God opened the hearts of the Bereans (compare 16:14), in verse 12 he records that "many of the Jews" believe the gospel. These people believe because they know God's Word. The situation in Berea differs from that in Thessalonica, where "some of the Jews were persuaded" (v. 4).

2. *Faith*. Like the Jews in Thessalonica, the Jews in Berea had welcomed the local Gentile population to their synagogue and had instructed them in the truths of Scripture. In both cities, many God-fearing Gentiles, men and women, came to the faith. And in both places, the Gentile women were prominent.[25] Luke displays evenhandedness in referring to men and women. Here he mentions the women first and then the men (compare 18:26). He repeatedly reports that prominent women in Jewish Gentile churches come to faith in Christ and give leadership. Luke even records names and relationships: Timothy's mother (16:1), Lydia of Thyatira (16:14–15), Damaris of Athens (17:34), Priscilla (18:2, 18, 26), and Philip's four daughters who prophesied (21:9). With the men, these women demonstrate faith in action.

Luke leaves the impression that a flourishing church arose at Berea. Nonetheless, he never indicates that Paul revisited the place. He relates that one of Paul's travel companions in Macedonia was Sopater son of Pyrrhus from Berea (20:4).

13. But when the Jews of Thessalonica learned that the Word of God was proclaimed by Paul also in Berea, they came even there, agitating and stirring up the crowds.

Probably Paul and his fellow missionaries labored in Berea for several months. But when unbelieving Jews from Thessalonica heard that Paul preached the gospel in Berea, they traveled to Berea. The Thessalonian Jews did the same thing the Jews in Pisidian Antioch and Iconium did when they followed Paul to Lystra (14:19). They traveled there and stirred up the crowds in an attempt to stop Paul from preaching the Word of God, that is, the gospel.[26] The plural *crowds* indicates that these Jews continued to agitate the people until they achieved their purpose: the removal of Paul. In fact,

---

25. A. N. Sherwin-White, *Roman Society and Roman Law in the New Testament* (1963; reprint ed., Grand Rapids: Baker, 1968), p. 174.

26. Refer to Acts 4:31; 8:14; 11:1; 12:24; 13:5, 7, 46; 17:13; 18:11.

they agitated the inhabitants of this noble town[27] until the Christians there provided safe conduct for Paul to go elsewhere.

Originally Paul was called to come over to Macedonia (16:9) to preach the gospel. But now he was forced to leave the province to shield himself from physical harm.

14. The brothers immediately sent Paul to travel to the sea, but Silas and Timothy remained in Berea. 15. The men who accompanied Paul brought him as far as Athens. They received instructions for Silas and Timothy to come to him as soon as possible, and then they departed.

The Christians in Berea care for Paul's safety and speedily send him on his way to the Aegean coast. Once again he is forced to leave a fledgling congregation (see 14:6, 20; 16:40; 17:10) and travel to other places. Perhaps Paul received divine instructions to go to Athens either by sea or by the coastal road. Luke is silent on this point, but indicates that the Berean Christians take only Paul to the coast. Silas and Timothy remain behind at Berea. They continue to preach the gospel there, although it is possible that they temporarily absented themselves from Berea until the turmoil ceased.

Paul's Berean friends accompany him all the way to Athens. Scholars aver that they traveled by boat, even though the Western text comments that Paul "passed by Thessaly, for he was prevented from proclaiming the word to them."[28] (Thessaly is the eastern region of Greece.) This comment seems to imply that Paul and his friends journeyed on foot along the coastal road to Athens. Also, Luke seems to depart from his custom of listing the port city from which Paul sails. In view of this omission, the interpretation that Paul traveled on foot to Athens is credible.

When Paul arrives at Athens, he realizes what a task it will be to preach the gospel to the educated Athenian citizens. He needs all the help he can possibly muster. Hence, he instructs his Berean friends to return to Berea and tell Silas and Timothy to come to Athens as soon as possible. From Paul's writings we know that these two missionaries promptly traveled to this city (I Thess. 1:1; 3:1). Paul, however, longs to be with the believers in Thessalonica. Because he is hindered from going there, he sends Timothy to learn about the spiritual well-being of the Thessalonian Christians (I Thess. 3:2). From Athens, Paul sends Silas back to Macedonia (Acts 18:5). Afterward Silas and Timothy return to Paul in Corinth.

Practical Considerations in 17:10–15

The Bible continues to be at the top of the bestseller list throughout the world. But at the same time the Bible continues to be the most neglected book in the lives of

---

27. Livy *History* 45.30.
28. Metzger, *Textual Commentary*, p. 455. One translation reads, "the brethren sent away Paul to go *as it were* to the sea" (KJV, italics added).

those who own a copy. The desire to possess it is not matched by the desire to know its message. In many homes the Bible gathers dust and is a forgotten book.

During the reign of Josiah king of Judah, the high priest discovered the Book of the Law in the temple of the Lord (II Kings 22:8). In a neglected corner of this building, the Word of God had been hidden from view, was forgotten, and consequently had no influence on the people. The Jews forsook Israel's God and turned to idol worship. But once the Scriptures were discovered, King Josiah literally changed the course of history. He read the Word of God to the people and had the worshipers pledge renewed obedience to the convenant which God had made with them (II Kings 23:1–3), thus averting God's anger and judgment.

We ought to read God's Word together as families and meditate on its meaning. By maintaining daily family devotions, we are able to build strong families that love the Lord. We must encourage one another to memorize portions of Scripture so that we make God's Word relevant in our lives. Furthermore, in our worship services the Bible ought to take a central place and our pastors should faithfully teach the entire Bible and all its doctrines.

By reading, learning, and knowing the Bible, we commune with God and hear him speak to us. By that Word he instructs us how to live for him. And when we prayerfully dedicate our lives to him, numerous blessings descend upon us.

Greek Words, Phrases, and Constructions in 17:10–15

Verse 10

διὰ νυκτὸς—"at night." As a genitive of time, the preposition is superfluous (see John 3:2; Acts 9:25).

ἀπῄεσαν—the imperfect active of ἄπειμι (I depart). The meaning of ἀπό (away) in the compound is supplanted by the preposition εἰς (into).

Verse 11

εὐγενέστεροι—the primary interpretation of this adjective is "well-born." Its secondary meaning refers to noble-mindedness. Here the secondary sense is applicable. The adjective is comparative and is succeeded by the genitive case.

οἵτινες—this indefinite relative pronoun (translated "who") has a causal connotation; it explains the noble character of the Bereans.

ἔχοι—here is the present optative in an indirect question. The verb *to have* in this idiomatic sentence signifies the verb *to be:* "whether these things were true."

Verses 12–13

The Western text (Codex Bezae) reads "and many of the Greeks and prominent men and women believed." Obviously, in this reading the significance of women has been lessened.

ἀπό—perhaps the choice of this preposition ("from") instead of ἐν (in) relates to the author's perspective of seeing Thessalonian Jews in Berea.

σαλεύοντες—the present participle of σαλεύω (I shake) denotes continued action together with the present participle of παράσσοντες (stirring up).

Verses 14–15

ἕως—the Textus Receptus has ὡς (as) instead of ἕως (as far as). Translators favor the second choice.

ὡς τάχιστα—here is the true superlative adverb, "as soon as possible."[29]

---

16 While Paul was waiting for them in Athens, he became agitated because he saw that the city was full of idols. 17 So he debated with the Jews and the God-fearing Greeks in the synagogue, and daily in the marketplace with those who happened to be present. 18 And some of the Epicurean and Stoic philosophers began to argue with him. Some of them said, "What does this babbler wish to say?" And others said, "He seems to be a proclaimer of foreign deities." They were saying this because Paul was proclaiming Jesus and the resurrection. 19 Having taken him, they brought him to the Areopagus and said: "May we learn this new teaching which you are presenting? 20 You are bringing to our ears some strange notions. Therefore, we want to know what they mean." 21 (All the Athenians and the foreigners living there used to spend their time doing nothing else but telling or listening to the latest ideas.)

22 Standing in the midst of the Areopagus, Paul said: "Men of Athens, I observe that you are very religious in every respect. 23 For while I was walking around and examining your objects of worship, I found an altar with this inscription:

TO AN UNKNOWN GOD

What, therefore, you worship in ignorance, this I am proclaiming to you. 24 The God who made the world and all things in it, because he is Lord of heaven and earth, does not dwell in manmade temples. 25 And he is not served by human hands as if he needs anything; rather, he gives to everyone life, breath, and all things. 26 He made from one person every nation of the human race to dwell on the whole face of the earth, and he determined the appointed times for these nations and the boundaries of their habitation. 27 They were to seek after God, if perhaps they might grope for him and find him, even though he is not far from each one of us. 28 'For in him we live and move and exist.' As even some of your own poets have said, 'We are his offspring.'

29 "Therefore, because we are the offspring of God, we ought not to think that the divine being is like an image of gold, silver, or stone made by man's skill and thought. 30 Having overlooked the times of ignorance, God is now commanding all men everywhere to repent. 31 For God has appointed a day on which he is going to judge the world in righteousness through a man whom he has appointed. He furnished proof to all men by having raised him from the dead."

32 When the audience heard about the resurrection of the dead, some began to sneer. Others said, "We want to hear you again concerning this." 33 So Paul went away from them. 34 But some men became disciples of him and believed. Among them were Dionysius the Areopagite and a woman named Damaris and others with them.

C. Greece
17:16–18:17

1. Athens
17:16–34

When Paul arrived in Athens, the intellectual center of the world, he realized that the Lord wanted him to teach the gospel where Greek philoso-

---

29. Robertson, *Grammar*, pp. 696, 974.

phy reigned supreme. In Athens, he met Epicurean and Stoic philosophers, professors from the city's renowned university, and numerous students from every part of the known world. Paul was at home in the academic arena of that day, for he was born in Tarsus, reared and educated in Jerusalem (22:3), and after his conversion spent many years in Tarsus (9:30). He was thoroughly acquainted with Stoic philosophy, which was taught in the university at Tarsus.

No longer a prosperous city, Athens had lost influence in the political and commercial world of that day. The Romans had conquered the city in 146 B.C. but wisely refrained from interfering with her local government. Enjoying a measure of independence, Athens rested on her reputation as a center of art, literature, philosophy, learning, and oratorical skill. Her culture, however, derived from Greece's golden age of the fifth and fourth centuries B.C.

Paul observed Greek culture wherever he went. In Athens, he saw the temples and altars, the sculptures and statues. For him, these artifacts were not mere artistic objects but objects of a pagan religion. In this idolatrous city, Paul had to introduce the gospel of Christ. Although the Jews had a synagogue where he could preach on the Sabbath, he knew that he had to confront the Athenian philosophers with the teachings of Christ in a presentation that had to be intelligible and direct.

a. Setting
17:16–18

16. While Paul was waiting for them in Athens, he became agitated because he saw that the city was full of idols. 17. So he debated with the Jews and the God-fearing Greeks in the synagogue, and daily in the marketplace with those who happened to be present.

1. *Waiting.* Paul was acquainted with idol worship and on an earlier occasion had experienced its effect in Lystra (14:11–20). In Athens, however, he encountered its influence everywhere.[30] In spite of its distinction of being the center of learning and artistry, this city exceeded all others in spiritual blindness and indulged in unrivaled idolatry. Even the name *Athens* had been chosen to honor the goddess Athena. And the place where Paul addressed the Athenian philosophers was called the Areopagus (vv. 19, 22), which according to one tradition was the hill of Ares (or Mars, in Latin), the god of war.[31]

While Paul waited for Silas and Timothy to come to Athens (see v. 15), he used his time to prepare himself for a formal encounter with Athenian philosophers. Paul did not visit Athens as a tourist who viewed monuments and artifacts, but as an apostle of Jesus Christ who proclaimed the

---

30. Josephus calls the Athenians "the most pious of the Greeks." *Against Apion* 2.11 [130] (LCL).
31. Consult Donald H. Madvig, "Areopagus," *ISBE*, vol. 1, p. 287.

message of salvation. Everywhere in Athens he was provoked by the idolatrous spirit of the Athenians. Satisfying a human need, he sought support and encouragement from fellow Jews and God-fearing Gentiles in the local synagogue. According to his custom (v. 2), Paul went to the Jew first and then to the Gentile.

2. *Debating.* "So he debated with the Jews and the God-fearing Greeks in the synagogue." The local Jews had introduced the teaching of the Scriptures to the Athenians and were successful in persuading some of them to accept these doctrines. We surmise that the membership of the synagogue in Athens was less than that of the synagogues in Berea and Thessalonica. Luke provides no indication that Paul was able to gain converts among the members of the synagogue, nor does he indicate that Paul was rebuffed or persecuted as he had been in other places.

"So he debated . . . daily in the marketplace with those who happened to be present." Paul did not limit his teachings to the Jews and the God-fearing Gentiles in the local synagogue on the Sabbath. During the rest of the week, he taught in the marketplace, where the people came to buy food and other merchandise. In the nearby buildings, the magistrates and other civic dignitaries would hear court cases. The senate met here to discuss political matters.[32]

Under the sheltered passageways, known as stoas, the philosophers gathered to give or listen to lectures. The public was permitted to listen to the lectures that were given, and as a result numerous learned debates took place in the marketplace. Here Paul went to debate with philosophers, their disciples, and others who came to listen to his account of the person, work, death, and resurrection of Jesus.

18. And some of the Epicurean and Stoic philosophers began to argue with him. Some of them said, "What does this babbler wish to say?" And others said, "He seems to be a proclaimer of foreign deities." They were saying this because Paul was proclaiming Jesus and the resurrection.

3. *Arguing.* Among the philosophers who listened to Paul and argued with him were those who belonged to two groups of thinkers: the Epicureans and the Stoics. Those of the first group were the followers of Epicurus (342–270 B.C.), who taught that death ought not to be feared; even the soul comes to an end when the body dies. Further, he taught that every being strives to attain pleasure by avoiding suffering and grief and by pursuing satisfaction and happiness.

The Stoics, who derived their name from visiting the Stoa Poikilē (the Painted Colonnade), were the disciples of the thinker Zeno (332–260 B.C.). This philosopher taught that man attains his highest aspiration when he subjects himself to the course of events, which divine necessity controls. When man submits to his lot, he reaches the state of happiness.

---

32. Lake and Cadbury observe, "It is, however, impossible to give a plan of Athens showing exactly where these buildings were." *Beginnings*, vol. 4, p. 210.

These philosophers were the intellectuals who engaged Paul in debate. With the tense of the Greek verb, Luke indicates that they continued their debate for a protracted period. Paul was a foreign visitor who came to the Athenian philosophers with strange ideas. These pundits, who were in charge of the debate, scorned Paul and his message by asking, "What does this babbler wish to say?" I have translated the Greek term *spermologos* as "babbler," but literally it means "seed picker."[33] Originally, the term described either the birds that picked up the seeds a farmer inadvertently sowed onto a path (Matt. 13:4) or men who picked up discarded items in the marketplace. In time, however, the word was used metaphorically as a derisive description of a plagiarist who would continually prate to anyone who paid him attention.[34]

4. *Proclaiming*. Paul preached the message of Jesus and his resurrection; except for the difference in audience, his presentation was the same as in the local synagogue, where he addressed both Jews and God-fearing Greeks.

Apart from the derisive question which the philosophers had asked, they regarded Paul with a measure of respect because his teaching related to the quality and essence of life: morality, death, judgment, and resurrection. Paul's teaching was a novelty to them, and they mistakenly thought that Paul was proclaiming a doctrine about two deities: Jesus and his feminine companion Anastasis (Greek for "resurrection"; see the NEB). They had not heard about Jesus and had no teaching on the resurrection; hence their comment that Paul "seems to be a proclaimer of foreign deities."[35] However, Paul preached the good news of Jesus and taught that he had risen from the dead. This was newsworthy and called for a formal address by Paul.

Greek Words, Phrases, and Constructions in 17:16–18

Verses 16–17

ἐκδεχομένου—the present participle with the proper noun *Paul* in the genitive case forms the genitive absolute construction. However, because the subject in the main sentence is the same as that of the genitive absolute clause, this construction is faulty. The present tense denotes durative action: "he continued to wait for."

παρωξύνετο—the imperfect middle expresses the inceptive idea: "Paul *became* agitated."

διελέγετο—the repeated use of the imperfect in this paragraph reveals the author's descriptive intent. The compound verb signifies "to debate, to enter a discussion."

---

33. Bauer, p. 762; Thayer, p. 584; Blass and Debrunner, *Greek Grammar*, #119.1.

34. Maurice A. Robinson opines that in the Athenian marketplace Paul preached the parable of the sower, in which he used the words *sperma* (seed) and *logos* (word). The contemptuous pun *spermologos* resulted from a misunderstanding of Paul's message. "Spermologos: Did Paul Preach from Jesus' Parables?" *Bib* 56 (1975): 231–40.

35. The phrase *foreign deities* is a subtle allusion to the trial of Socrates in 399 B.C.; the phrase occurs in reports of the trial. See Xenophon *Memorabilia* 1.1.1; Plato *Apology* 24b.

Verse 18

τῶν . . . φιλοσόφων—the noun is modified by the two adjectives *Epicurean* and *Stoic,* which are two distinct groups but here are taken together.

θέλοι—the present optative reflects classical usage of a conditional sentence with an implied protasis: *"if it were possible,* what would this babbler wish to say?"[36]

δοϰεῖ—here the personal construction ("he seems to be") is employed instead of the impersonal ("it seems").

---

b. Request
17:19–21

19. Having taken him, they brought him to the Areopagus and said: "May we learn this new teaching which you are presenting? 20. You are bringing to our ears some strange notions. Therefore, we want to know what they mean."

Translators face two problems in the first part of this text (v. 19). The first difficulty relates to the translation *having taken Paul,* which can be understood as "they invited him to accompany them" (JB). Other translations read "they took hold of him" (MLB, RSV), with the intimation that Paul was arrested because he preached about "foreign deities" in Athens. The Greek verb *epilambanomai* (I take hold of) may be translated two ways, and both senses of the verb occur in Acts.[37] The context, however, gives us no reason to think that Paul was arrested and formally charged with breaking the law in Athens.

Next, did the philosophers take Paul to a formal court session of the Areopagus? Indeed, the New English Bible translates the verse (19a) as follows: "So they took him and brought him before the Court of Areopagus." The expression *Areopagus* actually means "hill of Ares"; the hill, located nortwest of the Acropolis, was where the governing council of Athens met. Eventually the name *Areopagus* was applied to the meeting place and the council. In later times, the council held its meetings in the Royal Colonnade, located on the west side of the marketplace. We conjecture that the philosophers took Paul not to the hill but to the Royal Colonnade. Here, in an informal session, Paul faced the members of the court and the pundits who introduced him.[38]

One of the functions of the council "was that of supervising education,

---

36. C. F. D. Moule, *An Idiom-Book of New Testament Greek,* 2d ed. (Cambridge: Cambridge University Press, 1960), p. 151.

37. Acts 9:27; 23:19 for gently leading a person, and 16:19; 18:17; 21:30, 33 for arresting him.

38. Consult Colin J. Hemer, "Paul at Athens: A Topographical Note," *NTS* 20 (1973–74): 341–50; R. E. Wycherley, "St. Paul at Athens," *JTS* n.s. 19 (1968): 619–21; T. D. Barnes, "An Apostle on Trial," *JTS* n.s. 20 (1969): 407–19; Ned B. Stonehouse, *Paul Before the Areopagus and Other New Testament Studies* (Grand Rapids: Eerdmans, 1957), pp. 8–9; W. G. Morrice, "Where Did Paul Speak in Athens—on Mars' Hill or Before the Court of the Areopagus? Acts 17:19," *ExpT* 83 (1972): 377–78.

particularly of controlling the many visiting lecturers."[39] The members of the council wished to learn whether Paul's teaching constituted a threat to the state. Should the court be satisfied that Paul was harmless, he could continue to preach his message.

"May we learn this new teaching which you are presenting?" The philosophers presented no accusation against Paul but in the presence of the court they asked a penetrating question. They called Paul's teaching new, and in the Greek they indicated that this indeed is an "unprecedented, novel, uncommon, unheard-of [doctrine]."[40] Paul stood alone in the presence of brilliant teachers who wanted to know whether his views transcended their own. Before a completely pagan audience he had to present the message of Christ's gospel. No longer could he appeal to the Old Testament Scriptures as he did when he addressed synagogue audiences. In place of Jews and God-fearing Gentiles, Paul faced people who had never heard of Israel's God.

"You are bringing to our ears some strange notions. Therefore, we want to know what they mean." The philosophers state only that Paul is introducing "some strange notions." They do not feel that these notions are a threat to their philosophies; many intellectually curious philosophers express their desire to learn something from Paul. They emphasize gaining knowledge by listening to new ideas (vv. 19, 20, 21).[41] And this emphasis on knowledge gives Paul an opening to acquaint his audience with "strange notions."

21. (All the Athenians and the foreigners living there used to spend their time doing nothing else but telling or listening to the latest ideas.)

In this parenthetical statement, Luke portrays the life of a typical university city of that day. The academicians had the leisure to devote themselves to the pursuit of learning. They would not perform manual labor or fill any occupation other than that of debating concepts in the marketplace, for they strove to add the latest ideas to their store of knowledge. The professors and their students would spend their time debating theories they themselves had researched or had learned from foreigners, whose presence was commonplace. These strangers lived among the Athenians for longer or shorter periods and were invited to contribute to the process of learning new ideas. The invitation to address the Areopagus offered Paul a splendid opportunity to present the good news of Jesus Christ in the academic setting of Athens.

Greek Words, Phrases, and Constructions in 17:19–21

Verses 19–20

γνῶναι—note that this aorist infinitive occurs twice in these two verses. The emphasis is on the academician's learning process.

---

39. Bauer, p. 105.
40. Thayer, p. 317; Bauer, p. 394.
41. Refer to Gustav Stählin, *TDNT*, vol. 5, p. 7.

ξενίζοντα—this present active participle in the neuter plural with τινα (some) denotes the secondary meaning *to surprise,* not the primary meaning *to entertain a guest;* see ξένοι (foreigners, v. 21).

The Western text has added a few words to verse 19. The added words are italicized: "And *after some days* they took hold of him and brought him to the Areopagus, *inquiring and* saying. . . . "[42]

Verse 21

ἕτερον—the use of this adjective purposely contrasts the life of a scholar with that of other citizens. The Athenian scholar would pursue no interests other than debating new ideas. The meaning of the adjective is "different."

καινότερον—the comparative form of καινός (see v. 19) refers to "something newer than what they had recently heard."[43]

---

c. Introduction[44]
17:22–23

22. Standing in the midst of the Areopagus, Paul said: "Men of Athens, I observe that you are very religious in every respect. 23. For while I was walking around and examining your objects of worship, I found an altar with this inscription:

TO AN UNKNOWN GOD

What, therefore, you worship in ignorance, this I am proclaiming to you."

If we understand the word *Areopagus* to refer to the council, the phrase *in the midst of* fits perfectly. Conversely, if the term *Areopagus* refers to the hill, we have difficulty explaining how Paul could stand in the midst of a hill. Standing in the midst of council members, philosophers, students, and interested spectators, Paul seizes the occasion to teach the "latest ideas" about Jesus Christ.

"Men of Athens." Skillfully Paul addresses his audience with the same formula that had been used by the famous orator Demosthenes. With this address he touches the hearts of his hearers. Then he follows it with words of praise for their ostentatious religiosity. Paul needs a point of contact from which he gradually can lead his audience to a knowledge of eternal values in Christ. The presence of numerous temples, idols, and altars in Athens gives Paul a magnificent point of contact, notwithstanding that he himself is thoroughly provoked by the idolatry of this city (v. 16).

---

42. Metzger, *Textual Commentary,* p. 456.

43. Robertson, *Grammar,* p. 665.

44. Paul's speech is divided into three parts: introduction (vv. 22b–23), content (vv. 24–28), and application (vv. 29–31). For variations on this division, see Jacques Dupont, "Le discours à l'Aréopage (Ac 17, 22–31) lieu de rencontre entre christianisme et hellénisme," *Bib* 60 (1979): 530–46; Hans Conzelmann, *Acts of the Apostles,* trans. James Limburg, A. Thomas Kraabel, and Donald H. Juel (1963; Philadelphia: Fortress, 1987), p. 141.

For the sake of the gospel he is willing to accommodate his speech to the level of his audience.

Teaching a pantheistic doctrine, the Athenian philosophers had encouraged the people to erect places of worship for numerous gods. For that reason, Paul tells his audience that they are "very religious." This term can be understood either in a derogatory sense ("superstitious") or as a complimentary statement of fact. In the context of the speech, Paul uses the term affirmatively, because he is interested in gaining the attention of the Athenian crowd. To complete his commendation, he even adds the words *in every respect*. Of course, we should understand that Paul is not interested in endorsing the religiosity of the Athenians but desires to acquaint them with the doctrines of Christ. He indicates this desire by explicitly referring to Jesus' resurrection[45] and by placing the Christian faith over against the idols of Athens.

"For while I was walking around." Paul indicates that by daily traversing the city of Athens, he has taken note of the religious objects of worship. He has carefully examined the magnificent temples, altars, and idols. Among all these objects of adoration he has even found an altar with the inscription:

TO AN UNKNOWN GOD

He commends the Athenians for their thoughtfulness in constructing an altar even to a deity of whom they have no knowledge. In other words, they have expended efforts not to offend even an unknown deity. The Greek words *agnostos theos* can be translated either "unknown god" or "unknowable god." The first translation is preferable, for Paul's purpose is to teach that God, who created heaven and earth, is knowable.

In his speech Paul uses the inscription as a point of contact with the Athenians, who at this altar[46] worshiped an unknown god. By their act of worship, the audience has to admit that they are open to receiving instruction about an unknown god, and that they are unable to worship a new god unless they know him. John Calvin comments that it is far better to have knowledge of God than to worship without knowing him, for God cannot be worshiped reverently unless he first becomes known.[47]

"What, therefore, you worship in ignorance, this I am proclaiming to

---

45. H. Armin Moellering, "Deisidaimonia, a Footnote to Acts 17:22," *ConcThMonth* 34 (1963): 470.

46. No archaeological evidence of this altar has been discovered. But this does not disprove that an altar with the inscription in the singular ("to an unknown god") existed. The inscription in the singular, not the plural, may refer to an older form of altar, because Paul uses the Greek pluperfect tense *epegegrapto* (had been inscribed). See John Albert Bengel, *Gnomon of the New Testament*, ed. Andrew R. Fausset, 5 vols. (Edinburgh: Clark, 1877), vol. 2, p. 666. The literature on this particular subject is vast. For a current, though not exhaustive, list, consult F. F. Bruce, *The Book of the Acts*, rev. ed., New International Commentary on the New Testament series (Grand Rapids: Eerdmans, 1988), pp. 333–34 n. 47.

47. John Calvin, *Commentary on the Acts of the Apostles*, ed. David W. Torrance and Thomas F. Torrance, 2 vols. (Grand Rapids: Eerdmans, 1966), vol. 2, p. 111.

you." Paul transfers the concept *unknown* from the deity to the worshipers. They worship without knowledge, which in Athens, the bastion of learning, was a contradiction in terms. They concede that this unknown god exists, but they have no knowledge of him. And they must acknowledge that their approach to proper worship is deficient because of their ignorance. Paul, however, does not equate the unknown god of the Athenians with the true God. Notice that he says "what you worship," not "whom you worship."[48] Paul calls attention only to their lack of knowledge and thus takes the opportunity to introduce God as Creator and Judge of the universe. Paul intimates that the Athenians' ignorance of God is blameworthy and this ignorance demands swift emendation.

Paul speaks with absolute authority when he says, "This I am proclaiming to you." He speaks on behalf of God and thus his authority is representative and divinely derived. Paul, then, serves as a channel through whom God speaks to the Athenians. If they reject the message of Paul, then in effect they reject God himself.

Greek Words, Phrases, and Constructions in 17:22–23

Verse 22

σταθείς—the aorist passive participle of ἵστημι (I stand) should be interpreted as an intransitive active. No one placed Paul physically in the midst of the Areopagus; Paul stood.

δεισιδαιμονεστέρους—this adjective in the comparative means "more religious than I expected" or "more religious than ordinary."[49]

Verse 23

ἐπεγέγραπτο—the use of the pluperfect passive is perhaps an indication that the inscription belonged to earlier times.

ὅ—"what" (neuter), not ὅν (whom; masculine), expresses the impersonal nature of pagan religion.

---

d. Content
17:24–28

24. "The God who made the world and all things in it, because he is Lord of heaven and earth, does not dwell in manmade temples. 25. And he is not served by human hands as if he needs anything; rather, he gives to everyone life, breath, and all things."

The message Paul proclaims is thoroughly scriptural. Although the peo-

---

48. Some translations (κjv, νκjv, jb, and *Phillips*) follow the Majority Text and read "whom you worship."

49. Robertson, *Grammar*, p. 665; Robert Hanna, *A Grammatical Aid to the Greek New Testament* (Grand Rapids: Baker, 1983), p. 225.

ple in his audience are unaware of the references, Paul teaches that God, who is the creator of the heavens and the earth, gives life to all people. He does this by freely quoting the words of Isaiah:

> This is what God the LORD says—
> he who created the heavens and stretched them out,
>   who spread out the earth and all that comes out of it,
> who gives breath to its people,
>   and life to those who walk on it. [42:5, NIV]

Paul puts the teaching concerning God and his revelation in the place of the Stoic philosophy that sees deities in every aspect of the world but has no doctrine of creation. Paul teaches monotheism over against Stoic pantheism. He introduces God, who made the world and everything in it. The Greek word *kosmos* signifies the world arranged in orderly fashion "as the sum total of everything here and now."[50] When Paul adds to the term *kosmos* the phrase *and all things in it,* he stresses the orderliness of creation that finds its origin in one personal God. He says that this God is Lord of heaven and earth. Paul intimates that as Lord, God governs and cares for all that he has made, including this Athenian audience.

Incidentally, Paul's reference to creation has an echo in the speech he delivered in Lystra (14:15–17; compare Gen. 14:19, 22; Exod. 20:11). There he stressed that God provides the people with plenty of food and fills their hearts with joy. Now he asserts that God rules over everything in heaven and on earth.[51]

"[God] does not dwell in manmade temples." Again Paul proclaims the teachings of the Old Testament when he points out that God does not live in temples made by human hands (see 7:48; I Kings 8:27). Simple reasoning should convince the Athenians that God who has created heaven and earth cannot be restricted to the confines of a temple.

"And he is not served by human hands as if he needs anything." God is immeasurably greater than the human mind can ever fathom. Therefore, in the psalms God says that because everything in this world belongs to him, he has no need for bulls and goats as sacrificial animals (Ps. 50:8–13). To the point, God is not dependent on sacrifices that man brings to him. With this teaching, Paul finds a listening ear among the Athenian philosophers. "Here may be discerned approximations to the Epicurean doctrine that God needs nothing from human beings and to the Stoic belief that he is the source of all life. . . . "[52]

---

50. Bauer, p. 445. See also E. Fudge, "Paul's Apostolic Self-Consciousness at Athens," *JETS* 14 (1971): 193–98.

51. Consult Stonehouse, *Paul Before the Areopagus*, p. 26.

52. F. F. Bruce, *The Acts of the Apostles: The Greek Text with Introduction and Commentary*, 3d (rev. and enl.) ed. (Grand Rapids: Eerdmans, 1990), p. 506. See also Bertil Gärtner, *The Areopagus Speech and Natural Revelation*, trans. C. H. King (Lund: Gleerup, 1955), pp. 144–45.

"Rather, he gives to everyone life, breath, and all things." God is a personal God who not only creates but also sustains everything he has made. This self-sufficient God daily cares for man and for his great creation in the minutest details. God is the source of life, for he gives breath to all living creatures.[53] Note the striking contrast Paul makes in this verse (v. 25). He says that God, who does not "need anything," provides "all things" for everyone. In the Greek, the expression *all things* connotes that God in his support of man excludes absolutely nothing from the totality of creation. God gives man everything he needs and thus upholds him by his power.

26. "He made from one person every nation of the human race to dwell on the whole face of the earth, and he determined the appointed times for these nations and the boundaries of their habitation. 27. They were to seek after God, if perhaps they might grope for him and find him, even though he is not far from each one of us."

Notice these four points:

1. *Creation.* The Athenians divided the people of the world into two classes: the Greeks and the barbarians. Everyone not born in Greece was considered a barbarian. Paul challenges this theory by focusing attention on the origin of man. Without mentioning his source, he teaches the creation account of Genesis and states that God is man's creator (Gen. 2:7). Furthermore, out of one man, Adam, God made every nation on this earth.[54] God purposed to have the entire globe inhabited by the various nations that originated from this one man (Gen. 1:28; 9:1; 11:8–9). This means that the human race is integrally related as its members populate the entire earth (compare Mal. 2:10). Because of his common origin, a Jew ought not to despise a Gentile and an Athenian philosopher ought not to loathe a Jew. God, who created humanity, governs and provides for it. For that reason, man has to acknowledge him as Creator and Lord.

2. *Providence.* God rules his creation and especially the development of the races and nations. "He determined the appointed times for these nations and the boundaries of their habitation." That is, God himself is in full control by defining their epochs and their borders. The Greeks taught that they had originated from the soil on which they dwelled. Paul's teaching, therefore, conflicted with their own theory of origin; but Paul replaced their defective theory with God's revelation of man's descent.

What is the meaning of the phrase *the appointed times*? One view is that God determined once for all the seasons of the year (see 14:17; and Ps. 74:17).[55] Other interpreters understand the phrase to refer to "historical

---

53. The Greek term *pasi* (either masculine or neuter) refers to man; yet it does not exclude the rest of God's creation that has life and breath. Here is an inclusive translation: "He is himself the universal giver of life and breath and all else" (NEB).

54. The Western manuscripts and the Majority Text have the reading *from one blood* (KJV, NKJV). The word *blood* was either added by a reviser or was (accidentally) deleted.

55. Haenchen, *Acts*, p. 523.

epochs."[56] They base their explanation on the immediate context of Adam's creation and the nations that descended from him. Hence, they say that God has appointed to these nations periods of history in which they prosper. A third interpretation explains the word *times* with reference to individuals that make up the nations. In the past, God has appointed the exact times for every person and in the present he fulfills them.[57] Because the text speaks of nations, not of individual persons, I prefer the second choice and interpret the phrase as "historical epochs determined by God." Luke in his Gospel also uses the word *times* to mean epochs; there he notes that Jerusalem will be destroyed when "the times of the Gentiles are fulfilled" (Luke 21:24).

The second choice corresponds with the next clause: "[God determined] the boundaries of their habitation," which appears to be an echo of a line in the Song of Moses, "When the Most High gave the nations their inheritance, . . . He set the boundaries of the peoples" (Deut. 32:8, NASB). God, then, has determined the epochs for and the borders of the nations of this world. Borders often are geographic demarcations caused by either bodies of water (seas, lakes, rivers) or mountain ranges.[58] We know that God determines where the nations of the world are to reside.

3. *Search.* Paul says that God expressed a twofold purpose for the human race: to dwell on the earth and "to seek after God." These purposes are interrelated, for dwelling on this earth entails seeking after God. To put it differently, the second phrase is an explanation of the first phrase. God created man so that man might worship him. But how does a person seek after God? The Old Testament is replete with examples of people seeking God for the purpose of serving him. The Psalter records numerous references to seeking God, and the books of the prophets continually warn and exhort the people to seek and obey him.[59]

Paul qualifies his comment on people searching for God and states a wish: "if perhaps they might grope for him and find him." He hopes that people, even though blinded by sin, may grope for God their Maker— much as a sightless person reaches out to and touches a fellow human being without seeing him. The writer of Hebrews stresses this same truth but puts it in the context of true faith. Says he, "For without faith it is impossible to

---

56. Gärtner, *Areopagus Speech and Natural Revelation*, pp. 147–51; I. Howard Marshall, *The Acts of the Apostles: An Introduction and Commentary*, Tyndale New Testament Commentary series (Leicester: Inter-Varsity; Grand Rapids: Eerdmans, 1980), p. 288; Gerhard Delling, *TDNT*, vol. 3, p. 461.

57. F. W. Grosheide, *De Handelingen der Apostelen*, Kommentaar op het Nieuwe Testament series, 2 vols. (Amsterdam: Van Bottenburg, 1948), vol. 2, p. 149.

58. Martin Dibelius says that the boundaries are the five zones of this globe (two polar regions, two temperate zones, and the tropical zone) and, from his native perspective (Germany), avers that the temperate zones "differ favourably from the tropical and the two arctic zones." *Studies in the Acts of the Apostles* (London: SCM, 1956), p. 31.

59. E.g., Pss. 24:6; 27:8; 83:16; 105:3–4; Isa. 9:13; 31:1; 55:6; 65:1; Jer. 29:13–14. See also Édouard des Places, "Actes 17,27," *Bib* 48 (1967): 1–6.

please God. Because the one who comes to God must believe that he exists and that he is a rewarder of those who earnestly seek him" (Heb. 11:6).

4. *Presence.* Paul touches on a tenet of Stoic religion when, appealing to his pagan audience, he says: "[God] is not far from each one of us." He moves from the general concept of nations to the specific notion of the individual person by teaching that religion is a one-to-one relation between God and man. Every human being is personally responsible to his God. Paul diverges, however, from Stoic philosophy with its teaching that God, in an impersonal manner, is present everywhere. By contrast, Paul's teaching is that we are able to have a personal relationship with God, because God is near to his people (see Pss. 139:5–12; 145:18; Jer. 23:23).

28. " 'For in him we live and move and exist.' As even some of your own poets have said, 'We are his offspring.' "

Establishing rapport with his Athenian audience, Paul quotes verbatim from two Greek poets. Both writers extol the virtues of the god Zeus. The first one is the Cretan poet Epimenides (600 B.C.). The words of his poem occur in a ninth-century commentary, written in Syriac, by Isho'dad of Merw, who comments: "The Cretans said as truth about Zeus, that he was a lord; he was lacerated by a wild boar and buried; and behold! his grave is known amongst us; so therefore Minos, son of Zeus made a laudatory speech on behalf of his father; and he said in it,

> 'The Cretans carve a Tomb for thee,
> O Holy and high!
> liars, evil beasts, and slow bellies;
> for thou art not dead for ever;
> thou art alive and risen; for
> *in thee we live and are moved,*
> *and have our being.'* "[60]

The second quotation is from the poet Aratus (315–240 B.C.), who was a native of Cilicia in Asia Minor, and thus a compatriot of Paul. In the third century B.C., Aratus wrote a poem honoring Zeus in a composition called *Phainomena.* The fourth and fifth lines of the poem have the words: "In every way we have all to do with Zeus, for we are truly his offspring."[61]

The first citation presents a minor problem that relates to its source. Although Isho'dad of Merw attributes the words of the poem to Minos of Crete, Clement of Alexandria ascribes the lines "Cretans are always liars, evil beasts, lazy gluttons" (see Titus 1:12) to Epimenides.[62] In all probability, Minos quoted rather than wrote these words.

---

60. Margaret D. Gibson, ed., *The Commentaries of Isho'dad of Merw,* Horae Semiticae no. 10 (Cambridge: Cambridge University Press, 1913), p. 28. See also Kirsopp Lake, "Your Own Poets," *Beginnings,* vol. 5, pp. 246–51.

61. The words also occur in a *Hymn to Zeus* written by Cleanthes (331–233 B.C.). Clement of Alexandria refers to it in *Stromata* 1.19.91.4–5.

62. Clement of Alexandria *Stromata* 1.14.59.

By quoting these poets Paul is not intimating that he agrees with the pagan setting in which the citations flourished. Rather, he uses the words to fit his Christian teaching. From the Old Testament, he is able to draw the evidence that man derives his life, activity, and being from God (Job 12:10; Dan. 5:23). Paul uses the expression *in him* as a favorite term for the believer who is in Christ, but in many instances the names *Christ* and *God* are identical (e.g., "your life is hidden with Christ in God" [Col. 3:3]). And John states that God gives the believer life through his Son (I John 5:11). Accordingly, E. Margaret Clarkson gave poetic voice to these thoughts in her hymn:

> We come, O Christ, to Thee,
> True Son of God and man,
> By Whom all things consist,
> In Whom all life began:
> In Thee alone we live and move,
> And have our being in Thy love.

Greek Words, Phrases, and Constructions in 17:25–28

Verse 25

προσδεόμενος—the present participle denotes condition: "as if he needs anything." The use of the present also occurs in διδούς (he gives) to signify continued action.

ζωὴν καὶ πνοήν—"life and breath." English is unable to reproduce the assonance of the Greek. The German *Leben und Atem* and the Dutch *leven en adem* come close to the rhythm and similarity in sound.

τὰ πάντα—the addition of the definite article indicates that nothing is excluded from the totality of πάντα (all things).

Verse 27

εἰ ἄρα—these particles introduce a condition, "if perhaps," that is followed by two optatives in the aorist tense (ψηλαφήσειαν, they might grope, and εὕροιεν, they might find [him]).

ὑπάρχοντα—the present participle is concessive: "although he is." It is negated by οὐ instead of μή for emphasis.

Verse 28

καθ' ὑμᾶς—the preposition κατά appears in place of the personal pronoun ὑμῶν in the genitive case. This construction is a periphrase for the genitive pronoun.[63]

τοῦ—the definite article fills the place of the demonstrative pronoun τούτου (of this one).

---

63. Bauer, p. 408.

e. Application
17:29–31

29. "Therefore, because we are the offspring of God, we ought not to think that the divine being is like an image of gold, silver, or stone made by man's skill and thought."

With the adverb *therefore*, Paul indicates that he is ready to draw the conclusion and apply his message to the audience. On the basis of the two quotations from the Greek poets, he can freely assert: "We are the off-spring of God." Because this is so, Paul contends, we ought to regard God from a divine perspective, not a human perspective. That is, we should not picture God in the form of a man and thus worship him by fashioning images made of gold, silver, or stone. God is spirit (John 4:24) and cannot be portrayed in the form of an idol made by man.

God is man's Creator and, therefore, infinitely greater than man the creature. God cannot be compared to the precious commodities he himself has made: gold, silver, stone. In a sense, man stands between God and matter. When man, relying on his skills and thoughts, attempts to construct an image from metal or stone and worships it, he himself becomes odious to God. Man transgresses the divine command when he makes graven images and worships them (refer to Exod. 20:4–6; Deut. 5:8–10). By implication, Paul teaches his Gentile audience God's explicit command not to worship idols.[64] He so skillfully presents the argument that the philosophers are unable to oppose his teaching.

Paul carefully chooses his words when he says that "the divine being" is not made like an image of gold, silver, or stone. The term *divine being* is in the neuter and corresponds to the use of the relative pronoun *what* in the clause *what . . . you worship* (v. 23). He refrains from calling an idol "God," but classifies it with impersonal objects. Thus he clearly distinguishes between the living God and inanimate idols.

30. "Having overlooked the times of ignorance, God is now command-ing all men everywhere to repent. 31. For God has appointed a day on which he is going to judge the world in righteousness through a man whom he has appointed. He furnished proof to all men by having raised him from the dead."

1. *Overlook.* If the Gentiles choose to defend themselves by asserting that they acted in ignorance of God's commands, Paul tells them that God has overlooked their deeds of sinful ignorance (see 3:17; 13:27). That is, God has neither judged the people nor meted out due punishment for their sins but instead has looked the other way, so to speak. In two other instances Paul makes this same point.

First, in his speech to the people at Lystra, Paul states that in the past God allowed the Gentile nations to live their own way of life (14:16). That does

---

64. Compare Deut. 4:23, 28; Isa. 40:18–20; 44:9–20; Rom. 1:23; Wis. 13:10.

not mean that God excuses the nations, for he holds them responsible for their actions (Rom. 1:19–20). But when these Gentiles hear the proclamation of the gospel, their times of ignorance have come to an end.[65] If they hear the Good News but fail to repent, they forfeit God's offer of salvation and consequently suffer eternal punishment.

Second, in Romans 3:25 Paul writes that God tolerated the sins people committed in earlier times and thus overlooked them. But now that Christ has shed his blood for the sins of his people, God is ready to forgive these sins of the past, just as he forgives the sins of those people who repent and come to him now.[66]

Paul tells the Athenian philosophers that God presently commands "all men everywhere to repent." This is the divine command that no one can afford to ignore. Because Christ has shed his blood on the cross for remission of sin, all people of all nations, tribes, races, and tongues are told to repent, believe, and cease living in ignorance and sin as soon as they hear the gospel message proclaimed (compare, e.g., Luke 24:47).

2. *Judge*. Paul now comes to the heart of the matter: "For God has appointed a day on which he is going to judge the world in righteousness through a man whom he has appointed." Paul does not mention the name of Jesus Christ but continues to speak of the acts of God. He says that God has designated a certain day as the day of judgment. Paul's reference to divine judgment is a warning to the people to repent and thus avoid a day that leads to condemnation, doom, and destruction. The message of divine judgment causes people either to confess their sins and believe in Christ (10:42) or to harden their hearts and turn away from God (24:25–26).

On the judgment day God will judge the world in righteousness (Pss. 9:8; 96:13; 98:9). Paul teaches that God is both man's creator and his ultimate judge. Although Paul indirectly refers to Jesus Christ as "a man whom [God] has appointed," he intimates that this man is the second Adam. From one man (the first Adam) God made the entire human race (v. 26), and in the presence of another man (the second Adam) all of humanity will be judged (v. 31).[67] Jesus himself teaches that God has given him, the Son of man, the authority to judge the world (John 5:22, 27).

But the Athenians might ask whether this man, who remains nameless, possesses divine authority to judge the world. What proof can this man furnish that God has conferred on him the power to judge? Paul states affirmatively that God himself provides proof to all men, because he raised this man from the dead.

The Greeks undoubtedly had difficulty understanding how the resurrection of a man could be proof that God appointed him to judge the world.

---

65. Gärtner, *Areopagus Speech and Natural Revelation*, p. 233.

66. Refer to William Hendriksen, *Exposition of Paul's Epistle to the Romans*, New Testament Commentary series (Grand Rapids: Baker, 1980), p. 134.

67. Édouard des Places, "Actes 17,30–31," *Bib* 52 (1971): 531–32.

They taught the immortality of the soul and the destruction of the body, but they had no doctrine of the resurrection.

True to apostolic form, wherever Paul preaches the Good News, he teaches the resurrection of Jesus Christ. For the apostles, this doctrine is basic to the Christian faith and should be proclaimed to both Jews and Gentiles.[68] Therefore, Paul introduces this cardinal doctrine without apology and demonstrates that it is God's proof for appointing a man, namely, Jesus Christ, as supreme judge (compare I Thess. 1:9–10).

Paul's speech comes to an abrupt end when his audience refuses to accept the doctrine of the resurrection. After a lengthy introduction to establish rapport with his audience, Paul began to develop the main part of his speech: the good news of salvation. When he mentions the doctrine of resurrection, his audience no longer shows interest,[69] even though this is the topic Paul had been teaching in the marketplace before he was invited to address the Council of the Areopagus (v. 18). Paul's address does not mention Christ's death on the cross or his return; nonetheless, the speech sets forth some of the basic elements of the gospel: sin, repentance, judgment, and the resurrection.

Additional Note on the Areopagus Address

Strictly speaking, Paul's address in Athens is not a defense of the Christian faith. Rather, his speech is both a challenge to pagan religion and a proclamation of the gospel. When Paul addressed the Council of the Areopagus, he faced an audience that differed from those in the synagogue worship services. Standing before the Athenian philosophers, he could not assume that they had any knowledge of the Scripture or of Jesus, who fulfilled the prophecies in Scripture. Paul had to begin his speech by teaching his audience the doctrines of God and creation. He continued his teaching with the doctrine of man, for man is God's offspring. And he concluded his oration with the doctrines of judgment and the resurrection.

We affirm the historicity of Paul's visit to the Council of the Areopagus.[70] In that meeting, Paul the apostle to the Gentiles introduced his pagan audience to the teachings of the Christian faith. He commented that God created man, appointed a day for judgment, and overlooked man's sins of the past. The similarity between this speech and Paul's writing lends weight to the authenticity of this passage. For example, in his letter to the Romans, Paul mentions that God has

---

68. Acts 2:24, 32; 3:15, 26; 4:2, 10, 33; 5:30; 10:40; 13:34, 37; 17:31; 25:19.

69. Leland Ryken asserts that the construction of Paul's speech reveals that he intended to deliver a classical oration that was cut short. *Words of Life: A Literary Introduction to the New Testament* (Grand Rapids: Baker, 1987), p. 128. Stonehouse, however, thinks that the speech is complete. *Paul Before the Areopagus*, pp. 36–40.

70. F. F. Bruce, "Paul and the Athenians," *ExpT* 88 (1976): 11. Hans Conzelmann calls Paul's speech "not an extract from a missionary address, but a purely literary creation." See "The Address of Paul on the Areopagus," in *Studies in Luke-Acts: Essays Presented in Honor of Paul Schubert*, ed. Leander E. Keck and J. Louis Martyn (Nashville: Abingdon, 1966), p. 218.

made himself known in creation, that God judges men's secrets through Jesus Christ, and that God has shown his forbearance by leaving sins unpunished (Rom. 1:19–21; 2:16; 3:21–26).

Even though Paul alludes to an inscription ("to an unknown God") on an altar and quotes some lines from pagan sources, he nowhere indicates that the gospel occupies "common ground with pagan religion and philosophy."[71] Paul uses these pagan features as points of contact with his audience but refuses to accommodate and compromise the gospel message. In this respect, he is true to his God, who gives man the law not to have any gods before him. Whether Paul faces a Jewish audience or a pagan assembly, he faithfully teaches the uncompromising truth of God's revelation.

In his accounts of the three missionary journeys of Paul, Luke includes a discourse given on each journey. For the first excursion, he gives an account of Paul's sermon delivered in Pisidian Antioch. For the second he has the apostle's Areopagus address, and for the third Paul's farewell discourse to the Ephesian elders on the beach at Miletus.[72]

Luke portrays Athens as the world's cultural and intellectual center where the message of the gospel encounters the wisdom of the Greeks. The result of this encounter is that a prominent member of the council, a lady of note, and several others become Christians. The limited effect, however, should be attributed not to Paul's speech but to the refusal of the Athenians to listen to and accept the gospel. The lack of response is insignificant in comparison to the march of the gospel.

In a sense, Paul's encounter with the sophisticated Athenians in the middle of the first century is representative of the church's mission to the secular world of today. Should we consider Paul's mission in Athens a failure? Certainly not, because the church has a duty to proclaim the gospel in every area of life and to call people to repentance and faith in Jesus Christ.

Greek Words, Phrases, and Constructions in 17:29–31

Verses 29–30

τὸ θεῖον—literally "the divine [being]." The adjective is neuter and corresponds to the relative pronoun ὅ in verse 23.

ὑπεριδών—this aorist active participle from ὑπεροράω (I overlook) conveys a negative notion.[73]

Verse 31

ἐν ἀνδρί—the noun is either a dative of sphere ("in the person of a man") or an instrumental dative ("by a man"). The second translation is preferred.[74]

---

71. Thomas L. Wilkinson, "Acts 17: The Gospel Related to Paganism," *VoxRef* 35 (1980): 12.
72. Refer to Jacques Dupont, *Nouvelles Études sur les Actes des Apôtres*, Lectio Divina 118 (Paris: Cerf, 1984), p. 384.
73. Robertson, *Grammar*, p. 629.
74. Moule, *Idiom-Book*, p. 77.

f. Reaction
17:32–34

32. When the audience heard about the resurrection of the dead, some began to sneer. Others said, "We want to hear you again concerning this." 33. So Paul went away from them. 34. But some men became disciples of him and believed. Among them were Dionysius the Areopagite and a woman named Damaris and others with them.

Athenian philosophers, among them Plato, had developed a doctrine of the soul's immortality. They reasoned that the soul migrated to another place, but that death terminated man's physical existence. The philosophers in Paul's audience reject his teaching of a physical resurrection, for "the idea of a general resurrection at the end of the age is alien to the Greeks."[75] As a result some of Paul's listeners begin to sneer and thereby indicate that his message is unacceptable to them. To them, the doctrine of the resurrection is pointless. Others show an interest in the subject and inform Paul that they would like to listen to him again. Luke provides no evidence that there was a division between the two philosophical parties (the Epicureans and the Stoics) on this matter. Therefore, we are unable to determine who in Paul's audience desired to hear him again on this topic.

When Paul leaves the Council of the Areopagus, he realizes that his message has been rejected. Meeting both stinging ridicule and polite indifference, he knows that his stay in Athens must come to a close. He has been unable to penetrate the intellectual world of the Athenian philosophers with Christ's gospel. On his own accord he leaves the audience.

Yet Paul's labors are not in vain, for Luke reports that some people become his followers and believers in Christ. These may be the people who have asked him to address them again on the doctrine of the resurrection. Luke mentions two persons, one man and one woman. The first one is Dionysius, an Areopagite and obviously a member of the ruling council. The other is Damaris, of whom nothing else is revealed. Some scholars suggest that she was known by the name *Damalis* (which means "heifer"), was a foreigner, belonged to the educated class, and was given access to the public meetings of the council.[76]

In addition to Dionysius and Damaris, people who represented different backgrounds became Christians. We surmise that Paul stayed some time in Athens to instruct these believers in the gospel (compare I Thess. 3:1–2). But neither the New Testament nor the early church fathers refer to the

---

75. Albrecht Oepke, *TDNT*, vol. 1, p. 369. See also Colin Brown, *NIDNTT*, vol. 3, p. 261.
76. Ramsay, *St. Paul the Traveller*, p. 252. Codex Bezae has the reading: "among whom also was a *certain* Dionysius, *an* Areopagite of *high standing*, and others with them." The omission of the name *Damaris* is explained either as an indication of an antifeminist attitude or as an accidental omission of a line in the manuscript. Metzger, *Textual Commentary*, p. 459.

founding of a church in Athens. However, fourth-century church historian Eusebius writes:

> Dionysius, one of the ancients, the pastor of the diocese of the Corinthians [approximately A.D. 170], relates that the first bishop of the Church at Athens was that member of the Areopagus, the other Dionysius, whose original conversion after Paul's speech to the Athenians in the Areopagus Luke describes in Acts.[77]

And, last, when Paul writes that the members of the household of Stephanas in Corinth were the first converts in the province of Achaia (I Cor. 16:15), he undoubtedly had in mind not Athens but the Peloponnesian peninsula and Corinth as its provincial capital.

Summary of Chapter 17

Paul arrives at Thessalonica and preaches Christ in the local synagogue on three successive Sabbaths. He opens the Scriptures and explains that Christ had to suffer and rise from the dead. Some of the Jews and many God-fearing Greeks believe.

Jealous Jews in Thessalonica gather a mob to riot and to oppose Paul and Silas. They go to the house of Jason in search of the missionaries, but are unable to find them. They drag Jason and other believers before the magistrates, but Paul and Silas escape and travel to Berea. There the missionaries preach in the synagogue. The Bereans study the Scriptures to check the accuracy of Paul's preaching. Many Jews and prominent Greeks believe. The Thessalonian Jews come to Berea to persecute Paul, who with fellow Christians travels to the coast. From there Paul and his companions journey to Athens.

Paul is dismayed because of the widespread idolatry in Athens. He preaches to the Jews and God-fearing Greeks in the synagogue and teaches in the marketplace for the benefit of the public. Epicurean and Stoic philosophers ridicule Paul, but they bring him to a meeting of the Areopagus, the governing council. At this meeting Paul teaches the doctrine of creation and quotes Greek poets to prove the point that God has created man. He exhorts his listeners to repent, for he tells them that God has appointed a man to judge the world on a day God has set. As proof, Paul mentions the resurrection of the man whom God has appointed as judge. Some people in the audience sneer at Paul; others tell him that they wish to hear him again. Still others believe and become his followers.

---

77. Eusebius *Ecclesiastical History* 3.4.10; 4.23.3 (LCL).

18

The Second Missionary Journey, *part 4*

18:1–22

and The Third Missionary Journey, *part 1*

18:23–28

Outline (continued)

18:1–17	2. Corinth
18:1–3	a. Tentmaker
18:4–8	b. Preacher
18:9–11	c. Visionary
18:12–17	d. Accused
18:18–22	D. Return to Antioch
18:23–21:16	VIII. The Third Missionary Journey
18:23–28	A. To Ephesus

18 1 After this, Paul left Athens and went to Corinth. 2 And he met a certain Jew called Aquila, a native of Pontus, who had recently come from Italy with his wife, Priscilla, because Claudius had commanded all the Jews to leave Rome. Paul came to them, 3 and because he was of the same trade, he stayed with them. He worked, for they were tentmakers by trade.

4 Paul was reasoning in the synagogue every Sabbath, trying to persuade both Jews and Greeks. 5 When Silas and Timothy came down from Macedonia, Paul began to devote himself completely to preaching, testifying to the Jews that Jesus was the Christ. 6 But when the Jews resisted and insulted him, he shook out his garments and said to them, "Your blood be on your own heads! I am guiltless, and from now on I will go to the Gentiles." 7 And he left from there and went to the house of a man named Titius Justus, a worshiper of God, whose house was next door to the synagogue. 8 Crispus, the leader of the synagogue, with his entire household believed in the Lord. And when they heard him, many Corinthians believed and were baptized.

9 The Lord spoke to Paul in a vision at night: "Do not be afraid, but continue to speak and do not be silent. 10 For I am with you, and no one is going to attack you to harm you, because I have many people in this city." 11 Paul stayed there a year and a half, teaching the word of God among them.

12 While Gallio was proconsul of Achaia, the Jews rose up together against Paul and brought him before the judgment seat. 13 They said, "This man persuades the people to worship God contrary to the law." 14 When Paul was about to open his mouth, Gallio said to the Jews: "If it were a matter of a certain misdeed or serious crime to you Jews, I would be justified in accepting your complaint. 15 But if these are questions about words, names, and your own law, you look after it yourselves. I am unwilling to be a judge of these matters." 16 He drove them away from the judgment seat. 17 And they all took hold of Sosthenes, the leader of the synagogue, and began to beat him in front of the judgment seat. But these things were of no concern to Gallio.

---

2. Corinth
18:1–17

In Paul's day, Corinth, not Athens, was the capital of Achaia (Greece). As was his custom, Paul went primarily to principal cities and capitals. From Athens he traveled to the west-southwest for some fifty miles and within a day or two arrived in Corinth. Here he found lodging with a husband and wife who were tentmakers.

a. Tentmaker
18:1–3

1. After this, Paul left Athens and went to Corinth. 2. And he met a certain Jew called Aquila, a native of Pontus, who had recently come

from Italy with his wife, Priscilla, because Claudius had commanded all the Jews to leave Rome. Paul came to them, 3. and because he was of the same trade, he stayed with them. He worked, for they were tentmakers by trade.

Initially Paul received the urgent call to help the Macedonians (16:9), but because of persecution he traveled to Athens. When he realized that his work in Athens was stymied, he looked to Corinth, with a population estimated at two hundred thousand. Situated at the isthmus that divides the Peloponnesus from the mainland, Corinth became a thriving commercial center with a harbor at each end of the isthmus. Goods were transported from one harbor to the other along a specially constructed stone corridor. About two miles north of Corinth was the harbor of Lechaeum, which accommodated ships to and from Italy, Spain, and North Africa. The harbor of Cenchrea was located seven miles east of Corinth and facilitated sea traffic to and from Egypt, Phoenicia, and Asia Minor. From Paul's perspective, Corinth was an ideal mission center from which the gospel could spread by seafarers to east and west.

Corinth had enjoyed its golden age in the seventh century before Christ. Rivalry between Athens and Corinth contributed to a decline that was hastened by the Peloponnesian War (431–404 B.C.). Almost three centuries later, the Romans conquered Corinth. When a revolt broke out against Rome in 146 B.C., the Roman general Lucius Mummius had all the male inhabitants of Corinth killed and its women and children sold as slaves.

In 46 B.C., Julius Caesar gave Corinth the name *Colonia Laus Julia Corinthiensis* (the Corinthian colony is Julian praise), caused many Roman freedmen to take up residence there, and made Latin its official language (Greek was the common language). His successor, Augustus, made Corinth the capital of the province Achaia (27 B.C.). The commercial interests of Corinth once again flourished and attracted many Jews, who constructed a synagogue in this city.

The residents of Corinth worshiped Aphrodite, the goddess of love, and under the guise of religion engaged in unrestrained immorality. Corinth had a sizable number of temple prostitutes, who were in the employ of the religious authorities of the city. Throughout the Mediterranean world the expression *to Corinthianize* (to live immorally) became a byword. In God's plan, Corinth was the place where Paul had to preach the gospel and establish a church.

When Paul arrived in Corinth, he presumably sought contact with the local synagogue authorities and found lodging with a Jew named Aquila and his wife, Priscilla.[1] The name *Aquila* is Latin for "eagle," and Priscilla is a diminutive form of Prisca, which in Latin means "ancient" or "elderly." Aquila was a native of the province of Pontus in Asia Minor, but had moved to Rome. He and his wife were tentmakers who fashioned small tents out of

---

1. Refer to v. 26; Rom. 16:3–5; I Cor. 16:19; II Tim. 4:19.

leather, linen, or cloth woven from goats' hair. Travelers made use of this type of tent.[2] Paul, in his extensive travels, perhaps used these tents; certainly he knew how to make them.

Paul, Aquila, and Priscilla had more in common than being Jews and knowing the trade of tentmaking. All three were Christians. Aquila and Priscilla had recently come to Corinth from Rome, for the emperor Claudius had expelled the Jews from the imperial city in A.D. 49. The Roman historiographer Suetonius writes that Claudius "expelled the Jews because they were continually rioting at the instigation of Chrestus."[3] We suspect that he misspelled the name of Christ, which to him was meaningless. He also thought that Christ was personally present in Rome to instigate riots. As a result of repeated conflicts between Jews and Christians, both groups had to leave the imperial city. Some time later, however, Jews and Christians returned, as is evident from the travels of Aquila and Priscilla (Rom. 16:3–5).

Luke's reference to the imperial edict seems to indicate that Aquila and Priscilla were Christians when they left Rome. This assumption is strengthened by the fact that in his writings, Paul does not consider them his first converts in Achaia (I Cor. 16:15). Also, when Paul sought lodging in Corinth after arriving from Athens, he would have preferred to stay with Christians. For these reasons, we conjecture that Paul, Aquila, and Priscilla formed the nucleus of the Corinthian church.

Jewish fathers taught their sons the family trade, which remained in the family for many generations. Zebedee taught his sons James and John the intricacies of fishing. Jesus learned carpentry from Joseph in his workshop in Nazareth. And Paul was trained by his father in Tarsus in the trade of tentmaking, and probably the art of working with leather. The tools needed for this craft were relatively few in number and could easily be taken along wherever Paul went.[4] Many rabbis supported themselves by performing manual labor in the trade they had learned in their youth. Paul writes to the Corinthians that he worked with his own hands (I Cor. 4:12; see also 9:6) and to the Thessalonians that he worked night and day to support himself in his needs (I Thess. 2:9; see also Acts 20:34–35).

Practical Considerations in 18:3

Should a pastor have a tentmaking ministry and not be dependent on the support of the Christian community? Not necessarily, for the Lord has stipulated

---

2. Thayer, p. 578; Bauer, p. 755.

3. "Judaeos impulsore Chresto assidue tumultuantes Roma expulit." Suetonius *Claudius* 25.4. See also Dio Cassius *History* 60.6.6; Robert O. Hoerber, "The Decree of Claudius in Acts 18.2," *ConcThMonth* 31 (1960): 690–94.

4. Refer to Ronald F. Hock, *The Social Context of Paul's Ministry: Tentmaking and Apostleship* (Philadelphia: Fortress, 1980), p. 25. See Lake and Cadbury, *Beginnings*, vol. 4, p. 223.

that "those who proclaim the gospel should make their living from the gospel" (I Cor. 9:14; compare Matt. 10:10; Luke 10:7; I Tim. 5:18). Yet Paul writes that to avoid any hindrance to the spread of the gospel he will not avail himself of the right to receive material support (I Cor. 9:12b). Paul speaks about his own situation and has no intention of issuing an apostolic decree. The apostles in Jerusalem gave themselves completely to prayer and the ministry of the Word of God (6:2, 4). In a sense, they set the example for a full-time ministry that is free from material pressure.

In some situations, however, a minister or missionary may practice a trade and thus enter a world that is otherwise closed to the gospel. The particular trade then becomes a vehicle for teaching the Word of God to people who have not yet heard the message of salvation.

Greek Words, Phrases, and Constructions in 18:2–3

τῷ γένει—the dative noun expresses manner (see 4:36): "by nationality" or "a native of."[5]

ἠργάζετο—from ἐργάζομαι (I work), the imperfect tense denotes that Paul worked at his trade for some time.

The Western text embellishes these verses (the additions are italicized):

> [Aquila and Priscilla] had come out from Rome because Claudius *Caesar* had commanded all Jews to leave Rome; *and they settled in Greece*. And Paul *became known* to Aquila because he was of *the same tribe and* the same trade, and he stayed with them and worked; for they were tentmakers by trade.[6]

---

b. Preacher
18:4–8

4. Paul was reasoning in the synagogue every Sabbath, trying to persuade both Jews and Greeks. 5. When Silas and Timothy came down from Macedonia, Paul began to devote himself completely to preaching, testifying to the Jews that Jesus was the Christ.

Faithful to his practice, Paul worshiped in the local synagogue on the Sabbath (compare 13:14; 14:1). Invited to preach, Paul tried to persuade both the Jews and the God-fearing Gentiles to listen to the gospel and accept Jesus as their Messiah, who fulfilled the prophecies of Scripture. Every Sabbath, week after week, Paul seized the opportunity to confront the people with the Good News and sought to win them for Christ.

In 1898, archaeologists discovered a stone in Corinth on the Lechaeum Road that has the Greek letters *gōgē ebr*. Scholars have made the inscription

---

5. A. T. Robertson, *A Grammar of the Greek New Testament in the Light of Historical Research* (Nashville: Broadman, 1934), p. 530.

6. Bruce M. Metzger, *A Textual Commentary on the Greek New Testament*, 3d corrected ed. (London and New York: United Bible Societies, 1975), pp. 460–61.

intelligible with the addition of a few letters to form the words *synagōgē hebraiōn* (synagogue of the Hebrews). The inscription dates from the first century before Christ to the first two centuries after Christ and was the lintel above the doorway of the synagogue where Paul preached.

The Jews had reached out in the community by inviting Greeks to come to the synagogue, which was called the house of learning. Here the rabbis would teach the Gentiles about Israel's God. In time, a number of Greeks believed and became God-fearers.

At first, Paul labored in his trade during the week and taught in the synagogue on the Sabbath. But when Silas and Timothy arrived from Macedonia (Philippi, Thessalonica, and Berea), Paul gave himself entirely to preaching the gospel of salvation. His two companions brought him a monetary gift from the churches in Macedonia (II Cor. 11:9; Phil. 4:14–15), so that the need to perform manual work lessened. Paul learned from his companions that the believers in Thessalonica were doing well (I Thess. 3:6).

When Paul was in Athens, Timothy had come to him in response to Paul's instruction (17:15). But Paul had sent him back to Thessalonica (I Thess. 3:1–5). Perhaps Silas had gone back to the church in Philippi while Timothy returned to Thessalonica. When Timothy and Silas eventually arrived in Corinth, Timothy informed Paul about the spiritual welfare of the believers in Thessalonica (I Thess. 3:6). This prompted Paul to send his first epistle and, about half a year later, his second epistle to the Thessalonians. The tone of these letters is joyful and thankful, and Paul speaks of his longing to see these believers. Among the letters Paul wrote during the period that Luke covers in Acts are ten canonical epistles, yet surprisingly Luke never mentions Paul's correspondence.[7]

Luke writes that Paul, preaching and teaching full time, testified to the Jews that Jesus was the Messiah. The verb *testify* applies to the apostolic witness[8] and signifies that Paul as an apostle told the Jews in Corinth about his encounter with the risen Lord near Damascus. Paul singles out the Jews, not the God-fearing Greeks, for the Jews know the messianic prophecies of the Scriptures.

6. But when the Jews resisted and insulted him, he shook out his garments and said to them, "Your blood be on your own heads! I am guiltless, and from now on I will go to the Gentiles."

Of all the people on earth, the Jews should have been the first to acknowledge Jesus as the Christ. For centuries they possessed the prophecies about the coming of the Messiah. When Jesus eventually fulfilled all these prophecies, the Jews should have recognized and acclaimed him as the promised

---

7. On his second missionary journey, Paul composed Galatians and I and II Thessalonians. He wrote Romans and I and II Corinthians during his third missionary journey; and while he was imprisoned he authored Ephesians, Colossians, Philippians, and Philemon.

8. Acts 8:25; 20:21, 24; 23:11; 28:23.

Messiah. But when Jesus came to his own, his own people received him not (John 1:11).

Paul told the Corinthian Jews that he himself had seen and heard Jesus and that he was one of his apostles. But instead of accepting the message of the gospel, the Jews resisted the truth and began to speak abusively against Paul's message (13:45). They rejected the gospel, as is indicated by the Eighteen Petitions. The oldest prayer of Judaism, simply known as "the Prayer," was recited in the worship service by the leader of the synagogue. The Mishnah requires that every Jew recite it three times per day.[9] In the twelfth petition (Palestinian Recension) of this prayer we read:

> And for the apostates let there be no hope; and may the insolent kingdom be quickly uprooted, in our days. And may the Nazarenes and the heretics perish quickly; and may they be erased from the Book of Life; and may they not be inscribed with the righteous. *Blessed art thou, Lord, who humblest the insolent.*[10]

In the local synagogue, Paul shook out his cloak to symbolize his break with the Jews (see Neh. 5:13). We presume that he did not shake the dust off his sandals, because he had left them at the entrance of the synagogue.[11] Jesus had instructed his disciples to shake the dust off their feet when they saw that their listeners would not accept the gospel message (Matt. 10:14; compare Acts 13:51).

Paul explained his action by saying, "Your blood be on your own heads! I am guiltless, and from now on I will go to the Gentiles." He alluded to God's word spoken to Ezekiel concerning the watchman who blew the trumpet to warn the people of impending danger. If anyone failed to listen and was killed by the sword, his blood would be on his own head and the watchman would not be held accountable (Ezek. 33:4). Paul asserted that he had done his duty, and that hereafter the Jews would have to take full responsibility for their refusal to accept the gospel. He considered himself guiltless and absolved of God's judgment that eventually would come to the Jews (refer to 20:26).

Cognizant of his calling as the apostle to the Gentiles, Paul declared that he would leave the Jews and bring his message to the Gentiles in Corinth. The situation resembles what took place in Pisidian Antioch, where Paul left the local synagogue and went to the Gentiles of that city (13:46; cf. 28:28; Rom. 1:16; 11:11). Hence, the expression *from now on* should not be taken literally, for it applies only to the local scene. Paul continued his ministry to the Jews in other places (20:21).

---

9. Mishnah, *Berakhoth* 3.3; 4.1.

10. Emil Schürer, *The History of the Jewish People in the Age of Jesus Christ (175 B.C.–A.D. 135)*, rev. and ed. Geza Vermes and Fergus Millar, 3 vols. (Edinburgh: Clark, 1973–87), vol. 2, p. 461. See also SB, vol. 4, pt. 1, pp. 212–13.

11. H. J. Cadbury, "Dust and Garments," *Beginnings*, vol. 5, p. 274.

7. And he left from there and went to the house of a man named Titius Justus, a worshiper of God, whose house was next door to the synagogue. 8. Crispus, the leader of the synagogue, with his entire household believed in the Lord. And when they heard him, many Corinthians believed and were baptized.

Luke gives no indication that Paul left the home of Aquila and Priscilla to take up residence with Titius Justus.[12] Rather, he implies that Paul no longer worshiped with the Jews in the local synagogue, but held worship services in a house adjacent to it. Having no intention of aggravating the Jews, Paul nevertheless had to find a suitable location to preach, and the house of Titius Justus proved to be the place.

Jewish Christians and God-fearing Greeks began to meet for worship and instruction in the home of a person who probably was wealthy (his home could accommodate at least a small congregation) and a Roman citizen. Some translations give this man the name *Justus* (kjv, nkjv, jb), others have *Titus Justus* (nab, *Moffatt*), and still others read *Titius Justus* (rsv, neb, mlb, gnb, seb, niv, nasb). The difference results from the variants in the Greek manuscripts. As a Roman citizen, this person probably had three names: Gaius Titius Justus. Some scholars justifiably identify him with the Gaius to whom Paul refers as the believer who extended his hospitality to him and the whole church of Corinth (Rom. 16:23; and see I Cor. 1:14).[13] He should not be identified as Titus, who accompanied Paul to Jerusalem at the conclusion of Paul's first missionary journey and probably was a native of Antioch in Syria (Gal. 2:1).[14]

Both Jewish and Greek Christians attended the worship services in the house of Titius Justus. The first converts in Corinth were Stephanas and his household. Luke reports that the ruler of the synagogue, Crispus, and his entire household also became followers of Jesus Christ. (In Acts, Luke often uses the term *household*, which usually refers to a man's wife, sons and daughters, close relatives, and servants [see 11:14; 16:15, 31–34].) Crispus was a prominent figure in the Jewish community. His conversion to Christianity proved to be decisive to the growth of the local church. His successor or colleague in the synagogue, Sosthenes (v. 17), in time became a believer (I Cor. 1:1).

All of these persons, except Sosthenes, were baptized by Paul himself (I Cor. 1:16; 16:15), although, according to his own testimony, he normally did not baptize converts. It is possible that Stephanas, Crispus, Gaius, and the members of their families were baptized before Silas and Timothy arrived in Corinth and before the break with the Jews occurred. Perhaps

---

12. Henry Alford writes that Paul, "on leaving the synagogue, went no longer to the house of the Jew Aquila." *Alford's Greek Testament: An Exegetical and Critical Commentary*, 7th ed., 4 vols. (1877; Grand Rapids: Guardian, 1976), vol. 2, p. 202. But this is hardly the meaning of the text, because Paul's friendship with Aquila and Priscilla remained firm.

13. E.g., Edgar J. Goodspeed, "Gaius Titius Justus," *JBL* 69 (1950): 382–83.

14. Lake and Cadbury, *Beginnings*, vol. 4, p. 225.

the conversion of these prominent persons caused jealousy that erupted in sharp disputes and led to Paul's departure from the synagogue.

Paul continued his work of preaching in the home of Titius Justus. Many Corinthians, both Jews and Greeks, listened to Paul's instruction and believed. Among the members of the Corinthian church were Erastus, the city treasurer, and a person named Quartus (Rom. 16:23). In the Greek, Luke indicates that they regularly listened to Paul and that the baptism of converts was a common occurrence.

Greek Words, Phrases, and Constructions in 18:4–8

Verse 4

The Western text has added some phrases to give a smooth reading of the passage. The additions are italicized: "And *entering into* the synagogue each sabbath day, he held a discussion, *inserting the name of the Lord Jesus,* and persuaded *not only* Jews *but also* Greeks."[15]

διελέγετο—the use of the imperfect tense shows Paul's repeated attempt to debate with the Jews. Likewise, the imperfect tense of ἔπειθεν (he tried to persuade) indicates repeated and attempted action.

Verse 5

συνείχετο—the imperfect middle of συνέχομαι (I am occupied with) signifies "he was holding himself to [the preaching of] the word."[16]

εἶναι τὸν Χριστὸν Ἰησοῦν—the noun with the definite article serves as the subject of the infinitive, the noun without the article as the predicate. The Jews knew about the Messiah from the Scriptures, but they were not acquainted with Jesus. A literal translation is, "that the Christ is Jesus."

Verses 6–8

The Western text begins verse 6 with an introductory clause: "And after there had been much discussion, and interpretation of the scriptures had been given. . . . "[17]

ἐκτιναξάμενος—this compound middle participle in the aorist is reflexive and intensive: "shaking out his clothes from himself."[18] The idiomatic plural τὰ ἱμάτια refers to a person's upper garment.

ἐκεῖθεν—some Western manuscripts replace this adverb with the phrase *from Aquila.* Other witnesses combine these two: "from there from Aquila."

ἦν συνομοροῦσα—the past periphrastic construction with the verb *to be* and a present participle is equivalent to the simple construction *was next to,* so that the participle is an adjective.

---

15. Metzger, *Textual Commentary,* p. 461.
16. Refer to Robertson, *Grammar,* p. 808.
17. Metzger, *Textual Commentary,* p. 462.
18. Robertson, *Grammar,* p. 810.

The use of the imperfect tense in verse 8 describes repeated confessions of faith and occasions of baptism.

---

c. *Visionary*
18:9–11

While Paul, with the help of Silas and Timothy, devoted himself fully to the preaching and teaching of the gospel, the opposition from the Jews became increasingly powerful. Discouragement and fear became Paul's companions and hindered him in his ministry. Like many other saints who had preceded him, Paul needed a word of encouragement (compare Josh. 1:9; Isa. 41:10; 43:5; Jer. 1:8, 19).

9. The Lord spoke to Paul in a vision at night: "Do not be afraid, but continue to speak and do not be silent. 10. For I am with you, and no one is going to attack you to harm you, because I have many people in this city." 11. Paul stayed there a year and a half, teaching the word of God among them.

Paul is discouraged and fearful. He readily admits this in a subsequent letter to the Corinthians: "I was with you in a state of weakness, fear, and much trembling" (I Cor. 2:3). Prestigious citizens of Corinth regard him as a person without strength, influence, and privilege because of his trade as a tentmaker.[19] They place Paul on the level of a slave. The Jews want him to stop teaching the people about Jesus, and the threat to his personal safety is always present. The seemingly endless opposition to Paul's ministry begins to have a depressing effect on his spiritual life.

1. *Command.* When Jesus appears to Paul in a vision at night, Paul immediately recognizes him (compare 9:10, 12; 22:18; 23:11; 27:23–24). Jesus speaks directly to the problems Paul faces and gives him three short orders:

> Do not be afraid.
> Continue to speak.
> Do not be silent.

Acute fear in man's heart often debilitates. In extreme cases such fear can lead to death and in mild cases to a distortion of reality. Fear is used by Satan to make men subservient to him. By contrast, God continually tells his people not to be afraid. To illustrate, Jesus exhorts his disciples to take heart because he has overcome the world (John 16:33). So in a vision Jesus instructs Paul not to fear. The tense of the verb *to fear* indicates that Paul indeed suffers from this malady, but Jesus bids him to subdue this fear.

Moreover, Jesus orders Paul to keep talking. He is not referring to the content of Paul's speeches but to the act of his speaking. To this positive injunction Jesus adds the negative command, "Do not become silent." He is

---

19. Consult Hock, *Social Context of Paul's Ministry,* p. 60.

not saying that Paul is silent, but he warns him not to become quiet. Through the voice of Paul, Christ makes his gospel known to the people and, therefore, he forbids Paul to become reticent.

2. *Promise.* In the first verse of Acts, Luke writes that in his first book he told Theophilus all that Jesus began to do and to teach (1:1). He implies that in Acts Jesus continues his work. This is a vivid illustration of Jesus' direct involvement in the growth of the church. The first reason for Jesus' threefold order is that he is with Paul in Corinth (refer to Matt. 28:20). He assures Paul that no one is going to lay hands on him to harm him. Paul will not endure the physical hardships that characterized his stay in Philippi, Thessalonica, and Berea.

Jesus gives a second reason for issuing the three commands to Paul: "because I have many people in this city." What an encouragement for Paul! Jesus himself guarantees that Paul's labors in Corinth will bear fruit. God himself appoints his people to eternal life (13:48), opens their hearts to the gospel message (16:14), and brings them to salvation. Observes Leon Morris, "They had not yet done anything about being saved; many of them had not even heard the gospel. But they were God's. Clearly it is he who would bring them to salvation in due course."[20] God calls Jews and Gentiles to be his own people and builds the church in Corinth (compare II Cor. 6:16).[21]

3. *Response.* "Paul stayed there a year and a half, teaching the word of God among them." Luke relates little about Paul's ministry in Corinth, so we have to glean data from Paul's epistles. We know that God blessed Paul's ministry, because there were believers throughout the province of Achaia (II Cor. 1:1). In the harbor city of Cenchrea some believers founded a church in which Phoebe was a deaconess (Rom. 16:1). And Paul mentions by name some other believers in Corinth itself: Chloe and her household (I Cor. 1:11), Fortunatus and Achaicus (I Cor. 16:17), and Tertius (Rom. 16:22).

Paul describes the Corinthian worship services and notes that the church enjoyed "a variety of highly diversified ministries: there were apostles, prophets, teachers, miracle workers, healers, helpers, 'governments,' speakers with tongues."[22] The Corinthian church continued to expand and develop in the period after Paul's departure and the time he wrote his letters. But in light of the Lord's assurance that he had many people in Corinth, we dare say that Paul saw encouraging growth in the year and a half he spent in that city.

---

20. Leon Morris, *New Testament Theology* (Grand Rapids: Zondervan, Academie Books, 1986), p. 154.
21. Hans Bietenhard, *NIDNTT,* vol. 2, p. 800; Hermann Strathmann, *TDNT,* vol. 4, p. 54.
22. Richard B. Rackham, *The Acts of the Apostles: An Exposition,* Westminster Commentaries series (1901; reprint ed., Grand Rapids: Baker, 1964), p. 328.

Doctrinal Considerations in 18:10

The pastor, the evangelist, and the missionary should never forget that the Lord Jesus Christ is always with them. Jesus is the commander-in-chief who sends his servants into the world to be his ambassadors. Furthermore, he gives them the assurance that he will bless their labors.

Scripture teaches that God the Father has chosen his people from eternity (Eph. 1:4). Through the proclamation of God's Word and the power of his Spirit, he will bring his people to salvation in Christ. Therefore, preachers who faithfully proclaim the gospel message can put their full confidence in God and ask him for tangible results.

> In the midst of opposition,
>   Let them trust, O Lord, in Thee;
> When success attends their mission,
>   Let Thy servants humblest be.
>   Never leave them
> Till Thy face in heaven they see.
> —Thomas Kelly

Greek Words, Phrases, and Constructions in 18:9–10

Verse 9

δι' ὁράματος—"through [in] a vision." The prepositional phrase denotes both means and manner.

μὴ φοβοῦ—the present tense of the imperative reveals that Paul indeed is fearful, while the aorist tense of the subjunctive in μὴ σιωπήσῃς indicates that even though Paul is not reticent now, he should never become silent in the future.

Verse 10

τοῦ κακῶσαι—the aorist infinitive preceded by the definite article in the genitive singular denotes purpose that is dependent on the preceding verb and object ἐπιθήσεταί σοι ([no one] will attack you).

λαός—the context of this noun shows that God calls persons his own people even before they are converted. In the Septuagint, the word λαός frequently signifies God's covenant people. In this text, God applies the expression to the Christian community. From God's point of view, the church in Corinth, consisting largely of Gentiles, has assumed the place of the theocratic people of Israel.[23] The Christian church, therefore, constitutes the continuation of God's covenant people of the Old Testament era.

---

23. Thayer, p. 372; Bauer, p. 467.

d. Accused
18:12–17

When Jesus assured Paul that no one in Corinth would attack him, he did not mean that Paul would not have to endure opposition. The Corinthian Jews, antagonistic to Paul but restrained by Greek democracy, devised means to bring legal action against Paul. They took him to court with the intent of petitioning the proconsul, Gallio, to outlaw Christianity in the province of Achaia.

12. While Gallio was proconsul of Achaia, the Jews rose up together against Paul and brought him before the judgment seat. 13. They said, "This man persuades the people to worship God contrary to the law."

1. *Proconsul.* Inscriptions discovered near Delphi provide near certainty in establishing the exact time Gallio served as proconsul of Achaia. One inscription reveals that Claudius, in the twelfth year of his reign and acclaimed emperor for the twenty-sixth time,[24] mentions his friend Gallio, the proconsul of Achaia. From these data, we are able to deduce that Gallio served his term of office from July 51 to June 52. Imperial decree limited the proconsul's term in a given place to one year.

We conjecture that Paul came to Corinth in the autumn of A.D. 50 and for approximately half a year preached first in the synagogue and then in the house of Titius Justus. If Paul appeared before Gallio at the beginning of the proconsul's term, we have a firm date for the chronology of Paul's second missionary journey.[25]

Gallio was born in Córdoba, Spain, the son of Seneca, whose eldest son bore the same name. Gallio's given name was Marcus Annaeus Novatus, but when he eventually arrived in Rome, he was adopted by Lucius Junius Gallio and thus assumed the latter's family name. Gallio soon entered government service and served first as praeter for a period of five years. He then went to Achaia as proconsul for one year, and afterward attained the rank of consul. When his brother Seneca, who was the tutor and adviser of Nero, committed suicide by order of the emperor, Gallio asked that his own life might be spared.[26] Yet a short time later he, too, was killed. Seneca mentions Gallio a number of times. He notes that Gallio had health prob-

---

24. "Though in practice the emperors reigned for their life, they were acclaimed *imperator* at frequent but irregular intervals." Kirsopp Lake, "The Chronology of Acts," *Beginnings,* vol. 5, p. 462.

25. Consult Colin J. Hemer, "Observations on Pauline Chronology," in *Pauline Studies,* ed. Donald A. Hagner and Murray J. Harris (Exeter: Paternoster; Grand Rapids: Eerdmans, 1980), p. 8; see also his *Book of Acts in the Setting of Hellenistic History,* ed. Conrad H. Gempf (Tübingen: Mohr, 1989), pp. 168–69. For varying views, see B. Schwank, "Der sogenannte Brief an Gallio und die Datierung des 1 Thess.," *BZ* n.s. 15 (1971): 265–66; Klaus Haacker, "Die Gallio-Episode und die paulinische Chronologie," *BZ* n.s. 16 (1972): 252–55.

26. Tacitus *Annals* 15.60–65; 15.73.

lems, was an intelligent person who hated flattery, and was blessed with an "unaffectedly pleasant personality."[27]

2. *Accusation.* The Corinthian Jews were trying to use the proconsul for their own purpose: to ban Christianity from the province of Achaia. They took hold of Paul, not necessarily with force, and brought him to the Roman tribunal located near the marketplace. Having devised a united strategy, they brought Paul before Gallio to register the following accusation: "This man persuades the people to worship God contrary to the law." The brevity of the charge leaves the meaning of the term *law* open to interpretation. If the expression should refer to Roman law, they would have to prove that Paul was a security risk to Rome. If it concerned the religious law of the Jews, they would meet Gallio's refusal to hear evidence against Paul.

The Roman government allowed the Jews to worship their God as freely as other people worshiped pagan deities. When the populations of Alexandria, Antioch, and cities of Asia Minor sought to persecute the Jews because of their religion, Roman authorities always upheld "the religious freedom of the Jews, so long as they did not forfeit these rights (as in A.D. 66) through revolutionary action."[28]

To Gallio, the accusation the Jews leveled at one of their own countrymen must have seemed absurd. If they were unable to prove that Paul was a threat to the security of Rome, he would dismiss them forthwith. Further, the wording of the accusation referred to one God, namely, Israel's God, and not to pagan deities. In short, the Jews defeated their own purpose by their choice of words.

When the Jews appeared before Roman authorities, they usually sought legal protection. For example, if the Jews had complained that the civic magistrates in Corinth forbade them to worship on the Jewish Sabbath, Gallio would have to defend the Jews or risk Caesar's wrath.[29] But now that the Jews came as accusers, Gallio understood that they were talking not about Roman law but about internal matters related to their own religion.

14. When Paul was about to open his mouth, Gallio said to the Jews: "If it were a matter of a certain misdeed or serious crime to you Jews, I would be justified in accepting your complaint. 15. But if these are questions about words, names, and your own law, you look after it yourselves. I am unwilling to be a judge of these matters."

Gallio did not even give Paul a chance to defend himself before his accusers, because to him the matter had to do not with Roman law but with

---

27. Seneca *Natural Questions* 4a, preface 10–11; *Epistles* 104.2; and see Dio Cassius *Roman History* 61.35.

28. Schürer, *History of the Jewish People*, vol. 3, p. 132. See also Josephus *Antiquities* 19.5.3 [289]; 20.1.2 [10–14].

29. A. N. Sherwin-White, *Roman Society and Roman Law in the New Testament* (1963; reprint ed., Grand Rapids: Baker, 1978), p. 103.

the intricacies of Jewish religion (compare 23:29; 25:18–20). In Greek, Gallio used a conditional sentence that expresses a contrary-to-fact statement: "If you were bringing to my attention information about a misdeed or a serious crime (but you are not doing so), I would have been justified in listening to your accusation (but now I won't have to do so)."

The proconsul continued with a second conditional sentence, a statement that is true to fact. In effect he says, "If you bring to my attention questions pertaining to words, names, and your own religious law, not I but you must be the judge." The Jews are told that they have come to Gallio with an accusation that should be handled in the local synagogue, not before Gallio's tribunal.

The proconsul concluded by telling the Jews that he would not be party to their religious squabble. We are unable to gauge Gallio's tone of voice, but we surmise that his words conveyed disdain and scorn: "I am unwilling to be a judge of these matters."

16. He drove them away from the judgment seat. 17. And they all took hold of Sosthenes, the leader of the synagogue, and began to beat him in front of the judgment seat. But these things were of no concern to Gallio.

Undoubtedly Gallio had other legal business that needed his attention. But first he had to rid his court of the Jews who refused to leave. Thus he had to order his lictors: "Use your rods and clear the court." Luke is very brief in his report, so a number of interpretations are possible:

a. When they realized that they had lost their case, all the Jews took hold of Sosthenes. But would the Jews pounce on their own synagogue ruler?

b. The lictors beat Sosthenes because he was the spokesman of the Jews. But the adjective *all* is jarring to the context if it relates to two or three lictors.

c. The Western and Byzantine manuscripts read "all the Greeks" (KJV, NKJV). The Gentile population, then, vented its dislike for the Jews and gave Sosthenes a beating. But if the Greeks unleashed their anti-Semitic feelings, why did they single out one Jew? Perhaps Sosthenes, as the spokesman for the Jews, became their target.

d. According to the leading Greek manuscripts, Luke fails to provide a subject for the clause, "And they all took hold of Sosthenes."

For this reason, translators leave the question unresolved, even though commentators generally suggest that a mob attacked Sosthenes.

"But these things were of no concern to Gallio." The aftermath of the court case is bittersweet. On the one hand, Gallio's disinterest in maintaining public order is difficult to understand. Gallio acted wisely in respect to the accusation the Jews brought against Paul but indifferently toward Sosthenes, the ruler of the synagogue. He applied Roman law to protect religious freedom but failed to safeguard the physical welfare of one person. On the other hand, because of Gallio's ruling, Christianity continued to receive religious protection. In fact, because Rome made no distinction between Christianity and Judaism, Christianity was shielded by

Caesar's decree that recognized the legality of the Jewish religion in the Roman empire.

True to his word, Jesus shielded Paul from physical harm by thwarting Jewish opposition to the spread of the gospel. Accordingly, in the capital city of Corinth, the church began to grow and expand throughout Achaia (II Cor. 1:1; 11:10; I Thess. 1:7–8). The conclusion Gallio reached constituted a decisive victory for the church in Greece.

Greek Words, Phrases, and Constructions in 18:12–17

Verses 12–13

The Western text has a lengthy addition after the word Ἰουδαῖοι. The added words are italicized: "*having talked together among themselves* against Paul, *and having laid hands on him* they brought him *to the governor, crying out and* saying. . . . "[30]

τὸ βῆμα—"the judgment seat" was a raised platform on which the bench of a judge was placed. The judge transacted legal matters publicly (Matt. 27:19; John 19:13; Acts 18:12, 16–17; 25:6, 10, 17).

παρὰ τὸν νόμον—the preposition conveys the meaning *to go beyond* in the sense of "contrary to." Thus, the Jews charged, Paul was preaching in violation of the law.

Verse 14

μέλλοντος—this is the present active participle of μέλλω (I am about to) in a genitive absolute construction.

κατὰ λόγον—the combination of preposition and noun forms an idiom that means "reasonably" or "justly."

Verses 15–17

ὄψεσθε—the future indicative from the verb ὁράω (I see) expresses a command: "see to it." The pronoun αὐτοί (you yourselves) is emphatic.

ἔμελεν—this form is the imperfect of an incomplete verb (μέλει, it is a concern) that demonstrates Gallio's indifference. The Latin text of Codex Bezae reads: "Then Gallio acted as though he did not see him." The Greek text at this place in Codex Bezae has been erased, but "it is fair to assume that the text of D corresponded to this."[31]

---

18 Paul remained in Corinth for many days. He said farewell to the brothers and sailed to Syria with Priscilla and Aquila. He had his hair cut in Cenchrea, for he was keeping a vow. 19 They arrived at Ephesus, and he left Priscilla and Aquila there. But he himself entered the synagogue and reasoned with the Jews. 20 When they asked him to remain for a longer period, he declined. 21 But he departed and said, "I will return to you, God willing." Then he left Ephesus. 22 When he arrived at Caesarea, he went up and greeted the church and went down to Antioch.

---

30. Metzger, *Textual Commentary*, p. 463.
31. James Hardy Ropes, *Beginnings*, vol. 3, p. 176.

D. Return to Antioch
18:18–22

The next section is a summary of the concluding part of Paul's second missionary journey, his brief stay in Ephesus, his voyage to Caesarea and visit to Jerusalem, and his return to Antioch. In a few verses Luke presents an outline of a period in Paul's life about which we know little (see II Cor. 11:23–27).

18. Paul remained in Corinth for many days. He said farewell to the brothers and sailed to Syria with Priscilla and Aquila. He had his hair cut in Cenchrea, for he was keeping a vow.

a. "Paul remained in Corinth." After Gallio had spoken, Paul knew that Roman law protected him in Corinth. He also knew that at the conclusion of Gallio's proconsulship in Achaia, he would possibly face renewed opposition.[32] He preached the gospel and strengthened the church and stayed for a year and a half (v. 11). The expression *for many days* conceivably refers to part of that eighteen-month period. If Paul arrived in the autumn of A.D. 50, he departed in the spring of 52, before the proconsul left.

b. "He said farewell to the brothers." The flow of thought in this verse is disjointed. Paul said goodbye to the church in Corinth, yet as an afterthought Luke writes that Paul spent time in Cenchrea, the harbor town located a few miles to the east of Corinth. From Paul's epistle to the Romans, we know that Cenchrea had a thriving church in which Phoebe served as deaconess (Rom. 16:1). We assume that Paul was instrumental in the founding and nurturing of that church. Moreover, Silas and Timothy were Paul's fellow workers who apparently continued to labor in Corinth and Cenchrea after his departure.

c. "And sailed to Syria with Priscilla and Aquila." In 64 B.C., the Romans declared Syria a province; its boundaries extended from the Taurus Mountains in the north, the Euphrates River in the east, Palestine in the south, and the Mediterranean Sea to the west.[33] Since Antioch was the capital of that province, Paul's intention was to travel to that city and give the local church a report on his work (vv. 22–23; compare 14:26–27). But Paul had made a vow that compelled him to visit Jerusalem.

The voyage was completed in two stages in which Ephesus became the midway point. Priscilla and Aquila decided to accompany Paul on this first leg of the journey. Why they left Corinth and took up residence in Ephesus is not known. Perhaps Paul planned to begin a new phase of mission work in Ephesus and wanted the help of this husband-wife team.[34] Notice that the name of Priscilla precedes that of her husband (see also v. 26; Rom.

---

32. See Hemer, *Book of Acts*, pp. 255–56.
33. Bauer, p. 794; Thayer, p. 607.
34. Consult R. C. H. Lenski, *The Interpretation of the Acts of the Apostles* (Columbus: Wartburg, 1944), p. 762.

16:3; II Tim. 4:19; and compare I Cor. 16:19). Priscilla seems to have applied her keen mind to knowing and interpreting Scripture. For that reason, she obtained preeminence.

d. "[Paul] had his hair cut in Cenchrea, for he was keeping a vow." Although the Greek word order can mean that Aquila had made a vow, the context points to Paul as the main subject in this verse. Paul followed the Jewish practice of making a Nazirite vow which stipulated that a person cut his hair at the conclusion of a specified period. Within thirty days following this period, a sacrifice had to be offered in Jerusalem.[35] After Paul had made his vow, he was obligated to travel to Jerusalem and offer his locks with the sacrifice.[36] Paul made this vow to express his thanksgiving to God for protecting him in Corinth and for blessing his work. To the Jews, Paul remained a Jew even in keeping vows and bringing offerings to the temple (21:23–26).

19. They arrived at Ephesus, and he left Priscilla and Aquila there. But he himself entered the synagogue and reasoned with the Jews. 20. When they asked him to remain for a longer period, he declined. 21. But he departed and said, "I will return to you, God willing." Then he left Ephesus.

From the port of Cenchrea, the ship that carried Paul, Priscilla, and Aquila sailed across the Aegean Sea to Ephesus. Earlier, while traveling through Asia Minor, Paul had been prevented by the Holy Spirit from going to the Roman province of Asia (16:6), of which Ephesus was the capital and an important harbor city. Presently he considered this city the next base of operation.

Ephesus originally had been a Greek colony that served as a commercial center for the population of the rest of Asia Minor. Since the Roman conquest, a proconsul resided there to implement Roman rule. In this city the temple of the goddess Artemis annually drew multitudes of worshipers and provided a lucrative income for the craftsmen who made idols (19:23–27).

Paul left Aquila and Priscilla in Ephesus, presumably to draw people to Christ and form a nucleus of believers. For instance, this husband and wife met Apollos in the local synagogue and instructed him more accurately in the way of the Lord (v. 26). Although Paul himself attended the worship services in the Ephesian synagogue and reasoned with the Jews, he did not stay there.[37] In spite of the Jews' request that he spend more time with them and instruct them in the Scriptures, Paul declined because of his vow (see the comments on v. 18). He promised that he would return to Ephesus and

---

35. Refer to Num. 6:1–21; Josephus *War* 2.15.1 [313]; Mishnah, *Nazir* 1.1–9.5.

36. SB, vol. 2, p. 749.

37. Jews held local citizenship in Ephesus. See Josephus *Against Apion* 2.4 [39]; and Schürer, *History of the Jewish People*, vol. 3, pp. 22–23.

added, "God willing." Luke reveals that the Jewish population appreciated the work Paul performed and wanted him to continue his teaching. For this reason Paul told the Jews that he would return to them. But first he had to leave Ephesus and sail to Caesarea.

The Western and Majority texts have expanded verse 21: "But [Paul] took leave of them, saying, *'I must by all means keep this coming feast in Jerusalem; but* I will return again to you, God willing.' And he sailed from Ephesus" (NKJV; KJV). Because the italicized information is lacking in the major manuscripts, translators are of the opinion that a scribe has added this explanatory note. The addition, however, describes Paul's hurry to arrive in Jerusalem for the feast. If Paul intended to be there for the Passover feast in the first part of April, he had but a few days to find passage on a ship to Caesarea. After the passing of winter, shipping began on March 10.[38] Favorable winds from the northwest would soon bring a ship to the port of Caesarea.

22. When he arrived at Caesarea, he went up and greeted the church and went down to Antioch.

Luke is exceptionally brief in reporting Paul's voyage to Caesarea and subsequent journeys. Caesarea had a flourishing church (8:40; 10:1, 24), but all indications are that Paul did not greet the local church. He traveled sixty-five miles to the southeast to visit the church in Jerusalem. Even though the Greek manuscripts omit the location, numerous Bible translations insert the words *in* or *at Jerusalem.*[39]

The context provides a few indications that Paul indeed went to Jerusalem. First, the verb *went up* refers not to Caesarea (at sea level) but to the holy city (at a higher elevation). Next, Caesarea served as the international harbor for Jerusalem (see 9:30). Third, the verb *went down* can apply to Antioch if Paul started out from the heights of Jerusalem. Fourth, Paul had no cause to visit the congregation in Antioch but he had reason to go to the church of the apostles and elders in Jerusalem. Finally, the haste with which Paul left Ephesus can be explained only if he had to be in Jerusalem at a specified time. Conclusively, the text speaks of Paul's visit to the mother church.

After Paul had spent some time in Jerusalem, most likely with some apostles and James and the elders, he decided to travel to Antioch. Covering the three hundred miles on foot, he arrived in the capital city of Syria

---

38. Consult F. F. Bruce, *The Book of the Acts,* rev. ed. New International Commentary on the New Testament series (Grand Rapids: Eerdmans, 1988), p. 356. See also William M. Ramsay, *St. Paul the Traveller and the Roman Citizen* (1897; reprint ed., Grand Rapids: Baker, 1962), p. 264.

39. GNB, SEB, *Phillips,* LB, and some translations in Dutch, German, French, Spanish, and Portuguese. Jakob van Bruggen identifies Paul's visit to Jersualem with Gal. 2:1. *"Na Veertien Jaren": De Datering van het in Galaten 2 genoemde Overleg te Jeruzalem* (Kampen: Kok, 1973), pp. 114–17, 228–29.

and reported to the church what God had done through him and the other missionaries.

Practical Considerations in 18:18–22

If we plan to make a vow to the Lord, we do well to heed the words of the Preacher:

> When you make a vow to God, do not delay in fulfilling it. He has no pleasure in fools; fulfill your vow. It is better not to vow than to make a vow and not fulfill it. [Eccl. 5:4–5, NIV]

Scripture teaches that many of the vows that people made were bargaining actions with God. The worshiper asked God for a favor, and if God granted the request he would receive the worshiper's gift. At Bethel, Jacob asked God for protective care and pledged a tenth of his possessions if God would answer his prayer (Gen. 28:20–22). Hannah pleaded for a son, whom she would dedicate to the Lord if God granted her request (I Sam. 1:11, 27–28).

However, we ought to refrain from making a vow to God on the condition that he grant us our request. If God honors our petition, but we find that we are unable or unwilling to fulfill our obligation, we are but fools in his presence. Rather, we should render to him our vows of thanksgiving, praise, and service for the gift of salvation in his Son Jesus Christ (Rom. 12:1–2).

Greek Words, Phrases, and Constructions in 18:18–22

Verse 18

ἐξέπλει—the imperfect tense from ἐκπλέω (I sail away) reflects the duration of the voyage. The imperfect tense of εἶχεν (he was having) also reflects duration.

κειράμενος—this aorist middle participle from the verb κείρομαι (I cut my hair) describes both time and manner.

Verse 19

κατήντησαν—"they arrived." The Majority Text has the singular verb *he arrived* (compare NKJV, KJV).

αὐτός—the position of this personal (intensive) pronoun indicates that it receives emphasis.

Verses 21–22

πάλιν ἀνακάμψω—here is a case of redundancy that is attributed to a habit of speech: "I will return *again*."[40]

κατελθών—the aorist participle (having gone down) stands separate from the

---

40. Friedrich Blass and Albert Debrunner, *A Greek Grammar of the New Testament and Other Early Christian Literature,* trans. and rev. Robert Funk (Chicago: University of Chicago Press, 1961), #484.

other two aorist participles (ἀναβάς, having gone up, and ἀσπασάμενος, having greeted). The word order reveals a subtle reason for the sequence of events.

---

23 And having spent some time in Antioch, Paul departed and passed successively through the region of Galatia and Phrygia, strengthening all the disciples.
24 A certain Jew named Apollos, who was a native of Alexandria and very learned, arrived in Ephesus. He was skilled in the Scriptures. 25 Apollos had been instructed in the way of the Lord, and with burning zeal in spirit he was speaking and teaching correctly the things concerning Jesus. He was acquainted only with the baptism of John. 26 Apollos began to speak boldly in the synagogue. When Priscilla and Aquila heard him, they took him aside and more accurately explained to him the way of God. 27 When Apollos wanted to go to Achaia, the brothers encouraged him and wrote to the disciples to welcome him. When he arrived there, he greatly helped those who through grace had believed. 28 He vigorously refuted the Jews in public and demonstrated from the Scriptures that Jesus was the Christ.

VIII. The Third Missionary Journey
18:23–21:16

A. To Ephesus
18:23–28

In his writing, Luke refrains from giving the reader an outline of Paul's three missionary journeys. Indeed, he is terse in relating details of those events that conclude Paul's second journey and begin the third phase of the apostle's ministry.

23. And having spent some time in Antioch, Paul departed and passed successively through the region of Galatia and Phrygia, strengthening all the disciples.

Once again, Luke omits the details of Paul's stay in Antioch. We conjecture that Paul stayed there perhaps for half a year before he set out to visit the churches in Galatia and Phrygia. Whether Paul had travel companions on this lengthy journey is not known. Nor do we read how Paul was received by the church in Antioch (compare 14:27). Leaving Antioch, he followed the same route he had taken when he set out on his second missionary journey (16:1–6). That is, Paul visited the churches of Derbe, Lystra, Iconium, and Pisidian Antioch, and then decided to return to Ephesus (19:1).

"Paul . . . passed successively through the region of Galatia and Phrygia." This clause raises interesting questions. Why does Luke reverse the order from that mentioned earlier (16:6)? Did Paul receive news about the churches in that area that prompted him to visit the disciples in Galatia and Phrygia?

First, variation in word order should be understood as a variation in style from 16:6 (see the commentary). The adjectives *Galatia* and *Phrygia* describe the region located in the southern part of the Roman province of Galatia.[41]

---

41. Refer to Kirsopp Lake, "Paul's Route in Asia Minor," *Beginnings,* vol. 5, pp. 239–40.

Next, we suppose that after Paul had visited the churches in the Galatian and Phrygian region on his second journey, he wrote the letter to the Galatians from Corinth. He composed this letter after two visits (13:14–14:23; 16:1–6), as he seems to imply in Galatians 4:13.[42] When Paul came to the churches, his task was to strengthen all the believers, whom Luke calls "disciples," that is, learners. He strengthened them spiritually (14:22) but also taught them to put their newfound faith into practice. Paul reminded the Galatians of their obligation to support the poverty-stricken saints in Jerusalem (Gal. 2:10; see also I Cor. 16:1).

24. A certain Jew named Apollos, who was a native of Alexandria and very learned, arrived in Ephesus. He was skilled in the Scriptures. 25. Apollos had been instructed in the way of the Lord, and with burning zeal in spirit he was speaking and teaching correctly the things concerning Jesus. He was acquainted only with the baptism of John. 26. Apollos began to speak boldly in the synagogue. When Priscilla and Aquila heard him, they took him aside and more accurately explained to him the way of God.

Note the following characteristics of Apollos:

a. *Educated.* A Jew from the Egyptian city of Alexandria came to his fellow Jews in Ephesus. Scholars estimate that about one million Jews resided in Egypt, where they spoke the Greek language. In Alexandria, the Old Testament had been translated from the Hebrew into the Greek in an effort to help the Greek-speaking Jews understand the Scriptures. The Jews had built an enormous synagogue, which "was so large that the hazzan, or sexton, had to stand on a platform in the middle to signal with a flag so that those in the back would know when to join in the amens."[43] Alexandria was the second city of rank in the Roman empire and had the distinction of being a seat of learning. Here Jewish students received a thorough education.

The name of this Alexandrian Jew was Apollos, which is an abbreviated form of the common name *Apollonius* (II Macc. 3:5–7; 4:21; 5:24; 12:2). Apollos was a learned man who attended the Jewish and the Greek schools of Alexandria and was familiar with the literature of both cultures. Luke specifies that "he was skilled in the Scriptures." That is, Apollos was an expert in reading and interpreting the Old Testament writings. In brief, he was an intelligent and capable man, as both Luke and Paul demonstrate in Acts and the epistles.[44]

b. *Eloquent.* "Apollos had been instructed in the way of the Lord." Among the pilgrims at Pentecost were Jews from Egypt (2:10) who returned to

42. William Hendriksen, *Exposition of Galatians,* New Testament Commentary series (Grand Rapids: Baker, 1968), pp. 14–15.
43. J. Alexander Thompson, "Alexandria," *ISBE,* vol. 1, p. 91. And see Talmud, *Sukkah* 51b.
44. Acts 19:1; I Cor. 1:12; 3:4–6, 22; 4:6; 16:12; Titus 3:13. See G. D. Kilpatrick, "Apollos-Apelles," *JBL* 89 (1970): 77.

their homeland with the gospel Peter had proclaimed. Because of Luke's terseness, we are unable to tell whether Apollos heard the gospel from one of these pilgrims or from others. However, the Western text has the interesting addition and change (in italics) that "Apollos had been instructed *in his own country* in the *word* of the Lord." If this reading is correct, we have here the earliest indication that Christianity had come to Egypt during the first two decades of its existence.[45] To be precise, the perfect tense of the participle *instructed* intimates that the teaching which Apollos received had taken place in the past and continued to have lasting effect.

Next, the phrases *the way of the Lord* and *the word of the Lord* signify the same thing (see also v. 26; 9:2). Apollos had become acquainted with the teaching of the Way. With a burning desire in his soul, he eloquently spoke about Jesus. He was fervent in spirit (compare Rom. 12:11). Whatever he knew concerning the Messiah, he continued to teach accurately. The drawback was that "he was acquainted only with the baptism of John." John had proclaimed a baptism of repentance, not a baptism of faith in Jesus Christ. Although Apollos accurately articulated the facts about Jesus (his birth, ministry, death, and resurrection), he was not familiar with the work of the Holy Spirit, the progress of God's kingdom, and the way of God.[46] In short, through oral teaching Apollos had learned the content of the gospel.[47] But he had not grasped its significance and application.

c. *Teachable.* "Apollos began to speak boldly in the synagogue." The Jews in Ephesus had not shut out the teaching of the gospel. They had asked Paul to spend more time with them (v. 20), they welcomed Priscilla and Aquila (v. 19), and they invited Apollos to preach about Jesus. Because no opposition to Christianity had developed, Apollos was able to speak boldly and without hindrance.

Among the worshipers in the Ephesian synagogue were Priscilla and Aquila. When they listened to Apollos, they recognized a deficiency in his gospel presentation. Consequently, they invited him to come to their home for further instruction in the Christian faith.

"They took him aside and more accurately explained to him the way of God." Notice, first, that the name of Priscilla precedes that of her husband, Aquila. She and her husband taught the educated orator Apollos "the way of God," a term that means "the Christian gospel and its application." We imagine that Priscilla and Aquila showed Apollos the significance of God's work that followed the resurrection and ascension of Jesus Christ. Next, Apollos demonstrated remarkable restraint when he consented to come to the home of a tentmaker and his wife and to receive instruction not only

---

45. Lake and Cadbury, *Beginnings*, vol. 4, p. 233. However, Martin Hengel doubts the "historical value" of this reading. *Acts and the History of Earliest Christianity*, trans. John Bowden (Philadelphia: Fortress, 1980), p. 107.

46. Consult Rackham, *Acts*, p. 342.

47. Refer to Klaus Wegenast, *NIDNTT*, vol. 3, pp. 771–72; Hermann Wolfgang Beyer, *TDNT*, vol. 3, pp. 638–40.

from a humble craftsman but also from a woman.[48] Apollos was knowledgeable about the Old Testament Scriptures, yet he lacked understanding of
"the way of God." In brief, Priscilla and Aquila taught this great preacher to
teach the things concerning Jesus more accurately.

The text does not say anything about Apollos receiving the gift of the
Holy Spirit and Christian baptism. "If he had received John's baptism
before Pentecost, his baptism, like that of the Twelve, would be accepted as
valid."[49] The text intimates that from Priscilla and Aquila Apollos learned
the importance of Christian baptism: forgiveness of sin through the blood
of Christ and renewal of life through the indwelling power of the Holy
Spirit. Because of the brevity of Luke's account, questions concerning this
passage will remain.

**27. When Apollos wanted to go to Achaia, the brothers encouraged him
and wrote to the disciples to welcome him. When he arrived there, he
greatly helped those who through grace had believed. 28. He vigorously
refuted the Jews in public and demonstrated from the Scriptures that
Jesus was the Christ.**

a. "When Apollos wanted to go to Achaia." After some time had elapsed,
Apollos expressed to the believers in Ephesus his desire to go to the province of Achaia and its capital, Corinth (19:1). Paul's first epistle to the
Corinthians indicates that in the course of time, the congregations of Corinth and Ephesus developed an enduring bond (I Cor. 16:19). We do not
know much about the formation of the Ephesian church while Paul was
absent. Yet Luke seems to indicate that Priscilla and Aquila, with the help of
Apollos, had formed a nucleus of believers.

Priscilla and Aquila had told Apollos about the spiritual growth of the
church in Corinth. Together with the other believers in Ephesus, they
encouraged him to visit the Christians in Achaia. They even asked the
Corinthian believers to receive Apollos and to welcome him as a Christian
brother. Correspondence among churches and individuals was common, as
is evident from the letter of the Jerusalem Council (15:23–29) and the
numerous epistles of Paul, Peter, John, James, and Jude and the epistle to
the Hebrews.

b. "He greatly helped those who through grace had believed." Apollos
used his knowledge of the Scriptures and his oratorical talent to strengthen
the Christians in Corinth. As a result of his labors, the Corinthian church
even had a faction known as the followers of Apollos (I Cor. 1:12; 3:4).
Although he chides the Corinthians for the factions within the church, Paul
speaks favorably about Apollos's work of teaching and preaching the Scrip-

---

48. John Calvin, *Commentary on the Acts of the Apostles*, ed. David W. Torrance and Thomas F.
Torrance, 2 vols. (Grand Rapids: Eerdmans, 1966), vol. 2, p. 145.
49. D. Edmond Hiebert, "Apollos," *ZPEB*, vol. 1, p. 215. Compare G. W. H. Lampe, *The Seal
of the Spirit*, 2d ed. (London: SPCK, 1967), p. 66. Consult also C. K. Barrett, "Apollos and the
Twelve Disciples of Ephesus," in *The New Testament Age: Essays in Honor of Bo Reicke*, ed.
William C. Weinrich, 2 vols. (Macon, Ga.: Mercer University Press, 1984), vol. 1, p. 38.

tures to Jews and Gentiles and of strengthening the churches in Achaia (I Cor. 3:5–6; 4:6; 16:12).

c. "He vigorously refuted the Jews in public and demonstrated from the Scriptures that Jesus was the Christ." In the absence of Paul, the Corinthian Jews seemed to gain influence among the Christians with their interpretation of the Scriptures. But when Apollos arrived, he publicly debated the Jews and proved from the Old Testament Scriptures that Jesus was the Christ (compare v. 5). In God's providence, Apollos filled the place of Paul at Corinth, where he valiantly defended the Christian faith in the face of Jewish opposition. As Paul and Silas proclaimed Jesus as the Messiah, so Apollos in their absence continued that glorious task.

Greek Words, Phrases, and Constructions in 18:23–28

Verse 23

διερχόμενος—the present participle follows the main verb ἐξῆλθεν (he went out) and has a futuristic bent: "to go through."[50]

τὴν χώραν—in 16:6, the definite article with the noun χώραν (region) includes the two adjectives *Phrygian* and *Galatian*. In verse 23, the definite article is not repeated. "Hence, no absolute conclusions can be drawn from the one article."[51]

Verses 25–26

ἦν κατηχημένος—the perfect passive participle from the verb κατηχέω (I sound down upon, teach orally) with the imperfect form of the verb *to be* is a periphrastic construction. The use of the perfect participle instead of the present or aorist shows action that took place in the past but has effect in the present.

ζέων τῷ πνεύματι—the dative with the present participle has a locative sense and literally means "boiling over in his spirit."[52]

ἀκριβέστερον—note the repetition of the adverb ἀκριβῶς (v. 25) but now as a comparative: "more accurately."

Verse 27

The Western text expands and paraphrases this verse. The additions are in italics: *"Now certain Corinthians were staying at Ephesus, and having heard him* [i.e., Apollos] *urged him* to cross over *with them* to *their own country. And when he had consented the Ephesians* wrote to the disciples *in Corinth that they should* receive *the man*—he who *having stayed in Achaia* was of great help *to the churches*."[53]

βουλομένου—the genitive case of the participle is part of the genitive absolute construction. The present tense denotes continued action.

---

50. Blass and Debrunner, *Greek Grammar*, #339.2a.
51. Robertson, *Grammar*, p. 788.
52. Robert Hanna, *A Grammatical Aid to the Greek New Testament* (Grand Rapids: Baker, 1983), p. 227.
53. Metzger, *Textual Commentary*, pp. 467–68.

Verse 28

διακατηλέγχετο—from the verb διακατελέγχομαι (I refute), this compound (two prepositions with a verb) signifies perfection. The imperfect tense describes repeated action.

Summary of Chapter 18

Paul arrives in Corinth and meets Aquila and Priscilla, who, like Paul, are tentmakers. When Silas and Timothy come to him from Macedonia, he devotes himself completely to preaching the message that Jesus is the Christ. As some of the Jews oppose him, Paul breaks with them and is ready to go to the Gentiles. He teaches in the house of Titius Justus and baptizes the houschold of Crispus. Jesus appears to him in a vision and instructs him to stay in Corinth, to not be afraid, and to speak. The Lord promises him safety and adds that he has many people in that city.

The Jews accuse Paul of teaching a form of religious worship that is contrary to the law. However, Gallio, the proconsul, makes a distinction between criminal law and religious law and tells the Jews to settle the matter among themselves. Sosthenes, the ruler of the synagogue, receives a beating in front of Gallio, who fails to intervene.

In the company of Priscilla and Aquila, Paul travels to Ephesus, where he speaks in the synagogue. He continues his voyage and arrives in Caesarea; then he goes up to Jerusalem to visit the church. From there he journeys to Antioch and to the churches in Galatia and Phrygia.

An Alexandrian Jew, Apollos, who is skilled in interpreting the Scriptures, teaches about Jesus, but Apollos knows only the teachings of John the Baptist. When Priscilla and Aquila hear him, they invite him to their home for further instruction. Apollos travels to Achaia, refutes the Jews in public debate, and proves that Jesus is the Christ.

19

The Third Missionary Journey, *part 2*

19:1–41

Outline (continued)

19:1–41	B.	At Ephesus
19:1–7		1. John's Baptism
19:8–12		2. Paul's Ministry
19:13–20		3. Jesus' Name
19:21–22		4. Paul's Plan
19:23–41		5. Demetrius's Grievance
19:23–27		a. Grievance
19:28–31		b. Uproar
19:32–34		c. Confusion
19:35–41		d. Speech

19 1 While Apollos was in Corinth, Paul passed through the interior regions and came to Ephesus. There he found some disciples 2 and asked them, "Did you receive the Holy Spirit when you believed?" They replied, "No, we have not even heard that there is a Holy Spirit." 3 Paul asked, "How then were you baptized?" And they answered, "With the baptism of John." 4 Paul said, "John baptized the people with a baptism of repentance and told them to believe in the one coming after him, namely, Jesus." 5 When they heard this, they were baptized in the name of the Lord Jesus. 6 As Paul placed his hands on them, the Holy Spirit came on them. They began to speak in tongues and prophesy. 7 In all, they were twelve in number.

8 Paul entered the synagogue and for three months reasoned persuasively and spoke boldly about the kingdom of God. 9 But as some of them became hardened and disobedient, they spoke evil of the Way in the presence of the multitude. So Paul withdrew and took the disciples with him. Daily he held discussions in the school of Tyrannus. 10 And this lasted for two years, so that all who lived in the province of Asia, both Jews and Greeks, heard the word of the Lord.

11 God performed extraordinary miracles through Paul, 12 so that even the handkerchiefs and aprons that had touched Paul's skin were taken to the sick; their diseases left them and the evil spirits departed.

13 Some of the Jews who drove out evil spirits went about attempting to use the name of Jesus on those who were demon-possessed. They were saying, "I adjure you by the name of Jesus, whom Paul preaches, to come out." 14 Seven sons of Sceva, a Jewish high priest, were doing this. 15 But the evil spirit said to them, "I know Jesus, and I know about Paul, but who are you?" 16 And the demon-possessed man jumped on them. He subdued and so overpowered them all that they fled from that house naked and wounded. 17 This became known to all the Jews and Greeks living in Ephesus. They were all terrified and they began to hold the name of the Lord Jesus in high honor.

18 Many of those who had believed were coming to confess and report their evil deeds. 19 A number of those who practiced magic brought together their scrolls and burned them publicly. When they calculated their value, it came to fifty thousand drachmas. 20 So the word of the Lord grew in power and might.

21 After these things happened, Paul decided in the Spirit to go to Jerusalem by way of Macedonia and Achaia. He said, "After I have been there, I must visit Rome, too." 22 He sent two of his assistants, Timothy and Erastus, to Macedonia. Paul himself remained in Asia for a while.

23 At this time, concerning the Way a great disturbance arose. 24 For a silversmith named Demetrius, making silver shrines for Artemis, was bringing no little profit for the artisans. 25 He gathered them together with workmen of similar trades and said: "Men, you know that our prosperity depends on this business. 26 And you see and hear that not only in Ephesus but in nearly the whole province of Asia, this fellow Paul has persuaded and turned away a great number of people. He tells them that gods made with hands are no gods at all. 27 Not only do we run the risk of our trade falling into disrepute, but the temple of the great goddess Artemis will be regarded as nothing; and all who worship her in Asia and the whole world will suffer the loss of her magnificence."

28 When they heard this, the artisans became angry and began to shout, "Great is Artemis of the Ephesians!" 29 The whole city was filled with confusion. The people rushed together into the theater after they had seized both Gaius and Aristarchus, who were Paul's traveling companions from Macedonia. 30 The disciples did not allow Paul to appear before the crowd, even though he wanted to do so. 31 Even some of the deputies of the province of Asia who were friendly to Paul sent a message to him urging him not to venture into the theater. 32 Then some people were shouting one thing or another, for the assembly was in confusion. Most people did not even know why they had assembled there. 33 Some of the crowd advised Alexander to speak, for the Jews pushed him forward. Alexander motioned with his hand and desired to make a defense before the assembly. 34 But when they realized that he was a Jew, for about two hours they all shouted with one voice: "Great is Artemis of the Ephesians."

35 The town clerk calmed the crowd and said: "Men of Ephesus, who does not know that the city of the Ephesians is the guardian of the temple of the great Artemis and of the image that fell down from heaven? 36 Therefore, since these things are undeniable, you must be calm and not do anything that is rash. 37 For you have brought these men here, though they have neither robbed temples nor blasphemed our goddess. 38 If, then, Demetrius and the artisans with him have a complaint against anyone, the courts are in session and the proconsuls are available. Let them bring charges against each other. 39 But if there is anything further that you want to know, it should be settled in a legal assembly. 40 For indeed, we are running the risk of being accused of rioting concerning today's events. And there is no reason for it, because we will be unable to account for this uproar." 41 Having said this, he dismissed the assembly.

B. At Ephesus
19:1–41

1. John's Baptism
19:1–7

In these verses, Luke presents an extremely brief report on Paul's meeting with twelve disciples in Ephesus. Because of this brevity, Luke places the expositor in a quandary. To illustrate, in his Gospel Luke relates that John the Baptist began his ministry in the fifteenth year of the reign of Tiberius Caesar (see Luke 3:1–3). A probable date is A.D. 25–26. And within a brief period of time, John the Baptist was arrested and later beheaded by Herod Antipas (see Matt. 14:3–12). His ministry and influence had ended. But in Acts Luke reveals that, nearly three decades after John's death, some people who were baptized with John's baptism reside not in Judea but in Ephesus. Luke calls them disciples.

But what is the significance of the word *disciples* in respect to the Christian faith? And what is meant by "being baptized with the baptism of John"? Is the second baptism of the disciples unique? These are perplexing questions in this particular passage.

1. While Apollos was in Corinth, Paul passed through the interior regions and came to Ephesus. There he found some disciples 2. and asked them, "Did you receive the Holy Spirit when you believed?" They replied, "No, we have not even heard that there is a Holy Spirit." 3. Paul

asked, "How then were you baptized?" And they answered, "With the baptism of John."

a. *Ephesus.* Even though Luke introduces Apollos in the preceding chapter (18) and mentions his name in this chapter (19), he nowhere reveals that Paul and Apollos met each other. Luke only states that while Apollos was in Corinth, Paul traveled from Pisidian Antioch through the interior (according to the Greek text, the higher) regions of Asia Minor and arrived at Ephesus.

Paul had promised the Jews in Ephesus that he would return to them, the Lord willing, and give them further instruction (refer to 18:19–21). Although on an earlier occasion the Holy Spirit had prevented him from entering the province of Asia (16:6), Paul considered Ephesus crucial to the spread of the gospel.

Situated south of the Caÿster River and three miles inland from the Aegean Sea, Ephesus was a crossroad for the coastal highway that went from north to south and the highway that stretched east to Laodicea and to the region of Phrygia (Pisidian Antioch). In earlier centuries, Ephesus, where the traffic of the sea met the traffic of the land, had been the leading commercial center in the province of Asia. But in Paul's day, the harbor of Ephesus was so clogged with silt that ships had difficulty docking there and were forced to go elsewhere.

Although its silted harbor caused the city's inevitable decline in commercial influence, Ephesus had nonetheless surpassed Pergamum in significance when the Romans made it the provincial capital of Asia (western Turkey) toward the end of the first century B.C. In the middle of the first century A.D. the city may have had more than two hundred thousand inhabitants; archaeological excavations have unearthed the ancient theater, which seated an estimated twenty-four thousand people. Of greater significance was the temple of the goddess Artemis. The temple, which was the largest known building of that time and ranked among the seven wonders of the ancient world, drew crowds of worshipers to Ephesus. And here a flourishing business had been developed by silversmiths who fashioned silver shrines and images of Artemis.

b. *Disciples.* When Paul arrived in Ephesus, he undoubtedly met Priscilla and Aquila, who informed him about the work of Apollos in the local synagogue. Soon afterward, Paul met a group of twelve men whom Luke describes as disciples. The word *disciples,* which Luke in Acts uses to describe Christian believers, is usually a synonym for "followers of Christ." Paul seemed to give these people the benefit of the doubt, because he used the verb *to believe,* with the implication that they believed in Christ. He asked, "Did you receive the Holy Spirit when you believed?"

But these disciples answered Paul: "We have not even heard that there is a Holy Spirit." This statement in itself seems inconceivable, because the Old Testament teaches the doctrine of the Spirit. And the evidence of the Spirit's presence was obvious in John's life (compare Luke 1:15). The scribe of the Western text faced this problem and made the disciples say: "We have not even heard whether people are receiving the Holy Spirit."[1] But translators hesitate to adopt this reading, for the usual inclination of scribes is to revise the text and make it easier for the reader to understand. The harder reading, therefore, prevails: "that there is a Holy Spirit."

The fact that the disciples in Ephesus show ignorance of the Spirit's presence raises questions, because a Christian without the Spirit is a contradiction in terms. Faith (or, belief) without the Spirit is nothing more than nodding consent. Moreover, were these men followers of Christ? Had they been baptized in the name of Jesus? The New Testament teaches that "anyone who has not received Christian baptism does not belong to the community at all."[2]

Paul wanted to know more about the spiritual base of these disciples and asked, "How then were you baptized?" The disciples simply replied, "With the baptism of John." Their answer may indicate that they were indeed disciples of John the Baptist, had been baptized by their teacher or one of his followers, and had moved from Judea to Ephesus. Writes C. K. Barrett, "There is good, though hardly overwhelming, reason to think that groups of John's disciples did persist after their master's death, and even after the death and resurrection of Jesus."[3]

Notice the difference between Apollos and these disciples: Apollos knew only the baptism of John but taught accurately about Jesus with a thorough knowledge of the Scriptures (18:24–25); the disciples had John's baptism but lacked knowledge of the Holy Spirit. Although they were learning about Jesus, the men remained closely associated with John the Baptist. They missed the joyful assurance of the Spirit in their lives, had no living relationship with Christ, and were told that John's baptism was inadequate. They were in a phase that was introductory to the Christian faith. And because they were in this phase, Luke and Paul guardedly used the terms *disciples* (learners) and *believe* (consent).[4]

As Priscilla and Aquila taught Apollos about the gospel of Christ and strengthened him, so Paul led these followers of John to a saving knowledge of Jesus. Thus Paul affirmed the words that the Baptist spoke about

---

1. Bruce M. Metzger, *A Textual Commentary on the Greek New Testament*, 3d corrected ed. (London and New York: United Bible Societies, 1975), p. 469.

2. Ernst Käsemann, "The Disciples of John the Baptist in Ephesus," in *Essays on New Testament Themes*, Studies in Biblical Theology series 41 (London: SCM, 1964), p. 144. Consult C. K. Barrett, "Apollos and the Twelve Disciples of Ephesus," in *The New Testament Age: Essays in Honor of Bo Reicke*, ed. William C. Weinrich, 2 vols. (Macon, Ga.: Mercer University Press, 1984), vol. 1, p. 30. But see F. W. Norris, "Christians only, but not the only Christians (Acts 19:1–7)," *ResQ* 28 (1985–86): 97–105.

3. Barrett, "Apollos and the Twelve Disciples," p. 37. J. D. G. Dunn advises against calling these Ephesian disciples simply "disciples of John the Baptist." *Baptism in the Holy Spirit*, Studies in Biblical Theology, 2d series 15 (London: SCM, 1970), p. 84.

4. In Acts, the verb *believe* is used occasionally to signify consent without allegiance (see, e.g., 8:13).

the Christ in comparison to himself: "He must increase; I must decrease" (John 3:30).

4. Paul said, "John baptized the people with a baptism of repentance and told them to believe in the one coming after him, namely, Jesus."

The disciples reveal that they are not true to the teachings of John the Baptist, who made it known that he was the forerunner of the Messiah. They should have listened to the words of John and accepted Jesus as their Messiah. For that reason, Paul refers them to the ministry and the teachings of the Baptist (Matt. 3:11; Acts 1:5; 10:37; 13:24–25).

a. "A baptism of repentance." To provide a smooth translation in English, I have added the direct object *the people*. The Greek at this point is condensed: "John baptized a baptism of repentance." Actually, the word *baptized* has the connotation *preached* (see Mark 1:4). John called the people to repentance, and when they repented, he baptized them as a sign of spiritual cleansing. But John's preaching was preparatory to the coming of the Messiah, because not John but Jesus could cleanse the people from sin. In his preaching John pointed to the one coming after him who would baptize the people with the Holy Spirit (Matt. 3:11; Mark 1:8; Luke 3:16).

b. "Believe in the one coming after him." Paul instructs the men who had John's baptism not by telling them about the Holy Spirit but by acquainting them with Jesus, the one who came after John. His objective is that they come to faith in Jesus. By achieving this goal, Paul causes the ministry of the Baptist to yield effectively to Christ. And this was exactly the purpose of the Baptist's ministry. After this reference, John's name appears no more in Acts.

5. When they heard this, they were baptized in the name of the Lord Jesus.

Paul leads these disciples to Jesus Christ, in whom they put their trust. He points out to them the difference between the preparatory work of John and the mediatorial work of Jesus. The preaching and baptism of John demand repentance from sin. Obedience to the message of the gospel and a desire for baptism in the name of Jesus presume true faith in Christ. As the men listen to Paul's instruction, they hear and understand the message of the gospel. In faith they accept the word of salvation and ask for baptism in Jesus' name.

Was rebaptism necessary for these disciples? The New Testament is not explicit on this point; for example, Luke fails to report whether Apollos, who knew only John's baptism, was rebaptized (18:25). John Calvin, therefore, interprets the baptism of the disciples in Ephesus as the coming of the Holy Spirit upon them (v. 6). Says he, "I do deny that the baptism of water was repeated."[5] But the sequence in the narrative is that these men are baptized and then receive the laying on of hands, which is followed by the

---

5. John Calvin, *Commentary on the Acts of the Apostles*, ed. David W. Torrance and Thomas F. Torrance, 2 vols. (Grand Rapids: Eerdmans, 1966), vol. 2, p. 151.

outpouring of the Holy Spirit. Other interpreters see John's baptism as an introduction to baptism in the name of Jesus.[6] For instance, many of the three thousand Jews who repented and were baptized at Pentecost (2:41) presumably had already received the baptism of John in the Jordan. The baptism of John points toward Christ, but the baptism in the name of Jesus looks back to Christ's accomplished work.

In striking poetic form, Dora Greenwell has captured the thought of the forgiven sinner who looks to Christ and sings:

> I am not skilled to understand
> What God has willed,
>   what God has planned;
> I only know at his right hand
> Stands one who is my Saviour.

6. As Paul placed his hand on them, the Holy Spirit came on them. They began to speak in tongues and prophesy. 7. In all, they were twelve in number.

John preached about repentance and forgiveness but was unable to cleanse people from their sins. By contrast, Jesus forgives sinners and completely restores them. John told his audience about the baptism of the Holy Spirit but could not give anyone the gift of the Spirit. Jesus, however, promised the outpouring of the Holy Spirit, who at the proper time came upon the Jews in Jerusalem, the Samaritans in Samaria, and the Gentiles in Caesarea.

For the fourth time the Spirit is poured out on a group of people. Jews in Jerusalem, Samaritans, and Gentiles in Caesarea had had the Spirit poured out upon them; now the disciples in Ephesus receive the Spirit. The text further states that Paul places his hands on the disciples. In only three places in Acts do we read that the laying on of hands is accompanied by the outpouring of the Spirit: in 8:17, on the Samaritans; in 9:17, on Paul; and here, on John's disciples. In other instances the symbolic act of laying on of hands takes place in ordination ceremonies.[7]

The coming of the Holy Spirit on the disciples in Ephesus compares with the experiences of the apostles in Jerusalem (2:11) and the Gentiles in Caesarea (10:44–46). The disciples in Ephesus begin to speak in tongues and to prophesy. In Jerusalem, the apostles spoke in other (that is, known) languages and declared the wonders God had done; in Caesarea, the Gentiles expressed themselves in tongues and praised God; and in Ephesus, the disciples articulated in tongues and prophesied. The word *prophesy* in these contexts conveys the idea of glorifying the name of God and witnessing for Jesus.

---

6. J. K. Parratt, "The Rebaptism of the Ephesian Disciples," *ExpT* 79 (1967–68): 182–83; Henry Alford, *Alford's Greek Testament: An Exegetical and Critical Commentary*, 7th ed., 4 vols. (1877; Grand Rapids: Guardian, 1976), vol. 2, p. 211.

7. See Acts 13:3; I Tim. 4:14; 5:22; II Tim. 1:6; and refer to Heb. 6:2.

Note that Luke provides no explanation whether the converts in Caesarea and in Ephesus uttered known languages or ecstatic speech. In both instances (10:46; 19:6), there is no indication whether interpreters were needed to explain the words of the speakers. Because the evidence in Acts is inconclusive, a wise course of action is to refrain from being dogmatic on this point.

Luke adds the information that twelve men in this group were baptized and received the Holy Spirit. The reception of the Holy Spirit was the ultimate proof that they were Christians.[8] The number twelve in this text should not be taken symbolically or be compared with the twelve disciples of Jesus. That would be reading into the text something which it does not intend to teach.

Why was the Holy Spirit poured out on these twelve men in Ephesus? In keeping with Jesus' promise (1:8), the Spirit descended upon the Jews, the Samaritans, and the Gentiles. After the Spirit was poured out on the members of Cornelius's household (i.e., on Gentiles ["to the ends of the earth," 1:8]), the promise seems to have been fulfilled. How, then, do we account for the incident in Ephesus?[9]

A possible answer is to consider the extension of the church in Jerusalem, Samaria, and Caesarea as a first phase of mission work among Jews, Samaritans, and Gentiles. A second phase relates to the work of evangelizing persons who have an inadequate knowledge of Christ but are subsequently instructed in the truth of the gospel. If we consider the first phase to be extensive, then the second is intensive.

Doctrinal Considerations in 19:1–7

The four outpourings of the Holy Spirit recorded in Acts are confirmed by the apostles: in Jerusalem by the Twelve, in Samaria by Peter and John, in Caesarea by Peter, and in Ephesus by Paul.

Does Acts teach a Spirit-baptism that results in glossolalia? The answer is no. First, the outpouring of the Spirit in Ephesus is not a baptism in the Spirit but baptism in the name of Jesus. After this ceremony is complete, Paul puts his hands on the disciples of John and they receive the Holy Spirit. This is to confirm that now they are Christians who have had a true conversion experience. Next, numerous people were baptized but did not speak in tongues: the three thousand believers in Jerusalem on the day of Pentecost (2:41); the Ethiopian official (8:38–39); Paul in Damascus (9:18); Lydia and her household (16:15); and the Philippian jailer and his family (16:33). Third, many people who believe are filled with the Holy Spirit but do not speak in an ecstatic tongue: Peter facing the Sanhedrin (4:8); Stephen addressing the Sanhedrin (7:55); and Paul confronting Elymas (13:9).

---

8. Consult Dunn, *Baptism in the Holy Spirit*, p. 88.
9. F. F. Bruce sees Ephesus as "the new center for the Gentile mission" and the Spirit-filled disciples as "the nucleus of the Ephesian church." *The Book of the Acts*, rev. ed., New International Commentary on the New Testament series (Grand Rapids: Eerdmans, 1988), p. 365.

In brief, the New Testament fails to support the belief that reception of the Holy Spirit results in tongue-speaking.[10] On the contrary, the historical evidence in Acts shows that all those Christians who were filled with the Spirit witnessed intelligibly for Jesus Christ.

Greek Words, Phrases, and Constructions in 19:1–7

Verse 1

The Western text has a variant reading, given here in italics, for the first sentence: "And *although Paul wished, according to his own plan, to go to Jerusalem, the Spirit told him to return to Asia.* And having passed through the upper country he *comes* to Ephesus."[11]

The scribe of the Western text tried to link 19:1 (Paul returning to Ephesus as soon as possible) with 18:22, where Luke writes that Paul went to Caesarea and then "went up and greeted the church." But the information in 18:23 contradicts the variant reading.

Verse 2

εἰ—the first εἰ introduces a direct question. It is not translated and derives from the literal Septuagint translation of Hebrew syntax: "Did you receive . . . ?" The tense of the aorist participle πιστεύσαντες (when you believed) is simultaneous with that of the main verb ἐλάβετε (you received).[12] The second εἰ (if) is in an indirect question.

Verse 3

εἰς τί—"into what?" signifies "how?" The preposition εἰς in εἰς τό is the equivalent of the dative, "with."

Verse 6

The scribe of the Western text embellished the text at the end of the clause: "they began to speak in tongues." The addition is in italics: "*other* tongues, *and they* themselves *knew them, which they also interpreted for themselves; and certain* also prophesied."[13]

---

2. Paul's Ministry
19:8–12

When Luke writes that Paul entered the synagogue, he has no intention of saying that, upon his return to Ephesus, he first met with the twelve

---

10. Consult Anthony A. Hoekema, *Holy Spirit Baptism* (Grand Rapids: Eerdmans, 1972), pp. 44–45.

11. Metzger, *Textual Commentary*, p. 468.

12. A. T. Robertson, *A Grammar of the Greek New Testament in the Light of Historical Research* (Nashville: Broadman, 1934), p. 861.

13. Metzger, *Textual Commentary*, p. 470.

disciples of John (vv. 1, 7) and then went to the synagogue. Rather, Luke relates two separate historical incidents that could have happened at about the same time. He reports Paul's teaching ministry in respect first to the followers of John the Baptist and then to the people in the local synagogue.

8. Paul entered the synagogue and for three months reasoned persuasively and spoke boldly about the kingdom of God.

When Paul briefly stayed in Ephesus on his way to Jerusalem (18:19), he immediately went to the synagogue, where he reasoned with the Jews. His audience was pleased with his teaching and begged him to stay. Although he declined the invitation, he nevertheless promised that he would return. Luke conveys the impression that Paul and his Jewish audience had developed an amicable relationship. When Paul returned to Ephesus, he immediately went to the synagogue and took up a full-time teaching ministry. Because of the congenial associations he had with the Ephesian Jews, he was able to teach for a period of three months. Elsewhere Paul had been instructing the people in a synagogue for only a limited time, but in Ephesus he was allowed to continue for an entire season.

During this three-month period, Paul lectured on the kingdom of God. In Acts, to preach the kingdom of God means to proclaim the Word of the Lord, that is, the gospel.[14] For instance, in the same context (v. 10) Luke writes that the Jews and the Greeks heard "the word of the Lord"; in 20:24–25, he uses the terms *the gospel of grace* and *the kingdom* as synonyms; and in 28:30–31, he writes that Paul, a prisoner under house arrest in Rome, proclaimed both the kingdom of God and Jesus to all who visited him. In Ephesus, the clash between the kingdom of God and Satan's idolatrous rule became evident when the craftsmen of shrines and images instigated a riot (vv. 23–41). Even some of the Jews who had listened to Paul slandered the Christian faith (v. 9).

9. But as some of them became hardened and disobedient, they spoke evil of the Way in the presence of the multitude. So Paul withdrew and took the disciples with him. Daily he held discussions in the school of Tyrannus. 10. And this lasted for two years, so that all who lived in the province of Asia, both Jews and Greeks, heard the word of the Lord.

a. "But as some of them became hardened and disobedient." Paul continued his teaching ministry in the Ephesian synagogue, but at the end of three months he realized that opposition from a minority of the Jews impeded him. These people turned against Paul as they gradually hardened their hearts and demonstrated their disobedience to God and the teachings of his Word.

b. "They spoke evil of the Way in the presence of the multitude." These unbelieving Jews made their hatred public by maligning the teachings of the Christian faith. The Jews vilified the Way, Luke writes. The term *Way*

---

14. Consult George E. Ladd, *A Theology of the New Testament* (Grand Rapids: Eerdmans, 1974), p. 333; also see his "Kingdom of God (Heaven)," *BEB*, vol. 2, p. 1277. And refer to Donald Guthrie, *New Testament Theology* (Downers Grove: Inter-Varsity, 1981), p. 429.

was a self-designation for the church. Perhaps the Christians used it as a missionary term in the first few decades of the church's existence.[15] As an interesting parallel, Luke records that Paul before his conversion wanted to imprison persons who belonged to the Way (9:2). But years later, Paul himself had to endure the opposition of fellow Jews in Ephesus who slandered members of the Way.

c. "So Paul withdrew and took the disciples with him." Following a pattern, Paul withdrew his students from the synagogue school. Looking for another location, he learned that the lecture hall of a certain Tyrannus was available. We have no further knowledge of Tyrannus, whose name means Tyrant.[16] Probably this was a nickname given to him by his pupils.

The Western text adds the interesting note that Paul held discussions "from the fifth to the tenth hour," that is, from 11 A.M. to 4 P.M. Tyrannus used the lecture hall in the morning hours; when the heat of the day became oppressive, Paul could use the hall while the citizenry enjoyed the noon meal and rested. Presumably, Paul worked at his trade during the morning hours to support himself financially (see 18:3; 20:34; I Cor. 4:12). With gifts from other donors, he was able to pay the rental fee for the lecture hall, where he taught his disciples for five hours, with appropriate periods of rest.

There is reason to believe that the additional note of the Western text is authentic, yet translators hesitate to make it part of the New Testament text. They question why this piece of information, if it is genuine, has been deleted from the major manuscripts.

d. "Daily he held discussions in the school of Tyrannus." In Ephesus, Paul opened a school of theology to train future leaders for the developing church in the province of Asia. These students may have been employed on a regular basis from early morning until eleven o'clock and then engaged in religious instruction.[17] The long hours of work and study testify to the enthusiasm of the early Christians, and such testimony was not lost on the pagan world.

e. "This lasted for two years." Paul taught daily in the Ephesian lecture hall for two years. In round numbers (three months of teaching in the local synagogue and two years in the lecture hall), the entire course of study lasted nearly three years (20:31). And in the Jewish culture of Paul's day, part of a year was considered a full year. In conclusion, both teacher and students demonstrated an indomitable will to earn a living and to further the gospel.

---

15. Günther Ebel, *NIDNTT*, vol. 3, p. 941. S. V. McCasland concludes that the term *the Way* "as a designation of Christianity was derived from Isa[iah] 40:3 and that it is an abbreviated form of the 'way of the Lord.'" The idiom came to Christianity via Qumran and John the Baptist. "The Way," *JBL* 77 (1958): 230.

16. One of the bodyguards of Herod the Great also bore the name *Tyrannus*. Josephus *Antiquities* 16.10.3 [314].

17. Gerald F. Hawthorne, "Tyrannus," *ISBE*, vol. 4, p. 932.

f. "All who lived in the province of Asia, both Jews and Greeks, heard the word of the Lord." From Ephesus, the word of the Lord went forth to all the Jews and the Greeks who lived in the province of Asia. We assume that the students trained by Paul became pastors in developing congregations in western Asia Minor (compare, e.g., the reference to the seven churches [Rev. 1:11]). These disciples were instrumental in preaching Christ's gospel, that is, the word of the Lord, to both the Jews and the Greeks. For example, Epaphras was a faithful minister of the gospel in Colosse (Col. 1:7), Laodicea, and Hierapolis (Col. 4:12–13). He was with Paul in Rome during Paul's first imprisonment and became his fellow prisoner. Likewise Tychicus, a native of the province of Asia (20:4), was a close associate; Paul calls him a fellow servant (Col. 4:7) and a faithful minister (Eph. 6:21). Then there was Trophimus, who also was from Asia (20:4). Finally, Philemon and Archippus were fellow workers and fellow soldiers with Paul in Colosse (Philem. 1–2).[18]

Consider these points:

First, it is possible that the disciples (v. 9) who had been baptized with John's baptism were among Paul's students. Next, it is a fact that for decades Ephesus was the evangelistic center for the Christian church in western Asia Minor (compare Rev. 2:1–7). And last, Ephesus is the only place where Paul, during his missionary journeys, spent a three-year teaching ministry. His successor was Timothy (I Tim. 1:3), and in later years the apostle John served the church of Ephesus.

11. God performed extraordinary miracles through Paul, 12. so that even the handkerchiefs and aprons that had touched Paul's skin were taken to the sick; their diseases left them and the evil spirits departed.

We observe an interesting parallel in Acts. After the outpouring of the Holy Spirit on Pentecost, God performed extraordinary miracles through the apostles (2:43; and see 5:12). Before the Spirit came upon the Samaritans, God worked miraculous signs through Philip (8:6, 13). When the Holy Spirit descended on the disciples in Ephesus, God made his power known through miracles effected by Paul. Of course, God had given both Paul and Barnabas power to perform miraculous signs and wonders in Iconium during the first missionary journey (14:3).

Another parallel is obvious: Peter's shadow fell on the sick, who were healed when he passed by (5:15); Paul's handkerchiefs and aprons cured the sick. The reference in Paul's case is to cloths used to remove perspiration and to protective coverings that likely were soiled and stained from daily use in the workshop. These items were taken to the sick who, upon touching them, would be healed; evil spirits would leave demon-possessed people.

---

18. Consult Richard B. Rackham, *The Acts of the Apostles: An Exposition*, Westminster Commentaries series (1901; reprint ed., Grand Rapids: Baker, 1964), p. 352.

Note these observations on Paul's service to the Lord:

a. God is the miracle worker, not Paul. Admittedly, the people in Ephesus regarded Paul as having superhuman power to heal the sick. Yet Luke clearly writes that God performed miracles through Paul.

b. Luke, who by profession is a physician, calls these miracles extraordinary. Whatever the wonders may have been, they were astonishing in the eyes of the people. Countless sick were healed, became recipients of God's grace, and heard the gospel of salvation proclaimed publicly by Paul.

c. Besides teaching the gospel openly and performing healing miracles, Paul also taught the Good News from house to house (20:20). Addressing both Jews and Greeks, he admonished them to repent, to turn to God, and to have faith in Jesus Christ (20:21).

d. Paul contended for the unity of the church, which he regarded as the body of Christ.[19] At Ephesus he received information about factions and quarrels in the church at Corinth (I Cor. 1:11–12). A delegation of three people also communicated personally with Paul about the conditions in Corinth (I Cor. 16:17). In answer, Paul wrote the two canonical epistles to the Corinthians and two other letters no longer extant (see I Cor. 5:9; II Cor. 2:4). In addition, Paul himself decided to visit the church in Corinth, but this visit proved to be a painful experience for him (II Cor. 2:1).

Paul labored unceasingly for the advancement of God's kingdom, the growth and development of Christ's church, the proclamation of the gospel of God's grace, and the salvation of sinful man.

Doctrinal Considerations in 19:11–12

Reading the words in this particular passage, we invariably think that the people in Ephesus were superstitious. They expected to be healed from diseases by taking articles of clothing that had touched Paul's skin. They seemed to consider Paul to be nearly divine because of the healing powers he possessed.

However, Luke gives no indication that the people worshiped Paul or that they idolized his handkerchiefs and aprons. Calvin points out that worthless things were chosen so that the people might not fall into superstition and idolatry.[20]

The focus is on God, who heals the people physically and through the preaching of the gospel restores them spiritually. God performs "extraordinary miracles," as Luke writes. He demonstrates his power among the people so that they may turn to him in faith and obtain salvation. Miracles and faith are the two sides of the same coin. In the words of the writer of Hebrews, "This salvation, which was first announced by the Lord, was confirmed to us by those who heard him. God also testified to it by signs, wonders and various miracles, and gifts of the Holy Spirit distributed according to his will" (2:3–4, NIV).

---

19. I Cor. 12:12–27; Eph. 1:22–23; 4:12; Col. 1:18, 24.
20. Calvin, *Acts of the Apostles*, vol. 2, p. 155.

Greek Words, Phrases, and Constructions in 19:11

δυνάμεις τε οὐ τὰς τυχούσας—"miracles, not the common ones." Here is one of Luke's characteristic understatements in which he expresses the negative to accentuate the positive (compare v. 24). The use of the particle οὐ instead of μή, to negate the aorist participle τυχούσας, points to the extraordinary nature of the miracles.

---

3. Jesus' Name
19:13–20

Among the people who were healed by Paul in Ephesus were some who were demon-possessed. As Jesus had given the twelve disciples authority over evil spirits (Mark 6:7), so God endowed Paul with power to drive out demons from afflicted people. Paul entered Satan's domain and, with the sovereignty God had given him, told the devils to depart.

13. Some of the Jews who drove out evil spirits went about attempting to use the name of Jesus on those who were demon-possessed. They were saying, "I adjure you by the name of Jesus, whom Paul preaches, to come out." 14. Seven sons of Sceva, a Jewish high priest, were doing this.

a. *Exorcism.* In writing Acts, Luke often presents first the setting and then a specific incident. For example, he discloses the general information that the Lord did many miraculous signs and wonders through Paul and Barnabas (14:1–7). Then he relates the story of Paul healing the cripple at Lystra (14:8–10). Similarly, after describing the setting in Ephesus, Luke provides details of a distinctive instance of Jewish exorcists attempting to expel a demon.

From the Gospels we know that Jews in Israel were casting out demons (Matt. 12:27; Luke 11:19). Also, the Jewish historian Josephus reports that he saw a countryman driving out a demon from a possessed man in the presence of the Roman general Vespasian.[21] At times, Gentiles asked Jewish teachers to exorcise demons. Some of these teachers visited fellow Jews living in the dispersion and used magic formulas to adjure the evil spirits. Because the formulas often failed to achieve results, the magicians were forced to acquire new adjurations to enhance their craft.[22] A number of ancient manuscripts attest to a variety of incantations that Jewish exorcists employed, and as this account discloses, the city of Ephesus proved to be a storehouse of magical scrolls.

---

21. Josephus *Antiquities* 8.2.5 [46–49].
22. Adolf Deissmann translated a papyrus fragment that reads: "I adjure thee by the god of the Hebrews Jesu." Deissmann comments that the name *Jesu* is an insertion; "no Christian, still less a Jew, would have called Jesus 'the god of the Hebrews.'" *Light from the Ancient East*, rev. ed., trans. Lionel R. M. Strachan (New York: Doran, 1927), p. 260 n. 4.

The Jewish exorcists who saw Paul drive out demons in the name of Jesus Christ were intrigued. They realized that their own magical powers had failed them but that the words uttered by Paul were effective. The apostles healed people in the name of Jesus, not to practice magic but to demonstrate Jesus' authority (compare 3:6). The term *name* signifies the person, words, and works of Jesus, so that anyone who uses this name identifies completely with its bearer and becomes a true representative. Therefore, unbelievers can never use the power of Jesus' name.

The Jewish charlatans in Ephesus would say to evil spirits, "I adjure you by the name of Jesus, whom Paul preaches, to come out." Their adjuration is derivative, for it includes the name of Paul. Moreover, they expose themselves as unbelievers, for their adjuration shows that Paul, not the charlatans, serves Jesus. By contrast, consider the man who cast out demons in Jesus' name. Jesus commanded his disciples not to stop this man, for "whoever is not against you is for you" (Luke 9:50). The man evidently believed in Jesus and was his follower.

b. *Sceva*. Luke relates three facts about Sceva: He was a Jew, a chief priest, and the father of seven sons. Jewish magicians were influential during the first century (e.g., the Jewish sorcerer Bar-Jesus, who was an attendant of the proconsul Sergius Paulus [13:6–7]). We have no evidence that Sceva served as high priest at the temple in Jerusalem; therefore, we need not assume that he had a ruling position. Josephus indicates that some men who were called chief priests never ruled in that capacity.[23] It is plausible, however, that this Jew called himself a high priest for his own benefit and that of his sons living in the dispersion.[24] Still, Luke fails to indicate whether Sceva himself was present in Ephesus; he only notes that his seven sons were there. Because we lack solid evidence concerning the name and office of Sceva, we suggest that these sons belonged to a priestly family and practiced exorcism.[25] In fact, the Western text has the reading *priest* instead of "high priest."[26]

15. But the evil spirit said to them, "I know Jesus, and I know about Paul, but who are you?" 16. And the demon-possessed man jumped on them. He subdued and so overpowered them all that they fled from that house naked and wounded.

Luke's description of the evil spirit who talks through the mouth of the

---

23. Josephus *War* 2.20.4 [566]; 4.9.11 [574]; 5.13.1 [527]. From the writings of Josephus, Emil Schürer compiled a list of twenty-eight high priests who were appointed from 37 B.C. to A.D. 67–68. *The History of the Jewish People in the Age of Jesus Christ (175 B.C.–A.D. 135)*, rev. and ed. Geza Vermes and Fergus Millar, 3 vols. (Edinburgh: Clark, 1973–87), vol. 2, pp. 229–32.

24. Bruce, *Book of the Acts*, p. 368; Gary M. Burge, "Sceva," *ISBE*, vol. 4, p. 350.

25. Consult B. A. Mastin, "Scaeva the Chief Priest," *JTS* 27 (1976): 412.

26. Albert C. Clark asserts that because in the Greek New Testament the term *high priest* occurs far more often than the expression *priest*, "a scribe . . . would easily substitute the more familiar word for the rarer." *The Acts of the Apostles: A Critical Edition with Introduction and Notes on Selected Passages* (1933; Oxford: Clarendon, 1970), p. 370.

demon-possessed man parallels accounts in the synoptic Gospels (see Matt. 8:29; Mark 1:24; Luke 4:41). In these accounts, the demons acknowledge Jesus as the Son of God. In Ephesus, the demon, hearing the formula spoken by the exorcists, responds with full knowledge: "I know Jesus, and I know about Paul, but who are you?" In the Greek text, Luke uses two different words for the verb *to know*. Perhaps they serve to distinguish the heavenly Jesus from the earthly Paul. Yet these two verbs are virtually synonymous, for both relate to acquired, not innate, knowledge.[27] The demon has learned about Jesus and knows that the divine power flowing from Jesus to Paul can overpower him. He also detects the deception that the Jewish exorcists practice and knows that they are powerless. The question, "Who are you?" reveals the demon's contempt.

The demon then vents his wrath on the seven sons of Sceva. The possessed man, given superhuman strength, jumps on the seven men and subdues and overpowers them. At this point, some translations diverge from each other because of a variant in the Greek text. The better manuscripts have the reading *both*, which appears in one translation as "subdued both of them" (NASB) and in another as "and overpowered first one and then another" (JB). This reading clashes with the number seven (v. 14) if the word *both* is understood to apply to only two persons. But when more than two people are involved, the term can mean "all" (see 23:8), which most versions have.[28]

The demon-possessed man gives the seven exorcists such a beating that they narrowly escape from the house in which they were. Thankful to be alive, they emerge naked and wounded. The Greek indicates that the wounds lasted for a considerable period before they healed. On the one hand, these exorcists learned not to invoke the name of Jesus. On the other, the incident promoted the cause of the gospel.

17. This became known to all the Jews and Greeks living in Ephesus. They were all terrified and they began to hold the name of the Lord Jesus in high honor.

God confirms that he is in control of the situation. He thwarts Satan's strategy of usurping Jesus' power and he causes even the demon to advance God's kingdom in a Gentile world. Notice that Luke mentions first the Jews and then the Greeks living in Ephesus. The Ephesian Jews acknowledged the utter humiliation of their own countrymen. Next, the Greeks heard about the incident. The name of Jesus became the topic of conversation: "Paul used that name, and the demons were expelled; the exorcists used it, and were themselves crushed. What was back of that name?"[29]

---

27. The verbs *ginōskō* (I come to know, understand) and *epistamai* (I understand, know) are identical in meaning. See Günther Harder, *NIDNTT*, vol. 3, p. 122.

28. Bauer, p. 47. Consult Robertson, *Grammar*, p. 745.

29. R. C. H. Lenski, *The Interpretation of the Acts of the Apostles* (Columbus: Wartburg, 1944), p. 796.

Twice in this verse Luke employs the adjective *all:* "all the Jews and Greeks" and "they were all terrified." He stresses the all-encompassing nature of the incident. We see a parallel with the deaths of Ananias and Sapphira. At that time, "great fear came upon the whole church and all who heard these things" (5:11). In Jerusalem, the people were afraid when they saw divine punishment strike within the confines of the church itself (see 5:5). Similarly, in Ephesus both Jews and Greeks were frightened when they heard about the punishment that the seven sons of Sceva received. They had great respect for the name of Jesus, which revealed divine power and authority. Consequently, the local population highly respected the name of the Lord Jesus and many people repented and confessed their sins.

18. Many of those who had believed were coming to confess and report their evil deeds. 19. A number of those who practiced magic brought together their scrolls and burned them publicly. When they calculated their value, it came to fifty thousand drachmas. 20. So the word of the Lord grew in power and might.

a. "Many of those who had believed were coming to confess and report their evil deeds." Luke describes how the power of the gospel arrested the widespread influence of magic in Ephesus.[30] The general practice of magic was so pervasive that even the Christians were not immune. Luke refers to Christians who had come to faith in Christ but who continued to practice the magic arts. Having heard about the incident involving the sons of Sceva, these believers realized that such magic practices were "deviant and inconsistent with the Christian faith."[31]

The Greek text reveals that these Christians were gradually coming forward, probably in the worship services, where they first confessed and then reported that they were practicing magic.[32] Suddenly they realized that their conduct was unbecoming to a Christian lifestyle and that they had to put aside their evil deeds. What were their evil deeds? These people were practicing divination and sorcery, interpreting signs and omens, engaging in black magic, casting charms, or consulting the dead. Now they were told that long ago God had forbidden these detestable practices (Deut. 18:10–14). The Word of God convicted the Ephesian believers of their sin. As a result, they repented and turned from their evil deeds.

b. "A number of those who practiced magic brought together their scrolls and burned them publicly." Many Christians who publicly confessed that

---

30. The city was a center of the magic arts, as archaeological discoveries confirm. Numerous documents contain magical incantations, some of which were known as the Ephesian letters. The latter term relates to the magic charms that were used in the cultic worship of the goddess Artemis. Hans Dieter Betz, ed., *The Greek Magical Papyri in Translation: Including the Demotic Spells* (Chicago and London: University of Chicago Press, 1986), pp. 84, 89, 91.

31. David E. Aune, "Magic," *ISBE,* vol. 3, p. 219.

32. Consult Adolf Deissmann, *Bible Studies* (reprint ed.; Winona Lake, Ind.: Alpha, 1979), p. 323. See also Bauer, p. 646.

they had dabbled in the magic arts added the deed to the word. Resolutely they removed magic scrolls from their homes and brought them to a public place where, day after day, they burned them. The text fails to disclose whether the only people who burned these books were Christians. Possibly a number of Gentiles also added their parchments and scrolls to the fire to rid themselves of the tools of magic.

c. "When they calculated their value, it came to fifty thousand drachmas." The value of these books was substantial, although we are unable to determine the exact amount in today's currency. The Greek text has the words *silver coin,* which I have translated "drachmas." Walter Bauer avers that the worth of a drachma was "normally 18 to 20 cents, eight or nine pence."[33] Nor is it probable that the valuation was exaggerated, for the population of Ephesus in those days was more than two hundred thousand people. The public burning of the books was a clear sign that the people of Ephesus were turning away from magic and were embracing the gospel of Jesus Christ. The local church experienced phenomenal growth in the three-year period during which Paul ministered the Word in Ephesus (20:31). Conclusively, the Christian church advanced victoriously.

d. "So the word of the Lord grew in power and might." Throughout Acts, Luke employs a few summary statements. One of these is Luke's reference to "the word of the Lord" or "the word of God" (compare 6:7; 12:24; 13:49). He describes the growth of the church by pointing to the powerful influence of God's Word in the lives of the people. In this succinct statement, Luke conveys the information that the church increased numerically and that the believers applied the message of the gospel to their daily conduct. They strengthened their faith, showed obedience to God's Word, and lived godly lives.[34] The city of Ephesus experienced a transformation because of the living and powerful Word of God.

The city of Ephesus purged itself of bad literature by burning magic scrolls and became the depository of sacred literature that made up the canon of the New Testament.[35] While Paul resided in Ephesus, he penned his first epistle to the Corinthians. When Paul was under house arrest in Rome, he sent his epistle to the Ephesians. In later years, when Timothy was pastor in Ephesus, Paul dispatched the two epistles that bear Timothy's name. Some decades later, the apostle John composed his Gospel and his three epistles in Ephesus. In a manner of speaking, as the Jews had been entrusted with the Old Testament Scriptures (Rom. 3:2), so the Ephesians became the custodians of the New Testament books.

---

33. Bauer, p. 105.

34. Calvin, *Acts of the Apostles,* vol. 2, p. 159. A. W. Argyle suggests the following translation: "Thus by the might of the Lord the word increased and prevailed." See "Acts xix. 20," *ExpT* 75 (1964): 151. And see Édouard Delebecque, "La mésaventure des fils de Scévas selon ses deux versions (*Actes* 19, 13–20)," *RSPT* 66 (1982): 231.

35. John Albert Bengel, *Gnomon of the New Testament,* ed. Andrew R. Fausset, 5 vols. (Edinburgh: Clark, 1877), vol. 2, p. 680.

Practical Considerations in 19:17–20

When the gospel is proclaimed and people turn in faith to Christ, we wish to see immediate and lasting results. We expect recent converts to live in harmony with the message of the Bible and to abide by its teachings in everything they do and say. We realize that our expectations are high but we are also aware of human weakness and failure. Nevertheless, we continually strive to please our Creator and Redeemer. For that reason, we set priorities and trust that recent converts to the Christian faith and the world around us will benefit from our way of life and follow our example.

We seek to apply the principles of Christian conduct to every area of life. For instance, we expect that honesty and integrity are the guiding principles in business and the workaday world; justice and equity the enduring hallmarks in courts and in the assemblies of our legislatures; faithfulness and truthfulness the innate characteristics of every citizen.

On the other hand, we are fully cognizant of the fact that we live in a sinful, selfish, and corrupt world whose influence and power we must resist from day to day. In this world, the recent convert to the Christian faith faces daily temptations and distractions that try to make him live a dual life: following Christ in the Sunday worship service and following the world the rest of the week.

Yet the preaching of the gospel and the application of its message are powerful and effective weapons in opposing the forces of darkness. Indeed, through the inner working of the Holy Spirit, all obedient Christians gain victories. They see the forces of darkness retreat when the light of God's Word illumines the path of the righteous. Then as Christians with true faith in God we joyfully exclaim: "In your light we see light" (Ps. 36:9).

Greek Words, Phrases, and Constructions in 19:14–20

Verse 14

This is the reading of the Western text, in which the italics indicate additions:

In this connection also [seven] sons of a certain priest named Sceva *wished* to do *the same thing* (*they were accustomed to exorcize such persons*). And *they came in to one who was demon-possessed and began to invoke the Name, saying, "We command you, by Jesus* whom Paul preaches, *to come out.*"[36]

Verse 16

ἀμφοτέρων—"both" or "all." The Majority Text has the reading αὐτῶν (their). τετραυματισμένους—the perfect passive participle of the verb τραυματίζω (I wound) shows lasting effect.

ἐκφυγεῖν—the compound form of this aorist infinitive indicates that the men

---

36. Metzger, *Textual Commentary*, p. 471.

narrowly escaped with their lives. The participle ὥστε (so that) preceding the infinitive shows the result of an action.

Verses 18–20

Notice that all the main verbs in these three verses, except for the two verbs *to calculate* and *to come to* (v. 19), are in the imperfect tense. This tense is descriptive and portrays progression and repetition.

---

4. Paul's Plan
19:21–22

This segment of the chapter is rather brief: only two verses. But in these verses, Luke reveals Paul's intention to travel first in a northerly direction to Macedonia, then to Achaia, and last to Jerusalem. In the next chapter, he relates that Paul indeed went to Macedonia and Achaia (20:1–2). He not only visited Macedonia but also preached the gospel in or as far as Illyricum (modern Yugoslavia: see Rom. 15:19), wrote his letter to the Romans, presumably while he was in Corinth (Rom. 16:22–23), and collected monetary gifts for the saints in Jerusalem (I Cor. 16:1–3). These events probably took place in about two years.

21. After these things happened, Paul decided in the Spirit to go to Jerusalem by way of Macedonia and Achaia. He said, "After I have been there, I must visit Rome, too." 22. He sent two of his assistants, Timothy and Erastus, to Macedonia. Paul himself remained in Asia for a while.

a. "After these things happened." Luke's information on the travel plans of Paul forms a brief interlude between the burning of the books of magic and the riot that was instigated by Demetrius. Luke introduces the present segment with the clause *after these things happened* and obviously refers to the immediately preceding episode. The clause reflects the high point of Paul's work in Ephesus and indicates that the time of his departure is at hand.

During Paul's second missionary journey, the cities of Thessalonica and Corinth became Christian centers. And during his third journey, Ephesus became the focal point of Christianity. On every side of the Aegean Sea (north, east, and west), centers of the Christian faith dominated the scene. From these harbors the gospel spread throughout the Mediterranean basin. Still Paul was not content. His heart's desire was to visit Rome, the capital of the empire.

Throughout his Gospel Luke directs his attention to Jerusalem as the center where Jesus died, arose from the dead, and ascended to heaven. In Acts Luke directs his attention to Rome, from which the message of salvation would extend to the ends of the earth (1:8).

b. "Paul decided in the Spirit." Should the world *spirit* be spelled with or without a capital letter? Does the text speak about the human spirit or the Holy Spirit? If we interpret the expression to refer to the human spirit ("decide in his spirit"), we can compare it with a similar phrase, "decide in his heart,"[37] and take it as an idiom. A number of translators have chosen an equivalent expression: "made plans" or "made up his mind."[38]

Many translations interpret the word as a reference to the Holy Spirit: "Paul resolved in the Spirit."[39] That is, in the broader context, Paul's travel plans are at the direction of the Holy Spirit (20:22). Moreover, in verse 21 Luke uses the word *must* ("I must visit Rome"), which in the New Testament often denotes a divine directive. When the term *spirit* means the human spirit, Luke usually qualifies it with a possessive pronoun (in translation, "my spirit" [Luke 1:47] or "his spirit within him" [he became agitated; Acts 17:16]). But in verse 21, he refrains from delimiting the term. For all these reasons, several scholars have appropriately chosen to be guided by the context and, therefore, spell the word *Spirit* with a capital letter.

c. "To go to Jerusalem by way of Macedonia and Achaia." By either land or sea, the direct route from Ephesus to Jerusalem is east and southeast, not northwest and west. But Paul intended to visit the churches in Macedonia and Achaia, much as he had once again cared for the churches in Asia Minor on his second missionary journey (15:36; 16:1–5). His purpose was to strengthen the believers in the churches he had founded. After spending time with the Christians in Philippi, Thessalonica, Berea, and Corinth, he planned to travel to Jerusalem. His purpose for going to Jerusalem was to attend the Pentecost celebrations (20:16), to deliver financial gifts for the poor (Rom. 15:26–27; I Cor. 16:1–3; II Cor. 8:1–9), and to report to James and the elders (Acts 21:18–19).

d. "I must visit Rome, too." Note the wording of this short statement. First, after visiting Jerusalem, Paul is under divine obligation to visit the imperial city (compare 23:11). Paul is not a tourist but an ambassador of Jesus Christ. Next, the Greek text indicates that he must *see* Rome. Paul knew that the Roman Christians had a flourishing church, so that his purpose for going to Rome was to strengthen the believers in their faith (Rom. 1:11–12). He set his sights still further and planned to go to Spain (Rom. 15:24, 28).

e. "He sent two of his assistants, Timothy and Erastus, to Macedonia." Luke has failed to provide any details concerning the work of Timothy during Paul's stay in Ephesus, although Luke previously mentioned Timothy's name in relation to Corinth (18:5). We infer that Timothy had come to Ephesus to assist Paul. From Paul's epistles we learn that Timothy served as Paul's emissary at Corinth; he then returned to Paul in Ephesus (I Cor. 4:17; 16:10–11). Now Paul sends him and Erastus to Macedonia, presumably to Philippi and Thessalonica.

Apart from this text, the name *Erastus* appears twice in the New Testa-

---

37. Compare the Greek text in Luke 1:66; 21:14; Acts 5:4; II Cor. 9:7.
38. SEB; GNB, JB, NAB, NEB, respectively.
39. RSV, NKJV, MLB, *Moffatt*, with variations.

ment. Paul mentions Erastus in connection with Corinth and describes him as the city treasurer (Rom. 16:23). And in Paul's last epistle he remarks that Erastus stayed in Corinth (II Tim. 4:20). In 1930, archaeologists in Corinth discovered a slab of pavement stone that bears the inscription, "Erastus, commissioner of public works, sustained the cost for this pavement."[40] We do not know whether all these references are to the same person or to more than one man.

f. "Paul himself remained in Asia for a while." The discord in the Corinthian church kept Paul in Ephesus. He had written letters (among them First Corinthians) to the Corinthians and had dispatched Titus to Corinth to reconcile the differences.[41] He was waiting for Titus to bring him encouraging news. (Luke nowhere mentions Titus in Acts, just as he never mentions his own name. Perhaps Luke and Titus were related to each other, and the silence is a form of modesty. We do not know.) While he waited at Ephesus, Paul witnessed the riot instigated by Demetrius.

5. Demetrius's Grievance
19:23–41

The kingdom of God progresses and makes its influence felt in the province of Asia Minor. When God's kingdom advances, Satan must yield, but the prince of darkness does not capitulate without combat. He mobilizes the forces of idol worshipers in Ephesus and incites a riot. Luke includes the account of the riot in Ephesus to illustrate the power of Satan,[42] the progress of the gospel, and the wisdom of the city clerk. In great detail, Luke records an incident that had a profound effect on the development of the church in Ephesus.

a. Grievance
19:23–27

23. At this time, concerning the Way a great disturbance arose. 24. For a silversmith named Demetrius, making silver shrines for Artemis, was bringing no little profit for the artisans.

With the phrase *at this time*, Luke indicates that the incident occurred when Paul was about ready to leave the city (20:1). The key word in verse 23 is "disturbance." Luke qualifies it with one of his characteristic understatements that in a literal translation reads, "not a small one."[43] In this oriental city, the shock waves from the disturbance were of grave concern

---

40. H. J. Cadbury, "Erastus of Corinth," *JBL* 50 (1931): 42–58. See also Colin J. Hemer, *The Book of Acts in the Setting of Hellenistic History*, ed. Conrad H. Gempf (Tübingen: Mohr, 1989), p. 235.

41. II Cor. 2:13; 7:6, 13; 8:6, 16–18, 23; 12:18.

42. Consult Calvin, *Acts of the Apostles*, vol. 2, p. 161.

43. Luke has a penchant for understatements. Examples in the Greek text are 12:18; 14:28; 15:2; 17:4, 12; 19:23–24; 27:20.

to the members of the local church. Reflecting on this disturbance, Paul writes to the Corinthians that he fought wild beasts in Ephesus (I Cor. 15:32; see also II Cor. 1:8–11). If we take Paul's comment figuratively (that is, human beings who fought like wild beasts), then we begin to understand the fierce opposition the Christians had to endure in that city.[44]

Luke uses not the term *church* but the general expression *Way*, because the latter represents the Christian lifestyle (compare 9:2; 18:25, 26; 19:9; 22:4; 24:14, 22). Opposition to the Christian way of life came from the local silversmiths, whose livelihood depended on the worship of the goddess Artemis, known in Latin as Diana (see KJV, NKJV, JB, NEB).[45]

The temple of Artemis attracted worshipers who, before returning to their homes, bought small shrines and images depicting Artemis. These artifacts, used as objects of worship in private homes, were made and sold by the silversmiths in Ephesus. One of those silversmiths was Demetrius. (An inscription that dates from A.D. 57 describes a certain Demetrius as "warden of the temple," but we do not know if the inscription refers to the silversmith Luke mentions. The name *Demetrius* was common [see, e.g., III John 12].) Perhaps Demetrius designed the images and employed craftsmen to make them. In addition, he may have been the spokesman for the silversmiths' guild in Ephesus. We do know that he and other silversmiths had a lucrative enterprise, for Luke, using a characteristic understatement, writes, "Demetrius was bringing no little profit for the artisans." These artisans, incited by Demetrius, opposed anyone and anything that posed a threat to their trade. Under the guise of religion, they defended their source of income.

25. He gathered them together with workmen of similar trades and said: "Men, you know that our prosperity depends on this business. 26. And you see and hear that not only in Ephesus but in nearly the whole province of Asia, this fellow Paul has persuaded and turned away a great number of people. He tells them that gods made with hands are no gods at all."

a. "He gathered them together." Luke makes a distinction between the artisans and the workmen. The artisans are the skilled technicians; the workers represent the spin-off trades and businesses that depend on the manufacture of shrines and images. All these people derived their income from the

---

44. R. E. Osborne interprets the term *wild beasts* to mean the Jews who opposed Paul first in Ephesus and later in Jerusalem ("Paul and the Wild Beasts," *JBL* 85 [1966]: 225–30). Abraham J. Malherbe thinks that Paul refers to heretics ("The Beasts at Ephesus," *JBL* 87 [1968]: 71–80).

45. The worship of Artemis was widespread in Greece, where she was revered as the goddess of animals, nature, and hunting. In Asia Minor she was known as the goddess of fertility and childbirth (see William S. La Sor, "Artemis," *ISBE*, vol. 1, pp. 306–7). In 1956, archaeologists at Ephesus uncovered two statues of Artemis, each with more than twenty breasts (symbols of fecundity). Although the goddess was known as Artemis of the Ephesians (v. 34), the actual object of worship at her temple in Ephesus was a stone, probably a meteorite, that had fallen from the sky (v. 35).

cult of Artemis. Demetrius called them together, perhaps in an enclosed meeting place, and addressed them:

b. "Men, you know that our prosperity depends on this business." The address *men* was customary at the beginning of a speech. The Western text has the reading, "Men, fellow-craftsmen." Because this latter word appears nowhere else in the New Testament, scholars reject the authenticity of the reading. The verb *to know* signifies that Demetrius's listeners are well aware of their source of income. The business of manufacturing and selling images and shrines translates into prosperity for them. According to the Greek, Demetrius indicates that all of them are prospering financially. Thus when Demetrius refers to their earnings, he has their undivided attention.

c. "Not only in Ephesus but in nearly the whole province of Asia." The silversmiths, merchants, and workmen have observed and have heard of the fervor of the Christian faith that has gripped numberless people in Ephesus and western Asia Minor. These people have turned their backs on the worship of Artemis and no longer purchase the objects created and sold by the members of Demetrius's audience. Demetrius testifies to the fact that Paul's ministry in Ephesus and the province of Asia has borne fruit. I see no reason to interpret the words of Demetrius as "the most exaggerated statement possible."[46] The broader context reveals that because of the extraordinary miracles of God and the faithful preaching of the gospel by Paul, "the word of the Lord grew in power and might" (v. 20). Luke provides no report about Paul's work in the regions surrounding Ephesus; hence, we do not know if Paul founded any of the seven churches of Asia (Rev. 1:11) in addition to the church at Ephesus.

d. "This fellow Paul has persuaded and turned away a great number of people." Demetrius and his listeners know that Paul has been instrumental in reaching the people, especially in the city of Ephesus. Demetrius has nothing but contempt for Paul and therefore refers to him as "this fellow" (in the sense of "you know him just as well as I do").[47] He is acquainted with Paul's methodology, because he states that "Paul has persuaded" (see v. 8) the people to turn away from idol worship and serve the living God.

e. "[Paul] tells them that gods made with hands are no gods at all." Here is the crux of Paul's preaching to a Gentile audience. When Paul addressed the Athenian philosophers, he told them that God, who created heaven and earth, does not live in a manmade temple. God is not an image crafted by man from gold, silver, or stone (17:24, 29). In short, Demetrius had paid attention to Paul's message but, because his livelihood depended on idol worship, he rejected it and opposed Paul.

27. "Not only do we run the risk of our trade falling into disrepute, but

---

46. Lake and Cadbury, *Beginnings,* vol. 4, p. 246.
47. Refer to F. W. Grosheide, *De Handelingen der Apostelen,* Kommentaar op het Nieuwe Testament series, 2 vols. (Amsterdam: Van Bottenburg, 1948), vol. 2, p. 215.

the temple of the great goddess Artemis will be regarded as nothing; and all who worship her in Asia and the whole world will suffer the loss of her magnificence."

Demetrius cleverly changes the course of his address. He moves from the topic of material prosperity to that of the worship of Artemis and emphasizes not so much the craftsmen's affluence as interest in Artemis's temple. He points out the connection between their craft and the worship of the goddess and alerts his audience to the danger of Artemis losing her good name. If she is discredited, their source of income will dwindle. He is saying not that they already are seeing a decline in their trade but that the danger is imminent.

"The temple of the great goddess Artemis will be regarded as nothing." Of greater concern than their own future is the disregard people will have for the temple of Artemis. This temple, built of marble, "was of enormous proportions—about four times the size of the Parthenon."[48] It measured 425 feet by 220 feet, was 60 feet in height, and was surrounded by 127 columns. When Paul lived in Ephesus, he observed the temple in all its beauty. [49] After it burned in 356 B.C., it was restored to its full size and even surpassed its previous splendor. Archaeologists have discovered that this temple was located about a mile and half to the northeast of Ephesus.

The temple honored the great goddess Artemis. Not the temple but Artemis is described as great. Demetrius attests to her greatness by saying, "All who worship her in Asia and the whole world will suffer the loss of her magnificence." He accurately states that the worship of Artemis was universal,[50] and his statement constitutes a call to action. He sounds the trumpet, so to speak, and declares strident opposition to the Christian faith.

Practical Considerations in 19:25–27

Christians strive to penetrate all segments of an existing culture with their teaching and principles. In areas where the Christian faith is developing rapidly, its influence begins to change the surrounding culture; for example, literature, painting, and sculpture reflect Christian influence. This influence usually spreads during a number of decades, with the result that a city or even a country may be described as Christian. Believers generally wish to see that their faith influences the culture in which they live.

The forces within an existing culture, however, offer stiff resistance to the growing Christian persuasion. At times, fierce battles are fought for dominance in a

---

48. Lily Ross Taylor, "Artemis of Ephesus," *Beginnings*, vol. 5, p. 252.

49. Alford, *Alford's Greek Testament*, vol. 2, p. 217.

50. Larry J. Kreitzer surmises that commemorative Roman coins, minted at Ephesus, bearing the inscription and emblem of the temple of Diana, and dated at about A.D. 51, may indicate imperial support for the temple worship of Artemis. "A Numismatic Clue to Acts 19.23–41. The Ephesian Cistophori of Claudius and Agrippina," *JSNT* 30 (1987): 59–70.

given society, as history can eloquently testify. And if Christianity begins to wane, a non-Christian or even anti-Christian culture immediately predominates.

Wherever God in his providence has placed his people, there they must be vigilant in the service of the Lord. In the words of Isaac Watts, the Christian asks:

> Are there no foes for me to face?
> Must I not stem the flood?
> Is this vile world a friend to grace,
> To help me on to God?

> Since I must fight if I would reign,
> Increase my courage, Lord;
> I'll bear the toil, endure the pain,
> Supported by Thy Word.

Greek Words, Phrases, and Constructions in 19:24–27

Verse 24

ἀργυροκόπος—from ἄργυρος (silver) and κόπτω (I beat), this noun occurs only here in the New Testament and once in the Septuagint (Jer. 6:29). Together with the craftsmen, Demetrius formed a guild of silversmiths. Archaeologists have not yet found any silver shrines or images of Artemis in Ephesus.

Verse 26

Ἐφέσου . . . πάσης τῆς Ἀσίας —here is an example of the seldom-used genitive of place (see also Luke 5:19; 16:24; 19:4). To link the genitive case to the noun ὄχλον (people) poses a syntactical problem because of the location of this noun in the sentence.[51]

οὗτος—by his use of this demonstrative pronoun, Demetrius expresses contempt. For a similar use of this pronoun, see John 3:26.

Verse 27

εἰς ἀπελεγμὸν ἐλθεῖν—the phrase is idiomatic and means "to fall into disrepute."[52] The noun derives from the verb ἀπελέγχω (I repudiate) and its -μος ending denotes progressive action.

The present infinitive μέλλειν gives the present middle infinitive καθαιρεῖσθαι a future connotation: "the whole world will suffer the loss of her magnificence."

b. Uproar
19:28–31

Demetrius was successful in convincing his audience of the detrimental effect Christianity would have on their income. And he aroused the reli-

---

51. C. F. D. Moule, *An Idiom-Book of New Testament Greek*, 2d ed. (Cambridge: Cambridge University Press, 1960), p. 39.
52. Refer to G. D. Kilpatrick, "Act 19.27 *apelegmon*," *JTS* n.s. 10 (1959): 327.

gious sentiments of his listeners so that they began to proclaim the greatness of Artemis.

**28. When they heard this, the artisans became angry and began to
shout, "Great is Artemis of the Ephesians!"**

The Western text adds an interesting note to this text: "they ran out into
the street." If this reading is authentic, we would visualize Demetrius in a
room skillfully stirring up the crowd. The artisans became irate with the
forces that threatened them and rushed out into the street in search of their
foe.[53] The people milled through the city and kept on shouting, "Great is
Artemis of the Ephesians." The saying itself fits in with similar mottos of
earlier times.[54] It stirred the crowd to a frenzy; as Luke relates, they later
shouted the slogan for two hours (v. 34).

**29. The whole city was filled with confusion. The people rushed to-
gether into the theater after they had seized both Gaius and Aristarchus,
who were Paul's traveling companions from Macedonia.**

The inhabitants of Ephesus heard the recurring shout about the greatness
of Artemis of the Ephesians but did not know exactly why the crowds were
gathering. The uproar must have been extraordinary. Luke uses the word
confusion twice in this account (here and in verse 32: "the assembly was in
confusion. Most people did not even know why they had assembled there.").

The crowd converged on the open-air theater in the center of the city. By
all appearances they were nothing but a mob. We assume that the artisans
had tried to capture Paul, but because they were unable to find him, they
seized two of his traveling companions, Gaius and Aristarchus. The names
of these two men are Roman and Greek, respectively, and Luke discloses
that they hail from Macedonia. He provides no information about when
these two men had accompanied Paul and how long they had been in
Ephesus. We know that Aristarchus, who made his home in Thessalonica,
later accompanied Paul to Troas (20:4) and on his voyage to Rome (27:2).
Paul mentions Aristarchus as a fellow worker (Philem. 24) and prisoner
(Col. 4:10). The name *Gaius* was common, for it appears a number of times
in the New Testament (20:4; Rom. 16:23; I Cor. 1:14; III John 1). Luke
states that this Gaius came from Macedonia, while the Gaius who escorted
Paul to Jerusalem resided in Derbe (20:4). We surmise that both Gaius and
Aristarchus were Gentile Christians. If this is the case, then the crowd
attacked not Jews but fellow Gentiles who were visitors in Ephesus.

The phrase *rushed together* also occurs in the account of Stephen's death
(7:57). We imagine that the intention of the crowd in Ephesus matched that
of the Sanhedrists in Jerusalem. In brief, the lives of Gaius and Aristarchus
in particular and of Christians in general were in jeopardy.

---

53. F. Sokolowski ("A New Testimony on the Cult of Artemis of Ephesus," *HTR* 58 [1965]:
427–31) details an incident in which forty-five persons from Sardis were put to death. The
anger expressed in this incident and by the crowd in Ephesus is similar.

54. Xenophon Ephesius 1.11.15.

30. The disciples did not allow Paul to appear before the crowd, even though he wanted to do so.

The followers of Paul realized the threat to his life. For that reason, they exerted every possible effort to prevent him from appearing before the mob. Nonetheless, Paul wanted to defend the cause of Jesus Christ over against the pagan religion of Artemis. We should not misunderstand Paul's purpose. He considered himself an ambassador for Jesus Christ, thought that Gaius and Aristarchus needed support, and wanted to refute the charges made by Demetrius.

Paul's disciples knew that the artisans had wanted to capture Paul and that the mob would attack him. These disciples knew that Paul had survived a stoning in Lystra and a beating in Philippi, but they used common sense and prevented him from becoming a martyr. Luke uses the term *disciples* in a general sense, so that we do not necessarily have to think in terms of the students at the hall of Tyrannus or of the twelve men who had received John's baptism (vv. 1, 9).

31. Even some of the deputies of the province of Asia who were friendly to Paul sent a message to him urging him not to venture into the theater.

Luke seems to indicate that Paul was not easily dissuaded from going into the theater. He implies that Paul's disciples did not rely only on their powers, physical and mental, to cause Paul to yield to their collective wisdom. They also sought the help of the provincial government officials. Luke relates that some of these high-placed deputies, or Asiarchs, were Paul's friends. These men had civil power to protect Paul and kept on begging him not to go near the theater.

Who were these provincial deputies? The title *Asiarchs* (see NASB, NAB, JB, RSV) means "deputies of the provincial assembly of Asia." Some scholars assert that they were also high priests. But this may not be true of every Asiarch, because the two titles *high priest* and *Asiarch* were "sometimes differentiated."[55] These Asiarchs belonged to the wealthy class of society and were "delegates of individual cities to the provincial council (*Commune Asiae*) which regulated the worship of Rome and of the emperor. They were probably assembled at Ephesus, among other places, to preside over the public games and the religious rites at the festival, in honor of the gods and the emperor."[56] Indeed, we have difficulty explaining how some of these influential people, as rulers in certain civil and religious matters and as representatives of the Roman emperor, could have been friendly to Paul. They perhaps objected to the motives of the artisans who had instigated the riot and had unlawfully called a meeting in the theater (see v. 40). Thus, they favored Paul and begged him not to appear before this mob. Here is

---

55. Bauer, p. 116. A. N. Sherwin-White, *Roman Society and Roman Law in the New Testament* (1963; reprint ed., Grand Rapids: Baker, 1968), p. 90. And see Lily Ross Taylor, "The Asiarchs," *Beginnings*, vol. 5, pp. 256–62.

56. Morris O. Evans, "Asiarch," *ISBE*, vol. 1, p. 329.

another instance in which Roman officials were favorably disposed to the Christian faith.

Greek Words, Phrases, and Constructions in 19:30–31

βουλομένου—the genitive absolute construction features the participle in the present tense to stress continued action. The use of the verb βούλομαι expresses intent and purpose.

The verbs εἴων and παρεκάλουν are in the imperfect tense to show repeated and continued effect.

ὄντες—this present participle from εἰμί may have a causal connotation. Because they were Paul's friends, they begged him not to go to the theater.

δοῦναι ἑαυτόν—the meaning of the verb *to give* in this instance is equivalent to the verb τίθεναι (to place, put). Paul's friends tried to persuade him not to place himself in danger.

---

c. Confusion
19:32–34

32. Then some people were shouting one thing or another, for the assembly was in confusion. Most people did not even know why they had assembled there.

Describing this incident, Luke seems to have difficulty suppressing humor. A mob keeps on shouting one thing after another and chaos characterizes the scene. He relates that people have converged on the theater but no one there seems to know the reason for the assembly. In the Greek, the word *ekklēsia* (assembly) is used for the gathering in the theater. Elsewhere in Scripture, this word means "church" and connotes order and peace (compare I Cor. 14:28, 33 in its context). But here it connotes disorder and confusion.

33. Some of the crowd advised Alexander to speak, for the Jews pushed him forward. Alexander motioned with his hand and desired to make a defense before the assembly. 34. But when they realized that he was a Jew, for about two hours they all shouted with one voice: "Great is Artemis of the Ephesians."

The Greek at the beginning of verse 33 is cryptic, for it means either that some people in the crowd asked Alexander to speak or that they found Alexander in the crowd. In view of the interest the Jews had in this matter, I prefer the first choice and interpret the words *some of the crowd* to include the Jews.

Some Jews in the crowd find Alexander, lead him to the front, and ask him to address the multitude. Apparently this particular person had made a name for himself as an eloquent speaker. From the Jews and presumably from Demetrius and the artisans he receives information about the purpose of the meeting. We guess that the Jews wanted to clear themselves of any charge of opposing the worship of Artemis. At the same time they want to place Paul and his followers in a bad light (compare v. 9). For that reason, Alexander is about to speak on behalf of the Jews. The conclusion is that this man, a Jew, is in league with the artisans.

We are unable to ascertain whether Alexander the metalworker (II Tim. 4:14) was the same person as the orator in Ephesus or the one who, according to Paul, shipwrecked his faith (I Tim. 1:19–20).[57] Because the name *Alexander* was common throughout the ancient world, I judge that these were three different persons.

Alexander motions with his hand to the crowd and thus asks people to be silent so that he can speak (refer to 12:17; 13:16; 21:40). He intends to absolve the Jews of any accusation that they have shown disrespect to Artemis. Alexander no sooner opens his mouth and mentions the word *Jew* than the crowd begins to howl, "Great is Artemis of the Ephesians." The people see no difference between the religion of the Jews in the local synagogue and the Christian faith in the house churches. Both the Jews and the Christians refuse to worship the goddess Artemis and therefore are out of step with the general population of Ephesus and the province of Asia. For two hours, the people give vent to their religious feelings and shout their one-line chorus that proclaims the greatness of Artemis. The mob spirit provides the necessary enthusiasm to chant for that length of time. As Alexander is unable to speak, he wisely blends in with the crowd and disappears. But Gaius and Aristarchus remain captives of Demetrius and his fellow workers (see vv. 37–38).

Greek Words, Phrases, and Constructions in 19:32–34

Verse 32

ἄλλοι . . . ἄλλο—this is a classical idiom that signifies "*one* one thing, [and] *one* another."[58]

οἱ πλείους—the masculine adjective is a contraction of πλειόνες and in this instance means "the majority."

Luke uses two verbs in the pluperfect tense: ᾔδεισαν (from οἶδα, I know) and the compound συνεληλύθεισαν (from συνέρχομαι, I assemble). The pluperfect of οἶδα actually conveys the meaning of the imperfect tense.

Verse 33

ἐκ δὲ τοῦ ὄχλου—"some of the crowd." However, the aorist active participle in the genitive construction προβαλόντων (from προβάλλω, I thrust forward) has a causal meaning: "because they thrust him forward" (compare NASB, GNB, MLB).

---

57. Consult William Hendriksen, *Exposition of the Pastoral Epistles*, New Testament Commentary series (Grand Rapids: Baker, 1957), pp. 86–87, 323–25.

58. Robertson, *Grammar*, p. 747 (italics added).

Therefore, the participle influences the subject of the main verb συνεβίβασαν (they instructed, advised).

Verse 34

ἐπιγνόντες—the nominative aorist participle lacks a main verb in this sentence. In this syntactically difficult sentence, Luke is trying to say: "All the people cried out with one voice." The verb *to cry,* given here as the present participle κραζόντων, serves as the main verb. The genitive case of the participle is controlled by the preposition ἐκ (from).

---

d. Speech
19:35–41

35. The town clerk calmed the crowd and said: "Men of Ephesus, who does not know that the city of the Ephesians is the guardian of the temple of the great Artemis and of the image that fell down from heaven? 36. Therefore, since these things are undeniable, you must be calm and not do anything that is rash."

a. "The town clerk calmed the crowd." Demetrius has lost control of the movement he initiated, Alexander is prevented from speaking, and the crowd keeps on shouting a religious slogan. No one is able to change the situation until eventually the town clerk stands up before the people and addresses them.

The town clerk in Ephesus was an official whose position may be compared with that of the mayor of a modern city.[59] He served as the intermediary between the government of Rome and the city council of Ephesus. This man had authority and the people acknowledged it. When he motioned with his hand, the people became calm and were ready to listen to reason.

b. "Who does not know that the city of the Ephesians is the guardian of the temple of the great Artemis?" The town clerk knows his people and begins by addressing them as "men of Ephesus." Then he continues by stating an obvious truth which he skillfully puts in the form of a rhetorical question. With this question (to which he expects a negative answer) he deftly bypasses the issue raised by Demetrius and his fellow workers. The town clerk queries whether anyone is not acquainted with the fact that Ephesus is the guardian city of the temple of the great goddess Artemis. The answer is no.

The honorific title *guardian of the temple* usually was given to cities that

---

59. In his translation of the New Testament, Martin Luther rendered the Greek term *grammateus* (town clerk) as *Kanzler* (chancellor), which is the equivalent of a secretary or a minister in a government. Consult Theodor Zahn, *Die Apostelgeschichte des Lucas,* Kommentar zum Neuen Testament series, 2 vols. (Leipzig: Deichert, 1921), vol. 2, p. 697 n. 26.

built and maintained temples for the Roman emperor. In the case of Ephesus the honorific related to the goddess Artemis,[60] for the city was the guardian "of the image that fell down from heaven." This image probably was a meteorite that had the appearance of an icon (see n. 45).

c. "Therefore, since these things are undeniable, you must be calm and not do anything that is rash." The town clerk states these facts as incontrovertible evidence and then deftly invites the citizens to display dignity and proper decorum. By starting a riot in Ephesus, the people exhibited conduct that was the "reverse of the standard of a Greek gentleman."[61] With well-chosen words he challenges them to resort to reason and to use common sense.

37. "For you have brought these men here, though they have neither robbed temples nor blasphemed our goddess."

Throughout this entire ordeal, both Gaius and Aristarchus have been captives of the artisans. We surmise that the town clerk was acquainted with these men, knew that no charges had been pressed in the civil courts, and understood that Demetrius had provoked a riot. Accordingly, the town clerk argues for the release of the two captives because of lack of evidence against them. They are neither temple robbers nor blasphemers. As aliens in dispersion, Jews observed this rule: "Let none blaspheme the gods which other cities revere, nor rob foreign temples, nor take treasure that has been dedicated in the name of any god."[62] Even if Gaius and Aristarchus are Gentiles, not Jews, they have not robbed the temple treasury in Ephesus and they have not spoken blasphemous words against Artemis.

The town clerk overlooks the fact that the Jewish and Christian teachings exalt the living God over against lifeless idols. An able statesman, he disregards glaring inconsistencies in the interest of peace and order.[63] However, if Demetrius wishes to question his observation, the clerk has a recommendation for him and his men.

38. "If, then, Demetrius and the artisans with him have a complaint against anyone, the courts are in session and the proconsuls are available. Let them bring charges against each other. 39. But if there is anything further that you want to know, it should be settled in a legal assembly."

In front of all the people, the town clerk tells Demetrius and the artisans how to proceed in case they have a complaint against Gaius and Aristarchus. How humiliating for the members of the craftsmen's guild! Everyone knows that civil suits should be brought before the magistrates when the

---

60. Bauer, p. 537. Sherwin-White notes that the title *neokoros* (temple guardian) "appears on civic coins of Ephesus from the time of Trajan, though a generation later than on provincial coins." *Roman Society and Roman Law*, pp. 88–89.

61. Rackham, *Acts*, p. 369.

62. Josephus *Antiquities* 4.8.10 [207] (LCL); *Against Apion* 2.33 [237].

63. Consult Grosheide, *Handelingen der Apostelen*, vol. 2, p. 222.

courts are in session. Demetrius first loses control of the mob; next, he loses face when he is told to go to the courts and see the proconsuls.[64]

Both the civic and the imperial courts are the places where arguments are settled in the presence of either the city councilmen, magistrates, or proconsuls. In brief, the town clerk gives his audience a general directive: "Let the plaintiffs and the defendants go to our courts, where they can press charges in legal assemblies." The clerk uses technical terms, "bring charges" and "legal assembly." As a man of law and order, he stresses that charges must be pressed before a legally constituted court that convenes at stated times.[65] By implication he avers that the present gathering lacks every appearance of legality.

40. "For indeed, we are running the risk of being accused of rioting concerning today's events. And there is no reason for it, because we will be unable to account for this uproar."

In this last verse, the clerk is explicit when he warns his audience of the danger they are facing. If Roman authorities should investigate the events of the day, they would find that the Ephesians were guilty of rioting. Note the irony of the entire episode. Demetrius tells the members of his guild that they are in danger of seeing their trade decline and therefore he encourages the people to riot; the town clerk tells the Ephesians that they are in danger of being held accountable for having started a riot.

What are the dangers the Ephesians face? The clerk fails to spell them out, but we speculate that they pertain to the loss of privileges the Romans had given the city. For the rioting, the general population of Ephesus, not the Christian church represented by Gaius and Aristarchus, has to take full responsibility and face the consequences. The city clerk points out the predicament in which they find themselves. He says that there is no valid reason for assembling in the theater, and no one will be able to account for this uproar. (The strong term *uproar* in the Greek has the additional meaning of "conspiracy.")

41. Having said this, he dismissed the assembly.

Possibly the absence of an appointed proconsul in Ephesus (see n. 64)

---

64. The term *proconsul* fits the context because a Roman proconsul resided in the capital of the province to which he was assigned. Ephesus, capital of the province Asia, had one proconsul. The use of the plural in this instance perhaps refers to proconsuls as a class.

Another explanation for the use of the plural is that soon after Nero became emperor (October A.D. 54), his mother, Agrippina, plotted the death of Marcus Junius Silanus, the proconsul in Asia. She instructed two Romans, one a knight and the other a freedman, to poison the proconsul. The two officials, who were protected by Agrippina, functioned as comptrollers of the imperial revenues in Asia (Tacitus *Annals* 13.1; Dio Cassius *History* 61.6.4–5). Some scholars surmise that these men temporarily assumed the function of proconsul and thus that Luke's use of the word *proconsuls* is an allusion to these two officials. (Consult E. M. Blaiklock, *Cities of the New Testament* [Westwood, N.J.: Revell, 1965], p. 65; Rackham, *Acts*, p. 369; Hemer, *Book of Acts*, pp. 123, 169. But Bruce calls this suggestion "improbable." (*Book of the Acts*, p. 379.) However, because the information is insufficient, any conclusion on this matter is nothing more than a hypothesis.

65. Consult Lake and Cadbury, *Beginnings*, vol. 4, p. 251.

may explain why the Roman authorities failed to suppress a riot that lasted a few hours. The clerk alerts the people to possible consequences and then speaks the appropriate words for dismissing an audience.

Doctrinal Considerations in 19:35–41

a. Although neither Gaius, Aristarchus, nor Paul played an active role in the riot, the effect on them and on the local church was telling. In his second letter to the church in Corinth, Paul alludes to the hardships he and his companions had to endure in the province of Asia and even speaks of receiving the death sentence (II Cor. 1:8–9). Yet in the darkest hour when an entire city was in an uproar, God ruled in favor of his people through a town clerk. The cause of Christ continued to advance so that the church of Ephesus increased in strength, size, and stature.

b. When Paul left the Ephesian congregation for Macedonia (20:1), godly elders gave leadership and cared for the members as shepherds watch over the welfare of the sheep (20:28). Further, the church demonstrated unity and harmony by breaking down the wall of separation between Jewish and Gentile believers (Eph. 2:14–16).

c. The church of Ephesus became an evangelistic church that at first was consumed by a love for the Lord (Rev. 2:2–3).[66] It spread the gospel throughout the province of Asia and became a leader among the churches in that region. It became the recipient of Paul's circular Epistle to the Ephesians.

Greek Words, Phrases, and Constructions in 19:35–41

Verse 35

νεωκόρον—"temple guardian." The word literally connotes "temple sweeper," for it is a combination of ναός (temple) and κορέω (I sweep). It refers to someone who is in charge.

τοῦ διοπετοῦς—from the verb πίπτω (I fall) and διός (of the gods), this term needs the additional noun ἄγαλμα (image) to make the thought complete.[67]

Verses 36–37

ἀναντιρρήτων—this verbal adjective has a passive connotation, and with the present participle ὄντων forms the genitive absolute construction that expresses cause: "because it cannot be disputed."

βλασφημοῦντας—the present active participle in this setting denotes concession: "even though they do not blaspheme."

Verse 38

εἰ—this particle ("if") with the present indicative signifies a simple fact condition. That is, Demetrius and his men have a grievance.

ἀγοραῖοι—with the supplied noun ἡμέραι (days) or σύνοδοι (assemblies), the expression means "market days" or "assemblies held when there are markets."

---

66. Refer to Everett F. Harrison, *The Apostolic Church* (Grand Rapids: Eerdmans, 1985), p. 215.
67. Friedrich Blass and Albert Debrunner, *A Greek Grammar of the New Testament and Other Early Christian Literature,* trans. and rev. Robert Funk (Chicago: University of Chicago Press, 1961), #241.7; Thayer, p. 152.

Verse 40

Here is a report that is compressed into a single sentence. But this sentence "has become obscure through the attempt to say a great deal in a few words."[68] Because of the density of the sentence structure, the textual problems are substantial.

στάσεως—"uprising." Is the genitive case dependent on the preceding verb *to be accused of* or on the preposition περί (concerning)? If it is taken with the verb, it means "being charged with rioting today" (RSV). But if it is construed with the preposition, it means to be "called into question for today's uproar" (NKJV). Both readings are difficult. Translators generally supply a noun, given here in italics, to complete the prepositional phrase: "concerning this day's *event*."[69]

Summary of Chapter 19

Paul arrives in Ephesus and meets twelve disciples who have been baptized with John's baptism. He tells them to believe in Jesus, baptizes them in the name of Jesus, and places his hands on them. They receive the Holy Spirit, speak in tongues, and prophesy.

For three months Paul teaches in the local synagogue, but when he meets opposition from some Jews, he leaves. For two years he teaches his disciples in the hall of Tyrannus. God performs miracles through Paul. Paul's handkerchiefs and aprons are used to heal the sick.

The sons of Sceva, a Jewish high priest, try to cast out a demon in the name of Jesus. The demon overpowers them and severely beats them, so that they flee naked and bleeding from that house. Many people believe in Jesus, confess their sins, and burn their books on sorcery, which have the value of fifty thousand silver coins.

Paul plans to leave Ephesus, travel through Macedonia and Achaia, and go to Jerusalem. Before Paul leaves Ephesus, the silversmith Demetrius convenes the guild of artisans and other workers who make and sell silver shrines. He appeals to the economic and religious interests of his audience and denounces Paul and the Christians for saying that manmade idols are not gods. An uproar ensues. Gaius and Aristarchus are captured and taken to the theater, but Paul's friends prevent him from going there. Alexander tries to address the multitude, but because he is a Jew he is drowned out by the people shouting, "Great is Artemis of the Ephesians." The town clerk quiets the crowd, admonishes them, and warns them of the consequences that could result from the rioting. He then dismisses the crowd.

---

68. William M. Ramsay, *Pauline and Other Studies in Early Christian History*, Limited Editions Library (1906; reprint ed., Grand Rapids: Baker, 1970), p. 213.

69. Robert Hanna, *A Grammatical Aid to the Greek New Testament* (Grand Rapids: Baker, 1983), p. 230.

20

The Third Missionary Journey, *part 3*

20:1–38

Outline (continued)

20:1–21:16	C.	To Jerusalem
20:1–6		1. Through Macedonia
20:7–12		2. At Troas
20:13–38		3. At Miletus
20:13–16		a. Traveling
20:17–21		b. Declaring
20:22–24		c. Testifying
20:25–31		d. Warning
20:32–35		e. Committing
20:36–38		f. Leaving

20 1 After the turmoil had ended, Paul sent for the disciples and encouraged them. And when he had said good-by, he set out to go to Macedonia. 2 He went through those areas, encouraged the believers with many words, and arrived in Greece, 3 where he stayed three months. When the Jews plotted against him as he was about to sail for Syria, he decided to return by way of Macedonia. 4 He was accompanied by Sopater son of Pyrrhus from Berea, Aristarchus and Secundus from Thessalonica, Gaius from Derbe, and Timothy, Tychicus, and Trophimus from the province of Asia. 5 These men went ahead and waited for us in Troas. 6 But we sailed from Philippi after the Feast of Unleavened Bread, and within five days we came to them at Troas, where we stayed seven days.

C. To Jerusalem
20:1–21:16

1. Through Macedonia
20:1–6

Paul had already decided to leave Ephesus, visit the churches in Macedonia and Achaia, and travel to Jerusalem. By his own account (I Cor. 16:8), he decided to stay in Ephesus until Pentecost, which was probably in May of A.D. 55. Visiting and traveling apparently took considerable time; how long Paul ministered to the believers in the churches of Philippi, Thessalonica, and Berea is not known.

In Macedonia Paul waited for Titus to inform him about the situation in the Corinthian church (II Cor. 2:13; 7:6, 13), once again sent Titus to Corinth (II Cor. 8:6, 16–17), and composed his second epistle to the Corinthians. He then journeyed to Corinth, where he spent three months (20:3), perhaps the winter months (I Cor. 16:6) of A.D. 56–57. At Corinth, he wrote his letter to the Romans, collected monetary gifts for the poverty-stricken saints in Jerusalem (Rom. 15:26; I Cor. 16:2–3; II Cor. 8:2–4), traveled back through Macedonia, and after Passover sailed from Philippi to Troas (20:6). He intended to be in Jerusalem before Pentecost (20:16).

1. After the turmoil had ended, Paul sent for the disciples and encouraged them. And when he had said good-by, he set out to go to Macedonia.

The words of the town clerk in Ephesus brought an end to the noisy gathering in the theater (19:35–41). The people returned to their respective homes and places of work. But Paul realized that his days in Ephesus were numbered, even though he had already decided to leave (19:21). Paul spent

711

time with his disciples, that is, the believers and the students whom he had instructed in the lecture hall of Tyrannus (19:9). He would not see them again for many years. They would have to stand alone in times of persecution and hardship (Rev. 2:3), and they needed Paul's encouragement.

After saying farewell to the believers in Ephesus, Paul traveled to Macedonia. From another source we learn that he went to Troas first (II Cor. 2:12). Earlier he had been in this harbor city, but had not preached the gospel there (16:8). Nonetheless, the Lord had prospered his work of preaching the gospel of Christ, for we learn that there was a church in Troas. Here Paul waited in vain for Titus to come from Corinth with news about the conflicts in that congregation. Eventually he booked passage on a boat that took him to Macedonia. Perhaps Paul suffered either physical ailments or a mental depression (II Cor. 4:7–12).[1] The information on this point is scant; both Luke and Paul in their respective writings fail to enlighten us about Paul's afflictions. Paul relates that when he traveled through Macedonia, his body received no rest (II Cor. 7:5).

2. He went through those areas, encouraged the believers with many words, and arrived in Greece, 3. where he stayed three months. When the Jews plotted against him as he was about to sail for Syria, he decided to return by way of Macedonia.

a. "He went through those areas." In these particular verses Luke presents his shortest account of Paul's travels. We are not told where Paul went in Macedonia and how long he stayed. Some commentators think that Paul traveled to the northeast and preached the gospel in Illyricum, that is, modern Yugoslavia ("So that I have brought to completion the preaching of the gospel of Christ from Jerusalem all the way around to Illyricum" [Rom. 15:19]). Although this interpretation is acceptable, the text can also mean that Paul went as far as the border of Illyricum.[2] In Acts, Luke merely states that Paul "went through those areas." Whether he means that Paul went beyond the borders of the province of Macedonia cannot be determined. In later years, Paul sent Titus to Dalmatia (II Tim. 4:10), which is the southern part of Illyricum.

b. "[He] encouraged the believers with many words." Luke uses the verb *encourage* repeatedly to show that wherever Paul met believers he spoke words of encouragement (14:22; 15:32; 16:40). Paul was the spiritual father of the believers in the Gentile world and he addressed them as his spiritual children (I Cor. 4:14; Gal. 4:19; I Thess. 2:7, 11). Paul's first preaching tour in Macedonia had been relatively brief, but during his second visit he had stayed for a lengthy period.

---

1. Philip Edgcumbe Hughes provides a list of interpretations relating to Paul's physical and mental afflictions. *Paul's Second Epistle to the Corinthians: The English Text with Introduction, Exposition and Notes,* New International Commentary on the New Testament series (Grand Rapids: Eerdmans, 1962), pp. 17–18.

2. E.g., Everett F. Harrison, *Interpreting Acts: The Expanding Church,* 2d ed. (Grand Rapids: Zondervan, Academie Books, 1986), p. 326.

c. "[He] arrived in Greece." To indicate that considerable time had elapsed during Paul's Macedonian journeys, at least two translations add the word *finally* to this clause: "Finally [Paul] arrived in Greece" (NIV, NAB). Paul may have traveled along the west coast of Macedonia and then visited Nicopolis, a harbor in western Greece (Titus 3:12). When he eventually came to Greece, he spent three months in Corinth.

d. "When the Jews plotted against him as he was about to sail for Syria, he decided to return by way of Macedonia." The Jews in Corinth had not forgotten Paul, who had converted two of their synagogue rulers (Crispus and Sosthenes) and had founded a church next to their synagogue (18:7–8, 17; I Cor. 1:1, 14). They still remembered the humiliation of losing a court case when Gallio was proconsul (18:12–17). Hence, they formed a plot to attack Paul.[3] He became aware of their evil intentions, changed his plans to board ship to Syria, and traveled on foot to Macedonia instead.

Paul was not alone in Corinth. He had sent Timothy and Erastus from Ephesus to Achaia (19:22); on his way to Syria some of his followers from Macedonia and Asia Minor, including Luke, were Paul's travel companions.

The Western text adds interesting details, given in italics, to the account of Paul's stay in Corinth and his subsequent journey:

> And when he had spent three months there, *and when a plot was made against him by the Jews, he* wished *to sail for Syria,* but the Spirit told him to return through Macedonia. Therefore when he was about to go out, Sopater of Beroea, the son of Pyrrhus, and of the Thessalonians Aristarchus and Secundus, and Gaius of *Douberios,* and Timothy, went with him *as far as Asia;* but the *Ephesians Eutychus* and Trophimus. . . ."[4]

Paul abandoned his plan to set sail from the Corinthian harbor of Cenchrea. We assume that fellow Jews, who wanted to eliminate Paul, also had booked passage to Jerusalem. They could easily arrange for him to be drowned during the voyage.[5]

4. He was accompanied by Sopater son of Pyrrhus from Berea, Aristarchus and Secundus from Thessalonica, Gaius from Derbe, and Timothy, Tychicus, and Trophimus from the province of Asia.

Paul was no longer able to arrive in Jerusalem before Passover and consequently planned to be there for the Pentecost feast (v. 16). From the Macedonian churches he received monetary gifts for the members of the church in Jerusalem (II Cor. 8:2–3). Furthermore, representatives from some of the churches accompanied Paul. Although Luke mentions no representatives from the Corinthian and Philippian congregations, he himself may

---

3. See 9:23–24; 14:5; 20:19; 23:12, 15, 30; 25:3; II Cor. 11:26 for references to other plots.
4. Bruce M. Metzger, *A Textual Commentary on the Greek New Testament,* 3d corrected ed. (London and New York: United Bible Societies, 1975), p. 474.
5. Consult William M. Ramsay, *St. Paul the Traveller and the Roman Citizen* (1897; reprint ed., Grand Rapids: Baker, 1962), p. 287.

have represented Philippi. (During Paul's second missionary journey, Luke seems to have remained in Philippi.) Or perhaps Luke was in Corinth with Titus (II Cor. 8:18–19). Support for this suggestion can be inferred from Luke's use of pronouns: in verse 4 he does not use "we" and "us," but in verse 5 he does, thus indicating his own participation in the events recorded. (Incidentally, the "we" sections in Acts are 16:10–17; 20:5–15; 21:1–18; 27:1–28:16.) Throughout Acts, Luke nowhere mentions his own name or refers to Titus; again, one can infer that these two men could have been entrusted with carrying the churches' gifts for the Jerusalem saints.

Among the travel companions of Paul was Sopater, who is identified as the son of Pyrrhus and a native of Berea. Elsewhere Paul mentions Sosipater, which apparently is a variant spelling of Sopater (Rom. 16:21).

The two companions Aristarchus and Secundus are from Thessalonica. Luke mentions Aristarchus in two additional places (19:29; 27:2) to indicate the close relationship he had with Paul. Paul's epistles also speak of this closeness (Col. 4:10; Philem. 24). The name *Secundus* occurs only once in the New Testament. It is Latin for "second," as Tertius signifies "third" (Rom. 16:22) and Quartus "fourth" (Rom. 16:23).

Luke next lists Gaius, who comes from Derbe. The Western text gives the residence of Gaius as Douberios, which was a town near Philippi. Albert C. Clark adopts this reading and thus identifies Gaius as a Macedonian.[6] However, the manuscript support for this reading is weak and, furthermore, the logical sequence Luke presents demands the reading *Derbe*. The first travel companion is from Berea, the next two from Thessalonica, the following pair from Derbe and Lystra, and the last two from the province of Asia.[7] Gaius from Derbe is not the same person who was arrested in Ephesus (cf. 19:29). Luke lists only Timothy's name, but we know he was from Lystra (16:1).

Last, Tychicus and Trophimus are from the province of Asia. Both names recur in Paul's epistles and are associated with Ephesus and the surrounding area. We read that Tychicus served Paul as a messenger (courier),[8] and the presence of Trophimus in Jerusalem led to Paul's arrest (21:29). Years later Paul left Trophimus sick at Miletus (II Tim. 4:20).

The seven men, delegates from various churches, accompanied Paul to protect him from physical harm. Their numbers also safeguarded the money they were bringing to the Jerusalem church.

5. These men went ahead and waited for us in Troas.

Luke now reveals that he himself was a travel companion of Paul and

---

6. Albert C. Clark, *The Acts of the Apostles; A Critical Edition with Introduction and Notes on Selected Passages* (1933; Oxford: Clarendon, 1970), pp. xlix–1, 374–75.

7. Refer to Ernst Haenchen, *The Acts of the Apostles: A Commentary*, trans. Bernard Noble and Gerald Shinn (Philadelphia: Westminster, 1971), pp. 52–53; Lake and Cadbury, *Beginnings*, vol. 4, p. 254; Colin J. Hemer, *The Book of Acts in the Setting of Hellenistic History*, ed. Conrad H. Gempf (Tübingen: Mohr, 1989), p. 124.

8. Eph. 6:21–22; Col. 4:7–9; II Tim. 4:12; Titus 3:12.

that they remained in Philippi longer than did the seven other men.[9] Luke does not state the reason for the separation, but we surmise that Paul desired to stay in Philippi for the Passover feast, which may have been observed in a Christian setting as Easter. John Calvin thinks that Paul sought opportunities to teach during Passover because "the Jews were [then] more attentive to learning."[10] But when Paul came to Philippi on his second missionary journey, only women came together at a place of prayer (16:13–15), and we have no indication that Jews had settled there in the intervening years. For lack of evidence we are unable to explain Paul's separation from his travel companions.

6. But we sailed from Philippi after the Feast of Unleavened Bread, and within five days we came to them at Troas, where we stayed seven days.

Paul spent Passover in Philippi and afterward he and Luke sailed from Neapolis (the harbor city of Philippi) to Troas. With a favorable wind, the voyage across the northern tip of the Aegean Sea could be accomplished in two days (16:11). But in adverse conditions, the journey could last for five days and require stops at islands between the two ports.

Paul spent an entire week at Troas. The text does not specify a reason; perhaps, even though his travel companions had preceded Paul, they were unable to locate a ship that would sail from Troas to Syria.

Greek Words, Phrases, and Constructions in 20:2–4

Verses 2–3

τὴν Ἑλλάδα—here is the only New Testament instance of the designation *Greece*. This Roman province was officially known as Achaia, to which both Luke and Paul testify in their respective writings.

ἐπιβουλῆς—derived from the compound ἐπί (against) and βούλομαι (I decide), the word *plot* in the New Testament occurs only with reference to Paul (9:24; 20:3, 19; 23:30). The genitive case is part of the genitive absolute construction.

γνώμης—the verb ἐγένετο (he became) controls the genitive case of the noun *decision*. C. F. D. Moule queries whether the genitive construction is similar to the English "he became possessed of a decision."[11]

Verse 4

ἄχρι τῆς Ἀσίας—"as far as Asia." A few translations have adopted this reading that appears in a number of Greek, Latin, and Syriac manuscripts (see the KJV, NKJV,

---

9. The wording of verse 5 ("[they] waited for us") rules out Timothy as the author of Acts; Timothy and the other companions went to Troas while Luke stayed with Paul. Haenchen opines that only Tychicus and Trophimus went ahead to Troas while the rest stayed with Paul in Philippi. *Acts*, p. 583.

10. John Calvin, *Commentary on the Acts of the Apostles*, ed. David W. Torrance and Thomas F. Torrance, 2 vols. (Grand Rapids: Eerdmans, 1966), vol. 2, p. 168.

11. C. F. D. Moule, *An Idiom-Book of New Testament Greek*, 2d ed. (Cambridge: Cambridge University Press, 1960), p. 38.

RV, ASV). However, other leading manuscripts omit this phrase. Because the addition of the phrase is easier to explain than the deletion, scholars hesitate to accept the addition as original.

The Western text substitutes the word *Eutychus* for the name *Tychicus*. Probably scribes were influenced by verse 9.

---

7 On the first day of the week, we came together to break bread. Paul began to speak to them; because he intended to depart the next day, he continued to deliver his message until midnight. 8 And many lamps were in the upper room where we were meeting. 9 A young man named Eutychus, who was sitting on a windowsill, had sunk into a deep sleep while Paul kept on speaking. Eutychus was overcome by sleep, fell down from the third story, and was picked up dead. 10 Paul went down, threw himself on him, and embraced him. He said, "Don't be disturbed, for he is alive." 11 Then Paul went upstairs again, broke bread, and ate. He spoke with them until daybreak and then departed. 12 The audience took the young man home alive and they were greatly comforted.

---

2. At Troas
20:7–12

Paul had visited Troas on his second missionary journey and there had seen a vision of a Macedonian man who begged him to "come over . . . and help us" (16:9–10). At that time, Paul did not preach the gospel in Troas. But during his third missionary journey, he found a church there (II Cor. 2:12).

7. On the first day of the week, we came together to break bread. Paul began to speak to them; because he intended to depart the next day, he continued to deliver his message until midnight.

Luke, an eyewitness, provides almost a day-by-day chronology of the events that occurred while Paul traveled from Philippi to Jerusalem. In verse 6 he records that the voyage to Troas took five days and that Paul stayed there seven days. In this verse Luke is equally precise. He relates that on the first day of the week Paul attended the local worship service; on the next day he planned to leave Troas.

"On the first day of the week" (i.e., Sunday; this is the first New Testament reference to Sunday worship) the Christians gathered for the celebration of the Lord's Supper, which was followed by the communal meal, the "love feast."[12] In Acts, the expression *to break bread* means to celebrate communion (2:42; and see 2:46). The worship service began with the preaching of the Word, and Luke relates that Paul preached until midnight.

The believers gladly listened to Paul preach for an extended period, even though many of them probably had worked all day (see **Practical Considerations in 20:7–12**). They saw Paul's visit as an extraordinary opportunity to receive instruction from an apostle, and they knew that on the next morning (Monday) Paul and his companions would depart for Syria. Hence, they rejoiced to hear Paul explain the Scriptures.

---

12. Consult J. C. Lambert, "Agape," *ISBE*, vol. 1, p. 66.

8. And many lamps were in the upper room where we were meeting. 9. A young man named Eutychus, who was sitting on a windowsill, had sunk into a deep sleep while Paul kept on speaking. Eutychus was overcome by sleep, fell down from the third story, and was picked up dead.

Here is the account of an eyewitness who accurately describes the scene in a room on the third story. Luke writes that there were many lamps in the room; these lamps provided light for the people in attendance, but also increased the room temperature. We imagine that the meeting hall was full; no wonder that a young man named Eutychus had to find a seat in a window.[13] In those days a window was only a recessed opening in a wall. It was usually draped with a curtain, but when the curtain was removed, someone could take a seat on the windowsill.

Eutychus, whose name means "fortunate," probably had worked throughout the day and was fatigued. When Paul "talked on and on" (NIV), he could not keep awake any longer. Overwhelmed by sleep, Eutychus fell out of the third-floor window to his death. Whether other people fell asleep was insignificant to Luke. He intimates that the death of this young man changed joy and happiness into tragedy and sorrow. The members of the church picked him up dead; Luke, the physician, was able to verify this fact.

10. Paul went down, threw himself on him, and embraced him. He said, "Don't be disturbed, for he is alive." 11. Then Paul went upstairs again, broke bread, and ate. He spoke with them until daybreak and then departed. 12. The audience took the young man home alive and they were greatly comforted.

Note these points:

a. *Resurrection.* The preaching came to an abrupt end. Paul rushed downstairs and threw himself on Eutychus. Embracing him, Paul looked up at the weeping bystanders and said, "Don't be disturbed, for he is alive."

We find a parallel in the lives of two of the prophets, Elijah and Elisha.[14] Each prophet brought back to life an only son, and he did so by stretching himself out on the deceased person's body (I Kings 17:21; II Kings 4:34–35). A New Testament parallel is Peter raising Dorcas from the dead. To preserve propriety, Peter knelt down, prayed, and then told Dorcas to get up (refer to 9:40). Luke plainly records that both apostles raised people from the dead.

Paul brought Eutychus back to life and so told the people: "I know you are distressed, but you need not be because his breath of life is in him." When he raised Eutychus, he did so through the power Jesus gave him. By this miracle Paul demonstrated the reality of Jesus' presence in the midst of God's people.

---

13. Although Bauer (p. 534) states that the word *young man* refers to a person's age from "about the 24th to the 40th year," Eutychus was probably in his late teens. (The Greek word *pais* [see v. 12] can also mean "slave" or "servant.")

14. Lake and Cadbury remark that this parallelism "seems far-fetched" (*Beginnings*, vol. 4, p. 257). Their comment applies to a strict verbal comparison but not to the illustration.

b. *Communion.* In this passage, Luke mentions twice the breaking of bread, but he does not give a lucid presentation of the sequence and the meaning of this act. Often he introduces an incident or action which he explains in the succeeding context; for example, he briefly notes that the Jerusalem believers had all things in common (2:44–45), but in later passages he describes the generosity of Barnabas (4:36–37) and the deception of Ananias and Sapphira (5:1–11). Similarly, Luke's remark that the Christians in Troas came together to break bread (v. 7) probably is introductory. The comment that Paul broke bread and ate refers to the actual celebration of the Lord's Supper and the partaking of the love feast (v. 11). In the Greek text of verse 11, Luke writes the definite article before the word *bread* to demonstrate that this was a special event: Paul broke the bread of Holy Communion. After celebrating the Lord's Supper, Paul partook of the love feast (compare I Cor. 11:20, 33; II Peter 2:13; Jude 12).[15] The rest of the night he spent in conversation with the believers. At daybreak he left and traveled to Assos (v. 13).

c. *Joy.* Luke completes the account by reporting that the people "took the young man home alive and . . . were greatly comforted." This note reveals the effect of Eutychus's resurrection on the congregation. A literal translation of Luke's characteristic understatement describes the joy of the believers: "they were not moderately comforted."

Scripture records few instances of people who were raised from the dead: two in the Old Testament period in the time of Elijah and Elisha; three during the ministry of Jesus (the daughter of Jairus, the young man of Nain, and Lazarus); and two in the apostolic period (Dorcas and Eutychus). When a resurrection occurs, God himself confirms the testimony of his Word. And here that Word is clear: the Christians in Troas took Eutychus home alive, says Luke.

Practical Considerations in 20:7–12

Throughout the world people today observe a seven-day week. But in Paul's day only the Jews, God-fearers, and Christians kept a calendar in which the week had seven days. They did so in harmony with the creation account in the first two chapters of Genesis and the command in the Decalogue to keep the Sabbath after laboring six days (Exod. 20:8–11; Deut. 5:12–15). Moreover, the Greeks and the Romans did not have days of rest. In fact, the Roman author Seneca scoffed at the Jews and derided them for wasting time by resting one day out of every seven. When Paul preached the gospel to exclusively Gentile audiences (for example, in Lystra and in Athens), he began by teaching them the doctrine of creation. He had to teach them that God created heaven and earth in six days and rested on the seventh day.

---

15. F. F. Bruce relates the breaking of the bread to Holy Communion and eating bread to "the fellowship meal." *The Book of Acts,* rev. ed., New International Commentary on the New Testament series (Grand Rapids: Eerdmans, 1988), p. 385 n. 30.

The Jews designated five days of the week by ordinal numbers (the first day, the second, the third, the fourth, the fifth). These were followed by the day of preparation (Friday) and the Sabbath (Saturday). The early Christians adopted this nomenclature. But by the end of the first century, they called the first day of the week the Lord's Day to commemorate that Jesus rose from the grave on that day (Rev. 1:10; the first-century document *Didache* 14.1). Interestingly, the modern Greek calendar lists the days of the week as Lord's Day, second, third, fourth, fifth, day of preparation, and Sabbath. In Portuguese the days are Domingo (Sunday), second day (Monday), third (Tuesday), fourth (Wednesday), fifth (Thursday), sixth (Friday), and Sabado (Saturday).

Greek Words, Phrases, and Constructions in 20:7–12

Verse 7

τῇ μιᾷ τῶν σαββάτων—"the first day after the sabbath." If the plural *sabbaths* means "weeks," then it should be translated "the first day of the week."

ἡμῶν—the genitive absolute construction is completed with the perfect passive participle συνηγμένων (from συνάγω, I gather). The perfect tense denotes duration.

Verse 9

καταφερόμενος—from the verb καταφέρω (I bring down), this present passive participle has an intensive connotation. The present tense shows process.

διαλεγομένου—"discoursing." Note that the present tense of this participle (in a genitive absolute construction) intimates continued action.

κατενεχθείς—this is the aorist passive participle of καταφέρω. The aorist expresses single action, the preposition ἀπό cause or means (because of or by [sleep]), and the compound thoroughness.

Verses 11–12

ἐφ᾽ ἱκανόν—this idiomatic expression signifies "for a long time."

οὕτως—even though the adverb simply means "thus," it is difficult to convey the concept adequately with the verb *to depart*. Some translations delete the adverb; others render it "then."

The Western text changes the plural *they took* into the singular *Paul took:* "While they were saying good-by, Paul took the young man home alive."

---

13 We had gone ahead to the ship and set sail for Assos. There we intended to take Paul aboard, because he had arranged that he would travel that far on foot. 14 When he met us at Assos, we took him aboard and came to Mitylene. 15 And on the next day we sailed from there and arrived opposite Chios. On the following day we approached Samos, and the day after we came to Miletus. 16 For Paul had decided to sail past Ephesus so that he might not spend time in the province of Asia. He was hurrying to be in Jerusalem on the day of Pentecost, if possible.

17 From Miletus Paul sent word to Ephesus to summon the elders of the church. 18 And when they came to him he said: "You know how I was with you the whole time from the first day I set foot in the province of Asia. 19 I served the Lord with all humility, with tears and trials that came to me through the plots of the Jews. 20 I kept back nothing from that which is

good for you as I preached to you and taught you publicly and from house to house. 21 I testified to both Jews and Greeks that they turn in repentance to God and have faith in our Lord Jesus.

22 "And now, I am compelled by the Spirit to go to Jerusalem, though I do not know what will happen to me there, 23 except the Holy Spirit has told me that in every city imprisonments and afflictions await me. 24 However, I do not consider my life worthy of any account; I wish to finish the race and fulfill the ministry which I received from the Lord Jesus, namely, to testify to the gospel of God's grace.

25 "And I know that none of you among whom I went preaching the kingdom will see my face again. 26 Therefore I testify to you today that I am innocent of the blood of all men. 27 I did not hesitate to proclaim to you the whole purpose of God. 28 Keep watch over yourselves and the entire flock over which the Holy Spirit has made you overseers to shepherd God's church which he purchased with his own blood. 29 I know that after my departure, savage wolves will come in among you and will not spare the flock. 30 Even from among your number men will stand up to speak perverse things to draw away disciples after them. 31 So be alert and remember that for three years I did not stop warning each one of you night and day with tears.

32 "And now I commend you to God and to the word of his grace which is able to build you up and give you the inheritance among all those who are sanctified. 33 I have coveted no one's silver, gold, or clothes. 34 You yourselves know that these hands have ministered to my own needs and to those of the men who are with me. 35 In everything I showed you by working hard in this way that we must help the weak and remember the words of the Lord Jesus, who himself said, 'It is more blessed to give than to receive.' "

36 When he had said these things, he knelt down with everyone and prayed. 37 They began to weep aloud and they threw their arms around him and kissed him. 38 They were especially saddened by his statement that they would not see his face again. They accompanied him to the ship.

---

3. At Miletus
20:13–38

Luke gives us a page from his diary, so to speak, for he writes in the style of an eyewitness who records both events and conversations. He provides a day-to-day description of the journey from Troas to Miletus.

a. Traveling
20:13–16

13. We had gone ahead to the ship and set sail for Assos. There we intended to take Paul aboard, because he had arranged that he would travel that far on foot. 14. When he met us at Assos, we took him aboard and came to Mitylene.

For undisclosed reasons, Paul separated from his companions and decided to travel on foot to Assos. Commentators suggest that Paul was a bad sailor, that he was afraid of inimical Jews aboard ship, or that he wanted to be alone with God. We do not know his reason. The text seems to imply that as Paul's companions went ahead to the ship, he himself momentarily stayed behind in Troas. He knew that the ship would dock later that day (Monday) in Assos, which was located on a hill that stood seven hundred feet above sea level.

Luke seems to indicate that Paul boarded ship either before he arrived in

Assos or in Assos itself. That same day, the vessel sailed south along the island of Lesbos to a harbor town called Mitylene, which was located about fifty miles south of Troas. Here they spent the night.

William M. Ramsay provides an interesting observation:

> The ship evidently stopped every evening. The reason lies in the wind, which in the Aegean during the summer generally blows from the north, beginning at a very early hour in the morning; in the late afternoon it dies away; at sunset there is a dead calm, and thereafter a gentle south wind arises and blows during the night. The start would be made before sunrise; and it would be necessary for all passengers to go on board soon after midnight in order to be ready to sail with the first breath from the north.[16]

15. And on the next day we sailed from there and arrived opposite Chios. On the following day we approached Samos, and the day after we came to Miletus. 16. For Paul had decided to sail past Ephesus so that he might not spend time in the province of Asia. He was hurrying to be in Jerusalem on the day of Pentecost, if possible.

a. "And on the next day we sailed from there and arrived opposite Chios." The ship sailed again early in the morning of the next day (Tuesday). A northerly wind moved the vessel south-southwest across open water to the island of Chios. In the strait between the mainland and Chios, the travelers spent the night. On the following day (Wednesday), they sailed toward the southeast and, once more crossing open water, approached the island of Samos, situated to the west-southwest of Ephesus. Opposite the island on the mainland was a town named Trogyllium. According to the Western text and the Majority Text, Paul and his companions "stayed at Trogyllium."[17] This little detail is "natural and probable in a coasting voyage and geographically accurate."[18] The phrase was either deleted from some major Greek manuscripts or added to the Western and Majority texts.

The fourth day (Thursday), the ship sailed along the coast of western Asia Minor and landed at Miletus (compare II Tim. 4:20). This town was located nearly forty miles south of Ephesus in a straight line; but, because in apostolic times a traveler had to go around the Gulf of Priene, the total distance was much further. "Today this gulf is an inland lake, and the island of Lade, which once sheltered the harbor, has become a hill surrounded by a swampy alluvial plain."[19]

b. "For Paul had decided to sail past Ephesus so that he might not spend

---

16. Ramsay, *St. Paul the Traveller*, p. 293.

17. KJV, NKJV, JB, *Moffatt*.

18. William M. Ramsay, *The Church in the Roman Empire Before A.D. 170* (London: Hodder and Stoughton, 1907), p. 155.

19. Gerald L. Borchert, "Miletus," *ISBE*, vol. 3, p. 355.

time in the province of Asia." Notice that Luke portrays Paul as the one who makes decisions:[20]

Paul had arranged to travel on foot to Assos;

Paul decided not to spend time in the province of Asia;

Paul sent a messenger to Ephesus to ask the elders to come to Miletus.

He had opportunity to leave ship at Trogyllium and walk to Ephesus, but he stayed aboard until the vessel docked in the harbor of Miletus. Paul realized that a personal visit to Ephesus would be time-consuming, whereas a meeting with the Ephesian elders in Miletus would prove to be short. Further, having lost the opportunity to be in Jerusalem for the Passover feast, he now longed to be there for the celebration of Pentecost.

Luke reports how Paul filled the seven weeks between Passover and Pentecost: he spent five days traveling between Neapolis and Troas (20:6); he stayed a week in Troas (20:6); he took four days to travel from Troas to Miletus (20:13–16); he spent perhaps most of a week on the voyage from Miletus to Tyre (21:1–3); he remained a week in Tyre (21:4); and with stops in Caesarea, he needed at least a week to travel to Jerusalem (21:7–15). According to the record that Luke provides, Paul had some time to spare before Pentecost.

The captain of the ship presumably had decided to stay in the harbor of Miletus for a few days to load and unload cargo. During those days of waiting, Paul was able to meet with the elders from Ephesus and, perhaps in a worship service, to give his farewell address.

Greek Words, Phrases, and Constructions in 20:13–16

Verses 13–14

προελθόντες—the context supports this reading ("we went ahead") instead of προσελθόντες (we approached). The wording of the Western text ("we went down") appears to be a scribal modification.

διατεταγμένος—the perfect tense in this passive participle from διατάσσω (I order, command) reveals that Paul had not made a decision on the spur of the moment.

συνέβαλλεν—by use of the imperfect tense, Luke makes possible two translations: Paul boarded ship either near Assos or in Assos.

Verse 16

εἰ δυνατὸν εἴη—"if it were possible." Here is one of the few optatives in a conditional sentence. It is a parenthetical phrase resembling "if God wills" (18:21).

---

20. Compare J. Lambrecht, "Paul's Farewell-Address at Miletus (Acts 20, 17–38)," in *Les Actes des Apôtres: Traditions, Rédaction, Théologie*, ed. J. Kremer, Bibliotheca Ephemeridium Theologicarum Lovaniensium 48 (Louvain: Louvain University Press, 1979), pp. 329–30.

εἰς—not "into" but "in." After γενέσθαι (to be), it means "at Jerusalem" (see 21:17; 25:15).[21]

---

b. Declaring
20:17–21

Although Luke had recorded accurately the substance and phrasing of other sermons and speeches by Paul, the farewell address at Miletus is probably the one that Luke himself heard. The farewell address is in one of the "we" sections of Acts;[22] this account then is by an eyewitness, and the text records the words Paul spoke. By comparing the word choices in this address with the phraseology of Paul's epistles, we note striking similarities:

"serv[ing] the Lord with all humility" (v. 19 and Rom. 12:11; Eph. 4:2);

"that I may finish the race" (v. 24 and II Tim. 4:7);

"fulfill the ministry which I received from the Lord" (v. 24 and Col. 4:17);

the "inheritance among all those who are sanctified" (v. 32 and Col. 1:12).[23]

Although the speech can be read as a unit, some editors of the Greek New Testament and some translators use its recurring phrases ("you know" [v. 18], "and now" [vv. 22, 32], "and I know" [v. 25], "I know" [v. 29]) as logical points at which to divide the speech into four or five paragraphs.[24] The repetitive phrases are part of Paul's last will and testimony to the Ephesian elders. He informs them that with the passing of the apostolic era they have become the shepherds of Christ's flock. Paul uses the verb *to know* to stress those matters which they have in common:

"You know how I was with you" (v. 18);

"Though I do not know what will happen to me there" (v. 22);

"I know that none of you . . . will see my face again" (v. 25);

---

21. Friedrich Blass and Albert Debrunner, *A Greek Grammar of the New Testament and Other Early Christian Literature*, trans, and rev. Robert Funk (Chicago: University of Chicago Press, 1961), #205.

22. C. K. Barrett asks why Luke would write fiction and set the story in Miletus instead of "the great city and Pauline centre Ephesus." See "Paul's Address to the Ephesian Elders," in *God's Christ and His People: Studies in Honour of N. A. Dahl*, ed. Jacob Jervell and Wayne A. Meeks (Oslo, Bergen, and Tromsö: Universitetsforlaget, 1977), p. 109.

23. H. J. Cadbury, "The Speeches in Acts," *Beginnings*, vol. 5, p. 413. Recent literature on Paul's address at Miletus is voluminous; see especially Jacques Dupont, *Le Discours de Milet: Testament Pastoral de Saint Paul (Acts 20:18–36)*, Lectio Divina 32 (Paris: Cerf, 1962); Hans-Joachim Michel, *Die Abschiedsrede des Paulus an die Kirche Apg 20, 17–38: Motivgeschichtliche und theologische Bedeutung* (Munich: Kösel, 1973).

24. E.g., see Nes-Al, Merk; MLB, NIV, NEB. C. Exum and C. Talbert analyze the speech as a chiasm in which v. 25 serves as the center, vv. 22–24 balance vv. 26–30, and vv. 18–21 convey the same message as vv. 31–35. "The Structure of Paul's Speech to the Ephesian Elders (Acts 20,18–35)," *CBQ* 29 (1967): 233–36.

"I know that . . . savage wolves will come" (v. 29);

"You yourselves know that these hands have ministered to my own needs" (v. 34).[25]

The repeated use of this verb emphasized the bond between Paul and the elders and conveyed to them that Paul was leaving them in charge of the church. The elders of Ephesus received the legacy of being overseers and shepherds of the flock of Jesus Christ.

17. From Miletus Paul sent word to Ephesus to summon the elders of the church.

A messenger could cover the distance between Miletus and Ephesus in two days, and the elders needed an equal number of days to travel to Miletus. Perhaps Trophimus, who was a native of Ephesus (21:29), served as messenger and accompanied the elders when they came to Paul. We presume that Paul spent a day exhorting and instructing the elders. In later years, he wrote to Timothy and Titus the qualifications for elders, that is, overseers (I Tim. 3:1–7; 5:17; Titus 1:6–9).

Wherever Paul founded churches, he appointed elders to give leadership (compare 14:23; and see Titus 1:5). Luke calls these men "elders" in this verse, yet in his speech Paul describes them as "overseers" (v. 28). The word *elder* refers to office; the word *overseer* describes the task the person performed.

18. And when they came to him he said: "You know how I was with you the whole time from the first day I set foot in the province of Asia."

We trust that the elders came to Miletus without delay. They presumed that Paul's message would differ from the words of encouragement he spoke to the disciples when he left for Macedonia (v. 1). They came as governing and teaching elders to whom Paul would entrust a spiritual inheritance.

Paul recalls, in this first part of his speech, how he first came from Corinth (18:19), taught in the local synagogue, went to Jerusalem, and returned to Ephesus. When he came back to Ephesus, he taught for nearly three years. In no other place had he preached the gospel for as long a period. The elders knew that Paul had faithfully taught the word of the Lord to Jews and Gentiles in the province of Asia (19:10). They could testify that he had been in their midst as a true messenger of the gospel of Christ. Convinced of Paul's mission, they were witnesses of the veracity of the message he proclaimed. They had observed that Paul was completely devoted to serving his Lord.

19. "I served the Lord with all humility, with tears and trials that came to me through the plots of the Jews."

Note these points:

First, by saying "I served the Lord," Paul indicates in the Greek that he

---

25. Consult Jacques Dupont, *Nouvelles Études sur les Actes des Apôtres,* Lectio Divina 118 (Paris: Cerf, 1984), p. 439.

was a servant of Christ (compare Rom. 1:1; 12:11; Gal. 1:10; Phil. 1:1). He literally calls himself a slave. As a slave he looked up to his Lord, for he would consider it a sin to do less. Accordingly, Paul confesses that he served Jesus "with all humility."[26] He had learned to live in all humility as a servant of the Lord (see Phil. 4:12), and he exhorted the people not to look merely to their own advantage but also to promote that of others (Phil. 2:4; and see Eph. 4:2). Augustine captured the importance of humility by saying:

> For those who would learn God's ways,
> humility is the first thing,
> humility is the second,
> humility is the third.

Next, Paul served the Lord with tears. Twice in this address Paul confesses that he shed tears: when he was persecuted by his enemies (v. 19) and when he agonized over converts (v. 31). During his ministry, Paul gave himself completely to serve the Lord and the church. He wept not for the wounds and bruises he received as a servant of Christ. He cared for the members of the church when he wrote to the Corinthians to reveal his deep love for them (a letter not extant; see II Cor. 2:4). And he told the Philippians of his tears when he revealed that many people lived as enemies of the cross of Christ (Phil. 3:18). These tears testify to Paul's greatness.

Last, trials were formidable impediments in Paul's apostolic life. Paul relates that these trials were the plots of the Jews. Since his conversion near Damascus, Jewish plots against his life seemed to occur with amazing frequency, either in Damascus, Asia Minor, Macedonia, Greece, or Jerusalem.[27] His life always seemed to be in danger from bandits, Jews, or Gentiles (II Cor. 11:26), but the Lord protected him.

20. "I kept back nothing from that which is good for you as I preached to you and taught you publicly and from house to house. 21. I testified to both Jews and Greeks that they turn in repentance to God and have faith in our Lord Jesus."

a. "I kept back nothing." Even though he faced dangers everywhere, Paul fearlessly gave the believers everything they needed for their spiritual development. Actually he said, "I did not keep silent in fear of hiding something from you that might be beneficial" (compare v. 27). What then was advantageous to them? Their spiritual welfare. With unflagging devotion, Paul conveyed to the Ephesians the riches of salvation by preaching the Word of God.

b. "I preached to you and taught you." Paul proclaimed the gospel in the worship services, but he also taught daily in the lecture hall of Tyrannus (19:9). Moreover, his preaching was never done in secret. He publicly preached the Word in the city of Ephesus so that everyone had an opportu-

---

26. Refer to Hans-Helmut Esser, *NIDNTT*, vol. 2, p. 263; Walter Grundmann, *TDNT*, vol. 8, pp. 21–23.

27. See, e.g., 9:23–24, 29; 14:5; 20:3; 23:12; 25:3; II Cor. 11:26.

nity to listen to the message of salvation. His teaching was not limited to the daily lectures to his disciples; he also went from house to house to instruct the people in the riches of the Word. The word *house* undoubtedly refers to the numerous house churches that were formed (see Rom. 16:5; Col. 4:15; Philem. 2). In his work, Paul demonstrated that he was always and everywhere a minister of that Word.

c. "I testified to both Jews and Greeks." Paul was all things to all men so that he might win them for Christ. He was a Jew in the company of Jews and a Gentile with the Gentiles. He did everything possible to further the cause of the gospel (I Cor. 9:19–23). As it were, he lived in two different worlds, each with its own culture and customs. He never tried to use his calling of apostle to the Gentiles as an excuse not to preach to the Jews. Paul testified faithfully to both groups of people. The verb *to testify* occurs frequently in Acts and describes the preaching of the apostles Peter, John, and Paul.[28]

Luke indicates in the Greek text that Paul continually testified. What was the content of his testimony? Simply put, it is the summary of Christian doctrine: repentance and faith. In his speech, Paul says that he proclaimed to both Jews and Greeks

repentance	faith
to God	in our Lord Jesus

The nouns *repentance* and *faith* are the two sides of the same coin. Because Paul gives two aspects of one concept, we ought not to link repentance to the Gentile and faith to the Jew. Both Jews and Gentiles had to repent of their sins and both had to express their faith in Jesus. Further, repentance that lacks faith as its counterpart is useless, and faith without the prerequisite of repentance is futile. Indeed, "repentance and faith are tied together in an unbreakable connexion."[29]

Practical Considerations in 20:17–21

Numerous Sunday worshipers prefer to hear a sermon about heaven rather than a reference to hell. They want to hear pleasing words on the love of God, but refuse to accept the justice of God. They welcome a word of commendation but reject even an allusion to condemnation. From the doctrines of the Christian faith, they pick and choose those that are agreeable and gratifying. Consequently, they decline to listen to expositions on sin and repentance, unbelief and disobedience, hell and reprobation.

---

28. In Greek, it occurs nine times in Acts (2:40; 8:25; 10:42; 18:5; 20:21, 23, 24; 23:11; 28:23). It appears once in Luke's Gospel (16:28), four times in Paul's epistles (I Thess. 4:6; I Tim. 5:21; II Tim. 2:14; 4:1), and once in Hebrews (2:6).
29. Calvin, *Acts of the Apostles*, vol. 2, p. 176. For a suggestion of a chiasm, see Lake and Cadbury, *Beginnings*, vol. 4, p. 260; and John Albert Bengel, *Gnomon of the New Testament*, ed. Andrew R. Fausset, 5 vols. (Edinburgh: Clark, 1877), vol. 2, p. 687.

What is the task of the pastor who ministers the Word to people who have itching ears (II Tim. 4:3)? He must remember that he is a minister of God's Word, not a minister of the people. He ministers the Word to the people, but he is first a minister of that Word. To put it in the language of Scripture, God has given him the duty to blow the trumpet to prepare his people for the war on sin (I Cor. 14:8). But if the trumpet fails to produce a clear sound, no one will prepare for battle, and as a result everyone will become captive to sin.

Failure to preach the full message of salvation is cruel, for the results are destruction and death. The pastor who faithfully preaches the gospel never fails to include a call to repentance. He sounds a warning of impending doom if this call is ignored. He points out the narrow path that leads to life and warns his audience not to walk the wide road of sin that leads to eternal doom. A true preacher calls the sinner to repentance and faith. Said the noted evangelist D. L. Moody, "Repentance is the tear in the eye of faith."

Greek Words, Phrases, and Constructions in 20:18 and 20

Verse 18

ἀπὸ πρώτης ἡμέρας ἀφ' ἧς—the relative clause stands in sharp relief to the antecedent noun because the preposition is repeated.[30] Paul is emphatic in his speech and points to the first day he set foot in Ephesus.

τὸν πάντα χρόνον—"the whole time." The noun refers to calendar time and not an opportune time or moment.

Verse 20

ὑπεστειλάμην this verb from ὑποστέλλω (I withdraw) always shows that fear is the motivating force. It occurs twice in Acts (20:20, 27), once in Galatians (2:12), and once in Hebrews (10:38).

---

c. Testifying
20:22–24

22. "And now, I am compelled by the Spirit to go to Jerusalem, though I do not know what will happen to me there, 23. except the Holy Spirit has told me that in every city imprisonments and afflictions await me."

After reminding his audience of the work he had performed among them in earlier days, Paul in the second part of his speech tells them why he is on his way to Jerusalem.

a. "And now, I am compelled by the Spirit to go to Jerusalem." The Ephesian elders knew of Paul's desire to travel to Jerusalem, for while he was still teaching in the lecture hall of Tyrannus he had expressed a desire to proceed to that city (19:21). Probably they were amazed that instead of

---

30. A. T. Robertson, *A Grammar of the Greek New Testament in the Light of Historical Research* (Nashville: Broadman, 1934), p. 721.

going south and east toward Palestine, Paul instead went north and west to Macedonia and Greece (20:1).

The reason for sailing to Jerusalem, according to the nuances of the Greek text, was that for some time already Paul was bound, that is, under obligation to make the trip. Was it a desire within Paul's human spirit or was Paul prompted by the Holy Spirit?[31]

We try to answer this question by looking at the broader context. In Acts, Luke shows that the Holy Spirit worked in many people. Thus, the Spirit induced

Philip to approach the Ethiopian official (8:29),

Peter to accompany the men sent by Cornelius (10:20; 11:12),

the church in Antioch to commission Barnabas and Paul (13:2), and

Paul to bypass the regions of Asia and Mysia (16:6–7).

At times, Luke uses the word *spirit* when he refers to the human spirit (see 18:25). Often he shows precision when in Greek he delimits this word with a possessive adjective (e.g., *my* or *his* spirit; see Luke 1:47; Acts 17:16). In verse 22, Luke appears to indicate that he is alluding to the Spirit, especially when in the following verse (v. 23) he explictly writes, "the Holy Spirit." Conclusively, Paul is driven by the Holy Spirit to go to Jerusalem.[32]

b. "Though I do not know what will happen to me there." The Holy Spirit compels Paul to journey to Jerusalem, but Paul has not been told what awaits him there. Paul himself has no innate knowledge of future events. But he experiences that the Spirit is revealing details to him as he continues his travel. During the course of his voyage (to be precise, in both Tyre and Caesarea), Paul receives additional information. In Tyre, the Christians warn him not to continue to Jerusalem (21:4). And in Caesarea, the prophet Agabus reveals to Paul that in Jerusalem he will be bound and delivered to the Gentiles (21:10–11).

Three days after Paul's conversion, Jesus said to Ananias in Damascus that Jesus would show Paul how much he would have to suffer for the sake of Christ's revelation (9:16). Even though Paul had endured much suffering (see Paul's itemized list in II Cor. 11:23–29), he knows that he will be imprisoned and will suffer adversities in Jerusalem and elsewhere. As Paul himself says, "the Holy Spirit has told me that in every city imprisonments and afflictions await me." The closer he comes to Jerusalem, the more clearly the Spirit speaks to him about his impending sufferings.

---

31. Some translations print the word *spirit* in lower case to indicate that it was Paul's spirit and not the Holy Spirit (KJV, NKJV, NASB, JB). Others print the word with the capital *Spirit* (MLB, NAB, NEB, NIV, RSV). Still others add the word *Holy* to the text and have the reading *Holy Spirit* (GNB, SEB).

32. Compare F. F. Bruce, "The Holy Spirit in the Acts of the Apostles," *Interp* 27 (1973): 182. See also my commentary on 19:21.

The text gives no evidence that Paul delayed his journey to postpone or avoid the afflictions that await him. He does not resist the Spirit but obediently listens and permits him to govern his life. Hence, Paul explicitly states:

24. "However, I do not consider my life worthy of any account; I wish to finish the race and fulfill the ministry which I received from the Lord Jesus, namely, to testify to the gospel of God's grace."

Observe the following points:

a. *Variations.* If we consult a few translations, we notice variations in the first line of this verse:

"But none of these things move me; nor do I count my life dear to myself" (NKJV; see also KJV, MLB).

"But life to me is not a thing to waste words on" (JB).

"But I do not consider my life of any account as dear to myself" (NASB).

The reason for the differences lies, first, in Greek manuscript evidence and, second, in the use of idiomatic expressions. The Western and Majority texts have the expanded version that is reflected in the longer translations.[33] Further, the verse contains both a combination and a contraction of two expressions: "I have regard for nothing" and "I do not consider my life precious."[34] A more or less literal translation of the first part of verse 24 is, "But I make of no account my life, (as though) precious to myself."[35]

b. *Explanation.* Both in the presence of the believers in Caesarea and in his writings, Paul declares that he is ready to yield everything, including his life, to Jesus Christ (21:13; II Cor. 12:10; Phil. 1:20–21; 2:17; 3:8). Paul states that he is running a race to fulfill his ministry, a metaphor he repeats in his last epistle, which he wrote before his death: "I have finished the race" (II Tim. 4:7). Paul's conversion experience was the beginning of that race, which he now expects to end. He knows that the purpose of this race is to complete the work Jesus has given him to do, namely, the task of testifying to the good news of God's grace (compare II Cor. 5:18).

c. *Intention.* Paul's words should not necessarily be understood to mean that he expected his life's task to come to a speedy end in Jerusalem. Earlier he expressed his desire to travel to Rome (19:21), and in his epistle to the church in the imperial city he writes that he wishes to go to Spain (Rom. 15:24, 28). He saw his task expanding in widening circles from Jerusalem to the ends of the earth (1:8).

---

33. Consult Metzger, *Textual Commentary*, p. 479.

34. See Hans Conzelmann, *Acts of the Apostles*, trans. James Limburg, A. Thomas Kraabel, and Donald H. Juel (1963; Philadelphia: Fortress, 1987), p. 174.

35. Compare James Hardy Ropes, "The Text of Acts," *Beginnings*, vol. 3, p. 196; F. F. Bruce, *The Acts of the Apostles: The Greek Text with Introduction and Commentary*, 3d (rev. and enl.) ed. (Grand Rapids: Eerdmans, 1990), p. 570.

The gospel itself discloses God's grace to his people. In his farewell address, Paul uses this concept once again when he commends the elders to God and to the word of his grace (v. 32). Correspondingly, at the Jerusalem Council Peter said that the Gentiles are saved through the grace of Jesus (15:11). Salvation is God's gift of grace, which the sinner appropriates in faith.[36]

Greek Words, Phrases, and Constructions in 20:22–24

Verses 22–23

πορεύομαι—the present tense of this verb "describes an action that was already in progress, 'I am going to Jerusalem.' "[37]

δεσμά—this plural noun *chains* (i.e., imprisonment) appears three times in the New Testament, all in Luke's writings (Luke 8:29; Acts 16:26; 20:23). As a synonym of δεσμός (fetter), it vividly describes Paul's eventual imprisonment.

Verse 24

The first clause in this verse is awkward Greek because two idiomatic expressions are telescoped. The Western text has separated the expressions by expanding the text: οὐδενὸς λόγον ἔχω μοι (I have no reckoning [thought] of anything for myself) and οὐδὲ ποιοῦμαι τὴν ψυχήν μου τιμίαν ἐμαυτοῦ (I do not make my life precious to me). With modifications, the Textus Receptus and Majority Text have adopted this expanded reading.

τῆς χάριτος τοῦ θεοῦ—"the grace of God." With the noun *gospel*, this phrase is a subjective genitive, not the objective genitive. The gospel is a gift from God.

---

d. Warning
20:25–31

25. "And I know that none of you among whom I went preaching the kingdom will see my face again."

In the third part of Paul's farewell address to the Ephesian elders he predicts that they will never meet again. How should we interpret this verse, in view of the fact that Paul later returned to Ephesus (I Tim. 1:3; 3:14)? Various answers can be given:

1. When Luke composed Acts, he was not aware of Paul's intended visit to Ephesus. This is possible if we hold that Luke wrote Acts soon after Paul's release from house arrest in Rome.
2. Paul set his sights on visiting Rome and other lands; he had no inten-

---

36. The concepts *grace* and *faith* are closely linked. Consult Donald Guthrie, *New Testament Theology* (Downers Grove: Inter-Varsity, 1981), p. 617.
37. Robert Hanna, *A Grammatical Aid to the Greek New Testament* (Grand Rapids: Baker, 1983), p. 232.

tion of returning to Ephesus. This is a credible explanation if we assume that he visited Spain.[38]

3. Paul expected to travel to Rome, where he would die.[39] But Luke ends the Book of Acts on an optimistic note that describes Paul preaching the gospel without hindrance (28:31).

4. Paul was of the opinion that he would be put to death in Jerusalem. Only if we interpret this verse (v. 25) from a strictly human point of view can we say that Paul feared such a possibility.

5. When Paul eventually returned to his former parishioners in Ephesus, "almost *all* these persons [had] died or removed elsewhere."[40] But this is a mere guess.

The first two interpretations are the most plausible. Granted that Paul realized the significance of the Spirit's promptings, he nevertheless had a desire to preach the gospel elsewhere. Accordingly, he told the Ephesian elders who had heard the message of the kingdom (that is, the gospel [see 19:8]) that they would see his face no more. Paul would not return to Ephesus as their minister; he now commissioned the elders to take care of the local church (v. 28).

26. "Therefore I testify to you today that I am innocent of the blood of all men. 27. I did not hesitate to proclaim to you the whole purpose of God."

Paul concludes from the preceding statement that his task in Ephesus has ended. By using the verb *testify* (v. 21) once again, he attests to his faithfulness in preaching the gospel: "I am innocent of the blood of all men." Paul alludes to a prophecy in Ezekiel in which the watchman on the city wall blows the trumpet to warn the people of approaching danger. But if the inhabitants of the city ignore the warning, the watchman will not be held accountable if their blood is shed in the ensuing siege (Ezek. 33:4; and see 3:17–19). Paul referred to the same Old Testament passage when he departed from the Jewish leaders of the synagogue in Corinth (18:6).

Once more Paul repeats what he has stated earlier (v. 20): "I did not hesitate to proclaim to you the whole purpose of God." He did not hold back any truths of the gospel but proclaimed the full gospel to both Jew and Gentile. In addressing his audiences, Paul used tact and discretion but never compromised the message of salvation. The phrase *the whole purpose of God* refers to the complete revelation God has given in his Son Jesus Christ, through whom the believer appropriates salvation (compare 2:23; 4:28). Note that in his epistle to the Ephesians, Paul delineates how God realizes and fulfills his plan of salvation through Christ, "in whom we also

---

38. Clement of Rome says, "[Paul] reached the limits of the West." I Clem. 5.7 (LCL); see the Muratorian Canon, lines 34–39. Hemer supports the idea that Paul visited Spain but refrains from speculation. *Book of Acts,* p. 400.

39. Conzelmann sees one imprisonment in Rome, during which Paul died (*Acts,* p. 174). Tradition, however, holds that Paul was imprisoned twice and traveled widely in the interim.

40. Bengel, *Gnomon of the New Testament,* vol. 2, p. 688.

have been made heirs, having been predestined according to the purpose of him who works out all things after the counsel of his will" (1:11).

28. "Keep watch over yourselves and the entire flock over which the Holy Spirit has made you overseers to shepherd God's church which he purchased with his own blood."

a. "Keep watch over yourselves and the entire flock." Paul gives a charge to the Ephesian elders, who must assume pastoral responsibilities in the local church. He begins by telling them to keep watch over themselves; that is, they have to be spiritual examples for the members of the church. He exhorts them to put their minds to work in watching themselves (compare I Tim. 4:16).

In addition, the elders have the task of caring for the spiritual needs of "the entire flock." Paul uses imagery borrowed from the agricultural society of his day.[41] This is rather unusual for Paul, whose educational training kept him from any intimate knowledge of sheepherding. Yet he knew that Jesus had frequently alluded to the shepherd and the sheep.[42] And when Peter wrote his epistle, he called Jesus the Chief Shepherd under whom elders serve as overseers and shepherds of God's flock (I Peter 5:1–4).

b. "Over which the Holy Spirit has made you overseers." This clause introduces two significant points. First, Paul states that the Holy Spirit has appointed the elders as overseers. Perhaps Paul is referring to a specific ceremony that marked their appointment (compare 14:23). Next, he uses the term *overseers* as a synonym for "elders" (see v. 17). The task of the overseer is to be a shepherd (compare Num. 27:16–17) like Jesus Christ:

> Oversight means loving care and concern, a responsibility willingly shouldered; it must never be used for personal aggrandisement. Its meaning is to be seen in Christ's selfless service which was moved by concern for the salvation of men.[43]

Both Paul and Peter describe the responsibilities of an overseer in their respective epistles. Paul lists a number of qualifications for anyone who aspires to the office of elder/overseer (I Tim. 3:1–7; Titus 1:6–9), and Peter similarly specifies the duties of an elder (I Peter 5:1–4). Both apostles use the terms *elder* and *overseer* interchangeably.

c. "To shepherd God's church which he purchased with his own blood." This clause presents difficulties, for the expression *God's church* can be translated "church of God/Christ" or "church of the Lord." The first expression is common in the New Testament; it occurs twelve times apart from

---

41. In his epistles, Paul only once refers to a flock (I Cor. 9:7), and similarly to shepherds (pastors) once (Eph. 4:11).

42. E.g., Matt. 7:15; 10:6; 18:12; 25:32; 26:31; John 10:1–4, 11, 14, 16; 21:16–17.

43. Lothar Coenen, *NIDNTT*, vol. 1, p. 191. And see Hermann Wolfgang Beyer, *TDNT*, vol. 2, pp. 615–17.

Acts 20:28.[44] Conversely, although the reading *the Lord's church* does appear in a number of excellent Greek manuscripts, that reading occurs nowhere else in the New Testament and only seven times in the Septuagint. On the basis of the scriptural evidence, I am inclined to adopt the reading *the church of God.*

Another difficulty, however, remains. What is the meaning of the literal translation *with the blood of his own?* If we translate the phrase "with his own blood," which most translations have adopted, we confuse the meaning of the sentence. The context mentions the Holy Spirit and God, to whom the word *blood* fails to apply. Perhaps the suggestion to say that "his own" is a variant of "his beloved" or "his one and only [Son]" is a step toward solving the matter.[45]

d. "God's church which he purchased." God bought his universal church with the blood of his Son. He paid an incalculable price to save a people for himself through Christ's death on the cross. Writes Donald Guthrie, "The idea of the death of Christ being a purchase price is a distinctive emphasis in Paul's epistles."[46] Indeed, Paul tells the Corinthians, "You were bought at a price" (I Cor. 6:20; 7:23; and see Ps. 74:2; Rev. 5:9).

29. "I know that after my departure, savage wolves will come in among you and will not spare the flock. 30. Even from among your number men will stand up to speak perverse things to draw away disciples after them."

a. "I know." Again Paul employs the verb *to know.* He is fully cognizant of the perilous condition in which the believers will find themselves after he has left them. He speaks from innate knowledge: "Savage wolves will come in among you." Wolves are predators that attack the flock and slaughter many of the sheep (compare Matt. 7:15; 10:16; John 10:12).

b. "After my departure." Paul introduces the concept *departure* in general terms. After the departure of the apostles, many of the seven churches in the province of Asia showed spiritual lethargy (Rev. 2:1–3:22). Paul himself continued to warn the church of Ephesus through his pastoral epistles to Timothy (e.g., I Tim. 4:1; II Tim. 3:1–9).

c. "Savage wolves." The metaphor of wolves attacking the flock is a portrayal of false teachers who enter the church to deceive the members and lead them away from the faith. Both Peter and Jude oppose false teachers and scoffers who have furtively slipped into the church and led the people astray. For instance, these teachers deny the return of Christ, despise au-

---

44. The expression *church of Christ* occurs only in Rom. 16:16; other texts have *church of God* (I Cor. 1:2; 10:32; 11:16, 22; 15:9; II Cor. 1:1; Gal. 1:13; I Thess. 2:14; II Thess. 1:4; I Tim. 3:5, 15).

45. Lake and Cadbury, *Beginnings*, vol. 4, p. 262; Metzger, *Textual Commentary*, pp. 480–81. The versions (NEB, RSV, SEB) that accept the reading *the Lord's church* eliminate the difficulty with the translation *his own blood.*

46. Guthrie, *New Testament Theology*, p. 462; and see p. 481.

thority, reject Jesus Christ, repudiate Christian conduct, and live in immorality (see, e.g., II Peter 2; Jude 4–19).[47]

d. "Even from among your number." Not only do false teachers slip in
among the members of the church (compare Jude 4), but even within the
church the danger of heresy is real (see I John 2:18–19). Some people in
the church become false prophets, who at times disguise themselves as
angels of light (II Cor. 11:14). They purposely strive to draw believers away
from the truth of the gospel.

**31. "So be alert and remember that for three years I did not stop warn-
ing each one of you night and day with tears."**

Paul sounds the alarm: "Be alert" (compare Matt. 24:42; Mark 13:37).
He cautions the elders about the spiritual warfare they face, which no
member of the church can afford to take lightly.

During his three-year ministry in Ephesus, Paul tirelessly warned the members of the church to be on the alert. He did so night and day with tears. In
short, Paul gave himself heart, soul, and mind to the work of admonishing
the believers to follow the Lord. And in the shedding of his tears, he demonstrated his loving concern as a pastor of the Ephesian congregation.

Implicitly, Paul is exhorting the elders to follow his example as they
assume the responsibility of caring for the church of God. He intimates that
as he unceasingly toiled for their spiritual welfare, even to the point of
weeping for them, so they in turn should labor arduously for the Lord.
Paul reveals that during his ministry he has been a diligent pastor, because
he warned and instructed each member of the church (see I Cor. 4:14).

Moreover, the expression *night and day* is not merely a convenient idiom
that denotes continuity. It means that Paul pursued his trade (19:9) in the
morning, taught daily in the lecture hall of Tyrannus (19:9), and filled the
evening hours in teaching the people both in public and from house to
house (20:20).

Doctrinal Considerations in 20:28

Three points require our attention:

a. *Purchase.* God purchased for himself a people that is peculiarly his own. The
price he paid was the blood of his Son shed on Calvary's cross. However, the
metaphor of buying cannot be taken beyond this point, for there is no seller, so to
speak. God did not buy the church from anyone. In fact, the Greek word which I
have translated "purchased" (v. 28) means "to acquire, obtain, gain for oneself."[48]

---

47. Refer to Simon J. Kistemaker, *Exposition of the Epistles of Peter and of the Epistle of Jude,* New
Testament Commentary series (Grand Rapids: Baker, 1987), pp. 227–29, 357–58. See also
G. W. H. Lampe, " 'Grievous Wolves' (Acts 20:29)," in *Christ and Spirit in the New Testament:
Studies in Honour of C. F. D. Moule,* ed. Barnabas Lindars and Stephen S. Smalley (Cambridge:
Cambridge University Press, 1973), pp. 253–68.
48. Bauer, p. 650. See also Richard B. Rackham, *The Acts of the Apostles: An Exposition,* Westmin-
ster Commentaries series (1901; reprint ed., Grand Rapids: Baker, 1964), p. 392.

The word has nothing to do with buying and selling but rather with paying a price in a court of law. Through the meritorious work of his Son, God paid the penalty for sin. That is, the blood of Jesus shed at Golgotha covered the sins of his people.

b. *Trinity.* In his address to the Ephesian elders, Paul implicitly teaches the doctrine of the Trinity. He juxtaposes "repentance to God" and "faith in our Lord Jesus" (v. 21) and continues with a reference to the Spirit (v. 22) and Holy Spirit (v. 23). He also mentions the "Holy Spirit" who appointed overseers for the flock, "the church of God [the Father]," and the "blood of his own [Son]" (v. 28).

c. *Church.* Writing a letter to a group of believers, Paul at times addresses an individual church (e.g., the church in Thessalonica [I Thess. 1:1; II Thess. 1:1]). But in his speech at Miletus, he alludes to the universal church. He calls attention to the church of God, "which [God] made his own through the death of his Son" (GNB). "[T]his verse (v. 28) is one of the clearest assertions in the New Testament of the doctrine of the atonement."[49] In this text, Paul plainly teaches that Jesus Christ died for the people who constitute the church, that is, the elect (compare John 10:15; 17:9; Rom. 8:32–33).

Greek Words, Phrases, and Constructions in 20:25–30

Verses 25–26

διῆλθον—the use of the aorist must be seen as "a single fact without reference to its progress."[50]

διότι—in context, this compound particle means "and so."

Verse 27

ὑπεστειλάμην—this aorist is in the middle voice: "I withdraw myself."[51] It is followed by an infinitive construction (τοῦ μὴ ἀναγγεῖλαι). The genitive case depends on the preceding verb that expresses hesitation and fear. The negative particle μή strengthens the particle οὐ that negates the verb.

Verse 28

ποιμαίνειν—note the present tense, "to shepherd continually." The infinitive can express either command, as a substitute for the imperative, or purpose.[52] With the preceding verb ἔθετο (he appointed), the idea of purpose is preferred.

περιεποιήσατο—the compound aorist verb is in the middle voice: "he acquired for himself." The insertion ἑαυτῷ (for himself) of the Western text is superfluous.

τοῦ ἰδίου—"his own." We supply the noun *Son* to complete the phrase.[53]

---

49. David John Williams, *Acts*, Good News Commentaries series (San Francisco: Harper and Row, 1985), p. 351. Consult Louis Berkhof, *Systematic Theology*, 2d rev. ed. (Grand Rapids: Eerdmans, 1941), pp. 394–95.
50. F. D. Burton, *Moods and Tenses of New Testament Greek* (Edinburgh: Clark, 1898), #39(b).
51. Robertson, *Grammar*, p. 807.
52. Bruce, *Acts* (Greek text), p. 572.
53. Moule, *Idiom-Book*, p. 121.

Verse 30

ὑμῶν αὐτῶν—this combination usually expresses the reflexive meaning of the pronoun, but in this case it has more the sense of the intensive.[54]

διεστραμμένα—the perfect passive participle from the verb διαστρέφω (I make crooked). It is used "of objects that turn out as failures in the hands of a clumsy workman, and whose shape is therefore distorted."[55]

---

e. Committing
20:32–35

Luke reports the last part of Paul's speech to the Ephesian elders in a summary statement. Indeed, Luke telescopes a number of terms—grace, build up, inheritance, sanctified—without explaining them. Yet the intent is plain.

32. "And now I commend you to God and to the word of his grace which is able to build you up and give you the inheritance among all those who are sanctified."

Paul is making his concluding remarks and commits his audience both "to God and to the word of his grace." Similarly, Paul commended the elders in the churches of Pisidian Antioch, Iconium, Lystra, and Derbe to the Lord (14:23). Reporting Paul's gospel preaching in Iconium, Luke notes that the Lord himself "testified to the message of his grace" (14:3). The concept *grace* is typically Pauline, for Paul uses the word about one hundred times in his epistles. Simply put, the expression *the word of his grace* is a synonym for "gospel" (see v. 24).[56]

The gospel of Christ has innate power to strengthen and establish the Ephesian elders in their faith. By implication, we understand that the gospel receives its authority from the Lord Jesus. He demonstrates his power by confirming the believers through the spoken and written word (compare Rom. 16:25). To be precise, it is the gospel to which Paul commits the elders, and this gospel gives them a legacy. The church already had the Old Testament canon, but in due time it also received and acknowledged the New Testament books as canonical and thus inherited the word of God's grace.

When Paul alludes to the inheritance, he addresses the entire church. Notice he says that the gospel is able to "give you the inheritance among all those who are sanctified." The key word in this phrase is the preposition *among,* for Paul does not say that the word of grace will give an inheritance to the Ephesian elders. He says that these particular saints, who are entrusted to God and his Word, receive an inheritance *among* all the believers who are sanctified (see, e.g., I Cor. 1:2). That is, Paul emphasizes "the

---

54. Robertson, *Grammar,* p. 687.
55. Bauer, p. 189.
56. Hans-Helmut Esser, *NIDNTT,* vol. 2, p. 119.

corporate nature of the Church *within* which these believers have their place."[57] Hence Paul stresses the unity of the body of Christ.

33. "I have coveted no one's silver, gold, or clothes. 34. You yourselves know that these hands have ministered to my own needs and to those of the men who are with me."

a. "I have coveted no one's silver, gold, or clothes." Even though the Lord Jesus stated that those who preach the Good News should receive an income (Luke 10:7; cited in I Cor. 9:14; I Tim. 5:18), Paul never availed himself of that right. Instead, in his letters he discloses that he worked night and day with his own hands to support himself,[58] so that no one would ever be able to accuse him of depending on the hearers of the gospel for his material needs (compare I Sam. 12:3). He refused to be a burden to anyone in the churches he established. By performing manual labor, he provided for his financial needs. Paul received gifts from the believers in Philippi, as he himself reveals (Phil. 2:25; 4:16–18), yet he declares that he did not solicit those gifts.

b. "You yourselves know that these hands have ministered to my own needs." The Ephesian elders had observed Paul's ministry and physical work during his three-year stay. They were able to testify that he had never exploited anyone (II Cor. 7:2) but had always set an example of diligence and self-sufficiency, in the good sense of the word. He was a model to the believers and taught the rule: "If you will not work, you shall not eat" (II Thess. 3:10).

c. "And to those of the men who are with me." This is an interesting bit of information. It appears that Paul generated sufficient income to support not only himself but even his companions. Among his companions in Ephesus were Timothy and Erastus. We do not know whether these two men engaged in any type of physical labor or were completely dependent on Paul. Luke, however, indicates that on the arrival of Silas and Timothy in Corinth, Paul devoted himself exclusively to the preaching of the gospel. We assume that his companions had brought him financial gifts from the churches in Macedonia (18:5).

35. "In everything I showed you by working hard in this way that we must help the weak and remember the words of the Lord Jesus, who himself said, 'It is more blessed to give than to receive.' "

This verse raises five questions:

a. What is hard work? In every respect, says Paul to the elders of Ephesus, I taught you to work hard and with your earnings to help the weak. The phrase *by working hard* need not be limited to physical labor but can also mean mental and spiritual exertion. In the Greek New Testament, the verb *to labor* refers to both bodily labor (e.g., Matt. 6:28; Luke 5:5; 12:27) and

---

57. Hanna, *Grammatical Aid*, p. 233.
58. See I Cor. 4:12; I Thess. 2:9; II Thess. 3:8.

the efforts expended by teachers of the gospel and promoters of God's kingdom (I Cor. 15:10; 16:16).[59]

b. Who are the weak? The Gentile world of Paul's day lacked the virtues of love and mercy. No one cared for the poor, the destitute, the sick and physically weak persons. The Christians reached out to those in need because of the love and mercy they themselves had received from Christ. They cared for the poor, they visited the sick, and they helped the weak. They did so without remembering when, where, and whom they aided (see Matt. 25:37–40).

c. Was this saying known? Paul exhorts the Ephesian elders to obey the rule the Lord Jesus himself gave: "It is more blessed to give than to receive." Notice that Paul introduces this saying of the Lord with the command *remember the words*. During his ministry in Ephesus, Paul had faithfully taught the sayings of Jesus, so that the elders were well aware of their significance. And one of these sayings was the rule concerning the blessing of giving. The four evangelists have not recorded this saying in their respective Gospels, yet it is an authentic word from the Lord.

d. What is the meaning of this well-known proverb? We should not think that only the giver and not the recipient is blessed. The recipient receives a blessing through the gift. But the virtue of giving is a reflection of God's continuous activity. God's greatest desire is to give. When man follows God's example, he receives a divine blessing because he demonstrates that he is one of God's children.[60] What Jesus intimates in this proverb is that the act of giving, not that of taking or snatching something for oneself, is blessed.[61] The contrast in this saying is comparable to Jesus' remark that he came to serve, not to be served (Mark 10:45). The Christian must show his love for his neighbor by giving his goods cheerfully (see Luke 6:30; II Cor. 9:7b).

e. Is this a genuine word of Jesus? Popular sayings from Persian, Greek, and Jewish cultures are analogous to Jesus' statement; for example, "It is more becoming for a free man to give where he must than to receive where he must."[62] But analogies do not disprove the genuineness of Jesus' maxim. Jesus did not borrow the Golden Rule, "Do to others as you would have them do to you" (Luke 6:31 [NIV]), from Confucius. Whereas Jesus spoke positively, Confucius expressed himself negatively: "Whatever you do not wish that others should do unto you, do not do unto them."[63]

---

59. Thayer, p. 355; Bauer, p. 443.

60. Consult Joachim Jeremias, *Unknown Sayings of Jesus,* trans. Reginald H. Fuller (London: SPCK, 1957), p. 80.

61. The *Didache* (1.5) has an interesting parallel: "Blessed is he that gives. . . . Woe to him who receives; for if any man receive alms under pressure of need he is innocent; but he who receives it without need shall be tried as to why he took it and for what."

62. Aristotle *Ethica Nicomachea* 4.1.7. Compare Thucydides 2.97.4; and see Sir. 4:31.

63. Confucius *The Analects* 12.2.

Practical Considerations in 20:34–35

The New Testament teaches the dignity and significance of labor, whereby the worker is able to care for the needs of his family and people who are unable to work (I Thess. 4:11–12; I Tim. 5:8). The Christian community must always take care of the poor (Gal. 2:10; 6:10). Conversely, every able body should be engaged in suitable employment. In the words of the *Didache*, "Let everyone who 'comes in the Name of the Lord' be received. . . . If he has no craft [occupation] provide for him according to your understanding, so that no man shall live among you in idleness because he is a Christian."[64]

Greek Words, Phrases, and Constructions in 20:32 and 35

Verse 32

τῷ θεῷ—although some manuscripts have τῷ κυρίῳ, the textual evidence supports the reading *to God*.

τῷ δυναμένῳ—the dative case depends on the nearest antecedent, which is τῷ λόγῳ (the word).

Verse 35

πάντα—the accusative plural is an accusative of specification that has the sense of an adverb: "in every respect."[65]

ὅτι οὕτως—"in this way." This combination does not mean "thus—namely by toiling." It is a command (accompanied by forceful gesture): "look, thus must one work and toil."[66]

f. Leaving
20:36–38

Paul concludes his charge to the Ephesian elders with a saying attributed to Jesus and known to them from Paul's earlier teaching ministry in Ephesus. The elders realize that the responsibility of caring for the spiritual needs of the believers belongs to them. The time to say farewell to their beloved teacher has come.

36. When he had said these things, he knelt down with everyone and prayed.

Throughout his narrative, Luke reveals that Paul is fully in control of every situation. At the conclusion of his speech, Paul kneels down with the elders from Ephesus and fervently prays for each of them. In his address, he commended them to God; now, before his departure, he carries their needs and requests to God in prayer (compare 21:5).

64. *Didache* 12.1, 4–5 (LCL).
65. Bauer, p. 633.
66. Blass and Debrunner, *Greek Grammar*, #425.6.

37. They began to weep aloud and they threw their arms around him and kissed him.

The constant love Paul had given the Ephesians during his ministry is fully reciprocated by the elders, who, overcome by their emotions, begin to weep loudly. The intensity of their weeping demonstrates their affection for Paul. They embrace him and repeatedly kiss him. The Greek is descriptive: "Having fallen around his neck, they kept on kissing him" (compare Gen. 33:4; 45:14–15; and Luke 15:20).

38. They were especially saddened by his statement that they would not see his face again. They accompanied him to the ship.

In his address, Paul stated that the elders would never see him again (v. 25). Now he experiences the impact of that word, because the members of his audience say farewell to him with the understanding that they will never meet again on earth. The verb that is translated "see" actually means "to observe carefully." They realize that the end has come. They sadly accompany Paul to the ship that will carry him and his fellow travelers on their way toward Jerusalem. Yet in God's providence they meet again after Paul's release from imprisonment in Rome (I Tim. 1:3; 3:14).

Summary of Chapter 20

When the riot in Ephesus ends, Paul realizes that the time for his departure is near. He gathers his disciples, encourages them, and then leaves for Macedonia and Greece. After spending three months in Greece, he decides to travel to Syria. To foil a plot against his life, he detours through Macedonia with some companions.

From Philippi Paul sails to Troas, where he stays seven days, breaks bread on the first day of the week, and preaches the Word. While Paul preaches, Eutychus, "overcome by sleep," falls out of a window. Although Eutychus is dead, Paul revives him. Paul continues his journey by walking to Assos, where he boards ship and sails to Miletus. There he summons the elders from Ephesus, who come and listen to Paul's farewell address.

Paul reminds the elders of the work he performed among them by teaching publicly and from house to house. He informs them that the Holy Spirit is warning him that prison and hardship are awaiting him in Jerusalem. He tells them that they will see him no more. Paul states that he has proclaimed to them the complete message of God's word and charges the Ephesian elders to be watchful shepherds of God's church. He alerts them to the danger of ravenous wolves who will appear among the sheep. He exhorts them to follow his example and to labor hard. And last, he concludes his speech with a well-known word from the Lord Jesus.

After the address, the elders weep, embrace Paul, and kiss him. They accompany him to the ship.

21

The Third Missionary Journey, *part 4*

21:1–16

and In Jerusalem and Caesarea, *part 1*

21:17–40

Outline (continued)

21:1–16	4. Travel
21:1–6	a. To Tyre
21:7–9	b. At Caesarea
21:10–11	1) Prophecy
21:12–14	2) Reply
21:15–16	c. To Jerusalem
21:17–26:32	IX. In Jerusalem and Caesarea
21:17–23:22	A. At Jerusalem
21:17–26	1. Paul's Arrival
21:17–19	a. Reception
21:20–25	b. Advice
21:26	c. Vow
21:27–36	2. Paul's Arrest
21:27–29	a. Accusation
21:30–32	b. Confusion
21:33–36	c. Intervention
21:37–22:21	3. Paul's Address
21:37–40	a. Request

21 1 When we had parted from them, we set sail and headed straight to Cos; the next day we went to Rhodes and from there to Patara. 2 We found a boat that was crossing over to Phoenicia; we embarked and set sail. 3 We came within sight of Cyprus and leaving it on the left, we kept sailing toward Syria. We landed at Tyre, for there the ship was to unload its cargo. 4 Having found the disciples, we stayed there seven days. Through the Spirit, they told Paul not to go to Jerusalem. 5 But when our time was up, we departed and began our journey. When all of them with their wives and children escorted us outside the city, we knelt on the beach and prayed. 6 We said good-by to each other and boarded the ship while they returned home. 7 We continued our voyage from Tyre and landed at Ptolemais, where we greeted the brothers and stayed with them for a day. 8 On the next day we left, came to Caesarea, entered the house of Philip the evangelist, one of the Seven, and stayed with him. 9 He had four daughters who were virgins and who prophesied.

10 After we had been there several days, a prophet named Agabus came down from Judea. 11 And coming to us, he took Paul's belt and tied his own hands and feet. He said, "The Holy Spirit says: 'In this way, the Jews in Jerusalem will bind the man to whom this belt belongs and deliver him into the hands of the Gentiles.' " 12 When we heard this, we and the local residents began to beg Paul not to go up to Jerusalem. 13 Then Paul asked, "Why are you weeping and breaking my heart? I am ready not only to be bound but also to die in Jerusalem for the name of the Lord Jesus." 14 Because he could not be dissuaded, we gave up and said, "Let the will of the Lord be done."

15 After this interval, we got ready and went up to Jerusalem. 16 Some of the disciples from Caesarea accompanied us and took us to Mnason of Cyprus, a long-time disciple, with whom we stayed.

---

4. Travel
21:1–16

In his travel narrative, Luke presents nearly a day-by-day account of the incidents that happened on the journey from Miletus to Jerusalem. He notes that in both Tyre and Caesarea believers warn Paul through the Holy Spirit not to go to Jerusalem. In short, Luke introduces an apparent conflict: Paul being compelled by the Spirit to proceed to Jerusalem (20:22) and the believers through the Spirit warning him not to go.

a. To Tyre
21:1–6

1. When we had parted from them, we set sail and headed straight to Cos; the next day we went to Rhodes and from there to Patara. 2. We

found a boat that was crossing over to Phoenicia; we embarked and set sail.

We have no indication who traveled with Paul from Miletus to Jerusalem, but we presume that Luke and the travel companions who were listed in 20:4 are with him. Thus the pronoun *we* refers to nine men who say good-by to the elders of Ephesus. The Greek text describes the emotional farewell scene: Just before the men embark, they tear themselves loose from the embraces of the Ephesian elders.

The ship leaves the harbor of Miletus; propelled by a northerly wind, it hugs the coastline and sails south to the island of Cos. The travelers arrive in the evening and spend the night there. The next morning the crew hoists the sails. Cruising in a southeasterly direction, the ship reaches the town of Rhodes, located at the northern tip of the island of Rhodes, by the end of the second day. The vessel is rounding the curve of southwest Asia Minor; on the third day it heads for Patara, a city with an excellent harbor, in the province of Lycia.[1]

At Patara, Paul and his friends transfer to another ship. Even though Luke fails to give a reason for this transfer, we assume that the vessel that sailed along the western coast of Asia Minor functioned as a shuttle service. In the first century, most ships generally stayed close to shore, but larger vessels crossed the open sea from Patara to Tyre in Phoenicia. Measuring probably in excess of one hundred feet in length, these larger vessels were suited to venture far from land.[2] Some cargo ships accommodated numerous passengers; for instance, the one stranded at Malta had 276 people aboard (27:37). Furthermore, a ship that offered a nonstop crossing from Patara to Tyre (about four hundred miles) would be much faster than a vessel that went from port to port along the coastline.

3. We came within sight of Cyprus and leaving it on the left, we kept sailing toward Syria. We landed at Tyre, for there the ship was to unload its cargo.

Paul and his associates board a large ship that sails directly to Tyre. Possibly in the course of the third day, they begin to see the mountains of Cyprus as they approach the island and pass it to the south (contrast 27:4). Because Luke writes "we kept sailing," he seems to intimate that they have the benefit of a favorable wind. They arrive at the port of Tyre on either the fourth or the fifth day of the voyage. Luke adds that the ship stayed in the harbor to unload its cargo. With the Greek construction of the present participle *unloading,* he indicates that the task of emptying this vessel took time—seven days. This information confirms that Paul's voyage was aboard

---

1. According to the Western text, Paul and his companions voyaged to Myra. The other major manuscripts lack this reference, which may have been inserted in the Western text through assimilation to 27:5 or the Acts of Paul and Thecla. Consult Bruce M. Metzger, *A Textual Commentary on the Greek New Testament,* 3d corrected ed. (London and New York: United Bible Societies, 1975), p. 482.

2. Refer to Earle Hilgert, "Ships; Boats," *ISBE,* vol. 4, pp. 482–89.

a large freighter.[3] Paul apparently continued his voyage aboard this same vessel; otherwise he would not have had to stay in port for an entire week.

4. Having found the disciples, we stayed there seven days. Through the Spirit, they told Paul not to go to Jerusalem.

In Acts, the name *Tyre* occurs twice in this context (vv. 3, 7) and once in 12:20. The city was located in Phoenicia (modern Lebanon); Jewish believers who were scattered after the death of Stephen traveled as far as Phoenicia (11:19) and acquainted the people with Christ's gospel. When Paul and Barnabas traveled from Antioch to Jerusalem, they went through Phoenicia to tell the believers how God had brought Gentiles to faith (15:3). These believers were very happy to hear about the growth of the church among the Gentiles. The city of Tyre, which enjoyed colonial status in Roman times, may have had a Jewish-Gentile congregation when Paul came to visit. We know little about this church, but in postapostolic times Tyre became a major center of the Christian faith (the fulfillment of Ps. 87:4).

Tyre is approximately 110 miles to the north-northwest of Jerusalem and about 65 miles north-northeast of Caesarea. In other words, Paul could easily reach Jerusalem before the day of Pentecost (20:16). Even if he walked the entire distance, he would arrive in Jerusalem within a week. But now he has time to minister to the disciples in Tyre.

While the crew unloads the ship, Paul and his colleagues go into the city, where they try to find the members of the local church. They are successful in their search and stay for seven days (see 20:6). We presume that Paul used the time to teach these Christians, whom Luke calls disciples. Yet these believers are not necessarily recent converts. They receive instruction from Paul and in return have a word of warning for him.

Luke relates that the Christians in Tyre seek to dissuade Paul from going to Jerusalem. They have received a revelation from the Holy Spirit (compare I Cor. 14:32) that Paul is going to meet adversities there. This revelation supports Paul's comment that the Holy Spirit warned him about future imprisonment and hardship (20:23).

Is there a contradiction between the revelations Paul received from the Holy Spirit and those which the believers in Tyre obtained? No, not at all. The Christians in Tyre heard the Holy Spirit say that Paul would meet adversities, but they did not understand the purpose of Paul's future suffering. Conversely, Paul understood the warnings as confirmation that "he must suffer for [the Lord's] name" (9:16, NIV). He considered these divine revelations to be symbols of God's grace designed to prepare him for the immediate future.[4]

The church members in Tyre express a normal human reaction: they

3. Consult William M. Ramsay, *St. Paul the Traveller and the Roman Citizen* (1897; reprint ed., Grand Rapids: Baker, 1962), p. 300.

4. John Calvin, *Commentary on the Acts of the Apostles*, ed. David W. Torrance and Thomas F. Torrance, 2 vols. (Grand Rapids: Eerdmans, 1966), vol. 2, p. 193.

warn Paul not to go to Jerusalem. They want Paul to avoid the obvious afflictions that lie ahead. But Paul becomes increasingly determined to accept the foreordained sufferings as a true servant of his Lord and to set out for Jerusalem (see a parallel in Luke 9:51).

5. But when our time was up, we departed and began our journey. When all of them with their wives and children escorted us outside the city, we knelt on the beach and prayed.

a. "But when our time was up." The wording of this clause proves that the crew had finished unloading the cargo and was ready to continue the voyage. Hence, not Paul but the captain of the ship determined the duration of the stay in Tyre.

b. "All of them with their wives and children escorted us outside the city." Here follows another sketch of the closeness between Paul and the churches he served. At Miletus, the Ephesian elders embraced Paul and kissed him good-by (20:37). In Tyre nearly the entire congregation—husbands, wives, and children—accompanied Paul and his companions to the ship. The farewell at Tyre is less emotional than the one at Miletus; Paul had served in Ephesus almost three years and had been with the believers in Tyre for one week. Nevertheless, there is a parallel: at both Miletus and Tyre the believers pray together.

c. "We knelt on the beach and prayed." Although kneeling is an appropriate posture in prayer,[5] Scripture refrains from prescribing a particular pose. In the pastoral Epistles Paul speaks of lifting holy hands in prayer (I Tim. 2:8), and the Jews usually stand when they pray. On the beach at Tyre the entire congregation, Paul, and his friends knelt and prayed for each other. What a testimony to the Gentiles who witnessed the event! The content of the prayers that were offered on the beach at Tyre is unknown, but we imagine that Paul prayed for the growth of the local church. The church members in turn prayed for Paul's safety.

6. We said good-by to each other and boarded the ship while they returned home.

The members of the congregation accompany Paul and his companions to the ship docked along the pier. Here they take leave of one another: Paul and his friends board the vessel that has taken them to Tyre and now will take them to Ptolemais and Caesarea. The church members return to their respective homes.

Greek Words, Phrases, and Constructions in 21:1–6

Verses 1–2

ἀποσπασθέντας—the aorist passive participle (from ἀποσπάω, I tear away) should be understood as a reflexive and be given a literal interpretation: "we tore ourselves away."

---

5. See II Chron. 6:13; Ps. 95:6; Dan. 6:10; Acts 9:40.

διαπερῶν—this present active participle from διαπεράω (I cross over) "has a futuristic sense of purpose." The purpose expressed in the participle coincides with the action of the main verb or preceding participle: "We found a boat that was to cross over." This is also true of the present participle ἀποφορτιζόμενον (v. 3), "The ship was appointed to unload her cargo."[6]

Verse 3

ἀναφάναντες—from ἀναφαίνω (I light up; cause to appear), the aorist active participle means "we made it visible to ourselves by drawing near."[7]

ἐπλέομεν—the imperfect tense has a descriptive sense: "we kept sailing." It indicates that the winds were favorable throughout the voyage. By contrast, the aorist tense in κατήλθομεν (we landed) denotes single occurrence.

Verse 4

αὐτοῦ—an adverb of place ("there"), not the genitive case of the personal pronoun.[8]

ἔλεγον—the imperfect tense signifies repetition: "they kept on telling him not to go." μὴ ἐπιβαίνειν is a negative purpose clause with a present infinitive.

Verses 5–6

ἐξαρτίσαι—this aorist active infinitive from the verb ἐξαρτίζω (I finish, complete) probably is a nautical term.[9]

τὸ πλοῖον—the definite article appears to support the interpretation that Paul boarded the same vessel that brought him to Tyre.

τὰ ἴδια—the term is idiomatic: "to their own homes."

---

b. At Caesarea
21:7–9

7. We continued our voyage from Tyre and landed at Ptolemais, where we greeted the brothers and stayed with them for a day.

Luke reports that from Tyre the group continued the voyage to the port of Ptolemais. The distance between the two places is about twenty-seven miles; with a favorable wind a ship can readily cover it within part of a day. With minor differences many translations read, "When we had finished the voyage from Tyre."[10] The implication is that Paul debarked at Ptolemais and intended to walk the rest of the way. However, the Greek

---

6. A. T. Robertson, *A Grammar of the Greek New Testament in the Light of Historical Research* (Nashville: Broadman, 1934), pp. 891, 1115.

7. Consult Friedrich Blass and Albert Debrunner, *A Greek Grammar of the New Testament and Other Early Christian Literature,* trans. and rev. Robert Funk (Chicago: University of Chicago Press, 1961), #309.1.

8. Bauer, p. 124.

9. F. F. Bruce, *The Acts of the Apostles: The Greek Text with Introduction and Commentary,* 3d (rev. and enl.) ed. (Grand Rapids: Eerdmans, 1990), p. 580.

10. KJV, NKJV, RSV, NASB, MLB, JB, *Moffatt.*

verb *dianyo* (to complete) can also be interpreted "to continue," as is evident from Greek literature.[11] Paul, then, resumed his journey after a brief pause in Ptolemais.

The city of Ptolemais has a history that goes back to Old Testament times, when it was known as Acco (Judg. 1:31). But during the inter-testamental era after the death of Alexander the Great, the area was occupied by the Ptolemies of Egypt, who gave the city the name *Ptolemais* (see I Macc. 5:22; 10:39; 12:48). In Roman times, the city became a colony and kept the Egyptian name.[12] Later, the Semitic name came back in vogue, and today the city is known as Acre. We conjecture that when the gospel spread along the coast in the northerly direction to Phoenicia (11:19), it also reached Ptolemais.

While the crew of the ship loads and unloads cargo, the passengers have time to go ashore. Paul and his fellow travelers meet the members of the local church—the phrase *we greeted the brothers* has the same connotation as "having found the disciples" (v. 4). After staying with them for one day, Paul continues his journey to Caesarea, some thirty-five miles south.

8. On the next day we left, came to Caesarea, entered the house of Philip the evangelist, one of the Seven, and stayed with him. 9. He had four daughters who were virgins and who prophesied.

The Greek text gives no indication whether Paul traveled to Caesarea on foot or by boat. If we translate the verb in the preceding verse (v. 7) as "continued," it is logical to suppose Paul sailed from Ptolemais to Caesarea.

When Paul and his associates arrive in Caesarea,[13] he is no stranger in the city, for twice on his voyages to and from Jerusalem (9:30; 18:22) he visited it. Here Philip, one of the seven deacons in Jerusalem (6:5), lives. He is called "the evangelist" because of his evangelistic endeavors in Samaria (8:4–13) and along the Mediterranean coast from Azotus to Caesarea (8:40). In the two decades since his first public appearance, Philip had settled in the port city of Caesarea. Luke adds the interesting comment that Philip had four unmarried daughters who had the gift of prophecy. Unfortunately, he provides no details, so that we know nothing about the nature of their prophecies. The word *prophesied* should be interpreted in harmony with Paul's reference to the gifts of the Spirit (I Cor. 11:5; 14:1, 39). Evidently these four women were well versed in the Scriptures and, like their father, evangelized the Gentile society in which they lived.

From the church fathers of the second century we learn that Philip and

---

11. Bauer, p. 187. See the use of this verb in Xenophon Ephesius 1.11.2; 3.2.12; 5.1.5; 5.10.3; 5.11.1.

12. Refer to H. Porter, "Acco," *ISBE*, vol. 1, pp. 23–24.

13. At least two translations (kjv, nkjv), following the Majority Text, add the words given here in italics: "On the next day we *who were Paul's companions* departed." However, the major manuscripts do not support the addition.

his daughters eventually moved to the city of Hierapolis in western Asia Minor and were buried there.[14]

1) Prophecy
21:10–11

10. After we had been there several days, a prophet named Agabus came down from Judea. 11. And coming to us, he took Paul's belt and tied his own hands and feet. He said, "The Holy Spirit says: 'In this way, the Jews in Jerusalem will bind the man to whom this belt belongs and deliver him into the hands of the Gentiles.' "

a. "After we had been there several days." From the data Luke provides in his travel narrative, we can chart how Paul spent the time between Passover and Pentecost:

First week	Leave Philippi after Easter
	Travel to Troas (20:6; five days)
Second week	Spend seven days in Troas (20:6)
Third week	Travel to Miletus (20:13–16; four days)
Fourth week	Travel from Miletus to Tyre (21:1–3; seven days)
Fifth week	Spend seven days in Tyre (21:4)
Sixth week	Travel to Ptolemais (21:7; one day)
	Spend one day in Ptolemais (21:7)
	Travel to Caesarea (21:8; one day)
Seventh week	Spend several days in Caesarea (21:10, 15)
	Travel to Jerusalem (21:15; two or three days)
	Arrive in Jerusalem (21:17)

Paul was counting the days prior to Pentecost, for six weeks had passed since he had left Philippi. From Caesarea he would have to travel sixty-five miles to Jerusalem. And this journey would take two, if not three, days. Because of the numerous warnings Paul has received in many places (20:23), he is not interested in arriving early in Jerusalem. He wants to spend his time with Philip (who, incidentally, must have owned a large house to be able to accommodate Paul and his friends). In the meantime, Luke has opportunity to hear from Philip's lips the accounts of the baptisms of the Samaritans and the Ethiopian official and of his mission work along the coast.

b. "A prophet named Agabus came down from Judea." This is the second time Luke mentions the prophet Agabus (see also 11:28). Why Luke thinks

---

14. Clement of Alexandria *Stromata* 3.6.52; Eusebius quotes from Polycrates of Ephesus in *Ecclesiastical History* 3.31.3–5.

it necessary to introduce this person and his office once more is not clear; perhaps it is because this is the first time Luke meets Agabus.

In the preceding decade, Agabus had traveled from Jerusalem to Antioch, where he predicted the coming of a severe famine in the entire Roman world. Paul and Barnabas heard him prophesy in Antioch, and the believers there delegated them to carry gifts to the elders in Judea. Now once again Agabus meets Paul. As a prophet inspired by the Holy Spirit, Agabus comes from Judea, that is, the land of the Jews, with a personal message for Paul.[15]

c. "He took Paul's belt and tied his own hands and feet." Agabus follows the Old Testament example of the prophets Isaiah, Jeremiah, and Ezekiel, who used visual signs to warn the Israelites of their impending exile (see Isa. 20:2; Jer. 13:1–11; Ezek. 4:1–12). Agabus takes the belt that belongs to Paul and deftly ties his own hands and feet with it. The belt presumably was made of cloth and not of leather; a cloth belt would facilitate the process of tying oneself.

The difference between Old and New Testament prophets should not be overlooked. While the function of the Old Testament prophets was to reveal the coming of the Messiah, Agabus predicts immediate future events.[16]

d. "The Holy Spirit says: 'In this way, the Jews in Jerusalem will bind the man to whom this belt belongs.'" The Spirit speaks directly through Agabus and addresses Paul. By this visible sign the Holy Spirit is telling Paul the manner in which he will become a prisoner in Jerusalem. Of course, the facts should not be pushed to their logical extreme; the Jews in Jerusalem did not bind Paul with a belt. Instead, the Jews would have killed Paul if the Roman commander had not intervened. The commander rescued Paul and had him bound with two chains (vv. 31–33).

e. "And deliver him into the hands of the Gentiles." With these words, the Holy Spirit is alluding to Jesus, who predicted that he would be betrayed, condemned, and handed over to the Gentiles (Matt. 20:19; Mark 10:33). The Gentiles are the Roman authorities who, influenced by the Jewish hierarchy, crucified Jesus and soon will imprison Paul. Note, however, that the Holy Spirit predicts Paul's binding and incarceration but not his death. By implication, his gospel ministry will continue even in prison.

Doctrinal Considerations in 21:11

In Acts, the doctrine of the Holy Spirit is taught in many chapters. Because of this emphasis, the early church father Chrysostom referred to Acts as the Gospel of the

---

15. Located in the province of Judea, Caesarea was the Roman military and administrative center of Palestine and, in the eyes of the Jews, not part of Israel. Compare Josephus *Antiquities* 15.9.6 [331–41]; 16.5.1 [136–41].

16. Consult Donald Guthrie, *New Testament Theology* (Downers Grove: Inter-Varsity, 1981), p. 740.

Holy Spirit.[17] God's Spirit speaks directly through the prophets. In Antioch, the Holy Spirit uses Agabus to predict a worldwide famine (11:28). Through the prophets and in harmony with the Antiochean church, he makes his will known concerning the apostolic ministry of Paul and Barnabas (13:1–2). And in Caesarea, the Spirit once again employs the prophet Agabus to speak directly to Paul.

Paul experiences the compelling power of the Holy Spirit, who tells him to go to Jerusalem, where he will endure hardship and affliction. Paul obediently responds to the guidance of the Spirit. He also demonstrates his trust in God.

Sometime before Paul decided to travel to Jerusalem, he wrote his epistle to the Romans. In that epistle, he exhorted the Christians in Rome to pray to God on his behalf. He asked them to pray that he might be rescued from the unbelievers in Judea and that his service to the saints in Jerusalem might be acceptable. And he expected that in answer to this prayer he might visit the church in Rome (Rom. 15:30–32). Paul, then, trusted that the prayers of the saints would be answered and that the Holy Spirit would guide him through the difficulties he was about to face. In faith, he accepted the words of the Spirit spoken by Agabus as a detailed revelation of future events.[18]

---

2) Reply
21:12–14

12. When we heard this, we and the local residents began to beg Paul not to go up to Jerusalem. 13. Then Paul asked, "Why are you weeping and breaking my heart? I am ready not only to be bound but also to die in Jerusalem for the name of the Lord Jesus."

a. "We and the local residents began to beg Paul not to go up to Jerusalem." Paul's companions and the Christians in Caesarea want to shield him from harm and plead with him not to visit Jerusalem. At an earlier occasion in Ephesus, Paul's disciples and certain provincial officials had successfully restrained Paul from entering the theater to address the unruly crowd. Thus they rescued Paul from possible physical injury (19:30–31). But in Caesarea the situation has a different focus because Paul knows that the Holy Spirit compels him to travel to Jerusalem (19:21; 20:22). He sees every manifestation of the Spirit on this point as a confirmation of the mandate to demonstrate in Jerusalem the unity of Christ's expanding church.

Paul's fellow travelers must have been struck by the Spirit's recurring message in both Tyre and Caesarea. Observe the similar response of the two groups; the difference is that in Caesarea, the people accompany their plea with weeping.

b. "Then Paul asked, 'Why are you weeping and breaking my heart?' " Paul shows unflinching determination in the face of an emotional response

---

17. Chrysostom *Homilies on the Acts of the Apostles* 1.5.

18. Refer to E. Earle Ellis, "The Role of the Christian Prophet in Acts," in *Apostolic History and the Gospel,* ed. W. Ward Gasque and Ralph P. Martin (Exeter: Paternoster; Grand Rapids: Eerdmans, 1970), pp. 55–67.

from his own companions and the believers in Caesarea. Paul shows no obstinacy but rather obedience. For that reason, he perceives the well-intended efforts of the people as an obstacle. He rebukes them by asking what they are trying to do. With their weeping, they are breaking Paul's heart and are trying to dissuade him. But Paul objects to their crying, first, because he himself has an emotional proclivity that often makes him weep (20:19, 31), and second, because he wants to obey the prompting of the Holy Spirit.

c. "I am ready not only to be bound but also to die in Jerusalem for the name of the Lord Jesus." The Spirit gives Paul inner strength and enables him to withstand the temptation to escape. Immediately after his conversion in Damascus, Jesus told Paul that he would have to suffer much for the name of Christ (9:15–16).

Paul is unafraid, for he knows that God determines the outcome of all things. His attitude is completely free from fatalism; in full reliance on Christ, he accepts the message of the Holy Spirit and tells his audience that he is ready not only to be bound but also to die in Jerusalem (compare 20:24). In view of the suffering he already endured on behalf of Christ (see II Cor. 11:23–28), Paul has proved his willingness to die for the Lord Jesus. Conversely, Paul's statement should not be interpreted to mean that he expects his life to come to an end in Jerusalem. He still intends to extend the church to the ends of the earth.

14. Because he could not be dissuaded, we gave up and said, "Let the will of the Lord be done."

Luke writes that Paul could not be dissuaded. Luke ought to have known that at the end of his Ephesian ministry Paul had expressed his desire to go to Jerusalem (19:21). When he finally left Troas on his way south and east, Paul was in a hurry, for he had only one desire: to be in Jerusalem before Pentecost (20:16). Within sixty-five miles of his destination, Paul could not be persuaded to change his mind. He remained obedient to his Lord. Although he was apprehensive he, like his Master, set his face in the direction of Jerusalem.

Even Luke had joined the effort to dissuade Paul. But when he and the rest of the group perceived Paul's steadfast desire to obey God's will, they said, "Let the will of the Lord be done." This is not a pious statement but rather an echo of the third petition of the Lord's Prayer, "Your will be done."[19] We are confident that in the second half of the first century, the Lord's Prayer was widely used, certainly by the apostles and their helpers. Further, the words spoken by the people in Caesarea are reminiscent of Jesus' prayer uttered to his Father in Gethsemane: "Not my will, but . . . yours be done" (Luke 22:42).

---

19. Henry Alford, *Alford's Greek Testament: An Exegetical and Critical Commentary*, 7th ed., 4 vols. (1877; Grand Rapids: Guardian, 1976), vol. 2, p. 238.

Practical Considerations in 21:14

Luke portrays Paul as a true follower of Jesus Christ. As he reports on Paul's travel, Luke indirectly draws a number of parallels:

Paul wished to go to Jerusalem to attend Passover (Acts 20:3) or Pentecost (Acts 20:16)	Jesus traveled to Jerusalem for his last Passover feast (John 12:1; 13:1)
The Spirit warned Paul three times (Acts 20:23; 21:4, 11)	Jesus spoke of his passion three times (Luke 9:22, 44; 18:31–33)
Paul was bound by Roman soldiers (Acts 21:33)	Jesus was bound by soldiers (John 18:12)
Paul knelt down and prayed (Acts 20:36; 21:5)	Jesus knelt down and prayed (Luke 22:41)
"Let the Lord's will be done" (Acts 21:14)	"Let your will be done" (Luke 22:42)

Greek Words, Phrases, and Constructions in 21:12–14

Verses 12–13

τοῦ μὴ ἀναβαίνειν—the present infinitive with the definite article in the genitive case and the negative particle μή expresses negative purpose. For a comparable construction, see verse 4.

συνθρύπτοντες—the compound form of the present participle occurs only once in the New Testament. Similarly, the single verb θρύπτω (I break in small pieces) appears once in the New Testament (I Cor. 11:24). The compound verb is intensive and means "thoroughly break in pieces."

εἰς—the preposition in this context is equivalent to ἐν (at).

ἑτοίμως ἔχω—"I hold myself ready." This is an idiomatic expression that should be translated with the verb *to be*: "I am ready."

Verse 14

πειθομένου—this is the genitive absolute construction. The present participle of the verb πείθω (I persuade) indicates continued action; the passive implies that the audience is the agent.

εἰπόντες—following the main verb ἡσυχάσαμεν (we remained silent), the construction parallels the idiom *he answered and said.*

c. To Jerusalem
21:15–16

15. After this interval, we got ready and went up to Jerusalem. 16. Some of the disciples from Caesarea accompanied us and took us to Mnason of Cyprus, a long-time disciple, with whom we stayed.

After the believers give up their attempt to persuade Paul to stay away from Jerusalem, Paul and his travel companions make preparations to leave Caesarea. The Greek text literally says, "after these days" (that is, when they conclude their stay of several days). The time has come to complete the journey to Jerusalem. Luke fails to indicate whether the travelers walked or rode; the text only relates that they made preparations for the journey.[20] However, the reading of the Western text implies that the trip was completed in two days: Paul and his companions stayed overnight at the house of Mnason of Cyprus and departed for Jerusalem the next day.[21] To cover a distance of sixty-five miles within two days can best be done on horseback. If they walked, the travelers might have taken an extra day.

The church in Caesarea extended its care to Paul and his associates by sending a number of believers to accompany them part way to Jerusalem. Paul's party of nine people (seven companions [20:4] plus Luke) in addition to several Caesarean Christians must have formed an impressive group.

The Greek sentence construction in the latter part of verse 16 is ambiguous. Two different translations are possible. The first one is, "and brought with them one Mnason of Cyprus, an early disciple, with whom we were to lodge."[22] The second one is, "and took us to Mnason of Cyprus, a long-time disciple, with whom we stayed."[23] The sense of the passage favors the second translation, for it would seem strange to have Mnason as both a travel companion and a host.

Numerous travelers were on their way to Jerusalem for Pentecost, so lodging must have been difficult to find. However, Mnason (the name may be the Greek spelling of the Hebrew name *Manasseh*) provided shelter;[24] he must have been a man of means to own a house that could accommodate a large group of visitors. Luke's remark that Mnason, a native of Cyprus (compare 4:36), was a long-time disciple may mean that he was among the first converts at Pentecost.

Greek Words, Phrases, and Constructions in 21:15–16

Verse 15

μετὰ δὲ τὰς ἡμέρας ταύτας—the temporal phrase *after these days* refers directly to the clause *after we had been there several days* (v. 10).

---

20. Ramsay states that the verb *to make ready* means "to equip or saddle a horse." *St. Paul the Traveller*, p. 302. Because this verb appears only once in the New Testament (and twice elsewhere), the evidence supporting Ramsay's interpretation is slim.

21. Additions to the text are in italics; the Western text reads: "And these [the Caesarean disciples] brought us to those with whom we were to lodge; *and when we arrived at a certain village, we stayed* with Mnason of Cyprus, an early disciple. *And when we had departed* thence we came. . . ." See Metzger, *Textual Commentary*, p. 483.

22. With minor variations, KJV, NKJV, RV, ASV, NEB.

23. A few changes aside, JB, NASB, NAB, NIV, RSV, SEB, *Phillips*, and *Moffatt*.

24. Bruce, *Acts* (Greek text), p. 585.

ἐπισκευασάμενοι—"having made preparations." The Textus Receptus has ἀποσκευασάμενοι, which probably means "pack up and leave."[25]

Verse 16

τῶν μαθητῶν—to give meaning to the partitive genitive of this construction, we must supply the indefinite pronoun τινές (some).

ἄγοντες—this present participle from the verb *to bring* needs a direct object (ἡμᾶς, us) to complete the meaning of this transitive verb.

ξενισθῶμεν—the aorist passive subjunctive from ξενίζω (I receive as a guest) has a volitive sense, "we should lodge."[26] The preceding relative clause παρ' ᾧ (with whom) expresses purpose.

---

17 When we arrived in Jerusalem, the brothers joyfully welcomed us. 18 The next day Paul went with us to James, and all the elders were present. 19 Having greeted them, Paul began to relate in detail all the things God had done among the Gentiles through his ministry.

20 When they heard this, they began to glorify God and said to him: "You see, brother, how many thousands of Jews have come to believe, and all of them are zealous for the law. 21 They have been informed concerning you that you are teaching all the Jews who live among the Gentiles to abandon Moses, telling them not to circumcise their children and not to keep our traditions. 22 What shall we do? In fact, they will hear that you have arrived. 23 So do what we tell you. There are four men who have taken a vow. 24 Take these men, be purified with them, and pay their expenses, so that they will shave their heads. Then everyone will know that the things they have heard about you are not true, but that you yourself adhere to and keep the law. 25 Concerning the Gentile believers, we have sent our decision that they should abstain from meat sacrificed to idols, from blood, from strangled animals, and from sexual immorality."

26 The following day, Paul took the men and was purified with them. He entered the temple and gave notice of the time when the days of purification would be fulfilled and when the offering would be brought for each of them.

IX. In Jerusalem and Caesarea
21:17–26:32

A. At Jerusalem
21:17–23:22

After every missionary tour, Paul returned to the church in Jerusalem. When Paul and Barnabas had completed the first tour, they went to Jerusalem to give a report at the council (15:1–2, 4, 12; Gal. 2:1–2). Although Luke is extremely concise in the narrative about the conclusion of Paul's second tour, he seems to indicate that Paul went up to Jerusalem (18:22). And last, Paul came to the leaders of the church in Jerusalem to report what God had done during the third missionary journey.

Even though Antioch became the mission center of the early church and commissioned men to bring the message of the gospel to the Gentile world, the church in Jerusalem occupied a leading, albeit diminishing, role.

---

25. Bauer, p. 98.
26. Robertson, *Grammar*, p. 955.

1. Paul's Arrival
21:17–26

Jerusalem the golden, with milk and honey blessed,
Beneath thy contemplation sink heart and voice oppressed.
I know not, oh, I know not what joys await us there,
What radiancy of glory, what joys beyond compare!

In the twelfth century, Bernard of Cluny composed a hymn in which he described the joys of the heavenly Jerusalem. But when Paul arrived in the earthly Jerusalem, he experienced the joy of being warmly welcomed by the local Christians and the anxiety of being arrested by the Romans.

a. Reception
21:17–19

17. When we arrived in Jerusalem, the brothers joyfully welcomed us. 18. The next day Paul went with us to James, and all the elders were present. 19. Having greeted them, Paul began to relate in detail all the things God had done among the Gentiles through his ministry.

a. "The brothers joyfully welcomed us." After spending the night at the house of Mnason, the group arrives in Jerusalem the next day, probably late in the evening. When Paul and his friends reach Jerusalem, representatives of the church are on hand to extend to them a warm welcome. Luke calls these representatives "brothers," which is a term that signifies "fellow believers." Paul is safe in the presence of fellow Christians, but the repeated warnings from the Holy Spirit intensify his awareness of the dangers in this city (compare 9:29).

b. "James and all the elders were present." The next day, which may have been the Jewish Sabbath, James and the elders receive Paul and his companions. The leaders of the Jerusalem church thus acknowledge the seven representatives of the Gentile churches as brothers in Christ. They are able to see the bond of fellowship in the worldwide church of Jesus Christ. Although Luke does not specifically report that Paul's companions transmitted the gifts from the Gentile churches,[27] we assume that they did, and that James and the elders rejoiced in receiving those gifts.

In this verse Luke says nothing about the apostles; apparently they were elsewhere, and some perhaps had already died. He focuses on the elders and on James, who was Peter's successor in the Jerusalem church (see 12:17). James made the decisive speech at the Jerusalem Council (15:13–21) and was one of the three pillars who extended the right hand of fellowship to Paul and Barnabas (Gal. 2:9).

In this verse Luke also changes his use of pronouns. For literary purposes—to emphasize that Paul is the central figure in the account—he

---

27. See also Rom. 15:25–28; I Cor. 16:1–4; II Cor. 8:1–4.

shifts from the first person plural to the third person plural.[28] He resumes use of the first person plural in his account of Paul's voyage to Rome (27:1), on which Luke was a fellow traveler.

c. "[Paul] began to relate in detail all the things God had done among the Gentiles through his ministry." The purpose of Paul's visit is threefold: first, to deliver the monetary gift from the Gentile churches; next, to strengthen the bond between Jews and Gentiles by having James and the elders meet Gentile representatives; last, to give a report of the growth and influence of Gentile churches.

Paul presents a detailed account of his third missionary journey; to relate his narrative, he needs time. So James and the elders spend the greater part of the day listening to what God has done among the Gentiles through his servant Paul. These Jerusalem leaders must develop an understanding of the unity of the church universal. Luke stresses that God did the work and, therefore, he ascribes to God the praise and glory. *Soli Deo Gloria!* (to God alone the honor [I Tim. 1:17]).

Greek Words, Phrases, and Constructions in 21:17–19

γενομένων—the genitive absolute construction with a verb that expresses motion: "when we arrived." Hence, the preposition εἰς, although translated "in," can have the usual connotation, "toward."

εἰσῄει—this is the past (imperfect) tense of the verb εἴσειμι (I enter). See 3:3; 21:26; Hebrews 9:6. This verb lacks the aorist, so the imperfect has to do double duty.

ἐξηγεῖτο—notice the imperfect tense of the verb ἐξηγέομαι (I report). In this context, the imperfect denotes continued action. Further, the idiom καθ' ἓν ἕκαστον (one by one) indicates that Paul related his experiences in considerable detail and made known God's hand in the development of the church abroad.

---

b. Advice
21:20–25

20. When they heard this, they began to glorify God and said to him: "You see, brother, how many thousands of Jews have come to believe, and all of them are zealous for the law."

We make two observations:

a. *Glorify*. Hearing about the tremendous growth of the church in Asia Minor, Macedonia, Greece, Rome, and Illyricum and about Paul's intention to go to Spain, James and the elders keep on shouting hallelujah. They praise God for his marvelous work among the Gentiles and see the fulfillment of the Old Testament Scriptures that speak about the Gentiles coming to know the Lord. They are thankful that the negative reports they have

---

28. Consult Ernst Haenchen, *The Acts of the Apostles: A Commentary*, trans. Bernard Noble and Gerald Shinn (Philadelphia: Westminster, 1971), p. 608.

heard about Paul and his work among the Gentiles are incorrect. Neverthe-less, they feel constrained to inform Paul about the sentiments of numerous Jewish Christians in Jerusalem.

b. *Alert.* Paul comes to the elders to promote the unity of the church and expects them to accept Gentile Christians from abroad on a par with the Jewish Christians in Jerusalem. But the converse is also true, namely, that Paul pay due attention to those Jewish Christians who zealously keep the law. James and the elders involve Paul directly by saying to him, "You see, brother." The verb *to see* means to perceive something and thus to reflect and ponder. The word *brother* intimates that James and the elders consider Paul a brother in Christ. And they also distance themselves from those Jewish Christians who in their zeal have voided the decisions of the Jerusa-lem Council (15:19–21, 23–29).

James showed wisdom by inviting only the elders to come and listen to Paul. He wanted to maintain peace in the church and avoid any rift that might result from Paul's report of his work among the Gentiles. James also wished to alert Paul to the thinking and practices of the many thousands of Jewish believers. He desired that Paul would clear himself of the suspicions the Jewish Christians had, for Paul could not abandon all these people who, with the Gentile believers, formed the body of Christ.[29]

Multitudes of Jewish Christians in Jerusalem and Judea strictly observed the law and expected all believers to do the same. They were like the Judaizers who opposed Paul and Barnabas at the conclusion of their first missionary journey to Cyprus and Asia Minor (15:1, 5). Because of its zeal for the law the Jerusalem church had lost its zeal for missions. Whereas Paul had forged ahead by preaching the message of salvation to the Greco-Roman world, the Jews who came to faith in Christ sought to merit salva-tion by keeping their Jewish traditions and by observing the Mosaic law. In all fairness, we note that the decisions of the Jerusalem Council addressed Gentile Christians but allowed Jewish Christians to continue their adher-ence to the time-honored customs and rituals of Judaism.

We presume that the expression *thousands* includes all the Jewish Chris-tians who lived in Palestine. After the persecution following the death of Stephen, the believers were scattered throughout Judea and Samaria (8:1). More, the church in Jerusalem in the course of time began to grow, so that literally thousands of believers resided in the city and countryside.

21. "They have been informed concerning you that you are teaching all the Jews who live among the Gentiles to abandon Moses, telling them not to circumcise their children and not to keep our traditions. 22. What shall we do? In fact, they will hear that you have arrived."

a. "You are teaching all the Jews who live among the Gentiles to abandon Moses." While Paul proclaimed the gospel in Ephesus, news concerning his labors reached Jerusalem. The people in Jerusalem interpreted this news

---

29. Calvin, *Acts of the Apostles,* vol. 2, p. 199.

from their perspective, which differed considerably from that of Paul in Ephesus. The Christian Jews in Jerusalem placed the gospel within the context of Mosaic law and traditions, but Paul in Ephesus taught Gentile Christians that they were not obligated to abide by Mosaic regulations. Paul told the Gentiles about the decisions of the Jerusalem Council, which instructed them "to abstain from things sacrificed to idols, from blood, from strangled animals, and from fornication" (15:29). He taught the Jews in Ephesus the gospel of God's grace (20:24) and showed them that faith in Jesus Christ overshadowed Mosaic laws and customs (Gal. 3:25).

In Asia Minor, Macedonia, and Greece, Paul preached the gospel to both Jews and Greeks (20:21). To the Jew he was a Jew and to the Gentile he became a Gentile so that he might gain them both for Christ (I Cor. 9:20–22). Paul fully realized the difficulty he faced in preaching the gospel to two groups of people, yet his conscience was clear. He called both Jews and Greeks to repentance. Among the Jews in dispersion were those who disagreed with Paul's approach (see vv. 27–29). They registered complaints to the Jews and Jewish Christians in Jerusalem and said that Paul told all the Jews not to observe Jewish laws and customs.

b. "[You tell] them not to circumcise their children and not to keep our traditions." The Christian Jews in Jerusalem heard reports concerning Paul's mission activities and saw serious flaws in his work. On the basis of the reports they had received—that Paul did not require the Jews in dispersion to circumcise their children and observe Jewish customs—they considered Paul outside the mainstream. Although James and the elders knew that Paul applied the decisions of the Jerusalem Council, the multitude of Jewish Christians wanted Paul to stress circumcision and Jewish laws. They refused to realize that Gentiles had become more numerous than Jews in the church, and that they themselves would have to promote the unity of the body of Christ.

To Paul's credit, we should note that in his work and life he demonstrated his loyalty to the Jews by adhering to Jewish customs. For instance, he had Timothy circumcised at the very time when he was delivering the letter of the Jerusalem Council to the churches in Galatia (16:3–4). Next, he himself had taken a Nazirite vow that required cutting his hair and appearing at the Jerusalem temple before a specified date (18:18). And last, in his epistles, he never forbids Jews to circumcise their children.

c. "What shall we do? In fact, they will hear that you have arrived." The Majority Text has an expansion, shown in italics: "What then? *The assembly must certainly meet,* for they will hear that you have come."[30] The intent is obvious, for the difference between Gentile Christians and Jewish Christians could be resolved only in an assembly. Even though the addition appears to be original, scholars hesitate to include it in their translations.

---

30. NKJV; see also KJV, JB. The Greek addition can also mean "a mob will congregate." See Lake and Cadbury, *Beginnings,* vol. 4, p. 272; James Hardy Ropes, *Beginnings,* vol. 3, p. 205.

James and the elders supported Paul in his work and teachings, but they had to find a way to defuse the volatile atmosphere in Jewish Christian circles. If the Christian Jews in Jerusalem had a strong prejudice against Paul, "the non-Christian Jews were enraged in the highest degree."[31] With numerous Jews violently opposed to Paul, the situation was grave indeed. And the news of Paul's arrival in the city could not be kept secret, especially not when the Jewish Christians met the delegates from the Gentile churches (see vv. 17–19).

23. "So do what we tell you. There are four men who have taken a vow. 24. Take these men, be purified with them, and pay their expenses, so that they will shave their heads. Then everyone will know that the things they have heard about you are not true, but that you yourself adhere to and keep the law."

We make these observations:

a. *Advice.* The elders of the Jerusalem church offered a prudent proposal to Paul. They knew of four men, Christian Jews, who had taken a vow. We presume that they took a Nazirite vow prior to the feast of Pentecost. At the end of the month-long period of the vow, they were unable to pay the expenses involved with fulfilling the vow. According to Numbers 6:14–17, the Nazirite had to offer three animals (a male and a female lamb, and a ram), a grain and a drink offering, and a basket of bread.[32] The cost for the individual Nazirite was high but served as an expression of his undivided commitment to God.

b. *Vow.* During the period of his vow, a Nazirite might not use a razor on his head and had to let his hair grow. But when the period was over, he shaved off his hair, dedicated it to the Lord, and burned it together with the sacrifice for the fellowship offering (Num. 6:18).[33]

c. *Rites.* James and the elders advised Paul to take these four men, join in their purification rites, and pay their expenses. We should understand that James himself was acquainted with the Nazirite vow. Church historian Eusebius quotes from a book written by Hegesippus, who belonged to the generation that succeeded the apostles. In the quote, Hegesippus portrays James as a Nazirite.[34]

Although the four men had taken the Nazirite vow, Paul himself evidently had not. Therefore, the purification rites for the Nazirites and for himself could not be the same. Paul had come to Jerusalem from Gentile territory and was ceremonially unclean. He had to submit to Levitical purification before he could be the benefactor for the four Nazirites and partici-

---

31. William M. Ramsay, *Pictures of the Apostolic Church: Studies in the Book of Acts* (reprint ed.; Grand Rapids: Baker, 1959), p. 272.

32. Refer to SB, vol. 2, p. 755.

33. Compare Josephus *Antiquities* 4.4.4 [72]; 19.6.1 [294].

34. Eusebius *Ecclesiastical History* 2.23.4–6.

pate in their ceremonies. For him, the prescribed days of purification lasted one week. On the third day of the week, he was sprinkled with atonement water (v. 26); a second sprinkling took place on the seventh day (v. 27). Afterward, when the sacrifices were scheduled to be offered, Paul would then defray the expenses of the four Nazirites.[35] He could take part in the ceremonies only when he himself was Levitically clean. On the seventh day of Paul's cleansing, the time of abstentions for the Nazirites also had ended (compare Num. 6:3).[36] And if Paul sought to obtain ceremonial cleansing in a one-week period, he would not need to shave his hair.

d. *Proof.* By paying the expenses for four Nazirites, by going to the priest with them to set the time for the sacrifices, and by participating in the purification rites, Paul demonstrated that he was a law-abiding Jew. A discernible display of his integrity as a Jew would be much more effective than an extended explanation. He applied the old adage: "A picture is worth a thousand words."

The leaders of the church and Paul expected that the Christian Jews in Jerusalem would be able to see that the reports they had received about Paul's teaching were false. To pay the expenses for four Nazirites was considered an act of piety. The leaders anticipated that Paul's participation in the ceremonies, even if he himself were not a Nazirite, would convince the Christian Jews that Paul was a traditional son of Abraham. In brief, Paul's association with four Nazirites should be overwhelming evidence that he was a Jew dedicated to keeping the law of God in very respect.

25. "Concerning the Gentile believers, we have sent our decision that they should abstain from meat sacrificed to idols, from blood, from strangled animals, and from sexual immorality."

a. *Translation.* The Western text both adds and deletes material in this verse. The added words (in italics) are intended to show the difference between Jewish and Gentile Christians: "Concerning the Gentile believers, *they* [that is, the Jewish Christians] *have nothing to say to you, for* we sent and decreed *that they should observe nothing of the kind, except* to keep themselves from what is offered to idols, from blood and from sexual immorality." The expansion adds nothing to the meaning of the text and appears to be a paraphrase. For this reason, scholars delete the augments[37] and adopt the shorter version. Conversely, the Western text has omitted one of the stipulations of the Jerusalem Council: to abstain from eating the meat of strangled animals. For a discussion on this omission, see the **Textual Note on 15:20.**

---

35. See SB, vol. 2, pp. 757–58; Haenchen, *Acts,* p. 612.
36. Josephus *War* 2.15.1 [313]. We have difficulty believing that all four men simultaneously were defiled because of a death in their presence (Num. 6:9), just at the time when Paul made the necessary arrangements for his own purification rites.
37. But see kjv and nkjv.

b. *Intent.* James and the elders of the Jerusalem church wanted to avoid any misunderstanding about the issue at stake. They knew that the matter involved Jewish Christians who lived in the Dispersion, not Gentile Christians. Nonetheless, the elders thought it wise to repeat the decisions made by the Jerusalem Council so that everyone would realize that Gentile Christians were not required to observe Jewish ceremonial laws and customs. The repetition was not meant to instruct the Gentile Christian delegates.[38] They already had been instructed by Paul, were acquainted with the prescribed rules, and enjoyed their freedom in Christ. The leaders of the Jerusalem church reiterated the stipulations to imply that they had settled the Gentile Christian question but not the Jewish Christian question. Indeed, the church would have to convene another meeting to debate the matter of freedom in Christ for the Jewish believers.

Doctrinal Considerations in 21:20–25

Strengthened by the decisions of the Jerusalem Council, Paul returned to the Greco-Roman world on his second and third missionary journeys. He was determined to preach the gospel of Christian liberty to every Gentile who would listen to him. He instructed the Gentile that he would not have to become a Jew, for Christ had fulfilled the ceremonial laws of Judaism.

But in Jerusalem, Paul willingly accepted the advice of the Jerusalem elders to pay for sacrifices offered by four Nazirites and to submit to Levitical purification rites. Did Paul compromise his own teachings and beliefs? Should he have rejected the advice of the elders? No, not really. Paul maintained that Gentile Christians would sin if they were to observe Jewish ceremonial laws and customs, and Jewish Christians would sin if they kept the law for the purpose of meriting salvation. Observing the Jewish ceremonies in itself is not sinful.[39] Paul himself remained a Jew and continued to observe Jewish customs. Thus, he had made a vow in Cenchrea and had traveled to Jerusalem to fulfill it (18:18). In his defense before Governor Felix, Paul stated that he had come to Jerusalem to present offerings (24:17).

Paul's purpose for going to Jerusalem was to promote the unity of the church. He wanted to bring together representatives of the Gentile Christian churches abroad and those of the Jewish Christian church in Jerusalem. He himself would do everything in his power to maintain that unity, even if he had to undergo purification rites and pay for sacrifices.

---

38. Refer to I. Howard Marshall, *The Acts of the Apostles: An Introduction and Commentary,* Tyndale New Testament Commentary series (Leicester: Inter-Varsity; Grand Rapids: Eerdmans, 1980), p. 346. Marshall adds that "Luke failed to edit the [we-]source in the light of the earlier mention of the decree in chapter 15." This explanation has merit if we understand that the "we-source" is Luke's own diary.

39. F. W. Grosheide, *De Handelingen der Apostelen,* Kommentaar op het Nieuwe Testament series, 2 vols. (Amsterdam: Van Bottenburg, 1948), vol. 2, p. 267 n. 2.

Greek Words, Phrases, and Constructions in 21:20–25

Verse 20

ἐδόξαζον τὸν θεὸν εἶπόν—the imperfect and the aorist tenses indicate continuous action in the one case and single action in the other. "They praised God for some time and in various ways until they finally said."[40]

τοῦ νόμου—the genitive case is objective ("[zealous] for the law"). The influence and numerical increase of believers who "belonged to the party of the Pharisees" (15:5) seem to have been substantial. A literal translation from the Greek is "tens of thousands" but in idiomatic English "thousands."

Verse 21

διδάσκεις—the verb *to teach* takes a double accusative: one a thing (ἀποστασίαν, apostasy) and the other persons ('Ιουδαίους, Jews). The adjective πάντας (all), due to its place in the sentence, reveals a touch of exaggeration in the report concerning Paul. The word order throughout this sentence is awkward.

τοῖς ἔθεσιν—the dative of sphere signifies "according to our customs."[41]

Verses 23–24

ἡμῖν—the dative of possession. In translation the verb *to be* becomes *to have:* "we have four men."

ἐφ' ἑαυτῶν—"on themselves." The reading ἀφ' in at least two major manuscripts (Sinaiticus and Vaticanus) means "on their own initiative."

ἁγνίσθητι—the aorist passive imperative of ἁγνίζω (I purify) should be understood as a causative middle: "purify yourself."

ξυρήσονται—the ἵνα particle introduces a purpose clause, but in a number of leading manuscripts the verb appears in the future indicative instead of the aorist subjunctive. In the New Testament, the use of the future tense in place of the subjunctive is common (see, e.g., John 7:3; I Peter 3:1; Rev. 6:4). The passive is equivalent to a permissive middle: "so that they may have their heads shaved."[42]

Verse 25

ἐπεστείλαμεν—the external evidence for either this reading or ἀπεστείλαμεν is equally strong. The intent of the verse remains the same with either reading.

c. Vow
21:26

26. The following day, Paul took the men and was purified with them. He entered the temple and gave notice of the time when the days of

---

40. Blass and Debrunner, *Greek Grammar,* #327.
41. Robertson, *Grammar,* p. 524.
42. Bauer, p. 549; Robertson, *Grammar,* p. 809.

purification would be fulfilled and when the offering would be brought for each of them.

Within the compass of this one verse Luke compresses a number of details that need an explanatory footnote, so to speak. (In Acts, Luke repeatedly condenses information to the point that the clarity of a particular verse is affected [see, e.g., 6:13–14; 7:16; 18:22].) When he writes "the following day," Luke is referring to the third day of Paul's arrival in Jerusalem (see vv. 17–18). We venture to say that if Paul came to Jerusalem on a Friday and met with James and the elders on Saturday, then Sunday (the day of Pentecost) is the third day. For a full discussion, see the commentary on 24:11.

When Paul took the four Nazirites to a priest in the temple on that Pentecost Sunday, he had to subject himself to a week-long purification process in order to qualify as the sponsor for these four men. The priest sprinkled Paul with water of atonement on the third day of this purification process (Tuesday) and again on the seventh day (Saturday)—the days specified for purification were the third and the seventh days (see Num. 19:12). Paul himself could not take the Nazirite vow, but for one week he had to join these men in purification rites. Later, speaking in his own defense before Governor Felix, Paul testified that he was ceremonially clean. He had gone to the temple to bring gifts for the poor, that is, for his own people (24:17–18). From this information, we do not learn that Paul paid the expenses for the Nazirites from the gifts he brought to Jerusalem. We assume that he paid the expenses from his own resources. Moreover, with Paul paying their expenses, the Nazirites were able to complete the prescribed ceremonies. According to Jewish regulations, the presentation of sacrifices and the shaving of the heads lasted seven days.[43]

In short, Paul made the necessary provisions for the Nazirites by going to the priest in the temple, stating the duration of the days of purification, and scheduling the time for the sacrifices for each of the Nazirites. He also scheduled the shaving of their heads and the burning of their hair with the fellowship offering (Num. 6:18).

Greek Words, Phrases, and Constructions in 21:26

εἰσῄει—see the discussion of this verb in verse 18.

διαγγέλλων—from the verb *to give notice of,* this present participle expresses purpose.

ὑπέρ—the basic meaning of this preposition is singularly applicable in the present context: "in behalf of, for the sake of someone."[44]

---

43. Mishnah *Nazir* 3.6.
44. Bauer, p. 838; C. F. D. Moule, *An Idiom-Book of New Testament Greek,* 2d ed. (Cambridge: Cambridge University Press, 1960), p. 64.

27 When the seven days were almost fulfilled, the Jews from the province of Asia saw him in the temple, began to stir up the whole multitude, and seized him. 28 They shouted, "Men of Israel! Help us! This is the man who teaches all men everywhere against our people, the law, and this place. He even has brought Greeks into the temple and has defiled this holy place." 29 They had seen Trophimus of Ephesus with him in the city and supposed that Paul had brought him into the temple.

30 The whole city was aroused and the people rushed together. They took Paul and dragged him out of the temple, and immediately the doors were shut. 31 While they were trying to kill him, a report went to the commander of the occupation forces that all of Jerusalem was aroused. 32 At once he took some soldiers and officers and ran to the crowd. When the Jews saw the commander and his soldiers, they stopped beating Paul.

33 Then the commander approached Paul, arrested him, and had him bound with two chains. He asked who he was and what he had done. 34 But when some in the crowd shouted one thing and others something else, and because the commander was unable to discover the truth, he ordered Paul to be brought to the barracks. 35 As Paul reached the steps, the violence of the mob forced the soldiers to carry him. 36 The multitude of Jewish people kept following and shouted: "Away with him."

2. Paul's Arrest
21:27–36

For Paul, the temple was both the safest and the most perilous place in Jerusalem. It was safe because he had submitted himself to purification rites and so could not be accused of defiling the temple or breaking Jewish customs. But because the temple attracted the Jewish masses, especially during a festival, it was extremely dangerous for Paul to appear there.

a. Accusation
21:27–29

27. When the seven days were almost fulfilled, the Jews from the province of Asia saw him in the temple, began to stir up the whole multitude, and seized him.

The relationship between the Jews and the Jewish Christians in Jerusalem was harmonious, especially at the time of religious festivals. As long as the Jewish Christians continued to observe the customs and traditions of Judaism, the Jews were willing to overlook some aberrations.[45] In the Jews' opinion, the Christians were no threat. The persecution following Stephen's death belonged in the past.

Jews in the dispersion did not extend tolerance to Paul, however. Jews in Corinth had plotted to take Paul's life when he was about to sail for Jerusalem to celebrate the Passover (20:3), but Paul foiled their plot by traveling through Macedonia and arriving in Jerusalem for the feast of Pentecost. In Jerusalem, Jews from western Asia Minor, probably from Ephesus, recog-

---

45. Richard B. Rackham, *The Acts of the Apostles: An Exposition*, Westminster Commentaries series (1901; reprint ed., Grand Rapids: Baker, 1964), p. 411.

nized Paul, who had lived in that city for nearly three years. These Jews perhaps had waited to see if Paul would appear in Jerusalem to celebrate the feast; when he did, they saw an opportunity to eliminate him, which, in spite of their plotting (20:19), they had been unable to do.

For the first week of his stay in Jerusalem, Paul remained undetected by the crowds. The Jews in Jerusalem did not recognize him, because he had been absent from the city for more than two decades. But when he entered the temple precincts with four men whom they did not know, the Jews from Asia were outraged. They had seen him in the city with Trophimus, a Gentile from Ephesus, and assumed that Paul had brought Gentiles into the holy place. So these Jews stirred up the crowds in the temple courts. Luke specifies that the Jews, not the Jewish Christians, instigated the riot that resulted in Paul's arrest.

Why were the Jews so set against Paul? In their opinion, he represented a menace to Judaism: he allegedly taught the Jews in dispersion not to observe the customs and the ceremonial laws of Moses. The accusations against Paul parallel those brought against Stephen. The Jews charged Stephen with speaking against the law, God, and the temple (6:11, 13–14). The Jews from Asia accuse Paul of teaching against the law and the temple (vv. 28–29).

28. They shouted, "Men of Israel! Help us! This is the man who teaches all men everywhere against our people, the law, and this place. He even has brought Greeks into the temple and has defiled this holy place." 29. They had seen Trophimus of Ephesus with him in the city and supposed that Paul had brought him into the temple.

These are the significant points:

a. *Concern.* In the Greek Luke is able to record in one sentence a twofold charge which the Ephesian Jews level against Paul. In fact, when Paul makes his defense before Governor Felix in Caesarea, he challenges these Jews to come before the court and press their charges (24:19). What they have said in the courts of the temple can hardly be considered a charge!

The Dispersion Jews introduce the matter as a typical Jewish concern. Accordingly, they shout: "Men of Israel!" They consider themselves to be the watchmen on the walls of Zion; they are the defenders of the orthodox faith. They call on fellow Jews to lend a hand and cry out: "Help us!" But if they needed help, they should have summoned the captain of the temple guard and his officers (4:1; 5:24, 26; Luke 22:4).

b. *First charge.* The Jews from Asia begin their accusation against Paul with these words: "This is the man who teaches all men everywhere against our people, the law, and this place."

This part of the charge reveals exaggeration: "all men everywhere." The words *all men* are inclusive: Jews and Gentiles. If the allegation were true, then Paul should have been teaching in Jerusalem, too. Moreover, the accusation that Paul taught against the Jewish people simply cannot be substantiated; information from Acts and Paul's epistles shows that Paul preached the gospel first in the synagogues and that, despite rejection, Paul expressed concern for the Jews (e.g., Rom. 11:1–2a, 13–15). Although Paul instructed the Jewish people that the ceremonial laws were fulfilled by Jesus Christ, he stressed the meaning and application of the moral law. Lastly, the facts—that Paul was in the temple to be purified and that he paid the expenses for four Nazirites—confute the indictment that Paul spoke against the temple.

c. *Second charge.* The second part of the accusation ("He even has brought Greeks into the temple and has defiled this holy place") is also groundless. No Gentile would think of entering the sacred temple courts; according to Josephus, numerous signs in Greek and Latin forbade Gentiles to go beyond the Court of the Gentiles.[46] Anyone in the city of Jerusalem, whether Jew or Gentile, was acquainted with the posted inscription: "No Gentile may enter within the railing around the sanctuary and within the enclosure. Whoever should be caught will render himself liable to the death penalty which will inevitably follow."[47]

If Paul had brought Greeks into the specific temple area—the Court of the Women and the Court of the Israelites—that was forbidden to Gentiles, then the Jews would have had evidence: captured trespassers. But this is not at all the case. The angry Jews rely on assumptions and hearsay, not on facts.

d. *Explanation.* The Ephesian Jews had seen Paul a few days earlier in the city. At that time he was accompanied by Trophimus of Ephesus, whom they knew to be a Gentile who had become a Christian. They now saw Paul in the temple courts with four men. Not knowing who these men were, the Ephesian Jews presumed that they were Gentile Christians who had accompanied Paul to Jerusalem. But Paul stood with four Nazirites near the so-called chamber of the Nazirites, which was located in the southeast corner of the Court of the Women.[48] Here Paul and the Nazirites were making the final arrangements with a priest for offering their sacrifices and completing their vows.

The assumptions of the Jews from Asia do not match reality. If they had seen Trophimus in the temple area, they should have captured him without delay. Then they would have had incontrovertible proof that Paul had defiled the temple by taking Trophimus, a Gentile, into the Court of the Women and the Court of the Israelites. Then the temple guard (see 4:1) could have made an arrest.

---

46. Josephus *War* 5.5.2 [194]; 6.2.4 [124–26]; *Antiquities* 15.11.5 [417]. See also SB, vol. 2, pp. 761–62.

47. Harold G. Stigers, "Temple, Jerusalem," *ZPEB*, vol. 5, p. 650.

48. Refer to Shmuel Safrai and Michael Avi-Yonah, "Temple," *Encyclopaedia Judaica*, vol. 15, p. 966.

Greek Words, Phrases, and Constructions in 21:27–29

Verse 27

ἀπό—instead of the more appropriate preposition ἐκ (out of), Luke resorts to ἀπό (from). Compare 6:9.

συνέχεον—the imperfect tense of the verb συγχέω (I stir up) depicts a continued effort to confuse the crowd. The literal meaning of this verb is "to pour together."

Verse 28

τοῦ λαοῦ—notice the use of the definite article for this noun and for the words *law* and *place*. The Jews specify three distinct categories. The noun λαός means God's own people.

πάντας πανταχῇ—"everyone everywhere." This combination perhaps is an idiomatic expression.

εἰσήγαγεν—the aorist tense of εἰσάγω (I enter) denotes a single occurrence; but notice that the verb κεκοίνωκεν is in the perfect tense that shows continued effect and lasting consequences.[49]

Verse 29

ἦσαν γὰρ προεωρακότες—the perfect periphrastic construction of the verb *to be* with the perfect participle of προοράω (I see previously) indicates that the act of observing Trophimus in the city continued to upset the Ephesian Jews.

ἐνόμιζον—the imperfect tense of the verb νομίζω (I think) adds descriptive liveliness to the narrative.

---

b. Confusion
21:30–32

30. The whole city was aroused and the people rushed together. They took Paul and dragged him out of the temple, and immediately the doors were shut.

By word of mouth the people spread the accusation that Paul taught against the Jewish people, the law, and the temple. This accusation was sufficient to arouse the entire population of Jerusalem and the numerous visitors. At the time of a festival, the people were attuned to extraordinary reports. For instance, when Jesus made his triumphal entry into Jerusalem, the whole city was agitated (Matt. 21:10); when the Holy Spirit was poured out on the day of Pentecost, the crowd came together in confusion (2:6). Similarly, the people now amassed throughout the city and rushed to the temple area without knowing any precise details. This is typical of oriental cities, where even today large crowds gather in record time and are easily aroused to take up a chant and carry various placards and banners.

---

49. Blass and Debrunner, *Greek Grammar*, #342.4; Robertson, *Grammar*, p. 894.

The instigators of the riot, the Ephesian Jews, had apprehended Paul (v. 27). Now they and other men dragged him outside the temple courts. Luke fails to distinguish the different courts of the temple complex; for him, the temple included all the areas that could be closed off by gates and that were forbidden to the Gentiles. These were the temple proper, the Court of the Priests, the Court of the Israelites, and the Court of the Women. The unrestricted areas of the temple—the court of the Gentiles, Solomon's Colonnade (John 10:23; Acts 3:11; 5:12), and the Royal Portico, where the moneychangers and the merchants conducted their business— afforded ample room for thousands of people.

The captain of the temple guard and his men quickly moved to shut the doors between the Court of the Gentiles and the Court of the Women. The captain was in charge of maintaining order in and around the temple complex.[50] By shutting the doors, he prevented the crowd from rioting within the courts. If the crowd should kill Paul on the sacred temple grounds, his blood would defile the temple (II Kings 11:15–16; II Chron. 24:21).

31. While they were trying to kill him, a report went to the commander of the occupation forces that all of Jerusalem was aroused. 32. At once he took some soldiers and officers and ran to the crowd. When the Jews saw the commander and his soldiers, they stopped beating Paul.

Paul was in danger of losing his life, for he had no recourse to legal action. Anyone accused of defiling the temple could be killed instantly, without benefit of trial. The mob could have dragged Paul outside the city and stoned him to death, as they did Stephen (7:58). But they had no patience and, as Luke reports, already were trying to kill Paul. Only the intervention of the Roman military spared Paul.

The Romans had constructed Fortress Antonia and its adjacent barracks (v. 34) on "a rock fifty cubits [75 feet] high and on all sides precipitous."[51] The fortress itself was fifty feet high but had turrets that were at least a hundred feet high. From this elevated vantage point, the Romans were able to survey the crowds not only in the temple area but also in other parts of the city. If tumults should break out, the commander immediately would send in his troops to restore order.

Luke calls the commander a chiliarch (a leader of one thousand); today, such an officer would have the rank of major or colonel.[52] He was superior to a centurion and held equestrian rank in Roman society. This commander was well known in Jerusalem: Luke records his name, Claudius Lysias (23:26). When the commander heard from his sentry in the lookout tower that the entire city was in an uproar, he immediately took action. He

---

50. Emil Schürer, *The History of the Jewish People in the Age of Jesus Christ (175 B.C.–A.D. 135)*, rev. and ed. Geza Vermes and Fergus Millar, 3 vols. (Edinburgh: Clark, 1973–87), vol. 2, p. 278.

51. Josephus *War* 5.5.8 [238].

52. Bauer, p. 882; see also, e.g., John 18:12. There was a cohort of 760 foot soldiers and a squadron of 240 horsemen in Jerusalem. Consult Lake and Cadbury, *Beginnings*, vol. 4, p. 275.

noticed large crowds milling around, so he ordered some of his officers and soldiers—at least two hundred men—to accompany him. They ran into the crowds to arrest the troublemaker.

Immediately Paul's attackers stopped beating him, for they had no intention of being arrested with Paul. They would rather release him to the Roman commander than to be apprehended themselves and charged with rioting.

Doctrinal Considerations in 21:30–32

When Jesus died at Calvary, the curtain separating the Most Holy Place from the rest of the temple proper split from top to bottom (Matt. 27:51). By this supernatural incursion, God decisively showed that the Levitical priesthood and the temple were obsolete. Yet God gave the Jews forty years before he terminated the priesthood and destroyed the temple.

Throughout that forty-year period, the temple remained sacred to the Jewish people. Anyone who spoke words about the temple that could be understood negatively was put to death. For instance, both Jesus (Matt. 26:61) and Stephen (Acts 6:13) were accused of speaking against the temple and were killed. To the Jews, Israel was central to the nations of the world, Jerusalem was central to Israel, and the temple was central to everything.

Yet with the influx of Gentile Christians into the church, the Jewish Christians had to solve a problem of immense magnitude. They themselves continued to worship with the non-Christian Jews in the temple. But if they were to promote the unity of the universal church, they had to come to terms with temple worship which excluded Samaritan and Gentile Christians. Jesus had told the Samaritan woman that true worshipers would worship the Father in spirit and truth (John 4:21–24), but they would worship neither in Jerusalem nor on Mount Gerizim. Jesus, the promised Messiah, ushered in a new system of worship that is "not tied to any particular holy place."[53]

A Gentile Christian, Luke witnessed the arrest of Paul and the subsequent closing of the temple gates. From his perspective, the act of closing the gates symbolically signified that the temple was of no importance to the Gentile Christian church and within time—after A.D. 70—would be meaningless to the Jewish Christian segment as well.

> In the land of fadeless day
> 　Lies a city four-square;
> It shall never pass away,
> 　And there is no night there.
>
> And the gates shall never close
> 　To the city four-square;
> There life's crystal river flows,
> 　And there is no night there.
> 　　　　　—John R. Clements

---

53. Leon Morris, *The Gospel According to John,* New International Commentary on the New Testament series (Grand Rapids: Eerdmans, 1971), p. 270.

Greek Words, Phrases, and Constructions in 21:30–32

Verse 30

εἷλκον—the imperfect tense of ἕλκω (I drag) is descriptive and denotes process. But the aorist passive verb ἐκλείσθησαν (from κλείω, I shut) connotes single action. While the Jews were dragging Paul out of the Court of the Women and into the Court of the Gentiles, the temple guard shut the gates.

Verses 31–32

ζητούντων—the genitive absolute construction lacks the pronoun αὐτῶν in the genitive case. The pronoun is implied.[54] The verb ζητέω (I seek) conveys the unfavorable connotation of attempting to kill someone.

συγχύννεται—this is a variation of the present tense of συγχέω (I confuse). See verse 27.

κατέδραμεν—from κατατρέχω (I run down), this verb in the second aorist vividly depicts the commander running down the stairs toward the Court of the Gentiles.

---

c. Intervention
21:33–36

33. Then the commander approached Paul, arrested him, and had him bound with two chains. He asked who he was and what he had done.

From Luke's narrative we learn that Roman authorities were kindly disposed toward Paul. Except in Philippi (16:22), officials of the Roman government repeatedly favored and sheltered Paul. For instance, in Corinth the Roman proconsul acquitted Paul even before he had an opportunity to defend himself (18:14–15). In Ephesus, the Asiarchs advised Paul not to enter the theater (19:31). During the voyage to Rome, the centurion named Julius was kindly disposed toward Paul and allowed him to go ashore at Sidon to see his friends (27:3).

The commander in Jerusalem approached Paul, arrested him, and had him bound with two chains (compare 12:6).[55] By having Paul bound, the commander cut off any possible attempt to escape. (Paul realized that the prophecy of Agabus and his demonstration of being bound was fulfilled [21:10–11].) By intervening, the commander saved Paul from death. He began to ask the attackers about Paul's identity and transgressions. The tense of the Greek verb indicates that the commander asked the question repeatedly.

34. But when some in the crowd shouted one thing and others something else, and because the commander was unable to discover the truth, he ordered Paul to be brought to the barracks.

The commander demonstrated that he was fully in control of the situa-

---

54. Robertson, *Grammar*, p. 1126.
55. Compare Josephus *Antiquities* 18.6.7 [196]; see also Acts 28:20; Eph. 6:20; II Tim. 1:16.

tion. Whereas a few years earlier Governor Cumanus had ordered his troops to quell a riot and as a consequence killed thousands of Jews,[56] Claudius Lysias himself stood in the midst of the mob and tried to find out what had happened.

The crowd was unable to give an answer because they themselves had no idea why they were there (see 19:32 for a parallel). Some people shouted that Paul had led Jewish people astray, while others cried out that he had broken the law and still others declared that he had defiled the temple (v. 28). Consequently, when the commander received no satisfactory answers to his inquiry, he ordered his troops to take Paul into the barracks, where he personally would interrogate him (22:27–28).

35. As Paul reached the steps, the violence of the mob forced the soldiers to carry him. 36. The multitude of Jewish people kept following and shouted: "Away with him."

The attackers saw that the object of their hatred was being carried away in Roman custody and possibly would escape the death penalty which they longed to administer. When Paul, bound between two soldiers, reached the two flights of stairs that led to Fortress Antonia, the mob tried to prevent him from ascending these steps.[57] The press of the mob was so great that the soldiers had to lift Paul from the ground and carry him up the stairs.

The mob kept following the Roman soldiers, who undoubtedly tried to prevent the people from mounting the steps. When the multitude realized that they had lost their victim, they began to shout to the soldiers, "Away with him." This chant did not mean that the soldiers should take Paul inside the barracks but that they should kill him. Notice the similarity to the mob's chant when Pontius Pilate sought to release Jesus. Then the multitude screamed, "Away with him! Crucify him!" (John 19:15; and see Luke 23:18; Acts 22:22). Indeed Paul could affirm the truth of Jesus' words that no servant is greater than his master (Matt. 10:24; John 13:16).

Greek Words, Phrases, and Constructions in 21:33–36

Verse 33

αὐτοῦ—the genitive case of the pronoun depends on the aorist verb ἐπελάβετο (he arrested). Verbs that denote grasping, catching, and arresting govern the genitive case.

ἐπυνθάνετο—the imperfect tense depicts repeated questioning by the commander, who tried to learn the details about Paul as a person (τίς, who) and as the cause of the riot (τί, what).

εἴη—the present optative of the verb εἰμί (I am) with the perfect periphrastic construction of ἐστιν and the perfect participle πεποιηκώς. The use of the optative and the periphrastic construction probably reflect the very words spoken by the

---

56. Josephus *War* 2.12.1 [223–26]; *Antiquities* 20.5.3 [105–12].
57. Josephus *War* 5.5.8 [243]. Consult Schürer, *History of the Jewish People*, vol. 1, p. 366.

commander. Compare the frequent use of the optative in the relatively short speech of Governor Festus (25:16 [twice], 20).

Verse 34

ἄλλοι δε ἄλλο—"some one thing, some another." See 19:32 for this idiomatic expression.[58]

ἐπεφώνουν—the imperfect tense shows repetitive action; the compound verb reveals intensity: "they kept crying loudly."

δυναμένου δὲ αὐτοῦ—although the construction is the genitive absolute, it is not true to form because the subject of the main verb ἐκέλευσεν (he ordered) is the same as that of the genitive absolute.

Verses 35–36

συνέβη—this aorist from συμβαίνω (I meet, happen) is a stylistic variant of ἐγένετο (it happened). With the present infinitive βαστάζεσθαι (to carry), it describes Luke's amazement that Roman soldiers would carry Paul to safety.

ἠκολούθει—the imperfect tense of the verb ἀκολουθέω (I follow) shows the persistence of the crowd and their passionate hatred of Paul.

---

37 When Paul was about to be brought into the barracks, he asked the commander, "May I say something to you?" And the commander exclaimed, "Do you know Greek? 38 Then you are not the Egyptian who some time ago started a revolt and led four thousand assassins into the desert?" 39 Paul replied, "I am a Jew of Tarsus in Cilicia, a citizen of no unimportant city. Please allow me to speak to the people." 40 The commander gave him permission, so Paul stood on the steps and motioned to the people with his hand. The people became silent and Paul spoke to them in Aramaic.

---

3. Paul's Address
21:37–22:21

Paul is now a prisoner of Rome, and he remains a prisoner from this point in Acts to the end of the book. Yet by being in Roman custody, Paul takes his first steps on his way to the capital of the empire. Even though he is in chains, he eventually fulfills his intention to visit Rome (see 19:21).

Rome constituted the hub of the empire from which roads, like spokes issuing from the hub of a wheel, extended to the ends of the world. Accordingly, for Paul to reach Rome meant to fulfill the missionary mandate Jesus gave the apostles: "You will be my witnesses both in Jerusalem, in all Judea and Samaria, and to the ends of the earth" (1:8).

a. Request
21:37–40

37. When Paul was about to be brought into the barracks, he asked the commander, "May I say something to you?" And the commander ex-

---

58. Robertson, *Grammar*, p. 747.

claimed, "Do you know Greek? 38. Then you are not the Egyptian who some time ago started a revolt and led four thousand assassins into the desert?"

a. "Paul was about to be brought into the barracks." Having taken an interest in Paul, the commander stays next to him. His soldiers have prevented the multitude from climbing the steps and Paul is shielded from the brutal force of the mob. While the officers and soldiers are still on the steps outside the barracks, Paul, using excellent Greek, addresses a question to the commander.

b. "May I say something to you?" The commander is surprised to hear Paul speak fluent Greek and to be addressed courteously, for he had supposed Paul was an Egyptian Jew and a criminal. Further, the commander's attempt to make inquiries in the Court of the Gentiles had proved to be futile. Without giving Paul an answer, the commander reveals his amazement and in turn asks an obvious question, "Do you know Greek?" He probably wants to know whether Paul's native tongue is Greek and where he learned the language.

c. "Then you are not the Egyptian." The rhetorical question the officer poses demands a positive answer. He knows that the native tongue of an Egyptian Jew would be Greek. But Paul is not the Egyptian the commander has in mind, that is, the one who started a rebellion against Rome and led some four thousand dagger-carrying men into the desert a few years earlier.

d. "[The Egyptian] who some time ago started a revolt." Josephus relates that an imposter from Egypt who claimed to be a prophet had led a band of thirty thousand people from the desert to the Mount of Olives. This imposter claimed that at his command the walls of Jerusalem would fall. He intended to overthrow the Roman garrison in Fortress Antonia and then become a tyrant. But Governor Felix heard about the uprising and sent out his cavalry. His soldiers killed numerous Jews and made many others captives (compare 5:36). The Egyptian and a few followers escaped.[59]

e. "And led four thousand assassins into the desert." The discrepancy in numbers between Josephus's account and that of Acts probably stems from a scribal error. In ancient manuscripts, numbers are signified by abbreviated letter forms, whereby in Greek a capital D (Δ) equals four and a capital L (Λ) represents thirty. In Greek, the difference is only a short stroke of the pen.[60]

During the administration of Governor Felix, a terrorist group known as the Sicarii engaged in selective assassinations of Jewish leaders friendly toward the Romans. These assassins derived their name from the *sica* (dagger) which they concealed in their flowing robes.[61] Especially during Jewish festivals, they mingled with the crowds, swiftly struck down their opponents, joined the mourners, and thus escaped detection.

---

59. Josephus *War* 2.13.1 [261–63]; *Antiquities* 20.8.1 [169–72].
60. Lake and Cadbury, *Beginnings*, vol. 4, p. 277.
61. Josephus *Antiquities* 20.8.10 [186]. See Schürer, *History of the Jewish People*, vol. 1, p. 463; Terence L. Donaldson, "Zealot," *ISBE*, vol. 4, p. 1178.

No wonder the commander wants to know Paul's identity. He realizes that Paul is not a notorious murderer but an educated person from abroad.

39. Paul replied, "I am a Jew of Tarsus in Cilicia, a citizen of no unimportant city. Please allow me to speak to the people."

Standing on the steps with a seething mob below in the Court of the Gentiles, Paul wisely refrains from giving a lengthy explanation of his identity. He merely discloses that he is a Jew born in Tarsus in the province of Cilicia. Then he adds by way of clarification, "a citizen of no unimportant city." Paul's comment was not trifling; Tarsus was the capital of Cilicia (9:11; 22:3; 23:34) and a university city that ranked with Athens. It was known as the seat of learning for Stoic philosophers.[62]

The commander, however, is unimpressed by Paul's assertion that he hails from no insignificant city in Asia Minor. But when Paul subsequently reveals that he is a Roman citizen, the officer is intrigued and informs Paul that he paid a large sum of money to obtain his citizenship (22:28). Paul states that he was born a Roman citizen.

Paul asks permission to address the milling crowd below. By doing so, he identifies himself with the people who only moments earlier had tried to kill him. To address these unruly people shows boldness and character. Hence, Paul's request gains him the commander's respect, and the officer readily grants permission.

40. The commander gave him permission, so Paul stood on the steps and motioned to the people with his hand. The people became silent and Paul spoke to them in Aramaic.

When Paul receives permission to speak to the crowd, he motions to the crowd (see 12:17; 13:16; 19:33). And the crowd, seeing the gesture, gradually becomes silent and is ready to listen to what Paul has to say.

Paul shows tact and skill by addressing the crowd in Aramaic, the vernacular of the Jewish people. He wants to address the Jews to acquaint them with his background, training, conversion, and calling. For that reason, he communicates in the language of the people to gain their confidence in him. He takes this opportunity to tell the Jews about Jesus.

Greek Words, Phrases, and Constructions in 21:37–40

Verse 37

εἰ—when this particle introduces a direct question, it does not need to be translated (see 19:2).

γινώσκεις—the verb *to know* in this context means "to understand." However,

---

62. Refer to E. M. Blaiklock, *Cities of the New Testament* (Westwood, N.J.: Revell, 1965), p. 21; Ramsay, *St. Paul the Traveller*, pp. 31–32; and see Colin J. Hemer, "Tarsus," *ISBE*, vol. 4, pp. 734–36.

Lake and Cadbury assert that the present infinitive λαλεῖν should be added after γινώσκεις: "Do you know how to speak Greek?"[63]

Verses 39–40

μὲν . . . δέ—notice the contrast in this verse. With the particle μέν Paul answers the commander's question, and with δέ he poses a question.

σιγῆς—the genitive absolute construction: "when there was great silence." Luke corroborates this statement in the next chapter by saying: "they became even more quiet" (22:2).

Summary of Chapter 21

After leaving the Ephesian elders at Miletus, Paul and his companions board ship and sail via Cos and Rhodes to Patara. From there they cross over to Tyre, where they stay for a week with the Christians. These believers urge Paul not to go to Jerusalem, but he tells them that the Spirit compels him to do so. Before he leaves, they pray together on the beach. Afterward Paul and his associates go aboard ship and travel to Ptolemais and Caesarea. In Caesarea they are the guests of Philip the evangelist, whose four daughters prophesy.

The prophet Agabus travels from Judea to Caesarea with a prophecy for Paul. He takes Paul's belt, which he ties around his own hands and feet, and says that the Jews in Jerusalem will bind the owner of this belt and hand him over to the Gentiles. Even though his friends tearfully plead with him not to go to Jerusalem, Paul is determined to go for the sake of Jesus Christ. He and his friends leave Caesarea, stop overnight at the home of Mnason, and arrive in Jerusalem the following day.

The Christians in Jerusalem warmly welcome Paul, who meets with James and the elders of the church the following day. He reports all that God has done through his ministry. The elders advise him to dispel the rumors that he teaches the Jews in dispersion not to circumcise their children. They tell him to pay the expenses for four men who have made a Nazirite vow. By doing this, they say, everybody will know that the rumors they have heard are false.

Paul follows the elders' advice and submits to purification rites in the temple. Some Jews from the province of Asia see him there and seize him. They loudly call for help by saying that Paul has defiled the temple. They drag him from the temple and try to kill him. The Roman commander receives word that the whole city of Jerusalem is in an uproar. Backed by about two hundred soldiers, the commander arrests Paul and has him bound with two chains. As they ascend the steps to the barracks, Paul asks for permission to address the people. When the commander gives permission, Paul addresses them in Aramaic, the vernacular.

---

63. Lake and Cadbury, *Beginnings*, vol. 4, p. 276.

22

In Jerusalem and Caesarea, *part 2*

22:1–30

Outline (continued)

22:1–5	b. Training
22:6–11	c. Conversion
22:12–16	d. Restoration
22:17–21	e. Assignment
22:22–23:11	4. Paul's Trial
22:22–29	a. Appeal
22:30	b. Accusation

22 1 "Men, brothers and fathers, now listen to my defense before you." 2 When they heard Paul speak in Aramaic, they became even more quiet. He said: 3 "I am a Jew, born in Tarsus of Cilicia, but brought up in this city, and educated at Gamaliel's feet in the strict manner of the law of our fathers, being zealous for God just like all of you are today. 4 I persecuted the adherents of this Way to their death by binding both men and women and putting them in prisons. 5 Indeed, even the high priest and the whole council of elders can testify on my behalf that I received letters from them for the brothers in Damascus. I went there to bring those who were prisoners to Jerusalem to be punished."

Although the audience that Paul addresses from the steps of Fortress Antonia is Jewish, it is divided into Christians and non-Christians. He knows that both groups are zealous for the law (21:20). He also knows that both the Jews and the Christians in Jerusalem think that he teaches against the Jewish race, the law, and the temple (21:28). He wants to tell these people that he is one of them in race, training, and, as far as the Christians are concerned, in conversion. And he wishes to inform them about his commission as apostle to the Gentiles.

The accusations against Paul parallel those against Stephen, who was accused of speaking against God, the law, and the temple (6:11–14). Stephen defended himself by tracing Israel's history to show that the charges were unfounded; Paul recounts his personal history to prove the genuineness of his roots and his devotion to his Lord. In his speech, Paul refrains from absolving himself of the charge of desecrating the temple. Instead, the climax of his oration comes in his reference to the divine command to work among the Gentiles.[1]

Paul addresses the crowd in Aramaic, the vernacular of the Jewish people. From his writings, we infer that Luke was able to understand Aramaic sufficiently to translate Paul's speech into Greek. In addition, he was familiar with Paul's history, which he as a travel companion had heard a number of times from the apostle's lips. Accordingly, Luke encountered no difficulties in reconstructing the speech and accurately presented its content.

---

1. Consult Martin Dibelius, *Studies in the Acts of the Apostles* (London: SCM, 1956), p. 160.

b. Training
22:1–5

1. "Men, brothers and fathers, now listen to my defense before you."
The Jews who only moments earlier had intended to kill Paul now hear
him address them respectfully as brothers and fathers. To their amazement, Paul establishes rapport with them, not only by speaking in Aramaic
but also by saying that he is a son of the Jewish people. Paul shows respect
by using the word *fathers* (see 7:2); he calls his listeners brothers and fathers
and requests that they listen to his word of explanation.

Paul asks the assembled crowd to listen to his "defense," and with the use
of that term he by implication turns the situation into a court case. However, he fails to state the accusations against him and he ignores the
charges. Yet the Greek construction (verb and noun) here translated "defense" appears again in the speeches Paul makes before Felix and before
Festus and Agrippa.[2] In other words, Paul definitely considers his speech a
defense of his work, namely, the proclamation of the gospel to the Gentiles.
The apostle's speech is not a defense before a Roman commander, even if
Paul is his prisoner, but a justification of his work in the presence of his own
people, the Jews.[3]

**2. When they heard Paul speak in Aramaic, they became even more
quiet. He said: 3. "I am a Jew, born in Tarsus of Cilicia, but brought up in
this city, and educated at Gamaliel's feet in the strict manner of the law of
our fathers, being zealous for God just like all of you are today."**
Note these points:

a. *Language.* Paul wisely addresses the crowd in Aramaic, the vernacular
in Israel. He seeks to establish rapport with the people and, when they hear
Aramaic words coming from his lips, they listen. They believe that a Jew
from the Dispersion who speaks fluent Aramaic deserves their attention.
Luke describes the developing scene by saying, "They became even more
quiet." Paul skillfully reaches out and now begins his speech.

b. *Nurture.* The first item Paul touches on is his identity (see Phil. 3:5). He
calls himself a Jew and adds that he was born in Tarsus (9:11; 21:39), which
was the capital of the province of Cilicia. Paul says that he is a Dispersion
Jew but then immediately adds that he was reared in the city of Jerusalem.
To be precise, his parents moved from Tarsus to Jerusalem when Paul was
a child (compare 26:4).[4] The verb *to bring up,* which occurs in verse 3, refers

---

2. See 24:10; 25:8, 16; 26:1, 2, 24. And refer to Rom. 2:15; I Cor. 9:3; II Cor. 12:19; Phil. 1:7,
16; II Tim. 4:16.

3. Consult F. W. Grosheide, *De Handelingen der Apostelen,* Kommentaar op het Nieuwe Testament series, 2 vols. (Amsterdam: Van Bottenburg, 1948), vol. 2, p. 282. However, Jacob Jervell
thinks that the object of defense is the person of Paul rather than Paul's mission to the
Gentiles, the Christian community, or the gospel. "Paulus—der Lehrer Israels. Zu den
apologetischen Paulusreden in der Apostelgeschichte," *NovT* 10 (1968): 164–90.

4. W. C. van Unnik, *Tarsus or Jerusalem: The City of Paul's Youth,* trans. George Ogg (London:
Epworth, 1962), p. 44.

to the mental and physical nurture of a child[5] but differs from the verb *to educate*. Paul grew up speaking Aramaic and possibly Greek, for "Jewish students studied Greek in Jerusalem. Greek vocabulary and concepts found lodgment in the usage of many rabbis."[6]

c. *Education.* In Jerusalem, Paul continues, "[I was] educated at Gamaliel's feet in the strict manner of the law of our fathers." His teacher was Rabban Gamaliel the Elder, who was highly revered (see 5:34–39). He also was a teacher with the greatest respect for the law, so that after his death the rabbis used to say: "From the time that Rabban Gamaliel the Elder died, respect for the Torah ceased; and purity and abstinence died at the same time."[7] When Paul received his education, he and his fellow students would sit on the floor while their teacher sat on a platform. They literally sat at his feet.

As Paul mentions Gamaliel's name and reveals that he has been trained by this renowned teacher of the law, his words are effective. The Jews see him as a Pharisee and an expert in the law of their spiritual forefathers (see Gal. 1:14).

d. *Zeal.* Paul proceeds, calling himself a zealot for God and then adding, "just like all of you are today." The word *zealot* has overtones of "persecutor." Paul reflects on the zeal he had before his conversion, when he persecuted the church and thought that he was doing God a service (Phil. 3:6; compare John 16:2). As he writes concerning the Jews in his epistle to the Romans, "For I testify to them that they have a zeal for God but a zeal which is not on the basis of knowledge" (10:2).[8] Paul is direct and frank, stating that the Jews he is addressing, both Christian and non-Christian, have that same type of ill-directed zeal. They displayed their zeal for God moments earlier when they wanted to kill Paul in the Court of the Gentiles. Paul is not accusing them, for he knows that their zeal results from ignorance (see 3:17).

4. "I persecuted the adherents of this Way to their death by binding both men and women and putting them in prisons."

Paul now recalls his sinful past (see 8:3; 9:2). For a time, he was a persecutor who tried to destroy the church (Gal. 1:23). But notice that Paul uses the phrase *adherents of this Way* to describe the members of the church. Paul

---

5. Bauer, p. 62. The punctuation in this verse is decisive if we distinguish between the verbs *to bring up* and *to educate*. A few translations, however, take the verbs as synonyms: "brought up in this city at the feet of Gamaliel, educated according to the strict manner of the law of our fathers" (RSV; and see NKJV, ASV).

6. Everett F. Harrison, "Acts 22:3—A Test Case for Luke's Reliability," in *New Dimensions in New Testament Study*, ed. Richard N. Longenecker and Merrill C. Tenney (Grand Rapids: Zondervan, 1974), p. 256. See also Emil Schürer, *The History of the Jewish People in the Age of Jesus Christ (175 B.C.–A.D. 135)*, rev. and ed. Geza Vermes and Fergus Millar, 3 vols. (Edinburgh: Clark, 1973–87), vol. 2, p. 78.

7. Mishnah *Sota* 9.15. Consult SB, vol. 2, p. 763; Schürer, *History of the Jewish People*, vol. 2, p. 368.

8. Hans-Christoph Hahn, *NIDNTT*, vol. 3, p. 1167.

reverts to this name because it was among the earliest designations for the believers. He wants his audience to realize that he is speaking about events that occurred more than twenty years ago (9:2; and compare 19:9, 23; 24:14, 22).

"I persecuted [them] to their death." What the Jews in Paul's audience tried to do to him, Paul actually did to the early Christians. Paul openly and honestly confesses his sin of killing innocent men and women. Some scholars are of the opinion that Paul consented only to the death of Stephen (8:1a).[9] But this is hardly correct if we consider Paul's additional explanation before King Agrippa: "And this is just what I did in Jerusalem: not only did I lock up many of the saints in prisons because I received authority from the chief priests, but also I cast my vote against them when they were put to death" (26:10). Paul says that he bound both men and women and delivered them to prisons. This is a direct reference to the persecution that followed the death of Stephen. Luke reports that at that time Paul went from house to house and dragged off to prison both men and women (8:3).

In the church, men and women were active participants, as is evident from the greetings Paul conveys to the church at Rome (Rom. 16:3–23; see also Phil. 4:2–3; Col. 4:15; Philem. 1–2); in the temple and the synagogues men were prominent in religious matters. Yet when Paul behaved as a blind zealot, he made no distinctions and imprisoned both men and women.

5. "Indeed, even the high priest and the whole council of elders can testify on my behalf that I received letters from them for the brothers in Damascus. I went there to bring those who were prisoners to Jerusalem to be punished."

a. "Indeed, even the high priest." Granted that Paul left Jerusalem more than two decades earlier, some people in the crowd should be able to recall the times when the high priest and the council of elders commissioned Paul to persecute Christians in other cities. We know that when Paul refers to the high priest, he has in mind Caiaphas, who served in that capacity from A.D. 18 to 36 (see the commentary on 4:6 and 9:1). From Luke's account we learn that at the moment of Paul's address to his Jewish audience, Ananias, an exceptionally cruel man, was high priest (23:2). We surmise that this person who belonged to a high-ranking priestly family would have been present when Paul persecuted the Christians.

b. "And the whole council of elders can testify." The expression *council of elders* is another name for the Sanhedrin, which approved the task Caiaphas gave to Paul (compare Luke 22:66).[10] The Sanhedrin exercised its authority to send Paul to Damascus to arrest Jewish Christians and bring them as prisoners to the high priest.[11] Even if the present leaders of the Sanhedrin

---

9. Refer, e.g., to Lake and Cadbury, *Beginnings*, vol. 4, p. 279.
10. Lothar Coenen, *NIDNTT*, vol. 1, pp. 196–97. The Christians also used the term (I Tim. 4:14).
11. See also Schürer, *History of the Jewish People*, vol. 2, pp. 198, 218.

fail to recall Paul's former position, the records should indicate that at one time he was in the employ of the high priest.

c. "I received letters from them for the brothers in Damascus." Paul says that he went to Damascus with letters authorized by the Sanhedrin and addressed to the brothers there. Specifically, these brothers were leaders in the synagogues in Damascus (9:2); with other Jews they afterward plotted to kill him (9:23).

d. "I went there to bring those who were prisoners to Jerusalem to be punished." The Christians driven from Jerusalem after Stephen's death traveled to Judea, Samaria, Phoenicia, Antioch, and Cyprus (8:1b; 11:19). We presume that they also settled in Damascus. But not every believer in Damascus was a refugee, because the devout Ananias received reports about the persecution in Jerusalem (9:13). Paul recalls that he was on his way to Damascus to arrest Christians and bring them bound to Jerusalem, where they were to be punished. He uses the imperfect tense of the verb *to journey* to indicate that he was unable to complete his mission.

Practical Considerations in 22:1–5

Verses 1–3

When proclaiming or teaching the Word of God, the pastor should exercise tact and diplomacy. However difficult he may find the adjustment to a culture or a situation in which God has placed him, he ought to learn to address the people in words that touch their hearts. In communicating the gospel effectively, he must strive to gain a point of contact with the audience.

Verses 4–5

Throughout his Gospel, Luke shows no partiality; he mentions both men and women (e.g., Zechariah and Elizabeth, Joseph and Mary, Simeon and Anna). In Acts, Luke continues the theme of equality: the women and the apostles (1:13–14), Ananias and Sapphira (5:1–10), Aeneas and Dorcas (9:32–42), Aquila and Priscilla (18:2), Felix and Drusilla (24:24), Agrippa and Bernice (25:23).

The fact that Luke relates the account of Paul's conversion three times is sufficient proof that Paul freely admitted his part in persecuting the church. When he became a believer, he realized that he would suffer persecution for the sake of the Lord Jesus Christ. Even though this persecution came chiefly from the Jews, he still called them brothers.

Greek Words, Phrases, and Constructions in 22:1–5

Verses 1–2

μου—this unemphatic pronoun should be taken with the noun ἀπολογίας (defense) and not with the verb ἀκούω (to hear). The position of the pronoun is due to

783

the Greek custom of placing unemphatic pronouns as close as possible to the beginning of the sentence.[12]

Ἑβραΐδι—although the word means "Hebrew," the term in context refers to the Aramaic language spoken in Palestine (see 21:40; 26:14).

Verse 3

τῆς Κιλικίας—this noun ("Cilicia") is a descriptive genitive of place.[13]

ἀνατεθραμμένος—the perfect passive participle of ἀνατρέφω (I rear) discloses that Paul spent his youth in Jerusalem. The perfect tense shows lasting action.

ὑπάρχων—the participle in the present tense is a substitute for the present participle of εἰμί (I am).

Verse 5

μαρτυρεῖ—the context demands the use of the auxiliary verb *can,* that is, "the high priest can testify." Western witnesses add the noun Ἀνανίας (Ananias) after the term *high priest,* but the insertion is influenced by and derived from the next chapter (23:2).

ἄξων—the future participle of ἄγω (I lead, bring) expresses purpose.

---

6 "While I was on my way and approaching Damascus about noon, suddenly a bright light from heaven flashed around me. 7 I fell to the ground and heard a voice saying to me, 'Saul, Saul, why do you persecute me?' 8 But I asked, 'Who are you, Lord?' And he said to me, 'I am Jesus of Nazareth, whom you are persecuting.' 9 They who were with me saw the light but did not understand the voice of him who was speaking to me. 10 I asked, 'What shall I do, Lord?' And the Lord said to me, 'Get up and go to Damascus and there you will be told everything that has been arranged for you to do.' 11 Since I could not see because of the brightness of the light, my companions led me by the hand and I entered Damascus."

---

c. Conversion
22:6–11

6. "While I was on my way and approaching Damascus about noon, suddenly a bright light from heaven flashed around me. 7. I fell to the ground and heard a voice saying to me, 'Saul, Saul, why do you persecute me?' "

Paul relates his conversion experience; this account (22:6–11) differs from the earlier narrative (9:3–9) only in minor details. Paul reports that he was on his way to Damascus, and when he was approaching the city at about noon, he suddenly saw a bright light from heaven blazing around him. The addition in this account is the reference to time: "about noon."

---

12. Friedrich Blass and Albert Debrunner, *A Greek Grammar of the New Testament and Other Early Christian Literature,* trans. and rev. Robert Funk (Chicago: University of Chicago Press, 1961), #473.1.
13. A. T. Robertson, *A Grammar of the Greek New Testament in the Light of Historical Research* (Nashville: Broadman, 1934), p. 497.

When Paul speaks about a bright light flashing from heaven, he communicates to his Jewish audience that he experienced a divine encounter. The Jews knew from the Scriptures that light proceeds from God (Ps. 4:6; 44:3; 89:15) and that it is a feature God employs to reveal himself (see, e.g., Exod. 13:21–22; Neh. 9:12; Ps. 104:2; Dan. 2:22; Hab. 3:4).[14] In fact, the light of God's self-disclosure supersedes created light. In his speech before Agrippa, Paul says that the light which enveloped him was brighter than the sun (26:13).

Paul asserts that he was converted to Christianity not because believers persuaded him but because Jesus stopped him near Damascus. He recalls that he fell to the ground and heard a voice addressing him twice by his Hebrew name, Saul. From their knowledge of Scripture, the Jews knew that when God calls people, he often repeats their name. For instance, from the burning bush God said: "Moses, Moses" (Exod. 3:4), and in the tabernacle God called the boy Samuel and said: "Samuel, Samuel" (I Sam. 3:10). Paul, therefore, indicates that he was divinely called. The voice asked, "Why do you persecute me?"

8. "But I asked, 'Who are you, Lord?' And he said to me, 'I am Jesus of Nazareth, whom you are persecuting.' "

While he was blinded by the light, lying on the ground, and hearing a heavenly voice asking him a question—Paul remembers—he kept a clear mind. The voice that addressed Paul asked him why he was victimizing the speaker. Paul had to answer by asking the voice to identify himself. Thus he inquired, "Who are you, Lord?" And the surprising answer came back to him, "I am Jesus of Nazareth, whom you are persecuting." Note that in his address to the Jews, Paul mentions the clarifying noun *Nazareth*, which is lacking in the other two accounts (9:5; 26:15). In Acts, the appellation *Jesus of Nazareth* appears frequently and is the name by which Jesus was known to believing and unbelieving Jews.[15]

The Jews listening to Paul know that Jesus called him from heaven and indicated twice that Paul persecuted him. Paul refrains from further identifying Jesus but leaves the distinct impression that Jesus is divine. The Jews also learn from the dialogue between Jesus and Paul that Jesus completely identifies with the believers. Paul continues his account and says,

9. "They who were with me saw the light but did not understand the voice of him who was speaking to me."

The travel companions of Paul witnessed the brilliant light and saw Paul lying on the ground. Although they observed the phenomenon, the light did not blind them as it did Paul. Further, they heard a voice speaking but did not understand it, even though the voice addressed Paul in Aramaic (26:14). The voice was unintelligible to them. They were speechless because

---

14. Hans-Christoph Hahn and Colin Brown, *NIDNTT*, vol. 2, pp. 491, 495.
15. See 2:22; 3:6; 4:10; 6:14; 22:8; 26:9; and refer to 24:5.

of fright (9:7; see the commentary for a discussion).[16] Not they but Paul understood Jesus' words that led to Paul's conversion.

10. "I asked, 'What shall I do, Lord?' And the Lord said to me, 'Get up and go to Damascus and there you will be told everything that has been arranged for you to do.' "

The earlier account (9:5–7) differs slightly from the description Paul gives before his Jewish audience, for he supplies them with additional information. First, Paul relates that the men who accompanied him "saw the light." Next, Paul reveals a continued dialogue with Jesus. He asked him, "What shall I do, Lord?" This question and the sentence that introduces Jesus' response are lacking in the first report of Paul's conversion. And last, the instructions Jesus gave are more detailed in the second account than in the first. The clause *everything that has been arranged for you* has been added.

Three times in two verses (vv. 8, 10), Paul employs the term *Lord,* by which he demonstrates his respect for Jesus. At the same time, numerous persons in Paul's audience were Christian Jews (compare 21:20). Paul knows that he and they share a mode of addressing Jesus. But in order not to provoke the unbelieving Jews, he refrains from using the name *Jesus* and employs the expression *Lord* instead.

The Lord is fully in control of the calling and conversion of Paul, for already he has arranged a task for him. The clause *everything that has been arranged for you* signifies that Jesus has planned a career of service for Paul.[17] The tense of the Greek verb indicates that the arrangements had been made in the past but were put into effect at the time of Paul's conversion. That is, Jesus appointed Paul to be his servant and witness (26:16) and would send him forth as an apostle to the Gentiles (9:15).

11. "Since I could not see because of the brightness of the light, my companions led me by the hand and I entered Damascus."

Paul continues his account and describes being blinded by the brilliant light that had flashed around him (9:3). In this verse, he briefly reports his blindness and his dependence on his travel companions. Luke's earlier description, with minor variations, is the same in meaning (9:8). But Luke divulges that Paul was blind for three days and that during that time he fasted (9:9). Paul himself deletes this detail from his narrative. To be stricken with blindness, according to Scripture, was one of the curses God pronounced on the disobedient (Deut. 28:15, 28–29). But this does not apply to Paul, as he receives further instruction from the Lord in Damascus.

---

16. The Western and Majority texts feature an expansion. After the words *saw the light,* they add "and were afraid" (KJV, NKJV). Translators must decide whether the phrase was accidentally omitted from the text or was added. Most favor the second choice.

17. Consult J. I. Packer, *NIDNTT,* vol. 1, p. 476.

Greek Words, Phrases, and Constructions in 22:6–11

Verse 6

μοι—"for me." The case is a dative of advantage, followed by the descriptive present participles πορευομένῳ (going) and ἐγγίζοντι (approaching).

περὶ μεσημβρίαν—see the comment at 8:26.

Verse 7

ἤκουσα φωνῆς—"The class[ical] rule of the gen[itive] for the persons whom we hear, and the acc[usative] for the persons or things about whom or which we hear, is applied even more systematically in the N[ew] T[estament], where the acc[usative] tends to replace the more common class[ical] gen[itive] even in the case of hearing a sound, though the latter still occurs."[18]

Verse 10

τί ποιήσω—the deliberative subjunctive instead of the future indicative: "What am I to do?"

ἀναστάς—although the participle with a finite verb normally means "to get ready," for Paul lying prostrate on the ground the word has a literal connotation: "get up."

τέτακται—from τάσσω (I appoint), the perfect shows an action in the past with lasting results for the present.

Verse 11

ἀπό—in context, this preposition has a causal sense: "because of the brightness of the light."

---

12 "Someone named Ananias came to me. He was a devout man according to the law and respected by all the Jews living there. 13 He stood next to me and said, 'Brother Saul, receive your sight!' And I looked at him that very moment. 14 Ananias said: 'The God of our fathers has appointed you to know his will and to see the Righteous One and to hear a message from his mouth, 15 because you will be a witness for him to all men of the things you have seen and heard. 16 And now why are you delaying? Get up, be baptized, and wash away your sins by calling on his name.' "

---

d. Restoration
22:12–16

12. "Someone named Ananias came to me. He was a devout man according to the law and respected by all the Jews living there. 13. He stood next to me and said, 'Brother Saul, receive your sight!' And I looked at him that very moment."

---

18. Gerhard Kittel, *TDNT*, vol. 1, p. 216.

Once again, Paul is more concise than Luke in his account concerning Ananias. Luke describes Ananias's vision in which Jesus gave him the necessary information about Paul (9:10–16). By contrast, Paul reviews the incident from his own point of view. He remembers that a certain man named Ananias visited him. The name *Ananias* was rather common in Judaism, as is evident from Acts (see 5:1; 23:2) and apocryphal literature (which often lists the name with variant spellings).[19] Paul shrewdly relates that Ananias "was a devout man according to the law and respected by all the Jews living there." He desists from calling him a disciple or a follower of the Way. Instead he describes Ananias in terms that sound pleasing in the ears of a Jewish audience and are intended to place the entire conversion episode in a favorable light.[20]

Ananias devoutly kept the law, says Paul, so that in the city of Damascus he was highly respected by the Jewish residents. Paul emphasizes this point to show that Ananias, even though a Christian, was a law-abiding Jew in good standing with his fellow Jews. Incidentally, in a later verse Paul describes himself as a traditional Jew who worshiped in the temple (v. 17).

Paul recalls that Ananias came and "stood next to [him]." He disregards the fear that Ananias had to overcome to approach the persecutor of believers. Rather, Paul portrays his visitor as one who merely spoke the words, "Brother Saul, receive your sight," and Paul could see again. As Paul tells the story in a Jewish context, the word *brother* intimates the close bond between two Jews. Moreover, the audience realized that when Ananias spoke the word for Paul to regain his sight, a miracle occurred. From the prophecy of Isaiah they had learned that the coming Messiah would open the eyes of the blind (Isa. 35:5). And Jesus during his ministry had frequently healed the blind (e.g., Matt. 9:28–30; 11:5; 20:30–34). In brief, through the words of Ananias, Jesus restored Paul's sight. For apologetic purposes, however, Paul omits the words Luke recounts in the first report of Paul's conversion: "Brother Saul, the Lord Jesus, who appeared to you on the road by which you were coming, has sent me so that you may regain your sight and be filled with the Holy Spirit" (9:17). Now Paul uses a typical Jewish phrase, "the God of our fathers," which indirectly yet clearly refers to the Messiah.

14. "Ananias said: 'The God of our fathers has appointed you to know his will and to see the Righteous One and to hear a message from his mouth, 15. because you will be a witness for him to all men of the things you have seen and heard.' "

Reciting the words of Ananias, Paul explains what the Lord has arranged for him to do. By employing the expression *the God of our fathers*, Paul continues to affirm his Jewish identity. He demonstrates that the God who

---

19. I Esd. 5:16; 9:21, 29, 43, 48; Tob. 5:12; Song of the Three Young Men 66.
20. Lake and Cadbury, *Beginnings*, vol. 4, p. 280.

dealt graciously with the forefathers is the same God who appointed and called him.[21]

The expression is a vivid reminder of the time Moses stood at the burning bush in the Sinai desert and heard God saying to him: "The LORD, the God of your fathers—the God of Abraham, the God of Isaac and the God of Jacob—has sent me to you" (Exod. 3:15, NIV). Peter also used the expression in his sermon at Solomon's Colonnade (3:13) and in his speech before the Sanhedrin (5:30). Now Paul uses these words of Ananias to convince his audience that Israel's God appointed him (see 26:16). God set Paul apart from birth, as Paul himself writes (Gal. 1:15). Accordingly, Paul recognized that in his life God was working out his plan.[22] What is this plan?

a. "To know his will." For the Jews, to know God's will meant to obey his precepts. They understood that anyone who knows God's will, but disobeys, receives just punishment. It would be better for such a person if he had never known God's will.[23] Paul had tried to do God a service by persecuting the Christians, but God told him that his divine will was entirely different. Paul had to see God's will in relation to the Righteous One.

b. "To see the Righteous One." The term *Righteous One* is a messianic title that has its origin in the books of the prophets. For instance, Isaiah says, "By his knowledge my righteous servant will justify many" (53:11).[24] The apostles recognized these prophetic passages as messianic and ascribed them to Jesus. On the way to Damascus, Paul saw the resurrected Jesus and heard his voice.

c. "To hear a message from his mouth." Indeed, God revealed the Righteous One to Paul, but Jesus gave him additional instructions. Paul had heard one message from Jesus outside Damascus, but through Ananias received another message. Revealing to his audience that Jesus had spoken to Ananias (9:15), Paul avoided using Jesus' name.

d. "Because you will be a witness for him to all men of the things you have seen and heard." On the basis of seeing and hearing Jesus, Paul became an apostle (I Cor. 9:1; compare 4:20). When he saw Jesus and heard his voice, he understood the will of God: "You will be a witness for [Jesus]." For Paul, then, proclaiming the resurrected Jesus to all men everywhere became the equivalent of doing God's will. The words *all men* are purposely general, for they could refer to all the Jews who lived in the Dispersion. But because Jesus called Paul to be the apostle to the Gentiles, in this context the term obviously is all-inclusive.

---

21. Refer to Donald Guthrie, *New Testament Theology* (Downers Grove: Inter-Varsity, 1981), p. 89.

22. Leon Morris, *New Testament Theology* (Grand Rapids: Zondervan, Academie Books, 1986), p. 173.

23. Refer to Luke 12:47; Rom. 2:12; James 4:17; II Peter 2:21.

24. See also Jer. 23:5; 33:15; Zech. 9:9. For New Testament references see Acts 3:14; 7:52; I John 2:1.

16. "And now why are you delaying? Get up, be baptized, and wash away your sins by calling on his name."

Paul fails to say that for three days he fasted and was unable to see (9:10–12). When he received his sight and heard Jesus' message from Ananias, he had to be prodded. That is, Ananias asked him why he needed still more time, for Paul himself had to make the decision to follow Jesus.[25] Paul discloses that Ananias instructed him what steps to take:

> get up
> > be baptized and
> > > wash away your sins
> > > > by calling on his name.

The verb *get up* is more idiomatic than literal and means "get ready [to be baptized]." The Jews were acquainted with Levitical baptism and that of John the Baptist.[26] Christian baptism was visibly demonstrated at Pentecost, when three thousand Jews believed and were baptized (2:41), and numerous times afterward.

When Peter answered the query of the crowd, he told them to be baptized for the forgiveness of sins in the name of Jesus Christ (2:38). Ananias likewise instructed Paul to be baptized for the purpose of cleansing himself from sin and to do so by calling on Jesus' name. By persecuting the Christians, Paul had brought injuries on the church of Jesus and consequently on Jesus himself. He could receive remission from sin only by asking Jesus to forgive him. When Paul called for pardon in the name of Jesus Christ, he in turn was baptized in that name.[27] Paul's self-conscious act of confessing his sin displayed his faith in Jesus. The external rite of baptism sealed his union with Christ. In later years, Paul told the Corinthian believers that they were washed, sanctified, and justified in the name of Jesus Christ (I Cor. 6:11).

Paul avoids using the name of Jesus when he reports Ananias's words. Yet the nearest antecedent to which the expression *his name* exegetically can refer is "the Righteous One," namely, Jesus Christ. Throughout Paul's address to the Jews he does not use the name *Jesus*, with the exception of Jesus' self-identification (v. 8). We assume that the audience was acquainted with Christian baptism and understood that Paul had been baptized.

Greek Words, Phrases, and Constructions in 22:14–16

Verse 14

γνῶναι—the content of the aorist active of the verb γινώσκω (I know) is strengthened by the meaning of the aorist infinitives ἰδεῖν (to see) and ἀκοῦσαι (to hear).

---

25. Consult James D. G. Dunn, *Baptism in the Holy Spirit*, Studies in Biblical Theology, 2d series 15 (London: SCM, 1970), p. 74.

26. Consult W. H. T. Dau, "Baptism," *ISBE*, vol. 1, p. 425.

27. G. R. Beasley-Murray, *NIDNTT*, vol. 1, p. 146.

Verse 16

βάπτισαι—the aorist imperative of βαπτίζω (I baptize) and the aorist imperative of ἀπόλουσαι (from ἀπολούω, I wash away) are causative middle verbs: "get yourself baptized and get your sins washed away."[28]

---

17 "When I returned to Jerusalem and was praying in the temple, I fell into a trance. 18 I saw the Lord speaking to me, 'Hurry, get out of Jerusalem immediately, because they will not accept your testimony about me.' 19 And I said, 'Lord, they know that from one synagogue to another I was imprisoning and beating those who believe in you. 20 When the blood of your martyr Stephen was shed, I was approving and standing by, guarding the cloaks of those who were killing him.' 21 He said to me, 'Go! Because I will send you far away to the Gentiles.' "

---

e. Assignment
22:17–21

17. "When I returned to Jerusalem and was praying in the temple, I fell into a trance. 18. I saw the Lord speaking to me, 'Hurry, get out of Jerusalem immediately, because they will not accept your testimony about me.' "

Paul excludes details relating to his preaching in the Damascus synagogues (9:20–22), his extended stay in the Arabian desert (Gal. 1:17), and his escape in a basket over the city wall of Damascus (II Cor. 11:33). He ignores details concerning his return to Jerusalem, where he experienced rejection by the Christians, who were afraid of him, and by the Jews, who plotted to kill him (9:26–29). He mentions, however, aspects of his religious life that have no parallel in either 9:26 or 26:20.

a. "When I returned to Jerusalem and was praying in the temple." Paul speaks in general without indicating when he came back to the city.[29] He reveals the successive development of "everything that has been arranged for [him] to do" (v. 10). While he was in a trance, he says, he was receiving further instructions from Jesus.

Notice that Paul places no emphasis on the time of his return. What is important to him in his current address is that he came to the temple to pray. Skillfully he introduces this fact. Paul expects his listeners to under-

---

28. Robertson, *Grammar,* p. 808.

29. Some scholars reject the suggestion that Paul refers to his first visit after his conversion. They say this because they are unable to see a parallel with other passages (9:29–30; Gal. 1:17–2:2). Hans Conzelmann avers that Paul's trance (vv. 17–21) "forms a concurrent variant to the account of the call on the way to Damascus." *Acts of the Apostles,* trans. James Limburg, A. Thomas Kraabel, and Donald H. Juel (1963; Philadelphia: Fortress, 1987), p. 187. See also E. P. Blair, who places Paul's trance and call to the Gentiles during his visit to the Jerusalem Council. "Paul's Call to the Gentile Mission," *BibRes* 10 (1965): 19–33.

But Paul provides additional details about his stay in Jerusalem that indicate it followed his conversion experience. For example, the Lord commands him to leave Jerusalem forthwith because the Jews refuse to listen to the gospel. The reference fits with the Jewish plot to kill Paul (9:29).

stand that he clearly cannot be a desecrator of the temple, because he returned to pray there.

b. "I fell into a trance." In the Greek, Luke uses the word *ekstasis,* from which we have the derivative *ecstasy.* Peter had an ecstatic experience on the flat roof of Simon's house in Joppa, when he was in prayer at noon (10:9–10), and John was in the Spirit on the Lord's Day (Rev. 1:10). The apostles experienced ecstasy when their minds became so intensely concentrated in prayer that they entered the presence of Jesus. When that happened, Jesus gave them instructions that related to their individual ministries. The apostles were not dreaming or fantasizing, but were attentive to God's power that was transmitted to them both in sight and in sound.

c. "I saw the Lord speaking to me: 'Hurry, get out of Jerusalem immediately.'" A literal rendering of the Greek is simply, "I saw him speaking to me." The pronoun *him* evidently refers to Jesus, who addressed Paul on the road near Damascus. Here, then, is Paul's confirmation that the Lord who spoke to him near Damascus is the same risen Lord who appears to him in Jerusalem. The Lord himself is protecting Paul by giving him pertinent instructions about the immediate future. He knows the dangers that lurk in Jerusalem and therefore tells Paul to leave the city at once.

d. "Because they will not accept your testimony about me." The subject is lacking in this clause, because Paul tries to soften Jesus' reproach that the Jews in Jerusalem refused to listen to the good news of salvation. But Jesus' message actually is an understatement. It expresses an affirmative thought in negative terms; the intent is to heighten the effect of the words spoken by Jesus.[30] He actually means that the Jews would reject Paul's message of salvation and, like their fathers of old who persecuted the prophets, would plot to take Paul's life.

Paul the Jew wished to preach the gospel first to his own people, especially those residing in the city of Jerusalem. For a period of two weeks, Paul boldly spoke about Jesus by debating with Greek-speaking Jews. But the Jews rejected Paul's teaching and plotted to kill him. Jesus, however, prevented him from continuing his work among the Jews. Through the intervention of Christian brothers who took Paul from Jerusalem to Caesarea and put him aboard ship to Tarsus (9:30), Jesus caused Paul's ministry among the Jerusalem Jews to cease. This does not mean that Paul would not proclaim the gospel to Jews anymore, for during his missionary journeys he followed Jesus' exhortation to preach to the Jew first and then to the Gentile (Matt. 10:5–6; and see Rom. 1:16). In his speech to the Ephesian elders at Miletus, he averred that he had testified to both Jews and Greeks to turn to God in repentance and to believe in Jesus (20:21).

---

30. John Albert Bengel, *Gnomon of the New Testament,* trans. Andrew R. Fausset, 5 vols. (Edinburgh: Clark, 1877), vol. 2, p. 698. Bengel calls this literary device a tapeinosis or litotes. Louis Berkhof explains that "the litotes affirms a thing by the negation of the opposite." *Principles of Biblical Interpretation,* 2d ed. (Grand Rapids: Baker, 1952), p. 91.

19. "And I said, 'Lord, they know that from one synagogue to another I was imprisoning and beating those who believe in you. 20. When the blood of your martyr Stephen was shed, I was approving and standing by, guarding the cloaks of those who were killing him.' "

Instead of telling his audience what he did after leaving Jerusalem, Paul relates that he was determined to stay in the city and testify to his countrymen. In Damascus Paul had preached to the Jews in the local synagogues; when he came to Jerusalem, he again went to the Jews. He intimates that he was well qualified to impart the teachings of the Christian faith to the Jews; as an expert in Jewish law he would be able to lead the citizens of Jerusalem to Christ. He felt at home with Jewish people because they knew the Scriptures. Paul was able to debate with them and had an immediate point of contact (9:29). But the Lord had informed him, through Ananias in Damascus, that he would have to preach the gospel to the Gentiles (9:15). Jesus wanted to employ Paul's gifts and talents in the Gentile world so that the church indeed might become universal.

Paul enters into a dialogue with Jesus, although he does not call Jesus by name. Instead he uses the word *Lord,* which is a general term that can also refer to God. Paul says: "Lord, the Jews know that I went from one synagogue to another imprisoning and beating those people who believe in you" (see 8:3). He implies that when Paul returned to Jerusalem, the Jews would remember him as a persecutor of Christian men and women. By saying "they know," Paul suggests that the Jews should remember his past. Only three years before his return to Jerusalem (Gal. 1:18), Paul imprisoned and beat members of the Christian church.[31] In his response to Jesus' command to leave the city, Paul uses the personal pronoun *I* three times. With the frequent use of this pronoun, he divulges that he objected to going abroad. In other words, Paul would rather have continued his teaching ministry in the city, even at the risk of losing his life.

From the verb tenses in the Greek text we learn that a sustained period of time elapsed during which Paul imprisoned and beat the Christians. He went from synagogue to synagogue, where believers were brought before councils. When the Christians were found to be guilty of confessing Jesus' name, they were flogged (compare Matt. 10:17; 23:34). Paul admits that he himself lashed these believers.

"When the blood of your martyr Stephen was shed," Paul continues, "I was approving and standing by, guarding the cloaks of those who were killing him" (see 7:58; 8:1). The death of Stephen made a lasting impression on Paul. In effect, he became Stephen's successor in reaching out to Greek-speaking Jews (compare 6:8–10 and 9:29). Paul uses the word *martyr,* which derives from the Greek verb *martyreō* (to testify, to witness). While testifying for Jesus, Stephen was killed by his accusers with full approval of

31. The verb *to know* "expresses the result of a process of perception." Günther Harder, *NIDNTT,* vol. 3, p. 122.

the Sanhedrin. Luke provides no evidence that Paul at one time was a member of that Jewish council. Instead he conveys that Paul was commissioned by the Sanhedrin to persecute Christians. In this passage, Paul confesses that he himself consented to the death of Stephen. He guarded the outer garments of the men who hurled the stones at Stephen, the first Christian martyr.

On the one hand, Paul recalls his participation in the death of Stephen to show his identity with the true law-abiding Jews who guard the purity of the Jewish faith. On the other, he uses this incident to introduce the response of Jesus. If Paul had thought that he could convince Jesus to change his instructions, Paul was sadly mistaken. Jesus had told Paul to go preach his name before the Gentiles and reiterated his unaltered command.

21. "He said to me, 'Go! because I will send you far away to the Gentiles.'"

Paul comes to the climax of his address. Avoiding the use of the name *Jesus*, Paul nevertheless ascribes to Jesus the command that he had to leave Jerusalem. The Lord would send him far away to the Gentiles. At last the word *Gentiles* comes from the lips of Paul, although originally it was spoken by the Lord. This means, of course, that Paul's charge to preach the gospel to the Gentiles came not at his own initiative but by divine command. For Paul, Jesus' message was encouraging, because Jesus himself would send him forth to the Gentiles and thus provide for his physical and spiritual well-being (compare 26:17). Moreover, Jesus specifically told Ananias that Paul was his chosen instrument to serve him as his messenger to the Gentiles (9:15). Paul is unable to delete from his report the charge which Jesus gave him.

Additional Notes on 22:1-21

The differences between the first and second accounts of Paul's conversion (9:1–19 and 22:1–21) are obvious despite the fact that Luke composed both of them. The first report is a narrative description given by Luke as he traces Paul's life. The second, even though written by Luke, is a speech Paul delivered to the Jews as he was standing on the steps of Fortress Antonia. Although we do not expect to find a word-for-word transcription, we discover that Luke faithfully presents the content of Paul's address. Consider these aspects:

a. *Jewish emphases.* That Paul addressed the Jews in their native tongue (Aramaic) is significant, but also significant are his word choices, expressions, and descriptions, which are typically Jewish. See how Paul addresses the crowd: "Men, brothers and fathers" (v. 1); the address is paralleled by Stephen, who faced the members of the Sanhedrin (7:2). Paul resorts to using Jewish terms, including "the God of our fathers" and "the Righteous One" (v. 14). He identifies himself as a Jew, born abroad but reared and educated in Jerusalem, whose name is Saul. He stresses respect for the Mosaic law and, by his reference to zeal for God, identifies with any Jew listening to his address (v. 3). He calls Ananias a devout man according to the law (v. 12) and avoids referring to him as a disciple (see 9:10). And last, he depicts himself as a Jew who goes to the temple for prayer (v. 17).

b. *Omissions*. Apart from Jesus' self-identification, "I am Jesus of Nazareth" (v. 8), Paul deliberately avoids using that name and in the Greek alludes to him with personal pronouns. He uses the Greek for "Lord" four times (vv. 8, 10 [twice], 19), but this term was also used for God and presented no offense to the Jews. In the first account of Paul's conversion, Ananias informs Paul that the Lord Jesus sent him (9:17), but in Paul's address to the Jews these words are missing. More, Jesus instructs Ananias to go to Paul, who must proclaim Jesus' name to the Gentiles (9:15). But when Paul addresses the Jews, he reports that Ananias told him: "You will be a witness for [the Righteous One] to all men of the things you have seen and heard" (v. 15). Again, the wording *all men* is inoffensive.

c. *Additions*. In his account, Paul describes his dialogue with Jesus (vv. 10, 18–21). This information is absent in Luke's earlier account (9:5–7). In the Old Testament, God encourages dialogue with his people (e.g., see Isa. 1:18). The Jews exhibit this characteristic freedom of verbal exchange: Ananias (9:10–16), Peter (10:13–15), and Paul (22:8–10, 18–21).

When Jesus says to Paul, "You will be told everything that has been arranged for you to do" (v. 10), he develops his instructions for Paul in Damascus (9:15–16) and in Jerusalem (vv. 18, 21). Jesus keeps his promise and at various times informs Paul what to do next (see 18:9–10; 23:11).

d. *Conclusion*. Luke accurately portrays Paul as the speaker who tells his conversion experience "as a second variation of the Damascus event."[32] Luke assumes that the reader recalls the details of the first account and now he reports how Paul addressed the Jews in Jerusalem. Further, Luke ends Paul's speech with the words, "I will send you far away to the Gentiles" (v. 21), because the crowd raucously prevented Paul from continuing his discourse (v. 22). Martin Dibelius calls this "intentional interruption" a literary device that Luke employs to conclude the speeches in Acts.[33] But when it is subjected to careful scrutiny, this ingenious observation hardly holds true for Paul's speech in Jerusalem. For one thing, in its conclusion this speech lacks an exhortation to the audience.[34] In light of the development of and reaction to Paul's speech, we are not persuaded to doubt its historicity but to affirm that Luke gives a true-to-fact presentation.

Greek Words, Phrases, and Constructions in 22:17–21

Verses 17–18

προσευχομένου μου—"while I was praying." Because the subject of this genitive absolute is the same as that of the main clause, the grammatical construction is faulty.

παραδέξονται—this is the predictive future of the compound verb παραδέχομαι (I accept, acknowledge) in its perfective sense. With the negative particle οὐ (not), the verb actually means "to reject, spurn."

---

32. Paul Schubert, "The Final Cycle of Speeches in the Book of Acts," *JBL* 87 (1968): 14.
33. Dibelius, *Studies in the Acts of the Apostles,* p. 160.
34. Consult Thomas L. Budesheim, "Paul's *Abschiedsrede* in the Acts of the Apostles," *HTR* 69 (1976): 16–17.

Verse 19

ἤμην—with the two present participles φυλακίζων (imprisoning) and δέρων (beating), this imperfect of the verb εἰμί (I am) is a periphrastic construction which, perhaps, reflects Aramaic syntax.

κατά—the preposition expresses the distributive idea: "from one synagogue to another."

Verses 20–21

ἐξεχύννετο—note the descriptive use of the imperfect tense ("was being shed") to heighten the effect of an eyewitness account.

μακράν—this adjective modifies the supplied noun ὁδόν (way) and functions as an accusative of extent: "far away."

---

22 They listened to Paul up to that statement. They raised their voices, shouting, "Take this fellow from the earth. He is not fit to live!" 23 They shouted, threw off their cloaks, and hurled dust into the air. 24 The commander ordered that Paul be brought into the barracks. He said Paul should be examined by scourging so that he might learn the reason for the shouting of the Jews against Paul. 25 As they stretched him out for flogging, Paul said to the officer standing nearby, "Is it lawful for you to scourge a man who is a Roman citizen without a trial?" 26 When the officer heard this, he went to the commander and asked, "What are you intending to do? This man is a Roman citizen." 27 The commander went to Paul and said, "Tell me, are you a Roman citizen?" And Paul replied, "Yes." 28 The commander declared, "I acquired my citizenship with a large sum of money." But Paul said, "I was born a citizen." 29 Those who were about to question him immediately let him go. Even the commander was afraid when he learned that Paul was a Roman citizen, because he had put him in chains.

---

4. Paul's Trial
22:22–23:11

The crowd had assembled in the courts of the temple because the Jews had spread word that Paul taught Jewish people in dispersion to live like Gentiles (21:28). They also alleged that Paul had brought Gentiles into the temple court that was off limits to them (21:29). When the crowd heard Paul say that he was sent to the Gentiles, they concluded that he himself confirmed the reports they had heard.

a. Appeal
22:22–29

22. They listened to Paul up to that statement. They raised their voices, shouting, "Take this fellow from the earth. He is not fit to live!"

The audience standing at the steps that led to the Fortress Antonia listened attentively to the words Paul spoke. Although they accepted his speech that was couched in language pleasing to their ears, they turned against him when he mentioned that he had preached to the Gentiles. This one word, Gentiles, was sufficient for them to condemn Paul as a desecrator of the temple.

In the opinion of the Jews, Paul had forsaken the truth of Judaism and could no longer be considered orthodox. They felt that in his speech he tried to hide his efforts to gain Gentile converts.[35] They had no objections to Paul teaching Gentiles about Israel's God; indeed they encouraged God-fearing Gentiles to become converts (compare Matt. 23:15). But they regarded Paul's teaching contrary to their demand that the Gentiles obey the law. When Paul alluded to his divine commission to go to the Gentiles, he infuriated his listeners. They refused to acknowledge him as a missionary for the Jewish cause. To them, Paul's statement meant that he considered Jews and Gentiles equal before God. This was totally unacceptable to Paul's audience.[36]

The Jews interrupted Paul's speech and shouted at the top of their voices: "Take this fellow from the earth. He is not fit to live!" Nearly three decades earlier, a Jewish crowd had shouted almost the same words to Pontius Pilate (Luke 23:18; John 19:15; and see Acts 21:36). The Jews refused to identify Paul by name but derisively referred to him as "this fellow" or "such a person" (lit.). Their clamor about his physical removal from this earth and unfitness to live was tantamount to demanding the death penalty (see 25:24).

23. They shouted, threw off their cloaks, and hurled dust into the air.

Luke describes a typical oriental riot during which the people give vent to their emotions. He depicts the crowd shouting (probably one slogan after another), removing articles of clothing which they were either waving or tossing into the air, and picking up dust by the handful and throwing it into the air. The entire scene was one of turmoil and utter confusion.

We suspect that the Roman commander had been unable to understand Paul's speech. Even if he had known Aramaic, he still would not have been able to follow the theological reasoning that caused the uproar among the Jewish people. Although he had personally protected Paul from physical injury and possible death, he was now at a loss to know why the Jews were upset with Paul.

24. The commander ordered that Paul be brought into the barracks. He said Paul should be examined by scourging so that he might learn the reason for the shouting of the Jews against Paul.

When the commander realized that the crowd became increasingly hostile, he ordered his soldiers to take Paul into the barracks. By removing Paul from sight, he sought to end the riot. As commander of the armed forces in Jerusalem, he was responsible for maintaining the peace.

---

35. Refer to Lake and Cadbury, *Beginnings*, vol. 4, pp. 281–82.
36. Grosheide, *Handelingen der Apostelen*, vol. 2, pp. 296–97. A. J. Mattill, Jr., points out that the Jewish Christians from Judea and Galilee "may have been even more zealous for the Law than those of Jerusalem." See "The Purpose of Acts: Schneckenburg Reconsidered," in *Apostolic History and the Gospel*, ed. W. Ward Gasque and Ralph P. Martin (Exeter: Paternoster; Grand Rapids: Eerdmans, 1970), p. 116.

Perhaps the commander resented Paul's decision to address the crowd in Aramaic and not in Greek. Neither from the Jews nor from Paul had he learned the cause of the riot. Yet he had to discover what the sources of discontent were, so that he could take measures to deal with possible eruptions in the future.

The Roman officer commanded his soldiers to scourge Paul, for he assumed that when they applied the whip, Paul would answer questions about why the crowd was shouting at him (compare 21:34). Roman law permitted scourging as a means to question a lawbreaker or to punish slaves or criminals. The scourge was made of leather straps to which pieces of bone or metal were attached. Consequently, when the whip was applied to victims, they were often left with open wounds that exposed their bones.[37] At times the victims died on the spot or soon afterward.

25. As they stretched him out for flogging, Paul said to the officer standing nearby, "Is it lawful for you to scourge a man who is a Roman citizen without a trial?"

Paul realized that once more he was in mortal danger. According to his own testimony (II Cor. 11:23–25), he had been flogged more severely than any other apostle (compare Acts 5:40) and had repeatedly faced death. He recalled that on five different occasions he had received the thirty-nine lashes from the Jews as prescribed by the rabbis (see Deut. 25:1–3). These floggings probably were meted out in Jewish synagogues where Paul preached the gospel and met opposition. In three other instances, he had received severe beatings with rods—one of them in Philippi (16:22–23).

a. "As they stretched him out for flogging." The construction of this clause in the Greek allows for two interpretations. The clause can mean that either the soldiers stretched Paul's arms around a pole and exposed his back for a flogging or, tying his hands with thongs, hoisted him from the ground to administer the whipping. In either translation, the result remains the same.

b. "Is it lawful for you to scourge a man who is a Roman citizen without a trial?" Roman law exempted citizens from scourging, although in the days of Cicero a Roman citizen was beaten to death. But such procedures were highly unusual.[38] Roman citizens possessed inalienable rights that generally were strictly observed. Says Cicero, "To bind a Roman citizen is a crime, to flog him is an abomination, to slay him is almost an act of murder: to crucify him is—what? There is no fitting word that can possibly describe so horrible a deed."[39]

The laws protecting the rights of Roman citizens had been enacted dur-

---

37. Josephus *War* 2.21.5 [612]; 6.5.3 [304]. Consult David W. Wead, "Scourge," *ISBE*, vol. 4, p. 359.

38. Livy 10.9.4. Consult Conzelmann, *Acts*, p. 189; A. N. Sherwin-White, *Roman Society and Roman Law in the New Testament* (1963; reprint ed., Grand Rapids: Baker, 1968), p. 172; Mark Black, "Paul and Roman Law in Acts," *ResQ* 24 (1981): 209–18.

39. Cicero *Against Verres* 2.5.66 (LCL); see also *In Defence of Rabirius* 4:12–13.

ing the centuries preceding the apostolic age. In the days of Paul, these Roman laws were applied in all the provinces throughout the empire. Paul objected to being scourged without a trial; thus, he invoked these laws to his own advantage and stated that he was a Roman citizen. In later years he exercised his right to appeal to Caesar (25:11). By contrast, when both Paul and Silas were beaten with rods in Philippi (16:22–23), they did not invoke their rights as Roman citizens but suffered for the sake of the local congregation (16:37–40).

26. When the officer heard this, he went to the commander and asked, "What are you intending to do? This man is a Roman citizen."

The centurion in charge of the scourging understood the implications of Paul's question and rushed to Claudius Lysias. We assume that in some manner Paul could prove his Roman citizenship (see the commentary on 16:38). The evidence was sufficient for the centurion to halt the proceedings and to ask his superior whether he knew what he was doing. When the officer mentioned the expression *Roman citizen*, the commander went straight to Paul. To apply the scourge to a Roman citizen without giving him a proper trial would place the commander in serious difficulties with his superiors. He could be demoted or dismissed from the military.

27. The commander went to Paul and said, "Tell me, are you a Roman citizen?" And Paul replied, "Yes." 28. The commander declared, "I acquired my citizenship with a large sum of money." But Paul said, "I was born a citizen."

Roman citizenship could be obtained in various ways: being rewarded for a service rendered to Rome, purchasing the right, or being born into a family that possessed the privilege and passed it on to their children. The conversation between the Roman commander and the Jewish prisoner hinged on the expression *Roman citizen*. Claudius Lysias asked Paul whether he was able to claim this status. When Paul answered in the affirmative, the commander voluntarily explained, "I acquired my citizenship with a large sum of money." Luke provides no other details about Claudius Lysias's citizenship. However, the commander's name indicates that he obtained citizenship during the reign of Emperor Claudius, and the "large sum of money" was the bribe he paid the officials.[40] Luke leaves the distinct impression that to the commander, the claim to citizenship was extremely important.

When Paul added that he was a Roman citizen by birth, the commander had to acknowledge that Paul superseded him in status. Paul's ancestors obtained their citizenship in Tarsus, most likely for services rendered to

---

40. Scholars assume that Claudius Lysias was a Greek by birth; people who were Roman citizens by birth usually had three names rather than two. On the issue of bribes, see Dio Cassius *History* 60.17.5–6; Sherwin-White, *Roman Society and Roman Law*, pp. 154–55; F. F. Bruce, *The Acts of the Apostles: The Greek Text with Introduction and Commentary*, 3d (rev. and enl.) ed. (Grand Rapids: Eerdmans, 1990), p. 609.

Rome.[41] Upon receiving their citizenship, his ancestors stipulated that this privilege would be conferred on their descendants.

29. Those who were about to question him immediately let him go. Even the commander was afraid when he learned that Paul was a Roman citizen, because he had put him in chains.

At the command of Claudius Lysias, the centurion and the soldiers lost no time in setting Paul free. The commander was fully acquainted with the rights of a Roman citizen and realized that, even though he had not harmed Paul, he nevertheless was guilty of having him bound. Paul could have told the commander at the outset that he was a citizen not only of Tarsus (21:39) but also of Rome, but he waited until the soldiers had bound him and were ready to scourge him. He knew that the commander would be averse to breaking Roman law and, in an effort to redeem himself, would treat Paul deferentially.

The chains on Paul were visible tokens of his Roman imprisonment (21:33). Chaining a citizen was a direct violation of Roman law and could be used as evidence against the commander. Nonetheless, during his imprisonment in Caesarea and his house arrest in Rome, Paul was chained for a total of at least four years.[42]

Practical Considerations in 22:26 and 28

Verse 26

During his lifetime Paul exercises his rights as a Roman citizen twice directly (16:37–38; 22:26) and once by appealing to Caesar (25:11). For Paul, however, citizenship in the kingdom of heaven is of far greater importance than civil rights. He writes, "But our citizenship is in heaven" (Phil. 3:20, NIV). He does not point the Philippian believers to earthly citizenship (even though Philippi had special status [see the commentary on 16:12a]) but instead conveys the message that believers are residents in the city of God.[43]

Verse 28

In this verse, Luke indirectly refers to the time in which the event occurred. Claudius Lysias mentions the large sum of money he had to pay to obtain his Roman citizenship. During the reign of Emperor Claudius, officials were permitted to take substantial bribes from persons who wished to purchase citizenship. But when Nero became emperor in A.D. 54, he terminated the abuses and prescribed appropriate punishment for offenders. In brief, the remark of Claudius Lysias reflects the time of Emperor Claudius (A.D. 41–54) and not that of Nero.[44]

---

41. William M. Ramsay, *The Cities of St. Paul: Their Influence on His Life and Thought* (1907; reprint ed., Grand Rapids: Baker, 1963), pp. 197–98.
42. See Acts 26:29; 28:20, 30; Eph. 6:20; Phil. 1:13–14, 17; Col. 4:3, 18; Philem. 10, 13.
43. Hans Bietenhard, *NIDNTT*, vol. 2, p. 804.
44. Sherwin-White, *Roman Society and Roman Law*, p. 156.

Greek Words, Phrases, and Constructions in 22:24–29

Verses 24–25

εἴπας—this second aorist participle with a first aorist ending is equivalent to a coordinate verb ("he said"); that is, "the commander ordered . . . and said."

τοῖς ἱμᾶσιν—from the noun ἱμάς (thong), this dative plural can be interpreted as an instrumental dative ("with the thongs"). It can also signify a dative of purpose ("for the thongs"; that is, Paul was stretched out to be whipped). Translators prefer the second interpretation.[45]

εἰ—this particle introduces a direct question and is not translated.

Verses 28–29

κεφαλαίου—this is the second meaning of the noun κεφάλαιον (summary), which in context means "sum of money." The genitive is the genitive of price.

ὅτι—the first instance is the declarative "that," but the second has a causal meaning.[46]

ἦν δεδεκώς—the perfect periphrastic construction from the verb δέω (I bind) denotes action in the past with continued effect in the present.

---

30 On the next day, wishing to know exactly why Paul had been accused by the Jews, the commander released him and ordered the chief priests and all the Sanhedrin to assemble. And he brought Paul down and placed him before them.

---

b. Accusation
22:30

After Paul was set free from his bonds, the soldiers took him into the barracks and guarded him during the night. In the meantime, Claudius Lysias could reflect on the situation and find a way to solve the problem of an unwanted prisoner in his fortress. He realized that the matter that disturbed the Jews concerned theological issues. Therefore, on the following day he tried to settle the question by convening the Sanhedrin and placing Paul before this governing body of the Jewish people.

30. On the next day, wishing to know exactly why Paul had been accused by the Jews, the commander released him and ordered the chief priests and all the Sanhedrin to assemble. And he brought Paul down and placed him before them.

a. "Why Paul had been accused by the Jews." Claudius Lysias had to find out precisely why the Jews accused Paul of wrongdoing. He was the commander of the Roman forces stationed in Jerusalem and was account-

---

45. Bauer, p. 376.
46. Robert Hanna, *A Grammatical Aid to the Greek New Testament* (Grand Rapids: Baker, 1983), pp. 237–38.

able to his superior, Governor Felix (23:24), if turmoil erupted. By knowing the causes of the riot on the preceding day, he would be able to prevent a recurrence.

b. "The commander released him and ordered the chief priests and all the Sanhedrin to assemble." I understand the text to say that Claudius Lysias released Paul from custody and gave him the privilege of walking freely next to Roman soldiers. A day earlier the commander had set Paul free from his chains when he learned of Paul's citizenship (v. 29).[47]

Some scholars consider that this incident cannot be an actual historical event.[48] They think that the commander left Paul in chains during the night, and that instead of examining Paul the commander shirked his responsibilities by bringing him before the Sanhedrin. But these difficulties disappear when we accept the preceding verse (v. 29) at face value and see that the commander realized his error. He kept Paul in safe custody during the night and in the morning gave him complete freedom.[49] Moreover, because the conflict between Paul and the Jews was theological and not political, Claudius Lysias had a perfect right to take Paul to the Sanhedrin in an effort to gain precise information from Jewish theologians.

Did the commander have the authority to convene the Sanhedrin? Yes, indeed. In Israel, the Jewish Sanhedrin and the Roman court existed side by side. Although the Sanhedrin had the power to bring Paul to trial, the Roman commander, when he thought that the interests of Rome were at stake, exercised a higher authority than the Jewish court.[50] He not only ordered the members of the Sanhedrin to meet (v. 30), but also transported Paul to Caesarea to be tried in a Roman court (24:1–22).

c. "And he brought Paul down and placed him before them." The commander first informed the high priest (see the commentary on 4:6) about a meeting; the high priest in turn summoned the members of the court. Afterward he had Paul brought into the meeting room.

Gentiles were not permitted to enter any of the rooms in the temple complex. According to Josephus, the assembly hall of the Sanhedrin was situated to the west of the temple proper.[51] Here the commander brought

---

47. Boyd Reese notes the similar concern of the magistrates in Philippi (16:38) and the commander in Jerusalem (22:29). "The Apostle Paul's Exercise of his Rights as a Roman Citizen as Recorded in the Book of Acts," *EvQ* 47 (1975): 142.

48. Conzelmann, *Acts,* p. 191; see also Ernst Haenchen, *The Acts of the Apostles: A Commentary,* trans. Bernard Noble and Gerald Shinn (Philadelphia: Westminster, 1971), pp. 639–40.

49. Lake and Cadbury, *Beginnings,* vol. 4, p. 286. I. Howard Marshall is of the opinion that Paul was kept in bonds. *The Acts of the Apostles: An Introduction and Commentary,* Tyndale New Testament Commentary series (Leicester: Inter-Varsity; Grand Rapids: Eerdmans, 1980), p. 361.

50. Schürer, *History of the Jewish People,* vol. 1, pp. 377–78.

51. Josephus *War* 2.16.3 [344]; 5.4.2 [144]; 6.6.3 [354]. Consult Schürer, *History of the Jewish People,* vol. 2, pp. 223–24.

Paul and had him face the members of the Sanhedrin (compare 4:7; 5:27; 6:15).

Summary of Chapter 22

Paul addresses the Jewish people as he stands on the steps leading to the Fortress Antonia. In Aramaic he tells the Jews that he was born in Tarsus but reared in Jerusalem and educated by the respected teacher Gamaliel. He reveals that he was a persecutor of Christians and, supplied with letters from the high priest and the Sanhedrin, even went to Damascus to arrest these people.

Near Damascus, Paul relates, Jesus called him and instructed him to go into the city, where he would be told what to do. Blinded by the brilliant light from heaven, he was led into Damascus. There a devout Jew called Ananias came to him and restored his sight. Ananias told him to be a witness to all men, to be baptized, and to call on the name of the Lord.

Upon his return to Jerusalem, says Paul, he went to the temple to pray, fell into a trance, and heard Jesus warn him to leave Jerusalem immediately. Although Paul objected to this directive, the Lord commanded him to go far away to the Gentiles.

The audience had listened to Paul without interruption, but when they hear that Paul had to go to the Gentiles, they create an uproar. The Roman commander takes Paul to the barracks and orders his officer to examine Paul by administering a scourging. When the soldiers stretch him out to be flogged, Paul asks the officer if it is lawful to flog a Roman citizen. The officer informs the commander, who inquires whether Paul can claim citizenship. Paul answers in the affirmative and the commander, fearing adverse consequences for having chained a Roman citizen, sets him free. The next day Paul appears before the Sanhedrin.

23

In Jerusalem and Caesarea, *part 3*

23:1–35

Outline (continued)

23:1–5		c. Appearance
23:6–8		d. Assembly
23:9–11		e. Rescue
23:12–22		5. Paul's Protection
23:12–15		a. The Plot
23:16–22		b. Discovery
23:23–26:32	B. At Caesarea	
23:23–35		1. Paul's Transfer
23:23–24		a. Order
23:25–30		b. Letter
23:31–35		c. Arrival

23 1 Paul looked intently at the Sanhedrin and said, "Men and brothers, I have lived my life with a perfectly clear conscience before God to this day." 2 The high priest Ananias commanded those standing beside him to strike Paul on the mouth. 3 Then Paul said to him, "God is about to strike you, you whitewashed wall. You sit judging me according to the law, but by ordering me to be struck you yourself break the law." 4 Those who were standing nearby asked Paul, "Do you dare to insult the high priest of God?" 5 Paul answered, "I did not know, brothers, that he is the high priest, because it is written: 'Do not speak evil about the ruler of your people.'"

---

c. Appearance
23:1–5

Paul stood in the exact place where Stephen had stood more than twenty years earlier. Although Paul had stated that he was ready to die for Jesus in Jerusalem (21:13), he also knew that the Roman commander was responsible for his safe conduct. As a Roman citizen, Paul always had the right to request trial in a Roman court.

Because Paul is thoroughly acquainted with the organization of the Sanhedrin, he realizes that his appearance before this court only exacerbates the situation. He understands that the leaders of the Sanhedrin gladly complied with the commander's request to summon the members of the court. And he knows their refusal to present the truth of the matter and their intent to accuse him as a disturber of the peace. If this accusation is leveled against him before the Roman commander, the result will be detrimental to Paul's physical well-being.

Three inferences arise from the context. First, for the benefit of the Roman commander, Paul addressed the members of the court in Greek. This is in stark contrast to the previous day, when Paul sought to build rapport with the Jewish people by speaking to them in Aramaic (21:40; 22:2). Next, because of Paul's theological training in Jerusalem and his close association with the Sanhedrin (22:5), he was able to take control of the situation in the court and to turn the proceedings to his advantage. Last, many members of the Sanhedrin had listened to Paul's speech on the preceding day and thus did not need detailed information about Paul's life and ministry.

1. Paul looked intently at the Sanhedrin and said, "Men and brothers, I have lived my life with a perfectly clear conscience before God to this day."

a. "Paul looked intently at the Sanhedrin." We assume that customary opening remarks were made by the presiding officer, namely, Ananias the high priest, and that the commander asked the court to furnish information that would help him understand the theological differences between the Jews and Paul. Paul then received permission to speak.

Luke, who may have been a bystander at the session, records that Paul took his time and looked intently at the members of the court. The membership of the Sanhedrin had changed considerably since the time Paul had been commissioned to persecute the Christians in Jerusalem and Damascus. But Paul no doubt wanted to see whether he could recognize anyone.

b. "Men and brothers." When Paul begins to speak, he does not repeat his earlier address, "Men, brothers and fathers" (22:1), but says only, "Men and brothers." He seems to continue the speech he gave the previous day, because in his opening statement he fails to set forth his case. He continues at the point where he was interrupted in his earlier speech and states: "I have lived my life with a perfectly clear conscience before God to this day." This one sentence is filled with meaning.

c. "I have lived my life." Paul is not saying that his death is imminent (in contrast, see II Tim. 4:7). Rather, he means that his life is spent in harmony with religious principles. He has consciously tried to live a life of faith in God.[1]

d. "[I have] a perfectly clear conscience." This is a claim Paul makes consistently both in his defense before Governor Felix and in his epistles. In the presence of Felix, the high priest Ananias, and others he says, "I always do my best to maintain a blameless conscience before God and men" (24:16). And in his epistles he also speaks of a clear conscience: "The testimony of our conscience is this: that in holiness and sincerity . . . we have conducted ourselves in the world" (II Cor. 1:12; see also I Tim. 3:9; compare I Peter 3:16, 21).

e. "Before God to this day." What is the meaning in context of the word *conscience*? We first look at the two qualifiers, which I have translated "perfectly" and "clear." That is, Paul's conscience not only affected *every* aspect of his life but also was *good*. (In English idiom we speak of a clear conscience.) Before God, Paul could openly say that he had lived a moral and religious life. Sins committed before his conversion, including those of persecuting the Christians, Paul readily confessed. But in respect to the charges brought against him by the Jews, he considered himself blameless. He knew that he lived as a Jew who was faithful to his God and obeyed God's law to that very day.[2]

---

1. Consult Hans Bietenhard, *NIDNTT*, vol. 2, p. 804; Hermann Strathmann, *TDNT*, vol. 6, p. 534.

2. The literature on the concept *conscience* is extensive; a few representative works are Claude A. Pierce, *Conscience in the New Testament* (Naperville, Ill.: Allenson, 1955); Alfred Martin Rehwinkel, *The Voice of Conscience* (St. Louis: Concordia, 1956); N. H. G. Robinson, *Christ and Conscience* (London: Nisbet, 1956); Hans-Christoph Hahn and Colin Brown, "Conscience," *NIDNTT*, vol. 1, pp. 348–53.

2. The high priest Ananias commanded those standing beside him to strike Paul on the mouth.

The high priest rudely interrupted Paul's speech. On the basis of one remark, the high priest instructed the people standing next to Paul "to strike [him] on the mouth." To Ananias, Paul was a perverter of the Jewish religion who ought to be humiliated and condemned. His intense dislike for Paul became evident some days later when he personally traveled sixty-five miles from Jerusalem to Caesarea to bring charges against Paul before Governor Felix (24:1).

From Josephus we learn that Ananias, son of Nedebaeus, was appointed high priest by Herod, king of Chalcis (A.D. 44–48), presumably a decade before this incident. He served as high priest from A.D. 47 to 59.[3] Ananias, known for being vicious and violent, was both influential and wealthy, but his rapacity made him unpopular with the people. King Agrippa deposed him in A.D. 59; assassins murdered him in September A.D. 66, during the Jewish uprising.[4]

The command to smite Paul on the mouth has a parallel in John 18:22–23: Jesus, answering a question from the high priest Caiaphas, was struck in the face by one of the officials. Whether Ananias wanted Paul to be more respectful to the Sanhedrin or whether the slap served as a signal to Paul that he was put in his place is not clear.[5] What is plain is that the high priest disrupted proper courtroom procedure when he instructed the bystanders to discipline Paul for making an opening statement. By departing from the normal procedure, he unwittingly created confusion he was unable to remove.

3. Then Paul said to him, "God is about to strike you, you whitewashed wall. You sit judging me according to the law, but by ordering me to be struck you yourself break the law."

The slap in his face made Paul neither respectful nor silent. He immediately reacted. Jesus also reacted when an official hit him in the face, but he merely inquired whether he had said anything wrong and asked the official who struck him why he had done this (John 18:23). By contrast, Paul failed to follow his master's example. Paul asked God to strike the high priest; his request was actually a curse pronounced on Ananias.[6] (Incidentally, Paul spoke prophetically, because the curse he pronounced was fulfilled some years later when Ananias died at the hands of assassins.)

Moreover, Paul described Ananias with an insulting epithet: "you whitewashed wall." In other words, Ananias was like a tottering wall which had

---

3. Josephus *Antiquities* 20.5.2 [103]; 20.6.2 [131]. Consult Emil Schürer, *The History of the Jewish People in the Age of Jesus Christ (175 B.C.–A.D. 135)*, rev. and ed. Geza Vermes and Fergus Millar, 3 vols. (Edinburgh: Clark, 1973–87), vol. 2, p. 231.

4. Josephus *War* 2.12.6 [243]; 2.17.6 [429]; 2.17.9 [441–42]; *Antiquities* 20.8.11 [196]. See also SB, vol. 2, p. 766.

5. F. W. Grosheide, *De Handelingen der Apostelen,* Kommentaar op het Nieuwe Testament, 2 vols. (Amsterdam: Van Bottenburg, 1948), vol. 2, p. 305.

6. Refer to SB, vol. 2, p. 766.

an external coat of whitewash but an internal structure that lacked mortar to hold the stones together. If torrential rains lashed against it and the wind blew, that wall would tumble (compare Ezek. 13:10–12). Another comparison is that of a tomb whose whitewashed exterior hides the bones of the dead (Matt. 23:27). No doubt Paul's intent was to portray the character of Ananias; therefore, he resorted to a term "of general abuse."[7]

"You sit judging me according to the law, but by ordering me to be struck you yourself break the law." Paul, trained as an expert in the Mosaic law, put a legal question before Ananias. On the basis of the law, the high priest had no right to order that Paul be struck. If Ananias had admitted that he had broken the law (see Lev. 19:15, "Judge your neighbor fairly" [NIV]), he would have lost his authority to judge. The Pharisees and the experts in the law who were present in the court would have to agree with Paul, "for in Jewish law the rights of the defendant were carefully safeguarded."[8]

4. Those who were standing nearby asked Paul, "Do you dare to insult the high priest of God?" 5. Paul answered, "I did not know, brothers, that he is the high priest, because it is written: 'Do not speak evil about the ruler of your people.' "

For the bystanders—among them, perhaps, the one who had slapped Paul—this insult was too much. A cry of indignation arose: "Do you dare to insult the high priest of God?" Despite the high priest's ruthless and greedy character and his appointment by a secular king, the bystanders acknowledge him as "the high priest of God." Once again, notice the parallelism between Jesus and Paul. The official who struck Jesus asked, "Do you answer the high priest in this manner?" (John 18:22). The people standing next to Paul asked virtually the same question.

Paul's reply ("I did not know, brothers, that he is the high priest") is difficult to interpret. Various explanations, none of them satisfactory, have been given:

1. Because Paul had been absent from Jerusalem, he did not know that Ananias was high priest. But this hardly seems plausible, for Paul had been in Jerusalem at the end of his second missionary journey (18:22) and thus would have known about Ananias.

2. Paul refused to acknowledge Ananias as high priest and therefore expressed irony: "I did not know, brothers, that he is the high priest." But Paul was thoroughly familiar with Israel's history and knew that some of the past high priests had been equally wicked.

3. Paul had poor eyesight (Gal. 4:15; 6:11) and could not distinguish the

---

7. Lake and Cadbury, *Beginnings*, vol. 4, p. 287.

8. David John Williams, *Acts*, Good News Commentaries series (San Francisco: Harper and Row, 1985), p. 383. F. F. Bruce observes that "the Jewish law presumed innocence until guilt was proved." *The Acts of the Apostles: The Greek Text with Introduction and Commentary*, 3d (rev. and enl.) ed. (Grand Rapids: Eerdmans, 1990), p. 612.

high priest from the other members of the Sanhedrin. But he knew that the high priest presided in the Sanhedrin.

Whatever solutions commentators may choose, they meet objections. Perhaps we do well to understand that Luke sketches Paul as a human being, "warts and all." Paul lost his temper when he was rudely interrupted by the high priest and was slapped in the face. While trying to regain his composure, he made a remark that lacks clarity. It should be understood as a specious excuse for being discourteous to Ananias.

As an expert in the law, Paul immediately quoted the Mosaic law: "Do not speak evil about the ruler of your people" (Exod. 22:28 [22:27, LXX]). The wording follows the reading in the Septuagint, "Do not revile God and do not curse the ruler(s) of your people." To be precise, the rabbis understood the word *God* as "judges."[9] God wants his people to respect their rulers and obey the authorities he has appointed (see Rom. 13:1; I Peter 2:13–14). Paul knew that he had to show obedience to the spiritual authority of the high priest and thus quoted Scripture for the purpose of apologizing to Ananias and the court.

Greek Words, Phrases, and Constructions in 23:1–5

Verse 1

πάσῃ συνειδήσει ἀγαθῇ—this is the dative of manner. The two adjectives have been placed before and after the noun. The preceding adjective πάσῃ (in every respect, completely) and the succeeding adjective ἀγαθῇ (good; pure, clear) may be translated "perfectly clear." The noun derives from the preposition σύν (together) and the verb οἶδα (I know); it indicates joint knowledge or conscience.[10]

πεπολίτευμαι—preceded by the emphatic pronoun ἐγώ, the verb in the perfect middle (from πολιτεύομαι, I am a citizen) has a political connotation in many passages. Here, however, it means to live as a citizen in obedience to the law. The Greek of this verse is excellent.

Verse 3

κατὰ τὸν νόμον—"according to the law." Note the contrast in the use of the present active participle παρανομῶν (breaking the law). The participle denotes manner.

Verse 5

ᾔδειν—the pluperfect of the verb οἶδα (I know) as an imperfect means "I was unaware of the fact."

---

9. SB, vol. 2, p. 766; Lake and Cadbury, *Beginnings*, vol. 4, p. 288; Ernst Haenchen, *The Acts of the Apostles: A Commentary*, trans. Bernard Noble and Gerald Shinn (Philadelphia: Westminster, 1971), p. 638 n. 2.
10. Thayer, p. 602.

οὐκ ἐρεῖς—the imperatival future, common in the Septuagint, conveys a command: "do not speak [evil]."

---

6 But Paul knew that some were Sadducees and others Pharisees. He began to shout in the Sanhedrin: "Men and brothers, I am a Pharisee, a son of Pharisees. I am on trial for the hope in the resurrection of the dead." 7 When he had said this, dissension arose between the Pharisees and Sadducees and the assembly was divided. 8 The Sadducees say that there is neither resurrection, nor angels, nor spirits, while the Pharisees acknowledge them all.

---

d. Assembly
23:6–8

6. But Paul knew that some were Sadducees and others Pharisees. He began to shout in the Sanhedrin: "Men and brothers, I am a Pharisee, a son of Pharisees. I am on trial for the hope in the resurrection of the dead."
Luke portrays Paul as a man who saw his opportunity to take charge of the situation. Educated as a Pharisee under an able teacher and a member of the Sanhedrin, Gamaliel, Paul knew the factions in the court. He knew that the ruling minority party was the Sadducees, while the Pharisees, who made up the majority, exerted great influence, especially in theological matters. (See the commentary on 4:1–4 for a detailed discussion of the Sadducees and Pharisees.) In addition, Paul realized that the purpose of this meeting was to provide information useful to the Roman commander.

a. "Men and brothers, I am a Pharisee, a son of Pharisees." The text indicates that the noise in the assembly hall was so overwhelming that Paul had to shout to be heard. He unequivocally identified himself as a Pharisee, and in truth, he had been a member of that party in his student days (26:5; Phil. 3:5). Further, when he returned to Jerusalem at the conclusion of his third missionary journey, he learned that thousands of Christian Jews were zealous for the law (i.e., as Pharisees [21:20]). And, even though he differed with these Jewish Christians on some points, he, in deference to their concerns, submitted to purification rites and offered sacrifices at the temple (21:26). In doctrinal matters, Paul agreed with the Pharisees. Accordingly, we ought not to accuse him of misrepresenting the truth.[11]

Paul once again addressed the members of the Sanhedrin as "men and brothers." He adroitly played upon a partisan spirit and sided with the majority party of the court: "I am a Pharisee, a son of Pharisees." The phrase *son of* does not necessarily refer to Paul's ancestors but rather is a general term that was common among the Jews (e.g., "son of Abraham" and "son of David"). Here the phrase appears to mean that Paul supported the Pharisaic party.[12]

---

11. John Calvin, *Commentary on the Acts of the Apostles,* ed. David W. Torrance and Thomas F. Torrance, 2 vols. (Grand Rapids: Eerdmans, 1966), vol. 2, p. 230.
12. Bauer (p. 833) thinks that the expression "is prob[ably] a ref[erence] to direct descent."

b. "I am on trial for the hope in the resurrection of the dead." Paul touched a critical issue—namely, the doctrine of the resurrection—that united the Pharisees and the Christians but separated the Pharisees from the Sadducees. "In the early Jewish Christian church a person might become a Christian and remain a Pharisee, but a Sadducee would need to change his whole theological position."[13] When Peter and John preached "in Jesus the resurrection of the dead" (4:2), the Sadducees opposed them. The Sadducees rejected this doctrine and reacted vehemently when Paul stated that he was tried because of his hope in the resurrection of the dead.

In subsequent speeches, Paul again mentions the term *hope*. Before King Agrippa Paul eloquently explains the concept: "And now I stand on trial for the hope of the promise made by God to our fathers. This promise our twelve tribes hope to attain by earnestly serving God night and day. Concerning this hope, O king, I am being accused by the Jews. Why do you Jews consider it incredible that God raises the dead?" (26:6–8). And in his meeting with Jewish leaders in Rome, Paul explains that he is a prisoner because of "the hope of Israel" (28:20). This hope, then, is centered on the resurrection of the dead. Paul presents this belief in the resurrection as Christianity's "true continuation of the Jewish religion and of the people of God."[14] For that reason, he receives the support of both the Jewish Christians and the Pharisees. In Paul's presentations, Jesus' resurrection is inextricably related to the general resurrection, for to reject the one is to reject the other (compare 13:32–41; 17:31; 26:23).[15]

7. When he had said this, dissension arose between the Pharisees and Sadducees and the assembly was divided. 8. The Sadducees say that there is neither resurrection, nor angels, nor spirits, while the Pharisees acknowledge them all.

Paul presented himself as a Pharisee who promulgates and defends the doctrine of the resurrection. As soon as he had shouted this statement, the Pharisees and the Sadducees were at odds with one another. Luke uses the word *dissension*, which can mean "riot," but in this context refers to discord that degenerates into physical violence (see v. 10). The high priest Ananias lost control of the situation.

For the benefit of the readers, Luke clarifies the doctrinal differences between the Pharisees and the Sadducees. Indeed, he adds a parenthetical thought that is equivalent to a footnote. He says that the Sadducees reject the doctrines of the resurrection, angels, and spirits, but the Pharisees accept these beliefs. Because of their doctrinal affinity with the Jewish Christians on these tenets, the Pharisees were willing, for the moment, to

---

13. I. Howard Marshall, "The Resurrection in the Acts of the Apostles," in *Apostolic History and the Gospel*, ed. W. Ward Gasque and Ralph P. Martin (Exeter: Paternoster; Grand Rapids: Eerdmans, 1970), p. 97.

14. Robert J. Kepple, "The Hope of Israel, the Resurrection of the Dead, and Jesus," *JETS* 20 (1977): 240–41.

15. Consider also Peter's presentations: 2:24; 3:15; 4:2, 10; 5:30; 10:40.

claim Paul as one of their number and defend him against the attacks of the Sadducees.

When the Sadducees tried to test Jesus, they fabricated a story of seven brothers who successively married one woman. They asked to which of the seven brothers this woman would belong at the resurrection. Jesus shrewdly answered their query by comparing resurrected people with angels, who do not marry and are not given in marriage (Matt. 22:23–32). He confuted the Sadducees by teaching the doctrines of the resurrection and of angels.

Historical Considerations in 23:1–8

Looking at the descriptive details of the court proceedings, one writer is of the opinion that "the incident is historically impossible" and that Luke wrote this story in "anecdotal style."[16] We grant that at first glance Luke's account appears to be problematic, but the problems we face do not give us the liberty of saying that Luke fabricated anecdotes.

Because Paul was familiar with the parties and doctrinal differences in the Sanhedrin, he knew that he had to sow discord between the Pharisees and the Sadducees. He perceived that if they united to accuse him of disrupting the *pax Romana* he would lose the protection of the commander. In short, Paul was fighting for his life, and Luke's account reflects that fact.

If we look at Luke's style of reporting, we discover that he repeatedly compresses his accounts. Their brevity inevitably raises questions about their historical accuracy, but throughout Acts Luke has proven his trustworthiness. For example, the vivid narrative about Paul's nephew reporting the plot against his uncle forces the reader to conclude that it is an eyewitness account. Another example is the description of the militia that accompanied Paul from Jerusalem to Antipatris and Caesarea (v. 23). At least one scholar terms the account "sheer fantasy."[17] The truth is that the countryside was infested with Jewish guerrillas;[18] Josephus reports that these terrorists caused untold damage during the administration of Governor Felix.[19] This guerrilla activity—and the willingness of more than forty Jews to kill Paul—exemplified the disregard for and lack of order in that day. Such civil disorder would make the Roman commander particularly aware of his responsibility to provide safe conduct, in the form of 470 men, for Paul, a Roman citizen. Granted that Luke is succinct in his reports, he accurately presents the facts.

---

16. Hans Conzelmann, *Acts of the Apostles*, trans James Limburg, A. Thomas Kraabel, and Donald H. Juel (1963; Philadelphia: Fortress, 1987), pp. 191–92. See also Martin Dibelius, *Studies in the Acts of the Apostles* (London: SCM, 1956), p. 170.

17. Conzelmann, *Acts*, p. 194.

18. Consult E. M. Blaiklock, "The Acts of the Apostles as a Document of First Century History," in *Apostolic History and the Gospel*, ed. W. Ward Gasque and Ralph P. Martin (Exeter: Paternoster; Grand Rapids: Eerdmans, 1970), p. 48.

19. Josephus *War* 2.13.6 [264–65]; *Antiquities* 20.8.5–6 [160–72].

Greek Words, Phrases, and Constructions in 23:6 and 8

Verse 6

γνούς—the aorist participle from γινώσκω (I know) is constative. "This use of the aorist contemplates the action in its entirety."[20]

ἔκραζεν—the tense is the descriptive imperfect. Luke depicts Paul trying to raise his voice so he can be heard above the noise in the building.

ἐλπίδος καὶ ἀναστάσεως—"the co-ordination of two ideas, one of which is dependent on the other, serves in the New Testament to avoid a series of dependent genitives." The phrase, therefore, means "on account of the hope of the resurrection of the dead."[21]

κρίνομαι—"I am judged." Paul is not saying that he is judged in a legal assembly because the Sanhedrin had convened a court session. Rather, Paul refers to the teaching of the resurrection for which he is being judged.

Verse 8

μὲν . . . δέ—the contrast between the Sadducees and the Pharisees is sharpened with these two particles: "the one and the other."

τὰ ἀμφότερα—the primary meaning of this adjective in the neuter plural is "both"; the secondary meaning is "all" when more than two items are mentioned.[22]

---

9 Shouting increased and some of the scribes of the Pharisees stood up and began to argue vehemently, "We find nothing wrong with this man. Suppose a spirit or an angel has spoken to him?"

10 The dissension became violent to the point that the commander feared that Paul would be torn to pieces by them. He commanded the troops to go down and to take Paul away from them by force and bring him into the barracks. 11 The following night the Lord stood next to Paul and said, "Take courage! As you have witnessed about me in Jerusalem, so you must witness in Rome."

---

e. Rescue
23:9–11

9. Shouting increased and some of the scribes of the Pharisees stood up and began to argue vehemently, "We find nothing wrong with this man. Suppose a spirit or an angel has spoken to him?"

Luke continues the account by describing the argument between the two

---

20. H. E. Dana and Julius R. Mantey, *A Manual Grammar of the Greek New Testament* (1927; New York: Macmillan, 1967), p. 196.
21. Friedrich Blass and Albert Debrunner, *A Greek Grammar of the New Testament and Other Early Christian Literature*, trans. and rev. Robert Funk (Chicago: University of Chicago Press, 1961), #442.16.
22. Bauer, p. 47.

opposing groups. The Pharisees claim Paul as their protégé because he and they believe the same doctrinal tenets. But the Sadducees oppose these teachings and consequently wish to prosecute Paul. The shouts grow increasingly louder and, as Luke indicates, some of the scribes of the Pharisees are no longer able to keep calm. They rise and start vehement arguments with the Sadducees. We are unable to tell whether the Pharisees are seated separately from the Sadducees or whether the two parties mingle in the seating arrangement.

Some of the scribes of the Pharisees loudly declare Paul innocent of any wrongdoing: "We find nothing wrong with this man. Suppose a spirit or an angel has spoken to him?" Once more I call attention to the parallel between Jesus and Paul. When Pontius Pilate declared Jesus innocent, he repeatedly stated: "I find no basis for a charge against this man."[23] Some of the Pharisees utter the same judgment about Paul. In these circumstances, Paul could not help but notice similarities.

We ought to expect that numerous Pharisees considered Paul to be innocent. During Jesus' ministry many of them, among whom were Nicodemus and Joseph of Arimathea, agreed with him. In Acts, "Luke never disparages the Pharisees: to him they represent what is best in Judaism, and some of them on this occasion show themselves to be not far from the kingdom of God."[24]

The second half of the judgment made by the Pharisees is telling. Instead of mentioning the doctrine of the resurrection, they state two other doctrinal beliefs: "Suppose an angel or a spirit has spoken to him."[25] They surmised that a spirit or an angel had spoken to Paul at his conversion near Damascus. In context, we see that Luke provided his explanatory note to smooth the transition from the doctrine of the resurrection to that of spirits and angels (v. 8).

10. The dissension became violent to the point that the commander feared that Paul would be torn to pieces by them. He commanded the troops to go down and to take Paul away from them by force and bring him into the barracks.

The arguments become increasingly louder and the reaction that accompanies them reaches the point of physical violence. Even though the Pharisees try to shield Paul, the Sadducees attack him. He becomes an object that is in danger of being torn to pieces.

When the Roman commander surveys the precarious situation, he orders his soldiers to enter the assembly hall of the Sanhedrin and to rescue Paul from the physical violence that rages around him. Under military guard,

---

23. Luke 23:4, 14, 22; John 18:38.

24. F. F. Bruce, *The Book of the Acts*, rev. ed., New International Commentary on the New Testament series (Grand Rapids: Eerdmans, 1988), p. 429; Haenchen, *Acts*, p. 643.

25. The kjv and nkjv add a clause that lacks the support of major manuscripts. The added clause (in italics) perhaps was introduced from 5:39: "But if a spirit or an angel has spoken to him, *let us not fight against God.*"

Paul leaves the meeting and is escorted to the barracks at Fortress Antonia (see 21:34; 22:24). Meanwhile, the high priest Ananias and the Sadducees perceive that they have lost their opportunity to have Paul convicted, sentenced, and executed.

11. The following night the Lord stood next to Paul and said, "Take courage! As you have witnessed about me in Jerusalem, so you must witness in Rome."

a. "The following night the Lord stood next to Paul." We surmise that fears overwhelm Paul. He has no idea what is going to happen next. Twice in as many days, the Roman commander Claudius Lysias rescued him, first on the temple grounds and next in the assembly hall of the Sanhedrin. But when dangers surround Paul so that he feels hemmed in on every side, Jesus appears to him in a vision (compare 18:9; 22:18; 27:23; II Tim. 4:17).

During the following night, Paul has a vision in which he sees Jesus standing next to him and saying, "Take courage!"[26] This verb is one Jesus often used during his earthly ministry. For instance, when Jesus walked on the waves of the Lake of Galilee and the disciples were filled with fear, he told them to take courage (Matt. 14:27; Mark 6:50).[27] Here in Jerusalem, Jesus encourages Paul to be undaunted.

b. "As you have witnessed about me in Jerusalem, so you must witness in Rome." What an unshakable assurance! What a wonderful promise! Just when Paul sees himself at the end of the road, he receives a direct word from Jesus that as he preached in Jerusalem, so he will preach in Rome. Having completed his third missionary journey, Paul now obtains his next assignment: "go to Rome and preach there." The assignment assures him that Jesus will protect him. Note, however, that the Lord does not promise him freedom and a pleasant journey to the imperial city. Jesus assures Paul that he will arrive at his destination, but he refrains from informing him how long the journey will take and what kind of dangers Paul will meet along the way. In the words of a time-honored saying:

> God has not guaranteed an easy voyage,
> but he has promised a safe harbor.

Greek Words, Phrases, and Constructions in 23:9–11

Verse 9

διεμάχοντο—the imperfect tense denotes progressive action: "they began and continued to contend sharply." The compound form should be understood in the perfective sense.

εἰ—although translated "suppose," the particle introduces a conditional sentence

---

26. The addition of the name *Paul* (kjv and nkjv) is not supported by major manuscripts. Accordingly, translators delete the name.
27. See also the Greek text of Matt. 9:2; Mark 10:49; John 16:33.

that lacks the second half. The sentence should conclude with the apodosis, "what opposition could we make?"[28]

Verse 10

στάσεως—in this context στάσις no longer means "dissension" (v. 7), because the adjective πολλῆς modifies it to signal physical violence. The -σις ending of the noun connotes continued activity; the genitives form the genitive absolute construction.

διασπασθῇ—this aorist passive subjunctive is in a fear clause. The form is a compound from the preposition διά (through) and the verb σπάω (I draw) and means "to draw in two." The English noun *spasm* derives from this verb.

Verse 11

διεμαρτύρω—the aorist middle second person singular ("you testified") hardly differs in meaning from the aorist active infinitive μαρτυρῆσαι (to testify). The infinitive is introduced by δεῖ (it is necessary), which expresses a divine command.

εἰς—preceding the two nouns describing the cities of Jerusalem and Rome, this preposition is equivalent to ἐν and should be translated "at."

---

12 The following morning, the Jews formed a conspiracy and placed themselves under a curse saying that they would neither eat nor drink until they had killed Paul. 13 More than forty people made this vow. 14 They came to the chief priests and elders and said, "We have placed ourselves under a curse to taste nothing until we have killed Paul. 15 Now, therefore, you and the Sanhedrin suggest that the commander bring Paul to you as if you are going to determine his case by a more thorough investigation. But before Paul gets here, we are ready to kill him."

16 When the son of Paul's sister heard of the plot, he went to the barracks and told Paul. 17 Paul summoned one of the officers and said, "Take this young man to the commander. He has something to tell him." 18 Then the officer took the young man to the commander and said, "Paul the prisoner summoned me and asked me to take this young man to you because he has something to tell you." 19 The commander took the young man by the hand and drawing him aside began to ask, "What is it that you have to tell me?" 20 He replied, "The Jews have agreed to ask you to bring Paul to the Sanhedrin tomorrow as if it is going to investigate him more thoroughly. 21 So do not listen to them, because more than forty of them are ambushing him. They have placed themselves under a curse not to eat or drink until they have killed him. Now they are ready and waiting for word from you." 22 Then the commander dismissed the young man and instructed him, "Don't tell anyone that you have informed me about this."

---

5. Paul's Protection
23:12–22

After a night of peaceful rest, Paul knows that he eventually will see Rome. Even though he is aware that the Jews may plot to take his life, he trusts that the Roman military forces will keep him safe.

---

28. Blass and Debrunner, *Greek Grammar*, #482.

a. The Plot
23:12–15

12. The following morning, the Jews formed a conspiracy and placed themselves under a curse saying that they would neither eat nor drink until they had killed Paul. 13. More than forty people made this vow.

With Paul in Roman custody, the Jews rue the fact that he eluded their control. When they come together the next morning, they heatedly discuss the matter with some of the Sadducees, express their hatred toward Paul, and form a conspiracy to kill him at any cost. Luke uses the term *Jews* only as a general category, rather than to indicate that all Jews are involved in the plot. We assume that even terrorists, who were called Zealots (21:38) and were fiercely opposed to Roman occupation, are among them. These people want to trick the Roman commander into having Paul appear once more in public so that they can eliminate him.

The Jews who plot to kill Paul swear an oath. They ask God to curse them if they consume any food or liquid before they have assassinated Paul. They expect to murder Paul soon, for they are unable to live without water for more than about twenty-four hours. Thirst, not hunger, sets the limits of their endurance.

Luke proves to be a master narrator who, with a few strokes of his literary pen, describes the scene with undisguised humor. He delights in depicting the rash vow of the Jews to not eat or drink anything until they murder Paul. He adds that the participants in this plot are more than forty in number. By revealing that many radicals have taken a solemn oath, he hints that this plot cannot remain a secret.

14. They came to the chief priests and elders and said, "We have placed ourselves under a curse to taste nothing until we have killed Paul. 15. Now, therefore, you and the Sanhedrin suggest that the commander bring Paul to you as if you are going to determine his case by a more thorough investigation. But before Paul gets here, we are ready to kill him."

The number of people acquainted with the plot increases dramatically when the would-be assassins approach the high priests and the elders. They inform these leaders about the oath they have taken; in effect, they announce their plan to slay Paul[29] and ask the Sanhedrin to approve the plan. What is their scheme? They want the Sanhedrin, represented by these leaders, to ask Claudius Lysias to bring Paul before them once more for detailed questioning. The commander should understand that because of the turmoil on the preceding day, a proper inquiry could not be held. Therefore, another hearing would be advisable.

However, the request is a pretext for killing Paul before he ever comes to the assembly room of the Sanhedrin. In other words, if the commander accedes to their request, the plotters are willing to fight the Roman military,

---

29. Compare 4:23; 25:2, 15; and see Matt. 26:47.

if necessary, to achieve their goal. They also think that the Sanhedrin will agree to their proposal because the high priest and the Sadducees desire to have Paul killed. And if their plan fails, they can have their oath annulled on the grounds that they were unable to fulfill their obligations.[30] Even though oaths were irrevocable, the experts in the law annulled them when the oaths could not be fulfilled.

Greek Words, Phrases, and Constructions in 23:12 and 15

Verse 12

οἱ Ἰουδαῖοι—the Majority Text has the indefinite pronoun ("some") preceding this definite article and noun: "some of the Jews" (kjv, nkjv). The presence of the pronoun forms a smooth transition to the next verse (v. 13). But according to a textual rule, the more difficult reading is the better. The absence of the pronoun is harder than to explain its presence, and so its omission is preferred.

Verse 15

The Western text expands the beginning of this verse: "Now therefore *we ask you that you do this for us: Gather the Sanhedrin together and* give notice to the tribune." And the Western text adds a concluding clause to the verse: "even though we must die too."[31]

ἀκριβέστερον—this comparative adverb functions as a superlative and means "very accurately." See also verse 20.

---

b. Discovery
23:16–22

16. When the son of Paul's sister heard of the plot, he went to the barracks and told Paul. 17. Paul summoned one of the officers and said, "Take this young man to the commander. He has something to tell him."

The conspirators apparently make no attempt to keep their plot secret. Perhaps they are of the opinion that cultural and linguistic barriers would prevent the Romans from finding out about the plot. But they should have known that God rules and overrules. As Solomon observes, "There is no wisdom, no insight, no plan that can succeed against the Lord" (Prov. 21:30, niv; see also Isa. 8:10). God laughs at man's deliberations and thwarts his schemes.[32]

The vividness of the written story plainly shows the presence of an eyewitness. Luke relates that Paul's sister lives in Jerusalem, and that her son hears about the Jews' plot to kill Paul. This news alarms him, so he visits

---

30. Midrash *Nedarim* 3.3; 9.1. Consult Schürer, *History of the Jewish People*, vol. 2, p. 486.
31. Bruce M. Metzger, *A Textual Commentary on the Greek New Testament*, 3d corrected ed. (London and New York: United Bible Societies, 1975), p. 488.
32. Consult Calvin, *Acts of the Apostles*, vol. 2, p. 239.

Paul in the barracks to tell him about the plot that is afoot. According to the customs of that day, prisoners were dependent on their relatives and friends for food and other necessities (Heb. 10:34; 13:3). Consequently, the boy is readily admitted to see Paul. Perhaps Luke accompanied the boy; if so, the incident would be indelibly recorded in the writer's mind.

Paul, having had experience with other plots by the Jews (9:23, 29; 20:3), immediately acts. He calls one of the officers and instructs him to take the boy to Claudius Lysias. In harmony with the customs of that day, Paul communicates with a commander through an officer of lesser rank. Moreover, Paul's relationship with the centurions and the commander is cordial indeed; as a Roman citizen, Paul is treated with respect.

18. Then the officer took the young man to the commander and said, "Paul the prisoner summoned me and asked me to take this young man to you because he has something to tell you." 19. The commander took the young man by the hand and drawing him aside began to ask, "What is it that you have to tell me?"

The centurion takes the boy to Claudius Lysias and presents a typical military report. He correctly states who gave him orders, what the orders were, and the evidence to confirm the orders. He identifies Paul as the prisoner, even though the Romans treat Paul graciously and not at all as a captive. The officer says that Paul summoned him and requested that he take the boy to the commander. Then he explains that the young man has something to tell him. Luke employs various terms in Greek to describe Paul's nephew as a son (v. 16) and a young man (vv. 17, 18). But we receive the distinct impression that the boy is not even a teenager; no officer would take a teenager or an adult by the hand. Claudius Lysias wants the information he receives to remain confidential. He understands that if confidential material becomes public knowledge, he loses opportunity to act decisively. Having found privacy, the commander puts the boy at ease and in a friendly voice asks him to relate what is on his mind. In Greek, the tense of the verb *to ask* indicates that he engages in an extended conversation with the boy.

20. He replied, "The Jews have agreed to ask you to bring Paul to the Sanhedrin tomorrow as if it is going to investigate him more thoroughly. 21. So do not listen to them, because more than forty of them are ambushing him. They have placed themselves under a curse not to eat or drink until they have killed him. Now they are ready and waiting for word from you."

With childish candor and openness, the boy reports what he has heard about the scheming of the rebellious Jews. He begins with a description of the plot and then switches to direct speech in which he pleads with the commander not to listen to the Jews. Next, he reverts to recounting that which has already happened, and last, he states that the officer will have to take action.

The boy accurately conveys the information he has received about the plot (compare the wording of v. 15). The crux of the matter, of course, lies in the words *as if*. And this crux is sufficient reason for the young man to express his fears that the commander may not see through the pretext and thus may unwittingly place Paul in mortal danger. In a boyish way, Paul's nephew instructs the commander not to listen to the Jews who will come to him with their request. He informs Claudius Lysias that more than forty Jews will ambush Paul, for they are under oath not to eat or drink anything until they have killed him. He completes his report by stating that the Jews momentarily will be at the commander's door and will be waiting for his favorable reply.

Luke gives no indication whether the boy speaks only as a close relative of Paul or as a Christian who unofficially represents the church. In the final analysis, we see God's guiding hand as he protects Paul from harm by thwarting the plot of the Jews.

22. Then the commander dismissed the young man and instructed him, "Don't tell anyone that you have informed me about this."

Claudius Lysias accepts the boy's report at face value, for he perceives that the young man speaks the truth. The commander has to maintain law and order in Jerusalem, and any information to deflect restlessness and treachery he welcomes. He dismisses Paul's nephew with instructions not to tell anyone about the conversation they have had. The commander wishes to dispel any suspicions the Jews may have in regard to the actions he is going to take.

Practical Considerations in 23:15 and 20

In these two verses, the phrase *as if* reveals a deliberate attempt to deceive the unwary listener and to take advantage of his naiveté. The world is filled with deception: in the marketplace, in advertisements, in politics, in testimonies, to mention only a few areas. Misrepresentation of the truth is the order of the day, so that society readily loses trust in persons who deliberately distort facts in their own spheres of expertise. "The well-known credibility gap in all these areas has led to the demand for truth-in-advertising, truth-in-lending, truth-in-testimony laws."[33]

Greek Words, Phrases, and Constructions in 23:18–21

Verses 18–19

ἠρώτησεν—when this verb appears in the aorist, it is a form of request that must be obeyed. The verb ἐρωτάω (I request), not the verb αἰτέω (I ask, beseech), is used.

ἔχοντα—this is the present active participle of ἔχω (I have, hold) with a causal connotation: "because he has. . . ."

ἐπυνθάνετο—the imperfect tense of the verb πυνθάνομαι (I inquire) is descriptive and denotes an animated conversation.

---

33. Ralph E. Powell, "Deception," in *Baker's Dictionary of Christian Ethics*, ed. Carl F. H. Henry (Grand Rapids: Baker, 1973), p. 167.

Verse 20

ὅπως—with the verb καταγάγῃς (you bring down), this is a purpose clause that follows the articular aorist infinitive ἐρωτῆσαι, which also conveys purpose.

ὡς—the particle *as if* (see v. 15) is the focal point in the sentence. The neuter singular participle μέλλον (going to) agrees with the noun *Sanhedrin*.

Verse 21

μὴ πεισθῇς αὐτοῖς—the negative prohibition is in the aorist passive subjunctive: "do not be persuaded by them." The pronoun expresses the dative of agency.

---

23 The commander summoned two of his officers and said, "Prepare two hundred soldiers, seventy horsemen, and two hundred spearmen to go to Caesarea at nine this evening. 24 Provide horses, so that Paul can ride and you can take him safely to Felix the governor." 25 He wrote a letter having this form:

> 26 "Claudius Lysias, to His Excellency, Governor Felix, greetings. 27 I rescued this man who was taken by the Jews and was about to be killed by them. I came upon them with my troops because I learned that he is a Roman citizen. 28 Wanting to know the cause of their accusations against him, I brought him down to their Sanhedrin. 29 I found that he was accused concerning disputes of their law, but no accusation deserved death or imprisonment. 30 After it became known to me that there would be a plot against the man, I immediately sent him to you. I also instructed his accusers to bring charges against him before you."

31 So the soldiers, following their orders, took Paul and brought him by night to Antipatris. 32 In the morning, they left the horsemen to proceed with Paul and returned to the barracks. 33 When the horsemen arrived in Caesarea, they delivered the letter to the governor and presented Paul to him. 34 After he read the letter, he asked from what province Paul came. When he learned that he came from Cilicia, 35 he said, "I will give you a hearing when your accusers arrive." He commanded that Paul be kept under guard in Herod's palace.

B. At Caesarea
23:23–26:32

1. Paul's Transfer
23:23–35

Claudius Lysias was directly responsible to Governor Felix, who resided in Caesarea. Because Paul was a Roman citizen whose personal safety was in jeopardy in Jerusalem, the commander wisely decided to transfer him to Caesarea. There Felix would be able to decide Paul's case.

a. Order
23:23–24

23. The commander summoned two of his officers and said, "Prepare two hundred soldiers, seventy horsemen, and two hundred spearmen to go to Caesarea at nine this evening. 24. Provide horses, so that Paul can ride and you can take him safely to Felix the governor."

We make the following observations:

a. *Time.* Luke relates that the Jews formed their plot in the course of the morning and went to the chief priests and elders for approval. Paul's nephew presumably heard about the plot in the afternoon and rushed to the barracks. That same afternoon, the commander summoned two centurions and gave them the following instructions: "At nine o'clock this evening, under cover of darkness, be ready to leave here with two hundred soldiers, seventy horsemen, and two hundred spearmen and go to Caesarea. Take Paul along on horseback and deliver him safely to Governor Felix."

b. *Text.* The passage presents some difficulties. First, the Western text has a different reading (the changes are in italics):

> "Get ready soldiers to go to Caesarea, *a hundred* horsemen and two hundred spearmen," and *he commanded that they be ready to start at the third hour of the night. And he ordered the centurions* to provide mounts for Paul to ride, and bring him *by night* to Felix the governor; *for he was afraid that the Jews would seize him* [Paul] *and kill him, and afterwards he would incur the accusation of having taken money* [i.e., to allow Paul to be lynched].[34]

This reading indicates, first, that the total force consisted of three hundred men and, second, the reason for the extraordinary measures Claudius Lysias took. Should the terrorists assassinate Paul, the commander would be held responsible and would "incur the accusation of having taken money" (i.e., a bribe. The taking of bribes caused the recall of Governor Cumanus, the predecessor of Felix, and Felix himself hoped that Paul would give him a bribe [24:26].). But, in view of limited manuscript support for this reading, translators hesitate to adopt it.

c. *Interpretation.* A difficulty lies in the Greek word *dexiolaboi,* which literally means "throwing with the right [hand?]." The word occurs only here and in a few seventh- and tenth-century manuscripts, but nowhere else in all of known Greek literature. Scholars have presented many suggestions to clarify its meaning, but none are satisfactory.[35] Translators usually give the reading *spearmen,* because the spear was thrown with the right hand.[36] Others translate the word "auxiliaries" (JB) or "light-armed troops" (NEB). Whatever the translation, the meaning of the word remains uncertain.

d. *Questions.* Why did Claudius Lysias commit such a large force to protect one prisoner? He was unable to judge whether the forty would-be assassins had alerted other terrorists outside Jerusalem, and thus he wanted to be sure that his force was large enough that a group of assassins would not dare to attack it. Roman troop movements were common enough that a

---

34. Metzger, *Textual Commentary,* pp. 488–89.

35. Lake and Cadbury propose the translation "led horses"; *Beginnings,* vol. 4, p. 293. G. D. Kilpatrick suggests "spearmen from the local police force"; see his article, "Dexiolaboi," *JTS* 14 (1963): 393–94.

36. E.g., KJV, NKJV, NASB, GNB, NIV, SEB, RSV, NAB, *Phillips,* and *Moffatt.*

large segment of soldiers, cavalry, and spearmen could prepare to leave Jerusalem without arousing immediate suspicion among the Jews.

Why did Claudius order his officers to "provide horses, so that Paul can ride"? Were Paul's friends (Luke and Aristarchus) who accompanied him to Caesarea permitted to ride? We do not know. We do know that Aristarchus was Paul's companion from the time of the riot in Ephesus (19:29), the journey from Corinth via Macedonia to Jerusalem (20:4), and the voyage to Rome (27:2). In Paul's letters, he is called "a fellow prisoner" (Col. 4:10), and he sends greetings (Philem. 24).

Greek Words, Phrases, and Constructions in 23:23–24

Verse 23

δύο τινάς—the translation appears to be "a certain two" instead of "about two."[37]
δεξιολάβους—the word occurs here and in a few seventh- and tenth-century documents, and has an uncertain meaning: "taking [a spear] in the right hand." A soldier held a spear in his right hand and a shield with the left.[38]

Verse 24

κτήνη—from the verb κτάομαι (I possess), this noun refers to a person's property in the form of pack animals (horses or donkeys).
παραστῆσαι—this aorist infinitive from παρίστημι (I provide; place next to) serves as an imperative.
διασώσωσι—the compound verb in the aorist subjunctive is followed by the preposition πρός (toward) and is directive· "take [Paul] safely to [Felix]" and thus protect him from danger.

b. Letter
23:25–30

25. He wrote a letter having this form:

26. "Claudius Lysias, to His Excellency, Governor Felix, greetings."

We ought not to think that Luke had direct access to correspondence between a Roman commander and a governor. We conjecture that the essence of the letter was conveyed to Paul, who in turn informed Luke.[39] For this reason, Luke prefaces his paraphrase with the words, "he wrote a letter having this form."

---

37. A. T. Robertson, *A Grammar of the Greek New Testament in the Light of Historical Research* (Nashville: Broadman, 1934), p. 742.
38. Blass and Debrunner, *Greek Grammar*, #119.1; Robert Hanna, *A Grammatical Aid to the Greek New Testament* (Grand Rapids: Baker, 1983), p. 239.
39. Colin J. Hemer speculates that "the original letter was actually read in court in Paul's presence." *The Book of Acts in the Setting of Hellenistic History*, ed. Conrad H. Gempf (Tübingen: Mohr, 1989), p. 348.

Claudius addresses his letter to "His Excellency, Governor Felix." The governor's name is a matter of dispute; it could be either Tiberius Claudius Felix or Marcus Antonius Felix.[40] From Roman authors we learn that Felix and his brother Pallas were former slaves who ascended to positions of influence in the Roman government. In A.D. 52, Emperor Claudius appointed Felix governor of Caesarea and thus elevated him to a still higher level. Indications are that his administration lasted seven years and was less than distinguished. Indeed, Tacitus observed: "[He] practiced every kind of cruelty and lust, wielding the power of a king with the instincts of a slave."[41] After Felix had routed the followers of the Egyptian (21:38), gangs of rebellious forces roamed the countryside at will. They looted houses, burned villages, and assassinated leaders. The result was an unstable political and social climate throughout the country, especially in Jerusalem.[42]

27. "I rescued this man who was taken by the Jews and was about to be killed by them. I came upon them with my troops because I learned that he is a Roman citizen."

The letter, written in excellent Greek, is a military report in which a commanding officer acquaints his superior with a political problem. Claudius explains that he himself has done everything possible to solve the problem. (Notice the use of the pronoun *I*, which in my translation occurs seven times in four verses.) Claudius informs Felix that as a military commander, he ordered his soldiers to snatch Paul away from the Jews who were about to kill him. He adds that he did this because Paul told him of his Roman citizenship. Here Claudius places himself in a favorable light, for in actuality he did not learn about Paul's status until he had given orders to have him scourged. We imagine that the commander refrains from mentioning any facts that might cast aspersions on himself, and we understand that he presents the account in a condensed manner. We ought not necessarily to fault Claudius for shading the truth.

28. "Wanting to know the cause of their accusations against him, I brought him down to their Sanhedrin. 29. I found that he was accused concerning disputes of their law, but no accusation deserved death or imprisonment."

In a few sentences, Claudius describes the next action he took, namely, placing Paul before the Sanhedrin to learn the cause of the accusations that were leveled against Paul. He wisely refrains from commenting on the unruly proceedings in the assembly hall of the Sanhedrin. Instead he merely summarizes the legal issue by saying that the matter concerned controversies

---

40. Josephus *Antiquities* 20.7.1 [137]; Tacitus *History* 5.9; F. F. Bruce, "The Full Name of Procurator Felix," *JSNT* 1 (1978): 33–36; Colin J. Hemer, "The Name of Felix Again," *JSNT* 31 (1987): 45–49.

41. Tacitus *History* 5.9 (LCL).

42. Schürer, *History of the Jewish People*, vol. 1, pp. 460–65.

about Jewish law.[43] Viewing Paul as a Roman citizen, Claudius judges that the accusations by the Jews warrant neither death nor imprisonment.[44]

30. "After it became known to me that there would be a plot against the man, I immediately sent him to you. I also instructed his accusers to bring charges against him before you."

Claudius merely states that he heard of a plot to kill Paul and assumes that Felix will understand. Then he discloses that he told Paul's accusers to travel to Caesarea to present their accusation before the governor himself. By this course of action Claudius Lysias appeals to the governor to function as judge on behalf of a Roman citizen whom he is legally obligated to protect. In fact, the commander tells Felix that in his opinion Paul is no criminal and ought to be set free (compare 25:11, 25; 26:31–32; 28:18).

Greek Words, Phrases, and Constructions in 23:27 and 30

Verse 27

μαθών—the aorist participle from μανθάνω (I learn) denotes cause: "because he was a Roman citizen." Did Claudius Lysias distort the truth? C. F. D. Moule suggests that the wording of the commander "represents a diplomatic adjustment of the facts."[45]

Verse 30

ἔσεσθαι—this future infinitive of εἰμί (I am) depends on the aorist passive participle μηνυθείσης in the genitive absolute construction: "after it was revealed to me that there would be a plot."

ἔπεμψα—"I sent." Claudius Lysias uses the epistolary aorist and considers the point of view of the recipient, who sees the action as past tense.

---

c. Arrival
23:31–35

31. So the soldiers, following their orders, took Paul and brought him by night to Antipatris. 32. In the morning, they left the horsemen to proceed with Paul and returned to the barracks.

By order of the commander, the soldiers are Paul's guardians. They march from Jerusalem as far as Antipatris, forty miles to the northwest. When they arrive in Antipatris, only the seventy horsemen continue with Paul to Caesarea. The troops return to Jerusalem.

---

43. The Western text enhances the reading by adding a clause: "[of their law] of Moses and a certain Jesus."

44. Again, the Western text embellishes. At the end of the sentence, it adds, "with force, I hardly led him away."

45. C. F. D. Moule, *An Idiom-Book of New Testament Greek,* 2d ed. (Cambridge: Cambridge University Press, 1960), p. 100.

Questions have been raised concerning this incident. For instance, the original order to the two centurions was to ready the troops to take Paul safely to Caesarea (v. 23). But the soldiers go only to Antipatris; they then return to their barracks in Jerusalem and leave to the cavalry the responsibility of escorting Paul to Caesarea. A plausible explanation is that Luke reports a general command, not specific details. Furthermore, the seventy horsemen were able to deliver Paul safely to Felix in Caesarea.

Antipatris was a Roman military post used as a resting place between Caesarea and Jerusalem. Herod the Great had built the city and dedicated it to his father, Antipater.[46] For Paul, the trip from Jerusalem to Caesarea retraced the route he had taken about two weeks earlier (21:15–16).[47] For the soldiers, the excursion to Antipatris was merely another of their military exercises.

33. When the horsemen arrived in Caesarea, they delivered the letter to the governor and presented Paul to him.

We presume that upon their arrival in Antipatris, the soldiers and Paul rested before they continued their respective journeys the following day. Antipatris was about twenty-five miles from Caesarea, so Paul and his fellow riders could reach Caesarea before nightfall. When they arrived, the Roman officers delivered Claudius Lysias's letter to the governor and presented Paul as the person for whom the escort had been arranged. The military had fulfilled its task and returned to headquarters. Paul was now in the custody of Felix.

34. After he read the letter, he asked from what province Paul came. When he learned that he came from Cilicia, 35. he said, "I will give you a hearing when your accusers arrive." He commanded that Paul be kept under guard in Herod's palace.

Felix read the communication from Claudius Lysias and perceived that Paul was no criminal and no rioter. Felix wanted to know Paul's background, because he could legally send Paul to his native province for trial.[48] When Paul informed Felix that he was a native of Cilicia, the governor decided to try Paul in Caesarea instead of sending him to Tarsus. At the time Paul appeared before Felix, Ummidius Quadratus served as legate of the province of Syria-Cilicia.[49] We sense that Felix hesitated to bother the legate with a trivial court case. He also preferred not to antagonize the Jewish leaders by forcing them to travel from Jerusalem to Cilicia.

Felix told Paul that he would give him a thorough hearing when his

---

46. Josephus *War* 1.21.9 [417]; see also *Antiquities* 13.15.1 [390]; 16.5.2 [143].

47. Paul arrived in Jerusalem on the Friday before Pentecost, and about two weeks later stood before Felix. See the commentary on 24:11; see also Richard B. Rackham, *The Acts of the Apostles: An Exposition*, Westminster Commentaries series (1901; reprint ed., Grand Rapids: Baker, 1964), pp. 441–42.

48. A. N. Sherwin-White, *Roman Society and Roman Law in the New Testament* (1963; reprint ed., Grand Rapids: Baker, 1978), p. 55.

49. Bruce, *Acts* (Greek text), p. 625.

accusers arrived in Caesarea. He expected that a delegation of Jewish officials from Jerusalem would be present at a scheduled meeting of the court
(see 24:1). In the meantime he commanded his officers that Paul be kept
prisoner in Herod's palace, which had been constructed by Herod the
Great and was the governor's residence.[50] On the basis of Paul's citizenship,
Felix should have set him free. Instead he kept Paul under guard while he
waited for the Jews to arrive.

Greek Words, Phrases, and Constructions in 23:31–35

Verse 31

μὲν . . . δέ—these two particles show sequence of action rather than contrast: the
soldiers traveled to Antipatris and then returned to Jerusalem.

διὰ νυκτός—"by night." The preposition denotes that the journey lasted through
the night (compare 5:19; 16:9; 17:10). Without the preposition, the noun in the
genitive case generally means "at night."[51]

Verses 34–35

ἐκ—this preposition here is a stylistic variation of ἀπό (from).

ποίας—the interrogative pronoun depicts the quality of the noun it modifies. But
in this context it merely introduces a simple question and thus specifies location.

κελεύσας—although given in the form of an aorist participle, the word is translated as a finite verb: "he commanded."

Summary of Chapter 23

Paul faces the members of the Sanhedrin and begins to address them.
But after one sentence the high priest interrupts him and orders bystanders to strike Paul on the mouth. Paul reacts by calling the high priest a
whitewashed wall, receives a reprimand for this remark, and offers his
apologies. Knowing that some members of the Sanhedrin are Sadducees
and others Pharisees, Paul calls out that he is a Pharisee and believes in the
resurrection of the dead, a doctrine the Sadducees refuse to accept. The
Pharisees support Paul, a dispute breaks out, and the result is that Paul is
nearly torn to pieces. The Roman commander calls in his soldiers, who
rescue Paul and bring him to their barracks.

During the night the Lord appears to Paul in a vision and encourages
him with the announcement that he must preach the gospel in Rome.
Meanwhile the Jews plot to kill Paul. They ask the Sanhedrin to have Paul
appear once again in court, for they plan to assassinate him while he is
being transported from the Roman barracks to the Sanhedrin. Paul's

---

50. Josephus *Antiquities* 15.9.6 [331].
51. In the Greek, see Matt. 2:14; 28:13; Luke 2:8; John 3:2; 19:39; Acts 9:25.

nephew hears about the plot, runs to Paul, and tells him the news. The boy is taken to the Roman commander and relates that forty Jews have taken an oath not to eat or drink anything until they have killed Paul. The commander orders two centurions to ready their troops to accompany Paul to Caesarea that night. He writes a letter to Governor Felix and sends the soldiers on their way. The foot soldiers go only to Antipatris and then return to Jerusalem, while the cavalry travels to Caesarea with Paul. When they arrive, the officers deliver the letter and Paul to Felix, who places Paul under guard in Herod's palace.

24

In Jerusalem and Caesarea, *part 4*

24:1–27

Outline (continued)

24:1–27	2. Paul Before Felix
24:1–4	a. Introduction
24:5–9	b. Accusation
24:10–16	c. Response
24:17–21	d. Facts
24:22–27	e. Adjournment and Delay

24 1 After five days, the high priest Ananias went down to Caesarea with the elders and an attorney named Tertullus. They brought charges against Paul to the governor. 2 After Paul had been summoned, Tertullus began to accuse Paul, saying to Felix: "Since we have attained lasting peace through you, and reforms have been carried out in this nation by your foresight, 3 we acknowledge this with sincere thankfulness in every way and everywhere, most excellent Felix. 4 But not to weary you further, I beg you to be so kind as to hear us briefly. 5 We have found this man to be a troublemaker who stirs up riots among all the Jews throughout the world. He is a leader of the Nazarene sect. 6 He even tried to desecrate the temple, so we arrested him [6b and wanted to judge him according to our law. 7 But Lysias, the commander, came and with great violence took him out of our hands, 8a ordering his accusers to come to you.] 8 If you find out from him what has happened, you will be able to ascertain the complaints which we bring against him." 9 The Jews joined in the accusation and asserted that these things were true.

10 When the governor nodded, Paul replied: "I know that you have been a judge in this nation for many years, so I cheerfully make my defense. 11 You are able to ascertain that not more than twelve days ago I went up to Jerusalem to worship. 12 And neither in the temple nor in the synagogues nor in the city itself did my accusers find me arguing with anyone or causing a riot among the people. 13 They cannot prove to you the charges they now are bringing against me. 14 But this I admit to you: I serve the God of our fathers according to the Way, which they call a sect, and I believe everything that is written in the Law and the Prophets. 15 I hold to the same hope in God as these men have: there certainly will be a resurrection of both the righteous and the wicked. 16 Therefore I always do my best to maintain a blameless conscience before God and men. 17 But after several years, I returned to Jerusalem to bring gifts to my people and to present offerings. 18 While I was doing this, they found me purified in the temple—not in a crowd or a riot. 19 But some Jews from the province of Asia were there, who ought to be present before you to accuse me if they have anything against me. 20 Or else let these men themselves tell what crime they found in me when I stood before the Sanhedrin, 21 unless it was this one sentence that I shouted while standing among them: "I am on trial before you today concerning the resurrection of the dead."

22 But Felix, who understood the Way more accurately [than most people], adjourned the proceedings and said, "When the commander Lysias comes down, I will decide your case." 23 He commanded the officer that Paul be kept under guard but be allowed some freedom and that he permit his friends to be helpful to him.

24 Several days later, Felix came with his wife Drusilla, a Jewess. He summoned Paul and listened to him speak about faith in Christ Jesus. 25 As Paul was conversing with them about righteousness, self-control, and the judgment to come, Felix became afraid. "Go away for now," he said, "I will call for you when I have time." 26 At the same time, however, he was hoping that Paul would offer him a bribe. So he used to send for him quite often and talk with him. 27 After two years, Porcius Festus became the successor of Felix. But Felix wanted to do the Jews a favor, so he left Paul in prison.

2. Paul Before Felix
24:1–27

Paul's appearance before the Sanhedrin could not be called a successful trial (23:1–11). But when the commander Claudius Lysias sent him to Felix with an accompanying letter (23:26–30), he put the case before the governor and asked him to adjudicate the matter.

a. Introduction
24:1–4

1. After five days, the high priest Ananias went down to Caesarea with the elders and an attorney named Tertullus. They brought charges against Paul to the governor.

Luke writes as an eyewitness who has kept a detailed diary about Paul's arrest, imprisonment, and trial. Notice the reference to a lapse of five days before the trial could begin. After his arrest Paul had spent about a day and a half or two days in Jerusalem before he was taken to Caesarea. That journey took about one and a half or two days. After Paul's departure, Claudius Lysias told the Jewish leaders to present their accusations against Paul before Governor Felix in Caesarea (23:30). The leaders met to formulate their charges and asked a lawyer named Tertullus to go with them and speak for them in court. Without delay, they set out for Caesarea. By the time they arrived, at least five days had elapsed since Paul's arrest in Jerusalem.[1]

The high priest Ananias deemed the case against Paul of such importance that he himself, the chief ruler of the Jews, had to be present at the trial. Moreover, prudence told him to win the favor of the Roman authorities.[2] Some of the elders, representing the Sanhedrin, accompanied Ananias; we suspect that these particular elders supported the view of the Sadducees. These religious leaders refrained from stating the charges themselves but retained a lawyer named Tertullus as their spokesman.

The name *Tertullus* is a diminutive form of Tertius, which means "third" (compare Rom. 16:22). Tertullus may have been a Jew who was born and raised in the Dispersion.[3] He seems to have been trained in Roman law and probably could speak Latin.

2. After Paul had been summoned, Tertullus began to accuse Paul,

---

1. Another translation is, "Five days later . . . Ananias went to Caesarea" (GNB). This means that five days after Paul's arrival in Caesarea, Ananias appeared.

2. In the time of Ananias "Jewish client-kings (Herod of Chalcis and Agrippa II)" appointed the high priest, but in earlier times that prerogative belonged to Roman governors. See Emil Schürer, *The History of the Jewish People in the Age of Jesus Christ (175 B.C.–A.D. 135)*, rev. and ed. Geza Vermes and Fergus Millar, 3 vols. (Edinburgh: Clark, 1973–87), vol. 1, p. 377.

3. John Albert Bengel opines, "He seems to have been an Italian." *Gnomon of the New Testament*, ed. Andrew R. Fausset, 5 vols. (Edinburgh: Clark, 1877), vol. 2, p. 706. F. F. Bruce sees him as a Hellenist. *The Acts of the Apostles: The Greek Text with Introduction and Commentary*, 3d (rev. and enl.) ed. (Grand Rapids: Eerdmans, 1990), p. 627.

saying to Felix: "Since we have attained lasting peace through you, and reforms have been carried out in this nation by your foresight, 3. we acknowledge this with sincere thankfulness in every way and everywhere, most excellent Felix."

The arrival of the high priest, accompanied as he was by an orator and Jewish elders, impressed Governor Felix. These dignitaries had come in haste to Caesarea and wished to avoid a delay in convening the court. Thus, the governor obliged them and commanded a soldier to summon Paul to the courtroom.

By all appearances, Luke is present at the proceedings. Although he may not offer a word-for-word account, he accurately portrays Tertullus by depicting his flowery rhetoric. Tertullus first flatters Felix and then accuses Paul of sedition.

a. "Since we have attained lasting peace through you." The administration of Felix, which began five years earlier (A.D. 52), had not at all been characterized by lasting peace. Felix had routed a band of four thousand Jews led by an Egyptian who had promised to overthrow Roman rule and to drive the Roman garrison from the Fortress Antonia (see 21:38). He also had captured and had crucified an incalculable number of both insurgents and innocent citizens.[4] His repressive actions caused a backlash among the Jewish citizens who longed for independence from Rome. Rebels and assassins freely roamed the countryside, so that life in Israel was no longer safe for any person who was inclined to promote Roman rule. Only those people who were partial to the Romans praised the brutal measures of Governor Felix. Among them was the orator Tertullus, whose inordinate praise gratified Felix.

b. "And reforms have been carried out in this nation by your foresight." Tertullus employs flattery that has no congruity with reality. He uses the word *foresight,* a theological expression that in its Old Testament context refers to God's care for his people.[5] But the governor lacked the virtue of foresight. Indeed, Jews would be hard pressed to mention any beneficial reforms that Felix had initiated. His administration was so oppressive that Nero recalled him two years after Paul's trial (compare v. 27). Felix left Palestine in a state of civil disorder that later culminated in the Jewish war. During the war, Jerusalem and the temple were destroyed and the priesthood ceased.

c. "We acknowledge this with sincere thankfulness in every way and everywhere, most excellent Felix." Luke gives the reader a sample of the exaggerated praise Tertullus showered on the governor. The three qualifiers *sincere, every way,* and *everywhere* heighten the effect. Tertullus's praise is

---

4. Josephus *War* 2.13.2 [253]; *Antiquities* 20.8.5 [160]; Schürer, *History of the Jewish People,* vol. 1, p. 463.

5. Paul Jacobs and Hartmut Krienke, *NIDNTT,* vol. 1, p. 694; Johannes Behm, *TDNT,* vol. 4, pp. 1011–12.

undeserved; although the epithet *most excellent* is a title of respect, history shows that Felix did nothing to earn it.

4. "But not to weary you further, I beg you to be so kind as to hear us briefly."

Tertullus notes that his laudatory comments ostensibly are wearisome to the governor. As a preface to the accusations he is about to bring, Tertullus appeals to the gentleness of the governor and implores him to listen for a few moments. The irony of the situation is that the complaint against Paul is so flimsy that a lengthy oration of praise must give the charges the appearance of substance. By his own admission, Tertullus has little to say.

Greek Words, Phrases, and Constructions in 24:1–4

Verses 1–2

κατά—followed by a noun in the genitive case, the preposition in this context means "against."

κληθέντος—Luke employs a legal term, "summoned." It is the aorist passive participle from καλέω (I call) and with the pronoun αὐτοῦ forms the genitive absolute construction. The reference is to Paul.

πολλῆς εἰρήνης—the use of the adjective *great* to modify the word *peace* indicates gross exaggeration. The genitive depends on the present participle τυγχάνοντες (finding, experiencing).

Verses 3–4

ἀποδεχόμεθα—"we acknowledge." In Greek the verb lacks a direct object, which is supplied in translation. Luke reports all the grammatical inconsistencies uttered by the orator.

ἐγκόπτω—"I hinder, thwart." This verb "is understood by Syr[iac] and Armen[ian] versions to mean *in order not to weary you any further*."[6]

---

b. Accusation
24:5–9

In the next few sentences, Tertullus levels three charges: he portrays Paul as a rebellious fellow, a champion of the Nazarene sect, and a desecrator of the temple. He instructs Felix to investigate for himself if these charges are true.

5. "We have found this man to be a troublemaker who stirs up riots among all the Jews throughout the world. He is a leader of the Nazarene sect. 6. He even tried to desecrate the temple, so we arrested him."

Granted that Luke does not transcribe the speech, he nevertheless records the clumsy structure of the Greek sentence spoken by Tertullus. A wooden translation of the first sentence is, "Finding this man to be a trouble-

---

6. Bauer, p. 216.

maker who stirs up riots among all the Jews throughout the world." In brief, the sentence needs a main verb (compare the Greek text of Luke 23:2). Luke reports the grammatical errors of this orator with journalistic accuracy.[7] He wants to demonstrate that the orator is unable to convince the court.

The accusation is in three parts:

First, Tertullus contemptuously refers to Paul as "this man" and calls him a troublemaker. In Greek, the word *loimos* actually means a person who spreads a pestilence. Paul, then, endangers the public welfare and should be either quarantined or completely eliminated. The orator charges that Paul is stirring up riots among Jewish people everywhere in the world. Even though the allegation is exaggerated, from the viewpoint of the governor it is serious. Tertullus characterizes Paul as a seditious person who imperils the Roman state.

Second, the orator says that Paul is a ringleader of the Nazarene sect. In translation, the word *Nazarene* is usually rendered "of Nazareth."[8] The Jews identified Christians as followers of Jesus the Nazarene,[9] but why did Tertullus speak of the Nazarene sect? "It is conjectured that in pre-Christian times a Nazorean party of Jewish sectaries was known for a close observance of ascetic rules of conduct. Perhaps this party was taunted with the name *Nazoraioi* by orthodox Jews, who by Christian times applied the term of disrespect, knowingly or ignorantly, to the new Christian sect."[10] Tertullus attempts to portray the so-called Nazarene sect as a political party, but he fails, because Felix is acquainted with the Christian faith (v. 22).

Third, Tertullus says Paul tried to desecrate the temple, "but we arrested him." At best, the statement is a half-truth, because the Jews were intent on killing Paul when they seized him in the temple (21:27, 30).

[6b. "And wanted to judge him according to our law. 7. But Lysias, the commander, came and with great violence took him out of our hands, 8a. ordering his accusers to come to you."]

Consider these two points:

a. *Text.* This passage, relegated to a footnote in many translations,[11] is not in the major manuscripts. With the support of lesser manuscripts in the

---

7. James Hope Moulton states that "Luke cruelly reports the orator *verbatim*." *A Grammar of New Testament Greek*, vol. 1, *Prolegomena*, 2d ed. (Edinburgh: Clark, 1906), p. 224.

8. Linguistic difficulties remain with regard to the spelling; see Hans Heinrich Schaeder, *TDNT*, vol. 4, p. 879; Karl Heinrich Rengstorf, *NIDNTT*, vol. 2, pp. 332–34. From the Gospels we learn that the phrases *Jesus of Galilee* and *Jesus of Nazareth* are virtually synonymous (Matt. 26:69, 71), and the inscription on Jesus' cross featured the word *Nazareth* as a reference to his place of origin (John 19:19). The Jews, especially those in Jerusalem and Judea, considered Galilee a backward area and the term *Nazareth* one of derision (see John 1:46).

9. In Acts, see 2:22; 3:6; 4:10; 6:14; 22:8; 24:5; 26:9.

10. David H. Wallace, "Nazarene," *ISBE*, vol. 3, p. 500.

11. See, e.g., RSV, NASB, NEB, GNB, NIV.

Western text, it is included in some versions.[12] The interpretation of verse 8 ("If you find out from him what has happened") depends on whether one includes or deletes the passage.[13]

Some scholars think that the verses were added by a scribe to effect a smooth transition from verse 6a to verse 8b. They do not include the verses (see, e.g., NIV) and interpret the passage to mean that Felix will ask Paul about the charges brought by the Jews.

Other scholars, however, include the disputed passage in their translations. They contend that the broader context indicates Lysias is the person to be questioned by the governor (see v. 22), and they at least consider accepting the passage.[14]

b. *Explanation.* The word choice and syntax of the Western addition fit the structure of Tertullus's speech; without the addition, the speech seems to break off abruptly after the phrase *so we arrested him.*[15] The addition clearly is a protest against Lysias; Tertullus complains to the governor that the commander had exceeded his jurisdiction. The Romans had given the Jews the authority to execute anyone who desecrated their temple. Hence, by removing Paul from the temple court, the commander had blatantly violated Jewish prerogatives.

Tertullus continues to express his dissatisfaction by reminding Felix of Lysias's order that the Jewish leaders present their accusations against Paul before the governor (see 23:30). If it had not been for that order, the Jews would not have had to travel to Caesarea. The complaints noted by the orator appear to be justified.

It is one thing to say that a scribe noticed a break after the phrase *so we arrested him* and then constructed a transition. But it is quite another matter to explain the omission of this passage if it happens to be original.[16] Textual evidence aside, the Western reading has a ring of authenticity. Hence, I do not wish to bar its inclusion but judiciously place it within brackets.

8. "If you find out from him what has happened, you will be able to ascertain the complaints which we bring against him." 9. The Jews joined in the accusation and asserted that these things were true.

Without the Western addition, syntax dictates that the word *him* ("If you find out from him what has happened") refers to the nearest antecedent—

---

12. KJV, NKJV, JB, MLB. The Textus Receptus and the Vulgate also have this reading, but Arthur L. Farstad and Zane C. Hodges delete the passage. *The Greek Text According to the Majority Text* (Nashville: Nelson, 1982), p. 459.

13. Consult James Hardy Ropes, "The Text of Acts," *Beginnings,* vol. 3, p. 225.

14. See Albert C. Clark, *The Acts of the Apostles: A Critical Edition with Introduction and Notes on Selected Passages* (1933; Oxford: Clarendon, 1970), p. xlvii. Also consult F. F. Bruce, *The Book of the Acts,* rev. ed., New International Commentary on the New Testament series (Grand Rapids: Eerdmans, 1988), p. 441.

15. Lake and Cadbury aver: "On weighing the two sets of argument there seems a noticeable preponderance in favour of the Western text." *Beginnings,* vol. 4, p. 299.

16. Henry Alford, *Alford's Greek Testament: An Exegetical and Critical Commentary,* 7th ed., 4 vols. (1877; Grand Rapids: Guardian, 1976), vol. 2, p. 262.

that is, to Paul. In other words, Tertullus is telling Felix that he doubts that Paul is going to withhold information in the presence of the governor. He encourages Felix to interrogate Paul and thus learn whether the accusations the Jews level against him are true.

If the addition is accepted as the original reading, the nearest antecedent for the pronoun *him* is Lysias. This reading harmonizes with verse 22, which says that Felix adjourns the proceedings until Claudius Lysias arrives. Then it also follows that Tertullus intimates that the governor should investigate the complaints which the Jews bring against the commander. A difficulty with this interpretation is that the Jews are interested in having Felix investigate the charges they lodge against Paul.[17] Also, they wanted Felix to reprimand Lysias for interfering with their objectives and usurping their prerogatives. Although this interpretation demonstrates the peevishness of the Jews, it fails to clarify the overall context (v. 22). The textual evidence remains inconclusive; hence I have placed the text in brackets.

The speech delivered by the lawyer Tertullus reveals pompous oratory at the outset but inconclusive evidence at the end. By asking Felix to investigate all the charges against Paul, Tertullus implicitly admits the weakness of the evidence he has presented.

Luke concludes by saying that Ananias and the elders added their support to the speech of Tertullus. The irony of the incident is that Ananias, who prevented Paul from speaking in the assembly of the Sanhedrin (23:2), is now forced to listen to Paul's defense.

Greek Words, Phrases, and Constructions in 24:5 and 8

Verse 5

εὑρόντες—the aorist active participle ("finding"). Because the main verb is lacking, the sentence is incoherent. It should have featured the form εὕρομεν (we found).
στάσεις—"riots." The Majority Text has the singular "dissension" (NKJV).

Verse 8

ἀνακρίνας—this aorist active participle from the verb ἀνακρίνω (I question, examine) denotes condition: "If you find out."

---

c. Response
24:10–16

In reporting the speeches of both Tertullus and Paul, Luke devotes considerably more space to Paul's defense than to Tertullus's accusation.

---

17. Édouard Delebecque argues that on the basis of the larger context the reference must be to Paul. "Saint Paul avec ou sans le tribun Lysias en 58 à Césarée (Actes, XXIV, 6–8)," *RevThom* 81 (1981): 426–34.

With characteristic conciseness (compare 7:16; 20:24, 32) Luke telescopes the facts so that his references to both Lysias and Paul overlap.

Observe that Paul's words of respect to Felix are relatively brief (half a verse), while Tertullus's eulogy is lengthy (three verses).

10. When the governor nodded, Paul replied: "I know that you have been a judge in this nation for many years, so I cheerfully make my defense."

We should remember that Felix had received a letter from Claudius Lysias which provided him with a number of facts. He knew that Paul was a Roman citizen, that the charge against him concerned a matter of Jewish law, that the Jews wanted to kill Paul, and that Paul had done nothing to deserve the death penalty or imprisonment (23:27–29). He also knew that Lysias had heard of a Jewish plot against Paul.

When representatives of the Sanhedrin came before Felix with an orator who failed to produce convincing evidence, the governor became annoyed. With a nod in the direction of Paul, Felix gave him permission to speak.[18]

a. "I know that you have been a judge in this nation for many years." Paul refrains from praising Felix but instead merely states a neutral fact. He says that the governor has been a judge but he omits any qualifying adjectives. He notes that Felix has filled this post for many years (Felix succeeded Cumanus as governor in A.D. 52).[19] According to the Roman historiographer Tacitus, Ventidius Cumanus ruled Galilee from A.D. 48 to 52 and Felix ruled Samaria (and Judea) simultaneously until Cumanus was deposed in A.D. 52, when Felix became governor of the province of Judea.[20] We suggest that the expression *many years* should be taken literally, not rhetorically, to refer to his administration in the decade of the fifties.

b. "So I cheerfully make my defense." Paul intimates that Felix is acquainted with lawsuits in Judea and should be able to understand matters that relate to the differences between Judaism and Christianity. Paul, therefore, cheerfully begins his defense because he wants to set the record straight in the presence of a judge who has some knowledge of the Way (see v. 22). He trusts that Felix will prove to be an impartial judge.

11. "You are able to ascertain that not more than twelve days ago I went up to Jerusalem to worship. 12. And neither in the temple nor in the synagogues nor in the city itself did my accusers find me arguing with anyone or causing a riot among the people."

At the outset, Paul involves Felix in the trial by challenging him to ascertain that only twelve days had expired since Paul arrived in Jerusalem to celebrate the feast of Pentecost. He invites Felix to ask the Jewish leaders

---

18. The Western text enlarges the passage: "And when the governor had motioned for him *to make a defense for himself,* Paul answered; and *having assumed a godlike bearing,* he said. . . ." Bruce M. Metzger, *A Textual Commentary on the Greek New Testament,* 3d corrected ed. (London and New York: United Bible Societies, 1975), p. 491. (The additions are italicized.)

19. Josephus *War* 2.12.8 [247]; *Antiquities* 20.7.1 [137].

20. Tacitus *Annals* 12.54.3; Schürer, *History of the Jewish People,* vol. 1, p. 459 n. 15. But Ernst Haenchen seriously doubts the accuracy of Tacitus's report. He shows that Felix was not appointed governor until A.D. 52. *The Acts of the Apostles: A Commentary,* trans. Bernard Noble and Gerald Shinn (Philadelphia: Westminster, 1971), pp. 68–70.

when they had first seen Paul in the city. They realize that the governor knows exactly when Jewish festivals take place. They also know that Felix keeps in close contact with the military commander in Jerusalem.

a. "Not more than twelve days ago I went up to Jerusalem to worship." There are two interpretations of this sentence. Some scholars say that the twelve-day period extends from the time of Paul's arrival in Jerusalem to the moment of his defense before Felix. They assume that Paul arrived in Jerusalem on the Friday before Pentecost and count that as the first day. Then on Saturday he met with James and the elders (21:18). On Sunday Paul purified himself in the temple (21:26), and before the week of purification came to an end he was arrested (21:27). On the eighth day (Friday) he appeared before the Sanhedrin (22:30) and on the ninth day (Saturday) at nine in the evening was transported from Jerusalem to Caesarea, where he arrived on Monday, the eleventh day. The Jewish leaders came to Caesarea on Tuesday (the twelfth day), and the trial before Felix was held on Wednesday.[21] The difficulty with this view is that if Paul went to the temple for purification on Sunday, he would be sprinkled with the water of atonement on the third day following Sunday, namely, on Tuesday; and the second sprinkling would have occurred on the seventh day, namely, Saturday. In short, Paul would have been in Jerusalem longer than the time allotted by these scholars.

Other scholars take the twelve-day period to refer to the total period Paul spent in Jerusalem from arrival to departure. Following Adolf Schlatter, Ernst Haenchen extends Paul's week of purification from the third to the ninth day, places Paul's appearance before the Sanhedrin on the tenth day, and puts his transfer to Caesarea on the twelfth day.[22] The difficulty with this view is that Paul addresses Governor Felix and not the Jewish high priest about the twelve-day period. The high priest Ananias would know that Paul spent twelve days in Jerusalem, but Felix would perceive that this period continued to the moment Paul appeared before him in court.

We realize that an accurate accounting is perplexing, first, because we do not know the exact day when Paul was arrested in the temple court (21:27) and, second, because part of a day was generally counted as a full day. We are inclined to say, however, that the view to limit the twelve-day period to Paul's stay in Jerusalem has merit. In conclusion, the point Paul is making is that the time he spent in Jerusalem was short.

b. "Neither in the temple nor in the synagogues nor in the city itself." In view of the warnings Paul had received on his way to Jerusalem (20:23; 21:4, 11) and the advice of James and the elders when he was in the city

---

21. Consult Richard B. Rackham, *The Acts of the Apostles: An Exposition*, Westminster Commentaries series (1901; reprint ed., Grand Rapids: Baker, 1964), p. 441; Alford, *Alford's Greek Testament*, vol. 2, p. 263.

22. Haenchen, *Acts*, p. 654 n. 2. Bruce adopts this schedule but places Paul's arrival in Caesarea on day 12. *Acts* (Greek text), p. 631.

(21:20–24), Paul avoided public appearances. Except for making the proper arrangements for purification, he stayed away from the temple. He did not visit the local synagogues. Nowhere did Paul create any disturbance or riot. Instead, he says, "I went up to Jerusalem to worship." He wanted to be with the Jewish Christians and strengthen the bond of unity between them and Gentile believers. For him, to worship meant to serve Christ with his people.

c. "My accusers [did not] find me arguing with anyone or causing a riot among the people." The text is emphatic, as the use of three successive negative adverbs shows: "*neither* in the temple . . . *nor* in the synagogues *nor* in the city itself." In his defense, Paul refutes the charge that he is a trouble-maker who stirs up riots. He avers that this accusation lacks substance.

13. "They cannot prove to you the charges they now are bringing against me."

Paul puts Tertullus and the Jewish leaders on the defensive by challenging them to prove, in the presence of the governor, that Paul stirred up trouble in Jerusalem. According to Jewish law, an accusation had to be verified by two or three witnesses (Deut. 17:6; 19:15). Paul's opponents are unable to present evidence to support their accusation. For this reason, Paul turns from the first accusation of causing disturbances (a political offense) to the second allegation of being a leader in the Nazarene sect (v. 8; a religious issue).

14. "But this I admit to you: I serve the God of our fathers according to the Way, which they call a sect, and I believe everything that is written in the Law and the Prophets."

Paul's answer to the indictment that he is a Christian leader is straightforward: he openly admits to Felix that he is a Christian. He has no desire to hide this important fact. However, Paul blunts the significance of the Jews' accusation by putting his admission within the context of serving Israel's God. He wants the governor to know that the followers of the Way come forth from Judaism, which was a recognized legal religion within the Roman empire. Paul serves the God of his Jewish forefathers and he observes that the Christian religion has its roots in the religion of the Jews.

In the first century, Christianity was known as the Way. We understand from Paul's speech that the believers called themselves followers of the Way.[23] Sometimes they referred to their religion as "the way of the Lord" (18:25) or "the way of God" (18:26). Their adversaries, however, gave them the denigrating name *the Nazarene sect*. For the Christians, the Way was a way of life. To their Jewish opponents, it was a heresy.

Paul sets the record straight when he says that he serves "the God of our [Jewish] fathers according to the Way, which [my accusers] call a sect." He identifies himself with the Jewish people when he uses the personal pronoun *our* (but note, too, that he addresses Felix, who had married Drusilla,

---

23. Acts 9:2; 19:9, 23; 22:4; 24:14, 22.

a Jewess [v. 24]). The word *fathers* also is significant. It indicates that Paul has not forsaken the teachings of his spiritual and physical forefathers, for he serves the God of Abraham, Isaac, and Jacob (compare 22:3; 28:17).

How does Paul serve Israel's God? By believing "everything that is written in the Law and the Prophets." In other words, Paul is saying to Felix that he holds to the teachings of the Old Testament Scriptures (see 26:22; 28:23). By referring to the two parts of the Old Testament, Paul identifies with the Jews, whose religion, as Felix knows, is protected by Roman law. Conclusively, Paul proves that, although he is a leader in the Christian community, his activity breaks no Roman law.

15. "I hold to the same hope in God as these men have: there certainly will be a resurrection of both the righteous and the wicked. 16. Therefore I always do my best to maintain a blameless conscience before God and men."

We make these observations:

a. *Hope.* Paul states without compromise that he has the same hope in God as his accusers have. What is this hope in God? In brief, it is the doctrine of the resurrection of the dead. When Paul stood before the Sanhedrin and realized that the high priest Ananias refused to give him an impartial hearing, Paul cried out that he belonged to the Pharisaic party and was "on trial for the hope in the resurrection of the dead" (23:6). In the presence of Felix, Paul returns to this same topic: the hope of Israel, here called the hope in God. Once again the stage is set for a conflict between the Jews who accept the doctrine of the resurrection and those who do not. But because Paul's accusers are in the presence of the governor, they hold their peace.

b. *Resurrection.* In Old Testament times, the doctrine of the resurrection was taught (Dan. 12:2). Throughout the intertestamental period and the time of Jesus and the apostles, this doctrine was part of Israel's beliefs.[24] Paul, like the Pharisees, taught the doctrine of the resurrection, but the Sadducees rejected it.

In his epistles, Paul expounds his belief in the twofold resurrection of the dead: that of the righteous and the unrighteous.[25] (Consider that a number of Paul's letters were already written at the time of his trial and were circulating in the churches.) Writes Emil Schürer, "This idea was never commonly accepted; many continued to look only for a resurrection of the just."[26] Nevertheless, Jesus teaches that all people have to face the judgment (Matt. 25:31–46) and all the dead—those who have done good and those who have done evil—will be raised to be judged (John 5:28–30; see also Rev. 20:12). Concurring with Jesus' teachings on this point of doctrine,

---

24. See the literature of intertestamental times: II Macc. 7:9, 14, 23, 36; 12:43–44; Psalms of Solomon 3:11–12; 10:8; 14:10. And consult Josephus *War* 2.8.14 [163]; *Antiquities* 18.1.3 [14].

25. See I Cor. 15:23–26; I Thess. 4:16–17.

26. Schürer, *History of the Jewish People,* vol. 2, p. 494.

Paul refers to a resurrection of the just and the unjust that is followed by the judgment and the coming of Christ's kingdom (compare II Tim. 4:1).

For the apostles, the teaching of Jesus' resurrection was fundamental to the Christian faith. In their sermons and speeches before Jewish and Gentile audiences, both Peter and Paul proclaim this doctrine.[27] From this teaching, they deduced the tenet of the general resurrection of believers and unbelievers. Paul himself cherished the firm conviction that after his departure from this life, his body would be raised from the dead, he would face judgment, and he would be with Christ eternally.

c. *Conscience.* "Therefore I always do my best to maintain a blameless conscience before God and men." Paul says that he puts forth every effort to have a conscience unburdened by sin, without offense, and blameless.[28] He chooses the same words he uttered before the Sanhedrin a few days earlier, when he said, "I have lived my life with a perfectly clear conscience before God to this day" (23:1). For teaching the fundamental truth of the resurrection of the dead, he is facing trial (see v. 21). Yet his conscience is blameless before God and man because he constantly strives to do God's will: to proclaim his revealed truth.

Greek Words, Phrases, and Constructions in 24:10–16

Verse 10

νεύσαντος—the aorist active participle from νεύω (I nod) in the genitive case is part of the genitive absolute construction. The participle denotes time: "When the governor nodded to him."

ἐκ—with expressions of time, this preposition indicates a point of departure (i.e., the time when something began): "for many years."[29]

ὄντα—the present participle of the verb εἰμί (I am) in context conveys the meaning of the perfect tense ("you have been").

ἀπολογοῦμαι—here is a true middle that is translated "I make my defense."

Verse 11

δυναμένου—the present middle participle in the genitive case forms the genitive absolute construction with the pronoun σου (you). The participle introduces the complementary infinitive ἐπιγνῶναι (to learn, find out).

οὐ πλείους—"not more than." The genitive of comparison would normally be used instead of the nominative. "But it is an idiom of *comparison* and not limited to the Nominative as such."[30]

εἰσίν μοι—the pronoun is the dative of possession; in translation the verb *to be*

---

27. Acts 2:24, 32; 3:15; 4:10; 5:30; 10:40; 13:30, 33–34, 37; 17:31.

28. Bauer, p. 102; Thayer, p. 70.

29. A. T. Robertson, *A Grammar of the Greek New Testament in the Light of Historical Research* (Nashville: Broadman, 1934), p. 597.

30. C. F. D. Moule, *An Idiom-Book of New Testament Greek,* 2d ed. (Cambridge: Cambridge University Press, 1960), p. 31 n. 2.

becomes the verb *to have* and the pronoun *me* becomes "I": "I have not more than twelve days." In a smooth translation it reads, "not more than twelve days ago."[31]

προσκυνήσων—this is the future active participle of the verb προσκυνέω (I worship) and transmits the idea of purpose.

ἀφ' ἧς—the abbreviation of ἀφ' ἡμέρας ᾗ (from the day on which). The dative pronoun is attracted to the genitive noun and becomes ἧς.

Verse 14

οὕτως—although the adverb means "to such an extent," it is completely replaced by κατὰ τὴν ὁδόν (according to the Way) and therefore is not translated. The verb λατρεύω (I serve) relates to worship services (compare II Tim. 1:3; Heb. 12:28).

τῷ πατρῴῳ θεῷ—the adjective πατρῴῳ (of one's [fore]father) needs the possessive pronoun *my*.

γεγραμμένοις—the perfect passive participle from γράφω (I write) is a perfect with resultant state. That is, the Scriptures written in the past have lasting validity.

Verses 15–16

μέλλειν ἔσεσθαι—the two infinitives both express the future and thus one is redundant. Consult the comment on 11:28.

ἐν τούτῳ—this prepositional phrase does not mean "in this" but "for that reason."[32] It has a causal connotation.

διὰ παντός—see the explanation at 2:25.

---

d. Facts
24:17–21

In his trial Paul counteracts three accusations: a political charge that he is a troublemaker and two religious allegations, one that he is a leader of the Nazarene sect and another that he desecrated the temple. Having effectively refuted the first two indictments, he now proceeds to disprove the third charge.

17. "But after several years, I returned to Jerusalem to bring gifts to my people and present offerings. 18. While I was doing this, they found me purified in the temple—not in a crowd or a riot."

a. "But after several years, I returned to Jerusalem." Paul states that he had been away from Jerusalem for an extended period. His last visit to the city (at the conclusion of his second missionary journey [18:22]) had been made five years earlier. But if we think in terms of Paul's extended visit to the Jerusalem Council (15:4), the interval spans nearly a decade.

b. "To bring gifts to my people." Paul intimates that his absence from Jerusalem could not have contributed to riots. On the contrary, he tried to

---

31. Friedrich Blass and Albert Debrunner, *A Greek Grammar of the New Testament and Other Early Christian Literature*, trans. and rev. Robert Funk (Chicago: University of Chicago Press, 1961), #189.1.

32. Ibid., #219.3.

fulfill the apostolic mandate "to remember the poor" (Gal. 2:10) and to help all people (Gal. 6:10). Accordingly, he brought a collection of financial gifts from Gentile churches to the poverty-stricken Jewish Christians in Jerusalem. In his epistles, Paul mentions the collections for these people;[33] here is the only reference in Acts to Paul's delivering the gifts to the impoverished Christians in Jerusalem. For undisclosed reasons, both Paul and Luke refrain from providing additional information.

c. "And present offerings." What is the meaning of the expression *offerings*? The word lends itself to three possible interpretations. The first interpretation is that the terms *gifts* and *offerings* are synonyms. Paul dedicated these donations as thank offerings to God by giving them to the poor (compare II Cor. 8:19). A second interpretation is that Paul delivered the gifts to the poor and thereafter presented thank offerings to God as in response to a vow (compare 18:18). And the third interpretation is that Paul did not intend to come to Jerusalem to bring offerings, but on the advice of James and the elders he did pay the expenses of the four Nazirites (21:26). Since Luke often compresses material, the term *offering* is a shortened form meant to bring to mind the episode in the temple (21:26–27).

d. "While I was doing this, they found me purified in the temple." Paul obviously refers to the time when the days of purification were almost completed (21:27). Paul mentions this incident to Felix to refute Tertullus's accusation that he had tried to desecrate the temple.

e. "Not in a crowd or a riot." At the time the Jews discovered Paul in the temple, they found him privately and peacefully engaged in a ceremonial rite. They did not see him stirring up a crowd or provoking a riot. The high priest and his companions could say that they themselves were not present in the temple when Paul was arrested, but that others had brought the incident to their attention. Precisely for that reason, Paul becomes specific in relating the facts of the incident.

19. "But some Jews from the province of Asia were there, who ought to be present before you to accuse me if they have anything against me."

Paul specifies who his erstwhile accusers were: Jews from the province of Asia. They knew Paul from his travels and work in that part of the world and, after traveling to Jerusalem for Pentecost, had seen Paul in the temple. To be precise, they, not Paul, had stirred up the crowd and instigated a riot. If these Jews from the Dispersion had anything against him, they should have accused him in the presence of Governor Felix. But these accusers are not present. Therefore, Paul now involves the high priest and the elders in the trial. Thus far they have been silent and allowed the lawyer Tertullus to speak for them. If they themselves had learned of any crime Paul had committed while they questioned him in the Sanhedrin, let them speak now.

20. "Or else let these men themselves tell what crime they found in me when I stood before the Sanhedrin, 21. unless it was this one sentence that

---

33. See Rom. 15:25–28; I Cor. 16:1–4, 15; II Cor. 8:1–4.

I shouted while standing among them: 'I am on trial before you today concerning the resurrection of the dead.' "

a. "Or else let these men themselves tell what crime they found in me when I stood before the Sanhedrin." Paul now challenges Ananias and his companions to speak. Even if they themselves did not witness the incident in the temple, they were present the next day when Paul stood before the Sanhedrin. They had listened to Paul's words and should be capable of testifying whether they had discovered any crime Paul had committed. The orator Tertullus presumably had not been present at the Sanhedrin meeting; now, before Felix, Ananias himself must testify whether he had found Paul guilty. But the high priest remains silent.

b. "Unless it was this one sentence that I shouted while standing among them." Paul asks his accusers whether he had committed a crime. Should they choose to answer, they would have to admit: no, not at all!

Paul once more seizes the opportunity to refer to the resurrection (see v. 15). He prefaces his remark by saying that he shouted one sentence while he stood among the members of the Sanhedrin. The fact that he uses the verb *to shout* should not be understood as an apology for unseemly behavior before the ecclesiastical body. Rather, it provides evidence that the meeting had been unruly (see 23:1–10). Simply put, the comment placed Ananias, who had presided at that meeting, in an unfavorable light.

c. "I am on trial before you today concerning the resurrection of the dead." Paul states that when he was before the Sanhedrin he uttered only one critical sentence, and it pertained not to the political concerns of the Romans but to the theological concerns of Jews and Christians. This means that the point of conflict between Ananias and Paul is a theological issue that ought to be discussed in a Jewish ecclesiastical court. In brief, Paul expects the judge to dismiss the case, which had no place in a Roman civil court, and to set him free. In view of the fact that the theological tenet of the resurrection of the dead was shared by both Pharisees and Christians but not by the Sadducees, we realize that Paul alludes to the well-known controversy between Sadducees and Pharisees.

Paul addresses not only Felix but also Ananias and his companions. He says, "I am on trial before you [plural]." By using the plural pronoun *you*, in the Greek, he compels Ananias and the elders to speak on a theological issue that Felix refuses to accept as evidence in a Roman court.

Notice that whenever Paul sees an opportunity to mention the doctrine of the resurrection, he seizes it. For him, this doctrine is fundamental to the Christian faith and fearlessly he proclaims it everywhere.

Practical Considerations in 24:17–21

At different times, both Peter and Paul defend themselves in court. Both of them undauntedly present factual material to support their claims to innocence, both are fully in command of the proceedings, and both nudge the court to arrive at a verdict that is favorable to them. Peter and John stand trial before the Sanhedrin after healing the cripple at the temple gate (3:1–10), and Peter forthrightly speaks the truth (4:8–12, 19–20). He changes the trial from a criminal investigation to an inquiry about an act of mercy. Moreover, he puts the stress not on the cripple who was healed but on Jesus the Savior (4:12; see also 5:30–32). Lacking training in law and skill in courtroom procedures, Peter nevertheless answers all the charges against him. He demonstrates that the Holy Spirit guides him in presenting the truth.

Paul also takes control of courtroom proceedings. In front of his accusers and Governor Felix, Paul succinctly answers every allegation brought against him and demonstrates that the charges are unfounded. In this trial Paul twice introduces the doctrine of the resurrection, which is basic to the Christian faith. The Holy Spirit enables Paul to serve as his own lawyer.

Both Peter and Paul face Jewish leaders who profess to serve Israel's God. The apostles counteract the lie and Satan, the father of the lie. Today, men and women filled with the Holy Spirit skillfully and boldly advance the cause of Christ by establishing God's revealed truth. They know that in the face of error, truth eventually will triumph. They fearlessly expose the lie and oppose the father of the lie. As Martin Luther, referring to the devil, put it succinctly,

One little Word shall fell him.

Greek Words, Phrases, and Constructions in 24:17–21

Verse 17

πλειόνων—the comparative of πολύς is translated "several." It is comparative, not positive or superlative, even though it signifies "many."

ποιήσων—the future active participle expresses purpose. The idiom in English is "to *give* alms," not "to *do* alms."

τὸ ἔθνος—"the [Jewish] nation." Paul employs this term instead of λαός (people) in addressing a Gentile governor. With this term, he includes Jews and Jewish Christians.

Verse 18

ἐν αἷς—the relative pronoun relates to the feminine plural noun προσφοράς (offerings), which is its nearest antecedent. Some lesser manuscripts feature the neuter plural οἷς (among which [circumstances]), which is harder to explain and thus deserves consideration as being the original reading.

ἡγνισμένον—the perfect passive participle from ἁγνίζω (I purify) shows lasting result. The passive has its agent in the dative case of the noun *offerings*.

Verse 19

τινὲς . . . Ἰουδαῖοι—in this clause the verb *to be* must be supplied. Its absence does not connote incoherence.

ἔδει—the imperfect of δεῖ (it is necessary) conveys moral obligation. The Asian Jews ought to have been present in court.

ἔχοιεν—the optative in the protasis of a conditional sentence shows a degree of flexibility. "If they (really) had any complaint (which they have not)."[34]

Verses 20–21

ἐπί—"before." This preposition with the genitive case occurs "in the language of lawsuits."[35] (See also 23:30; 25:10.) The reading ἐφ' ὑμῶν (before you) is preferred by most translators.[36] Others follow the reading ὑφ' ὑμῶν (by you).[37]

μιᾶς ταύτης φωνῆς—"this one utterance." The demonstrative pronoun *this* has been placed between the numerical adjective *one* and the noun *utterance* for emphasis. ἧς is the genitive of attraction.

---

e. Adjournment and Delay
24:22–27

After Paul had defended himself, Felix explained that he would wait for the arrival of Claudius Lysias before deciding Paul's case. In view of Paul's defense, he should have dismissed the case for lack of evidence. Instead he adjourned the court.

22. But Felix, who understood the Way more accurately [than most people], adjourned the proceedings and said, "When the commander Lysias comes down, I will decide your case."

Luke portrays the spread of the gospel and reports that Governor Felix had appreciable knowledge of Christianity. He writes that Felix "understood the Way more accurately," to which I add the phrase *than most people*. How Felix learned about the Christian faith Luke fails to disclose. Possibly, the believers in Caesarea were instrumental in teaching this Roman official the doctrines of the faith. About two decades earlier, the Holy Spirit had been poured out on Gentile believers in Caesarea (10:44–46); among them was Cornelius, an officer in the Roman army. Or perhaps Felix gained religious knowledge from his wife Drusilla, who was a Jewess (v. 24), a daughter of Herod Agrippa I (see 12:1–23), and a sister to Agrippa II (25:13). Both Felix and Drusilla revealed an interest in the Christian faith, as is evident from their desire to hear Paul preach the gospel (v. 24).

Luke presents a summary statement of the manner in which Felix brought the trial to a conclusion. The governor, employing the tactic of delay, dismissed the high priest and elders and told them that he would decide the case when the commander Lysias came down from Jerusalem. With his characteristic brevity, Luke chooses not to offer any information about Lysias's visit.

---

34. Moule, *Idiom-Book*, p. 150.
35. Bauer, p. 286.
36. NAB, NASB, NEB, NIV, RSV, JB, *Moffatt,* and *Phillips.*
37. KJV, NKJV, GNB, MLB.

23. He commanded the officer that Paul be kept under guard but be allowed some freedom and that he permit his friends to be helpful to him.

The governor should not have kept Paul in custody, for the charges against him did not involve any point of Roman law. Felix perhaps desired both to appease the Jews and to protect a Roman citizen. He instructed an officer to guard Paul but to allow him a measure of freedom, as if he were living in his own house (compare 28:30).[38] Felix allowed Paul's friends to bring him food, drink, and other commodities to make his life comfortable. The friends who visited him probably were members of the church in Caesarea (see 21:8–14).

Mission Headquarters

During his mission career, Paul had spent considerable time in Antioch before and after his first missionary journey, in Corinth during his second journey, and afterward in Ephesus. Now Caesarea becomes his residence. In the protective custody of the Roman military, he is free to receive friends. We imagine that delegations come to him from various churches in Palestine, and that Paul, a seasoned missionary, strengthens these friends. But Paul did more than receive visitors. For example, his conversations with soldiers who guarded him undoubtedly were evangelistic in nature. We expect that a number of these soldiers became believers; when they were transferred to other parts of the Roman empire, they would spread the knowledge of Jesus far and wide.

It is reasonable to suppose that during Paul's two-year stay in Caesarea, Luke busied himself in collecting pertinent data for the writing of his two books, the Gospel and Acts. He received his information from "eyewitnesses and ministers of the word" (Luke 1:2) in Jerusalem, Judea, Samaria, and Galilee. Further, he had ample time to write these books. He probably completed the Gospel during Paul's imprisonment and sent it forth into the Greco-Roman world. In his pastoral Epistles, written after his release, Paul quotes Luke's Gospel and calls it Scripture: "The worker deserves his wages" (Luke 10:7, quoted in I Tim. 5:18). Paul, then, was acquainted with Luke's literary activities and used these writings in his missionary task.

---

24. Several days later, Felix came with his wife Drusilla, a Jewess. He summoned Paul and listened to him speak about faith in Christ Jesus.

Among the first to listen to Paul were Governor Felix and his wife Drusilla. They came to hear the gospel, which Luke describes as objective "faith in Christ Jesus." Luke gives no indication that the governor and his wife demonstrated subjective faith.

The expression *came* need not be interpreted that Felix had returned to Caesarea after having been away. Rather, the term in context signifies that

---

38. Josephus relates that Herod Agrippa I was imprisoned in Rome at the time of Emperor Tiberius's death. He had been moved from a military prison camp "to the house where he had lived before his imprisonment." *Antiquities* 18.6.10 [235] (LCL).

both Felix and Drusilla left the governor's mansion and proceeded to the place where Paul was kept in custody. The governor ordered the military officer to bring Paul to him. Then at leisure he and his wife listened to Paul preach the gospel.

This couple, interested in learning more about the Way, had a marital history that was tainted by promiscuity. The Roman historiographer Suetonius relates that Drusilla was the third wife of Felix.[39] Drusilla likewise had her share of husbands. Born in Rome, Drusilla was brought by her father to Caesarea, where she spent her childhood.[40] Six-year old Drusilla was promised in marriage to Epiphanes, the son of King Antiochus of Commagene.[41] But Epiphanes refused to submit to the Jewish rite of circumcision, and so the marriage was never consummated. When Drusilla was fourteen, her brother, Agrippa II, gave her in marriage to Azizus king of Emesa in northern Syria; however, Drusilla left him to become the wife of Felix.[42] Through an intermediary, the governor had promised Drusilla a life of happiness, which she lacked at the court of Azizus.[43] By marrying Felix, the Jewess Drusilla defied the Old Testament law that forbade her to become the spouse of a Gentile. Yet she was sufficiently interested to come to Paul and listen to him preach the gospel of Jesus Christ.

The Western text indicates that Drusilla persuaded Felix to let her listen to Paul: "Felix came with his wife Drusilla, who was a Jewess, *who asked to see Paul and hear the word. Wishing therefore to satisfy her,* he summoned Paul."[44]

25. As Paul was conversing with them about righteousness, self-control, and the judgment to come, Felix became afraid. "Go away for now," he said, "I will call for you when I have time."

Although he has considerable knowledge of the Way, Felix sees an opportunity to receive accurate information about Christianity from one of its foremost leaders. Drusilla, acquainted with the teachings of Scripture and Jewish traditions, also wants to hear the teachings of the Christian faith. Both husband and wife are attracted to the gospel as a moth is to the light that dispels the darkness.

True to form, Paul preaches the gospel and speaks to them about righteousness.[45] He uses this particular term thirty-three times in his letter to the Romans, which he wrote a few months earlier while he was still in Corinth and before he commenced his journey to Jerusalem. By contrast,

---

39. Suetonius *Claudius* 28.

40. Herod Agrippa I erected a statue of her in Caesarea. Josephus *Antiquities* 19.9.1 [357].

41. Josephus *Antiquities* 19.9.1 [354–55].

42. Drusilla married Felix in A.D. 54. Consult Schürer, *History of the Jewish People*, vol. 1, pp. 461–62.

43. Josephus *Antiquities* 20.7.1–2 [139–43].

44. Metzger, *Textual Commentary*, p. 491 (the additions are italicized); Clark, *Acts*, pp. 155, 381.

45. The word *dikaiosunē* (righteousness) is one of Paul's favorite expressions: it occurs fifty-six times in all his epistles. John features it seven times in his writings, Matthew seven times, the author of Hebrews six times, James three times, and Luke (in his Gospel) once.

the word *righteousness* occurs only four times in Acts: Peter uses it once in his sermon preached in Caesarea (10:35); Paul calls Elymas an "enemy of all righteousness" (13:10), mentions the word in his Areopagus address (17:31), and again uses it in Caesarea when he preaches to the governor and his wife (24:25).

We should not think that Paul gives this couple an abstract theological lecture. Rather, he presents the gospel to them in terms of living according to the principles of the Way. That is, Paul teaches them about knowing right from wrong, the virtues of self-control and chastity, and an unavoidable day of judgment. He tells them that they must become followers of Jesus to be able to walk in the Way.[46]

Felix and Drusilla become uneasy when Paul explains the word *self-control*.[47] In the mirror of Paul's explicit teaching, the governor and his spouse see themselves. And when the speaker adds that they eventually must face the divine Judge to receive their verdict, Felix is filled with fear. He himself has been appointed to judge Paul, but Paul informs the governor that he must appear before the judgment seat of Jesus Christ (10:42; 17:31).

Enough is enough for Felix, especially when Paul's teaching reflects on the governor's moral and ethical conduct. Like the Athenian philosophers who informed Paul that they would hear him again sometime (17:32), Felix terminates Paul's teaching with the polite excuse that he will listen to him again when time permits. The governor is afraid of the coming judgment, but he refuses both to repent of his evil ways and to turn in faith to Jesus.

26. At the same time, however, he was hoping that Paul would offer him a bribe. So he used to send for him quite often and talk with him.

Felix kept Paul in jail because he hoped to receive a bribe from his prisoner.[48] The practice of keeping prisoners in jail until they paid a bribe, although forbidden by Roman law, was common.[49]

We surmise that when Felix heard that Paul had brought monetary gifts to the people of Jerusalem (v. 17), his greedy mind immediately conceived a plan to exact a price for Paul's release. When numerous friends visited Paul to provide for his daily needs, Felix was convinced that they could help in paying a bribe for Paul's release.

Luke writes that Felix would frequently call for Paul to have a chat with him. This information indicates that the relationship between Felix and

---

46. Consult J. Pathrapankal, "Christianity as a 'Way,'" in *Les Actes des Apôtres: Traditions, Rédaction, Théologie*, ed. J. Kremer, Bibliotheca Ephemeridium Theologicarum Lovaniensium 48 (Louvain: Louvain University Press, 1979), pp. 537–38.

47. Literature of that era discloses that the word frequently denoted sexual purity that is maintained by exercising restraint in one's conduct. See, for instance, I Cor. 7:9 (the verb *control*); Gal. 5:23; Polycarp to the Philippians 4:2; Testament of Naphtali 8:8.

48. The KJV and NKJV, following the Majority Text, have an additional phrase, "that he might loose [release] him."

49. Albinus, the governor who succeeded Porcius Festus (v. 27), on two different occasions freed only those prisoners who paid him a bribe. Josephus *War* 2.14.1 [273]; *Antiquities* 20.9.5 [215].

Paul was amicable, yet these talks never resulted in any significant action. Felix used them to fill some of his idle moments, but Paul remained under arrest. The governor could legally keep Paul in custody because Paul had not yet exercised the right of a Roman citizen: to appeal to the emperor. As soon as an appeal was made, the governor was obliged to send Paul under military guard to Rome, where he would have to stand trial before the emperor. In short, Felix was within the bounds of the law.[50]

27. After two years, Porcius Festus became the successor of Felix. But Felix wanted to do the Jews a favor, so he left Paul in prison.

Two years later, Emperor Nero recalled Felix to Rome. The recall was prompted by political conditions in Palestine. Felix had intervened militarily when Jewish and Syrian inhabitants of Caesarea started throwing rocks at each other in a dispute over civil rights. The soldiers killed a number of Jews, imprisoned others, and looted houses in which these people had hoarded substantial sums of money.[51] As a result, writes Josephus, "when Porcius Festus was sent by Nero as successor to Felix, the leaders of the Jewish community of Caesarea went up to Rome to accuse Felix."[52] Fortunately for Felix, his well-to-do brother Pallas pleaded for him in the presence of Nero and had him exonerated.

However, Luke writes, "Felix wanted to do the Jews a favor, so he left Paul in prison." The word Luke uses for "favor" conveys the meaning *quid pro quo* (something for something).[53] Felix knew that he would be questioned about disturbances that had occurred in Caesarea. He wanted to gain the support of the Sanhedrin in Jerusalem by keeping Paul imprisoned and thus to counteract the accusations of the Caesarean Jews. The Western text, however, states that Felix kept Paul in prison "on account of Drusilla." As Herodias bore a grudge against John the Baptist (Mark 6:19), so Drusilla despised Paul for criticizing her marital life. She could not have him killed, but she was instrumental in keeping him imprisoned.

Greek Words, Phrases, and Constructions in 24:22–27

Verse 22

ἀκριβέστερον—the comparative of ἀκριβῶς (accurately) can be understood as a superlative ("very accurately"). However, because the object of comparison is implied in the context, interpreting the adverb as a comparative is acceptable and valid.[54]

---

50. Consult A. N. Sherwin-White, *Roman Society and Roman Law in the New Testament* (1963; reprint ed., Grand Rapids: Baker, 1978), p. 63.
51. Josephus *War* 2.13.7 [266–70]; *Antiquities* 20.8.7 [173–78].
52. Josephus *Antiquities* 20.8.9 [182].
53. In the Greek, the word is in the plural. Luke uses the same expression in 25:9, but in the singular.
54. Consult Robert Hanna, *A Grammatical Aid to the Greek New Testament* (Grand Rapids: Baker, 1983), p. 241.

εἰδώς—the perfect active participle of οἶδα (I know) conveys the present tense and has a causal meaning.

Verses 23–24

τηρεῖσθαι—"to be watched." Note the present tense in the series of four successive infinitives. The Majority Text adds the words ἤ προσέρχεσθαι (or to come to) after the verb ὑπηρετεῖν (to be helpful).

ἰδίᾳ—the presence of this adjective ("one's own") is superfluous; the definite article τῇ is sufficient.

Verses 25–26

διαλεγομένου—the genitive absolute construction features the present participle with a temporal connotation ("while he was conversing"). By contrast, the participle γενόμενος is in the aorist to disclose that Felix's fear was momentary. The attributive participle ἔχον with τὸ νῦν, meaning "for the time being," is difficult to explain.[55]

πυκνότερον—this comparative adverb can be interpreted as a superlative ("very often") or as a comparative ("more often").

ἅμα καὶ ἐλπίζων—the combination of adverb, conjunction, and present participle means "at the same time also in the expectation."[56]

Verse 27

διετίας—"a period of two years." The noun occurs only twice in the New Testament (here and in 28:30). The genitive case is part of the genitive absolute construction.

δεδεμένον—the perfect passive participle of the verb δέω (I bind). The perfect tense signifies an extended period. The participle need not denote that Paul was kept in chains, for he was given "some freedom" (v. 23). But according to Paul's own testimony, he was in chains during the administration of Felix (26:29).

Summary of Chapter 24

The high priest Ananias, along with some of the elders and a lawyer named Tertullus, comes to Caesarea to be present at Paul's trial before Governor Felix. Tertullus praises and thanks the governor for the changes he has effected in the nation. Then he registers his accusations against Paul by calling him a troublemaker, a leader of the Nazarene sect, and a desecrator of the temple.

Paul responds by denying that he stirred up a crowd either in the synagogues or elsewhere in Jerusalem. He declares that he worships Israel's God, subscribes to the teachings of the Scriptures, and believes in the resurrection. He informs Felix that he came to Jerusalem to bring gifts to the poor and to present offerings. He says that if the Jews from the province of

---

55. Moule, *Idiom-Book*, p. 160.
56. Blass and Debrunner, *Greek Grammar*, #425.2.

Asia, who are absent, or the delegation from Jerusalem have any charges, they should state them before Felix.

Felix dismisses the proceedings and announces that he will make a decision when the military commander Lysias arrives. He orders that Paul be kept in custody but have the freedom to receive friends.

Felix and Drusilla visit Paul for the purpose of hearing Paul preach about the Christian faith. When Paul discusses righteousness, self-control, and judgment, Felix terminates the meeting with the promise of summoning Paul some other time. He summons Paul frequently but expects to receive a bribe from him. After a two-year period has ended, Felix is succeeded by Porcius Festus and Paul remains a prisoner.

25

In Jerusalem and Caesarea, *part 5*

25:1–27

Outline (continued)

25:1–12	3. Paul Before Festus
25:1–5	a. Jerusalem
25:6–8	b. Caesarea
25:9–12	c. Appeal
25:13–27	4. Paul and Agrippa II
25:13–14a	a. Visitors Identified
25:14b–22	b. Problem Explained
25:23–27	c. Paul Introduced

25 1 Festus, then, three days after arriving in the province, went up to Jerusalem from Caesarea. 2 There the chief priests and Jewish leaders appeared before him and were bringing charges against Paul. 3 They were asking that he favor them instead of Paul, namely, that Festus summon Paul to Jerusalem; meanwhile they were plotting an ambush to kill him along the way. 4 Festus replied, "Paul is being kept in Caesarea and I myself am about to go there soon. 5 Therefore, let some of your leaders accompany me, and if they find anything morally wrong in this man, let them press charges against him."

6 After Festus spent no more than eight or ten days among them, he went down to Caesarea. The next day, he took his place in the courtroom and ordered that Paul be brought before him. 7 When Paul arrived, the Jews who had come down from Jerusalem stood around him and brought many serious charges against him, which they were unable to support. 8 Then Paul defended himself: "I have not sinned against either the Jewish law, the temple, or Caesar."

9 But Festus, wishing to do the Jews a favor, asked Paul, "Are you willing to go up to Jerusalem and there stand trial before me on these things?" 10 Paul, however, said: "I am now standing in Caesar's court, where I should be tried. I have done nothing wrong against the Jews, as you yourself very well know. 11 If, then, I am in the wrong and have done something worthy of death, I do not refuse to die. But if there is no truth to the accusations of these Jews, then no one has the right to hand me over to them. I appeal to Caesar." 12 When Festus had conferred with his council, he said: "You appealed to Caesar; to Caesar you will go."

---

3. Paul Before Festus
25:1–12

Unlike Felix, a freed slave who had climbed the political ladder until he became governor, Festus was a member of one of the noble families in Rome. Whereas Felix had been greedy and evil, Festus was wise and honorable. From Felix he inherited a nation that was marked by the absence of law and order. In an effort to restore a semblance of security and peace, Festus eliminated the so-called daggermen, who had become increasingly bold in the last years of Felix's administration.[1] These daggermen were Jewish assassins who mingled among the crowds on festive days. With daggers hidden in their cloaks, they would murder their opponents and then disappear. When bystanders gathered around a fallen leader, the daggermen would reappear, join the mourners, and so escape detection.[2]

---

1 Josephus *Antiquities* 20.8.10 [185–88].
2. Consult Emil Schürer, *The History of the Jewish People in the Age of Jesus Christ* (175 B.C.–A.D. 135), rev. and ed. Geza Vermes and Fergus Millar, 3 vols. (Edinburgh: Clark, 1973–87), vol. 1, p. 463.

Festus also inherited the problem of determining the guilt or innocence of Paul, the prisoner. Lacking experience in Jewish religious matters, Festus immediately went to Jerusalem to learn about Jewish law, worship, and customs.

a. Jerusalem
25:1–5

1. Festus, then, three days after arriving in the province, went up to Jerusalem from Caesarea. 2. There the chief priests and Jewish leaders appeared before him and were bringing charges against Paul.

a. *Time.* Both time references ("three days" [25:1] and "two years" [24:27]) provide no indication what year Porcius Festus came to Judea and how long he was governor. To find clues, let us look at information that historiographers supply.

The beginning of Festus's rule cannot be determined accurately because we do not know exactly when Felix was recalled. We can make an estimate, using as a starting point a comment made by Claudius Lysias. When he questioned Paul, the commander referred to the Egyptian who revolted against Rome "some time ago" (21:38). This incident occurred during Nero's rule, when the emperor had reigned for some time. Lysias's remark must be interpreted to refer to a time much later than Nero's accession to the throne (October 13, A.D. 54).[3] And after his arrest, Paul had spent two years in prison. It is likely that Felix governed Palestine from A.D. 52 to 59,[4] and that Nero recalled him in 59. Festus probably would have arrived in Caesarea in 59 or 60.

We do know that Festus died in office and that his successor, Albinus, came to Judea in A.D. 62. Josephus relates that Albinus was governor at the time of the Feast of Tabernacles in the autumn of the year; presumably he had assumed his duties a few months earlier.[5]

b. *Moment.* "Festus, then, three days after arriving in the province, went up to Jerusalem from Caesarea." When Porcius Festus arrived in Caesarea, he knew that only the Jewish leaders would be able to help him reverse the tide of political and social unrest in Judea. He immediately traveled to Jerusalem, where he met the high priest Ishmael, son of Phabi, who had been appointed by Agrippa II in A.D. 59.[6] Luke writes that the chief priests and Jewish leaders appeared before Festus in Jerusalem, probably in Fortress Antonia. But note that he writes the plural form *chief priests.* Even

---

3. Josephus *War* 2.13.5 [261–63]; *Antiquities* 20.8.6 [169–72]. See Schürer, *History of the Jewish People,* vol. 1, p. 465 n. 42.

4. For an early date for Felix's departure from Caesarea, see Kirsopp Lake, "The Chronology of Acts," *Beginnings,* vol. 5, pp. 464–67. Compare Colin J. Hemer, *The Book of Acts in the Setting of Hellenistic History,* ed. Conrad H. Gempf (Tübingen: Mohr, 1989), p. 171.

5. Josephus gives the date as "four years before the war" (*War* 6.5.3 [300]) and "seven years and five months" before the destruction of Jerusalem [308] (LCL).

6. Josephus *Antiquities* 20.8.8 [179]; Schürer, *History of the Jewish People,* vol. 2, p. 231. Ananias (see 23:2; 24:1) had been deposed.

though Ananias had been deposed, he continued to exert enormous influence. He possibly was among the Jewish leaders who acquainted Festus with the grievances of the people. Other members of the high-priestly family were also present (compare 4:6).

c. *Charges.* "[They] were bringing charges against Paul." Luke is not interested in the political unrest of that day but rather calls attention to the charges the Jews brought against Paul (refer to 24:5–8). Although two years had passed since Paul had defended himself before Felix (24:10–21, 27), the Jews had not forgotten their charges against their enemy Paul. For two years, Paul had been safe in the custody of the Roman military (see 24:23, 27) and could not be touched by the Jewish authorities. In their opinion, Paul represented a menace to Judaism and had to be eliminated.

3. They were asking that he favor them instead of Paul, namely, that Festus summon Paul to Jerusalem; meanwhile they were plotting an ambush to kill him along the way.

a. "They were asking that he favor them instead of Paul." The Jerusalem leaders understood that the new governor might choose to release Paul. If Paul should travel west to Rome and Spain (see Rom. 15:23–24, 28), they would be unable to eliminate him. So the chief priests and elders curried Festus's goodwill and repeatedly asked him to extend them a favor by not listening to any pleas from Paul. They suggested that Festus summon Paul to Jerusalem, where the governor could conduct a trial with the Jewish leaders present. Their request seemed perfectly logical, because Festus was already in Jerusalem. He would only have to send a messenger to Caesarea with the summons for Paul and then rule whether Paul was guilty or innocent of the charges against him.

b. "Meanwhile they were plotting an ambush to kill him along the way." Luke adds that the Jews were plotting an ambush in case Festus agreed to their request. They planned to station a number of people somewhere between Caesarea and Jerusalem; these people would assassinate Paul and the Roman soldiers assigned to escort him (compare 23:12, 21).

4. Festus replied, "Paul is being kept in Caesarea and I myself am about to go there soon. 5. Therefore, let some of your leaders accompany me, and if they find anything morally wrong in this man, let them press charges against him."

If we suppose that Claudius Lysias was still commander in Jerusalem, Festus would have received pertinent information from him about Paul and the earlier Jewish plot (compare 23:12–22). Further, if Luke could write about the Jews planning another ambush, we presume that the news of the plot also came to the attention of Festus. As the Roman governor he had to guarantee Paul's safety and therefore he refused the request of the Jews.

In addition, the Jewish leaders indirectly tried to weaken Festus's authority by having him move his judgment seat from Caesarea, where the Roman governor had his residence and headquarters, to Jerusalem, the center of Jewish influence. Festus reacted negatively to this encroachment on his power and thus rejected the suggestion for a change of venue. He stated that Paul was under guard in Caesarea and that he himself would go there soon. Festus's refusal saved Paul's life, for in Caesarea Paul had no fear of physical harm. There the Jews were unable to harm him, but on the way to Jerusalem or in the city itself Paul would be in mortal danger.

Suddenly the Jews learned that the governor had turned the tables on them. Instead of having Paul brought to Jerusalem, Festus told the Jews, "Let some of your leaders [lit., powerful ones] accompany me." That is, let the high priest and his associates come to Caesarea. Normally, the plaintiff comes to the courthouse; the judge and jury do not come to the plaintiff.[7]

"If they find anything morally wrong in this man, let them press charges against him." Festus made it known to the Jewish hierarchy that he had no knowledge of their religious laws, but if they could prove that Paul had committed a crime, he would be willing to judge the matter. Therefore, he said, let them come with their accusations.

Greek Words, Phrases, and Constructions in 25:2–5

Verse 2

οἱ πρῶτοι—"the most prominent men." This word is a synonym for "elders" (Luke 19:47; Acts 28:17).[8]

παρεκάλουν—the imperfect tense of παρακαλέω (I appeal to, entreat, request) discloses the repeated action of the Jewish hierarchy.

Verse 3

αἰτούμενοι—the present tense denotes persistent and continued action. The verb αἰτέω (I ask) is in the middle voice, which is the common mode in the New Testament for describing business transactions.[9]

χάριν—in the singular (see 24:27 for the plural), the word *favor* reveals a *quid pro quo* (something for something) exchange.

Verse 4

μὲν οὖν—this combination signifies the adversative *however*. The definite article and noun ὁ Φῆστος (Festus) signal a change in subject; the construction conveys a shift in speakers.[10]

εἰς—the preposition in this context is equivalent to ἐν (at).

---

7. John Albert Bengel, *Gnomon of the New Testament*, ed. Andrew R. Fausset, 5 vols. (Edinburgh: Clark, 1877), vol. 2, p. 710.

8. Josephus *Antiquities* 11.5.3 [141].

9. A. T. Robertson, *A Grammar of New Testament Greek in the Light of Historical Research* (Nashville: Broadman, 1934), p. 805; Friedrich Blass and Albert Debrunner, *A Greek Grammar of the New Testament and Other Early Christian Literature*, trans. and rev. Robert Funk (Chicago: University of Chicago Press, 1961), #316.2.

10. C. F. D. Moule, *An Idiom-Book of New Testament Greek*, 2d ed. (Cambridge: Cambridge University Press, 1960), p. 163.

Verse 5

δυνατοί—"powerful ones." The adjective refers not to capability but to influence and authority.[11]

εἴ τί ἐστιν—"if there is anything." Notice that the governor uses the present indicative instead of the subjunctive. The indicative conveys fact and certainty but the subjunctive probability and uncertainty.

---

b. Caesarea
25:6–8

A few matters call for attention. First, Governor Festus exercises his authority in regard to the Jews. Next, the Jewish leaders decide to travel to Caesarea to press charges against Paul. And last, Luke relates that the judicial procedure reflects haste.

6. After Festus spent no more than eight or ten days among them, he went down to Caesarea. The next day, he took his place in the courtroom and ordered that Paul be brought before him.

Luke describes the events that preceded Paul's trial before Festus on a day-to-day basis. He mentions that within three days after arriving in Caesarea, Festus went to Jerusalem (v. 1). There he spent eight to ten days with the Jewish leaders (v. 6) and, after he returned to Caesarea, convened the court the next day (v. 6).

We receive the impression that the Jewish leaders accompanied Festus from Jerusalem to Caesarea, which took two days of traveling. The very next day Festus convened the court session with the Jerusalem dignitaries as plaintiffs, Paul as the defendant, and the governor as the judge (see the parallel in 22:30).

7. When Paul arrived, the Jews who had come down from Jerusalem stood around him and brought many serious charges against him, which they were unable to support.

The case before the court is extraordinary. Two years earlier, Felix had listened to Tertullus's accusations and Paul's defense but had failed to pronounce a verdict. Felix left the case unresolved and kept Paul imprisoned.

At the insistence of the Jerusalem Jews, Festus agreed to resolve the case. He ordered a soldier to summon Paul; when Paul appeared in court, he stood in the midst of the members of the Sanhedrin. This arrangement must have contributed to a volatile atmosphere in the courtroom, for the Jews suddenly stood next to their archenemy, Paul.

Then Festus gave the Jews permission to state their grievances, and these were numerous and serious. Under cross-examination, however, the Jews were unable to prove any of the charges. We suspect that they repeated the accusations they leveled against Paul during his trial before Felix (24:2–9). But the Jews from the province of Asia (21:27) could not be called as

---

11. Compare Josephus *War* 1.12.4 [242]; *Antiquities* 14.13.1 [324].

eyewitnesses after a lapse of two years. Consequently, none of the accusations against Paul could be verified by reliable witnesses.

Listening to the accusations, Festus soon realized that Paul was not a criminal but that the charges related to the religious laws and customs of the Jews. He had to judge a man who was a Roman citizen and had not offended Caesar in word or deed. Moreover, he allowed a man who was innocent to be his own lawyer and to refute the allegations of the Jews.

8. Then Paul defended himself: "I have not sinned against either the Jewish law, the temple, or Caesar."

Luke condenses Paul's defense at this point to one sentence. Even though the charges were many and serious, the Jews failed to bring any new ones. The allegations were identical to the ones Tertullus made at the first trial (24:5–6). The verb *defended* (in the original, it is present tense) indicates that Paul repeatedly vindicated himself. He refuted the charges that he had sinned against the Jewish law, had desecrated the temple, and had shown contempt for Caesar. By saying that he had not sinned, he stated that he was innocent of any offense against the Jews, the Jerusalem temple, and Roman authority.

Paul's attitude toward the Romans was positive (see Rom. 13:1–7). In his relations with officials who represented the Roman government, Paul had always shown courtesy and respect. And the Romans were usually considerate of Paul, especially when he claimed his right as a Roman citizen (16:37; 22:25). Nevertheless, as he stood in the midst of angry Jews who hurled insults and accusations at him in Festus's courtroom, Paul knew that he could not expect to receive a fair trial. The newly appointed governor might decide to support the Jews to gain their goodwill.

Greek Words, Phrases, and Constructions in 25:6–8

Verses 6–7

ἤ—this particle means "or" between the words *eight* and *ten*. It should not be taken as part of the comparative πλείους (more [than]) in the sense of "than."

βήματος—Festus sat on the judgment seat and thereby made the court session an official trial on behalf of the Roman government. See Matthew 27:19; John 19:13; Acts 18:12.

αἰτιώματα—"charges." This word occurs once in the New Testament. The usual term is αἰτία (accusation).

Verse 8

ἀπολογουμένου—from the verb ἀπολογέομαι (I make a defense, defend myself), this present middle participle shows, first, continued action; next, reflexive action, with Paul serving as his own lawyer; and last, the genitive case as part of the genitive absolute construction. This construction is faulty; the subject in the clause and the main sentence is the same.[12]

---

c. Appeal
25:9–12

In these verses Luke portrays an interesting power play between a Roman governor and a Roman citizen. Festus wants to please the Jews and win their favor by having Paul tried in Jerusalem, but Paul, claiming his rights of citizenship, insists on being tried in a Roman court, states his innocence, and appeals to Caesar.

9. But Festus, wishing to do the Jews a favor, asked Paul, "Are you willing to go up to Jerusalem and there stand trial before me on these things?"

a. *Assent.* This verse reveals that the word *favor* is the key to understanding the change in Festus. In Jerusalem, he had exercised his power as the Roman governor and refused to grant the Jewish leaders the courtesy of a change of venue for Paul's trial. But when these leaders traveled to Caesarea, they placed him in their debt. If he wanted their help in restoring law and order throughout the land and curbing the power of the Zealots, he would have to do the leaders a favor. And the favor which the Jews desired was to have Paul tried in Jerusalem. There they could charge him with desecrating the temple and convict and execute him. The Romans would be unable to intervene and Paul's citizenship would be of no avail.

Festus, however, informed Paul that in Jerusalem the governor would be the judge. The question is whether Festus would be accompanied by his own council (v. 12) or permit the Sanhedrin to serve as his council. Would he listen to both the Jewish prosecutors and Paul and then render impartial judgment? Would he serve as a mediator between the Jews and Paul?[13]

Paul considered his options and feared that

1. Festus would use the members of the Sanhedrin as his council, and thus the proceedings would lack objectivity;[14]
2. the governor wanted to ingratiate himself with the Jews and therefore would be partial in his judgments;
3. if Festus should declare him innocent and set him free, Paul would no longer enjoy the protection of the Roman military and thus would risk his life on the streets of Jerusalem and the roads of Judea;

---

12. J. de Zwaan has tabulated ninety-five occurrences of the genitive absolute construction in Acts and shows that twenty of these are faulty. "The Use of the Greek Language in Acts," *Beginnings*, vol. 2, p. 42.

13. A few Greek manuscripts have inserted the comparative conjunction *or* to have the text read, "and there stand trial *or* before me."

14. A. N. Sherwin-White, *Roman Society and Roman Law in the New Testament* (1963; reprint ed., Grand Rapids: Baker, 1978), p. 67.

4. the Jews would plot to assassinate him on his way to or from Jerusalem (9:23–24, 29; 20:3, 19; 23:12, 15, 30; 25:3; II Cor. 11:26).

When Governor Festus asked Paul to travel to Jerusalem and stand trial there, Paul refused to accede to his request. Paul treasured his Roman citizenship (see 22:25–29; 23:27) and through it he sought immunity from Jewish prosecution in Judea.

10. Paul, however, said: "I am now standing in Caesar's court, where I should be tried. I have done nothing wrong against the Jews, as you yourself very well know."

b. *Immunity.* Both Felix and Festus had tried Paul. Both governors should have released him for lack of evidence, but they curried the favor of the Jews and kept Paul in prison. When Festus suggested that Paul be tried for a third time, before a (religious) court in Jerusalem, Paul promptly invoked his rights as a Roman citizen. He called the governor's attention to the fact that a Roman citizen should be tried in a Roman court.

Paul displayed his integrity and innocence when he called Festus to task and reminded him that the governor was Caesar's representative and therefore had to insure justice on behalf of a Roman citizen. Paul forced Festus to acknowledge his innocence, which the governor already had determined (vv. 4–8). Paul also touched the governor's conscience.[15] When Paul said that he had not wronged the Jews in any way, he contrasted his innocence with Festus's questionable attempt to show favoritism to the Jews.

11. "If, then, I am in the wrong and have done something worthy of death, I do not refuse to die. But if there is no truth to the accusations of these Jews, then no one has the right to hand me over to them. I appeal to Caesar."

c. *Innocence.* Paul frankly states that he is either guilty or innocent. In the presence of Festus, the judge, he places himself under the law and voices two parallel sentences that express simple fact conditions.

In the first sentence Paul tells the governor that if indeed he is guilty and has committed a crime that calls for the verdict of capital punishment, he refuses to find ways to escape execution. Thus, he places the challenge before Festus and his council (v. 12) to prove his guilt. The second sentence is not only the exact opposite of the first but also specifies that the charges against him were formulated by the Jews. He could have made a declarative statement about his integrity, even though Festus was well acquainted with his innocence. Instead, Paul states the simple fact of his guiltlessness in conditional form: "If there is no truth to the accusations, [and you know that these charges are unfounded,] then no one has the right to hand me over to [the Jews]."

During the administration of Felix, Paul avoided appealing his case to the

---

15. Bengel, *Gnomon of the New Testament*, vol. 2, p. 711.

Roman emperor. Felix had not yet pronounced a verdict but at any time could have declared him innocent and released him. When, however, Felix was recalled to Rome and Festus appeared on the scene, Paul realized that his future became precarious if the new governor wished to favor the Jews by having Paul tried in Jerusalem. Now Paul has to fight for his life and therefore he resorts to his last option: as a Roman citizen he exercises his right to appeal to Caesar.

When Paul declares that no one has the right to hand him over to the Jews, he directly addresses Festus. At this point we face a legal question that derives from the general context: Did Festus, and for that matter Felix, lack the authority to pass a verdict if Paul had the right to appeal to Caesar? Festus freely admits to Agrippa his inability to formulate charges against Paul (v. 27). And Agrippa concludes that Paul "could have been set free if he had not appealed to Caesar" (26:32). The context discloses that Paul's appeal prevents the governor from delivering a verdict of innocence should he belatedly choose to do so.[16] In short, the appeal to Caesar grants Paul a status that puts him above prosecution from either the Sanhedrin in Jerusalem or Festus's court in Caesarea.

With the short statement *I appeal to Caesar,* Paul relieves Festus of his judicial duties to him. (In both Latin and Greek, the statement *I appeal to Caesar* consists of only two words: *Caesarem appello* [Latin] and *kaisara epikaloumai* [Greek]. The Greek verb in the middle means "I call upon Caesar in my behalf.")[17] At the same time, Paul places the governor in the unenviable position of having to justify sending Paul to Nero without any specific charges. Nero and his officials would not take kindly to a governor who showed incompetence in judging trivial matters. Paul appealed to Caesar for three reasons: first, the appeal saved his life; next, it would bring him to Rome, as Jesus had foretold (23:11); and last, in Rome he would preach the gospel to the members of Nero's entourage (see Phil. 1:13; 4:22) and perhaps receive official recognition for Christianity.[18]

12. When Festus had conferred with his council, he said: "You appealed to Caesar; to Caesar you will go."

d. *Appeal.* From the beginning of the Roman empire, citizens had the right to appeal to the emperor capital verdicts by local judges. This privilege was limited to citizens within the walls of Rome and as far as a mile beyond them. In the provinces, H. J. Cadbury writes, governors had no authority to try and condemn citizens. With respect to charges that carried the death penalty, governors in effect functioned not as judges but as prosecutors who presented the cases, along with the accused citizens, to the

---

16. H. J. Cadbury, "Roman Law and the Trial of Paul," *Beginnings,* vol. 5, pp. 310–11; Schürer, *History of the Jewish People,* vol. 1, p. 369 n. 76.

17. Consult Robertson, *Grammar,* p. 809.

18. Refer to J. M. Gilchrist, "On What Charge Was St. Paul Brought to Rome?" *ExpT* 78 (1967): 264–66; Sherwin-White, *Roman Society and Roman Law,* pp. 57–70.

emperor.[19] Roman emperors honored this right of the citizens. Aided by their officials, they judged the cases according to the full descriptions supplied them by governors and consuls. (Paul exercised his rights during the first part of Nero's reign [A.D. 54–62], which is usually called the emperor's golden age.)

When Festus heard Paul say, "I appeal to Caesar," he immediately conferred with his council. Realizing full well that only exceptional cases could be sent to the emperor and that Paul had not committed any offense at all against the Roman state, Festus sought advice from the members of his council, who "included both the higher officials of his court and the younger men who accompanied him to gain experience in provincial administration."[20]

To Festus's credit, the governor accepted Paul's appeal and agreed to send him to Rome. He resisted the temptation to mislead Paul in one way or another. Festus kept his word and within a short time made preparations for Paul to sail to the imperial city.

Greek Words, Phrases, and Constructions in 25:9–11

Verse 9

χάριν—"favor." Notice the similar construction in 24:27, where the form χάριτα occurs. The word *favor* predominates in this context: as a noun in verses 3 and 9, and as a verb (χαρίζομαι, I give as a favor) in verses 11 and 16.

θέλεις—this is a simple present verb ("are you willing?"), because it appears in an interrogative sentence.[21]

Verses 10–11

Καισαρός—the word *Caesar* is prominent in this chapter (vv. 8, 10, 11, 12, 21).

κάλλιον—the superlative adverb of καλῶς (well, commendably) is translated "very well."

ἀδικῶ—although present in form ("I am wrong"), this verb is close to the perfect tense, much the same as πέπραχα (I have done). A. T. Robertson defines the latter verb as "a perfect of broken continuity."[22]

---

13 When several days had passed, King Agrippa and Bernice arrived at Caesarea to welcome Festus. 14 After they had stayed there for many days, Festus presented Paul's case to the king and said: "Felix left a certain man here, a prisoner. 15 When I was in Jerusalem, the chief

---

19. Cadbury, "Roman Law and the Trial of Paul," p. 315. The appeal was called the *provocatio*, which signified the "right of a citizen to appeal against the verdict of a magistrate" (p. 313).

20. F. F. Bruce, *The Acts of the Apostles: The Greek Text with Introduction and Commentary*, 3d (rev. and enl.) ed. (Grand Rapids: Eerdmans, 1990), p. 645.

21. Robert Hanna, *A Grammatical Aid to the Greek New Testament* (Grand Rapids: Baker, 1983), p. 242.

22. Robertson, *Grammar*, p. 896.

priests and elders of the Jews brought charges against him and demanded a guilty verdict. 16 I answered them that it is not customary for the Romans to hand over any man before the accused meets his accusers and has an opportunity to defend himself against the charges. 17 When the Jews had come here, I did not postpone the matter but on the next day I took my place in court and ordered that the man be brought before me. 18 His accusers stood up and began to bring an accusation against him, but not of such crimes I was suspecting. 19 They only had some points of disagreement with him concerning their own religion and concerning a certain dead man, Jesus, whom Paul claimed to be alive. 20 Being at a loss how to investigate this, I asked Paul if he would be willing to go to Jerusalem and there stand trial on these matters. 21 When Paul had made his appeal to be kept in custody for the Emperor's decision, I ordered that he be kept until I could send him to Caesar." 22 Then Agrippa said to Festus, "I myself wish to hear this man." And Festus replied, "Tomorrow you will hear him."

23 Then, on the next day, Agrippa and Bernice entered the auditorium with great pageantry, accompanied by the commanders and the prominent men of the city. Festus commanded that Paul be brought before them. 24 Festus said, "King Agrippa and all you gentlemen here with us. You see this man about whom all the Jews have appealed to me both in Jerusalem and here, and shouted that he should not live any longer. 25 But I find that he committed nothing worthy of death. Since he appealed to Caesar, I decided to send him there. 26 But I have nothing definite to write about him to His Majesty. Therefore, I have brought him before you and especially before you, King Agrippa, so that after the investigation, I may have something to write. 27 For dispatching a prisoner without indicating any charges against him seems absurd to me."

---

4. Paul and Agrippa
25:13–27

Festus faced an immense problem. He knew that he had to honor Paul's appeal to Caesar, yet the governor was perplexed in regard to sending a legal description of Paul's case to Rome. He was unable to formulate a charge against Paul because the accusations of the Jews pertained to religious matters that had nothing to do with Roman law.

Much to the relief of Festus, King Agrippa II and Bernice came to Caesarea to pay their respects. Agrippa was of Jewish descent, had been educated at Rome, and was ruler of a kingdom. He would be able to give pertinent advice to Festus and help him out of his predicament.

a. Visitors Identified
25:13–14a

13. When several days had passed, King Agrippa and Bernice arrived at Caesarea to welcome Festus. 14a. After they had stayed there for many days, Festus presented Paul's case to the king.

For a few days Festus was at a loss to formulate a proper description of Paul's case for the emperor. Just at that time, King Agrippa and Bernice arrived in Caesarea to welcome Festus to his new assignment as governor of Judea. They made their appearance at the palace of Governor Festus and stayed with him many days. A polite friendship developed between these two rulers. Festus realized that Agrippa had been trained at the court of Claudius and had a clear understanding of the Jewish religion.

Moreover, Emperor Claudius had given Agrippa II the position of cura-
tor of the Jerusalem temple and the right to appoint its high priests.[23]
After a few days Festus made his predicament known to Agrippa and
asked him for advice.

Additional comments on Agrippa II and the Herodian dynasty

Agrippa, Bernice, and Drusilla were the children of King Herod Agrippa I (see
the genealogical chart).

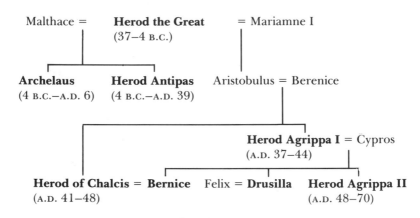

KEY
numbers in parentheses refer to years in office
boldface type indicates persons mentioned in text
= indicates marriage

When Herod died in A.D. 44, Agrippa II was seventeen; Bernice, sixteen; and
Drusilla, six. At the time, Agrippa II was in Rome. He hoped that the emperor
Claudius would grant him his father's crown, but Claudius thought that a youth
of seventeen lacked the maturity to rule Palestine, beset as it was by nationalistic
and religious interests, problems, and conflicts. In A.D. 50, Claudius did entrust
to Agrippa the kingdom of Chalcis (in the Lebanon valley), which had belonged
to Herod Agrippa's brother.[24] Three years later, however, Claudius offered
Agrippa II the tetrarchy of Philip (Batanaea, Trachonitis, and Gaulanitis), the
tetrarchy of Lysanias (Abilene), and the territory of Varus (Acra) in exchange for
the kingdom of Chalcis.[25] In the first year of Nero's reign (A.D. 54), the emperor

---

23. Josephus *Antiquities* 20.5.2 [103]; 20.9.4, 7 [213, 222–23].

24. Josephus *War* 2.12.1 [223]; *Antiquities* 20.5.2 [104]; see also Schürer, *History of the Jewish People*, vol. 1, pp. 562–63, 571–73.

25. Compare Luke 3:1; refer to Josephus *War* 2.12.8 [247]; *Antiquities* 20.7.1 [138].

gave Agrippa II a number of leading cities and villages in both Galilee and Perea.[26]

Agrippa II, then, ruled the northern half of Palestine. Expanding the capital city of Caesarea Philippi, he renamed it Neronias in honor of Emperor Nero.[27] Although he called himself "Great King, pious Friend of Caesar and Friend of Rome," he nonetheless tried to promote the Jewish cause. He was known as an expert in Jewish customs and conflicts (26:3), and he was well versed in the Hebrew Scriptures (26:27). Agrippa traced his Jewish roots to his great-grandmother Mariamne, the second wife of Herod the Great.

Agrippa showed his allegiance to Rome by visiting Festus soon after his arrival in Caesarea. From a moral perspective, however, the presence of his sister Bernice was an embarrassment. At the age of thirteen, she had married her uncle, Herod of Chalcis, and bore him two sons during their seven-year marriage. When Herod died in A.D. 48, Bernice began to live with her brother, who became king of Chalcis two years later. Bernice functioned as queen, while Agrippa II remained unmarried. Josephus and the Roman author Juvenal note that the rumor of an incestuous relationship between Agrippa and Bernice was widespread.[28] To suppress this rumor, Bernice married Polemo, king of Cilicia, presumably after A.D. 64. But soon afterward she deserted him and returned to her brother.

Agrippa and Bernice exerted themselves to avert the bloodshed that resulted from the Jewish revolt, which culminated in the fall of Jerusalem in A.D. 70. Both Agrippa and Bernice were supporters of the Roman general Titus and stayed in his company. "And when Titus sponsored magnificent games at great expense in Caesarea Philippi to celebrate the conquest of Jerusalem, King Agrippa was no doubt also present, rejoicing as a Roman in the defeat of his people."[29] Furthermore, Bernice engaged in a love affair with Titus and expected him to marry her when they eventually came to Rome in A.D. 75. But because the public opposed the marriage, Titus dismissed Bernice. Agrippa, the last member of the Herodian dynasty, died in A.D. 100.

Throughout the Gospels and Acts, the writers of Scripture show the reaction that members of the Herodian dynasty displayed toward Christ or his cause. Herod the Great wanted to kill the infant Jesus (Matt. 2:13, 16). In the next generation, his son Archelaus ruthlessly ruled Judea, thereby forcing Joseph, Mary, and the infant Jesus to settle in Nazareth instead of Bethlehem (Matt. 2:22–23). Another son, Herod Antipas, beheaded John the Baptist (Matt. 14:10). One generation later, Herod the Great's grandson King Agrippa I killed the apostle James and arrested Peter (Acts 12:2). And in Acts 25, Luke depicts the great-grandson, King Agrippa II, participating in the investigation of Paul's case. Unlike his forebears, this king was kindly disposed toward the cause presented by Paul. He heard the gospel and subsequently declared that Paul should have been set free.[30]

---

26. Josephus *War* 2.13.2 [252]; *Antiquities* 20.8.4 [159].
27. Josephus *Antiquities* 20.9.4 [211].
28. Josephus *Antiquities* 20.7.3 [145]; Juvenal *Satires* 6.156–60.
29. Schürer, *History of the Jewish People*, vol. 1, p. 477, see also Josephus *War* 7.2.1 [23–24].
30. Compare Richard B. Rackham, *The Acts of the Apostles*, Westminster Commentaries series (1901; reprint ed., Grand Rapids: Baker, 1964), p. 457–58.

Greek Words, Phrases, and Constructions in 25:13–14a

διαγενομένων—this compound participle in the genitive absolute construction actually means "some days came in *between* (διά)."[31]

ἀσπασάμενοι—the use of the aorist participle is abnormal in a setting that demands the future participle to express purpose ("to welcome"). Grammarians consider the action indicated by the aorist participle to be coincident with that of the main verb.[32]

κατά—this preposition with the accusative case is more expressive than the mere genitive of the phrase *Paul's case*. It signifies "the things pertaining to Paul."

---

b. Problem Explained
25:14b–22

Presuming that the conversation between Festus and Agrippa was private, we suspect that Luke in his account presents the main ideas of the discussion. "Luke's form of composition is inferential rather than based on sources."[33] We are unable to indicate how and from which source Luke obtained the content of this private conversation that took place between two rulers. Nevertheless, the Greek in this speech is classical and free from any Semitic influences. Festus speaks as an educated Roman official who addresses Agrippa in excellent Greek.

14b. [Festus] said: "Felix left a certain man here, a prisoner. 15. When I was in Jerusalem, the chief priests and elders of the Jews brought charges against him and demanded a guilty verdict. 16. I answered them that it is not customary for the Romans to hand over any man before the accused meets his accusers and has an opportunity to defend himself against the charges."

With the use of the perfect tense (in the Greek), Festus testifies to the fact that Paul had been a prisoner for an extended period. He notes that his predecessor, Felix, had left Paul without passing a verdict and that the matter subsequently came to Festus's attention when he appeared in Jerusalem. There the Jewish religious hierarchy immediately informed him about Paul, whom they accused of breaking the law. They demanded that Festus pass a guilty verdict on Paul. Festus expressly states that the Jews were not asking for a trial in which Paul's guilt or innocence could be determined; on the contrary, they demanded a guilty verdict.

Festus reports that he objected to this patently biased procedure, for as a

---

31. Robertson, *Grammar,* p. 580.

32. Blass and Debrunner, *Greek Grammar,* #339.1; Moule, *Idiom-Book,* p. 100. Consult also Bruce M. Metzger, *A Textual Commentary on the Greek New Testament,* 3d corrected ed. (London and New York: United Bible Societies, 1975), p. 492.

33. Hemer, *Book of Acts,* p. 348.

judge representing the Roman emperor he would have to judge a Roman citizen according to Roman practice and law. The Jews wanted Festus not only to declare Paul guilty but also to hand him over to them as a favor. The governor reveals his integrity in his explanation to Agrippa. According to Roman civil law, no one should be condemned without his case being heard and without being given the opportunity to defend himself in court.[34]

17. "When the Jews had come here, I did not postpone the matter but on the next day I took my place in court and ordered that the man be brought before me. 18. His accusers stood up and began to bring an accusation against him, but not of such crimes I was suspecting."

The Greek text seems to imply that the Jews traveled with Festus to Caesarea. When they arrived, the governor immediately convened his court and ordered Paul to be brought before him. The circumstances of having the Jewish delegation at hand and Festus's determination to hold the trial in Caesarea contributed to avoiding any delay. Festus undoubtedly thought that Paul's trial was of great significance and wanted to bring the matter to a conclusion. Much to his surprise, he soon realized that Paul was not a criminal who had broken Roman law. The governor, appointed to uphold civil law and punish evildoers and those who rebelled against Rome, was at a loss to adjudicate Jewish disputes on religious matters. If Festus had wanted to bring Paul's trial to a satisfactory conclusion from a Roman perspective, he should have declared Paul innocent and set him free. But the governor, like his predecessor, wanted to do the Jews a favor and kept Paul a prisoner.

19. "But they only had some points of disagreement with him concerning their own religion and concerning a certain dead man, Jesus, whom Paul claimed to be alive."

The governor admits his lack of expertise on "some points of disagreement" relating to the Jewish religion. The Roman government had given the religion of the Jews legal status and maintained a policy of noninterference in the religious laws and practices. But when the Jews asked Roman governors to judge a fellow Jew on the basis of Jewish law, these officials were unable to comply with their requests.

Yet Festus reveals at least a surface knowledge of the Jewish dispute that concerns the resurrection of Jesus. Although Festus fails to identify Paul by name but only refers to him as a man who is a prisoner, in the context of Jesus' resurrection he mentions the names of both Jesus and Paul. Here is the crucial point that causes the Jews to clamor for a guilty verdict against Paul before Festus: Jesus' resurrection from the dead. Festus informs Agrippa II that the issue was "concerning a certain dead man, Jesus, whom

---

34. Before the Roman Senate and Cicero, Senator Piso declared: "Our law, Senators, requires that the accused shall himself hear the charge preferred against him and shall be judged after he has made his own defence." Appian *Civil Wars* 3.54 (LCL). See also Tacitus *Histories* 1.6; Jacques Dupont, *Études sur les Actes des Apôtres*, Lectio Divina 45 (Paris: Cerf, 1967), pp. 527–52.

Paul claimed to be alive." John Calvin remarks that Festus, an unbeliever and a worshiper of idols, had to be Paul's judge and mediator in the presence of Paul's Jewish adversaries.[35] In spiritual ignorance, the governor had to pass judgment on God's truth pertaining to Christ's resurrection. However, because of personal pride Festus resolutely rejected Paul's teaching concerning Christ's death and resurrection (see 26:22–24).

20. "Being at a loss how to investigate this, I asked Paul if he would be willing to go to Jerusalem and there stand trial on these matters. 21. When Paul had made his appeal to be kept in custody for the Emperor's decision, I ordered that he be kept until I could send him to Caesar."

In respect to religious matters of Jews and Christians, Festus frankly confesses to "being at a loss." The Greek text shows that he uses the personal pronoun *I* to indicate that he himself does not know how to proceed. What he withholds from Agrippa, however, is the fact that he wanted to do the Jews a favor by changing the venue from Caesarea to Jerusalem (v. 9). He reports only that he asked Paul whether he would be willing to stand trial in Jerusalem and bases his request on the fact that he is incapable of ruling on religious matters. His admission foretells that Paul would not receive a favorable verdict should he agree to travel to Jerusalem. But Festus's royal guest perfectly understands the entire situation and is not at all surprised to hear the governor say that Paul appealed to Caesar.[36]

Festus informs Agrippa that he has issued the order to keep Paul in custody in Caesarea until proper arrangements can be made to send him to Rome. But Festus first has to compose a legal document that must accompany Paul to the emperor. And he is able to send Paul only when a sufficient number of prisoners can be accompanied to Rome by a centurion and soldiers of the Imperial Regiment (27:1). In the meantime, Paul will stay in Caesarea.

22. Then Agrippa said to Festus, "I myself wish to hear this man." And Festus replied, "Tomorrow you will hear him."

Festus has aroused Agrippa's curiosity, for from Paul Agrippa will be able to gain direct information about the Christians and their religion. We see a parallel between Agrippa, who desires to meet Paul, and Agrippa's great-uncle Herod Antipas, who wanted to see Jesus (Luke 9:9; 23:8). On an earlier occasion, Agrippa's sister Drusilla had the opportunity to listen to Paul present the teachings of Christ (24:24–26).

In aptly chosen words, Agrippa voices his desire to hear Paul. He could have bluntly stated that he wanted to hear him, but with the tense of the verb

---

35. Consult John Calvin, *Commentary on the Acts of the Apostles*, ed. David W. Torrance and Thomas F. Torrance, 2 vols. (Grand Rapids: Eerdmans, 1966), vol. 2, p. 266.

36. In current English, this title would be the same as "His Majesty." The speaker apparently uses several (synonymous) titles for Nero, calling him either Caesar (v. 21), Emperor (vv. 21, 25; the word *emperor* in the Greek text is *Sebastos*, which is the Latin equivalent of "Augustus"), or His Majesty (v. 26). Lake and Cadbury, *Beginnings*, vol. 4, p. 312. Consult Bauer, pp. 745–46; Thayer, p. 572.

to wish he conveys a polite request ("I was at the point of wishing").[37] Festus's reply to this request is short and to the point: "Tomorrow you will hear him."

Historical Considerations in 25:10–21

When Rome conquered Israel in 63 B.C., the Roman government wisely left intact the religious substratum of the Jewish people. The Jewish religion was given legal status so that throughout the Roman empire Jews could worship according to their own laws and customs. Rome even gave the Jews in Jerusalem the right to impose the death penalty on any non-Jew who entered the temple area that was forbidden to Gentiles.

For at least the first thirty years of its existence, the Christian church was considered part of the Jewish religion acknowledged by the Roman state. But the widespread development of the church together with the increased hostility of the Jews against Christianity caused a rift between the Christian faith and Judaism. This rift the Romans could not ignore, for they either had to grant equal rights to the church or brand its existence illegal. Jews who were violently opposed to the Christians ardently strove to have the Romans outlaw the church.

When Paul appealed to Caesar in the presence of Governor Festus, Rome came face to face with the Christian religion. At Caesar's court, Rome eventually had to make a decision relative to the church's existence. (Paul's appeal to Caesar was not an evangelistic effort to present the gospel in the imperial city. Indeed, the church of Rome was already thriving and expanding many years before Paul composed his Epistle to the Romans in A.D. 57.) Even though he was a prisoner, Paul could raise the issue of the legal status of Christianity before Caesar. Festus was unable to adjudicate the matter and had to send Paul to the emperor. In Rome, Paul declared that he was a prisoner on account of the hope of Israel, which consisted of the coming of God's kingdom and his Messiah and the doctrine of the resurrection. In brief, Paul was a prisoner in Rome for the sake of Christ's gospel. Although Luke provides no evidence, tradition holds that Paul was released from house arrest in Rome. Luke reveals that Paul boldly preached the gospel without hindrance from the state (compare 28:31).

Greek Words, Phrases, and Constructions in 25:14b–22

Verses 14b–15

καταλελειμμένος—with the verb *to be* in the present tense, this is a periphrastic construction ("has been left behind"). The perfect tense in the participle denotes lasting effect and the use of the compound signifies abandonment.

οἱ . . . οἱ—the appearance of two definite articles before two nouns signals two distinct groups: the chief priests and the elders.

καταδίκην—"guilty verdict." The Majority Text has adopted the reading δίκην (judgment). In view of the phrase κατ' αὐτοῦ (against him), however, scholars prefer καταδίκην, a compound noun that repeats the preposition.

---

37. Refer to Robertson, *Grammar*, p. 919.

Verse 16

πρὶν ἤ—this combination is common in Koine Greek; in Attic Greek the single form πρίν occurs. Both forms mean "before." Here and in Luke 2:26 the combination is followed by the finite verb in an indirect discourse construction. The two optatives ἔχοι (has) and λάβοι (receives) denote future possibilities.

Verses 18–19

ἔφερον—note the increased use of the descriptive imperfect in verses 18–20: "were bringing," "was suspecting," "was claiming," and "was asking."

πονηρῶν—"of the crimes." Manuscripts of the Majority Text omit this word, perhaps in the interest of a smoother reading.

δεισιδαιμονίας—in the New Testament, this word occurs only here. It is used objectively; that is, in a favorable sense meaning "religion." See 17:22 for the use of the adjective.

Verse 20

εἰ βούλοιτο—instead of the present indicative θέλεις (v. 9), Festus uses the optative ("whether he would like") "to soften the force of the actual command and consequently to conceal the original motive for this question."[38]

---

c. Paul Introduced
25:23–27

When Festus had Paul brought before King Agrippa, it is reasonable to assume that Luke was present. During Paul's imprisonment, his friends were permitted to visit him and take care of his needs (24:23); it seems unlikely that they would be denied access to this event. Moreover, the words of Festus ("all you gentlemen here with us," 25:24) imply that persons other than the invited nobility and dignitaries were present.[39] And Luke attended the earlier trials of Paul. He would want to be near his friend on this occasion also. Any information concerning Paul that circulated in and around Festus's palace would have come to Luke's attention.

Throughout his presentation, Luke gives Paul a leading role in the developing account. He considers important not the presence of royalty and the display of military and administrative might, but the quiet dignity of Paul.

23. Then, on the next day, Agrippa and Bernice entered the auditorium with great pageantry, accompanied by the commanders and the prominent men of the city. Festus commanded that Paul be brought before them.

Why did Festus invite royalty and dignitaries to his auditorium? The meeting obviously was not a formal trial, for Paul already had been tried before Festus and his accusers had returned to Jerusalem. Moreover, the

---

38. Hanna, *Grammatical Aid*, p. 243.

39. Theodor Zahn, *Die Apostelgeschichte des Lucas*, Kommentar zum Neuen Testament series, 2 vols. (Leipzig: Deichert, 1921), vol. 2, p. 814.

meeting took place not in the courtroom (v. 6) but in the audience room of the governor.[40] And to be precise, Paul's appeal to Caesar precluded any trial at this time.

Nevertheless, Festus had not completed his work on Paul's case. He was obliged to write a legal document for the benefit of Nero, but Festus publicly admitted his puzzlement (v. 27). For this reason, the governor convened Agrippa and Bernice, military officers, and city officials to give him advice (v. 26) on stating his justification for sending Paul to Rome. At the heart of the matter was the gospel which Paul eventually presented.

Some scholars have questioned the historicity of Luke's comment about pageantry. Writes Hans Conzelmann, "The display of ostentation is Luke's creation and is without a historical core."[41] But the historicity of Luke's account certainly is not at stake. What took place was Festus's attempt to honor King Agrippa. The governor provided for Agrippa the occasion to display his royal power; yielded to him the judge's seat so that the king could give Paul permission to speak (26:1); allowed the king to rise first (26:30); and granted him the privilege of making the closing statement on Paul's case (26:32).[42]

King Agrippa II clothed himself in exquisite raiment, just as his father Herod Agrippa had decked himself in royal robes (12:21). To impress Governor Festus and the other notables, Agrippa II exhibited his royalty by the clothes he wore for the occasion. Bernice, even though she was not the queen, did likewise. And the high-ranking Roman army officers, five in number,[43] came to the meeting in their finest military attire out of respect for the visiting king. The prominent leaders of the city dressed accordingly.

Among the "prominent men of the city" were perchance Jews, but we conjecture that the majority of those attending were Gentiles. When all the honored guests were seated, Governor Festus ordered a soldier to fetch Paul. And mindful of Jesus' word that he would be brought before governors and kings on account of Jesus, Paul seized the opportunity to witness to the Gentiles (Matt. 10:18).

24. Festus said, "King Agrippa and all you gentlemen here with us. You see this man about whom all the Jews have appealed to me both in Jerusalem and here, and shouted that he should not live any longer. 25. But I find that he committed nothing worthy of death. Since he appealed to Caesar, I decided to send him there."

Before Festus yields his authority to Agrippa II, he presents Paul to the

---

40. Bauer, p. 33.

41. Hans Conzelmann, *Acts of the Apostles,* trans. James Limburg, A. Thomas Kraabel, and Donald H. Juel (1963; Philadelphia: Fortress, 1987), p. 207. And Ernst Haenchen avers: "Anyone who . . . conceives of such a presentation as a historically reliable report . . . must of necessity make a botch of his own correct insights." *The Acts of the Apostles: A Commentary,* trans. Bernard Noble and Gerald Shinn (Philadelphia: Westminster, 1971), p. 679.

42. Consult Rackham, *Acts,* p. 461.

43. Josephus mentions five cohorts, each of which had a commander. *Antiquities* 19.9.2 [365].

audience. With deference, he addresses Agrippa as king and welcomes everyone in the audience. According to the custom of that day, he speaks only to the men, even though Bernice is in attendance.

Festus calls attention to Paul and then, with a touch of exaggeration, declares that "all the Jews have appealed to me both in Jerusalem and here." He evidently refers to the Jewish leaders and not to every Jew living in these two places. He stresses the seriousness of the matter by saying that the Jews are not merely petitioning but are shouting that Paul ought not to live any longer (compare 21:36; 22:22). In the original the negative adverb *not* appears with the expression *no longer* as a reinforcement of the petition: "he should not live any longer." The Jews are adamant in their desire for Paul's death.

The governor reveals to his audience that he examined Paul and found that Paul had committed no deed worthy of capital punishment. At this point, Festus continues, Paul appealed to the emperor (see the discussion on v. 21). What the governor fails to reveal is the immediate cause for Paul's appeal. He passes over his suggestion that the trial be held in Jerusalem as a favor to the Jews (see vv. 9, 20).

To fill this gap, the Western text adds to the text (vv. 24–25; the additions are italicized) considerably:

> *that I should hand him over to them for punishment without any defense. But I could not hand him over because of the orders that we have from the Emperor. But if anyone was going to accuse him,* I said that he should follow me to Caesarea, where he [Paul] was being held in custody. *And when they came,* they cried out that *he should be put to death. But when I heard both sides of the case,* I found that he was in no respect guilty of death. *But when I said, "Are you willing to be judged before them in Jerusalem?"* he appealed to Caesar.[44]

The time-honored rule that the shorter text is more likely to be the original reading applies in this case. The expansion appears to be the work of a scribe who wished to present a smoother reading of the text.

The governor speaks as a judge and reveals that he has made a ruling relative to Paul's appeal that he be sent to Rome. This decision is final, but now Festus needs help in writing an accompanying report.

26. "But I have nothing definite to write about him to His Majesty. Therefore, I have brought him before you and especially before you, King Agrippa, so that after the investigation, I may have something to write. 27. For dispatching a prisoner without indicating any charges against him seems absurd to me."

a. "But I have nothing definite to write about him to His Majesty." Although court records of Paul's earlier trial are available to the governor, he knows that he has to write his own report. Festus openly confesses that he is

---

44. Metzger, *Textual Commentary*, p. 494. Refer to Albert C. Clark, *The Acts of the Apostles: A Critical Edition with Introduction and Notes on Selected Passages* (1933; Oxford: Clarendon, 1970), pp. 158–59, 381–82. And see Bruce, *Acts* (Greek text), p. 651.

at a loss in respect to the wording of the report. He has determined that the charges laid against Paul are unsubstantiated, yet he is unable to understand the cause for the raging anger of the Jews against him. Hence, he says that he has nothing definite to write about Paul. In some respects, we see a parallel between Claudius Lysias, who wanted to learn from the Jewish leaders in the Sanhedrin the reason for their anger (22:30), and Governor Festus, who is asking Agrippa II, an expert in Jewish matters (26:3), to help him understand the hatred the Jews have for Paul.

Festus refers to Emperor Nero as "His Majesty." The Greek word is *kyrios,* which is translated "lord." So the governor actually says that he has nothing to write to *the lord.* Both Augustus and Tiberius declined to be addressed by this title, but Caligula and all the emperors who followed him accepted it. Archaeological evidence has incontestably proved that Nero especially desired to be called "lord." He valued the title and demanded that his subjects throughout the empire use it. "Everywhere, down to the remotest village, the officials called Nero *Kyrios.*"[45]

The earliest Christian confession is "Jesus is Lord" (I Cor. 12:3). This declaration stood diametrically opposed to the slogan *Caesar is Lord.*[46] In his address before Agrippa Paul boldly calls Jesus "Lord" (26:15). For followers of Christ, only Jesus deserves that name.

b. "Therefore, I have brought him before you and especially before you, King Agrippa." Festus now looks to his audience for help in his predicament. He understands that the Christian religion, represented by Paul, has placed him in this plight. He expects that, of all people in the audience, Agrippa will furnish him with a solution to his problem. And he hopes that at the conclusion of the investigation, after Paul's speech and Agrippa's evaluation, he will have substantive material for his report.

c. "For dispatching a prisoner without indicating any charges against him seems absurd to me." This remark is an understatement. Festus implies that should he send Paul to the emperor without providing written charges, he would be in serious trouble. Nero did not waste his time on matters that should have been handled by his officials in the provinces. With the word *absurd* the governor means to say that no one in his right mind would do such a thing.

Greek Words, Phrases, and Constructions in 25:23–26

Verse 23

φαντασίας—the Greek noun ("pomp, pageantry") derives from the verb φαντάζω (I become visible). An English derivative is "fantasy."

---

45. Adolf Deissmann, *Light from the Ancient East,* rev. ed., trans. Lionel R. M. Strachan (New York: Doran, 1927), p. 353.
46. Polycarp was asked to say "Lord Caesar" and be saved from being burned at the stake (A.D. 155). He refused. *Martyrdom of Polycarp* 8.2.

κατ᾽ ἐξοχήν—"par excellence." The idiom applies to the prominent men in the city of Caesarea.

Verses 24–25

ἐνέτυχον—"they appealed." The plural form appears, even though the subject πλῆθος (multitude) is singular.

δεῖν—the infinitive is part of an indirect command: "shouting that he *should* not live any longer."

κατελαβόμην—from the verb καταλαμβάνω (I seize), this is the middle which, as a reflexive, means "I grasp, find, understand."

Verse 26

τι γράψαι—"something to write." Note the repetition of τί γράψω (what am I to write). In the first instance, Festus states a fact with the use of the indefinite pronoun τι (something) and the aorist infinitive. In the second instance, he employs the interrogative pronoun τί (what?) and the aorist subjunctive first person singular. The subjunctive is deliberative.

Summary of Chapter 25

Festus takes the place of Governor Felix and within three days of his arrival in Caesarea travels to Jerusalem, where he meets the chief priests and elders. They press charges against Paul, who is kept prisoner in Caesarea, and ask Festus to have Paul tried in Jerusalem. Festus refuses and schedules a trial in Caesarea, where he summons Paul and listens to numerous charges which the Jews are unable to prove. Paul asserts that he has neither acted contrary to the law of the Jews or of Caesar nor desecrated the temple. When Festus asks him whether he is willing to stand trial in Jerusalem, Paul reminds the governor that he ought to be tried in a Roman court. Defending his rights, Paul appeals to Caesar. Festus declares that Paul will go to Caesar.

King Agrippa and Bernice arrive in Caesarea to welcome Festus, who relates to the king the case of Paul. Agrippa states that he wishes to hear Paul, and Festus assures him that his wish will be granted the following day. With great pomp Agrippa, Bernice, military officers, and prominent leaders of the city gather in Festus's audience room. When Paul has been summoned, Festus introduces him and asks the audience, especially Agrippa, to give the governor something to write to Caesar concerning the charges leveled against Paul.

26

In Jerusalem and Caesarea, *part 6*

26:1–32

Outline (continued)

26:1–32	5. Paul's Speech	
26:1		a. Permission
26:2–3		b. Acknowledgment
26:4–8		c. Background
26:9–11		d. Purpose
26:12–14		e. Conversion
26:15–18		f. Commission
26:19–23		g. Testimony
26:24–29		h. Persuasion
26:30–32		i. Conclusion

26 1 Agrippa said to Paul, "You are permitted to speak for yourself." Then Paul motioned with his hand and began to defend himself. 2 "King Agrippa, I consider myself fortunate that I am about to defend myself before you today regarding all the things of which the Jews accuse me. 3 I beg you to listen to me patiently, especially because you are an expert in all the customs and disputes of the Jews.

4 "All the Jews know my way of life from my childhood on, which I spent from the beginning in my own nation and in Jerusalem. 5 They have known me for a long time and can testify, if they are willing, that I have lived according to the strictest sect of our religion as a Pharisee. 6 And now I stand on trial for the hope of the promise made by God to our fathers. 7 This promise our twelve tribes hope to attain by earnestly serving God night and day. Concerning this hope, O king, I am being accused by the Jews. 8 Why do you Jews consider it incredible that God raises the dead?

9 "So then I thought that I myself should do as many things as possible against the name of Jesus of Nazareth. 10 And this is just what I did in Jerusalem: not only did I lock up many of the saints in prisons because I received authority from the chief priests, but also I cast my vote against them when they were put to death. 11 Often I had them punished as I went from synagogue to synagogue, and I tried to force them to blaspheme. I was so enraged at them that I even persecuted them in foreign cities.

12 "While doing this, I was going to Damascus with the authority and commission of the chief priests. 13 At noon, O king, while I was on the road, I saw from heaven a light brighter than the brilliance of the sun shining around me and those traveling with me. 14 When all of us had fallen to the ground, I heard a voice saying to me in Hebrew, 'Saul, Saul, why do you persecute me? It is hard for you to kick against the goads.' 15 So I asked, 'Who are you, Lord?' And the Lord said: 'I am Jesus, whom you are persecuting. 16 Now get up and stand on your feet. For this reason I appeared to you: to appoint you as a servant and a witness not only to the things you have seen of me but also to the things I will show you. 17 I am rescuing you from the Jewish people and from the Gentiles. I am sending you to them 18 to open their eyes, to turn them from darkness to light and from the power of Satan to God. I do so that they may receive forgiveness of sins and an inheritance among those who have been sanctified by faith in me.'

19 "So then, King Agrippa, I was not disobedient to the heavenly vision. 20 But I kept declaring first to those in Damascus, then in Jerusalem, and then throughout all Judea, and even to the Gentiles that they should repent, turn to God, and practice works worthy of repentance. 21 For this reason, the Jews arrested me while I was in the temple and tried to kill me. 22 Therefore, having obtained help from God to this very day I stand here witnessing to both great and small and declaring nothing but what the prophets and Moses said would happen. 23 They declared that the Christ must suffer and, because of his resurrection from the dead, would be the first to proclaim light to both the Jewish people and the Gentiles."

24 While Paul was saying these things in his defense, Festus shouted in a loud voice, "Paul, you are out of your mind. Your great learning is driving you insane." 25 Then Paul replied, "I am not out of my mind, most excellent Festus. But I utter words that are true and reasonable. 26 The king understands these things, so I speak confidently to him. I am persuaded that none of this has escaped his notice, for it has not been done in a corner. 27 Do you believe the prophets, King Agrippa? I know you do."

28 Agrippa answered Paul, "In a short time you are trying to persuade me to act as a Christian." 29 Paul said, "I pray to God that whether in a short or a long time not only you but also all who hear me today may become what I am, except for these chains."

30 The king, Bernice, the governor, and those who were sitting with them stood up. 31 While they withdrew, they began to talk to one another, saying, "This man is not doing anything worthy of death or imprisonment." 32 Then Agrippa said to Festus, "This man could have been set free if he had not appealed to Caesar."

---

5. Paul's Speech
26:1–32

The purpose of this ostentatious gathering is to have King Agrippa II give advice about the charges against Paul. Festus has honored Agrippa by yielding the gavel to the king. Luke records only summary statements from and about Agrippa; in Luke's account, Paul is the main character.

a. Permission
26:1

1. Agrippa said to Paul, "You are permitted to speak for yourself." Then Paul motioned with his hand and began to defend himself.

King Agrippa is kindly disposed to Paul. The king does not ask for an explanation of the charges; instead, he grants Paul complete freedom to speak. Obviously, the king realizes that, because Paul has appealed to Caesar, the present gathering is not a formal court session. By permitting Paul to address the audience without interruption or rebuttal, Agrippa places him at ease and thus receives a comprehensive account of Paul's teachings.

Agrippa avoids even the impression of having a semblance of authority over Paul. He wisely employs the passive voice when he says, "You are permitted to speak for yourself," instead of, "I give you permission to speak." By saying that Paul may speak for himself, he provides Paul with a wonderful opportunity to preach the gospel. He himself had indicated that he wanted to hear Paul preach (25:22).

"Then Paul motioned with his hand and began to defend himself." The motion of his hand is a common gesture of a first-century orator. When Luke writes that Paul speaks in his own defense, he is indicating that the words Paul utters are a defense of the gospel in the presence of King Agrippa (see the immediate context of v. 24). As a prisoner, Paul wears shackles (v. 29) while standing in front of his distinguished listeners. The contrast between the dazzling garb of the high and mighty and the humble clothes of the chained prisoner suddenly becomes meaningless, for Paul displays the quiet dignity of a man with a message.[1]

---

1. The Western text reads, "confident, and encouraged by the Holy Spirit, Paul motioned with his hand." However, the addition appears only in Latin, which Albert C. Clark has reconstructed in Greek. *The Acts of the Apostles: A Critical Edition with Introduction and Notes on Selected Passages* (1933; Oxford: Clarendon, 1970), pp. 159, 232.

No speech, either by Paul or by any other speaker in Acts, is as personal in tone as Paul's address before Agrippa (see especially v. 27). Paul speaks engagingly to King Agrippa throughout his discourse, addressing him by his title, his name, and the personal pronoun *you*.[2] This speech sparkles with the beauty of its direct gospel appeal.

Paul fits his choice of words to his audience. That is, his use of the language approaches classical Greek and is on the level of his address to the Areopagus (17:22–31). At the same time, we hear in this speech the same tone of Paul's other discourses.

In this speech before Agrippa, Paul again recounts his conversion experience (compare 22:1–21; and see 9:1–19). The three conversion accounts differ, but in each case Paul emphasizes those elements that suit his present purposes. He is free to choose his own wording to describe the event.

Although Paul addresses Agrippa, who is of Jewish descent and is "an expert in all the customs and disputes of the Jews" (v. 3), the speech is not a one-sided gospel appeal directed only to Agrippa (see, for instance, v. 8). Paul presents the doctrine of Christ's resurrection as a light to the Jewish people and to the Gentiles (v. 23).[3]

Greek Words, Phrases, and Constructions in 26:1

ἐπιτρέπεται—"it is now permissible." The use of the imperfect tense is punctiliar.[4] The passive voice of the verb with the pronoun in the dative case is equivalent to the active ("you are permitted").

περί—with the pronoun σεαυτοῦ in the genitive case, the phrase means "on account of yourself."

ἀπελογεῖτο—the imperfect tense is inchoative and is translated "he began to defend himself."[5]

---

b. Acknowledgment
26:2–3

2. "King Agrippa, I consider myself fortunate that I am about to defend myself before you today regarding all the things of which the Jews accuse me. 3. I beg you to listen to me patiently, especially because you are an expert in all the customs and disputes of the Jews."

a. "I consider myself fortunate." Paul means every word he utters to Agrippa. He expresses his joy for the opportunity the king gives him to pre-

---

2. Refer to vv. 2, 3, 7, 13, 19, 27.

3. Compare Klaus Haacker, "Das Bekenntnis des Paulus zur Hoffnung Israels nach der Apostelgeschichte des Lukas," *NTS* 31 (1985): 437–51.

4. C. F. D. Moule, *An Idiom-Book of New Testament Greek*, 2d ed. (Cambridge: Cambridge University Press, 1960), p. 7.

5. A. T. Robertson, *A Grammar of the Greek New Testament in the Light of Historical Research* (Nashville: Broadman, 1934), p. 885.

sent the gospel. Paul addresses not a Gentile ruler but a Jewish king who is versed in the Old Testament Scriptures.[6] With respect to Agrippa, Paul has a spiritual point of contact which he lacks with Festus. Agrippa is able to understand the doctrines of the Christian faith and can give his evaluation to Festus.

b. "I am about to defend myself before you today regarding all the things of which the Jews accuse me." Paul can relate to King Agrippa his background, conversion experience, divine mandate, and arrest in Jerusalem. And he trusts that the king will understand that, from a Jewish point of view, Paul is in complete accord with Israel's hope for the fulfillment of Old Testament prophecies (see v. 7). This hope centers on the Jewish teaching of the resurrection of the dead (vv. 8, 23).

Paul fails to enumerate the accusations which the Jews have brought against him, but in his discourse he refutes the charges that have vexed him since his arrest in Jerusalem.[7] His primary intent is to further the cause of the gospel, but a secondary consideration is to clear himself. In the absence of his Jewish accusers, Paul can freely speak his mind without fear of altercations. When Festus eventually breaks into Paul's discourse, the governor expresses disbelief but no animosity (v. 24).

c. "I beg you to listen to me patiently." Paul employs the oratorical formalities of his day when he implores Agrippa to listen to him. At Paul's trial before Governor Felix, the orator Tertullus spoke similar words (see 24:4). However, Paul should not be accused of insincerity. He means every word he speaks and wants Agrippa to pay close attention to the theological message he is going to hear.

d. "Especially because you are an expert in all the customs and disputes of the Jews." Because Agrippa is acquainted with the Jewish faith, Paul intends to show him that Christianity has its roots in Judaism. A literal translation of the text is, "because you are especially expert" (see the NASB margin). Paul means to say that, of all the rulers, King Agrippa is best qualified to understand Jewish customs and disputes. He politely pays the king a compliment by calling him an expert in Jewish matters.

Greek Words, Phrases, and Constructions in 26:2–3

Ἰουδαίων—the omission of the definite article is common wherever names of people are mentioned in Greek lawsuits.[8]

---

6. Consult Emil Schürer, *The History of the Jewish People in the Age of Jesus Christ* (*175 B.C.–A.D. 135*), rev. and ed. Geza Vermes and Fergus Millar, 3 vols. (Edinburgh: Clark, 1973–87), vol. 1, p. 475; R. F. O'Toole, *The Christological Climax of Paul's Defense*, Analecta Biblica 78 (Rome: Biblical Institute, 1978), p. 17.

7. Refer to John J. Kilgallen, "Paul Before Agrippa (Acts 26, 2–23): Some Considerations," *Bib* 69 (1988): 170–95.

8. Friedrich Blass and Albert Debrunner, *A Greek Grammar of the New Testament and Other Early Christian Literature*, trans. and rev. Robert Funk (Chicago: University of Chicago Press, 1961), #262.

ἥγημαι—this is the perfect of the verb ἡγέομαι (I think, consider), which has lost its middle function and therefore needs the pronoun ἐμαυτόν to complete the meaning of the verb ("I consider myself"). The perfect has the sense of the present.

ἀπολογεῖσθαι—the middle voice is expressed as a reflexive: "to defend myself."

ὄντα σε—"you are." This is a dangling participle. "A lack of congruence in participles is not confined to the least educated writers of the New Testament."[9]

---

c. Background
26:4–8

The introductory part of Paul's speech varies in content from the discourse he delivered from the steps of Fortress Antonia some two years earlier (22:3). The difference is that in the presence of King Agrippa, Paul stresses the doctrine of the resurrection from the dead. He notes that he is on trial because of this teaching (vv. 6–8).

4. "All the Jews know my way of life from my childhood on, which I spent from the beginning in my own nation and in Jerusalem. 5. They have known me for a long time and can testify, if they are willing, that I have lived according to the strictest sect of our religion as a Pharisee."

a. "All the Jews know my way of life." With the use of the adjective *all*, Paul speaks in generalities. He means that his opponents in Jerusalem and elsewhere know his identity and are able to examine his personal life. They know his origin (see 22:3; Gal. 1:13; Phil. 3:5). When he was still a child, his parents moved from Tarsus in Cilicia to Jerusalem. In this city he was reared and educated. Paul employs the phrases *from my childhood on, from the beginning,* and *for a long time* to support his claim that the Jews are acquainted with his way of life. In addition, Paul's opponents had come to know his background through the addresses he delivered in Jerusalem and in Caesarea (22:1–21; 24:10–21).

Paul states that he spent his time in his "own nation." He uses the customary Greek term *ethnos* (nation), not the Greek noun *laos*, which usually refers to Israel as God's covenant people.[10] His audience is mostly Gentile, so Paul carefully avoids giving any offense and accordingly chooses the customary term *ethnos*. While the term *nation* is broad, the reference to Jerusalem is specific. Here Paul lived for several decades until he left for Damascus (9:1–3) and subsequently for Tarsus (9:30). His protracted sojourn in Jerusalem clearly identified Paul with the Jewish religion.

b. "They have known me for a long time and can testify, if they are

---

9. Nigel Turner, *A Grammar of New Testament Greek,* 4 vols. (Edinburgh: Clark, 1963), vol. 3, p. 316.

10. In several instances in both his Gospel and Acts, Luke describes the people of Israel as *ethnos* (e.g., Luke 7:5; 23:2; Acts 10:22). The context determines the exact meaning of the Greek term *ethnos*. Consult Hans Bietenhard, *NIDNTT,* vol. 2, p. 793.

willing." Paul declares that the Jews had known him since his youth.[11] By race, education, and zeal he is one of them, but the Jews refuse to acknowledge Paul's training in and dedication to the Jewish religion. The Jews' knowledge of Paul would compel them to testify on his behalf, but he doubts that they will do so. Paul puts the onus to testify onto the Jews.

c. "I have lived according to the strictest sect of our religion as a Pharisee." If the Jews decline to testify, Paul himself will. He identifies himself with the law-abiding Jews of his day, for the Pharisees were known to obey God's commands according to the letter of the law. Paul describes the Pharisees as "the strictest sect of our religion." No one, Paul implies, is able to accuse him of flouting God's law, for his roots are in the strictest sect of Judaism.

The verb *I have lived* refers to Paul's youth and the duration of his training in Jerusalem. Paul could justifiably call himself "a Pharisee, a son of Pharisees"(23:6). If anyone would defend Paul in a Jewish court of law, the Pharisees should be the first to speak for him.

Paul knows that Agrippa has authority to appoint the high priest, who belongs to the party of the Sadducees. Paul refrains from making an issue of the difference between the Sadducees and the Pharisees, but he wants the king to understand that in respect to the doctrine of the resurrection, the Pharisees ought to support Paul.

And with the term *religion* Paul is specifically referring to the worship of Israel's God. He testifies that he and the king share in this worship. Yet Agrippa would have to acknowledge that Paul is the more faithful worshiper.

6. "And now I stand on trial for the hope of the promise made by God to our fathers."

In a sense, verses 6, 7, and 8 form a parenthetical thought that briefly interrupts the self-identification of Paul, a Pharisee (v. 5) who expresses his previous opposition to Jesus of Nazareth (v. 9).[12] Paul clearly explains that the reason for his trial is spiritual and pertains to Israel's religion: "the hope of the promise made by God to our fathers." Once more (see v. 5) Paul includes Agrippa among the Jewish people.

What is the hope that Paul shares with the nation Israel? Throughout his preaching and speaking ministry to predominantly Jewish audiences, Paul repeatedly mentions the word *hope* (23:6; 24:15; 28:20) and often links it to both Jesus and the resurrection of the dead. Hope refers to the promise that God made to Israel's spiritual forefathers through the prophets in the Old Testament era. And God fulfilled this promise in the resurrection of Jesus Christ.[13]

---

11. Josephus writes the same verb ("to know from times past") when he describes the ruined landscape surrounding Jerusalem. It could not be recognized by anyone who had known its beauty in earlier days. *War* 6.1.1 [8].

12. John Albert Bengel, *Gnomon of the New Testament*, ed. Andrew R. Fausset, 5 vols. (Edinburgh: Clark, 1877), vol. 2, p. 714.

13. Consult Robert J. Kepple, "The Hope of Israel, the Resurrection of the Dead, and Jesus," *JETS* 20 (1977): 231–41.

The refusal of Paul's opponents to recognize the fulfillment of Israel's hope causes the apostle to proclaim and teach even more earnestly the actuality of this hope.[14] Indeed, Paul wants his countrymen to acknowledge Jesus' resurrection from the dead (compare Rom. 9:4–5; Phil. 3:11). By doing so they will graduate from expecting fulfillment of the promise to realizing that it has been fulfilled.

7. "This promise our twelve tribes hope to attain by earnestly serving God night and day. Concerning this hope, O king, I am being accused by the Jews."

a. "This promise our twelve tribes hope to attain by earnestly serving God night and day." The expression *our twelve tribes* occurs only here and in Paul's letters, although other New Testament writers use a similar expression in Greek (see Matt. 19:28; Luke 22:30; James 1:1; Rev. 7:4–8; 21:12). The term serves as a synonym for "Israel" and provides no information on postexilic history.[15]

Paul wisely states the positive aspects of Israel's hope. He speaks complimentary words and stresses that the people of Israel are trying to bring about the fulfillment of God's promise by serving him night and day. Although Paul explains in his epistles that the Jews' zeal for keeping God's law cannot possibly ensure their salvation (see, e.g., Rom. 10:2–3), here he omits doctrinal explanations and only makes an observation. He affirms that the nation Israel earnestly worships God and expects God to fulfill his promise that the Messiah will restore Israel. This hope is basic to the Jewish religion.

In a subtle manner Paul demonstrates that the hope he cherishes originates in the Jewish religion and that both the Jews and he foster the same hope, but that the Jews have brought him to trial because of this hope in Jesus and the resurrection. Here, then, is the incongruity Agrippa faces as he listens to Paul's defense.

b. "Concerning this hope, O king, I am being accused by the Jews." Paul addresses the king once again (see v. 2) because he wants Agrippa to pay close attention to this crucial point: the Jews drag Paul into court for espousing a doctrine they themselves teach. We must add, however, that for Paul the hope as such has become reality in the coming and resurrection of Jesus Christ. For the apostle the preaching of this hope is a message of fulfillment. In brief, the expression *this hope* represents the proclamation of the gospel.

8. "Why do you Jews consider it incredible that God raises the dead?"

The change from the preceding verse (v. 7) to the present verse is abrupt and can be understood only by someone whose heritage is Jewish. The connection between the hope that God will fulfill his promise to the fathers (v. 6) and the fact that God raises the dead (v. 8) would not be evident to a

---

14. Some translations personalize the concept *hope* by having Paul say "my hope." See JB, NAB, NIV.

15. At least two manuscripts of I Clem. 55:6 (Codex Alexandrinus and Codex Constantinopolitanus) have the reading *the twelve tribes*.

Gentile. Therefore, Paul usually refrained from giving Gentile audiences a detailed exposition of the doctrine of the resurrection. He made an exception in Athens, where he addressed the learned philosophers (17:31–32). But whenever he spoke with Jews, he knew that he had a common basis, namely, God's promise to the fathers concerning the Messiah and the resurrection from the dead.

Paul's listeners in the governor's mansion were military officers and prominent citizens of Caesarea (25:23). We are confident that most of these people were Gentiles, yet among the prominent leaders of Caesarea were Jews. Now Paul directs his attention away from King Agrippa and channels it toward the Jews in his audience. He disregards the Gentiles and candidly asks the Jews who are present: "Why do you Jews consider it incredible that God raises the dead?"

From their Old Testament heritage the Jews knew that God indeed raised people from the dead.[16] They also had to admit that Jesus did the same, as did the apostles by the power Jesus gave them. And last, they knew the Christian teaching that Jesus rose from the grave. The Pharisaic Jews accepted the doctrine of the resurrection, but they refused to believe that God raised Jesus from the dead. If God could bring back to life the son of the widow of Zarephath and the son of the Shunammite woman, would he not be able to raise Jesus?

Doctrinal Considerations in 26:6–8

The Old Testament discloses a gradual development of the doctrine of the resurrection. After man's fall into sin, God placed a limit on man's physical life. The genealogy from Adam to Noah, for example, has a recurring refrain for every person that is listed: "and he died" (Gen. 5:5, 8, 11, 14, etc.). The exception is Enoch, who "was no longer here, for God took him" (Gen. 5:24, NAB). God also took Elijah to heaven (II Kings 2:11). These two people were translated to heaven but did not experience a resurrection. The prophets Elijah and Elisha were instrumental in raising young men from the dead (I Kings 17:23; II Kings 4:35), but in the course of time the widow's son in Zarephath died again, and so did the son of the Shunammite woman. Likewise, the dead man who was thrown into Elisha's grave and came back to life died again, in the course of time (II Kings 13:21).

The doctrine of the resurrection becomes more distinct in Job, the psalms, and the prophets. In these books a number of allusions to the resurrection appear. Job declares that after death he will see his Redeemer with his own eyes (Job 19:25–27). David asserts that God's Holy One (or: faithful one) will not be abandoned to the grave and see decay (Ps. 16:10). Isaiah records a hymn in which these lines occur:

---

16. John Calvin, *Commentary on the Acts of the Apostles,* ed. David W. Torrance and Thomas F. Torrance, 2 vols. (Grand Rapids: Eerdmans, 1966), vol. 2, p. 272; Haacker, "Das Bekenntnis des Paulus," pp. 437–51.

But your dead will live;
  their bodies will rise.
You who dwell in the dust,
  wake up and shout for joy.
Your dew is like the dew of the morning;
  the earth will give birth to her dead. [26:19, NIV]

Daniel prophesies: "Multitudes who sleep in the dust of the earth will awake: some to everlasting life, others to shame and everlasting contempt" (Dan. 12:2, NIV). The prophet Hosea invites the people to return to the Lord, who will revive them after two days and restore them on the third day (Hos. 6:2). And Ezekiel relates his vision of the dry bones that come to life again (Ezek. 37:1–14).

In the New Testament era, Martha reveals that she believes in the resurrection of the dead. She responds to Jesus' assurance that Lazarus will live by confessing, "I know that he will rise again in the resurrection at the last day" (John 11:24, NIV). Martha demonstrates that as a member of the Jewish community she is acquainted with the doctrine of the resurrection, which she accepts in faith. Jesus' reply to her, "I am the resurrection" (John 11:25), is the fulfillment of man's longing for restoration. This teaching, therefore, has become one of the basic doctrines of Christianity.

Greek Words, Phrases, and Constructions in 26:4–8

Verse 4

μὲν . . . οὖν—"so then." This combination is contrasted by that of καὶ νῦν (and now), which introduces a parenthetical comment (vv. 6–8).

ἴσασιν—the Attic form of the third plural οἴδασιν (they know) occurs only here. Paul uses classical Greek in the presence of government officials, military commanders, and prominent citizens.

Verse 5

ἐὰν θέλωσιν—the use of the subjunctive ("in case they wish") expresses uncertainty and doubt. It also indirectly shows the Jews' animosity toward Paul.

ἔζησα—"I lived." Here is the culminative use of the aorist tense. Paul looks back on a period in his life when he practiced his religion as a Pharisee.

Verses 7–8

ἐν ἐκτενείᾳ—the expression has the force of an adverb and signifies "earnestly." An approximate parallel appears in I Thessalonians 3:10.

ἧς—this relative pronoun is similar to a demonstrative pronoun and should be translated "this hope."[17]

παρά—the preposition παρά with the dative conveys a metaphorical sense: "Why is it judged incredible in your eyes?"[18]

---

17. Blass and Debrunner, *Greek Grammar*, #458.
18. Moule, *Idiom-Book*, p. 52.

εἰ—the meaning of this particle in the context of the sentence is the equivalent of ὅτι (that).

---

d. Purpose
26:9–11

After a brief doctrinal explanation (vv. 6–8), Paul resumes his biographical sketch. He informs his audience how he used to oppose the teachings of Jesus of Nazareth.

9. "So then I thought that I myself should do as many things as possible against the name of Jesus of Nazareth."

The introductory words *so then* connect this sentence with Paul's earlier train of thought (vv. 2–5). As a Pharisee he consciously decided to negate the influence of the Christian church—indeed, to destroy it. Paul intimates that no one ordered him to oppose Jesus Christ; he himself made this decision.

Moreover, Paul indicates that he felt a moral obligation to counter the spread of Christianity with all the resources at his disposal. Even though he believed in the resurrection of the dead, he refused to believe that God had raised Jesus of Nazareth. Blinded by unbelief, he thought that he was serving God by opposing the name of Jesus Christ (compare John 16:2). The term *name* must be understood in the broad sense of Jesus' teachings and ministry, that is, his revelation. Paul identifies Jesus not as the Christ but with reference to his residence, Nazareth (see the commentary on 22:8 and 24:5). As an ardent Pharisee he opposed Jesus in numerous ways. For Paul, thwarting the cause of Christ became a way of life.

10. "And this is just what I did in Jerusalem: not only did I lock up many of the saints in prisons because I received authority from the chief priests, but also I cast my vote against them when they were put to death."

Here is Paul's candid confession about his former life as persecutor of Christ's followers. Subsequent to Stephen's death, Paul victimized the residents of Jerusalem who believed in Christ. He went from house to house and, dragging away both men and women, he put them in jail (8:3). Note that Paul identifies these victims as saints (lit.: the holy ones).[19] By using this explicit term, the former persecutor not only openly admits that he inflicted injuries on innocent people but also ascribes to them the attribute of holiness. In short, he regards them highly.[20]

At other places, Luke reports that Paul "dragged away men and women and put them in prison" (8:3; and see 9:2; the term *prison* probably refers to the jails that at one time housed the apostles [4:3; 5:18]). Paul's obsession

---

19. In Acts, the term *holy ones* occurs only four times: those harmed by Paul (9:13); the Christians in Lydda (9:32); the believers in Joppa (9:41); and the imprisoned saints in Jerusalem (26:10). The first and the last references are to the same group of Christians.

20. Paul employs the term *holy ones* at least thirty-seven times in his epistles, where it is synonymous with the expressions *called, elect,* and *faithful.* See Hans Seebass, *NIDNTT,* vol. 2, p. 229; H. J. Cadbury, "Names for Christians and Christianity in Acts," *Beginnings,* vol. 5, pp. 380–81.

had blinded him. He showed respect for neither men nor women. Making no distinction, he had both incarcerated. And at the trials of these people, Paul was present. He confesses that he cast his vote against them when they received the death penalty, although the Jews did not have the right to administer capital punishment (John 18:31).[21]

From the information in Acts we know of only one person whom the Jews stoned to death, namely, Stephen, and perhaps Paul has in mind this first martyr. But in the unsettled times during Pontius Pilate's last year in office and his recall to Rome in A.D. 36, the Jews not only continued their attacks on the Christians but even executed some of them (see 22:4). How many Christians were put to death is not known.

We know next to nothing of the process of appointing new members to the Sanhedrin, although Emil Schürer states that "rabbinical learning [functioned] as the sole test of a candidate's eligibility."[22] But age may also have been a factor, for Paul is portrayed as a young man at the time of Stephen's death (7:58). Therefore, he may have had to wait before he could join the ranks of the Sanhedrin. Filling the role of prosecutor for the Sanhedrin, Paul voted for the execution of the imprisoned Christians.

11. "Often I had them punished as I went from synagogue to synagogue, and I tried to force them to blaspheme. I was so enraged at them that I even persecuted them in foreign cities."

The point Paul tries to make in his address to King Agrippa is that he was a most zealous Jew who served the governing body, the Sanhedrin, in Jerusalem. In that capacity, he aided the forces that opposed the rise of Christianity by persecuting those who adhered to this faith. The Christians were part of the local synagogues. Thus, Paul could easily lay his hands on them and have them tried and punished by the judicial courts of these synagogues (compare Matt. 10:17). These lower courts meted out floggings (see Matt. 23:34; II Cor. 11:24). When Christians stayed away from the synagogue worship services, Paul would go to their homes and drag them before the courts.

Paul openly confesses that he was so filled with rage against the followers of Jesus that he tried to force them to blaspheme. He fails to specify what the word *blaspheme* entails, but the context implies the cursing of Jesus' person, teaching, and work (I Cor. 12:3).

Terrorizing the Christian community in Jerusalem and Judea failed to satisfy Paul. He sought permission from the high priest to persecute Christians in foreign cities and take them as captives to Jerusalem. He knew that the Sanhedrin exercised authority over synagogues outside of Israel, and that with proper credentials he could travel to cities where numerous Jews had settled. Damascus was one of these places.

---

21. Ernst Haenchen understands the text to mean that the Sanhedrin had the *ius gladii* (the authority of the sword). *The Acts of the Apostles: A Commentary*, trans. Bernard Noble and Gerald Shinn (Philadelphia: Westminster, 1971), p. 684 n. 5.
22. Schürer, *History of the Jewish People*, vol. 2, p. 211.

Greek Words, Phrases, and Constructions in 26:9–11

Verses 9–10

μὲν οὖν—in context, this combination probably is the equivalent of the English colloquial idiom *Why,* or, "Why, I myself thought."[23]

ὅ—the relative pronoun in the neuter accusative singular (see 11:30) actually refers to the entire preceding verse (v. 9): "and this is just what I did."

ἀναιρουμένων—the present passive participle of the verb ἀναιρέω (I destroy) alludes to the act of executing someone.[24] The present tense denotes repeated occurrence, the genitive case is the genitive absolute construction, and the use of the passive serves to hide the identity of the executioners.

Verse 11

ἠνάγκαζον—from the verb ἀναγκάζω (I force), the imperfect tense should be interpreted in the conative sense: "I tried to force." Paul admits that, in spite of his efforts, he failed.

περισσῶς—the adverb meaning "exceedingly" can be translated "very."

---

e. Conversion
26:12–14

This account of his conversion varies from the one Paul delivered to the Jews in Jerusalem (22:6–21). We can hardly fault Paul for presenting his own experience in two slightly different versions; the setting and purpose of each account contribute to the differences.

12. "While doing this, I was going to Damascus with the authority and commission of the chief priests. 13. At noon, O king, while I was on the road, I saw from heaven a light brighter than the brilliance of the sun shining around me and those traveling with me."

Paul relates that he continued persecuting Jesus' followers, even in foreign cities. In the presence of the king, Paul employs official terms. On an earlier occasion, he said that he had received letters from the high priest and the council (22:5). Now he speaks formally and says that he went to Damascus with "the authority and commission of the chief priests." The expression *chief priests* points to members of priestly families who occupied a seat in the Sanhedrin (see the commentary on 4:6).

At this juncture in his address, Paul tells Agrippa about his conversion to Christianity. Near the city of Damascus the unexpected happened. Paul points out that it was high noon while he was traveling. Suddenly a light that surpassed the brightness of the sun enveloped him and his travel companions (compare Luke 2:9), as those companions could attest (22:9; in

---

23. Moule, *Idiom-Book,* p. 163.
24. Bauer, p. 54.

short, Paul did not suffer an epileptic spell, a heatstroke, or a hallucination). He states that the light originated in heaven, so that Agrippa has to realize the supernatural characteristics of the event.

14. "When all of us had fallen to the ground, I heard a voice saying to me in Hebrew, 'Saul, Saul, why do you persecute me? It is hard for you to kick against the goads.' "

The two earlier accounts (9:4 and 22:7) and this one differ at several points.

In verse 14 Paul reveals that everyone in the group fell to the ground, but the other reports state that Paul alone was prostrate. (The Western text adds a clause [the addition is in italics]: "When all of us had fallen to the ground *because of fear, only I myself* heard. . . .") How do we explain such an obvious variation? We need not see an obstacle if we accept the interpretation that Paul's companions were prostrate but soon got to their feet again. They were not blinded by the light as Paul was and, although they heard the sound, they could not understand the words that Jesus spoke (9:7; 22:9).

Next, only here do we read that Jesus addressed Paul in the Hebrew tongue.[25] We surmise that Paul wanted to communicate to Agrippa that the heavenly voice spoke to him in the language of the sacred Scriptures of the Old Testament. The Greek text shows that Jesus called Paul by his Hebrew name (*Saoul*) and not by the Greek form (*Saulos*).

And last, the first two narratives disclose that Jesus briefly asks: "Saul, Saul, why do you persecute me?" (9:4; 22:7). But here Jesus continues and states, "It is hard for you to kick against the goads" (see the comments on the Greek text at 9:5). Paul undoubtedly tells Agrippa more of Jesus' words than he told his Jewish audience in Jerusalem. This illustration, borrowed from an agricultural setting, was well known as a proverb throughout the Mediterranean world.[26] King Agrippa was no stranger to it.

What is the meaning of the proverb? The saying illustrates an ox delivering a swift kick, only to experience the sharp pain caused by the point of a goad. The ox's unwillingness to serve its master leads only to pain. But when the animal docilely performs the required task, the master can put the goad away. Metaphorically, this proverb applies to a man who resists God's call to serve him. Jesus wanted to use Paul's talent and training for the purpose of extending God's kingdom and proclaiming the gospel, but Paul persecuted the church. His efforts resulted in pain. After his conversion he repeatedly speaks about his sin of persecuting the church (I Cor. 15:9; Gal. 1:23). He calls himself a former blasphemer, persecutor, and

---

25. Most translations follow the Greek text, which has the word *Hebraidi* (Hebrew). See KJV, NKJV, NASB, NAB, RSV, JB, GNB, *Phillips*, and *Moffatt*. A few versions (NIV, SEB) read "Aramaic," because that was the language spoken at that time in Palestine. Bauer, p. 213.

26. F. F. Bruce remarks that this "proverb has not been found in any Aram[aic] source, but it is the sort of saying that might be current in any agricultural community." *The Acts of the Apostles: The Greek Text with Introduction and Commentary*, 3d (rev. and enl.) ed. (Grand Rapids: Eerdmans, 1990), p. 660.

violent man (I Tim. 1:13). Conclusively, this proverb informs Agrippa about the turning point in Paul's life. Instead of being Jesus' enemy, he has become his servant.

Greek Words, Phrases, and Constructions in 26:12–14

Verses 12–13

ἐν οἷς—"while doing this." The use of the prepositional phrase appears to have a resumptive meaning equivalent to "and so, well then."[27]

ἡμέρας μέσης—the combination ("middle of the day") denotes the Roman way of reckoning time. The case is the genitive of time.

Verse 14

καταπεσόντων—from the verb καταπίπτω (I fall down), the aorist active participle is part of the genitive absolute construction.

ἤκουσα φωνήν—"I heard a voice." See the commentary on 9:7.

κέντρα—the plural probably refers to the double-pointed goad.[28]

---

f. Commission
26:15–18

15. "So I asked, 'Who are you, Lord?' And the Lord said: 'I am Jesus, whom you are persecuting. 16. Now get up and stand on your feet. For this reason I appeared to you: to appoint you as a servant and a witness not only to the things you have seen of me but also to the things I will show you.' "

a. "Who are you, Lord?" The meaning of verse 15 has already been explained in the context of the earlier accounts (9:5; 22:8). A slight variation occurs here, where Jesus identifies himself but omits his place of origin, Nazareth.

b. "Now get up and stand on your feet." Of the three reports of Paul's conversion only this one states that he must stand on his feet. The command at first seems redundant, but further reflection shows that it conveys a dual message. The first and obvious message is that Paul must arise from his prone position, stand in the presence of Jesus, his Lord, and accept his new task. The second message hinges on the fact that the words are a direct quotation from one of the Old Testament prophets. God told Ezekiel to stand on his feet and called him to be his prophet. Similarly, Jesus appointed Paul to be a prophet. Agrippa believed the writings of the prophets (see v. 27) and now he understood that Paul, too, was divinely called to a prophetic office.

---

27. Moule, *Idiom-Book,* p. 131.
28. Turner, *Grammar of New Testament Greek,* vol. 3, p. 27.

c. "For this reason I appeared to you." The resurrected and glorified Jesus appeared to Paul and then personally called him to fulfill a task. In other words, Paul's calling had a divine origin that was personal and direct.

d. "To appoint you as a servant."[29] In the first two accounts of Paul's conversion, Jesus instructs Paul to enter the city of Damascus, where he will be told what to do (9:6; 22:10). Here, however, Jesus shows the purpose for appearing to Paul: "to appoint you as a servant and a witness." The verb *to appoint* is significant because in Greek it has a combined form that includes the meaning *beforehand*.[30] That is, God separated Paul before his birth to the task of preaching the gospel (compare 22:14; Gal. 1:15). In his speech before the Jews in Jerusalem, Paul discloses that God appointed him, but now he says that Jesus did so.

e. "[To appoint you] a witness not only to the things you have seen of me but also to the things I will show you." Paul must be a witness both as a person who saw Jesus during the encounter near Damascus (compare I Cor. 9:1) and as a proclaimer of Christ's gospel. After Paul's conversion, Jesus repeatedly revealed himself to Paul in visions.[31] Paul, then, became an eyewitness and a minister of the word (compare Luke 1:2) and fulfilled the requirements for apostleship (1:21–22). Jesus designated Paul a witness of Christ's resurrection and a herald of what he heard from his Lord.

17. " 'I am rescuing you from the Jewish people and from the Gentiles. I am sending you to them 18. to open their eyes, to turn them from darkness to light and from the power of Satan to God. I do so that they may receive forgiveness of sins and an inheritance among those who have been sanctified by faith in me.' "

We make these observations:

a. *Rescue.* The words of Jesus that Paul conveys to King Agrippa are based on Old Testament passages from the prophets and the psalms. God tells Jeremiah not to be afraid of the people because he himself will rescue the prophet (Jer. 1:8, 19). And in his psalm of thanks, David cries out to God for deliverance from the nations (I Chron. 16:35; Ps. 106:47).

Paul's life testifies to the fact that he needed deliverance from both the Jewish people and the Gentiles. On numerous occasions the Jews wanted to kill him, as did the Gentiles (see II Cor. 11:24–27). The irony is that Paul, the former persecutor of Christ's disciples, was persecuted by Jew and Gentile alike. Yet the Lord repeatedly rescued him.

b. *Apostle.* When Jesus said to Paul, "I am sending you to them," he indirectly used the words God spoke to Jeremiah and Ezekiel when he commissioned them as prophets (see Jer. 1:7; Ezek. 2:3). Believing the

---

29. Translators hesitate to take the Greek passive infinitive *to appoint* as a true passive whereby the direct object *you* becomes the subject of the infinitive: "you are appointed to be my servant" (see, e.g., *Phillips*).

30. Consult Peter Schmidt, *NIDNTT*, vol. 1, pp. 475–76; Wilhelm Michaelis, *TDNT*, vol. 6, pp. 862–64.

31. See 18:9; 22:17–18; 23:11; II Cor. 12:1; Gal. 1:12.

prophets, Agrippa would have to admit that Paul stood in the line of the Old Testament prophets. To be precise, Jesus commissioned Paul as a witness to both the Jews and the Gentiles (20:21) but especially as an apostle to the Gentiles (9:15; Rom. 15:15–16; Gal. 2:8).

Note that the words Jesus spoke to Paul near Damascus and which Paul now recalls in the presence of King Agrippa are all allusions to the writings of the prophets. When Paul says, "to open their eyes, to turn them from darkness to light," Agrippa should know that Jesus is referring especially to Isaiah 42:7. This part of Isaiah's prophecy is known as one of the servant songs depicting the coming of the Messiah.[32] The work of opening the spiritual eyes of the people belongs to the Holy Spirit. The Spirit empowers God's servants to preach the gospel and grants them the joy of seeing the effect of their preaching.[33] Paul points out that he works among Jews and Gentiles on behalf of the Messiah. As an apostle of Christ he preaches the gospel. The Good News opens the eyes of those who are spiritually blind and turns the people from darkness to the light of God's Word (I Peter 2:9).

c. *Purpose.* In respect to the people, Jesus specifies three spiritual objectives for Paul: first, to open their eyes; next, to turn them from darkness to light; and last, to turn them from the power of Satan to God. When a person opens his spiritual eyes and comes to conversion, he leaves his world of darkness and enters the light of the gospel. He is no longer Satan's slave but serves the living God.

To the Jews, the imagery of stumbling like blind men in darkness appropriately depicted the condition of the Gentiles. But God had entrusted his holy oracles to the Jews (Rom. 3:2), so that they might live in his light. The Jews, however, had refused to accept God's Word and thus were spiritually blind (John 9:39–41). Both the Jews and the Gentiles had to turn from darkness into light. In his epistles to the Gentile churches, Paul frequently uses the metaphor of darkness and light.[34] Darkness characterizes the realm of Satan, which Jesus here describes as the power of Satan. (In Acts, the name *Satan* appears twice, here and in a question Peter asked: "Ananias, why has Satan filled your heart?" [5:3].) Paul meets the power of Satan wherever he proclaims the gospel (see, e.g., 13:10; 16:16; 19:15).

d. *Salvation.* The words Paul speaks are not his own but those of Jesus. This becomes clear from the first person pronouns that predominate in Jesus' words, especially in the last sentence: "I do so that they may receive forgiveness of sins and an inheritance among those who have been sanctified by faith in me." The Greek places emphasis on the last word in the sentence, which in this case is "me." Salvation comes to expression when the

---

32. See also Isa. 29:18; 32:3; 35:5.
33. Calvin, *Acts of the Apostles,* vol. 2, p. 276.
34. Rom. 13:12; II Cor. 4:6; Eph. 5:8–14; Col. 1:13; I Thess. 5:5.

sinner repents, is cleansed from sin, and takes his place among those who obtain their spiritual inheritance through faith in Christ. The believer receives his inheritance when Jesus, having declared him holy, embraces him and welcomes him into the fellowship of the saints.

Practical Considerations in 26:12–18

A word aptly spoken
is like apples of gold in settings of silver. [Prov. 25:11, NIV]

Addressing the Jews from the steps of Fortress Antonia in Jerusalem, Paul disclosed that after his conversion a Damascene Jew named Ananias came to see him. He added that Ananias "was a devout man according to the law and respected by all the Jews living there" (22:12). Paul used this description to mollify his listeners and prove that he was welcomed in Damascus by a highly respected Jew. In addition, he carefully avoided using the name of Jesus so that he would not give offense.

Standing before King Agrippa, Paul refrained from mentioning Ananias. Instead he chose to relay the words of Jesus who, by appointing Paul his servant and witness, placed him in the line of the Old Testament prophets and New Testament apostles.[35] Paul conveyed Jesus' words that echoed the Old Testament prophecies. He knew that Agrippa believed these prophecies and therefore Paul wanted to persuade him to accept the truth of Jesus' message.

Paul preached the gospel to both the Jews in Jerusalem and King Agrippa in Caesarea. In both instances he recalled his conversion experience. From that same incident he wisely chose different words and emphasized different aspects in his effort to bring the gospel to each party: the words of Ananias for the Jews in Jerusalem, the words of Jesus for Agrippa. Paul was all things to all men in order to win some for Christ (I Cor. 9:20–23).

Greek Words, Phrases, and Constructions in 26:16–17

ὀφθήσομαι—from the verb ὁράω (I see), this future passive verb has an ingressive connotation: "I will begin to appear."[36]

ἐξαιρούμενος—in the passive, the verb αἰρέω means "to choose," but the meaning *to deliver* or *to save* is preferred.[37]

οὕς—the nearest antecedent is the neuter plural ἐθνῶν (nations). Together with the noun λαοῦ ([Jewish] people) the neuter noun effects a change of gender in the relative pronoun from the neuter to the masculine.

ἀποστέλλω σε—"I am sending you." The phrase is followed by a series of three aorist infinitives that express purpose: to open, to turn, and to receive.

---

35. Consult P. Boyd Mather, "Paul in Acts as 'Servant' and 'Witness,'" *BibRes* 30 (1985): 23–44.
36. Robertson, *Grammar,* p. 871.
37. Bauer, p. 272.

g. Testimony
26:19–23

Paul's gospel presentation before King Agrippa gradually leads to a climax. The apostle offers a testimony of his obedience to the divine commission he received. Paul becomes increasingly personal, as is evident from his use of the first person singular in nearly every sentence.[38]

19. "So then, King Agrippa, I was not disobedient to the heavenly vision. 20. But I kept declaring first to those in Damascus, then in Jerusalem, and then throughout all Judea, and even to the Gentiles that they should repent, turn to God, and practice works worthy of repentance."

a. "So then, King Agrippa." Skillfully preaching the gospel as if to one man, Paul addresses King Agrippa three times by name (vv. 2, 19, 27) and six times by his royal title (vv. 2, 7, 13, 19, 26, 27). He involves the king in a personal way to win him for the cause of Christ.

b. "I was not disobedient." After citing the words of Jesus, the apostle now reveals his reaction to his divine appointment. He chooses the double negative construction to stress his immediate response: "I was not disobedient to the heavenly vision." (This reference includes Jesus' subsequent revelations.) Paul omits any reference to the three days of soul-searching when he was in a state of physical blindness. Rather, he indicates that he promptly began to preach Christ's gospel in the synagogues of Damascus (9:20). When he was forced to flee from that city, he returned to Jerusalem and continued to speak boldly in the name of Jesus Christ, especially to the Greek-speaking Jews (9:28–29). Paul believed in bringing the message of salvation first to the Jews and then to the Gentiles (see, e.g., Rom. 1:16).

c. "Then throughout all Judea, and even to the Gentiles." At this point, the grammatical construction of the Greek text is awkward. For instance, we would have expected the sequence *in Damascus, in Jerusalem,* and *in Judea.* But Paul never preached in the cities and villages of Judea. He spent only fifteen days in Jerusalem (Gal. 1:18) and he states categorically that he was unknown to the churches of Judea (Gal. 1:22). But through a change in the Greek grammar of the sentence, which I translate with the preposition *throughout,* he notes the effect of his preaching.

Paul preached the gospel

in Damascus,
in Jerusalem,
throughout Judea,
to the Gentiles.

---

38. Refer to Paul Schubert, "The Final Cycle of Speeches in the Book of Acts," *JBL* 87 (1968): 1–16; Jacob Jervell, "Paulus—der Lehrer Israels. Zu den apologetischen Paulusreden in der Apostelgeschichte," *NovT* 10 (1968): 164–90.

The emphasis is not on Paul's presence in Judea but on the fact that he, a former persecutor of 'the church, preached the gospel. This astonishing news spread throughout the rural areas of Judea.[39] Further, Paul's special calling was to bring the gospel *to* the Gentiles (Rom. 15:16; Gal. 2:8), which he did on his journeys to Cyprus, Asia Minor, Macedonia, and Achaia. Paul indeed fulfilled the missionary mandate Jesus gave the apostles before his ascension: to be his witnesses in Jerusalem, Judea, Samaria, and to the ends of the earth (1:8; Rom. 15:19).

d. "They should repent, turn to God, and practice works worthy of repentance." Like John the Baptist (Matt. 3:2, 8), Paul preached the gospel of repentance. He called both the Jews and the Gentiles to turn to God in repentance (20:21). His objective was to have both of these groups acknowledge Jesus Christ as their Savior.

For Paul, the acts of repenting and turning to God must be followed by deeds that show the reality of repentance. To be precise, repentance denotes that the whole person with heart, mind, and soul is turned around from sin to service. Repentance for everyone, regardless of age, race, or nationality, marks a moral and religious orientation to a new way of life.[40] In the words of Jesus: "So then, you will recognize them by their fruits" (Matt. 7:20; and see James 2:14–17).[41]

21. "For this reason, the Jews arrested me while I was in the temple and tried to kill me."

Disregarding the accusations of the Jews (21:26–29) and the charges leveled by Tertullus (24:5–6), Paul states that the Jews arrested him for preaching about repentance. He refrains from presenting details, for he realizes that in the presence of King Agrippa he is not a defendant in court but a herald of Christ's gospel. Nevertheless, in passing he refers to the violence directed against him in Jerusalem: "the Jews arrested me while I was in the temple and tried to kill me." The expression *to kill* actually means "to manhandle in such a way that death is inevitable" (see 5:30). When the Jews attempted to stop Paul from preaching the gospel, they deliberately chose to oppose God. However, in their fight against God, they eventually would be losers and Paul through God's grace the victor.[42]

22. "Therefore, having obtained help from God to this very day I stand

---

39. R. C. H. Lenski, *The Interpretation of the Acts of the Apostles* (Columbus: Wartburg, 1944), p. 1044. See also David John Williams, *Acts,* Good News Commentaries series (San Francisco: Harper and Row, 1985), p. 423.

40. I. Howard Marshall, *Luke: Historian and Theologian* (Grand Rapids: Zondervan, 1971), p. 193.

41. In Paul's epistles, the Greek noun and verb for "repentance" and "to repent" (*metanoia* and *metanoeō,* respectively) occur only five times (Rom. 2:4; II Cor. 7:9, 10; 12:21; II Tim. 2:25; but see II Cor. 3:16; Gal. 4:9; I Thess. 1:9 for the Greek verb *epistrephō*). Paul employs the terminology of faith: "to be in Christ" or "to put on the new man." Consult Jürgen Goetzmann, *NIDNTT,* vol. 1, p. 359.

42. See II Chron. 13:12; Job 9:4; Prov. 21:30; Acts 5:39; 11:17.

here witnessing to both great and small and declaring nothing but what the prophets and Moses said would happen."

Paul saw the hand of God in his deliverance from Philippian imprisonment, mob violence in Thessalonica and in Ephesus, and the rioters in the temple area of Jerusalem. God had protected Paul from evil men while he remained obedient to his calling: to proclaim the gospel of salvation. Paul had received Jesus' word that he must testify for the Lord in Rome, and he knew that God would shield him from danger (23:11).

As a prisoner Paul received the necessities of life from numerous friends and acquaintances. These members of the Christian community in turn received the gospel and spiritual counsel from the apostle. Other visitors, both great and small on the social scale, also heard the proclamation of the Good News. Not only the high and mighty (Roman governors and a Jewish king), but also the lower class of society (the common laborer and the soldier) attended to Paul's words.

What was the content of Paul's gospel proclamation? It was the same gospel that Jesus taught the men of Emmaus and his disciples in the upper room. Jesus opened the Scriptures for them by beginning with the books of Moses and continuing through the prophetic writings and the psalms (Luke 24:27, 44).[43] Paul uses not the threefold division of the Old Testament but the twofold (the books of Moses and the prophets) and places the word *Moses* at the end for emphasis (compare 28:23).

Paul tells King Agrippa that the Old Testament canon is his source of information for preaching the gospel. Because the king himself believes the writings of this same canon, Agrippa will have to conclude that Paul preaches the gospel within the parameters of Judaism and is innocent of any wrongdoing (see v. 32).

23. "They declared that the Christ must suffer and, because of his resurrection from the dead, would be the first to proclaim light to both the Jewish people and the Gentiles."

Paul asserts that the Old Testament prophecies disclose the suffering, death, and resurrection of the Messiah. Further, these prophecies teach that the Messiah would shine his light on Jew and Gentile alike. Both the psalmists (Pss. 2:6–7; 16:10; 22:1–21; 118:27) and the prophet Isaiah (42:6; 49:6; 53:3–11; 60:3) speak about the task, life, death, and resurrection of the Messiah.

For the Jews, the doctrine that the Messiah would suffer and die was difficult to accept.[44] Even though Jesus and his apostles turned to the Scriptures that taught this doctrine, the Jews displayed their reluctance to accept it. In fact, Jesus pointedly (and rhetorically) asked the men of Em-

---

43. Consult Jacques Dupont, "La Mission de Paul d'après Actes 26.16–23 et la Mission des Apôtres d'après Luc 24.44–9 et Actes 1.8," in *Paul and Paulinism: Essays in Honour of C. K. Barrett,* ed. M. D. Hooker and S. G. Wilson (London: SPCK, 1982), p. 296.
44. Refer to SB, vol. 2, pp. 273–99.

maus whether the prophets said that the Christ must suffer and enter his glory (Luke 24:26). Paul, in his sermons in the synagogue at Thessalonica, taught and proved from the Scriptures that "the Christ had to suffer and rise from the dead" (17:3). And in one of his epistles, he teaches the heart of the gospel: Christ died, was buried, and was raised on the third day according to the Scriptures (I Cor. 15:3–4). But because the Jews rejected this teaching, they arrested Paul and were ready to kill him.

Christ came to cause the light of the gospel to shine on both the Jewish people and the Gentiles. Jesus is the light of the world (see John 8:12) who calls both the Jew and the Gentile to leave the darkness and enter his light. The apostles as Christ's servants continue the task of dispelling darkness and causing the light to shine (see 13:47).

Greek Words, Phrases, and Constructions in 26:19–23

Verses 19–20

ὅθεν—as an adverb, the word introduces a coordinate sentence that expresses cause: "because of this."[45]

ἐν—the preposition denoting place governs the two nouns *Damascus* and *Jerusalem*.

πᾶσαν—"all of Judea." This is the accusative of extent that indicates how far the news of Paul's preaching had spread.

τοῖς ἔθνεσιν—the dative of the indirect object separates the Gentiles from the Jews living in the places just mentioned.

πράσσοντας—modifying the understood subject of the preceding infinitives, the present tense of this participle shows continued action. The verb πράσσω points to a habitual lifestyle: "they practice."

Verse 23

εἰ—this particle takes the place of the conjunction *that*.

παθητός—a verbal adjective from the verb παθεῖν (to suffer). In the light of Luke's practice of expressing the necessity of Christ's suffering (see Luke 24:26, 46; Acts 3:18; 17:3), this verbal adjective should be interpreted as "must suffer."[46]

---

h. Persuasion
26:24–29

Throughout his address, Paul speaks directly to King Agrippa. But Governor Festus is also present and listens attentively. The subject matter and the word choice prove to be too much for him. Being unfamiliar with the Scriptures and ignorant of the Christian faith, he reacts adversely to Paul's word concerning Christ's resurrection.

---

45. Robertson, *Grammar*, p. 962.
46. Bauer, p. 602; Blass and Debrunner, *Greek Grammar*, #65.3; Lake and Cadbury, *Beginnings*, vol. 4, p. 321.

24. While Paul was saying these things in his defense, Festus shouted in a loud voice, "Paul, you are out of your mind. Your great learning is driving you insane."

a. "Paul, you are out of your mind." The word *defense* should be construed as a defense of the gospel and not as a defense in a court case (see the commentary on v. 1). Paul was so caught up in preaching the gospel that Festus considered Paul to be beside himself. The outburst of Festus actually conveys the idea that the governor considers Paul to be overly enthusiastic and lacking sound judgment.[47] Paul's emotional address had affected Festus, who as a consequence suddenly shouted in a loud voice and interrupted Paul's presentation of the gospel. When a person is unable to fathom spiritual truths because of unbelief and ignorance, he is apt to remark that the speaker is out of his mind. Elsewhere Paul observes, "For the message of the cross is foolishness to those who are perishing, but to us who are being saved it is the power of God" (I Cor. 1:18, NIV). Incidentally, many of the Jews accused Jesus of being demon-possessed and raving mad (John 10:20).

b. "Your great learning is driving you insane." Paul's speech, delivered in excellent Greek, showed him to be an educated man. When Paul opened the Scriptures for his audience, Festus knew that he was unable to understand Paul's message. Being unfamiliar with the Old Testament and the teaching of Jesus, the governor realized that he would not gain any information for his letter to Nero. To maintain his own prestige, he resorted to describing Paul as a man whose higher learning had driven him to eccentricity. In Festus's opinion, Paul held untenable positions, especially in regard to the doctrine of the resurrection (compare 17:32).

25. Then Paul replied, "I am not out of my mind, most excellent Festus. But I utter words that are true and reasonable. 26. The king understands these things, so I speak confidently to him. I am persuaded that none of this has escaped his notice, for it has not been done in a corner."

Notice these two points:

a. *Festus.* Paul is fully in control of the situation. He first speaks directly to Festus and then, while continuing to address the governor, engagingly speaks about the intellectual capabilities of King Agrippa. In brief, he involves both Festus and Agrippa in understanding his gospel presentation.

The first thing Paul stresses is his mental state: he is in his right mind. He calls the governor by name and addresses him by a title of respect ("most excellent"). This appellation was commonly used as a designation for persons of high social rank, including those in governing positions (see 23:26; 24:3; and compare Luke 1:3).

The next thing Paul emphasizes is that the words he has spoken thus far are to be characterized as true and reasonable. Words spoken in a frenzy usually are exaggerated and sometimes false. By contrast, the words Paul

---

47. Bauer, p. 486.

has uttered are based on historical facts that can be verified. Words uttered by someone who is out of his mind fail to communicate reasonableness. But Paul's address is rational and demonstrates sound judgment and self-control. During the delivery of his speech, and particularly toward the end, Paul exhibited enthusiasm and fervor for the sake of Christ. Yet, no one is able to fault Paul for displaying a measure of zeal for a cause that is near to his heart.

b. *Agrippa.* While answering Festus, Paul cleverly involves Agrippa to keep the king's attention. In his reply to the governor, he sketches a picture of Agrippa and places him in a favorable light. According to Paul, the king comprehends the speech Paul delivered. Agrippa is acquainted with the Old Testament Scriptures and thus Paul can confidently preach the gospel to him. Paul is actually saying that he can do so boldly, that is, freely and openly.

Agrippa hears Paul paying him a compliment, for Paul says that the king is exceptionally observant regarding religious issues in Israel. He says, "I am persuaded that none of this has escaped his notice." Paul avers that Agrippa is fully aware of the fact that Christianity is the fulfillment of the Old Testament messianic prophecies. After Pentecost in A.D. 30, the gospel of Christ has been proclaimed openly and boldly in Israel and throughout the Greco-Roman world. And Agrippa, while spending his childhood years in Caesarea, certainly had learned about the growth of the Christian church among the Jews and the members of the household of Cornelius, the Roman centurion.

"For it has not been done in a corner." The adherents of the Christian faith did not hide in secret places. They carried the message of salvation to every major city. They were present everywhere in Judea, Samaria, and Galilee (9:31); they had traveled as far as Phoenicia, Cyprus, and Antioch (11:19); they founded churches throughout Asia Minor, Macedonia, and Achaia; and they had taken the gospel as far as Rome. Christianity had become a world religion. Paul had spoken fearlessly before Epicurean and Stoic philosophers in Athens (17:16–33), had lectured publicly for more than two years in Ephesus (19:8–10), and had defended himself before Felix and Festus (24:10–21; 25:8–11). Nothing was done secretly in a corner.[48] Paul ingeniously quotes words which philosophers pejoratively used for uneducated teachers. These teachers tried to gain a following among people of the lower classes of society but were unable and unwilling to present their teaching among scholars. By citing this adage, Paul effectively refutes Festus's accusation of insanity.

27. "Do you believe the prophets, King Agrippa? I know you do."

Once more turning his attention directly to Agrippa, Paul asks him a personal question that immediately follows his compliment to the king. Paul inquires whether Agrippa believes the prophets, which is an oblique

---

48. Consult Abraham J. Malherbe, " 'Not in a Corner': Early Christian Apologetic in Acts 26:26," *SecCent* 5 (1985–86): 193–210.

reference to the canon of the Old Testament. With this question, he causes
the king to face a dilemma: if Agrippa answers negatively, he incurs the
wrath of the Jewish people; if the king replies affirmatively, he loses face if
Paul asks him to believe the gospel. Before he is able to respond, Paul
already has formulated the answer for him: "I know you do." Indeed,
Paul's reply is so positive that it conveys the meaning "I intuitively know
that you do."

**28. Agrippa answered Paul, "In a short time you are trying to persuade
me to act as a Christian."**

a. *Translations.* Variants in the Greek text are reflected in divergent translations of this verse:

"You almost persuade me to become a Christian" (NKJV).

"You with a few words are trying to persuade me to be a Christian" (MLB).

"In a short time you will persuade me to become a Christian" (NASB).

"Do you think that in such a short time you can persuade me to be a
    Christian?" (NIV).

"In a short time you think to make me a Christian" (RSV).

The readings differ in respect to three points. First, does the Greek text refer
to time ("in a short time") or means ("with a few words")? Next, should the
text be translated "persuade" or "think"? And last, do we adopt the reading *to
become* [*be*] *a Christian* or *to make me Christian*? The technical problems are
discussed in other sources; here I wish to point out the wisdom of accurately
understanding idiomatic expressions in Greek instead of providing a literal,
but wooden, translation.[49] This idiom in Paul's speech connotes, "In a short
time you are trying to persuade me to act as a Christian."

b. *Interpretation.* Before, throughout, and even after Paul's speech, Agrippa
is kindly disposed toward Paul. We should interpret Agrippa's remark,
therefore, as neither an attempt to ridicule the speaker nor a witty reply to
evoke laughter from the audience.[50]

Agrippa sees that Paul's penetrating question concerning belief in the
writings of the prophets would lead to a further query on believing the
truth of the gospel. He evasively counters Paul's probe by asking whether
the apostle expects "an instantaneous response to preaching."[51] Like Felix,
who dismissed Paul when the topic of personal ethics became too personal

---

49. A similar example is in the Greek text of III Kings 20:7 (that is, I Kings 21:7 in our Bibles),
in which the verb *to make* means "to act the part of." Queen Jezebel taunts King Ahab and tells
him to "act as king over Israel." Refer to A. Nairne, "En oligō me peitheis Christianon
poiēsai—Acts xxvi.28," *JTS* 21 (1919–20): 171–72; Lake and Cadbury, *Beginnings,* vol. 4,
p. 323; Bruce, *Acts* (Greek text), pp. 666–67.

50. Compare Lenski, *Acts,* p. 1055.

51. Malherbe, " 'Not in a Corner,' " p. 210.

(24:25), Agrippa resorts to a delaying tactic: a half-hour is too short a time to make a commitment! Furthermore, he does not want to be identified as a Christian. During the first century, the name *Christian* elicited derision and scorn (see I Peter 4:16). In the presence of a governor, high-ranking military officers, and prominent leaders, Agrippa is not interested in declaring that he acknowledges the truth of Christ's gospel and wishes to follow Jesus. With a question that betrays a lack of earnestness, he answers Paul and considers the matter closed.

29. Paul said, "I pray to God that whether in a short or a long time not only you but also all who hear me today may become what I am, except for these chains."

The apostle takes the opportunity to make his closing statement. In elegant Greek, he utters a wish that applies both to the king and to all the members of his audience. Paul expresses his wish in the form of a prayer to God. He is literally saying that at the moment he would pray to God if the circumstances were conducive for prayer. The meeting has come to an end, for immediately after Paul has spoken the king arises. This action signals adjournment.

Paul's wish, regardless of the time involved, is to see everyone who listened to his speech become like he is. He does not use the word *Christian,* but his desire is for everyone to follow Jesus Christ, because in him is salvation full and free. Having intimated as much, Paul has the last word and quickly adds, "except for these chains." With this last clause, he reminds the king and the governor that he has not received proper justice, that he longs to be free, and that he has appealed his case to Caesar.

Practical Considerations in 26:28

When David became king of Israel and set the example to serve Israel's God, the people flourished spiritually and materially. If King Agrippa had put his faith in Jesus Christ, he would have set an example for the citizens of his kingdom. Agrippa, who received a personal invitation to express his faith but declined to accept it, considered being a follower of Jesus Christ below his dignity. Christianity flourished among the lower classes of society and therefore was scorned by the elite. However, the gospel of Jesus Christ is for all classes of society, for the high and mighty as well as the poor and powerless.

In Acts, Luke demonstrates that Christ's gospel reached men and women of influence. He mentions people of note who became Christians: a royal treasurer (8:27), a centurion (10:1), a foster brother of Herod Antipas (13:1), a proconsul (13:7), and prominent Greek men and women (17:4, 12). Some of the women were rich (12:12), in the business world (16:14), and able to teach (18:26) and prophesy (21:9). Christ's followers are at every level of society, where Christ places them to advance the cause of his church and kingdom. Jesus' teachings are open to the world (John 18:20) and should never be banned from public life.

Greek Words, Phrases, and Constructions in 26:24–29

Verse 24

μεγάλη τῇ φωνῇ—the adjective is in a predicate position with the result that it is the equivalent of a relative clause: "with the voice elevated."[52]

σε—the personal pronoun appears in the first part of the sentence; in the Greek, the placement probably is meant to express emphasis.

γράμματα—the noun refers to letters or books. However, it "can also mean *higher learning.*"[53]

Verse 26

λανθάνειν—note that the present tense of this infinitive denotes continual action: "to continually escape notice."

οὐ—this particle does not negate the verb πείθομαι (I persuade) but belongs to the infinitive λανθάνειν as a double negative.[54]

ἐστιν πεπραγμένον—this is the periphrastic construction with the perfect passive participle of the verb πράσσω (I do, practice). The stress is on the punctiliar aspect of this construction; that is, the action is viewed from the beginning until the present.

Verse 28

ἐν ὀλίγῳ—this phrase probably connotes time ("quickly"). If it is understood as a dative of means, the noun λόγῳ (word) or a similar substantive should be supplied.

πείθεις—it is the conative use of this verb in the present tense. The conative points to an act that is begun but interrupted: "you are trying to persuade me."[55] The reading in the present passive πείθῃ (you are persuaded, trust, think) has the support only of Codex Alexandrinus. It may indicate a scribe's attempt to smooth the reading of the text.[56]

ποιῆσαι—"to make, do, act." Supported by leading manuscripts (P[74]; codices Sinaiticus, Alexandrinus, and Vaticanus), this reading appears to be more difficult to explain than the reading γενέσθαι (to become), which is sustained by the Byzantine text. The rule that the more difficult text is original has merit in this case. Also, the possibility is not remote that inclusion of the infinitive γενέσθαι was influenced by the reading of verse 29.

Verse 29

εὐξαίμην ἄν—with an implied protasis ("if only it were possible") the optative connotes "I could pray."[57]

---

52. Robertson, *Grammar,* p. 789.
53. Bauer, p. 165.
54. Moule, *Idiom-Book,* pp. 167–68.
55. Turner, *Grammar of New Testament Greek,* vol. 3, p. 63.
56. Consult Bruce M. Metzger, *A Textual Commentary on the Greek New Testament,* 3d corrected ed. (London and New York: United Bible Societies, 1975), p. 496.
57. Moule, *Idiom-Book,* p. 151.

ὁποῖος καὶ ἐγώ—"as even I." The conjunction means "as."[58]

---

i. Conclusion
26:30–32

30. The king, Bernice, the governor, and those who were sitting with them stood up. 31. While they withdrew, they began to talk to one another, saying, "This man is not doing anything worthy of death or imprisonment."

King Agrippa, who presided over this august gathering, stands up and thus signals that the meeting has ended. All the other dignitaries, including Bernice and the governor, do the same. While walking out of the room, the members of the audience engage in spirited conversation about Paul's imprisonment and his speech. We surmise that Luke was present (see the comment at 25:23) and overheard the remarks that were made concerning Paul. He heard the dignitaries say that Paul had done nothing that deserved incarceration or death (compare 23:29; 25:25). On the basis of Paul's speech, the speakers were implying that the preaching of Christ's gospel was no threat to the Roman empire and, therefore, was no offense worthy of punishment.

32. Then Agrippa said to Festus, "This man could have been set free if he had not appealed to Caesar."

In response to Governor Festus's request for help in composing a letter to Emperor Nero, Agrippa provided him the necessary information. After consulting the dignitaries who were present, Festus perhaps communicated to Paul the wording of the letter that would be sent to Rome. Agrippa had told the governor that if Paul had not appealed to Caesar, he could have been released from prison. The blame for his imprisonment, then, is attributed to Paul's decision to appeal to the emperor. Not the governor but Paul must take the blame!

Agrippa's counsel to Festus characterizes the king's fairness to Paul. As a Jew, Agrippa could have sided with the Jews, but on the basis of his knowledge of the Old Testament Scriptures and the teachings of Christianity he declares Paul innocent of any wrongdoing. As a king appointed by the Roman emperor, he had to abide by Roman law and honor Paul's request to be tried in Rome. Festus concurred with Agrippa, and Paul waited for transport to the imperial city.

Summary of Chapter 26

Paul receives permission to speak. He informs Agrippa and the rest of the audience that he counts himself fortunate to make his defense before the king, who is acquainted with the customs and controversies of the Jews.

---

58. Blass and Debrunner, *Greek Grammar*, #442.13.

He identifies himself as a Jew who came to Jerusalem, who lived as a Pharisee, and who is accused by the Jews for believing in the teaching of the resurrection. He relates that he opposed the name of Jesus, oppressed the saints, went to numerous synagogues to have them punished, and traveled abroad to persecute them.

Paul recounts his conversion experience near Damascus, his appointment as servant and witness, and his commission to preach the gospel. He describes how he obeyed the heavenly voice, proclaimed the message of salvation, and was arrested by the Jews, who tried to kill him.

Governor Festus interrupts Paul's discourse and accuses Paul of being out of his mind. Paul denies that he is insane and asks Agrippa to affirm his faith in the writings of the prophets. Agrippa refuses to answer this personal question and adjourns the meeting. He comments that Paul could have been released had he not appealed to Caesar.

27

Voyage to and Stay in Rome, *part 1*

27:1–44

Outline

27:1 – 28:31   X.   Voyage to and Stay in Rome

27:1–44   A.   Caesarea to Malta

27:1–12   1.   To Crete

27:1–2   a.   Boarding Ship

27:3–8   b.   Sailing to Crete

27:9–12   c.   Waiting at Crete

27:13–44   2.   The Storm

27:13–20   a.   The Northeaster

27:21–26   b.   Revelation

27:27–32   c.   Soundings

27:33–38   d.   Encouragement

27:39–44   e.   Shipwreck

27 1 When it was decided that we would sail to Italy, Paul and some other prisoners were entrusted to an officer named Julius, who belonged to the Imperial Regiment. 2 We boarded an Adramyttian ship about to sail for ports of the province of Asia. We set out to sea and were accompanied by Aristarchus, a Macedonian from Thessalonica. 3 On the following day we arrived at Sidon; Julius treated Paul kindly and allowed him to go to friends to take care of his needs. 4 From there we set out to sea again and sailed under the shelter of Cyprus because the winds were against us. 5 And having crossed the open sea along the coast of Cilicia and Pamphylia, we arrived at Myra of Lycia. 6 There the officer found an Alexandrian ship sailing for Italy; he made us board the ship. 7 For many days we sailed slowly and with difficulty arrived at Cnidus. The wind did not permit us to go farther, so under the shelter of Crete we sailed opposite Salmone. 8 With difficulty we sailed along the coast of Crete to a place called Fair Havens, which was near the town of Lasea.

9 When much time had passed and the voyage had become dangerous because the season in which the Fast [the Day of Atonement] was observed had passed, Paul warned them, 10 saying, "Men, I perceive that the voyage will be disastrous and will be a great loss not only to the cargo and the ship but also to our lives." 11 But the officer was persuaded more by the pilot and the captain of the ship than by what Paul said. 12 Because the harbor was unsuitable for winter quarters, the majority decided to sail from Fair Havens, hoping to reach Phoenix and spend the winter in that harbor of Crete, which faced both southwest and northwest.

13 When a moderate south wind came up, they thought that they had achieved their purpose. They lifted the anchor and began to sail as close as possible along the coast of Crete. 14 But before very long, a violent wind, called the "northeaster," rushed down from the island. 15 The ship was caught and was unable to sail against the wind; we were carried away and let ourselves be driven along. 16 Running under the shelter of a small island called Cauda, we were scarcely able to fasten the lifeboat. 17 After they had lifted it up, they used supporting cables to undergird the ship. Because they feared they might run aground at the sandbars of Syrtis, they had let down the sea anchor, and thus the ship was carried along. 18 Since we were violently beaten by a storm, they began to throw out the cargo the next day. 19 On the third day, they threw the tackle overboard with their own hands. 20 Because neither sun nor stars appeared for many days and no small storm lay upon us, we gradually gave up all hope of being saved.

21 When they had gone without food for a long time, Paul stood up among them and said: "Men, you should have followed my advice and not sailed from Crete; you would have avoided this damage and loss. 22 And now I advise you not to lose courage. No one of you, but only the ship, will perish. 23 This very night an angel of the God to whom I belong and whom I serve stood beside me 24 and said, 'Do not be afraid, Paul; you must stand trial before Caesar. Moreover, God has granted to you all those who are sailing with you.' 25 Therefore, men, be courageous, for I believe in God that it will happen exactly as I have been told. 26 But we must run aground on some island."

27 On the fourteenth night while we were being driven across the Sea of Adria, about midnight the sailors began to sense that they were approaching some land. 28 They took soundings and discovered the water was a hundred and twenty feet deep. A little farther, they took another sounding and found the water to be ninety feet deep. 29 Fearing that we might

run aground on the rocks, they let down four anchors from the stern and wished for daylight. 30 The sailors were trying to escape from the ship and had lowered the lifeboat into the sea under the pretense of intending to let down anchors from the bow. 31 Paul said to the officer and soldiers, "Unless these men remain in the ship, you yourselves cannot be saved." 32 Then the soldiers cut the ropes of the lifeboat and let it fall away.

33 Until the day began to dawn, Paul continued to urge everyone to take some food. He said, "Today is the fourteenth day you have been on watch. You have been without food; you have taken nothing. 34 Therefore, I urge you to take some food. This is for your own survival, for none of you will lose a single hair from his head." 35 When he had said this, he took bread and gave thanks to God before them all. He broke it and began to eat. 36 All of them were encouraged and they themselves took some food. 37 Altogether on board we numbered 276 people. 38 When they were filled, they began to lighten the ship by throwing the grain into the sea.

39 When daylight came, they did not recognize the land. But they noticed a bay with a beach onto which they decided to run the ship, if possible. 40 After they cast off the anchors and left them in the sea, they loosened the ropes of the rudders, hoisted the foresail to the wind and headed for the beach. 41 They struck a reef and ran the ship aground. The bow stuck fast and remained immovable, but the stern began to break up by the pounding of the waves. 42 The soldiers planned to kill the prisoners so that no one might escape by swimming away. 43 But the officer wanted to spare Paul and prevented the soldiers from carrying out their plan. He commanded that those who were able to swim should jump overboard first and get to land. 44 And the rest were to reach land on planks or on various parts of the ship. Thus everyone arrived safely on land.

X. Voyage to and Stay in Rome
27:1–28:31

A. Caesarea to Malta
27:1–44

Except for fishermen, the Jews were not seafaring people. Only when necessity forced him to travel by ship would the Jew make an extended voyage across the sea. He had an innate fear of the unpredictable power of the wind and waves. When John writes that he saw the new heaven and new earth appear, "the sea was no longer there" (Rev. 21:1). For him, the disappearance of the sea was a source of comfort. Now he could expect peace and tranquility.

Paul had sailed the waters of the Aegean and the Mediterranean on more than one occasion. He was acquainted with the dangers of the sea, for he writes that three times he suffered shipwreck and that he spent a night and a day on the open waters of the sea (II Cor. 11:25). Once more Paul had to board ship, but now as a prisoner sent under guard to Rome. He was accompanied by Luke, who has written a detailed account of the harrowing experience of sailing from Caesarea to Italy. The account begins with the passage from Caesarea to Crete.

1. To Crete
27:1–12

Throughout this chapter and the next, the writer again (see 16:10–17; 20:5–21:18) uses the first person plural pronoun to indicate that he accom-

914

panied Paul from Caesarea to Rome.[1] He mentions names of places—and some are rather obscure—that scholars have identified as being accurate; he describes climatic conditions that can best be understood as the observations of an eyewitness.[2] We favor the view that the vivid details presented in this account are the work of an eyewitness who experienced the storm and subsequent shipwreck.

a. Boarding Ship
27:1–2

1. When it was decided that we would sail to Italy, Paul and some other prisoners were entrusted to an officer named Julius, who belonged to the Imperial Regiment.

a. "When it was decided." The sentence shows the author's desire to introduce a measure of anonymity, because the subjects for the verbs *decided* and *entrusted* are lacking. Even though Festus gave the order to have Paul transported to Rome, the fulfillment of his order depended on a number of factors and people. For instance, the governor would not send to Rome one prisoner accompanied by a centurion and a band of soldiers. He would wait until a group of prisoners from various parts of Palestine and the interior could be sent by ship to Italy. The authorities would have to wait for a ship that was able to accommodate a sizeable company. (Note that the ship that was wrecked carried 276 people [v. 37].) Transportation was by means of a fairly large freighter that would sail along the coast to deliver and receive freight and provide passage for voyagers.

b. "We would sail to Italy." When Paul was imprisoned in Caesarea, his friends might visit him and supply his daily needs. But could Luke accompany Paul on a ship? The same thing can be asked concerning Aristarchus, who is identified as a Macedonian from Thessalonica (v. 2; 19:29; 20:4). These men are Paul's friends and travel companions.[3] We conjecture that they paid their own fare and so could accompany Paul and attend to his needs. Prisoners had to depend on friends and relatives for food, clothing, and other necessities.[4]

Note that Luke writes they sailed for Italy, not Rome. Travelers to Rome

---

1. Hans Conzelmann doubts that Luke was present and calls the use of the personal pronoun "a literary device." *Acts of the Apostles,* trans. James Limburg, A. Thomas Kraabel, and Donald H. Juel (1963; Philadelphia: Fortress, 1987), p. 215.

2. Consult Colin J. Hemer, *The Book of Acts in the Setting of Hellenistic History,* ed. Conrad H. Gempf (Tübingen: Mohr, 1989), pp. 330–31; see also his article, "First Person Narrative in Acts 27–28," *TynB* 36 (1985): 79–109.

3. William M. Ramsay is of the opinion that Luke and Aristarchus were permitted to accompany Paul as his slaves. *St. Paul the Traveller and the Roman Citizen* (1897; reprint ed., Grand Rapids: Baker, 1962), p. 316. F. F. Bruce suggests that Luke signed on as the ship's physician. *The Acts of the Apostles: The Greek Text with Introduction and Commentary,* 3d (rev. and enl.) ed. (Grand Rapids: Eerdmans, 1990), p. 672.

4. Consult Jean Rougé, "Actes 27, 1–10," *VigChr* 14 (1960): 193–203.

often journeyed by ship to the southern part of Italy and then walked to the imperial city.

c. "Paul and some other prisoners were entrusted to an officer named Julius." The significant person in this account is not Luke but Paul; except for the use of the pronouns *we* and *us*, the writer cloaks himself in anonymity. Paul is set apart from another group of men who are prisoners, writes Luke. That is, the other men presumably are criminals. But the centurion regards Paul as a person of stature who receives due respect and to whom people listen (see especially vv. 21–26, 31, 33–35).

The Roman officer in charge of the prisoners was a centurion named Julius. Luke describes him as an officer who belonged to the Imperial Regiment.[5] With the aid of his soldiers, Julius served as a military courier with special authority to escort and protect prisoners.[6] Presumably he was a member of Nero's bodyguard who had been sent on a special mission to Caesarea and now was returning to Rome.

2. We boarded an Adramyttian ship about to sail for ports of the province of Asia. We set out to sea and were accompanied by Aristarchus, a Macedonian from Thessalonica.

Governor Festus apparently was unable to find suitable means to send Paul along Roman roads from Caesarea to Troas, then across the Aegean Sea to Macedonia, along the Via Egnatia to the west coast of Macedonia, and then by ship across the Adriatic Sea to Italy. Instead, he believed that confinement on a ship would make escape difficult, if not impossible. For the transport of prisoners by vessel, he had to rely on freighters that plied the coastal waters. The ships that carried Egyptian grain from Alexandria to Italy did not stop at the harbor of Caesarea, but sailed to the coast of Asia Minor. Festus put Julius, his soldiers, and the prisoners aboard a freighter that stopped at various places until it reached its home port of Adramyttium. This harbor city was located along the northwest coast of Asia Minor to the east of Troas and Assos and opposite Mitylene (see 20:13–14).

Luke writes that Aristarchus accompanied Paul on his voyage. Paul later writes in one of his prison epistles that Aristarchus is his fellow prisoner, so we may conclude that this person traveled with Paul the entire distance to Rome (Col. 4:10). There he stayed with the apostle in a rented house. He probably volunteered to be with Paul and share his imprisonment.[7]

---

5. Another translation is "a centurion of the Augustan cohort" (NASB). In the first century, a regiment by that name was stationed in Syria and Batanea (east of Galilee). T. R. S. Broughton, "The Roman Army," *Beginnings*, vol. 5, pp. 443–44.

6. Refer to A. N. Sherwin-White, *Roman Society and Roman Law in the New Testament* (1963; reprint ed., Grand Rapids: Baker, 1968), pp. 109–10. Consult Henry Alford, *Alford's Greek Testament: An Exegetical and Critical Commentary*, 7th ed., 4 vols. (1877; Grand Rapids: Guardian, 1976), vol. 2, p. 285.

7. William Hendriksen, *Exposition of Colossians and Philemon*, New Testament Commentary series (Grand Rapids: Baker, 1964), p. 187.

Greek Words, Phrases, and Constructions in 27:1–2

Verse 1

ἐκρίθη—the aorist passive has the articular infinitive τοῦ ἀποπλεῖν as subject: "it was determined that we should sail for Italy."[8] The construction, however, is unusual. The third person singular construction is indefinite.

The Western text has provided an expansion (the additions are in italics): "*So then the governor decided to send him to Caesar; and the next day he called* a centurion named Julius of the Augustan Cohort, and delivered to him Paul with the other prisoners. *And beginning to sail for Italy* we embarked in a ship."[9]

παρεδίδουν—the use of the imperfect of the verb παραδίδωμι (I deliver) is descriptive.[10]

Verse 2

ὄντος—the present active participle is part of a genitive absolute construction.

ἀνήχθημεν—the verb ἀνάγω (I bring up) in the middle and passive is a nautical term (compare 13:13; 16:11; 18:21; 27:12; 28:11) and means "put out to sea." Luke employs no fewer than fourteen different verbs to express the progress of a ship. All these nautical terms are peculiar to his Gospel and Acts; they are not found in the other New Testament books.[11]

---

b. Sailing to Crete
27:3–8

3. On the following day we arrived at Sidon; Julius treated Paul kindly and allowed him to go to friends to take care of his needs.

If the winds were favorable, the captain of the ship could easily sail the seventy nautical miles between Caesarea and Sidon in a day, but Luke makes no remarks about the wind (contrast the following verse). At Sidon they docked to load and unload cargo. Because this work was time-consuming, Julius gave Paul permission to go ashore to visit friends in the city. Julius apparently knew that Paul was a Roman citizen and not a criminal, and for this reason he was kindly disposed toward him. Luke seems to indicate that throughout the voyage Paul was not chained. By contrast,

---

8. A. T. Robertson, *A Grammar of the Greek New Testament in the Light of Historical Research* (Nashville: Broadman, 1934), p. 1424.

9. Bruce M. Metzger, *A Textual Commentary on the Greek New Testament,* 3d corrected ed. (London and New York: United Bible Societies, 1975), p. 496.

10. Friedrich Blass and Albert Debrunner, *A Greek Grammar of the New Testament and Other Early Christian Literature,* trans. and rev. Robert Funk (Chicago: University of Chicago Press, 1961), #327.

11. Consult James Smith, *The Voyage and Shipwreck of St. Paul,* 3d ed. (London: Longmans, Green, 1866), pp. 27–28.

when Paul eventually arrived in Rome and was under house arrest, Luke
mentions that Paul was bound with a chain (28:20).

Although Luke fails to identify Paul's friends, we conjecture that they
were believers who belonged to the church in Sidon. Luke provides indirect
evidence that Christians were present there, for he writes that the people
who were scattered following the death of Stephen traveled as far as Phoenicia (11:19). Moreover, Paul and Barnabas traveled through Phoenicia on
their way to the Jerusalem Council and told the brothers about the conversion of Gentiles (15:3).

**4. From there we set out to sea again and sailed under the shelter of
Cyprus because the winds were against us.**

On an earlier voyage from Patara to Tyre, when the ship had sailed to
the south of Cyprus (21:1–3), Luke had seen the island from the south
and west sides. But on this voyage the winds were adverse (from the west),
he writes, and the ship sailed under the shelter of the island—that is, east
of the island in a northerly direction. "Now, a sailor or a person accustomed to these seas would not have thought of making any explanation,
for the course of the ship was the normal one."[12] However, Luke perhaps
was not "accustomed to these seas" and writes as an eyewitness who describes exact details.[13]

We are not told whether the ship made additional stops at harbors
along the coast of Syria and Cilicia. By staying close to the shoreline, the
captain and his crew would take advantage of the protective shelter of
land areas. But the time came for them to move west and face the northwesterly breezes.

**5. And having crossed the open sea along the coast of Cilicia and
Pamphylia, we arrived at Myra of Lycia.**

Sailing in a westerly direction, the men aboard the ship could see the
mountains of Cyprus disappear behind the horizon. The crew knew they
were on the open sea and that they would do well to navigate within sight of
the two adjoining southern provinces, Cilicia and Pamphylia. The sailors
were acquainted with the current that runs west along the southern coast of
Asia Minor.

Even though Luke condenses his story, we surmise that the northwesterly
winds caused the ship to make slow progress over an extended period of
about two weeks. With favorable winds the estimated traveling time from
Patara to Tyre was four to five days (21:3), but with adverse winds a return

---

12. Ramsay, *St. Paul the Traveller*, p. 317.
13. Vernon K. Robbins contends that the writer received his material from oral tradition and
written sources. "By Land and By Sea: The We-Passages and Ancient Sea Voyages," in *Perspectives on Luke-Acts*, ed. Charles H. Talbert (Edinburgh: Clark, 1978), p. 241. See the analysis of
Hemer, *Book of Acts*, pp. 317–20; and "First Person Narrative," pp. 81–86. See also C. K.
Barrett, "Paul Shipwrecked," in *Scripture: Meaning and Method*, ed. Barry P. Thompson (Hull,
England: Hull University Press, 1987), pp. 51–56.

trip could last five times longer.[14] The voyage from Caesarea to Myra took three if not four weeks and probably occurred during the last week of August and the first half of September (see the additional comments at v. 9), when the prevailing winds are from the northwest.

Eventually the ship arrived at the port city of Myra, located in the province of Lycia. This was a major harbor, similar to Patara, where passengers booked voyages on ships going to various parts of the Mediterranean basin. Julius and his men could have stayed aboard the freighter to Adramyttium, crossed the Aegean Sea, and traveled over land to the west coast of Macedonia. But Julius chose to transfer the prisoners and his soldiers to a vessel that would go directly to Italy.

6. There the officer found an Alexandrian ship sailing for Italy; he made us board the ship.

In the first century, Rome depended on Egypt for its grain supply; in consequence, the Roman government developed a merchant marine that transported large quantities of grain from the Egyptian harbor of Alexandria to Puteoli in southern Italy. Relying on westerly winds, these ships sometimes crossed the Mediterranean Sea from Alexandria directly to Myra, which lies due north. But if the winds blew from the northwest, they would sail to Phoenicia and then to either Patara or Myra in Asia Minor. From there they would continue their voyage toward the island of Rhodes and to Crete. They proceeded along Crete's southern coast and, sailing across the Mediterranean, continued westward to Malta and Sicily.

Using his military authority, Julius arranged passage for the prisoners, his soldiers, and himself on an Alexandrian ship that was bound for Italy. All these people left the Adramyttian craft and, as Luke says, boarded the Alexandrian ship. (The adjective *Alexandrian* reveals that the vessel carried cargo and grain from Egypt [see vv. 18, 38].) Incidentally, even though Julius had used his military power to secure passage for his men, the relationship between this Roman officer and the captain of the ship appears to have been cordial.

By the standards of the day, the grain freighters were immense, measuring 180 feet in length, 45 in width, and 43 in depth.[15] Some of the passengers on these vessels were given small cabins, but most of them had to stay on the open deck, where they made their own shelters. Conditions on board were excessively crowded, as Josephus relates.[16]

7. For many days we sailed slowly and with difficulty arrived at Cnidus. The wind did not permit us to go farther, so under the shelter of Crete we

---

14. For literature on this subject, see Hemer, *Book of Acts*, p. 134 n. 102. The Western text adds "for fifteen days" after the words *having crossed the open sea*.

15. Lucian *Navigium* 5.

16. During the governorship of Felix, he traveled to Rome; suffering shipwreck, he and his "company of some six hundred souls had to swim all that night." Eighty of these people were taken aboard a ship of Cyrene. Josephus *Life* 3 [13–15].

sailed opposite Salmone. 8. With difficulty we sailed along the coast of Crete to a place called Fair Havens, which was near the town of Lasea.

The large vessel, loaded with cargo, grain, and 276 people, set out in a westerly direction. Because of the strong winds from the west and northwest, the ship had to hug the coastline and take advantage of its shelter. Yet it made little progress. After many days the craft arrived at Cnidus, a city located on the tip of a long peninsula that juts from the coast in a westerly direction. When the vessel came to Cnidus, it no longer received protection from the mainland and the advantage of the westerly current. The ship was forced to go nearly straight south toward Crete. With the northwesterly wind blowing in its sails, the vessel moved to the lee of Crete near Cape Salmone, a promontory situated on the northeast corner of the island. The name itself may suggest that Salmone was a "refuge from exposure to the wind."[17]

The eastern shore of Crete is relatively short. Within a matter of hours, the crew faced the task of turning the vessel westward and sailing along the southern coast. Luke indicates that they expended much toil in doing so. The crew eventually moved the ship toward a place that was called Fair Havens, located near the village of Lasea, where they cast anchor.

Not much is known of these two places. Lasea was situated about five miles east of Fair Havens.[18] At Fair Havens vessels were relatively safe from the northwest winds; the area had two adjoining bays that in their own way were attractive, as their name indicates. Although they were protected by several insignificant offshore islands, the bays faced the open sea, and the suitability of wintering there for four months proved questionable.

Greek Words, Phrases, and Constructions in 27:4–8

Verses 4–5

ὑπεπλεύσαμεν—this compound in the aorist active signifies "we sailed close by."[19]
τε—the adjunct particle unites verses 4 and 5.
τήν—notice that one definite article precedes the two nouns *Cilicia* and *Pamphylia*. The construction indicates proximity and unity (compare 9:31).

Verses 7–8

προσεῶντος—from the verb προσεάω (I permit to go farther), the present active participle is part of the genitive absolute construction. The preposition πρός in the compound is directive, not intensive.
μόλις—"with difficulty." The adverb occurs twice, once with the aorist participle γενόμενοι (arrived) and again with the present participle παραλεγόμενοι (sailing).

---

17. Hemer, *Book of Acts*, p. 135.
18. Consult Smith, *Voyage and Shipwreck*, pp. 83–85, 259–60.
19. Robertson, *Grammar*, p. 634.

c. Waiting at Crete
27:9–12

9a. When much time had passed and the voyage had become dangerous because the season in which the Fast [the Day of Atonement] was observed had passed.

a. *Time.* In the last week of September, the ship anchored in one of the bays of Fair Havens. There it was detained, possibly because of adverse winds blowing from the northwest. If the crew decided to leave Fair Havens, they would have to navigate around Cape Matala (a few miles further west) and then face the open sea. At Cape Matala, the shoreline moves sharply to the north for a number of miles. The ship would be unable to stay close to shore with a wind from the northwest.

Luke merely states the passing of time. Everyone aboard ship knew that a day spent waiting in the harbor meant shortening the time that was favorable for sailing the high seas. The season for navigating the high seas was rapidly coming to an end.

b. *Danger.* Luke writes that sailing across the Mediterranean Sea had become dangerous. In ancient times, sailing the high seas after September 15 was not advisable.[20] By then, cloudy weather set in; the cloud cover made it impossible for seafarers to observe the stars, by which they navigated. And from November 11 to March 10 all seafaring ships stayed in port. The Jewish rabbis advised people to travel by sea only between Passover and the Feast of Tabernacles (observed five days after the Fast on the fifteenth of Tishri).[21] We know that along the southern shores of Italy, coastal traffic began to sail again in the first week of February.

c. *Fast.* Luke mentions the Fast, which is the Jewish Day of Atonement, observed in the last part of September or first part of October (according to the lunar calendar; see Lev. 16:29–34; 23:26–32). We are compelled to take the latest possible date for the observance of the Fast because of the time indications Luke provides in the sequence of his account. The latest date for the Fast (the tenth of Tishri) fell on October 5 in A.D. 59.[22] While the ship was at Fair Havens, Paul and his friends observed the Fast. A few days later, the captain decided to lift anchor and sail to the harbor of Phoenix (v. 12). After leaving Crete, the ship spent two weeks on the high seas before being shipwrecked (vv. 27, 41) in the last week of October. Thereafter, Paul waited for three months on the island of Malta (November, December, and January) before he boarded an-

---

20. Vegetius *De Re Militari* 4.39. Consult Lionel Casson, *Ships and Seamanship in the Ancient World* (Princeton: Princeton University Press, 1971), p. 270.

21. SB, vol. 3, p. 771.

22. Hemer, *Book of Acts,* pp. 137–38, 333; F. F. Bruce, *The Book of the Acts,* rev. ed., New International Commentary on the New Testament series (Grand Rapids: Eerdmans, 1988), p. 481; Ramsay, *St. Paul the Traveller,* p. 322.

other ship and landed at Puteoli (28:11, 13). By that time it was the middle of February.

If we conjecture that the Adramyttian vessel left Caesarea in the last week of August and that Paul landed at Puteoli in the middle of February, we have some notion about the beginning and the end of his voyage. We lack absolute proof, but the corroborative evidence in the account seems to illustrate that Paul came to Italy in February of A.D. 60.

9b. Paul warned them, 10. saying, "Men, I perceive that the voyage will be disastrous and will be a great loss not only to the cargo and the ship but also to our lives."

Paul was an experienced traveler who, according to his own testimony, had suffered shipwreck three times (II Cor. 11:25). He knew that a decision had to be made regarding where to spend the winter months.

What authority did Paul have to advise the pilot, the captain of the ship, and the centurion? We do not know, but his experience, demeanor, and insight did not go unnoticed during the voyage. When Paul spoke, the people listened to what he had to say (vv. 21–26, 33–34). The sum and substance of Paul's advice was that continuing the voyage meant facing the danger of losing the ship, its cargo, and even the lives of crew and passengers. (The tense of the verb *to warn* indicates that Paul repeatedly advised a number of people not to leave the harbor [see v. 21].) Paul and his friends had humbled themselves before God on the day of the Fast (Lev. 16:29) and were hesitant to risk leaving port to face the inevitable danger of the sea. This risk they perceived as tempting God.[23]

11. But the officer was persuaded more by the pilot and the captain of the ship than by what Paul said. 12. Because the harbor was unsuitable for winter quarters, the majority decided to sail from Fair Havens, hoping to reach Phoenix and spend the winter in that harbor of Crete, which faced both southwest and northwest.

Julius had authority in this matter, for he was a military officer in charge of both prisoners and grain bound for Rome.[24] He listened to Paul, but he also had to consider what the pilot and the captain of the ship had to say. The pilot and the captain were not unfamiliar with the coast of Crete. They knew that Fair Havens was not a harbor that would provide protection from winter storms. They also knew that if they could sail approximately forty miles west to the harbor of Phoenix, they would have a more suitable place for spending the winter months.

Luke relates that Phoenix had a harbor that faced both the southwest and the northwest. At this place, Cape Mouros juts out into the sea to the south and to the west. It provides two bays: one on the east side of the cape and the other on the west side. Along the shores of the western bay

---

23. John Calvin, *Commentary on the Acts of the Apostles,* ed. David W. Torrance and Thomas F. Torrance, 2 vols. (Grand Rapids: Eerdmans, 1966), vol. 2, p. 288.

24. Hemer, "First Person Narrative," p. 94.

lies a village that today bears the name *Phoinika,* while the village of Loutro is located along the shore of the eastern bay. Not only in ancient times but even today sailors prefer the western bay during the winter months; "the boatmen of Loutro are said to regard the harbor on the Loutro side as unsafe from November to February."[25] In the western bay was the harbor of Phoenix, where the crew of the Alexandrian ship wanted to spend the winter.

Commentators have a problem explaining how a harbor on the south side of Crete can face the northwest. The reading seems logically absurd. However, archaeological research has shown that in Paul's day the western bay had two harbors. As the map below indicates, harbor A faces the south and harbor B the northwest. The topography of Crete has changed since ancient times. Earthquakes have raised the western part of Crete as much as twenty feet in some places and probably thirteen and a half feet at Loutro. Harbor B has become dry land. "The line of shells, marking the limit of the raised beaches here and right round the bay, is about 14 feet above present sea-level."[26] Also, since ancient times the rocky projection of the west promontory of Cape Mouros has decreased by about fifty to a hundred yards and consequently offers less protection from the sea than in former days.

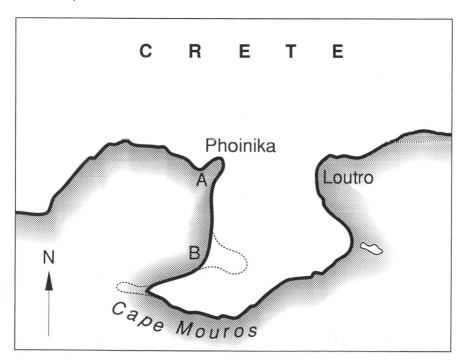

25. Jack Finegan, *The Archeology of the New Testament: The Mediterranean World of the Early Christian Apostles* (Boulder, Colo.: Westview; London: Croom Helm, 1981), p. 197.
26. R. M. Ogilvie, "Phoenix," *JTS* n.s. 9 (1958): 312.

Practical Considerations in 27:9–12

In Acts, Luke records the festive days of the Jewish calendar. For instance, he refers twice to the feast of Pentecost (2:1; 20:16), twice to the Passover feast (also called the Feast of Unleavened Bread; 12:4; 20:6), and once to the Fast (27:9). The references occur because Luke writes about Peter and Paul, who observed the festive days of this calendar. In the harbor of Fair Havens, Paul's observance of the Fast coincided with the Day of Atonement that was celebrated in Jerusalem.

The Christian church has constructed its own festive calendar that begins for some believers with Epiphany. All Christians observe Good Friday and Easter, Ascension Day (forty days after Easter, 1:3), Pentecost (seven weeks after Easter), and Christmas. The church has composed hymns and cantatas to be sung and played for these occasions. Believers are urged to celebrate these holy days and to express their joy and happiness. Conversely, the world lacks a storehouse of hymns and looks enviously at Christians when they celebrate their special days.

Greek Words, Phrases, and Constructions in 27:9–12

Verses 9–10

The genitives in the first half of verse 9 twice form the genitive absolute construction. This construction is followed by the causal use of the articulate infinitive in the perfect active mode παρεληλυθέναι (to have passed). In a grammatically concise manner, three times in succession Luke expresses the idea that time has elapsed.

παρῄνει—from παραινέω (I advise, recommend, warn), the imperfect tense connotes repeated action.

μέλλειν ἔσεσθαι—the infinitive construction is introduced by the conjunction ὅτι (that). The syntax, however, is cumbersome and probably due to an inadvertent slip by the author.[27]

Verse 12

εἴ πως—the combination of two particles introduces a purpose clause which, by implication, has the indirect discourse.[28]

δύναιντο—"if by any means they could." Here is the present optative in an implied indirect discourse construction. The apodosis is lacking but can be deduced from the protasis.

2. The Storm
27:13–44

Paul's voyage to Rome is a compelling story in the Book of Acts, and the section on the storm must be considered the best part of this story. Luke

27. C. F. D. Moule, *Idiom-Book of New Testament Greek*, 2d ed. (Cambridge: Cambridge University Press, 1960), p. 154.
28. Robertson, *Grammar*, p. 1021.

proves to be an excellent chronicler, an eyewitness who uses the first person pronoun *we*. With a few strokes of his masterful pen, he depicts drama on the high seas and composes literature that ranks among the classic stories of all times.

a. The Northeaster
27:13–20

13. When a moderate south wind came up, they thought that they had achieved their purpose. They lifted the anchor and began to sail as close as possible along the coast of Crete.

The sailors waited until they detected a change in the direction of the wind. Instead of a northwest breeze, a gentle wind from the south or southwest began to blow. The crew saw the opportunity which they had awaited and, without losing any time, they lifted anchor to sail the forty miles to Phoenix.

For three or four miles they sailed straight west until they rounded Cape Matala. At that moment, they had to move north for about twelve miles and then proceed in a west-northwesterly direction. All along they hugged the coast for fear that a sudden storm would drive them into the open sea. If the wind should stay in force from the south, they would reach the safety of Phoenix in a few hours.

14. But before very long, a violent wind, called the "northeaster," rushed down from the island.

Before the crew could properly turn the rudder and steer the ship to the north, the wind unexpectedly turned and began to blow from the northeast. In the Greek, Luke writes that the south wind was blowing underneath, which seems to indicate that the skies above were far from cloudless. A storm swept down from the island and caused the ship to drift away from the land and out onto the open sea. James Smith graphically describes the changing weather conditions in the eastern Mediterranean: "The sudden change from a south wind to a violent northerly wind is a common occurrence in these seas. The term '*typhonic*,' by which it is described, indicates that it was accompanied by some of the phenomena which might be expected in such a case, namely, the agitation and whirling motion of the clouds caused by a meeting of the opposite currents of air when the change took place."[29]

The wind is called the "northeaster," which in the Greek is *Euraquilon*. The word is a nautical term that derives from the Greek word *euros* (east wind) and the Latin expression *aquilo* (north wind).[30] At a place named Thugga in proconsular Africa, archaeologists have discovered a twelve-point wind rose that was chiseled into the pavement. The names of the

---

29. Smith, *Voyage and Shipwreck*, p. 101.

30. The KJV and NKJV have the reading *Euroclydon*, which actually means "the Southeast wind that stirs up waves" (Bauer, p. 325). But a wind from the southeast would have caused the ship to reach the harbor of Phoenix and not the island Cauda (v. 16).

winds begin with the north and move clockwise to the east, south, and west. For the northeast wind, the name *euraquilo* appears.[31]

15. The ship was caught and was unable to sail against the wind; we were carried away and let ourselves be driven along.

The word choice that describes the fury of the hurricane is striking. Luke says that the ship was torn away and "unable to face the eye of the wind" (lit.). The storm swooped over the mountains of Crete to the sea and struck the vessel with a violent wind from the east-northeast. The crew did everything possible to stay close to shore as they tried to use the wind to their advantage, but they realized that the force of the wind would not allow the ship to stay on course. The ship began to drift. The men could do no more than yield to the wind and let the ship drift in a southwesterly direction.[32]

Although Luke himself was not a sailor, he nevertheless became so personally involved in the tension and uncertainty of the voyage that he wrote this verse and the succeeding sentences in the first person plural.

16. Running under the shelter of a small island called Cauda, we were scarcely able to fasten the lifeboat.

The northeast wind blew the ship on a west-southwesterly course from Cape Matala toward a small island named Cauda (modern Gaudos or Gozzo).[33] The ship covered the distance between Cauda and Crete, which is about twenty-three miles, within a few frantic hours. The men managed to steer the vessel into the shelter of the island. With the protection of the land, they had an opportunity to prepare the ship for worse things to come. The first task was to secure the lifeboat that normally drifted along behind the ship. The howling wind was about to knock the lifeboat against the vessel. The sailors (and, apparently, the passengers, including Luke himself), had great difficulty hauling it toward the ship.

17. After they had lifted it up, they used supporting cables to undergird the ship. Because they feared they might run aground at the sandbars of Syrtis, they had let down the sea anchor, and thus the ship was carried along.

The sailors had three tasks to perform:

a. *Lifeboat.* The ship had passed the east side of the island; the crew avoided the west side with its dangerous reefs. Now, with the ship's sails trimmed and its stem to the wind to minimize drifting, the crew managed to hoist the lifeboat aboard ship.

b. *Ropes.* As soon as they had accomplished the one task, the seamen began the next. They wanted to put ropes underneath and around the ship to undergird and strengthen it. How this was done cannot be ascertained,

---

31. Hemer, *Book of Acts*, pp. 141–42. See also his "Euraquilo and Melita," *JTS* n.s. 26 (1975): 100–11.

32. The Western text expands the text: "We gave way to [the wind] *which was blowing, and having furled the sails* we were driven." Metzger, *Textual Commentary*, p. 497.

33. The spelling of the name varies from Cauda to Clauda and Clauden. Perhaps *Cauda* may be the Latin spelling and *Clauda* the Greek.

because the Greek words in the text are obscure. Probably ropes were drawn tightly around the hull of the ship to keep the planks against the timbers and thus prevent leakage. This procedure is called frapping; it refers to running ropes across and around the ship at various places from stem to stern.[34] Other suggestions are that the ropes stretched lengthwise from the front to the back of the vessel or along the outside of the ship from fore to aft.[35] Whatever the procedure may have been, the objective was to fortify the ship against the battering wind and waves.

c. *Anchor.* As soon as they had arrived in the lee of the island Cauda, the crew had lowered the sea anchor in an attempt to keep the vessel stationary. The Greek word *skeuos,* which I have translated "sea anchor," is a general term that can mean "thing, object, vessel, instrument." This object may have been a drift anchor or a floating anchor.[36] The context dictates that the *skeuos* served to slow the drifting of the ship. The sailors knew that if the northeaster drove the vessel toward the southwest, eventually the ship would strike the dreaded sandbanks of Syrtis (the Gulf of Sidra on the coast of Libya. The lesser Syrtis is the Gulf of Gabes off the east coast of Tunisia.). These sandbars of greater Syrtis, as the sailors knew, were extremely dangerous.[37] Hence, the men were doing everything in their power to prevent shipwreck on the quicksands of Syrtis.

Anchoring at Cauda proved to be impossible because the harbor of the island was on the east-northeast side and thus offered no protection from the storm. The ship had to leave the lee of Cauda and move into the open sea. With the aid of storm sails, the sailors could exert some control and keep the ship steady. The use of the sails prevented the craft from drifting toward Syrtis.[38] Even though the vessel drifted, with the help of the storm sails it slowly moved westward.[39]

18. Since we were violently beaten by a storm, they began to throw out the cargo the next day. 19. On the third day, they threw the tackle overboard with their own hands.

Mariners in ancient times lacked navigational instruments and had to rely on the sun, moon, and stars to determine direction. But overcast skies made it impossible for them to get their bearings, and during the storm the crew of the Alexandrian ship was unable to check their course. When winds of hurricane force blew, and rain and spray from tempestuous waves

---

34. Consult H. J. Cadbury, "Hypozōmata," *Beginnings,* vol. 5, p. 348; Smith, *Voyage and Shipwreck,* pp. 107–8; Hemer, *Book of Acts,* p. 143 n. 120.

35. See Casson, *Ships and Seamanship,* pp. 91–92.

36. Refer to Ernst Haenchen, *The Acts of the Apostles: A Commentary,* trans. Bernard Noble and Gerald Shinn (Philadelphia: Westminster, 1971), p. 703 n. 2. See Jean Rougé, *Ships and Fleets of the Ancient Mediterranean,* trans. Susan Frazer (Middletown, Conn.: Wesleyan University Press, 1981), p. 66.

37. Vergil *Aeneid* 4.40–41; Strabo *Geography* 2.5.20; 17.3.16–17.

38. Smith, *Voyage and Shipwreck,* p. 114.

39. Lake and Cadbury, *Beginnings,* vol. 4, p. 333.

greatly diminished visibility, the crew panicked. Although Luke gives a day-by-day report, he leaves to the imagination of the reader how the crew and passengers coped during the night. It is no wonder that the frightened seamen took drastic measures the next morning.

We have difficulty explaining why the sailors threw cargo and tackle overboard, except to say that the vessel would be lightened. But an empty ship rides much higher on the waves than a loaded vessel and catches more wind. Perhaps the crew was of the opinion that an empty ship would clear the sandbars if it entered the greater Syrtis.

The word *cargo* is a general term; accordingly, we should understand that the crew threw overboard the extra cargo stacked on deck and in the ship's hold (compare Jon. 1:5).[40] Luke relates that about two weeks later, when shipwreck was almost certain, the crew threw the grain into the sea (v. 38).

The next day (that is, the third day since they left the coast of Crete), the sailors with their own hands cast the ship's tackle into the sea. Some manuscripts have the reading *we threw*,[41] which would indicate that all the members of the crew and the passengers were needed to throw overboard the mainmast that was as tall as a full-grown tree. Discarding this heavy spar would lighten the ship considerably. The Greek word *skeue* is general and refers to not just the mainmast but the ship's equipment, namely, its rigging.[42] Equipment which the sailors thought should be jettisoned they threw away with their own hands. The mainsail attached to the yardarm was cast overboard and, when tied to the ship's stern, served as a brake. With these few words, Luke depicts the panic that gripped the crew.

20. Because neither sun nor stars appeared for many days and no small storm lay upon us, we gradually gave up all hope of being saved.

In plain terms Luke describes the scene aboard ship. As if the reader might have missed the point, the writer restates the obvious. The crew and passengers were unable to see the sun by day and the stars by night. Thus, lost at sea, they were fearful of striking land. If they had been stationary near land, the storm would have passed. But on the high seas, they stayed with the storm that began at Crete and ended at Malta.

Luke characteristically expresses himself with a negative understatement: "no small storm lay upon us." The tempest raged about them day and night, hour after hour. Not surprisingly, the men despaired of their lives. Luke frankly admits, "We gradually gave up all hope of being saved." We are not told whether the ship was taking on water because of leakage, rain, and surging waves, but an increasing volume of water in the hold of the ship may have been one of the reasons for discarding cargo and tackle.

---

40. Rougé comments that the practice of carrying cargo on deck was common. *Ships and Fleets*, p. 70.

41. The Majority Text, reflected in the kjv and nkjv.

42. D. J. Clark translates: "The violent storm continued, so on the next day, they tried to hoist the ship's heavy equipment overboard; on the third day, by manhandling it, they succeeded." "What Went Overboard First?" *BibTr* 26 (1975): 144–46.

Greek Words, Phrases, and Constructions in 27:13–20

Verse 13

Every sentence in this verse and the following verses (14–20) begins with one or two genitive absolute constructions. This usage appears to be a characteristic literary device of the author.

κεκρατηκέναι—the perfect active infinitive of κρατέω (I attain) takes the genitive προθέσεως (purpose) as a direct object. The perfect tense reveals that the sailors had planned their action for a long time.

ἄραντες—from αἴρω (I lift), the aorist active participle is supplemented by an understood noun and verb: "having lifted the anchor, they sailed."

ἆσσον—although this comparative adverb of ἄγχι (near) means "nearer," it should be perceived as a superlative: "they began to sail as near to the land as possible." The verb παρελέγοντο (v. 8) is the inchoative imperfect.

Verses 14–16

ἔβαλεν κατ' αὐτῆς—the aorist is effective; it signifies that the wind "beat down from it [Crete]," not "against it."[43]

ἀντοφθαλμεῖν—the present infinitive is a compound of the preposition ἀντί (against) and the noun ὀφθαλμός (eye). The ship was unable to face the wind.

τῷ ἀνέμῳ—"the wind." This noun in the dative can be taken with the preceding infinitive *to face* or the succeeding aorist participle ἐπιδόντες (surrendered). Most translators construe the noun with both the infinitive and the participle (e.g., JB, NAB, NIV, RSV).

ὑποδραμόντες—from ὑποτρέχω (I run, sail under), this aorist participle descriptively shows that the ship sailed south of the island to find shelter from the storm.

ἰσχύσαμεν—the aorist is ingressive: "we began to succeed."

Verses 17–18

μή—after verbs expressing fear, the negative clause appears with μή and the subjunctive. The aorist subjunctive ἐκπέσωσιν (they ran aground) has the meaning of the passive form of ἐκβάλλω (I throw out).[44]

ἐκβολὴν ἐποιοῦντο—the noun denotes jettisoning; the verb is the inchoative imperfect: "they began to lighten."

Verse 20

λοιπόν—an adverbial expression that signifies "at last." It is akin to the French idiom *enfin*.

τοῦ σῴζεσθαι—the articular infinitive complements the noun ἐλπίς (hope): "all hope of being rescued."

---

43. Moule, *Idiom-Book*, p. 60.
44. Robertson, *Grammar*, p. 802.

---

b. Revelation
27:21–26

Describing the tension-filled scene of coping with the hurricane (vv. 13–20), Luke leaves Paul entirely out of the picture. Yet Paul was with and among the people. When despair crushed the hearts of everyone aboard and no one uttered a word of hope or encouragement, Paul brought a spiritual message of rescue.

21. When they had gone without food for a long time, Paul stood up among them and said: "Men, you should have followed my advice and not sailed from Crete; you would have avoided this damage and loss."

Despair has a debilitating effect on the mind and, by extension, on the body of man. Despair causes a person to not feel hunger pangs, with the consequence that the body becomes weakened. Anxiety caused the crew and passengers to not eat for a long time. Besides, cooking had become nearly impossible, and the food supply may have been damaged by seawater.

In these dismal circumstances, Paul stood up to address the men who were sitting listlessly and waiting for disaster to strike. Paul took a place in the midst of the crowd. And these people, broken in spirit because of the hopelessness of their situation, were ready to listen to his words. He said,

a. "Men, you should have followed my advice and not sailed from Crete." Earlier Paul had advised the Roman centurion, the pilot, and the captain of the ship (v. 10) not to continue the voyage. But they rejected Paul's counsel. Within hours, they knew that they had foolishly risked the ship, its cargo, and the lives of crew and passengers.

b. "To avoid this damage and loss." Everyone aboard knew about Paul's earlier advice, and many of the passengers had assisted the crew in casting cargo and equipment into the sea. This loss could have been averted if they had stayed at the port of Fair Havens. The price they paid for the rash decision to set sail was damage to the ship and loss of goods, not to mention the anguish and discomfort of the passengers. In their desperation the people looked to Paul. If Paul had a word of encouragement to help them in their desperate plight, they were eager to hear him.

22. "And now I advise you not to lose courage. No one of you, but only the ship, will perish. 23. This very night an angel of the God to whom I belong and whom I serve stood beside me 24. and said, 'Do not be afraid, Paul; you must stand trial before Caesar. Moreover, God has granted to you all those who are sailing with you.'"

a. "And now I advise you not to lose courage." Paul takes pride not in his own personal strength but rather in Jesus Christ, who gives him strength to endure (compare Phil. 4:13). He knows that he will have to testify for Jesus in Rome (23:11), and on that basis he is able to advise the men not to lose courage. However, he needs definite information about the outcome of the voyage to make his words meaningful. Unless God communicates pertinent information to him, he will lack certainty in predicting that no one will perish.

b. "This very night an angel of the God to whom I belong and whom I serve stood beside me." In season and out of season (see II Tim. 4:2), Paul takes every opportunity to acquaint people with his God and the message of truth. After gaining the confidence of his audience, he tells the men that he has received good news from an angel of God concerning their physical safety and well-being. Although he had earlier warned that ship, cargo, and lives would be lost (v. 10), now he can assure the men that their lives, but not the ship, will be spared.

Paul adds that he himself belongs to God and is God's servant. Notice that Paul is addressing Gentiles who were polytheistic in their religious conceptions and superstitions. But Paul unreservedly speaks about belonging to one God and serving that God. He has to oppose and correct the Gentile idea that if a person serves God, then God is obligated to reward him with favors.[45] He shows the men that he has put his full trust in God, who has proven repeatedly that he will never fail Paul. For this reason, he conveys to them the exact words of the angel.

c. "Do not be afraid, Paul; you must stand trial before Caesar." We suspect that on an earlier occasion the crew, soldiers, and prisoners had learned that Paul had appealed to Caesar. Now the men understand that if an angel of God spoke directly to Paul, he must be a righteous man. In their opinion, he cannot be a criminal, even though he will stand trial before Caesar.

God appears to Paul neither in a vision nor in a dream. He sends his angel with a special communication to corroborate Jesus' assurance that Paul will arrive in Rome. In the middle of the storm, when everyone is giving up hope of being saved, God sends a special messenger to Paul to reinforce the earlier message of Jesus (23:11). Moreover, the angel told Paul:

d. "God has granted to you all those who are sailing with you." Paul is God's servant and, by implication, his spokesman. He presents himself as God's representative who presumably asked his God to spare the lives of all the people aboard ship. Now, through an angel, God informs Paul that his prayer has been answered and that the lives of all the men aboard ship belong to him. That Paul is in charge becomes evident when he instructs the centurion to keep all the men in the ship (v. 31). Even the centurion himself, in submission to God's providence and in deference to Paul, spared the lives of all the prisoners (v. 43).[46]

25. "Therefore, men, be courageous, for I believe in God that it will happen exactly as I have been told. 26. But we must run aground on some island."

---

45. F. W. Grosheide, *De Handelingen der Apostelen,* Kommentaar op het Nieuwe Testament series, 2 vols. (Amsterdam: Van Bottenburg, 1948), vol. 2, p. 404.

46. John Albert Bengel, *Gnomon of the New Testament,* ed. Andrew R. Fausset, 5 vols. (Edinburgh: Clark, 1877), vol. 2, p. 725.

For the second time (see v. 22) Paul urges his listeners to be courageous. He links courage to faith when he declares that he believes in God. Implicitly Paul invites the men to follow his example and trust God, who controls not only the weather but also everything else. He affirms that he fully trusts God to save both himself and everyone else aboard, but that the ship itself will be lost. Here is a man who demonstrates his unshakable faith in his God. Paul's faith was anchored in God. Priscilla J. Owens communicates this thought in these words:

> Will your anchor hold in the storms of life,
> When the clouds unfold their wings of strife?
> When the strong tides lift, and the cables strain,
> Will your anchor drift, or firm remain?
>
> We have an anchor that keeps the soul
> Steadfast and sure while the billows roll,
> Fastened to the Rock which cannot move,
> Grounded firm and deep in the Saviour's love.

Paul reveals that the ship will run aground on some island. This cannot be a guess on his part. It is revelation given to him by the angel of God, so that no one can say later that the landing at Malta was by chance. As God's representative, Paul vouches that the prediction he has received will come true.[47]

Doctrinal Considerations in 27:22–26

God wants his people to be the salt of the earth and to let their influence pervade the society in which he in his providence has placed them. Indeed, he urges his people to pray for the well-being of society. From Scripture we learn that

God blessed all the nations on earth because of Abraham (Gen. 12:3; 18:18; 22:18);

God blessed the household of Potiphar for Joseph's sake (Gen. 39:5);

God spared the crew and passengers who accompanied Paul on his voyage (vv. 22, 24).

For the sake of his elect, God grants blessings to unbelievers. In spite of God's promise of safety, some of the sailors demonstrated their lack of faith by attempting to leave the ship under a pretense (v. 30).

> Blind unbelief is sure to err
>   And scan His work in vain;
> God is His own Interpreter
>   And He will make it plain.
>   —William Cowper

---

47. Calvin, *Acts of the Apostles*, vol. 2, p. 293.

Greek Words, Phrases, and Constructions in 27:22–24

Verse 22

τὰ νῦν—this is an adverbial expression that signifies "as far as the present situation is concerned."[48]

πλήν—"except." The adverb serves as an improper preposition that governs the genitive case.

Verses 23–24

The word order is striking and stresses the sequence *God, Paul,* and *an angel.* The definite article in τοῦ θεοῦ must be translated into English, for it points to the special God Paul is serving.[49]

κεχάρισται—the perfect tense of the infinitive conveys the idea that God has granted Paul the lives of the crew and the passengers for the duration of the voyage.

c. Soundings
27:27–32

27. On the fourteenth night while we were being driven across the Sea of Adria, about midnight the sailors began to sense that they were approaching some land.

a. *Time.* As Luke has shown in other parts of his book, he keeps accurate count of the days that pass. Here he mentions the fourteenth night of the voyage (i.e., since the ship left Crete). According to Smith, the distance between the islands of Cauda and Malta is about 476.6 nautical miles. He calculates that a first-century ship drifting at a rate of a mile and a half per hour with an east-northeast wind could cover this distance in thirteen days.[50] The drift across the Mediterranean Sea appears to have been in a straight line rather than in the zigzag pattern often portrayed in sketches.

b. *Location.* The designation *Sea of Adria* in New Testament times refers to "that portion of the Mediterranean which extends from Malta to Crete."[51] The name derived from the Italian city Atria in Etrusca and is used by the historiographer Strabo.[52] Medieval sailors used the name *Adriatic* for "the whole Eastern half of the Mediterranean" (with the exception of the Aegean Sea).[53] Luke, then, employs the geographical terminology of his day.

c. *Land.* The sailors begin to sense that the ship is approaching land. The text literally says that land is approaching them, for from the seafarer's point

---

48. Bauer, p. 546.
49. Robertson, *Grammar*, p. 758.
50. Smith, *Voyage and Shipwreck*, pp. 124–26.
51. George H. Allen and Donald H. Madvig, "Adria," *ISBE*, vol. 1, p. 58.
52. Strabo *Geography* 5.1.8.
53. Ramsay, *St. Paul the Traveller*, p. 334.

of view, the land and not the ship is in motion. The men hear the noise of the breakers on the rocky promontory called the Point of Koura, a barrier located along the northeast shore of Malta. Driven by northeasterly gales, breakers crashing on these rocks can be heard at a distance of a quarter of a mile. In the middle of the night, the sailors are unable to see anything, but they hear the noise and know that a rocky shore is near. The wind is no longer of hurricane force and, as they drift in a west-northwesterly direction, they hear the sound from the southeast. With terror in their hearts they imagine being shipwrecked on a rocky shore.

28. They took soundings and discovered the water was a hundred and twenty feet deep. A little farther, they took another sounding and found the water to be ninety feet deep.

The members of the crew throw the fathom lines overboard to determine the depth of the sea. At first they learn that the water is 120 feet deep. And when they go a little farther, the depth is only 90 feet. Because the original text has only the word *little,* many translators supply the word *while* and understand the term in a temporal sense (compare Luke 22:58).[54] Other scholars take the term to mean distance.[55]

29. Fearing that we might run aground on the rocks, they let down four anchors from the stern and wished for daylight. 30. The sailors were trying to escape from the ship and had lowered the lifeboat into the sea under the pretense of intending to let down anchors from the bow.

Within a quarter of a mile from shore, the sailors try to prevent the ship from crashing against the rocks. They cast four anchors from the stern of the vessel and thus prevent it from completely swinging around with its stem to the wind. These four anchors, two on each side of the ship,[56] hold the ship in place while the crew wishes for daybreak.

The temptation to find safety ashore proves too much for some or all of the crew. They decide to leave the ship under the pretense of letting down anchors from the bow. To do so they have to lower the lifeboat (see v. 16), which presumably has been kept in the prow of the ship. Now the passengers, among them Paul and Luke, see the intentions of the sailors. The passengers realize that they lack the nautical skills to maneuver the ship safely toward harbor and thus will face great difficulties. We surmise that the pilot and the captain of the ship are among the sailors. They have abdicated their responsibility and now try to forsake the soldiers, prisoners, and other passengers.

31. Paul said to the officer and soldiers, "Unless these men remain in the ship, you yourselves cannot be saved." 32. Then the soldiers cut the ropes of the lifeboat and let it fall away.

---

54. GNB, JB, NEB, NIV.

55. MLB, NAB, RSV, KJV, NKJV.

56. Haenchen writes that "ancient anchors weighed only 55 lbs." *Acts,* p. 705 n. 7. Smith observes "that ships of the ancients were fitted to anchor by the stern." *Voyage and Shipwreck,* p. 132.

According to the message Paul received from the angel, the lives of all the people aboard have been given to Paul. He is in charge and therefore immediately addresses the officer and his soldiers. He tells them that if the sailors are allowed to leave the ship, they themselves will not be saved. Although Paul had given them a message from God that promised not one life would be lost, in the face of treachery he now warns the military that they no longer have the guarantee of safety. This is the third time during the course of the voyage that Paul speaks. Julius and the soldiers know by now that Paul's word is true and ought not to be taken lightly. Hence they listen to Paul's word. As Julius and the soldiers take over, the sailors abandon their attempt to flee. Then the soldiers take the drastic measure of cutting the ropes and letting the dinghy fall into the sea. Both sailors and soldiers are prone to follies; the one group wishes to use the lifeboat for selfish purposes and the other group thoughtlessly abandons it. The loss of the lifeboat means that all the passengers are exactly the same: each one will have to go through the water to get to shore.

Greek Words, Phrases, and Constructions in 27:27–30

Verse 27

προσάγειν—"to approach." The awkwardness of the text is reflected in the rise of at least four variants, of which the infinitive προσηχεῖν (to resound) is interesting. The present infinitive *to approach,* which in context means "was approaching them," remains the preferred reading.

Verses 29–30

φοβούμενοι—see the comment on verse 17.

ηὔχοντο—the imperfect tense of this verb indicates continued action: "they kept on wishing."

ὡς—with the preceding participle χαλασάντων (letting down), which is the aorist active in the genitive absolute construction, the particle introduces alleged reason: "as pretext."

---

d. Encouragement
27:33–38

33. Until the day began to dawn, Paul continued to urge everyone to take some food. He said, "Today is the fourteenth day you have been on watch. You have been without food; you have taken nothing."

The eventful and eerie night is a time of waiting. While the storm has moderated and the ship lies at anchor, Paul takes the opportunity to exhort the crew and passengers to take some food before going on shore. He has given them the word of God's angel that no one would be lost and that they would land on some island. Paul is in control of the situation and now urges the people to eat so that they may have strength and confidence to face the unknown challenges of the day. He realizes that the men have been on watch for the duration of the voyage, that they have lacked proper appetite for two weeks because of uncertainty and anxiety, and that they have not eaten a decent meal. They are physically exhausted and weak. But if they take some food, they will gain strength and will be able to go on shore.

34. "Therefore, I urge you to take some food. This is for your own survival, for none of you will lose a single hair from his head."

Paul sets the example of being filled with hope, expectation, faith, and courage. He knows that everyone will be rescued and thus he looks forward to the developments of the day that lies before them. He says, "I urge you to take some food. This is for your own survival." They are facing not death but salvation. As he told them earlier (v. 22), no one aboard ship will be lost. He even goes a bit further, adding a Jewish saying: "None of you will lose a single hair from his head."[57] Paul repeats the exact words spoken by Jesus in the discourse on the last things (Luke 21:18). These words are now applied to the seafarers, who in the course of the morning will all reach the shore in safety (v. 44). They need words of encouragement, but they also need to eat; the food will give them strength to act on Paul's words of encouragement.

35. When he had said this, he took bread and gave thanks to God before them all. He broke it and began to eat. 36. All of them were encouraged and they themselves took some food. 37. Altogether on board we numbered 276 people.

The words of verse 35 resemble those of Jesus at the feeding of the five thousand (Matt. 14:19) and the institution of the Lord's Supper (Matt. 26:26). Paul follows the Jewish custom of uttering a prayer before a meal.[58] In the presence of the people, Paul worships God in an act of thanksgiving. This practice he observes aboard ship and, by implication, encourages the people to adopt. He shows that he belongs to God and serves him (v. 23).

Identification of Paul's act of worship and the celebration of Holy Communion is ruled out immediately on the basis of several points.

First, the text merely mentions prayer and the breaking and eating of bread; it does not say anything about drinking wine, the second element in the Lord's Supper.

Second, Paul would not celebrate communion in the presence of unbelievers. The Western text expands verse 35 after the clause [*he*] *began to eat* by adding the words [*and*] *gave also to us.* Perhaps the pronoun *us* refers to Luke and Aristarchus.[59] But the scene itself is inappropriate for celebrating the sacrament of the Lord's Supper, which is observed in a worship service and is restricted to professing Christians who have engaged in proper self-examination (I Cor. 11:28).

Third, Paul prays, breaks bread, and eats without any trace of secrecy.

---

57. See I Sam. 14:45; II Sam. 14:11; I Kings 1:52.

58. Jews would not eat until they had thanked God for their food (SB, vol. 1, pp. 685–87). Christians also thank God for the daily provision of food.

59. Metzger, *Textual Commentary*, p. 499.

Inviting the seafarers to follow his example is not to say that everyone present understood Paul's words and actions. His example to pray before eating demonstrated Paul's relationship with his God. All the seafarers witnessed Paul's devoutness and some may have been influenced by his example to give thanks to God.

Fourth, in his discussion on the celebration of the Lord's Supper Paul makes a clear distinction between bread eaten to satisfy hunger and bread that is taken at communion (see I Cor. 11:20–34). Aboard ship the purpose of eating is to strengthen man's physical body.[60]

When Paul breaks the bread and eats it, the others follow his example. Luke notes that they are encouraged and take some of the food. Thus we conclude that Paul has achieved his spiritual, psychological, and practical objectives. At this particular junction, Luke adds that the total number of persons aboard ship is 276.[61] We are unable to say why Luke supplies that information here. Perhaps the captain and the centurion wished to have a final roll call before leaving the ship.

38. When they were filled, they began to lighten the ship by throwing the grain into the sea.

The captain and his crew believe Paul's word that the ship will be wrecked even though everyone will be saved. Because they no longer have the use of the skiff, the ship itself has to serve as their lifeboat. And because of the storm, the ship may have taken on a great quantity of seawater. After the meal, the men go to work with renewed zeal and decide to lighten the vessel by dumping the cargo of wheat (see v. 18). Riding higher on the waves, the ship will perhaps be able to cross sandbars or reefs and reach land. All this happens while it is still night.

We suspect that the grain was transported loose in the hold of the ship. It had been carried aboard in sacks that were emptied in the hold; now the grain was put back in sacks to be dumped overboard. The task of scooping the grain into sacks and carrying them to the deck was laborious; the men undoubtedly formed a brigade to facilitate the work. The crew used the foremast for loading and unloading cargo and in a relatively short period was able to lighten the load of the ship.[62]

Doctrinal Considerations in 27:33–38

Paul, the prisoner, is the man who is fully in control of the situation. He informs the crew and passengers that everyone will be saved (although the ship will be

---

60. Theodor Zahn, *Die Apostelgeschichte des Lucas,* Kommentar zum Neuen Testament series, 2 vols. (Leipzig: Deichert, 1921), vol. 2, p. 837 n. 94.

61. Manuscripts show a few variations; e.g., Codex Vaticanus has the reading *about seventy-six.* This reading results from the duplication of one of the Greek letters that represented the number.

62. Refer to Haenchen, *Acts,* p. 707 n. 5; see also Rougé, *Ships and Fleets,* p. 74.

destroyed) and that they will land on an island (vv. 22–26). He commands the centurion and the soldiers to prevent the crew from leaving the ship (v. 31). And he tells the men to take courage, break their fast, and eat (vv. 33–34). In the eyes of the sailors and soldiers, Paul, who survives a snakebite (28:5) and heals the sick (28:8), must be divine.

Nowhere in the account is there any hint that Paul considers himself to be divine. On the contrary, he is a servant of his God (v. 23); he worships God (v. 35); and, even though the storm rages, he firmly believes every word God has revealed to him. In the midst of the hurricane, Paul is a rock of faith. His trust in God is unshakable. He believes God and his Word and he challenges everyone to emulate his example.

Greek Words, Phrases, and Constructions in 27:33–38

Verses 33–34

ἄχρι οὗ—the conjunction serves as a preposition and governs the genitive case of the relative pronoun. The relative has an antecedent in the supplied noun χρόνου (time): "until the time when."

προσδοκῶντες—"expecting." Translations vary for the clause in which this present participle appears. The clause is an idiom that signifies "today is the fourteenth day you have been on watch."[63]

ὑμετέρας—instead of the personal pronoun ὑμῶν, Paul uses the possessive adjective for emphasis: "your own."

Verse 38

ἐκούφιζον—the imperfect tense of the verb *to lighten* is inceptive: "they began to lighten."[64]

---

e. Shipwreck
27:39–44

39. When daylight came, they did not recognize the land. But they noticed a bay with a beach onto which they decided to run the ship, if possible. 40. After they cast off the anchors and left them in the sea, they loosened the ropes of the rudders, hoisted the foresail to the wind, and headed for the beach.

Malta was outside the shipping lanes of that day. If vessels passed the island at all, they would do so along the southern coast or would dock at the harbor of Valletta. When morning came and the seamen could distinguish the contours of the land, they were unable to identify the coastline. They could not recognize any of the features: the bay, the beach, and the shores.

---

63. Blass and Debrunner, *Greek Grammar,* #161.3. See also Robert Hanna, *A Grammatical Aid to the Greek New Testament* (Grand Rapids: Baker, 1983), p. 249.

64. Compare H. E. Dana and Julius R. Mantey, *A Manual Grammar of the Greek New Testament* (1927; New York: Macmillan, 1967), p. 190.

They noticed that the bay had a sandy flat beach which, in their opinion, would be a safe place to land the vessel. A sandy beach was much preferred to the rocky coast that would smash the ship to pieces.

From the vantage point aboard ship, the sailors could not determine if there were sandbars or reefs in the bay. They would have to determine how to avoid them when they entered the bay itself. In fact, they were unable to see that at the northeast entrance of the bay was the island Salmonetta. Only after entering the bay did they see a channel between Salmonetta and Malta. The water flowing through the channel "of not more than a hundred yards in breadth" met the water of the bay.[65] The Greek word *dithallason* (v. 41) actually means "lying between two seas." Luke clearly notes that the site of the shipwreck was at "a place where two seas met" (v. 41, NKJV). Incidentally, here is a clear indication that Luke was an eyewitness who accurately reported the exact spot where the shipwreck occurred.[66] He presents his personal observations of these topographical details. Modern translators, however, interpret the word *dithallason* in terms of the result, namely, the reef created by the two seas. Today, at the traditional site where the seafarers landed, the waves have washed away the sandbar.

The crew chose a wise course of action by cutting the ropes that anchored the ship. They wanted to keep the prow facing the entrance of the bay; they could ill afford to see the vessel swing toward the rocky shore if they lifted one anchor before the other one. Thus, they cut the ropes and left the anchors at the bottom of the sea. Simultaneously they loosened the rudders that ropes had held in place during the storm. On each side of the ship was a rudder in the form of a steering oar that was let down into the water through a hawsehole. These oars were lifted out of the water when the ship was at anchor to "keep them from banging about."[67] At the same time the men hoisted the sail on the foremast and steered the ship toward the beach. All this work had to be done with utmost precision.

41. They struck a reef and ran the ship aground. The bow stuck fast and remained immovable, but the stern began to break up by the pounding of the waves.

Once inside the bay the ship struck a reef and ran aground. Conceivably the crew either lacked the time to maneuver the vessel around the reef or thought that the tide would carry the ship over it. In what is today called Saint Paul's Bay, sand and clay particles are moved by the currents and form deposits of mud. At the point where the two currents met ("at the place where the two seas met"; see the comment on v. 40), a reef had formed and the front of the ship became immovably stuck in the clay. But

---

65. Smith, *Voyage and Shipwreck*, p. 140.

66. Conzelmann asserts that Luke took his material from a travel journal "from a companion of Paul." *Acts*, p. 221. In *Acts*, p. 710, Haenchen agrees. Martin Dibelius notes "that a secular description of the voyage and shipwreck served as a pattern, basis or source." *Studies in the Acts of the Apostles* (London: SCM, 1956), p. 205.

67. Casson, *Ships and Seamanship*, p. 228.

the stern, exposed to the pounding of the waves, could no longer withstand the battering and began to break up. The men rushed to the front of the ship to find safety and keep dry. Yet each one knew that he had to abandon the wreck and swim to shore.

42. The soldiers planned to kill the prisoners so that no one might escape by swimming away. 43. But the officer wanted to spare Paul and prevented the soldiers from carrying out their plan. He commanded that those who were able to swim should jump overboard first and get to land.

In ancient times, soldiers were told that when they were assigned to guard condemned prisoners, they had to forfeit their own lives should a prisoner escape (see, e.g., 12:19). Roman law stipulated that if a prisoner escaped, his guard had to suffer the punishment of that prisoner.[68] So in the confusion of the shipwreck, the soldiers think in terms of their personal safety when they eventually will have to report in Rome. Calvin says "the soldiers' ingratitude was far too cruel" as they contemplate killing Paul.[69] He had given them the good news that their lives would be spared; he had encouraged them when all had lost hope of being saved; and he had given them sound advice and an exhortation to eat. These soldiers demonstrated ruthlessness by planning to kill the prisoners.

God rules and overrules. He moves Julius, the centurion, to stop the soldiers from executing the prisoners. Luke relates that Julius wanted to spare Paul. Throughout this chapter and the next (chap. 28), Luke indicates that the officer was kindly disposed to Paul. Julius had allowed Paul to leave ship in Sidon to visit friends (v. 3) and permitted him to stay a week with Christians in Puteoli before going on to Rome (28:14). Luke does not indicate that Julius became a believer, yet we may suppose that the centurion wished to express his thanks to Paul for giving leadership in the midst of the storm. Julius had seen the literal fulfillment of the divine prophecy that everyone aboard would find safety on an island even though the ship would be destroyed. He knew that God had granted Paul the lives of all the men on the ship (v. 24). Sparing Paul's life meant sparing the lives of the other prisoners.

Thus, Julius told his soldiers not to kill anyone. Instead he instructed those prisoners who could swim to jump into the sea and head for shore. He knew that no one would be able to escape from an island. We assume that the distance to shore was relatively short and that the storm had abated.

44. And the rest were to reach land on planks or on various parts of the ship. Thus everyone arrived safely on land.

Everyone aboard ship who could not swim tried to find items that remained afloat. Clinging to these pieces of wreckage, they kept their heads above water and let the wind drive them to the shore. Luke mentions the

---

68. Recorded in Justinian's Code (9.4.4). See Bruce, *Acts* (Greek text), p. 388; Hemer, *Book of Acts,* p. 152.

69. Calvin, *Acts of the Apostles,* vol. 2, p. 296.

word *planks*. These planks probably came out of the hold of the ship, where they were placed on top of the loose grain to keep it in place.[70] When the ship began to disintegrate, the planks became available to the shipwrecked people, who used them as rafts to reach safe ground.

After his brief description of leaving the ship, Luke merely states that everyone landed safely on shore. Thus, the word of the angel (vv. 22–26) was literally fulfilled. An interesting question to which we have no answer is, how did Luke keep his writing material dry?

Greek Words, Phrases, and Constructions in 27:39–44

Verse 39

κατενόουν—the use of the imperfect refers not to the object perceived but to the persons who observe: "one after the other noticed."

ἐξῶσαι—the aorist infinitive from the verb ἐξωθέω (I propel, drive) is a nautical term meaning "to drive a ship to shore."

Verse 40

εἴων—from the verb ἐάω (I allow, permit, let), this imperfect denotes voluntary action: "they let them [be]."

ἅμα—the adverb indicates simultaneous action: "at the same time."

τῇ πνεούσῃ—the noun αὔρᾳ (morning air) should be supplied: "the blowing morning wind."

κατεῖχον—this is a nautical term with τὴν ναῦν (the ship). The verb signifies "to head the ship." The imperfect is inceptive.

Verses 43–44

ἐκώλυσεν—"he prevented." The aorist connotes single action with immediate effect. The verb is followed by the genitive construction τοῦ βουλήματος (the plan) because verbs of preventing and hindering govern the genitive case.

τινων—this indefinite pronoun in the neuter is understood to refer to the pieces of debris floating near the ship. If it is taken as a masculine, it means that swimmers placed nonswimmers on their backs. The preposition ἐπί governs the dative case of "planks" and the genitive case of "some."[71]

Summary of Chapter 27

Paul and other prisoners are placed aboard a ship that is about to sail for ports along the coast of the province of Asia. A centurion named Julius is in charge of the prisoners but allows Paul to visit friends in Sidon. From there the ship passes the east coast of Cyprus and continues its voyage to the harbor of Myra in Lycia. Here the centurion finds passage for his troops

---

70. Rougé, *Ships and Fleets*, p. 71.
71. Consult Bruce, *Acts* (Greek text), p. 695.

and prisoners on a ship that sails for Italy. The ship proceeds slowly to Cnidus and then, taking advantage of the wind, sails to the south side of Crete and docks in the harbor called Fair Havens. Because the season for safe sailing is past, Paul advises the centurion, the pilot, and the captain of the ship to stay there. His advice is ignored and the crew decides to sail west to the port of Phoenix.

A hurricane, called the "northeaster," sweeps across Crete, falls upon the ship, and drives it in a southwesterly direction toward the island of Cauda. Here the crew secures the lifeboat by hoisting it aboard the ship, girds the ship with ropes, and eventually throws cargo and tackle overboard. When the storm rages for many days, the people aboard ship give up all hope of being rescued.

Paul admonishes the men to be of good courage. He reports that an angel of the God to whom he belongs and whom he serves has informed him that Paul will stand trial before Caesar in Rome. He predicts that the ship will be destroyed but that they will come ashore on an island.

The sailors realize that the ship is approaching land and cast the anchors overboard. Under the pretense of letting down anchors from the bow, they lower the lifeboat and attempt to escape. Paul alerts the centurion; the soldiers cut the ropes and so prevent the escape. Paul exhorts the people to eat, gives thanks to God for the bread he breaks, and sets the example of eating. The crew lightens the ship by throwing the grain into the sea.

At daybreak, the men fail to recognize the land. They see a bay, cut the ropes that hold the anchors, hoist the foresail, and steer the vessel into the bay. The ship strikes a reef, is stuck in the sand, and begins to disintegrate as the waves batter it. The centurion prevents the soldiers from killing the prisoners, allows those who are able to swim to jump into the water and go ashore, and tells the rest to head for the beach on planks and other parts of the ship. Everyone comes safely to the shore.

28

Voyage to and Stay in Rome, *part 2*

28:1–31

Outline (continued)

28:1–31	B.	Malta to Rome
28:1–10		1. At Malta
28:1–6		a. Kindness Expressed
28:7–10		b. Kindness Returned
28:11–16		2. To Rome
28:17–31		3. Roman Imprisonment
28:17–20		a. Paul's Statement
28:21–22		b. Reply from the Jews
28:23–28		c. Paul's Explanation
28:30–31		d. Conclusion

28

1 When we were safe, we found out that the island was called Malta. 2 The islanders showed us unusual kindness by welcoming all of us. They lit a fire because it was cold and had begun to rain. 3 When Paul had gathered a bundle of sticks and put it on the fire, a viper came out because of the heat and fastened itself on his hand. 4 When the islanders saw the snake hanging from his hand, they said to each other, "Obviously, this man is a murderer. Although he has been saved from the sea, Justice has not allowed him to live." 5 However, Paul shook the snake from his hand into the fire and suffered no harm. 6 But they expected him to swell up or suddenly fall dead. After waiting a long time and seeing nothing unusual happen to him, they changed their minds and began to say that Paul was a god.

7 Nearby that place were fields belonging to Publius, the chief of the island. He welcomed us and kindly hosted us for three days. 8 The father of Publius was ill with fever and dysentery and he was lying down. Paul went to see him and, after praying and laying his hands on the man, healed him. 9 When this had occurred, the rest of the people on the island who had diseases came to Paul and were cured. 10 And they honored us with many items of respect; when we were ready to set sail, they supplied us with everything we needed.

11 After three months, we set sail in an Alexandrian ship that had wintered at the island and was marked by the insignia of the Twin Brothers. 12 We put in at Syracuse and stayed there for three days. 13 From there we set sail and arrived at Rhegium. The next day a south wind came up, and on the following day we reached Puteoli. 14 There we found some brothers who invited us to stay with them for seven days. And so we started for Rome. 15 The brothers in Rome had heard news about us and came as far as the Forum of Appius and the Three Taverns to meet us. Paul saw them, thanked God, and was encouraged. 16 When we arrived at Rome, Paul was allowed to live alone with a soldier guarding him.

17 After three days, Paul summoned the leaders of the Jews. When they had assembled, he said to them: "Men and brothers, I had done nothing against our people or the customs of our fathers, yet I was delivered as a prisoner out of Jerusalem into the hands of the Romans. 18 They examined me and wanted to release me because they found no reason to put me to death. 19 When the Jews objected, I was forced to appeal to Caesar, not that I had any accusation against my people. 20 For this reason I invited you, to see you and speak with you, for I am bearing this chain because of the hope of Israel." 21 The Jews said to Paul: "We have not received any letters from Judea concerning you. None of the brothers who have come here have reported or said anything bad about you. 22 We desire to hear from you the views that you hold. We know that everywhere people are objecting to this sect."

23 They set a day for Paul and came to him at his lodging in large numbers. He explained and testified to them about the kingdom of God. And from morning to evening, he tried to persuade them from the Law of Moses and the Prophets concerning Jesus. 24 Some were convinced by what he said, while others would not believe. 25 The Jews did not agree with one another and began to leave after Paul had spoken one last word: "The Holy Spirit rightly spoke through Isaiah the prophet to your fathers, 26 saying,

'Go to this people and say:
"You will keep on hearing but never understand;
You will keep on seeing but never perceive."

945

27 For the heart of this people has become dull,
they hardly hear with their ears,
and they have closed their eyes.
Otherwise they might see with their eyes
and hear with their ears
and understand with their heart
and turn again, and I would heal them.'

28 "Therefore, let it be known to you that this salvation of God has been sent to the Gentiles; they will listen!"

30 Paul stayed for two full years in his own rented house and welcomed all who came to him. 31 Boldly and unhindered he was preaching the kingdom of God and teaching the things concerning the Lord Jesus Christ.

B. Malta to Rome
28:1–31

In about one-third of this chapter, Luke describes two incidents in which Paul takes a leading role. He relates Paul's encounter with a snake (vv. 3–6) and Paul's healing ministry to those who were sick (vv. 7–9). Of the rest of Paul's three-month stay on the island of Malta Luke provides no further information.

1. At Malta
28:1–10

The inhabitants of Malta were descended from Phoenicians who had settled there in preceding centuries. Like the Phoenician settlers on the neighboring islands Gozo and Comino, they had prospered from trade. According to the historiographer Diodorus, the Phoenicians sailed their mercantile ships as far as the western ocean (the Atlantic) and used Malta's excellent harbors as a place of refuge.[1] The island is between Sicily and the African coast, some 60 miles from the former and 180 from the latter. It measures 18 miles in length from northwest to southeast and has a breadth of 8 miles.[2]

In fact, the word *Melita* (Malta) in Semitic languages, spoken in a Phoenician dialect by the islanders, may have been a translation for the expression *a place of refuge*. From the sixth to the third centuries, the people of Carthage ruled this island. In 218 B.C. the Romans took control of it and made it part of the province of Sicily. They left the local administration intact, but during the reign of Augustus a procurator ruled Malta. In the settled parts of the island, the population spoke Latin in addition to their Phoenician

---

1. Diodorus Siculus 5.12.

2. Attempts to link the word *Melita* with an island called Mljet in the Adriatic Sea prove to be unconvincing. See the discussions by Angus Acworth, "Where Was St. Paul Shipwrecked? A Reexamination of the Evidence," *JTS* n.s. 24 (1973): 190–93; and Colin J. Hemer, *The Book of Acts in the Setting of Hellenistic History*, ed. Conrad H. Gempf (Tübingen: Mohr, 1989), p. 141 n. 115.

dialect. (People who spoke an unfamiliar language were generally called barbarians. This term, however, was not used pejoratively.)

a. Kindness Expressed
28:1–6

1. When we were safe, we found out that the island was called Malta. 2. The islanders showed us unusual kindness by welcoming all of us. They lit a fire because it was cold and had begun to rain.

The fact that Luke and the rest of the men landed unscathed at Malta must have made a deep impression on the author. He expressly writes about the physical safety of the people and uses the first person pronoun *we*, perhaps to suggest only his Christian companions, Paul and Aristarchus.[3] Luke implies that when Paul and his friends came ashore, they asked the native people the name of the island. The answer they received was *Melita* (refuge), which sounded pleasing in the ears of the seafarers from the wrecked Alexandrian freighter.[4] It is probable that the Semitic languages Hebrew and Aramaic and the Phoenician dialect were similar enough that Paul was able to converse with the islanders.

In ancient times, survivors of a shipwreck who managed to land on unknown shores expected to face either death or slavery. This was not so on Malta, because since 218 B.C. the island had belonged to Rome. When the islanders saw a centurion and soldiers coming to the island, they had the wisdom to show hospitality and kindness to representatives of Rome. Luke reports that "the islanders showed us unusual kindness by welcoming all of us." This statement becomes meaningful if we remember that the native population had to meet the physical needs of 276 guests (27:37) for three months (v. 11). Incidentally, the translated word *islanders* is a dynamic equivalent for the Greek term *barbaroi*. The Greek differs from the English derivative *barbarians*, which has a decidedly negative connotation. The Greeks referred to all foreigners as *barbaroi*. Luke's use of this term for the inhabitants of Malta must be understood in that light and is free from any derogatory slant.

As the wind blew from the northeast and the rain came down, the people clothed in drenched garments stood shivering on the beach that particular morning in late October. Seeing the wretched condition of these people, the islanders took pity on them and lit a huge bonfire so that everyone could dry his clothes and warm himself.

3. When Paul had gathered a bundle of sticks and put it on the fire, a viper came out because of the heat and fastened itself on his hand.

---

3. In succeeding verses, the pronouns *we* and *us* seem to refer to believers (vv. 7, 10). The KJV and NKJV, on the basis of the Majority Text, have the translation *they* in v. 1.

4. Consult Theodor Zahn, *Die Apostelgeschichte des Lucas*, Kommentar zum Neuen Testament series, 2 vols. (Leipzig: Deichert, 1921), vol. 2, pp. 841, 844. See also A. M. Honeyman, "Two Semitic Inscriptions from Malta," *PEQ* 93 (1961): 151–53.

A wood fire has to be supplied continually with more fuel. Paul sets an example, gives leadership, and shows his willingness to help the islanders by finding and collecting tree branches which he throws onto the fire. The people immediately notice that Paul is bitten by a snake hidden among the sticks. The snake, warmed by the heat of the fire, defends itself by biting the hand that is casting it into the flames.

Although at present Malta has no venomous snakes, in Paul's day poisonous serpents undoubtedly lived in wooded parts of the island. The question remains whether the snake that fastened itself on Paul's hand was venomous. Some scholars think that the reptile was a common grass snake that, although it may strike a man, does not harm him. The reaction of the natives is different, for they expect Paul to die.

4. When the islanders saw the snake hanging from his hand, they said to each other, "Obviously, this man is a murderer. Although he has been saved from the sea, Justice has not allowed him to live."

a. "The islanders saw the snake hanging from his hand, [and] said to each other." In this verse, Luke records the comments of the islanders. We expect that, if Paul indeed was able to communicate with them, the native population paid close attention to him. Because Paul was guarded by soldiers, they knew that he was a prisoner on his way to Rome. There is no evidence that Paul was chained during his voyage and stay at Malta. For this reason, the islanders would have to receive their knowledge of Paul's status from other indications.[5]

b. "Obviously, this man is a murderer." The Maltese make a hasty evaluation of Paul's predicament. In their eyes, this engaging Jew must be a criminal guilty of manslaughter. They speak reproachfully about Paul when they call him "this man."

c. "Although he has been saved from the sea, Justice has not allowed him to live."[6] The natives conclude that their goddess Justice is meting out divine punishment on an evildoer. This criminal may have escaped death at sea but is unable to avoid the poison of a reptile. (Perhaps the islanders are acquainted with a story concerning a shipwrecked sailor who, after landing safely on a Libyan beach, was fatally bitten by a snake.)[7] In their opinion, Paul will soon die now that he has received his sentence from the goddess Justice.

5. However, Paul shook the snake from his hand into the fire and suffered no harm. 6. But they expected him to swell up or suddenly fall dead. After waiting a long time and seeing nothing unusual happen to him, they changed their minds and began to say that Paul was a god.

---

5. John Albert Bengel asserts that the islanders "saw his chains." *Gnomon of the New Testament*, ed. Andrew R. Fausset, 5 vols. (Edinburgh: Clark, 1877), vol. 2, p. 728.

6. Hans Conzelmann doubts the historical accuracy of the account; he writes that "the author puts these words into the mouth of the natives." *Acts of the Apostles*, trans. James Limburg, A. Thomas Kraabel, and Donald H. Juel (1963; Philadelphia: Fortress, 1987), p. 223.

7. Statyllius Flaccus *Palatine Anthology* 7.290.

Paul is a man who fully trusts his God to protect him from all danger. He knows the word of Jesus: he has authority to trample on snakes and nothing will harm him (Luke 10:19; see Mark 16:18). He believes that he will stand trial before Caesar in Rome. A snakebite will not deter him.

To the sailors and passengers of the shipwrecked Alexandrian freighter, Paul had proved to be a man of God when he predicted that everyone would safely land on an island but the ship would be destroyed. Now, in the presence of the native population of Malta, Paul shows that he is a man of God by shaking the viper from his hand into the fire and suffering no harm. Both at sea and on the land Paul performs extraordinary feats to indicate that he is a servant of God.[8] The snakebite is not a freak accident but a divinely directed incident in which God displays his power and might.

When a venomous snake strikes, its poison enters the bloodstream, breaks down the capillaries, and causes massive internal hemorrhage. The affected area begins to swell and, if the poison is sufficiently powerful, the victim will die almost instantaneously. Therefore, the people standing around the fire closely observe Paul and quietly wait to see what the effect of the snakebite will be. But nothing happens to Paul, who continues to warm himself at the fire and dry his clothes. After waiting a long time and seeing nothing unusual in Paul's physical condition, the people around the fire begin to change their minds. The islanders no longer see Paul as a criminal or even an ordinary person, but as a god. In this respect they differ little from the Gentiles in Lystra who, after Paul had healed a crippled man, considered Paul and Barnabas to be Greek gods (14:12). The difference between the episode in Lystra and that on Malta is the absence of adoration and worship. Should the Maltese have demonstrated any misplaced reverence to Paul, he certainly would have rebuked them and told them to worship God alone.

Doctrinal Considerations in 28:1–6

The sailors and soldiers aboard ship fail to express themselves in religious terms as did the seafarers in Jonah's day. By contrast, the inhabitants of Malta reveal their religious devotion when they refer to their goddess Justice, mention divine retribution, and consider Paul to be a god. Everett F. Harrison queries why it did not seem odd to the islanders to see a god in human custody.[9]

The writers of the New Testament generally link faith to the performance and effect of miracles. That is, a miracle occurs when a person in faith performs it and when the witnesses respond to it in faith. On the island of Malta Paul demonstrates his faith in God's protective power, but Luke fails to report whether those who

---

8. Consult John Calvin, *Commentary on the Acts of the Apostles*, ed. David W. Torrance and Thomas F. Torrance, 2 vols. (Grand Rapids: Eerdmans, 1966), vol. 2, p. 298.

9. Everett F. Harrison, *Interpreting Acts: The Expanding Church*, 2d ed. (Grand Rapids: Zondervan, Academie Books, 1986), p. 424.

witnessed the event came to faith in Christ. We conjecture that Paul used every opportunity given to him to teach the people the gospel of Jesus Christ. Nevertheless, we have no evidence that he founded a church at Malta.

Greek Words, Phrases, and Constructions in 28:1–6

Verses 1–2

διασωθέντες—the miraculous delivery from the tempestuous sea must have made an impact on Luke. He repeatedly uses the compound verb διασῴζω (I rescue) to note that Paul and his fellow prisoners were spared (27:43), all arrived safely (27:44), Luke and his friends were safe (28:1), and Paul was saved from the sea (28:4).

Μελίτη—some manuscripts have the reading Μελιτήνη, which may be the result of duplicating two letters in context.[10]

οὐ τὴν τυχοῦσαν—this is a common vernacular phrase (19:11) that means "not the common," hence, the unusual. The participle is in the aorist (from τυγχάνω, I happen to be).

ἐφεστῶτα—the perfect active participle of ἐφίστημι (I am on hand) indicates that it threatened to and eventually began to rain.

Verses 4–5

τὸ θηρίον—the diminutive form of θήρ (beast) is used to refer to snakes of ancient and modern times in Greece.[11]

μὲν οὖν—"however, nay rather." This combination here expresses an adversative meaning.[12]

Verse 6

προσεδόκων—the imperfect tense of προσδοκάω (I expect, wait for) implies repeated action and lapse of time. This is reinforced by the phrase ἐπὶ πολύ (after a long time) and the present participle of the verb.

πίμπρασθαι—a medical term in the passive infinitive that means either "burn up with fever" or "swell up." In the New Testament it occurs only here, but see Numbers 5:21, 27 (LXX).

---

b. Kindness Returned
28:7–10

Luke records two incidents that illustrate kindness at Malta. One is the welcome the islanders gave to the drenched crew and passengers. The Maltese extended kindness to Paul, his friends, and others. The second incident

---

10. Bruce M. Metzger, *A Textual Commentary on the Greek New Testament,* 3d corrected ed. (London and New York: United Bible Societies, 1975), p. 500.

11. Bauer, p. 361; Lake and Cadbury, *Beginnings,* vol. 4, p. 342.

12. C. F. D. Moule, *An Idiom-Book of New Testament Greek,* 2d ed. (Cambridge: Cambridge University Press, 1960), p. 163.

concerns the healing ministry Paul extended to the sick on the island. In a sense, Paul returned the kindness by restoring the sick to health.

7. Nearby that place were fields belonging to Publius, the chief of the island. He welcomed us and kindly hosted us for three days. 8. The father of Publius was ill with fever and dysentery and he was lying down. Paul went to see him and, after praying and laying his hands on the man, healed him.

Note these points:

a. *The man.* We do not know how much time elapsed between the welcome on the beach (vv. 1–6) and the invitation to the chief's home (v. 7). Luke gives the impression that immediately after his arrival, Paul was introduced to the leading person on the island. Apparently, Paul and his friends were taken directly to the chief's house.

The name *Publius* is a first name and not a family name, for a Roman citizen normally had three names. It is possible (but cannot be proven) that Publius and Luke developed a relationship so close that they called each other by their first names.[13] Most likely, people in the culture of that day were known by their first names. This is the case in many parts of the world today.

Publius is called the first (man) of the island. The term *first* means that he is the highest authority on the island. The expression need not be interpreted to be a title of a Roman government official but instead can refer to a benefactor of various philanthropic causes.[14] Publius seemed to have filled the role of a benefactor by welcoming Paul and his companions to his home and by hosting them for three days.

Publius was a man of means who owned fields that surrounded the beach where the men had landed. He must have possessed dwellings and other buildings where the stranded crew and passengers could find shelter. Even though he belonged to the well-to-do class of society, Publius was not expected to provide accommodation and meals for 276 guests. Luke indicates that Publius's hospitality to Paul and his friends lasted three days. After that time, the rest of the islanders had made arrangements for sheltering them.

b. *The father.* The kindness of the islanders in general and of Publius in particular finds an echo in Paul and his companions. We assume that Luke in his profession as physician found plenty to do on the island. And Paul employs his gift of healing when he hears that Publius's father is sick with fever and dysentery. In Greek, Luke uses the plural form of "fever" to point out that the patient suffered repeated feverish attacks. (The ailment, now known as Malta fever, is caused by the milk of Maltese goats. Medical authorities have been able to prescribe proper treatment and preventive measures.)

---

13. See Zahn, *Apostelgeschichte des Lucas,* vol. 2, p. 846 n. 5.

14. Colin J. Hemer, "First Person Narrative in Acts 27–28," *TynB* 36 (1985): 79–109, esp. p. 100. See also his *Book of Acts,* p. 153 n. 152.

Paul heals the father of Publius by praying for him and laying his hands on him. In other words, not Paul but Jesus, whose name Paul invoked, heals the ailing father (compare Luke 4:38). Paul follows the practice of praying for restoration (see 9:40). Once again, a miracle takes place on the strength of Paul's faith in Christ. Luke does not elaborate about the man's response to this miracle. He only relates that Publius's father receives healing.

9. When this had occurred, the rest of the people on the island who had diseases came to Paul and were cured.

The news concerning the healing of Publius's father went from mouth to mouth with the result that many sick people came to the house where Paul was staying. We are unable to estimate how many patients came to Paul, but we see a direct parallel to the account of Jesus healing Peter's mother-in-law in Capernaum (Mark 1:30–31). After Jesus had healed her, in the evening of that day all the sick and demon-possessed people of Capernaum came to him for help and healing (Mark 1:32–34). As Jesus had a healing and teaching ministry, so Paul in his ministry healed the sick and preached the Word of God. We know that these miracles were effective means in leading people to a knowledge of God. And we know that the act of preaching the gospel is not futile but achieves God's purposes (Isa. 55:11).

10. And they honored us with many items of respect; when we were ready to set sail, they supplied us with everything we needed.

The people who had been healed wished to express their appreciation to Paul and his companions. Thus the islanders paid them respect (compare I Tim. 5:17), not by paying fees for Paul's healing ministry, but rather by bringing gifts.

When Paul and his friends arrived in Malta, they had nothing more than their sea-drenched clothes on their backs. We expect that the Maltese brought them numerous gifts of clothing and provisions, so that they could continue their travels in comfort. In brief, when the time came for Paul, Luke, and Aristarchus to depart, the Maltese had supplied them with everything they needed for the remainder of the journey. Thus, the islanders expressed their appreciation for all that Paul and his friends had done and said while they were guests on Malta.

Greek Words, Phrases, and Constructions in 28:7–10

Verse 7

τοῖς—the noun μέρεσιν (parts) should be supplied. The sentence itself is wordy: "now in the parts around that place," which really means, "now in the neighbourhood of that place."[15]

ἡμέρας—this is the accusative of time or duration: "for three days."

---

15. Moule, *Idiom-Book*, p. 62.

Verse 8

συνεχόμενον—the present passive participle literally means "being held by" or "being tormented by." The grammatical construction makes the malady the subject and the sufferer the object. Our idiom is the reverse; it makes the patient the subject and the affliction the object. That is, we have a fever, a cold, or a headache.

Verse 10

τιμαῖς ἐτίμησαν—"they honored us with honors." The verb and noun are from the same root. The combination, although not common, appears elsewhere.[16]

A few manuscripts add the phrase *as long as we were guests* after the first clause in the verse. The phrase, however, is an addition that is redundant.

---

2. To Rome
28:11–16

Near the end of Paul's stay in Ephesus, he expressed his desire to visit Rome (19:21; see Rom. 1:11, 15). He did not realize that he would have to endure imprisonment and shipwreck before he arrived there. But when he had spent three months on the island of Malta, he knew that the day had come for him to complete the last part of his journey to Rome.

11. After three months, we set sail in an Alexandrian ship that had wintered at the island and was marked by the insignia of the Twin Brothers.

The shipwrecked crew and passengers spent the months of November, December, and January on Malta. When the south wind began to blow in the first week of February,[17] ships that had taken refuge in the harbors of Malta dared to make the sixty-mile voyage from Malta to the port of Syracuse in Sicily. That voyage would be relatively safe and of short duration, because the passage could be made in a single day. With a favorable south wind, a vessel could maintain a speed of about four to six nautical miles per hour.

Julius had made inquiries in a harbor that had given shelter from the winter storms to an Alexandrian ship. With the advent of good weather in the first week of February, the captain of the ship wished to deliver his grain cargo as soon as possible. He would take his passengers to Putcoli and the grain to Portus, which was a new harbor of Ostia at the mouth of the Tiber River.[18] He was willing to take Julius, the soldiers, and the prisoners aboard and sail as soon as an advantageous wind blew from the south.

In passing, Luke mentions that the ship bore the insignia of the Twin Brothers. The Greek word *dioskouroi* (sons of Zeus) refers to Castor and Pollux, who were the twin sons of Leda and the Greek god Zeus. Sailors regarded these two brothers as patron deities who would protect them

---

16. Compare Josephus *Antiquities* 20.3.3 [68].
17. Consult Pliny the Elder *Natural History* 2.122. February 7 or 8 was the earliest date for coastal sailing.
18. Hemer, *Book of Acts*, p. 154.

from the dangers of the sea. Why Luke mentions these names cannot be determined. Although Paul and his friends objected to idol worship, we must assume that other ships on which Paul had been a passenger had similar insignia.

12. We put in at Syracuse and stayed there for three days. 13. From there we set sail and arrived at Rhegium. The next day a south wind came up, and on the following day we reached Puteoli.

The fact that the ship stayed in the port of Syracuse for three days probably points to adverse weather conditions. In the month of February, the weather remains unstable, so ships would make coastal runs from one safe harbor to the next, preferably in one-day spans. Accordingly, the distance from Syracuse to Rhegium had to be covered in one day with the help of a south wind. Some of the time in the harbor of Syracuse would have been spent loading and unloading cargo.

The town of Rhegium (modern Reggio) is located at the Straits of Messina and faces the island of Sicily. To make the passage through these straits (known for the whirlpool of Charybdis and the rock of Scylla) to the harbor of Puteoli, sailors would need a favorable wind to carry them there in twenty-four hours. Puteoli (Pozzuoli), a harbor in the Bay of Naples, is about 120 miles southeast of Rome.

14. There we found some brothers who invited us to stay with them for seven days. And so we started for Rome.

In Paul's day, Puteoli was a busy harbor that thrived on the commerce Rome conducted with the rest of the inhabited world, especially the ports in the eastern Mediterranean. Before Ostia's new harbor, Portus, was constructed during the reign of Emperor Claudius, Puteoli was the only harbor for Rome. Travelers coming from the east would go through this port to proceed to the Eternal City. After Julius, his soldiers, and his prisoners disembarked, the centurion planned to travel to Rome on foot. This distance could be covered in about five days.

The journey to Rome, however, was delayed for an entire week. If Luke had expanded his account, we would know why Julius stayed in the port city of Puteoli for seven days. Luke does reveal that Paul was welcomed by brothers, that is, Christians. We know that in the commercial city of Puteoli the Jews had formed their own community.[19] We conjecture that the "visitors from Rome" (2:10) were Jews who heard the gospel from Peter and returned to Rome via Puteoli. In this port city, the Christian community may have formed simultaneously with that in Rome. When in A.D. 49 Claudius expelled Jews (including Christians) from the imperial city, many of them stayed in Puteoli or passed through it on their way to other cities.

Upon disembarking, Paul and his companions contacted the Christians who resided in Puteoli. The Christians invited Paul, with permission from

---

19. Josephus *War* 2.7.1 [104]; *Antiquities* 17.12.1 [328]. The Greeks called the harbor city Dicaearchia. See Josephus *Life* 16; Strabo *Geography* 5.4; 17.1.

Julius (compare 27:3) and presumably under guard, to stay with them for seven days. What joy for these believers to have Paul in their midst for preaching and teaching, especially on the Lord's Day (see 20:6–7)! The believers also sent word to the Christians in Rome that Paul would undertake the last lap of his journey within a week (see v. 15).

"And so we started for Rome." Translators usually render this short sentence "and so we came to Rome." The verb *came* in the clause *we came to Rome* signifies "we started for Rome."[20] (A parallel is found in John 20:3, where we read that Peter and John set out for the tomb. The text has the verb *to come*, but the meaning in context is that the two disciples "started for the tomb" [NIV].)

The emphasis in the sentence is on the first two words *and so*. Paul and his companions were refreshed by the local Christians and knew that fellow believers in Rome had been told of their imminent arrival. In turn, the Christians there would welcome Paul and provide for him.

15. The brothers in Rome had heard news about us and came as far as the Forum of Appius and the Three Taverns to meet us. Paul saw them, thanked God, and was encouraged.

The messenger from Puteoli had alerted the Christians in Rome that Paul was on the way to the imperial city. Thus, two groups of believers set out to meet him halfway.[21] One party traveled as far as the Forum of Appius, which is about forty miles southeast of Rome; the other came to a place called Three Taverns, some thirty miles southeast of the city.

The Forum of Appius was a marketplace where people rested from their travels along the Appian Way. The road was named after the censor Appius Claudius, who began its construction in 312 B.C. The Roman poet Horace described the Forum of Appius as "crammed with boatmen and stingy tavern-keepers."[22] These boatmen were not sailors but men employed on boats that transported passengers along a canal through the Pontine marshes. The Forum of Appius was not known for law and order. The second place was called Three Taverns; the term *tavern* denotes not only an inn but also a shop or a store. From his writings we know that Cicero at times lodged at this resting place.[23]

When Paul met the brothers from Rome, he began to thank God and took courage as he continued his journey to Rome. He realized that God was true to his word by sending him to the capital of the Roman empire. At the end of his journey, he was surrounded and supported by Christian brothers who welcomed him to the imperial city. Paul had continued to

---

20. Compare the following translations: "Then on to Rome we went" (MLB), "And so to Rome" (NEB), "And so we went toward Rome" (NKJV).

21. Josephus writes that the entire Jewish community in Rome went out to meet an impostor who claimed to be Alexander, son of Herod the Great. *Antiquities* 17.12.1 [324–31].

22. Horace *Satires* 1.5.4 (LCL).

23. Cicero *Letters to Atticus* 1.13.1.; 2.10; 2.12.2; 2.13.1.

pray for the Christians in Rome ever since he wrote to them about three years earlier (Rom. 1:9–10). And he had asked the believers there to pray for his safety in Jerusalem and his travel to Rome (Rom. 15:31–32). We have no idea how many believers met Paul on the Appian Way, but we imagine that the joyful meeting at both the Forum of Appius and the Three Taverns must have made an impression on Julius.

16. When we arrived at Rome, Paul was allowed to live alone with a soldier guarding him.

For almost two days, the Christians accompanied Paul to Rome. When they arrived there, their way parted because Paul had to be taken into custody. Julius must have interceded for Paul with the authorities when he delivered the prisoners.[24]

The evidence from Festus's report, which Julius presented to the Roman authorities, stresses three points: that Paul was innocent of any wrong-doing, that he had appealed to Caesar, and that the reason for his impris-onment concerned a religious dispute with the Jews. In addition, Julius himself perhaps commented on Paul's conduct during the voyage from Caesarea to Rome. In his concise manner, Luke writes that "Paul was allowed to live alone with a soldier guarding him." In a later verse, he adds that Paul lived in a house he rented for the duration of his imprisonment, namely, two years (v. 30). Nonetheless, Paul was chained (v. 20) and a soldier guarded him (compare 24:23). Paul's citizenship may have influ-enced the authorities to allow him to live in a rented house. We imagine that the Christians in Rome and other places paid the rent and supplied Paul's food, clothing, and other necessities (see Phil. 2:25; 4:10).

Greek Words, Phrases, and Constructions in 28:11–14

Verse 11

παρασήμῳ Διοσκούροις—this phrase does not mean "marked by the Dioscuri." Rather, because the construction is a dative absolute, it should be translated "a ship, insignia the Dioscuri," in conformity with the registration data of a ship.[25]

Verses 13–14

περιελόντες—some manuscripts have the reading περιελθόντες, which in transla-tion means "circled around" (NKJV, and see NAB, NEB, RSV). Without the letter ϑ, the

---

24. The Western text has an expansion that the Majority Text adopts: "When we arrived at Rome, the centurion delivered the prisoners to the captain of the guard" (NKJV; KJV). See Metzger, *Textual Commentary*, p. 501; Albert C. Clark, *The Acts of the Apostles: A Critical Edition with Introduction and Notes on Selected Passages* (1933; Oxford: Clarendon, 1970), pp. 386–88; William M. Ramsay, *St. Paul the Traveller and the Roman Citizen* (1897; reprint ed., Grand Rapids: Baker, 1962), pp. 347–48, 362.

25. Friedrich Blass and Albert Debrunner, *A Greek Grammar of the New Testament and Other Early Christian Literature*, trans. and rev. Robert Funk (Chicago: University of Chicago Press, 1961), #198.7.

participle is the aorist from περιαιρέω and, as a nautical term, signifies "having lifted the anchors on both sides of the ship." In brief, the meaning is "the ship set sail." It is possible that this particular reading is responsible for the variants.[26]

παρεκλήθημεν—as a compound verb, this is the aorist passive in the intensive sense: "we were invited." Translators prefer this version to the one that reads, "we were comforted by staying."

---

3. Roman Imprisonment
28:17–31

The Jews of Asia Minor had been responsible for Paul's arrest in Jerusalem (21:27–29), where the Jewish leaders vehemently opposed Paul. They even traveled to Caesarea to accuse Paul at his trial before Felix (24:1) and two years later before Festus (25:7). When Paul arrived in Rome, he had no knowledge of accusations that the local Jews might bring before Caesar. He boldly called together Jewish leaders in an effort to learn from them whether they were acquainted with his case. He also subtly prepares them to hear the gospel.

a. Paul's Statement
28:17–20

17. After three days, Paul summoned the leaders of the Jews. When they had assembled, he said to them: "Men and brothers, I had done nothing against our people or the customs of our fathers, yet I was delivered as a prisoner out of Jerusalem into the hands of the Romans. 18. They examined me and wanted to release me because they found no reason to put me to death."

Within a period of three days, Paul already had contacted the leaders of the Jews in Rome and asked them to come to his house. Who were these Jewish leaders? On the basis of information provided by Roman and Jewish historiographers (Suetonius, Tacitus, and Josephus), we can estimate that as many as forty thousand Jews lived in the imperial city in the middle of the first century.[27] From inscriptions we know that there were at least ten synagogues in Rome with influential leaders.[28] These leaders, then, met with Paul to hear him state the reason for his imprisonment.

Paul addresses these leaders as "men and brothers," which was a common greeting in Jewish circles.[29] He intimates that he, a fellow Jew, is their brother. He vows that he has done nothing against the Jewish people or

---

26. Refer to Metzger, *Textual Commentary*, p. 501.

27. Consult George A. Van Alstine, "Dispersion," *ISBE*, vol. 1, pp. 964–65; Leo Levi, "Italy," *Encyclopaedia Judaica*, vol. 9, p. 1116.

28. Emil Schurer, *The History of the Jewish People in the Age of Jesus Christ (175 B.C.–A.D. 135)*, rev. and ed. Geza Vermes and Fergus Millar, 3 vols. (Edinburgh: Clark, 1973–87), vol. 3, pp. 96–100.

29. See the Greek text of 2:29, 37; 7:2, 26; 13:15, 26, 38; 15:7, 13; 22:1; 23:1, 6; 28:17.

their customs (25:8). Paul declares that although he is innocent of any wrongdoing, the Jews in Jerusalem nevertheless handed him over to the Romans as a prisoner. He refrains from giving precise details, from mentioning names, and from accusing the Jews in Jerusalem of treating him unjustly. He wisely avoids any negative remarks so that he is able to gain the goodwill of these leaders and make them receptive to the gospel on another occasion (vv. 23–28).

Paul even has a kind word for the Romans, saying that they examined him in a trial and were unable to find him guilty of any crime that deserved the death sentence. He omits the fact that both Felix and Festus wanted to please the Jews: Felix kept Paul in prison for two years, and Festus wanted him to be tried in Jerusalem. Instead Paul says that they were ready to release him (see 26:32). In an effort to advance the cause of the gospel, he wishes to avoid any hint of confrontation between either the Jews and the Christians or the Jews and the Romans. And, in keeping with his usual practice, Paul presented the gospel "first to the Jew and then to the Greek" (Rom. 1:16). He had always observed that rule during his ministry in Cyprus (13:5, 7), Pisidian Antioch (13:14, 46), Corinth (18:6), and Ephesus (20:21); now he applies it in Rome.

Consistent with his purpose in writing Acts, Luke shows the spread of the gospel, even in the capital. When Paul will be in Rome, he plans to defend the cause of Christ so that the gospel can freely spread throughout the empire.

19. "When the Jews objected, I was forced to appeal to Caesar, not that I had any accusation against my people."

Paul states only the fact and not the cause of the opposition to his release. He lets the emphasis fall on the words *I was forced*; by using the passive voice he avoids telling his audience who compelled him to appeal to Caesar, even though the context points to the Jews in Jerusalem.

When Paul mentions that he appealed to Caesar, he indirectly reveals that he is a Roman citizen. He also implies that he desires a trial in the presence of Caesar. Yet Paul is careful not to dwell on the privileges which accompany his Roman citizenship.[30] He realizes the political overtones and the possibility that he might be accused of forsaking his Jewish heritage.

Paul emphatically asserts that his appeal to Caesar was not because he sought to bring any accusation against the Jews as a nation. With this statement, he assures the Jewish leaders in Rome that he will not cause them trouble. He will be true to his people and present no accusation against them in court.

The Western text has expanded the verse in an effort to complete it and provide balance: "When the Jews objected *and were shouting 'Away with our enemy!'*, I was forced to appeal to Caesar, not that I had any accusation against my people, *but that I might deliver my soul from death.*" Translators are

---

30. A. N. Sherwin-White, *Roman Society and Roman Law in the New Testament* (1963; reprint ed., Grand Rapids: Baker, 1968), p. 66.

of the opinion that the origin of the shorter text is easier to explain than that of the longer. They point to the fact that scribes were more inclined to add than to delete words.

20. "For this reason I invited you, to see you and speak with you, for I am bearing this chain because of the hope of Israel."

Paul concludes his general statement. He demonstrates his love for the Jewish people by inviting their leaders to visit him in his rented house. He desires to explain to his countrymen in Rome the causes for his appeal to Caesar, his imprisonments in Caesarea and in Rome, and his refusal to incriminate the Jews. He expects the Jewish leaders to have questions about his imprisonment, which is evidenced by the chain he is wearing and the presence of a Roman soldier in the house. He also wants them to know that he is interested in a spiritual dialogue, summarizing both purposes by saying, "I am bearing this chain because of the hope of Israel."

This statement in itself is rather brief, and we infer from his words that Paul at this time postponed a detailed discussion of the matter. The Jewish leaders understood the expression *Israel's hope* as a reference to the Messiah. In a subsequent meeting Paul would introduce the messianic teaching concerning Jesus the Messiah. Paul told the Jewish leaders that the cause for being chained was rooted in their common hope.

In this last remark, Paul calls attention to his house arrest with the use of the word *chain* (singular). Apparently he had sufficient freedom to be able to move around in the house. Note that when the commander in Jerusalem at first arrested Paul, he had bound him with two chains (21:33) but removed them when he heard of Paul's Roman citizenship (22:29).

Greek Words, Phrases, and Constructions in 28:17–20

Verse 17

τοὺς ὄντας—the articular participle with the adjective πρώτους (first) has a technical sense: "the local leaders of the Jews" (compare 5:17).

οὐδέν—this negative adjective is a substantive that is used as a direct object of the participle ποιήσας (having done nothing [wrong]).[31]

Verses 19–20

οὐχ ὡς—"not as if" (see II John 5). The negative adverb precedes the participle *having*, which is unusual, but the distance between the adverb and the participle probably accounts for the use of οὐ instead of μή.

τοῦ ἔθνους—in fourteen places in the New Testament, the Jewish people are called ἔθνος (nation)—a word normally used for Gentiles (see, e.g., 10:22).

ὑμᾶς—the personal pronoun serves a direct object for the main verb *I invited* and for the two infinitives *to see* and *to talk with*.

---

31. Robert Hanna, *A Grammatical Aid to the Greek New Testament* (Grand Rapids: Baker, 1983), p. 251.

b. Reply from the Jews
28:21–22

21. The Jews said to Paul: "We have not received any letters from Judea concerning you. None of the brothers who have come here have reported or said anything bad about you. 22. We desire to hear from you the views that you hold. We know that everywhere people are objecting to this sect."

The Jewish leaders remember that only a decade earlier (A.D. 49), Emperor Claudius had expelled them from Rome because of riots. Those riots had been instigated by a person called Chrestos (Christos), according to the Roman historiographer Suetonius.[32] Presumably the non-Christian Jews clashed with the Christian Jews. Unable to distinguish the differences between the two groups, Claudius expelled both. Now, facing a leader of the Christian faith, the Jewish leaders are cautious yet fair in their response.

"We have not received any letters from Judea concerning you." This is an honest admission of justifiable ignorance. The fact that the Jerusalem hierarchy had not sent word to either the Jews or the Roman authorities supported Paul's claim of innocence. After Paul appealed to Caesar and was sent to Rome, the Jewish authorities in Jerusalem were of the opinion that he was too far removed from Israel to do any harm. In addition, while time erased the memory of Paul's arrest in Jerusalem, opposition to Rome itself became the issue of the day.

Moreover, a Roman judge would consider the absence of an accuser or an accusation a punishable offense.[33] The Jews in Rome wish to be absolved of any such blame and consequently are open in their response to Paul. They honestly admit, "None of the brothers who have come here have reported or said anything bad about you." The Jews in Rome are saying that they have not heard anything about Paul. In itself, such a statement appears incongruous, for we know that Paul sent his letter to the Christians in Rome three years earlier. But the contacts between Jews and Christians may not have been intimate enough for the Christians to share this information.

Yet the Jewish leaders are interested in learning the theological views of Paul himself. They are open to hearing Paul teach the gospel and explain it to them in detail. Their request pleases Paul beyond measure, for it fulfills Jesus' word that as Paul had testified for Jesus in Jerusalem, so he would have to testify in Rome (23:11). Here he has the opportunity to proclaim the message of salvation to Jewish leaders who, if they accept the gospel, can influence their people in the local synagogues.

"We know that everywhere people are objecting to this sect." Luke presents a condensed version of the request the Jews make. When these lead-

---

32. Suetonius *Claudius* 25.4.
33. Consult Sherwin-White, *Roman Society and Roman Law*, p. 52.

ers use the word *sect,* they have in mind the Christian church (see 24:5, 14). The word by itself is not derogatory. It means "party" or "school of thought," as is evident from Acts and the writings of Josephus; it is used to describe the Sadducees (5:17) and the Pharisees (15:5).[34] The Jewish leaders speak in generalities and observe that people, namely the Jews, are opposed to the teaching of the Christian church. But the leaders are willing to listen to what Paul has to say to them.

c. Paul's Explanation
28:23–28

23. They set a day for Paul and came to him at his lodging in large numbers. He explained and testified to them about the kingdom of God. And from morning to evening, he tried to persuade them from the Law of Moses and the Prophets concerning Jesus. 24. Some were convinced by what he said, while others would not believe.

Luke is interested in reporting that Paul preached to a large number of Jews in the capital city. He is true to his purpose in writing the Book of Acts (see 1:8). But in the process he neglects to describe details concerning the size of Paul's rented quarters, the freedom Paul evidently enjoyed to meet with large numbers of people, and the reaction of the Christians in Rome. These aspects are immaterial to Luke's purpose. We venture to say that the Jewish leaders encouraged their people to come to Paul's house on a given day, that permission for this meeting had been granted by the Roman authorities, and that many of the Jews were coming and going.

The focus is again on Paul, who takes this opportunity to preach the gospel from morning to evening. We expect this may be from sunrise to sunset. He appears to have boundless energy for speaking for hours without a break (see 20:7, 11). We are reminded of Jesus and his disciples, who at one time were surrounded by a crowd and were not even able to eat (Mark 3:20).

Paul teaches the people about God's kingdom, which is equivalent to teaching them Christ's gospel. For instance, when Paul taught in the synagogue of Ephesus and in the lecture hall of Tyrannus, he taught the people about "the kingdom of God" and "the word of the Lord" (19:8, 10).[35] In Paul's farewell address to the Ephesian elders, the phrases *gospel of God's grace* and *preaching the kingdom* signify the same thing (20:24–25). Likewise, in Rome Paul preached "the kingdom of God" to the people and tried to persuade them "concerning Jesus" (see 28:23, 31).

Schooled in the Law of Moses and the Prophets, Paul opened the Scriptures for his listeners and tried to explain to them that Jesus of Nazareth is indeed the Messiah. As Jesus opened the Old Testament (the Law and the

---

34. Josephus *Antiquities* 13.5.9 [171]; *Life* 10; 12; 191.

35. These two expressions appear to be synonymous in Acts. See Donald Guthrie, *New Testament Theology* (Downers Grove: Inter-Varsity, 1981), p. 429.

Prophets) to the men on the way to Emmaus, so Paul tried to persuade the Jews that Jesus fulfilled the messianic prophecies in the Scriptures (compare Luke 24:27). The men of Emmaus believed Jesus' word when their spiritual eyes were opened, but many Jews in Rome were not to be persuaded.

The Jews in Rome were acquainted with and applied the doctrine of works but not the doctrine of grace (compare, e.g., Rom. 4:4; 11:6). When Paul taught the Jews that entrance in the kingdom of God is not by works but by grace, he met opposition and eventual rejection. It was Paul's desire that his countrymen might be saved and that their zeal for God might be expressed not in terms of righteousness by the law but through faith in Christ (Rom. 10:1–6).

Teaching about the birth, life, death, and resurrection of Jesus, Paul had to show from the Scriptures that God promised the coming of the Messiah. He introduced the Messiah as the One who would

atone for man's sin;

reconcile God to mankind;

purchase eternal righteousness;

fashion men after the image of God;

regenerate his people with his Spirit;

make his faithful servants heirs with Christ.[36]

To his credit, Paul was able to keep the attention of his audience from morning until evening. Some of the Jews accepted Jesus as the Messiah, but others continued in their unbelief. Throughout his ministry, in places as diverse as Pisidian Antioch, Thessalonica, and Corinth, Paul had experienced the same thing: some believe in Jesus while others reject him (see 13:43–46; 17:4–5; 18:6–8, respectively).

25. The Jews did not agree with one another and began to leave after Paul had spoken one last word: "The Holy Spirit rightly spoke through Isaiah the prophet to your fathers."

a. "The Jews did not agree with one another." The text implies that the audience is divided on the proper interpretation of the Scriptures. Those who do not believe are at variance with those who do believe. Luke indicates that their disagreement was not of a momentary nature but continued to divide them. Those who disagree with the believers reject not Paul but rather Jesus Christ the Son of God and the Scriptures that testify of him. On the other hand, the Jews who believe become part of the existing churches in Rome and thus strengthen the Christian community.

b. "[They] began to leave after Paul had spoken one last word." Gradually the people begin to depart. Yet Paul wishes to address the unbelieving

---

36. Refer to Calvin, *Acts of the Apostles*, vol. 2, p. 309.

Jews with a last word from the Scriptures. Hence, not Paul but God himself has the decisive word with the hardened Jews.

c. "The Holy Spirit rightly spoke through Isaiah the prophet to your fathers." Paul attributes the word he is going to speak, not to the prophet Isaiah, but to the Holy Spirit, who is the primary author of the Scriptures. If the Jews reject the Scriptures, they not only are spurning Isaiah but also are defying the Holy Spirit. In his Word, God has given them the messianic prophecies and has sent his servant Paul to explain to them that Jesus has fulfilled these prophecies.

When the Jews have received all the evidence and then refuse to accept the truth of God's Word, they are defying the living God. For this reason, Paul boldly asserts that the Holy Spirit rightly addressed the forefathers through a word from Isaiah the prophet. The term *forefathers* allows the Jews to reflect on the historical setting. This word that Isaiah delivered to his contemporaries is now addressed to Paul's contemporaries in Rome.

At the same time, Paul separates himself from the Jews and their ancestors with the use of the possessive pronoun *your*.[37] When Paul first called the Jews to his house, he spoke of *our* fathers (v. 17). Now he purposely refrains from identifying himself with the unbelieving Jews, much as Stephen did before the Sanhedrin. Stephen at first expressed his identity with his audience by using the inclusive pronoun *our* in the phrase *our fathers* (7:11, 12, 15, 38, 39, 44, 45). When he realized that his audience rejected his presentation, he separated himself and spoke of *your* fathers (7:51, 52).

> **26.** " 'Go to this people and say:
> "You will keep on hearing but never understand;
> You will keep on seeing but never perceive."
> **27.** For the heart of this people has become dull,
> they hardly hear with their ears,
> and they have closed their eyes.
> Otherwise they might see with their eyes
> and hear with their ears
> and understand with their heart
> and turn again, and I would heal them.' "

Observe these salient points:

a. *Setting.* The Jews in Rome know that Paul quoted from Isaiah 6:9–10 and are familiar with the historical setting of these words. They understand that God told Isaiah to go to the Israelites whose hearts were hardened because of unbelief and disobedience. They know that the divine words spoken by Isaiah only drove the people of Israel further away from salvation.

God told Isaiah to go to Israel and inform the people that they were always hearing but failing to understand and always seeing but never perceiving. This was hardly a compliment. In fact, it was a stern rebuke that

---

37. On the basis of the Majority Text, the KJV and NKJV have the pronoun *our*.

ultimately terminated in judgment on Israel and resulted in destruction of cities, devastation of fields, and exile of the people (Isa. 6:11–12). Isaiah's task would be disheartening, yet the Lord promised that out of a stump God would raise up his holy seed (Isa. 6:13).

b. *Application.* The evangelists Matthew, Mark, and Luke report that Jesus taught the parable of the sower. In response to his disciples' question about why he taught in parables (Matt. 13:10; Mark 4:10; Luke 8:9), Jesus quoted the words of Isaiah 6:9–10 and applied them to the unbelieving Pharisees and teachers of the law (Matt. 12:24; Mark 3:22). John relates that despite all the miracles Jesus performed, the Jews refused to believe in Jesus. He quotes Isaiah 6:10 to explain why the Jews were unable to believe (John 12:40). Jesus observed the hardness of man's heart and thus could apply the words and setting of Isaiah to the Jews of his day. And Paul turns to this passage when he encounters unbelieving Jews who, after they have heard a full exposition of the Scriptures, refuse to accept Jesus as the Messiah (compare the content of Rom. 9–11).

Through Isaiah the prophet, God is saying to Israel that the people have permitted their hearts to become calloused, have let their hearing become impaired, and have allowed their eyesight to become dim. They purposely have cut themselves off from the possibility of repentance. If this were not so, they would turn to God and he would restore them. By quoting the passage from Isaiah, Paul tells his listeners that in terms of spirituality they are similar to Isaiah's contemporaries.

c. *Text.* The wording of this lengthy quotation comes directly from the Septuagint. The words are the same in Matthew 13:14–15, while Mark, Luke, and John in their respective Gospels have an abbreviated version of the passage from Isaiah. The Gospel according to Matthew, however, is addressed to Jewish readers and therefore has the full text. Likewise, Paul addressed the Jews of Rome and wanted them to hear the entire passage from the prophecy of Isaiah.

28. "Therefore, let it be known to you that this salvation of God has been sent to the Gentiles; they will listen!"

Paul adds his own conclusion to his teaching. On the basis of Isaiah's prophecy he actually says, "You Jews should know that salvation is first for the Jew and then for the Gentile. But you have rejected God's assurance of salvation and now God offers it to the Gentiles."

We observe two things. First, God called Paul to be an apostle to the Gentiles (9:15; 22:21; Gal. 1:15–16; 2:8). Next, throughout his ministry Paul adhered to the rule to present the gospel first to the Jew and then to the Gentile. Wherever the Jews rejected the preaching of the gospel, Paul turned to the Gentiles (see, e.g., 13:46; 18:6). The gospel has a universal message for all people. Accordingly, the Book of Acts ends not on a negative note of unbelieving Jews refusing to accept the gospel. To the contrary, the last word of Paul is positive. He states that the Gentiles will listen to the gospel of salvation and by believing in Jesus will be saved.

Doctrinal Considerations in 28:23-28

If we look at the historical setting of Isaiah proclaiming God's message to the people of Israel (Isa. 6:9–10) and consider the backdrop of Jesus' healing and teaching ministry, we notice a remarkable parallel. God had blessed Israel in many ways, yet the more he showed his love to the people the more they turned away from him. But God's love that was designed to bless the Israelites changed to divine wrath when they had filled up the measure of their sins. Observes Franz Delitzsch, "For just as in all the good that men do, the active principle is the love of God; so in all the harm that they do, the active principle is the wrath of God."[38] God's wrath culminated in shutting the way to repentance and delivering the people to their own destruction.

When Jesus in his healing ministry gave sight to the blind, he fulfilled Isaiah's prophecy that he was the Messiah (see Isa. 35:5; John 9:6–7, 35–38). But the Jews refused to believe. When he cast out demons, the experts in the law and the Pharisees said that he did so in the name of Beelzebub, the prince of the demons. In effect, they accused Jesus of being in league with Satan (Matt. 12:22–24; Mark 3:22). Then Jesus taught the doctrine of the sin against the Holy Spirit. He intimated that the Jews who attributed his healing miracles to Satan instead of acknowledging the power of the Holy Spirit committed the unpardonable sin (Matt. 12:32; Mark 3:29). Jesus said that these people were on the outside (Mark 4:11) and implied that they would be excluded from being instructed in the secrets of God's kingdom.[39] In this setting, Jesus quoted the words of Isaiah 6:9–10.

Paul expounded the Scriptures to the Jews in Rome and at the end of the day realized that many Jews refused to adopt the messianic truths fulfilled in Jesus Christ. He knew that these people would continue to harden their hearts and cut themselves off from the living God. In his opinion, these Jews could be compared with natural olive branches that were broken off—the olive tree stands for the true Israel—because they had died a spiritual death. Paul says that because of unbelief they were broken off (Rom. 11:20). Persistent unbelief leads to hardening of the heart. Hardening of the heart leads to apostasy and the sin that leads to death (I John 5:16).

Greek Words, Phrases, and Constructions in 28:23-29

Verse 23

τὴν ξενίαν—the primary meaning is "hospitality" or "entertainment." The secondary meaning is "guest room," which is the preferable translation for the two places in which this word occurs in the New Testament (here and Philem. 22).

ἐξετίθετο—the imperfect middle of the verb ἐκτίθημι (I explain) is followed by two participles that express manner or mode: διαμαρτυρόμενος (by testifying) and

---

38. Franz Delitzsch, *Biblical Commentary on the Prophecies of Isaiah*, trans. James Martin, 2 vols. (1877; Grand Rapids: Eerdmans, 1954), vol. 1, p. 201.
39. William L. Lane, *The Gospel According to Mark*, New International Commentary on the New Testament series (Grand Rapids: Eerdmans, 1974), p. 159.

πείθων (by persuading). The imperfect denotes continued action. Its use predominates in this section (see vv. 24 and 25).

Verses 26–27

The reading of the Septuagint differs slightly from the Hebrew text in the introductory sentence: "Go and tell this people" (Isa. 6:9) and "Go to this people and say" (v. 26).

The clauses in verse 27 are in the literary sequence *a b c, c b a*. The sequence serves to emphasize the message.

The use of the future tense ἰάσομαι (I will heal) instead of the aorist active subjunctive ἰάσωμαι is due to confusion of the Greek vowels o and ω. These two letters are quite similar in sound.

Verses 28–29

γνωστὸν ἔστω—"let it be known." This solemn phrase is common in formal speeches. See 2:14; 4:10; 13:38.

The Majority Text adopted the expansion of the Western text in verse 29: "And when he had said these words, the Jews departed and had a great dispute among themselves" (nkjv; see kjv). Translators favor the exclusion of this verse.

---

d. Conclusion
28:30–31

Throughout the second half of Acts, Luke portrays Paul as the leading figure. The reader would be tempted to think that Luke has written a biography of this apostle. This is not the case, for the book fails to relate the demise of Paul. Luke composes a history, not of Paul, but of the spread of the gospel. He concludes the Book of Acts by showing that Paul presented the teachings of Jesus boldly and without hindrance.

30. Paul stayed for two full years in his own rented house and welcomed all who came to him. 31. Boldly and unhindered he was preaching the kingdom of God and teaching the things concerning the Lord Jesus Christ.

a. "Paul stayed for two full years." With the time reference, Luke provides the last biographical note on Paul. He fails to disclose Paul's release, subsequent travels, second imprisonment, and death. We know from his epistles that Paul expected to be released from prison (see Phil. 1:19, 25; 2:24) and would need lodging in Colosse (Philem. 22). The pastoral Epistles include references to places that are not mentioned in Acts. Hence we conclude that Paul must have traveled to Ephesus and Macedonia (I Tim. 1:3; 3:14), Nicopolis (Titus 3:12), and Troas (II Tim. 4:13). And finally, in his last epistle he writes that his execution is at hand (II Tim. 4:6).

If Luke had known of Paul's return to the congregation at Ephesus, he certainly would have written a different ending to the emotional farewell of the Ephesian elders (20:38). Luke apparently composed Acts during Paul's imprisonment and completed it soon after his release (see the Introduction for the date of Acts).

We are unable to say why Paul was imprisoned for two years in the capital city. Scholars have suggested that, because his accusers failed to come to Rome for Paul's trial within a two-year period, Paul was released.[40] But we have no evidence that his case was dropped by default. "Roman tradition . . . is that the prosecutor must prosecute. The protection of the accused person lay not in any provision for an automatic release if his accusers were absent, but in the severity of the sanctions against defaulting prosecutors."[41] Further, in case of a "just cause" or the death of a prosecutor, the accused could request dismissal of the charges against him. Even then, Roman lawmakers were reluctant to cancel charges.[42] In other words, if Paul's accusers never presented themselves in Rome, Paul would remain a prisoner. At the end of the two years, Nero may have released him.

b. "[Paul stayed] in his own rented house and welcomed all who came to him." Another translation reads "at his own expense" (RSV). The Vulgate has the same rendering: *in suo conducto* (on his own resources). The crux of the matter lies in the Greek word *misthōma*, which means either "rent" (active) or "what is rented" (passive).[43]

Luke writes that Paul stayed and not that he lived, by which he implies that Paul remained a prisoner in separate living quarters. Paul fulfilled his task of preaching and teaching the gospel to all the people who came to visit him. He simply lacked the time to supply his financial needs, for which, we presume, he depended on his friends.

c. "Boldly, he was preaching the kingdom of God and teaching the things concerning the Lord Jesus Christ." Luke completes the Book of Acts on a note of triumph. Paul preaches the kingdom of God and teaches about Jesus to anyone coming to his house. In addition to some of the Jews in Rome, numerous Gentiles came to him. Indeed, he was the appointed apostle to the Gentiles.

The word *boldly* signifies that Paul enjoyed complete freedom to preach and teach Christ's gospel. Filled with the Holy Spirit, he could speak with authority to all his visitors and expect to see results in his ministry. The two clauses ("preaching the kingdom of God" and "teaching the things concerning the Lord Jesus Christ") are synonymous and support each other. With the combination *Lord Jesus Christ,* Luke gives voice to the early Christian confession that Jesus is Lord (I Cor. 12:3), in opposition to the Roman

---

40. Consult, e.g., H. J. Cadbury, "Roman Law and the Trial of Paul," *Beginnings,* vol. 5, pp. 325–36.

41. Sherwin-White, *Roman Society and Roman Law,* p. 114.

42. Sherwin-White (ibid., p. 117) argues that Cadbury (*Beginnings,* vol. 5, p. 330) fails to prove his point.

43. Bauer, p. 523.

maxim *Caesar is Lord.* And with respect to the Jews, he testifies that Jesus is the Christ.

d. "Unhindered." This word, the last in the original text, is telling. Luke suggests that the Roman government placed no restrictions on the spread of the gospel throughout Rome and the empire. With this word, which because of its place in the Greek text is emphatic, Luke describes the openness of the state toward the church. Paul was vindicated and the charges leveled against him by the Jews were false.[44] From Paul's rented house the gospel went forth to the end of the world. And after his release, he continued his travels for the sake of the gospel.

Mission Headquarters[45]

I am sure that while Paul lived in his house with a soldier guarding him that his daily conversation was not about the weather. Instead he introduced the soldier to Jesus Christ, taught him the truths of Christ's gospel, and instilled in him a saving knowledge of Jesus. As in any army, a soldier in the Roman army was frequently transferred. If we assume that the soldier who guarded Paul became a Christian and was posted to another part of the Roman empire, Paul would indeed send forth a missionary (compare Phil. 1:13; 4:22).

How many soldiers guarded Paul in that two-year period? And how many missionaries did Paul send into the world? We are not told, but we are confident that Paul's rented house in Rome indeed became mission headquarters. Friends and acquaintances from many parts of the world were allowed to visit Paul. He sent them forth with the gospel of Christ (see the parallel in II Tim. 4:9–12). He also wrote the so-called prison Epistles: Colossians, Philemon, Ephesians, and Philippians.

A last observation. The commissioning of missionaries from Rome to the ends of the earth proved to be the fulfillment of Jesus' mandate to be "witnesses both in Jerusalem, in all Judea and Samaria, and to the ends of the earth" (1:8).

Greek Words, Phrases, and Constructions in 28:30–31

The Western text adds these words to verse 30: "both Jews and Greeks." And to the end of verse 31, Latin manuscripts add: "saying that this is Christ Jesus, the Son of God, through whom the whole world is to be judged." The hand of a well-meaning scribe is obvious in both additions.

Summary of Chapter 28

With the crew and passengers of the wrecked freighter, Paul arrives safely on the island of Malta. Here the native people light a fire so that

---

44. Refer to Gerhard Delling, "Das Letzte Wort der Apostelgeschichte," *NovT* 15 (1973): 193–204.

45. Compare the similar section in the commentary on 24:23.

those drenched by the sea and chilled by wind and rain can warm themselves. Paul gathers a bundle of branches which he throws into the flames; a snake, driven out by the heat, puts its fangs in Paul's hand. Paul shakes the reptile off into the fire. The islanders expect him to swell up or fall dead; when nothing happens to Paul, they regard him as a god.

Paul heals the father of Publius from fever and dysentery. As a consequence, many sick people come to Paul and he heals them. After waiting for three months and receiving many supplies from the islanders, Paul and his friends board an Alexandrian vessel and sail to Italy. They land at Puteoli, where Paul stays with Christian friends for one week. Then they travel on foot to the Forum of Appius and to the Three Taverns. At these two places Christians from Rome come to welcome Paul. When they arrive in Rome, Paul is permitted to live separately with a soldier guarding him.

After three days, Paul invites the Jewish leaders in Rome to his dwelling. He informs them about his arrest in Jerusalem and his imprisonment by the Romans. The leaders tell him that they have not received any letters or messengers concerning charges against Paul. They are willing to learn about the religion of the Christians. With numerous fellow Jews they come to Paul's quarters. Paul explains to them the teachings of the kingdom of God and of Jesus and tries to convince them from the Scriptures. Some believe, but others reject his instruction. Paul quotes from the prophecy of Isaiah and tells the unbelieving Jews that God's salvation is now sent to the Gentiles, who will listen to the gospel. For two years Paul stays in his rented house and without hindrance teaches the gospel to everyone who visits him.

Select Bibliography*

Commentaries

Alford, Henry. *Alford's Greek Testament: An Exegetical and Critical Commentary*. 4 vols. 7th ed. 1877. Grand Rapids: Guardian, 1976.

Arrington, French L. *The Acts of the Apostles: An Introduction and Commentary*. Peabody, Mass.: Hendrickson, 1988.

Bengel, John Albert. *Gnomon of the New Testament*. Edited by Andrew R. Fausset. 5 vols. Edinburgh: Clark, 1877.

Bruce, F. F. *The Acts of the Apostles: The Greek Text with Introduction and Commentary*. 3d (rev. and enl.) ed. Grand Rapids: Eerdmans, 1990.

————. *The Book of the Acts*. New International Commentary on the New Testament series. Rev. ed. Grand Rapids: Eerdmans, 1988.

Calvin, John. *Commentary on the Acts of the Apostles*. Edited by David W. Torrance and Thomas F. Torrance. 2 vols. Grand Rapids: Eerdmans, 1966.

Carter, Charles W., and Ralph Earle. *The Acts of the Apostles*. Grand Rapids: Zondervan, 1959.

Clark, Albert C. *The Acts of the Apostles: A Critical Edition with Introduction and Notes on Selected Passages*. 1933. Oxford: Clarendon, 1970.

Conzelmann, Hans. *Acts of the Apostles*. Translated by James Limburg, A. Thomas Kraabel, and Donald H. Juel. 1963. Philadelphia: Fortress, 1987.

Delebecque, Édouard. *Les Actes des Apôtres: Texte Traduit et Annoté*. Paris: Les Belles Lettres, 1982.

Delitzsch, Franz. *Biblical Commentary on the Psalms*. Translated by Francis Bolton. 3 vols. Reprint. Grand Rapids: Eerdmans, 1955.

de Zwaan, J. *De Handelingen der Apostelen*. Het Nieuwe Testament series. 2d ed. Groningen: Wolters, 1932.

Dibelius, Martin. *Studies in the Acts of the Apostles*. London: SCM, 1956.

Dupont, Jacques. *Les Actes des Apôtres*. Bible de Jérusalem. 2d ed. Paris: Cerf, 1954.

Fee, Gordon D. *The First Epistle to the Corinthians*. New International Commentary on the New Testament series. Grand Rapids: Eerdmans, 1987.

Findlay, J. A. *The Acts of the Apostles*. London: SCM, 1936.

Foakes Jackson, F. J. *The Acts of the Apostles*. Moffatt New Testament Commentary. London: Hodder and Stoughton, 1931.

---

*Consult the Index of Authors and the footnotes for references to the numerous books and articles considered in the commentary.

Gibson, Margaret D., ed. *The Commentaries of Isho'dad of Merw.* Horae Semiticae no. 10. Cambridge: Cambridge University Press, 1913.

Gispen, W. H. *Bible Student's Commentary: Exodus.* Translated by Ed van der Maas. Grand Rapids: Zondervan; St. Catharines: Paideia, 1982.

Greeven, Heinrich. *Studies in the Acts of the Apostles.* London: SCM, 1956.

Grosheide, F. W. *De Handelingen der Apostelen.* Kommentaar op het Nieuwe Testament series. 2 vols. Amsterdam: Van Bottenburg, 1942, 1948.

―――. *De Handelingen der Apostelen.* Korte Verklaring der Heilige Schrift series. Kampen: Kok, 1950.

Haenchen, Ernst. *The Acts of the Apostles: A Commentary.* Translated by Bernard Noble and Gerald Shinn. Philadelphia: Westminster, 1971.

Hanson, R. P. C. *The Acts of the Apostles.* New Clarendon Bible. Oxford: Clarendon, 1967.

Harrison, Everett F. *Interpreting Acts: The Expanding Church.* 2d ed. Grand Rapids: Zondervan, Academie Books, 1986.

Hemer, Colin J. *The Book of Acts in the Setting of Hellenistic History.* Edited by Conrad H. Gempf. Tübingen: Mohr, 1989.

Hendriksen, William. *Exposition of Colossians and Philemon.* New Testament Commentary series. Grand Rapids: Baker, 1964.

―――. *Exposition of Galatians.* New Testament Commentary series. Grand Rapids: Baker, 1968.

―――. *Exposition of the Pastoral Epistles.* New Testament Commentary series. Grand Rapids: Baker, 1957.

―――. *Exposition of Paul's Epistle to the Romans.* New Testament Commentary series. Grand Rapids: Baker, 1980.

―――. *Exposition of Philippians.* New Testament Commentary series. Grand Rapids: Baker, 1962.

Hughes, Philip Edgcumbe. *Paul's Second Epistle to the Corinthians: The English Text with Introduction, Exposition and Notes.* New International Commentary on the New Testament series. Grand Rapids: Eerdmans, 1962.

Kistemaker, Simon J. *Exposition of the Epistle to the Hebrews.* New Testament Commentary series. Grand Rapids: Baker, 1984.

―――. *Exposition of the Epistle of James and the Epistles of John.* New Testament Commentary series. Grand Rapids: Baker, 1986.

―――. *Exposition of the Epistles of Peter and of the Epistle of Jude.* New Testament Commentary series. Grand Rapids: Baker, 1987.

Knowling, R. J. *The Acts of the Apostles.* Vol. 2 of the *Expositor's Greek Testament.* Edited by W. R. Nicoll. 1900. Grand Rapids: Eerdmans, 1951.

Krodel, Gerhard A. *Acts.* Augsburg Commentary on the New Testament. Minneapolis: Augsburg, 1986.

Lake, Kirsopp, and H. J. Cadbury. *English Translation and Commentary* [on Acts]. Vol. 4 of *The Beginnings of Christianity.* Reprint. Grand Rapids: Baker, 1965.

Lane, William L. *The Gospel According to Mark.* New International Commentary on the New Testament series. Grand Rapids: Eerdmans, 1974.

Lenski, R. C. H. *The Interpretation of the Acts of the Apostles.* Columbus: Wartburg, 1944.

Longenecker, Richard N. *Acts of the Apostles.* In vol. 9 of *The Expositor's Bible Commentary,* edited by Frank E. Gaebelein. 12 vols. Grand Rapids: Zondervan, 1981.

Luedemann, Gerd. *Das frühe Christentum nach den Traditionen der Apostelgeschichte: ein Kommentar.* Göttingen: Vandenhoeck und Ruprecht, 1987.

Marshall, I. Howard. *The Acts of the Apostles: An Introduction and Commentary.* Tyndale New Testament Commentaries series. Grand Rapids: Eerdmans; Leicester: Inter-Varsity, 1980.

Meyer, H. A. W. *Critical and Exegetical Handbook to the Acts of the Apostles.* Kritisch-Exegetischer Kommentar. 3 vols. 4th ed. 1870. Edinburgh: Clark, 1877.

Munck, Johannes. *The Acts of the Apostles.* Anchor Bible. Vol. 31. Garden City, N.Y.: Doubleday, 1967.

Neil, William. *The Acts of the Apostles.* New Century Bible. London: Oliphants, 1973.

Packer, J. W. *The Acts of the Apostles.* Cambridge Bible Commentary on the New English Bible. Cambridge: Cambridge University Press, 1966.

Rackham, Richard B. *The Acts of the Apostles: An Exposition.* Westminster Commentaries series. 1901. Grand Rapids: Baker, 1964.

Ridderbos, J. *De Kleine Propheten: Hosea, Joël, Amos.* Korte Verklaring der Heilige Schrift series. 2d ed. Kampen: Kok, 1952.

Roloff, Jürgen. *Die Apostelgeschichte.* Das Neue Testament Deutsch series. Vol. 5. Göttingen: Vandenhoeck und Ruprecht, 1981.

Schille, G. *Die Apostelgeschichte des Lukas.* Theologischer Hand-Kommentar zum Neuen Testament. Vol. 5. Berlin: Evangelische Verlagsanstalt, 1983.

Schlatter, A. *Die Apostelgeschichte.* Erläuterungen zum Neuen Testament. Vol. 4. Stuttgart: Calwer Verlag, 1948.

Schmithals, W. *Die Apostelgeschichte des Lukas.* Züricher Bibelkommentar. Vol. 3.2. Zürich: Theologischer Verlag, 1982.

Schneider, Gerhard. *Die Apostelgeschichte.* Herders Theologischer Kommentar zum Neuen Testament series. Freiburg: Herder, 1980.

Stählin, Gustav. *Die Apostelgeschichte.* Das Neue Testament Deutsch. Vol. 5. Göttingen: Vandenhoeck und Ruprecht, 1962.

Walker, T. *The Acts of the Apostles.* 1910. Chicago: Moody, 1965.

Weiser, A. *Die Apostelgeschichte.* Ökumenischer Taschenbuch-Kommentar zum Neuen Testament. Vol. 5.1, 2. Gütersloh: Mohn; Würzburg: Echter Verlag, 1980, 1985.

Williams, C. S. C. *A Commentary on the Acts of the Apostles.* Black's (Harper's) New Testament Commentaries. New York: Harper, 1957.

Williams, David John. *Acts.* Good News Commentaries series. San Francisco: Harper and Row, 1985.

Williams, R. R. *The Acts of the Apostles.* Torch Biblical Commentaries. London: SCM, 1953.

Young, Edward J. *The Book of Isaiah.* New International Commentary on the Old Testament series. 3 vols. Grand Rapids: Eerdmans, 1972.

Zahn, Theodor. *Die Apostelgeschichte des Lucas.* Kommentar zum Neuen Testament series. 2 vols. Leipzig: Deichert, 1921.

Studies

Achtemeier, Paul J. *The Quest for Unity in the New Testament Church: A Study in Paul and Acts.* Philadelphia: Fortress, 1987.

Augustine. *Augustine: The Later Works,* in vol. 8, *On the Holy Spirit and the Letter.* Translated by John Burnaby. The Library of Christian Classics. 13 vols. Philadelphia: Westminster, 1955.

————. *Confessions of St. Augustine.* Translated by W. Watts. Loeb Classical Library series. 2 vols. Cambridge: Harvard University Press, 1977–79.

Barrett, C. K. "Apollos and the Twelve Disciples of Ephesus." In *The New Testament Age: Essays in Honor of Bo Reicke,* edited by William C. Weinrich. 2 vols. Macon, Ga.: Mercer University Press, 1984.

————. *Luke the Historian in Recent Study.* London: Epworth, 1961.

————. *New Testament Essays.* London: SPCK, 1972.

————. "Paul's Address to the Ephesian Elders." In *God's Christ and His People: Studies in Honour of N. A. Dahl,* edited by Jacob Jervell and Wayne A. Meeks. Oslo, Bergen, and Tromsö: Universitetsforlaget, 1977.

Betz, Hans Dieter, ed. *The Greek Magical Papyri in Translation: Including the Demotic Spells.* Chicago and London: University of Chicago Press, 1986.

Bishop, E. F. F. *Apostles of Palestine.* London: Lutterworth, 1958.

Black, M. *An Aramaic Approach to the Gospels and Acts.* 3d ed. Oxford: Clarendon, 1967.

Blaiklock, E. M. *Cities of the New Testament.* Westwood, N.J.: Revell, 1965.

Bousset, Wilhelm. *Kyrios Christos: A History of the Belief in Christ from the Beginnings of Christianity to Irenaeus.* Translated by John E. Steely. Nashville: Abingdon, 1970.

Bultmann, Rudolf. *Theology of the New Testament.* Translated by Kendrick Grobel. 2 vols. New York: Charles Scribner's Sons, 1951.

Cadbury, H. J. *The Book of Acts in History.* New York: Harper; London: A. and C. Black, 1955.

————. *The Making of Luke-Acts.* 1927. Naperville, Ill.: Allenson; London: SPCK, 1958.

————. *The Style and Literary Method of Luke.* 2 vols. Cambridge: Harvard University Press, 1919–20.

Casson, Lionel. *Ships and Seamanship in the Ancient World.* Princeton: Princeton University Press, 1971.

Conzelmann, Hans. *History of Primitive Christianity.* Translated by John E. Steely. Nashville: Abingdon, 1973.

————. *The Theology of St. Luke.* Translated by Geoffrey Buswell. New York: Harper; London: Faber, 1960.

Cullmann, Oscar. *The Early Church.* London: SCM, 1956.

————. *Peter: Disciple-Apostle-Martyr.* London: SCM, 1953.

Dalman, Gustaf. *The Words of Jesus.* Translated by D. M. Kay. Edinburgh: Clark, 1909.

Deissmann, Adolf. *Light from the Ancient East.* Translated by Lionel R. M. Strachan. Rev. ed. New York: Doran, 1927.

Dibelius, Martin. *Paul.* Edited by W. G. Kümmel. London: Longmans, 1953.

————. *Studies in the Acts of the Apostles.* London: SCM, 1956.

Dodd, C. H. *The Apostolic Preaching and Its Developments.* 1937. New York and Evanston: Harper, 1964.

Dunn, James D. G. *Baptism in the Holy Spirit.* Studies in Biblical Theology. 2d series 15. London: SCM, 1970.

Dupont, Jacques. *Études sur les Actes des Apôtres.* Lectio Divina 45. Paris: Cerf, 1967.

————. *Nouvelles Études sur les Actes des Apôtres.* Lectio Divina 118. Paris: Cerf, 1984.

————. *The Salvation of the Gentiles: Essays on the Acts of the Apostles.* Translated by John R. Keating. New York: Paulist, 1979.

————. *The Sources of the Acts.* Translated by Kathleen Pond. New York: Herder and Herder, 1964.

Ellis, E. Earle. *The Gospel of Luke*. New Century Bible. London: Oliphants, 1974.

————. "The Role of the Christian Prophet in Acts." In *Apostolic History and the Gospel*, edited by W. Ward Gasque and Ralph P. Martin. Exeter: Paternoster, 1970.

Epp, Eldon J. *The Theological Tendency of Codex Bezae Cantabrigiensis in Acts*. Cambridge: Cambridge University Press, 1966.

Foakes Jackson, F. J. *The Life of St. Paul*. London: Jonathan Cape, 1927.

————. *Peter: Prince of Apostles*. London: Hodder and Stoughton, 1927.

Foakes Jackson, F. J., and Kirsopp Lake. *The Beginnings of Christianity*. Vols. 1–5. London: Macmillan, 1920–33.

Gärtner, Bertil. *The Areopagus Speech and Natural Revelation*. Translated by C. H. King. Lund: Gleerup, 1955.

Gasque, W. Ward. *A History of the Criticism of the Acts of the Apostles*. Beiträge zur Geschichte der biblischen Exegese 17. Tübingen: Mohr, 1975.

Gasque W. Ward, and Ralph P. Martin, eds. *Apostolic History and the Gospel*. Exeter: Paternoster, 1970.

Goulder, M. D. *Type and History in Acts*. London: SPCK, 1964.

Hagner, Donald A., and Murray J. Harris, eds. *Pauline Studies*. Exeter: Paternoster; Grand Rapids: Eerdmans, 1980.

Harnack, A. *The Acts of the Apostles*. London: Williams and Norgate, 1909.

————. *Date of the Acts and of the Synoptic Gospels*. London: Williams and Norgate, 1911.

Harrison, Everett F. *The Apostolic Church*. Grand Rapids: Eerdmans, 1985.

Hengel, Martin. *Acts and the History of Earliest Christianity*. Translated by John Bowden. Philadelphia: Fortress, 1980.

————. *Between Jesus and Paul*. Translated by John Bowden. Philadelphia: Fortress, 1983.

Hobart, W. K. *The Medical Language of St. Luke*. Dublin: Hodges, Figgis; London: Longmans, Green, 1882.

Hock, Ronald F. *The Social Context of Paul's Ministry: Tentmaking and Apostleship*. Philadelphia: Fortress, 1980.

Hochner, Harold W. *Chronological Aspects of the Life of Christ*. Grand Rapids: Zondervan, 1976.

Hoekema, Anthony A. *Holy Spirit Baptism*. Grand Rapids: Eerdmans, 1972.

Hollander, Harm W. *Joseph as an Ethical Model in the Testaments of the Twelve Patriarchs*. Leiden: Brill, 1981.

Hooker, M. D., and S. G. Wilson. *Paul and Paulinism: Essays in Honour of C. K. Barrett*. London: SPCK, 1982.

Hyldahl, Niels. *Die Paulinische Chronologie*. Leiden: Brill, 1986.

Jeremias, Joachim. *Jerusalem in the Time of Jesus*. Philadelphia: Fortress, 1969.

————. *Unknown Sayings of Jesus*. Translated by Reginald H. Fuller. London: SPCK, 1957.

Jervell, Jacob. *Luke and the People of God: A New Look at Luke-Acts*. Minneapolis: Augsburg, 1972.

————. *The Unknown Paul*. Minneapolis: Augsburg, 1984.

Jewett, Robert. *A Chronology of Paul's Life*. Philadelphia: Fortress, 1979.

Judge, E. A. *The Social Pattern of Christian Groups in the First Century*. London: Tyndale, 1960.

Kaiser, Walter C. *The Uses of the Old Testament in the New*. Chicago: Moody, 1985.

Käsemann, Ernst. "The Disciples of John the Baptist in Ephesus." In *Essays on New Testament Themes*. Studies in Biblical Theology series 41. London: SCM, 1964.

Keck, Leander E., and J. Louis Martyn, eds. *Studies in Luke-Acts: Essays Presented in Honor of Paul Schubert*. Nashville: Abingdon, 1966.

Kilgallen, John J. *The Stephen Speech: A Literary and Redactional Study of Acts 7, 2–53*. Analecta Biblica 67. Rome: Biblical Institute, 1976.

Kistemaker, Simon J. *The Psalm Citations in the Epistle to the Hebrews*. Amsterdam: Van Soest, 1961.

Knox, John. *Chapters in a Life of Paul*. New York and Nashville: Abingdon-Cokesbury, 1950.

Lampe, G. W. H. " 'Grievous Wolves' (Acts 20:29)." In *Christ and Spirit in the New Testament: Studies in Honour of C. F. D. Moule*, edited by Barnabas Lindars and Stephen S. Smalley. Cambridge: Cambridge University Press, 1973.

———. *The Seal of the Spirit*. 2d ed. London: SPCK, 1967.

———. *St. Luke and the Church of Jerusalem*. London: Athlone, 1969.

Lohfink, Gerhard. *The Conversion of St. Paul: Narrative and History in Acts*. Translated and edited by Bruce J. Malina. Chicago: Franciscan Herald Press, 1976.

Long, William R. "The Trial of Paul in the Book of Acts: Historical, Literary, and Theological Considerations." Ph.D. diss., Brown University, 1982.

Longenecker, Richard N. *The Christology of Early Jewish Christianity*. Studies in Biblical Theology. 2d series 17. London: SCM, 1970.

Longenecker, Richard N., and Merrill C. Tenney, eds. *New Dimensions in New Testament Study*. Grand Rapids: Zondervan, 1974.

Luedemann, Gerd. *Paul, Apostle to the Gentiles: Studies in Chronology*. Translated by F. Stanley Jones. Philadelphia: Fortress, 1984.

———. *Paulus der Heidenapostel: Antipaulinismus im frühen Christentum*. Forschungen zur Religion und Literatur des Alten und Neuen Testaments 130. Göttingen: Vandenhoeck und Ruprecht, 1983.

MacDonald, William G. "Glossalalia in the New Testament." In *Speaking in Tongues: A Guide to Research on Glossolalia*, edited by Watson E. Mills. Grand Rapids: Eerdmans, 1986.

Maddox, R. *The Purpose of Luke-Acts*. Edinburgh: Clark, 1982.

Marshall, I. Howard. *Luke: Historian and Theologian*. Grand Rapids: Zondervan, 1971.

Martin, Ralph P. *Mark: Evangelist and Theologian*. Grand Rapids: Zondervan, 1972.

Michel, Hans-Joachim. *Die Abschiedsrede des Paulus an die Kirche Apg 20, 17–38: Motivgeschichtliche und theologische Bedeutung*. Munich: Kösel, 1973.

Mills, Watson E., ed. *Speaking in Tongues: A Guide to Research in Glossolalia*. Grand Rapids: Eerdmans, 1986.

Morris, Leon. *New Testament Theology*. Grand Rapids: Zondervan, Academie Books, 1986.

Ogg, George. *The Chronology of the Life of Paul*. London: Epworth, 1968.

O'Neill, J. C. *The Theology of Acts in Its Historical Setting*. London: SPCK, 1970.

Orosius, Paulus. *The Seven Books of History Against the Pagans*. Fathers of the Church series. Translated by Roy J. Deferrari. Washington, D.C.: Catholic University Press, 1964.

O'Toole, R. F. *The Christological Climax of Paul's Defense*. Analecta Biblica 78. Rome: Pontifical Institute, 1978.

Pathrapankal, J. "Christianity as a 'Way'." In *Les Actes des Apôtres: Traditions, Rédac-*

tion, Théologie, edited by J. Kremer. Bibliotheca Ephemeridium Theologicarum Lovaniensium 48. Lovain: Lovain University Press, 1979.

Pierce, Claude A. *Conscience in the New Testament.* Naperville, Ill.: Allenson, 1955.

Praeder, Susan M. "The Narrative Voyage: An Analysis and Interpretation of Acts 27–28." Ph.D. diss., Graduate Theological Union, 1980.

Puskas, Charles B., Jr. "The Conclusion of Luke-Acts: An Investigation of the Literary Function and Theological Significance of Acts 28:16–31." Ph.D. diss., St. Louis University, 1980.

Ramsay, William M. *The Church in the Roman Empire Before A.D. 170.* London: Hodder and Stoughton, 1907.

———. *The Cities of St. Paul: Their Influence on His Life and Thought.* 1907. Grand Rapids: Baker, 1963.

———. *Pauline and Other Studies in Early Christian History.* Limited Editions Library. 1906. Grand Rapids: Baker, 1970.

———. *Pictures of the Apostolic Church: Studies in the Book of Acts.* 1910. Grand Rapids: Baker, 1959.

———. *St. Paul the Traveller and the Roman Citizen.* 1897. Grand Rapids: Baker, 1962.

Rehwinkel, Alfred Martin. *The Voice of Conscience.* St. Louis: Concordia, 1956.

Ridderbos, Herman N. *The Speeches of Peter in the Acts of the Apostles.* London: Tyndale, 1962.

Robinson, J. A. T. *Redating the New Testament.* London: SCM, 1976.

———. *Twelve New Testament Studies.* Studies in Biblical Theology 34. London: SCM, 1962.

Robinson, N. H. G. *Christ and Conscience.* London: Nisbet, 1956.

Rougé, Jean. *Ships and Fleets of the Ancient Mediterranean.* Translated by Susan Frazer. Middletown, Conn.: Wesleyan University Press, 1981.

Ryken, Leland. *Words of Life: A Literary Introduction to the New Testament.* Grand Rapids: Baker, 1987.

Sanders, J. T. *The Jews in Luke-Acts.* London: SCM, 1987.

Scharlemann, Martin H. *Stephen: A Singular Saint.* Analecta Biblica 34. Rome: Biblical Institute, 1968.

Sherwin-White, A. N. *The Roman Citizenship.* 2d ed. Oxford: Clarendon, 1973.

———. *Roman Society and Roman Law in the New Testament.* 1963. Grand Rapids: Baker, 1978.

Smallwood, E. M. *The Jews under Roman Rule.* Leiden: Brill, 1976.

Smith, James. *The Voyage and Shipwreck of St. Paul.* 3d ed. London: Longmans, Green, 1866.

Stonehouse, Ned B. *Paul Before the Areopagus and Other New Testament Studies.* Grand Rapids: Eerdmans, 1957.

Suhl, A. *Paulus und seine Briefe: Ein Beitrag zur paulinischen Chronologie.* Gütersloh: Mohn, 1975.

Talbert, Charles H. *Literary Patterns, Theological Themes and the Genre of Luke-Acts.* Missoula, Mont.: Scholars, 1974.

———, ed. *Perspectives on Luke-Acts.* Edinburgh: Clark, 1978.

———, ed. *Luke-Acts: New Perspectives from the Society of Biblical Literature Seminar.* New York: Crossroad, 1984.

Taylor, Vincent. *The Names of Jesus.* London: Macmillan, 1953.

Thompson, Barry, ed. *Scripture: Meaning and Method.* Hull, England: Hull University Press, 1987.

van Unnik, W. C. *Tarsus or Jerusalem: The City of Paul's Youth.* Translated by George Ogg. London: Epworth, 1962.

van Veldhuizen, A. *Markus. De Neef van Barnabas.* Kampen: Kok, 1933.

Wilcox, Max. *The Semitisms of Acts.* Oxford: Clarendon, 1965.

Williams, C. S. C. *Alterations to the Text of the Synoptic Gospels and Acts.* Oxford: Blackwell, 1951.

Zehnle, Richard F. *Peter's Pentecost Discourse: Tradition and Lukan Reinterpretation in Peter's Speeches of Acts 2 and 3.* Society of Biblical Literature Monograph series 15. Edited by Robert A. Kraft. Nashville: Abingdon, 1971.

Tools

Aland, Kurt, ed. *Synopsis Quattuor Evangeliorum.* 4th rev. ed. Stuttgart: Württembergische Bibelanstalt, 1967.

Archer, Gleason L., Jr. *Encyclopedia of Bible Difficulties.* Grand Rapids: Zondervan, 1982.

Bauer, Walter. *A Greek-English Lexicon of the New Testament and Other Early Christian Literature.* 4th revised and augmented edition by F. Wilbur Gingrich and Frederick W. Danker from Walter Bauer's 5th edition. Chicago and London: University of Chicago Press, 1979.

Berkhof, Louis. *Principles of Biblical Interpretation.* 2d ed. Grand Rapids: Baker, 1952.

———. *Systematic Theology.* 2d rev. ed. Grand Rapids: Eerdmans, 1941.

Blass, Friedrich, and Albert Debrunner. *A Greek Grammar of the New Testament and Other Early Christian Literature.* Translated and revised by Robert Funk. Chicago: University of Chicago Press, 1961.

Bromiley, Geoffrey W., ed. *The International Standard Bible Encyclopedia.* Rev. ed. 4 vols. Grand Rapids: Eerdmans, 1979–88.

Brown, Colin, ed. *New International Dictionary of New Testament Theology.* 3 vols. Grand Rapids: Zondervan, 1975–78.

Bruce, F. F. *New Testament History.* 1969. Garden City, N.Y.: Doubleday, 1971.

Burton, E. D. *Moods and Tenses of New Testament Greek.* Edinburgh: Clark, 1898.

Charlesworth, James H., ed. *The Old Testament Pseudepigrapha.* 2 vols. Garden City, N.Y.: Doubleday, 1983.

Dana, H. E., and Julius R. Mantey. *A Manual Grammar of the Greek New Testament.* 1927. New York: Macmillan, 1967.

Danby, Herbert, ed. *The Mishnah.* London: Oxford University Press, 1933.

Deissmann, Adolf. *Bible Studies.* Reprint ed. Winona Lake, Ind.: Alpha, 1979.

Elwell, Walter A., ed. *Baker Encyclopedia of the Bible.* 2 vols. Grand Rapids: Baker, 1988.

———, ed. *Evangelical Dictionary of Theology.* Grand Rapids: Baker, 1984.

Epstein, Isidore, ed. *The Babylonian Talmud.* 18 vols. London: Soncino, 1948–52.

Eusebius. *Ecclesiastical History.* Translated by J. E. L. Oulton. Loeb Classical Library series. 2 vols. Cambridge: Harvard University Press, 1980.

Farstad, Arthur R., and Zane C. Hodges. *The Greek New Testament According to the Majority Text.* Nashville: Nelson, 1982.

Finegan, Jack. *The Archeology of the New Testament: The Mediterranean World of the Early Christian Apostles.* Boulder, Colo.: Westview; London: Croon Helm, 1981.

Goold, E. P., ed. *The Apostolic Fathers*. Translated by Kirsopp Lake. Loeb Classical Library series. 2 vols. Cambridge: Harvard University Press; London: Heinemann, 1976.

―――, ed. *Appian's Roman History*. Translated by Horace White. Loeb Classical Library series. 4 vols. Cambridge: Harvard University Press; London: Heinemann, 1979.

―――, ed. *Eusebius*. Translated by Kirsopp Lake. Loeb Classical Library series. 2 vols. Cambridge: Harvard University Press; London: Heinemann, 1980.

Guthrie, Donald. *New Testament Introduction*. 3d ed. Downers Grove: Inter-Varsity, 1971.

―――. *New Testament Theology*. Downers Grove: Inter-Varsity, 1981.

Hanna, Robert. *A Grammatical Aid to the Greek New Testament*. Grand Rapids: Baker, 1983.

Hennecke, Edgar. *New Testament Apocrypha*. Edited by Wilhelm Schneemelcher. 2 vols. Philadelphia: Westminster, 1963–64.

Henry, Carl F. H., ed. *Baker's Dictionary of Christian Ethics*. Grand Rapids: Baker, 1973.

Huck, Albert. *Synopsis of the First Three Gospels*. Revised by Hans Lietzmann. 9th ed. Oxford: Blackwell, 1957.

Josephus, Flavius. *Antiquities*. Loeb Classical Library series. London: Heinemann; New York: Putnam, 1966–76.

―――. *Life* and *Against Apion*. Loeb Classical Library series. London: Heinemann; New York: Putnam, 1966–76.

―――. *Wars of the Jews*. Loeb Classical Library series. London: Heinemann; New York: Putnam, 1966–76.

Kittel, Gerhard, and Gerhard Friedrich, eds. *Theological Dictionary of the New Testament*. Translated by Geoffrey W. Bromiley. 10 vols. Grand Rapids: Eerdmans, 1964–76.

Ladd, George E. *A Theology of the New Testament*. Grand Rapids: Eerdmans, 1974.

Mattill, A. J., and M. B. Mattill. *A Classified Bibliography of Literature on the Acts of the Apostles*. New Testament Tools and Studies 7. Leiden: Brill, 1966.

Metzger, Bruce M. *A Textual Commentary on the Greek New Testament*. 3d corrected ed. London and New York: United Bible Societies, 1975.

―――, ed. *The Oxford Annotated Apocrypha of the Old Testament*. New York: Oxford University Press, 1965.

Mills, Watson E. *A Bibliography of the Periodical Literature on the Acts of the Apostles, 1962–84*. Novum Testamentum Supplement 58. Leiden: Brill, 1986.

Morris, Leon. *New Testament Theology*. Grand Rapids: Zondervan, Academie Books, 1986.

Moule, C. F. D. *An Idiom-Book of New Testament Greek*. 2d ed. Cambridge: Cambridge University Press, 1960.

Moulton, James Hope. *A Grammar of New Testament Greek*. Vol. 1, *Prolegomena*. Edinburgh: Clark, 1906.

Nestle E., and Kurt Aland. *Novum Testamentum Graece*. 26th ed. Stuttgart: Deutsche Bibelstiftung, 1981.

Roberts, Alexander, and James Donaldson, eds. *The Ante-Nicene Fathers: Translations of Writings of the Fathers down to A.D. 325*. 14 vols. Grand Rapids: Eerdmans, 1899–1900.

Robertson, A. T. *A Grammar of the Greek New Testament in the Light of Historical Research*. Nashville: Broadman, 1934.

Ropes, James Hardy. *The Text of Acts.* Vol. 3 of *The Beginnings of Christianity.* Reprint. Grand Rapids: Baker, 1965.

Roth, Cecil, ed. *Encyclopaedia Judaica.* 16 vols. New York: Macmillan, 1972.

Schürer, Emil. *The History of the Jewish People in the Age of Jesus Christ (175 B.C.–A.D. 135).* Revised and edited by Geza Vermes and Fergus Millar. 3 vols. Edinburgh: Clark, 1973–87.

Strack, H. L., and P. Billerbeck. *Kommentar zum Neuen Testament aus Talmud und Midrasch.* 5 vols. Munich: Beck, 1922–28.

Tenney, Merrill C., ed. *The Zondervan Pictorial Encyclopedia of the Bible.* 5 vols. Grand Rapids: Zondervan, 1975.

Thayer, Joseph H. *A Greek-English Lexicon of the New Testament.* New York, Cincinnati, and Chicago: American Book Co., 1889.

Trench, R. C. H. *Synonyms of the Greek New Testament.* 1854. Grand Rapids: Eerdmans, 1953.

Turner, Nigel. *A Grammar of New Testament Greek.* Vol. 3. Edinburgh: Clark, 1963.

———. *Grammatical Insights into the New Testament.* Edinburgh: Clark, 1965.

Index of Authors

Acworth, Angus, 7 n. 11, 946 n. 2
Aland, Kurt, 90 n. 32, 270 n. 65, 539 n. 9
Alden, Robert L., 255n
Alford, Henry, 47 n. 5, 53 n. 15, 84, 91n, 93 n. 36, 111n, 193, 194 n. 24, 202 n. 36, 224 n. 7, 228 n. 17, 241 n. 6, 258 n. 42, 262 n. 52, z297 n. 23, 306n, 352 n. 43, 357n, 374 n. 11, 386 n. 30, 392n, 422 n. 32, 445 n. 29, 525 n. 43, 549 n. 27, 554 n. 40, 585 n. 20, 653 n. 12, 680 n. 6, 698 n. 49, 752n, 838 n. 16, 841 n. 21, 916 n. 6
Allen, George H., 933 n. 51
Appian, 873n
Archer, Gleason L., Jr., 243 n. 12, 433 n. 7
Argyle, A. W., 691 n. 34
Aristotle, 738 n. 62
Augustine, 313 n. 56
Aune, David E., 298 n. 26, 690 n. 31
Avi-Yonah, Michael, 767 n. 48

Baehr, Jürgen, 165n
Baltensweiler, Hans, 312 n. 54
Barnard, L. W., 13 n. 25
Barnes, T. D., 628 n. 38
Barrett, C. K., 155 n. 19, 669 n. 49, 678, 723 n. 22, 918 n. 13
Bauer, Walter, 46 n. 1, 64 n. 39, 105 n. 59, 113 n. 77, 156 n. 20, 158 n. 28, 161 n. 32, 169 n. 51, 177n, 187n, 198 n. 32, 200n, 223n, 245 n. 14, 265 n. 54, 266 n. 58, 273 n. 71, 280 n. 84, 311 n. 51, 334 n. 9, 348 n. 34, 350 n. 41, 359n, 448 n. 38, 489n, 505 n. 6, 515 n. 29, 525 n. 45, 542 n. 14, 569 n. 71, 588 n. 28, 595 n. 41, 614 n. 10, 616n, 627 n. 33, 629 nn. 39, 40, 633 n. 50, 637n, 649 n. 2, 657n, 662 n. 33, 689 n. 28, 690 n. 32, 691, 701 n. 55, 705 n. 60, 717 n. 13, 734 n. 48, 736 n. 55, 738 n. 59, 739 n. 65,

747 n. 8, 748 n. 11, 755 n. 25, 763 n. 42, 764 n. 44, 769 n. 52, 781 n. 5, 801 n. 45, 812 n. 12, 815 n. 22, 836n, 844 n. 28, 849 n. 35, 874 n. 36, 877 n. 40, 894 n. 24, 895 n. 25, 899 n. 37, 903 n. 46, 904n, 908 n. 53, 925 n. 30, 933 n. 48, 950 n. 11, 967 n. 43
Beasley-Murray, G. R., 790 n. 27
Beck, Hartmut, 393 n. 44
Behm, Johannes, 835 n. 5
Bengel, John Albert, 3 n. 2, 53 n. 14, 66 n. 43, 86n, 136 n. 29, 161 n. 34, 207 n. 44, 258 n. 41, 259 n. 44, 276, 276n, 318, 318 n. 65, 371 n. 5, 377 n. 16, 394 n. 48, 398 n. 57, 399n, 455 n. 5, 470 n. 36, 472, 517n, 541, 591, 631 n. 46, 691 n. 35, 726 n. 29, 731 n. 40, 792n, 834 n. 3, 862 n. 7, 866n, 888 n. 12, 931 n. 46, 948 n. 5
Benoit, P., 427 n. 42
Berkhof, Louis, 105 n. 60, 735 n. 49, 792n
Bertram, Georg, 593 n. 38
Best, Ernest, 456 n. 9
Beyer, Hermann Wolfgang, 668 n. 47, 732 n. 43
Bietenhard, Hans, 77 n. 4, 102 n. 53, 125n, 168 n. 48, 198 n. 30, 271 n. 69, 419 n. 26, 551 n. 31, 656 n. 21, 800 n. 43, 808 n. 1, 887 n. 10
Billerbeck, P., 46 n. 2, 58 n. 29, 75 n. 2, 83 n. 15, 84 n. 19, 139 n. 33, 146 n. 2, 210 n. 49, 211 n. 52, 222n, 228 n. 16, 242n, 253 n. 35, 262 n. 51, 289 n. 6, 296 n. 21, 313 n. 56, 376n, 387 n. 31, 441 n. 23, 472 n. 42, 483 n. 59, 578 n. 2, 652 n. 10, 663 n. 36, 760 n. 32, 761 n. 35, 767 n. 46, 781 n. 7, 809 nn. 4, 6, 811 n. 9, 902 n. 44, 921 n. 21, 936 n. 58
Black, Mark, 798 n. 38

Blackman, E. C., 220 n. 3

Blaiklock, E. M., 228 n. 19, 341, 341 n. 20, 422, 459n, 509 n. 17, 523n, 706 n. 64, 775n, 814 n. 18

Blair, E. P., 791 n. 29

Blass, Friedrich, 33, 110 n. 70, 163 n. 37, 164 n. 38, 172 n. 54, 250n, 252 n. 32, 273 n. 72, 342 n. 24, 402 n. 67, 448 n. 37, 457 n. 11, 464 n. 23, 499 n. 89, 520 n. 36, 526 n. 49, 581 n. 10, 607 n. 63, 615 n. 12, 627 n. 33, 665n, 670 n. 50, 707 n. 67, 723 n. 21, 739 n. 66, 747 n. 7, 763 n. 40, 768n, 784 n. 12, 815 n. 21, 818n, 825 n. 38, 845 nn. 31, 32, 854 n. 56, 862 n. 9, 872 n. 32, 886 n. 8, 891 n. 17, 903 n. 46, 909n, 917 n. 10, 938 n. 63, 956 n. 25

Blinzler, J., 433 n. 6

Borchert, Gerald L., 589 n. 31, 721 n. 19

Bornkamm, Günther, 427 n. 43

Bousset, Wilhelm, 102 n. 54, 419 n. 28

Bowers, W. P., 584n

Bratcher, Robert G., 94 n. 39, 336 n. 13

Braun, Michael A., 552 nn. 36, 37, 554 n. 40

Brinkman, J. A., 82 n. 13

Brock, S. P., 176n

Bromiley, Geoffrey W., 302 n. 34

Broughton, T. R. S., 370 n. 2, 916 n. 5

Brown, Colin, 135 n. 25, 155 n. 18, 260 n. 45, 295 n. 16, 373n, 393 n. 44, 475 n. 48, 507 n. 11, 512 n. 22, 546 nn. 19, 20, 556 n. 44, 642 n. 75, 785 n. 14, 808 n. 2

Bruce, F. F., 16 n. 35, 17 n. 39, 26 n. 61, 28n, 32 n. 70, 33, 33 n. 73, 67n, 81 n. 11, 82 n. 14, 115n, 126 n. 12, 224 nn. 8, 9, 249 n. 24, 262, 262 n. 50, 279n, 302 n. 35, 332n, 346 n. 32, 348, 348 n. 36, 349 nn. 38, 39, 364 n. 64, 370 n. 3, 435 n. 11, 474 n. 46, 514 n. 25, 535 n. 5, 552 n. 34, 554 n. 42, 571n, 580 n. 9, 588 n. 27, 600 n. 48, 601 n. 50, 620 n. 24, 631 n. 46, 633 n. 52, 640 n. 70, 664 n. 38, 681 n. 9, 688 n. 24, 706 n. 64, 718n, 728 n. 32, 729 n. 35, 735 n. 52, 747 n. 9, 754 n. 24, 799n, 810 n. 8, 816 n. 24, 826 n. 40, 828 n. 49, 834 n. 3, 838 n. 14, 841 n. 22, 868 n. 20, 878n, 895 n. 26, 906 n. 49, 915 n. 3, 921 n. 22, 940 n. 68, 941 n. 71

Büchsel, Friedrich, 556 n. 44

Budesheim, Thomas L., 795 n. 34

Bultmann, Rudolf, 102 n. 54

Burge, Gary M., 688 n. 24

Burton, E. D., 735 n. 50

Cadbury, H. J., 8 n. 17, 11 n. 22, 20n, 135 n. 26, 189 n. 11, 220 n. 3, 241 n. 8, 245, 245 n. 16, 247 n. 20, 275n, 294, 294 n. 15, 296 n. 21, 321 n. 70, 343 n. 26, 360 n. 57, 362 n. 61, 382 n. 24, 423 n. 34, 432 n. 1, 437 n. 17, 454 n. 3, 464 n. 22, 470 n. 36, 488 n. 66, 496n, 524n, 540n, 549 n. 26, 587 n. 25, 588 n. 28, 594 n. 39, 595 n. 42, 605 n. 58, 615 n. 14, 617 n. 17, 626n, 649 n. 4, 652 n. 11, 653 n. 14, 668 n. 45, 695 n. 40, 697 n. 46, 706 n. 65, 714 n. 7, 717 n. 14, 723 n. 23, 726 n. 29, 733 n. 45, 759n, 769 n. 52, 774 n. 60, 776, 782 n. 9, 788 n. 20, 797 n. 35, 802 n. 49, 810 n. 7, 811 n. 9, 824 n. 35, 838 n. 15, 867, 874, 892 n. 20, 903 n. 46, 906 n. 49, 927 nn. 34, 39, 950 n. 11, 967 nn. 40, 42

Calvin, John, 49 n. 8, 59n, 88 n. 26, 99 n. 49, 108 n. 65, 115, 123 n. 9, 130 n. 19, 148 n. 7, 153 n. 16, 173 n. 56, 183 n. 4, 210 n. 50, 243 n. 11, 258 n. 41, 259 n. 43, 274 n. 75, 278 n. 80, 298 n. 24, 299 n. 28, 304 n. 38, 309, 309 n. 48, 331n, 361, 362 n. 59, 372 n. 7, 374 n. 11, 383 n. 26, 437 n. 18, 444n, 446 n. 35, 456 n. 9, 464 n. 21, 472 n. 43, 494 n. 81, 496n, 518n, 545 n. 17, 552 n. 36, 556, 569 n. 70, 591n, 593 n. 37, 603 n. 53, 631 n. 47, 669 n. 48, 679, 686 n. 20, 691 n. 34, 695 n. 42, 715, 726 n. 29, 745 n. 4, 758n, 812 n. 11, 820 n. 32, 874, 890n, 898 n. 33, 922 n. 23, 932n, 940, 949 n. 8, 962n

Campbell, Robert C., 570 n. 74

Capper, B. J., 183 n. 5

Carter, Charles W., 519 n. 35

Casey, Robert P., 296 n. 20

Casson, Lionel, 921 n. 20, 927 n. 35, 939 n. 67

Catchpole, David R., 556 n. 44

Charlesworth, James H., 168 n. 46

Cheetham, F. P., 114 n. 79

Chrysostom, 750

Cicero, 604 n. 56, 620 n. 23, 798, 955 n. 23

Clark, Albert C., 32, 32 n. 69, 688 n. 26, 714, 838 n. 14, 851 n. 44, 878n, 884n, 956 n. 24

Clark, D. J., 928 n. 42

Clement of Alexandria, 3 n. 1, 20, 636 nn. 61, 62, 749n

Clement of Rome, 22, 22 n. 55

Coenen, Lothar, 54 n. 19, 427 n. 43, 526 n. 48, 732 n. 43, 782 n. 10

Cohn, H., 214 n. 56

Confucius, 738 n. 63

Conzelmann, Hans, 7 n. 13, 15 n. 28, 18 n. 45, 22 n. 54, 593 n. 36, 598n, 630 n. 44, 640 n. 70, 729 n. 34, 731 n. 39, 791 n. 29, 798 n. 38, 802 n. 48, 814 nn. 16, 17, 877, 915 n. 1, 939 n. 66, 948 n. 6
Currie, Stuart D., 400 n. 63

Dahl, Nils A., 551 n. 33
Dalman, Gustaf, 296 n. 21
Dana, H. E., 97 n. 43, 186n, 398 n. 58, 410 n. 8, 416 n. 14, 449 n. 41, 499 n. 91, 572 n. 77, 815 n. 20, 938 n. 64
Dau, W. H. T., 790 n. 26
Dayton, Wilber T., 147 n. 4
de Waard, J., 553 n. 38
de Zwaan, J., 31 n. 66, 865 n. 12
Debrunner, Albert, 110 n. 70, 163 n. 37, 164 n. 38, 172 n. 54, 250n, 252 n. 32, 273 n. 72, 342 n. 24, 402 n. 67, 448 n. 37, 457 n. 11, 464 n. 23, 499 n. 89, 520 n. 36, 526 n. 49, 581 n. 10, 607 n. 63, 615 n. 12, 627 n. 33, 665n, 670 n. 50, 707 n. 67, 723 n. 21, 739 n. 66, 747 n. 7, 763 n. 40, 768n, 784 n. 12, 815 n. 21, 818n, 825 n. 38, 845 nn. 31, 32, 854 n. 56, 862 n. 9, 872 n. 32, 886 n. 8, 891 n. 17, 903 n. 46, 909n, 917 n. 10, 938 n. 63, 956 n. 25
Decock, P. B., 316 n. 61
Deissmann, Adolf, 140 n. 35, 176, 176n, 295 n. 17, 526 n. 48, 687 n. 22, 690 n. 32, 879 n. 45
Delebecque, Édouard, 581 n. 12, 691 n. 34, 839n
Delitzsch, Franz, 63 n. 37, 97 n. 41, 965 n. 38
Delling, Gerhard, 47 n. 4, 635 n. 56, 968 n. 44
Denzinger, Heinrich J. D., 302 n. 33
Derrett, J. Duncan M., 304 n. 37
des Places, Édouard, 635 n. 59, 639 n. 67
Dibelius, Martin, 7 n. 13, 9 n. 19, 557 n. 46, 598n, 635 n. 58, 779n, 795, 814 n. 16, 939 n. 66
Dio Cassius, 15 n. 29, 17 n. 36, 425 n. 38, 649 n. 3, 659 n. 27, 706 n. 64, 799n
Diodorus Siculus, 4 n. 4, 587 n. 24, 946 n. 1
Dodd, C. H., 393 n. 46
Donaldson, Terence I., 774 n. 61
Dulon, Günter, 93 n. 37
Dunn, James D. G., 75 n. 2, 77 n. 5, 134 n. 23, 297 n. 22, 301 n. 32, 303n, 678 n. 3, 681 n. 8, 790 n. 25
Dupont, Jacques, 5 n. 7, 34 n. 75, 47 n. 4, 454 n. 2, 466 n. 28, 485 n. 61, 525 n. 44, 551 n. 33, 630 n. 44, 641 n. 72, 723 n. 23, 724n, 873n, 902 n. 43

Earle, Ralph, 519 n. 35
Ebel, Günther, 330 n. 4, 684 n. 15
Edwards, David Miall, 181n
Eichler, Johannes, 614 n. 11
Ellis, E. Earle, 751 n. 18
Enroth, Ronald M., 298 n. 25
Epp, Eldon J., 33 n. 71
Esser, Hans-Helmut, 725 n. 26, 736 n. 56
Eusebius, 5, 5 n. 9, 15 n. 29, 20, 22 n. 54, 68 n. 46, 281n, 288 n. 2, 425 n. 38, 440n, 446 n. 33, 550 n. 28, 597 n. 43, 643, 749n, 760
Evans, Morris O., 701 n. 56
Ewing, William, 358 n. 54
Exum, C., 723 n. 24

Farstad, Arthur L., 493 n. 78, 567 n. 66, 838 n. 12
Fee, Gordon D., 563 n. 56
Feinberg, Charles L., 269n
Fensham, F. Charles, 99 n. 47
Finegan, 923 n. 25
Finn, T. M., 371 n. 4
Foerster, Werner, 393 n. 44, 592n
France, Richard T., 129 n. 16
Friedrich, Gerhard, 454 n. 2
Fudge, E., 633 n. 50
Fürst, Dieter, 613 n. 7

Gapp, Kenneth S., 425 n. 40
Gärtner, Bertil, 633 n. 52, 635 n. 56, 639 n. 65
Gasque, W. Ward, 7 n. 12, 9 n. 19
Gess, Johannes, 316 n. 60
Gilchrist, J. M., 867 n. 18
Gispen, W. H., 251 n. 28
Glasser, Arthur F., 75 n. 2
Glasson, T. F., 9 n. 19
Glombitza, Otto, 475 n. 47, 585 n. 20
Glover, Richard, 454 n. 4
Goetzmann, Jürgen, 105 n. 59, 372 n. 6, 901 n. 41
Goldsmith, D., 484n
Goodspeed, Edgar J., 653 n. 13
Gordon, A. B., 62 n. 35
Gordon, R., 474 n. 45
Goulder, M. D., 29 n. 65, 509 n. 18
Gray, J., 266 n. 59
Green, E. M. B., 561n
Grelot, Pierre, 495n

Grosheide, F. W., 31 n. 67, 52n, 79n, 92 n.
34, 159n, 163 n. 36, 193 n. 22, 211 n. 52,
243 n. 12, 270 n. 64, 288 n. 3, 332n, 335 n.
12, 349 n. 37, 379n, 395 n. 53, 410 n. 7,
437 n. 15, 463 n. 19, 488 n. 67, 507 n. 12,
514 n. 26, 524n, 525 n. 44, 545 n. 16, 551
n. 32, 568 n. 69, 593 n. 37, 635 n. 57, 697
n. 47, 705 n. 63, 762 n. 39, 780 n. 3, 797 n.
36, 809 n. 5, 931 n. 45
Grundmann, Walter, 156 n. 20, 725 n. 26
Günther, Ebel, 684 n. 15
Günther, Walther, 191 n. 19
Guthrie, Donald, 23 n. 57, 26 n. 61, 48, 48 n.
6, 56 n. 23, 89 n. 28, 103 n. 55, 133n, 141
n. 38, 166 n. 42, 169 n. 49, 183 n. 3, 194 n.
26, 261 n. 48, 293 n. 11, 301, 301 n. 31,
343 n. 25, 346 n. 32, 391 n. 42, 414n,
473n, 492 n. 75, 496n, 505 n. 5, 538n, 547
n. 23, 559 n. 51, 584n, 591n, 683n, 730 n.
36, 733, 750 n. 16, 789 n. 21, 961 n. 35
Güting, E., 82 n. 13

Haacker, Klaus, 658 n. 25, 885 n. 3, 890n
Haenchen, Ernst, 7 n. 13, 18 n. 45, 84 n. 20,
94 n. 39, 97 n. 42, 155 n. 19, 174 n. 58,
185 n. 6, 190 n. 13, 194 n. 25, 316 n. 61,
346 n. 30, 363 n. 62, 436 n. 14, 486 n. 64,
515 n. 28, 525 n. 45, 579 n. 7, 598n, 616n,
634 n. 55, 714 n. 7, 715 n. 9, 757n, 761 n.
35, 802 n. 48, 811 n. 9, 816 n. 24, 840 n.
20, 841, 877 n. 41, 893 n. 21, 927 n. 36,
934 n. 56, 937 n. 62, 939 n. 66
Hagner, Donald A., 146 n. 3, 200n, 498 n.
88, 521 n. 39
Hahn, Hans-Christoph, 170 n. 53, 305 n. 39,
781 n. 8, 785 n. 14, 808 n. 2
Hanna, Robert, 55 n. 20, 103 n. 56, 110 n.
69, 122n, 138n, 169 n. 50, 245 n. 15, 260
n. 46, 317 n. 63, 364 n. 66, 542 n. 12, 607
n. 61, 632 n. 49, 670 n. 52, 708 n. 69, 730
n. 37, 737 n. 57, 801 n. 46, 825 n. 38, 853
n. 54, 868 n. 21, 876 n. 38, 938 n. 63, 959n
Harder, Günther, 689 n. 27, 793n
Harrison, Everett F., 80n, 89 n. 29, 102 n. 52,
158 n. 29, 191 n. 18, 205n, 295 n. 17, 334
n. 10, 342 n. 22, 361n, 377 n. 15, 417 n.
22, 455 n. 7, 507 n. 12, 525 n. 45, 566 n.
62, 578 n. 3, 579 n. 7, 613 n. 6, 707 n. 66,
712 n. 2, 781 n. 6, 949
Harrison, Roland K., 358 n. 54
Hasel, Gerhard F., 147 n. 19
Hawthorne, Gerald F., 125n, 578 n. 3, 684 n.
17

Hedrick, C. W., 330 n. 5
Hemer, Colin J., 5 n. 8, 7 n. 11, 11 n. 24, 17
n. 39, 19 n. 49, 371 n. 4, 462 n. 18, 467 n.
30, 477n, 509 n. 17, 534 n. 1, 583 n. 14,
588 n. 27, 628 n. 38, 658 n. 25, 662 n. 32,
695 n. 40, 706 n. 64, 714 n. 7, 731 n. 38,
775n, 825 n. 39, 826 n. 40, 860 n. 4, 872 n.
33, 915 n. 2, 918 n. 13, 919 n. 14, 920 n.
17, 921 n. 22, 922 n. 24, 926 n. 31, 927 n.
34, 940 n. 68, 946 n. 2, 951 n. 14, 953 n.
18
Hendriksen, William, 352 n. 44, 465 n. 25,
534 n. 2, 568 n. 68, 580 n. 8, 600 n. 49,
639 n. 66, 667 n. 42, 703 n. 57, 916 n. 7
Hengel, Martin, 4 n. 4, 419 n. 26, 534 n. 3,
547 n. 23, 668 n. 45
Hennecke, Edgar, 514 n. 27
Herntrich, Volkmar, 554 n. 41
Herodotus, 46 n. 1
Hess, Klaus, 455 n. 6
Hiebert, D. Edmond, 181n, 669 n. 49
Hilgert, Earle, 744 n. 2
Hill, David, 443n
Hock, Ronald F., 649 n. 4, 655n
Hodges, Zane C., 493 n. 78, 567 n. 66, 838 n.
12
Hoehner, Harold W., 75 n. 1
Hoekema, Anthony A., 401 n. 64, 682 n. 10
Hoerber, Robert O., 649 n. 3
Holwerda, David E., 55 n. 22, 112 n. 75
Honeyman, A. M., 947 n. 4
Horace, 955 n. 22
House, Colin, 380n
Howard, David M., Jr., 112 n. 74
Huck, Albert, 417 n. 18
Hughes, Philip Edgcumbe, 712 n. 1
Hunter, S. F., 462 n. 17

Irenaeus, 3 n. 1, 20, 295 n. 19, 320 n. 69
Irvin, Dorothy, 590n

Jackson, F. J. Foakes, 9 n. 20
Jacobs, Paul, 835 n. 5
Jamieson, Howard M., 363 n. 63
Jeremias, Joachim, 121 n. 6, 129 n. 16, 165n,
220 n. 1, 261 n. 48, 316 n. 60, 443n, 738 n.
60
Jerome, 20
Jervell, Jacob, 780 n. 3, 900n
Jewett, Robert, 19 n. 48
Josephus, 4 n. 4, 15 nn. 29, 30, 31, 32, 16 n.
33, 17, 18, 18 nn. 40, 41, 43, 19, 19 nn. 48,
50, 22, 23, 23 n. 58, 46 n. 2, 83, 83 nn. 16,

17, 18, 88 n. 27, 98 n. 46, 120 n. 3, 121 n.
5, 127 n. 13, 146 nn. 1, 2, 149 n. 8, 150,
150 n. 11, 151 nn. 12, 13, 174 n. 58, 211
nn. 51, 53, 220 n. 1, 225, 225 n. 12, 228 n.
14, 240 n. 5, 241 n. 8, 248 nn. 22, 23, 252
n. 30, 254n, 280 nn. 85, 86, 281n, 292n,
311 n. 53, 329 n. 3, 356 nn. 49, 50, 358 n.
54, 360 n. 56, 370 n. 1, 382 n. 22, 408 n. 2,
417 nn. 19, 20, 425 nn. 38, 40, 432 nn. 2,
3, 4, 435 n. 12, 437 n. 16, 445 n. 30, 446 n.
32, 447 n. 49, 471, 472, 475 n. 49, 497 n.
85, 583 n. 15, 625 n. 30, 659 n. 28, 663 nn.
35, 37, 684 n. 16, 687, 688 n. 23, 705 n. 62,
750 n. 15, 760 n. 33, 761 n. 36, 767 n. 46,
769 n. 51, 771 n. 55, 772 nn. 56, 57, 774
nn. 59, 61, 798 n. 37, 802 n. 51, 809 nn. 3,
4, 814 n. 19, 826 n. 40, 828 n. 46, 829 n.
50, 835 n. 4, 840 n. 19, 843 n. 24, 850n,
851 nn. 40, 41, 43, 852 n. 49, 853 nn. 51,
52, 859 n. 1, 860 nn. 3, 5, 6, 862 n. 8,
863n, 870 nn. 23, 24, 25, 871 nn. 26, 27,
28, 29, 877 n. 43, 888 n. 11, 919, 953 n. 16,
954n, 955 n. 21, 957, 961
Judge, E. A., 354n, 465 n. 26, 617 n. 19
Justin Martyr, 292n, 295, 295 n. 18
Juvenal, 417 n. 21, 871 n. 28

Kaiser, Walter C., Jr., 99 n. 50, 552 n. 35, 553
n. 39
Käsemann, Ernst, 678 n. 2
Kaye, B. N., 560 n. 52
Kepple, Robert J., 813 n. 14, 888 n. 13
Kilgallen, John J., 13 n. 26, 886 n. 7
Kilpatrick, G. D., 82 n. 12, 667 n. 44, 699 n.
52, 824 n. 35
Kistemaker, Simon J., 113 n. 76, 131n, 154n,
253 n. 36, 268 n. 62, 483 n. 59, 485 n. 62,
550 n. 29, 734 n. 47
Kittel, Gerhard, 300n, 787n
Klappert, Bertold, 409 n. 3
Klijn, A. F. J., 13 n. 25
Knapp, Gary L., 197 n. 29
Koivisto, R. A., 249 n. 24
Kraabel, A. T., 371 n. 4
Kreitzer, Larry J., 698 n. 50
Krienke, Hartmut, 191 n. 19, 835 n. 5

Ladd, George E., 56 n. 24, 78 n. 7, 133n, 169
n. 49, 683n
Laertius, Diogenes, 4 n. 4
Lake, Kirsopp, 6n, 9 n. 20, 16 n. 34, 121, 121
n. 4, 135 n. 26, 189 n. 11, 222n, 241 n. 8,
245, 245 n. 16, 247 n. 20, 275n, 294, 294

n. 15, 296 n. 21, 321 n. 70, 343 n. 26, 349
nn. 38, 39, 360 n. 57, 362 n. 61, 374 n. 10,
382 n. 24, 432 n. 1, 437 n. 17, 464 n. 22,
470 n. 36, 488 n. 66, 492 n. 74, 496n,
524n, 540n, 549 n. 26, 558 n. 49, 587 n.
25, 588 n. 28, 595 n. 42, 605 n. 58, 615 n.
14, 617 n. 17, 626n, 636 n. 60, 649 n. 4,
653 n. 14, 658 n. 24, 666n, 668 n. 45, 697
n. 46, 706 n. 65, 714 n. 7, 717 n. 14, 726 n.
29, 733 n. 45, 759n, 769 n. 52, 774 n. 60,
776, 782 n. 9, 788 n. 20, 797 n. 35, 802 n.
49, 810 n. 7, 811 n. 9, 824 n. 35, 838 n. 15,
860 n. 4, 874 n. 36, 903 n. 46, 906 n. 49,
927 n. 39, 950 n. 11
Lambert, J. C., 716n
Lambrecht, J., 722n
Lampe, G. W. H., 669 n. 49, 734 n. 47
Lane, William L., 965 n. 39
Lang, Friedrich, 77 n. 4
LaSor, William S., 127 n. 13, 220, 220 n. 2,
228 n. 18, 509 n. 15, 696 n. 45
Lenski, R. C. H., 88 n. 25, 92 n. 34, 104n,
135 n. 27, 139 n. 33, 161 n. 35, 174 n. 59,
244n, 278 n. 79, 319n, 354n, 393 n. 45,
409 n. 5, 441 n. 22, 478 n. 53, 504 n. 3,
507 n. 12, 525 n. 44, 555n, 589 n. 32, 597
n. 45, 662 n. 34, 689 n. 29, 901 n. 39, 906
n. 50
Lerle, E., 519 n. 34
Levi, Leo, 957 n. 27
Link, Hans-Georg, 136 n. 29, 156 n. 20, 546
n. 20, 613 n. 9
Livy, 588, 604, 612 n. 2, 622 n. 27, 798 n. 38
Lohfink, Gerhard, 330 n. 5
Lohse, Eduard, 525 n. 45
Longenecker, Richard N., 65 n. 40, 76n, 97
n. 42, 101n, 102 n. 53, 106 n. 62, 141 n.
38, 174 n. 58, 206n, 241 n. 8, 261 n. 48,
316 n. 60, 340 n. 19, 394 n. 50, 417 n. 21,
419 n. 28, 427 n. 42, 466 n. 29, 475 n. 47,
483 n. 59, 485 n. 62, 554 n. 42, 579 n. 6
Lucian, 919 n. 15
Luedemann, Gerd, 15 n. 28, 17 n. 38
Luther, Martin, 115

MacDonald, William G., 78 n. 6, 107n
Mack, Edward, 156 n. 24
Madvig, Donald H., 613 n. 5, 625 n. 31, 933
n. 51
Maher, M., 546 n. 20
Malherbe, Abraham J., 696 n. 44, 905n, 906
n. 51

Mantey, Julius R., 97 n. 43, 186n, 398 n. 58, 410 n. 8, 416 n. 14, 449 n. 41, 499 n. 91, 572 n. 77, 815 n. 20, 938 n. 64

Mare, W. Harold, 185 n. 7

Marshall, I. Howard, 26 n. 62, 49 n. 9, 87 n. 24, 106 n. 61, 161 n. 33, 182n, 228 n. 17, 318 n. 66, 321 n. 70, 409 n. 6, 548n, 552 n. 34, 635 n. 56, 762 n. 38, 802 n. 49, 813 n. 13, 901 n. 40

Martin, Ralph P., 440n

Masson, C., 350 n. 40

Mastin, B. A., 688 n. 25

Mather, P. Boyd, 899 n. 35

Mattill, A. J., Jr., 797 n. 36

McCasland, S. V., 684 n. 15

Meeks, Wayne A., 296 n. 20

Merk, 723 n. 24

Merkel, Friedemann, 97 n. 42

Merrill, Eugene H., 471 n. 39

Metzger, Bruce M., 32, 32 n. 69, 33 n. 71, 51 n. 12, 57 n. 26, 64 n. 39, 82 n. 13, 85n, 115n, 149 n. 9, 167 n. 44, 204 n. 39, 212n, 230 n. 21, 232n, 252 n. 32, 270 n. 66, 294 n. 13, 308 n. 47, 315 n. 59, 317 n. 64, 320, 320 n. 68, 333n, 347n, 356 n. 48, 383 n. 25, 386 n. 29, 389 n. 37, 398 n. 60, 409 n. 4, 416 n. 15, 419 n. 27, 424 n. 36, 427 n. 44, 437 n. 17, 448, 449 n. 39, 474 n. 45, 476 n. 51, 483 n. 58, 490 nn. 69, 71, 491 n. 73, 506 n. 8, 508 n. 13, 510n, 519 n. 33, 521 n. 38, 539 n. 8, 549 n. 26, 558 n. 48, 566 n. 64, 572 n. 79, 581 n. 12, 586 n. 22, 588 n. 28, 600 n. 48, 603 n. 55, 605 n. 60, 615 n. 13, 622 n. 28, 630 n. 42, 642 n. 76, 650 n. 6, 654 nn. 15, 17, 661 n. 30, 670 n. 53, 678 n. 1, 682 nn. 11, 13, 692n, 713 n. 4, 729 n. 33, 733 n. 45, 744 n. 1, 754 n. 21, 820 n. 31, 824 n. 34, 840 n. 18, 851 n. 44, 872 n. 32, 878n, 908 n. 56, 917 n. 9, 926 n. 32, 936 n. 59, 950 n. 10, 956 n. 24, 957 n. 26

Michaelis, Wilhelm, 330 n. 4, 897 n. 30

Michel, Hans-Joachim, 723 n. 23

Michel, Otto, 129 n. 16

Moehring, H. R., 336 n. 13

Moellering, H. Armin, 631 n. 45

Morrice, W. G., 628 n. 38

Morris, Leon, 25, 25n, 26 n. 60, 401 n. 65, 415n, 478, 512 n. 21, 551 n. 30, 562n, 613 n. 9, 656 n. 20, 770n, 789 n. 22

Moule, C. F. D., 57 n. 26, 58 n. 28, 66 n. 44, 109 n. 68, 157 n. 27, 164 n. 39, 195n, 204 n. 40, 216n, 220 n. 3, 245 n. 15, 251 n. 29, 261 n. 47, 293 n. 12, 303n, 307 n. 43, 310n, 317 n. 62, 345 n. 28, 355 n. 46, 382 n. 24, 390 n. 39, 410 n. 10, 434 n. 10, 439 n. 19, 476 n. 51, 506 n. 9, 528 n. 50, 542 nn. 12, 13, 559 n. 50, 567 n. 65, 572 n. 76, 581 n. 11, 586 n. 21, 588 n. 29, 594 n. 40, 603 n. 54, 607 n. 61, 628 n. 36, 641 n. 74, 699 n. 51, 715, 735 n. 53, 764 n. 44, 827, 844 n. 30, 849 n. 34, 854 n. 55, 862 n. 10, 872 n. 32, 885 n. 4, 891 n. 18, 894 n. 23, 896 n. 27, 908 nn. 54, 57, 924 n. 27, 929 n. 43, 950 n. 12, 952n

Moulton, James Hope, 260 n. 46, 364 n. 65, 381 n. 21, 837 n. 7

Moyer, James C., 280 n. 83

Müller, Dietrich, 48 n. 7

Mullins, E. Y., 302 n. 34

Mundle, Wilhelm, 556 n. 44

Nairne, A., 906 n. 49

Navonne, John, 8 n. 17

Neirynck, F., 398 n. 57

Nes-Al, 723 n. 24

Nestle, Eberhard, 90 n. 32, 270 n. 65, 539 n. 9

Nock, Arthur Darby, 461 n. 14

Nolland, John, 547 n. 21

Norris, F. W., 678 n. 2

North, Robert, 590n

Oepke, Albrecht, 136 n. 29, 642 n. 75

Ogg, George, 523n

Ogilvie, R. M., 923 n. 26

Olevianus, Caspar, 115

O'Neill, J. C., 22 n. 53

Origen, 20

Orosius, Paulus, 17, 17 n. 37

Osborne, R. E., 442 n. 24, 696 n. 44

O'Toole, Robert F., 467 n. 32, 886 n. 6

Overman, J. A., 371 n. 4

Ovid, 513 n. 23

Packer, J. I., 62 n. 34, 786 n. 17

Parker, Pierson, 23 n. 56, 535 n. 4

Parratt, J. K., 680 n. 6

Pathrapankal, J., 852 n. 46

Payne, David F., 121 n. 6

Payne, J. Barton, 185 n. 7

Peisker, Carl Heinz, 454 n. 2

Pelletier, A., 264n

Petersen, Lorman M., 583 n. 13

Philo, 46 n. 1, 240 n. 5, 241 n. 8, 248 n. 22, 252 n. 31

Pierce, Claude A., 808 n. 2

Plato, 46 n. 1, 627 n. 35

Pliny the Elder, 423 n. 33, 612 n. 3, 953 n. 17

Polycarp, 879 n. 46

Porter, H., 748 n. 12

Powell, Ralph E., 822n

Rackham, Richard B., 79n, 109, 109 n. 67, 147 n. 5, 158 n. 29, 209 n. 47, 227n, 239 n. 2, 315 n. 58, 335 n. 11, 378n, 385n, 395 n. 51, 420n, 456 n. 10, 469n, 492 n. 75, 493 n. 77, 525 n. 47, 585 n. 18, 613 n. 8, 656 n. 22, 668 n. 46, 685n, 705 n. 61, 706 n. 64, 734 n. 48, 765n, 828 n. 47, 841 n. 21, 871 n. 30, 877 n. 42

Rainey, Anson F., 311 n. 53

Ramsay, William M., 422 n. 31, 465–66, 466 n. 27, 497 n. 84, 503n, 509 n. 16, 521 n. 39, 523n, 599, 618 n. 21, 642 n. 76, 664 n. 38, 708 n. 68, 713 n. 5, 721, 745 n. 3, 754 n. 20, 760 n. 31, 775n, 800 n. 41, 915 n. 3, 918 n. 12, 921 n. 22, 933 n. 53, 956 n. 24

Reese, Boyd, 604 n. 56, 802 n. 47

Rehwinkel, Alfred Martin, 808 n. 2

Rengstorf, Karl Heinrich, 48 n. 7, 68 n. 47, 507 n. 10, 837 n. 8

Richard, E., 241 n. 7, 265 n. 56

Ridderbos, Herman N., 65 n. 42, 90 n. 31, 129 n. 17, 153 n. 15, 465 n. 25, 568 n. 68, 583 n. 13

Ridderbos, J., 265 n. 57

Riesenfeld, Harald, 398 n. 57

Robbins, Vernon K., 594 n. 39, 918 n. 13

Robertson, A. T., 51 n. 11, 55 n. 21, 57 n. 27, 103 n. 57, 122n, 126 n. 11, 132n, 141 n. 39, 156 n. 25, 157 n. 26, 160, 160n, 164 n. 39, 172 n. 55, 175n, 190 n. 12, 202 n. 35, 208 n. 45, 213n, 230, 230 n. 20, 233n, 252 n. 33, 253 n. 34, 257 n. 39, 277n, 290n, 294 n. 14, 299 n. 27, 308 n. 46, 322n, 336 n. 14, 342 n. 23, 348 n. 35, 355 n. 46, 356 n. 51, 374 n. 13, 381 n. 20, 382 n. 23, 398 n. 59, 410 n. 9, 416 n. 17, 421n, 449 n. 41, 457 n. 12, 464 n. 24, 468n, 476 n. 50, 482n, 490 n. 70, 491 n. 72, 493 n. 79, 499 n. 90, 506 n. 7, 508 n. 14, 520 n. 37, 526 n. 49, 564 n. 59, 572 n. 78, 597 n. 44, 607 n. 62, 615 n. 15, 619n, 624n, 630 n. 43, 632 n. 49, 641 n. 73, 650 n. 5, 654 nn. 16, 18, 670 n. 51, 682 n. 12, 689 n. 28, 703 n. 58, 727n, 735 n. 51, 736 n. 54, 747 n. 6, 755 n. 26, 763 nn. 41, 42, 768n, 771 n. 54, 773n, 784 n. 13, 791 n. 28, 825 n. 37, 844 n. 29, 862 n. 9, 867 n. 17, 868, 872 n. 31, 875n, 885 n. 5, 899 n. 36, 903 n. 45, 908 n. 52, 917 n. 8, 920 n. 19, 924 n. 28, 929 n. 44, 933 n. 49

Robertson, O. Palmer, 553 nn. 38, 39, 554 n. 42

Robinson, Maurice A., 627 n. 34

Robinson, N. H. G., 808 n. 2

Robinson, William Childs, 68 n. 47, 342 n. 22

Roloff, Jürgen, 11 n. 24

Ropes, James Hardy, 33, 33 n. 71, 661 n. 31, 729 n. 35, 759n, 838 n. 13

Ross, Alexander, 57 n. 25

Rougé, Jean, 915 n. 4, 927 n. 36, 928 n. 40, 937 n. 62, 941 n. 70

Ryan, Rosalie, 590n

Ryken, Leland, 509 n. 18, 640 n. 69

Safrai, Shmuel, 767 n. 48

Schaeder, Hans Heinrich, 837 n. 8

Scharlemann, Martin H., 13 n. 25, 239 n. 3

Schlier, Heinrich, 170 n. 53

Schmidt, Peter, 897 n. 30

Schneider, Gerhard, 140 n. 37, 200n, 346 n. 30

Schneider, Johannes, 312 n. 54, 475 n. 48

Schneider, Walter, 546 n. 19

Schoonheim, P. L., 370 n. 3

Schrenk, Gottlob, 121 n. 6, 613 n. 7

Schubert, Paul, 795 n. 32, 900n

Schürer, Emil, 14n, 19 n. 49, 146 n. 1, 165n, 200n, 228 n. 16, 329 n. 1, 349 n. 38, 371 n. 4, 376n, 387 n. 32, 467 n. 32, 547 n. 22, 557 n. 47, 652 n. 10, 659 n. 28, 663 n. 37, 688 n. 23, 769 n. 50, 772 n. 57, 774 n. 61, 781 nn. 6, 7, 782 n. 11, 802 nn. 50, 51, 809 n. 3, 820 n. 30, 826 n. 42, 834 n. 2, 835 n. 4, 840 n. 20, 843, 851 n. 42, 859 n. 2, 860 nn. 3, 6, 870 n. 24, 871 n. 29, 886 n. 6, 893 n. 22, 957 n. 28

Schwank, B., 658 n. 25

Schwartz, D. R., 192n

Schweizer, Eduard, 135 n. 25

Scott, J. Julius, Jr., 239 n. 3

Seebass, Hans, 892 n. 20

Seesemann, Heinrich, 546 n. 19, 570 n. 72

Seneca, 658–59, 659 n. 27

Shea, William H., 251 n. 27

Sherwin-White, A. N., 6n, 595 n. 42, 604 n. 57, 605 n. 59, 621 n. 25, 659 n. 29, 701 n. 55, 705 n. 60, 798 n. 38, 799n, 800 n. 44,

828 n. 48, 853 n. 50, 865 n. 14, 867 n. 18, 916 n. 6, 958n, 960 n. 33, 967 nn. 41, 42

Siede, Burghard, 47 n. 4

Simon, M., 563 n. 57

Singer, Charles Gregg, 302 n. 33

Smallwood, E. M., 17 n. 38, 19 n. 47

Smith, Gary V., 89 n. 29

Smith, James, 917 n. 11, 920 n. 18, 925, 927 nn. 34, 38, 933 n. 50, 934 n. 56, 939 n. 65

Smith, Robert H., 26 n. 62

Sokolowski, F., 700 n. 53

Sorg, Theo, 544n

Stählin, Gustav, 629 n. 41

Statyllius Flaccus, 948 n. 7

Stigers, Harold, 127 n. 14, 150 n. 10, 767 n. 47

Stonehouse, Ned B., 106 n. 63, 628 n. 38, 633 n. 51, 640 n. 69

Strabo, 927 n. 37, 933 n. 52, 954n

Strack, H. L., 46 n. 2, 58 n. 29, 75 n. 2, 83 n. 15, 84 n. 19, 139 n. 33, 146 n. 2, 210 n. 49, 211 n. 52, 222n, 228 n. 16, 242n, 253 n. 35, 262 n. 51, 289 n. 6, 296 n. 21, 313 n. 56, 376n, 387 n. 31, 441 n. 23, 472 n. 42, 483 n. 59, 578 n. 2, 652 n. 10, 663 n. 36, 760 n. 32, 761 n. 35, 767 n. 46, 781 n. 7, 809 nn. 4, 6, 811 n. 9, 902 n. 44, 921 n. 21, 936 n. 58

Strathmann, Hermann, 54 n. 19, 228 n. 15, 455 n. 6, 656 n. 21, 808 n. 1

Suetonius, 15 n. 29, 16 n. 34, 17, 17 n. 36, 18 n. 42, 382 n. 22, 408 n. 1, 423 n. 33, 425 n. 38, 445 n. 31, 617 n. 18, 649 n. 3, 851, 957, 960

Tacitus, 15 n. 29, 18, 18 nn. 43, 44, 46, 228 n. 14, 423 n. 33, 425 n. 38, 658 n. 26, 706 n. 64, 826 nn. 40, 41, 840 n. 20, 873n, 957

Talbert, C., 723 n. 24

Taylor, Lily Ross, 698 n. 48, 701 n. 55

Taylor, Vincent, 102 n. 53

Tertullian, 3 n. 1, 20

Thayer, Joseph H., 105 n. 59, 114 n. 78, 156 n. 20, 158 n. 28, 161 n. 32, 208 n. 46, 249 n. 25, 265 n. 54, 308 nn. 44, 45, 313 n. 57, 334 n. 9, 350 n. 42, 374 n. 12, 388 n. 34, 416 n. 16, 424 n. 37, 434 n. 9, 565 n. 60, 614 n. 10, 627 n. 33, 629 n. 40, 649 n. 2, 657n, 662 n. 33, 707 n. 67, 738 n. 59, 811 n. 10, 844 n. 28, 874 n. 36

Thiede, C. P., 441 n. 23

Thompson, J. Alexander, 667 n. 43

Thompson, W. Ralph, 75 n. 1

Thornton, L. S., 302 n. 33

Thornton, T. C. G., 271 n. 70

Thucydides, 9, 9 n. 18, 13, 738 n. 62

Tiedtke, Erich, 156 n. 20, 613 n. 9

Trench, R. C., 64 n. 38, 98 n. 44

Turner, Nigel, 336 n. 15, 345 n. 28, 427 n. 45, 528 n. 51, 887 n. 9, 896 n. 28, 908 n. 55

Unger, M. F., 498 n. 87

Ursinus, Zacharias, 53, 115, 307, 424

Van Alstine, George A., 289 n. 4, 957 n. 27

van Bruggen, Jakob, 535 n. 4, 664 n. 39

van der Horst, P. W., 193 n. 23

Van Elderen, Bastiaan, 461 n. 16, 467 n. 30, 523n

van Unnik, W. C., 29 n. 64, 34 n. 74, 311 n. 52, 394 n. 50, 780 n. 4

Van Veldhuizen, A., 439 n. 20

VanGemeren, Willem A., 519 n. 35

Vegetius, 921 n. 20

Vergil, 927 n. 37

Vos, Howard F., 587

Walker, W. O., 578 n. 4

Wallace, David H., 837 n. 10

Wead, David W., 68 n. 46, 798 n. 37

Wegenast, Klaus, 668 n. 47

Wenham, John, 442 n. 24

Wilcox, Max, 10n, 62 n. 35, 371 n. 4, 477n, 497 n. 85

Wilkinson, Thomas L., 641 n. 71

Williams, David John, 54 n. 17, 59n, 84 n. 20, 135 n. 26, 246 n. 18, 278 n. 79, 299 n. 28, 309 n. 49, 321 n. 70, 372 n. 8, 535 n. 6, 612 n. 1, 735 n. 49, 810 n. 8, 901 n. 39

Windisch, Hans, 419 n. 26

Woudstra, Marten H., 546 n. 18

Wright, J. Stafford, 592n

Wycherley, R. E., 628 n. 38

Xenophon, 4 n. 4, 627 n. 35, 700 n. 54, 748 n. 11

Yadin, Y., 168 n. 47

Yaure, L., 462 n. 17

Young, Edward J., 495n

Youngblood, Ronald F., 209 n. 48, 566 n. 63

Zahn, Theodor, 488 nn. 66, 67, 704n, 876 n. 39, 937 n. 60, 947 n. 4, 951 n. 13

Zehnle, Richard F., 87 n. 23

Index of Scripture

Genesis

1:28—634
2:7—57, 634
2:17—94
3:1—182
3:5—298
3:15—552
3:17-18—94
5:5—890
5:8—890
5:11—890
5:14—890
6:20—377
9:1—634
9:4—556
11:1-9—79
11:8-9—634
11:26—240
11:31—240
11:32—240
12:1—240, 241
12:1-3—496
12:3—140 n. 36, 391, 932
12:4—240
12:6—242
12:7—241 n. 9
13:15—241 n. 9
13:17—241 n. 9
14:15—329
14:19—633
14:22—633
15:2—329
15:5—250
15:7—240, 250
15:13 242, 245, 254, 470
15:13-14—242
15:14b—242
15:18—140, 241 n. 9
15:18-21—470
17:1—241, 244

17:2—140
17:2-21—243
17:4—140
17:5—125, 555
17:7—107, 140, 264, 379, 545
17:8—241 n. 9, 269
17:9-14—243, 545
17:11-12—417
17:12—243
17:17—241
17:21—243
18:18—140 n. 36, 391, 932
18:25—396 n. 55
19:11—296
21:10—473
22:18—140, 391, 932
23:15—248
23:17-18—241
26:4—140 n. 36, 391
28:14—140 n. 36
28:20-22—665
30:24—246
33:4—740
33:19—248
37:2—247
37:12-36—246
39:2—246
39:5—932
39:21—246
39:23—246
41:25-36—246
41:37-43—246
41:46—247
41:53—247
41:54—247
41:56-57—247
42:1-3—247
42:2—250
45:5—247
45:6—248
45:7—247, 248

45:8—246
45:14-15—740
46:27—248 n. 21
46:28—248
48:4—242
48:5—246
49:10—472
50:5—248
50:13—248
50:20—249
50:25—248
50:26—250

Exodus

1:5—248 n. 21
1:7—250
1:11—251
1:15-16—251
1:17—205
1:20—469
1:22—250, 251
2:1-2—251
2:2—251
2:10—252
2:11—253
2:12—254
2:13—255
2:15—255
2:16-22—255
2:22—245
3—339
3:1—255, 262
3:2—257, 260
3:2-5—77
3:4—136, 785
3:5-6—258
3:6—128, 149
3:7—257
3:12—243, 257
3:15—128, 205, 789
3:16—152
4:10—252

4:19—259
5:5—469
6:1—470 n. 35
6:6—260, 470 n. 35
7:7—253
8:8—309
8:15—134
8:28—309
9:28—309
10:17—309
12:36—242
12:37—250
12:40-41—242
13:3—470 n. 35
13:19—248
13:21—258
13:21-22—785
14:19—198
15:22-27—546
16:29—58 n. 29
16:35—470
17:6—470
17:7—546
17:8-13—470
18:3-4—256
18:17-26—221
19:1—75
19:11-13—257
19:18—258
20:1—262, 275
20:1-4—264
20:1-17—262
20:3-4—386
20:4-6—638
20:5—446, 447
20:8-11—718
20:11—166, 517, 633
22:28—811
23:16—75
24:1-8—264
24:3-8—137, 140
24:9-11—264
25:8—240

25:9—268
25:22—268 n. 61
25:40—268
26:30—268
26:33–34—268 n. 61
27:8—268
27:21—268
28:30—68
31:1–6—268
31:18—262, 268 n. 61
32:1—263
32:6—264
32:9—273 n. 73
32:15—268 n. 61
32:20—264
32:23—263
32:34—551
33:2—446 n. 34
33:3—273
33:5—273
33:13—469
34:9—273 n. 73
34:15—556 n. 44
34:15–16—387 n. 31
34:29—268 n. 61
34:29–30—233
40:34–35—56, 240

Leviticus

2:2—373
2:9—373
2:16—373
3:17—556
5:12—373
7:26—556
10:1–2—184, 448
10:2—184
10:4—185
10:5—186
11—377
16:29—922
16:29–34—921
17:10—556
17:13—556
17:13–14—556
19:15—810
23:15–16—75
23:26–32—921
23:29—137
24:16—230, 279
26:4—518
26:41—274 n. 74

Numbers

1:46—250
1:50—268 n. 61
5:21—950
5:27—950

6:1–21—663 n. 35
6:3—761
6:9—761 n. 36
6:14–17—760
6:18—760, 764
8:10—225
11:16–17—150
11:26—91
12:3—254
12:8—137
14:4—263
14:21–23—188
14:22—470
15:30–31—133
15:37–41—467
17:7—268 n. 61
18:20—176
19:11—186
19:12—764
22:16—364
22:22—198
26:55—68
27:16–17—732
27:16–18—222
27:23—225
28:26—75
35:5—58 n. 29

Deuteronomy

1:6—257
1:31—470, 474
2:5—242
4:10—262
4:19—265 n. 55
4:23—638n
4:28—638n
4:34—470 n. 35
4:37—369
5:4—262
5:7–8—264, 386
5:8–10—638
5:9—446, 447
5:12–15—718
5:15—470 n. 35
6:4—102, 279, 346
6:4–9—467
6:5—173 n. 57
6:16—188, 546
7:1—470
7:8—470 n. 35
8:4—470
9:6—273 n. 73
9:10—262
9:13—273 n. 73
9:26—470 n. 35
9:29—470 n. 35
10:9—176, 305 n. 40
10:12—173 n. 57

10:15—469
10:16—273 n. 73, 274
10:17—391
10:22—248 n. 21
11:13—173 n. 57
11:13–21—467
12:5—271 n. 68
12:11—271 n. 68
12:12—305 n. 40
12:21—271 n. 68
13:3—173 n. 57
13:5—280 n. 82
13:6–18—433
13:15—433
14:3–21—377–78
14:23—271 n. 68
14:27—305 n. 40
15:1–11—112
15:4—121, 173
15:4b—174 n. 59
15:7–8—121
15:11—360, 536
16:9–12—75
17:3—265 n. 55
17:6—842
17:6–7—231, 280
17:7—280
17:14–17—471 n. 40
17:19—433
18:1—305 n. 40
18:10–14—295, 690
18:15—256
18:15–20—136
18:18—136, 256
19:15—480, 842
19:19—280 n. 82
21:21—280 n. 82
21:23—94, 185, 186,
  205, 280 n. 82, 479,
  481, 614
23:1—312
24:7—280 n. 82
25:1–3—798
25:2–3—213
26:16—173 n. 57
28:15—786
28:28–29—786
29:5—470
29:18—306
29:29—52
30:2—173 n. 57
30:6—173 n. 57, 274
30:10—173 n. 57
30:19–20—262
31:27—273 n. 73
32:4—463 n. 20
32:5—108
32:8—635
32:21—516n

32:46–47—262
32:49—269
34:7—253
34:10–12—137

Joshua

1:9—655
2:15—349
3:4—58 n. 29
3:10—470
3:14–17—269
5:1–12—182
5:15—258
7:1—181
7:16–18—68
14–21—470
14:2—68
15:1—68
18:1—269
23:9—269
24—239 n. 1
24:2—240
24:11—470
24:18—269
24:20—265
24:32—248

Judges

1:31—748
2:15—463
2:16—471
3:9—475
3:15—475
6:11–24—198
11:27—396 n. 55

I Samuel

1:11—665
1:27–28—665
2:35—471
3:1–14—136
3:10—332, 785
3:19—139
3:20—471
4:3—269
5:1—321
7:1—269
7:2—472
8:6–7—471 n. 40
10:6—91
10:10—91
10:19—471 n. 40
10:20–21—68
12:3—737
12:15—463
12:17—471 n. 40
12:19—471 n. 40
13:1—472

13:14—139 n. 34, 472, 473, 474 n. 46
14:45—936 n. 57
15:23—472
15:28—139 n. 34
16:1—472
16:13—139 n. 34, 472
21:1—269
28:17—139 n. 34

II Samuel

5:6–7—470
6:3—269
6:7—184
6:17—269
7:1–2—269
7:12–13—474
7:12–14—139
7:12–16—99 n. 48
7:13—269
7:14—346, 483
8:6—329
8:17—149
14:11—936 n. 57
15:24–36—149
22:6—94
22:31—463 n. 20
22:51—474

I Kings

1:32—149
1:52—936 n. 57
2:19—278
2:35—149
3:2—271 n. 68
4:30—252
5:11—445 n. 28
6:1—471
7:51—270
8:17–19—269
8:27—270, 271, 633
8:41–43—312
11:24–25—329
14:21—271 n. 68
16:13—516n
16:26—516n
17:19—360
17:19–23—362
17:21—717
17:23—890
18:12—321 n. 72
18:24—258
18:38—77, 258
19:10—274
19:14—274
20:35—140 n. 35
21:7—906 n. 49

II Kings

2:3—140 n. 35
2:5—140 n. 35
2:7—140 n. 35
2:11—77, 890
2:16—321 n. 72
4:10—360
4:21—360
4:32–35—362
4:34–35—717
4:35—890
5:15–16—305
5:23–27—305
6:17—279
11:15–16—769
12:1—364
13:21—890
17:15—516n
17:24–41—295
19:4—554
19:14–37—205
19:35—446
21:3—265 n. 55
21:5—265 n. 55
22:8—623
23:1–3—623
23:11—265 n. 55

I Chronicles

2:30—245
2:32—245
5:2—246
6:54—68
11:4–8—470
16:35—897
16:39—269
17:1—269
17:11–14—474
22:8—269
25:3—89
28:3—269

II Chronicles

2:6—270, 270 n. 67
2:16—360
6:13—746n
11:24–27—897
12:13—271 n. 68
13:12—212, 901 n. 42
24:21—275, 769
26:16–21—448
36:15–21—266
36:16—274
36:23—287

Ezra

2:36–39—225 n. 12

3:7—445 n. 28

Nehemiah

3:16—98 n. 46
5:13—652
7:39–42—225 n. 12
9:5–37—239 n. 1
9:6—166
9:7—240
9:12—785
9:26—274
10:34—68
11:1—68

Esther

1:3—82
1:18–19—82

Job

9:4—901 n. 42
12:10—637
19:25–27—97, 890
34:19—391 n. 41

Psalms

2—167, 168, 169, 170, 484
2:1–2—166, 167, 167 n. 45, 168
2:2—167
2:6—167
2:6–7—902
2:7—167 n. 45, 346, 473, 482, 483, 484
2:9—168
3:5—435
4:6—785
9:8—639
11:7—97
16—98, 101, 486
16:8—96, 97 n. 42
16:8–11—95, 101, 167 n. 45
16:9–11—97
16:9b—96
16:10—30, 95, 96, 97, 98, 99, 129, 167 n. 45, 485, 487, 890, 902
16:11—96
17:15—97
17:26—167–68
18:4—94
18:6—95
18:30—463 n. 20
19:7—489
19:14—260, 261

22—63
22:1—97 n. 42
22:1–21—902
22:22—473
24:6—635 n. 59
27:8—635 n. 59
27:14—322
29:1–2—240 n. 4
31:6—516n
35:5–6—446 n. 34
35:16—278
36:9—692
37:14—112 n. 75
42:8—598
44:3—785
50:8–13—633
51—472
55:16–17—120
55:17—376
63:2—278
65:9–13—518
69—63, 63 n. 36
69:9a—63
69:9b—63
69:22–23—63 n. 36
69:25—63, 167 n. 45
73:23—96
73:23–26—97
74:2—733
74:17—634
77:15—470 n. 35
78—239 n. 1
78:35—260, 261
78:37—305
78:49—446 n. 34
81:8–10—298
83:16—635 n. 59
87:4—745
89:3–4—99 n. 48
89:15—785
89:20—472
89:35–36—99 n. 48
91:11—441, 442
95:6—746n
95:7–11—188, 473
96:13—639
98:9—639
104:2—785
105—239 n. 1
105:3–4—635 n. 59
105:20–22—246
105:24—250
106—239 n. 1
106:33—274
106:47—897
109:8—63, 65, 167 n. 45
109:31—96
110—101

110:1—101, 167 n. 45, 206, 419
110:5—96
115:4–8—517
116:3—94, 95
118:15—470 n. 35
118:22—154, 155, 156
118:22–23—154
118:27—902
119:105—97
121:5—96
132:4–5—269
132:11–12—99, 474–75
136:12—470 n. 35
139:5–12—636
139:7–16—270 n. 67
145:9—518
145:18—636
146:5–6—167 n. 45
146:6—166, 517
148:10—411
150—272

Proverbs

15:3—184
16:33—67
21:30—212, 820, 901 n. 42
25:11—899

Ecclesiastes

5:4–5—665
12:1–7—519

Isaiah

1:2—469
1:18—795
2:2–4—554
5:26—54
6:1—278
6:1–13—136
6:8a—586
6:8b—586
6:9—966
6:9–10—963, 964, 965
6:10—964
6:11–12—964
6:13—964
8:10—820
8:14—156
9:13—635 n. 59
11:2—91
11:4—184
20:2—750
26:19—891
28:16—156
29:18—898 n. 32
31:1—635 n. 59

32:3—898 n. 32
33:24—397n
35:5—788, 898 n. 32, 965
35:5–6a—124
37:4—554
37:16—166
37:16–20—166
40:3—684 n. 15
40:9—483
40:18–20—638n
41:10—655
41:14—129
42–53—318
42:5—633
42:6—495, 496, 902
42:7—898
43:5—655
44:3—91
44:9–20—638n
45:15—475
45:21—555
48:15–17—475
49:6—495, 496, 902
49:6a—495
49:6b—495
49:15–16—598
50:6—134
52:7—392, 483
52:13—129
52:13–15—169
52:13–53:12—128, 141 n. 38, 318, 478
53—35, 318
53:1–12—169
53:3–11—902
53:3–12—134
53:5–6—397n
53:7—316
53:7–8—315
53:8—316
53:9—479
53:10–11—397n
53:11—129, 275, 789
53:12—129
55:3—98, 484, 485, 490
55:3–5—554
55:6—635 n. 59
55:11—952
56:3—387
56:3–7—312
56:7—271
57:6—305
58:6—307
60:3—902
61:1—169, 321, 394
63:10—265, 274
65:1—635 n. 59
65:16—256

66:1—271 n. 70
66:1–2—239, 270 n. 67, 271
66:2b—271
66:19–21—554

Jeremiah

1:4–19—136
1:7—897
1:8—655, 897
1:19—655, 897
2:5—516n
2:30—274
3:16—256, 271
3:19–20—346
4:4—274
5:24—518
6:29—699
7:18—265 n. 55
8:2—265 n. 55
8:19—516n
9:25–26—274 n. 74
10:8—516n
13:1–11—750
14:10—551
14:14–16—461
19:13—265 n. 55
20:9—162
23:5—129, 275, 789 n. 24
23:23—636
23:24—270 n. 67
29:13–14—635 n. 59
31:33—101
31:34—89, 215, 397n
33:8—397n
33:15—129, 275, 789 n. 24
50:20—397n

Ezekiel

1:1–3—136
2:3—897
3:14—321 n. 72
4:1–12—750
4:14—379
8:3—321 n. 72
13:10–12—810
20:33—470 n. 35
27:17—445 n. 28
29:10—312
33:4—652, 731
37:1–14—891
37:9—76
37:14—76
38:10—256
39:29—91
40:45–46—149

40:46—146
44:7—274 n. 74
44:9—274 n. 74
44:15–16—146
44:15–17—149
48:11—146, 149

Daniel

2:22—785
5:23—637
5:28—82
6:8—82
6:10—376, 746n
6:12—82
6:15—82
7:13–14—279
8:20—82
9:26—316
10:7—334
12:2—843, 891

Hosea

6:2—891
11:1—346
14:9—463 n. 20

Joel

2:28—77
2:28–32—91, 92, 106
2:30—111
2:32—107, 114

Amos

1:3–5—329
3:8—162
5:25–27—265, 265 n. 57
5:26—265
9:1–10—553
9:11–12—552, 553
9:11–15—553 n. 38

Jonah

1—339
1:3—360
1:5—928
3:1–3—162

Micah

2:1–2—112
5:2—474

Habakkuk

1:5—489
3:4—785

Zephaniah

1:5—265 n. 55

Zechariah

2:7-9—445
3:8—475
9:9—129, 275, 789 n. 24
14:4—58
14:16—554

Malachi

2:10—634

Matthew

1:1-17—474
1:16—60n
1:18—60n
1:20—60n, 89 n. 30
1:20-24—198 n. 31
1:21—125, 155, 206, 475
2:1—432
2:2—139
2:5-6—474
2:11—60n
2:12—89 n. 30
2:13—198 n. 31, 871
2:14—829 n. 51
2:16—251, 443, 871
2:19—198 n. 31
2:22-23—871
3:1—66
3:2—50, 104, 901
3:7—149
3:7-12—475
3:8—901
3:11—50, 76, 105, 400, 416, 679
3:16—53, 169, 394
3:17—379
4:1-11—345 n. 29
4:7—188
4:12—394 n. 49
4:17—50, 104, 206
4:24—393
5:2—391 n. 40
5:3—112
5:12—163, 214, 275
5:17—99, 232
5:44—351
5:45—518
6:1-2—121
6:9-10—125
6:24—184
6:28—737
7:15—732 n. 42, 733

7:20—901
7:22—125
7:29—147
8:8—387
8:11—128
8:16—195
8:29—689
8:34—605
9:2—817 n. 27
9:9—65
9:22—512 n. 21
9:25—362 n. 60
9:28-30—788
9:37—266
10:1—195
10:2-4—59
10:3—59
10:4—60, 211
10:5—65, 292
10:5-6—80, 494, 792
10:6—101, 140, 378, 732 n. 42
10:8—111, 305, 308, 362
10:9-10—123
10:10—650
10:14—498 n. 86, 652
10:16—733
10:17—214, 290, 793, 893
10:17-20—36
10:18—877
10:19-20—152, 202
10:20—50n, 207, 229, 494
10:24—772
10:27—421
10:40—332
10:45—738
11:1—65 n. 41
11:3—476
11:4-5—394
11:5—93, 124, 788
11:28-30—546
12:18—128
12:22-24—965
12:24—133, 964
12:27—687
12:29—51
12:31-32—133
12:32—965
13:4—627
13:10—964
13:14-15—964
13:21—307
13:35—391 n. 40
13:41—446 n. 34
13:55—60, 60n
14:1-12—454

14:3—329
14:3-12—676
14:9—168
14:10—871
14:19—936
14:21—148
14:27—817
15:6—232
15:11—380
16:1—149
16:6—149
16:18—27, 91, 94, 189
17:1—119
17:1-8—336
17:5—56, 136 n. 30, 138, 379
18:10—441, 442
18:12—732 n. 42
18:17—27, 189
18:20—272, 340 n. 18
19:21—112
19:28—65 n. 41, 889
20:19—750
20:21—52
20:30-34—788
21:9—521
21:10—768
21:11—137n, 394
21:23—147, 151
21:25-26—201
21:42—156
21:43-44—154
22:12—183
22:23—147, 149, 209
22:23-32—814
22:32—128
22:41-44—419
22:41-46—101
22:44—102 n. 52
22:46—147
23:4—546
23:7—388
23:8-11—388
23:15—410, 492, 797
23:27—810
23:31—275
23:34—793, 893
23:35—275
24—24
24:2—232
24:8—94
24:14—136
24:15—232
24:36—52, 136
24:42—734
25:31-46—843
25:32—732 n. 42
25:37-40—738
25:45—332

25:46—496
26:3—150, 329 n. 2
26:11—360
26:26—936
26:28—137
26:31—732 n. 42
26:42—381
26:47—819n
26:57—150
26:57-66—149
26:59-66—230
26:60-61—231
26:60-63—315
26:61—51, 770
26:63—346
26:64—102 n. 52, 278, 296
26:65—279, 336
26:69—837 n. 8
26:71—92, 158, 443n, 837 n. 8
26:73—81 n. 10
27:3-10—62
27:5—62
27:6—62
27:19—89 n. 30, 129, 661, 864
27:23—479n
27:24—203
27:25—203
27:32—83, 228, 418n, 454
27:35—68
27:37—139
27:40—231
27:45—90
27:51—770
27:57-59—185
27:57-60—479
27:63—203n
28:1-10—480n
28:2—198 n. 31
28:3—389 n. 37
28:9-10—48
28:10—50, 60
28:13—154, 829 n. 51
28:16-20—48, 60, 480
28:18—103, 279, 393, 484
28:19—34, 107, 140, 301, 396
28:19-20—51, 105, 109, 223, 287, 369, 378, 542
28:20—47, 57, 110, 162, 340 n. 18, 396, 656
28:20b—167

Mark

1:1—66
1:4—105, 206, 487, 679
1:7—476
1:8—105, 400, 414,
   416, 679
1:14—394 n. 49
1:22—110, 147
1:23–26—293
1:24—129 n. 17, 593,
   689
1:27—594
1:30–31—952
1:31—124
1:32–34—952
1:41—225 n. 10
2:16—410
3:7–8—194
3:16–19—59
3:18—59, 60
3:20—961
3:21—60
3:22—133, 964, 965
3:29—965
4:10—964
4:11—965
5:7—593 n. 38
5:20—329
5:34—512 n. 21, 566 n.
   63
5:41—362
6:3—60, 60n
6:7—120, 593, 687
6:11—498 n. 86
6:14—168
6:14–29—454
6:17—329
6:19—853
6:22—168
6:25–27—168
6:50—817
6:56—193, 195
7:31—329
8:9—148
9:4—136 n. 30
9:7—136 n. 30
9:11—410
9:24—585
9:28—410
9:35—388
9:39—125
10:16—225 n. 10
10:33—750
10:45—738
10:49—817 n. 27
10:52—512 n. 21
11:1—58
11:14—307

11:17—271
12:14—391 n. 41
12:26–27—128
12:30—173
12:31—173
12:42–44—222
13—24
13:8—94
13:37—734
14:13–15—440
14:33—120
14:53—152
14:61–62—102
14:63—515 n. 29
14:64—336
14:70—81 n. 10
15:7—129
15:21—228
15:24—68
16:5—389 n. 37
16:7—50
16:9–11—48, 480n
16:12—48
16:14–18—48
16:15—396
16:18—191 n. 16, 949
16:19—47 n. 4

Luke

1:1—9
1:2—5, 24, 87, 159,
   850, 897
1:3—21, 47, 904
1:4—34
1:5—393 n. 47
1:8—146
1:11—56, 198 n. 31
1:11–20—339
1:13—372
1:15—91, 677
1:23—455
1:27—60n
1:30—60n, 372
1:32—593 n. 38
1:32–33—99, 474
1:34—60n
1:35—194, 593 n. 38
1:38—60n
1:39—60n
1:41—60n, 91
1:46—60n
1:47—694, 728
1:56—60n
1:66—694 n. 37
1:67—91
1:76—593 n. 38
1:80—345 n. 29
2:2—211

2:4—474
2:5—60n
2:8—829 n. 51
2:9—198 n. 31, 894
2:10—206
2:11—102
2:16—60n
2:19—60n
2:21—332
2:25—80
2:26—876
2:29—166
2:32—495
2:34—60n
2:49—613
3:1—66, 432, 454, 870
   n. 25
3:1–2—533
3:1–3—676
3:2—151, 329 n. 2
3:7–20—415, 475
3:10—104
3:16—50, 76, 105, 400,
   416, 679
3:19—329
3:23—5
4:14—394 n. 49
4:16—612
4:18—394
4:20—374, 460, 469
4:22—521
4:29—521
4:38—952
4:41—689
4:43—613
4:44—393 n. 47
5:5—737
5:19—699
6:12–16—61
6:14–16—59
6:17–19—194
6:18—194
6:20—112
6:30—738
6:31—738
6:35—593 n. 38
7:1–6—370
7:5—83, 887 n. 10
7:6—387
7:11–17—362 n. 60
7:16—137n
7:17—393 n. 47
7:22—93, 124
7:39—136 n. 30, 137n
7:50—512 n. 21, 566 n.
   63
8:1—221n
8:2–3—59
8:9—964

8:10—191
8:28—593 n. 38
8:29—730
8:48—512 n. 21, 566 n.
   63
9:1—221n
9:5—498 n. 86
9:9—874
9:12—221n
9:22—753
9:35—469
9:44—753
9:50—688
9:51—746
9:54—300
10:1—65
10:2—266
10:7—304, 650, 737,
   850
10:11—498 n. 86
10:17—65, 68 n. 46,
   125, 131
10:18—51
10:19—949
11:15—133
11:19—687
11:46—546
12:10—233
12:27—737
12:47—789 n. 23
13:16—394
13:33—613
15:4–32—522
15:10—602
15:18—233
15:20—740
16:13—184
16:20—443n
16:24—699
16:28—726 n. 28
17:15—124
17:19—512 n. 21
17:21—50
18:31—221n, 479
18:31–33—753
18:37—93
18:42—512 n. 21
19:4—699
19:41–44—24
19:42–44—28, 265
19:43–44—22, 24, 232
19:47—862
20:37–38—128
21:5–36—24, 28
21:14—694 n. 37
21:15—158, 229
21:18—936
21:20–24—22, 24
21:24—635

21:27—56
22:1—433
22:3—182, 221n
22:4—146, 200, 766
22:8—120
22:12—58
22:30—889
22:31–32—182
22:37—129
22:41—753
22:42—752, 753
22:44—434 n. 8
22:47—221n
22:52—146, 200
22:56—158, 374
22:58—934
22:59—81 n. 10
22:66—782
23:2—618, 837, 887 n. 10
23:4—129, 479n, 816 n. 23
23:5—393 n. 47
23:8—874
23:12—168
23:13–19—129
23:14—129, 479n, 816 n. 23
23:18—772, 797
23:21—108, 521
23:22—203, 479n, 816 n. 23
23:26—228
23:34—68, 133, 281, 478
23:35—469
23:43—97 n. 42
23:46—97 n. 42, 281
23:49—59
23:55–56—59
24—29
24:1—59
24:4—56, 389 n. 37
24:9–10—59
24:13–32—48
24:13–49—480n
24:19—137n
24:21—260
24:25—134, 136 n. 30
24:25–27—613
24:26—613, 903
24:26–27—133
24:27—315, 902, 962
24:30—111, 395
24:34—48
24:35—111
24:36–43—48, 49
24:42–43—29, 395
24:42–53—29

24:44—26, 902
24:44–46—613
24:44–49—207
24:45—134, 590
24:45–46—133
24:46—903
24:47—54, 125, 206, 396, 639
24:48—29
24:49—29, 50, 58, 106–07
24:49a—54
24:50—29, 55
24:50–51—55
24:50–53—47
24:51—29
24:52—29, 56, 57, 214
24:53—29, 76

John

1:11—129, 256, 494, 652
1:19–21—261
1:19–27—476
1:21—136 n. 30, 137
1:25—137
1:26—416
1:27—476
1:29—94, 316
1:33—105
1:35–51—65
1:36—316
1:43—394 n. 49
1:45—394
1:46—837 n. 8
2:1—394 n. 49
2:17—63
2:18—147
2:19—231, 232
3:2—93, 199, 623, 829 n. 51
3:8—76
3:16—490
3:26—699
3:30—476, 679
3:34—91
4:2—401
4:9—297
4:20—292
4:20–23—563
4:21–24—232, 770
4:24—272, 638
4:35—266
4:39–42—292
4:40–42—563
4:53—372, 412–13
4:54—381
5:22—396 n. 55, 639

5:25—362
5:27—396 n. 55, 639
5:28–29—147
5:28–30—843
5:45–46—137
5:46—136 n. 30
6:14—137n
6:67–68—198
6:69—129 n. 17
6:70—65 n. 41
7:3—763
7:5—60, 442
7:15—158
7:39—91, 100
7:40—137, 261
7:42—474
7:50—159
8:12—903
8:44—463
9:1—120
9:6–7—965
9:8—120
9:16—203n
9:24—203n
9:35–38—965
9:39—396 n. 55
9:39–41—898
10:1–4—732 n. 42
10:11—732 n. 42
10:12—733
10:14—732 n. 42
10:15—735
10:16—732 n. 42
10:20—904
10:22—127
10:23—769
10:28—130, 496
10:30—394
10:33—230
10:38—93, 394
11:18—55
11:24—891
11:25—891
11:44—362 n. 60
11:47—203n
11:47–53—150
11:49—329 n. 2
11:50—149
12:1—753
12:8—115
12:20—312
12:21—317
12:32—316
12:40—964
12:41—278
13:1—753
13:2—182
13:13—601 n. 51
13:16—772

13:27—182
14:2–3—57
14:6—155, 393
14:9–10—394
14:13–14—125
14:16–17—50n
14:26—50, 50n, 100, 125, 207, 414
15:13—606
15:16—125
15:26—50n, 54, 100
15:26–27—207
16:2—328, 781, 892
16:3—478
16:7–8—50n
16:12–13—50n
16:13—315
16:23–24—125
16:33—655, 817 n. 27
17:2—496
17:9—735
17:22—571
18:5—93
18:7—93
18:12—753, 769 n. 52
18:13—150, 151
18:13–14—329 n. 2
18:14—149, 150
18:16—158
18:16–17—440
18:20—907
18:22—810
18:22–23—809
18:23—809
18:24—150, 151, 329 n. 2
18:28—150, 329 n. 2, 378, 410
18:31—277, 280, 893
18:36—99, 617
18:38—479n, 816 n. 23
19:4—479n
19:6—479n
19:12–16—129
19:13—661, 864
19:15—618, 772, 797
19:19—93, 123, 837 n. 8
19:24—68
19:25—59
19:31—185
19:38–39—479
19:39—829 n. 51
20:3—955
20:11–18—48
20:12—56, 389 n. 37
20:19–23—48
20:19–25—480n
20:21—53

20:22—48, 53
20:22–23—91
20:23—306
20:24–29—48
20:26–31—480n
21:1–23—48, 480n
21:13—396
21:16—381
21:16–17—732 n. 42
21:25—47

Acts

1—3, 29, 48, 69
1–15—8
1:1—3, 7, 21, 28, 29, 46
  n. 1, 51, 550, 656
1:1–2—51
1:1–5—46, 51
1:1–8—46
1:1–26—46
1:2—47, 47 n. 4, 56, 67
1:3—50, 51, 58, 395 n.
  52, 480, 524, 924
1:3–5—51
1:3–8—480n
1:4—29, 51, 58, 75, 106
1:4–5—27, 615
1:4–14—29
1:5—13, 78, 105, 400,
  414, 679
1:6—49, 55
1:6–8—51, 55
1:7—52
1:8—28, 29, 34, 35, 52,
  54 n. 18, 55, 66, 77,
  90, 162, 207 n. 43,
  287, 299, 300, 373,
  393 n. 47, 399, 456,
  494, 681, 693, 729,
  773, 901, 961, 968
1:9—29, 55
1:9–11—4, 47, 55, 57
1:10—57, 278, 374, 389
  n. 37
1:10–11—55, 57
1:11—28, 47 n. 4, 58,
  90, 732
1:12—29, 55, 448 n. 39
1:12–14—58
1:12–15—91
1:13—60, 76, 433, 440
1:13–14—60, 783
1:13–15—165
1:14—29, 60, 60n, 61 n.
  32, 111, 166, 171,
  192, 222, 223, 442
1:15—59, 64, 75, 108,
  115, 189

1:15–20—60, 64
1:15–22—204
1:15–26—60
1:16—27, 61 n. 33, 62,
  64, 65, 98, 98 n. 45,
  167, 167 n. 45, 169
1:16–22—8 n. 15
1:17—64
1:17–18—345
1:18—64, 351
1:18–19—351
1:19—31, 64
1:20—64, 167 n. 45
1:21—66, 67
1:21–22—54, 65, 66,
  341, 353, 480, 507,
  897
1:22—47 n. 4, 50, 54 n.
  18, 66, 148, 174, 207
  n. 43, 395
1:23—31, 560
1:23–26—67, 525
1:24—26, 69, 224
1:24–26—69
1:25—69
1:26—68, 69, 75, 224
2—116
2:1—13, 79, 115, 924
2:1–4—3, 75, 79, 90,
  302, 399, 544
2:1–11—433
2:1–13—75
2:1–41—456
2:1–47—75
2:1–8:1a—75
2:2—76, 78, 79, 80, 171
2:4—27, 48, 77, 78, 79,
  91, 106, 171, 399,
  400
2:5—84, 85, 93, 289,
  550
2:5–11—80, 84, 85, 220
2:6—78, 81, 85, 768
2:7—85
2:8—78, 81, 85
2:9—79, 85, 393 n. 47
2:9–11—4, 80
2:10—228, 418n, 465,
  583, 667, 954
2:11—27, 78, 81, 171,
  400, 492 n. 74, 680
2:12—86, 101, 202
2:12–13—85, 86
2:13—79, 86, 127
2:14—75, 79, 88, 92,
  153, 157, 618, 966
2:14–21—87
2:14–36—8 n. 15, 30,
  468

2:14–39—204
2:14–41—87
2:15—86
2:17—77, 91, 92, 102
2:17–21—91, 92
2:19—111, 191 n. 17
2:21—92, 107, 114, 340
  n. 18
2:22—26, 88, 93, 100,
  128, 191 n. 17, 477,
  785 n. 15, 837 n. 9
2:22–24—25, 92, 102
2:22–36—90
2:23—10, 93, 95, 100,
  102, 169, 204 n. 38,
  395, 478, 479, 564 n.
  58, 591, 731
2:23–24—95, 130 n. 18,
  154
2:24—93, 95, 100, 147,
  148 n. 6, 206, 487,
  614, 640 n. 68, 813
  n. 15, 844 n. 27
2:25—97, 167 n. 45,
  600, 845
2:25–27—97
2:25–28—95, 97, 167 n.
  45
2:27—96, 98, 129, 486
2:28—96
2:29—61 n. 33, 88, 98
  n. 45, 104, 167 n. 45,
  170 n. 52, 477, 494
  n. 80, 957 n. 29
2:29–32—96
2:29–35—486
2:29–36—98
2:30—99, 102, 103, 139
2:30–36—103
2:30b—32 n. 68
2:31—99, 103, 486
2:32—54 n. 18, 93, 94
  n. 38, 100, 102, 103,
  147, 148 n. 6, 614,
  640 n. 68, 844 n. 27
2:32–36—25
2:33—47 n. 3, 50, 100,
  103, 107, 206, 282
2:34—167 n. 45, 282,
  419
2:34–35—167 n. 45,
  206
2:36—26, 91, 93, 100,
  102, 103, 174, 214,
  478
2:37—61 n. 33, 75, 88,
  98 n. 45, 109, 209,
  957 n. 29
2:37–38—487

2:37–39—109
2:37–41—104
2:38—30, 78, 79, 84,
  106, 109–10, 123 n.
  8, 134, 164, 185, 206,
  260, 300, 301, 320,
  340 n. 18, 378, 401,
  403, 414, 487n, 790
2:38–39—8 n. 15, 28,
  207
2:38–41—106
2:39—106, 110
2:40—79, 726 n. 28
2:40–41—109
2:41—79, 189, 225,
  363, 680, 681, 790
2:41–42—120
2:42—28, 48, 59, 109,
  111, 113, 115, 219,
  222, 480, 566, 716
2:42–43—110
2:42–45—115
2:42–47—110, 190
2:43—119, 185, 191,
  685
2:44—111, 115, 189
2:44–45—115, 123,
  173, 175, 183, 718
2:44–47—112, 115, 355
2:45—116, 175
2:46—112, 114, 716
2:46a—113
2:47—108 n. 66, 111,
  114 n. 79, 116, 120,
  174, 189, 225, 419,
  580
3—142
3:1—3, 14, 111, 122,
  371, 376
3:1–5—119, 122
3:1–10—30, 119, 194,
  456, 511, 848
3:1–5:16—119
3:2—122, 163, 511
3:3—757
3:3–7—130
3:4—122, 374, 512
3:5—122, 505
3:6—23, 92 n. 35, 109,
  121, 123 n. 8, 125,
  131, 153, 203, 301 n.
  30, 359, 464, 593,
  688, 785 n. 15, 837
  n. 9
3:6–7—148, 293 n. 10
3:6–10—123
3:7—125, 191 n. 16
3:7–10—125
3:8—121, 125–26

3:10—126
3:11—113, 121, 132, 191, 769
3:11–16—126, 132
3:11–26—126
3:12—132, 374, 477
3:12–26—8 n. 15, 204, 468
3:13—26, 141, 169, 789
3:13–15—25, 204 n. 38
3:14—26, 130, 132, 275, 789 n. 24
3:14–15—478
3:15—54 n. 18, 94, 94 n. 38, 130, 148 n. 6, 154, 174, 198, 206, 395, 480, 487, 640 n. 68, 813 n. 15, 844 n. 27
3:16—9, 119, 122, 130, 131, 132, 203, 511
3:17—138, 477, 478, 638, 781
3:17–18—94
3:17–19—731
3:17–23—132, 138
3:18—93, 136, 169, 903
3:19—105, 134 n. 24, 138, 141, 415, 487n
3:19–20—28
3:19–21—10
3:20—26, 138, 469
3:21—138, 613
3:22—25, 26, 138, 141, 261
3:22b—138
3:23—138
3:24—141
3:24–26—139, 141
3:25—391
3:26—26, 128, 141, 169, 174, 199, 494, 640 n. 68
3:36—464
4—177
4:1—149, 200, 290, 335, 766, 767
4:1–2—197
4:1–4—145, 433, 812
4:1–7—194
4:1–21—149, 196
4:1–22—145
4:2—174, 601, 640 n. 68, 813, 813 n. 15
4:3—191, 192, 197, 294, 435, 892
4:3–21—522
4:4—108 n. 66, 119, 159, 165, 173, 189,

220, 225 n. 11, 363, 464
4:5—152, 526
4:5–7—149, 152
4:5–22—200
4:6—165, 197, 329 n. 2, 782, 802, 861, 894
4:7—86, 152, 159, 803
4:8—77, 157, 681
4:8–12—8 n. 15, 152, 204, 232, 275, 848
4:9—152, 156
4:9–12—156
4:10—23, 25, 26, 92 n. 35, 94, 109, 123 n. 8, 130 n. 18, 148 n. 6, 151, 157, 174, 203, 206, 301 n. 30, 362, 395, 478, 487, 640 n. 68, 785 n. 15, 813 n. 15, 837 n. 9, 844 n. 27, 966
4:10–11—204 n. 38
4:11—156, 157
4:12—153, 155 n. 18, 157, 160, 206, 278, 512, 848
4:13—126, 146, 147, 160, 170, 494 n. 80
4:13–17—157, 160
4:14—151
4:15—210
4:17—109, 203, 348
4:17–18—301 n. 30
4:17–20—146
4:18—109, 123 n. 8, 163–64, 170, 194, 214, 600
4:18–22—161, 163
4:19—30, 164, 204
4:19–20—8 n. 15, 848
4:20—164, 789
4:21—163, 164, 174, 192, 201, 213, 496
4:22—122, 158, 164
4:23—153, 189, 819n
4:23–24a—165
4:23–31—165, 440
4:24—167 n. 45, 222
4:24–30—171, 191
4:24b–28—166
4:25—27, 166, 167 n. 45, 169
4:25–26—167 n. 45
4:25–27—169
4:27—26, 128, 141, 168, 169, 299, 454
4:27–28—94
4:28—93, 169, 591, 731

4:29—170, 171–72, 199, 409 n. 3, 494 n. 80, 505 n. 4
4:29–31—170, 171
4:30—26, 123 n. 8, 128–29, 141, 169, 170, 172, 174, 191 n. 17, 301 n. 30, 419
4:31—27, 76, 77, 170, 171, 172, 199, 203, 409 n. 3, 494 n. 80, 505 n. 4, 598, 621 n. 26
4:32—175, 183, 189
4:32–35—173, 175, 190, 355 n. 47
4:32–37—172
4:33—65, 174, 175, 227, 640 n. 68
4:34—28
4:34–35—123, 175, 183
4:34a—112
4:34b–35—113
4:35—175
4:36—177, 418n, 421, 459, 569, 571, 650, 754
4:36–37—176, 303, 352, 718
5—196, 216
5:1—181n, 337, 788
5:1–2—123
5:1–6—181, 185
5:1–10—783
5:1–11—4, 181, 294, 303, 306, 718
5:2—186
5:2–6—186
5:3—184, 186, 214, 463, 898
5:3–4—185
5:4—113, 183, 187, 694 n. 37
5:5—111, 188, 690
5:6—187
5:7—189
5:7–9—189
5:7–11—187
5:8—189–90
5:9—184, 185, 187, 190, 321
5:11—111, 185, 189 n. 10, 190 n. 15, 690
5:12—111, 113, 191, 193, 197, 293 n. 10, 505, 560, 564 n. 58, 685, 769
5:12–16—190, 355 n. 47

5:12a—190, 190 n. 15, 191
5:12b—190, 190 n. 15
5:12b–14—190, 193
5:13—174, 190, 191
5:14—108 n. 66, 148, 189, 190, 193, 194, 195, 220, 225 n. 11, 297, 363
5:14–16—195
5:15—190, 192, 193, 195, 685
5:15–16—293 n. 10
5:16—195, 293
5:17—198–99, 388, 616, 959, 961
5:17–18—149
5:17–20—196, 198
5:17–42—196
5:18—86, 294, 435, 892
5:18–40—522
5:19—260, 371, 434, 436 n. 13, 598, 829
5:19–20—199, 435
5:20—215, 222
5:21—202, 393
5:21–26—199, 202
5:21b—199
5:22—335
5:24—8 n. 14, 146, 165n, 200, 202, 766
5:25—435, 444
5:26—31, 146, 191, 197, 202, 335, 766
5:27—204, 803
5:27–28—202
5:27–32—202, 207
5:28—109, 204, 348
5:29—30, 162, 207, 208, 212
5:29–32—8 n. 15, 204, 208, 232, 275
5:30—94, 94 n. 38, 154, 205, 208, 395, 398, 479, 640 n. 68, 789, 813 n. 15, 844 n. 27, 901
5:30–32—25, 130 n. 18, 848
5:31—26, 100, 130, 208, 260, 415, 487n
5:32—54 n. 18, 208, 212, 562
5:33—194, 278, 280, 282
5:33–34—209, 210
5:33–40—208
5:34—159, 280
5:34–39—781

5:34–40—147
5:35—213
5:35–39—8, 210, 213
5:36—213, 774
5:37—211
5:38—171
5:38–39—162, 212, 213
5:39—328, 816 n. 25, 901 n. 42
5:40—86, 109, 123 n. 8, 213, 301 n. 30, 798
5:41—216, 225, 330, 561
5:41–42—214, 215, 216
5:42—26, 171, 216, 222, 566
6—226, 233–34
6:1—108, 108 n. 66, 110 n. 72, 113, 220, 222, 223, 225 n. 11, 226, 353, 363, 419 n. 24
6:1–4—219, 223
6:1–6—28, 525
6:1–7—219, 244
6:1–8:1a—219
6:2—65 n. 41, 110 n. 72, 220, 223, 409 n. 3, 566, 650
6:3—229, 300
6:4—59, 221, 222, 223, 226, 650
6:5—6, 21n, 27, 223, 278, 282, 417, 421, 492 n. 74, 566, 748
6:5–7—223, 226
6:6—68
6:7—108 n. 66, 110 n. 72, 208, 220, 225, 363, 409 n. 3, 419, 447, 580, 691
6:8—191 n. 17, 226, 229, 293 n. 10, 505
6:8–10—27, 222, 227, 793
6:8–11—229
6:8–15—226
6:9—83, 230, 353, 418n, 768
6:9–10—291
6:10—229, 278
6:10–11—230
6:11—233, 240, 268, 766
6:11–14—779
6:11–15—230, 233
6:13—54 n. 18, 230, 268, 547, 770
6:13–14—243, 764, 766

6:14—23, 92 n. 35, 233, 267, 785 n. 15, 837 n. 9
6:15—233, 278, 374, 803
7—13, 226, 229, 282–83
7:1—244–45
7:1–8—239, 244
7:1–51—276
7:1–53—239
7:2—61 n. 33, 98 n. 45, 244, 245, 780, 794, 957 n. 29
7:2–8—244
7:2–53—8, 12, 469
7:3—244, 245
7:4—245
7:4–5—31
7:5—244, 245
7:6—245, 481
7:6–7—244, 245
7:7—242, 245
7:8—244, 245
7:9–15—246
7:9–16—245, 249
7:10—229
7:11—249, 268 n. 60, 963
7:11–13—249
7:12—268 n. 60, 963
7:12–13—250
7:14—248 n. 21
7:14–15—248
7:15—268 n. 60, 963
7:16—764, 839n
7:16b—249
7:17—252
7:17–22—250, 252
7:19—252, 268 n. 60
7:21—260
7:21–22—253
7:22—229
7:23—256
7:23–27—256
7:23–29—253, 256
7:24—257
7:25—564 n. 58
7:26—957 n. 29
7:26–27—257
7:27—256, 259, 263
7:29—481
7:30—198, 260
7:30–36—257, 260
7:30–38—310
7:31—257, 260
7:32—128, 257, 260
7:33—260
7:34—260–61

7:35—256, 257, 261, 263, 276
7:35–40—261
7:36—191 n. 17, 261
7:37—136, 256, 261, 276
7:37–43—261
7:38—189 n. 10, 261, 268, 268 n. 60, 275, 547, 963
7:39—256, 257, 268 n. 60, 963
7:39–43—266
7:41—267
7:41–43—267
7:42—267
7:43—267
7:44—267, 268 n. 60, 963
7:44–50—240, 267, 272
7:45—167 n. 45, 268 n. 60, 963
7:46—273
7:46–48—273
7:47—270
7:48—273, 593 n. 38, 633
7:48–49—231
7:51—277, 963
7:51–52—268
7:51–53—268, 273, 277
7:52—26, 129 n. 17, 276, 277, 789 n. 24, 963
7:53—262 n. 51, 277, 547
7:54—209
7:54–55—282
7:54–60—282, 433, 522
7:54–8:1a—277
7:55—47 n. 3, 336, 374, 421, 681
7:56—26, 281, 282, 332
7:57—700
7:57–58—209
7:58—54 n. 18, 86, 150, 229, 281, 282, 328, 769, 793, 893
7:59—47 n. 3
7:59–60—282
7:60—148, 294, 486
8—322–23
8:1—175, 189 n. 10, 328, 355, 432, 506, 524, 540, 758, 793
8:1–4—148, 416
8:1a—280, 281, 351, 521, 782

8:1b—108, 290, 294, 339, 783
8:1b–3—287, 290
8:1b–11:18—287
8:2—80
8:2–3—290
8:3—89, 189 n. 10, 192, 328, 781, 782, 793, 892
8:4—293
8:4–7—293
8:4–8—292
8:4–13—748
8:4–25—101, 244, 291
8:4–40—291
8:5—26, 292, 294, 300
8:5–25—6
8:6—222, 226, 294, 299, 685
8:7—31, 195, 294
8:8—113
8:9—298–99
8:9–11—298
8:9–13—294, 298, 303
8:10—299
8:11—299
8:11–17—302
8:12—49, 105, 123 n. 8, 192, 301, 301 n. 30, 307, 320, 464, 524
8:13—185, 305, 307, 678 n. 4, 685
8:14—3, 120, 303, 364, 409 n. 3, 420, 496, 506, 569, 621 n. 26
8:14–17—27, 299, 303, 378, 456
8:15—303
8:15–17—399, 401
8:16—123 n. 8, 401
8:16–17—78, 303
8:17—3, 77, 90, 106, 225 n. 10, 321, 680
8:18—307
8:18–19—592
8:18–23—303, 307
8:18–24—456
8:19—297
8:20—8 n. 14, 106, 307–08
8:20–23—462
8:21—297, 308
8:22—185, 308, 415
8:23—308
8:24—32, 308, 309
8:24–25—308, 309
8:25—310, 356, 448 n. 39, 569, 651 n. 8, 726 n. 28

8:26—198, 309, 310, 313, 319, 321, 371, 436 n. 13, 787
8:26–28—313
8:26–29—310
8:26–40—6, 310
8:27—313, 907
8:28—313
8:29—310, 382, 728
8:30—317
8:30–33—313, 316, 317
8:31—8 n. 14, 317
8:33—317
8:34–35—317
8:34–40—322
8:35—391 n. 40
8:36—319, 322, 401
8:36–39—302
8:36–40—319, 322
8:37—32 n. 68, 320
8:38—226, 320, 344
8:38–39—681
8:39—113, 310, 382, 455 n. 8, 464, 603
8:40—322, 358, 360, 370, 373, 664, 748
9—365
9:1—110 n. 72, 220, 289 n. 7, 331, 349, 782
9:1–2—331
9:1–3—328, 887
9:1–9—328, 336
9:1–19—30, 330, 331, 341, 411, 507, 794, 885
9:1–19a—346
9:1–31—328
9:2—192, 215, 225, 329, 331, 477, 668, 684, 696, 781, 782, 783, 842n, 892
9:3—331, 786
9:3–9—784
9:4—333, 336, 895
9:4–6—331, 333
9:4–9—335
9:5—47 n. 3, 333, 372, 785, 895, 896
9:5–7—786, 795
9:5b–6a—32 n. 68
9:6—333, 615, 649, 897
9:7—233n, 279, 334, 336, 786, 895, 896
9:7–9—333, 336
9:8—331, 337, 786
9:8–18—463
9:9—335, 337, 786

9:10—89 n. 30, 110 n. 72, 181n, 220, 328, 585 n. 17, 655, 795
9:10–12—337, 790
9:10–16—47 n. 3, 788, 795
9:10–17—182
9:10–19—335
9:10–25—337
9:11—335, 338n, 775, 780
9:11–16—371
9:12—89 n. 30, 336, 343, 371, 585 n. 17, 655
9:13—337, 340 n. 17, 358, 783, 892 n. 19
9:13–14—339
9:14—91, 165n, 329
9:15—333, 336, 341, 342, 369, 469, 507, 786, 789, 793, 794, 795, 898, 964
9:15–16—340, 342, 752, 795
9:16—215, 333, 342, 349, 615, 728, 745
9:17—77, 302, 332, 342, 345, 456, 462, 680, 788, 795
9:17–18—335
9:17–19a—342, 345
9:18—344, 345, 681
9:19—110 n. 72, 220, 328, 345
9:19a—345
9:19b—346, 348
9:19b–22—345, 346
9:19b–25—351
9:20—26, 347, 348, 900
9:20–21—348
9:20–22—791
9:21—165n, 289 n. 7, 347, 348
9:22—85, 329, 614
9:23—346, 350, 783, 821
9:23–24—713 n. 3, 725 n. 27, 866
9:23–25—14, 346, 348, 350, 562
9:24—350, 715
9:25—110 n. 72, 350, 508, 620, 623, 829 n. 51
9:26—110 n. 72, 288, 329, 354–55, 791
9:26–28—346, 354
9:26–29—533, 791

9:26–30—350, 354
9:27—123 n. 8, 170 n. 52, 301 n. 30, 332, 355, 422, 494 n. 80, 569, 571, 628 n. 37
9:27–28—505 n. 4
9:28—170 n. 52, 355, 494 n. 80
9:28–29—900
9:29—220,.227, 351, 419 n. 24, 432, 725 n. 27, 756, 791 n. 29, 793, 821, 866
9:29–30—426, 791 n. 29
9:30—338n, 346, 370, 422, 508, 625, 664, 748, 792, 887
9:31—108 n. 66, 189 n. 10, 225 n. 11, 355, 356, 363, 419, 455 n. 8, 580, 905, 920
9:32—340 n. 17, 358, 359, 892 n. 19
9:32–34—359
9:32–35—357
9:32–38—321
9:32–42—783
9:32–11:18—357
9:34—47 n. 3, 359
9:35—108 n. 66, 358, 363
9:36—31, 329, 364
9:36–39—364
9:36–42—30, 511
9:36–43—360
9:38—110 n. 72, 329, 364
9:39—364
9:40—31, 148, 717, 746n, 952
9:41—191 n. 16, 340 n. 17, 358, 892 n. 19
9:42—108 n. 66, 363
9:43—373, 411n
9:44—213
10—385, 403
10:1—83, 664, 907
10:1–2—47
10:1–3—369
10:1–6—374
10:1–8—369
10:1–11:18—6, 34, 376, 407
10:2—312, 372, 375, 477, 590, 614, 781
10:3—89 n. 30, 371, 436 n. 13, 585 n. 17
10:3–6—339, 411n

10:4—371, 374, 389
10:4–6—372, 374, 412
10:5–6—374, 390
10:6—363, 411n
10:7—371, 383
10:7–8—375
10:9—375
10:9–10—792
10:9–13—376, 378–79
10:9–16—30, 319, 339, 411n
10:9–23a—376
10:10—337, 384
10:10–16—371
10:13–15—47 n. 3, 795
10:14—380–81, 387
10:14–15—380
10:14–16—379
10:15—381
10:17—8 n. 14, 382, 411n, 443n, 585 n. 17
10:17–20—381, 382
10:18—382
10:19—383, 455 n. 8, 585 n. 17
10:20—728
10:21–23a—383
10:22—222, 372, 384, 390, 411n, 887 n. 10, 959
10:23—375
10:23–29—388
10:23b—388
10:23b–29—385, 388
10:23b–48—385
10:24—322, 375, 664
10:24–25—388
10:24–48—101, 319
10:25–26—600
10:25–48—557
10:26—515
10:27–28—388–89
10:28—25, 30, 409
10:30—375, 385, 390
10:30–32—411n
10:30–33—8, 389, 390
10:31–32—412
10:32—363, 411n
10:33—390
10:34—10, 388 n. 33, 398
10:34–35—390, 400
10:34–42—25
10:34–43—8 n. 15, 390, 397, 398
10:35—477, 852
10:36—26, 398
10:36–37—10

10:36–38—391, 398
10:36–43—409
10:37—66, 398, 679
10:38—92 n. 35, 169, 398
10:38–40—23
10:39—54 n. 18, 94, 205, 398
10:39–41—130 n. 18, 391
10:40—94 n. 38, 148 n. 6, 640 n. 68, 813 n. 15, 844 n. 27
10:40–41—49
10:41—26, 54 n. 18, 100, 398, 403
10:42—10, 28, 399, 639, 726 n. 28, 852
10:42–43—391
10:43—155, 206, 399, 487n
10:44—27, 90, 300, 391, 402, 415, 455 n. 8, 464
10:44–45—78
10:44–46—3, 77, 399, 680, 849
10:44–47—302
10:44–48—302, 399, 402
10:45—106, 385, 396, 403, 409, 528
10:45–46—301
10:46—27, 88, 400, 603, 681
10:47—319, 403, 538
10:48—105, 123 n. 8, 301, 320, 403
11—427–28, 432
11:1—400 n. 62, 410, 496, 621 n. 26
11:1–3—408, 410
11:1–18—385, 407
11:2—410
11:2–3—387
11:3—378, 410
11:4—188
11:4–10—411
11:5—585 n. 17
11:5–10—30, 411n
11:5–17—8 n. 15
11:6—374, 412
11:11—383, 413
11:11–14—412, 413
11:12—382, 385, 400, 402, 412, 728
11:13—411n
11:13–14—413

11:14—390 n. 38, 602n, 653
11:15—399, 400, 415
11:15–18—413, 415
11:16—50, 319, 400, 415–16, 567
11:17—27, 106, 107, 299, 400, 416, 601 n. 51, 901 n. 42
11:17–18—542
11:18—378, 400 n. 62, 415, 416, 496, 539, 544
11:19—21n, 287, 339, 378, 419, 453n, 459, 540, 745, 748, 783, 905, 918
11:19–20—454
11:19–21—417
11:19–26—557
11:19–30—416, 453
11:19–13:3—416
11:20—21n, 65, 83, 220, 419 n. 24, 453n
11:20–21—287, 419
11:21—108 n. 66, 421
11:22—5, 21, 21n, 189 n. 10, 426, 453n, 454, 457
11:22–23—421, 538
11:22–24—420
11:23—492
11:24—5, 108 n. 66, 352
11:24–25—569
11:25—338n
11:25–26—353, 421, 424, 454, 571
11:26—21, 21n, 110 n. 72, 112, 189 n. 10, 358, 423–24, 453, 453n, 454, 566
11:27—21n, 453n
11:27–28—14, 32
11:27–30—424, 453, 533, 534, 535, 536
11:28—27, 425, 427, 749, 751, 845
11:28–30—427
11:29—14, 110 n. 72, 425
11:29–30—15, 427
11:30—364, 420, 426, 427, 447, 526, 534, 536, 564 n. 58, 894
12—432, 449
12:1—189 n. 10, 424, 434
12:1–5—432, 434

12:1–19—431
12:1–23—849
12:2—15, 65, 433, 442, 871
12:2–4—15
12:3—434
12:3–11—30
12:3–17—15
12:4—435, 924
12:4–10—198
12:5—189 n. 10, 435
12:6—438, 771
12:6–11—435, 438, 511
12:7—598
12:7–8—439
12:7–10—198, 310, 371
12:9—89 n. 30, 585 n. 17
12:10—32, 439, 441
12:11—439
12:12—6, 59, 176, 288, 569, 907
12:12–17—439
12:13—6
12:14—443
12:14–17—443
12:15—442
12:17—4, 328, 443, 468, 535, 540, 549 n. 26, 550, 703, 756, 775
12:18—542, 695 n. 43
12:18–19—443
12:19—16, 434, 437, 444, 599, 940
12:19b–23—533
12:20—16, 448, 745
12:20–25—444, 448
12:21—16, 877
12:21–23—15, 447, 516
12:23—198, 310, 356, 436 n. 13, 444
12:24—225 n. 11, 419, 445, 580, 621 n. 26, 691
12:25—16, 447, 448–49, 448 n. 39, 460, 533, 534, 536, 569
13—466, 499–500
13–14—534
13:1—6, 21n, 83, 189 n. 10, 410, 418n, 425, 453n, 454, 455, 457, 566, 569, 907
13:1–2—27, 457, 751
13:1–3—447, 453, 456, 507, 525, 527

13:2—328, 341 n. 21, 364, 382, 455, 457, 494, 499, 539, 728
13:2–3—225, 455
13:3—455, 680 n. 7
13:4—462
13:4–5—418n, 440, 459
13:4–12—459
13:4–14:28—459, 464
13:5—346 n. 31, 409 n. 3, 447, 460, 467 n. 31, 603, 612, 621 n. 26, 958
13:6—31, 299
13:6–7—688
13:6–12—456, 460, 549
13:7—6, 16, 409 n. 3, 461, 569, 621 n. 26, 907, 958
13:7–8—592
13:8—225, 299
13:9—77, 374, 462, 681
13:10—463, 464, 852, 898
13:11—419
13:12—16
13:13—83, 440, 448 n. 39, 468, 526, 569, 917
13:13–15—465, 468
13:13–52—464
13:14—11, 346 n. 31, 591, 650
13:14–15—468
13:14–14:23—667
13:15—61 n. 33, 98 n. 45, 469, 478, 489, 565 n. 61, 957 n. 29
13:16—372, 441, 469, 473, 477, 491, 590, 703, 775, 958
13:16–22—468, 473
13:16–41—8 n. 16, 30, 613
13:17–37—25
13:18—470, 473–74
13:19–20a—474
13:19b–20a—471
13:20—139, 471
13:22—167 n. 45, 472, 474, 486
13:23—206, 477, 483
13:23–24—476
13:23–25—474, 476
13:24–25—679
13:25—476
13:26—61 n. 33, 98 n. 45, 372, 481, 494, 590, 957 n. 29

13:26–31—476, 481
13:27—94, 133, 479, 481–82, 638
13:28—482
13:28–31—130 n. 18
13:29—205, 479, 481
13:30—94 n. 38, 100, 148 n. 6, 614, 844 n. 27
13:30–31—482
13:31—54, 54 n. 18
13:32—480, 490
13:32–41—482, 490, 813
13:33—148 n. 6, 167 n. 45, 168, 490, 614
13:33–34—100, 844 n. 27
13:34—94 n. 38, 148 n. 6, 167 n. 45, 448 n. 38, 490, 614, 640 n. 68
13:34–35—490
13:35—95, 167 n. 45, 485
13:36—167 n. 45, 486
13:36–37—96
13:37—94 n. 38, 100, 148 n. 6, 614, 640 n. 68, 844 n. 27
13:38—30, 61 n. 33, 98 n. 45, 153, 157, 206, 957 n. 29, 966
13:38–39—490–91
13:39—11, 489, 547
13:40–41—491
13:42—493
13:42–45—491, 493
13:43—372, 421
13:43–46—962
13:43–48—614
13:44—409 n. 3, 493, 496, 603
13:45—492, 493–94, 616, 652
13:46—141, 170 n. 52, 341 n. 21, 409 n. 3, 466, 494 n. 80, 499, 621 n. 26, 652, 958, 964
13:46–52—494, 499
13:47—903
13:48—25, 113, 400, 400 n. 62, 409 n. 3, 499, 591, 603, 656
13:49—691
13:50—192, 288, 372, 469, 477, 508, 522, 590

13:50–51—11
13:51—498 n. 86, 652
13:52—77, 110 n. 72, 113, 498–99
14—466, 529
14:1—108 n. 66, 346 n. 31, 419, 419 n. 25, 467 n. 31, 505–06, 650
14:1–3—503, 505
14:1–4—170
14:1–7—503, 509–10, 687
14:2—506
14:3—170 n. 52, 191 n. 17, 494 n. 80, 503, 506, 511, 564 n. 58, 685, 736
14:4—506, 508, 516
14:4–5—506, 508, 616
14:4–6—11
14:5—508, 520, 522, 713 n. 3, 725 n. 27
14:6—510, 577, 580, 622
14:6–7—508, 510
14:7—510
14:8—512, 577
14:8–10—30, 456, 511, 512, 549, 687
14:8–18—128
14:8–20a—511
14:9—374, 511
14:9–10—124, 512–13
14:10—125
14:11—81
14:11–12—448
14:11–13—513
14:11–20—625
14:12—509, 949
14:13—515
14:13–15—448
14:14—341, 456, 462, 506, 549 n. 25, 601
14:14–15—386
14:14–18—515, 519
14:15—520, 555, 571
14:15–17—8 n. 16, 468, 633
14:15–18—520
14:16—638
14:16–17—520
14:17—634
14:18—520, 521
14:18–19—521
14:19—11, 497, 521, 522, 562, 616, 621
14:19–20—522
14:19–20a—520, 522

14:20—515, 577, 622
14:20a—521, 522
14:20b–25—523
14:20b–28—523
14:21—108 n. 66, 448 n. 39
14:21–23—519
14:21–24—497
14:21–25—456
14:22—49, 421, 492, 504, 521, 524, 526–27, 618 n. 20, 667, 712
14:22–23—526
14:23—28, 189 n. 10, 427, 455, 521, 527, 724, 732, 736
14:25—465
14:26—21n, 453n
14:26–27—662
14:26–28—527
14:27—189 n. 10, 342, 400 n. 62, 455, 466, 528, 541, 666
14:27–28—528
14:28—529, 542, 566, 695 n. 43
15—534, 539, 535, 536, 553, 572–73
15:1—387, 542, 544, 562, 568, 758
15:1–2—534, 539, 755
15:1–5—537, 541–42
15:1–21—537
15:1–35—459, 533
15:2—427, 539, 542, 559 n. 51, 566, 695 n. 43
15:3—113, 189 n. 10, 539, 542, 565, 745, 918
15:4—27, 189 n. 10, 379, 528, 533, 534, 535, 559 n. 51, 755, 845
15:4–5—543
15:5—197 n. 28, 410, 534, 538, 543, 562, 565, 758, 763, 961
15:6—559 n. 51
15:6–7—534
15:6–11—543, 547, 549
15:7—31, 61 n. 33, 98 n. 45, 400 n. 62, 548, 567, 957 n. 29
15:7–10—25
15:7–11—8 n. 15, 387, 442, 548
15:8—67, 619

15:8–9—548
15:8–11—399
15:9—10, 555
15:10—579
15:10–11—548
15:11—730
15:12—27, 191 n. 17, 400 n. 62, 462, 535, 541, 548, 549–50, 566, 755
15:12–22—543
15:13—61 n. 33, 98 n. 45, 534, 606, 957 n. 29
15:13–21—8, 442, 550, 756
15:14–15—558
15:14–20—553 n. 38
15:14–21—558
15:15—549 n. 26
15:16—167 n. 45
15:16–18—552
15:17—554, 558
15:18—32 n. 68
15:19—558–59, 579
15:19–20—379
15:19–21—758
15:20—414, 535, 558, 559, 563, 564, 579, 761
15:21—478, 559
15:22—6, 21n, 27, 67, 189 n. 10, 453n, 535, 559, 559 n. 51, 560, 564, 567, 570, 572
15:22–35—559
15:23—21n, 353, 410, 453n, 559 n. 51, 564, 572
15:23–29—8, 560, 563, 564, 669, 758
15:24—541
15:24–25—564
15:25—548, 564
15:27—364, 564
15:28—27, 539, 555, 564
15:28–29—414, 559
15:29—556, 558, 563, 564–65, 567, 579, 759
15:30—21n, 453n, 566–67
15:30–33—566
15:30–35—565
15:32—6, 425 n. 39, 524, 560, 567, 571, 584, 712
15:33—566, 567

15:34—32 n. 68, 566
15:35—21n, 453n, 527
15:36—572, 694
15:36–41—568, 571, 572
15:36–16:5—567
15:36–18:22—567
15:37—569
15:37–38—572
15:37–39—466
15:37–40—440
15:38—572
15:39—568, 572
15:40—11
15:41—27, 189 n. 10, 229, 354, 422, 503, 524, 561, 572
15:41–16:1—524
16—607–08
16–28—8
16:1—419 n. 25, 524, 594, 621, 714
16:1–2—580
16:1–3—11, 509
16:1–5—577, 580, 694
16:1–6—666, 667
16:2—222, 580
16:3—419 n. 25
16:3–4—581, 759
16:4—535, 559 n. 51, 561, 565, 567, 572
16:5—27, 108 n. 66, 189 n. 10, 225 n. 11, 419, 524, 581
16:6—83, 586, 663, 666, 670, 677
16:6–7—27, 728
16:6–9—586
16:6–10—582, 586
16:6–17:15—582
16:7—27, 47 n. 3, 48, 321
16:8—583, 712
16:9—585 n. 17, 586, 622, 648, 829
16:9–10—716
16:10—579 n. 7, 585 n. 17
16:10–17—5 n. 6, 21, 585 n. 19, 714, 914
16:11—585, 588, 715, 917
16:11–12a—587, 588
16:11–40—586
16:12—612
16:12a—588, 800
16:12b—591, 595
16:12b–15—588, 591
16:13—591, 592

16:13–15—715
16:14—6, 374, 492 n. 74, 591, 592, 614, 621, 656, 907
16:14–15—392, 601, 621
16:15—412, 590, 592, 602, 602n, 653, 681
16:16—195, 594, 898
16:16–18—293, 592, 593, 594
16:17—593 n. 38, 594
16:18—123 n. 8, 301 n. 30, 594
16:19—577, 628 n. 37
16:19–21—594
16:19–40—6
16:20—589
16:20–21—617 n. 18
16:22—597, 771
16:22–23—798, 799
16:22–24—596, 597
16:24—597
16:25–28—511
16:25–30—598
16:26—171, 730
16:26–30—30
16:27—443, 596
16:29—601
16:29–30—601
16:30—32, 104, 599, 600–01
16:30–34—302
16:31—65, 372, 602n
16:31–32—603
16:31–34—412, 601, 603, 653
16:32—409 n. 3
16:33—601, 681
16:33–34—603
16:34—113, 372
16:35—596
16:35–40—603, 606
16:35–49—606
16:36—566 n. 63, 606
16:36–40—606
16:37—422, 560, 571, 587, 596, 607, 864
16:37–38—30, 800
16:37–40—799
16:38—596, 799, 802 n. 47
16:39–40—607
16:40—590, 622, 712
17—643
17:1—467 n. 31, 615
17:1–4—611, 614–15
17:1–9—11, 611

17:2—346 n. 31, 467 n. 31, 620, 626
17:2–3—615
17:3—26, 903
17:4—89, 372, 374, 392, 419 n. 25, 492 n. 74, 497, 542, 615, 621, 695 n. 43, 907
17:4–5—962
17:5—619
17:5–9—616, 619
17:6—15, 619
17:7—619
17:8—619
17:9—619
17:10—346 n. 31, 467 n. 31, 622, 623, 829
17:10–15—619, 622, 623
17:11—8 n. 14, 245, 496, 623
17:12—89, 108 n. 66, 392, 542, 621, 695 n. 43, 907
17:12–13—623
17:13—409 n. 3, 621 n. 26
17:14–15—624
17:15—625, 651
17:16—570, 630, 694, 728
17:16–17—627
17:16–18—625, 627
17:16–33—905
17:16–34—624
17:16–18:17—624
17:17—346 n. 31, 372, 467 n. 31, 492 n. 74
17:18—8 n. 14, 628, 640
17:19—625, 628, 629, 630
17:19–20—629–30
17:19–21—628, 629
17:19a—628
17:20—86, 629
17:21—629, 630
17:22—625, 632, 876
17:22–23—630, 632
17:22–31—8 n. 16, 468, 519, 885
17:22b–23—630 n. 44
17:23—632, 638, 641
17:24—270 n. 67, 273, 697
17:24–28—516, 630 n. 44, 632
17:24–31—25
17:25—634, 637

17:25–28—637
17:26—639
17:27—8 n. 14, 637
17:28—637
17:29—697
17:29–30—641
17:29–31—630 n. 44, 638, 641
17:30—517
17:31—26, 28, 94 n. 38, 100, 148 n. 6, 396, 614, 639, 640 n. 68, 641, 813, 844 n. 27, 852, 890
17:32—28, 395, 852, 904
17:32–34—642
17:34—621
18—671, 677
18:1–2—6
18:1–3—647
18:1–17—647
18:2—11, 17, 533, 589, 621, 783
18:2–3—650
18:3—613, 649–50, 684
18:4—346 n. 31, 419 n. 25, 467 n. 31, 504 n. 2, 654
18:4–8—650, 654
18:5—26, 560, 622, 654, 670, 694, 726 n. 28, 737
18:6—495, 498, 654, 731, 958, 964
18:6–8—654–55, 962
18:6–10—25
18:7—6, 67, 372, 374, 492 n. 74
18:7–8—392, 713
18:8—6, 11, 372, 412, 602n, 655
18:9—47 n. 3, 56, 89 n. 30, 585 n. 17, 657, 817, 897 n. 31
18:9–10—331, 657, 795
18:9–11—655
18:10—657
18:11—409 n. 3, 621 n. 26, 662
18:12—6, 17, 461, 661, 864
18:12–13—661
18:12–17—533, 657, 661, 713
18:14—661
18:14–15—771
18:15–17—661
18:16–17—661

18:17—6, 11, 628 n. 37, 653, 713
18:18—621, 663, 665, 759, 762, 846
18:18–22—662, 665
18:19—346 n. 31, 467 n. 31, 665, 668, 683, 724
18:19–21—677
18:20—668
18:21—664, 722, 917
18:21–22—665–66
18:22—4, 21n, 189 n. 10, 453n, 682, 748, 755, 764, 810, 845
18:22–23—662
18:23—83, 453n, 465, 524, 527, 670, 682
18:23–28—666, 670
18:23–21:16—666
18:24—11
18:24–25—678
18:24–26—6
18:25—670, 679, 696, 728, 842
18:25–26—670
18:26—89, 170 n. 52, 467 n. 31, 494 n. 80, 621, 648n, 663, 668, 696, 842, 907
18:27—670
18:28—319, 671
19—677, 708
19:1—567, 666, 667 n. 44, 669, 682, 683, 701
19:1–6—77, 475
19:1–7—27, 105, 302, 676, 681–82
19:1–12—583
19:1–41—676
19:2—682, 775
19:3—682
19:5—105, 123 n. 8, 301, 320, 401
19:6—3, 27, 78, 88, 90, 225 n. 10, 301, 302, 400, 425 n. 39, 679, 681, 682
19:6–7—680
19:7—683
19:8—49, 170 n. 52, 297, 346 n. 31, 467 n. 31, 494 n. 80, 505 n. 4, 524, 618 n. 20, 697, 731, 961
19:8–10—905
19:8–12—682

19:9—32, 215, 330, 685, 696, 701, 703, 712, 725, 734, 782, 842n
19:10—419 n. 25, 504 n. 2, 683, 724, 961
19:11—564 n. 58, 687, 950
19:11–12—686
19:12—193, 293
19:13—123 n. 8, 301 n. 30, 461
19:13–16—131
19:13–20—687
19:14—689, 692
19:14–20—692
19:15—195, 898
19:16—692
19:17—111, 123 n. 8, 185, 301 n. 30, 419 n. 25, 504 n. 2
19:17–20—692
19:18–20—693
19:19—693
19:20—225 n. 11, 419, 447, 697
19:21—694, 711, 727, 728 n. 32, 729, 751, 752, 773, 953
19:21–22—693
19:22—364, 713
19:23—215, 330, 542, 695, 782, 842n
19:23–24—695 n. 43
19:23–27—663, 695
19:23–41—683, 695
19:24—542, 687, 699
19:24–27—699
19:25–27—8, 698–99
19:26—564 n. 58, 699
19:27—699
19:28–31—699
19:29—700, 714, 825, 915
19:30–31—702, 751
19:31—771
19:32—85, 189 n. 10, 700, 703, 772, 773
19:32–34—702, 703
19:33—468, 616n, 702, 703, 775
19:34—696 n. 45, 700, 704
19:35—616n, 696 n. 45
19:35–40—8
19:35–41—704, 707, 711
19:36–37—707
19:37–38—703

19:38—461, 707
19:39—189 n. 10
19:40—701, 708
19:41—189 n. 10
20—740
20:1—695, 707, 724, 728
20:1–2—693
20:1–6—711
20:1–15—585 n. 19
20:1–21:16—711
20:2–3—715
20:2–4—715
20:3—6, 567, 711, 715, 725 n. 27, 753, 765, 821, 866
20:4—6, 524, 577, 616, 621, 685, 700, 714, 715, 744, 754, 825, 915
20:4–5—585
20:5—714, 715 n. 9
20:5–6—584, 606
20:5–15—714
20:5–21:18—5 n. 6, 21, 914
20:6—7, 587, 711, 716, 722, 745, 749, 924
20:6–7—955
20:7—7, 718, 719, 961
20:7–12—716, 718, 719
20:9—716, 719
20:9–12—30, 511
20:11—111, 718, 961
20:11–12—719
20:12—717 n. 13
20:13—718
20:13–14—722, 916
20:13–16—720, 722, 749
20:13–38—720
20:15–16—7
20:16—8 n. 14, 79, 694, 711, 713, 722, 745, 752, 753, 924
20:17—189 n. 10, 427, 732
20:17–21—723, 726–27
20:18—723, 727
20:18–20—727
20:18–21—723 n. 24
20:18–35—8 n. 16
20:19—12, 713 n. 3, 715, 723, 725, 752, 766, 866
20:20—686, 727, 731, 734
20:21—65, 419 n. 25, 504, 544, 651 n. 8,

652, 686, 726 n. 28, 731, 735, 759, 792, 898, 901, 958
20:22—562, 694, 723, 728, 735, 743, 751
20:22–23—730
20:22–24—723 n. 24, 727, 730
20:23—726 n. 28, 728, 730, 735, 745, 749, 753, 841
20:24—12, 65, 651 n. 8, 723, 726 n. 28, 729, 730, 736, 752, 759, 839n
20:24–25—683, 961
20:25—22, 22 n. 54, 49, 297, 618 n. 20, 723, 731, 740
20:25–26—735
20:25–30—735
20:25–31—730
20:26—652
20:26–30—723 n. 24
20:27—725, 727, 735
20:27–28—25
20:28—28, 189 n. 10, 707, 724, 731, 733, 734–35
20:29—723, 724
20:30—736
20:31—29, 349, 684, 691, 725, 752
20:31–35—723 n. 24
20:32—171, 505, 723, 730, 739, 839n
20:32–35—736, 739
20:33–35—305
20:34—684, 724
20:34–35—649, 739
20:35—47 n. 3, 65, 739
20:36—753
20:36–38—739
20:37—746
20:38—22, 966
21—776
21–26—7
21:1–2—746
21:1–3—722, 749, 918
21:1–6—743, 746
21:1–8—7
21:1–16—743
21:1–18—585 n. 19, 714
21:3—745, 747, 918
21:4—722, 728, 747, 748, 749, 753, 841
21:5—739, 753
21:5–6—747

21:6—448 n. 39
21:7—745, 748, 749
21:7–9—747
21:7–15—722
21:8—6, 224, 226, 292, 344, 749
21:8–9—321
21:8–14—850
21:9—89, 621, 907
21:9–10—425 n. 39
21:10—749, 754
21:10–11—27, 425, 728, 749, 771
21:11—382, 750–51, 753, 841
21:12–13—753
21:12–14—751, 753
21:13—123 n. 8, 301 n. 30, 729, 807
21:14—753
21:15—749, 754
21:15–16—753, 754, 828
21:16—418n, 754, 755
21:17—723, 749
21:17–18—5, 764
21:17–19—28, 550, 756, 757, 760
21:17–26—756
21:17–23:22—755
21:17–26:32—755
21:18—594, 764, 841
21:18–19—694
21:19—442, 541
21:20—363, 496, 548, 763, 779, 786, 812
21:20–21—535
21:20–24—842
21:20–25—8, 757, 762, 763
21:21—232, 763
21:23–24—763
21:23–26—663
21:25—556, 558, 763
21:26—757, 761, 763, 764, 812, 841, 846
21:26–27—846
21:26–29—901
21:27—85, 761, 768, 769, 771, 837, 841, 846, 863
21:27–29—759, 765, 768, 957
21:27–36—765
21:27–40—146
21:28—231, 419 n. 25, 548, 768, 772, 779, 796

21:28–29—539, 557, 766
21:29—714, 724, 768, 796
21:30—628 n. 37, 771, 837
21:30–32—768, 770, 771
21:30–36—23, 281
21:31—85
21:31–32—771
21:31–33—750
21:33—8 n. 14, 628 n. 37, 753, 772, 800, 959
21:33–36—771, 772
21:34—769, 773, 798, 817
21:35–36—773
21:36—797, 878
21:37—775
21:37–40—773, 775
21:37–22:21—773
21:38—23, 819, 826, 835, 860
21:39—338, 338n, 422, 780, 800
21:39–40—776
21:40—437, 441, 468, 703, 784, 807
22—803
22:1—61 n. 33, 98 n. 45, 239, 794, 808, 957 n. 29
22:1–2—783
22:1–3—783
22:1–5—780, 783
22:1–21—8 n. 16, 23, 341, 507, 794–95, 885, 887
22:2—776, 807
22:3—209, 280, 338, 338n, 422, 625, 775, 780, 784, 794, 843, 887
22:3–16—30, 411
22:4—215, 289 n. 7, 330, 696, 842n, 893
22:4–5—783
22:4–16—330, 331
22:5—329, 784, 807, 894
22:6—311, 331, 787
22:6–11—784, 787
22:6–21—341, 894
22:7—336, 787, 895
22:7–10—47 n. 3

22:8—23, 92 n. 35, 785 n. 15, 786, 790, 795, 837 n. 9, 892, 896
22:8–10—795
22:9—334, 336, 894, 895
22:10—104, 786, 787, 791, 795, 897
22:11—787
22:12—80, 222, 289 n. 5, 337, 795, 899
22:12–16—787
22:13—344
22:14—26, 128, 129 n. 17, 275, 332, 469, 790, 794, 897
22:14–16—344, 790
22:15—54 n. 18, 795
22:16—340 n. 18, 345, 791
22:17—448 n. 39, 788, 795
22:17–18—351, 377, 795, 897 n. 31
22:17–21—331, 791, 791 n. 29, 795
22:18—655, 795, 817
22:18–21—47 n. 3, 795
22:19—289 n. 7, 795, 796
22:20—54 n. 18, 233
22:20–21—796
22:21—341 n. 21, 507, 795, 964
22:22—772, 795, 878
22:22–29—796
22:22–23:11—796
22:24—817
22:24–25—801
22:24–29—801
22:25—864
22:25–28—30
22:25–29—866
22:26—800
22:27–28—772
22:28—338, 422, 775, 800
22:28–29—801
22:29—802, 802 n. 47, 959
22:30—165n, 801, 802, 841, 863, 879
22:30–23:5—182
22:30–23:10—152
23—829–30
23:1—61 n. 33, 98 n. 45, 374, 811, 844, 957 n. 29
23:1–5—388, 807, 811

23:1–8—814
23:1–10—847
23:1–11—834
23:2—150, 181n, 337, 782, 784, 788, 839, 860 n. 6
23:3—811
23:5—98 n. 45, 811
23:6—61 n. 33, 98 n. 45, 541, 815, 843, 888, 957 n. 29
23:6–8—149, 197, 812
23:7—818
23:8—147, 198, 689, 815, 816
23:9—817
23:9–11—815, 817
23:10—813, 818
23:11—47 n. 3, 615, 651 n. 8, 655, 694, 726 n. 28, 795, 818, 867, 897 n. 31, 902, 930, 936, 960
23:12—713 n. 3, 725 n. 27, 820, 861, 866, 931
23:12–15—819
23:12–22—818, 861
23:13—820
23:14—153, 165n
23:15—713 n. 3, 820, 821, 822, 823, 866
23:16—349, 351, 821
23:16–22—820
23:17—821
23:18—821
23:18–19—822
23:18–21—822
23:19—628 n. 37
23:20—820, 822, 823
23:21—823, 861
23:22—615
23:23—364, 620, 814, 825, 828
23:23–24—823, 825
23:23–35—823
23:23–26:32—823
23:24—802, 825
23:25–30—825
23:26—21, 46, 769, 904
23:26–30—834
23:27—827, 866
23:27–29—840
23:27–30—8
23:29—660, 909
23:30—349, 713 n. 3, 715, 827, 834, 838, 849, 866
23:31—620, 829

23:31–35—827, 829
23:32—448 n. 39
23:34—775
23:34–35—829
24—854-55
24:1—809, 829, 860 n. 6, 957
24:1–2—836
24:1–4—834, 836
24:1–22—802
24:1–27—834
24:2—18
24:2–8—8
24:2–9—863
24:3—21, 46, 904
24:3–4—836
24:4—886
24:5—92 n. 35, 197 n. 28, 423, 785 n. 15, 837 n. 9, 839, 892, 961
24:5–6—864, 901
24:5–8—839, 861
24:5–9—836
24:6b—838
24:6b–8a—32 n. 68
24:8—839, 842
24:8a—838
24:9—245
24:10—18, 780 n. 2, 844
24:10–16—839, 844
24:10–21—8 n. 16, 861, 887, 905
24:11—764, 844
24:12—410
24:14—197 n. 28, 215, 330, 548, 696, 782, 842n, 845, 961
24:15—847, 888
24:15–16—845
24:16—808
24:17—51, 426n, 762, 848, 852
24:17–18—764
24:17–21—845, 847-48
24:18—848
24:19—8 n. 14, 766, 848
24:20–21—849
24:21—844
24:22—215, 330, 696, 782, 837, 838, 839, 840, 842n, 853
24:22–27—849, 853
24:23—854, 861, 876, 956, 968 n. 45
24:23–24—854
24:24—783, 843, 849

24:24–26—874
24:25—396, 852, 907
24:25–26—639, 854
24:26—824
24:27—18, 533, 835, 852 n. 49, 854, 860, 861, 862, 868
25—872, 880
25:1—19, 860, 863
25:1–5—860
25:1–12—859
25:2—819n, 862
25:2–5—862
25:3—713 n. 3, 725 n. 27, 862, 866, 868
25:4—862
25:4–8—866
25:5—863
25:6—19, 661, 863, 877
25:6–7—864
25:6–8—863, 864
25:7—957
25:8—548, 780 n. 2, 864, 868, 958
25:8–11—905
25:9—853 n. 53, 868, 874, 878
25:9–11—868
25:9–12—865
25:10—661, 849, 868
25:10–11—868
25:10–21—875
25:11—799, 800, 827, 868
25:11–12—341
25:12—865, 866, 868
25:13—849
25:13–14a—869, 872
25:13–22—19
25:13–27—869
25:14b–15—875
25:14b–22—872, 875
25:15—153, 165n, 723, 819n
25:16—8 n. 14, 773, 780 n. 2, 868, 876
25:17—661
25:18–19—876
25:18–20—660, 876
25:19—640 n. 68
25:20—8 n. 14, 773, 876, 878
25:21—341, 868, 874 n. 36, 878
25:22—884
25:23—783, 880, 890, 909
25:23–26—880
25:23–27—876

25:24—797, 876
25:24–25—878, 880
25:24–27—8
25:25—341, 827, 874 n. 36, 909
25:26—874 n. 36, 877, 880
25:27—867, 877
26—909-10
26:1—441, 468, 780 n. 2, 877, 884, 885, 904
26:1–32—884
26:2—780 n. 2, 885 n. 2, 889, 900
26:2–3—885, 886-87
26:2–5—892
26:2–18—507
26:2–23—8 n. 16
26:3—871, 879, 885, 885 n. 2
26:4—780, 891
26:4–8—887, 891
26:5—197 n. 28, 541, 812, 888, 891
26:6—888
26:6–8—813, 887, 890-91, 892
26:7—885 n. 2, 886, 888, 889, 900
26:7–8—891
26:8—885, 886, 888, 889
26:9—23, 92 n. 35, 123 n. 8, 301 n. 30, 785 n. 15, 837 n. 9, 888, 894
26:9–10—894
26:9–11—892, 894
26:9–18—411
26:10—165n, 289, 328, 340 n. 17, 358, 782, 892 n. 19
26:10–11—289 n. 7
26:11—493, 894
26:12—165n, 329
26:12–13—896
26:12–14—894, 896
26:12–18—30, 330, 331, 341, 899
26:13—331, 785, 885 n. 2, 900
26:13–14—333
26:14—332, 333, 784, 785, 895, 896
26:14–17—47 n. 3
26:15—332, 785, 879, 896
26:15–18—896

26:16—54 n. 18, 786, 789
26:16–17—507, 899
26:16–18—342
26:17—794
26:18—463, 487n
26:19—885 n. 2, 900
26:19–20—903
26:19–23—900, 903
26:20—555, 791
26:22—843
26:22–24—874
26:23—813, 885, 886, 903
26:24—28, 780 n. 2, 884, 886, 908
26:24–29—903, 908
26:25—21, 46
26:25–27—8 n. 16
26:26—170 n. 52, 494 n. 80, 548, 900, 908
26:27—871, 885, 885 n. 2, 896, 900
26:28—341, 423, 908
26:29—8 n. 14, 800 n. 42, 854, 884, 908
26:30—877
26:30–32—909
26:31–32—827
26:32—341, 867, 877, 902, 958
27—34, 940, 941-42
27–28—7
27:1—757, 874, 917
27:1–2—915, 917
27:1–12—914
27:1–44—914
27:1–28:16—5 n. 6, 21, 585 n. 19, 714
27:1–28:31—914
27:2—700, 714, 825, 915, 917
27:3—771, 940, 955
27:3–6—946
27:3–8—917
27:4—744
27:4–5—920
27:4–8—920
27:5—744 n. 1
27:7—83, 350
27:7–8—920
27:7–9—946
27:8—929
27:9—533, 919, 924
27:9–10—924
27:9–12—921, 924
27:10—930, 931
27:12—8 n. 14, 917, 921, 924

27:13—929
27:13–20—925, 929, 930
27:13–44—924
27:14–16—929
27:14–20—929
27:16—925 n. 30, 934
27:17—935
27:17–18—929
27:18—919, 937
27:20—695 n. 43, 929
27:21—922
27:21–26—8 n. 16, 916, 922, 930
27:22—171, 932, 933, 936
27:22–24—933
27:22–26—932, 938, 941
27:23—198 n. 31, 436 n. 13, 817, 936
27:23–24—655, 933
27:24—932, 940
27:27—915, 921, 935
27:27–30—935
27:27–32—933
27:29–30—935
27:30—932
27:31—916, 931, 938
27:33–34—922, 938
27:33–35—916
27:33–38—935, 937–38
27:35—936, 938
27:37—744, 947
27:38—919, 928, 938
27:39—8 n. 14, 941
27:39–44—938, 941
27:40—939, 941
27:41—921, 939
27:42—443, 599
27:43—23, 931, 950
27:43–44—941
27:44—936, 950
28—23, 34, 940, 968–69
28:1—947 n. 3, 950
28:1–2—950
28:1–6—949–50, 951
28:1–10—946
28:1–31—946
28:4—950
28:4–5—950
28:5—938
28:6—950
28:7—947 n. 3, 951, 952
28:7–10—950, 952
28:8—191 n. 16, 225 n. 10, 938, 953

28:10—947 n. 3, 953
28:11—917, 922, 947, 956
28:11–14—956
28:11–16—953
28:13—922
28:13–14—956
28:14—940
28:15—955
28:16—435 n. 12, 594
28:16b—32 n. 68
28:17—61 n. 33, 98 n. 45, 843, 862, 957 n. 29, 959, 963
28:17–20—8 n. 16, 957, 959
28:17–31—957
28:18—827
28:19—341
28:19–20—959
28:20—771 n. 55, 800 n. 42, 813, 888, 918, 956
28:21–22—960
28:22—197 n. 28
28:23—49, 297, 524, 618 n. 20, 651 n. 8, 726 n. 28, 843, 902, 961, 965
28:23–28—958, 961, 965
28:23–29—965
28:24—966
28:25—27, 966
28:26—966
28:26–27—966
28:27—966
28:28—153, 157, 487, 652
28:28–29—966
28:29—32 n. 68, 966
28:30—21, 22, 800 n. 42, 850, 956, 968
28:30–31—23, 683, 966, 968
28:31—23, 29, 49, 170 n. 52, 225 n. 11, 297, 494 n. 80, 505 n. 4, 524, 618 n. 20, 731, 875, 961, 968

Romans

1:1—725
1:4—102
1:9–10—956
1:11—494, 953
1:11–12—694
1:15—953

1:16—140, 393, 419, 494, 652, 792, 900, 958
1:19–20—517, 519, 639
1:19–21—641
1:23—638n
1:24—265
1:26—265
1:28—265
2:4—901 n. 41
2:9—494
2:10—140
2:11—388 n. 33, 391 n. 41
2:12—789 n. 23
2:14–15—519
2:15—780 n. 2
2:16—396 n. 55, 641
2:28–30—274
3:2—140, 494, 520, 691, 898
3:20–21—11 n. 24
3:21–26—641
3:25—639
3:28—11 n. 24
4:4—962
5:1—392
5:5—302
5:10—512
6:1–4—105
6:9—484
6:17—544
7:12–13—490
8:9—301
8:9–11—302
8:29–30—496
8:32–33—735
9–11—964
9:4—140
9:4–5—494, 889
9:33—156
10:1–6—962
10:2–3—889
10:4—99
10:9—106, 601
10:10—96
10:12—393, 545
10:13—90, 340 n. 18
10:14—223
10:17—464
11:1—471, 494
11:1–2a—767
11:6—962
11:9–10—63 n. 36
11:11—652
11:13—341 n. 21
11:13–15—767
11:17–21—494
11:20—965

12:1–2—665
12:6—425 n. 39
12:11—12, 668, 723, 725
13:1—163, 811
13:1–7—864
13:12—898 n. 34
14:9–10—396 n. 55
14:14—380
14:17—618 n. 20
15:3—63
15:15–16—341 n. 21, 898
15:16—901
15:19—693, 712, 901
15:23–24—861
15:24—22, 694, 729
15:25–28—426n, 756n, 846n
15:26—711
15:26–27—694
15:27—426
15:28—22, 694, 729, 861
15:30–32—751
15:31—426n
15:31–32—956
16:1—656, 662
16:3—11, 662–63
16:3–5—648n, 649
16:3–23—782
16:5—726
16:7—507
16:16—733 n. 44
16:21—454, 714
16:22—656, 714, 834
16:22–23—693
16:23—653, 654, 695, 700, 714
16:25—736
18:26—662

I Corinthians

1:1—6, 11 n. 23, 653, 713
1:2—340 n. 18, 733 n. 44, 736
1:11—413, 602n, 656
1:11–12—686
1:12—11 n. 23, 442, 667 n. 44, 669
1:14—6, 11 n. 23, 401, 653, 700, 713
1:14–16—344, 590
1:15—401
1:16—401, 413, 602n, 653
1:17—344

1:18—904
1:23—481
2:3—655
2:8—240 n. 4
3:4—11 n. 23, 669
3:4–6—667 n. 44
3:5—11 n. 23
3:5–6—670
3:6—11 n. 23
3:9—322
3:16—302
3:22—11 n. 23, 442, 667 n. 44
4:6—11 n. 23, 667 n. 44, 670
4:12—649, 684, 737 n. 58
4:14—712, 734
4:17—578 n. 1, 694
4:20—618 n. 20
5:8—438
5:9—686
6:9—556, 618 n. 20
6:10—618 n. 20
6:11—790
6:18—556
6:19—107, 302
6:20—733
7:9—852 n. 47
7:14—590
7:19—579
7:23—733
8:1—556 n. 44
8:4—556 n. 44
8:4–10—563
8:7—556 n. 44
8:10—556 n. 44
8:13—563
9:1—342, 789, 897
9:1–3—507
9:1–6—456
9:3—780 n. 2
9:4—304
9:5—357, 442
9:6—507, 570
9:7—732 n. 41
9:12b—650
9:14—123, 650, 737
9:19–23—579, 726
9:20–22—759
9:20–23—899
10:1–22—563
10:14—556
10:16—111
10:19—556 n. 44
10:32—733 n. 44
11:5—748
11:16—733 n. 44
11:19—197 n. 28

11:20—115, 718
11:20–22—113
11:20–34—937
11:22—733 n. 44
11:24—753
11:25—137
11:28—936
11:33—718
12:3—65, 106, 301, 601 n. 51, 618, 879, 893, 967
12:8–11—106
12:9—131
12:10—425 n. 39
12:12–27—686 n. 19
12:28—131
12:28–31—106
12:30—131
13:2—425 n. 39
13:5—570
13:8—425 n. 39
14—78
14:1—748
14:1–2—106
14:3—425 n. 39
14:6—425 n. 39
14:8—727
14:23—115
14:27—301
14:28—549 n. 26, 702
14:29–32—454
14:29–37—425 n. 39
14:30—549 n. 26
14:32—745
14:33—702
14:34—549 n. 26
14:39—748
15:3–4—903
15:4—395
15:5—48
15:5–7—480n
15:5–9—507
15:6—48, 60, 355, 395
15:7—48, 60, 442
15:8—65
15:9—333, 462, 733 n. 44, 895
15:10—738
15:12–18—147
15:14—436 n. 14
15:23–26—843 n. 25
15:24—136, 618 n. 20
15:24–28—51
15:25—57
15:30—562
15:32—696
15:50—618 n. 20
15:55–56—94
16:1—426n, 667

16:1–3—693, 694
16:1–4—756n, 846n
16:2–3—711
16:6—711
16:8—79, 711
16:9—528
16:10–11—694
16:11—566 n. 63
16:12—11 n. 23, 667 n. 44, 670
16:15—643, 649, 653, 846n
16:16—738
16:17—656, 686
16:19—11, 648n, 663, 669

II Corinthians

1:1—656, 661, 733 n. 44
1:8–9—707
1:8–11—696
1:12—808
1:19—11, 560, 570 n. 73
2:1—686
2:4—686
2:12—528, 584, 712, 716
2:13—578 n. 4, 695 n. 41, 711
2:14–16—496
2:16—209
2:24—725
3:7—374
3:13—374
3:16—901 n. 41
4:6—898 n. 34
4:7–12—712
4:17—215
5:16—332
5:18—729
6:14—578
6:16—656
7:2—737
7:5—712
7:6—578 n. 4, 695 n. 41, 711
7:9—901 n. 41
7:10—901 n. 41
7:13—578 n. 4, 695 n. 41, 711
7:14—578 n. 4
8:1–4—756n, 846n
8:1–6—426n
8:1–9—694
8:2–3—713
8:2–4—711

8:6—578 n. 4, 695 n. 41, 711
8:16—578 n. 4
8:16–17—711
8:16–18—695 n. 41
8:18–19—714
8:19—525, 846
8:23—578 n. 4, 695 n. 41
9:7—115, 183, 426, 499, 694 n. 37
9:7b—738
11:7—305
11:9—651
11:10—661
11:14—734
11:23–25—798
11:23–27—662
11:23–28—752
11:23–29—282, 349, 728
11:24—213, 893
11:24–27—897
11:25—11, 521, 596, 914, 922
11:26—466, 526, 713 n. 3, 725, 725 n. 27, 866
11:32—329
11:32–33—14, 346, 349, 350
11:33—349, 350, 508, 620, 791
12:1—897 n. 31
12:2—321
12:4—321
12:7—466
12:7–9—131
12:9—131
12:10—729
12:12—191 n. 17
12:18—578 n. 4, 695 n. 41
12:19—780 n. 2
12:21—556, 901 n. 41

Galatians

1:1—341, 459
1:6–7—524
1:7—561
1:10—725
1:12—331, 353, 897 n. 91
1:12–17—507
1:13—289 n. 7, 333, 347, 733 n. 44, 887
1:13–14—331
1:14—781

1:15—789, 897
1:15–16—964
1:16—341 n. 21, 347, 456
1:16–24—345
1:17—83, 346, 791
1:17–2:2—791 n. 29
1:18—68, 348, 352, 353, 533, 534, 793, 900
1:18–19—346, 352
1:19—442
1:21—346, 353
1:22—351, 900
1:23—209, 289 n. 7, 333, 347, 781, 895
2—535, 536
2:1—51, 426, 427 n. 42, 533, 534, 540, 578 n. 4, 653, 664 n. 39
2:1–2—68, 353, 536, 755
2:1–10—536, 543
2:2—342, 486, 534
2:3—534, 578 n. 4, 579
2:6—391 n. 41
2:6–7—534
2:7–8—341 n. 21
2:7–9—544
2:7–10—68
2:8—898, 901, 964
2:9—120, 442, 534, 540, 756
2:9–10—507
2:10—115, 536, 667, 739, 846
2:11—21, 453
2:11–12—567 n. 67
2:11–14—402 n. 66, 442, 535
2:12—550, 568, 727
2:12–13—580
2:12–14—378
2:13—568, 570
2:16—488
3:8—140 n. 36
3:10–12—567 n. 67
3:13—94, 185, 205, 479, 614
3:16—11 n. 24, 140
3:17—242
3:19—262 n. 51, 275
3:25—759
4:9—901 n. 41
4:13—466, 667
4:14—513
4:15—810
4:19—712
4:28–29—274

4:30—473
5:1—546, 579
5:2–3—567 n. 67, 579, 580
5:2–6—545
5:6—579
5:10—561
5:13–14—579
5:19—556
5:20—197 n. 28, 295
5:21—618 n. 20
5:22—293, 498
5:22–23—307
5:23—852 n. 47
6:9–10—360
6:10—115, 739, 846
6:11—810
6:12—567 n. 67, 580
6:15—579
6:17—521

Ephesians

1:4—657
1:13—302
1:22–23—686 n. 19
2:3—191
2:8–9—415
2:9—11 n. 24
2:11–22—387
2:13—107
2:14—545
2:14–16—707
2:17—107, 393
2:20—156
3:8—462
4:2—12, 723, 725
4:11—425, 454, 732 n. 41
4:12—686 n. 19
4:30—302
5:5—618 n. 20
5:8–14—898 n. 34
5:19—598
6:5–9—89
6:9—388 n. 33, 391 n. 41
6:15—393
6:20—435 n. 12, 771 n. 55, 800 n. 42
6:21—685
6:21–22—714 n. 8

Philippians

1:1—222, 226, 601, 725
1:7—606, 780 n. 2
1:13—36, 867, 968
1:13–14—800 n. 42
1:16—780 n. 2

1:17—800 n. 42
1:19—606, 966
1:20–21—729
1:25—966
1:29–30—606
2:4—725
2:9–11—103
2:11—601 n. 51
2:12–13—415, 496, 615
2:15—108
2:16—198
2:17—729
2:24—966
2:25—600, 737, 956
2:27—131
3:5—351, 471, 541, 780, 812, 887
3:6—333, 781
3:8—729
3:11—889
3:18—725
3:20—800
4:2—589, 601
4:2–3—782
4:10—956
4:12—725
4:13—930
4:14–15—651
4:14–18—600
4:16—612
4:16–18—737
4:18—600
4:19—606
4:22—36, 867, 968

Colossians

1:7—685
1:12—723
1:13—898 n. 34
1:18—686 n. 19
1:24—686 n. 19
2:11–12—546
3:3—637
3:16—598
3:22–4:1—89
3:25—388 n. 33, 391 n. 41
4:3—528, 800 n. 42
4:7—685
4:7–9—714 n. 8
4:10—176, 439, 440, 569, 570, 700, 714, 825, 916
4:11—67, 618 n. 20
4:12–13—685
4:14—7, 20, 21, 417, 569, 585
4:15—726, 782

4:16—24
4:17—12, 723
4:18—800 n. 42

I Thessalonians

1:1—11, 570 n. 73, 622, 735
1:5—616
1:7–8—661
1:8—612
1:9—517, 613, 901 n. 41
1:9–10—640
2:2—596
2:7—712
2:9—613, 649, 737 n. 58
2:11—620, 712
2:14—618, 733 n. 44
2:14–16—11, 616
2:18—618
3:1—622
3:1–2—642
3:1–5—651
3:2—622
3:2–3—618
3:6—651
3:10—891
4:6—726 n. 28
4:11–12—739
4:13—191
4:16—618
4:16–17—843 n. 25
5:5—898 n. 34
5:6—191
5:17—59
5:27—24

II Thessalonians

1:1—11, 570 n. 73, 735
1:4—214, 733 n. 44
1:5—618 n. 20
2:8—618
2:13—301
3:5—544
3:8—613, 737 n. 58
3:10—737

I Timothy

1:2—578 n. 1
1:3—685, 730, 740, 966
1:13—478, 896
1:17—757
1:18—578 n. 1, 579 n. 5
1:19–20—703
2:8—746
3:1–2—526
3:1–7—724, 732

3:1–13—226
3:3—539
3:5—733 n. 44
3:8–13—222, 226
3:9—808
3:14—22, 730, 740, 966
3:15—733 n. 44
3:16—47 n. 4
4:1—733
4:12—578
4:14—225 n. 10, 579 n. 5, 680 n. 7, 782 n. 10
4:16—732
5:1—185
5:3–16—222
5:8—739
5:17—388, 526, 724, 952
5:18—650, 737, 850
5:21—726 n. 28
5:22—225, 680 n. 7
6:1–2—89

II Timothy

1:2—578 n. 1
1:3—845
1:5—577
1:6—225 n. 10, 680 n. 7
1:6–7—579 n. 5
1:16—435 n. 12, 771 n. 55
2:9—148
2:14—726 n. 28
2:15—317
2:24—539
2:25—415, 901 n. 41
3:1–9—733
3:8—462
3:10–11—578
3:11—11, 521, 523
3:15—577
3:16—473
4:1—396 n. 55, 726 n. 28, 844
4:2—931
4:3—727
4:6—966
4:7—12, 723, 729, 808
4:9–12—968
4:10—21, 578 n. 4, 712
4:11—7, 21, 22, 440, 570
4:12—714 n. 8
4:13—584, 966
4:14—703
4:16—780 n. 2
4:17—817
4:19—11, 648n, 663

4:20—131, 695, 714, 721

Titus

1:4—578 n. 4
1:5—83, 427, 724
1:5–7—526
1:6–9—724, 732
1:12—636
2:1–6—185
2:9–10—89
3:5—301
3:12—713, 714 n. 8, 966
3:13—11 n. 23, 667 n. 44

Philemon

1–2—685, 782
2—726
10—800 n. 42
13—800 n. 42
22—965, 966
24—7, 21, 440, 569, 700, 714, 825

Hebrews

1:3—278
1:5—139, 168, 473, 483
1:13—278
1:14—437
2:2—262 n. 51, 275
2:3–4—686
2:4—505
2:6—726 n. 28
2:10—130
2:11—485
2:12—473
3:5–6—137
3:7—473
3:16–19—188
4:12—262
5:5—168, 483
6:2—680 n. 7
6:4—512
8:2—268
8:5—268
8:11—89
8:13—137
9:6—757
9:11—268
9:14—546
9:24—268
9:28—247
10:29—186
10:31—186
10:34—821
10:38—727

11—239 n. 1
11:3—519
11:6—519, 636
11:9—242
11:13—410
11:23—251
11:24—253
11:24–25—253
11:26—253
12:2—130, 335
12:15—306
12:21—258
12:28—845
13:3—821
13:17—388

James

1:1—60, 289, 889
1:2—560 n. 53
1:16—560 n. 53
1:19—560 n. 53
1:27—222
2:1—240 n. 4, 388 n. 33, 391 n. 41, 560 n. 53
2:2—189
2:5—560 n. 53
2:6—595
2:7—555
2:14—560 n. 53
2:14–17—901
2:16—566 n. 63
2:17—504
3:1—560 n. 53
3:10—560 n. 53
3:12—560 n. 53
4:11—560 n. 53
4:17—789 n. 23
5:7—560 n. 53
5:9—560 n. 53
5:10—560 n. 53
5:12—560 n. 53
5:13—598
5:14—131
5:15—131, 512
5:16—434 n. 8
5:17—516
5:19—560 n. 53

I Peter

1:1—83, 289, 584
1:2—10, 93, 301
1:10—621
1:10–11—274
1:10–12—134, 136
1:11—98, 167, 207
1:17—10, 391 n. 41
1:19—316

1:20—93
2:4—154
2:6—156
2:6–8—154
2:9—898
2:13—618
2:13–14—811
2:17—163, 618
2:18–21—89
2:20—597
2:21—597
2:24—205
3:1—763
3:14—597
3:15—115
3:16—808
3:21—808
4:3—517
4:5—10, 396 n. 55
4:11—10
4:13—214
4:13–16—597
4:16—423, 907
5:1—207 n. 43
5:1–4—732
5:2—305
5:4—90
5:5—185
5:8–9—183
5:12—160, 570 n. 73
5:13—440, 570

II Peter

1:17—56
1:19–21—136
1:20–21—61
1:21—167, 207, 473
2—734
2:1—166, 197 n. 28
2:13—64, 113, 718
2:15—64
2:21—789 n. 23
3:4—90
3:5b–6—10
3:10–13—90
3:11b–12a—10
3:12—135

I John

1:1—54
1:1–3—480
1:3—421
1:3–4—97
2:1—57, 129 n. 17, 789 n. 24
2:18–19—734
4:18—354
5:11—637
5:16—965

II John

5—959

III John

1—700
5—959
5–8—542
7—215
12—696

Jude

1—60
4—166, 734

4–19—734
12—113, 718

Revelation

1:9–20—336
1:10—719, 792
1:11—229, 589, 685, 697
1:18—487
2:1–7—685
2:1–3:22—733
2:2–3—707
2:3—712
2:6—224

2:14—556 n. 44, 558
2:15—224
2:18—589
2:20—556 n. 44, 558
2:24—589
2:26–27—168
5:6—278 n. 80
5:9—733
6:4—763
6:10—166
7:4–8—889
7:5–8—65 n. 41
11:13—191 n. 19
12:17—191 n. 19
16:5—98

17:14—103
19:10—386, 515
19:15—168
19:16—51, 103
20:12—843
21:1—914
21:8—295
21:12—65 n. 41, 889
21:14—65 n. 41
21:16—65 n. 41
21:21—65 n. 41
22:8–9—386, 515
22:15—295, 461

Extrabiblical References

Apocrypha

I Esdras

5:16—181n, 788 n. 19
9:21—181n, 788 n. 19
9:29—788 n. 19
9:43—788 n. 19
9:48—788 n. 19

Tobit

5:12—181n, 788 n. 19
11:12–13—344n
12:12–15—442 n. 25
12:19—396 n. 54

Judith

4:9—434 n. 8

8:1—181n

Sirach

4:31—738 n. 62
35:6—373 n. 9
38:11—373 n. 9
45:16—373 n. 9

Wisdom

13:10—638 n. 64

Song of the Three Young Men

66—788 n. 19

I Maccabees

5:22—748
10:39—748
12:48—748

II Maccabees

3:5–7—667
4:21—667
5:24—667
7:9—843 n. 24
7:14—843 n. 24
7:23—843 n. 24
7:36—843 n. 24
9:9—446
12:2—667
12:43–44—843 n. 24

Pseudepigrapha

Jubilees

6:17—75 n. 2
46:8—248 n. 23

IV Maccabees

16:25—246 n. 17

Psalms of Solomon

3:11–12—843 n. 24
10:8—843 n. 24
14:10—843 n. 24

Testimony of Naphtali

8:8—852 n. 47

Jewish Writings

Babylonian Talmud

Berachoth

1.1–2—120 n. 3
4.1—120 n. 3

Megillah

25b—264n

Sanhedrin

1.2a—589 n. 30

6.6—289 n. 6

Shabbath

17a—264n
75a—461 n. 15

Sopherim

35a—264n

Sukkah

51b—667 n. 43

Mishnah

Aboth

3.6—589 n. 30

Berakhoth

3.3—652 n. 9
4.1—652 n. 9

Nazir

1.1–9:5—663 n. 35
3.6—764 n. 43

Sanhedrin

1.2a—589 n. 30
4.3—151 n. 4

Sota

7.8—433 n. 5
9:15—781 n. 7

Midrash

Nedarim

3:3–3—820 n. 30
9:1—820 n. 30

Early Christian Writings

I Clement

5.7—22 n. 55, 731 n. 38
55:6—889 n. 15

Didache

1.5—738 n. 61
2.2—461 n. 15

12.1—739 n. 64
12.4–5—739 n. 64
14:1—719
15.1—525 n. 46

Polycarp to the Philippians

4:2—852 n. 47